W9-BOA-866

Fodor's
ESSENTIAL
AUSTRALIA

WELCOME TO AUSTRALIA

A vast island continent, Australia teems with natural and cultural treasures. Relax on gorgeous beaches along the sprawling coastline, or plunge below the water in Queensland to explore the Great Barrier Reef. Nature enthusiasts revel in exciting adventures in the interior, from trekking around majestic Uluru to spotting wildlife in tropical rain forests. But there's more to life down under than outdoor activities. Cosmopolitan cities like Sydney and Melbourne entice with thriving dining and arts scenes, while world-class vineyards abound.

TOP REASONS TO GO

★ **Cool Cities:** Vibrant Sydney, artsy Melbourne, laidback Brisbane, far-flung Perth.

★ **Beaches:** From Bondi to the Gold Coast, stylish strands cater to all tastes.

★ **Food and Wine:** Mod Oz cuisine, top-notch whites and reds, and, of course, the barbie.

★ **Untamed Nature:** Adventures await in the Great Barrier Reef, the Outback, and Tasmania.

★ **Aboriginal Culture:** A rich heritage of music, art, and stories continues to thrive.

★ **Unique Wildlife:** From kangaroos to koalas, the wildlife here is sure to delight.

Fodor's ESSENTIAL AUSTRALIA

Publisher: Amanda D'Acierno, *Senior Vice President*

Design: Tina Malaney, *Associate Art Director*; Erica Cuoco, *Production Designer*

Photography: Jennifer Arnow, *Senior Photo Editor*; Mary Robnett, *Photo Researcher*

Maps: Rebecca Baer, *Senior Map Editor*; David Lindroth, Mark Stroud (Moon Street Cartography), *Cartographers*

Production: Angela L. McLean, *Senior Production Manager*

Sales: Jacqueline Lebow, *Sales Director*

Marketing & Publicity: Heather Dalton, *Marketing Director*; Katherine Punia, *Publicity Director*

Business & Operations: Susan Livingston, *Senior Vice President, Strategic Business Planning*; Sue Daulton, *Vice President, Operations*

Fodors.com: Megan Bell, *Executive Director, Revenue & Business Development*; Yasmin Marinaro, *Senior Director, Marketing & Partnerships*

Copyright © 2017 by Fodor's Travel, a division of Penguin Random House LLC

Writers: Lee Atkinson, Fleur Bainger, Tess Curran, Narrelle Harris, Leah McLennan, Tim Richards, Merran White

Editors: Luke Epplin and Margaret Kelly

Production Editor: Carrie Parker

1st Edition

ISBN 978-1-101-87987-0

ISSN 2470-9409

SPECIAL SALES

This book is available at special discounts for bulk purchases for sales promotions or premiums. For more information, e-mail specialmarkets@penguinrandomhouse.com.

PRINTED IN THE UNITED STATES OF AMERICA

10 9 8 7 6 5 4 3 2

CONTENTS

Fodor's Features

MAPS

ABOUT THIS GUIDE

Fodor's Recommendations

Everything in this guide is worth doing—we don't cover what isn't—but exceptional sights, hotels, and restaurants are recognized with additional accolades. Fodor's Choice★ indicates our top recommendations. Care to nominate a new place? Visit Fodors.com/contact-us.

Trip Costs

We list prices wherever possible to help you budget well. Hotel and restaurant price categories from $ to $$$$ are noted alongside each recommendation. For hotels, we include the lowest cost of a standard double room in high season. For restaurants, we cite the average price of a main course at dinner or, if dinner isn't served, at lunch. For attractions, we always list adult admission fees; discounts are usually available for children, students, and senior citizens.

Hotels

Our local writers vet every hotel to recommend the best overnights in each price category, from budget to expensive. Unless otherwise specified, you can expect private bath, phone, and TV in your room. For expanded hotel reviews visit Fodors.com.

Top Picks	Hotels & Restaurants
★ **Fodor's** Choice	
	🏨 Hotel
Listings	⤹ Number of rooms
✉ Address	
✉ Branch address	⍾ Meal plans
☎ Telephone	✕ Restaurant
🖷 Fax	⟁ Reservations
⊕ Website	🏛 Dress code
✉ E-mail	⊟ No credit cards
✉ Admission fee	$ Price
☉ Open/closed times	**Other**
M Subway	⇨ See also
⊹ Directions or Map coordinates	☞ Take note
	𝌂 Golf facilities

Restaurants

Unless we state otherwise, restaurants are open for lunch and dinner daily. We mention dress code only when there's a specific requirement and reservations only when they're essential or not accepted.

Credit Cards

The hotels and restaurants in this guide typically accept credit cards. If not, we'll say so.

EUGENE FODOR

Hungarian-born Eugene Fodor (1905–91) began his travel career as an interpreter on a French cruise ship. The experience inspired him to write *On the Continent* (1936), the first guidebook to receive annual updates and discuss a country's way of life as well as its sights. Fodor later joined the U.S. Army and worked for the OSS in World War II. After the war, he kept up his intelligence work while expanding his guidebook series. During the Cold War, many guides were written by fellow agents who understood the value of insider information. Today's guides continue Fodor's legacy by providing travelers with timely coverage, insider tips, and cultural context.

EXPERIENCE
AUSTRALIA

WHAT'S WHERE

1 Sydney. One of the most naturally beautiful cities in the world, Sydney blends beachside cool with corporate capitalism and Victorian-era colonial architecture. Arts, tourism, and business thrive around Sydney Harbour.

2 New South Wales. Southeastern Australia displays most of the continent's rural and coastal variations: historic towns, mountains, dramatic beaches, and world-class vineyards. The nation's spacious capital showcases myriad Australian national monuments.

3 Melbourne. Melbourne is Australia's most European city and a cultural melting pot; you can see that in its fantastic food and café scene.

4 Victoria. Rugged coastline, historic towns, wineries, fairy penguins, and national parks are reason enough to explore the Victorian countryside.

5 Tasmania. From Freycinet Peninsula to wild South West National Park, Tasmania's natural beauty testifies to Australia's topographic diversity. Don't miss the relics of the island's volatile days as a penal colony.

6 Brisbane and Its Beaches. Name your pleasure and you'll find it in sunny Queensland: nearly deserted beaches, lush rain forests, great restaurants, and easy access to family-friendly parks.

7 The Great Barrier Reef. Queensland's crown jewel is the 2,600-km-long (1,616-mile-long) Great Barrier Reef. More than 3,000 individual reefs and 900 islands make up this vast aquatic universe.

8 Adelaide and South Australia. Well-planned and picturesque Adelaide has many charms, including its famous biennial festival of the arts. Be sure to take a tour of the region's renowned wine country, and then unwind on a Murray River cruise.

9 The Outback. This region stuns with its diversity. In the country's vast, central desert region are Uluru and Kata Tjuta, monoliths of deep significance to the local Aboriginal people. Darwin is the gateway to World Heritage wetlands, monster cattle ranches, and rock art.

10 Perth and Western Australia. This is a remote, awe-inspiring region and the producer of much of Australia's mineral wealth. It includes the country's sunniest capital, Perth, and top-notch wine valleys.

Banda Sea

DILI
EAST
TIMOR

INDONESIA

PAPUA
NEW GUINEA

Solomon Sea

Arafura Sea

Torres Strait

PORT
MORESBY

Timor Sea

DARWIN

Gulf of
Carpentaria

CAPE YORK PENINSULA

Coral Sea

GREAT BARRIER REEF

Katherine

Wyndham
Kununurra

Daly
Waters

BARKLY TABLELANDS

Cooktown
Port Douglas
Cairns
Ingham
7
Townsville

Airlie Beach
Mackay

Tennant Creek

9
NORTHERN
TERRITORY

Mount
Isa

Cloncurry

QUEENSLAND

Alice Springs

Longreach
Emerald

Rockhampton
Gladstone
Bundaberg
Maryborough

Yulara
Kata Tjuta
Uluru
(Ayers Rock)

SIMPSON DESERT

Charleville

SUNSHINE COAST
6
BRISBANE
GOLD COAST

GREAT VICTORIA DESERT

Coober Pedy

SOUTH
AUSTRALIA

Bourke
Wilcannia
Nyngan

Moree

Ballina
Grafton
Kempsey

Ceduna

Port
Augusta

8
Peterborough

NEW SOUTH
WALES

Dubbo

2

Taree
Newcastle

Great Australian Bight

Cowell
Port Lincoln

Port Pirie

Mildura

Hay

Narrandera

1
SYDNEY

Nowra

ADELAIDE

Ouyen

Bendigo

Albury

CANBERRA

KANGAROO
ISLAND

Kingston

4

VICTORIA

3

Eden

Coonawarra
Warrnambool
Apollo Bay

MELBOURNE

Southern Ocean

KING ISLAND

FLINDERS ISLAND

TASMANIA

5
HOBART
Port Arthur

0 ____ 300 mi

0 ____ 300 km

NEED TO KNOW

AUSTRALIA
Canberra

AT A GLANCE

Capital: Canberra

Population: 23,889,955

Currency: Australian dollar

Money: ATMs are common; credit cards accepted

Language: English

Country Code: 61

Emergencies: 000; 112 from a mobile phone

Driving: Left

Electricity: 230-40V/50Hz; wall outlets take slanted three-prong plugs and plugs with two flat prongs set in a V

Time: 14 hours ahead of New York

Documents: U.S. citizens can apply for a free e-visa good for 90-day entries and valid for 12 months.

Mobile Phones: GSM

Major Mobile Companies: Telstra, Optus, Virgin Mobile, Vodafone

WEBSITES

Tourism Australia:
⊕ www.australia.com

Immigration and Border Protection: ⊕ www.immi.gov.au/Visit/Pages/Visit

Australian Travel and Tourism Network:
⊕ www.atn.com.au

GETTING AROUND

✈ **Air Travel:** Sydney (Kingsford Smith); Melbourne (Tullamarine)

🚌 **Bus Travel:** City-to-city by bus is relatively easy. Greyhound Australia is the national service provider. Save 5% by booking online. Passes are available.

🚗 **Car Travel:** Hertz, Avis, and Budget allow for one-way rentals. Review insurance conditions, particularly the deductible and whether you're covered off-road.

🚆 **Train Travel:** Rail service is run by each state's individual provider. Great Southern Railways operates the three major long-haul routes.

PLAN YOUR BUDGET

	HOTEL ROOM	MEAL	ATTRACTIONS
Low Budget	A$150	A$20	West MacDonnell National Park, free
Mid Budget	A$200	A$25	Art Gallery of NSW, A$10
High Budget	A$300	A$35	Great Barrier Reef snorkel trip, A$200

WAYS TO SAVE

Eat Asian. Australia's cities have top-notch Asian fare that's inexpensive and far healthier than those tempting sausage rolls.

Rent a flat. Costs are high in the big cities and a flat gives you more space, a kitchen, and, if you're lucky, a local host.

Rent a car. If you're in a group of three or more, renting a car is more economical than individual rail or bus tickets, and gives you more freedom.

Get outside. Most outdoor sites country-wide are free. Ogle Uluru, laze on Sydney's Bondi Beach, and drive the Great Ocean Road.

WHEN TO GO

High Season: School break is mid-December through end of January. Hot, sunny days mean beach resorts are packed. In the northern half of the country, June, July, and August are dry and in the upper 80s F.

Low Season: May, June, and late July through September, airfare from the United States is at its lowest. Low season in Sydney is May through August, with temperatures in the mid-60s F. In Melbourne, June through August sees temperatures in the upper 50s F. This is Australia's winter so prices are more reasonable.

Value Season: Between March and May (fall) and September and November (spring), Melbourne has temperatures mid-70s F and 60s F, respectively. In Sydney, late September to early December, and late February to April, the weather is in the mid- to upper 70s F.

BIG EVENTS

March: Melbourne Food and Wine Festival: Celebrate the city's food culture with over 300 events. ⊕ *www. melbournefoodandwine.com.au*

June: Vivid Sydney: For 18 days, the sails of the Opera House glow with performances. ⊕ *www.vividsydney.com*

January: Australia Day: Ring it in with barbecues and fireworks country-wide. ⊕ *www.australiaday.org.au*

January: Sydney Festival: Celebrate all things Sydney for 2½ weeks, with art installations, family events, and performances. ⊕ *www.sydneyfestival.org.au*

READ THIS

■ *The Slap,* Christos Tsiolkas. At a barbecue, a man hits a child who is not his own.

■ *Cloudstreet,* Tim Winton. Two working class families live together and bond, from 1943 to 1963.

■ *Picnic at Hanging Rock,* Joan Lindsay. In 1900, a group of students go missing while picnicking.

WATCH THIS

■ *The Castle.* An iconic comedy of a suburban family fighting to save their home from airport development.

■ *Rabbit-Proof Fence.* A touching story of three young Aboriginal girls' 1,500-mile trek to return home.

■ *Muriel's Wedding.* Socially awkward Muriel pursues her dreams.

EAT THIS

■ **Meat pies:** A hand-size pie is stuffed with mince-meat and gravy.

■ **Vegemite:** A salty, bitter, malty spread made from brewers' yeast extract.

■ **Lamingtons:** Squares of sponge cake coated in chocolate and rolled in shredded coconut.

■ **Anzac biscuit:** Crispy cookies made with coconut, rolled oats, and syrup.

ESSENTIAL AUSTRALIA
TOP ATTRACTIONS

Australia has more cultural and natural treasures than is fair to many other countries. It also, fortunately, has the wealth and resolve to protect them as best it can. Eighteen sites across the country, including two offshore territories in sub-Antarctic waters, have been World Heritage listed.

Tasmanian Wilderness

(A) Harsh glacial action over millions of years has put the wild in the Tasmanian Wilderness. Remote and subject to extreme weather, this vast World Heritage area—it covers a fifth of Australia's island state—protects one of the few expanses of temperate rain forest on Earth. Here, too, are stunning landforms fashioned by complex geology, diverse habitats for flora and fauna found nowhere else, and evidence of tens of thousands of years of Aboriginal occupation. Angling, white-water rafting, and hiking national park walking trails are some favorite activities in the Tasmanian Wilderness World Heritage Area.

Fraser Island

(B) Remnant rain forest, shifting sand dunes, and half of the world's perched lakes (lakes that are isolated above the groundwater table by rock or organic material) contributed to Fraser Island's World Heritage listing in 1992. The largest sand island on Earth, Fraser lies just off Queensland's coast, about 200 km (124 miles) north of Brisbane. This exquisite island is both ecologically precious and extremely popular for soft-adventure holidays—a sometimes problematic combination. Fraser's dingo population is one of Australia's purest, but be aware that visitors have had fatal interactions with these wild dogs. Humpback whales frequent Fraser's west-coast waters June to November, and the spring tailor fish run lures anglers to the island's wilder ocean shore. Four-wheel-drives barrel along the 122-km (76-mile) ocean beach, which is Fraser Island's unofficial main highway.

Sydney Opera House

(C) One of Australia's recent World Heritage properties is the country's most recognizable building. A realization of visionary design and 20th-century technological innovation, the Sydney Opera House was listed in 2007 as a masterpiece of human creative genius. It is also a structure of extraordinary beauty. Danish architect Jorn Utzon's interlocking vaulted "shells" appear to hover like wind-filled sails on their Sydney Harbour promontory. Floodlighting at night increases the sense of movement.

Awarded the project in 1957 by an international jury, Jorn Utzon never saw his creation finished. Utzon resigned and left Australia in 1966, amid funding controversies and political change, and his architectural sculpture was completed by others. Familiar to people around the world, the Sydney Opera House is a world-class performing arts venue.

Greater Blue Mountains Area

(D) Sunlight refracting off a mist of eucalyptus oil gives the Blue Mountains, west of Sydney, their famous hue. The 91 varieties of eucalypts (commonly called gum trees) across this mountain range's varied habitats was integral to its World Heritage listing. The 1.03 million hectares of sandstone country encompass the Blue Mountains National Park. There are significant numbers of rare species and "living fossils" such as the Wollemi pine, which was discovered in 1994.

Great Barrier Reef

(E) While its name suggests otherwise, Australia's most famous World Heritage site is not a single reef. The 2,600-km-long (1,616-mile-long) Great Barrier Reef is actually the world's largest collection of reefs. This fragile natural wonder contains 400 types of coral and 1,500 fish species of every size and almost every conceivable color combination. The giant clam, with its voluptuous purple, green, or blue mantle (algae dictate the color) is one of the 4,000 mollusks the reef supports.

Uluru-Kata Tjuta National Park

(F) What you see projecting from the sandy plains of Australia's Red Centre is just the tip, but this majestic monolith still packs a physical and spiritual punch well above its weight. Uluru (also called Ayers Rock) and Kata Tjuta, the seemingly sculpted rock domes clustered 55 km (34 miles) to the west, are deeply significant to the park's traditional owners, the Anangu Aboriginal people.

The Anangu ask visitors not to climb Uluru. Some controversy continues, however, about whether this is because the climb is the traditional route of the ancestral Mala men or because the Anangu think the ascent is just too dangerous. At least 35 people have died on the steep, exposed climb. Independent walks, ranger-guided walks, and Anangu-guided walks (fees apply) offer fascinating cultural perspectives of Uluru and Kata Tjuta from the ground.

Wet Tropics of Queensland

(G) Verdant and ancient, the Wet Tropics of Queensland are the hothouse of Australian flora and fauna. Three thousand plant species, hundreds of mammal types, and more than half the country's recorded birds inhabit the tangled rain forests north, south, and west of Cairns, on Australia's far northeastern coast. The remarkable tree kangaroo and the green possum are found only in this World Heritage area. Reptile residents of the Wet Tropics vary in size from inches-long geckos to 7-meter-long (23-foot-long) amethystine pythons. A shorter but considerably meaner local is the estuarine crocodile, or salty as it is commonly called.

Purnululu National Park

(H) Geological history is written large across this World Heritage site in Australia's northwest Kimberley region. Twenty million years of erosion and weathering have deeply dissected the Bungle Bungle Range into banded, beehive-shape sandstone towers. Other examples of cone karst in sandstone, as this remarkable phenomenon is called, are found around the world. None of these sites rival Purnululu for the diversity, size, and grandeur of formations.

Purnululu means sandstone in the Kija Aboriginal language, and spectacularly sculpted sandstone is the highlight of the park. Hard-edged gorges softened by fan palms separate the orange-and-black striped towers, however. Wild budgerigars are among the 100-plus bird species in the park. Wallabies, too, are sometimes spotted among the rocks.

Kakadu National Park

(I) X-ray paintings of barramundi, long-necked turtles, and other native animals festoon the main gallery at Ubirr Rock in Kakadu National Park. This menu-in-ocher is one of more than 5,000 art sites in the park that collectively date back 20,000 years. Archaeologists have put human habitation at twice that long. Ongoing and uninterrupted connection with Top End Aboriginal peoples was a key factor in Kakadu's World Heritage listing. So were the park's diverse habitats and natural beauty. Estuarine crocodiles prowl the Alligator River. Red-billed jabiru, Australia's only stork, stroll the flood plains. Waterfalls cannon off the Arnhem Land escarpment. Nowhere else in Australia are cultural and ecological significance so richly intertwined.

IF YOU LIKE

Beautiful Beaches

Whether you want to bake in the sun, see and be seen, or try body- or board-surfing in the white-capped waves, Australia has an abundance of beautiful beaches. Miles and miles of pristine sand line the coastline, so you can choose to join the crowd or sunbathe in blissful solitude.

■ **Bondi Beach.** On the edge of the Tasman Sea, trendy Bondi Beach is perhaps the most famous in all of Australia. You can take a surfing lesson here or just immerse yourself in the delights of suburban sand and water. Don't miss the Coast Walk from Bondi to Bronte Beach—it's a breathtaking 2½-km (1½-mile) path that will take you along dramatic coastal cliffs to a string of eastern beaches. The walking track continues beyond Bronte Beach to Waverley Cemetery, where many famous Australians are buried in cliff-top splendor.

■ **Queensland's Gold Coast and Islands.** Warm, moderate surf washes the 70-km (43-mile) stretch of Gold Coast beaches, which are perfect for board riding, swimming, or just collecting shells at sunset. Beach bums, however, know to head north to the Great Barrier Reef islands for less crowded, tropical stretches of sand.

■ **West Coast.** Fringing the Indian Ocean between Perth and South Fremantle are 19 wide beaches with good breaks, but head down to the south coast for a dip in the crystal clear waters of the deserted, sandy white beaches around Margaret River.

■ **Whitehaven.** The Whitsunday Islands are home to arguably Australia's most beautiful beach. The near-deserted arc of Whitehaven Beach has some of the whitest and most powdery sand on Earth.

Wine

Australian wines are among the best in the world, a judgment that international wine shows consistently reinforce. Australians are very proud of their wine. You'll be hard-pressed to find anything but Australian wines on the menus at most places, so take this opportunity to expand your palate beyond the export brands you may have tried at home, like Rosemount, Jacob's Creek, and Penfolds.

■ **Hunter Valley.** The largest grape-growing area in New South Wales, Hunter Valley has more than 120 wineries and a reputation for producing excellent wines. Expect some amazing Semillons and Cabernets.

■ **Margaret River.** In Western Australia the Margaret River region produces just 1% of the country's total wine output. Yet 25% of Australia's premium and ultra-premium wines come from this small area. Margaret River's Bordeaux-like climate helps producers grow excellent Cabernet-Merlot blends, since these grapes originally came from that region.

■ **South Australia.** The Barossa Valley, about an hour's drive northeast of Adelaide, produces some of Australia's most famous Syrah (or Shiraz, as they call it Down Under). You might recognize the Penfolds label, as makers of the renowned Grange Shiraz blend. In the nearby Clare Valley, German immigrants planted Riesling many decades ago and the grape has met with great success there.

■ **Yarra Valley.** More than 70 wineries fill the floor of the Yarra Valley, where Pinot Noir thrives.

Incredible Wildlife

Australia's diverse habitats are home to countless strange and amazing creatures.

■ **Birds.** Australia has many wild and wonderful creatures of the nonmarsupial variety. The waterholes at Kakadu National Park in the Northern Territory attract more than 280 species of birds, including the stately jabiru, Australia's only stork, as well as crocodiles, the ubiquitous creatures of Australia's Top End. The much friendlier and cuter fairy penguins draw nighttime crowds at **Philip Island** in Victoria, and North Queensland's Daintree Rainforest boasts hundreds of feathered species.

■ **Creatures of the Deep.** The Great Barrier Reef gets plenty of attention for its underwater wildlife, but Western Australia has two phenomenal spots of its own. The dolphins at Shark Bay in Monkey Mia, Western Australia, can be hand-fed, while Ningaloo Reef, off the Exmouth Peninsula, is home to humpback whales and whale sharks.

■ **Koalas and Kangaroos.** No trip to Australia would be complete without an encounter with Australia's iconic animals: kangaroos and koalas. The Lone Pine Koala Sanctuary in Brisbane is one of many wildlife parks around Australia that let you take a picture with a cuddly koala or hand-feed a mob of kangaroos. If you're lucky, you'll also spot them in the wild.

■ **Platypus.** This unusually beaked mammal, which lays eggs and lives underwater, can be found in small streams and rivers along Australia's east coast. Some of the best areas to spot platypi include Lake St. Clair in Tasmania's Cradle Moutain and Lake Elizabeth on Victoria's Great Ocean Road.

Water Sports

With 36,735 km (22,776 miles) of coast bordering two oceans and four seas, Australians spend a good deal of their time in and on the water. Opportunities abound for scuba diving, snorkeling, surfing, waterskiing, windsurfing, sailing, and just mucking about in the waves. Prime diving seasons are September–December and mid-March–May.

■ **Diving.** Avid divers will want to visit the resort islands of the Great Barrier Reef, which provide upscale accommodation and access to some of the country's top diving spots. Cod Hole, off the Lizard Island reef, in far north Queensland, ranks high among them. You can do a one-day introductory or resort dive, and four-day open-water dive certification courses, or if fins and oxygen tanks aren't your speed, opt for snorkeling off the island beaches. Diving expeditions are a specialty of the Cairns area, with carriers like Quicksilver and Tusa Dive running day trips to the reef for diving and snorkeling.

■ **Sailing.** Sailors love the Whitsunday Islands off the mid-north Queensland coast. Almost all the 74 islands in this group are national parks, and only 7 have resorts on them, making this an ideal spot to drop anchor and moor for a few days, or to try a vacation on a live-aboard boat or yacht. You can also experience the swashbuckling romance of olden-day sailing on multiday tall-ship cruises.

QUINTESSENTIAL
ESSENTIAL AUSTRALIA

Go Bush

When Aussies refer to the bush, they can mean either a scrubby patch of ground a few kilometers outside the city or the vast, sprawling desert Outback. In most cases, it's a way to describe getting out of the daily routine of the city and getting in touch with the natural landscape of this incredibly diverse country.

With 80% of its population living on eastern shores, and with all of its major cities (except Canberra) on or near the coast, most of Australia's wild, wonderful interior is virtually empty. Whether you find yourself watching the sun rise (or set) over Uluru, taking a camel trek through the Kimberley, or sleeping under the stars in a swag (traditional Australian camping kit), there are countless ways to go bush and see Australia's most natural, rural, and stunning sights.

Sports Fanatics

From world-class sporting events like the Australian Open tennis to national obsessions like the Australian Football League (AFL) Grand Final, Aussies love their sports.

Aussie Rules Football (or footy) is a popular, fast-paced, and rough-and-tumble sport that's played without padding and uses what looks like an American football through four 25-minute quarters. Rugby League Football is a 13-a-side game that is played internationally. Cricket test matches are the sport of summer, though the pace is much slower in these games than in footy matches. Spectators get to soak up the sun and drink a lot of beer while watching the Australians duel international teams in matches that can go for one to five days.

Aussies refer to authentic or genuine things as *fair dinkum*. The folks Down Under are a fun-loving bunch, so don't be shy. Here are a few ways to experience Australia like the locals do.

Hit the Beach

Australians love their beaches as much as they love their barbies, so put on your bathers or your cossie (slang for bathing costume) and slather on good sunblock—the damage to the ozone layer above Australia is very severe.

Many Australian beaches are patrolled by volunteer members of the Surf Lifesaving Association (SLSA), who post red and yellow flags to demarcate the safest areas to swim on any beach. The SLSA was formed in 1907, and its tan, buff lifesavers make the *Baywatch* team look like amateurs—it's rumored that no one has ever drowned while swimming in the areas that they patrol. Of course, these hunky heroes can't be everywhere all the time, so use caution when swimming on those picturesque deserted beaches you're bound to come across in your travels. The undertow or rip can be strong and dangerous.

The Barbie

Paul Hogan, aka Crocodile Dundee, showed the world laid-back Australian hospitality by inviting visitors to say "G'day," then throw another shrimp on the barbie, or barbecue. But it's unlikely you'll find shrimp on a barbie in Australia. What you will find is Aussies cooking up steak, sausages (often called snags), beef, chicken, and lamb on gas grills all over the country.

Barbies are so ubiquitous in Australia that almost every public park or beach will have a barbecue area set up for people to come and grill at will. The tools required for "having a barbie" the traditional Aussie way are newspaper and butter. The newspaper helps wipe the barbie clean from the previous grilling, and butter greases it back up again before putting the meat on. Sometimes an onion instead of a newspaper is used to clean off the grill—a slightly more hygienic system.

AUSTRALIA TODAY

Government

Australia is a constitutional monarchy, and the Queen of England is Australia's Queen as well. Her only role under the constitution, however, is to appoint her representative in Australia, the Governor-General, which she does on advice from Australia's Prime Minister. In 1975 the Governor-General caused a political crisis when he sacked the Prime Minister and his government and installed the Opposition minority as caretaker until new elections could be held. The Governor-General retains that power, but his or her duties are primarily ceremonial. Australia's government is elected for three-year terms, with no limit on how many terms a Prime Minister can serve. Controversially, Australia has had five Prime Ministers between 2010 and 2015. Voting is compulsory for all citizens 18 years and older, and failure to vote can result in a fine.

Economy

Australia is a major exporter of wheat and wool, iron-ore and gold, liquefied natural gas and coal. The major industries are mining, industrial and transport equipment, food processing, chemicals, steel manufacturing, and international education. The services sector dominates the domestic economy.

Abundant natural assets and massive government spending initially softened the impact of the global financial crisis that started in 2008. Demand for Australia's commodities from China and India has dipped, and mining has slowed. These developments have led to a slowdown in the country's economic growth.

Tourism

On- and offshore wonders, unique wildlife, beach culture, indigenous history, and multicultural cuisines help maintain Australia's multibillion-dollar tourism industry. The major challenges are keeping Australia on travelers' radars as other countries gain popularity, and protecting the most fragile attractions. Climate change has already affected the Great Barrier Reef, a World Heritage site on most visitors' must-see lists, and programs are in place to try to minimize the impact of rising sea temperatures and nearby mining sites. Contentious logging of old-growth forests for pulp, particularly in Tasmania, continues, and the opening of new mines rarely fits comfortably with conservation and cultural issues.

Religion

Australia's first settlers were predominantly English, Irish, and Scottish Christians. Now, almost two-thirds of Australians call themselves Christians (64%), with Buddhism a distant second (2.5%), and Islam third (2.2%); however, more than one-fifth of the population (22.9%) ticked "no religion" on the 2011 census. Active church worship has declined over recent decades, and many religions struggle to attract members.

Literature

Life Down Under has bred contemporary writers who speak with distinctly Australian voices. Tim Winton's book *Breath* brilliantly evokes the power of surfing and the angst of adolescence, while Kate Grenville's acclaimed *The Secret River* explores Australia's brutal colonial past and its effect on indigenous people. Look out for award-winning authors Richard Flanagan, Peter Carey, Christos Tsiolkas, David Malouf, and Helen Garner, among others. Morris Gleitzman and Paul Jennings write (mostly) laugh-out-loud books for children and the young at heart.

BEACHGOING IN AUSTRALIA

With more than 85% of Australians living less than one hour from the coastline, the beach has always held a special place in Australia's national identity. The country boasts some of the finest beaches on the planet, and they're places where Australians and tourists alike come to relax, sunbathe, and swim.

The coastline stretches for almost 37,000 km (22,940 miles) and encompasses more than 11,000 beaches. While many of these beaches are deserted, others closer to the major cities and towns are often treated as extensions of the typical Australian family's house or backyard.

Aussie Beach Culture

Going to the beach is a way of life for most Australians, as routine as grilling on the barbie or enjoying a cold beer with mates. It's an integral part of the Aussie lifestyle and a place where people spend their weekends and annual holiday celebrations such as Christmas, New Year's Eve, and Australia Day.

Australians look after their beaches, which are generally clean and pollution-free, and almost always of a high quality. Some people go to the beach for the sun and the surf; others choose to fish, sail, snorkel, or scuba dive. Whatever the reason, the beach unites Australians from all walks of life on a regular basis.

The Top Beaches

With so many top-notch beaches across the country, Australians are spoiled for choice. In Sydney, Bondi Beach is arguably Australia's most iconic strand, only minutes' driving distance from the city. It attracts more than 40,000 people on Christmas Day alone. Bells Beach in Victoria is well known for its annual surfing festival; it lures in world-famous surfers and international travelers alike.

The border between northern New South Wales and southern Queensland is where the renowned beaches at Byron Bay, Burleigh Head, and the Gold Coast and Surfers Paradise come together. Farther afield, the Whitsunday Islands consist of dazzling white sands and warm azure waters. These islands are home to many of Australia's ultimate beach retreats. In Western Australia, Perth's Cottesloe Beach is the region's most popular strand to visit.

Beach Safety in Australia

Although Australia has some of the most beautiful beaches in the world, it's necessary to take certain precautions when visiting. At any given beach, you might find large waves, rip currents, and shifting sandbars in the water, along with harsh UV rays on land.

It's common practice to never stray from an unpatrolled beach in Australia unless you're an experienced swimmer. Thousands of trained volunteer surf lifesavers don their red swimsuits and red-and-yellow swim caps every summer to keep the most popular swimming and surfing beaches around Australia safe.

Pay close attention to the flags raised on beaches, and only swim in areas patrolled by lifeguards. If you get caught in a rip, the standard advice is never to swim against it, as you rapidly become exhausted. Instead, try to relax and float parallel to the shore. Always bring plenty of suntan lotion and water to the beach, and protect your eyes with good-quality sunglasses.

GREAT ITINERARIES

FIRST TIMER'S ITINERARY: SYDNEY, THE GREAT BARRIER REEF, ULURU

This classic 10-day journey takes in three of Australia's most natural treasures, including the Blue Mountains, the Great Barrier Reef, and Uluru.

Days 1–2: Exploring Sydney

On your first day in Australia's largest city, visit the world-renowned **Sydney Opera House,** stopping for lunch at the Opera Bar with its sweeping views of the cityscape and Harbour Bridge. In the afternoon, take a guided walking tour through the historic **Rocks** area beyond **Circular Quay.** After some much-needed rest, start the second day with a harbor cruise. You can enjoy the best vantage points for seeing this spectacular city and its magnificent waterfront setting. In the afternoon, head over to **Sydney Harbour Bridge,** where a trek up the stairs of the South East Pylon rewards you with an unbeatable harbor panorama.

Day 3: Day trip to the Blue Mountains

Leave Sydney in the morning on a day trip to the Blue Mountains, approximately one hour away by car or bus. Head for **Katoomba** at the peak of the Blue Mountains National Park, where the **Three Sisters** await, an unusual rock formation representing three sisters who were turned to stone according to Aboriginal legend. Head to neighboring **Scenic World** and choose the scenic skyway, walkway, railway, or cableway to experience the majesty of the Jamison Valley. On your way back, make a small detour in the pretty garden village of **Leura,** with its many fine coffee shops, restaurants, and galleries. Return to Sydney for dinner and stay the night there.

Day 4: Wine Tour of the Hunter Valley

Take an organized day trip from Sydney to the **Hunter Valley Wine Region,** 150 km (93 miles) north of Sydney, and spend the day experiencing a selection of more than 150 wineries and cellar doors. Discover the region's finest Shiraz or Chardonnay and taste some of the freshest produce and best cheeses that Australia has to offer. Return to Sydney at night for dinner.

Day 5: Flight to Cairns

Fly to Cairns, a tropical city nestled in North Queensland and the gateway to the Great Barrier Reef. Relax after your three-hour flight from Sydney with a visit to the **Cairns Tropical Zoo** to cuddle a koala. At night, take in the atmosphere by strolling along the **Esplanade,** or beat the heat by taking a dip in the pristine **Cairns Lagoon.**

Day 6: Kuranda Village and Tjapukai Aboriginal Cultural Park

Take a full-day tour of nearby **Kuranda** village and the surrounding rain forest. Experience one of Australia's most scenic rail journeys, the **Skyrail Rainforest Cableway,** for a bird's-eye view over the forest. After lunch, head to the **Tjapukai Aboriginal Cultural Park** to watch traditional Aboriginal dances and listen to music and informational talks—perhaps even try your hand at throwing a boomerang or playing the didgeridoo!

Day 7: Cruise to the Great Barrier Reef

Book a full-day cruise from Cairns to the **Great Barrier Reef** and get up close and personal with the abundant sea life of the world's largest coral reef system. With some of the best snorkeling and diving on the planet, nothing beats getting in the water and swimming with groupers, clown fish, and rays. Then revel in the fact you're experiencing one of the seven wonders of the natural world firsthand.

INDIAN OCEAN

Gulf of Carpentaria

Coral Sea

Kuranda Village and Tjapukai Aboriginal Cultural Park

Great Barrier Reef

NORTHERN TERRITORY

Cairns

Uluru (Ayers Rock)

QUEENSLAND

WESTERN AUSTRALIA

SOUTH AUSTRALIA

NEW SOUTH WALES

Hunter Valley

Blue Mountains

Sydney

VICTORIA

SOUTHERN OCEAN

TASMANIA

Days 8–9: Two Days in Uluru

Rise and shine early to catch the 3-hour flight inland to the physical and spiritual heart of Australia: World Heritage–listed **Uluru**, the iconic symbol of the Australian Outback. Once you arrive and check in at Ayers Rock Resort, book a seat at the **Sounds of Silence** dinner, where you can feast on a barbecue buffet of kangaroo, crocodile, and barramundi and marvel at the immense desert sky.

Wake up before dawn the next morning to catch the majestic sunrise over Uluru (Ayers Rock). See the magnificence of Uluru as its surface changes color with the rising sun, from pink to blood red to mauve throughout the day. Afterward, walk around Uluru's base with a guide and learn about how this sacred site was created by spirit ancestors in the Dreamtime. In the afternoon, sign up for a tour of **Kata Tjuta** (the Olgas), the nearby rock domes over which you can watch the sun set.

Day 10: Back to Sydney

Once you return to Sydney, take the short ferry ride to **Taronga Zoo** and stroll around the zoo's harborside location, spying kangaroos, koalas, and other animal natives. If you have time, a short bus or train ride to the world famous Bondi Beach is in order for a taste of Sydney's much

TIPS

■ If driving around Sydney, avoid traveling at peak times. Either leave early or head off later, once the commuter traffic has died down.

■ Cairns has a wide range of hotels and resorts to suit any budget—a romantic getaway, weekend escape, or family vacation. It's worth booking ahead and finding somewhere central to the city.

■ When visiting the Great Barrier Reef for a dive or snorkel experience, the best time of year is in the winter months when marine stingers aren't present in the water and there is less need for a protective wet suit.

heralded beach life. Spend early evening at the Bondi Icebergs club, where you can enjoy a glass of Australian wine while gazing out over the picturesque southern end of the beach.

GREAT ITINERARIES

THE SOUTHERN EXPERIENCE: MELBOURNE, TASMANIA, KANGAROO ISLAND

Taking in the best of the south of the country, this 11-day trip combines Australia's second-largest city, Melbourne, and the surrounding region with the great Tasmanian outdoors and South Australia's Kangaroo Island.

Days 1–2: Melbourne

Start off in Australia's cultural capital, **Melbourne,** with its world-class shopping and thriving arts scene. No visit to Melbourne is complete without a freshly made espresso. Some of the best are on **Degraves Street,** directly off Flinders. Sit down at one of the RMB Café Bar's outdoor tables and enjoy delicious eggs Benedict with your coffee. Jump on the free city circle tram to get an overview of the city. It offers good hop-on, hop-off transportation for visitors and locals alike.

Day 3: Yarra Valley Wine Region

Leave the sights and sounds of Melbourne for a day of wine tasting at the **Yarra Valley.** It's within easy driving distance of the city, but your best bet is to go with a winery tour, which often provide transfers from the CBD. These generally include visits to four or five wineries and lunch. Return to Melbourne for dinner.

Day 4: Melbourne and Phillip Island

Explore the farther reaches of the city by visiting the trendy suburbs of **Richmond, St Kilda, Fitzroy,** or **Prahran.** All offer great café and shopping strips with a more laid-back feel than in downtown Melbourne. Take an evening tour to nearby **Phillip Island** to see the **Little Penguin Parade,** when the world's smallest penguins come ashore after a day's fishing.

Days 5–6: Hobart

Fly direct from Melbourne to **Hobart** (one-hour flight) to explore Tasmania, Australia's natural state. In the harbor capital, sate your Tasmanian appetite with a mix of history and contemporary art and culture. Start at **Salamanca Place** on the harbor-front and browse the galleries, art studios, cafés, and restaurants lining the quaint waterfront in original 19th-century warehouses. Then make your way up the hill to Battery Point and wander streets where grand colonial houses face out over the Derwent River. If time permits, the **Museum of Old and New Art (MONA)** is a must-see for art lovers and visitors alike, and is only a 15-minute drive from the center of Hobart.

Day 7: Port Arthur

Hire a car and make the 90-minute drive to **Port Arthur** on the Tasman Peninsula or join the cruise from Hobart to Port Arthur aboard the MV Marana, which takes approximately 2½ hours. Experience Australia's most intact convict site with more than 30 buildings, ruins, and restored homes. Hop on board a short cruise to the **Isle of the Dead** to join a guided tour of the settlement's island burial ground and learn about the lives of the people who lived in Port Arthur. On your return to Hobart, grab a bite to eat at Salamanca Place and enjoy some art, crafts, music, and theater at the Salamanca Arts Centre.

Day 8: Back to Melbourne

Fly back to Melbourne in the morning, and then it's time for shopping. A great place to start is at the **Queen Victoria Market** on Elizabeth Street, a shopping institution that showcases a wide range of quality food, clothing, jewelry, new-age products, and souvenirs. For more upmarket items, head to **Emporium Melbourne, QV Retail,** or **Melbourne GPO.** If you're feeling shopped out, take a trip to the **Eureka Skydeck 88** for impressive and expansive views of the city from the Southern Hemisphere's highest viewing platform.

Day 9: The Dandenong Ranges

You've tried the Yarra Valley but haven't yet explored the Dandenong Ranges, a tranquil region of towering rain forests and quaint mountain villages, just a short half-hour drive or one-hour train ride from Melbourne city (disembark at Hurstbridge, Lilydale, or Belgrave station, where you'll find connecting buses). You can hike through the **Dandenong Ranges National Park** and enjoy incredible views of Melbourne's skyline from the Skyhigh, perched on top of Mt. Dandenong. Afterward, explore your creative interests among the shops, galleries, and tearooms of nearby Olinda, Belgrave, and Sassafras. Overnight at one of the many quaint B&Bs nestled in the mountains, or make the brief journey back to Melbourne.

Days 10–11: Kangaroo Island

Visiting the southern tip of Australia wouldn't be complete without a trip to **Kangaroo Island,** Australia's third-largest island. The island is a pristine wilderness located southwest of Adelaide and home to some of the largest untouched populations of native Australian animals.

Take the short flight to **Adelaide** from Melbourne and then a further flight or ferry ride across to the Island. **Sealink Ferries** offers a range of single- and multi-day tours and accommodation packages, showcasing the best of the region's wildlife, coastline, and speciality food and wine.

If adventure is your thing, Kangaroo Helicopters offers a Heli Experience and Scenic Flight or, for wildlife enthusiasts, options include guided tours within the Seal Bay or Kelly Hill Conservation Parks. Fly via Adelaide back to Melbourne or on to the next stage of your journey.

GREAT ITINERARIES

ROAD TRIP: FROM SYDNEY TO BRISBANE

Drive along one of the most glorious and seductive stretches of land in northern New South Wales. It's a big trip—1,100 km (687 miles)—so allow a minimum of seven days if you decide to drive the entire route.

Day 1: Sydney to Pokolbin, 175 km (109 miles)

Start the journey heading north out of Sydney, with the famed Harbour Bridge in your rearview mirror. Take the Sydney–Newcastle (F3) Freeway about 75 km (47 miles) north to the Peats Ridge Road exit, and wind through the forested hills to Wollombi, a delightful town founded in 1820. Browse the antiques shops, sandstone courthouse, and museum. Next, head northeast to Cessnock and Pokolbin, the hub of the Lower Hunter, and spend the day tasting—and buying—fine wines and artisanal cheeses. Know that Australia has a zero tolerance policy for drinking and driving. Be sure to choose a designated driver or, better yet, take one of our recommended wine-tasting tours.

Day 2: Pokolbin to Port Macquarie, 271 km (168 miles)

Get up early with the birds and drive east via Cessnock to the Pacific Highway. Turn north for the long drive to Port Macquarie, Australia's third-oldest settlement. Have a well-earned lunch break in the café at Sea Acres Rainforest Centre and then stroll the elevated boardwalk—or take a guided tour—through centuries-old cabbage tree palms. Make a quick visit to the Koala Hospital in Port Macquarie for feeding time (3 pm), and then head into town for a lazy afternoon on a beach. The most pressing question is: Which of the 13 regional beaches should you laze on?

Day 3: Port Macquarie to Coffs, 260 km (162½ miles)

After a rest and an alfresco breakfast, resume driving up the Pacific Highway. Leave the highway 140 km (88 miles) north at the exit to Bellingen, one of the prettiest towns on the New South Wales north coast. It's a nice place to stop for lunch and a quick peek into a few galleries. Continue inland up onto the Dorrigo Plateau. Dorrigo National Park is one of about 50 reserves and parks within the World Heritage–listed Gondwana Rainforests of Australia. Stopping into the Dorrigo Rainforest Centre to learn about the area is gratifying, as is the forest canopy Skywalk. Back in your car, drive on to Dorrigo town and turn right onto the winding, partly unpaved, but scenic road to Corumba and Coffs Harbour. Now you've earned a two-night stay in Coffs.

Day 4: Coffs, no driving

Scuba dive on the Solitary Isles? Whitewater raft the Nymboida River? Or kick back on a beach? However you spend your day, don't miss an evening stroll to Muttonbird Island from Coffs Harbour marina. From September to April you can watch muttonbirds (or shearwaters) returning to their burrows. When the whales are about, it's also a good humpback viewing spot.

Day 5: Coffs to Byron Bay, 247 km (154 miles)

Drive north again, past Coffs Harbour's landmark Big Banana and up the coast to Byron Bay.

There is just too much to do in Byron: kayak with dolphins; dive with gray nurse sharks; go beachcombing and swimming; tread the Cape Byron Walking Track; or tour the lighthouse atop Cape Byron, which is mainland Australia's easternmost

QUEENSLAND

Brisbane ✪

GOLD COAST

Mt. Warning ◆ ○ Murwillumbah

Byron Bay ○

SOLITARY ISLANDS

Dorrigo
Dorrigo National Park ◆ ○ ○ Coffs
Bellingen

NEW SOUTH
WALES

○ Port Macquarie
◆ Sea Acres Rainforest Centre

Pokolbin ○
Wollombi ○ ○ Cessnock

Sydney ✪

point. It's best to decide over lunch at open-air Byron Bay Beach Café, a local legend. When the sun sets, wash off the salt and head out for some great seafood and then overnight in Byron Bay—there's everything from hostels to high-end villas.

Day 6: Byron Bay to Murwillumbah, 53 km (33 miles)

Catch up on the Byron Bay you missed yesterday before driving north to Murwillumbah and its remarkable natural landmark. Mt. Warning is the 3,800-foot magma chamber of an extinct shield volcano. From the top, on a clear day, there is a 360-degree view of one of the world's largest calderas, with mountainous rims on three sides and the Tweed River running through its eroded east rim. Climb this mountain (four hours round-trip), then reward yourself with a night at Crystal Creek Rainforest Retreat (bookings essential).

Day 7: Murwillumbah to Brisbane, 50 km (31 miles)

Relaxed and reinvigorated, you should make your way over the New South Wales border to Queensland and Australia's most developed stretch of coastline. With Brisbane just 90 minutes' drive farther north, you can spend as much or as little time as you want on the Gold Coast. Visit

TIPS

■ Unleaded petrol, diesel, and LPG are available at gas stations along most of this route.

■ Motel rooms are easy to find, except during school holidays and long weekends. To avoid driving around after a day at the wheel, book ahead. The staff at your previous night's accommodation should be able to help you arrange the next night.

■ If hiring a car for the trip, check that it contains a GPS. In case of technological failures, pick up a good road map or touring atlas before heading out of Sydney.

■ Mobile speed radars are used throughout Australia, and fines are high. Stick to the speed limits.

theme parks; toss dice at the casino; ride waves in gorgeous sunshine. Don't miss feeding the lorikeets at Currumbin Wildlife Sanctuary before Brisbane beckons.

GREAT ITINERARIES

ROAD TRIP: GREAT OCEAN ROAD

Arguably one of the country's most spectacular drives, the iconic Great Ocean Road hugs the windswept, rugged coastline just west of Melbourne. Allow six days for this 900-km (562-mile) road trip and be prepared to enjoy some of Victoria's best.

Day 1: Melbourne to Apollo Bay, 187 km (117 miles)

Having escaped Melbourne, drive down the Princes Freeway for about 75 km (47 miles) to the Torquay/Great Ocean Road turnoff. A quarter hour more at the wheel brings you to Torquay, Australia's premier surfing and windsurfing resort town. On your way out of town, detour to Bell's Beach, the setting for Australia's principal surfing competition each Easter. The renowned Great Ocean Road officially starts 30 km (19 miles) beyond Bell's Beach, but the dramatic splendor of Victoria's southwest coast reveals itself sooner.

Stop in Lorne, at the foot of the lush Otway Ranges, for lunch. Once you're back on the road, slow down and enjoy it. The winding Great Ocean Road is narrow; don't pass unless you can see far ahead, and don't pull onto the shoulder to admire the view! There are designated pull-over areas where you can safely enjoy the vista.

Drive the 45 km (28 miles) to Apollo Bay for dinner and the night.

Day 2: Apollo Bay to Port Fairy, 234 km (146 miles)

The 91-km (57-mile) Great Ocean Walk starts just west of Apollo Bay in Marengo. Here the Great Ocean Road heads inland. Stay on the main road to Lavers Hill; then detour about 17 km (11 miles) east to the Otway Fly. This 1,969-foot-long elevated treetop walk takes you up into the rain-forest canopy for a bird's-eye view of giant myrtle beech, blackwood, and mighty mountain ash. Backtrack to Lavers Hill and the Great Ocean Road. The road's most famous landmarks lie along a 32-km (20-mile) stretch of coast within Port Campbell National Park.

First stop is the Twelve Apostles—there are now only eight of these offshore limestone stacks, but who's counting? Take a helicopter flight for a jaw-dropping view of the eroded and indented coast. Next stop is Loch Ard Gorge, named after the iron-hulled clipper that hit a reef and sank here in 1878. Loch Ard is a natural gallery of sea sculpture, where you could wander for hours on a sunny day. Don't stay in your car if the sun doesn't show, though. Only when a howling wind is roughing up the Southern Ocean will you fully appreciate why this is called the Shipwreck Coast. Leaving the Great Ocean Road now, drive to the maritime village of Port Fairy for the night. In whale season (June–November), divert to Logan's Beach, in Warrnambool, where southern right cows and calves often loll just off the beach.

Day 3: Port Fairy to Halls Gap, 146 km (91 miles)

Take a leisurely postbreakfast promenade around Port Fairy, Victoria's second-oldest town and widely considered to be its prettiest. Then backtrack 7 km (4½ miles) to the Penshurst/Dunkeld Road and drive 74 km (46 miles) north to Dunkeld, on the edge of the Grampians National Park. Stop for lunch before undertaking the 60-km (37-mile) drive to Halls Gap, the main accommodation base. Be sure to slow down and enjoy one of the most picturesque drives in the Grampians; pull in at the Brambuk Cultural Centre, just before Halls Gap, and learn about the park's rich Aboriginal history.

Check into your Halls Gap accommodation for two nights.

Day 4: Grampians National Park, no driving

Spend a day exploring on foot. Walks of varied grades showcase the Grampians' extraordinary geology; don't miss the Pinnacle Walk, just out of Halls Gap, the valley and ranges view from Chatauqua Peak, and Hollow Mountain in the park's north.

Day 5: Halls Gap to Ballarat, 140 km (88 miles)

Drive out of Halls Gap to Ararat, on the Western Highway, and follow the highway east to the famous gold town of Ballarat. Spend the rest of the morning among the gold-rush-era Victorian architecture on Sturt and Lydiard streets. Visit the Ballarat Fine Art Gallery, if only to see the tattered remains of the Southern Cross flag that the rebels flew during the 1854 Eureka uprising over mine license fees. Spend the afternoon at Sovereign Hill, where you can pan for gold, ride a horse-drawn stagecoach through dusty streets, and stick your teeth together with old-fashioned candy.

TIPS

■ Unleaded petrol, diesel, and LPG are available at gas stations in major centers; however, LPG is rare in small country towns.

■ There is a petrol price cycle in Victoria, which authorities can't—or won't—explain; try to fill up on Tuesday and Wednesday, and avoid buying fuel on Friday.

■ Choosing accommodation as you go gives you flexibility in when and where you stop. For peace of mind, though, you might prefer to prebook.

Day 6: 111 km (69 miles)

Have close and not-so-close encounters with saltwater crocodiles, snakes, wombats, kangaroos, and other Australian fauna at Ballarat Wildlife Park. After that, continue your journey or head back to Melbourne.

ABORIGIN
PAST

Today's Australian Aboriginals are guardians of the world's oldest living culture. Most experts agree that it was about 50,000 years ago (possibly as many as 80,000) when the continent's first inhabitants migrated south across a landmass that once connected Australia to Indonesia and Malaysia. These first Australians brought with them a wealth of stories, songs, tribal customs, and ceremonies—many of which are still practiced today.

By Sarah Gold

AL ART,
AND PRESENT

All Aboriginal ideology is based upon the creation period known as The Dreaming. During this primordial time, totemic ancestors (who were associated with particular animals, plants, and natural phenomena) lived on and journeyed across the earth. The legends of these ancestors—what they did, where they traveled, who they fought and loved—are considered sacred, and have been passed down among Aboriginal tribes for thousands of years. Though these stories are largely shared in secret rituals, they have also been documented through the creation of unique, highly symbolic artworks.

This is why Aboriginal art, despite traditional beginnings as rock carvings and ochre paintings on bark, now hang in some of the world's finest museums. These works aren't just beautiful; they're also profound cultural artifacts—and a window into humanity's oldest surviving civilizaion.

(top right) Nourlangie Rock, Kakadu; (top left) Art by Emily Kame Kngwarreye; (bottom left) Work from Papunya Tula; (bottom right) Maningrida Art and Culture, Darwin

EARLY ABORIGINAL ART

Petroglyph

"X-ray" style pictograph

While dot paintings are the most widely recognized Aboriginal artworks today, they're only the latest incarnation of a creative legacy that stretches back thousands of years. The achievements of Australia's earliest artists can still be seen—etched right onto the sacred landscapes that inspired them.

PETROGLYPHS

The earliest Aboriginal artworks were petroglyphs—engravings carved into flat rock surfaces or faces of cliffs (most likely using pointed stones or shards of shell). Some surviving etchings show lines and circles similar to those in modern-day paintings; others depict animals, fish, birds, and human or spirit figures. The oldest known engravings on the continent, at Pilbara in Western Australia and Olary in South Australia, are estimated to be 40,000 years old. Perhaps the most visited, though, are those in Ku-rin-gai Chase National Park, less than an hour's drive north of Sydney.

PROTECTING ROCK-ART SITES

Given the centuries of weathering they've endured, it's remarkable that so many ancient rock art sites remain intact. In many places, the longevity of the artworks can be attributed to local Aboriginal tribes, who consider it a sacred responsibility to preserve and repaint fading images. Help preservation efforts by staying on marked paths, not touching the artwork, and taking a tour of the site with an indigenous guide.

Freehand pictograph

Stencil painting

PICTOGRAPHS

Other early Aboriginal artists chose to paint images rather than etch them. Using ochres and mineral pigments, and employing sticks, feathers, and their own fingers as brushes, these ancient painters chose sheltered spots—like the insides of caves and canyons—for their mural-like images. Protection from the elements allowed many of these ancient rock paintings to survive; today they're still found all over Australia.

REGIONAL STYLES

The styles of painting varied by region. In the Northern Territory, in Arnhem Land and what is now Kakadu National Park, early Aboriginal people painted "X-ray" portraits of humans and animals with their skeletons and internal organs clearly displayed. The Kimberley and Burrup Peninsula in Western Australia are rich repositories of elegant freehand paintings portraying human, animal, and ancestral Dreaming figures. And Queensland, especially the area that is now Carnarvon National Park, is known for its stencil paintings, in which the artists sprayed paint from their mouths.

EARTH TONES (LITERALLY)

Early Aboriginal artists used the earth to make pigments. Red, yellow, and brown were made from mineral-rich clays. Black was created with charcoal or charred tree bark; white from crushed gypsum rock; and grey from ashes left over from cooking fires. Modern artists may mix their pigments with oil or acrylic, but the traditional palette remains the same.

DECIPHERING "DOT PAINTINGS"

An artist uses a small, straight stick dipped in paint to create a dot painting. Ancient symbols and intricate dot motifs combine to create powerful works of art.

To a visitor wandering through a gallery, Aboriginal artwork can seem deceptively simple. Many traditional paintings feature basic designs—wavy lines, concentric circles—comprised of myriad tiny dots. They look as though they were created with the end of a paint-covered stick (and indeed, most were).

But the swirling motifs in these "dot paintings" aren't just abstractions—they're visual representations of ancestral legends.

According to Aboriginal beliefs, as the ancestors lived their lives during the Dreaming, they also gave shape to the landscape. In each spot where the ancestor shot an arrow, danced, or gave birth, an enduring mark was left on the topography: a hill, a ravine, a rock spire. As they conjured these geographical features, they sang out their names—composing singing maps of the territory they covered. Each is known as a "songline," and they criss-cross the entire continent.

Now thousands of years old, these songs are still memorized and sung by many of today's Aboriginal peoples. Songlines are the basis of all indigenous traditions and tribal laws; learning and teaching the songs are considered sacred—and very secret—duties. Over many centuries, however, artists have revealed parts of the songlines through the symbology of dot paintings.

The symbols may seem cryptic, but many are recurring and give clues to the ancestral stories they depict. Shapes punctuating dot paintings usually correspond to landmarks: bodies of water, rock formations, campsites, or resting places. The lines that surround the shapes and connect them represent the tracks of the ancestors as they moved from place to place. Each dot painting is, in effect, a sacred walking map that plots an ancestor's journey.

COMMON SYMBOLS IN ABORIGINAL ART

woman

emu tracks

four women
sitting around
a campfire

ants, fruits,
flowers, or eggs

well or
main campsite

water, fire,
smoke, lightning,
or bushfire

holes, clouds,
or nests

Honey ant

Coolamon
(wooden dish)

kangaroo
tracks

star

meeting place

traveling paths
or heavy rain

running water
connecting
two waterholes

man

Witchetty grub

possum tracks

boomerang

snake

spear

cloud, rainbow,
sandhill, or cliff

people sitting

THE DAWNING OF ABORIGINAL ART APPRECIATION

(left) Contemporary painting done in earth tones by a member of the Papunya Tula Artists collective; (top right) artwork from the Warlukurlangu Artists Aboriginal Corporation; (bottom right) Papunya Tula artwork.

IN THE BEGINNING . . .

It took a long time for Aboriginal art to gain the recognition it enjoys today. Australia's first European colonists, who began arriving in the late 18th century, saw the complex indigenous cultures it encountered as primitive, and believed that, as "nomads," Aboriginal people had no claim to the land. Consequently, expansion into tribal lands went unchecked; during the 19th and early 20th centuries, most Aboriginal people were forced onto white-owned cattle stations and missionary outposts.

Aboriginal land rights weren't formally acknowledged until 1976, when the first legislation was passed granting claim of title to natives with "traditional association" to the land. This watershed decision (called the Aboriginal Land Rights Act) allowed for the establishment of tribal land councils, which—in partnership with the Australian government—today manage many of the country's national parks and sacred ancient sites.

BREAKING GROUND

The growing awareness of Aboriginal heritage brought with it an increased interest in indigenous art. Before the 1970s, there had been only one celebrated Aboriginal artist in Australia—Albert Namatjira, who grew up on a Lutheran mission in Hermannsburg (in what is now the Northern Territory). In the 1930s, Namatjira studied under a white Australian artist and learned to paint sophisticated watercolor landscapes. Though these had almost nothing in common with traditional indigenous artworks, they won Namatjira enormous fame (by the 1950s, he was listed in *Who's Who*)

Curators often provide relevant historical context.

which reinforced an idea that was already burgeoning in the country: that Aboriginal creativity should receive the same attention and scholarship as non-Aboriginal forms of art.

ABORIGINAL ART CENTERS

Perhaps the single most significant event in modern Aboriginal art history occurred in 1973, with the formation of the Aboriginal Arts Board. The advent of this agency, as part of the government-funded Australia Council for the Arts, heralded a new level of respect for indigenous art. Its aim was to establish a standardized support system for Aboriginal artists through grant money.

But early board members (who came from both European and Aboriginal backgrounds) found this to be another challenge. Aboriginal artists were scattered all over the continent, many of them in isolated, far-flung communities surrounded by vast desert or impenetrable rainforests. How was the organization to find these artists, decide which of them deserved funds, and then dispense those funds in an organized way?

The solution was to set up art centers at specific Aboriginal communities around

Renouned artist David Malangi, Central Arnhem Land

the country—helmed by art-industry specialists who could both cultivate connections with local artists and manage their nuts-and-bolts requirements (like arranging for deliveries of art supplies, and for transport of finished artworks to exhibitors and buyers).

The plan worked, and is still working. There are some 50 Aboriginal art centers in Australia today (most in the Northern Territory and Western Australia), and they collectively represent more than a thousand artists. These centers are the conduit by which most modern Aboriginal works get to art dealers—and then on to galleries, museums, auction houses, and private collectors.

PAPUNYA TULA

Brenda Nungarrayi Lynch, well-known Western Desert artist

The founding members of the Aboriginal Arts Board were inspired by the example of a particular Northern Territory desert settlement, Papunya Tula. Here, with the help of a white Australian art teacher, residents had begun to create and then sell "Dreaming paintings" (what are known today as dot paintings) to nearby galleries. By 1972, the community had established its own thriving and successful

art collective, Papunya Tula Artists.

Today Papunya Tula Artists (which has never been government-subsidized) is the most famous Aboriginal art center in the country. The highly acclaimed dot paintings of its artists have hung in New York's Metropolitan Museum of Art and Paris's Musée du Quai Branly; their annual dollar sales are in the millions.

ABORIGINAL ART TODAY

(left) Art by Emily Kame Kngwarreye, Utopia Central Australia; (right) Papunya Tula

Over the past 30 years, the art world's regard for Aboriginal works has sky-rocketed—not just in Australia, but all over the world. Ancient etchings and modern dot paintings now hang in museums from London's British to the Chicago Art Institute; gallerists and art dealers vie to represent rising Aboriginal art stars; and many artists who got their start at art centers in the 1980s (such as Dorothy Napangardi, Michael Nelson Tjakamarra, and Paddy Stewart Tjapaljarri) are near-celebrities today. A few of these pioneers of the modern Aboriginal art movement (like Rover Thomas and David Malangi) were in their seventies and eighties by the time their canvases began decorating exhibit halls and commanding six-figure auction bids.

Some of Australia's most celebrated Aboriginal artists, though, never got to see just how popular their work became. Clifford "Possum" Tjapaltjarri, for example, whose painting *Warlugulong* sold at a Sotheby's auction in 2007 for $2.4 million—the highest price ever paid for a piece of Aboriginal art—died five years beforehand. And Emily Kame Kngwarreye died in 1996, a dozen years before the National Museum of Australia mounted a huge solo exhibition of her work.

The new generation of Aboriginal artists faces its own set of obstacles. The appetite among art dealers for a steady supply of works to sell has led some of them to cut exploitative deals directly with artists (rather than working through the relative safety net of art centers). Other opportunists have mass-produced paintings and then sold them as "authentic"—thus tainting the integrity of the real Aboriginal art market.

But even these problems, unsavory though they are, can be seen from a certain angle as signs of positive change. It was only decades ago, after all, that the phrase "Aboriginal artist" seemed oxymoronic for many Australians. Today, those "primitive" assemblages of lines, circles, and dots account for almost 75 percent of the country's art sales. They have, in effect, helped put Australia on the map.

Today, symbols might be just half the story: colors can range from calm and subdued to bright and vibrant.

TIPS FOR WHERE AND HOW TO BUY ART

The most easily accessible sources for buying Aboriginal art are galleries. When considering a purchase, ascertain the art's authenticity and ethicality. The Australian Indigenous Art Trade Association recommends asking:

■ Is the artwork documented with a certificate of authenticity from a reputable source, or by photos of the artist with the art?

■ How did the artwork get to the gallery? Is the artist represented by a recognized art center, cooperative, or respected dealer?

■ Is it clear that the artist was treated fairly and paid a fair price for putting the artwork on the market?

MUSEUM AND GALLERY COLLECTIONS

Australia has hundreds of galleries and museums at least partially devoted to Aboriginal artworks. Here are some of the best:

PERMANENT COLLECTIONS

The Australian Museum, Sydney
australianmuseum.net.au

The National Gallery of Australia, Canberra
nga.gov.au

Queensland Art Gallery, Brisbane
www.qagoma.qld.gov.au

National Gallery of Victoria, Melbourne
www.ngv.vic.gov.au

National Museum Australia, Canberra
www.nma.gov.au

The Art Gallery of NSW, Sydney
www.artgallery.nsw.gov.au

Museum of Art Gallery of the Northern Territory, Darwin
www.magnt.net.au

AUSTRALIA MADE EASY

Do U.S. citizens need a visa to visit Australia?

Yes. For visits of up to 90 days, U.S. visitors must obtain a free Electronic Travel Authority (601) visa online at ⊕ *www. border.gov.au*. A service charge of A$20 applies.

What's the best way to travel between long distances in Australia? Is it worth it to rent a car?

It depends on which regions you are planning to visit. Long driving distances and cheap airfares make it more economical to fly between major cities and regional hubs, and public transportation is good in most urban areas. But Australia is also a great road-trip country; traveling by car is an excellent way to explore the densely populated east coast. For more remote and rugged areas it's almost always wiser to fly and then rely on tours and charters to get around.

Any tips for a first-time trip into the Outback?

The golden rule of outback travel is: be prepared. Do your research, listen to advice from local guides, and always have safety measures in place. Remember that towns are few and far between in the Outback, so if you're driving, stock up on supplies. Have the relevant emergency information on hand, carry maps and communication equipment, and always let someone know where you are and where you're going. Pack a well-stocked first-aid kit, always wear sunscreen and insect repellent, and use caution after dark when animals such as snakes are about. Make sure you have the relevant permits for national parks and indigenous areas, and avoid swimming in unmarked waters. Always take crocodile warnings seriously. If all this feels too onerous, consider a tour so that you can take in the beauty of the Outback stress-free.

Australia sounds expensive. How can I save on sightseeing, food, accommodations, and travel?

Accommodation is a big cost in any trip, so book online in advance to take advantage of specials and multinight deals. Australia has plenty of Asian restaurants and eateries that offer cheap, healthy lunches and dinners. Flights between Australian cities can be inexpensive when booked online through budget carriers such as Jetstar and Tigerair. If you're planning on driving long distances, fill up the gas tank in urban areas and on Tuesday or Wednesday, when petrol is usually at its cheapest. Once at your destination, save on sightseeing by finding companies that offer multitour or multi-entry passes for theme parks, attractions, and tours. And remember, Australia is a place of great natural beauty, so many of its best attractions are free.

Do I need to tip in Australia?

No. Unlike in the United States, tipping is not customary in Australia—unless you feel so inclined, of course.

Can I use my cell phone in Australia?

Generally, yes, but beware steep charges. It's best to rely on text messaging, or purchase a prepaid SIM card from a local carrier (Telstra, Optus, Vodafone, or Virgin Mobile) for cheap calls and data usage.

What should I pack for a trip to Australia?

Warm, cold, and wet weather gear, a wide-brimmed hat, good walking shoes, a bathing suit, sunscreen, a reusable water bottle, smart-casual clothing for restaurants and city attractions, and a camera.

SYDNEY

WELCOME TO SYDNEY

TOP REASONS TO GO

★ **A Harbor Sail:** Take a ferry, sail a yacht, or paddle a kayak, but make sure you get out into Sydney Harbour. It's a glorious sight. Check out the Sydney Harbour section for tours of the harbor by boat.

★ **A Night at the Opera:** From rock to rap, theater to tap dancing, there's always something interesting happening at the world's most famous playhouse.

★ **Exquisite Dining:** Sydney restaurants are among the finest eateries in the world. Don't miss out on the fresh seafood and top-notch Mod Oz and Asian cuisines.

★ **Glorious Beaches:** Sydneysiders are besotted by the beach, and you'll be, too. With 40 to choose from, you can watch surfers ride the waves or paddle around the calmer waters of a sheltered harbor beach.

★ **National Parks and Wildlife:** Sydney's untamed beauty is close at hand. See native birds and colorful wildflowers just a few miles from the city.

1 Sydney Harbour. This spectacular waterway has a 240-km (149-mile) shoreline of bays, headlands, and quiet beaches. It's the city's jewel.

2 The Rocks. Sydney's oldest area, The Rocks, is full of restored 19th-century warehouses and pubs with great views of the famous bridge.

3 Domain and Macquarie Street. This stately quarter of town contains Parliament House, formal gardens, and the Domain, where rallies and concerts are staged.

4 The Opera House and the Royal Botanic Gardens. The white "sails" of the Opera House dominate the harbor; the neighboring Royal Botanic Gardens are an oasis on the harbor's edge.

5 Darling Harbour. Occupying a former goods yard on the city's western edge, Darling Harbour now houses museums, the aquarium, restaurants, and hotels.

6 Sydney City Center. Dominated by 880-foot Sydney Tower, the city center is packed with historic and modern shopping arcades.

7 Inner Sydney and the Eastern Suburbs. A few miles east of the city you'll find palatial harborside homes, beaches, and café-culture, bohemian-chic enclaves.

SYDNEY HARBOUR

2

Port Jackson

ennelong
Point

◆ **Sydney Opera
House**

Garden
Island
Naval
Dockyard

*Farm
Cove*

uay

4

**ROYAL
BOTANIC
GARDENS**

**THE
DOMAIN**

◆ **Parliament House**

acquarie St.

3

ueens
quare

WOOLLOOMOOLOO

**HYDE
PARK**

◆ Anzac
Memorial

William St.

76

**EAST
SYDNEY**

iverpool St.

**SURRY
HILL**

Reservoir St.

Albion St.

**GREATER
SYDNEY**

8

**POTTS
POINT**

Billyard Ave.

*Elizabeth
Bay*

*Challis
Ave.*

**BEARE
PARK**

Greenknowe

Orwell St.

**ELIZABETH
BAY**

**RUSHCUTTERS
BAY PARK**

7

**KINGS
CROSS**

**INNER
SYDNEY**

Kings Cross Rd.

DARLINGHURST

Surrey

Liverpool St.

11

PADDINGTON

0 — 1/8 mile

0 — 200 meters

8 **Greater Sydney.**
National parks, beautiful
beaches, and relics of
Sydney's colonial past can
all be explored within an
hour of the city center.

GETTING ORIENTED

Sydney is built around its huge harbor. The city center and main attractions are on the south shore. Harbour Bridge connects The Rocks on the south side with Milsons Point on the north side. Greater Sydney is vast, some 80 km (50 miles) from north to south and 70 km (43 miles) from east to west; however, the city center is relatively small. From the Opera House and Circular Quay the city stretches south for about 3 km (2 miles), and east to west for about 2 km (1 mile). It's relatively flat, making it easy to walk around. Beyond the harbor, the city center is essentially a business and shopping precinct, with colonial and modern buildings. The restaurant and nightlife suburbs of Kings Cross, Darlinghurst, and Surry Hill flank the city's eastern and southern edges.

Updated by
Lee Atkinson

Sydney belongs to the exclusive club of cities that generate excitement. At the end of a marathon flight there's renewed vitality in the cabin as the plane circles the city, where thousands of yachts are suspended on the dark water and the sails of the Opera House glisten in the distance. Blessed with dazzling beaches and a sunny climate, Sydney is among the most beautiful cities on the planet.

With 4.8 million people, Sydney is the biggest and most cosmopolitan city in Australia. A wave of immigration from the 1950s has seen the Anglo-Irish immigrants who made up the city's original population joined by Italians, Greeks, Turks, Lebanese, Chinese, Vietnamese, Thais, and Indonesians. This intermingling has created a cultural vibrancy and energy—and a culinary repertoire—that was missing only a generation ago.

Sydneysiders embrace their harbor with a passion. Indented with numerous bays and beaches, Sydney Harbour is the presiding icon for the city, and urban Australia. Captain Arthur Phillip, commander of the 11-ship First Fleet, wrote in his diary when he first set eyes on the harbor on January 26, 1788: "We had the satisfaction of finding the finest harbor in the world."

Although a visit to Sydney is an essential part of an Australian experience, the city is no more representative of Australia than Los Angeles is of the United States. Sydney has joined the ranks of the great cities whose characters are essentially international. What Sydney offers is style, sophistication, and great looks—an exhilarating prelude to the continent at its back door.

WHEN TO GO

The best times to visit Sydney are in late spring and early fall (autumn). The spring months of October and November are pleasantly warm, although the ocean is slightly cool for swimming. The summer months of December through February are typically hot and humid, February being the most humid. In the early autumn months of March and April weather is typically stable and comfortable, outdoor city life is still in full swing, and the ocean is at its warmest. Even the coolest winter months of July and August typically stay mild and sunny, with average daily maximum temperatures in the low 60s.

PLANNING YOUR TIME

You really need three days in Sydney to see the essential city center, while six days would give you time to explore the beaches and inner suburbs.

Start with an afternoon **Harbour Express Cruise** for some of the best views of the city. Follow with a tour of **The Rocks,** the nation's birthplace, and take a sunset walk up onto the **Sydney Harbour Bridge.** The following day, take a tour of the famous **Sydney Opera House** and a stroll through the **Royal Botanic Gardens** to visit **Mrs. Macquarie's Chair** for a wonderful view of the harbor icons. Spend some time exploring the city center and another spectacular panorama from the top of **Sydney Tower.** Include a walk around Macquarie Street, a living reminder of Sydney's colonial history, and, if you have time, the contrasting experience of futuristic Darling Harbour, with its museums, aquarium, and cafés, and colorful, aromatic **Chinatown.**

On your third day make your way to **Bondi,** Australia's most famous beach, and if the weather is kind follow the clifftop walking path to Bronte Beach. The next day catch the ferry to **Manly** to visit its beach and the historic Quarantine Station. From here, take an afternoon bus tour to the northern beaches, or return to the city to shop or visit museums and galleries. Options for the last day include a trip to the **Blue Mountains** west of the city or a wildlife park such as **WILD LIFE Sydney Zoo** at Darling Harbour or **Taronga Zoo,** on the north side of the harbor.

GETTING HERE AND AROUND

AIR TRAVEL

Sydney's main airport is Kingsford–Smith International, 8 km (5 miles) south of the city. Kingsford–Smith's international (T1) and domestic terminals (T2 and T3) are 3 km (2 miles) apart. To get from one to the other, take a taxi for about A$22, use the Airport Shuttle Bus (called the TBus) for A$5.50 (it takes 10 minutes), or take the Airport Link train, A$5.80, which takes two minutes. Destination New South Wales has two information counters in the arrival level of the international terminal. One provides free maps and brochures and handles general inquiries. The other books accommodations and tours, and sells travel insurance. Both counters are open daily from approximately 6 am to 11 pm. You can convert your money to Australian currency at the Travelex offices in both the arrival and departure areas.

AIRPORT TRANSFERS Airport Link rail travels to the city center in 15 minutes. A one-way fare is A$17. Taxis are available outside the terminal buildings. Fares are about A$45 to A$55 to city and Kings Cross hotels. There are a couple of shuttle-bus services from the airport that drop passenger at hotels in the city center, Kings Cross, and Darling Harbour for around A$15 to A$17 one-way and A$28 round-trip. ■ TIP➜ Passengers with only a little luggage can save money by taking the state government run bus

No. 400, to Bondi Junction. The fare is a mere A$5 for the hour-long bus ride, and is ideal for those staying at nearby Bondi Beach.

BUS TRAVEL

Bus travel in Sydney is slow due to congested streets and the undulating terrain. Fares are calculated in sections; the minimum section fare (A$2.20) applies to trips in the inner-city area, such as between Circular Quay and Kings Cross, or from Bondi Junction railway station to Bondi Beach. Bus information can be found at ⊕ *www.sydneybuses.info*.

CAR TRAVEL

With the assistance of a good road map you shouldn't have too many problems driving in and out of Sydney, thanks to the decent freeway system. However, driving a car around Sydney is not recommended because of congestion and lack of parking space. If you decide to drive a rental car, it costs between A$75 and A$85 per day. Local operator Bayswater Car Rental has cars from as little as A$25 per day (on a seven-day rental plan) for a one-year-old vehicle. Camper-vans that sleep two people can be hired from operator Jucy Rentals for A$75 a day and A$130 in the January peak season.

CRUISE TRAVEL

There are two cruise ship terminals in Sydney. The Overseas Passenger Terminal (OPT) is on the western side of Circular Quay in the heart of The Rocks; White Bay Cruise Terminal is in Rozelle, 6 km (4 miles) west of the city center. There is a taxi stand near the White Bay terminal, and it's the best way to get into the city center for sightseeing, as the nearest public bus stop is around 3 km (2 miles) away—a taxi ride to the city costs around A$20, A$50 to the airport.

TAXI TRAVEL

Taxis charge A$2.19 per km (½ mile), plus a flag fall (hiring charge) of A$3.60. Extra charges apply to baggage weighing more than 55 pounds, telephone bookings, and Harbour Bridge and tunnel tolls. Fares are 20% higher between 10 pm and 6 am, when the numeral "2" will be displayed in the tariff indicator on the meter, plus an additional A$2.50 flag fall surcharge.

TRAM AND TRAIN TRAVEL

The Sydney Light Rail is an efficient link between Central Station, Darling Harbour, the Star City casino/entertainment complex, Sydney fish markets, and two inner western suburbs. The modern trams operate at 10- to 30-minute intervals 24 hours a day. One-way tickets are A$3.80. The main terminal for long-distance, intercity, and Sydney suburban trains is Central Station. There are a number of good-value train passes including the Backtracker Pass, which at A$298 (for three months) allows unlimited travel between Sydney, Canberra, Melbourne, and Brisbane. Sydney's suburban train network, City Rail, links the city with dozens of suburbs as well as Blue Mountains and South Coast towns. Tickets start from A$4 one-way and are sold at all City Rail stations. Off-peak day return tickets are the best option.

DISCOUNTS AND DEALS

For the price of admission to two or three main attractions, the **Sydney Unlimited Attractions Pass** (☎ *1300/366476* ⊕ *seesydneypass.iventurecard. com*) gets you into 40 Sydney sights and attractions, including the Opera House, Sydney Aquarium, and harbor cruises. Several different cards are available, including three- and seven-day versions. Some cards can even include public transportation. Prices start at A$239 for a three-day adult card without transportation. Cards are available from the Sydney Visitor Centre at The Rocks.

NSW Transport operates all of the Sydney trains, buses, and ferries and sells the **MyZone tickets** (☎ *13–1500* ⊕ *www.transportnsw.info*), which include MyBus, MyTrain, andMyFerry tickets. A daily ticket is A$24; a weekly is A$48 for Zone 1. The AirportLink rail service and sightseeing buses are not included in the price. If you are planning on using public transport for more than two or three trips consider buying an opal card (it's similar to Oyster in London or Octopus in Hong Kong), which covers buses, trains, ferries and light rail—tap it against the card reader at wharves, stations, and on buses and tap off again at the end of your journey. You can buy an opal card at most convenience stores and newsagents (from A$10) and top it up at machines at train stations, wharves, and light rail stops, online at ⊕ *www.opal.com.au*, or by calling ☎ *13–6725*.

RESTAURANTS

Sydney is blessed with excellent dining. Its 4,000-plus restaurants range from ultrahip and expensive celebrity chef venues overlooking the harbor to über-cool eateries in the fringe suburbs of Darlinghurst and Surry Hills to neighborhood Italian and Asian joints loved by locals.

HOTELS

Sydney hotels range from the international five-star properties with stunning views over Sydney Harbour to boutique hotels in heritage buildings and historic pubs in The Rocks. Harborside hotels are modern and large with executive levels, pools, and day spas. Smaller hotels and apartment hotels are located on the city fringes, in Surry Hills, Darlinghurst, and Kings Cross/Potts Point, with easy access to the city center and harbor. *Hotel reviews have been shortened. For full information, visit Fodors.com.*

WHAT IT COSTS (IN AUSTRALIAN DOLLARS)			
$	$$	$$$	$$$$
Restaurants Under A$36	A$36–A$45	A$46–A$65	over A$65
Hotels Under A$201	A$201–A$300	A$301–A$450	over A$450

Restaurant prices are the average cost of a main course at dinner or, if dinner isn't served, at lunch. Hotel prices are the lowest cost of a standard double room in high season.

TOURS

SIGHTSEEING TOURS

FAMILY **City Sightseeing Sydney.** This fleet of brightly colored double-decker buses (with open tops) follows two routes: the Sydney route has 25 stops, and the Bondi and Bays has 10 stops. Both trips take 90 minutes. Sydney trips depart Circular Quay at 8:30 am daily (last bus departs at 7:30 pm); the Bondi bus departs Eddy Avenue, Central Station at 9 am daily (last bus at 7:30 pm). ■TIP→ **These days the operators are adding the Bondi and Bays trip at no extra charge—meaning the two trips will cost A$40 if taken in a 24-hour period, which is good value, and A$60 if taken over a 48-hour period.** ⊠ *Sydney* ☏ *02/9567–8400* ⊕ *www.theaustralianexplorer.com.au* ✉ *From A$40.*

Mount 'n Beach Safaris. This operator runs tours to the Blue Mountains and minicoaches around Sydney and the Hunter Valley, from A$118. The company's most popular tour, The Blue Mountains 4WD Canyon and Wildlife Discovery (A$251), provides the opportunity to see koalas and kangaroos, have morning tea in the bush, and explore the highlights of the Blue Mountains. ⊠ *Sydney* ☏ *02/9972–0899* ⊕ *www.mountnbeachsafaris.com.au* ✉ *From A$118.*

Oz Jet Boating. These bright red boats are the most distinctive of the jet boats operating on Sydney Harbour. The bow is painted with huge white teeth to resemble a shark. The 30-minute rides, at 75 kph (47 mph), zip past the Opera House, Harbour Bridge, and Clark and Shark islands, and perform 270-degree spins. Despite passengers being issued hooded raincoats, they always get wet. At least two trips run every day (at noon and 3) and more on the weekends and in summertime. Rides are A$79, and occasional discounts (for Internet bookings) are offered in the winter and spring. ⊠ *Sydney Harbour, Circular Quay, Eastern Pontoon, Sydney Harbour* ☏ *02/9808–3700* ⊕ *www.ozjetboating.com.au* ✉ *From A$79.*

SPECIAL-INTEREST TOURS

Aboriginal Heritage Tour. The Aboriginal Heritage Tour (A$38) is a tour of the Royal Botanic Gardens' display of plants that were growing before Europeans arrived on Sydney's shores in 1788. The tour, which operates Friday at 10 am (1½ hours duration), is led by an Aboriginal guide who explains the plants and their uses and bush foods. ⊠ *Royal Botanic Gardens, Mrs. Macquaries Rd., Circular Quay* ✛ *Tours depart from info booth outside Garden Shop at Palm Grove Centre* ☏ *02/9231–8134,* ⊕ *www.rbgsyd.nsw.gov.au/What-s-On/Aboriginal-heritage-tours* ✉ *From A$38.*

Bass and Flinders Cruises. You can go whale-watching from Sydney Harbour with Bass and Flinders Cruises. Boats leave from mid-May to early December, venturing a few miles outside Sydney Heads. Two-, three-, and four-hour cruises are available, and tours start from A$65, although online discounts are often available. ⊠ *Cockle Bay Marina, Darling Harbour* ☏ *02/9583–1199* ⊕ *www.whalewatchingsydney.net* ✉ *From A$65 (A$58.50 online).*

Bonza Bikes. Bonza Bikes lets you see the best Sydney sights without having to worry about heavy traffic. The half-day Classic Sydney Tour cruises past the Opera House, winds around the harbor, and cycles through the Royal Botanic Gardens. A bike and helmet are included on all tours. ⊠ *30 Harrington St., The Rocks* ☎ *02/9247–8800* ⊕ *www.bonzabiketours.com* ✉ *From A$119.*

Fodor's Choice
★
BridgeClimb. This unique tour affords the ultimate view of the harbor and city center from Sydney Harbour Bridge. The hugely popular tours take 3½ hours and start at A$218, with sunrise, day, sunset, and night-time tours available. They are all worth doing, but for sheer romance, the night tour is hard to beat—and the cheapest full-climb experience. An option for those on a budget or with a fear of heights is the 90-minute BridgeClimb Sampler, which takes climbers within the bridge's inner arch to a point around halfway to the top. Prices are higher during the peak season December 25–January 14 inclusive. ⊠ *5 Cumberland St., The Rocks* ☎ *02/8274–7777* ⊕ *www.bridgeclimb.com* ✉ *From A$148.*

Easyrider Motorbike Tours. Ride as a passenger on a Harley-Davidson on an exciting chauffeur-driven Harley-Davidson tour to the city's landmarks, the beaches, and rural areas. A 15-minute ride is A$35, and a two-hour tour is A$190 per person; a six-hour trip taking in the Blue Mountains' best views is A$350, while an eight-hour trip to the South Coast and the lovely town of Berry starts at A$410. ⊠ *The Rocks Market, George St., at Hickson Rd., The Rocks* ☎ *1300/882065* ⊕ *www.easyrider.com.au* ✉ *From A$35.*

Fodor's Choice
★
Sydney Pub Tours. This tour lets visitors drink in Sydney's history at five historic—and unique—pubs in The Rocks, and dine on some unusual pizzas during a 3½-hour jaunt. Operated by history-lover Gary West—a man who relishes handcrafted beers—the walking tour sets off from the Mercantile Hotel at 6 pm. It is designed for those who want to learn more about The Rocks' fascinating history (rather than party-types). Gary regales folks with tales of 19th-century rum smuggling and the quirky characteristics of each watering hole. There's a visit to one of the cellars, which is normally off-limits to the public. Adventurous diners might like to order the kangaroo or even crocodile pizza at the Australian Heritage Hotel. Nonbeer drinkers are offered wine or a soft drink at each pub. ⊠ *Mercantile Hotel, 25 George St., The Rocks* ☎ *0419/669–832 Gary's mobile* ⊕ *www.sydneypubtours.com* ✉ *A$125* ⊘ *Tours depart weekdays 6 pm.*

Sydney Seaplanes. A flight on Sydney Seaplanes is a wonderful way to see Sydney's sights and soar over beaches. Short flights taking in the harbor, Bondi Beach, and Manly cost from A$200 per person. The seaplanes take off from Rose Bay. ⊠ *1 Vickery Ave., Rose Bay* ☎ *02/9388–1978, 1300/732752* ⊕ *www.seaplanes.com.au* ✉ *From A$200.*

SYDNEY BY BOAT

Aboriginal Culture Cruise. Former Sydney tugboat the *Mari Nawi* is owned by the Tribal Warrior Association, an organization committed to empowering disadvantaged Aboriginal people. They operate cultural cruises year-round, showing passengers the sights and telling stories associated with tribes including the Eora, Cadigal, and Wangal, who inhabited areas around Sydney Harbour. After departing from Circular Quay, the cruises head to Clark Island for a traditional welcoming ceremony and dance performance. Back on board, passengers are shown cultural landmarks, fishing spots, and ancient rock carvings. The two-hour cruises cost A$60 per person and depart Saturdays April–September at 1 pm and October–March at 3 pm. The cruise departs from Eastern Pontoon, Circular Quay. ⊠ *Eastern Pontoon, Circular Quay, Sydney Harbour* ☎ *02/9699–3491* ⊕ *www.tribalwarrior.org* ⏍ *From $A60.*

Aussie Water Taxis. A fun, fast, but somewhat expensive way to get around is by water taxi. (Circular Quay to Manly, for example, costs A$180 for four people, and A$10 for each extra person.) One company, Aussie Water Taxis, runs a taxi shuttle between Darling Harbour and the Opera House for A$15 one-way, A$25 return. Minitours of the harbor in these little yellow taxi boats begin at A$35 per person for 45 minutes. ⊠ *Cockle Bay Wharf, Darling Harbour* ☎ *02/9211–7730* ⊕ *www.aussiewatertaxis.com* ⏍ *From $15.*

Fodor's Choice ★ **Captain Cook Cruises.** The best introduction to Sydney Harbour is Captain Cook's two-hour Harbour Story Cruise (A$39), which follows the southern shore to Watsons Bay, crosses to the north shore to explore Middle Harbour, and returns to Circular Quay. Other options include breakfast, lunch, and dinner cruises; and the popular 24-hour Hop-on-Hop-Off ferry service (A$40) to nine stops around the harbor. ☎ *02/9206–1111* ⊕ *www.captaincook.com.au* ⏍ *From A$30.*

Fodor's Choice ★ **Manly Ferry.** There is no finer introduction to the city than a trip aboard one of the commuter ferries that ply Sydney Harbour. The hub of the ferry system is Circular Quay, and ferries dock at the almost 30 wharves around the harbor between about 6 am and 11:30 pm. One of the most popular sightseeing trips is the Manly Ferry, a 30-minute journey from Circular Quay that provides glimpses of harborside mansions and the sandstone cliffs and bushland along the north shore. The one-way Manly Ferry fare is A$7.60, and the Manly Fast Ferry, operated by a private company (⊕ *www.manlyfastferry.com.au*), costs A$17 return, although cheaper if a SmartCard is purchased. ⊠ *Wharf 2, Circular Quay* ☎ *13–1500* ⊕ *www.transportnsw.info* ⏍ *From A$7.60.*

WALKING TOURS

Ghost Tours. The Rocks' dark alleyways can be scary, and The Rocks Ghost Tours make sure people are suitably spooked, as the guides, dressed in long black cloaks and carrying lanterns, regale them with stories of the murders and other nasty goings-on in the early days of the colony. Tours depart nightly at 6:45 (April–September) and 7:45 (October–March) from Cadmans Cottage. ⊠ *Cadmans Cottage, George and Argyle Sts., Circular Quay* ☎ *02/9241–1283* ⊕ *www.ghosttours.com.au* ⏍ *A$45.*

Rocks Walking Tours. Discover Sydney's first European settlement, with an emphasis on the buildings and personalities of the convict period on tours with this operator. The 1½-hour tours leave daily at 10:30 and 1:30. ⊠ *Clocktower Sq., Argyle and Harrington Sts., Shop 4a, The Rocks* ☎ *02/9247–6678* ⊕ *www.rockswalkingtours.com.au* ⏍ *$A25.*

VISITOR INFORMATION

There are information kiosks at locations throughout the city, including Circular Quay (Alfred and Pitt streets), Martin Place (at Elizabeth Street), and Town Hall (at George and Bathurst streets). The Sydney Harbour Foreshore Authority, which manages The Rocks, Darling Harbour, and other harbor precincts, also has an informative website.

The Sydney Visitor Centre is the major source of information for Sydney and New South Wales. There are two locations: The Rocks and Darling Harbour.

Contacts Sydney Harbour Foreshore Authority. ⊠ *Sydney* ☎ *02/9240–8500* ⊕ *www.shfa.nsw.gov.au.* **Sydney Visitor Centre.** ⊠ *Level 2, The Rocks Centre, Argyle and Playfair Sts., The Rocks* ☎ *02/9240–8788, 1800/067676* ⊕ *www. therocks.com.*

EXPLORING

Sydney is a giant, stretching nearly 80 km (50 miles) from top to bottom and about 70 km (43 miles) across. The harbor divides the city into northern and southern halves, with most of the headline attractions on the south shore. Most travelers spend their time on the harbor's south side, within an area bounded by Chinatown in the south, Harbour Bridge in the north, Darling Harbour to the west, and the beaches and coastline to the east. North of Harbour Bridge lie the important commercial center of North Sydney and leafy but somewhat bland suburbs. Ocean beaches, Taronga Zoo, Ku-ring-gai Chase National Park, and great shopping in the village of Mosman are the most likely reasons to venture north of the harbor.

Within a few hours' drive of Sydney are the World Heritage–listed Blue Mountains and the renowned Hunter Valley vineyards. Although both these spots are worthy of an overnight stay, they're also close enough to visit on day trips from the city.

SYDNEY HARBOUR

On a bright sunny day there's no more magical sight than glistening Sydney Harbour. The white sails of the Opera House are matched by the dozens of sailing boats skimming across the blue expanse. It's both a hive of activity and blissfully peaceful: It's easy to get away from the bustle in one of this area's many remote little corners. Explore by taking a ferry, walking across the bridge, or hiking around its native bushland edges. But whatever you do, get up close and enjoy the view.

GETTING HERE AND AROUND

Sydney is well served by public transport. Buses travel from a base in Circular Quay through the city center to the inner suburbs of Kings Cross, Darlinghurst, and Surry Hills and to the eastern suburb beaches. Trains travel from Central Station through the city on a circle line (calling at Circular Quay and Town Hall), out to Bondi Junction, over the bridge to the north shore and out to the west. Ferries leave Circular Quay for

Manly, Balmain, Darling Harbour, and other suburbs, while the free 555 shuttle bus does a circuit through the city, calling at the main sights.

TOP ATTRACTIONS

Fort Denison. For a brief time in the early days of the colony, convicts who committed petty offenses were kept on this harbor island, where they existed on such a meager diet that the island was named Pinchgut. Fortification of the island began in 1841, but was abandoned when cash ran out. It was finally completed in 1857, when fears of Russian expansion in the Pacific spurred the government on. Today the firing of the fort's cannon doesn't signal imminent invasion, but merely the hour—one o'clock. New South Wales National Parks and Wildlife Service runs half-hour tours at Fort Denison. Purchase tickets from either the NSW National Parks office (☎ 1300/072757) or at Captain Cook Cruises' booth at Jetty 6, Circular Quay; the ferries depart for the island from 10:30 am to 4 pm daily from Jetty 6. Those arriving on the island by water taxi or other boat transport have the option to buy tour-only tickets, on a stand-by basis, for A$15.50. The island also has a restaurant, open daily from 11:30 to 3 (☎ 02/9361–5208). ✉ Circular Quay, Alfred St., Jetty 6, Sydney Harbour ☎ 1300/072757 ⊕ www.nationalparks.nsw.gov.au; www.fortdenison.com.au ⬛ Tours from A$15.50 ⊙ Tours run daily at 11, 12:15, 1:45, and 2:45.

Giraffes at the Sydney's world-class Toronga Zoo.

Quarantine Station. From the 1830s onward, ship passengers who arrived with contagious diseases were isolated on this outpost in the shadow of North Head until pronounced free of illness. You can access the station as part of a guided tour, and now stay overnight in the four-star hotel and cottage accommodation known as Q Station; there are also two waterfront restaurants. There are day tours and five different evening ghost tours (the station reputedly has its fair share of specters) that depart from the visitor center at the Quarantine Station, and a "ghostly sleep-over" for those who want to spent the night in reputedly haunted rooms. Tours are led by rangers from NSW National Parks and involve a fair bit of walking, so good shoes are a must. Reservations are essential. ■ TIP→ Visitors can also visit the site without taking a tour, however, if you want to dine, you must make prior restaurant reservations. ⊠ *North Head, North Head Scenic Dr., Manly ⊹ Take ferry to Manly from Circular Quay, then Bus 135 to site. Or catch Q Station's complimentary bus shuttle near taxi rank on Belgrave St. opposite Manly Wharf* ☎ *02/9466–1500, 02/9466–1551 tour bookings* ⊕ *www.qstation.com.au* ✉ *Day tour A$15, ghost tours A$38–A$125, Quarantine Story A$35* ⊙ *Visitor center and museum open daily 10 am; Quarantine Story tour weekends 2 pm; adult ghost tours Wed., Thurs., and weekends 8 pm; family ghost tour Fri. at 6 pm.*

Fodor'sChoice
★ **Sydney Harbour National Park.** This massive park is made up of 958 acres of separate foreshores and islands, most of them on the north side of the harbor. To see the best areas, put on your walking shoes and head out on the many well-marked trails. The Hermitage Foreshore Walk skirts through bushland around Vaucluse's Nielsen Park. On the north side of

the harbor, Bradleys Head and Chowder Head Walk is a 5-km (3-mile) stroll that starts from Taronga Zoo Wharf. The most inspiring trail is the 9½-km (6-mile) Manly Scenic Walkway, which joins the Spit Bridge with Manly by meandering along sandstone headlands, small beaches, and pockets of rain forest, and past Aboriginal sites and the historic Grotto Point Lighthouse. You can take day tours of two harbor islands, Fort Denison and Goat Island, which have interesting colonial history and buildings. Call The New South Wales National Parks and Wildlife Service for tickets. You can also visit Shark Island (off Rose Bay) on a cruise with Captain Cook Cruises (A$20) departing daily from Jetty 6 at Circular Quay. The other two islands in the harbor park—Rodd and Clark—are recreational reserves that can be visited with permission from the NSW Parks and Wildlife and payment of a landing fee of A$7 per person. Visitors are allowed on these islands in small groups only, between 9 am and sunset or until 8 pm in summer. As there is no public transport, access is via private vessel, or water taxi. Water taxi fares cost around A$80 to A$120 for six passengers one-way. ■TIP➔ The landing fee is included when you book a tour or a Captain Cook Cruises ferry tour. ⊠ *Jetty 6, Alfred St., The Rocks* ☎ *1300/072757* ⊕ *www. nationalparks.nsw.gov.au.*

FAMILY **Taronga Zoo.** Sydney's zoo, in a natural bush area on the harbor's north shore, houses an extensive collection of Australian fauna, including everybody's favorite marsupial, the koala. The zoo has taken great care to create spacious enclosures that simulate natural habitats. The hillside setting is steep in parts, and a complete tour can be tiring, but you can use the map distributed free at the entrance gate to plan a leisurely route. The views of the harbor are stunning. Use of children's strollers (the basic model) is free. The best way to get here from the city is by ferry from Circular Quay or Darling Harbour. From Taronga Wharf a bus or the cable car will take you up the hill to the main entrance. The ZooPass, a combined ferry-zoo ticket (A$53) is available at Circular Quay. You can also stay overnight at the zoo in what's billed as the "wildest slumber party in town." The "Roar and Snore" program includes a night tour, two behind-the-scenes tours, drinks, dinner, breakfast, and luxury tent accommodation at A$288 per adult on weeknights and A$320 per adult on Friday/Saturday. Other special programs include being a "Keeper for a Day." ⊠ *Bradleys Head Rd., Mosman* ☎ *02/9969–2777* ⊕ *www.taronga.org.au* ⊠ *A$46* ⊙ *Sept.– Apr., daily 9:30–5; May–Aug., daily 9:30–4:30.*

■ NEED A BREAK? **Nielsen Park Kiosk & Restaurant.** Hikers completing the Hermitage Foreshore Walk can pull up a chair at the lovely Nielsen Park Kiosk & Restaurant to soak in fabulous harbor views and watch the sailing boats. Both kiosk and restaurant are open daily; the former serves casual takeaway snacks such as fish-and-chips, sandwiches, coffee, and pastries (which can be eaten at the kiosk's outside tables or in the park). The adjacent upscale restaurant is open for breakfast and lunch and specializes in seafood—Atlantic salmon with coconut broth or seafood chowder may grace the seasonal menu. A more casual dining option during summer is the takeaway Twilight Fish and Chips (Friday to Sunday from 4 pm until sunset) at the park's Shark Beach Kiosk. Take the 325 bus from Circular Quay (which will be signposted to Watsons Bay) and tell the driver where you want to get off. ⊠ *Greycliffe Ave., Vaucluse* ☎ *02/9337–7333* ⊕ *www. nielsenpark.com.au* ☯ *Tues.–Fri. 8:30–4, weekends 8–4.*

Vaucluse. The palatial homes in this glamorous harbor suburb provide a glimpse of Sydney's high society. The small beaches at Nielsen Park and Parsley Bay are safe for swimming and provide wonderful views. Both beaches are packed with families in summer. ⊠ *Vaucluse.*

Vaucluse House. The suburb takes its name from the 1803 Vaucluse House, one of Sydney's most illustrious remaining historic mansions. The 15-room Gothic Revival house and its lush gardens, managed by Sydney Living Museums (previously called Historic Houses Trust), are open to the public. The tearooms, built in the style of an Edwardian conservatory, are popular spots for lunch and afternoon tea on weekends. Events are regularly held at the "House" including vintage Sundays (where visitors can picnic in the grounds and dress up in costumes from various eras, such as Victorian and Edwardian) and Christmas-carol singing. ⊠ *Wentworth Rd., Vaucluse* ✛ *Take Bus 325 from Circular Quay bus stand* ☎ *02/9388–7922* ⊕ *www.vauclusehousetearooms. com.au* ☐ *A$8* ☯ *Feb.–late Dec., Fri.–Sun. 11–4; Jan. and NSW school holidays, daily 11–4.*

WORTH NOTING

Garden Island. Although it's still known as an "island," this promontory was connected with the mainland in 1942. During the 1941–45 War of the Pacific (WWII and a number of preceding conflicts), Australia's largest naval base and dockyard was a frontline port for Allied ships. Part of the naval base is now open to the public. Access, seven days a week, to the site is via ferry from Circular Quay (take the Watsons Bay ferry). Visitors can view the museum and picnic on the hill. The Naval Historical Society runs tours to the "secure" section of Garden Island and these must be booked well in advance. The 90-minute tours (A$15) run every Thursday and include morning tea and a video. Bookings are made by calling the society or through the website. ⊠ *Garden Island* ✛ *Take ferry from Circular Quay to Watsons Bay and ask to be let off at Garden Island. No buses go directly to Garden Island. To walk, catch train from Central or Town Hall to Kings Cross station, then walk down either Macleay or Victoria street toward harbor (or north). At end of Victoria St. is flight of stone steps that leads down to Woolloomooloo, near Garden Island* ☎ *02/9359–2003* ⊕ *www.navyhistory.org.au.*

Kirribilli. Residences in this attractive suburb opposite the city and Opera House have million-dollar views—and prices to match. Two of Sydney's most important mansions stand here. The more modest of the two is **Kirribilli House,** the official Sydney home of the prime minister, which, along with Admiralty House, is open to the public once a year. ⊠ *Kirribilli.*

Admiralty House. Next door and far more prominent is Admiralty House—the Sydney residence of the governor-general, the Queen's

The boardwalk around Sydney Cove on a typical sunny day

representative in Australia. This impressive residence is occasionally open for inspection. Both houses can be viewed (from the water) during harbor cruises. ⊠ *Kirribilli Ave., Kirribilli* ⊕ *Both Kirribilli and Admiralty House are at harbor end of Kirribilli Ave.; to get there take ferry from Circular Quay to either Kirribilli Wharf or Milson's Point Wharf, or take train from Town Hall to Milson's Point Station. The No. 267 bus does a loop from McMahon's Point to North Sydney via Kirribilli. There is no public access to either of these grand houses.*

Middle Harbour. Except for the yachts moored in the sandy coves, the upper reaches of Middle Harbour are almost exactly as they were when the first Europeans set eyes on Port Jackson more than 200 years ago. Tucked away in idyllic bushland are tranquil suburbs just a short drive from the city. ⊠ *Middle Harbour* ⊕ *The focal point of Middle Harbour is Spit Bridge. To get there, take train from either Central or Town Hall station to Milson's Point then take Bus 229 to Spit Bridge. From Spit Bridge walk to Manly and view most of beautiful Middle Harbour.*

Middle Head. Despite its benign appearance today, Sydney Harbour once bristled with armaments. In the mid-19th century, faced with expansionist European powers hungry for new colonies, the authorities erected artillery positions on the headlands to guard harbor approaches. One of Sydney's newest open spaces, Headland Park, has opened on a former military base. A walking track winds past fortifications, tunnels, and heritage buildings, several of which are now used as cafés, including the Tea Room Gunners' Barracks. The Sydney Harbour Federation Trust runs guided tours of the park on the first Sunday of the month at 10:45 am. ⊠ *1200 Middle Head Rd., Mosman* ⊕ *Several buses travel from* *central Sydney to Mosman, Balmoral, and Chowder Bay, which are all suburbs within Middle Head area and close to Headland Park. They include Buses 244, 245, 246, and 247 ☎ 02/8969–2100 Harbour Trust ⊕ www.harbourtrust.gov.au ☑ Free; A$8 for guided tour.*

NEED A BREAK?

Tea Room Gunners Barracks. Housed in a beautiful sandstone building that served a number of military purposes for over 130 years, the Tea Room Gunners Barracks has breathtaking views of the harbor and the surrounding gardens and bushland. Their traditional afternoon tea (A$45) is a great way to relax after exploring the armaments of Middle Head. ✉ *202 Suakin Dr., Mosman* ☎ *02/8962–5900* ⊕ *www.gunnersbarracks.com.au* ⊙ *Tea from 10 am daily; lunch weekdays.*

Rose Bay. This large bay, the biggest of Sydney Harbour's 66 bays, was once a base for the Qantas flying boats that provided the only passenger air service between Australia and America and Europe. The last flying boat departed from Rose Bay in the 1960s, but the "airstrip" is still used by floatplanes on scenic flights connecting Sydney with the Hawkesbury River and the central coast. It's a popular place for joggers, who pound the pavement of New South Head Road, which runs along the bay. ✉ *New South Head Rd., Rose Bay* ⊹ *Take Bus 325 from Circular Quay, or take ferry to Watsons Bay (it stops at Rose Bay).*

Fodor'sChoice
★

Sydney Cove. Bennelong Point and the Sydney Opera House to the east and Circular Quay West and The Rocks to the west enclose this cove, which was named after Lord Sydney, the British home secretary at the time the colony was founded. The settlement itself was to be known as New Albion, but the name never caught on. Instead, the city took its name from this tiny bay. ✉ *Sydney Cove* ⊹ *Take train from Central or Town Hall to Circular Quay railway station; or take any number of buses to Circular Quay from all over Sydney. Ferries travel to Circular Quay from many different parts of Sydney, including north side of harbor, Rose Bay, Balmain, and Parramatta. Circular Quay is right in middle of Sydney Cove.*

Fodor'sChoice
★

Watsons Bay. Established as a military base and fishing settlement in the colony's early years, Watsons Bay is a charming suburb, with a popular waterfront pub, that has held on to its village ambience despite the exorbitant prices paid for tiny cottages here. Unlike Watsons Bay's tranquil harbor side, the side that faces the ocean is dramatic and tortured, with the raging sea dashing against the sheer, 200-foot sandstone cliffs of The Gap. ✉ *Military Rd., Watsons Bay.*

Macquarie Lighthouse. When the sun shines, the 15-minute cliff-top stroll along South Head Walkway between The Gap and the Macquarie Lighthouse affords some of Sydney's most inspiring views. Convict-architect Francis Greenway (jailed for forgery) designed the original lighthouse here, Australia's first, in 1818. Visitors climb the 100 stairs to the top of the lighthouse on guided tours (20 minutes duration; A$5) that are run every two months by the Sydney Harbour Federation Trust. Call or check the website for dates and bookings. ✉ *Old South Head Rd., Vaucluse* ⊹ *To reach Watsons Bay either take ferry from Circular Quay or Bus 324 or 325 from Circular Quay. Bus 324 goes past lighthouse* ☎ *02/8969–2100* ⊕ *www.harbourtrust.gov.au.*

THE ROCKS

The Rocks is the birthplace not just of Sydney, but of modern Australia. Here the 11 ships of the First Fleet, the first of England's 800-plus ships carrying convicts to the penal colony, dropped anchor in 1788. This stubby peninsula enclosing the western side of Sydney Cove became known simply as The Rocks.

Most of the architecture here dates from the Victorian era, by which time Sydney had become a thriving port. Warehouses lining the waterfront were backed by a row of tradesmen's shops, banks, and taverns, and above them, ascending Observatory Hill, rose a tangled mass of alleyways lined with the cottages of seamen and wharf laborers. By the late 1800s The Rocks was a rough and squalid area. Conditions were so bad that as late as 1900 the black plague swept through The Rocks, prompting the government to offer a bounty for dead rats in an effort to exterminate their disease-carrying fleas.

Today The Rocks is hardly the run-down area it once was. Since the 1970s it's been transformed into a hot spot of cafés, restaurants, and quaint boutiques, and it's one of the city's most popular destinations. And because it's Sydney's most historic area, the old architecture has been beautifully maintained.

GETTING HERE AND AROUND

You can take the train or any number of buses to Circular Quay and then walk to The Rocks. From Bondi and Paddington, take the 380, 382, or 333 bus to Circular Quay via Elizabeth Street. From Clovelly, take the 339 bus all the way to The Rocks, via Central Station. Once there, the best way to get around is on foot—there are quite a few sandstone steps and narrow alleyways to navigate, and your feet are your best friends.

TOP ATTRACTIONS

Argyle Cut. Argyle Street, which links Argyle Place and George Street, is dominated by the Argyle Cut and its massive walls. In the days before the Cut (tunnel) was made, the sandstone ridge here was a major barrier to traffic crossing between Circular Quay and Millers Point. In 1843 convict work gangs hacked at the sandstone with hand tools for 2½ years before the project was abandoned due to lack of progress. Work restarted in 1857, when drills, explosives, and paid labor completed the job. On the lower side of the Cut an archway leads to the **Argyle Stairs,** which begin the climb from Argyle Street up to the Sydney Harbour Bridge walkway. There's a spectacular view from the South East Pylon. ⊠ *Argyle Pl., Millers Point.*

Campbell's Cove. Robert Campbell was a Scottish merchant who is sometimes referred to as the "father of Australian commerce." Campbell broke the stranglehold that the British East India Company exercised over seal and whale products, which were New South Wales's only exports in those early days. The cove's atmospheric sandstone **Campbell's Storehouse,** built from 1838 onward, now houses waterside restaurants. The pulleys that were used to hoist cargoes still hang on the upper level of the warehouses. The cove is also the mooring for Sydney's

The Rocks and Sydney Harbour Bridge

fully operational tall ships, which conduct theme cruises around the harbor. ⊠ *Campbell's Storehouse, 7–27 Circular Quay West, The Rocks.*

Fodor's Choice
★

Sydney Harbour Bridge. Despite its nickname "the coat hanger," the bridge has a fond place in all Sydneysiders' hearts. Its opening on March 19, 1932 (during the height of the Great Depression), lifted the spirits of citizens and provided some very unexpected theater. As NSW Premier Jack Lang waited to cut the ribbon, Captain Francis de Groot, a member of the paramilitary New Guard, galloped up on his horse, drew his sword, and slashed the ribbon first.

There are several ways to experience the bridge and its spectacular views. One way is through the South East Pylon. To reach this city-side pylon of the Sydney Harbour Bridge, walk along the bridge's pedestrian pathway. Access is from stairs on Cumberland Street, The Rocks (near BridgeClimb). This structure houses a display on the bridge's construction, and you can climb the 200 steps to the lookout and its unbeatable harbor panorama.

A second (more expensive) way is through the BridgeClimb tour. Not for those afraid of heights, the BridgeClimb tour takes you on a guided walking tour to the very top of Harbour Bridge, 439 feet above sea level. The cost is A$218 per person for a night climb midweek and A$258 for a day climb, with slightly higher prices on weekends.

EXPLORING THE ROCKS ON FOOT

Begin at Circular Quay, the lively waterfront ferry terminal, and walk west toward Harbour Bridge, passing the Museum of Contemporary Art, and climb the few stairs into George Street. Pass the historic Fortune of War pub, then as you round the corner head down the sandstone stairs on the right to **Campbell's Cove** and its warehouses. The waterfront restaurants and cafés are pleasant spots for a drink or meal. Continue along Hickson Road toward the Sydney Harbour Bridge until you are directly beneath the bridge's massive girders. Walk under the bridge to **Dawes Point Park** for excellent views of the harbor, including the Opera House and the small island of Fort Denison. Now turn your back on the bridge and walk south and west, via Lower Fort Street. Explore Argyle Place and continue walking south, past the **Sydney Observatory**. While you're in the neighborhood, be sure to pick up brochures and city information at the **Sydney Visitor Centre at The Rocks**, on the corner of Argyle and Playfair streets. Turn right at **Nurses Walk**, another of the area's historic and atmospheric backstreets, then left into Surgeons Court, and left again onto George Street. On the left is the handsome sandstone facade of the former Rocks Police Station, now a crafts gallery. From this point, Circular Quay is only a short walk away.

The third option is to walk to the midpoint of the bridge to take in the views free of charge, but be sure to take the eastern footpath, which overlooks the Sydney Opera House. Access is via the stairs on Cumberland Street (near the BridgeClimb meeting point) and close to the Shangri-La Hotel. ⊠ *Cumberland St., The Rocks.*

NEED A BREAK?

Lord Nelson Brewery Hotel. While in the west end of Argyle Place, consider the liquid temptations of the Lord Nelson, which with at least one other contender claims to be Sydney's oldest hotel. (It has been licensed to serve alcohol since 1841.) The sandstone pub has its own brewery on the premises. One of its specialties is Quayle Ale, named after the former U.S. vice president, who "sank a schooner" (drank a beer) here during his 1989 visit to Australia, or try Nelson's Blood (for those who like Irish stouts). ⊠ *19 Kent St., at Argyle St., Millers Point* ☎ *02/9251–4044* ⊕ *www. lordnelsonbrewery.com.*

WORTH NOTING

Argyle Place. With all the traditional requirements of an English green—a pub at one end, a church at the other, and grass in between—this charming enclave in the suburb of Millers Point is unusual for Sydney. Argyle Place is lined with 19th-century houses and cottages on its northern side and overlooked by Observatory Hill to the south. ⊠ *Argyle Pl., Millers Point.*

Cadman's Cottage. Sydney's oldest building, completed in 1816, has a history that outweighs its modest dimensions. John Cadman was a convict who was sentenced for life to New South Wales for stealing a horse. He later became superintendent of government boats, a position that entitled him to live in the upper story of this house. The water once practically lapped at Cadman's doorstep, and the original seawall still stands at the front of the house. The small extension on the side of the cottage was built to lock up the oars of Cadman's boats, since oars would have been a necessity for any convict attempting to escape by sea. The cottage can only be viewed from the outside. ⊠ *110 George St., The Rocks* ☎ *1300/072757* ⊕ *www.environment.nsw.gov.au.*

Customs House. The last surviving example of the elegant sandstone buildings that once ringed Circular Quay, this former customs house now features an amazing model of Sydney under a glass floor. You can walk over the city's skyscrapers, all of which are illuminated by fiber-optic lights. The Customs House has an excellent two-level library, art galleries, and ground-floor bar. The rooftop Café Sydney, the standout in the clutch of restaurants and cafés in this late-19th-century structure, overlooks Sydney Cove. The building stands close to the site where the British flag was first raised on the shores of Sydney Cove in 1788. ⊠ *Customs House Sq., 31 Alfred St., Circular Quay* ☎ *02/9242–8551* ⊕ *www.sydneycustomshouse.com.au* ⊙ *Weekdays 10–7, weekends 11–4.*

Dawes Point Park. The wonderful views of the harbor (and since the 1930s, the Harbour Bridge) have made this park and its location noteworthy for centuries. Named for William Dawes, a First Fleet marine officer and astronomer who established the colony's first basic observatory nearby in 1788, this park was also once the site of a fortification known as Dawes Battery. The cannons on the hillside pointing toward the Opera House came from the ships of the First Fleet. ⊠ *Hickson Rd., The Rocks.*

Lower Fort Street. At one time the handsome Georgian houses along this street, originally a rough track leading from the Dawes Point Battery to Observatory Hill, were among the best addresses in Sydney. Elaborate wrought-iron lacework still graces many of the facades. ⊠ *Lower Fort St., The Rocks.*

Museum of Contemporary Art. This ponderous art deco building houses one of Australia's most important collections of modern art, as well as two significant collections of Aboriginal art, a sculpture garden, and continually changing temporary exhibits. Free tours, talks, and hands-on art workshops are conducted regularly. ⊠ *140 George St., The Rocks* ☎ *02/9245–2400* ⊕ *www.mca.com.au* ⊠ *Free* ⊙ *Fri.–Wed. 10–5, Thurs. 10–9.*

Nurses Walk. Cutting across the site of the colony's first hospital, Nurses Walk acquired its name at a time when "Sydney" and "sickness" were synonymous. Many of the 736 convicts who survived the voyage from Portsmouth, England, aboard the First Fleet's 11 ships arrived suffering from dysentery, smallpox, scurvy, and typhoid. A few days after he landed at Sydney Cove, Governor Phillip established a tent hospital to care for the worst cases. ⊠ *Between Harrington and George Sts., The Rocks* ⊕ *www.therocks.com.*

Observatory Hill. The city's highest point, at 145 feet, was known originally as Windmill Hill, since the colony's first windmill occupied this

breezy spot. Its purpose was to grind grain for flour, but soon after it was built the canvas sails were stolen, the machinery was damaged in a storm, and the foundations cracked. The signal station at the top of the hill was built in 1848. This later became an astronomical observatory. This is a great place for a picnic with a view. ⊠ *Upper Fort St., The Rocks.*

Overseas Passenger Terminal. Busy Circular Quay West is dominated by this multilevel steel-and-glass port terminal, which is often used by visiting cruise ships. There are several excellent waterfront restaurants in the terminal, all with magnificent harbor views. Even if you're not dining in the terminal, it's worth taking the escalator to the upper deck for a good view of the harbor and Opera House. ⊠ *Circular Quay West, The Rocks* ⊕ *www.therocks.com.*

Suez Canal. So narrow that two people can't walk abreast, this alley acquired its name before drains were installed, when rainwater would pour down its funnel-like passageway and gush across George Street. Lanes such as this were once the haunt of the notorious late-19th-century Rocks gangs, when robbery was rife in the area. ⊠ *Harrington and George Sts., The Rocks* ⊕ *www.therocks.com.*

FAMILY **Sydney Observatory.** Originally a signaling station for communicating with ships anchored in the harbor, this handsome building on top of Observatory Hill is now an astronomy museum. During evening observatory shows you can tour the building, watch videos, and get a close-up view of the universe through a 16-inch mirror telescope. The digital Sydney Planetarium showcases the virtual night sky to just 20 visitors at a time in a small theater. Reservations are required for the evening shows only. ⊠ *Watson Rd., Millers Point* ☎ *02/9921–3485* ⊕ *www. sydneyobservatory.com.au* 🗏 *Museum free, daytime show A$10, evening show A$18; Sydney Planetarium A$10* ⊙ *Daily 10–5.*

Sydney Visitor Centre at the Rocks. Known as The Rocks Centre, this ultra-modern space is packed with free maps and brochures, and the friendly staff dispenses valuable information and will book tours, hotel rooms, and bus travel. It's near the popular Löwenbräu Keller, where many tourists gather for a beer. ⊠ *The Rocks Centre, Argyle and Playfair Sts., The Rocks* ☎ *02/9240–8788, 1800/067676* ⊕ *www.therocks.com* ⊙ *Daily 9:30–5:30.*

Upper George Street. The restored warehouses and Victorian terrace houses that line this part of George Street make this a charming section of the Rocks. The covered **Rocks Market** takes place here on weekends. ⊠ *George St., The Rocks.*

DOMAIN AND MACQUARIE STREET

Some of Sydney's most notable Victorian-era public buildings, as well as one of its finest parks, can be found in this area. In contrast to the simple, utilitarian stone convict cottages of The Rocks, these buildings were constructed at a time when Sydney was experiencing a long period of prosperity thanks to the gold rushes of the mid-19th century and an agricultural boom. The sandstone just below the surface of

CLOSE UP

Building Sydney

Descended from Scottish clan chieftains, Governor Lachlan Macquarie was an accomplished soldier and a man of vision. Macquarie, who was in office from 1810 to 1821, was the first governor to foresee a role for New South Wales as a free society rather than an open prison. He laid the foundations for that society by establishing a plan for the city, constructing significant public buildings, and advocating that reformed convicts be readmitted to society.

Macquarie's policies of equality may seem perfectly reasonable today, but in the early 19th century they marked him as a radical. When his vision of a free society threatened to blur distinctions between soldiers, settlers, and convicts, Macquarie was forced to resign. He was later buried on his Scottish estate, his gravestone inscribed with the words "the Father of Australia."

Macquarie's grand plans for the construction of Sydney might have come to nothing had it not been for Francis Greenway. Trained as an architect in England, where he was convicted of forgery and sentenced to 14 years in New South Wales, Greenway received a ticket of prison leave from Macquarie in 1814 and set to work transforming Sydney. Over the next few years he designed lighthouses, hospitals, convict barracks, and many other government buildings, several of which remain to bear witness to his simple but elegant eye. Greenway was eventually even depicted on one side of the old A$10 notes, which went out of circulation early in the 1990s. Only in Australia, perhaps, would a convicted forger occupy pride of place on the currency.

many coastal areas proved an ideal building material—easily honed into the ornamentation so fashionable during the Victorian era. Macquarie Street is Sydney's most elegant boulevard. It was shaped by Governor Macquarie, who planned the transformation of the cart track leading to Sydney Cove into a stylish street of dwellings and government buildings. An occasional modern high-rise breaks up the streetscape, but many of the 19th-century architectural delights here escaped demolition.

GETTING HERE AND AROUND

The area is served by two train stations—Martin Place and St. James—but they are not on the same line. You can catch trains to both stations from Central and Town Hall. St. James is right next to Hyde Park, and Martin Place has an exit on Macquarie Street. From Macquarie Street it's a short walk to the Domain via the passageway that cuts through Sydney Hospital. A number of buses (including the 380/382 and 333 from Bondi Beach and 555 free shuttle) travel along Elizabeth Street.

TOP ATTRACTIONS

Fodor's Choice
★

Art Gallery of New South Wales. Apart from Canberra's National Gallery, this is the best place to explore the evolution of European-influenced Australian art, as well as the distinctly different concepts that underlie Aboriginal art. All the major Australian artists of the last two centuries are represented in this impressive collection. The entrance level,

Domain and
Macquarie Street

KEY

⊢——⊢ Rail Lines

– – – Monorail

where large windows frame spectacular views of the harbor, exhibits 20th century art. Below, in the gallery's major extensions, the Yiribana Gallery displays one of the nation's most comprehensive collections of Aboriginal and Torres Strait Islander art. There are monthly free audio tours and free talks. ⊠ *Art Gallery Rd., The Domain* ☏ *02/9225–1700, 1800/679278* ⊕ *www.artgallery.nsw.gov.au* ✉ *Free; fee for special exhibits* ⊙ *Thurs.–Tues. 10–5, Wed. 10–10.*

Hyde Park Barracks. Before Governor Macquarie arrived, convicts were left to roam freely at night. Macquarie was determined to establish law and order, and in 1819 he commissioned convict-architect Francis Greenway to design this restrained, classically Georgian-style building. Today the Barracks houses compelling exhibits that explore behind the scenes of the prison. For example, a surprising number of relics from this period were preserved by rats, which carried away scraps of clothing and other artifacts for their nests beneath the floorboards. A room on the top floor is strung with hammocks, exactly as it was when the building housed convicts. The barracks are part of the Sydney Living Museums collection of 12 historic buildings. ⊠ *Queens Sq., Macquarie St., The Domain* ☏ *02/8239–2311* ⊕ *www.sydneylivingmuseums.com. au* ✉ *A$10* ⊙ *Daily 10–5.*

Museum of Sydney. This museum
built on the site of the original
Government House documents
Sydney's early period of European
colonization. Aboriginal culture,
convict society, and the gradual
transformation of the settlement
at Sydney Cove are woven into an
evocative portrayal of life in the
country's early days. A glass floor
in the lobby reveals the foundations
of the original structure. One of the
most intriguing exhibits, however,
is outside (and free): the striking
Edge of the Trees sculpture, where
Koori (Aboriginal) voices recite

> **ART AND ANGST**
>
> If you like a bit of controversy
> with your culture, head to the
> Art Gallery of New South Wales
> to view the finalists in the
> annual **Archibald Prize** (⊕ *www.*
> *thearchibaldprize.com.au*). Each
> year since 1921, the competition
> has attracted plenty of drama as
> everyone debates the merits of
> the winners. Prizes are announced
> in early March, and the exhibition
> hangs until mid-May.

Sydney place names as you walk around and through the collection
of 29 wood, iron, and sandstone pillars. ⊠ *Bridge and Phillip Sts.,*
The Domain ☎ *02/9251–5988* ⊕ *www.sydneylivingmuseums.com.au*
🖼 *A$10* ☉ *Daily 10–5.*

WORTH NOTING

Garden Palace Gates. These gates are all that remain of the Garden Palace, a massive glass pavilion that was erected for the Sydney International Exhibition of 1879 and destroyed by fire three years later. On the
arch above the gates is a depiction of the Garden Palace's dome. Stone
pillars on either side of the gates are engraved with Australian wildflowers. ⊠ *Macquarie St., between Bridge and Bent Sts., The Domain.*

NEED A BREAK?

Hyde Park Barracks Café. On a sunny day the courtyard tables of the
Hyde Park Barracks Café provide one of the city's finest places to enjoy an
outdoor lunch or morning or afternoon tea. The café and indoor restaurant
serve light fare, full meals, and delicious desserts such as the Belgian milk
chocolate and Grand Marnier Ganache tart pudding with espresso gelato.
There's also an extensive Australian wine list. ⊠ *Queens Sq., Macquarie*
St., The Domain ☎ *02/9222–1815* ⊕ *www.hydeparkbarrackscafe.com.au*
☉ *Weekdays 8–3, weekends 9–3.*

St. James' Church. Begun in 1819, the colonial Georgian–style St. James'
is the oldest surviving church in the City of Sydney, and another fine
Francis Greenway design. Now lost among the skyscrapers, the church's
tall spire once served as a landmark for ships entering the harbor.
Plaques commemorating Australian explorers and administrators cover
the interior walls. Half-hour lunchtime concerts are presented every
Wednesday from late February to late December at 1:15. ⊠ *Queens Sq.,*
173 King St., Hyde Park ☎ *02/8227–1300* ⊕ *www.sjks.org.au* ☉ *Week-*
days 10–4, Sat. 9–1, Sun. 7:30–4.

State Library of New South Wales. This large complex is based around
the Mitchell and Dixson libraries, which make up the world's largest
collection of Australiana. Enter the foyer through the classical portico

to see one of the earliest maps of Australia, a copy in marble mosaic of a map made by Abel Tasman, the Dutch navigator, in the mid-17th century. Through the glass doors lies the vast Mitchell Library reading room, but you need a reader's ticket (establishing that you are pursuing legitimate research) to enter. You can, however, take a free escorted history and heritage tour weekdays at 10:30 am. The library continuously runs free exhibitions, and the opulent Shakespeare Room is open to the public Tuesday 10–4. Inquire at the reception desk of the general reference library on Macquarie Street. ⊠ *Macquarie St., between Royal Botanic Gardens and Parliament House, The Domain* ☎ *02/9273–1414* ⊕ *www.sl.nsw.gov.au* ☼ *Mon.–Thurs. 9–8, Fri. 9–5, weekends 10–5 (Mitchell Library closed Sun.).*

State Parliament House. The simple facade and shady verandas of this Greenway-designed 1816 building, formerly the Rum Hospital, typify Australian colonial architecture. From 1829, two rooms of the old hospital were used for meetings of the executive and legislative councils, which had been set up to advise the governor. These advisory bodies grew in power until New South Wales became self-governing in the 1840s, at which time Parliament occupied the entire building. The Legislative Council Chamber—the upper house of the parliament, identifiable by its red color scheme—is a prefabricated cast-iron structure that was originally intended to be a church on the goldfields of Victoria.

State Parliament generally sits between mid-February and late May, and again between mid-September and late November. You can visit the public gallery and watch the local version of the Westminster system of democracy in action. When parliament is not sitting, you can take a free escorted tour (they are conducted on the first Thursday of the month at 1 pm) or walk around at your leisure and view the large collection of portraits and paintings. You must reserve ahead for tours and to sit in the public gallery. ⊠ *6 Macquarie St., The Domain* ☎ *02/9230–2111* ⊕ *www.parliament.nsw.gov.au* ☼ *Weekdays 9–5; hrs vary when Parliament is in session—call ahead.*

Sydney Hospital. Completed in 1894 to replace the main Rum Hospital building, which had stood on the site since 1811, this institution provided an infinitely better medical option. By all accounts, admission to the Rum Hospital was only slightly preferable to death itself. Convict nurses stole patients' food, and abler patients stole from the weaker. The kitchen sometimes doubled as a mortuary, and the table was occasionally used for operations.

In front of the hospital is a bronze figure of a boar. This is *Il Porcellino*, a copy of a statue that stands in Florence, Italy. According to the inscription, if you make a donation in the coin box and rub the boar's nose, "you will be endowed with good luck." Sydney citizens seem to be a superstitious bunch, because the boar's nose is very shiny indeed. ⊠ *8 Macquarie St., The Domain* ☎ *02/9382–7111.*

Sydney has enough museums and art galleries to appeal to just about every taste.

THE OPERA HOUSE AND THE ROYAL BOTANIC GARDENS

Bordering Sydney Cove, Farm Cove, and Woolloomooloo Bay, this section of Sydney includes the iconic Sydney Opera House, as well as extensive and delightful harborside gardens and parks.

The colony's first farm was established here in 1788, and the botanical gardens were laid out in 1816. The most dramatic change to the area occurred in 1959, however, when ground was broken on the site for the Sydney Opera House at Bennelong Point. This promontory was originally a small island, then the site of 1819 Fort Macquarie, later a tram depot, and finally the Opera House, one of the world's most striking modern buildings. The area's evolution is an eloquent metaphor for Sydney's own transformation.

GETTING HERE AND AROUND

The best way to get to the Opera House is to take one of the many ferries, buses, or trains that go to Circular Quay and then walk the pedestrian concourse. Some buses travel down Macquarie Street to the Opera House, which involves a slightly shorter walk. To get to the Royal Botanic Gardens, take the CityRail suburban train from the Town Hall, Central, or Bondi Junction station to Martin Place station, exit on the Macquarie Street side, and walk a few hundred yards.

TOP ATTRACTIONS

Farm Cove. The shallow bay east of the Opera House is called Farm Cove. The original convict-settlers established their first gardens on this bay's shores. The enterprise was not a success: the soil was too sandy for agriculture, and most of the crops fell victim to pests, marauding

The Opera House and the Royal Botanic Gardens

animals, and hungry convicts. The long seawall was constructed from the 1840s onward to enclose the previously swampy foreshore. The area is now home to the Royal Botanic Gardens, a wonderful place to escape the city bustle. ⊠ *Sydney* ✚ *Enter Botanic Gardens through gates near Opera House and in Macquarie St. From Opera House, turn right and walk along harbor foreshore (seawall is on your left, Botanic Gardens on your right). To enter Macquarie St. gates, take train to Martin Pl. railway station, exit station, turn left, and walk few hundred yards down Macquarie St.*

Fodor'sChoice
★
Royal Botanic Gardens. More than 80 acres of sweeping green lawns, groves of indigenous and exotic trees, duck ponds, greenhouses, and some 45,124 types of plants—many of them in bloom—grace these gardens. The elegant property, which attracts strollers and botany enthusiasts from all over the country, is a far cry today from what it once was: a failed attempt by convicts of the First Fleet to establish a farm. Though their early attempts at agriculture were disastrous, the efforts of these first settlers are acknowledged in the Pioneer Garden, a sunken garden built in their memory.

Among the many other feature gardens on the property are the Palm Grove—home to some of the oldest trees in Sydney, the Begonia Garden, and the Rare and Threatened Plants Garden. Not to be missed is a cutting from the famous Wollemi Pine, a plant thought to be extinct until it was discovered in a secluded gully in the Wollemi National Park in the Blue Mountains in 1994. Plants throughout the gardens have various blooming cycles, so no matter what time of year you visit, there are sure to be plenty of flowers. The gardens include striking sculptures and hundreds of species of birds. There are spectacular views over the harbor and the Opera House from the garden's sea wall and two lovely restaurants are open for lunch and snacks. ■TIP➜ For those who don't want to walk, the ChooChoo Express toylike train offers a 25-minute ride through the gardens, making four stops (A$10).

Completed in 1843, the Government House, in a Gothic Revival building in the Royal Botanic Gardens, served as the residence of the Governor of New South Wales—who represents the British crown in local matters—until the government handed it back to the public in 1996. Prominent English architect Edward Blore designed the two-story building without ever having set foot in Australia. The sandstone house's restored stenciled ceilings are its most impressive feature. Paintings hanging on the walls bear the signatures of some of Australia's best-known artists. You are free to wander on your own around Government House's gardens, which lie within the Royal Botanic Gardens, but you must join a free guided tour to see the house's interior. Tours take 45 minutes and run every 30 minutes from 10:30 am to 3 pm. Only 20 visitors are allowed on each tour. There are also maps available for a variety of themed, self-guided walks. ⊠ *Mrs. Macquaries Rd., The Domain* ☎ *02/9231–8111* ⊕ *www.rbgsyd.nsw.gov.au; www.choochoo.com.au* ✆ *Free* ☉ *Royal Botanic Gardens daily 7–dusk; tours daily 10:30 am.*

Fodor's Choice **Sydney Opera House.** Sydney's most famous landmark (listed as a World
★ Heritage site in 2007) had such a long and troubled construction phase that it's almost a miracle that the building was ever completed. In 1954 the state premier appointed a committee to advise the government on the building of an opera house. The site chosen was Bennelong Point (named after an early Aboriginal inhabitant), which was, until that time, occupied by a tram depot. The premier's committee launched a competition to find a suitable plan, and a total of 233 submissions came in from architects the world over. One of them was a young Dane named Joern Utzon.

His plan was brilliant, but it had all the markings of a monumental disaster. The structure was so narrow that stages would have minuscule wings, and the soaring "sails" that formed the walls and roof could not be built by existing technology.

Nonetheless, Utzon's dazzling, dramatic concept caught the judges' imagination, and construction of the giant podium began in 1959. From the start, the contractors faced a cost blowout; the building that was projected to cost A$7 million and take four years to erect would eventually require A$102 million and 15 years. Construction was financed by an intriguing scheme. Realizing that citizens might be hostile to the use of public funds for the controversial project, the state government raised the money through the Opera House Lottery. For almost a

The Sydney Opera House at night, viewed from The Rocks side of Circular Quay

decade, Australians lined up to buy tickets, and the Opera House was built without depriving the state's hospitals or schools of a single cent.

Initially it was thought that the concrete exterior of the building would have to be cast in place, which would have meant building an enormous birdcage of scaffolding at even greater expense. Then, as he was peeling an orange one day, Utzon had a flash of inspiration. Why not construct the shells from segments of a single sphere? The concrete ribs forming the skeleton of the building could be prefabricated in just a few molds, hoisted into position, and joined together. These ribs are clearly visible inside the Opera House, especially in the foyers and staircases of the Concert Hall.

In 1966 Utzon resigned as Opera House architect and left Australia, reportedly embittered by his dealings with unions and the government. He never returned to see his masterpiece, although he had been invited on several occasions.

A team of young Australian architects carried on, completing the exterior one year later. Until that time, however, nobody had given much thought to the *interior.* The shells created awkward interior spaces, and conventional performance areas were simply not feasible. It's a tribute to the architectural team's ingenuity that the exterior of the building is matched by the aesthetically pleasing and acoustically sound theaters inside. Joern Utzon died in Denmark on November 29, 2008, aged 90. Then Prime Minister Kevin Rudd paid tribute to Utzon's genius in speeches, while the lights of the Opera House sails were dimmed and flags on the Harbor Bridge were flown at half-mast as a mark of respect.

Sydney Opera House showcases all the performing arts in its five theaters, one of which is devoted to opera. The Australian Ballet, the Sydney Dance Company, and the Australian Opera Company also call the Opera House home. The complex includes two stages for theater, two smaller performance venues—the Playhouse and the Studio—and the 2,700-seat Concert Hall, where the Sydney Symphony Orchestra and the Australian Chamber Orchestra perform. The box office is open Monday to Saturday 9–8:30.

Although you can access the building throughout the day and early evening, all you really get to see, unless you have ticket to a performance, is the main foyer area, which is less than inspiring. To see the best of "the house" join one of the guided tours, which include the one-hour Sydney Opera House Tour, departing daily from the lower forecourt level between 9 and 5; the two-hour backstage tour, departing daily at 7 am; and the Tour & Tasting Plate, which is the general tour followed by a three-tier plate of goodies such as Wagyu burgers and fresh seafood from Opera Kitchen restaurant. All tours include discount show tickets. Call in advance for bookings. ⊠ *2 Macquarie St., Circular Quay* ☎ *02/9250–7111, 02/9250–7250 tour bookings* ⊕ *www. sydneyoperahouse.com* ⊠ *General tour A$37, backstage tour A$165, Tour & Tasting Plate A$76.*

WORTH NOTING

FAMILY **Andrew (Boy) Charlton Pool.** This heated saltwater eight-lane swimming pool overlooking the navy ships tied up at Garden Island has become a local favorite. Complementing its stunning location is a radical design in glass and steel. The pool also has a chic terrace café above Woolloomooloo Bay. It's open from September 1 until April 30. ⊠ *1C Mrs. Macquarie's Rd., The Domain* ☎ *02/9358–6686* ⊕ *www.abcpool.org* ⊠ *A$6.20* ◷ *6 am–7 pm (until 8 pm Oct.–late Mar.).*

Mrs. Macquarie's Chair. During the early 1800s, Elizabeth Macquarie often sat on the point in the Domain at the east side of Farm Cove, at the rock where a seat has been hewn in her name. The views across the harbor are sensational. ⊠ *Mrs. Macquarie's Rd., Royal Botanic Gardens.*

NEED A BREAK?

Botanic Gardens Restaurant. Botanic Gardens Restaurant is a lovely place to have lunch during the week or brunch on the weekend. Wide verandas provide tranquil views over the gardens, and the sound of birdsong fills the air. The menu changes seasonally and may include starters such as grilled quail with roast quince, and main dishes of fettuccini with pine forest mushrooms and macadamia nuts. The downstairs café serves lighter more casual fare and is open daily from 8:30 am to 4 (and later in summer). The restaurant is open for lunch from noon weekdays and brunch on the weekends from 9:30, where decadent eggs Benedict is best accompanied by a glass of bubbly. ■TIP→ The restaurant is within the Royal Botanic Gardens; it can be accessed from either the Palace Gate on Macquarie Street or from Lion Gate on Mrs. Macquarie's Road. ⊠ *Royal Botanic Gardens, Mrs. Macquarie's Rd., Royal Botanic Gardens* ☎ *02/9241–2419* ⊕ *www.botanicrestaurant.com.au.*

Mrs. Macquarie's Point. The inspiring views from this point, to the east of Bennelong Point (site of the Opera House), combine with the shady lawns to make this a popular place for picnics. The views are best at dusk, when the setting sun silhouettes the Opera House and the Harbour Bridge. ⊠ *Mrs. Macquarie's Rd., Royal Botanic Gardens.*

DARLING HARBOUR

Until the mid-1980s this horseshoe-shape bay on the city center's western edge was a wasteland of disused docks and railway yards. Then, in an explosive burst of activity the whole area was redeveloped and opened in time for Australia's bicentenary in 1988. Now there's plenty to take in at the Darling Harbour complex: the National Maritime Museum, SEA LIFE Sydney Aquarium, WILD LIFE Sydney Zoo, and the gleaming Exhibition Centre, whose masts and spars recall the square-riggers that once berthed here. At the harbor's center is a large park shaded by palm trees. Waterways and fountains lace the complex together.

GETTING HERE AND AROUND

Take the train to either Town Hall or Central Station. From Town Hall it's a short walk down Druitt Street; from Central you walk through Haymarket and Chinatown. The Light Rail tram (A$3.80 one-way; day pass A$9.60) connects Central Station with Darling Harbour and The Star casino a little farther to the west.

TOP ATTRACTIONS

FAMILY **Australian National Maritime Museum.** The six galleries of this soaring, futuristic building tell the story of Australia and the sea. In addition to figureheads, model ships, and brassy nautical hardware, there are antique racing yachts and the jet-powered *Spirit of Australia,* current holder of the world water speed record, set in 1978. The USA Gallery displays objects from such major U.S. collections as the Smithsonian Institution, and was dedicated by President George Bush Sr. on New Year's Day 1992. An outdoor section showcases numerous vessels moored at the museum's wharves, including the HMAS *Vampire,* a retired Royal Australian Navy destroyer, and the historic tall ship the *James Craig.* You can also climb to the top of the 1874 Bowling Green lighthouse. ⊠ *Maritime Heritage Centre, 2 Murray St., Wharf 7, Darling Harbour* ☎ *02/9298–3777* ⊕ *www.anmm.gov.au* ⊠ *A$7* ☉ *Daily 9:30–5 (until 6 in Jan.).*

Chinatown. Bounded by George Street, Goulburn Street, and Paddy's Market, Chinatown takes your senses on a galloping tour of the Orient. Within this compact grid are aromatic restaurants, traditional apothecaries, Chinese grocers, clothing boutiques, and shops selling Asian-made electronics. The best way to get a sense of the area is to take a stroll along Dixon Street, now a pedestrian mall with a Chinese Lion Gate at either end. Sydney's Chinese community was first established here in the 1800s, in the aftermath of the gold rush that originally drew many Chinese immigrants to Australia. For the next few years the area will be getting a major face-lift that will include new lighting, artwork, and more pedestrian walkways. Most Sydneysiders come here regularly to dine, especially on weekends for dim sum (called *yum cha*). ⊠ *Dixon St., Haymarket.*

Madame Tussauds Sydney. Hugh Jackman as Wolverine, songstress Kylie Minogue, and Olympic champion Cathy Freeman are among the contingent of Australian wax figures at the Madame Tussauds Sydney, the only version of the well-known museum in Australia. Located between SEA LIFE Sydney Aquarium and WILD LIFE Sydney Zoo at Darling Harbour, the museum has nine interactive themed areas where patrons can, for example, jump on a surfboard with world champion female surfer Layne Beachley or sing in the band with legendary Aussie rocker Jimmy Barnes. The 70 figures are grouped in themes such as world leaders, cultural icons, and music and film stars. ■TIP➔ Save more than A$12 on the "walk up" price by buying single-entry tickets or combination tickets (which include any of four other attractions) online. ⊠ *Aquarium Wharf, near Wheat St., Darling Harbour* ☎ *02/8251–7800* ⊕ *www.madametussauds.com/sydney* ⊡ *A$40* ☾ *Daily 9:30–8.*

FAMILY   **SEA LIFE Sydney Aquarium.** Bay of Rays and Shark Valley are among 14 themed areas at SEA LIFE Sydney Aquarium at Darling Harbour. Home to some 13,000 creatures, the huge aquarium also has two of only five dugongs (large, rare marine mammal [similar to a manatee] mainly found off the coast of northern Australia) that are on display anywhere in the world. The Sydney Harbour exhibit shows you what's underneath Sydney's huge expanse of water, while the new open coral tank is dazzlingly colorful. Fish and mammal feedings take place throughout the day, along with talks on some of these amazing creatures. A behind-the-scenes tour is a good value at A$18 over the online admission price. The aquarium is part of the Merlin Entertainments group and good combination ticket deals are available for the company's other attractions that include WILD LIFE Sydney Zoo, the new Madame Tussauds (both located next door to the Aquarium), and the Sydney Tower Eye (A$63). ■ TIP➔ Buy tickets online to save around A$12 on single-entry and various combo deals. ⊠ *Aquarium pier, 1–5 Wheat Rd., Darling Harbour* ☎ *1800/199657* ⊕ *www.sydneyaquarium.com.au* ⊠ *A$40* ☉ *Daily 9:30–7.*

FAMILY **WILD LIFE Sydney Zoo.** This recently renamed Sydney attraction brings thousands of Australian animals right to the heart of Sydney. Kangaroos, koalas, and dozens of other species come together under the one huge roof—in nine separate habitats—next door to the SEA LIFE Sydney Aquarium and the new Madame Tussauds. All three attractions are run by the same operator, Merlin Entertainments, and all are able to be visited on one combination ticket. In Devil's Den you'll see the famed Tasmanian devils; in Wallaby Cliffs there are yellow-footed wallabies and hairy-nosed wombats, while you can walk among the eastern grey kangaroos and agile wallabies with their joeys and the spiky echidnas in Kangaroo Walkabout. Watch out for Rex, the 16-foot saltwater crocodile in the Kakadu Gorge habitat. A popular spot is Gum Tree Alley where you'll meet koalas, while the endangered (and very cute) Greater Bilby is in the Nightfall nocturnal zone. Those who really want to get up close to the critters should book the Breakfast with the Koalas tour (A$55) that takes place on weekend mornings at 7:15 am. It includes zoo entry, private guided tour, hot breakfast on the rooftop surrounded by the furry creatures, and a chance to pose for photographs. ■ TIP➔ The best deals for stand-alone tickets or combination tickets with other Merlin Entertainment attractions are online. There are savings of around A$12 for a single ticket, while the current combo ticket is A$69. ⊠ *Aquarium Pier, Wheat Rd., Darling Harbour* ☎ *1800/206158* ⊕ *www.wildlifesydney.com.au* ⊠ *A$40* ☉ *Apr.–Sept., daily 9:30–5; Oct.–Mar., daily 9:30–6.*

WORTH NOTING

Barangaroo Reserve. This headland park west of Walsh Bay and The Rocks is part of a massive redevelopment of an old wharf area once known as "The Hungry Mile," which refers to the men who, during the Great Depression of the 1930s, went from wharf to wharf in search of work each day. The new name honors a powerful indigenous woman, who was also the wife of Bennelong—an important Aboriginal historical figure. When construction finishes on the adjacent hotel and casino complex (opening in stages 2016–19), you will be able to walk along the water's edge from Darling Harbour, around the Barangaroo headland, past the historic piers of Walsh Bay, underneath the Harbour Bridge and around Circular Quay to the Opera House and all the way to the Royal Botanic Gardens. Even if you don't do the walk, the headland park has lovely views of the western harbor and is a welcome expanse of open green space just behind The Rocks. ✉ *Millers Point* ⊕ *www. barangaroo.sydney.*

Chinese Garden of Friendship. Chinese prospectors came to the Australian goldfields as far back as the 1850s, and the nation's long and enduring links with China are symbolized by the Chinese Garden of Friendship, the largest garden of its kind outside China. Designed by Chinese landscape architects, the garden includes bridges, lakes, waterfalls, sculptures, and Cantonese-style pavilions—the perfect place for a refreshing cup of tea from the café. Free 35-minute guided tours run daily. ✉ *38 Harbour St., Darling Harbour* ☎ *02/9240–8888* ⊕ *www. darlingharbour.com* ✑ *A$6* ⊙ *Daily 9:30–5 (5:30 in summer)* ☞ *Tours run daily 10:30 and 2:30 Oct.–Apr., noon May–Sept.*

Cockle Bay Wharf. Fueling Sydney's addiction to fine food, most of this sprawling waterfront complex, on the city side of Darling Harbour, is dedicated to gastronomy, as well as a few bars and nightclubs. If you have a boat you can dock at the marina—and avoid the hassle of parking a car in one of the city's most congested centers. ✉ *201 Sussex St., Darling Harbour* ☎ *02/9269–9800* ⊕ *www.cocklebaywharf.com.*

NEED A BREAK?

Blackbird Café. Blackbird Café is great place to take a break while exploring Darling Harbour. The weekday lunch specials are all under A$20 and a good value, while happy hour (3–6 pm) has beers and cocktails at similarly affordable prices. There are great views from the balcony, so try and nab a table there. The à la carte menu includes starters of haloumi and vegetable stack or grilled prawns and crab, and there's a wide range of pizza, pasta, burgers, and grills. ✉ *Cockle Bay Wharf, 201 Sussex St., Balcony level, Darling Harbour* ☎ *02/9283-7385* ⊕ *www.blackbirdcafe.com.au.*

FAMILY **LG IMAX Theatre.** Both in size and impact, this eight-story-tall movie screen is overwhelming. One-hour presentations take you on astonishing, wide-angle voyages of discovery under the oceans and to the summit of the world's highest mountains. ✉ *Southern Promenade, 31 Wheat Rd., Darling Harbour* ☎ *02/9281–3300* ⊕ *www.imax.com.au* ✑ *A$23–A$33.50* ⊙ *Daily 10–10.*

FAMILY **Powerhouse Museum.** Learning the principles of science is a painless process with this museum's stimulating, interactive displays ideal for all ages. Exhibits in the former 1890s electricity station that once powered Sydney's trams include a whole floor of working steam engines, space modules, airplanes suspended from the ceiling, state-of-the-art computer gadgetry, and a 1930s art deco–style movie-theater auditorium. The museum also stages many excellent exhibitions that are not science-based on everything from fashion and crochet and jewelry to computer games. ✉ *500 Harris St., Ultimo, Darling Harbour* ☎ *02/9217–0111* ⊕ *www.powerhousemuseum.com* ✑ *A$15* ⊙ *Daily 10–5.*

Pyrmont Bridge. Dating from 1902, this is the world's oldest electrically operated swing-span bridge. The structure once carried motor traffic, but it's now a walkway that links Darling Harbour's western side with Cockle Bay on the east. The center span still swings open to allow tall-masted ships into Cockle Bay, which sits at the bottom of the horseshoe-shape shore. ⊠ *Darling Harbour.*

OFF THE
BEATEN
PATH **Sydney Fish Market.** Second in size only to Tokyo's giant Tsukiji fish market, Sydney's is a showcase for the riches of Australia's seas. An easy 10-minute walk from Darling Harbour (and with its own stop on the Metro Light Rail network), the market is a great place to sample sushi, oysters, octopus, spicy Thai and Chinese fish dishes, and fish-and-chips at the waterfront cafés overlooking the fishing fleet. Behind the scenes guided tours, including the auction, begin at 6:40 am and run until 8:30 am on Monday, Wednesday, Thursday, and Friday ($A35). They also offer cooking classes. Call ahead for advance reservations or book on the website. ⊠ *Pyrmont Bridge Rd., at Bank St., Pyrmont West* ☎ *02/9004–1100* ⊕ *www.sydneyfishmarket.com.au* ⊘ *Daily 7 am–4 pm.*

SYDNEY CITY CENTER

Shopping is the main reason to visit Sydney's city center, but there are several buildings and other places of interest among the office blocks, department stores, and shopping centers.

GETTING HERE AND AROUND

Buses from the eastern suburbs run along Elizabeth Street on the western side of Hyde Park; buses from the inner western suburbs such as Balmain travel to and from the Queen Victoria Building. The main train stations are Town Hall and Martin Place, while Hyde Park is served by both St. James and Museum Station on the City Circle rail line. The free shuttle bus (No. 555) completes a circuit around the city center, stopping at the main attractions.

TOP ATTRACTIONS

FAMILY **Australian Museum.** The strength of this natural history museum, a well-respected academic institution, is its collection of plants, animals, geological specimens, and cultural artifacts from the Asia-Pacific region. Particularly notable are the collections of artifacts from Papua New Guinea and from Australia's Aboriginal peoples. One of the most popular exhibits is "Dinosaurs" on Level 2, containing 10 complete skeletons, 8 life-size models and interactive displays, while "Surviving Australia" (about Australian animals) and "Indigenous Australia" are the most popular with overseas visitors. There are behind-the-scenes tours (A$98), an excellent shop, and a lively café. ⊠ *6 College St., near William St., Hyde Park* ☎ *02/9320–6000* ⊕ *www.australianmuseum. net.au* ⊠ *A$15* ⊘ *Daily 9:30–5* ☞ *Free guided tours daily, usually at 11 and 2 although subject to change.*

Hyde Park. Declared public land by Governor Phillip in 1792 and used for the colony's earliest cricket matches and horse races, this area was turned into a park in 1810. The gardens are formal, with fountains, statuary, and tree-lined walks, and its tranquil lawns are popular with office workers at lunchtime. The park has two sections, with Park Street (a traffic street) dividing the two halves. Several events, such as the Night Noodle Markets (open-air Asian food markets) in October,

Sydney City Center

Martin Pl.

Macquarie St.

Art Gallery Rd.

Elizabeth St.

Castlereagh St.

Pitt St.

Strand
Arcade

Queens Square

St. Mary's Rd.

York St.

Clarence St.

Kent St.

Market St.

George St.

The Great
Synagogue

HYDE PARK

College St.

Haig Ave.

Druitt St.

Park St.

William St.

Bathurst St.

Elizabeth St.

Sussex St.

Castlereagh St.

Pitt St.

Anzac
Memorial

EAST SYDNEY

Yurong St.

0 — 1/8 mile

0 — 200 meters

Liverpool St.

Liverpool St.

Commonwealth Ave.

**Chinese Garden
of Friendship**

Goulburn St.

Wentworth

KEY

⊢—⊢ Rail Lines

HAYMARKET

are held in the park. ⊠ *Elizabeth, College, and Park Sts., Hyde Park* ⊕ *www.cityofsydney.nsw.gov.au* ⊙ *Daily 24 hrs.*

Anzac Memorial. In the southern section of Hyde Park (near Liverpool Street) stands the 1934 art deco Anzac Memorial, a tribute to the Australians who died in military service during World War I, when the acronym ANZAC (Australian and New Zealand Army Corps) was coined. The 120,000 gold stars inside the dome represent each man and woman of New South Wales who served. The lower level exhibits war-related photographs, and a beautiful, poignant sculpture of an ANZAC soldier and shield. ⊠ *Hyde Park, Hyde Park* ☎ *02/9267–7668* ⊙ *Daily 9–5.*

Fodor's Choice   **Sydney Tower.** Short of taking a scenic flight, a visit to the top of this
★   309-meter (1,000 foot) golden-turret-topped spike is the best way to see Sydney's spectacular layout. This is the city's tallest building, and the views from its indoor observation deck encompass the entire Sydney metropolitan area. You can often see as far as the Blue Mountains, more than 80 km (50 miles) away. You can view it all from the Sydney Tower Eye Observation Deck 820 feet above the city streets, or for the real adrenaline don a safety harness and do the Sky Walk, a guided walk around the outside of the golden turret some 880 feet above the city. Walkers are attached to the tower's superstructure by harness lines.

The fountain in Hyde Park with the Australian Museum in the background

A combination ticket for Sky Walk, the Eye Observation Deck (which includes a 4-D cinema), and three other Sydney attractions—including SEA LIFE Sydney Aquarium—is a great deal at A$99 when purchased online. The building houses two restaurants in the turret. ⊠ *100 Market St., between Pitt and Castlereagh Sts., City Center* ☏ *02/9333–9222* ⊕ *www.sydneytowereye.com.au* ✉ *Observation deck A$26.50, Sky-Walk A$70; cheaper tickets available online* ⊘ *Sydney Tower: daily 9 am–9:30 pm (10 pm in summer). Skywalk: daily 9:30–8:45.*

WORTH NOTING

NEED A BREAK?

Marble Bar. Stop in at the Marble Bar to experience a masterpiece of Victorian extravagance. The 1890 bar was formerly in another building that was constructed on the profits of the horse-racing track, thus establishing the link between gambling and majestic public architecture that has its modern-day parallel in the Sydney Opera House. Threatened with demolition in the 1970s, the whole bar was moved—marble arches, color-glass ceiling, elaborately carved woodwork, paintings of voluptuous nudes, and all—to its present site in the basement of the Hilton Sydney Hotel. There is live music at night from Thursday to Saturday. ⊠ *Hilton Sydney, 488 George St., City Center* ☏ *02/9265–6026* ⊕ *www.marblebarsydney.com.au* ⊘ *Daily 4 pm–late.*

Martin Place. Sydney's largest pedestrian precinct, flanked by banks, offices, and shopping centers, is the hub of the central business district. There are some grand buildings here—including the beautifully refurbished Commonwealth Bank and the 1870s Venetian Renaissance–style General Post Office building with its 230-foot clock tower (now a Westin hotel). Toward the George Street end of the plaza the simple 1929 cenotaph war memorial commemorates Australians who died in World War I. ⊠ *Between Macquarie and George Sts., City Center* ⊕ *www.cityofsydney.nsw.gov.au.*

Queen Victoria Building (QVB). Originally the city's produce market, this huge 1898 sandstone structure was handsomely restored with sweeping staircases, enormous stained-glass windows, and the 1-ton Royal Clock, which hangs from the glass roof. The clock chimes the hour from 9 am to 9 pm with four tableaux: the second shows Queen Elizabeth I knighting Sir Frances Drake; the last ends with an executioner chopping off King Charles I's head. The complex includes more than 200 boutiques and restaurants including the lovely Tea Room on level 3. Boutiques on the upper floors are generally more upscale. Guided tours cost A$15 and depart Tuesday, Thursday, and Saturday at 11:30 am; bookings are essential. ⊠ *455 George St., City Center* ☎ *02/9264–9209* ⊕ *www. qvb.com.au* ⊙ *Mon.–Wed., Fri., and Sat. 9–6, Thurs. 9–9, Sun. 11–5.*

St. Andrew's Cathedral. The foundation stone for Sydney's Gothic Revival Anglican cathedral—the country's oldest—was laid in 1819, although the original architect, Francis Greenway, fell from grace soon after work began. Edmund Blacket, Sydney's most illustrious church architect, was responsible for its final design and completion—a whopping 50 years later in 1868. Notable features of the sandstone construction include ornamental windows depicting Jesus's life and a great east window with images relating to St. Andrew. ⊠ *George and Bathurst Sts., next to Town Hall, City Center* ☎ *02/9265–1661* ⊕ *www.sydneycathedral. com* ⊙ *Mon.–Sat. 10–4, Sun. for services only 8:30 am, 10:30 am, and 5 pm; Wed. healing service 6 pm; tours by arrangement.*

St. Mary's Cathedral. The first St. Mary's was built here in 1821, but fire destroyed the chapel. Work on the present cathedral began in 1868. The spires weren't added until 2000, however. St. Mary's has some particularly fine stained-glass windows and a terrazzo floor in the crypt, where exhibitions are often held. The cathedral's large rose window was imported from England.

At the front of the cathedral stand statues of Cardinal Moran and Archbishop Kelly, two Irishmen who were prominent in Australia's Roman Catholic Church. Due to the high proportion of Irish men and women in the convict population, the Roman Catholic Church was often the voice of the oppressed in 19th-century Sydney, where anti-Catholic feeling ran high among the Protestant rulers. Call ahead for tours. Separate tours take in the cathedral, the crypt, and the bell tower. Free guided tours depart after Sunday mass. ⊠ *College and Cathedral Sts., Hyde Park* ☎ *02/9220–0400* ⊕ *www.stmaryscathedral.org.au* ▧ *Tours free* ⊙ *Weekdays 6:30 am–6:30 pm, Sat. 8–7:30, Sun. 6:30 am–7:30 pm; tours operate at various times.*

Sydney Town Hall. Sydney's Town Hall—an elaborate sandstone structure—is one of the city's most ornate Victorian buildings. A centerpiece of the building is the massive 8,000-pipe Grand Organ, one of the world's most powerful, which is used for lunchtime concerts. Tours, conducted by the "Friends of Town Hall" for A$5, can be booked through the website. Mingle with locals on the marble steps of the front entrance. ⊠ *483 George St., City Center* ☎ *02/9265–9198 general inquiries* ⊕ *www.cityofsydney.nsw.gov.au* ☏ *Free* ⊙ *Weekdays 8–6.*

INNER CITY AND THE EASTERN SUBURBS

Sydney's inner city and eastern suburbs are truly the people's domain. They are the hip zones of Sydney featuring the foodie precincts as well as some of the most expensive real estate, great shopping, and the most accessible beaches. Architecture ranges from the mansions of the colonial aristocracy and the humble laborers' cottages of the same period to the modernized terrace houses of Paddington, one of Sydney's most charming and most desirable suburbs. A good way to explore the area is to take the Bondi & Bays Explorer bus that stops at 10 sites including Bondi Beach, Double Bay, Paddington, and Rose Bay.

GETTING HERE AND AROUND

The inner city and eastern suburbs are well served by buses, although the journey out to the eastern suburbs beaches can be quite long in peak hour. Most depart from Circular Quay (Alfred Street). Travel to Paddington and Bondi is on Nos. 380, 333, and 382; and to Watsons Bay and Vaucluse (via Double Bay and Rose Bay) on Nos. 323, 324, and 325. Buses 380, 382, and 333 travel along Oxford Street, the main artery of the alternative (and gay) neighborhood of Darlinghurst. It is quicker to take the train to Edgecliff or Bondi Junction stations to connect with buses traveling to many of the eastern suburbs including Coogee and Clovelly. A ferry operates between Circular Quay and Watsons Bay, calling at Garden Island, Darling Point, Double Bay, and Rose Bay. It is an easy walk to Darlinghurst and Surry Hills from the city center, while Kings Cross has its own train station, just one stop from the city center.

TOP ATTRACTIONS

Elizabeth Bay. Much of this densely populated but still-charming harborside suburb was originally part of the extensive Elizabeth Bay House grounds. Wrought-iron balconies and French doors on some of the older apartment blocks give the area a Mediterranean flavor. During the 1920s and 1930s this was a fashionably bohemian quarter, and it remains a favorite among artists and writers. ⊠ *Elizabeth Bay Rd., Elizabeth Bay.*

Elizabeth Bay House. This 1835–39 mansion was regarded in its heyday as the "finest house in the colony." It retains little of its original furniture, although the rooms have been restored in Georgian style. The most striking feature is an oval-shaped salon with a winding staircase, naturally lighted by glass panels in the domed roof. The view from the front-facing windows across Elizabeth Bay is stunning. A variety of soirees and talks are held in the house throughout the year. ⊠ *7 Onslow Ave., Elizabeth Bay* ☎ *02/9356–3022* ⊕ *sydneylivingmuseums.com.au/elizabeth-bay-house* ☏ *A$8* ⊙ *Fri.–Sun. 11–4.*

Sydney Jewish Museum. Artifacts, interactive displays, and audiovisual displays chronicle the history of Australian Jews and commemorate the 6 million killed in the Holocaust. Exhibits are brilliantly arranged

2

on eight levels, which lead upward in chronological order, from the handful of Jews who arrived with the First Fleet in 1788 to the 30,000 concentration-camp survivors who came after World War II—one of the largest populations of Holocaust survivors to be found anywhere. A free 40-minute guided tour starts at noon on Monday, Wednesday, Friday, and Sunday. ✉ *148 Darlinghurst Rd., Darlinghurst* ☎ *02/9360–7999* ⊕ *www.sydneyjewishmuseum.com.au* ✉ *A$10; free admission on 1st Sun. of month* ☽ *Sun.–Thurs. 10–4, Fri. 10–2.*

WORTH NOTING

Centennial Park. More than 500 acres of palm-lined avenues, groves of Moreton Bay figs, paperbark tree–fringed lakes, and cycling and horse-riding tracks make this a popular park and Sydney's favorite workout circuit. In the early 1800s the marshy land at the lower end provided Sydney with its fresh water. The park was proclaimed in 1888, the centenary of Australia's founding as a colony. The Centennial Park Café is often crowded on weekends, but a mobile canteen between the lakes in the middle of the park serves snacks and espresso. Bikes and blades can be rented from the nearby Clovelly Road outlets, on the eastern side of the park. The Moonlight Cinema screens movies during the summer months. ✉ *Oxford St., at Centennial Ave., Centennial Park* ☎ *02/9339–6699* ⊕ *www.centennialparklands.com.au* ☽ *Daily dawn–dusk.*

OFF THE
BEATEN
PATH

Harry's Café de Wheels. The attraction of this all-day dockyard food stall is not so much the delectable meat pies and coffee served as the clientele. Famous opera singers, actors, and international rock stars have been spotted here rubbing shoulders with shift workers and taxi drivers. This "pie cart" has been a Sydney institution since 1945, when the late Harry "Tiger" Edwards set up his van to serve sailors from the nearby Garden Island base. Drop in any time from 8:30 am (9 am on weekends) until the wee hours for a Tiger Pie, made with mushy peas, mashed potatoes, and gravy. Harry's now has nine other locations in Sydney. ✉ *1 Cowper Wharf Rd., Woolloomooloo* ☎ *02/9357–3074* ⊕ *www.harryscafedewheels.com.au.*

Paddington. Most of this suburb's elegant two-story terrace houses were built during the 1880s, when the colony experienced a long period of economic growth following the gold rushes that began in the 1860s. The balconies are trimmed with decorative wrought iron, sometimes known as Paddington lace, which initially came from England and later from Australian foundries. Rebuilt and repainted, the now-stylish Paddington terrace houses give the area its characteristic village-like charm. The Oxford Street shopping strip is full of upscale and funky boutiques, cafés, and several good pubs. ✉ *Oxford St., between Boundary and Queen Sts., Paddington.*

NEED A
BREAK?

Royal Hotel. The Royal Hotel is an enjoyable Victorian pub with leather couches and stained-glass windows. It's a good place to stop for something cool to drink. The top floor has a balcony restaurant that's popular on sunny afternoons. ✉ *237 Glenmore Rd., Paddington* ☎ *02/9331–2604* ⊕ *royalhotel.com.au.*

Victoria Barracks. If you're curious about the Australian military, you'll enjoy the free tours of this Regency-style barracks (built from 1841), which take place every Thursday at 10 am sharp. The tour includes entry to the Army Museum of New South Wales, which has exhibits covering Australia's military history from the days of the Rum Corps to the Malayan conflict of the 1950s. ✉ *Oxford St., at Oatley Rd., Paddington* ☎ *02/8335–5330* ⊕ *www.armymuseumnsw.com.au* 🎟 *Tours free, museum A$2* ⊙ *Museum: Thurs. 10–1, 1st Sun. of month 10–4.*

GREATER SYDNEY

The Greater Sydney area has numerous attractions that can be easily reached by public transport. These include historic townships, the Sydney 2000 Olympics site, national parks where you can explore and enjoy the Australian bush, and wildlife and theme parks that appeal to children.

Other points of interest are the north-side beaches, particularly Manly, and the historic city of Parramatta, founded in 1788 and 26 km (16 miles) to the west; and the magnificent Hawkesbury River, which winds its way around the city's western and northern borders. The waterside suburb of Balmain has pubs and restaurants, an atmospheric Saturday flea market, and backstreets full of character.

GETTING HERE AND AROUND

Trains travel from Central Station to Parramatta daily, and directly to Sydney Olympic Park on weekdays. To reach Olympic Park on weekends, take the train to Lidcombe and then change trains for the short ride to Olympic Park station. The RiverCat ferry travels from Circular Quay to Parramatta, calling at Sydney Olympic Park on the way. Trains depart from Central Station for the Hawkesbury River (alight at Hawkesbury River station in the town of Brooklyn). They also travel to the Royal National Park (alight at Engadine or Heathcote stations, or Loftus, where a tram travels from the station to the park on Sunday only).

TIMING

Each of the sights here could easily fill the better part of a day. If you're short on time, try a tour company that combines visits within a particular area—for example, a day trip west to the Olympic Games site, Featherdale Wildlife Park, and the Blue Mountains.

TOP ATTRACTIONS

FAMILY **Featherdale Wildlife Park.** This is the place to see kangaroos, dingoes, wallabies, and echidnas (and even feed some of them) in native bush settings 40 km (25 miles) west of Sydney. You can have your picture taken with a koala for free. The daily crocodile feeding sessions are very popular. Take the train to Blacktown station and then board the 725 bus for the park. ■TIP➜ The park is on the way to the Blue Mountains. ✉ *217 Kildare Rd., Doonside* ☎ *02/9622–1644* ⊕ *www.featherdale. com.au* ✉ *A$29.50* ⊗ *Daily 9–5.*

Parramatta. This bustling satellite city 26 km (16 miles) west of Sydney is one of Australia's most historic precincts. Its origins as a European settlement are purely agrarian. The sandy, rocky soil around Sydney Cove was too poor to feed the fledgling colony, so Governor Phillip looked to the banks of the Parramatta River for the rich alluvial soil they needed. In 1789, just a year after the first convicts-cum-settlers arrived, Phillip established Rosehill, an area set aside for agriculture. The community developed as its agricultural successes grew, and several important buildings survive as outstanding examples of the period. The two-hour self-guided Harris Park Heritage Walk, which departs from the River-Cat Ferry Terminal, connects the key historic sites and buildings. The ferry departs at frequent intervals from Sydney's Circular Quay, and is a relaxing, scenic alternative to the drive or train ride from the city. A free shuttle bus travels in a loop around Parramatta. ■TIP➜ A good place to start discovering Parramatta is the Heritage Centre at 346A Church Street. ✉ *Parramatta* ⊕ *www.discoverparramatta.com* ⊗ *Visitor center open daily 9–5.*

Elizabeth Farm. The oldest European building in Australia, Elizabeth Farm was built by John and Elizabeth Macarthur in 1793. With its simple but elegant lines and long, shady verandas, the house became a template for Australian farmhouses that survives to the present day. It was here, too, that the merino sheep industry began, since the Macarthurs were the first to introduce the tough Spanish breed to Australia. Although John Macarthur has traditionally been credited as the father of Australia's wool industry, it was Elizabeth who largely ran the farm

while her husband pursued his official and more-lucrative unofficial duties as an officer in the colony's Rum Corps. Inside are personal objects of the Macarthur family, as well as a re-creation of their furnishings. Free tours are at 11, noon, 1, and 2 each day. ☒ *70 Alice St., Rosehill* ☎ *02/9635–9488* ⊕ *sydneylivingmuseums.com.au/elizabeth-farm* ☲ *A$8* ☉ *Weekends 10:30–3:30.*

Experiment Farm. The site of the first private land grant in Australia, Experiment Farm was settled in 1789 by James Ruse, a former convict who was given 1½ acres by Governor Phillip on condition that he become self-sufficient—a vital experiment if the colony was to survive. Luckily for Phillip, his gamble paid off. The bungalow, with its wide verandas, was built by colonial surgeon John Harris in the 1830s; it contains a fine collection of Australian colonial furniture, and the cellar now houses an exhibition on the life and work of James Ruse. The surrounding ornamental garden is most beautiful in early summer, when the floral perfumes are strongest. ☒ *9 Ruse St., Harris Park* ☎ *02/9635–5655* ⊕ *www.nationaltrust.org.au* ☲ *A$8, combined ticket with* Old Government House *A$15* ☉ *Wed.–Sun. 10:30–3:30, last guided tour at 3.*

Old Government House. On the bank of the Parramatta River, Old Government House (which was the country residence of Sydney's 10 early governors) is Australia's oldest surviving public building, and the World Heritage–listed building is a notable work from the Georgian period. Built by governors John Hunter and Lachlan Macquarie, the building has been faithfully restored in keeping with its origins, and contains the nation's most significant collection of early Australian furniture. In the 260-acre parkland surrounding the house are Governor Brisbane's bathhouse and observatory and the Government House Dairy. The house is often home to special exhibitions. ☒ *Inside Parramatta Park, Parramatta* ✛ *Pitt St. entrance* ☎ *02/9635–8149* ⊕ *www.nationaltrust.org.au* ☲ *A$16* ☉ *Tues.–Sun. 10–4, last guided tour at 3:30.*

NEED A BREAK?

Parramatta Park Café. After visiting Old Government House, amble down to the bank of the river and pull up a seat in this shady spot, which was the park's former visitors' center. It's open for all-day breakfast, brunch, and lunch daily with a menu of gourmet burgers, soup, pastas, and sweet treats. ☒ *Parramatta Park, Byrnes Ave., Parramatta* ☎ *02/9630-0144.*

Royal National Park. Established in 1879 on the coast south of Sydney, the Royal has the distinction of being the first national park in Australia and the second in the world, after Yellowstone National Park in the United States. Several walking tracks traverse the grounds, most of them requiring little or no hiking experience. The Lady Carrington Walk, a 10-km (6-mile) trek, is a self-guided tour that crosses 15 creeks and passes several historic sites. Other tracks take you along the coast past beautiful wildflower displays and through patches of rain forest. You can canoe the Port Hacking River upstream from the Audley Causeway; rentals are available at the Audley boat shed on the river. The Illawarra train line, from Central Station, stops at Loftus,

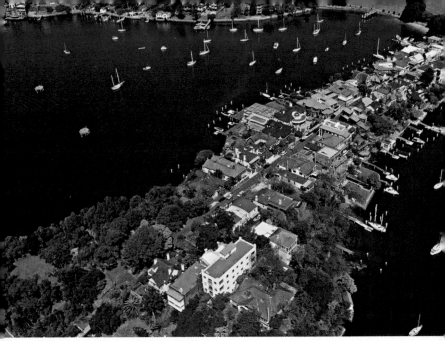

A bird's-eye view of the boats in Parramatta River

Engadine, Heathcote, Waterfall, and Otford stations, where most of the park's walking tracks begin. There are three campsites in the park. ⊠ *Royal National Park* ✢ *Royal National Park Visitor Centre, 35 km (22 miles) south of Sydney via Princes Hwy. to Farnell Ave., south of Loftus, or McKell Ave. at Waterfall* ☎ *02/9542–0648 visitor center, 1300/072757 campsite reservations* ⊕ *www.nationalparks.nsw.gov.au* ✉ *A$12 per vehicle per day, overnight camping A$10–A$28; booking required* ⊗ *Daily 7 am–8:30 pm.*

WORTH NOTING

FAMILY **Koala Park Sanctuary.** At this private park in Sydney's northern out-skirts you can feed a kangaroo or cuddle a koala. (Koala presentations are daily at 10:20, 11:45, 2, and 3.) The sanctuary also has dingoes, wombats, emus, penguins, and wallaroos. There are sheep-shearing and boomerang-throwing demonstrations. ⊠ *84 Castle Hill Rd., West Pennant Hills* ☎ *02/9484–3141* ⊕ *www.koalapark.com.au* ✉ *A$27* ⊗ *Daily 9–5.*

Ku-ring-gai Chase National Park. Nature hikes here lead past rock engrav-ings and paintings by the Guringai Aboriginal tribe, the area's original inhabitants for whom the park is named. Created in the 1890s, the park mixes large stands of eucalyptus trees with moist, rain-forest-filled gullies where swamp wallabies, possums, goannas, and other creatures roam. The delightful trails are mostly easy or moderate, including the compelling 3-km (2-mile) Garigal Aboriginal Heritage Walk at West Head, which takes in ancient rock-art sites. From Mt. Ku-ring-gai train station you can walk the 3-km (2-mile) Ku-ring-gai Track to Appletree Bay, while the 30-minute, wheelchair-accessible Discovery Trail is an excellent introduction to the region's flora and fauna. Leaflets on all of the walks are available at the park's entry stations and from the Wildlife Shop at Bobbin Head.

The park is 24 km (15 miles) north of Sydney. Railway stations at Mt. Ku-ring-gai, Berowra, and Cowan, close to the park's western border, provide access to walking trails. On Sunday, for example, you can walk from Mt. Ku-ring-gai station to Appletree Bay and then to Bobbin Head, where a bus can take you to the Turramurra railway station. By car, take the Pacific Highway to Pymble. Then turn into Bobbin Head Road or continue on the highway to Mt. Colah and turn off into the park on Ku-ring-gai Chase Road. You can also follow the Pacific Highway to Pymble and then drive along the Mona Vale Road to Terry Hills and take the West Head turnoff.

For more information on the park, contact the Sydney North Region Information Centre, which is located in the historic Bobbin Inn. ✉ *Ku-ring-gai Chase National Park, Bobbin Head Rd., Mount Colah* ☎ *02/9472–8949* ⊕ *www.nationalparks.nsw.gov.au* 💲 *A$12 per vehicle, per day* ⊙ *Daily 6 am–dusk.*

FAMILY **Sydney Olympic Park.** The center of the 2000 Olympic and Paralympic Games lies 14 km (8½ miles) west of the city center. Sprawling across 1,900 acres on the shores of Homebush Bay, the site is a series of majestic stadiums, arenas, and accommodation complexes. Among the park's sports facilities are an aquatic center, archery range, tennis center, and the centerpiece: the 85,000-seat ANZ Olympic Stadium. Since the conclusion of the 2000 Games it has been used for major sporting events like the 2003 Rugby World Cup and concerts for international acts including The Rolling Stones. The Explore interactive stadium tour, costing A$28.50 per person, takes you behind the scenes to sit in the media room and have your photo taken on the winners' dais. The new Gantry Tour (A$49) also includes a trip to the gantry (where the sound equipment and spotlights are kept, 140 feet above the stadium).

Don't miss the adjacent Bicentennial Park, made up of 247 acres of swamps, lakes, and parks dotted with picnic grounds and bike trails. The area, a former quarry, was developed to commemorate Australia's Bicentennial celebrations in 1988. The most scenic and relaxing way to get to Sydney Olympic Park is to take the RiverCat from Circular Quay to Homebush Bay. You can also take a train from Central Station, Sydney, to Olympic Park. ✉ *1 Herb Elliot Ave., Homebush Bay* ☎ *02/9714–7888* ⊕ *www.sydneyolympicpark.com.au; www.anzstadium.com.au* ⊙ *Daily dawn–dusk.*

BEACHES

Sydney is paradise for beach lovers. Within the metropolitan area there are more than 30 ocean beaches, all with golden sand and rolling surf, as well as several more around the harbor with calmer water for safe swimming. If your hotel is on the harbor's south side, the logical choice for a day at the beach is one of the southern ocean beaches between Bondi and Coogee. On the north side of the harbor, Manly is easily accessible by ferry, but beaches farther north involve a longer trip by car or public transportation.

Lifeguards are on duty at most of Sydney's ocean beaches during summer months, and flags indicate whether a beach is being patrolled. "Swim between the flags" is an adage that is drummed into every Australian child, with very good reason: the undertow can be very dangerous. If you get into difficulty, don't fight the current. Breathe evenly, stay calm, and raise one arm above your head to signal the lifeguards.

Although there's no shortage of sharks inside and outside the harbor, the risk of attack is reasonably low. These species are not typically aggressive toward humans, and shark nets protect many Sydney beaches. A more common hazard is jellyfish, known locally as bluebottles, which inflict a painful sting—with a remote risk of more serious complications (including severe allergic reactions). The staff at most beaches will supply a spray-on remedy to help relieve the pain, which generally lasts about 24 hours. Many beaches will post warning signs when bluebottles are present, but you can also determine the situation yourself by looking for the telltale bright-blue, bubble-like jellies washed up along the waterline.

Topless sunbathing is common at many Sydney beaches, but full nudity is permitted only at a couple of locations, including Lady Jane Beach, close to Watsons Bay on the south side of the harbor.

Details of how to reach the beaches by bus, train, or ferry are provided below.

> **RUN FOR YOUR LIFE**
>
> Pack your jogging shoes for the biggest footrace in the country. **City to Surf** (⊕ *city2surf.com. au*) attracts more than 50,000 people each August—some taking it very seriously, others donning a gorilla suit or fairy outfit. The race starts at Hyde Park and winds through the eastern suburbs 14 km (9 miles) to Bondi Beach, via the notorious "Heartbreak Hill" at Rose Bay. For some reason, it never seems to rain on the second Sunday in August.

INSIDE THE HARBOR

Balmoral Beach. This 800-yard-long, rarely crowded beach—among the best of the inner-harbor beaches—is in one of Sydney's most exclusive northern suburbs. There's no surf, but it's a great place to learn to windsurf (sailboard rentals are available). The Esplanade, which runs along the beachfront, has a handful of upscale restaurants, as well as several snack bars and cafés that serve award-winning fish-and-chips. In summer you can catch performances of Bard on the Beach. You could easily combine a trip to Balmoral with a visit to Taronga Zoo. To reach Balmoral, take the ferry from Circular Quay to Taronga Zoo and then board Bus 238. Or take Bus 247 from the city (near Wynyard Station) to Mosman and then walk down Raglan Street hill to the Esplanade, the main street running along Balmoral Beach. **Amenities:** food and drink; showers; toilets. **Best for:** swimming; walking; windsurfing. ⊠ *Raglan St., Balmoral.*

Sydney
Beaches

Camp Cove. Just inside South Head, this crescent beach is where Sydney's fashionable people come to watch and be seen. The gentle slope and calm water make it a safe playground for children. A shop at the northern end of the beach sells salad rolls and fresh fruit juices. The grassy hill at the southern end of the beach has a plaque to commemorate the spot where Captain Arthur Phillip, the commander of the First Fleet, first set foot inside Port Jackson. Parking is limited, and keep in mind it's a long walk to the beach. Dive company Abyss (☎ 02/9588–9662) operates an easy dive off the beach here. Take Bus 324 or 325 from Circular Quay to Watsons Bay and walk along Cliff Street. **Amenities:** food and drink; toilets. **Best for:** solitude; sunset; swimming. ⊠ *Cliff St., Watsons Bay.*

Lady Jane. Officially called Lady Bay, Lady Jane is the most accessible of the nude beaches around Sydney. It's also a popular part of Sydney's gay scene. Only a couple of hundred yards long and backed by a stone wall, the beach has safe swimming with no surf. From Camp Cove, follow the path north and then descend the short, steep ladder leading down the cliff face to the beach. Take Bus 234 or 325 from Circular Quay to Watsons Bay. From there walk along Cliff Street toward Camp Cove. **Amenities:** toilets. **Best for:** nudists; solitude; swimming. ⊠ *Cliff St., Watsons Bay.*

Nielsen Park. By Sydney standards, this beach at the end of the Vaucluse Peninsula is small, but behind the sand is a large, shady park that's ideal for picnics. The headlands at either end of the beach are especially popular for their magnificent views across the harbor. The beach is protected by a semicircular net, so don't be deterred by the beach's correct name, Shark Beach. The casual café is open daily and sells drinks, snacks, and meals; there is also a more upscale restaurant open for lunch daily. Parking is often difficult on weekends. Historic Greycliffe House—built in 1840 and now used as National Park offices—is in the park, while the more elaborate and stately Vaucluse House is a 10-minute walk away. Take Bus 325 from Circular Quay. **Amenities:** food and drink; showers; toilets. **Best for:** swimming; walking. ⊠ *Greycliffe Ave., off Vaucluse Rd., Vaucluse.*

SOUTH OF THE HARBOR

Fodor's Choice
★

Bondi Beach. Wide, wonderful Bondi (pronounced *bon*-dye) is the most famous and most crowded of all Sydney beaches. It has something for just about everyone, and the droves that flock here on a sunny day give it a bustling, carnival atmosphere unmatched by any other Sydney beach. Facilities include toilets, open-air showers for rinsing sandy feet and salty bodies, and a kiosk on the beach that rents out sun lounges, beach umbrellas, and even swimsuits. Cafés, ice-cream outlets, restaurants, and boutiques line Campbell Parade, which runs behind the beach. Families tend to prefer the calmer waters of the northern end of the beach. Surfing is popular at the south end, where a path winds along the sea-sculpted cliffs to Tamarama and Bronte beaches. Take Bus 380, 382, or 333 all the way from Circular Quay, or take the train from the city to Bondi Junction and then board Bus 380, 381, 382, or

333. **Amenities:** food and drink; lifeguards; parking (fee); showers; toilets; water sports. **Best for:** partiers; sunrise; surfing; swimming; walking. ⊠ *Campbell Parade, Bondi Beach.*

FAMILY

Fodor'sChoice

★

Bronte Beach. If you want an ocean beach that's close to the city and has a terrific setting, with both sand and grassy areas, this one is hard to beat. A wooded park of palm trees and Norfolk Island pines surrounds Bronte. The park includes a playground and sheltered picnic tables, and excellent cafés are in the immediate area. The breakers can be fierce, but swimming is safe in the sea pool at the southern end of the beach. Take Bus 378 from Central Station, or take the train from the city to Bondi Junction and then board Bus 378. Bus 362 runs between Bondi and Coogee beaches, stopping at Bronte Beach and Tamarama on the weekends only. **Amenities:** food and drink; lifeguard; showers; toilets. **Best for:** sunrise; surfing; walking. ⊠ *Bronte Rd., Bronte.*

FAMILY

Clovelly. Even on the roughest day it's safe to swim at the end of this long, keyhole-shape inlet, which makes it a popular family beach. There are toilet facilities, a kiosk, and a café. This is also a popular snorkeling spot that usually teems with tropical fish. Take Bus 339 from Argyle Street, Millers Point (the Rocks), Wynyard, or Central Station; or a train from the city to Bondi Junction, then board Bus 360. **Amenities:** food and drink; lifeguards; parking (fee); showers; toilets. **Best for:** snorkeling; sunrise; swimming. ⊠ *Clovelly Rd., Clovelly.*

FAMILY

Coogee. A reef protects this lively beach (pronounced *kuh*-jee), creating calmer swimming conditions than those found at its neighbors. A grassy headland overlooking the beach has an excellent children's playground. Cafés in the shopping precinct at the back of the beach sell ice cream, pizza, and the ingredients for picnics. Take Bus 373 or 374 from Circular Quay or Bus 372 from Central Station. **Amenities:** food and drink; lifeguards; parking (fee); showers; toilets. **Best for:** sunrise; swimming; walking. ⊠ *Coogee Bay Rd. and Arden St., Coogee.*

Tamarama. This small, fashionable beach—aka "Glam-a-rama"—is one of Sydney's prettiest, but the rocky headlands that squeeze close to the sand on either side make it less than ideal for swimming. The sea is often hazardous here, and surfing is prohibited. A café in the small park behind the beach sells sandwiches, fresh juices, and fruit whips. Take the train from the city to Bondi Junction and then board Bus 360 or 361, or walk for 10 minutes along the cliff path from the south end of Bondi Beach. **Amenities:** food and drink; lifeguard; showers; toilets. **Best for:** sunrise; surfing. ⊠ *Tamarama Marine Dr., Tamarama.*

NORTH OF THE HARBOR

Dee Why–Long Reef. Separated from Dee Why by a narrow channel, Long Reef Beach is remoter and much quieter than its southern neighbor. However, Dee Why has better surfing conditions, a big sea pool, and several good restaurants. To get here, take Bus 136 from Manly. **Amenities:** food and drink; lifeguard; parking (fee); showers; toilets. **Best for:** swimming; walking. ⊠ *The Strand, Dee Why.*

Sydneysiders have more than 30 beaches to choose from.

Fodor's Choice
★

Manly Beach. The Bondi Beach of the north shore, Manly caters to everyone except those who want to get away from it all. On sunny days Sydneysiders, school groups, and travelers from around the world crowd the 2-km-long (1-mile-long) sweep of white sand and take to the waves to swim and ride boards. The beach is well equipped with changing and toilet facilities and lockers. The promenade that runs between the Norfolk Island pines is great for people-watching and rollerblading. Cafés, souvenir shops, and ice-cream parlors line the nearby shopping area, the Corso. Manly also has several non-beach attractions, including Oceanworld, an aquarium about 200 yards from the ferry wharf. The ferry ride from the city makes a day at Manly feel more like a holiday than just an excursion to the beach. Take a ferry or the Manly Fast Ferry from Circular Quay. From the dock at Manly the beach is a 10-minute walk. The visitor center is located on the Forecourt of Manly Wharf. The Novotel Sydney Pacific Hotel and the Sebel Manly Beach Hotel are two upscale properties located on the beachfront. **Amenities:** food and drink; lifeguards; parking (fee); showers; toilets. **Best for:** sunrise; surfing; swimming; walking. ⊠ *Steyne St., Manly* ⊕ *www.manlyaustralia. com.au* ☉ *Manly Visitor and Information Centre weekdays 9–5, weekends 10–4.*

Fodor's Choice
★

Palm Beach. The golden sands of Palm Beach glitter as much as the bejeweled residents of the stylish nearby village. The beach is on one side of the peninsula separating the large inlet of Pittwater from the Pacific Ocean. Bathers can easily cross from the ocean side to Pittwater's calm waters. You can take a circular ferry trip around this waterway from the wharf on the Pittwater side. The view from the lighthouse at the northern end of the beach is well worth the walk. Shops and cafés sell light snacks and meals. North Palm Beach is only patrolled by lifeguards in summer (December to February). Take Bus 190 or L90 from Wynyard bus station. **Amenities:** food and drink; lifeguards; showers; toilets. **Best for:** surfing; swimming. ⊠ *Ocean Rd., Palm Beach.*

SPORTS AND THE OUTDOORS

Given its climate and its taste for the great outdoors, it's no surprise that Sydney is addicted to sports. In the cooler months rugby league dominates the sporting scene, although these days the Sydney Swans, the city's flag bearer in the national Australian Rules Football (AFL) competition, attract far bigger crowds. In summer cricket is the major spectator sport, and nothing arouses more passion than international test cricket games—especially when Australia plays against England, the traditional enemy. Sydney is well equipped with athletic facilities, from golf courses to tennis courts, and water sports come naturally on one of the world's greatest harbors.

Ticketek. This is the place to buy tickets for major sports events: the telephone line is notorious for being constantly busy, so try online first. ⊠ *Sydney* ☎ *13–2849* ⊕ *premier.ticketek.com.au.*

AUSTRALIAN RULES FOOTBALL

Sydney Cricket Ground. A fast, demanding game in which the ball can be kicked or punched between teams of 22 players, Australian Rules Football has won a major audience in Sydney, even though the city has only one professional team—the Sydney Swans—compared to the dozen that play in Melbourne—the home of the sport. Sydney Cricket Ground (SCG) hosts games April to September. ⊠ *Centennial Park, Moore Park Rd., Paddington* ☎ *02/9360–6601* ⊕ *www.sydneycricketground.com.au.*

BICYCLING

Sydney's favorite cycling track is Centennial Park's Grand Parade, a 3¾-km (2¼-mile) cycle circuit around the perimeter of this grand, gracious eastern suburbs park.

Centennial Park Cycles. Rent bicycles here for around A$20 per hour, A$70 per day. There is an additional location inside Centennial Park on Grand Drive. ⊠ *50 Clovelly Rd., Randwick* ☎ *02/9398–5027* ⊕ *www. cyclehire.com.au.*

Clarence Street Cyclery. This is a major store for all your cycling needs. Plus, you can rent hybrid bikes (an all round leisure bike) for A$29 for half day and A$49 full day; road and mountain bikes go for A$99 (half) and A$149 (full). ⊠ *104 Clarence St., City Center* ☎ *02/9295–0000* ⊕ *www.cyclery.com.au.*

Surf Lifesaving Clubs

The world's first Surf Lifesaving club was formed at Bondi Beach on February 21, 1907. Other clubs formed in quick secession, and today there are more than 300 clubs in Australia, with 38 in Sydney and 129 in New South Wales.

In the last century more than 500,000 swimmers have been rescued from patrolled beaches around the country, and more than 1 million swimmers have received first aid.

Lifesavers are Australian icons; volunteers undertake their five-hour beach patrols on a rostered basis during the summer season from September to April. In addition to the thousands of volunteers across Australia, there are also permanent, paid lifeguards who are employed by the local councils and are on duty year-round.

Lifesavers arrive at the beach bright and early, check the beach conditions, erect the red and yellow flags to indicate the safe swimming areas, and keep an eye on swimmers throughout their patrol. It's easy to spot a surf lifesaver—he or she wears the bright red-and-yellow cap and matching red-and-yellow uniform.

Bondi Beach lifesavers are the busiest in Australia. Each year about 2.5 million people come for a swim: some 2,500 rescues take place in an average year. The worst day in Bondi's history was February 6, 1938, known as Black Sunday. Lifesavers plucked 300 people from the huge surf. Five lives were lost.

It's not all work for Surf Lifesaving clubs. They hold competitions and surf carnivals throughout the summer months at numerous beaches. Events include surf swims, crew boat races (man-powered by oarsmen), surf ski races, and the macho-named "iron man" races where men (and women in separate events) perform all manner of endurance tests. Surf Lifesaving clubs opened their doors to women and children several decades ago.

BOATING AND SAILING

EastSail. Rent bareboat sailing and motored yachts from this operator for A$655 per half day (four hours); a manned yacht costs around A$915 for four hours and includes the skipper. It also conducts sailing schools. ⊠ *D'Albora Marina, New Beach Rd., Rushcutters Bay, Eastern Suburbs* ☎ *02/9327–1166* ⊕ *www.eastsail.com.au.*

Fodor'sChoice ★ **Sydney Harbour Kayaks.** Sydney Harbour Kayaks rents one- and two-person kayaks. The location beside Spit Bridge has calm water for novices, as well as several beaches and idyllic coves. Prices per hour start from A$25 for a one-person kayak and A$50 for a double. Guided 4-hour tours depart every Saturday and Sunday at 8:30 am (A$99 per person). Novices can take part in three-hour free lessons (A$50 for kayak hire). ⊠ *81 Parriwi Rd., Mosman* ☎ *02/9969–4590* ⊕ *www.sydneyharbourkayaks.com.au.*

Surf school at Bondi Beach

CRICKET

Cricket is Sydney's summer sport, and it's often played in parks throughout the nation. For Australians the pinnacle of excitement is the Ashes, when the national cricket team takes the field against England. It happens every other summer, and the two nations take turns hosting the event. Cricket season runs from October through March.

Sydney Cricket Ground. International and interstate games are played at the Sydney Cricket Ground (commonly called the SCG). ⊠ *Centennial Park, Moore Park Rd., Paddington* ☎ *02/9360–6601* ⊕ *www.sydneycricketground.com.au.*

HIKING

Fine walking trails can be found in the national parks in and around Sydney, especially in **Royal National Park** and **Ku-ring-gai Chase National Park** (32 km [20 miles] south and 25 km [15 miles] north of the city center, respectively) and **Sydney Harbour National Park**, which hugs the harbor shores. The **Bondi-to-Bronte Coast Walk** is a lovely 3½-km (2-mile) cliff walk, popular with just about everyone in the eastern suburbs. Signage explains the flora and Aboriginal history, and the area is the venue for the hugely popular Sculpture by the Sea outdoor art display (held every October and November). The **Federation Cliff Walk** from Dover Heights (north of Bondi Beach) to Vaucluse, and on to Watsons Bay, winds past some of Sydney's most exclusive suburbs. At Diamond Bay you can soak in great views of the 20-million-year-old sandstone cliffs from the steps and boardwalks.

RUGBY LEAGUE

Sydney Football Stadium. Known locally as football (or footy), rugby league is Sydney's winter addiction. This is a fast, gutsy, physical game that bears some similarities to North American football, although the action is more constant and the ball cannot be passed forward. The season falls between March and September. Sydney Football Stadium (now known by its corporate sponsorship name of Allianz Stadium) is the home ground of the Sydney Roosters. Other games are played at ANZ Stadium (Sydney Olympic Park) and stadiums throughout the suburbs. ⊠ *Centennial Park, Moore Park Rd., Paddington* ☎ *02/9360–6601* ⊕ *www.sydneycricketground.com.au.*

SCUBA DIVING

Dive Centre Manly. Located at the popular northern Sydney beach, Dive Centre Manly runs all-inclusive shore dives each day, which let you see weedy sea dragons and other sea creatures. PADI certification courses are also available. The cost for a shore dive is A$125 and A$145 for two dives. Night dives are A$125. ⊠ *10 Belgrave St., Manly* ☎ *02/9977–4355* ⊕ *www.divesydney.com.au.*

Pro Dive. Pro Dive is a PADI operator conducting courses and shore- or boat-diving excursions around the harbor and city beaches. Some of the best dive spots—with coral, rock walls, and lots of colorful fish—are close to the eastern suburb beaches of Clovelly and Coogee. The company also has a center in Manly. A four-hour boat dive with a guide costs around A$199, including rental equipment; a four-dive learn-to-dive course is A$399. Check the website for specials. ⊠ *27 Alfreda St., Coogee* ☎ *02/8116–1199* ⊕ *www.prodive.com.au.*

SURFING

All Sydney surfers have their favorite breaks, but you can usually count on good waves on at least one of the city's ocean beaches.

Lets Go Surfing. This is a complete surfing resource for anyone who wants to hang five with confidence. Lessons are available for all ages and you can rent or buy boards and wet suits. The two-hour beginner surfer lesson, in a small group, is A$99. ⊠ *128 Ramsgate Ave., North Bondi* ☎ *02/9365–1800* ⊕ *www.letsgosurfing.com.au.*

Manly Surf School. This company conducts courses for adults and children, and provides all equipment, including wet suits. Adults can join a two-hour group lesson (four per day) for A$70. Private instruction costs A$100 per hour. Stand-up paddling (on a board) lessons are also available, and are held on the calm waters of Balmoral and Narrabeen lakes. ⊠ *North Steyne Surf Club, North Steyne, Manly Beach, Manly* ☎ *02/9932–7000* ⊕ *www.manlysurfschool.com.*

Rip Curl. This store has a huge variety of boards and surfing supplies, incuding cool clothes. It's right at Bondi Beach. ⊠ *82 Campbell Parade, Bondi Beach* ☎ *02/9130–2660* ⊕ *www.ripcurl.com.au.*

Surfection Bondi Beach. Here is every surfer's idea of retail heaven: surfboards and cool clothing all housed in one huge sparkling store. ✉ *31 Hall St., Bondi Beach* ☎ *02/9130–1051.*

Swellnet. This website has surf reports and weather details. ☎ *1800/793556* ⊕ *www.swellnet.com.au.*

SWIMMING

Sydney has many heated Olympic-size swimming pools, some of which go beyond the basic requirements of a workout. Many Aussies, however, prefer to do their "laps" in ocean pools at Bondi and Manly.

FAMILY **Andrew (Boy) Charlton Pool.** Andrew (Boy) Charlton Pool isn't just any heated Olympic-size saltwater pool. Its stunning outdoor location overlooking the ships at Garden Island, its radical glass-and-steel design, and its chic terrace café above Woolloomooloo Bay make it an attraction in itself. Admission is A$6.20, and it's open September–April, daily 6 am–7 pm. ✉ *Mrs. Macquarie's Rd., The Domain* ☎ *02/9358–6686* ⊕ *www.abcpool.org.*

Cook and Phillip Park Aquatic and Fitness Centre. Cook and Phillip Park Aquatic and Fitness Centre includes wave, hydrotherapy, children's, and Olympic-size pools in a stunning high-tech complex on the eastern edge of the city center near St. Mary's Cathedral. There's also a complete fitness center and classes. Admission is A$7.20 to swim and A$19.80 for the gym, which includes pool entry. Open weekdays 6 am–10 pm, weekends 7 am–8 pm. ✉ *College St., City Center* ☎ *02/9326–0444* ⊕ *www.cookandphillip.org.au.*

TENNIS

Cooper Park Tennis Centre. This complex includes eight synthetic-grass courts and a café in a park surrounded by native bushland, about 5 km (3 miles) east of the city. Court fees are A$30 per hour from 6 am to 5 pm on weekdays, and A$34 per hour from 5 pm to 10 pm (weekdays) and on weekends 6 am to 7 pm. ✉ *Cooper Park, 1 Bunna Pl., off Suttie Rd., Woollahra* ☎ *02/9389–3100* ⊕ *www.cptennis.com.au.*

Parklands Sports Centre. Parklands Sports Centre has 11 courts in a shady park approximately 2½ km (1½ miles) from the city center. The weekday cost is A$25 per hour 9–5 and A$28 per hour 5–10 pm Monday–Thursday and until 7 pm on Friday; it's A$28 per hour 8 am–6 pm on weekends. Many buses travel past the site including the 339, 394, 396, and 397 from Circular Quay. ✉ *Moore Park, Lang Rd., at Anzac Parade, Centennial Park* ☎ *02/9662–7033* ⊕ *www.parklandssports. com.au.*

WINDSURFING

Balmoral Windsurfing, Sailing, and Kayak School. Balmoral Windsurfing, Sailing, and Kayak School runs classes from its base at this northside harbor beach. Private windsurfing lessons are A$135 per hour, sailing from A$297 for four hours of lessons over a two-day period.

Stand-up paddle boards and kayaks can be rented out for A$30 and A$25 per hour respectively. ⊠ *The Esplanade, Balmoral* ☎ *02/9960– 5344* ⊕ *www.sailingschool.com.au.*

Rose Bay Aquatic Hire. Rose Bay Aquatic Hire has joined forces with kayak operator Oz Paddle. They now rent motorboats, kayaks, and stand-up paddleboards. Motorboats are A$100 for the first two hours; kayaks are A$25 an hour, as are paddleboards. Whatever mode of transport chosen, an hour or two on Sydney's beautiful harbor is time well spent. ⊠ *1 Vickery Ave., Rose Bay* ☎ *0416/239–543, 0416/123–339* ⊕ *www.rosebayaquatichire.com.*

WHERE TO EAT

Sydney's dining scene is as sunny and cosmopolitan as the city itself, and there are diverse and exotic culinary adventures to suit every appetite. Mod Oz (modern-Australian) cooking flourishes, fueled by local produce and guided by Mediterranean and Asian techniques. Look for such innovations as tuna tartare with flying-fish roe and wasabi; emu prosciutto; five-spice duck; shiitake mushroom pie; and sweet turmeric barramundi curry. A meal at Tetsuya's or Rockpool constitutes a crash course in this dazzling culinary language. A visit to the city's fish markets at Pyrmont, five minutes from the city center, will also tell you much about Sydney's diet. Look for rudderfish, barramundi, blue-eye, kingfish, John Dory, ocean perch, and parrot fish, as well as Yamba prawns, Balmain and Moreton Bay bugs (shovel-nose lobsters), sweet Sydney rock oysters, mud crab, spanner crab, yabbies (small freshwater crayfish), and marrons (freshwater lobsters).

There are many expensive and indulgent restaurants in the city center, but the real dining scene is in the inner city, eastern suburbs, and inner-western suburbs of Leichhardt and Balmain. Neighborhoods like Surry Hills, Darlinghurst, Paddington, and beachside suburb Bondi are dining destinations in themselves. Plus, you're more likely to find a restaurant that will serve on a Sunday night in one of these places than in the central business district (the city center)—which can become a bit of a ghost town after offices close during the week. Circular Quay and The Rocks are always lively, and the Overseas Passenger Terminal (on the opposite side of the harbor from the Opera House) has several top-notch restaurants with stellar views.

Use the coordinate (⊕ 1:B2) at the end of each listing to locate a site on the corresponding map.

SYDNEY HARBOUR

$$$

AUSTRALIAN

Fodor's Choice

★

✕ **Bathers' Pavilion.** Balmoral Beach is blessed. Not only does it have an inviting sandy beach and great water views, but it also has one of the best eating strips north of the Harbour Bridge. Queen of the strip is Bathers' Pavilion, which includes a restaurant, café, and lavish private dining room. Serge Dansereau cooks with one hand on the seasons and the other on the best local ingredients at the acclaimed restaurant, but for a casual breakfast, lunch, afternoon tea or dinner it's hard to beat the café ($). There's a choice of salad, wood-fired pizzas, and seafood dishes for around A$30. Breakfast dishes are a little on the expensive side with most around A$20. No reservations taken for the café. $ *Average main: A$50* ⊠ *4 The Esplanade, Balmoral* ☎ *02/9969–5050* ⊕ *www.batherspavilion.com.au* ⌲ *Reservations essential* ✛ *2:C1.*

$ ✕ **The Deck.** If you've wanted to know just what's inside that giant face on the north side of the harbor under the bridge, well this is your chance. The Deck is located in a swanky refurbished space just as you step through the giant mouth of Luna Park, Sydney's long-established fun park. The stunning view, however, across the harbor with the Opera House right in your sights, is the real draw. The restaurant and cocktail bar are above a live venue that cranks up on the weekend, so expect a fun night out rather than a quiet tête-à-tête. You may have the place to yourself at a midweek lunch. There's a selection of seafood and non-seafood tasting plates to share, while wonderful classics such as paella and bouillabaisse are on the menu. Sweet treats include orange and cardamom crème brûlée with brandied kumquats. $ *Average main: A$34* ⊠ *Luna Park, 1 Olympic Dr., Milsons Point* ☎ *02/9033–7670* ⊕ *www.thedecksydney.com.au* ⊘ *Closed Mon. and Tues. No dinner Sun.* ✛ *2:A2.*

MODERN
AUSTRALIAN

THE ROCKS

$$ ✕ **Altitude.** The lure of this decadent restaurant high above Sydney Harbour on the 36th floor of the luxurious Shangri-La Hotel, is the view through the floor-to-ceiling windows, but the food is equally impressive. Chef Nathan Griffin presents an enticing menu of Mod Oz dishes with a strong European influence. Seafood lovers find ample selection among such dishes as Western Australian swordfish loin or Hiramasa Kingfish with celeriac, yuzu gel, and black garlic foam. For a special occasion, gather a dozen friends to dine in the opulent, egg-shaped private dining room, or indulge in the seven-course degustation (A$150; A$215 with matching wines). On weekends the adjoining bar can be a little noisy as the night wears on, so it might be a good idea to beat it early or join in the fun. $ *Average main: A$42* ⊠ *Shangri-La Hotel, 176 Cumberland St., level 36, The Rocks* ☎ *02/9250–6123* ⊕ *www.36levelsabove.com.au/altitude* ⊘ *Closed Sun. No lunch* ⌲ *Reservations essential* ✛ *1:B2.*

MODERN
AUSTRALIAN

$$$$ ✕ **Aria.** With windows overlooking the Opera House and Harbour Bridge, Aria could easily rest on the laurels of its location. Instead, celebrity chef Matthew Moran creates a menu of extraordinary dishes that may be your best meal down under. It doesn't come cheap, though; two courses are A$105, three A$130, four A$155. Lunch is a little less expensive at A$89 for three courses. Make a reservation before you even get on the plane and look forward to the Peking duck consommé with duck dumplings, shaved abalone, and mushrooms; or the barramundi with smoked dulse (a kind of seaweed), which will change the way you feel about cabbage forever. If you really want to splurge, the seasonal tasting menu is A$300 for eight courses, and a pretheater menu is also available. $ *Average main: A$105* ⊠ *1 Macquarie St., Circular*

AUSTRALIAN

Quay ☎ *02/9240–2255* ⊕ *www.ariarestaurant.com* ⊗ *No lunch weekends* ⌖ *Reservations essential* ⌂ *Jacket required* ✢ *1:C1.*

$$$$　✕**Bennelong.** One of Australia's most renowned chefs, Peter Gilmore,
AUSTRALIAN　oversees the kitchen at possibly the most superbly situated dining room
Fodor's Choice　in town. Tucked into the side of the Opera House, the restaurant affords
★　views of Sydney Harbour Bridge and the city lights. Gilmore's creations
are as special as the view and showcase the best of Australia's produce
with a focus on terroir: try the suckling pig from the Macleay Valley,
the roasted Holmbrae duck, or the superb King George whiting with
sea scallops and native parsley. Whatever you do, leave room for the
cherry jam lamington, a clever interpretation of an Australian classic,
although the pavlova (another iconic Australian dessert) shaped like the
Opera House is hard to resist for the wow factor alone. Three courses
are A$130 and pretheater dining is available if you are going to a per-
formance in the Opera House. ⑤ *Average main: A$130 three courses*
⊠ *Bennelong Point, Sydney Opera House, Circular Quay* ☎ *02/9240–
8000* ⊕ *www.bennelong.com.au* ⊗ *No lunch Sat.* ⌖ *Reservations essential* ⌂ *Jacket required* ✢ *1:C1.*

$$$$　✕**Quay.** In his take on Mod Oz cuisine, celebrity chef Peter Gilmore,
MODERN　(who also looks after Bennelong at The Opera House), masterfully
AUSTRALIAN　crafts a four-course à la carte menu with dishes like mud crab congee
Fodor's Choice　with split rice porridge, quail breasts with shallots and truffle-infused
★　milk custard, and slow-cooked suckling pig. Desserts are sublime—
Gilmore's "snow egg," which changes with the seasons and can include
white nectarine, apple, and jackfruit, had fans lining up to try it just
hours after it stole the show on MasterChef Australia. Glass walls
afford wonderful views of the bridge and Opera House. ⑤ *Average
main: A$175* ⊠ *West Circular Quay, Overseas Passenger Terminal,
Upper Level, The Rocks* ☎ *02/9251–5600* ⊕ *www.quay.com.au* ⊗ *No
lunch Mon.–Thurs.* ⌖ *Reservations essential* ✢ *1:C1.*

$　✕**Sailors Thai.** Aussies love their Thai food and this stylish restaurant
THAI　has been delivering some of the best in the city for 18 years. In a charming mid-19th-century sandstone building in The Rocks, there's a dining room on the lower level and a casual canteen, where you dine at a
long shared table, on the upper floor. Start with the shredded chicken
wrapped in organic egg nets with creamy coconut sauce and then move
on to the slow-cooked Massaman curry of Tasmanian Cape Grim beef
ribs. Everything on the five-course tasting menu (A$75) is delicious, or
choose one of the small plates, such as the soft-shell crab spiced with
garlic lime and fish sauce, from the à la carte menu. Finish your meal
off with deep-fried coconut ice cream and tamarind caramel sauce.
⑤ *Average main: A$35* ⊠ *106 George St., Lower level, The Rocks*
☎ *02/9251–2466* ⊕ *www.sailorsthai.com.au* ⊗ *No lunch weekends*
⌖ *Reservations essential* ✢ *1:C1.*

$　✕**Theatre Bar at the End of the Wharf.** Most people come to this buzzy
MODERN　bar at the end of Pier 4 for a quick bite before a show at the adjacent
AUSTRALIAN　Sydney Theatre Company, but the views of the Harbour Bridge are so
spectacular that it's worth coming here any time. It gets busy before a
show starts, but then the crowd vanishes, leaving it a pleasant place to
linger over a quiet glass of wine or cocktail and soak in the amazing

view. The menu is a mix of small plates designed to share and larger meals, with Middle Eastern and Mediterranean flavors mingling with crowd-pleasing favorites like fish and thick-cut chips and slow-cooked pork belly with crackling. A bonus is that the food and wine is half the price of other harborside restaurants, and the restaurant often runs promotions with all meals heavily discounted after 8 pm. ⑤ *Average main: A$25* ⊠ *Hickson Rd., End of Pier 4, Walsh Bay* ☎ *02/9250– 1761* ⊕ *www.sydneytheatre.com.au* ⊙ *Closed Sun.* ⌒ *Reservations not accepted* ✛ *1:B1.*

DARLING HARBOUR

$ ✕ **BBQ King.** You can find better basic Chinese food elsewhere in town,
CHINESE   but for duck and pork, barbecue-loving Sydneysiders know that this is the place to come. The poultry hanging in the window are the only decoration at this small Chinatown staple, where the food is so fresh you can almost hear it clucking—make sure you sample the duck pancakes. Barbecued pork is the other featured dish, and the suckling pig is especially delicious. It's open from 11 am until late at night, when the average customers are large groups of mates sprawled at the Formica tables feeding their drunken munchies, or Chinatown chefs kicking back after a day in the kitchen. The service can be a little brusque, but it's all part of the low-budget charm. ⑤ *Average main: A$33* ⊠ *18–20 Goulburn St., Haymarket* ☎ *02/9267–2586* ✛ *1:C5.*

$ ✕ **Golden Century.** For two hours—or as long as it takes for you to con-
CHINESE   sume delicately steamed prawns, luscious mud crab with ginger and shallots, and *pipis* (triangular clams) with black-bean sauce—you might as well be in Hong Kong. This place is heaven for seafood lovers, with wall-to-wall fish tanks filled with crab, lobster, abalone, and schools of barramundi, parrot fish, and coral trout. You won't have to ask if the food is fresh: most of it is swimming around you as you eat. Come for the big-ticket seafood or a simple meal of deep-fried duck. Supper is served until 4 am so it's popular with late-night revelers. It's not the prettiest of places and service can be hit and miss, but it has a legion of fans. ■TIP➔ Make a reservation for early in the evening, otherwise you'll encounter a long queue. ⑤ *Average main: A$30* ⊠ *393–399 Sussex St., Haymarket* ☎ *02/9212–3901* ⊕ *www.goldencentury.com.au* ✛ *1:B5.*

$ ✕ **The Malaya.** The cocktails (all A$17.50) are legendary, the view is cap-
MALAYSIAN   tivating, and the food, a traditional Chinese/Malay fusion, is extraordinary. After 50 years in the business (first opened in 1963), in different venues around Sydney, this modern Asian restaurant still does a roaring trade. Signature dishes include beef Rendang (Indonesian-style beef curry), and the spanner crab san choy bow, a fabulous twist on a classic dish. Szechuan eggplant is so good, it may be the food of the gods. Try one of the four set menus (for a minimum of three people and starting at A$58 per person) for a true feast on the extensive menu's flavor combinations. ⑤ *Average main: A$30* ⊠ *39 Lime St., King Street Wharf, Darling Harbour* ☎ *02/9279–1170* ⊕ *www.themalaya.com.au* ⊙ *No lunch Sun.* ✛ *1:B3.*

Continued on page 116

Australia's
Modern
Cuisine

It may be referred to as the land down under, but the culinary movement that's sweeping Australia means this country has come out on top. Modern Australian cuisine has transformed the land of Vegemite sandwiches and shrimp-on-the-barbie into a culinary Promised Land with local flavors, organic produce, and bountiful seafood, fashioned by chefs who remain unburdened by restrictive traditions.

Australia is fast proving to be one of the most exciting destinations in the world for food lovers. With its stunning natural bounty, multicultural inspirations, and young culinary innovators, it ticks off all the requisite foodie boxes.

In Sydney, chefs are dishing up new twists on various traditions, creating a Modern Australian (Mod Oz) cuisine with its own compelling style. Traditional bush tucker, for example, has been transformed from a means of survival into a gourmet experience. Spicy Asian flavors have been borrowed from the country's neighbors to the north, and homage has been paid to the precision and customs brought by Australia's early European settlers.

The diversity of the modern Australian culinary movement also means that it is more than just flavors: it's an experience. And one that can be obtained from the award-winning luxury restaurant down to the small Thai-style canteens, pubs, and outdoor cafés.

While purists might argue that Mod Oz cuisine is little more than a plagiarism of flavors and cultures, others will acknowledge it as unadulterated fare with a fascinating history of its very own. Either way, it still offers a dining experience that's unique from anywhere else in the world.

MENU DECODER

Barbie: barbeque | **Snags:** sausages | **Chook:** chicken | **Vegemite:** salty yeast spread | **Lamington:** small chocolate sponge cake with coconut | **Pavlova:** meringue dessert topped with cream and fruit | **Floater:** meat pie with mushy peas and gravy | **Damper:** simple bread cooked on a campfire | **Sanga:** sandwich | **Cuppa:** cup of tea | **Tucker:** food | **Chips:** French fries | **Tomato sauce:** ketchup | **Muddy:** mud crab | **Prawn:** shrimp

Seared tuna with avocado, cilantro, and black sesame seeds, topped with caviar

BUSH TUCKER

Bush Tucker food; Tropical rainforest fruits on paper bark

BACK THEN

Native Australian plants and animals have played a vital role in the diets of the Aboriginal people for more than 50,000 years. Generally referred to as bush tucker, these native fruits, nuts, seeds, vegetables, meats, and fish are harvested around the country—from arid deserts to coastal areas and tropical rainforests.

Once little more than a means of survival, today they're touted as gourmet ingredients. And you certainly don't need to go "walkabout" to find them.

RIGHT NOW

Bush tucker has undergone much transformation over the decades, experiencing a renaissance in recent years. Heavily influenced by multicultural cooking techniques, game meats such as emu and wallaby have been elevated from bush-stew ingredients to perfectly seared cuts of meat garnished with seasonal herbs and vegetables. Kangaroo is making its way into stir-fries and curries,

while crocodile—once cooked over coals on the campfire—is now served as carpaccio, tempura, or curry, among the many preparations. Seafood, like rock lobster and barramundi, can be found in humble fish-and-chip shops and top-notch eateries.

Of course, bush tucker isn't just about the protein. Native spices, wild fruits, and indigenous nuts have found favor in countless culinary applications. Lemon myrtle leaves lend a lemony flavor to baked goods and savory dishes. Alpine pepper, a crushed herb, gives foods a fiery zing. Quandong is a wild plum-like fruit with subtle apricot flavor. It once was dried as a portable energy source but now is made into jams and pie fillings. Kakadu plums are made into "super" juices with enormous vitamin C content. Bush tomatoes also have become popular in jams and sauces, and are available in supermarkets. Native nuts include the bunya nut, which is chestnut-like with pine notes, the shells of which are

Witchetty grub

Tandoori kangaroo

INDIGENOUS MEATS

CAMEL: With some one million camels in Australia, camel is fast being served up on many menus, though most are in the Northern Territory. The meat is often compared to mutton and has a similar taste and texture to beef.

CROCODILE: This meat may be fish-like in texture and appearance, but it tastes similar to chicken. The most popular cut is the tail, however legs and meat from the body are also consumed. Crocodile is growing in popularity because of its delicate flavor and versatility. It is often fried and grilled, but may be served raw in carpaccio or sushi rolls.

EMU: Although it's fowl, emu meat is similar in texture and flavor to beef with a light flavor and slight gamey tones on the palate. The meat is high in iron and very low in fat and cholesterol. Typical cuts include rump, strip loin, and oyster filet. It may be served pan-seared or lightly grilled.

KANGAROO: A dark red meat, it is extremely lean with only about 2% fat. The filet or rump is best eaten rare to medium rare, and is typically seared, barbecued, or stir-fried. Young kangaroo meat tastes like beef, while aged cuts take on a gamier flavor.

WALLABY: A cousin to the kangaroo, this meat has a somewhat milder flavor. It is a rich burgundy color and is best prepared with simple, delicate cooking styles, such as barbecuing or pan frying.

WITCHETTY GRUB: The larvae of ghost moths, these grubs are eaten raw or barbecued. People describe the taste as similar to egg, with the texture of a prawn.

used for smoking meat. Macadamia nuts, meanwhile, are among the country's biggest exports.

WHERE TO FIND IT

Despite the presence of numerous bush ingredients in Sydney restaurants, the modern bush tucker dining experience is more prominent in the northern parts of the country. You are most likely to find dishes such as kangaroo, and occasionally crocodile, on the menu of restaurants in the city's main tourist precincts of The Rocks and Circular Quay.

In Queensland and the Northern Territory, you'll find full degustation menus combining local meats and seafood with native herbs, spices, and berries. Some even offer tasting tours of their kitchen gardens where you can sample popular flavors like lemon myrtle, tarragon, and hibiscus flower straight from the bush.

Simple meal of grilled camel with vegetables

2

IN FOCUS AUSTRALIA'S MODERN CUISINE

UPDATED EUROPEAN FARE

Seafood Salad

BACK THEN

Although the foundation of Mod Oz cuisine stems from the arrival of early British settlers, the food scene has certainly steamed ahead since the days of boiled beef and damper.

The real progression of modern Australian food came after World War II, when European immigrants brought a new wave of cooking to the country. It was the French and Italians who really opened the eyes of Australians with their distinguished flavors, commitment to freshness, and masterful culinary techniques. They also laid the foundations for some of the finest vineyards and cheese makers in the country.

RIGHT NOW

Though small, there are still degrees of British influence in modern Australian cooking, albeit slightly updated. The quintessential English meat pie is now filled with ingredients such as Murray cod, lamb, bush tomato, and kangaroo. Traditional Sunday roasts and

fish-and-chips spring up in pubs and cafes, but often with a twist. And tea is still a staple on the breakfast table with a true Aussie favorite, Vegemite on toast.

Poaching, roasting, and braising are now popular methods to cook everything from reef fish and yabbies to lamb, suckling pig, and rabbit. Omelettes, cassoulets, and soufflés as well as pasta, risotto, and gnocchi are very well suited to the country's prize-winning meats, vegetables, and seafood. And the rigorous use of garlic, saffron, basil, and tarragon is common in many kitchens.

Greeks, Germans, and Spaniards have also greatly influenced dining, with tapas bars, tavernas, and schnitzel houses well represented throughout the country. Middle Eastern and North African flavors are also beginning to leave their marks.

Even casual pubs are updating dishes to reflect ethnic influences and local products. It's not unusual to see items like

Aussie meat pie

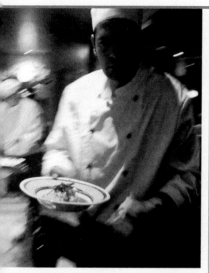

AUSTRALIA'S NATURAL BOUNTY

CHEESE FRUIT: Grown in tropical areas, this fruit high in vitamin C has long been used for medicinal purposes. It's eaten while still green since it has a distinct rotting cheese smell when ripe. Leaves can also be eaten raw or cooked.

ILLAWARRA PLUMS: Usually used in jams and chutneys or as a rich sauce to accompany kangaroo, venison, or emu. High in antioxidants, they have a subtle plum flavor with a hint of pine.

LEMON MYRTLE: A native tree with a citrus fragrance and flavor. Leaves can be used fresh or dried and ground in sweet and savory styles of cooking.

MACADAMIA NUTS: Known as Kindal Kindal by native Australians, the macadamia is a round white nut with a hard brown shell and creamy flavor.

MUNTRIES: Small berry-like fruit that have a distinct apple flavor. Also known as emu apples, they can be eaten fresh in salads or added to desserts.

PAPER BARK: Papery leaves from the Mellaluca tree, used to cook meat and seafood.

QUANDONG: A bright red fruit similar to a native peach. It's commonly used to make jams and sauces.

WARRIGAL GREENS: A herb-like vegetable with a flavor similar to spinach. They must be well cooked to eliminate their toxic oxalate content.

WATTLESEED: Also known as acacia seeds. They have a nutty to coffee-like flavor and are very high in protein. Often ground down and used in baking.

spicy chorizo pizza and Peking Duck pizza on their menus.

Another hallmark of Mod Oz cuisine—and one that parallels America's current culinary trends—is its fascination with seasonal vegetables and organic meats. Specialist farms raising free-range poultry and livestock have become extremely popular with many restaurants throughout the country. Menus often cite an ingredient's producer, i.e. "Blackmore's wagyu bresaola," and also note whether ingredients are "pasture-raised" or "locally grown."

The "paddock to plate" philosophy is getting more attention from top restaurateurs. This means a restaurant aims to source its produce from farmers and producers within their community, ensuring transport miles stay low while food is fresh and region-specific. Some establishments go a step further by growing and harvesting produce on-site in their own kitchen gardens.

Meringue topped with fresh fruit

ASIAN FUSION

Thai-style kangaroo curry

BACK THEN

Much has changed in the way of Asian food in Australia. Sixty years ago sushi didn't exist in the vocabulary, now there are Japanese restaurants on almost every street.

The Gold Rush of the mid-19th century brought an influx of Chinese immigrants to Australia, prompting Asian cuisine's humble beginnings here. Thai, Vietnamese, Indian, Malaysian, and Japanese migrants followed in various waves in the 20th century. Before long, a cuisine that had started out in family-run restaurants in the outer suburbs of Sydney had become a burgeoning new trend. And by the late 1990s the children of the first wave of immigrants had formed the new guard.

RIGHT NOW

Traditional Chinese, Thai, and Japanese restaurants are very popular in Australia. But Asian fusion restaurants are leading the charge in creating Australia-specific taste innovations. Asian fusion cuisine combines the traditional flavors of Thai, Chinese, Japanese, and Vietnamese cooking, using local Australian ingredients and Western culinary techniques. Chic contemporary interiors, often with long communal tables and shared dishes, are the latest trend. Robust herbs such as mint and coriander, fiery chili, zesty black vinegar, ginger, and pickled vegetables are core ingredients, often wok-fried with fresh Australian ingredients such as Barossa Valley chicken, Thirlmere duck, or Bangalow pork.

Leading the charge is world-renowned, Sydney-based chef Tetsuya Wakuda. His signature dish, a confit of Petuna Tasmanian Ocean Trout with konbu, apple, daikon, and wasabi is a prime example of Asian fusion, uniquely blending French techniques with his Japanese heritage and excellent Australian products.

Yet, smaller modern canteen-style eateries are also serving up contemporary Asian fare that pro-

Red chile peppers

Rock lobsters

LOCAL FISH AND SEAFOOD

ABALONE: A large sea snail with an edible muscular foot. It has a firm, rubbery texture with a very delicate flavor and can retail for about $100 per kilogram. Abalone are often seared or fried.

BALMAIN OR MORETON BAY BUGS: A smaller relative of the rock lobster with a short tail, flat head, and bug-like eyes. They have a sweet taste and a medium texture. A favorite served cold in salads and seafood platters, or split down the middle and grilled.

BARRAMUNDI: A member of the perch family, it's a highly versatile fish with a medium to firm flesh and white to light pink tones. Native to Australia, it lives in both fresh and salt waters and is farmed as well as caught in the wild.

ROCK LOBSTERS: A spiny lobster with long antennae and no claws. The four main types—eastern, southern, western, and tropical—each offer slightly different flavours and textures. The tropical are excellent as sashimi, while the eastern, southern and western lend themselves to baking and barbecue.

SYDNEY ROCK OYSTERS: Despite their name, these bivalves are commonly found throughout the east coast. They're prized for their distinct rich and creamy flavor, and are smaller in size than Pacific oysters. Try eating them raw with a squirt of lemon.

YABBIES: A fresh-water crayfish with firm white flesh and a sweeter taste than rock lobster. Small in size, they can be tricky to eat but are worth the effort. They're often cooked simply in a pot of salted, boiling water.

vides excellent quality at a fraction of the price. It's in these bustling restaurants that flavors and dishes such as shucked oyster with chili and galangal vinaigrette, roasted duck in coconut curry, wagyu-beef hotpot, soft-shell crab with chili jam, and green curry of barramundi bounce off their plates.

While the majority of Asian fusion food in Australia relies heavily on light cooking styles and fresh ingredients, clay pot cooking as well as heavier-style Malaysian and Indian curries, such as rendang and vindaloo made with local lamb and beef, are also becoming popular.

Asian influences have also made their mark on traditional seafood restaurants, where ginger, lime, coriander, and chili add extra zing to alfresco menus. Exquisite dishes include Japanese-inspired butter-grilled scallops, steamed mussels in Thai-style coconut broth, or ocean trout grilled with garlic, soy, and chili.

Salad of yabby tails

SYDNEY CITY CENTER

$$ ✕ **Bambini Trust.** It's hidden behind huge black doors in one of the city's
ITALIAN   historic sandstone buildings, but once you're inside you'd swear you
were in Paris. Dark-wood paneling, black-and-white photographs, and
mirrors bearing the day's specials in flowing script lend a bistro feel.
The fare is predominately Italian with a sprinkling of French and Mod
Oz dishes. Being in the heart of the city, it's also popular at breakfast
where the delicious crab omelet makes an exotic start to the work
day. At dinner you can't go wrong with the popular cracked pepper
spaghettini with a sauté of Yamba prawns, chili, and garlic. A pre- or
postmeal drink in the marble-lined, chandeliered Bambini Wine Room
is a must. $ *Average main: A$38* ⊠ *185 Elizabeth St., City Center*
☎ *02/9283–7098* ⊕ *www.bambinitrust.com.au* ⊗ *Closed Sun. No
breakfast or lunch Sat.* ✛ *1:C4.*

$$$$ ✕ **Est.** This elegant, pillared dining room is the perfect setting for show-
MODERN   ing off chef Peter Doyle's modern, light touch with Mod Oz cuisine.
AUSTRALIAN   Anything Doyle cooks with scallops is divine as is his salad of span-
ner crab, cauliflower, white radicchio, and nasturtiums. Seafood lovers
will relish the Murray cod with shaved abalone, or they can opt for
the tantalizing caramelized pork belly teamed with a bug tail (that's a
small crayfish). Finish off with a dessert of intriguing tastes—Earl Grey
ice cream with blood orange citrus curd doughnuts and blood orange
sorbet. The seven-course tasting menu (A$180) is a heavenly experi-
ence. There's also a four-course chef's menu (A$155) and various two-,
three-, and four-course lunch options, but no à la carte menu. $ *Aver-
age main: A$105* ⊠ *Establishment Hotel, 252 George St., City Center*
☎ *02/9240–3000* ⊕ *www.merivale.com.au/est* ⊗ *Closed Sun. No lunch
Sat.* ⊛ *Reservations essential* ✛ *1:C2.*

$$$$ ✕ **Rockpool.** A meal at Rockpool is a crash course in what Mod Oz cook-
MODERN   ing is all about, conducted in a glamorous, long dining room with a cat-
AUSTRALIAN   walk-like ramp. Chefs Neil Perry and Phil Wood weave Thai, Chinese,
Fodor's Choice   Mediterranean, and Middle Eastern influences into their repertoire with
★   effortless flair and originality. The seasonal 10-course dinner tasting
menu (A$185) constantly dazzles and may include mud crab with stir-
fried milk and Jerusalem artichoke or snapper with sour orange curry,
cashew, and coconut. Don't miss the date tart for dessert—it's been a
Rockpool favorite since 1984. The Classic Lunch Menu, of two set
courses, is a great value at A$49. $ *Average main: A$185* ⊠ *11 Bridge
St., City Center* ☎ *02/9252–1888* ⊕ *www.rockpool.com* ⊗ *Closed Sun.
No lunch Sat.* ⊛ *Reservations essential* ⋔ *Jacket required* ✛ *1:C2.*

$$ ✕ **Spice Temple.** The culinary focus of this chic basement eatery—another
CHINESE   of the restaurants owned by Neil Perry of Rockpool fame—is regional
China. There are dishes from far-flung Yunnan, Hunan, and Sichuan
provinces, and as the names suggests, they all have a kick. The food is
meant to be shared, so pass around the ginger shallot crab, the pork
belly, or the extra spicy hot and numbing crispy duck. ■ **TIP➜ The hottest dishes are marked in red on the menu.** It's a busy, trendy eatery
(down a somewhat steep flight of stairs), so if you have to wait at the bar
for a table, grab a cocktail and a spicy pork bun and take in the opium
den ambience. Cocktails are named after the Chinese Zodiac; if you're

2

born in the Year of the Dragon you might like to sip on a refreshing mix of lemongrass and rose soda, citrus, and Tanqueray gin. $ *Average main: A$40 ⊠ 10 Bligh St., City Center* ☎ *02/8078–1888* ⊕ *www. rockpool.com/spicetemplesydney* ⊙ *Closed Sun. No lunch Sat.* ✛ *1:C3.*

$$$$
MODERN
AUSTRALIAN
Fodor's Choice
★

✕ **Tetsuya's.** It's worth getting on the waiting list—there's *always* a waiting list—to sample the unique blend of Western and Japanese-French flavors crafted by Sydney's most applauded chef, Tetsuya Wakuda. The serene, expansive dining room's unobtrusive Japanese aesthetic leaves the food as the true highlight. Confit of ocean trout served with unpasteurized ocean-trout roe is a signature item on the set 11-course degustation menu (A$220 and A$110 extra for matching wines), while other dishes may include New Zealand Scampi with chicken liver parfait, or roasted breast of quail with quail leg rillettes. The menu changes often but never fails to dazzle. Views of a Japanese garden—complete with bonsai and a waterfall—make this place feel miles from the city center. It's open for dinner from Tuesday to Saturday, and lunch on Saturday only. $ *Average main: A$220* ⊠ *529 Kent St., City Center* ☎ *02/9267–2900* ⊕ *www.tetsuyas.com* ⊙ *Closed Sun. and Mon. No lunch Tues.–Fri.* ⚖ *Reservations essential* ✛ *1:B5.*

INNER SYDNEY AND THE EASTERN SUBURBS

DARLINGHURST

$
CAFÉ
Fodor's Choice
★

✕ **bills.** Named after celebrity chef and cookbook author Bill Granger, this sunny corner café is so addictive it should come with a health warning. It's a favorite hangout of everyone from local nurses to semidisguised rock stars, and you never know who you might be sitting next to at the newspaper-strewn communal table. If you're not interested in the creaminess of what must be Sydney's best scrambled eggs, try the ricotta hotcakes with fresh banana and honeycomb butter or the corn fritters. The coconut-poached chicken sandwich with cucumber and lime mayonnaise makes an ideal lunch. Dinner selections at the Surry Hills location (359 Crown Street) are similarly gourmet comfort food. $ *Average main: A$25* ⊠ *433 Liverpool St., Darlinghurst* ☎ *02/9360– 9631* ⊕ *www.bills.com.au* ⊙ *No dinner* ✛ *1:E5.*

$
CAFÉ

✕ **The Goods.** Griddle pan dishes are the draw at this friendly, and slightly noisy, organic café and food store on the city fringe. Served in cast iron skillets and topped with two baked eggs, the griddle choices include creamed corn with chorizo or their own home-cured smoky bacon. Cakes and baked goods are made on the premises; diners return time and time again for the coconut cake to savor with a great cup of tea or coffee. It's a perfect break after shopping in nearby trendy Darlinghurst. Much of the produce on the shelves are ingredients used in the meals, and the tea and coffee are grown on organic or biodynamic farms. Here's a place you can happily (and healthily!) browse. $ *Average main: A$16* ⊠ *253 Crown St., Darlinghurst* ☎ *02/9357–6690* ⊙ *No dinner* ✛ *1:D5.*

KINGS CROSS AND POTTS POINT

$$ × **Billy Kwong.** Locals rub shoulders while eating no-fuss Chinese food
CHINESE at TV chef Kylie Kwong's trendy restaurant. Kwong prepares the kind
Fodor's Choice of food her family cooks, with Grandma providing not just the inspira-
★ tion but also the recipes. The prawn wontons with brown rice vinegar
are always popular, but the standout dish is the poached chicken with
a dressing of tamari, chili, and coriander. If you have a big appetite,
indulge in a variety of dishes with the seven-course banquet (A$75).
⑤ *Average main: A$38* ⊠ *1/28 Macleay St., Elizabeth Bay* ☎ *02/9332–
3300* ⊕ *billykwong.com.au* ☽ *No lunch* ✛ *1:D6.*

$$ × **Mere Catherine.** You won't find the number of this little hole-in-the-
FRENCH wall restaurant in any trendy young thing's speed dial, but it is beloved
by legions of fans who rejoiced when it reopened a couple of years ago.
The design is retro 1970s, and the dishes are classic French—onion
soup, pâté, escargots, duck a l'orange, tarragon chicken, wonderful
chateaubriand, and crème caramel for dessert. It only seats 18 in a
tiny space that is akin to dining in some French family's home. The
windows have lace curtains and the tables are candlelit, so come with
someone you love and soak in the romantic atmosphere to the strains
of Edith Piaf in the background. ⑤ *Average main: A$42* ⊠ *166 Victoria
St., Potts Point* ☎ *02/9358–2000* ▭ *No credit cards* ☽ *No lunch Sun.
and Mon.* ✛ *1:E4.*

$$ × **Red Lantern on Riley.** Owned by Vietnamese TV chef Luke Nguyen,
VIETNAMESE this restaurant is popular with his legions of TV fans. Diners should
always start with the country's great export, rice paper rolls. Here you
can have them filled with roast duck, enoki mushrooms, and herbs;
or prawns and pork. Another ultra tasty dish is *go chien don*—crispy
skinned chicken slowly poached in master stock with ginger, shallot,
and oyster sauce. An unusual but yummy dessert is the black sesame
seed dumplings with black sesame seed ice cream. For the full range
of flavors, there's a tasting menu of nine dishes starting at A$70 per
person (desserts an extra A$10). ⑤ *Average main: A$38* ⊠ *60 Riley St.,
Darlinghurst* ☎ *02/9698–4355* ⊕ *www.redlantern.com.au* ☽ *No lunch
Sat.–Wed.* ✛ *1:D6.*

WOOLLOOMOOLOO

$$ × **Otto Ristorante.** Few restaurants have the magnetic pull of Otto, a
ITALIAN place where radio shock jocks sit side by side with fashion-magazine
editors and confirmed foodies. Yes, it's a scene, but fortunately one with
good Italian food prepared by chef Richard Ptacnik. The homemade
pastas are menu standouts; try the strozzapreti pasta with prawns or
the saffron fettucine with rabbit ragout. The fennel crusted swordfish,
potato confit with heirloom carrots and pencil leek is also delicious.
The selection of Italian wines is expensive but rarely matched this far
from Milan. ⑤ *Average main: A$44* ⊠ *Wharf at Woolloomooloo, Area
8, 6 Cowper Wharf Rd., Eastern Suburbs* ☎ *02/9368–7488* ⊕ *www.
ottoristorante.com.au* ⌱ *Reservations essential* ✛ *1:E3.*

Map 2: Where to Eat and Stay in Bondi Beach and the Eastern Suburbs

BALMORAL

Middle Head

Bathers' Pavilion

South Head

Sebel Manly Beach

CLIFTON GARDENS

Watsons Bay

NEUTRAL BAY

NORTH SYDNEY

Cremorne Pt.

VAUCLUSE

The Deck KIRRIBILLI

Bradleys Head

Shark Pt.

Port Jackson

Sydney Harbour Bridge

Potts Pt.

Pt. Piper

BALMAIN

SYDNEY

Darling Pt.

Catalina Restaurant

ROSE BAY

Park William St.

BONDI

GLEBE

Oxford St.

Elizabeth St.

Ocean St.

EDGECLIFF

Porch and Parlour Sean's Panaroma
Brown Sugar

WOOLLAHRA

Adina Apartment Hotel The Bucket List
Bondi Beach

Pyrmont Bridge Rd.

South Dowling St.

Birrell St.

Bondi Rd.

Icebergs Dining Room and Bar

CENTENNIAL PARK

BRONTE

0   1 mi

KEY

☐ Hotels
■ Restaurants
✦ following restaurant and hotel reviews indicates a map-grid coordinate

Bronte Belo

0   2 km

Crowne Plaza Coogee Beach

PADDINGTON

$$$ ✕ **Buon Ricordo.** Walking into this happy, bubbly place is like turning
ITALIAN up at a private party in the backstreets of Naples. Host, chef, and sur-
rogate uncle Armando Percuoco invests classic Neapolitan and Tuscan
techniques with inventive personal touches to produce such dishes as
warmed figs with Gorgonzola and prosciutto, truffled egg pasta, and
scampi with saffron sauce and black-ink risotto. The snapper fillet on
a bed of zucchini flowers, mint and zucchini is heaven for seafood
lovers. Everything comes with Italian-style touches that you can see,
feel, smell, and taste. Leaving the restaurant feels like leaving home,
especially if you've partaken of the wonderful six-course degustation
menu (A$140). ⑤ *Average main: A$48* ✉ *108 Boundary St., Padding-*
ton ☎ *02/9360–6729* ⊕ *www.buonricordo.com.au* ◷ *Closed Sun. and*
Mon. No lunch Tues.–Thurs. ⌂ *Reservations essential* ✦ *1:F5.*

$$ ✕ **Four in Hand.** At this cute, popular little pub in Paddington, chef
AUSTRALIAN Colin Fassnidge (an Irishman who emerged as the most controversial
guest judge on Australian TV cooking show "My Kitchen Rules") has
been wowing patrons for years with his shared dish for two of slow-
braised lamb shoulder with kipfler potatoes, baby carrots, and salsa
verde. His whole suckling pig is also a popular Sunday long-lunch treat.
Starters and mains change monthly, and the restaurant's popularity has

seen it open for lunch and dinner six days a week. $ *Average main: A$39* ⊠ *105 Sutherland St., Paddington* ☎ *02/9362–1999* ⊕ *www. fourinhand.com.au* ☺ *Closed Mon.* ✛ *1:G5.*

WOOLLAHRA

$$ ✕ **Bistro Moncur.** This bistro in the Woollahra Hotel spills over with
FRENCH   happy-go-lucky patrons—mostly locals from around the leafy suburb of
Woollahra—who have been coming back for more than 18 years now.
The best dishes are inspired takes on Parisian fare, like the grilled Sirloin
Café de Paris, french onion soufflé gratin, and port sausages with potato
puree and Lyonnaise onions, although the signature dish you must try is
the much-loved, twice-cooked souffle. The casual café and bar, Moncur
Terrace, serves mains such as Wagyu beef burgers (A$19) and gourmet
pizzas (A$20). $ *Average main: A$42* ⊠ *Woollahra Hotel, 116 Queen
St., Woollahra* ☎ *02/9327–9713* ⊕ *woollahrahotel.com.au* ✛ *1:H6.*

$ ✕ **Chiswick.** Few central Sydney restaurants have access to their own home-
MODERN   grown produce, but here in trendy and leafy Woollahra—just a few kilo-
AUSTRALIAN   meters east of the city—is an all-white and refreshingly bright restaurant
surrounded by formal gardens and a large kitchen garden. Chiswick is all
about stylish casual dining using the freshest of produce and a wonderful
place to linger over a long lunch on a sunny day. There are small plates
for sharing, such as the char-grilled scallops; large plates for sharing with
a group of four (try the lamb from celebrity chef Matt Moran's own farm);
and main courses such as wood-fired pork chops with celeriac, apple, and
the house mustard. $ *Average main: A$34* ⊠ *65 Ocean St., Woollahra*
☎ *02/8388–8688* ⊕ *www.chiswickrestaurant.com.au* ✛ *1:H6.*

SURRY HILLS

$ ✕ **Four ate Five.** This buzzy little café serves some of the best breakfasts
CAFÉ   in Surry Hills, which is really saying something as there is plenty of
stiff competition in this part of town. Come here for the house-made
muesli and organic yogurt or fuel up with the 485—egg, hummus, feta,
pilpelchuma chili paste, Israeli pickles, and red cabbage salad on a bagel
or pretzel—and wash it down with some ginger turmeric kombucha.
Or if you like to start your day with a sugar hit try the white choco-
late pancakes with berry compote and creamed coconut yogurt. They
also do great sandwiches and a wicked double espresso coffee frappe.
$ *Average main: A$16* ⊠ *485 Crown St., Surry Hills* ☎ *02/9698–6485*
⊕ *fouratefive.com* ☺ *No dinner* ✛ *1:D6.*

$$ ✕ **Longrain.** It's always a fun night at this fashionable post-industrial Thai
THAI   eatery because you never know who you'll end up meeting at the large
Fodor's Choice   communal table. The generous-size innovative mains—some say the best
★   Thai food in town—are designed to be shared. Begin with a simple starter
of either betel nut leaf with prawn-toasted coconut or a freshly shucked
oyster with red chili and coriander. Mains include the stir-fried pork belly
with chili and ginger, while egg nets—lacy omelets filled with prawns,
pork, peanuts, and bean sprouts—are also a popular choice. Longrain's
cocktails are legendary for their generous pours; try the ping pong—a
luscious mix of passion fruit, lychee, and vodka. ■ **TIP➔ Sign up for one
of the monthly cocktail classes to learn the barman's secrets.** $ *Aver-
age main: A$36* ⊠ *85 Commonwealth St., Surry Hills* ☎ *02/9280–2888*
⊕ *www.longrain.com* ☺ *No lunch Sat.–Thurs.* ✛ *1:C5.*

2

$$$$ ✕ **Marque.** Chef Mark Best insists on exemplary service and great food
FRENCH at this elegant Surry Hills restaurant. Few chefs approach French fla-
Fodor's Choice vors with such passion and dedication (and stints alongside three-star
★ demigods Alain Passard in Paris and Raymond Blanc in England haven't
done any harm either). Best's creative fare (which has been called "too
adventurous" by some diners) includes blue swimmer crab with almond
jelly, almond gazpacho, and sweet corn; and roasted Muscovy duck
with carrots, Kimchi pear, and nori. The chef is most famous for chaud-
froid egg and grissini, which will change the way you think about boiled
eggs and toast soldiers forever. The dinner degustation (A$115 for four
courses, A$165 for eight) will transport you to heaven. The best deal
in town, though, is the Friday-only, set-menu, three-course lunch for
A$49. There are no à la carte prices and a minimum of three courses.
$ *Average main: A$115* ⊠ *4/5 355 Crown St., Surry Hills* ☎ *02/9332–
2225* ⊕ *marquerestaurant.com.au* ⊗ *Closed Sun. No lunch Sat.–Thurs.*
⌸ *Reservations essential* ☞ *Sat. night, eight-course menu only* ✛ *1:D6.*

BONDI BEACH

$ ✕ **Bronte Belo.** One of eight or nine eateries in the buzzy café strip oppo-
BRAZILIAN site Bronte Beach, this is a great place to refuel after the Bondi-to-Bronte
clifftop walk. All share the same postcard-perfect view, but Bello is
worth seeking out for its consistently good coffee and spicy sticky chai.
It has a little more elbow space between tables than some of its neighbors. The menu has all the standard breakfast and brunch selections,
many with a slight Brazilian twist, like the poached eggs served with
a spicy tomato ragu. Lunch is even more Brazilian with Coxinha (croquettes filled with spicy chicken), Feijoada (black bean and meat stew)
and Moqueca (fish stew with coconut milk) alongside seafood pastas,
burgers, and hot sandwiches. $ *Average main: A$23* ⊠ *469 Bronte Rd.,
Bronte* ☎ *02/9369–5673* ⊕ *www.brontebelo.com.au* ✛ *2:D3.*

$$ ✕ **Brown Sugar.** You have to seek out this Bondi Beach restaurant, as it's
MODERN situated several hundred feet back from the beach. You'll quickly find
AUSTRALIAN out, however, why locals love this place: organic, seasonal, handcrafted
food. This daytime café and evening bistro is small, hip, and always
buzzing. Weekend breakfasts, brunches, and lunches are popular espe-
cially if you like Moroccan eggs (slow-cooked with English spinach,
chorizo, spiced peppers, and tomatoes) and sweet treats such as mouth-
watering buttermilk pancakes. It's a popular place for dinner, too, so
book ahead. Main course favorites include fish pie with leek and truffle
oil, while the hazelnut chocolate fondant with honey malt ice cream has
to be experienced. $ *Average main: A$35* ⊠ *106 Curlewis St., Bondi
Beach* ☎ *02/9130–1566* ⊕ *www.brownsugarbondi.com.au* ⊗ *Closed
Mon. No breakfast or lunch Tues.–Thurs.* ✛ *2:D3.*

$ ✕ **The Bucket List.** In the famous buttercup-yellow Bondi Pavilion, this
SEAFOOD beachfront restaurant has broad appeal—there are gatherings of fami-
FAMILY lies having brunch; lunchers enjoying the spectacular views; twenty-
somethings in for an early evening cocktail at the swanky bar; and
couples tucking into seafood under the stars. The grilled haloumi with
shaved zucchini and the grilled chorizo with lemon are there to be
shared; larger dishes include fish-and-chips, John Dory fish burger with
fries, and slipper lobster spaghetti with cherry tomatoes, spinach, chili,

and lemon. And, yes, the cutlery comes in colorful little buckets and the beachy interior includes surfboards and funky fish artwork. $ *Average main: A$29* ✉ *Shop 1, Bondi Pavillion, Queen Elizabeth Dr., Bondi Beach* ☎ *02/9365–4122* ⊕ *www.thebucketlistbondi.com* ⊗ *No dinner Mon. and Tues.* ☞ *No bookings taken for outside areas* ✛ *2:D3.*

$$$ ✕ **Catalina Restaurant.** This harbor-front restaurant occupies the site of
SEAFOOD the old "airport" (back in the days when the fastest way to get to England was by flying boat), and has ringside views of the harbor and Shark Island. Patrons can watch modern seaplanes take off and land just meters away while dining on fine seafood. Perched on piers over the water, with a distinctive white profile, Catalina has been one of Sydney's standout fine-dining establishments since it opened in 1994. A unique concept for Sydney, the restaurant kitchen is open from midday to midnight (except on Sunday), allowing diners to turn up at any time; patrons can also pop in for a drink and graze on a casual bar menu. Seafood lovers relish the oysters, sushi, and sashimi created by the sushi master chef, while the signature dish of roasted suckling pig with braised red cabbage and raisins (A$110) is sensational. The views from the floor-to-ceiling windows, the open deck, and the cozy fire in winter make this a restaurant for all seasons. $ *Average main: A$48* ✉ *Lyne Park, New South Head Rd., Rose Bay* ☎ *02/9371–0555* ⊕ *www.catalinarosebay.com.au* ⊗ *No dinner Sun.* ✛ *2:C2.*

$$$ ✕ **Icebergs Dining Room and Bar.** The fashionable and famous (including
ITALIAN celebrities like Mick Jagger and Paris Hilton) just adore perching like
Fodor's Choice seagulls over the swimming pool at the south end of Australia's most
★ famous beach. It is one of the must-visit restaurants in Sydney, for both the sensational view and the exquisite food. Take a seat on a low-back suede chair, check your reflection in the frosted glass, and prepare to indulge in sophisticated Mediterranean creations like buffalo mozzarella air-freighted from Campania, wood-fried artichoke hearts, aged Sicilian salted anchovies, and ligurina olives served with bruschetta and an array of fresh seafood pasta dishes. If you're a hearty party of eight, tuck into the whole roasted suckling pig on bay leaves with grilled peppers (with 48 hours notice). Those who just want to drink in the view, and a cocktail or two, can enjoy delicious morsels—such as oysters and mini-ciabattas—in the bar. $ *Average main: A$48* ✉ *1 Notts Ave., Bondi Beach* ☎ *02/9365–9000* ⊕ *idrb.com* ⊗ *Closed Mon.* ☖ *Reservations essential* ✛ *2:D3.*

$ ✕ **Porch and Parlour.** You'll probably have to wait to get one of the tiny
CAFÉ tables in this rustic hole-in-the-wall café and wine bar on the northern end of Bondi Beach, but it's worth waiting for one of the best (and healthiest) breakfasts in Bondi. Once you've got a seat and a cup of the fabulous coffee, the service is fast and efficient. Breakfasts range from porridge with flaxseed, amaranth, and quinoa to bowls of kale, spinach, coriander, mint, and avocado, with a couple of eggs thrown in for good measure. A more decadent option is the "devil's breakfast," with crispy pork belly, bean mole, roasted sweet potato and chili and paprika coated eggs. Lunch and dinner are also popular, with lots of delicious salads and seafood. After sundown, the café morphs into a hip little wine bar. $ *Average main: A$22* ✉ *110 Ramsgate Ave., Bondi*

Beach ☎ *02/9300–0111* ⊕ *www.porchandparlour.com.au* ☽ *No dinner Mon. and Tues.* ⌂ *Reservations not accepted* ✛ *2:D3.*

$$
AUSTRALIAN
✕ **Sean's Panaroma.** North Bondi Beach wouldn't be the same without Sean's Panaroma ("Sean's" to locals), perched on a slight rise a stone's throw from the famous beach. It's been there since the mid-1990s and owner Sean Moran loads his menu with fresh produce grown on his farm in the Blue Mountains, aptly named "Farm Panaroma." Dishes change regularly and are only featured on a blackboard: they may include backed snapper with red bell pepper, olives, eggplant, and tomato; or a ravioli of zucchini, mozzarella, and lemons. The many fans in Sydney means it can be difficult to secure a table, and some the say the service is hit-and-miss (if not a bit arrogant), so be warned. ⑤ *Average main: A$45* ✉ *270 Campbell Parade, Bondi Beach* ☎ *02/9365–4924* ⊕ *www.seanspanaroma.co* ☽ *No dinner Sun.–Tues. No lunch Mon.– Thurs.* ✛ *2:D2.*

WHERE TO STAY

From grand hotels with white-glove service to tucked-away bed-and-breakfasts, there's lodging to fit all styles and budgets in Sydney. The best addresses in town are undoubtedly in The Rocks, where the tranquil setting and harbor views are right near major cultural attractions, restaurants, shops, and galleries. The area around Kings Cross is another hotel district, with a good collection of boutique and backpacker lodgings. Keep in mind, however, that this is also the city's major nightlife district, and the scene can get pretty raucous after sunset.

Use the coordinate (✛ 1:B2) at the end of each listing to locate a site on the corresponding map.

THE ROCKS

$$
HOTEL
Fodor'sChoice
★
▦ **Harbour Rocks Hotel.** Formerly a wool-storage facility, this four-story hotel is an Accor MGallery property, which is a select portfolio of distinctive and individual hotels in Australia. **Pros:** great location near harbor; ultrastylish; unique courtyard in the city. **Cons:** heritage rooms could be larger; Wi-Fi is an additional charge. ⑤ *Rooms from: A$299* ✉ *34 Harrington St., The Rocks* ☎ *02/8220–9999* ⊕ *www. harbourrocks.com.au* ⌲ *57 rooms, 2 suites* ⏵ *Breakfast* ✛ *1:B2.*

$$
HOTEL
▦ **Holiday Inn Old Sydney.** Even though it's been around for a few decades, this hotel with its low-key facade is still a bit of a secret. **Pros:** fantastic location near harbor; good value; top story pool. **Cons:** still has a dated look; street-facing rooms very noisy. ⑤ *Rooms from: A$300* ✉ *55 George St., The Rocks* ☎ *1800/007697* ⊕ *www.holidayinn.com* ⌲ *174 rooms* ⏵ *No meals* ✛ *1:C2.*

$$$
HOTEL
Fodor'sChoice
★
▦ **The Langham Sydney.** More English country manor than inner-city hotel, this gorgeous property feels like a decadent, luxurious sanctuary. **Pros:** sumptuous, good location; excellent in-house restaurant; afternoon teas; complimentary Wi-Fi. **Cons:** lack of views. ⑤ *Rooms from: A$450* ✉ *89–113 Kent St., The Rocks* ☎ *02/9256–2222* ⊕ *www.sydney. langhamhotels.com.au* ⌲ *79 rooms, 21 suites* ⏵ *Breakfast* ✛ *1:B2.*

$
B&B/INN
 Lord Nelson Brewery Hotel. If your idea of heaven is sleeping above a pub that brews its own boutique beers (or ales, as they're rightly called), this is the place. **Pros:** great location near harbor; fun pub; cheap rates; free Wi-Fi. **Cons:** may be noisy on weekend nights; some rooms are small. $ *Rooms from: A$180* ⊠ *19 Kent St., The Rocks* ☎ *02/9251–4044* ⊕ *www.lordnelsonbrewery.com* ⟿ *9 rooms* ⦿ *Breakfast* ✣ *1:B2.*

$$$$
HOTEL
Fodor's Choice
★
 Park Hyatt Sydney. A multimillion-dollar total rebuild, which included the addition of an entire top floor, has seen the iconic Park Hyatt Sydney reemerge as Sydney's best address. **Pros:** fantastic location; gorgeous views. **Cons:** expensive. $ *Rooms from: A$1030* ⊠ *7 Hickson Rd., The Rocks* ☎ *02/9241–1234* ⊕ *www.sydney.park.hyatt.com* ⟿ *144 rooms, 11 suites* ⦿ *No meals* ✣ *1:C1.*

$$$
HOTEL
 Rendezvous Hotel Sydney The Rocks. Situated in the heart of the historic Rocks precinct, the lodging has a boutique-hotel style. **Pros:** great location; good value; spacious rooms. **Cons:** simply appointed rooms; no restaurant or bar; discreet street entrance can be difficult to find. $ *Rooms from: A$350* ⊠ *75 Harrington St., The Rocks* ☎ *02/9251–6711* ⊕ *www.tfehotels.com/brands/rendezvous-hotels/rendezvous-hotel-sydney-the-rocks* ⟿ *61 apartments, 7 terrace houses* ⦿ *No meals* ✣ *1:B2.*

$$
HOTEL
 The Russell. For charm, character, and central location, it's hard to beat this ornate Victorian hotel. **Pros:** location; personal service; warm ambience; includes breakfast. **Cons:** not all rooms have en suite bathrooms; near a pub and busy area, so can be noisy. $ *Rooms from: A$275* ⊠ *143A George St., The Rocks* ☎ *02/9241–3543* ⊕ *www.therussell.com.au* ⟿ *30 rooms, 20 with en suites* ⦿ *Breakfast* ✣ *1:B2.*

$$$$
HOTEL
Fodor's Choice
★
 Shangri-La Hotel Sydney. Towering above Walsh Bay from its prime position alongside the Sydney Harbour Bridge, this sleek hotel is *the* place for a room with a bird's-eye view. **Pros:** breathtaking views; soothing ambiance; great in-house restaurant. **Cons:** impersonal and busy feel at times. $ *Rooms from: A$460* ⊠ *176 Cumberland St., The Rocks* ☎ *02/9250–6000* ⊕ *www.shangri-la.com* ⟿ *525 rooms, 40 suites* ⦿ *No meals* ✣ *1:B2.*

DARLING HARBOUR

$$
HOTEL
 1888 Hotel. This former wool warehouse has been turned into one of Sydney's most cutting-edge designer hotels. **Pros:** great design; free Wi-Fi; free phone calls (in Australia). **Cons:** small rooms. $ *Rooms from: A$245* ⊠ *139 Murray St., Darling Harbour* ☎ *02/8586–1888* ⊕ *www.1888Hotel.com.au* ⟿ *88 room, 2 suites* ⦿ *Breakfast* ✣ *1:A4.*

SYDNEY CITY CENTER

$$$
HOTEL
 Fraser Suites Sydney. This serviced-apartment hotel is one of Sydney's swankiest places to stay. **Pros:** cutting-edge design; well priced for longer stays; free Wi-Fi throughout. **Cons:** minimalist design may not be to everyone's taste. $ *Rooms from: A$365* ⊠ *488 Kent St., City Center* ☎ *02/8823–8888* ⊕ *sydney.frasershospitality.com* ⟿ *55 rooms, 146 suites* ⦿ *No meals* ✣ *1:C5.*

$$$
HOTEL
 Hilton Sydney. At this landmark hotel in downtown Sydney you enter a spacious, light-filled lobby displaying a stunning four-story sculpture.

2

Pros: excellent service; lavishly appointed rooms; hip bar. **Cons:** impersonal, at-times busy feel; extra charge for fast Wi-Fi. ⑤ *Rooms from: A$430 ✉ 488 George St., City Center ☎ 02/9266–2000 ⊕ www. hiltonsydney.com.au ⤴ 550 rooms, 27 suites ⫯⦿⫯ No meals ✢ 1:C4.*

$$$ ⊡ **QT Sydney.** This hotel is the answer for those seeking color and quirki-
HOTEL ness, teamed with style and super-efficient service. **Pros:** great location; catchy design; stylish bars; historic restored building. **Cons:** funkiness may not be to all tastes; super-soft beds. ⑤ *Rooms from: A$330 ✉ 49 Market St., at George St., City Center ☎ 02/8262–0000 ⊕ www. qtsydney.com.au ⤴ 181 rooms, 19 suites ⫯⦿⫯ No meals ✢ 1:C4.*

$$$ ⊡ **Westin Sydney.** The Westin hotel chain is renowned for its heavenly
HOTEL beds—in Sydney it has heavenly service, too. **Pros:** in-room entertainment systems; great service; free Wi-Fi in public areas. **Cons:** slightly corporate feel; Wi-Fi extra for multiple devices. ⑤ *Rooms from: A$430 ✉ 1 Martin Pl., City Center ☎ 02/8223–1111 ⊕ www.westin.com/ sydney ⤴ 400 rooms, 16 suites ⫯⦿⫯ No meals ✢ 1:C3.*

$ ⊡ **Y Hotel Hyde Park.** Comfortable and affordable lodgings in a prime
HOTEL city location means that rooms here are often booked months in advance. **Pros:** great value; excellent location; free Wi-Fi. **Cons:** have to book well in advance; basic design. ⑤ *Rooms from: A$165 ✉ 5–11 Wentworth Ave., near corner of Hyde Park and Oxford St., City Center ☎ 02/9264–2451, 1800/994994 ⊕ www.yhotel.com.au ⤴ 104 rooms, 11 dorm rooms with shared baths, 6 studios ⫯⦿⫯ Breakfast ✢ 1:D5.*

INNER SYDNEY AND THE EASTERN SUBURBS

PADDINGTON

$ ⊡ **Arts Hotel Sydney.** On a quiet stretch in the trendy shopping precinct
HOTEL of Paddington, this small, friendly, family-run hotel has simple accommodations at an outstanding price. **Pros:** great value; personal service; warm feel. **Cons:** simply appointed rooms. ⑤ *Rooms from: A$185 ✉ 21 Oxford St., Paddington ☎ 02/9361–0211 ⊕ www.artshotel.com. au ⤴ 64 rooms ⫯⦿⫯ No meals ✢ 1:E6.*

DARLINGHURST

$$$ ⊡ **Medusa.** If you're tired of the standard travelers' rooms, this renovated
HOTEL Victorian terrace house may be just the tonic. **Pros:** good location; flashy design; warm service; kichenettes in every room; entry to off-site pool and gym; pet-friendly. **Cons:** urban location may get noisy. ⑤ *Rooms from: A$310 ✉ 267 Darlinghurst Rd., Darlinghurst ☎ 02/9331–1000 ⊕ www.medusa.com.au ⤴ 18 rooms ⫯⦿⫯ No meals ✢ 1:E5.*

KINGS CROSS

$ ⊡ **Hotel 59 & Cafe.** In its character as well as its dimensions, this friendly
B&B/INN B&B on a quiet part of a bar- and club-lined street is reminiscent of a European *pensione.* Simple, tastefully outfitted rooms come with high-quality beds and linens, as well as wooden blinds over the windows. **Pros:** comfortable rooms, recently repainted; free Wi-Fi and a cooked breakfast. **Cons:** simply appointed; half-hour to the city center. ⑤ *Rooms from: A$135 ✉ 59 Bayswater Rd., Kings Cross ☎ 02/9360– 5900 ⊕ www.hotel59.com.au ⤴ 9 rooms ⫯⦿⫯ Breakfast ✢ 1:F4.*

POTTS POINT

$ ▦ **De Vere Hotel.** "Simply comfortable and affordable" is the slogan at
HOTEL this 1920s-style hotel at the leafy end of Potts Point, and it's hard to dis-
agree on either count. **Pros:** good value; spacious rooms; friendly staff.
Cons: breakfast, although available on-site, is no longer included in rate.
⑤ *Rooms from: A$127* ⊠ *44–46 Macleay St., Potts Point* ☎ *02/9358–
1211* ⊕ *www.devere.com.au* ➔ *117 rooms, 1 suite* ⑩ *No meals* ✛ *1:F3.*

$ ▦ **Quest Serviced Apartments Potts Point.** This stylish, early 1920s–style
HOTEL boutique hotel is tucked down a laneway in hip Potts Point on the eastern
fringe of the city, an ideal base for exploring the eastern suburbs. **Pros:**
funky rooms, some with amazing views; good location; free Wi-Fi. **Cons:**
neighboring parts of Kings Cross can be seedy and noisy. ⑤ *Rooms from:
A$199* ⊠ *15 Springfield Ave., Potts Point* ☎ *02/8988–6999* ⊕ *www.
questapartments.com.au* ➔ *69 apartments* ⑩ *No meals* ✛ *1:E4.*

$$ ▦ **Simpsons of Potts Point.** This luxurious boutique hotel is the gem of
HOTEL inner Sydney. **Pros:** friendly, elegant, and cozy; free Wi-Fi and use of
Fodor's Choice computers; limited free parking; 20-minute walk to city center. **Cons:**
★ no elevator. ⑤ *Rooms from: A$255* ⊠ *8 Challis Ave., Potts Point*
☎ *02/9356–2199* ⊕ *www.simpsonshotel.com.au* ➔ *11 rooms, 1 suite*
⑩ *Breakfast* ✛ *1:E3.*

RUSHCUTTERS BAY

$$ ▦ **Vibe Hotel Rushcutters.** This good value hotel fronting a lovely harbor-
HOTEL side park is a more peaceful alternative to staying in Kings Cross, but
still within walking distance of the restaurants and bars of the buzzy
nightlife strip. **Pros:** bayside location; quieter alternative to Kings Cross;
good value. **Cons:** small rooms. ⑤ *Rooms from: A$230* ⊠ *100 Bay-
swater Rd., Potts Point* ☎ *02/8353–8988* ⊕ *www.tfehotels.com* ➔ *231
rooms, 14 suites* ⑩ *No meals* ✛ *1:F4.*

WOOLLOOMOOLOO

$$$$ ▦ **BLUE Sydney.** This ultrahip hotel occupies a former warehouse. **Pros:**
HOTEL DVDs and iPod docking stations in all rooms; trendy bar, trendier location. **Cons:** charge for Wi-Fi. ⑤ *Rooms from: A$459* ⊠ *Wharf at Wool-
loomooloo, 6 Cowper Wharf Rd., Woolloomooloo* ☎ *02/9331–9000*
⊕ *www.bluehotel.com.au* ➔ *100 rooms, 36 suites* ⑩ *No meals* ✛ *1:E3.*

BONDI BEACH

$$$ ▦ **Adina Apartment Hotel Bondi Beach.** This hotel apartment complex, sev-
HOTEL eral hundred feet from Bondi Beach, includes more than a dozen restau-
rants, bars, and stores. **Pros:** great location; spacious apartments; part
of a trendy complex. **Cons:** fee for room Wi-Fi and parking. ⑤ *Rooms
from: A$349* ⊠ *69–73 Hall St., Bondi Beach* ☎ *02/9300–4800* ⊕ *www.
adinahotels.com.au* ➔ *55 rooms, 56 apartments* ⑩ *No meals* ✛ *2:D3.*

COOGEE

$$$ ▦ **Crowne Plaza Coogee Beach.** Live like a local at Coogee Beach, which
HOTEL is just as gorgeous as nearby Bondi, but without the crowds. **Pros:** great
location; some rooms have balconies with ocean views; good value
for beachfront accommodations. **Cons:** fee for room Wi-Fi and parking. ⑤ *Rooms from: A$345* ⊠ *242 Arden St., Coogee* ☎ *02/9315–7600*
⊕ *www.crowneplazacoogee.com.au* ➔ *198 rooms, 11 suites* ⑩ *No
meals* ✛ *2:D3.*

GREATER SYDNEY

MANLY

$$ 🛏 **Sebel Manly Beach.** Right on the beachfront of beautiful Manly, this
HOTEL boutique hotel is a mixture of studios and one- and two-bedroom suites,
all with private balconies; the more-spacious accommodations have
hot tubs, kitchenettes, and high-tech goodies. **Pros:** beachside locale;
well-appointed rooms. **Cons:** busy place; expect crowds in summer; no
Wi-Fi in rooms. ⑤ *Rooms from: A$240* ✉ *8–13 South Steyne, Manly*
☎ *02/9977–8866* ⊕ *www.thesebelmanlybeach.com.au* ⤳ *42 rooms, 41
apartments* �🍽 *No meals* ✛ *2:D1.*

NIGHTLIFE AND PERFORMING ARTS

PERFORMING ARTS

Although Sydney's contemporary theater pays tribute to the giants of
drama, it's also driven by distinctly Australian themes: multicultural-
ism, the troubled relations between Aboriginal and white Australia, and
the search for national identity, characterized by the famous Australian
irreverence. Dance, music, and the visual arts are celebrated with equal
enthusiasm. At their best, Sydney's artists and performers bring a new
slant to the arts, one that reflects the unique qualities of their homeland
and the city itself. Standouts on the Sydney arts scene include the Syd-
ney Dance Company, the Museum of Contemporary Art, the Sydney
Opera House, and Belvoir Street Theatre. The most comprehensive
listing of upcoming events is in "The Shortlist" section of the *Sydney
Morning Herald,* published on Friday. On other days, browse through
the entertainment section of the paper.

Ticketek. Ticketek is the major ticket reservations agency, covering most
shows and performances. ☎ *13–2849* ⊕ *premier.ticketek.com.au.*

BALLET, OPERA, AND CLASSICAL MUSIC

Fodor's Choice **Sydney Opera House.** This venue showcases all the performing arts in its
★ five theaters, one of which is devoted to opera. The Australian Ballet,
the Sydney Dance Company, and the Australian Opera Company also
call the Opera House home. The complex includes two stages for theater
and the 2,700-seat Concert Hall, where the Sydney Symphony Orches-
tra and the Australian Chamber Orchestra perform. The box office is
open Monday to Saturday 9–8:30 and until 5 on Sunday. ✉ *Bennelong
Point, Circular Quay* ☎ *02/9250–7777* ⊕ *www.sydneyoperahouse.com.*

DANCE

Fodor's Choice **Bangarra Dance Theatre.** An acclaimed Aboriginal modern dance com-
★ pany, Bangarra Dance Theatre celebrated its 25th anniversary in 2015.
The company stages dramatic productions based on contemporary
Aboriginal social themes. The performances are described as a fusion
of contemporary dance and storytelling; some will have you transfixed
by the sheer energy, lighting, and special effects. ✉ *Pier 4, 15 Hickson
Rd., Walsh Bay* ☎ *02/9251–5333* ⊕ *www.bangarra.com.au.*

Sydney Dance Company. Sydney Dance Company is an innovative contemporary dance troupe with an international reputation. Spanish choreographer Rafael Bonachela is the artistic director. The company performs in Sydney at the Wharf Theatre, the Sydney Opera House, and the new Sydney Theatre and also runs casual drop-in dance classes for A$22: see the website for class schedules. ⊠ *The Wharf, Pier 4, Hickson Rd., Walsh Bay* ☎ *02/9221–4811* ⊕ *www.sydneydancecompany.com.*

THEATER

Belvoir Street Theatre. Belvoir Street Theatre has two stages that host innovative and challenging political and social drama. The smaller downstairs space showcases a lineup of brave new Australian drama. The theater is a 10-minute walk from Central Station. ⊠ *25 Belvoir St., Surry Hills* ☎ *02/9699–3444* ⊕ *www.belvoir.com.au.*

Capitol Theatre. This century-old city landmark was refurbished with such modern refinements as fiber-optic ceiling lights that twinkle in time to the music. The 2,000-seat theater specializes in Broadway blockbusters, such as the Lion King and Mary Poppins, and also hosts pop and rock concerts. Guided behind-the-scenes tours are available (A$28.50); bookings are essential. ⊠ *13 Campbell St., Haymarket* ☎ *02/9320–5000* ⊕ *www.capitoltheatre.com.au.*

Fodor's Choice ★ **State Theatre.** State Theatre is the grande dame of Sydney theaters. It operates as a cinema in June each year, when it hosts the two-week-long Sydney Film Festival; at other times this beautiful space hosts local and international performers. Built in 1929 and restored to its full-blown opulence, the theater has a vaulted ceiling, mosaic floors, marble columns and statues, and brass and bronze doors. A highlight of the magnificent theater is the 20,000-piece chandelier that is supposedly the world's second largest, which Robin Williams once likened to "one of Imelda Marcos's earrings." Even if you don't see a show here, it's worth popping into the lobby for a look around, or join a guided tour to get a good look at the theater's many treasures (A$22.50). ⊠ *49 Market St., City Center* ☎ *02/9373–6655* ⊕ *www.statetheatre.com.au* ☞ *Guided tours Mon.–Wed. 10 am and 1 pm.*

SWB Stables Theatre. This small 120-seat venue is home of the Griffin Theatre Company, which specializes in new Australian writing. ⊠ *10 Nimrod St., Kings Cross* ☎ *02/9361–3817* ⊕ *www.griffintheatre.com. au.*

Sydney Lyric. At The Star casino and entertainment complex, Sydney Lyric is one of the city's most spectacular performing-arts venues. Despite its size, there's no better place to watch big-budget musicals. Every seat in the lavishly spacious, 2,000-seat theater is a good one. ⊠ *20–80 Pyrmont St., Pyrmont, Darling Harbour* ☎ *1300/795267 tickets* ⊕ *sydneylyric.com.au.*

Fodor's Choice ★ **Wharf Theatre.** Wharf Theatre, on a redeveloped wharf in the shadow of Harbour Bridge, is the headquarters of the Sydney Theatre Company (STC), one of Australia's most original and highly regarded performance groups. Contemporary British and American plays and the latest shows from leading Australian playwrights such as David Williamson and Nick Enright are the main attractions. The company also performs at the Sydney Opera House and at the new Sydney Theatre just a few doors away, located opposite Pier 6/7 at No. 22 Hickson Road. ⊠ *Pier 4, Hickson Rd., Walsh Bay* ☎ *02/9250–1777* ⊕ *sydneytheatre.com.au.*

NIGHTLIFE

The *Sydney Morning Herald*'s daily entertainment section is the most informative guide to the city's pubs and clubs. For club-scene coverage—who's been seen where and what they were wearing—pick up a free copy of *The Music* magazine (⊕ *www.themusic.com.au*) available at just about any Oxford Street café or pub. The Ever Guide (⊕ *www.everguide.com.au*) is another good online source of entertainment information.

All bars and clubs listed here are open daily unless noted. Entry is free unless we list a cover charge.

SYDNEY HARBOUR
BARS AND DANCE CLUBS
The Oaks. For a northern Sydney landmark, The Oaks encapsulates the very best of the modern pub. The immensely popular watering hole, named after the huge oak tree in the center of the large beer garden, is big and boisterous. The pub has a restaurant and several bars with varying levels of sophistication. It's packed on Friday and Saturday nights. ⊠ *118 Military Rd., Neutral Bay* ☎ *02/9953–5515* ⊕ *www.oakshotel.com.au.*

THE ROCKS
BARS AND DANCE CLUBS
Blu Bar on 36. Blu Bar on 36 has a stellar view! Situated on the 36th floor of the Shangri-La Hotel, this is a sophisticated place to relax after work or enjoy a late-night drink while taking in the sweeping views of Sydney Harbour and the Opera House. Get here early (just after 5 pm) for a ringside seat. ⊠ *Shangri-La Hotel, 176 Cumberland St., The Rocks* ☎ *02/9250–6000* ⊕ *www.shangri-la.com.*

Fodor's Choice ★ **Opera Bar.** Perched beneath the concourse of the Opera House and at eye level with Sydney Harbour, Opera Bar has the best location in all of Sydney. Cozy up for a drink in the enclosed bar area or grab a waterside umbrella table and take in the glimmering skyline. Live music plays under the stars nightly from either 5:30 or 8 pm on weeknights, and from 2 pm on weekends. The bar has a full menu, though the attraction here is the scenery, not the cuisine. ⊠ *Sydney Opera House, Circular Quay* ☎ *02/9247–1666* ⊕ *operabar.com.au.*

A SEA OF TALENT

Sculpture by the Sea. A steel whale's tail sticking out of the ocean and retro kettles cunningly disguised as penguins strapped to a huge rock being lashed by waves are some of the imaginative artworks that have wowed visitors to the annual show called Sculpture by the Sea. Since 1996, artists have positioned more than 100 sculptures on and under rocky outcrops and on hilltops along the much-trodden Bondi-to-Bronte Coastal Walk. This free exhibition runs for two weeks beginning in late October. ⊠ *Bondi-to-Bronte Coastal Walk, Bondi Beach* ⊕ *www.sculpturebythesea.com.*

JAZZ CLUBS

The Basement. A Sydney legend, The Basement is the premier venue for top local and international jazz, rock, and blues musicians. Lunch and dinner are served daily, but you don't really come here for the food, although booking dinner and show package ensures you get a great seat rather than having to stand at the back. Performances begin around A$35 (standing room), while a two-course meal is A$60 on top of the ticket price. ⊠ *7 Macquarie Pl., Circular Quay* ☎ *02/9251–2797* ⊕ *www.thebasement.com.au.*

PUBS WITH MUSIC

Mercantile Hotel. In the shadow of Harbour Bridge, Mercantile Hotel is Irish and very proud of it. Fiddles, drums, and pipes rise above the clamor in the bar, and lilting accents rejoice in song seven nights a week from 8:30 pm until late and on weekends from 3 pm. ⊠ *25 George St., The Rocks* ☎ *02/9247–3570* ⊕ *www.themercantilehotel.com.au.*

DARLING HARBOUR

BARS AND DANCE CLUBS

Bungalow 8. With its primo waterside location at the northern end of King Street Wharf, and famous mussels from its open kitchen, Bungalow 8 invites a night of posing and partying. This is the place to be seen bobbing your head to the spinning of several ultracool resident DJs. ⊠ *King St. Wharf, 3 Lime St., Darling Harbour* ☎ *02/8070–2424.*

Marquee - The Star Sydney. Nightclubbers are heading to Marquee—on the top level of the relaunched casino and entertainment complex, The Star Sydney—to dance the night away. The huge nightclub heaves with 1,500 twentysomethings who take to the dance floors in the Main Room and the smaller Boom Box, or chill out in the opulent Library bar. R&B artists and local and international DJs perform on weekends, with tickets from A$15 if you get in before 11 pm. When it's time to cool down, there are great outdoor balconies overlooking the city and Darling Harbour. ⊠ *80 Pyrmont St., Darling Harbour* ☎ *02/9657–7737* ⊕ *www.marqueesydney.com* ▨ *A$35.*

SYDNEY CITY CENTER

BARS AND DANCE CLUBS

Fodor's Choice ★ **The Arthouse Hotel.** A former School of the Arts building, The Arthouse Hotel has been renovated into a modern, belle epoque–style hot spot, with four bars and a restaurant spread over three cavernous floors. Art is the focus here, whether it's visual—life-drawing classes are given on Monday, a burlesque drawing class biweekly on Tuesday—aural, or edible, and there is a full-time curator dedicated to programming music, events, and exhibitions. ⊠ *275 Pitt St., City Center* ☎ *02/9284–1200* ⊕ *www.thearthousehotel.com.au.*

Fodor's Choice ★ **Bambini Wine Room.** Bambini Wine Room is a sparkling little jewel box encased in marble-clad walls and topped with lovely chandeliers. You can sip cocktails (A$16) and any number of fine wines late into the night and feast on affordable bar snacks. ⊠ *185 Elizabeth St., City Center* ☎ *02/9283–7098* ☾ *Closed Sun.*

Hemmesphere. One of a string of swanky venues in the area, Hemmesphere is still drawing a hip crowd more than a decade after it first opened. Named for Justin Hemmes, son of iconic 1970s fashion designers Jon and Merivale Hemmes, this is where Sydney's hippest pay homage to cocktail culture from low, leather divans. The mood is elegant and sleek, and so are the well-dressed guests, who often include whichever glitterati happen to be in town. It's on the fourth level of the Establishment Hotel complex and draws those seeking an escape from the rowdy action downstairs. ⊠ *Level 4, 252 George St., City Center* ☎ *02/9240–3100* ⊕ *merivale.com.au/hemmesphere* ☾ *Closed Sun.*

Ivy. This multilevel complex of bars, pubs, and eateries is in an ultra-hip George Street complex. Cocktails are great but expensive, and the crowd varies depending on the night. If you don't fancy this bar, then there's the decadent Pool bar on the top floor, where if you get there early you can recline in your own cabana overlooking the swimming pool. Also on-site are the Den (a lavish bar with chaise longue furniture, chandeliers, and cigar menu), the casual Royal George pub, and the Ash Street Cellar bistro. ⊠ *330 George St., City Center* ☎ *02/9240–8100* ⊕ *merivale.com.au/ivy* ☾ *Closed Sun.*

Lobo Plantation. This Cuban-themed bar is a hit in Sydney. Patrons love the palm trees, the cane furniture, and the wall lined with Cuban bank notes. Cocktails (from around A$18) have a 1950s theme so you could try an Esther Williams, a Nuclear Daiquiri, or a Message in a Bottle, which comes with its own miniature bottle, or go all out and take a one-hour "rum flight," sipping your way through seven different rums (from A$60; bookings essential). The affordable bar menu, which runs from tamales to black bean stew and pork crackling, helps soak up the alcohol. ⊠ *209 Clarence St., basement, City Center* ☎ *02/9279–4335* ⊕ *www.thelobo.com.au* ☾ *Closed Sun.*

Fodor's Choice ★ **O Bar and Dining.** This is the place to come at sunset for the view, tapas, and cocktails—and the '70s kitsch of a revolving restaurant. Located on level 47 of the Australia Square building, O Bar has floor-to-ceiling windows, so no matter which seat you have, the view is great, and constantly changing. It's perfect for a predinner drink, or dinner, too. It's open daily from 5 pm and Friday lunch. ⊠ *Australia Sq., 264 George St., level 47, City Center* ☎ *02/9247–7777* ⊕ *obardining.com.au.*

INNER SYDNEY AND THE EASTERN SUBURBS
BARS AND DANCE CLUBS

Beach Road Hotel. This Bondi institution is famous for its Sunday Sessions, when locals come to enjoy a barbecue, drink, and dance in the outdoor courtyard. There's music every night in summer (except Monday), good affordable food, and a A$20 roast with all the trimmings on Sunday night. ⊠ *71 Beach Rd., Bondi Beach* ☎ *02/9130–7247* ⊕ *www.beachroadbondi.com.au.*

Fodor's Choice ★ **Eau de Vie.** You might have to seek them out but speakeasy-style bars are the new thing in Sydney. Eau de Vie, at the rear of the trendy Kirketon Hotel in Darlinghurst, perfectly fits the bill, especially with its cocktail menu. It's designed with the decades in mind, with drinks that fit into themes such as "1920s—The Train from Paris to Milan" and "1930s—The Boat to Cuba and Caribbean." Onboard the Paris locomotive you can try the Absinthe Frappe (A$20), a mix of La Fee Absinthe, maraschino liqueur, and honey and lemon squeezed over fresh ice. Drinks are a little pricey, but the bar staff and the patrons are friendly and the jazz-infused music takes the pain out of the bill. There's a bar snack menu, too. ✉ *229 Darlinghurst Rd., Darlinghurst* ☎ *04/2226–3226* ⊕ *www.kirketon.com.au.*

COMEDY CLUBS

Sydney's Comedy Store. The city's oldest comedy club is in a plush 300-seat theater in the Entertainment Quarter, which most people still refer to as Fox Studios (its former name). The difficult-to-find theater is at the rear of the complex, close to the parking lot. Shows are Thursday–Saturday at 8:30 pm, and admission is usually around A$30. ✉ *Entertainment Quarter, 122 Lang Rd, Bldg. 207, Centennial Park* ☎ *02/9357–1419* ⊕ *www.comedystore. com.au.*

GAY AND LESBIAN BARS AND CLUBS

Most of the city's gay and lesbian venues are along Oxford Street, in Darlinghurst. The free *Sydney Star Observer,* available along Oxford Street, has a roundup of Sydney's gay and lesbian goings-on, or check the magazine's website (⊕ *www.starobserver.com.au*). A monthly free magazine, *Lesbians on the Loose* (⊕ *www.lotl.com*), lists events for women, and the free *SX* online magazine (⊕ *www.gaynewsnetwork. com.au*) lists bars and events.

ARQ. Sydney's biggest, best-looking, and funkiest gay nightclub, ARQ attracts a clean-cut crowd who like to whip off their shirts as soon as they hear the beat. (Some women head here, too.) There are multiple dance floors, a bar, and plenty of chrome and sparkly lighting. It's open from 9 pm until whenever Thursday through Sunday; a Thursday night drag contest is free, while shows have a cover charge ranging from A$15 to A$25 (and sometimes a little more). ✉ *16 Flinders St., Darlinghurst* ☎ *02/9380–8700* ⊕ *www.arqsydney.com.au.*

The Midnight Shift. The Midnight Shift is Sydney's hard-core party zone, a living legend on the gay scene for its longevity and its take-no-prisoners approach. If anything, the upstairs nightclub, with drag acts and shows every night of the week and DJs every other night, is a little quieter than the ground-floor bars, where most of the leather-loving men go to shoot pool. Opening hours are weekdays from 4 pm until late; weekends from 2 pm. ✉ *85 Oxford St., Darlinghurst* ☎ *02/9358–3848* ⊕ *www. themidnightshift.com.au.*

HAVE A GAY OLD TIME

If you're in Sydney in late February and early March, you'll think the whole city has gone gay. The Sydney Gay and Lesbian Mardi Gras parade, which began as a gay rights protest march in 1978, is one of Australia's major events. Dozens of floats covered with buff dancers make their way from College Street, near St. Mary's Cathedral, up Oxford Street to Taylor's Square. Thousands of spectators watch this amazing party parade.

2

JAZZ CLUBS

The Vanguard. The Vanguard is Sydney's answer to a New Orleans jazz joint, and purposely built by its music-loving owners to mimic the U.S. model. Australian and international jazz, blues, and roots performers love this intimate venue with its 1920s decor and friendly vibe, although you'll often find other music styles here as well. Ticket prices range from around A$30 (some performances are free); it's advised to book a dinner and show package to get the best seats in the house. ⊠ *42 King St., Newtown* ☎ *02/9557-9409.*

PUBS WITH MUSIC

Harold Park Hotel. This is a great comedy venue that also serves up excellent jazz, pop, rock, and blues performances on Sunday afternoon, often featuring artists playing in Australia's top world music and blues festivals when they are in town. Often the performances are free. Comedy nights (around A$10 to A$15 for a performance) are held on Tuesday and Friday at 8 pm; international comedy stars have been known to drop into the pub when they're in town (and do a spot of stand-up). ⊠ *70A Ross St., Glebe* ☎ *02/9660-4745.*

Unity Hall Hotel. This quaint pub in the left-of-center suburb of Balmain declares itself the "spiritual home of jazz and live music for the past 40 years." Its resident jazz band has been playing there since 1970, and you can hear them for free each Sunday at 4 pm (except for the first Sunday of the month, when another jazz band takes their place). A variety of live music including pop, rock, swing, and blues is also on the bill. Music cranks up on Friday and Saturday nights from 9 pm. The pub attracts a friendly, unpretentious crowd and supports up and coming bands. ⊠ *292 Darling St., Balmain* ☎ *02/9810-1331* ⊕ *www. unityhallhotel.com.au.*

SHOPPING

Sydney's shops vary from those with international cachet to Aboriginal art galleries, opal shops, craft bazaars, and weekend flea markets. If you're interested in buying genuine Australian products, look carefully at the labels. Stuffed koalas and didgeridoos made anywhere but in Australia are a standing joke.

Aboriginal art includes historically functional items, such as boomerangs, wooden bowls, and spears, as well as paintings and ceremonial implements that testify to a rich culture of legends and dreams. Although much of this artwork remains strongly traditional in essence, the tools and colors used in Western art have fired the imaginations of many Aboriginal artists. Works on canvas are now more common than works on bark. Much of the best work of Arnhem Land and the Central Desert Region (close to Darwin and Alice Springs, respectively) finds its way into Sydney galleries.

Australia has a virtual monopoly on the world's supply of opals. The least expensive of these fiery gemstones are triplets, which consist of a thin shaving of opal mounted on a plastic base and covered by a plastic, glass, or quartz crown. Doublets are a slice of mounted opal without the capping. The most expensive stones are solid opals, which cost anywhere from a few hundred dollars to a few thousand. You can pick up opals at souvenir shops all over the city, but if you want a valuable stone you should visit a specialist. Sydney is also a good hunting ground for other jewelry, from the quirky to the gloriously expensive.

THE ROCKS

MARKETS

Fodor'sChoice ★ **The Rocks Market.** This sprawling covered bazaar transforms the upper end of George Street into a multicultural collage of music, food, arts, crafts, and entertainment. It's open weekends 10–5. Be sure to check out the new Rocks Foodies Market with delicious fare, on Friday 9–3. ⊠ *Upper George St., near Argyle St., The Rocks* ⊕ *www.therocks.com/things-to-do/the-rocks-markets.*

DARLING HARBOUR

MARKETS

Paddy's Market. Paddy's Market is a huge fresh produce and flea market held under the Market City complex near the Sydney Entertainment Centre in the Chinatown precinct. There has been a market on this site since 1834, and much of the historic exterior remains. The Metro Light Rail stops at the door. ⊠ *9–13 Hay St., Haymarket* ⊕ *www.paddysmarkets.com.au* ⊙ *Wed.–Sun. 9–6.*

SYDNEY CITY CENTER

BOOKS

Ariel Booksellers. This is a large, bright browser's delight, and the place to go for literature, pop culture, avant garde, and art books. They also hold book readings and other literary events. ⊠ *42 Oxford St., City Center* ☎ *02/9332–4581* ⊕ *www.arielbooks.com.au.*

Dymocks. This big, bustling bookstore is packed to its gallery-level coffee shop and is the place to go for all literary needs. ⊠ *424 George St., City Center* ☎ *02/9235–0155* ⊕ *www.dymocks.com.au.*

CLOTHING

Mountain Designs. In the middle of Sydney's "Rugged Row" of outdoor specialists, this store sells camping and climbing gear and dispenses the advice necessary to keep you alive and well in the wilderness. ⊠ *499 Kent St., City Center* ☎ *02/9267–3822* ⊕ *www.mountaindesigns.com.au.*

Fodor'sChoice ★ **Paddy Pallin.** This should be the first stop for serious bush adventurers heading for wild Australia and beyond. Maps, books, and mounds of gear are tailored especially for the Australian outdoors. ⊠ *507 Kent St., City Center* ☎ *02/9264–2685* ⊕ *www.paddypallin.com.au.*

Fodor'sChoice ★ **R. M. Williams.** The place to go for riding boots, Akubra hats, Drizabone raincoats, and moleskin trousers—the type of clothes worn by Hugh Jackman and Nicole Kidman in the movie *Australia.* ⊠ *389 George St., City Center* ☎ *02/9262–2228* ⊕ *www.rmwilliams.com.au.*

DEPARTMENT STORES AND SHOPPING CENTERS

Fodor's Choice ★ **David Jones.** The city's largest department store maintains a reputation for excellent service and high-quality goods. Clothing by many of Australia's finest designers is on display here, and the store also sells its own fashion label at reasonable prices. ⊠ *Elizabeth and Market Sts., City Center* ☎ *02/9266–5544* ⊕ *www.davidjones.com.au.*

Pitt Street Mall. The heart of Sydney's shopping area includes the Mid-City Centre, the huge Westfield Sydney Shopping Centre, Skygarden, Myer, and the charming and historic Strand Arcade—five multilevel shopping plazas crammed with more than 500 shops, from mainstream clothing stores to designer boutiques. ■TIP→ Just a short walk away is the iconic David Jones store on Elizabeth Street. ⊠ *Between King and Market Sts., City Center.*

Fodor's Choice ★ **Queen Victoria Building.** This is a splendid Victorian-era building with more than 200 boutiques, cafés, and antiques shops. The building is open 24 hours, so you can window-shop even after the stores have closed. Guided history tours, which run 45 minutes, cost A$15 and depart 11:30 am Tuesday, Thursday, and Saturday. Book at the concierge on the ground floor. ⊠ *George, York, Market, and Druitt Sts., City Center* ☎ *02/9265–6800* ⊕ *www.qvb.com.au.*

Fodor's Choice ★ **Strand Arcade.** This ornate three-story shopping arcade built in 1891 runs between George Street and Pitt Street Mall and is one of Sydney's most elegant shopping strips. Beautiful Victorian-era floor tiles, magnificent cedar staircases, and charmingly old-fashioned shopfronts help make the shopping here refreshingly chain-store free. The upstairs galleries are home to high-end Australian fashion designers and jewelers, while the ground floor has a charming mix of cozy speciality tea and cake shops, beauty and gift stores, and fashion boutiques. Strand Hatters is the best men's hat store in the city and the place to buy an Akubra or Fedora. The arcade is bookended by two of the country's iconic chocolate stores—Haigh's Chocolates at George Street and Koko Black on Pitt Street—and both are virtually irresistible. ⊠ *412–414 George St.* ☎ *02/9265–6800* ⊕ *www.strandarcade.com.au.*

JEWELRY AND ACCESSORIES

Dinosaur Designs. This fun store sells luminous bowls, plates, and vases, as well as fanciful jewelry crafted from resin and Perspex in eye-popping colors. There's another location at 339 Oxford Street in Paddington. ⊠ *Strand Arcade, George St., Shop 77, City Center* ☎ *02/9223–2953* ⊕ *www.dinosaurdesigns.com.au.*

The National Opal Collection. This is the only Sydney opal retailer with total ownership of its entire production process—mines, workshops, and showroom—making prices very competitive. In the Pitt Street showroom, you can prearrange to see artisans at work cutting and polishing the stones or visit the on-site museum and learn about the process of opal development and opalized fossils. ⊠ *60 Pitt St., City Center* ☎ *02/9247–6344* ⊕ *www.nationalopal.com.*

Paspaley Pearls. The jewelers here order their exquisite material from pearl farms near the remote Western Australia town of Broome. Prices start high and head for the stratosphere, but if you're serious about a high-quality pearl, this gallery requires a visit. ⊠ *Paspaley Bldg., 2 Martin Pl., City Center* ☎ *02/9232–7633, 1300/888080* ⊕ *www. paspaleypearls.com.*

Percy Marks Fine Gems. Here you'll find an outstanding collection of high-quality Australian gemstones, including dazzling black opals, pink diamonds, and pearls from Broome. ⊠ *62–70 Elizabeth St., City Center* ☎ *02/9233–1355* ⊕ *www.percymarks.com.au.*

Rox Gems and Jewellery. Come here for serious one-off designs at the cutting edge of lapidary chic. ⊠ *Shop 31, Strand Arcade, George St., City Center* ☎ *02/9232–7828* ⊕ *www.rox.com.au.*

MUSIC

Birdland Records. This institution for music lovers has an especially strong selection of jazz, blues, African, and Latin American music in multiple formats, including vinyl and super audio CDs, as well as an authoritative staff ready to lend some assistance. ⊠ *Level 4, Dymocks Bldg., 428 George St., City Center* ☎ *02/9231–1188* ⊕ *www.birdland. com.au.*

INNER SYDNEY AND THE EASTERN SUBURBS

ART AND CRAFT GALLERIES

Cooee Aboriginal Art. This gallery, open Tuesday–Saturday 10–5, exhibits and sells high-end Aboriginal paintings, sculptures, and limited-edition prints. It's a five-minute walk from Bondi Beach. ⊠ *31 Lamrock Ave., Bondi Beach* ☎ *02/9300–9233* ⊕ *www.cooeeart.com.au.*

BOOKS

Gertrude & Alice Café Bookshop. Need something to read on Bondi Beach? Take a stroll to Gertrude & Alice Café Bookshop, named in honor of lovers Gertrude Stein and Alice B. Toklas. Always buzzing with people, it's a great place to sip coffee or chai lattes, or have lunch while perusing the mostly secondhand books. ⊠ *46 Hall St., Bondi Beach* ☎ *02/9130–5155.*

CLOTHING

Belinda. This is where Sydney's female fashionistas go when there's a dress-up occasion looming. From her namesake store that scores high marks for innovation and imagination, former model Belinda Seper sells nothing but the very latest designs off the catwalks. ⊠ *8 Transvaal Ave., Double Bay* ☎ *02/9328–6288* ⊕ *www.belinda.com.au.*

Scanlan & Theodore. This is the Sydney outlet for one of Melbourne's most distinguished fashion houses. Designs take their cues from Europe, with superbly tailored women's knitwear, suits, and stylishly glamorous evening wear. ⊠ *122 Oxford St., at Glenmore Rd., Paddington* ☎ *02/9380–9388* ⊕ *www.scanlantheodore.com.*

Aboriginal paintings are visual representations of ancestral stories from "The Dreaming."

DEPARTMENT STORES AND SHOPPING CENTERS

Oxford Street. Nicknamed the "Style Mile," Paddington's main artery, from South Dowling Street east to Queen Street, Woollahra, is dressed to thrill. Lined with boutiques, home-furnishings stores, and cafés, it's a perfect venue for watching the never-ending fashion parade. Take Bus No. 380, 382, or 333 from Circular Quay. ⊠ *Oxford St., Paddington.*

MARKETS

Fodor's Choice ★ **Bondi Markets.** This relaxed and friendly beachside market at Bondi is the place to go for clothes—vintage and by up-and-coming designers—plus handmade jewelry, organic cosmetics, art, retro furniture, and secondhand goods. Look closely at the faces in the crowd, you'll often find visiting celebrities lurking behind messy bed hair and dark glasses. The markets are on every Sunday 10–4. ⊠ *Bondi Beach Public School, Campbell Parade, Bondi Beach* ☎ *02/9315–7011* ⊕ *www.bondimarkets.com.au.*

Fodor's Choice ★ **Paddington Markets.** About 200 stalls crammed with clothing, plants, crafts, jewelry, and souvenirs fill this busy churchyard market (sometimes called Paddington Bazaar). Distinctly New Age and highly fashion conscious, the market is an outlet for a handful of avant-garde clothing designers. Go early as it can get very crowded. ⊠ *Paddington Uniting Church, 395 Oxford St., Paddington* ☎ *02/9331–2923* ⊕ *www.paddingtonmarkets.com.au.*

GREATER SYDNEY

ART AND CRAFT GALLERIES

Kate Owen Gallery + Studio. This gallery showcases quality indigenous art over three levels in Rozelle, a suburb about 15 minutes west of the city center. Take the M50 or M52 bus from the bus station behind the Queen Victoria Building; alight at the corner of Victoria Road and Darling Street. ⊠ *680 Darling St., at Victoria Rd., Rozelle* ☎ *02/9555–5283* ⊕ *www.kateowengallery.com.*

DEPARTMENT STORES AND SHOPPING CENTERS

Birkenhead Point. A factory outlet with more than 100 clothing, shoe, and housewares stores on the western shores of Iron Cove, about 7 km (4 miles) west of Sydney, Birkenhead Point is a great place to shop for discounted labels including Alannah Hill, Witchery, Bendon (Elle Macpherson's lingerie range), Rip Curl, and David Jones warehouse. Take Bus 504, 506, 518, or the M52 from Druitt Street near Town Hall station and also Circular Quay. Water taxis depart from the site for Circular Quay and Darling Harbour. ⊠ *Roseby St., near Iron Cove Bridge, Drummoyne* ☎ *02/9182–8800* ⊕ *www.birkenheadpoint.com.au.*

MARKETS

Balmain Market. In a leafy churchyard less than 5 km (3 miles) from the city, Balmain Market has a rustic quality that makes it a refreshing change from city-center shopping. Crafts, handmade furniture, plants, bread, toys, tarot readings, and massages are among the offerings at the 140-odd stalls. Inside the church hall you can buy international snacks. Take Bus No. 442 from the Queen Victoria Building in York Street. ⊠ *St. Andrew's Church, Darling St., Balmain* ☎ *04/1876–5736* ⊕ *www.balmainmarket.com.au.*

Glebe Markets. Handmade and secondhand are the order of the day at this colorful market at the top end of Glebe Point Road. One of the best markets for lovers of all things vintage, Glebe also hosts live music on the lawn and good food stalls as well. The markets are open every Saturday 10–4. ⊠ *Glebe Public School, Derby Pl. and Glebe Point Rd., Glebe* ⊕ *www.glebemarkets.com.au.*

NEW SOUTH
WALES

WELCOME TO NEW SOUTH WALES

TOP REASONS TO GO

★ **Getting in Touch with Nature:** Exotic birds are prolific in the Blue Mountains and North Coast regions, and Canberra isn't known as the "Bush Capital" for nothing.

★ **The Great Australian Bite:** There are lots of fine restaurants in the Hunter Valley and in the North Coast towns of Coffs Harbour and Byron Bay. Fish-and-chips on the beach is a must.

★ **Outdoor Adventure:** The region's mountains and national parks offer opportunities for walks and hikes, horseback riding, rappelling, canyoning, and rock climbing.

★ **World-Class Wineries:** The Hunter Valley has an international reputation for producing excellent Chardonnay, Shiraz, and a dry Sémillon.

★ **Deserted Beaches:** The coastline has some of the most beautiful white-sand beaches in the country. Most of them are wonderfully undeveloped and crowd-free, with hardly a skyscraper in sight.

1 The Blue Mountains. Sydneysiders flock to this UNESCO-protected wilderness region with its majestic mountain peaks and deep green valleys sprinkled with charming country guesthouses. The famous sandstone rock formations known as the Three Sisters are the area's best-known attraction.

2 Hunter Valley Wine Region. This is one of the oldest and best-known wine regions in Australia, with vineyards dating back to the 1830s. Oenophiles shouldn't miss a trip to this thriving and perennially busy destination. We also like the food, historic towns, and tranquil countryside.

3 The North Coast. This region has some of the most glorious and seductive stretches of beach in Australia—and that's saying something when you consider the competition. The almost continuous line of beaches is interspersed with lively towns and harbors, with the Great Dividing Range rising to the west.

GETTING ORIENTED

3

New South Wales, with the country's capital city Canberra and the A.C.T. carved out in an area half the size of Rhode Island, covers the southeast corner of the country. Despite this being Australia's most populous state, the rich variety of landscapes is its biggest selling point. The Blue Mountains, a World Heritage site, lie approximately 100 km (60 miles) to the west of Sydney; the Hunter Valley is about 160 km (100 miles) or two hours north of Sydney. The North Coast is exactly where its name suggests, while Lord Howe Island is offshore, 700 km (435 miles) northeast of Sydney. Canberra is 288 km (180 miles) southwest of Sydney.

4 Canberra and the A.C.T.
The nation's capital and its environs may be quiet and a little too well-mannered for some, but its museums and galleries are the best in the country, and its diverse range of parks and gardens is a major draw.

Updated by
Lee Atkinson

For many travelers Sydney is New South Wales, and they look to the other, less-populous states for Australia's famous wilderness experiences. However, New South Wales contains many of Australia's natural wonders. High on the list are the subtropical rain forests of the North Coast, lush river valleys, warm seas, golden beaches, the World Heritage areas of Lord Howe Island, and some of Australia's finest vineyards. Many travelers overlook Canberra, but history buffs and art aficionados love its selection of galleries and museums, which rank among the nation's finest.

Today, with approximately 7.3 million people, New South Wales is Australia's most populous state—it's home to about one-third of the nation's population. Although it's crowded by Australian standards, keep in mind that New South Wales is larger than every U.S. state except Alaska. In the state's east, a coastal plain reaching north to Queensland varies in width from less than a mile to almost 160 km (100 miles). This plain is bordered on the west by a chain of low mountains known as the Great Dividing Range, which tops off at about 7,300 feet in the Snowy Mountains in the state's far south. On this range's western slopes is a belt of pasture and farmland. Beyond that are the western plains and Outback, an arid, sparsely populated region that takes up two-thirds of the state.

PLANNER

WHEN TO GO

For visitors from the northern hemisphere the Australian summer (approximately December–February) has great pull. The best times to visit the Hunter Valley are during the February–March grape harvest season and the June Hunter Food and Wine Festival. Spring and autumn are also ideal times to visit Canberra; from March to May, autumn leaves paint the city with amber hues. The spring flower celebration, Floriade, lasts from mid-September to mid-October. The North Coast resort region is often booked solid between Christmas and the first half of January, but autumn and spring are good times to visit.

PLANNING YOUR TIME

It's wise to decide in advance whether you'd like to cover a lot of ground quickly or choose one or two places to linger a while. If you have less than four days, stick close to Sydney. In a busy four- to seven-day period you could visit the Blue Mountains and the Hunter Valley as well.

Start with a visit to the **Blue Mountains.** You could arrange a round-trip itinerary from Sydney in a fairly hectic day or, preferably, spend a night in **Katoomba, Blackheath,** or **Leura** and make it a two-day excursion. Return to Sydney, and then head north to the **Hunter Valley.** A two-day/one-night driving visit here allows you enough time to see the main sights and spend time touring the wineries before traveling back to Sydney on the second day. An alternative would be a quick visit to the Blue Mountains, then two days in Canberra to see the city's excellent museums and galleries.

If you have more time in the region, continue to the North Coast. In three days of driving you won't likely get much farther than **Coffs Harbour** (with overnights there and in **Port Macquarie**), and this requires rushing it, but it's possible to fly back to Sydney from Coffs. Alternatively, travel southwest to sedate **Canberra** and have a leisurely few days exploring gems like the National Portrait Gallery, Parliament House, and the Australian War Memorial, while stretching your legs walking or biking around Lake Burley Griffin.

GETTING HERE AND AROUND

AIR TRAVEL

New South Wales is peppered with airports, so flying is the easiest way to get around if you're traveling long distances. You can score the best fares during the quieter seasons. From Sydney, REX (Regional Express) Airlines services Ballina and Lismore (both about 30 minutes from Byron Bay). Qantas flies into Canberra, Port Macquarie, Coffs Harbour, and Lord Howe Island; its low cost subsidiary Jetstar flies into Ballina, while Virgin Australia goes to Newcastle, Canberra, Port Macquarie, Ballina, and Coffs Harbour.

Airline Contacts Jetstar. ☎ *13–1538* ⊕ *www.jetstar.com.* **Qantas Airways.** ☎ *13–1313* ⊕ *www.qantas.com.au.* **REX Airlines.** ☎ *13–1713* ⊕ *www.rex.com. au.* **Virgin Australia.** ☎ *13–6789* ⊕ *www.virginaustralia.com.*

CAR RENTAL

Hiring your own car is the most convenient way of getting around the region. The scenic Blue Mountains and Hunter Valley routes and attractions are outside the towns, so having your own set of wheels is helpful. When visiting the wine country, be aware that Australia has very strict rules against drunk driving. Most towns have major car-rental companies. You can pick up a car at one point and drop off at another for an extra fee.

TRAIN TRAVEL

As in the States, most people drive here, so train services aren't brilliant and can often cost more than other options. It is possible to travel by train to the Blue Mountains with the Sydney Trains (aka CityRail) commuter network. NSW TrainLink (aka CountryLink) connects Sydney to towns in the Hunter Valley and along the North Coast. Canberra is not conveniently reached by train; it's quicker to drive, fly, or catch a bus.

Train Information NSW TrainLink. ☎ *13–2232, 02/4907–7501* ⊕ *www.nswtrainlink.info.* **Sydney Trains.** ☎ *13–1500* ⊕ *www.sydneytrains.info.*

RESTAURANTS

Dining varies dramatically throughout New South Wales, from superb city-standard restaurants to average country-town fare. As popular weekend retreats for Sydneysiders, the Blue Mountains have a number of fine restaurants and cozy tea rooms that are perfect for light meals. In the Hunter Valley several excellent restaurants show off the region's fine wines. Unsurprisingly, seafood dominates on the North Coast, and again, thanks to holidaying Sydneysiders with high standards, you should be able to tuck into some memorable meals. The eclectic selection of eateries in Canberra reflects the city's cosmopolitan residents, so despite the city's size, dining spots here hold their own against the restaurants of Sydney and Melbourne, although the feeling is generally more casual.

HOTELS

Accommodations include everything from run-of-the-mill motels and remote wilderness lodges to historic, cliff-perched properties and expansive seaside resorts. Rates are often much lower on weekdays, particularly in the Blue Mountains and the Hunter Valley, as traffic from Sydney is heavier on weekends. The North Coast is popular during summer and Easter school holidays, so book as far ahead as possible. Hotels in Canberra, with one or two notable exceptions, don't have the character that other places do. But there are plenty of upscale chain hotel options and self-catering apartments. *Hotel reviews have been shortened. For full information, visit Fodors.com.*

WHAT IT COSTS IN AUSTRALIAN DOLLARS			
$	**$$**	**$$$**	**$$$$**
Restaurants	Under A$21	A$21–A$35	A$36–A$50	over A$50
Hotels	Under A$151	A$151–A$200	A$201–A$300	over A$300

Restaurant prices are the average cost of a main course at dinner or, if dinner is not served, at lunch. Hotel prices are the lowest cost of a standard double room in high season, including tax and service.

THE BLUE MOUNTAINS

Sydneysiders have been doubly blessed by nature. Not only do they have a magnificent coastline right at their front door, but a 90-minute drive west puts them in the midst of one of the most spectacular wilderness areas in Australia—World Heritage Blue Mountains National Park. This rippling sea of hills is covered by tall eucalyptus trees and dissected by deep river valleys—the area is perfect terrain for hiking and adventure activities.

Standing 3,500-plus feet high, these "mountains" were once the bed of an ancient sea. Gradually the sedimentary rock was uplifted until it formed a high plateau, which was etched by aeons of wind and water into the wonderland of cliffs, caves, and canyons that exists today. Now the richly forested hills, crisp mountain air, cool-climate gardens, vast sandstone chasms, and little towns of timber and stone are supreme examples of Australia's diversity. The mountains' distinctive blue coloring is caused by the evaporation of oil from the dense eucalyptus forests. This disperses light in the blue colors of the spectrum, a phenomenon known as Rayleigh Scattering.

VISITOR INFORMATION

Blue Mountains Visitor Centre–Glenbrook. ⊠ *Great Western Hwy., Glenbrook* ☎ *1300/653408* ⊕ *www.bluemountainscitytourism.com.au.* **Blue Mountains Visitor Centre–Katoomba.** ⊠ *Echo Point Rd. and Panorama Dr., Katoomba* ⊹ *At the Three Sisters* ☎ *1300/653408* ⊕ *www.bluemountainscitytourism.com.au.*

WENTWORTH FALLS

95 km (59 miles) west of Sydney.

This attractive township is home to the Blue Mountains' most stunning natural waterfalls and bush walking trails. The Falls themselves straddle the highway, but most points of interest and views of the Jamison Valley and Blue Mountains National Park are a short way south.

GETTING HERE AND AROUND

From Sydney, head west onto Parramatta Road, then take the M4, following signs to the Blue Mountains. You'll pay a toll at the end of the motorway. It's also easy to catch a train to Wentworth Falls; the journey from Sydney Central Station takes 1¾ hours, with trains leaving roughly every hour. The Blue Mountains Bus Company (☎ *02/4751–1077* ⊕ *www.bmbc.com.au*) connects towns within the region with Routes 685 and 695, connecting Wentworth Falls to Leura and Katoomba.

EXPLORING

EN ROUTE

Norman Lindsay Gallery and Museum. If driving from Sydney, be sure to stop at the National Trust–listed Norman Lindsay Gallery and Museum, dedicated to the Australian artist and writer. Considered one of the cultural highlights of the Blue Mountains, Lindsay lived in this house during the latter part of his life until he died in 1969. Lindsay is best known for his paintings, etchings, and drawings (many of voluptuous nudes), but he also built model boats, sculpted, and wrote poetry and children's books, among which *The Magic Pudding* has become an Australian classic. The delightful landscaped gardens contain several of Lindsay's sculptures, and you can also take a short but scenic bushwalk beyond the garden or take refreshments in the café. Daily tours of Lindsay's studios run from 10:30 am to 2:30 pm and are included in the price, while dedicated art fans can stay in the cottage on the grounds for A$175 a night midweek or A$220 a night Friday, Saturday, and Sunday. ⊠ *14 Norman Lindsay Crescent, Faulconbridge* ☎ *02/4751–1067* ⊕ *www.normanlindsay.com.au* ✉ *A$15* ⊙ *Daily 10–4.*

SPORTS AND THE OUTDOORS

HIKING

Falls Reserve. From a lookout in Falls Reserve, south of the town of Wentworth Falls, you can take in magnificent views both out across the Jamison Valley to the Kings Tableland and of the 935-foot-high **Wentworth Falls** themselves. To find the best view of the falls, follow the trail that crosses the stream and zigzags down the sheer cliff face, signposted "national pass." If you continue, the trail cuts back across the base of the falls and along a narrow ledge to the delightful Valley of the Waters, where it ascends to the top of the cliffs, emerging at the Conservation Hut. The complete circuit takes at least three hours and is a moderately difficult walk. ⊠ *End of Falls Rd.*

WHERE TO EAT

$$ ✕ **Conservation Hut.** From its prime spot in Blue Mountains National
AUSTRALIAN Park, on a cliff overlooking the Jamison Valley, this spacious, mud-brick bistro serves simple, savory fare. Lovely brunch dishes include herbed mushrooms with a poached egg and roasted tomatoes on toast. For

lunch, dig into hearty soups, beef pies, or seared tuna with warm potato salad. Be sure to save room for the dessert cakes. An open balcony is a delight on warm days, and a fire blazes in the cooler months. A hiking trail from the bistro leads down into the Valley of the Waters, one of the splendors of the mountains. It's a wonderful pre- or post-meal walk. ⑤ *Average main: A$27* ✉ *88 Fletcher St.* ☎ *02/4757–3827* ⊕ *www.conservationhut.com.au* ⊗ *No dinner.*

$$ ✕ **2773.** In Glenbrook, one of the

MODERN first Blue Mountains towns you'll

AUSTRALIAN reach coming from Sydney, this is a great place for breakfast or a relaxing lunch before continuing to Wentworth Falls, about a 30-minute drive west. Dinner, served Thursday through Saturday, includes dishes like beer-brined baby spatchcock and organic meats from the Lithgow Valley (on the other side of the mountains). The best value is the A$36 Plank, featuring a little bit of just about everything on the menu. 2773 serves only fair-trade tea, coffee, and chocolate and uses many organically grown ingredients and locally sourced beer and wine. Live music on Sunday afternoon is a great way to enjoy the weekend. Kids love meeting the pigs out the back. ⑤ *Average main: A$28* ✉ *19 Ross St., Glenbrook* ☎ *02/4739–5908* ⊕ *www.2773glenbrook.com.au* ⊗ *No dinner Mon.– Wed. and Sun.*

> **BLOOMIN' BEAUTIFUL**
>
> **Leura Garden Festival.** When spring is in the air in the mountains, one of the most beautiful places to be is Leura. Dozens of cherry blossoms line the main street, and private gardens are open for viewing. Make a date for the weeklong Leura Garden Festival in early October. The gardens are adorned with the work of local artists keen to win the annual art prize. A village fair caps off the celebrations. One ticket (A$25) buys entrance to all the gardens on show. ✉ *Leura* ☎ *0431/095–279* ⊕ *www. leuragardensfestival.com.au.*

LEURA

5 km (3 miles) west of Wentworth Falls.

Leura, the prettiest and chicest of the mountain towns, is bordered by bush and lined with excellent cafés, restaurants, and gift shops. From the south end of the main street (the Mall), the road continues past superb local gardens as it winds down to the massive cliffs overlooking the Jamison Valley. The dazzling 19-km (12-mile) journey along Cliff Drive skirts the rim of the valley—often only yards from the cliff edge—providing truly spectacular Blue Mountains views.

GETTING HERE AND AROUND

The train station at Leura is one stop beyond Wentworth Falls, and the station is walking distance from all the town's shops and galleries. By car, Leura is a few kilometers west of Wentworth Falls on the Great Western Highway. Alternatively, catch a Blue Mountains Bus Company bus—Routes 685 and 695 connect the town with Wentworth Falls and Katoomba.

EXPLORING

Everglades Historic House and Gardens. Everglades Gardens, a National Trust–listed, cool-climate arboretum and nature reserve established in the 1930s, is one of the best public gardens in the Blue Mountains region. This former home of a Belgian industrialist is surrounded by 13 acres of native bushland and exotic flora, a rhododendron garden, an alpine plant area, and formal European-style terraces. The views of the Jamison Valley are magnificent. ⊠ *37 Everglades Ave.* ☎ *02/4784–1938* ⊕ *www.everglades.org.au* ⊠ *A$13* ⊙ *Oct.–Mar., daily 10–5; Apr.–Sept., daily 10–4.*

FAMILY   **Leuralla.** This imposing 1911 mansion still belongs to the family of Dr. H. V. ("Doc") Evatt (1894–1965), the first president of the General Assembly of the United Nations and later the leader of the Australian Labor Party. A 19th-century Australian art collection and a small museum dedicated to Dr. Evatt are inside the home. Baby boomers and their children (and grandchildren) will love the collection in the New South Wales Toy and Railway Museum, which is both inside the house and in the gardens. The museum is comprised of an extensive collection of railway memorabilia, antique curios from yesteryear (including lots of dolls depicting the Alice in Wonderland scenes), and exhibitions on iconic dolls like Barbie. Directly across the street from the mansion are the Leuralla Public Gardens (entry A$2), with spectacular views of the Jamison Valley. ⊠ *36 Olympian Parade* ☎ *02/4784–1169* ⊕ *www.toyandrailwaymuseum.com.au* ⊠ *A$15, gardens only A$10* ⊙ *Daily 10–5.*

Sublime Point Lookout. This viewpoint just outside Leura lives up to its name with a great view of the Jamison Valley and the generally spectacular Blue Mountains scenery. It's a quiet vantage point that provides a different perspective from that of the famous **Three Sisters** lookout at nearby Katoomba. ⊠ *Sublime Point Rd.*

WHERE TO EAT AND STAY

$$ ✕ **Leura Garage.** This buzzy eatery housed in an old garage opposite the
EUROPEAN   railway station in Leura serves top-notch food in a delightfully informal
Fodor's Choice   setting. Dishes are designed to share and although might sound simple
★   in the name, are simply astounding—the burrata (a handmade ball of mozzarella cheese with fresh tomato) will make you swoon when you cut into it and the soft center oozes out onto the plate. The menu changes seasonally, but long-time favorites include the salted anchovy pizza with potato and confit garlic, and Wagyu meatballs from the nearby Lithgow Valley. Most of the produce is local and all of the wine is sourced from nearby Mudgee or Orange district. One of the few places in the mountains, other than traditional cafés, to have all-day dining, the restaurant is also a great value, with a two-person, six-course tasting menu for just A$55 per person. ⑤ *Average main: A$25* ⊠ *84 Railway Parade* ☎ *02/4784–3391* ⊕ *leuragarage.com.au.*

$$$ ✕ **Silk's Brasserie.** Thanks to its Sydney-standard food, wine, and service,
AUSTRALIAN   Silk's still rates as one of the finest Blue Mountains restaurants after
Fodor's Choice   more than 20 years. The menu here changes seasonally, but popular
★   dishes include the pan-seared scallops with tomato confit, asparagus, pancetta, and a chicory-watercress salad with honey-mustard-seed

Continued on page 157

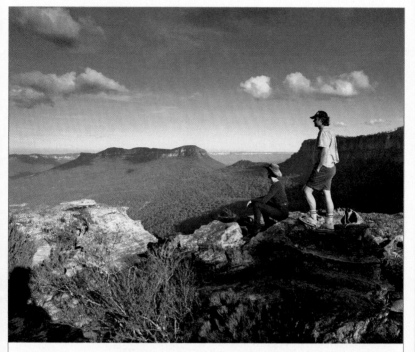

3

HIKING THE BLUE MOUNTAINS

Kanangra Falls

Head west of Sydney along the M4, or simply hop a bus or train, and within an hour you'll be on a gradual climb along a traditional Aboriginal pathway into the heart of the Blue Mountains—a sandstone plateau formed 150 million years ago that tops out at 3,600 feet. Dramatic valleys, canyons, and cliff faces to the north and south of the main road have been carved by wind and water over millennia. And the blue? That's light refracting off the fine oil mist from the world's most ecologically diverse tract of eucalypt forest.

(top) Looking out over the Jamison Valley.

A WORLD HERITAGE WONDERLAND

Part of the Greater Blue Mountains World Heritage Area, Blue Mountains National Park encompasses 2,678 sq km (1,034 sq ft) of prime hiking country. Most tracks skirt the cliff edges or run along the bottom of the canyons; paths that connect the two levels are often at points along the cliff that offer breathtaking panoramas of the Jamison, Megalong, or Grose Valleys.

While the geological landscape is worth the trip alone, the flora and fauna are some of the country's most unique. Within just a few square miles, the world's widest variety of eucalypts in one contiguous forest have evolved to thrive in everything from open scrub plains to dense valley rainforests. The Wollami pine, a tree that grew alongside dinosaurs, can only be found in a few small areas

here. Then there are the rare or threatened creatures like the Blue Mountains water skink, the yellow-bellied glider, and the long-nosed potoroo. It seems only fitting that both Charles Darwin and John Muir visited here. In 1932 it became one of the first formally protected tracts of land in Australia.

Towns dot the main highway through the Blue Mountains, but Katoomba is the unofficial capital, fully outfitted with resources for visitors and the starting point for some of the most iconic walks. Less-bustling Blackheath, minutes up the road from Katoomba, has our favorite eco-lodges and is closest to the best walks of the Grose Valley. You can get a feel for the region on a day trip from Sydney, but if your schedule permits, stay a night (or three) to fit in a few different hikes.

HIKING LITE: THREE WAYS TO SEE THE JAMISON VALLEY WITHOUT BREAKING A SWEAT

Scenic Skyway

SCENIC CABLEWAY
Less crowded than the Scenic Railway, the world's steepest cable car feels gentle in comparison. The enclosed gondola glides between the valley floor and the cliff rim with views of the Three Sisters.

SCENIC SKYWAY
This Swiss-style, glass-bottom cable car takes you on a 720 m (1/2 miles) long journey 270 m (886 ft) above the gorge for great 360 degree views across the Jamison Valley, the Katoomba Falls, and the famous Three Sisters.

KATOOMBA SCENIC RAILWAY
An incline of 52 degrees makes this former coal-haul railway the world's steepest. Grab a seat in the front. Be prepared for lines at peak visiting times. The railway runs every 10 minutes until 4:50 pm.

Claustral Canyon

BLUE MOUNTAIN TRAIL OVERVIEW

Lookout at Echo Point

KATOOMBA-ECHO POINT	TRAIL TIPS	HIGHLIGHTS
ECHO POINT TO SCENIC RAILWAY: This may not be a long walk, but thanks to the 900 steps of the Giant Staircase, don't underestimate it.	This route is very popular, especially on weekends, so set off early. Be aware that the last railway and cable car up leave at 4:50 pm. If you miss them, you'll have to walk.	• Expansive views across the Jamison Valley and beautiful forest vistas. • Brings you right up against the Three Sisters. • Scenic Railway boarding area is at the end of the trail, so you don't have to walk back up.
PRINCE HENRY CLIFF WALK: Start at the Leura Cascades picnic area and head up the mountain to Echo Point. This is a tough hike and not for the faint of heart.	Olympian Rock and Elysian Rock are perfect spots to picnic.	• Thanks to the level of difficulty, you'll be able to escape the crowds at Katoomba. • Spot lyre birds, kookaburras, and glossy black cockatoos.
BLACKHEATH	TRAIL TIPS	HIGHLIGHTS
GRAND CANYON WALK: Possible for anyone who's reasonably fit (though there are some steps) and well worth the effort.	A great choice for hot days: the canyon's cool temperatures will come as welcome relief.	• A winding path through lush vegetation and around plummeting waterfalls. • Spectacular views of gorges, forest, and cliff lines at Evans lookout.
PERRY'S LOOKDOWN TO BLUE GUM FOREST: This track starts at Perry's Lookdown parking lot, 9 km (5.5 miles) northeast of Blackheath, and takes you down a steep track into the lovely Blue Gum Forest.	Stop by the Heritage Centre in nearby Blackheath for excellent information on historic sites and hiking trips.	• Experience for yourself why the ecologically unique Blue Gum Forest attracted conservationists' attention in Australia. • You might spot possums, gliders, bandicoots, brown antechinuses, and swamp wallabies.
GLENBROOK	TRAIL TIPS	HIGHLIGHTS
RED HANDS CAVE TRACK: This moderately difficult circuit walk goes up the Red Hands Creek Valley along a creek and through the rainforest.	It's best to park at the Visitors Centre on Bruce Road and then walk for 10 minutes following the signs to the Glenbrook causeway, as there is no easy parking at the causeway itself.	• Bring your binoculars, because there are many birdwatching opportunities. • See the Blue Mountains' most sacred Aboriginal site, Red Hands Cave. The cave is named after the displays of Aboriginal hand stencils on its walls.

KATOOMBA

ECHO POINT TO SCENIC RAILWAY
Distance: 5 km
Start: Three Sisters Lookout
Finish: Scenic Railway

PRINCE HENRY CLIFF WALK
Distance: 6 km
Start: Leura Cascades picnic area
Finish: Echo Point

Waratah St.

Ada St.

Dalley St.

Warwick St.

Kurra St.

Martin St.

Katoomba St.

Cliff Dr.

Peckmans Rd.

Albert St.

Gordon Rd.

Balmoral Rd.

Leura

Lyrebird Dell Walk

Pool of Siloam

Gordon Falls Lookout

Tarpeian Rock

Round Walk

Bridal Veil Lookout

Leura Cascades

Fern Bower Circuit

Katoomba

Katoomba Falls

Reids Plateau

Witches Leap

Cliff View Lookout

Scenic Railway

Allambie Lookout

Prince Henry Cliff Walk

Honeymoon Lookout

Dardanelles Pass

Minnamurra Lookout

Federal Pass

Tallawarra Lookout

Three Sisters

Lady Game Lookout

Echo Point

Oreades Lookout

Giant staircase

Federal Pass

Katoomba River

BLUE MOUNTAINS NATIONAL PARK

0   1/2 mi
0   1/2 km

BLACKHEATH

PERRY'S LOOKDOWN TO BLUE GUM FOREST
Distance: 4.5 km
Start: Perrys Lookdown
Finish: Blue Gum Forest

Perry's Lookdown

Blue Gum Forest

Grose River

GROSE VALLEY

Pulpit Rock

BLUE MOUNTAINS NATIONAL PARK

Govett's Leap Lookout

Heritage Centre

32

Blackheath

Braeside Walk

Evans Lookout

Lockleys Route

GRAND CANYON WALK
Distance: 5.5km
Start: Neates Glen car park
Finish: Evans Lookout

Grand Canyon Track

0   1 mi
0   1 km

Blackheath

BLUE MOUNTAINS NATIONAL PARK

32

Katoomba

Glenbrook

KATOOMBA

View of Three Sisters from Echo Point lookout

ECHO POINT TO SCENIC RAILWAY

In the 1930s, the **Giant Staircase** was hewn out of the cliff by teams of park rangers. The top of the steps are near **Three Sisters Lookout** and the walk down is very steep and narrow in places. It's difficult going but the views make it all worthwhile. Look out for the encouraging half way sign. At the bottom, keep your eyes peeled for echidnas, brush-tailed and ring-tail possums, bandicoots, quolls, and grey-headed flying foxes. If you're keen for more exertion once you've reached the Railway, take the **Furber Steps**. It's a challenging but rewarding track that offers great views of **Katoomba Falls** and **Mt. Solitary** across the valley.

PRINCE HENRY CLIFF WALK

If you prefer to hike in the mountains rather than along the forest floor, you'll enjoy this section of the Cliff Walk with its superb vistas across the valley. From the picnic area, the trail descends beside Leura Cascades creek towards **Bridal Veil lookout**. Be sure to slow down and take in the great views over the **Leura Forest**. Continue on Prince Henry Drive; at **Tarpeian Rock** you can see Mt. Solitary.

Keep going uphill towards Olympian Rock and Elysian Rock. From here, follow the cliff line to **Millamurra** and **Tallawarra Lookouts**. The last part of the climb to the **Three Sisters** is perhaps the most challenging but also the most rewarding. Take a few minutes and savor the sweeping views of the valley.

QUICK BITES/SUPERMARKETS FOR PICNIC GOODIES

You can stock up at either Coles or ALDI supermarkets in Katoomba or Woolworths supermarket in Leura. Scenic World has two restaurants. For gourmet treats visit Carrington Cellars at the rear of the Carrington Hotel, or stop at Brown's Siding Store & Café at Medlow Bath for breakfast, lunch, and goodies.

STAY HERE IF:

On weekends tour buses descend on the town, but once they've headed back to Sydney, the place isn't over-run with vistors. Katoomba has a very relaxed feel helped in no small part by a small hippy community. It also has plenty of nice old pubs and cafés, cute vintage shops, and rural versions of big department stores.

BLACKHEATH

Mount Hay, Grose Valley

GRAND CANYON WALK

From the parking lot, 4.5 km (2.8 miles) from Blackheath, follow the Grand Canyon track signs as the path zig-zags down the hillside and the vegetation becomes more like a rainforest. The trail takes you down into the canyon and over a creek. It winds past a few overhanging rocks, then starts a steep decline towards a sandy overhang called the **Rotunda**. After a break here, follow the signs to **Evans Lookout**, which will lead you through a tunnel and past two waterfalls. You eventually reach the 10-meter-tall (33 ft) **Beauchamp Falls** in the center of the creek. From here head up through a gap in the cliffs, weaving through boulders, again following signs to Evans Lookout. From Evans Lookout, you can do a 6.5-km (4-mile) Cliffside walk to **Pulpit Rock** along the Cliff Top Track.

PERRYS LOOKDOWN
TO BLUE GUM FOREST

From the parking lot, follow the signs pointing out the trail down the hill to **Perrys Lookdown**. You'll have fine views over the **Grose Valley** with its sheer sandstone cliffs with the Blue Gum Forest below. Next, head down the hill and do a quick detour to **Docker's Lookout** with its view of Mt. Banks to the north. Head back following the Perrys Lookdown–Blue Gum Forest walk signs. The descent to **Blue Gum Forest** will take about 90 minutes. Once you've explored the forest floor and its dense canopy, head back up the steep track to Perrys Lookdown.

QUICK BITES/SUPERMARKETS
FOR PICNIC GOODIES

Blackheath has something of a gourmet reputation. A particular highlight is **Ashcrafts** (18 Govetts Leap Rd.). There's also a small IGA supermarket.

STAY HERE IF:

Blackheath is smaller and less-visited than Katoomba, but the old weatherboard houses give it a similar feel. There's also enough quirky shops and quaint cafes and restaurants to keep it entertaining. Several Sydney restaurateurs relocated here, so there's a breadth of excellent dining venues.

GLENBROOK

Glenbrook Gorge

An echidna

Kookaburras

RED HANDS CAVE TRACK

Red Hands Cave has some well preserved Aboriginal hand stencillings. The stencils are behind Plexiglas (called Perspex here) to protect them from graffiti. There are a few good placards explaining the history and describing the artifacts found in the area. The walk starts on the southern side of the causeway, and after about 2 km (1.2 miles) of gentle steps down the gully, the well-defined track forks: take the right-hand path just after a large rocky outcrop near the edge of a gully. ■ TIP→ Take care near the edge, there's a significant dropoff. Up the hill near **Camp Fire Creek**, keep an eye out for axe grinding grooves (oval-shaped indentations in sandstone outcrops that Aboriginal peoples used to shape and sharpen stone axes). The trail passes through several types of forest, including dry eucalypt forest, so there's a good variety of birds in the area. Watch for echidnas in the open forest and chestnut-rumped heathwrens and rock warblers in the sandstone area near the Red Hands Cave.

RED HANDS CAVE TRACK
Length: 6 km
Start: Glenbrook
Visitor Centre
Finish: Red
Hands Cave

Glenbrook

Great Western Hwy

32

Lapstone

Blue Pool Track

Red Hands Cave

Fire Creek

Car Park

Camp

Nepean River

Euroka-Nepean River Track

The Oaks Trail

Euroka

BLUE MOUNTAINS NATIONAL PARK

QUICK BITES/SUPERMARKETS FOR PICNIC GOODIES

Glenbrook doesn't have the same variety of food and lodging options as Katoomba and Blackheath, but there's a small supermarket on Park Street. Ross Street has a few nice cafes; check out **Mash Café's** delicious breakfasts.

dressing, and the main course of corn-fed chicken on bok choy with shiitake mushrooms, soy-ginger broth, and wild-wasabi mayonnaise. A favorite dessert is the warm bittersweet chocolate fondant with vanilla-bean Chantilly cream and black cherries. The restaurant is housed in a Federation-era building, and in colder months a log fire warms the century-old simple but elegant interior, where yellow ocher walls reach from black-and-white checkerboard floor to sky-high ceiling. $ *Average main: A$37* ✉ *128 The Mall* ☎ *02/4784–2534* ⊕ *www.silksleura.com.*

$$
B&B/INN
Bygone Beautys Cottages. These two country cottages, at Wentworth Falls and in the nearby village of Bullaburra, provide self-contained accommodations for couples, families, or small groups. **Pros:** antiques collectors love the connected tearoom (at Leura); very romantic surroundings. **Cons:** traditional old-world design isn't for everyone; bathrooms can be chilly in winter. $ *Rooms from: A$195* ✉ *Grose and Megalong Sts.* ☎ *02/4784–3117* ⊕ *www.bygonebeautys.com.au* 🔁 *2 cottages* ⌖ *Breakfast.*

SHOPPING

Josophan's. This gorgeous chocolate boutique in Leura's main shopping street has fast become *the* place to stop for luscious handmade chocolates and drinking chocolate. You can also take part in classes (how does making chocolate truffles sound?) and take away lovely gift boxes of sweets. For a light snack and yummy chocolate desserts, walk across the road to Cafe Madeline (*187a The Mall*), which is also owned by Josophan's proprietor and chocolatier Jodie Van der Velden. ✉ *132 The Mall* ☎ *02/4784–2031* ⊕ *www.josophans.com.au.*

KATOOMBA

2 km (1 mile) west of Leura.

The largest and busiest town in the Blue Mountains, Katoomba developed in the early 1840s as a coal-mining settlement, turning its attention to tourism later in the 19th century. The town center on Katoomba Street has shops, restaurants, and cafés, but the marvels at the lower end of town are an even greater draw.

GETTING HERE AND AROUND

Katoomba is just a few minutes' drive from Leura on the Great Western Highway. A train station connects the town with the rest of the region, as does the Blue Mountains Bus Company. A$40 buys a day's access to the red double-decker Explorer buses that travel around Katoomba and Leura stopping at 29 places (⊕ *www.explorerbus.com.au*).

TOURS

Blue Mountains Adventure Company. The well-established Blue Mountains Adventure Company runs abseiling (rappelling), rock-climbing, canyoning, bushwalking, and mountain-biking trips. Lunch, snacks, and all the equipment are generally included. Introductory and intermediate canyoning tours go to such places as Empress Falls or Serendipity Canyon. ✉ *84A Bathurst Rd.* ☎ *02/4782–1271* ⊕ *www.bmac.com.au* 🔁 *From A$220.*

Blue Mountains Explorer Bus. This company operates the signature red buses coming out of Katoomba and running at regular intervals throughout the region, stopping at 29 sites. You can hop on and off as often as you like. Multiple pass types are available, including some that combine with entry to popular attractions. ⊠ *283 Main St.* ☎ *1300/300915* ⊕ *www.explorerbus.com.au* ⊠ *From A$40.*

High n Wild. This outfitter conducts rappelling, canyoning, rock-climbing, and mountain-biking tours throughout the year. Half-day rappelling trips cost A$135; one-day trips are A$175; combination rappelling and canyoning tours cost A$225. The company's office is based at the YHA youth hostel, a short walk from the station. ⊠ *207 Katoomba St.* ☎ *02/4782–6224* ⊕ *www.high-n-wild.com.au* ⊠ *From A$135.*

Trolley Tours. These purple hop-on, hop-off trolleys operate on a convenient circuit throughout Katoomba and Leura, visiting 29 stops, in a vehicle that resembles a San Francisco streetcar. Tickets are available at the Trolley Shoppe near Katoomba railway station. ⊠ *Main St.* ☎ *1800/801577* ⊕ *www.trolleytours.com.au* ⊠ *A$25.*

ESSENTIALS

Visitor Information Blue Mountains Visitor Information Centre. ⊠ *Echo Point Rd.* ☎ *1300/653408* ⊕ *www.bluemountainscitytourism.com.au.*

EXPLORING

Fodor's Choice ★ **Echo Point.** Overlooking the densely forested Jamison Valley and three soaring sandstone pillars, this lofty promontory has the best views around Katoomba. The formations—called the Three Sisters—take their name from an Aboriginal legend that relates how a trio of siblings was turned to stone by their witch-doctor father to save them from the clutches of a mythical monster. The area was once a seabed that rose over a long period and subsequently eroded, leaving behind tall formations of sedimentary rock. From Echo Point—where the visitor center is located—you can clearly see the horizontal sandstone bedding in the landscape. There is a wide viewing area as well as the start of walks that take you closer to the Sisters. At night the Sisters are illuminated by floodlights. There are cafés and a visitor information center near the site. ⊠ *Echo Point Rd., off Katoomba St.*

FAMILY **Fodor's Choice** ★ **Scenic World.** Thrill-seekers can choose their own adventure on the Scenic Railway, whose trains descend 1,000 feet down the mountainside—the seats allow passengers to adjust the incline angle from 52 to a hair-raising 64 degrees. The railway is one of three attractions at Scenic World, which has carried more than 25 million passengers to the valley floor since it opened in 1945. Once at the base, visitors can hike on easy trails through the Rain forest or make the 20-minute hike to Cableway, a huge cable car that whisks passengers back up the mountain. You can also hike back up, but it's a steep, strenuous climb. The third attraction is Scenic Skyway, a glass-enclosed and -floored cabin that travels from one cliff to another, some 920 feet above the ravines below. The A$35 day pass provides unlimited rides on all three attractions. ⊠ *Cliff Dr., at Violet St.* ☎ *02/4780–0200* ⊕ *www.scenicworld.com.au* ⊠ *From A$35* ⊙ *Daily 9–5.*

CLOSE UP

Great Hikes in Katoomba

ECHO POINT TO SCENIC RAILWAY

In the 1930s, the **Giant Staircase** was hewn out of the cliff by teams of park rangers. The top of the steps are the **Three Sisters Lookout** and the walk down is very steep and narrow in places. It's difficult going but the views make it all worthwhile. Look out for the encouraging half-way sign. At the bottom, keep your eyes peeled for echidnas, brush-tailed and ring-tail possums, bandicoots, quolls, and grey-headed flying foxes. If you're keen for more exertion once you've reached the Railway, take the **Furber Steps**. It's a challenging but rewarding track that has great views of **Katoomba Falls and Mt. Solitary** across the valley.

PRINCE HENRY CLIFF WALK

If you prefer to hike in the mountains rather than along the forest floor, you'll enjoy this section of the Cliff Walk with superb vistas across the valley. From the Leura Cascades picnic area on Cliff Drive, the trail descends beside Leura Falls creek toward **Bridal Veil Falls**. Be sure to slow down and take in the great views over the **Leura Forest**. Continue on Prince Henry Drive; at **Tarpeian Rock** you can see Mt. Solitary. Keep going uphill toward Olympian Rock and Elysian Rock. From here, follow the cliff line to **Millamurra** and **Tallawarra Lookouts**. The last part of the climb to the **Three Sisters** is perhaps the most challenging but also the most rewarding. Take a few minutes and savor the sweeping views of the valley.

SPORTS AND THE OUTDOORS

A good hiking brochure can be picked up at Blue Mountains Visitor Centre at Echo Point, which lists walks varying in length from ½ hour to three days.

ECO-TOURS

Tread Lightly Eco Tours. This eco-minded company operates small-group tours of Blue Mountains National Park and guided day and night walks, as well as four-wheel-drive tours and breakfast trips to view wildlife. Half- and full-day walking tours take in such areas as Fern Bower, Blue Gum Forest, and the Ruined Castle. ⊠ *102 Great Western Hwy., Medlow Bath* ☏ *04/1497–6752* ⊕ *www.treadlightly.com.au* ✉ *From A$65.*

HIKING

Blue Mountains Guides. Single-day, overnight, and three-day walks are available through this guiding company. The half-day Grand Canyon Walk near Blackheath (A$155) is a great way to experience the rain forest if time is short. A four-wheel-drive trip, which includes breakfast with wild kangaroos, is another good choice. ⊠ *33 Portland Rd., Medlow Bath* ☏ *1300/300755* ⊕ *www.bluemountainsguides.com.au* ✉ *From A$145.*

Blue Mountains Walkabout. Experience the Blue Mountains from an Aboriginal perspective on this outfitter's challenging one-day walks, which follow a traditional walkabout song line. Indigenous guides take you on a 7-km (4½-mile) off-track walk through rain forests, while giving some background on Aboriginal culture. You'll also taste bush tucker (food). The walk involves some scrambling, so you need to be fit. The tours depart from Faulconbridge Railway Station (near Springwood, in the lower Blue Mountains), about a 30-minute drive east of Katoomba. ✉ *Springwood* ☎ *0408/433–822* ⊕ *www.bluemountainswalkabout.com* ☜ *A$95.*

WHERE TO EAT

$ ✗ **Brown's Siding Store & Cafe.** A great spot to stop for breakfast or lunch when driving across the mountains, this unassuming little café and food store in a former post office opposite the railway station at Medlow Bath has a loyal local fan base. The Reuben (corned beef on rye with cheese and spicy slaw) and steak sandwiches receive particular praise here, and the toasted fig and cranberry bread is worth trying. There is a range of gourmet produce on sale as well. ⑤ *Average main: A$20* ✉ *1 Railway Parade, Medlow Bath* ☎ *02/4788–1555* ☉ *Closed Mon. and Tues. No dinner.*

$ ✗ **Paragon Cafe.** With its chandeliers, gleaming cappuccino machine,
CAFÉ and bas-relief figures above the booths, this wood-paneled, art deco café opened in 1916 was a favorite Blue Mountains eatery in its heyday. There are much better places to eat nearby these days, but it's still worth dropping in for a coffee or one of 52 varieties of homemade chocolates, and to marvel at the opulence of the interior. A variety of events are staged on weekends throughout the year, including Regency dances, 1920s tango nights, and screenings of classic movies; most include dinner. ⑤ *Average main: A$15* ✉ *65 Katoomba St.* ☎ *02/4782–2928.*

WHERE TO STAY

$$$ 🏨 **The Carrington.** Established in 1880, this is one of the grande dames of
HOTEL the Blue Mountains, a Victorian-era relic that, in its heyday, was considered one of the four great hotels of the British Empire. **Pros:** drinks on their veranda are a pleasant way to end the day; breakfast included; free Wi-Fi in rooms. **Cons:** the newer rooms lack character; some rooms have shared bathrooms. ⑤ *Rooms from: A$250* ✉ *15–47 Katoomba St.* ☎ *02/4782–1111* ⊕ *www.thecarrington.com.au* ↦ *59 rooms, 49 with bath, 6 suites, 1 apartment* ¶⊙| *Breakfast; Some meals.*

$$$$ 🏨 **Echoes Boutique Hotel & Restaurant.** Perched on the edge of the Jamison
HOTEL Valley, this stylish boutique hotel has one of the best views in the Blue Mountains. **Pros:** spectacular views from the terrace; slick, contemporary design. **Cons:** a little pricey. ⑤ *Rooms from: A$525* ✉ *3 Lilianfels Ave.* ☎ *02/4782–1966* ⊕ *www.echoeshotel.com.au* ↦ *14 suites* ¶⊙| *Breakfast.*

$$$$ 🏨 **Lilianfels Blue Mountains Resort & Spa.** Teetering close to the brink of
HOTEL Echo Point, this glamorous boutique hotel adds a keen sense of manor-
Fodor's Choice house style to the standard Blue Mountains guesthouse experience.
★ **Pros:** luxurious and restful bathrooms; friendly five-star service; lovely drawing room with views. **Cons:** 19th-century style is not for everyone; restaurant is very expensive. ⑤ *Rooms from: A$475* ✉ *5–19 Lilianfels Ave., at Panorama Dr.* ☎ *02/4780–1200* ⊕ *www.lilianfels.com.au* ✍ *Reservations essential* ↦ *81 rooms, 4 suites* ¶⊙| *Breakfast.*

$$ **Lurline House.** This historic little B&B is arguably the town's best.
B&B/INN   **Pros:** rooms have four-poster beds; warm and welcoming. **Cons:**
Fodor'sChoice younger trendsetters might find the place not to their taste. $ *Rooms*
★   *from: A$180 ⊠ 122 Lurline St. ☎ 02/4782–4609 ⊕ www.lurlinehouse.*
com.au ⤳ 7 rooms, 1 cottage ⊙ Breakfast.

$$$ **Melba House.** If Dame Nellie, Dame Joan, and Dame Edna are new
B&B/INN to you, you'll certainly be well acquainted with the ladies after a stay
in beautiful Melba House, as the three guestrooms bear their names.
Pros: genial host; located minutes away from great walking trails. **Cons:**
no year-round dining area (except in summer when the veranda is an
option, breakfast is served in rooms). $ *Rooms from: A$280 ⊠ 98*
Waratah St. ☎ 02/4782–4141 ⊕ www.melbahouse.com ⤳ 3 suites
⊙ Breakfast ⌨ Minimum 2-night stay on weekends.

$$$ **Mountain Heritage Hotel & Spa.** This hotel overlooking the Jamison Val-
HOTEL ley is steeped in history: it served as a "coffee palace" during the temper-
ance movement, a rest-and-relaxation establishment for the British navy
during World War II, and a religious retreat in the 1970s. **Pros:** friendly
service; manicured gardens; public areas are charming with great valley
views. **Cons:** furniture is a little dated. $ *Rooms from: A$228 ⊠ Apex*
and Lovel Sts. ☎ 02/4782–2155 ⊕ www.mountainheritage.com.au
⤳ 37 rooms, 4 suites ⊙ Breakfast.

$$$ **Hydro Majestic Blue Mountains.** This iconic and much-loved cliff-top
HOTEL hotel in Medlow Bath, reopened in late 2014 after being closed for
Fodor'sChoice several years, has beautifully recaptured its former art deco splendor.
★   **Pros:** most rooms have amazing views; heritage glamour and living
history; lots of dining options. **Cons:** rooms are small. $ *Rooms from:*
A$269 ⊠ Great Western Hwy., Medlow Bath ☎ 02/4782–6885 ⊕ www.
hydromajestic.com.au ⤳ 54 rooms, 3 suites ⊙ No meals.

BLACKHEATH

12 km (7½ miles) north of Katoomba.

Magnificent easterly views over the Grose Valley—which has outstanding hiking trails—delightful gardens, good restaurants, and antiques
shops head the list of reasons to visit the village of Blackheath, at the
3,495-foot summit of the Blue Mountains.

GETTING HERE AND AROUND

Blackheath is an easy drive north from Katoomba, traveling on the
Great Western Highway, passing Medlow Bath on the way. There's also
a train station on the Blue Mountains line, and the town is also serviced
by Blue Mountains Bus Company on Route 698 between Katoomba
and Mount Victoria.

ESSENTIALS

Visitor Information Blue Mountains Heritage Centre. ⊠ *Govetts Leap Rd., at*
Mel Ave. ☎ 02/4787–8877 ⊕ www.nationalparks.nsw.gov.au.

EXPLORING

Govetts Leap Lookout. Blackheath's most famous view is from the Govetts
Leap Lookout, with its striking panorama of the Grose Valley and Bridal
Veil Falls. Govett was a surveyor who mapped this region extensively in

CLOSE UP

Great Hikes in Blackheath

GRAND CANYON WALK

From the parking lot at Evans Lookout, 4.5 km (2.8 miles) from Blackheath, follow the Grand Canyon signs as the path zigzags down the hillside, and the vegetation becomes more like a rain forest. The trail takes you down into the canyon and over a creek. It winds past a few overhanging rocks, then starts a steep decline toward a sandy overhang called the **Rotunda.** After a break here, follow the signs to **Evans Lookout,** which leads you through a tunnel and past two waterfalls. You eventually reach the 33-foot **Beauchamp Falls** in the center of the creek. From here head up through a gap in the cliffs, weaving through boulders, again following signs to Evans Lookout. From Evans Lookout, you can follow a 6.5-km (4-mile) cliffside walk to **Pulpit Rock** along the Cliff Top Track. The entire loop is 6 km (3.75 miles) and takes around 3½ hours.

PERRYS LOOKDOWN TO BLUE GUM FOREST

This is a hard, but rewarding, four-hour walk. From the Perry Lookdown parking lot (turn east into Hat Hill Road from the Great Western Highway at Blackheath), follow the signs pointing out the trail down the hill to **Perrys Lookdown.** You'll have fine views over the **Grose Valley** with its sheer sandstone cliffs with the **Blue Gum Forest** below. Next, head down the hill and do a quick detour to **Docker's Lookout** with its view of Mt. Banks to the north. Head back following the Perrys Lookdown-Blue Gum Forest walk signs. The descent to Blue Gum Forest will take about 90 minutes. Once you've explored the forest floor and its dense canopy, head back up the steep track to Perrys Lookdown.

---

the 1830s. This lookout is the start or finish of several excellent bush-walks. Brochures are available at the Blue Mountains Heritage Centre. ⊠ *End of Govett's Leap Rd.* ⊕ *www.nationalparks.nsw.gov.au.*

FAMILY **Trains, Planes and Automobiles.** Children and adults will enjoy a browse around this store that bills itself as the best antique toyshop in the world. ⊠ *50 Govetts Leap Rd.* ☎ *02/4787–7974* ⊕ *www.antiquetoys. com.au* ⊙ *Thurs.–Mon. 10–5.*

SPORTS AND THE OUTDOORS

HIKING

Auswalk. This environmentally conscious company, which also leads walks in other parts of Australia, has three-, five-, and seven-day self-guided or guided hiking tours through the region, staying at historic inns along the way, with all meals and admission to some local attractions included. The seven-day walk is A\$1,595 per person (double occupancy). The owners advise that you be in reasonable shape before starting. ☎ *03/5350–8800* ⊕ *www.auswalk.com.au* ✉ *From A\$1225.*

HORSEBACK RIDING

Megalong Australian Heritage Centre. This rural farm in a deep mountain valley off the Great Western Highway is the place to saddle up and explore the many mountain and valley trails. Both adults and children can go horseback riding around the farm's 2,000 acres, with prices ranging from A$50 for an hour's wilderness ride to A$95 for the most popular two-hour ride to A$395 for a full-day ride with breakfast and lunch. ✉ *993 Megalong Rd., Megalong* ⊹ *15 km (9 miles) south of Blackheath* ☎ *02/4787–8188* ⊕ *www.megalongcc.com.au* ⊠ *From A$50* ⊙ *Daily 9–5.*

WHERE TO EAT AND STAY

$$$ ✗ **Ashcrofts.** Amid the antiques and vintage shops of Blackheath village,
MODERN this acclaimed restaurant looks a little like a Parisian bistro, although
AUSTRALIAN the black-and-white photographs on the wall are of prominent Australians. Sydneysiders and locals turn up for Sunday lunch or dinner to feast on the six-course (A$90) tasting menu, although you can also order à la carte. You might start with a spring salad of honey-baked beetroot, house-made labneh, candied walnuts with tea-soaked muscats, and hibiscus vinaigrette, or the Egyptian-spice quail on Cape Malay carrot remoulade with sticky-eggplant jam. Mains include fish pie with wild sea scallops, tiger prawns, and fennel-infused snapper velouté, and slow-roasted crispy-skin duck with Persian aromatics and citrus flavors. ⑤ *Average main: A$38* ✉ *18 Govetts Leap Rd.* ☎ *02/4787–8297* ⊕ *www.ashcrofts.com* ⊙ *Closed Mon.–Wed. No lunch Wed.–Sat.*

$$ ✗ **Vesta.** Melt-in-your-mouth, slow-cooked food is the draw at this
EUROPEAN popular fine dining restaurant in Blackheath. Most of the rustic dishes, like the lamb shoulder braised for 12 hours, are cooked in a historic 120-year-old Scotch oven that baked the township's bread when the building was Blackheath's bakery in the 19th century. The oven was rediscovered 100 years later during renovations behind a false wall. The restaurant (which occupies the site of the former Vulcans, a renowned Blue Mountains dining destination) also offers the entire menu for takeaway, a popular option with travelers who don't feel like cooking in the self-contained cottages ⑤ *Average main: A$30* ✉ *33 Govetts Leap Rd.* ☎ *4787–6899* ⊕ *vestablackheath.com.au* ⊙ *Closed Mon. and Tues. No lunch Wed.–Fri.* ⚏ *Reservations essential.*

$$$ ⊡ **Jemby Rinjah Eco Lodge.** Designed for urbanites seeking a wilderness
B&B/INN experience, these rustic, self-contained wooden cabins and lodges are set deep in the bush. **Pros:** private and tranquil; hearty and healthy mountain fare at the restaurant. **Cons:** some might find the eco-toilet disconcerting; the lodges can be booked out by groups, who can get noisy; minimum two-night stay. ⑤ *Rooms from: A$240* ✉ *336 Evans Lookout Rd.* ☎ *02/4787–7622* ⊕ *www.jemby.com.au* ↪ *10 cabins, 3 lodges* ⊠ *No meals.*

MOUNT VICTORIA

7 km (4½ miles) northwest of Blackheath.

The settlement of Mount Victoria is the highest point in the Blue Mountains, and there's a Rip Van Winkle air about it—drowsy and only just awake in an unfamiliar world. A walk around the village reveals many atmospheric houses, stores, a charming old post office, and a stately old hotel with the patina of time spelled out in the fading paint of these buildings. Mount Victoria is at the far side of the mountains at the western limit of this region, and the village serves as a good jumping-off point for a couple of out-of-the-way attractions.

GETTING HERE AND AROUND

Mount Victoria is an easy drive north of Blackheath on the Great Western Highway, and it's also on the main Blue Mountains railway line linking Sydney with Lithgow. The 698V bus route connects the village with Katoomba, but only on weekdays.

EXPLORING

Hotel Imperial. The pink circa-1878 Hotel Imperial was one of several historic Blue Mountains inns built a few years after the railway line was opened from Sydney. It's worth popping in for a drink to have a look at the fading grand old dame. ⊠ *1 Station St.* ☎ *02/4787–1878* ⊕ *www. hotelimperial.com.au.*

FAMILY

Fodor's Choice

★

Jenolan Caves. Stalactites, stalagmites, columns, and lacelike rock on multiple levels fill the fascinating Jenolan Caves, a labyrinth of vast limestone caverns sculpted by underground rivers. There are as many as 320 caves in the Jenolan area. Two caves (Nettles Cave and Devil's Coachhouse) near the surface can be explored on your own, but a guide is required to reach the most intriguing formations. Standard tours lead through the most popular caves—many say that Orient Cave is the most spectacular, while the more rigorous adventure tours last up to seven hours. The one- to two-hour walks depart every 15 to 30 minutes, on weekends less frequently. Prices range from A\$35 for a standard tour to A\$220 for the full-day Mammoth Cave Adventure Tour where you squeeze through ancient passageways—it includes a bit of rappelling and is not for the claustrophobic. Concerts and murder mystery nights are also held in this spooky environment. Cave House, on the same site, is a nostalgic retreat and has been providing lodging since 1887. To get here, follow the Great Western Highway north out of Mount Victoria, then after Hartley, turn southwest toward Hampton. ⊠ *4655 Jenolan Caves Rd, 59 km (37 miles) southwest of Mount Victoria, Jenolan Caves* ☎ *1300/763–311* ⊕ *www.jenolancaves.org.au* ▭ *From A\$35* ⊙ *Daily 9:30–5:30.*

OFF THE
BEATEN
PATH

Mount Tomah Botanic Garden. This is the cool-climate branch of Sydney's Royal Botanic Gardens (30 km [19 miles] northeast of Mount Victoria). The garden is 3,280 feet above sea level, and is a spectacular setting for native and imported plants. You'll find beautiful rhododendrons and European deciduous trees, as well as plants that evolved in isolation for millions of years in the Gondwana Forest. The famous Wollemi Pine (once thought to be extinct) is also here. There are picnic grounds, a café with views of the ranges, and a daily guided tour at 11:30 am. Admission is free. ⊠ *Bells Line of Rd., Mount Tomah* ☎ *02/4567–3000* ⊕ *www.mounttomahbotanicgarden.com.au* ⊙ *Weekdays 9–5:30, weekends 9:30–5:30.*

The Hunter Valley Wine Region

THE HUNTER VALLEY WINE REGION

To almost everyone in Sydney, the Hunter Valley conjures up visions of one thing: wine. The Hunter is the largest grape-growing area in the state, with more than 120 wineries producing excellent varieties. The Hunter is divided into seven subregions, each with its own unique character. The hub is the Pokolbin/Rothbury region, where many of the large operations are found, along with several boutique wineries.

The Hunter Valley covers an area of almost 25,103 square km (9,692 square miles), stretching from the town of Gosford north of Sydney to 177 km (110 miles) farther north along the coast, and almost 300 km (186 miles) inland. The meandering waterway that gives this valley its name is also one of the most extensive river systems in the state.

POKOLBIN AND NEARBY

163 km (100 miles) north of Sydney.

The Lower Hunter wine-growing region is centered on the village of Pokolbin, where there are antiques shops, good cafés, and dozens of wineries. In peak season, wineries are very busy with tour groups, so if you can visit midweek or off-season, all the better.

GETTING HERE AND AROUND

A car is the best way to visit the wineries and off-the-beaten-path attractions unless you are on a guided tour. Leave Sydney via the Harbour Bridge or Harbour Tunnel and get onto the Pacific Highway (keep following the signs for Newcastle). Just before Hornsby the road joins the Sydney–Newcastle Freeway, known as the M1. Take the exit from the freeway signposted "Hunter Valley vineyards via Cessnock." From Cessnock, the route to the vineyards is clearly marked. Allow 2½ hours for the journey.

TOURS

Any tour of the area's vineyards should begin at Pokolbin's **Hunter Valley Wine Country Visitors Information Centre,** which has free maps of the vineyards, brochures, and a handy visitor's guide.

AAT Kings. From Sydney, AAT Kings operates a daylong wine-tasting bus tour of the Hunter Valley and another to Hunter Valley Gardens. Buses collect passengers from city hotels from 7 am. ☎ *1300/228546* ⊕ *www.aatkings.com.au* ✉ *From A$180.*

Heidi's Hunter Valley. Local operator Heidi's Hunter Valley operates personalized day tours to the wineries and restaurants in a sleek four-wheel-drive vehicle. Heidi Duckworth, who worked for the Hunter Valley Wine Tourism organization for 12 years, knows all the best places in the valley. ☎ *0408/623–136* ⊕ *www.heidishuntervalley.com. au* ✉ *From A$350 for up to 4 guests.*

Rover Coaches. To avoid driving after sampling too many wines, hop aboard one of the Wine Rover buses, which will pick you up from most accommodations in Pokolbin or Cessnock to visit several wineries. Rover also runs an Ale Trail tour, visiting several Hunter Valley breweries. ✉ *231–233 Vincent St., Cessnock* ☎ *02/4990–1699* ⊕ *www. rovercoaches.com.au* ✉ *From A$55.*

ESSENTIALS

Visitor Information Hunter Valley Visitors Information Centre. ✉ *455 Wine Country Dr., Pokolbin* ☎ *02/4993–6700, 1300/6948–6837* ⊕ *www. huntervalleyvisitorcentre.com.au.* **Maitland Hunter Valley Visitor Information Centre.** ✉ *New England Hwy., at High St., Maitland* ☎ *02/4931–2800* ⊕ *www. mymaitland.com.au.*

EXPLORING
TOP ATTRACTIONS

Briar Ridge Vineyard. In a delightful rural corner of the Mount View region, this is one of the Hunter Valley's most prestigious small wineries. It produces a limited selection of sought-after reds, whites, and sparkling wines. The Sémillon, Chardonnay, Shiraz, and intense Cabernet Sauvignon are highly recommended. The vineyard is on the southern periphery of the Lower Hunter vineyards, about a five-minute drive from Pokolbin. ✉ *593 Mt. View Rd., Mount View* ☎ *02/4990–3670* ⊕ *www.briarridge.com.au* ☼ *Daily 10–5.*

Lindeman's Ben Ean Winery. This has been one of the largest and most prestigious winemakers in the country since the early 1900s. In addition to its Hunter Valley vineyards, the company owns property in South

Australia and Victoria, and numerous outstanding wines from these vineyards can be sampled in the tasting room. Try the Shiraz, Sémillon, or Chardonnay. The winery has its own museum, displaying vintage winemaking equipment; the 1843 Harvest Cafe; and two picnic areas, one near the parking lot and the other next to the willow trees around the dam. ⊠ *McDonalds Rd., just south of DeBeyers Rd., Pokolbin* ☎ *02/4993–3700* ⊕ *www.lindemans.com.au* ⊗ *Daily 10–5.*

Margan Family Winegrowers. A leading light in the new wave of Hunter winemakers, Margan Family Winegrowers produces some of the valley's best small-volume wines. Try their full-bodied Verdelho, rosé-style Saignée Shiraz, and Certain Views Cabernet Sauvignon. A riper-than-most Sémillon is the flagship. Many items on the fine-dining lunch menu in the restaurant are sourced from the chef's vegetable and herb garden on-site, along with fresh eggs. Tasting plates are a great way to sample many of the dishes, such as pancetta-wrapped quail. ⊠ *1238 Milbrodale Rd., Broke* ☎ *02/6579–1372 cellar door* ⊕ *www.margan. com.au* ⊗ *Daily 10–5.*

Matilda Bay Brewhouse Hunter Valley. There are 12 craft beers produced in this boutique brewery, including the brewer's acclaimed "three-hop" beers: premium lager, premium light lager, and pilsner, along with its alcoholic ginger beer. You can order a chef's beer tasting "paddle" with small glasses of each, complete with tasting notes. Soak up the alcohol with fish-and-chips, meatballs, pizzas, and other light fare, and there's live music most days. It's part of a large complex that includes the resort, a wine school, cooking school, candy making classes, day spa, horseback riding, and Segway tours. ⊠ *Hermitage Rd. and Mistletoe La., Pokolbin* ☎ *02/4998–7777* ⊕ *www.hunterresort.com.au* ⊗ *Daily noon–9.*

McWilliams Mount Pleasant Estate. At this estate, part of Australia's biggest family-owned wine company, chief winemaker Jim Chatto (only the fourth since the winery was founded in 1921) continues the tradition of producing classic Hunter wines. The flagship Maurice O'Shea Shiraz and Chardonnay, and the celebrated Elizabeth Sémillon, are among the wines that can be sampled in the huge cellar door. ⊠ *401 Marrowbone Rd., Pokolbin* ☎ *02/4998–7505* ⊕ *www.mountpleasantwines.com.au* ⊠ *Tours A$5, tastings free* ⊗ *Daily 10–4.*

Fodor's Choice ★ **Roche Estate.** You can't miss this ultramodern facility in the heart of Pokolbin. This futuristic winery is a joint venture between two leading Hunter Valley families: the Roches (owners of Hunter Valley Gardens) and the McGuigans, who have made wine for four generations. The winery is best known for its Pinot Gris; however, you can sample a wide variety, including Sémillon, Sauvignon Blanc, Chardonnay, and Shiraz in the stylish tasting room. There's also a Goldfish Wine Bar and Oishii, an on-site fine-dining Japanese-Thai restaurant. If you can, stop in at the winery's branch of the Hunter Valley Smelly Cheese Shop. In the summer the winery hosts major concerts in its 10,000-seat amphitheater—past performers have included Elton John, Rod Stewart, and the Beach Boys. ⊠ *Broke and McDonalds Rds., Pokolbin* ☎ *02/4993–3999 cellar door* ⊕ *www.rocheestate.com.au* ⊗ *Daily 9–5.*

One of the hundreds of vineyards that dot the Hunter Valley

Tyrrell's Wines. Founded in 1858, Tyrrell's Wines is one of the Hunter Valley's oldest family-owned vineyards. This venerable establishment crafts a wide selection of wines, and was the first to produce Chardonnay commercially in Australia. Its famous Vat 47 Chardonnay is still a winner. Enjoy the experience of sampling fine wines in the rustic tasting room, or take a picnic lunch to a site overlooking the valley. Guided tours (A\$5) are given daily at 10:30. ⊠ *1838 Broke Rd., Pokolbin* ☎ *02/4993–7028* ⊕ *www.tyrrells.com.au* ⊗ *Mon.–Sat. 9–5, Sun. 10–4.*

WORTH NOTING

Bimbadgen Winery. This winery is particularly well-known for its very popular Day on the Green concerts, which are held several times between October and March. Artists have included Tom Jones and Leonard Cohen. Beyond the shows, the winery also produces some very good wines—try the signature Chardonnay or Sémillon. It is also home to one of the Hunter's best restaurants, Esca, which has fantastic views across the vineyards towards the Brokenback Mountains. If you have a sweet tooth, you'll love the Bimbadgen Dessert Experience (A\$35, from 3 pm, bookings essential) where you can try three desserts, each paired with a different dessert wine. The restaurant serves lunch every day and dinner Wednesday through Saturday. The cellar door is open daily for tastings. ⊠ *790 McDonalds Rd., Pokolbin* ☎ *02/4998–4650 cellar door, 02/4998–4666 restaurant* ⊕ *www.bimbadgen.com.au* ⊗ *Sun.–Thurs. 10–5, Fri. and Sat. 10–7.*

Binnorie Dairy. Drop by this cheesemaker at Tuscany Wine Estate to sample and buy Simon Gough's irresistible, handcrafted soft cow and goat cheeses made from locally sourced milk. You'd be hard-pressed to find a tastier marinated feta outside Greece—or even in it. ⊠ *Tuscany Wine Estate, Hermitage Rd. at Mistletoe La., Pokolbin* ☏ *02/4998–6660* ⊕ *www.binnorie.com.au* ☉ *Tues.–Sat. 10–5, Sun. 10–4.*

FAMILY

Fodor's Choice

★

Hunter Valley Gardens. Garden lovers and those who admire beauty in general should flock to the Hunter Valley Gardens, in the heart of the Pokolbin wine-growing district. The 12 separate gardens occupy 50 acres and include European formal gardens, a Chinese Moongate garden, and a delightful children's storybook garden featuring characters such as the Mad Hatter and Jack and Jill. The gardens have a dazzling Christmas lights display each year; the park is open at night during the holiday season (mid-November–late January) from 6 to 10. The adjacent complex houses restaurants, a popular pub, a hotel, a cute wedding chapel, the underground **Hunter Cellars,** and a selection of boutiques selling gifts as well as wonderful chocolates and fudge. ⊠ *2090 Broke Rd., Pokolbin* ☏ *02/4998–4000* ⊕ *www.hvg.com.au* ☒ *A$28* ☉ *Daily 9–5.*

McGuigan Wines. Adjoining the Hunter Valley Gardens is the cellar-door complex of McGuigan Wines, one of the most well-known wine labels in the Hunter Valley. Here you can taste and buy wines, such as Vineyard Select and Personal Reserve labels, that are not available in suburban wine shops. Winery tours depart at noon every day. While you're there try some of the superb cheeses at the adjacent **Hunter Valley Cheese Company**—look out for the washed-rind Hunter Valley Gold and the deliciously marinated soft cows'-milk cheese. You can also see the cheeses being made by hand. There is a cheese talk daily at 11. ⊠ *Broke and McDonalds Rds., Pokolbin* ☏ *02/4998–7402* ⊕ *www.mcguiganwines.com.au* ☉ *Daily 9–5.*

SPORTS AND THE OUTDOORS

BICYCLING

Hunter Valley Cycling. Your bike, helmet, and a map of the area will be delivered to your hotel door by owner Mark or one of his friendly staff. Half-day rentals are A$25, and full-day costs A$35. ⊠ *266 De Beyers Rd., Pokolbin* ☏ *0418/281–480* ⊕ *www.huntervalleycycling.com.au.*

HELICOPTER TOURS

Slattery Helicopter Charter. Soaring over a patchwork of wineries and the dramatic Brokenback Range is a thrilling experience—and can be a relatively inexpensive one (as helicopter rides go) with flights starting at A$80 per person for eight minutes, although you can splurge out A$500 for a one-hour flight to the beaches of Newcastle and the Central Coast. All flights require a minimum of two people. ⊠ *230 Old Maitland Rd., Hexham* ☏ *0408/649–696,* ⊕ *www.slatteryhelicoptercharter.com.au* ☒ *From A$80.*

HORSEBACK RIDING

Hunter Valley Horse Riding and Adventures. These friendly folks welcome equestrians of all levels and ages and have a nice selection of guided rides around the valley, from a one-hour ride to the popular sunset ride (A$80), when you're most likely to see wildlife. ⊠ *288 Talga Rd., Rothbury* ☏ *02/4930–7111* ⊕ *www.huntervalleyhorseriding.com.au* ☒ *From $A60.*

HOT-AIR BALLOONING

Fodor'sChoice **Balloon Aloft Hunter Valley.** It's an early start to the day, but drifting above
★ the vineyards at sunrise in a hot air balloon is an absolutely magical way
to see the Hunter Valley. Balloon Aloft has been operating since the late
'70s and runs hour-long sunrise flights, which culminate with a celebra-
tory Champagne breakfast at Petersons Winery. ⊠ *Wine Country Dr.,
Pokolbin* ✛ *Meet at Petersons Champagne House* ☎ *02/4991–1955,
1300/723279* ⊕ *www.balloonaloft.com* ✈ *From A$339.*

WHERE TO EAT

$$$ ✕**Bistro Molines.** Local French-born celebrity chef Robert Molines, who
FRENCH used to run Roberts Restaurant, has a restaurant on the grounds of
Fodor'sChoice the lovely Tallavera vineyard, which has one of the best views in the
★ valley. Make sure you nab a table on or near the veranda. Food isn't
overly complicated or styled, which fits nicely with the relaxed (but
professional) service. The twice-roasted Hunter duckling on braised
cabbage is delicious, while seafood fans love the fillet of Red Emperor
with Hervey Bay scallops. Those who want a nap after a long lunch, or
don't want to drive home, might want to book into the two-bedroom
cottage (operated by Robert and his wife Sally) that's just a stroll from
the restaurant. ⑤ *Average main: A$42* ⊠ *Tallavera Grove, 749 Mount
View Rd., Mount View* ☎ *02/4990–9553* ⊕ *www.bistromolines.com.
au* ☉ *Closed Tues. and Wed. No dinner Mon. and Thurs.* ⌂ *Reserva-
tions essential.*

$$ ✕**Cafe Enzo.** This breakfast and lunch café is at Peppers Creek Village,
CAFÉ a charming little shopping and dining enclave in Pokolbin with a vil-
lage green atmosphere. Housed in a sandstone building, with a lovely
attached sun-drenched courtyard overlooking a fountain, this is a great
spot for a hearty lunch after a visit to neighboring David Hooks winery
and the clothing and antiques shops. Meals are substantial and may
include handmade linguine with tiger prawns and fresh chili or zucchini
and corn fritters with beetroot-cured Atlantic salmon. It's a popular
place in the warmer months, and even breakfast can be booked out
on weekends. ⑤ *Average main: A$30* ⊠ *Peppers Creek Village, Broke
and Ekerts Rds., Pokolbin* ☎ *02/4998–7233* ⊕ *www.enzohuntervalley.
com.au* ☉ *No dinner.*

$$$$ ✕**Circa 1876.** This restaurant in grapevine-covered, 1876-built Pepper
MODERN Tree Cottage wins the ambience award hands down. The seasonal Mod
AUSTRALIAN Oz menu draws inspiration from regional recipes of France and Italy
and applies it to local game, seafood, beef, and lamb. A good choice
is the chef speciality duck breast roulade with ham or the blue-eye tra-
valla served with Thai green curry and mussels. Opt for the A$75 two-
course menu or splurge on the A$120 five-course Chefs Tasting Menu.
The cozy fireside lounge is perfect for enjoying after-dinner liqueurs,
or another wine from the extensive wine list. ⑤ *Average main: A$75*
⊠ *88 Halls Rd., Pokolbin* ☎ *02/4998–4998* ⊕ *theconventhuntervalley.
com/circa-1876* ⌂ *Reservations essential.*

$$$$ ✕**Leaves & Fishes.** A rustic boathouse-style café with a deck that projects
ASIAN FUSION over a fish-stocked dam and a lovely garden, this is the place to savor
delicious seafood with an Asian twist, and share antipasto dishes. Fish
comes straight from farm to plate, and wines are from local vineyards.

You could start with the mussels and prawn hot pot with chorizo or go straight to the hearty seafood chowder. Those who are not fans of seafood can tuck into the crispy skin duck with steamed asparagus and confit of potato. Desserts from the specials board might include mango and coconut pudding with fresh papaya. Reservations are recommended, especially on weekends, and it's a two-course minimum (A$68) at both lunch and dinner. There is also boathouse-style accommodation on the property, ideal for couples. ⑤ *Average main: A$68* ✉ *737 Lovedale Rd., Lovedale* ☎ *02/4930–7400* ⊕ *www.leavesandfishes.com. au* ☉ *Closed Mon.–Wed. No dinner Thurs. and Sun.*

WHERE TO STAY

$$$ 🏨 **Carriages Boutique Hotel.** On 36 acres at the end of a quiet country
B&B/INN lane, this rustic-looking but winsome guesthouse, set on a small vineyard, is all about privacy. **Pros:** romantic in winter with roaring fireplaces in some rooms; lovely verandas overlooking the grounds. **Cons:** no children allowed; wedding groups sometimes book out most of the place. ⑤ *Rooms from: A$275* ✉ *112 Halls Rd., Pokolbin* ☎ *02/4998–7591* ⊕ *www.thecarriages.com.au* ⭷ *2 rooms, 8 suites* ⑩ *Breakfast.*

$$$$ 🏨 **Cedars Mount View.** This property nestled in the hills above the valley
B&B/INN might tempt you to forget about wine tasting for a few days. **Pros:** private and luxurious; bathrooms have decadent sunken whirlpool baths. **Cons:** location a bit too remote for some. ⑤ *Rooms from: A$485* ✉ *60 Mitchells Rd., Mount View* ☎ *02/4990–9009* ⊕ *www.cedars.com.au* ⭷ *4 villas, 1 cottage* ⑩ *Breakfast.*

$$$ 🏨 **The Cooperage Bed and Breakfast.** This lovely B&B is in the heart of
B&B/INN Kelman Vineyards Estate, a working vineyard with a cellar door just a stone's throw from the rooms. **Pros:** big comfy beds; guesthouse rooms have private decks; free Wi-Fi. **Cons:** not suitable for children under 10; can be booked out months ahead. ⑤ *Rooms from: A$278* ✉ *41 Kelman Vineyards, off Oakey Creek Rd., Pokolbin* ☎ *02/4990–1232* ⊕ *www. huntervalleycooperage.com* ⭷ *5 rooms* ⑩ *Breakfast.*

$$$ 🏨 **Mercure Resort Hunter Valley Gardens.** This good value hotel is hard
HOTEL to beat when it comes to location: it's next door to the Hunter Valley Gardens and boutiques and within walking distance to half a dozen wineries, including Roche and Hope estates, which both host big-name musicians such as Elton John and Fleetwood Mac at regular concert events. **Pros:** great location; walking distance to major wineries; rooms have balconies or terraces. **Cons:** can get busy with conference groups; more business hotel than resort in style. ⑤ *Rooms from: A$250* ✉ *2090 Broke Rd., Pokolbin* ☎ *02/4998–2000* ⊕ *www.mercurehuntervalley. com.au* ⭷ *68 rooms, 4 suites* ⑩ *No meals.*

$$$ 🏨 **Peppers Convent.** This former convent, built in 1909 and transported
B&B/INN 605 km (375 miles) from its original home in western New South Wales, is ideal for those who love traditional guesthouses. **Pros:** romantic and secluded; balconies are a superb place to watch the sunset. **Cons:** standard rooms are on the small side; a bit noisy. ⑤ *Rooms from: A$300* ✉ *88 Halls Rd., Pokolbin* ☎ *02/4998–4999* ⊕ *www.peppers.com.au* ⭷ *17 rooms* ⑩ *No meals.*

THE NORTH COAST

The North Coast is one of the most glorious and seductive stretches of terrain in Australia, stretching almost 680 km (422 miles) from Newcastle up to the Queensland border. An almost continuous line of beaches defines the coast, with the Great Dividing Range rising to the west the farther you travel north. These natural borders frame a succession of rolling green pasturelands, mossy rain forests, towns dotted by red-roof houses, and waterfalls that tumble in glistening arcs from the escarpment.

A journey along the coast leads through several rich agricultural districts, beginning with grazing country in the south and moving into plantations of bananas, sugarcane, mangoes, avocados, and macadamia nuts. Dorrigo National Park, outside Bellingen, and Muttonbird Island, in Coffs Harbour, are two parks good for getting your feet on some native soil and for seeing unusual birdlife.

NEWCASTLE

160 km (100 miles) north of Sydney.

Once known as the Steel City, today Newcastle is one of Australia's hippest cities. It's flanked by the Pacific Ocean and six beaches on its eastern side and a harbor on its west side. Gentrification began when the steel mills closed in 1999. Nowadays the old wharves and warehouses form part of the lively riverside Honeysuckle precinct, which buzzes with hotels, cafés, and restaurants.

GETTING HERE AND AROUND

This city of about 500,000 is easy to navigate, as the harbor area and city center are just 3 km (2 miles) from the beaches, and buses run between them. Hunter Street—the main artery—runs parallel to the harbor, and it's only a five-minute walk from harbor to downtown. Trains from Sydney stop at Hamilton and Broadmeadow, and shuttle buses take you into the city center. Buses also travel from Hunter Street to Darby Street, the main shopping and dining area.

EXPLORING

Fort Scratchley. This was one of several forts built on headlands along Australia's shore in the mid-to-late 19th century to defend the colony against a possible Russian attack. Built in 1882, its guns had never been fired in anger until June 8, 1942, when the fort returned fire from Japanese submarines in a little-known World War II confrontation called "the shelling of Newcastle"—the city sustained 34 shells but neither damage nor loss of life. The fort, situated on Flagstaff Hill in Newcastle's east end (not far from the railway station), was occupied by the Australian Army until 1972, after which it became a historic site. Although admission is free, a tour of the fort's tunnels is A$12.50, and a tunnel and fort tour is A$16. Tours run from 10:30, with the last one at 2:30. ⊠ *Nobby's Rd.* ⊕ *www.fortscratchley.org.au* ☯ *Wed.–Mon. 10–4.*

The North Coast

BRISBANE

A2

QUEENSLAND

Warwick

M1

1

Southport

13

Coolangatta
Point Danger

Kingscliff

Woodenbone

Mt Warning

Uki

Murwillumbah

Mullumbimby

Cape Byron Lighthouse
Cape Byron

Byron Bay

Kyogle

The Channon

Byron Bay Hinterland

Bangalow

Lennox Head

Stanthorpe

Texas

Tabulam

44

Lismore

Casino

Ballina

42

15

Bonshaw

44

Tenterfield

Baryulgil

91

Evans Head

1

Deepwater

Cangai

Maclean

Angourie Point

38

Dundee

38

Jackadgery

Brooms Head

Inverell

Glen Innes

Grafton

Minnie Water

NORTH SOLITARY ISLAND

91

Woolgoolga

SOLITARY ISLANDS

Big Banana

The Promised
Land

Muttonbird Island

Coffs Harbour

Guyra

Dorrigo

Armidale

*Round
Mountain* ▲

Dorrigo
National Park

Ebor

Bellingen

Nambucca Heads

Macksville

Scotts Head

NEW ENGLAND RANGE

Bellbrook

South West Rocks

Trial Bay Gaol

Walcha

Willawarrin

Hat Head

Tamworth

Kempsey

Crescent Head

34

Crescent Head

Point Plomer

1

Sea Acres Rainforest Centre

Port Macquarie

Tacking Point

Nowendoc

Laurieton

Wingham

Crowdy Head

**Lord Howe
Island** ◄►

Gloucester

Taree

cone
Aberdeen

Krambach

Nabiac

Cape Hawke

Muswellbrook

Forster

15

Dungog

TO
↓ SYDNEY

Stroud

Bulahdelah

Seal Rocks

34

Singleton

BROUGHTON ISLANDS

9

Branxton

Raymond

Tea Gardens

Maitland

Terrace

Nelson Bay

Newcastle

South Pacific Ocean

0   40 mi

0   40 km

Fodor's Choice **Merewether Baths.** The largest ocean baths (swimming pools) in the
★ Southern Hemisphere, Mereweather Baths are a Newcastle icon per-
fect for swimming and splashing all year-round. Opened in 1935 at
one of the city's six fabulous beaches, they comprise two pools, with
one suitable for children. Complete with barbecues and picnic tables,
the baths are the ideal place for a family outing. ■ TIP➔ The baths are
patrolled by lifeguards during the summer months only, from around
late September to late April. ⊠ *Henderson Parade* 🖻 *Free* ☉ *Summer
6 am–9 pm, winter 6–6.*

FAMILY **Newcastle Museum.** In the former headquarters of the Great Northern
Railway, right on Newcastle Harbour, this museum tells the story of
the city's coal mining and steel production. Visitors can don a hard hat
to witness the Fire and Earth exhibition, which re-creates life in a steel
mill complete with furnaces, theatrical drama, and interactive displays
that shed light on the workers' challenging lives. Newcastle's other
faces are captured with exhibits on Aboriginal history, the gorgeous
beaches, and the earthquake that struck the city in 1989. A popular
draw for kids, the Supernova Hands-on Science Centre explains how a
heavy car is lifted, a tornado occurs, and magnetic fields work. ⊠ *Workshop Way* 🖀 *02/4974–1400* ⊕ *www.newcastlemuseum.com.au* 🖻 *Free*
☉ *Tues.–Sun. 10–5.*

WHERE TO EAT

$$ ✕ **The Landing Bar & Kitchen.** Enjoy the passing parade of tugboats and
MODERN tankers coming and going in Newcastle Harbour from this buzzy bar
AUSTRALIAN and restaurant on the Honeysuckle strip. Locals come here for casual
catch-ups over cocktails, pizzas, and shared plates on the deck, but
the serious foodies head inside for the larger Mod Oz plates, mostly
designed to share. The restaurant is famous for its charcuterie board and
other dishes featuring locally grown meats, but the fish is just as good,
especially the Landing seafood pie. ⑤ *Average main: A$28* ⊠ *1 Honey-
suckle Dr.* 🖀 *02/4927–1722* ⊕ *thelanding.com.au* ☉ *Closed Mon. and
Tues., no lunch Wed. and Thurs.*

$$ ✕ **Merewether Surfhouse.** Opened on the site of the Merewether Beach's
MODERN original surfhouse (a lifeguard station), this stunning three-story venue
AUSTRALIAN has fantastic ocean views from all three of its eateries. The ground floor
café, pizza, and gelato bar are steps from the beach, while the top-level
restaurant has expansive panoramas and is open for lunch and dinner.
You might begin with the local Port Stephens oysters with shallot vinegar before moving on to pan-roasted trout or roasted butternut squash
ravioli for main. Desserts include the mouthwatering gingerbread and
rhubarb pudding. The café is open for all-day breakfast and lunch
daily, offering burgers and salads. ⑤ *Average main: A$30* ⊠ *Henderson
Parade* 🖀 *02/4918–0000* ⊕ *www.surfhouse.com.au* ☉ *Closed Mon. and
Tues.; no dinner Sun.*

$$$ ✕ **Scratchleys on the Wharf.** This swank establishment is as close as New-
MODERN castle comes to having an iconic restaurant. Enclosed on three sides by
AUSTRALIAN glass and perched over the harbor on the busy esplanade, Scratchley's
opened not long after the Honeysuckle precinct transformed Newcastle
into a hip and happening place more than a decade ago. The restaurant
has one of the best views in Newcastle and an extensive menu to please

all-comers. Starters include seafood chowder, oysters, and prawn salad, while several dishes—king prawn linguine, and prawn satay with spicy peanut sauce—are available in either starter or main sizes. Non-seafood fans have steaks, lamb cutlets, and corn-fed chicken breast dishes to consider, and a range of vegetarian options and Hunter Valley cheeses to sustain them. $ *Average main: A$39* ✉ *200 Wharf Rd.* ☎ *02/4929–1111* ⊕ *www.scratchleys.com.au.*

$$$$
MODERN
AUSTRALIAN
Fodor's Choice
★

✕ **Subo Newcastle.** A bright, intimate star in Newcastle's dining scene, Subo has quickly become the hot spot in town and is often booked out weeks ahead. A stylish bistro in the central business district, Subo serves an A$85 five-course tasting plate that changes every six weeks and might include prawn carpaccio and foie gras, confit of chicken wings with blackened corn, Wagyu beef with smoked leeks, and chocolate-orange mousse with rum-and-orange syrup cake. $ *Average main: A$85* ✉ *551D Hunter St.* ☎ *02/4023–4048* ☉ *Closed Mon. and Tues.* ⌕ *Reservations essential.*

WHERE TO STAY

$$$
HOTEL

⌂ **Chifley Executive Suites Newcastle.** One block from the harbor, this hotel has a mix of apartments and suites, all fully equipped with kitchens, washer and dryer, Wi-Fi, LCD TVs, DVD player and DVD library, and minibar. **Pros:** great location. **Cons:** expensive on-site parking; central location can be noisy on weekends. $ *Rooms from: A$225* ✉ *111 Scott St.* ☎ *02/4040–1200* ⊕ *www.silverneedlehotels.com/chifley/newcastle-suites* ⇋ *39 suites, 2 studio apartments* ⎜○⎜ *No meals.*

$$$
HOTEL

⌂ **Crowne Plaza Newcastle.** Newcastle's most upscale hotel, the Crowne Plaza, is in the trendy Honeysuckle Precinct and has the best location of any hotel in town. **Pros:** great location; free Wi-Fi. **Cons:** parking is expensive. $ *Rooms from: A$245* ✉ *Merewether and Wharf Sts.* ☎ *02/4907–5000* ⊕ *www.crowneplazanewcastle.com.au* ⇋ *175 suites* ⎜○⎜ *No meals.*

$$
HOTEL

⌂ **Ibis Newcastle.** Set about a kilometer from Newcastle's downtown, the Ibis is a value-priced chain hotel with parking and a restaurant. **Pros:** good location; good price. **Cons:** not on beach or waterfront; expensive in-room Wi-Fi; small rooms with very small bathrooms. $ *Rooms from: A$159* ✉ *700 Hunter St.* ☎ *02/4925–2266* ⊕ *www.ibis.com* ⇋ *97 rooms* ⎜○⎜ *No meals.*

PORT MACQUARIE

390 km (243 miles) northeast of Sydney.

Port Macquarie was founded as a convict settlement in 1821 and is the third-oldest settlement in Australia. Set at the mouth of the Hastings River, the town was chosen for its isolation to serve as an open jail for prisoners convicted of second offenses in New South Wales. By the 1830s the pace of settlement was so brisk that the town was no longer isolated, and its usefulness as a jail had ended.

Today's Port Macquarie has few reminders of its convict past and is flourishing as a vacation area. With its pristine rivers and lakes and 13 regional beaches, including beautiful Town Beach and Shelley Beach, which both have sheltered swimming, it's a great place to get into water sports, catch a fish for dinner, and watch migrating humpback whales in season, usually May to August and September to November.

GETTING HERE AND AROUND

It's a five-hour drive from Sydney heading north on the Pacific Highway. Greyhound and Premier Motor Service run coaches from Sydney Central Station. NSW TrainLink trains operate three services daily between Sydney and the North Coast, though there is no direct train to Port Macquarie. Passengers depart at Wauchope station and then take a bus to Port Macquarie (a 20-minute journey). Timetables are available at the Greater Port Macquarie Visitor Centre or online. Qantas and Virgin Australia have flights from Sydney; Virgin Australia also flies to and from Brisbane.

ESSENTIALS

Visitor Information Visitor Information Centre. ⊠ *The Glasshouse, Clarence and Hay Sts.* ☎ *02/6581–8000, 1300/303155* ⊕ *www.portmacquarieinfo.com.au.*

EXPLORING

FAMILY
Fodor'sChoice
★
Koala Hospital. Operated by the Koala Preservation Society of New South Wales, the town's Koala Hospital is both a worthy cause and a popular attraction. The Port Macquarie region is home to many of these extremely appealing marsupials, and the hospital cares for 250 to 300 sick and injured koalas each year. The staff is passionate about their furry patients and happy to tell you about the care the animals receive. You can walk around the grounds to view the recuperating animals; you can even adopt one (but you can't take it home). Try to visit during feeding times at 8 in the morning or 3 in the afternoon. There are guided tours daily at 3. ⊠ *Macquarie Nature Reserve, Lord St.* ☎ *02/6584–1522* ⊕ *www.koalahospital.org.au* ⊠ *Donation requested* ⊗ *Daily 8–4:30.*

Port Macquarie Historical Museum. Housed in a two-story convict-built house dating from 1836, this eclectic museum displays period costumes, memorabilia from World Wars I and II, farm implements, antique clocks and watches, and relics from the town's convict days. ⊠ *22 Clarence St.* ☎ *02/6583–1108* ⊕ *www.port-macquarie-historical-museum.org.au* ⊠ *A$7* ⊗ *Mon.–Sat. 9:30–4:30.*

Fodor'sChoice
★
Sea Acres Rainforest Centre. This interpretive center comprises 178 pristine acres of coastal rain forest on the southern side of Port Macquarie. There are more than 170 plant species here, including 300-year-old cabbage-tree palms, as well as native mammals, reptiles, and prolific birdlife. An elevated boardwalk allows you to stroll through the lush environment without disturbing the vegetation. The center has informative guided tours, as well as a gift shop and a pleasant rain-forest café, a lovely place for a bite to eat while listening to the birdsong. ⊠ *Pacific Dr., near Shelley Beach Rd.* ☎ *02/6582–3355* ⊕ *www.environment.nsw. gov.au* ⊠ *A$8* ⊗ *Daily 9–4:30.*

St. Thomas Church. This 1828 church, the country's fifth-oldest house of worship, was built by convicts using local cedar and stone blocks cemented together with powdered seashells. ⊠ *Hay and William Sts.* ☎ *02/6584–1033* ⊗ *Tues.–Fri. 9:30–noon and 2–4.*

Orange fungi growing on the Rainforest Tree at Dorrigo National Park

SPORTS AND THE OUTDOORS

Unsurprisingly, most of the outdoor activities in this area revolve around the town's crystal-clear waters.

FISHING

Ocean Star. Deep-sea anglers will enjoy the day-long trips on this 40-foot custom Randel charting boat. Typical catches include snapper, pearl perch, dolphin fish, and grouper. If you have cooking facilities, the crew is happy to clean, ice, and pack your catch. ⊠ *Town Wharf, 74 Clarence St.* ☎ *0416/240–877* ⊕ *www.portmacquariefishingcharters.com.au.*

HORSEBACK RIDING

Bellrowan Valley Horseriding. Thirty minutes' drive inland from Port Macquarie, Bellrowan welcomes experts and beginners with short trail rides and overnight treks. The two-day Great Aussie Pub Ride ends the day's ride in some of the region's most interesting pubs and costs A$395 with all meals and accommodation. A two-hour trail ride is A$90. ⊠ *Crows Rd., Beechwood* ☎ *02/6587–5227* ⊕ *www.bellrowanvalley. com.au* ⊠ *From A$65.*

SURFING

Port Macquarie Surf School. Head back to school and learn to ride the waves from some very competent coaches, all of whom are fully accredited, licensed, and insured with Surfing Australia. There are daily group lessons (A$45 for two hours), or you can opt for one-on-one tutoring (A$70 per hour). Surfboards, wet suits, rash vests, and sunscreen are provided. ⊠ *46 Pacific Dr.* ☎ *02/6584–7733* ⊕ *www. portmacquariesurfschool.com.au* ⊠ *From A$45.*

WHALE-WATCHING

Port Macquarie Cruise Adventures. Majestic humpback whales migrate past Port Macquarie nonstop from May to the end of November, and Cruise Adventures gets you up close with great-value cruises (A$39) for up to two hours, depending on how far off-shore the whales are. The company also has both long and short cruises to see local bottle-nose dolphins, which can be spotted year-round. ⊠ *Short St. Wharf* ☎ *1300/555890* ⊕ *www.cruiseadventures.com.au* ⊡ *From A$15.*

WHERE TO EAT AND STAY

$$

AUSTRALIAN

✕ **The Corner.** This stylish, contemporary café packs in the crowds, thanks to its fabulously tasty meals, though you may need to exercise a little patience, as service can be a bit slow at times. Try the Corner Breakfast (A$22), which has everything from eggs the way you like them to hamhock-braised beans. Return for dinner to sample the Yamba grouper, baby beetroot, corn puree, and jamon. As the name suggests, it sits on a corner and is part of the Macquarie Waters Hotel & Apartments complex. $ *Average main: A$33* ⊠ *Clarence and Munster Sts.* ☎ *02/6583–3300* ⊕ *www.cornerrestaurant.com.au* ☽ *No dinner Sun.*

$$$

MODERN
AUSTRALIAN
Fodor's Choice
★

✕ **The Stunned Mullet.** Opposite Town Beach, Port Macquarie's best restaurant also has the best views, but don't let that distract you from the food. With so much sea in front of you it's only natural that the menu also features lots of seafood—all of it sustainably line caught or farmed—but other dishes worth trying, if they are on the menu when you visit, include the venison with tamarillo and juniper berry or the confit duck leg. Desserts are equally show-stopping; macarons will never taste the same after you've had one here, with coconut sorbet, white chocolate and candied chili. The wine list is suitably impressive. $ *Average main: A$39* ⊠ *24 William St.* ☎ *02/6584–7757* ⊕ *thestunnedmullet.com.au* ⟋ *Reservations essential.*

$$$

RESORT

🛏 **Beachcomber Resort.** This self-catering resort opposite Town Beach is a great option if you are staying for a few days or traveling with a family. **Pros:** well-maintained BBQ area; great location opposite the beach; swimming pool with kid's wading pool. **Cons:** no elevators; design a bit dated and tired. $ *Rooms from: A$205* ⊠ *54 William St.* ☎ *02/6584–1881, 1800/001320* ⊕ *www.beachcomberresort.com.au* ⟋ *39 apartments* ⥄ *No meals.*

$$$

HOTEL

🛏 **Best Western Plus HW Boutique Hotel.** Although the building dates from the late 1960s—when its sawtooth shape was considered very stylish—it's filled with up-to-the-minute amenities: designer furnishings, luxurious linens, marble bathrooms, and private balconies with ocean and river views. **Pros:** a good continental breakfast is brought to your room; toasters in rooms; beautiful breakfast room on the top floor with ocean views; free Wi-Fi. **Cons:** some street noise; a few rooms overlook car park. $ *Rooms from: A$249* ⊠ *1 Stewart St.* ☎ *02/6583–1200* ⊕ *www.hwboutique.com.au* ⟋ *45 rooms* ⥄ *No meals.*

$$$

HOTEL
Fodor's Choice
★

🛏 **The Observatory.** The most stylish digs in Port Macquarie are just a short walk across leafy parkland to the city's main beach. **Pros:** close to beach; great restaurants. **Cons:** packed with families in summer. $ *Rooms from: A$220* ⊠ *40 William St.* ☎ *02/6586–8000* ⊕ *www.observatory.net.au* ⟋ *81 rooms, 2 penthouses* ⥄ *No meals.*

Trial Bay Gaol. Trial Bay Gaol, a jail dating from the 1870s, occupies a dramatic position on the cliffs overlooking the seaside village of South West Rocks, 100 km (62 miles) north of Port Macquarie. The building, now partly in ruins, was used to teach useful skills to the prisoners who constructed it, but the project proved too expensive and was abandoned in 1903. During World War I the building served as an internment camp for some 500 Germans. It's free to walk around the outside of the ruins and visit the beach; the A$10 admission includes entry to a small museum. To get there, travel north through Kempsey and turn off to South West Rocks and follow the signs. The Trial Bay Kiosk Restaurant is a wonderful spot for lunch with a glass of wine while enjoying the stunning views across the bay—the fresh local seafood is always superb—but it's also open for breakfast (daily) and dinner on Friday and Saturday. ⊠ *Arakoon National Park, Cardwell St., South West Rocks* ☎ *02/6566–6168* ⊕ *www.nationalparks.nsw.gov.au* ⊠ *A$10* ⊙ *Daily 9–4:30.*

BELLINGEN

210 km (130 miles) north of Port Macquarie, 520 km (323 miles) from Sydney.

In a river valley a few miles off the Pacific Highway, artsy Bellingen is one of the prettiest towns along the coast. Many of Bellingen's buildings have been classified by the National Trust, and the museum, cafés, galleries, and crafts outlets are favorite hangouts for artists, craft workers, and writers. You'll find food, entertainment, and 250 stalls at the community markets that take place on the third Sunday of every month.

GETTING HERE AND AROUND

It's a seven-hour drive from Sydney along the Pacific Highway, but the town is just 30 minutes from Coffs Harbour and its airport. NSW TrainLink trains run from Sydney to Brisbane twice daily, stopping at Urunga, 10 km (6 miles) away. Both Greyhound and Premier Motor Service also run buses between Sydney and Urunga. From Urunga, either catch a taxi or a local Busways bus to Bellingen—though the bus is quite infrequent. There is also a Busways bus service from Coffs Harbour to Bellingen.

ESSENTIALS

Visitor Information Waterfall Way Visitor Centre. ⊠ *29–31 Hyde St.* ☎ *02/6655–1522, 1800/705735* ⊕ *www.visitnsw.com/ visitor-information-centres/waterfall-way-visitor-centre-bellingen.*

EXPLORING

Fodor's Choice ★ **Dorrigo National Park.** From Bellingen a meandering and spectacular road leads inland to Dorrigo and then travels back east eventually reaching the Pacific Highway, close to Coffs Harbour. This circular scenic route, beginning along the Bellinger River, climbs more than 1,000 feet up the heavily wooded escarpment to the Dorrigo Plateau. At the top of the plateau is Dorrigo National Park, a small but outstanding subtropical rain forest that is included on the World Heritage list. Signposts along the main road indicate walking trails. The Satinbird Stroll is a short rain forest walk, and the 6-km (4-mile) Cedar Falls Walk leads to the most spectacular of the park's many waterfalls, but the most dramatic of all is the free Skywalk lookout, a 230-foot boardwalk above the canopy that has panoramic views out to the coast. The adjacent Rainforest Centre has a good display on the natural heritage of the park and a small café that serves good coffee. The national park is approximately 31 km (19 miles) from Bellingen. ✉ *Dorrigo Rainforest Centre, Dome Rd., Dorrigo* ☎ *02/6657–2309* ⊕ *www.nationalparks.nsw.gov.au* ✉ *A$2 donation to visit Rainforest Centre* ⊗ *Rainforest Centre 9–4:30.*

SPORTS AND THE OUTDOORS

CANOEING

Bellingen Canoe Adventures. Rent a canoe or join an organized expedition on the Bellinger River, which meanders its way through some of the most spectacular and picturesque areas in the area. This company, which emphasizes safety above everything else, has a wide range of options including one-hour sunset tours (A$25), a half-day tour on calm water with tea (A$48), or full-day tours that promise the thrill of rapids and provide lunch as well (A$90). ✉ *4 Tyson St.* ☎ *02/6655–9955* ⊕ *www.canoeadventures.com.au* ✉ *From A$25.*

HORSEBACK RIDING

FAMILY **Valery Trails.** This large equestrian center is 10 km (6 miles) from Bellingen on the edge of Bongil Bongil National Park. They have 45 horses, and a variety of treks through the local rain forests. Choose from the popular two-hour rides (A$65), breakfast and afternoon barbecue rides, and a two-day ride to Bellingen to stay in the Federal Hotel for (A$450). ✉ *758 Valery Rd., Valery* ☎ *02/6653–4301* ⊕ *www.valerytrails.com. au* ✉ *From A$60.*

OFF THE
BEATEN
PATH

The Promised Land. If you have an hour to spare (and a set of wheels), cross the river at Bellingen and take an 18-km (11-mile) excursion on the Bellingen–Gleniffer Road to the village of Gleniffer. This tranquil, rambling journey leads through farmlands and wooded valleys and across the evocatively named Never Never River to—believe it or not—the Promised Land, a peaceful, pastoral region with spots for picnics and swimming. Author Peter Carey once lived in this vicinity, and the river and its surroundings provided the backdrop for his novel *Oscar and Lucinda.*

Promised Land Retreat. If you want to stay overnight in the area, the three chalets at the 100-acre Promised Land Retreat are lovely self-contained sanctuaries. ✉ *934 Promised Land Rd.* ☎ *02/6655–9578* ⊕ *www.promisedlandretreat.com.au* ✉ *From A$250 per night.*

WHERE TO STAY

$$ 🏠 **Koompartoo Retreat.** These self-contained hardwood cottages on a hill-
B&B/INN side overlooking Bellingen are superb examples of local craftsmanship, particularly in their use of timbers from surrounding forests. **Pros:** from the chalet verandas you can see kookaburras and black cockatoos; each cottage has small library. **Cons:** no wheelchair access; heating is noisy. Ⓢ *Rooms from: A$195* ✉ *Rawson and Dudley Sts.* ☎ *02/6655–2326* ⊕ *www.koompartoo.com.au* ➥ *4 cottages* ⦿ *No meals.*

COFFS HARBOUR

35 km (22 miles) northeast of Bellingen via the Pacific Hwy., 103 km (64 miles) from Bellingen via the inland scenic route along the Dorrigo Plateau, 534 km (320 miles) from Sydney.

The area surrounding Coffs Harbour is the state's "banana belt," where long, neat rows of banana palms cover the hillsides. Set at the foot of steep green hills, the town has great beaches and a mild climate. This idyllic combination has made it one of the most popular vacation spots along the coast. Coffs is also a convenient halfway point on the 1,000-km (620-mile) journey between Sydney and Brisbane.

GETTING HERE AND AROUND

Coffs Harbour is a comfortable 7½-hour drive from Sydney and a 6-hour drive from Brisbane. Regular Greyhound and Premier Buses connect the town to Sydney. There is a train station with daily NSW TrainLink services to and from Sydney and Brisbane. And the local airport, 6 km (4 miles) from the central Ocean Parade, is served by Qantas, Virgin Australia, and Tigerair. For more information, contact the visitor center, which is open 9–5 daily.

Airport Information Coffs Harbour Airport. ⊠ *Hogbin Dr.* 🕾 *02/6648–4767* ⊕ *www.coffsharbourairport.com.*

ESSENTIALS

Visitor Information Coffs Coast Visitors Information Centre. ⊠ *351 Pacific Hwy., at the Big Banana* 🕾 *02/6648–4990* ⊕ *www.coffscoast.com.au.*

EXPLORING

FAMILY
Fodor's Choice
★

The Big Banana. Just north of the city, impossible to miss, is the Big Banana—the symbol of Coffs Harbour. This monumental piece of kitsch has stood at the site since 1964. It welcomes visitors to the Big Banana complex, which takes a fascinating look at the past, present, and future of horticulture. There's a multimedia display called "World of Bananas" and a walkway that meanders through the banana plantations and banana packing shed. The park is fantastic for kids and has varied rides all with different prices, including toboggan rides (A$6), a waterslide (A$19.50 for 90 minutes), an ice-skating rink (A$14.50), and laser tag (A$9.90). There's a café on the premises, as well as the Banana Barn, which sells the park's own jams, pickles, fresh tropical fruit, and frozen chocolate-covered bananas on a stick. ⊠ *351 Pacific Hwy.* 🕾 *02/6652–4355* ⊕ *www.bigbanana.com* 🖾 *Entry to Big Banana free; rides and tours extra* ⊙ *Daily 9–4:30.*

FAMILY
Dolphin Marine Magic. Near the port in Coffs Harbour, the Dolphin Marine Magic aquarium includes colorful reef fish, turtles, seals, penguins, baby crocodiles, and dolphins. Shows take place daily at 10 and 1, and visitors are advised to arrive 30 minutes earlier to get a good seat and receive free "dolphin kisses" from the cute critters before each show. Children may help feed and "shake hands" with dolphins, as well as interact with the seals. You can swim, pat, and play ball with the dolphin and seals in special group encounters if you book in advance. These sessions vary in price depending on time of year—during peak holiday season, seal encounters cost A$260 per person and dolphin encounters

run around A$420 per person. The company's official name is Dolphin Marine Magic but many of the locals still call it by its old name, the Pet Porpoise Pool. ⊠ *65 Orlando St., beside Coffs Creek* ☎ *02/6659–1900* ⊕ *www.dolphinmarinemagic.com.au* ⊠ *A$35* ☽ *Daily 9–4.*

Muttonbird Island. The town has a lively and attractive harbor in the shelter of Muttonbird Island, and a stroll out to this nature reserve is delightful in the evening. To get here, follow the signs to the Coffs Harbour Jetty, then park near the marina. A wide path leads out along the breakwater and up the slope of the island. The trail is steep, but the views from the top are worth the effort. The island is named after the muttonbirds (also known as shearwaters) that nest here between September and April. Between June and September Muttonbird Island is also a good spot for viewing migrating humpback whales. ⊠ *Coffs Harbour* ⊕ *www.nationalparks.nsw.gov.au.*

SPORTS AND THE OUTDOORS
SCUBA DIVING
The warm seas around Coffs Harbour make this particular part of the coast, with its moray eels, manta rays, turtles, and gray nurse sharks, a scuba diver's favorite. Best are the Solitary Islands, 7 km–21 km (4½ miles–13 miles) offshore.

Jetty Dive Centre. This outfitter rents gear, schedules scuba and snorkeling trips, and hosts certification classes. A double-dive trip costs A$125; a one-day learn-to-dive course is A$249. There are also whale and dolphin watching cruises from June to October from A$59. ⊠ *398 Harbour Dr.* ☎ *02/6651–1611* ⊕ *www.jettydive.com.au.*

WHITE-WATER RAFTING
Wildwater Adventures. This highly regarded company conducts half-day, one-day, and two-day rafting trips down the Nymboida River. Trips begin from Bonville, 14 km (9 miles) south of Coffs Harbour on the Pacific Highway, but pickups from the Coffs Harbour and Bellingen region can be arranged. Half-day trips are A$80, one-day trips are A$185, and two-day trips cost A$430 per person including snacks and meals. Overnight trips feature camping on the river bank, breakfast, and dinner. ⊠ *16 Prince St.* ☎ *02/6653–2067* ⊕ *www.coffscentral.com/wildwater* ⊠ *From A$80.*

WHERE TO EAT AND STAY

$
SEAFOOD
Fodor's Choice
★

✕ **Fishermen's Co-op.** Fish-and-chips don't come any fresher than those served at the fisherman's co-op near the breakwall on the northern side of the harbor in Coffs—everything on the menu is straight off the trawler, literally. Although most of the retail space is given to sales of fresh seafood, you can buy freshly cooked (grilled, battered, or crumbed) fish-and-chips here, as well as calamari, fish cocktails, and salads. There's a few tables on a covered deck out front, but the best place to eat is perched on a rock on the nearby breakwall, staring out to sea. ⑤ *Average main: A$15* ⊠ *69 Marina Dr.* ☎ *02/6652–2811* ⊕ *coffsfishcoop.com.au* ⚲ *Reservations not accepted.*

$$
ECLECTIC

✕ **Shearwater Restaurant.** This waterfront restaurant with views of Coffs Creek (which is spotlighted at night—look for stingrays swimming by) is open for breakfast, lunch, and dinner, and leaves no culinary stone unturned in its search for novel flavors. The menu in the open-air dining room includes lunch dishes like prawn and scallop red curry. If you want a table on the deck in summer, book ahead. Service is friendly and attentive. $ *Average main: A$32* ⊠ *The Promenade, 321 Harbour Dr.* ☎ *02/6651–6053* ⊕ *www.shearwaterrestaurant.com.au* ⊗ *No dinner Sun.–Tues.*

$$ ⊞ **BreakFree Aanuka Beach Resort.** Teak furniture and antiques collected
RESORT from Indonesia and the South Pacific fill the accommodations at this
FAMILY resort, which sits amid palms, frangipani, and hibiscus. **Pros:** brilliant setting in a private beachfront cove; great value for families. **Cons:** some rooms need updating; kid-phobes might not appreciate all the families. $ *Rooms from: A$186* ⊠ *11 Firman Dr.* ☎ *02/6652–7555* ⊕ *www.aanukabeachresort.com.au* ⇗ *27 studios, 39 suites, 12 villas* ⦿| *Breakfast.*

$$$$ ⊞ **Smugglers on the Beach.** Five minutes' drive north of Coffs Harbour's
RESORT busy city center is this small resort with just 16 self-contained 1- to 3-bedroom apartments, some with hot tubs, spread out among tropical gardens. **Pros:** resort has fishing equipment and a BBQ, so you can catch your dinner; beautiful beachside location; good deals if staying for more than five nights. **Cons:** two-night minimum, check-out is at 9:30 am. $ *Rooms from: A$310* ⊠ *36 Sandy Beach Rd.* ☎ *02/6653–6166* ⊕ *www.smugglers.com.au* ⇗ *16 apartments* ⦿| *No meals.*

BYRON BAY

247 km (154 miles) north of Coffs Harbour, 772 km (480 miles) north of Sydney.

Byron Bay is the easternmost point on the Australian mainland, and perhaps earns Australia its nickname the "Lucky Country." Fabulous beaches, storms that spin rainbows across the mountains behind the town, and a sunny, relaxed and somewhat hippy style cast a spell over practically everyone who visits. For many years Byron Bay lured surfers with abundant sunshine, perfect waves on Watego's Beach, and tolerant locals who allowed them to sleep on the sand. These days a more upscale crowd frequents Byron Bay.

Byron Bay is also one of the must-sees on the backpacker circuit, and the town has a youthful energy that fuels late-night partying. There are many art galleries and crafts shops, a great food scene, and numerous adventure tours. The town is at its liveliest on the first Sunday of each month, when Butler Street becomes a bustling market.

GETTING HERE AND AROUND

Byron is the North Coast's most popular destination, and is well served by buses and trains from Sydney and Coffs Harbour. If driving, the journey takes 11 hours from Sydney and 3½ hours from Coffs Harbour. The closest airports are at Ballina and Lismore, both a 30-minute drive away. Virgin Australia, Jetstar, and REX fly to Ballina; REX also flies from Sydney to Lismore. All the usual car companies are there, or you can get a taxi into Byron or take a Ballina-Byron shuttle bus (operated by Byron Easy Bus) for A$20 one-way.

There's no shortage of activities in Byron Bay.

Airport Shuttle Byron Easy Bus. ✉ *Byron Bay* ☎ *02/6685–7447* ⊕ *www. byronbayshuttle.com.au.*

ESSENTIALS

Visitor Information Byron Visitor Centre. ✉ *Old Station Master's Cottage, 80 Jonson St.* ☎ *02/6680–8558* ⊕ *www.visitbyronbay.com.*

EXPLORING

Cape Byron Lighthouse. The most powerful beacon on the Australian coastline, Cape Byron Lighthouse dominates the southern end of the beach at Byron Bay and attracts huge numbers of visitors, who want to tick standing at Australia's most easterly point off their bucket list. You can tour the lighthouse (no children under five) daily from 10 am, with the last tour departing at 3 pm. The tours are led by volunteers, and while there's no entry charge, a donation is appreciated. Whale-watching is popular between June and September, when migrating humpback whales come close to shore. Dolphins swim in these waters year-round, and you can often see pods of them from the cape. You can stay in either of the two six-person assistant lightkeeper's cottages for A$360 a night in low season; prices rise from mid-December to late January and a two-week period over Easter (book well in advance during this period). There's a three-night minimum stay. ✉ *Lighthouse Rd.* ☎ *02/6620–9300* ⊕ *www.byronbaylighthouse.com* 🖃 *Free, suggested donation for tours* ☉ *Daily 8:30–sunset (summer), 9–sunset (winter).*

Cape Byron Walking Track. This popular trail circumnavigates a 150-acre reserve, passes through grasslands and rain forest, and has sensational seas views as you circle the peninsula and the lighthouse. From several vantage points along the track you may spot dolphins in the waters below. The track begins east of the town on Lighthouse Road. ⊠ *Off Lighthouse Rd.* ⊕ *www.nationalparks.nsw.gov.au.*

**OFF THE
BEATEN
PATH**

Byron Bay Hinterland. Inland from Byron Bay is some of the most pictur-esque country in Australia. Undulating green hills that once boasted a thriving dairy industry are dotted with villages with a New Age vibe. There are small organic farms growing avocados, coffee, fruits, and macadamia nuts, and cafés in most villages. The best way to discover this gorgeous part of the world—nicknamed the Rainbow Region—is to grab a map and drive. From Byron, take the road toward the regional town of Lismore for about 15 km (9 miles) to the pretty village of **Bangalow.** Walk along the lovely main street lined with 19th-century storefronts. Carefully follow your map and wind your way northwest for about 20 km (13 miles) to **Federal.** Meander, via the cute towns of **Rosebank** and **Dunoon,** to **The Channon,** where on the second Sunday of every month you'll find a wonderful market with dozens of stalls and entertainment. ⊠ *Byron Bay* ⊕ *www.tropicalnsw.com.au.*

BEACHES

Several superb beaches lie in the vicinity of Byron Bay. In front of the town, Main Beach provides safe swimming, and Clarks Beach, closer to the cape, has better surf. The most famous surfing beach, however, is Wategos', the only entirely north-facing beach in the state. To the south of the lighthouse Tallow Beach extends for 6 km (4 miles) to a rocky stretch of coastline around Broken Head, which has a number of small sandy coves. Beyond Broken Head is lonely Seven Mile Beach. Topless sunbathing is popular on many Byron Bay beaches.

Main Beach. As the name suggests Main Beach is right in the heart of Byron Bay, across the road from the much-loved Beach Hotel (a popular pub that has good restaurants and accommodation). It stretches south-ward for some 3 km (2 miles) where its name changes to Clarke's Beach and then The Pass, the latter a legendary surfing spot. Always busy in the summer months, the beach is most easily reached on foot from the city center. There's a sea wall and swimming pool at the northern end, and about 300 feet offshore lies the wreck of the *Tassie II,* a small ammunition supply boat that sunk around the end of Word War II. Swimmers should always swim beside the flags as rips and currents can make this beach hazardous at times—an average of about nine swim-mers annually require rescue. There are barbecues and picnic tables in the leafy park flanking the beach. **Amenities:** food and drink; lifeguards (summer only); showers; toilets. **Best for:** snorkeling; swimming; walk-ing. ⊠ *Jonson and Bay Sts.*

Watego's Beach. Named for a farming family who grew bananas and veg-etables in the hinterland (now a residential area) just behind the beach, Watego's is a lovely 2,000-foot strip of golden sand backed by panda-nus palms. It's sheltered from the winds and popular with all comers. If you fancy a walk it, you can reach the beach from the city center via the 4-km (2½-mile) Cape Byron Track. Otherwise, drive here and look for parking in the lot or on the street (it can be challenging during busy times). Coin-operated barbecues and picnic tables make this a perfect spot for do-it-yourself lunching, all in the shadow of the majestic Cape Byron Lighthouse, which looms over the beach. The upscale boutique hotel, Rae's of Watego's, is nearby. **Amenities:** lifeguards (summer only); parking (fee); toilets. **Best for:** swimming; sunrise. ⊠ *Marine Parade, off Palm Valley Dr.*

SPORTS AND THE OUTDOORS

KAYAKING

Go Sea Kayak. Owned and operated by local surf lifesavers (volunteer lifeguards), this new company runs three-hour kayak tours in two-person kayaks that venture out into the open ocean in search of viewing bottlenose dolphins, sea turtles, and even whales in the season. Guides weave in local Aboriginal history and point out the sights. ⊠ *Apex Park, Opposite 56 Lawson St.* ☎ *1800/732529* ⊕ *www.goseakayakbyronbay. com.au* ⊠ *From A$69.*

SCUBA DIVING

The best local diving is at Julian Rocks Marine Reserve, some 3 km (2 miles) offshore, where the confluence of warm and cold currents supports a profusion of marine life and is one of the few sites south of the Great Barrier Reef where you can snorkel with both tropical fish and deep-water animals from the Southern Ocean.

Byron Bay Dive Centre. This dive center runs snorkeling and scuba-diving trips for all levels of experience, plus gear rental and instruction. The five-hour introductory diving course costs A$160; a single dive with all equipment and guide and some 50 minutes of diving near Julian Rocks costs A$99. A 60-minute snorkel trip, complete with wet suit, is A$65. ⊠ *9 Marvel St.* ☎ *02/6685–8333, 1800/243483* ⊕ *www. byronbaydivecentre.com.au* ⊠ *From A$60.*

Sundive. This PADI dive center has courses for all level of divers, as well as boat dives and snorkel trips. The first dive, with all equipment, is A$95; snorkeling trips are available, too. ⊠ *9–11 Middleton St.* ☎ *02/6685–7755, 1800/008755* ⊕ *www.sundive.com.au* ⊠ *From A$70.*

WHERE TO EAT AND STAY

$$ ✗ **Byron Bay Beach Café.** A Byron Bay legend, this open-air café is a
CAFÉ   perfect place to sit in the morning sun and watch the waves. Breakfast runs the gamut from wholesome (award-winning locally produced Brookfarm Macadamia muesli with yogurt and banana) to hearty (corned-beef hash, sautéed spinach, fried egg with Béarnaise sauce). For lunch, try the steamed mussels in Thai broth or the mini Wagyu burgers. The café is open for cocktails and dinner during the summer months of December and January and has an attached take-away section for those who want to have light meals on the run. Reservations are recommended during the summer. $ *Average main: A$32* ⊠ *Clarks Beach, Near parking lot at end of Lawson St.* ☎ *1300/583766* ⊕ *www. byronbeachcafe.com.au* ◷ *No dinner Feb.–Nov.*

$$$$ ✗ **Fig Tree Restaurant & Rooms.** In this century-old farmhouse with distant
AUSTRALIAN   views of Byron Bay the draw is upmarket Mod Oz cuisine blending
Fodor's Choice   Asian and Mediterranean flavors. Produce fresh from the owners' farm
★   is featured in the weekly seven-course menu (A$75),along with locally

produced Bangalow duck, Bangalow pork belly, and Binna Burra sirloin steak. As the name suggests, the restaurant also has accommodations: the Dairy and the Sunrise House, two cottages with wonderful views, can both sleep up to eight people; prices are from A$600 a night in the holiday season of Christmas, January and Easter with a minimum stay of three nights. The restaurant and rooms are 5 km (3 miles) inland from Byron Bay at Ewingsdale. $ *Average main: A$75* ✉ *4 Sunrise La., Ewingsdale* ☎ *02/6684–7273* ⊕ *www.figtreerestaurant.com.au* ⊗ *Closed Mon.–Wed. No dinner Sun. No lunch Thurs.–Sat.*

$$$$
B&B/INN
🏠 **Byron Bay Beach Bure.** Three luxury bures—the Fijian word for cabin—may be only 650 feet from the city center, but the lush, peaceful setting makes it feel like a private oasis. **Pros:** perfect for a romantic getaway; two elevated bures have beach views. **Cons:** can book up early. $ *Rooms from: A$380* ✉ *36 Lawson St.* ☎ *02/6680–8483* ⤶ *3 bures* ❑ *Breakfast.*

$$$
B&B/INN
🏠 **Julian's Apartments.** These studio apartments just opposite Clarkes Beach are neat, spacious, and well equipped. **Pros:** perfect for families (cots and baby supplies can be rented), this is the quiet end of Byron Bay town. **Cons:** taxi, or hike into town, required; popular, so book early. $ *Rooms from: A$240* ✉ *124 Lighthouse Rd.* ☎ *02/6680–9697* ⊕ *www.juliansbyronbay.com* ⤶ *11 apartments* ❑ *No meals.*

$$$$
B&B/INN
🏠 **Rae's on Wategos.** If a high-design boutique hotel is your cup of tea, you'd be hard-pressed to do better than this luxurious Mediterranean-style villa surrounded by a tropical garden. **Pros:** perfect for a romantic break; superb food and spa. **Cons:** have to take a taxi to town; breakfast prices too high. $ *Rooms from: A$550* ✉ *Watego's Beach, 8 Marine Parade* ☎ *02/6685–5366* ⊕ *raesonwategos.com* ⤶ *7 suites* ❑ *No meals.*

NIGHTLIFE

For a small town, Byron rocks by night. Fire dancing—where bare-chested men dance with flaming torches—is a local specialty. Bars and clubs are generally open until about 2 am on weekends and midnight on weekdays.

Arts Factory Village. Head to this legendary complex—also known as the Piggery—to catch a movie at the Pighouse Flicks, grab a bite, have a beer brewed at the on-site Byron Bay Brewery, or see a live band at the Buddha Bar. A Nomads backpackers lodge is attached to the venue, so expect a lively crowd especially at the weekly talent show. ✉ *1 Skinners Shoot Rd., corner of Gordon St.* ☎ *02/6685–7709* ⊕ *www. pighouseflicks.com.au.*

Beach Bar. This lounge in the iconic Beach Hotel often hosts live bands. ✉ *Bay and Jonson Sts.* ☎ *02/6685–6402* ⊕ *www.beachhotel.com.au.*

Cocomangas. This lively bar-restaurant-nightclub is a favorite of carousing backpackers, often hosting themed dance parties. ✉ *32 Jonson St.* ☎ *02/6685–8493.*

Hotel Great Northern. Bands perform most evenings at this old-school pub. ✉ *Jonson and Byron Sts.* ☎ *02/6685–6454* ⊕ *www.thenorthern.com.au.*

Railway Friendly Bar. Live music rocks this pub, known locally as The Rails, every night; it's built on the old railway station site. ⊠ *Jonson St. Railway Station* ☎ *02/6685–7662* ⊕ *www.therailsbyronbay.com.*

SHOPPING

Byron Bay is one of the state's arts-and-crafts centers, with many innovative and high-quality articles for sale, such as leather goods, offbeat designer clothing, essential oils, natural cosmetics, and ironware. The community market, held on the first Sunday of every month, fills the Butler Street reserve with more than 300 stalls selling art, crafts, and local produce.

Byron Bay Hat Co. This local shopping institution carries great hats and bags perfect for the beach. ⊠ *4 Jonson St.* ☎ *02/6685–8357* ⊕ *byron-bayhatcompany.com.*

LORD HOWE ISLAND

Fringed by the world's southernmost coral reef as well as gorgeous, sheltered beaches, dominated by two dramatic peaks, and inhabited by just around 400 permanent residents—Lord Howe Island is a secluded slice of paradise that lies about 600 km (370 miles) east of mainland Australia. As a UNESCO World Heritage island, it welcomes just 400 visitors at any time, so it never feels overcrowded. It's a great place for a digital detox—there is no mobile phone coverage anywhere on the island and Internet access is patchy at best. Most visitors rent bicycles and spend their time snorkeling in the lagoon, hand-feeding fish, hiking, and bird-watching, while hardy types climb the summit of 875-meter (2,870-foot) Mt. Gower for sensational views.

GETTING HERE AND AROUND

Qantas subsidiary Qantas Link flies to Lord Howe Island from Sydney, Brisbane, and Port Macquarie. The flight from Sydney is 1 hour and 50 minutes. Flights from the other destinations are 10 minutes or so shorter. As Qantas is the only carrier, and only 400 tourists can visit the island, fares can be quite high—typically more than A\$400 one-way. The most economical way to travel to Lord Howe is with an air-and-hotel package deal.

Just 10 km (6 miles) long and with a width varying from 1,000 feet to 2 km (1 mile), crescent-shape Lord Howe Island is compact and easy to navigate. The lagoon hugs the western shore of the island. The town, known as Old Settlement, is midway along the lagoon, and most accommodations are within an easy cycle ride or walk from there. The airport is slightly south of the town, and the two volcanic peaks—Mt. Lidgbird and Mt. Gower—dominate the island's southeast extremity. Good beaches are spread along the lagoon shore and on the eastern coast just a kilometer or two from town.

BEACHES

FAMILY
Fodor's Choice
★

Ned's Beach. This beautiful beach on the northeast side of the island is a mecca for fish because fishing bans protect them here. Brightly colored tropical creatures, such as parrot fish and their less-spectacular mullet mates (which are occasionally chased by a harmless reef shark), swim up

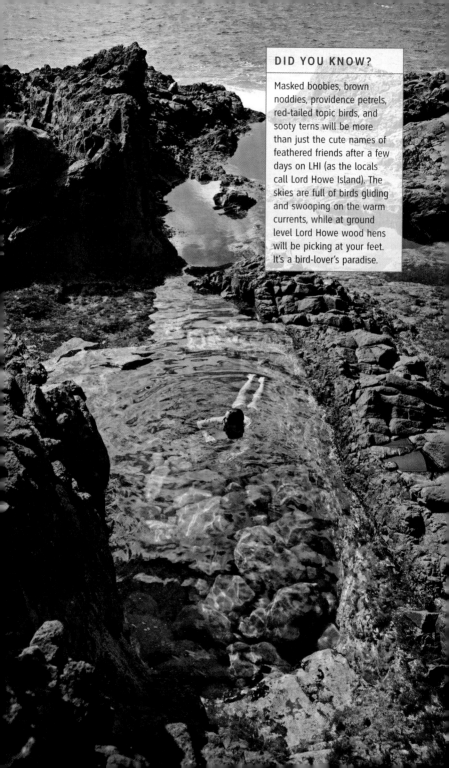

to shore and greet visitors at the daily 4 pm fish feed. However, visitors can also feed them at other times—you can buy fish food to toss to them from a beach kiosk. This feeding frenzy is fun to watch. Bring snorkel gear to explore the coral a little farther out, or bring a picnic and relax on this beach that's one of the cleanest in Australia. The beach is an easy drive, cycle, or walk from town and the northern hotels. **Amenities:** none. **Best for:** snorkeling; sunrise; swimming; walking. ⊠ *Ned's Beach Rd., Ned's Beach* ⊕ *www.lordhoweisland.info.*

SPORTS AND THE OUTDOORS

DIVING AND SNORKELING

Lord Howe Island Marine Park. UNESCO World Heritage lists Lord Howe Island's beautiful lagoon, which is sheltered by the world's southernmost coral reef, stretching for some 6 km (4 miles) along the western coast. Contained within Lord Howe Island Marine Park, the lagoon harbors some 500 species of fish and 90 species of coral. There are several ways to explore the lagoon and the coral-filled beaches of the eastern coast, which are only about 3 km (2 miles)—by glass-bottom boat, snorkeling, or scuba diving. Ned's Beach, the site of the island's fish-frenzy, is perfect for snorkelers. Another great spot is the wreck of the ship *The Favourite*, at North Bay, the lagoon's northernmost point. Divers have more than 50 sites to choose from, ranging from shallow resort dives near the beach, to spectacular trenches, caves, and volcanic drop-offs. Experienced divers love the waters around Ball's Pyramid, which abound with kingfish and Galapagos sharks up to 14 feet long. ■ **TIP→ If you don't bring your own snorkeling gear, you can rent it from local resorts.** ⊠ *Lord Howe Island Visitor Center, Middle and Lagoon Rds.* ☎ *02/6563–2114* ⊕ *www.lordhoweisland.info.*

FISHING

Fishing at Ball's Pyramid. Towering some 1,800 feet above the ocean, Ball's Pyramid is a unique rock stack and one of the world's tallest monoliths in water. Located 23 km (14 miles) south of Lord Howe Island, it's part of the pristine Lord Howe Island Marine Park, in which commercial fishing is banned and huge species of fish abound, making it a top destination for sportfishing. The boat trip to Ball's Pyramid takes 75 minutes and is a perfect way to soak up stunning views back toward the island before you start reeling in the catch. Several dedicated fishing charter operators, including Blue Billie (a fifth-generation family of fishermen), run tours to the pyramid, offering half- and full-day expeditions with rates starting from around A$200 per person. ⊠ *Lord Howe Island Marine Park* ⊕ *www.lordhoweisland.info.*

HIKING

Fodor's Choice **Mt. Gower.** The larger of the two volcanic peaks located at the southern
★ end of Lord Howe Island, Mt. Gower rises 875 meters (2,870 feet) above sea level. The hike to the summit is arduous and can only be undertaken with a guide. Covering a distance of about 14 km (9 miles) round-trip and taking about 8½ hours to complete, it's a wonderful experience and affords sensational views across the island, the reef, and out to Ball's Pyramid, 23 km (14 miles) away. Along the way, guides point out rare plants and birdlife. Fifth-generation islander Jack Shick, of Lord Howe Island Tours, is a highly experienced guide and takes

tours twice a week (Monday and Thursday); the cost is about A\$70 per person. ⊠ *Lord Howe Island* ☎ *02/6563–2218 Jack Shick* ⊕ *www.lordhoweislandtours.net* ⊠ *A\$70.*

WHERE TO EAT

\$\$\$\$
MODERN
AUSTRALIAN
Fodor'sChoice
★

✕ **Arajilla.** Dining at Arajilla Retreat at least once during a stay on Lord Howe Island is a must. The cuisine, which changes daily, uses fish straight from the ocean and lovely homegrown vegetables. Begin with a drink at the cozy bar, decked out just a little like a gentlemen's club with leather armchairs, and then take a seat at the restaurant with its white walls and one dramatic burgundy-color feature wall. The three-course menu changes often: recent choices have included baby beetroot salad with goat cheese and toasted almonds; a grilled kingfish with potato rosti, asparagus, and egg-yolk ravioli for main; and grilled Mediterranean vegetables with polenta chips and Parmesan cheese. Desserts are irresistible and may include black sticky rice with lychee sorbet, toasted coconut, and kaffir lime. ■**TIP➜ In-house guests take precedent over those not staying at the resort, so bookings are essential.** ⑤ *Average main: A\$95* ⊠ *Lagoon Rd., Old Settlement Beach* ⊕ *www.arajilla.com.au* ⊗ *Only dinner open to nonguests* ⌂ *Reservations essential.*

\$\$
SEAFOOD

✕ **Greenback's Eatery.** Named after a Lord Howe Island fishing vessel, Greenback's Eatery naturally specializes in fresh fish. This casual spot, basically a veranda attached to boat owner Dave Gardiner's house, is open only on Thursday night (from 6:30), and the only choice on the menu is the catch of the day, but at least you know it's super fresh. You can bring your own wine or beer, although it is licensed. It's small and popular with locals, so book ahead. Dave also sells fresh sashimi packs to take away. ⑤ *Average main: A\$30* ⊠ *Middle Beach, 2 Skyline Dr.* ☎ *02/6563–2208* ⊕ *www.fishlordhowe.com.au* ▬ *No credit cards* ⊗ *Closed Fri.–Wed. No lunch* ⌂ *Reservations essential.*

\$\$
AUSTRALIAN
Fodor'sChoice
★

✕ **Lord Howe Golf Club.** This is a fine place to socialize with the locals and tourists and enjoy some honest, unpretentious food. The on-site Sunset Bar & Grill is open for dinner on Tuesday, Friday, and Sunday, and the menu includes a variety of roasts (such as roast chicken or lamb), steak with garlic butter, schnitzel, fish, and salads, plus pizza on Sunday nights. Friday night is the "big night out" on the island, when almost everyone turns up for the sunset barbecue—try the barbecue kingfish and grab an ice-cold beer. Desserts include what appears to be the island staple—sticky-date pudding—and ice cream. It's best to come early to take in the view over the golf links and the lagoon beyond. Sunday morning only, breakfast is served. ⑤ *Average main: A\$25* ⊠ *Lord Howe Island* ☎ *02/6563–2179* ⊕ *www.lordhowegolf.com.au* ⊗ *Closed Mon., Wed., Thurs., and Sat. No lunch.*

\$\$
MALAYSIAN

✕ **Pandanus.** This lovely indoor-outdoor restaurant specializes in Italian and Malaysian fare, with an emphasis on seafood. Start with the salt-and-pepper squid or the Asian spring rolls. A bit spicier is the Malaysia seafood curry, which brims with shrimp, squid, fish, potatoes, and rice. Succulent pork belly and Asian-style chicken and basil please those not keen on fish, while seafood lovers relish the fresh-caught kingfish, yellowfin tuna, deep-sea cod, and trevally. Note the many blackboard specials, too. Regulars rave about the coconut-custard pie with ice cream. ⑤ *Average main: A$25* ⊠ *Pandanus Lodge, Anderson Rd.* ☎ *02/6563–2400* ☽ *No lunch.*

WHERE TO STAY

$$$$
RESORT
Fodor'sChoice
★
🏨 **Arajilla Lord Howe Island.** One of the most luxurious accommodations on Lord Howe, Arajilla Retreat contains 10 spacious suites and two two-bedroom suites. **Pros:** exclusive and secluded; rates include all meals, minibar and predinner drinks; free bike use. **Cons:** expensive. ⑤ *Rooms from: A$700* ⊠ *Old Settlement Beach, Lagoon Rd.* ☎ *02/6563–2002* ⊕ *www.arajilla.com.au* ☞ *12 suites* ⦿ *All-inclusive.*

$$$$
B&B/INN
🏨 **Capella Lodge.** In the shadow of Mt. Gower, Capella Lodge is Lord Howe Island's most posh lodging. **Pros:** great location; fantastic views; pure luxury; rates include breakfast, dinner, and drinks. **Cons:** steep rates. ⑤ *Rooms from: A$750* ⊠ *Lagoon Rd.* ☎ *02/6563–2008* ⊕ *www.lordhowe.com* ☞ *9 suites* ⦿ *Some meals.*

$$$$
HOTEL
🏨 **Pinetrees Lodge.** Right on Lagoon Beach and a short walk from the popular bowling club, the Pinetrees Lodge has a terrific location and is the largest accommodation on Lord Howe Island—with motel rooms, suites, and garden cottages. **Pros:** great amenities; excellent location; good five-night packages available online. **Cons:** can be noisy with families in peak times. ⑤ *Rooms from: A$790* ⊠ *Lagoon Rd.* ☎ *02/9262–6585* ⊕ *www.pinetrees.com.au* ☞ *34 rooms, 4 suites* ⦿ *All-inclusive.*

CANBERRA AND THE A.C.T.

As the nation's capital, Canberra is sometimes maligned by outsiders, who see the city as lacking the hipness of Melbourne or the glamour of Sydney. But Canberra certainly has charms of its own, with its world-class museums (the majority of which are free), leafy open spaces, and the huge Lake Burley Griffin.

When Australia federated in 1901, both Sydney and Melbourne vied to be the nation's capital. But in the spirit of compromise, it was decided that a new city would be built, and Canberra and the Australian Capital Territory (A.C.T.) were created when New South Wales ceded land to build a federal zone, based on the model of America's District of Columbia.

From the beginning this was to be a totally planned city. Walter Burley Griffin, a Chicago architect and associate of Frank Lloyd Wright, won an international design competition. Griffin arrived in Canberra in 1913 to supervise construction, but progress was slowed by two world wars and the Great Depression. By 1947 Canberra, with only 15,000 inhabitants, was little more than a country town.

Development increased during the 1950s, and the current population of more than 367,000 makes Canberra by far the largest inland city in Australia. The wide, tree-lined avenues and spacious parklands of present-day Canberra have largely fulfilled Griffin's original plan. The major public buildings are arranged on low knolls on either side of Lake Burley Griffin, the focus of the city. Satellite communities—using the same radial design of crescents and cul-de-sacs employed in Canberra—house the city's growing population.

GETTING HERE AND AROUND
AIR TRAVEL

Canberra Airport is 7 km (4½ miles) southeast of the city center. Flights are about a half hour to Sydney, an hour to Melbourne, and two hours to Brisbane. Qantas, Tiger Airways, and Virgin Australia fly to and from the capital, but there are no direct international flights. A taxi into the city is about A$30. A shuttle bus operated by Airport Express runs regularly between the airport and the city for A$12 per person. The buses run approximately every 45 minutes.

BUS TRAVEL

Canberra is served by two major bus lines, Greyhound Australia and Murrays Australia. One-way fares to Sydney start from A$40, and the trip takes just over three hours. Cheap Web deals can bring the price down to A$24.

The ACTION bus network operates weekdays 6:30 am–11:30 pm, Saturday 7 am–11:30 pm, and Sunday 8–7. There's a flat fare of A$4.60 per ride. A one-day unlimited-travel ticket costs A$8.80.

Bus Contacts ACTION Buses. ✉ *Canberra City* ☎ *13–1710* ⊕ *www.action. act.gov.au.* **Greyhound Australia.** ☎ *1300/473946* ⊕ *www.greyhound.com. au.* **Murrays Australia.** ☎ *13–2251* ⊕ *www.murrays.com.au.* **Qcity Transit.** ☎ *02/6299–3722* ⊕ *qcitytransit.com.au.*

CAR TRAVEL

Canberra can be difficult to negotiate by car for first-time visitors, given its radial roads, erratic signage, and often considerable distances between suburbs. Still, because sights are scattered about and not easily connected on foot or by public transportation, a car is a good way to see the city itself, as well as the sights in the Australian Capital Territory.

Taxi and Shuttle Contacts Canberra Elite. ☎ *13–2227* ⊕ *www.canberracabs. com.au.*

TRAIN TRAVEL

The Canberra railway station is about 6 km (4 miles) southeast of the city center. NSW TrainLink (aka CountryLink) trains make the four-hour trip between Canberra and Sydney twice daily. A daily bus-rail service by NSW TrainLink makes the nine-hour run between Canberra and Melbourne.

Train Contacts Canberra Railway Station. ✉ *Corner of Wentworth Ave. and Bourke Crescent, Kingston* ☎ *02/6208–9700.* **NSW TrainLink.** ☎ *13–2232* ⊕ *www.nswtrainlink.info.*

TOURS

Canberra Day Tours. A convenient (and fun!) way to see the major sights of Canberra is with the Canberra Explorer Bus, operated by Canberra Day Tours, which makes a regular circuit around the major attractions. Tickets are sold on the bus, and you can hop on and off all day. ✉ *Canberra* ☎ *0418/455–099* ⊕ *www.canberradaytours.com.au* ◪ *A$30.*

Canberra Ghost & History Tours. Canberra resident and crypto-naturalist (a student of strange and hidden phenomena) Tim the Yowie Man (the name he's legally chosen) runs ghost tours of the city and its environs.

Tours vary, but most last around two hours or so and include refreshments. ⊠ *Canberra* ☎ *04/0776–9980* ☎ *From A$70.*

ESSENTIALS

Visitor Information Canberra and Region Visitor Centre. ⊠ *330 Northbourne Ave., Dickson* ☎ *1300/554114* ⊕ *www.visitcanberra.com.au.*

EXPLORING

Canberra's most important public buildings stand within the Parliamentary Triangle. Lake Burley Griffin wraps around the northeast edge, while Commonwealth and Kings avenues radiate from Capital Hill, the city's political and geographical epicenter, to form the west and south boundaries. The triangle can be explored comfortably on foot, but a vehicle is required to see the rest of this area. The monuments and other attractions within the Parliamentary Triangle and around Lake Burley Griffin are not identified by street numbers, but all are clearly signposted.

CENTRAL CANBERRA

You can visit virtually all of central Canberra's major attractions by car, but in some places parking and walking may be more convenient. Around town you can use the local ACTION buses, which stop at most of the other sights, or join the hop-on, hop-off Canberra Day Tours bus.

TOP ATTRACTIONS

Fodor's Choice ★ **Australian War Memorial.** Both as a moving memorial to Australians who served their country in wartime and as a military museum, this is a shrine of great national importance and the most popular attraction in the capital. The museum explores Australian military involvement from the late 19th century through the 1970s and Vietnam up to Iraq and Afghanistan today. Displays include a Lancaster bomber, a Spitfire, tanks, landing barges, and sections of two of the Japanese midget submarines that infiltrated Sydney Harbour during World War II, as well as more interactive displays in the Anzac Hall. Anzac is an acronym for the Australian and New Zealand Army Corps, formed during World War I. One of the most moving places is the domed Tomb of the Unknown Soldier that stands above the Pool of Reflection and the Roll of Honour, which are two walls of names honoring the thousands of Australians who have died in all military conflicts. There are a range of free guided tours, led by volunteers, throughout the day. You can best appreciate the impressive facade of the War Memorial from the broad avenue of **Anzac Parade.** The avenue is flanked by several memorials commemorating the Army, Navy, Air Force, and Nursing Corps, as well as some of the campaigns in which Australian troops have fought, including the Vietnam War. ■**TIP➔ At closing time a bugler or bagpiper plays the emotive Last Post outside the Tomb of the Unknown Soldier.** ⊠ *Treloar Crescent, off Anzac Parade, Campbell* ☎ *02/6243–4211* ⊕ *www.awm. gov.au* ☎ *Free* ⊙ *Daily 10–5.*

Museum of Australian Democracy at Old Parliament House. This museum is inside the Old Parliament House. Curators use stories of real people and events to trace the history of democracy both in Australia and

Canberra

abroad. The museum features five exhibits, as well as the opportunity to see the original chambers and prime minister's office. There are free 45-minute guided tours every day starting at 9:45 am, with the last at 3:45 pm. While you're in the area, take a stroll through the delightful **Rose Gardens** on both sides of the Old Parliament House building. Across the road from the entrance, visit the controversial **Aboriginal Tent Embassy,** established in 1972 to proclaim the Aboriginal people as Australia's "first people" and to promote recognition of their fight for land rights. ⊠ *18 King George Terr., Parkes* ☎ *02/6270–8221* ⊕ *www. moadoph.gov.au* ⊡ *A$2* ⊙ *Daily 9–5.*

National Film & Sound Archive. Housed in one of Canberra's most beautiful art deco buildings, this museum displays Australia's audio-visual cultural history. Among the many exhibits are costumes from films including *Muriel's Wedding, The Adventures of Priscilla Queen of the Desert,* and *Ned Kelly,* along with vintage film, sound equipment, and a film still collection of more than 300,000 images. You can relax in the small theatrette (designed along early 20th-century theater lines) and watch some of the country's early news reels and short films (some are very funny). Watch arthouse movies (at an extra cost of around A$5–A$25) in the beautiful Arc cinema, which regularly screens classic movies and other nonmainstream cinematic gems. ⊠ *McCoy Circuit, Acton* ☎ *02/6248–2000* ⊕ *www.nfsa.gov.au* ⊡ *Free* ⊙ *Weekdays 9–5* ☞ *Open some weekends for special events.*

Fodor's Choice **National Gallery of Australia.** The most comprehensive collection of Australian art in the country is on exhibit in the nation's premier art gallery, including superlative works of Aboriginal art and paintings by such famous native sons as Arthur Streeton, Sidney Nolan, and Arthur Boyd. The gallery also contains a sprinkling of works by European and American masters, including Rodin, Picasso, Pollock, and Warhol, as well as art and artifacts from closer to home, Southeast Asia. Free guided tours on a variety of topics with excellent guides begin in the foyer each day—check the website for details. A new wing, containing 13 galleries, is dedicated to indigenous art. The gallery extends outside into the Sculpture Garden, and the innovative Fog Sculpture takes place (outdoors) from 12:30 to 2 pm daily. ⊠ *Parkes Pl., Parkes* ☎ *02/6240–6411* ⊕ *www.nga.gov.au* ⊡ *Free* ⊙ *Daily 10–5.*

NEED A BREAK? **Bookplate. A good spot to catch your breath amid the Parliamentary Triangle's mix of history, culture, and science is Bookplate, in the foyer of the National Library. It has lovely stained glass windows and extends out onto a patio overlooking the lake. Sandwiches, salads, cakes, warming soup and curry in the winter, and tea and coffee are served weekdays 7:30–5 (until 4 on Friday) and weekends 9–4.** ⊠ *Parkes Pl., Parkes* ☎ *02/6262–1154* ⊕ *bookplate.com.au.*

National Library of Australia. Constructed loosely on the design of the Parthenon in Athens, this library houses more than 5 million books and 500,000 photographs, maps, drawings, and recordings of oral history. Don't miss the state-of-the-art Treasures Gallery, which displays 80 of the library's prized pieces, such as Captain James Cook's journal of the

Endeavour and Australia's only complete original convict uniform. A free Treasures Gallery tour takes place daily at 11:30 am, and a behind-the-scenes tour takes place on Thursday at 2 pm. The café has a wonderful view, and the bookshop is a browser's and buyer's delight. ⊠ *Parkes Pl., Parkes* ☎ *02/6262–1111* ⊕ *www.nla.gov.au* ⊠ *Free* ☉ *Mon.–Thurs. 10–8, Fri. and Sat. 10–5, Sun. 1:30–5.*

FAMILY
Fodor'sChoice
★

National Museum of Australia. This unstuffy museum is spectacularly set on Acton Peninsula, thrust out over the calm waters of Lake Burley Griffin. The museum highlights the stories of Australia and Australians by exploring the key people, events, and issues that shaped and influenced the nation. Memorabilia include a carcass of the extinct Tasmanian tiger, the old Bentley beloved by former Prime Minister Robert Menzies, and the black baby garments worn by dingo victim Azaria Chamberlain (whose story was made famous in the Meryl Streep film *A Cry in the Dark*). *Circa*, a 12-minute movie, gives a fascinating snapshot of Australian history and should be your first port of call. Children love the KSpace display, an exhibit where they can use computers and 3-D technology to design a space-age city of the future. The highlights and First Australians tours cost A$10 each, while a tour package that includes a meal and a glass of wine in the restaurant is A$35. ⊠ *Lawson Crescent, off Lennox Crossing, Acton* ☎ *02/6208–5000, 1800/026132* ⊕ *www.nma.gov.au* ⊠ *Free* ☉ *Daily 9–5.*

National Portrait Gallery. This terrific space is dedicated to portraits of people who have shaped Australia and who in some way reflect the national identity. Look out for famous faces like pop star Kylie Minogue and Olympic champion Cathy Freeman, as well as priceless portraits of Captain James Cook. The building on the south shore of Lake Burley Griffin caused some controversy, but most architecture fans like its simple, clean design. The gallery also has a good arts program, with talks and film screenings, and the café's outdoor terrace has lovely views. ⊠ *King Edward Terr., Parkes* ☎ *02/6102–7000* ⊕ *www.portrait. gov.au* ⊠ *Free* ☉ *Daily 10–5.*

Fodor'sChoice
★

Parliament House. Much of this vast futuristic structure is submerged, covered by a domed glass roof that follows the contours of Capital Hill. You approach the building across a vast courtyard with a central mosaic titled *Meeting Place*, designed by Aboriginal artist Nelson Tjakamarra. Native timber has been used almost exclusively throughout the building, and the work of some of Australia's finest contemporary artists hangs on the walls.

Parliament generally sits Monday to Thursday mid-February to late June and mid-August to mid-December. Both chambers have public galleries, but the debates in the House of Representatives, where the prime minister sits, are livelier and more newsworthy than those in the Senate. Free 40-minute guided tours take place at 9:30, 11, 1, 2, and 3 daily. ⊠ *Parliament Dr., Capital Hill* ☎ *02/6277–5399* ⊕ *www.aph.gov. au* ⊠ *Free* ☉ *Daily 9–5, later when Parliament is session.*

Question Time. The best time to observe the House of Representatives is during Question Time, starting at 2, when the Government and the Opposition are most likely to be at each other's throats. To secure

The Australian War Memorial, Canberra

a ticket for Question Time, contact the sergeant-at-arms' office until 12:30 pm on the day you require a ticket. ✉ *Parliament Dr., Capital Hill* ☎ *02/6277–4889 sergeant-at-arms' office* ⊕ *www.aph.gov.au.*

WORTH NOTING

Australian National Botanic Gardens. Australian plants and trees have evolved in isolation from the rest of the world, and these delightful gardens on the lower slopes of Black Mountain display the continent's best collection of this unique flora. The rain forest, rock gardens, Tasmanian alpine garden, and eucalyptus lawn—with more than 600 species of eucalyptus—number among the 125-acre site's highlights. Two self-guided nature trails start from the rain-forest gully, and free guided tours depart from the visitor center daily at 11 and 2. Prebooked and more individualized guided tours cost A$5 per person. ✉ *Clunies Ross St., Acton* ☎ *02/6250–9540* ⊕ *www.anbg.gov.au* ✄ *Free* ☉ *Daily 8:30–5, weekends in Jan. 8:30–8 pm, visitor center 9:30–4:30.*

High Court of Australia. As its name implies, this gleaming concrete-and-glass structure is the ultimate court of law in the nation's judicial system. The court of seven justices convenes only to determine constitutional matters or major principles of law. Inside the main entrance, the public hall contains a number of murals depicting constitutional and geographic themes. Each of the three courtrooms over which the justices preside has a public gallery, and you can observe the proceedings when the court is in session. ✉ *Parkes Pl., off King Edward Terr., Parkes* ☎ *02/6270–6811* ⊕ *www.hcourt.gov.au* ✄ *Free* ☉ *Weekdays 9:45–4:30, Sun. noon–4.*

National Capital Exhibition. Photographs, plans, audiovisual displays, and a laser model inside this lakeside pavilion illustrate the past, present, and future development of Canberra. Exhibits cover the time of the early settlers, Walter Burley Griffin's winning design for the city, and plans for the coming decades. From the pavilion's terrace there are sweeping views of the Parliamentary Triangle across the lake. ⊠ *Regatta Point, Barrine Dr., Commonwealth Park* ☎ *02/6272–2902* ⊕ *www.nationalcapital.gov.au* ⊇ *Free* ⊙ *Weekdays 9–5, weekends 10–4.*

FAMILY

Fodor'sChoice

★

Questacon—The National Science and Technology Centre. This interactive science facility is the city's most entertaining museum, especially for kids. About 200 hands-on exhibits in seven galleries use high-tech computer gadgetry and everything from pendulums to feathers to illustrate principles of mathematics, physics, and human perception. There are daily stage shows (about such things as rockets and natural disasters), puppet shows, and talks. Staff members explain the scientific principles behind the exhibits. The free-fall slide (with a drop of 20 feet) and the 360-degree swing are huge hits with all ages. It's pricey, but kids (and their parents) love it. ⊠ *King Edward Terr., at Mall Rd. W, Parkes* ☎ *02/6270–2800, 1800/020603* ⊕ *www.questacon.edu.au* ⊇ *A$23* ⊙ *Daily 9–5.*

AROUND CANBERRA AND THE A.C.T.

TOP ATTRACTIONS

FAMILY

Cockington Green Gardens. You'll feel like Gulliver walking through this miniature village and gardens 15 km (9 miles) northwest of the center of Canberra. Named after a small town in England, this site is a big hit with children who love wandering past the football stadium and hearing the roar of the crowd, and seeing classic structures such as Stonehenge, a miniature turf maze, windmills, and a cricket match on the village green. They'll also love taking a ride on the miniature train through the gardens. Cockington Green began as a miniature museum for all things English (country cottages, village church, etc.) more than 30 years ago; however, many international miniature buildings—such as the Tenochtitlan Temple in Mexico, the Chateau Bojnice in Slovakia, and India's Red Fort—have been added over the years. It is near Gold Creek Village shopping center; take the Barton Highway and head toward Yass. ⊠ *11 Gold Creek Rd., Nicholls* ☎ *02/6230–2273* ⊕ *www.cockingtongreen.com.au* ⊇ *A$19.50* ⊙ *Daily 9:30–5, last entry 4:15.*

SPORTS AND THE OUTDOORS

BICYCLING

Canberra has almost 160 km (100 miles) of cycle paths, and the city's relatively flat terrain and dry, mild climate make it a perfect place to explore on two wheels. One of the most popular cycle paths is the 40-km (25-mile) circuit around Lake Burley Griffin.

Mr. Spokes Bike Hire. This shop rents several different kinds of bikes as well as tandems and baby seats. Bikes cost A$20 for the first hour, including helmet rental, locks, and a map of cycle routes. A half-day rental (4 hours) is A$30, and full-day costs A$40. ⊠ *Acton Ferry Terminal, Barrine Dr., Acton* ☎ *02/6257–1188* ⊕ *www.mrspokes.com.au.*

The Australian Federal Parliament, Canberra

BOATING

Southern Cross Cruises. This tour company runs a number of one-hour sailings (A$15) around Lake Burley Griffin on the MV *Southern Cross* as well as a two-hour cruise that includes a tour of Government House gardens (A$23). Three-course Thursday dinner cruises and Sunday lunch cruises cost A$70. ⊠ *Southern Cross Club, Lotus Bay, 1 Mariner Pl. off Alexandrina Dr., Yarralumla* ☎ *02/6273–1784* ⊕ *www.cscc. com.au* 🖅 *From A$15.*

HIKING

Namadgi National Park. Covering almost half the total area of the Australian Capital Territory's southwest, this national park has a well-maintained network of walking trails across mountain ranges, trout streams, and some of the most accessible subalpine forests in the country. The park's boundaries are within 35 km (22 miles) of Canberra, and its former pastures, now empty of sheep and cattle, are grazed by hundreds of eastern gray kangaroos in the early morning and late afternoon. Car-based tent camping is permitted in three designated campgrounds: Orroral, Honeysuckle Creek, and Mount Clear. Bookings are essential and can be made online (⊕ *www.accesscanberra.act. gov.au*) or by phone. Snow covers the higher altitudes June–September. ■ TIP ➔ **Bushfires are a constant threat in summertime, so check ahead for conditions.** ⊠ *Visitor center, Naas–Boboyan Rd., Tharwa* ✛ *3 km (2 miles) south of Tharwa* ☎ *02/6207–2900, 13–2281* ⊕ *www.tams. act.gov.au* 🖅 *Free* ☺ *Visitor center weekdays 9–4, weekends 9–4:30.*

FAMILY

Fodor's Choice

★

Tidbinbilla Nature Reserve. A good place to see native wildlife in a natural setting—including lots of kangaroos—this extensive bushland reserve features walking trails, wetlands, and animal exhibits, as well as good picnic facilities. The park is 40 km (25 miles) southwest of Canberra. Tours, including "platypus pursuit" and boomerang throwing, are run on weekends—some of these require a small fee. ⊠ *Tidbinbilla Ring Rd. or Paddy's River Rd., Tidbinbilla Nature Reserve* ☎ *02/6205–1233, 13–2281* ⊕ *www.tidbinbilla.act.gov.au* ⊠ *A$11.50 per car per day (free for pedestrians and cyclists)* ☉ *Visitor center, daily 9–5. Reserve grounds 7:30–8 during daylight saving time, 7:30–6 other times.*

3

WHERE TO EAT

The main restaurant precincts are around the city center and in the trendy suburbs of Manuka and Kingston. However, many fine eateries are tucked away in such suburban centers as Griffith, Ainslie, Belconnen, and Woden. In Dickson, Canberra's Chinatown, a line of inexpensive, casual eateries along Woolley Street includes many little spots serving Vietnamese, Malaysian, Chinese, Turkish, and Italian cuisine.

Use the coordinate (⊕ B2) at the end of each listing to locate a site on the corresponding map.

CENTRAL CANBERRA AND NORTHERN SUBURBS

$$

ITALIAN

✕ **Bicicletta.** Its name is Italian for bicycle and the motif is carried through his funky restaurant housed in the hip Peppers Gallery Hotel, with two-wheeled images on the big umbrella-shape light fittings and pieces of memorabilia. The popular dining spot for lunch, dinner, and weekend breakfasts was once a student dormitory, and the interior's distressed look (featuring old bathroom tiles and shabby walls) has been left to add to the venue's funky feel. The menu features antipasti, pasta, a long list of pizzas, salads, and a smattering of meat and fish dishes. Start with the yummy large olives stuffed with savory mince, crumbed and lightly fried; or try the slow-cooked pork and veal meatballs. Thin-crust pizzas include the "fantasia": mozzarella, spinach, sausage, cherry tomatoes, and gorgonzola. Pop in early for great pastries and good coffee and use the free Wi-Fi while you eat. ⑤ *Average main: A$35* ⊠ *15 Edinburgh Ave., Canberra City* ☎ *02/6262–8683* ⊕ *www.bicicletta.com.au* ⊕ *B3.*

$$

ASIAN FUSION

Fodor's Choice

★

✕ **The Chairman and Yip.** The menu at this longtime fusion favorite garners universal praise for its innovative mix of Asian and Western flavors against a backdrop of artifacts from Maoist China. Menu standouts include the sesame-crusted salmon with cinnamon-infused soy, and pork chops with red dates, ginseng, and honey. Finish with a delicious dessert, such as cinnamon-and-star anise crème brûlée. Watch for the special deals, such as the two-course lunch for $39.50, and lunch and dinner banquets from A$62.50 for seven courses. The service and wine list are outstanding, and you're welcome to bring your own bottle as well. ⑤ *Average main: A$32* ⊠ *108 Bunda St., Canberra City* ☎ *02/6248–7109* ⊕ *chairmangroup.com.au/chairmanyip* ☉ *Closed Sun. and Mon. No lunch Sat.* ⚑ *Reservations essential* ⊕ *C2.*

Where to Eat and Stay in Canberra

A

B

C

D

1

TO WOOLLEY ST.
DICKSON
Wattie St.
O'CONNOR
Macarthur Ave.
Majura Ave.
Tyson St.
Aria Hotel
AINSLIE
Moorhouse St.
David St.
Northbourne Ave.
Lonsdale St.
Duffy St.

2

Barry Dr.
TURNER
Greenway St.
BRADDON
Limestone Ave.
Chisholm St.
CANBERRA NATURE PARK
Australian National Botanic Gardens
Clunies Ross St.
University Ave.
Marcus Clarke St.
Italian and Sons
Courgette
East Row
Donaldson St.
Ainslie Ave.
Treloar Crescent
The Chairman and Yip
ACTON
Liversidge St.
McCoy
Thirst Wine Bar & Eatery
City Hill
CITY CENTRE
REID
TO AIRPORT
Bicicletta
Peppers Gallery Hotel
ACTON PARK
London Ct.
Crowne Plaza Hotel Canberra
Binara
Constitution Ave.
Anzac Parade
CAMPBELL

3

Springbank Island
Commonwealth Avenue Bridge
Barrine Dr.
Parkes Way
Regatta Pt.
Russell Dr.
CANBERRA NATURE PARK
NATIONAL MUSEUM
Flynn Dr.
Commonwealth Ave.
NATIONAL LIBRARY
Parkes Pl.
PARKES
Waters Edge
NATIONAL GALLERY
RUSSELL

4

Coronation Dr.
Hyatt Hotel Canberra
King Edward Terr.
King Geo. Terr.
Kings Ave.
Kings Ave. Bridge
Hotel Kurrajong
Perth Ave.
State Circle
PARLIAMENT HOUSE
Capital Hill
BARTON
Brisbane Ave.
CANBERRA NATURE PARK
YARRA-LUMLA
Adelaide Ave.
State Circle
Hotel Realm

5

Hopetoun Circuit
Melbourne Ave.
FORREST
Empire Circuit
MANUKA
Manuka Circle
Jardine
Giles St.
Wentworth Ave.
Silo Bakery
Kennedy St.
Oxley St.
Canberra Ave.
RAILWAY STATION
KINGSTON
McMillan Crescent

6

Red Hill
Federal Golf Course
CANBERRA NATURE PARK
Mugga Way
Monaro Circuit
Flinders Way
Captain Cook Crescent
Barrallier St.
GRIFFITH
Rubicon
NARRA-BUNDAH

0 ___ 1 mile
0 ___ 1 km

KEY
□ Hotels
■ Restaurants
↕ following reviews indicates a map-grid coordinate

A

B

C

D

\$\$\$\$
FRENCH FUSION
Fodor's Choice
★

✕ **Courgette.** Creative food served in spacious, sedate surroundings is the specialty of this popular restaurant on the city's outer edge. The seasonal four-course menu (A\$88) has such dreamy dishes as prosciutto-wrapped pan-seared scallops for starter, or, for a main, the crispy-skin snapper, fennel puree, and Balmain-bug-filled zucchini (also known as courgette) flower. Leave room for the decadent warm Belgian chocolate fondant with raspberries and vanilla bean ice cream. The restaurant also serves a three-course lunch menu for A\$66, which is a bargain for a restaurant of this acclaim, and one with such an impressive wine list. ⑤ *Average main: A\$88 ⊠ 54 Marcus Clarke St., Canberra City* ☎ *02/6247–4042* ⊕ *www.courgette.com.au* ⊗ *Closed Sun.* ⌲ *Reservations essential* ✛ *B2.*

\$\$\$
ITALIAN

✕ **Italian and Sons.** This lively restaurant calls itself a modern version of the traditional Roman trattoria. It serves regional Italian cuisine using local produce, much of it from the owner's farm. Sit among the hanging salamis at tables covered in white paper and feast on antipasti such as chili and garlic prawns. Move on to one of the delicious pizzas (Sicilian anchovy, black olive, and baby caper are standouts), or one of the dishes of the day, like wood-roast suckling pig with apple and sage. Finish with Ligurian honey panna cotta, or one of the imported Italian cheeses. Buon appetito. ⑤ *Average main: A\$36 ⊠ 7 Lonsdale St., Canberra City* ☎ *02/6162–4888* ⊕ *www.italianandsons.com.au* ⊗ *Closed Sun. No lunch Sat. or Mon.* ✛ *B2.*

\$\$
THAI

✕ **Thirst Wine Bar & Eatery.** This busy Thai restaurant in the heart of Canberra draws its inspiration from the street-food stalls of Thailand. Waitstaff does an excellent job of suggesting just the right wines for your meal from an acclaimed, although small, wine list. The crispy-fish salad is a specialty, a mix of crisp fried-fish pieces with green mango, coriander, mint, roasted peanuts, and a chili dressing (have it with the Thirst Riesling). The main dish of green curry with ocean trout dumplings is not only intriguing but delicious. A tasting plate featuring such delights as corn fritters, Thai sausages, and popular Thai fish cakes is A\$28.90 for two, while the "two-for-one" deals on Monday and Tuesday nights pulls in droves of locals—arrive early or expect a wait. ⑤ *Average main: A\$25 ⊠ Melbourne Bldg., 20 West Row, Canberra City* ☎ *02/6257–0700* ⊕ *www.thirstwinebar.com.au* ⊗ *Closed Sun. No lunch Sat.–Tues.* ✛ *B3.*

SOUTHERN SUBURBS

\$\$\$
AUSTRALIAN

✕ **Rubicon.** Everything about this cozy romantic restaurant speaks of attention to detail. Savor the melded flavors of prawns, clams, and crab chowder to start things off, then consider the duck confit and Toulouse sausage or pork belly cassoulet among the mains. Later you can linger over such delicious desserts as honey-rum panna cotta with baby figs and ginger ice cream. You can build your own degustation menu from the à la carte menu, choosing from four to seven courses. The four-course, for example, is A\$60, or A\$95 with paired wines. ⑤ *Average main: A\$36 ⊠ 6A Barker St., Griffith* ☎ *02/6295–9919* ⊕ *www.rubiconrestaurant.com.au* ⊗ *Closed Sun. No lunch Sat.* ✛ *C6.*

\$\$
CAFÉ

✕ **Silo Bakery.** It's not unusual to find a queue of hungry Canberrians waiting to take away some of the delectable homemade pastries (try the black-currant and Cabernet tart) and breads. It's also possible to sit down for breakfast, brunch, or lunch at one of the few tables. The eggs with chili jam are popular, as are the asparagus and smoked eel omelet with horseradish salsa and mouthwatering thin, crisp sourdough pizza topped with a mixture of mushrooms and hint of blue cheese. Many people complain about the rude staff, but don't let it keep you from going—the food, especially those pastries, can make you forget the brusque service. Still, don't expect a place where you can linger for hours over brunch and the papers. $ *Average main: A$22* ✉ *36 Giles St., Kingston* ☎ *02/6260–6060* ⊕ *www.silobakery.com.au* ☉ *Closed Sun. and Mon. No dinner* ☞ *Reservations recommended for lunch* ✛ *C5.*

$$$ ✕ **Waters Edge.** At this swanky eatery tables are set with fine linens and
ECLECTIC   crystal, and huge windows look out over the sparkling waters of Lake Burley Griffin. The menu cleverly blends French and Mod Oz influences with dishes such as duck breast and pressed leg confit with potatoes and rosemary gratin and sautéed sweet cabbage, and a luscious dessert of passion-fruit soufflé and coconut–and–kaffir lime sorbet. An impressive wine list has many by-the-glass vintages. $ *Average main: A$36* ✉ *Commonwealth Pl., 40 Parkes Pl., Parkes* ☎ *02/6273–5066* ⊕ *www. watersedgecanberra.com.au* ☉ *Closed Mon. and Tues.* ⌂ *Reservations essential* ✛ *C4.*

WHERE TO STAY

CENTRAL CANBERRA AND NORTHERN SUBURBS

$$$ ⌂ **Aria Hotel.** This contemporary, spick-and-span hotel is convenient for
HOTEL   travelers with a car, as it's just over 2 km (1 mile) north of the city, but it's also accessible from central Canberra via the Action buses. **Pros:** quiet; good for long stays. **Cons:** a little out of the center of town. $ *Rooms from: A$228* ✉ *45 Dooring St., Dickson* ☎ *02/6279–7000* ⊕ *www.ariahotel.com.au* ⇝ *51 rooms, 7 suites, 70 apartments* ¶◎¶ *No meals* ✛ *C1.*

$$$ ⌂ **Crowne Plaza Hotel Canberra.** In a prime location between the city
HOTEL   center and the National Convention Centre, this atrium-style hotel has a touch of luxury. **Pros:** excellent gym and pool; gambling fans enjoy being next door to the casino. **Cons:** hotel bars can be noisy; expensive parking. $ *Rooms from: A$243* ✉ *1 Binara St., Canberra City* ☎ *02/6247–8999, 1300/662218* ⊕ *www.crowneplaza.com.au* ⇝ *290 rooms, 6 suites* ¶◎¶ *No meals* ✛ *C3.*

$$$ ⌂ **Peppers Gallery Hotel.** In a city lacking in funk factor, the Peppers Gal-
HOTEL   lery Hotel stands out thanks to its groovy blend of art deco chic exterior
Fodor's Choice   and quirky interior. **Pros:** a good array of restaurants and bars for a
★   hotel of this size; beautifully landscaped modern gardens. **Cons:** bar and restaurants close early; cheaper rooms are on the small side. $ *Rooms from: A$209* ✉ *15 Edinburgh Ave., Canberra City* ☎ *02/6175–2222* ⊕ *www.peppers.com.au/gallery* ⇝ *79 rooms, 1 suite, 5 apartments* ¶◎¶ *No meals* ✛ *B3.*

SOUTHERN SUBURBS

$$$
HOTEL

Hotel Kurrajong. Stay here for a chance to immerse yourself in Canberra's political history and be within walking distance of Parliament House and the National Gallery. **Pros:** great location; stylish; lots of history; fresh off an extensive refurbishment. **Cons:** limited off-street parking A\$15 per night. $ *Rooms from: A\$239* ✉ *8 National Circuit, Barton* ☎ *02/6234–4444* ⊕ *www.hotelkurrajong.com.au* ⊃ *143 rooms, 4 suites* ⊘ *No meals* ✛ *C4.*

$$$
HOTEL
Fodor's Choice
★

Hotel Realm. This modern hotel is set among a new development of residential apartments and trendy eateries, and is close to all the attractions of the Parliamentary Triangle. **Pros:** modern; good location; trendy dining options; good value. **Cons:** can feel a bit geared to corporate travelers. $ *Rooms from: A\$255* ✉ *18 National Circuit, Barton* ☎ *02/6163–1888* ⊕ *www.hotelrealm.com.au* ⊃ *60 rooms, 103 suites* ⊘ *No meals* ✛ *C5.*

$$$$
HOTEL
Fodor's Choice
★

Hyatt Hotel Canberra. Occupying a National Heritage building dating from 1924, this elegant hotel has been restored to its original art deco splendor. **Pros:** friendly and unobtrusive service; superb location; free Wi-Fi. **Cons:** expensive breakfasts; can be very busy. $ *Rooms from: A\$405* ✉ *120 Commonwealth Ave., Yarralumla* ☎ *13–1234, 02/6270–1234* ⊕ *www.canberra.hyatt.com* ⊃ *231 rooms, 18 suites* ⊘ *No meals* ✛ *B4.*

NIGHTLIFE AND PERFORMING ARTS

Canberra's nightlife has had an adrenalin injection in recent years, and there are great wine bars, pubs, and music venues. Most venues are clustered in the city center and the fashionable southern suburbs of Manuka and Kingston. Except on weekends, few places showcase live music.

The Thursday edition of the *Canberra Times* has a "What's On" section (in the *Times Out* supplement) listing performances around the city. The Saturday edition's Arts pages also list weekend happenings.

PERFORMING ARTS

MUSIC

Llewellyn Hall. The Australian National University's School of Music has classical recitals and modern-style concerts on-campus at Llewellyn Hall. The Australian Chamber Orchestral also performs here six times a year. ✉ *100 William Herbert Pl., Acton* ☎ *02/6125–5767* ⊕ *llewellynhall. anu.edu.au.*

THEATER

Canberra Theatre Centre. The city's main live performance space has two different theaters that host productions by the Australian Ballet Company, touring theater companies, and overseas and local artists. ✉ *Civic Sq., Canberra City* ☎ *02/6275–2700* ⊕ *www.canberratheatrecentre. com.au.*

Erindale Theatre. Smaller stage and musical companies perform at neighborhood venues like this one. ✉ *McBryde Crescent, Wanniassa* ☎ *02/6142–2948.*

Interior of the National Museum of Australia, Canberra

The Street Theatre. This theater near the Australian National University campus showcases the best in local talent with excellent productions ranging from musicals to avant-garde plays. ✉ *15 Childers St., at University Ave., Canberra City* ☎ *02/6247–1223* ⊕ *www.thestreet.org.au.*

NIGHTLIFE

BARS AND CLUBS

The Academy Club. Canberra's liveliest nightspot draws hip crowd to its stylish, glitzy premises. The main room hosts DJs, live bands, and fun theme party nights. A roving photographer snaps partygoers and dancers. ✉ *50 Bunda St., Canberra City* ☎ *02/6253–2091* ⊕ *www.academyclub.com.au.*

Tilley's Devine Café Gallery. This 1940s-style club was once just for women, but now anyone can sit at the wooden booths and enjoy a relaxing meeting with friends or a meal at this arty café that does a great breakfast; in fact the kitchen is open all day. Established in 1984, the café stages a full range of cultural events from poetry readings to live music, particularly jazz and blues. Check the website for details. ✉ *Wattle and Brigalow Sts., Lyneham* ☎ *02/6247–7753* ⊕ *tilleys.com.au* ♡ *Mon.–Sat. 7:30 am–10 pm, Sun. 9–6.*

CASINOS

Casino Canberra. The European-style gaming room beside the National Convention Centre forgoes slot machines in favor of more sociable games like roulette, blackjack, poker, and keno. There are 40 gaming tables here, and the complex includes a restaurant (which has live music) and two bars. The Galaxy Club Retro is open Saturday nights and stages vintage dance parties. ✉ *Glebe Park, 21 Binara St., Canberra City* ☎ *02/6257–7074* ⊕ *www.casinocanberra.com.au.*

Experiencing Aboriginal Culture

The Ngunnawal people were the first inhabitants of the area now known as Canberra and the A.C.T., and the name "Canberra" comes from the Ngunnawal word "Kambera." In NSW the Cammeraygal, Eora, Kamilaroi, Tharawal, Wiradjuri, and Wonnarua peoples were some of the original inhabitants, each grouping speaking a different language and practicing a culture that stretched back thousands of years.

Muru Mittigar Aboriginal Cultural Centre near Penrith, an hour's drive from Sydney, tells the story of the Darug people. You can try bush tucker and boomerang throwing, or learn about the native plants used for medicine and food. (⊠ *89–151 Old Castlereagh Rd., Castlereagh, New South Wales 2749* ☎ *02/4730–0400* ⊕ *www.murumittigar.com.au*).

3

SHOPPING

Canberra has quite a diverse range of shopping opportunities, including the large 300-store Canberra Centre on Bunda Street in the heart of the city, and the well-to-do inner suburbs of Manuka and Kingston, where designer clothes and home wares can be had. There are also a number of high-quality arts-and-crafts outlets where you are likely to come across some unusual gifts and souvenirs. The galleries and museums sell interesting and often innovative items designed and made in Australia.

Beaver Galleries. This space has four exhibition galleries and a sculpture garden, where works by contemporary Australian artists are showcased. ⊠ *81 Denison St., Deakin* ☎ *02/6282–5294* ⊕ *www.beavergalleries. com.au* ☙ *Tues.–Fri. 10–5, weekends 9–5.*

Bungendore Wood Works Gallery. Thirty minutes out of the city, the Bungendore Wood Works Gallery exhibits the work of Australian wood artists, whose sculpture and contemporary furniture are made from the finest native timbers. ⊠ *22 Malbon St., Bungendore* ☎ *02/6238–1682* ⊕ *www.bwoodworks.com.au.*

Gold Creek Village. The charming streets of this shopping precinct on the city's northern outskirts are lined with all sorts of fun little places to explore. Peek into art galleries and pottery shops, browse through clothing boutiques and gift stores, and nosh at several eateries. ⊠ *O'Hanlon Pl., Nicholls* ⊕ *goldcreek.com.au.*

Fodor's Choice ★ **Old Bus Depot Markets.** South of Lake Burley Griffin, this lively Sunday market is in the former Kingston bus depot. Handmade crafts are the staples here, and buskers and inexpensive exotic food enliven the shopping experience. The markets also run on Saturday throughout December leading up to Christmas. When you've had your fill, wander across the road to the Canberra Glassworks to watch artisans at work. ⊠ *21 Wentworth Ave., Kingston Foreshore, Kingston* ☎ *02/6295–3331* ⊕ *www.obdm.com.au* ☙ *Sun. 10–4.*

WINERIES AROUND CANBERRA

Wineries began popping up everywhere around Canberra in the late 1990s, once it was discovered that the cool climate was optimal for producing Chardonnays, Rieslings, Cabernets, Shirazes, Merlots, and Pinot Noirs. There are now about 140 vineyards, about 35 of which have cellar doors, set in the peaceful rural countryside surrounding the city—mostly small operations, where visiting the cellar door usually involves sampling the wines in the tasting room. There is no charge for tastings.

Most are a maximum of 30 minutes from the city and are concentrated in the villages of Hall and Murrumbateman and in the Lake George area and Bungendore. Many are open to visits on weekends only. If you want to explore the wineries on your own, pick up a copy of *The Canberra District Wineries Guide* from the Canberra and Region Visitor Centre, or check out the websites ⊕ *www.canberrawines.com.au* and ⊕ *www.yassvalley.com.au*.

EXPLORING: WINERIES ALONG THE BARTON HIGHWAY

From Canberra take the Barton Highway (25) in the direction of Yass. After 20 km (12 miles) you'll pass the village of Hall and reach a handful of wineries, several of which are quite impressive.

Brindabella Hills Winery. It's worth heading to the cellar door at this winery (weekends only) to taste the Reserve Shiraz, one of the varieties that this family-run operation specializes in. The vineyard is ringed by the lovely Brindabella Range, providing a gorgeous setting on a sunny day for a picnic or barbecue. Light lunches are served on weekends, often accompanied by a jazz band. The vineyard is 25 km (16 miles) north of Canberra. ⊠ *156 Woodgrove Close, Wallaroo* ☎ *02/6230–2583* ⊕ *www.brindabellahills.com.au* ⊗ *Weekends 10–5.*

Fodor's Choice ★ **Poachers Pantry & Wily Trout Vineyard.** This favorite among gourmands is 25 minutes from Canberra. Here you'll find a tasting room offering good examples of Pinot Noir and Shiraz, and fabulous food and smoked goods offered by Poachers Pantry and the award-winning Smokehouse Cafe. Stock up on picnic-style smoked meats, poultry, and vegetables at the Pantry, or visit the Cafe for a memorable countryside dining experience in a historic cottage. Poachers Panty is one of the 25 operators who make up the Poacher's Way (⊕ *www.thepoachersway.com.au*), a collective of food emporiums, wineries, restaurants, galleries, and experiences that are loosely linked by a trail and that provide memorable regional experiences. ⊠ *431 Nanima Rd., Springrange* ☎ *02/6230–2487* ⊕ *www.poacherspantry.com.au* ⊗ *Cellar door daily 10–5.*

Surveyor's Hill Winery. Stop here to taste the Riesling, Chardonnay, Sauvignon Blanc, Rosé, and some dessert and sticky wines. In addition to the simple cellar door, the owners offer light meals to go with their wines. They make ample use of olives from their trees and other produce sourced from the property's gardens; seasonal produce is also sold. Guests can also stay overnight at the winery's B&B, which can accommodate up to 12 people in both the original family homestead and the new, more-modern apartments. ⊠ *215 Brooklands Rd., Wallaroo* ☎ *02/6230–2046* ⊕ *www.survhill.com.au* ⊗ *Cellar door weekends 10–5.*

EXPLORING: WINERIES ALONG THE FEDERAL HIGHWAY

From Canberra take the Federal Highway (23) for about 30 km (19 miles) north toward Sydney. There are a few wineries off the highway between Canberra and Lake George and a few not far from the lake.

Lambert Vineyards. You either like the style of this modern complex with cellar door or you don't—it provokes strong opinions on the Canberra wine trail. Its wines are generally popular, however. As it is more than 2,600 feet above sea level, it produces mostly red cool-climate varieties. After your tasting, don't miss the barrel room, which holds approximately 250 barrels of maturing wine. ⊠ *810 Norton Rd., Wamboin* ☎ *02/6238–3866* ⊕ *www.lambertvineyards.com.au* ⊗ *Weekends 11–4.*

Lark Hill Winery. This family-run enterprise overlooking (the usually bone-dry) Lake George specializes in biodynamic Riesling, Chardonnay, and Pinot Noir varieties. After your tasting, have lunch at the restaurant (weekends only, bookings essential) and sit out on the deck that looks out over the vines. ⊠ *Bungendore and Joe Rocks Rds., Bungendore* ☎ *02/6238–1393* ⊕ *www.larkhillwinery.com* ⊗ *Wed.–Mon. 11–4.*

Lerida Estate Wines. About 45 km (28 miles) out of Canberra, this highly respected winery is as famous for its design by Pritzker Prize–winning architect Glenn Murcutt as it is for its mid-price bottles. Try the Proprietor's Selection if its available at the cellar door—the Chardonnay is excellent. The tasting room and adjoining café, which serves light seasonal meals, enjoy lovely views over the often dry Lake George. Visitors, in groups of six or more, who make an appointment in advance can take either a 40-minute or 60-minute tour of the winery followed by tutored wine tasting priced from A$7.50 to A$12.50 per person. ⊠ *Federal Hwy., Lake George* ☎ *02/6295–6640* ⊕ *www.leridaestate. com* ♡ *Cellar door daily 10–5.*

MELBOURNE

WELCOME TO MELBOURNE

TOP REASONS TO GO

★ **Fabulous Markets:** Melbourne has nearly a dozen major markets. The huge Queen Victoria Market has more than 1,000 stalls.

★ **International Cuisine:** Melbourne's dining scene is a vast smorgasbord of cuisines.

★ **Sizzling Nightlife:** Melbourne's nightlife centers on King Street and Flinders Lane, with dozens of retro-style bars and clubs. The city's famous live music scene can be viewed in historic pubs in Fitzroy, Collingwood, and Brunswick.

★ **Sports Galore:** Melburnians, like Aussies in general, do love a good match. The Melbourne Cup horse race in November brings the entire city to a standstill. The same is true of Australian Rules Football.

★ **Arts and Culture:** Melbourne is renowned for its rich and lively arts scene. Live performances range from small, experimental theater productions to international comedy, fashion, and theater festivals.

1 City Center. Why come? For arts, funky back alleys, shopping, and Australia's best food. Explore the Southgate development, the arts district around the National Gallery of Victoria, and the King's Domain.

2 Richmond. Heaven for foodies and fashionistas in need of retail therapy. Come here for a new wardrobe, a Vietnamese soup kitchen, a Korean barbecue, a Laotian banquet, or a Thai hole-in-the-wall.

3 East Melbourne. The harmonious streetscapes in this historic enclave of Victorian houses, which date from the boom following the gold rushes of the 1850s, are a great excuse for a stroll.

4 St. Kilda. Dozens of alfresco restaurants overflow into the streets and the cafés and bars are buzzing with young fashionistas.

5 Fitzroy. Come here if you're looking for an Afghan camel bag, a secondhand paperback, or live music and a beer in a backstreet beer garden.

GETTING ORIENTED

The Yarra River cuts through the city center; the main business district is on the northern side, the southern side has arts, entertainment, and restaurant precincts. Several exclusive suburbs hug the southeastern shore of the bay. The Yarra Valley wineries and the Dandenong Ranges are an hour's drive to the east. The beaches and vineyards of the Mornington Peninsula are a 90-minute drive south. The Great Ocean Road begins at Torquay and continues along the Southern Ocean coast to Portland, about 350 km (217 miles). The goldfields, spa country, and Grampians are between one and two hours northwest of Melbourne; the Murray River Region and its wineries is about a three-hour drive north to northeast.

Updated by
Tim Richards
and Narrelle
Harris

Consistently rated among the "world's most livable cities" in quality-of-life surveys, Melbourne is built on a coastal plain at the top of the giant horseshoe of Port Phillip Bay. The city center is an orderly grid of streets where the state parliament, banks, multinational corporations, and splendid Victorian buildings that sprang up in the wake of the gold rush still stand. This is Melbourne's heart, which you can explore at a leisurely pace in a couple of days.

In Southbank, one of the newer precincts south of the city center, the sprawling Crown Melbourne entertainment complex and the Southgate Centre's bars, restaurants, and shops have refocused Melbourne's vision on the Yarra River. Once a blighted stretch of factories and run-down warehouses, the southern bank of the river is now a vibrant, exciting part of the city, and the river itself is finally taking its rightful place in Melbourne's psyche.

Just a hop away, Federation Square—with its host of restaurants, galleries, and museums—has become a civic hub for both Melburnians and visitors. A subtler city icon, its "laneways" thread the city center between major streets and are home to fascinating bars, cafés, shops, and art galleries.

Melbourne's inner suburbs have a character all their own. Stroll along the Esplanade in St. Kilda, amble past the elegant houses of East Melbourne, enjoy the shops and cafés of Fitzroy or Carlton, rub shoulders with locals at the Queen Victoria Market, nip into the Windsor for afternoon tea, or rent a canoe at Studley Park to paddle along one of the prettiest stretches of the Yarra—and you may discover Melbourne's soul as well as its heart.

PLANNER

WHEN TO GO

Melbourne and Victoria are at their most beautiful in autumn, from March to May. Days are crisp, and the foliage in parks and gardens is glorious. Melbourne winters can be gloomy, although the wild seas and leaden skies from June to August provide a suitable backdrop for the dramatic coastal scenery of the Great Ocean Road. By September the weather begins to clear, and the football finals are on. Book early to visit Melbourne during the Spring Racing Carnival and the Melbourne International Festival (late October/early November) and during mid-January when the Australian Open tennis tournament is staged.

PLANNING YOUR TIME

The free City Circle Tram is an easy hop-on/hop-off way to see many of the city's sights in a short time without exhausting yourself. The Parliament House tram stop goes to the Princess Theatre, the grand Windsor Hotel, Parliament House, the "Paris End" of Collins Street, and St. Patrick's Cathedral. Get off at Flinders Street to take a peek at the infamous *Chloe* painting in Young and Jackson's pub, and then walk over the Princes Bridge. There you can stroll the banks of the Yarra, looking back at Federation Square, before checking out the restaurants, shops, and the casino in the Southbank precinct. A trip to the Eureka Skydeck, the southern hemisphere's highest viewing platform, puts the city into perspective, and from there you can decide whether to head northeast to Fitzroy for an amble along groovy Brunswick Street, or north to Carlton to immerse yourself in Little Italy.

You might squeeze in a bit more exploring at the Treasury Gardens and Captain Cook's Cottage in the adjoining Fitzroy Gardens, or meet the sharks at the Melbourne Aquarium, opposite Southbank. On your second day, stroll through the Royal Botanic Gardens and see the Shrine of Remembrance. Afterwards, take a tram along St. Kilda Road to the hip Acland Street area, in the suburb of St. Kilda, for dinner. On Day 3, tour Chapel Street's shops, restaurants, and bars.

GETTING HERE AND AROUND

Melbourne is most easily reached by plane, as it's hours by car from the nearest big city. International airlines flying into Melbourne include Air New Zealand, United, Singapore Airlines, Emirates, Etihad, Thai Airways, Malaysia Airlines, Virgin Australia, and Qantas.

BUS AND TRAM TRAVEL

To use public transportation in Melbourne, you need a ticket called a Myki (a stored-value smart card). It can be purchased (A$6 for the card itself) at 7-Eleven stores, train stations, vending machines at major tram stops, and the Melbourne Visitors Centre at Federation Square. Each time you enter a train station, or hop on a tram or bus, you must touch the Myki card to a validator. The standard two-hour fare of A$3.76 is activated the first time you touch on, and you can change between any bus, tram, or train during this period. Daily travel is capped at two, two-hour fares (A$7.52), at which point you can travel as much as you like without extra charge. Trams run until midnight (1 am on Friday and Saturday) and can be hailed wherever you see a green-and-white tram-stop sign.

CAR TRAVEL

Melbourne's regimented layout makes it easy to negotiate by car, but two unusual rules apply because of the tram traffic. At intersections in the city center, trams should be passed by swinging to the far left before turning right (known as the "hook turn"); and when a tram stops to allow passengers to disembark across a roadway to the curb, the cars behind it also must stop. Motorists using various tollways have 72 hours to pay the toll after using the highway. To pay by credit card, call☎ 132–629. Alternatively, you can buy passes at the airport before using the tollways. A weekend pass is around A$16.50.

TRAIN TRAVEL

The main entrance to Southern Cross Railway Station is at Spencer and Little Collins streets. From here the statewide V/Line rail company sells tickets for 11-hour rail trips to Sydney, as well as services to many regional centers in Victoria. V/Line buses connect with the trains to provide transport to coastal towns; take the train to Geelong to connect with a bus to Lorne, Apollo Bay, and Port Campbell, or travel by train to Warrnambool and take a bus to Port Fairy.

CRUISE TRAVEL TO MELBOURNE

Cruise ships stopping in Melbourne dock in Port Melbourne at Station Pier. Tour buses, taxis, and a shuttle bus can collect visitors, and the terminus of tram 109 is just beyond the start of the pier. Frequent trams take passengers from here directly to the city center. The area around Station Pier has numerous restaurants and attractive water views. The lively entertainment and dining hub of St. Kilda is a pleasant 5-km (3-mile) walk southeast from here, alongside attractive bay beaches.

RESTAURANTS

Melbourne teems with top-quality restaurants, particularly in St. Kilda, South Yarra, Fitzroy, and Southbank. Lygon Street is still a favorite with those who love great coffee, pasta, and Italian bakeries, while the city center also has many back alleys (known as "laneways") containing popular cafés that serve meals as well as good coffee (a Melbourne trademark). Reservations are generally advised (though not possible for some places). Although most places are licensed to sell alcohol, the few that aren't usually allow you to bring your own. Many places serve food throughout the day, but lunch menus usually operate noon–2:30 pm, and dinner is usually served 7–10:30 pm. Tipping is not customary in Australia, but if you receive good service a 10% tip is welcome. Note there may be a corkage fee in restaurants, which allows you to bring in your own alcoholic drinks.

HOTELS

Staying in the heart of Melbourne, on Collins or Flinders streets and their nearby laneways, or at Southbank, is ideal for those who like dining and shopping. Another fashionable area, a little out of town, is South Yarra, which has excellent shopping. Wherever you stay, make sure you're near a tram or train line. *Hotel reviews have been shortened. For full information, visit Fodors.com.*

WHAT IT COSTS (IN AUSTRALIAN DOLLARS)			
$	$$	$$$	$$$$
Restaurants	Under A$21	A$21–A$35	A$36–A$50	over A$50
Hotels	Under A$151	A$151–A$200	A$201–A$300	over A$300

Restaurant prices are the average cost of a main course at dinner or, if dinner isn't served, a lunch. Hotel prices are the lowest cost of a standard double room in high season, excluding service.

TOURS

The free City Circle tram operates every 12 minutes from 10 to 9 Monday–Saturday and 10–6 Sunday around the edge of the Central Business District and Docklands, with stops on Flinders, La Trobe, Victoria, and Spring streets, and Harbour Esplanade. Look for the burgundy-and-cream trams. A red tourist bus (the Melbourne Visitor Shuttle, A$10 for two days) does a loop around central and inner Melbourne suburbs daily, every 30 minutes between 9:30 and 3:45, stopping at 13 destinations including Federation Square, Docklands, South Yarra, and the Botanic Gardens. Metropolitan buses operate daily until around 9 pm to all suburbs, while the NightRider bus service runs between 1:30 am and 4:30 am on Saturday and 1:30 am and 5:30 am on Sunday.

AAT Kings. This tour agency runs a half-day Magnificent Melbourne tour (A$65) that explores historical sights, gardens, and the Queen Victoria Market. The company also organizes longer tours outside Melbourne. ⊠ *Federation Sq., Flinders and Russell Sts., City Center* ☎ *1300/228546* ⊕ *aatkings.com* ✉ *From A$69.*

FAMILY **Chocoholic Tours.** Chocoholic Tours runs tours every day of the week for chocolate lovers, including the weekend Chocolate and Sweet Temptation tour, which focuses on organic and fair trade chocolate. The Spoil Yourself Chocolate Tour includes a gift at each stop. On weekdays, Melbourne's Chocolate Wonderland Tour goes for 2½ hours. Other tours are available, including private ones. Bookings are essential, and all tours depart from the Little Collins Street entrance of Reader's Feast Bookstore. ⊠ *195 Little Collins St., City Center* ☎ *03/9650–0795* ⊕ *www.chocoholictours.com.au* ✉ *From A$99.*

Golden Mile Heritage Trail. Hidden Secrets Tours runs guided walks of Melbourne's Golden Mile Heritage Trail, visiting the city's architectural and historic sites. The two-hour tours depart daily at 10 am from Federation Square and finish at the Melbourne Town Hall on weekdays and the Melbourne Museum on weekends. ⊠ *Melbourne* ☎ *03/9663–3358* ✉ *From A$29.*

Gray Line. Explore Melbourne and its environs on Gray Line's guided bus and boat tours. The Melbourne Morning City Tour visits the city center's main attractions and some of the surrounding parks. The 3½-hour tour departs daily at 8:20 am. ⊠ *Federation Square East, Flinders and Russell Sts., City Center* ☎ *1300/858687* ⊕ *www.grayline. com.au* ✉ *From A$62.*

Melbourne's Best Day Tours. The tour company runs half-day tours around Melbourne as well as taking visitors farther afield on three- and four-day treks. ⊠ *Federation Sq., Flinders and Russell Sts., City Center* ☎ *1300/130550* ⊕ *www.melbournetours.com.au* ⊠ *From A$70.*

Melbourne Greeters. The Melbourne Greeter service, a Melbourne Information Centre program, provides a free orientation walking tour, guided by a knowledgeable local volunteer. Tours are available in languages other than English. Book tours 24 hours ahead, and depart from the Melbourne Visitor Centre. ⊠ *Federation Sq., Flinders and Swanston Sts., City Center* ☎ *03/9658–9658 weekdays, 03/9658–9942 weekends* ⊕ *www.melbourne.vic.gov.au/greeter* ⊠ *Free.*

Melbourne River Cruises. One of the best ways to see Melbourne is from the deck of a boat on the Yarra River. Melbourne River Cruises' fleet of modern, glass-enclosed boats operate 1- and 2½-hour Yarra River cruises daily (A$23 and A$29, respectively), traversing either west through the commercial heart of the city or east through the parks and gardens, or a combination of the two. Cruises run roughly every half hour from 10 to 4, depending on weather and tide conditions. ⊠ *Vault 11, Banana Alley, 367 Flinders St., City Center* ☎ *03/8610–2600* ⊕ *www.melbcruises.com.au* ⊠ *From A$23.*

Queen Victoria Market Food Tour. The two-hour, guided Hunt and Gather food tour is conducted at Queen Victoria Market, where you'll taste your way around the market while learning some of its history. This tour runs Tuesday and Thursday to Saturday from January to November each year. Other tours include a meal or focus on history and gifts. ⊠ *Queen Victoria Market, Queen and Elizabeth Sts., City Center* ☎ *03/9320–5822* ⊕ *www.qvm.com.au* ⊠ *Hunt and Gather Tour A$49; others from A$40.*

Vietnam on a Plate. Take guided walking tours of the Asian food markets of Footscray and Springvale, visiting traditional herbalists, food stalls, and spice and herb specialists. These tours are designed for aspiring cooks and focus on sourcing and selecting the ingredients needed for authentic Asian cooking. A substantial Vietnamese lunch is included. Tours are usually given Saturday 9:30–2, for a minimum of four people. Other days can be arranged in advance. Reservations on all tours are essential. ⊠ *Footscray Market, Hopkins and Leeds Sts., Footscray* ☎ *03/9332–6848, 0411/578–641 mobile* ⊕ *www.vietnamonaplate.com.au* ⊠ *From A$77.*

VISITOR INFORMATION

The Melbourne Visitor Centre at Federation Square provides touring details in six languages. Large-screen videos and touch screens add to the experience, and permanent displays follow the city's history. Daily newspapers are available, and there's access to the Melbourne website (⊕ *www.visitmelbourne.com*). The center is open daily 9–6. The Best of Victoria Booking Service here can help if you're looking for accommodations. It also has cheap Internet access.

City Ambassadors, who provide information, can be identified by their bright red uniforms and found mainly along Swanston Street.

A free bus route map is available from the Melbourne Visitor Centre.

Visitor Information Best of Victoria Booking Service. ✉ *Melbourne Visitor Centre, Federation Sq., Flinders and Swanston Sts., City Center* ☎ *03/9928–0000, 1300/780045 toll-free in Australia* ⊕ *www.bestof.com.au/vic.* **City of Melbourne Ambassadors Program.** ✉ *City Center* ☎ *03/9658–9658.* **Melbourne Visitor Centre.** ✉ *Federation Sq., Flinders and Swanston Sts., City Center* ☎ *03/9658–9658* ⊕ *www.visitmelbourne.com.*

EXPLORING MELBOURNE

CITY CENTER

The City Center (CBD) is designed in a grid formation, with myriad alleyways twisting between them, often containing restaurants, galleries, and bars. The CBD is bounded by Spring Street in the east, Victoria Street to the north, Flinders Street to the South, and Spencer Street to the West. The Federation Square area, opposite the Flinders Street Station, is considered the CBD's heart and is an ideal starting point. The most popular shopping areas are the elegant eastern end of Collins Street and the busy pedestrian mall of Bourke Street. Spring Street holds many of the city's historic buildings from the mid-1800s.

GETTING HERE AND AROUND

Melbourne and its suburbs are well served by trams, trains, and buses. The free City Circle tram is perfect for sightseeing, but often crowded. Trams run east–west and north–south across the city, and travel to the popular St. Kilda and Docklands. The Metro train network operates a City Loop service with stops at Flinders Street, Parliament, Flagstaff, Melbourne Central, and Southern Cross stations, where you'll find connections with a network of trains to outer areas, including the Dandenong Ranges.

TOP ATTRACTIONS

Fodor's Choice
★ **The Arts Centre.** Melbourne's most important cultural landmark is the venue for performances by the Australian Ballet, Opera Australia, Melbourne Theatre Company, and Melbourne Symphony Orchestra. It encompasses Hamer Hall, the Arts Centre complex, the original National Gallery of Victoria, and the outdoor Sidney Myer Music Bowl. A 60-minute tour of the five floors of the complex, plus the current gallery exhibition and refreshment at the café, takes place Monday to Saturday at 11 am. On Sunday a 90-minute backstage tour begins at 11 am. Neither tour is suitable for children under 12 and both must be booked in advance. At night, look for the center's spire, which creates a magical spectacle with brilliant fiber-optic cables. ✉ *100 St. Kilda Rd., City Center* ☎ *03/9281–8000, 1300/182183 bookings* ⊕ *www. artscentremelbourne.com.au* ⬚ *Tours A$20* ⊗ *Mon.–Sat. 9 am–11 pm, Sun. 10–5.*

Block Arcade. Melbourne's most elegant 19th-century shopping arcade dates from the 1880s, when "Marvelous Melbourne" was flush with the prosperity of the gold rushes. A century later, renovations scraped back the grime to reveal a magnificent mosaic floor. Tours (A$15) operate on Tuesday and Thursday at 1 pm, and include afternoon tea at

Melbourne City Center

Queen Victoria Market

CARLTON

Royal Exhibition Building ◆

Melbourne Museum ◆

CARLTON GARDENS

Leicester St.

Bouverie St.

Swanston St.

Cardigan St.

Lygon St.

Grattan St.

Barkly St.

Argyle Pl.

Queensberry St.

Pelham St.

Earl St.

Drummond St.

Rathdowne St.

Nicholson St.

Therry St.

Victoria St.

Franklin St.

Elizabeth St.

RMIT University ●**19**

A' Beckett St.

Little La Trobe St.

Bowen St.

Gertrude St.

Regent St.

Princes St.

Fitzroy St.

Brunswick St.

Victoria Parade

Melbourne Central Complex

State Library of Victoria

La Trobe St.

Little Lonsdale St.

Lonsdale St.

Spring St.

Nicholson St.

Albert St.

Victoria Parade

Russell St.

Cohen Pl.

Little Bourke St.

Market La.

GPO Melbourne Complex

●**18**

Bourke St.

Exhibition St.

Parliament Station

State Parliament House

●**13**

Cathedral Pl.

St. Andrews Pl.

Gisborne St.

Lansdowne St.

●**12**

Swanston St.

Elizabeth St.

Little Collins St.

Alfred Pl.

●**17**

●**16**

Collins St.

Macarthur St.

Flinders La.

Melbourne Visitor Centre

Treasury Pl.

●**14**

TREASURY GARDENS

FITZROY GARDENS

●**9**

30

●**10** ●**11**

●**6** ●**8**

Flinders St.

●**7**

Wellington Parade

30

Wellington Parade South

Batman Ave.

Wellington Parade

●**15**

Jolimont Rd.

Yarra River

Riverside Ave.

Southbank Blvd.

City Rd.

●**1**

●**2**

●**3**

2

●**4**

3

ALEXANDRA GARDENS

●**5**

CARLTON GARDENS

0 _____ 1/8 mile

0 _____ 200 meters

the Charles Dickens Tavern. ⊠ *282 Collins St., City Center* ☎ *03/9654–5244* 🖼 *$A15.*

Federation Square. Encompassing a whole city block, the bold, abstract-style landmark was designed to be Melbourne's official meeting place, with a variety of attractions and restaurants within it. The square incorporates the second branch of the National Gallery of Victoria (Ian Potter Centre), which exhibits only Australian art, as well as the Australian Centre for the Moving Image; the Deakin Edge amphitheater, a contemporary music and theater performance venue; the Koorie Heritage Trust, which runs exhibitions, programs, and tours relating to Aboriginal Melbourne; and the Melbourne Visitor Centre. Regular events are held in the square and along the path beside the Yarra River. Crowds often gather to watch events on the giant "Fed TV" in the center of the square. ⊠ *Flinders St., between Swanston and Russell Sts., City Center* ☎ *03/9655–1900* ⊕ *www.fedsquare.com* 🖼 *Free* ☉ *Daily 10–5.*

FAMILY **Fitzroy Gardens.** This 65-acre expanse of European trees, manicured lawns, garden beds, statuary, and sweeping walks is Melbourne's most popular central park. Among its highlights is the **Avenue of Elms,** a majestic stand of 130-year-old trees that is one of the few in the world that has not been devastated by Dutch elm disease. ⊠ *Lansdowne St., at Wellington Parade, City Center* ⊕ *www.fitzroygardens.com* 🖼 *Free* ☉ *Daily sunrise–sunset.*

Flinders Street Station. Much more than just a train station, Flinders Street Station is a Melbourne icon and a popular meeting place. The term "meet me under the clocks" is widely known and used, indicating the time pieces on the front of this grand Edwardian hub of Melbourne's suburban rail network. When it was proposed to replace them with television screens, an uproar ensued. Today there are both clocks and screens. ⊠ *Flinders St. and St. Kilda Rd., City Center.*

The Hotel Windsor. Not just a grand hotel, the Windsor is home to one of Melbourne's proudest institutions—the ritual of afternoon tea (A$69 midweek), which is served noon–2 pm, and 2:30–4:30 from Wednesday to Friday. An even more indulgent dessert buffet (A$89), complete with chocolate fountain and other goodies, is added on weekends. Although the Grand Ball Room—a Belle Époque extravaganza with a gilded ceiling and seven glass cupolas—is reserved for private functions, occasionally afternoon tea is served there, so it's best to call first to check. ⊠ *111 Spring St., City Center* ☎ *03/9633–6000* ⊕ *www.thewindsor.com.au.*

Fodor's Choice ★ **Ian Potter Centre: NGV Australia.** The Australian art collection of the National Gallery of Victoria hangs on the walls of this gallery. Covering

---

EXPLORING THE THEATERS

Melburnians love their theater, and major shows often open in Melbourne first. If you want to take in Broadway or West End–style theater in grand surroundings, check out what's playing at the Regent and the Princess. Both are owned by Marriner Theatres, which lovingly restored the Regent for its reopening in the mid-1990s. For performances, check out ⊕ *www.marrinertheatres.com.au.*

The picturesque Yarra River is lined with picnic spots, fishing jettys, and bike paths.

the 19th and 20th centuries, it includes paintings from the famous Heidelberg school, such as Frederick McCubbin's *Lost* and Tom Roberts' *Shearing the Rams*. Other displays include textiles, sculpture, and photography. A gallery highlight is the indigenous collection, which changes every six months and includes both traditional and contemporary art. ⊠ *The Atrium, Federation Sq., Flinders and Russell Sts., City Center* 🕾 *03/8620–2222* ⊕ *www.ngv.vic.gov.au* 🖾 *Free; special exhibitions have varying ticket prices* ☉ *Tues.–Sun. 10–5.*

OFF THE BEATEN PATH **King's Domain Gardens.** This expansive stretch of parkland includes Queen Victoria Gardens, Alexandra Gardens, the Shrine of Remembrance, the Pioneer Women's Garden, the Sidney Myer Music Bowl, and the Royal Botanic Gardens. The temple-style **Shrine of Remembrance** is designed so that a beam of sunlight passes over the Stone of Remembrance in the Inner Shrine at 11 am on Remembrance Day—the 11th day of the 11th month, when in 1918 the armistice marking the end of World War I was declared. ⊠ *Between St. Kilda and Domain Rds., Anderson St., and Yarra River, City Center.*

National Gallery of Victoria International. This massive, moat-encircled, bluestone-and-concrete edifice houses works from renowned international painters, including Picasso, Renoir, and Van Gogh. It also hosts international blockbuster exhibitions that require tickets. In the Great Hall, it's considered perfectly reasonable to stretch out on the floor in order to properly appreciate the stained glass ceiling by Leonard French. A second branch of the National Gallery, in Federation Square in the city center, exhibits only Australian art. ⊠ *180 St. Kilda Rd., City*

Center ☎ *03/8620–0222* ⊕ *www.ngv.vic.gov.au* ☒ *Free* ☉ *Daily 10–5; ground level only on Tues.; closed Christmas Day and Good Friday.*

Royal Arcade. Opened in 1870, this is the country's oldest shopping arcade, and despite alterations it retains an airy, graceful elegance that often transfixes passersby. Walk about 30 feet into the arcade to see the statues of Gog and Magog, the mythical monsters that toll the hour on either side of **Gaunt's Clock.** ☒ *335 Bourke St., City Center* ☎ *03/9670–7777* ⊕ *www.royalarcade.com.au.*

St. Patrick's Cathedral. Construction of the Gothic Revival building began in 1858 and took 82 years to finish. Ireland supplied Australia with many of its early immigrants, especially during the Irish potato famine in the mid-19th century. A statue of the Irish patriot Daniel O'Connell stands in the courtyard. ☒ *Cathedral Pl., City Center* ☎ *03/9662–2233* ⊕ *www.cam.org.au/cathedral* ☉ *Weekdays 7–5, Sat. 8–7, Sun. 8–7:30.*

St. Paul's Cathedral. This 1892 headquarters of Melbourne's Anglican faith is one of the most important works of William Butterfield, a leader of the Gothic Revival style in England. In 2006 the cathedral underwent a massive restoration. Outside is a statue of Matthew Flinders, the first seaman to circumnavigate Australia, between 1801 and 1803. ☒ *Flinders and Swanston Sts., City Center* ☎ *03/9653–4333* ⊕ *www. stpaulscathedral.org.au* ☉ *Weekdays 8–6, Sat. 9–4, Sun. 7:30–7:30.*

FAMILY **SEA LIFE Melbourne Aquarium.** Become part of the action as you stroll through a transparent tunnel surrounded by water and the denizens of the deep on the prowl. Or press your nose to the glass in the Antarctica exhibition and watch King and Gentoo penguins waddling around on ice and darting through water. You can also don snow gear and sit among the penguins. If you're feeling brave, do a shark dive—they're held daily, include scuba equipment, and are led by an instructor. The aquamarine building illuminates a previously dismal section of Yarra River bank, opposite Crown Casino. ☒ *Flinders and King Sts., City Center* ☎ *03/9620–0999, 1800/026576* ⊕ *www.melbourneaquarium. com.au* ☒ *Entry A$38; shark dives A$299; Penguin Passport A$199 weekdays, A$290 weekends* ☉ *Daily 9:30–6; last admission at 5.*

Southgate. On the river's edge next to the Arts Centre, Southgate is a prime spot for lingering—designer shops, classy restaurants, bars, and casual eating places help locals and visitors while away the hours. The promenade links with the forecourt of Crown Casino and its hotels. ☒ *Maffra St., at City Rd., City Center* ☎ *03/9686–1000* ⊕ *www. southgatemelbourne.com.au.*

WORTH NOTING

Athenaeum Theatre and Library. The first talking picture show in Australia was screened in 1896 at this beautiful theater. Today the building houses three venues—a membership library, a theater for live performances, and the Last Laugh Comedy Club. ☒ *188 Collins St., City Center* ☎ *03/9650–3100* ⊕ *www.melbourneathenaeum.org.au* ☒ *Library: free* ☉ *Mon., Tues., and Thurs. 10–6, Wed. 10–8, Fri. 10–4, Sat. 10–2.*

NEED A
BREAK?

Journal. Next to the City Library, the café has leather couches, bookcases filled with magazines and newspapers, and communal tables where you can enjoy bruschetta, salads, antipasto platters, and selections from an excellent wine list from A$8 a glass. Journal Canteen, upstairs, serves a short lunch and dinner selection of delicious European courses. There is no obvious sign giving the café's name, but you will hear the buzz as you near it. ✉ *253 Flinders La., City Center* ☎ *03/9650–4399* ⊕ *journalcafe.com.au.*

Cook's Cottage. Once the on-leave residence of the Pacific navigator Captain James Cook, this modest two-story home, built in 1755 by Cook senior, was transported stone by stone from Great Ayton in Yorkshire, England, and rebuilt in the lush Fitzroy Gardens in 1934. It's believed that Cook lived in the cottage between his many voyages. The interior is simple, a suitable domestic realm for a man who spent much of his life in cramped quarters aboard sailing ships. ✉ *Fitzroy Gardens, Lansdowne St. and Wellington Parade, City Center* ☎ *03/9658–9658* 🖃 *A$6.20* ⊙ *Daily 9–5; last entry 4:45 pm.*

Eureka Skydeck 88. Named after the goldfields uprising of 1854, the Eureka Tower (which houses the 88th-level Eureka Skydeck 88) is the tallest residential building in the southern hemisphere. The funky-shape blue-glass building with an impressive gold cap is the place to get a bird's-eye view of Melbourne and overcome your fear of heights, especially on the Skydeck. An enclosed all-glass cube, known as the Edge (A$12 additional charge), projects 3 meters (9.84 feet) out from the viewing platform—here you can stand, seemingly suspended, over the city on a clear glass floor. ✉ *7 Riverside Quay, City Center* ☎ *03/9693–8888* ⊕ *www.eurekaskydeck.com.au* 🖃 *A$19.50* ⊙ *Daily 10–10.*

Old Melbourne Gaol Crime and Justice Experience. This blue-stone building, the city's first jail, is now a museum that has three tiers of cells with catwalks around the upper levels and is rumored to be haunted. Its most famous inmate was the notorious bushranger Ned Kelly, who was hanged here in 1880. On Saturday afternoon between 12 and 2, actors portray his story in free performances. The Hangman's night tours (reservations essential) are a popular, if macabre, facet of Melbourne nightlife. Museum entry now includes "being arrested" next door at the City Watch House, where guides walk visitors through the experience of being incarcerated. It is run by the Victorian branch of the National Trust. ✉ *Russell between LaTrobe and Victoria Sts., City Center* ☎ *03/8663–7228* ⊕ *www.oldmelbournegaol.com.au* 🖃 *A$25, night tours A$38* ⊙ *Daily 9:30–5; night tours: Wed., Fri., and Sat. at 7:30 pm.*

Young and Jackson's Hotel. Pubs are not generally known for their artwork, but climb the steps to the top-floor bar here to see *Chloe*, a painting that has scandalized and titillated Melburnians for many decades. The larger-than-life nude, painted by George Lefebvre in Paris in 1875, has adorned the walls of Young and Jackson's Hotel (which now specializes in Australian microbrew beers) since 1909. ✉ *1 Swanston St., opposite Flinders St. Station, City Center* ☎ *03/9650–3884* ⊕ *www.youngandjacksons.com.au.*

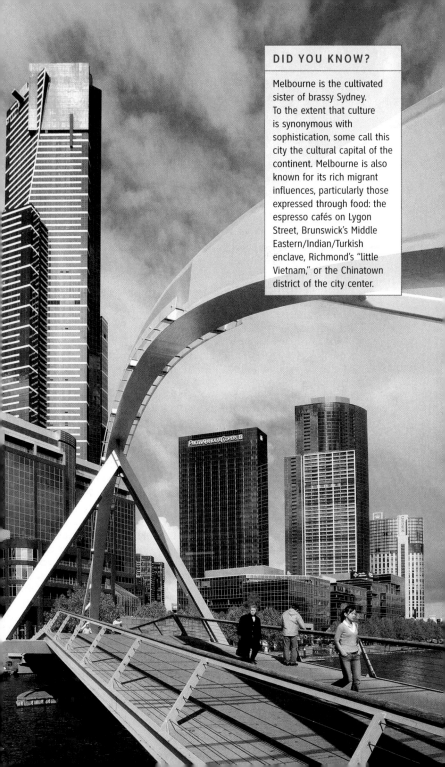

RICHMOND

Home of Victoria Street—Melbourne's "little Vietnam"—and the lively discount shopping stretch of Bridge Road, Richmond is 2 km (1 mile) east of the city center (take Tram 48 or 75 from Flinders Street for Bridge Road, or Tram 109 from Collins Street for Victoria Street). If you're looking for a new wardrobe, a Vietnamese soup kitchen, a Korean barbecue, a Laotian banquet, or a Thai hole-in-the-wall, this is the place to come.

GETTING HERE AND AROUND

Several tram lines connect central Melbourne with Richmond. Take Tram 70 from Flinders Street Station to Swan Street, Richmond, or take Tram 109 from Collins Street to Victoria Street. Trams 48 and 75 take you from Flinders Street to Bridge Road, while Tram 78 travels along Chapel Street (in South Yarra) north through the heart of Richmond. Trains connect Flinders Street Station with several useful local stations: Richmond, East Richmond and Burnley (for Swan Street), West Richmond (for Bridge Road), and North Richmond (for Victoria Street). If driving, or even walking, proceed east along Flinders Street, which becomes Wellington Parade, past the prominent Melbourne Cricket Ground, then cross Hoddle Street.

Bridge Road. Once a run-down area of Richmond, this street is now a bargain shopper's paradise. It's chockablock with clothing shops, cafés, and factory outlets selling leather goods, shoes, and gourmet foods. Take Tram 48 or 75 from the city. ⊠ *Bridge Rd., Richmond* ⊕ *www.bridgerd.com.au.*

Victoria Street. One of Melbourne's most popular "eat streets," this 2-km (1-mile) stretch has restaurants ranging from simple canteens to tablecloth-and-candlelight dining spots. The street also features Vietnamese grocers, kitchenware stores, several art galleries, and several chichi drinking spots. Once a year at Tet, Vietnamese New Year (in January and February but the exact date varies from year to year), the street comes to life with a day-long Lunar Festival, with dragon dances, music, and more food! ⊠ *Victoria St., Richmond.*

> ### WALTZING MATILDA
>
> Shopping mixes with history and a touch of patriotism at Melbourne Central shopping center. The main attraction, apart from the stores, is the historic brick shot tower, rising 165 feet above the center and encased in a glass cone. Built in 1890, the shot tower was used to make "shot" or bullets. Also suspended from the roof is a huge fob-watch that entertains shoppers on the hour with a musical rendition of Australia's unofficial national anthem, "Waltzing Matilda." You'll find this huge shopping mall on the corner of La Trobe and Swanston streets.

EAST MELBOURNE

The harmonious streetscapes in this historic enclave of Victorian houses, which date from the boom following the gold rushes of the 1850s, make East Melbourne a great neighborhood for a stroll.

4

GETTING HERE AND AROUND

East Melbourne's attractions are an easy walk from the city center. The Free City Circle tram travels along Spring Street, stopping at Parliament House and the Old Treasury building. The free, red-color Melbourne Visitor Shuttle bus also does a loop and stops at the Sports Precinct, which is a short walk from the MCG and Fitzroy Gardens. Trams 48 and 75 travel along Flinders Street and Wellington Parade to East Melbourne sights: Fitzroy Gardens is on the north side of Wellington Parade, and the MCG is on the south side.

Melbourne Cricket Ground (MCG). A tour of this complex is essential for an understanding of Melbourne's sporting obsession. You can get the stories behind it all at the new National Sports Museum. The site is a pleasant 10-minute walk from the city center or a tram ride (Nos. 48 and 75) to Jolimont Station. ⊠ *Jolimont Terr., East Melbourne* ☎ *03/9657–8888* ⊕ *www.mcg.org.au* 🖃 *A$30* ⊙ *Tours: daily every ½ hr 10–3, except on event days. Museum: 10–5 on nonevent days.*

ST. KILDA

Most nights of the week, the streets of this Victorian seaside suburb come alive with visitors, and its many restaurants, cafés, and bars buzz with energy. The holiday atmosphere continues on Sunday at open-air markets on the beach, while the tree-lined promenade and pier extending into Port Phillip Bay are perfect for strolling and people-watching. The quaintly named St. Kilda Sea Baths (now a modern swimming pool–spa complex) are housed in a turn-of-the-20th-century building. Although no one wanted to live there in the 1970s and '80s, St. Kilda is now a very smart address. Many visitors choose to stay here and hop on a tram to the city center.

GETTING HERE AND AROUND

Several trams travel to St. Kilda from central Melbourne. Trams 96 (from Bourke Street) and 12 (from Collins Street) head east–west through the city center, then go all the way south to St. Kilda. Tram 16 runs to St. Kilda from Melbourne University along Swanston Street, as does Tram 3A at weekends. A good place to board these latter two trams is the stop between Flinders Street Station and Federation Square. It's a pleasant ride down St. Kilda Road into Fitzroy Street and past the bay.

Acland Street. An alphabet soup of Chinese, French, Italian, and Lebanese eateries—along with a fantastic array of cake shops—lines the sidewalk of St. Kilda's ultra-hip restaurant row. The street faces Luna Park. ⊠ *Acland St., between Barkly St. and Shakespeare Grove, St. Kilda.*

Luna Park. A much-photographed Melbourne landmark, the park's entrance is a huge, gaping mouth, swallowing visitors whole and delivering them into a world of ghost trains, pirate ships, and carousels. Built in 1912, the **Scenic Railway** is the park's most popular ride. It's said to be the oldest continually operating roller coaster in the world. The railway is less roller coaster and more a relaxed loop-the-loop, with stunning views of Port Phillip Bay between each dip and turn. Luna Park is a five-minute stroll southeast of St. Kilda. ⊠ *Lower Esplanade, St.*

Melbourne Suburbs

KEY
+—+ Rail Lines
- - - Tram Line

0   1/4 mi
0   400 m

Kilda ☎ *03/9525–5033, 1300/888272* ⊕ *www.lunapark.com.au* ✉ *Free entry, A$10.95 per ride, A$46.95 for unlimited rides* ☉ *Summer (late Oct.–Apr. 27): Fri. 7 pm–11 pm, Thurs. and Sat., school holidays, and public holidays 11–11, Sun.–Wed. 11–8. Winter (Apr. 28–late Oct.): weekends and public holidays 11–6.*

FITZROY

Melbourne's bohemian quarter is 2 km (1 mile) northeast of the city center. If you're looking for an Afghan camel bag or a secondhand paperback, or perhaps to hear some tunes while sipping a pint in a backstreet beer garden, Fitzroy is the place. Take Tram 11 or 86 from the city.

GETTING HERE AND AROUND

Fitzroy is an easy place to access, both from the city and nearby suburbs. From the city, take the No. 11 from Collins Street. It will take you all the way up Brunswick Street. From Bourke Street, hop on the No. 86 tram for a ride to Gertrude Street.

Brunswick Street. Along with Lygon Street in nearby Carlton, Brunswick Street is one of Melbourne's favorite places to dine. You might want to step into a simple kebab shop serving tender meats for less than A$12, or opt for dinner at one of the stylish, highly regarded bar-restaurants. The street also has many galleries, bookstores, bars, arts-and-crafts shops, and clothes shops (vintage fashion is a feature). ✉ *Brunswick St., between Alexandra and Victoria Parades, Fitzroy.*

> ### A DAY AT THE RACES
>
> The usually serene atmosphere of Albert Park is turned into motor-head heaven every March, when Melbourne stages the Australian Grand Prix. It's the opening event of the Formula One season, with four full-throttle days of excitement on and off the track. Drivers scream around Albert Park Lake to the delight of fans and the horror of some nearby residents. Albert Park is 3 km (2 miles) south of the city center. ⊕ *www.grandprix.com.au.*

BRUNSWICK

Just 4 km (2 miles) north of the city center, Brunswick is Melbourne's multicultural heart. Here Middle Eastern spice shops sit next to avant-garde galleries, Egyptian supermarkets, Turkish tile shops, Japanese yakitori eateries, Lebanese bakeries, Indian haberdasheries, and secondhand bookstores. Take Tram 19 from the city.

GETTING HERE AND AROUND

Tram 19 travels from Flinders Street Station in the city along Elizabeth Street and Brunswick's main thoroughfare, Sydney Road. You can also catch a train to Brunswick; take the Upfield Railway Line from Flinders Street Station and alight at either Jewell, Brunswick, or Anstey stations—they're all in Brunswick.

FAMILY **CERES Community Environment Park.** On the banks of the Merri Creek in East Brunswick, this award-winning sustainability center is home to a permaculture and bushfood nursery. Buy local produce and crafts here, eat at the Merri Table Cafe, and explore the green technology

The groovy cafés of St. Kilda

displays. ✉ *45 Roberts St., at Stewart St., Brunswick East* ☎ *03/9389–0100* ⊕ *ceres.org.au* ✉ *Free* ☉ *Daily dawn–dusk.*

Sydney Road. Cultures collide on Sydney Road as Arabic mingles with French, Hindi does battle with Bengali, and the muezzin's call to prayer argues with Lebanese pop music. Scents intoxicate and colors beguile. Cafés serving everything from pastries to *tagines* (Moroccan stews) to Turkish delight sit shoulder-to-shoulder along the roadside with quirky record shops, antiques auction houses, and Bollywood video stores. ✉ *Sydney Rd. between Brunswick Rd. and Bell St., Brunswick.*

CARLTON

To see the best of Carlton's Victorian-era architecture, walk along Drummond Street, with its rows of gracious terrace houses (notably Rosaville at No. 46, Medley Hall at No. 48, and Lothian Terrace at No. 175), and Canning Street, which has a mix of workers' cottages and grander properties.

GETTING HERE AND AROUND
Carlton is served by the many Swanston Street tram routes that terminate at Melbourne University (located in Parkville, just west of Carlton). Trams 1 and 8 extend north beyond the university, turning into the top end of Lygon Street. Alternatively, catch a bus (No. 200 or 207) from Lonsdale Street to Carlton.

Carlton Gardens. Forty acres of tree-lined paths, artificial lakes, and flower beds in this English-style 19th-century park are the backdrop for the outstanding Melbourne Museum, and the World Heritage–listed

Royal Exhibition Building, erected in 1880. ✉ *Victoria Parade, at Nicholson, Carlton, and Rathdowne Sts., Carlton.*

Lygon Street. Known as Melbourne's Little Italy, Lygon Street is a perfect example of the city's multiculturalism: where once you'd have seen only Italian restaurants, there are now Thai, Malay, Caribbean, and Greek eateries. The city's famous café culture was also born here, with the arrival of Melbourne's first espresso machine at one of the street's Italian-owned cafés in the 1950s. ✉ *Lygon St. between Victoria and Alexandra Parades, Carlton.*

FAMILY **Melbourne Museum.** A spectacular, postmodern building (in Carlton Gardens) houses displays of the varied cultures around Australia and the Pacific Islands. The Bunjilaka exhibit explores the traditions of the country's Aboriginal groups, while the Australia Gallery focuses on Victoria's heritage (and includes the preserved body of Australia's greatest racehorse, Phar Lap). There's plenty for kids, too, with the wooded Forest Gallery, Children's Gallery (housed in what looks like a giant Rubik's Cube), Mind and Body Gallery, and Science and Life Gallery. The museum regularly hosts touring blockbuster exhibitions (additional fee). ✉ *Carlton Gardens, 11 Nicholson St., Carlton* ☎ *131–102 local, 03/8341–7777 international* ⊕ *www.museumvictoria.com.au/MelbourneMuseum* ✉ *A$12, children free* ☉ *Daily 10–5.*

SOUTH YARRA–PRAHRAN

One of the most chic and fashion-conscious areas to be on any given day (or night) is in South Yarra–Prahran. The area is chock-full of bars, eateries, and upscale boutiques.

GETTING HERE AND AROUND
Several trams, including Nos. 6, 8, 72, and 78, travel to either South Yarra or Prahran or both. No. 6 comes down St. Kilda Road from Flinders Street Station and turns into High Street, Prahran, while No. 8 turns into Domain Road (just south of the Royal Botanic Gardens) and then travels down Toorak Road. Tram 78 travels down Chapel Street from Richmond. You can also catch a train to both South Yarra and Prahran; take the Sandringham Line from Flinders Street Station.

Fodor's Choice **Chapel Street.** The heart of the trendy South Yarra–Prahran area, this
★ long road is packed with pubs, bars, notable restaurants, and upscale boutiques—more than 1,000 shops can be found within the precinct. Australian designers showcase their original designs at the fashion-conscious, upscale Toorak Road end of the street (nearest to the city). Walk south along Chapel Street to Greville Street and visit a small lane of hip bars, clothing boutiques, and record stores. Past Greville Street, at the south end of Chapel Street, it's grungier, with pawnshops and kitschy collectibles stores. ✉ *Chapel St. between Toorak and Dandenong Rds., Prahran* ☎ *03/9529–6331* ⊕ *www.chapelstreet.com.au.*

FAMILY **Royal Botanic Gardens.** Within its 100 acres are 12,000 species of native and imported plants and trees, sweeping lawns, and ornamental lakes populated with ducks and swans that love to be fed. The Children's Garden is a fun and interactive place for kids to explore. Summer brings alfresco performances of classic plays, usually Shakespeare, and children's classics like *Wind in the Willows,* as well as the popular Moonlight Cinema series. The present design and layout were the brainchild of W.R. Guilfoyle, curator and director of the gardens from 1873 to 1910. ⊠ *Birdwood Ave., South Yarra* ☎ *03/9252–2300* ⊕ *www.rbg. vic.gov.au* ⊠ *Free* ☼ *Daily 7:30–sunset. Children's Garden: Wed.–Sun. 10–sunset (closed mid-July–early Sept. for maintenance).*

OFF THE BEATEN PATH

Melbourne Zoo. Verdant gardens and open-environment animal enclosures are hallmarks of this world-renowned zoo, which is 4 km (2½ miles) north of the city center. A lion park, reptile house, and butterfly pavilion, where more than 1,000 butterflies flutter through the rain-forest setting, are onsite, as is a simulated African rain forest where a group of Western Lowland gorillas lives. The spectacular Trail of the Elephants, home of seven Asiatic elephants, has a village, tropical gardens, and a swimming pool. The orangutan sanctuary and baboon outlook are other highlights. It's possible to stay overnight with the Roar 'n' Snore package (A$199 per adult) and enjoy dinner, supper, breakfast, close encounters with animals, and a behind-the-scenes look at the zoo's operations. Twilight jazz bands serenade visitors on summer evenings. ⊠ *Elliott Ave., Parkville* ☎ *03/9285-9300, 1300/966784 bookings* ⊕ *www.zoo.org.au* ⊠ *A$31.60, children free* ☼ *Daily 9–5, select summer evenings to 9 or 9:30.*

BEACHES

Unlike Sydney, Melbourne is not known for its beaches. Nonetheless, there are several popular beaches on the shores of Port Phillip Bay. The best known are St. Kilda and Middle Brighton Beach. The latter is extremely picturesque, adorned with a colorful row of "bathing boxes" that runs along its shore. These vividly decorated little sheds are basically privately owned changing rooms—many dating back to the 1940s—but can sell for as much as a house in some parts of the city.

The absence of waves fails to provide the conditions for surfing; however, the brisk winds that whip across Port Phillip Bay make most of these beaches ideal for windsurfing and kitesurfing.

Middle Brighton Beach. Most commonly known for its 82 colorful and culturally significant bathing boxes, Brighton Beach is also ideal for families, since it's location in a cove means that it's protected from the wind. Perfect for those looking for a quieter spot to bathe than St. Kilda Beach, the Middle Brighton Baths is a nice place to view the boats and have a bite to eat. **Amenities:** parking (fee); toilets. **Best for:** solitude; swimming. ⊠ *Esplanade, Brighton.*

St. Kilda Beach. While there is no surf to speak of, this half-mile stretch of sand still remains one of the country's liveliest beaches as it's close to bars, restaurants, and hotels. While most people like to hang out on the sand, windsurfing, sailing, rollerblading, and beach volleyball are other popular activities. Two iconic landmarks—St. Kilda Baths and St. Kilda Pier—are close by and give visitors something to do on those blistering hot summer afternoons. The Sunday foreshore market is just minutes away as well. **Amenities:** food and drink; parking (fee); toilets. **Best for:** partiers; swimming; windsurfing. ⊠ *Marine Parade, St. Kilda.*

SPORTS AND THE OUTDOORS

AUSTRALIAN RULES FOOTBALL

This fast, vigorous game, played between teams of 18, is one of four kinds of football Down Under. Aussies also play Rugby League, Rugby Union, and soccer, but Australian Rules, widely known as "footy," is the one to which Victoria, South Australia, the Northern Territory, and Western Australia subscribe. It's the country's most popular spectator sport.

Despite its name, novice observers frequently ask the question: "What rules?" The ball can be kicked or punched in any direction, but never thrown. Players make spectacular leaps vying to catch ("mark") a kicked ball before it touches the ground, for which they earn a free kick. The game is said to be at its finest in Melbourne, where it was invented in the mid-19th century.

Melbourne Cricket Ground. The Melbourne Cricket Ground is the prime venue for AFL games. ⊠ *Brunton Ave., Yarra Park* ☎ *03/9657–8867* ⊕ *www.mcg.org.au.*

Ticketmaster7. Tickets for Australian Rules Football are available through Ticketek (MCG games) or Ticketmaster (Etihad Stadium) or at the playing fields. ☎ *1300/136–122 Ticketmaster, 132–849 Ticketek* ⊕ *www.ticketmaster.com.au.*

BICYCLING

Melbourne and its environs contain more than 100 km (62 miles) of bike paths, including scenic routes along the Yarra River and Port Phillip Bay. The Beach Road Trail extends 19 km (12 miles) around Port Phillip Bay from Elwood Beach to Sandringham; the new Docklands area of Melbourne can be cycled around—start on the Southbank Promenade, travel west, and then cross over the new Webb Street to Docklands Park and Harbour Esplanade; you can join the Main Yarra Trail bicycle route at the mouth of the Yarra River, just north of the West Gate Bridge or at Southbank. You can then follow the Yarra River for 35 km (22 miles) until it meets up with the Mullum Mullum Creek Trail in Templestowe in Melbourne's eastern suburbs. Information on paths can be found on the websites for each council area, or via VicRoads (⊕ *www.vicroads.vic.gov.au*). Bicycle Network can also give some advice.

The City of Melbourne has a bike share scheme around the city. Hire begins at A$2.90 for half an hour, but daily and weekly hire is also available. See ⊕ *www.melbournebikeshare.com.au* for the details. Note that under Australian law, all cyclists must wear helmets.

Bicycle Network. This company can provide advice on cycling in Melbourne and Victoria, including information about the road rules in relation to cyclists. The office sells some maps and books for cycling tours. Its website has trail maps. ⊠ *4/246 Bourke St., City Center* ☎ *03/8376–8888* ⊕ *www.bicyclenetwork.com.au.*

Real Melbourne Bike Tours. The daily bike tours offered by this company promise to show the best of Melbourne. The four-hour rides (which depart at 10 am) include coffee and cakes in Little Italy and lunch. The company also rents bicycles from A$15 an hour (A$35 per day), and provides a map of five top rides, with suggestions of where to eat and drink. It's on the edge of the Yarra River just near Princes Bridge and Federation Square. ⊠ *Vault 14, Federation Sq., City Center* ✛ *On riverbank level, near Princes Walk* ☎ *0417/339–203* ⊕ *www.rentabike. net.au* 🖃 *From A$110.*

BOATING

Studley Park Boathouse. Studley Park Boathouse, which opened in 1864, rents canoes, kayaks, and rowboats for journeys on a peaceful stretch of the lower Yarra River, about 7 km (4½ miles) east of the city center. Rentals are A$36 per hour for a two-person canoe or rowboat and A$44 per hour for a four-person rowboat. The boathouse is open daily 9–5 and has a café (lunch and weekend breakfast) and restaurant (weekends) with lovely river views. ⊠ *1 Boathouse Rd., Kew* ☎ *03/9853– 1828* ⊕ *www.studleyparkboathouse.com.au.*

CAR RACING

Australian Formula 1 Grand Prix. Australian Formula 1 Grand Prix is a popular—but increasingly controversial—fixture on Melbourne's calendar of annual events. It's held every March in the suburb of Albert Park, a small neighborhood 4 km (2½ miles) south of the city that encompasses the area surrounding Albert Park Lake. ⊠ *220 Albert Rd., South Melbourne* ☎ *03/9258–7100* ⊕ *www.grandprix.com.au.*

GOLF

Melbourne has the largest number of championship golf courses in Australia.

Albert Park Golf Course. Four kilometers (2½ miles) south of the city, Albert Park Golf Course is an 18-hole, par-72 course beside Albert Park Lake, where the Formula 1 Grand Prix is held in March. Clubs, buggies, and carts can be hired at the course. Golf lessons for everyone from beginners to advanced players, starting at A$65 for a half-hour lesson for a single player. ⊠ *Queens Rd., Albert Park* ☎ *03/9510–5588* ⊕ *www. albertparkgolf.com.au* 🖃 *Weekdays: 18 holes A$34, 9 holes A$25; weekends: 18 holes A$39, 9 holes A$25* ⅃ *18 holes, 6280 yards, par 72.*

Brighton Public Golf Course. The 18-hole, par-67 Brighton Public Golf Course has lovely scenery, with trees and wetlands, but is quite busy on weekends and midweek mornings. The first nine holes are considered more challenging than the last nine. Club rental is available for A$20, and carts are available for A$40. The course allows unlimited playing after 4 pm in winter and after 5:30 pm in summer in its Twilight Golf Specials (A$15). ⊠ *230 Dendy St., Brighton* ☎ *03/9592–1388* ⊕ *www. brightongolfcourse.com.au* 🖃 *18 holes A$31, 9 holes A$22* ⅃ *18 holes, 5335 yards, par 67.*

Sandringham Golf Links. Five minutes from the beach, Sandringham Golf Course is one of the better public courses, and one of several in Melbourne's renowned (coastal) Sand Belt. Located opposite the Royal Melbourne Golf Club, Sandringham is an 18-hole, par-72 course. The course contains a picnic area with a coin-operated barbecue for players to use before or after their round. A licensed café also operates on-site. ⊠ *Cheltenham Rd., Sandringham* ☎ *03/9598–3590* ⊕ *www.sandringhamgolfcourse.com.au* 🖭 *18 holes A$34, 9 holes A$22* ⚐ *18 holes, 6174 yards, par 72.*

FAMILY **Yarra Bend Golf Course.** Despite being just 4 km (2½ miles) northeast from the city, this challenging course seems a world away, due to long length and surrounding parkland. Ten thousand bats have also made it their home on the back 9. A newly built golf range is ideal to practice your game before the round. The course even has a 36-hole adventure mini golf course (A$25), suitable for children and adults. ⊠ *Yarra Bend Rd., Fairfield* ☎ *03/9481–3729* ⊕ *www.yarrabendgolf.com* 🖭 *Weekdays: 18 holes A$32, 9 holes A$25; weekends: 18 and 9 holes, A$38* ⚐ *18 holes, 6056 yards, par 70.*

HORSE RACING

Melbourne is the only city in the world to declare a public holiday for a horse race—the Melbourne Cup—held on the first Tuesday in November since 1861. The Cup is also a fashion parade, and most of Melbourne society turns out in full regalia. The rest of the country comes to a standstill, with schools, shops, offices, and factories tuning in to the action.

The city has four top-class racetracks.

Caulfield Race Course. Caulfield Race Course, 10 km (6 miles) from the city, runs the Blue Diamond Stakes in February and the Caulfield Cup in October. ⊠ *Station St., Caulfield* ☎ *03/9257–7200* ⊕ *www.melbourneracingclub.net.au* 🖭 *From A$10.*

Champions: Thoroughbred Racing Gallery. Horse-racing information, displays, and a mini-shrine to Australia's most famous race house, Phar Lap, take center stage at this gallery in the National Sports Museum. ⊠ *Melbourne Cricket Ground, Brunton Ave., Gate 3, Yarra Park* ☎ *03/9657–8879* ⊕ *www.nsm.org.au* 🖭 *A$30* 🕓 *10–5 on nonmatch days.*

Flemington Race Course. Australia's premier racecourse, 3 km (2 miles) outside the city, is home to the Melbourne Cup each November. ⊠ *448 Epsom Rd., Flemington* ☎ *1300/727–575* ⊕ *www.flemington.com.au* 🖭 *From A$12.*

Moonee Valley Race Course. Moonee Valley Race Course is 6 km (4 miles) from town and hosts the Cox Plate race in October. ⊠ *McPherson St., Moonee Ponds* ☎ *03/9373–2222 international, 1300/843825 local* ⊕ *www.thevalley.com.au* 🖭 *From A$10.*

William Hill Park. This park, also known as Sandown Race Track, hosts the Zipping Classic each November. ⊠ *Corrigan Rd. and Princes Hwy., Springvale* ☎ *03/9518–1300* ⊕ *www.sandown.net.au* 🖭 *From A$10.*

TENNIS

Fodor's Choice   **Australian Open.** The Australian Open, held in January, is one of the
★   world's four Grand Slam tournaments. You can buy tickets at the event
or from Ticketek. ⊠ *Batman Ave.* ☎ *03/9039–9407 tickets* ⊕ *www.*
australianopen.com.

Fawkner Park Tennis Centre. Play tennis here on six synthetic-grass outdoor
courts. ⊠ *Fawkner Park, Toorak Rd. W, South Yarra* ☎ *03/9820–0611*
⊕ *www.fawknerparktenniscentre.com* ⌨ *Court hire from A$25 an hr.*

Melbourne Park Tennis Centre. This center has 26 outdoor and 12 hard
indoor Rebound Ace courts, plus 8 Italian Clay Courts. Play is canceled
during the Australian Open in January. ⊠ *Batman Ave., City Center*
☎ *1300/836647* ⊕ *www.mopt.com.au* ⌨ *Court hire from A$15 an hr.*

Powlett Reserve Tennis Centre. This center has five synthetic-grass outdoor
courts. ⊠ *Powlett Reserve, Albert St., East Melbourne* ☎ *03/9417–6511*
⊕ *powlettreservetenniscentre.com* ⌨ *Court hire from A$20 an hr.*

WHERE TO EAT

Melbourne has fabulous food, and is known in some circles as Australia's
food capital. The restaurants themselves are often exceptionally stylish
and elegant—or totally edgy and funky in their own individual way.
Some are even deliberately grungy. The dining scene is a vast array of
cuisines and experiences that's constantly evolving. The swankiest (and
most expensive) restaurants all have five- to eight-course degustation
menus (with the opportunity to wine-match each course), but newer
restaurants are opting for tapas-style or grazing plates. Flexibility is the
new word in dining—restaurants are often also funky bars and vice versa.

Use the coordinate (✛ B2) at the end of each listing to locate a site on
the corresponding map.

CITY CENTER

$$$ ✕ **Becco.** Every city center needs a place like this, with a drop-in bar
ITALIAN   and lively dining room. At lunchtime no-time-to-dawdle business types
tuck into gnochi osso bucco with gremolata, while those with a sweet
tooth will go weak at the knees over a decadently refreshing mixed
gelato with almond praline. Things get a little moodier at night, when
a Campari and soda at the bar is an almost compulsory precursor
to dinner. ⑤ *Average main: A$38* ⊠ *11–25 Crossley St., City Center*
☎ *03/9663–3000* ⊕ *www.becco.com.au* ⊗ *Closed Sun. No lunch Sat.*
⌨ *Reservations essential* ✛ *1:B4.*

$$ ✕ **Chin Chin.** Shared plates of Asian dishes, from Thai papaya salad to
ASIAN   rendang curry and gado-gado, form the basis of Chin Chin's popular
menu. Modeled on hawker-style dining, the restaurant doesn't take
reservations, so you may have a short wait for a table. Come for an
early or late lunch to avoid the rush, or kill some time at the attached
Go Go Bar. ⑤ *Average main: A$25* ⊠ *125 Flinders La., City Center*
☎ *03/8663–2000* ⊕ *www.chinchinrestaurant.com.au* ⌨ *Reservations*
not accepted ⊟ No credit cards ✛ *1:B5.*

$$$$
MODERN
AUSTRALIAN
✕ **ezard.** Chef Teage Ezard's adventurous—and often exhilarating—take on fusion pushes the boundaries between Eastern and Western flavors. Some combinations may appear unusual, like the pan-fried sesame-crusted John Dory with gnocchi, nettle, black rice paper, Jerusalem artichoke, and chestnut custard, but everything works deliciously at this spot in the funky Adelphi hotel. And as with all upscale restaurants these days, there's an eight-course tasting menu (A$165 per person) featuring mouthwatering steamed spanner crab dumplings with Yarra Valley salmon roe, chervil cress, and coconut *tom kha*. A three-course lunch express menu (includes glass of wine) is great value at A$55. The dessert menu by itself is a celebration of indulgence. $ *Average main: A$53 ⊠ Adelphi Hotel, 187 Flinders La., City Center* ☎ *03/9639–6811* ⊕ *www.ezard.com.au* ☾ *Closed Sun. No lunch Sat.* ♨ *Reservations essential* ✛ *1:A5.*

$$$
CANTONESE
✕ **Flower Drum.** Superb Cantonese cuisine is the hallmark of one of Australia's truly great Chinese restaurants, which is still receiving awards after opening in 1975. The restrained elegance of the design, deftness of the service, and intelligence of the wine list puts most other restaurants to shame. Those in the know don't order from the menu at all but simply ask the waiter to bring the specials, which often changes between lunch and dinner with the arrival of produce fresh from suppliers; the Cantonese roast duck is one of the highlights. A delicious finish to the meal is the sweetened double-boiled almond soup. $ *Average main: A$40 ⊠ 17 Market La., City Center* ☎ *03/9662–3655* ⊕ *flowerdrum. melbourne* ☾ *No lunch Sun.* ♨ *Reservations essential* ☞ *No jacket or tie required, but men must wear shirt with collar* ✛ *1:B4.*

$$$$
ITALIAN
✕ **Grossi Florentino.** Since 1928, dining at Florentino has meant experiencing the pinnacle of Melbourne hospitality. After taking a seat in the famous mural room, with its huge chandeliers, wooden panels, and Florentine murals, you can sample dishes like suckling pig, and duck tortellini. At lunch, the upstairs restaurant serves two courses for A$65; the three-course dinner menu is A$130. The five-course tasting menu, called the Gran Tour (A$150), is also a popular option. Downstairs, the Grill has more businesslike fare, while the Cellar Bar is perfect for a glass of wine and pasta of the day. $ *Average main: A$65 ⊠ 80 Bourke St., City Center* ☎ *03/9662–1811* ⊕ *www.grossiflorentino.com* ☾ *Closed Sun.* ♨ *Reservations essential* ✛ *1:B4.*

$$$
JAPANESE
✕ **Hanabishi.** Touted as the city's best Japanese restaurant, Hanabishi sits in slightly seedy King Street, an area known for its bars, club venues, and occasionally unsavory clientele. With wooden floors, blue walls, and traditional ceramic serving trays, Hanabishi is the playground of Osakan chef Akio Soga, whose seasonal menu includes such gems as abalone sashimi and aburi salmon. There are long lists of hot and chilled sake and wines, ranging from reasonable to pricey. The bento boxes, which are culinary works of art, feature Wagyu beef and are a favorite with the lunchtime crowd. $ *Average main: A$40 ⊠ 187 King St., City Center* ☎ *03/9670–1167* ⊕ *www.hanabishi.com.au* ☾ *Closed weekends* ♨ *Reservations essential* ✛ *1:A3.*

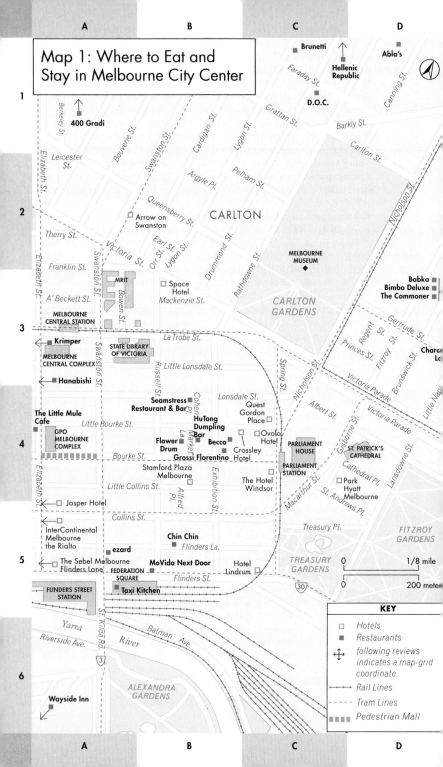

Map 1: Where to Eat and Stay in Melbourne City Center

A

B

C

D

Brunetti

Abla's

400 Gradi

Hellenic Republic

Berkeley St.

Leicester St.

Faraday St.

Grattan St.

D.O.C.

Canning St.

Barkly St.

Carlton St.

Bouverie St.

Swanston St.

Cardigan St.

Lygon St.

1

Elizabeth St.

Argyle Pl.

Pelham St.

Queensberry St.

CARLTON

Arrow on Swanston

Therry St.

Earl St.

Orr St.

Lygon St.

Drummond St.

Rathdowne St.

Nicholson St.

MELBOURNE MUSEUM

Babka
Bimbo Deluxe
The Commoner

2

Elizabeth St.

Franklin St.

A' Beckett St.

Victoria St.

Swanston St.

MRIT

Space Hotel

Mackenzie St.

CARLTON GARDENS

Gertrude St.

MELBOURNE CENTRAL STATION

Bowen St.

Regent St.

Princes St.

Fitzroy St.

Brunswick St.

Charc
Lo

3

Krimper

MELBOURNE CENTRAL COMPLEX

Hanabishi

STATE LIBRARY OF VICTORIA

La Trobe St.

Swanston St.

Russell St.

Little Lonsdale St.

Spring St.

Nicholson St.

Victoria Parade

Gisborne St.

Little Nap

The Little Mule Cafe

GPO MELBOURNE COMPLEX

Little Bourke St.

Seamstress Restaurant & Bar

HuTong Dumpling Bar

Cohen Pl.

Lonsdale St.

Quest Gordon Place

Albert St.

Victoria Parade

4

Elizabeth St.

Little Bourke St.

Flower Drum

Market La.

Becco

Grossi Florentino

Ovolo Hotel

Crossley Hotel

PARLIAMENT HOUSE

ST. PATRICK'S CATHEDRAL

Lansdowne St.

Bourke St.

Stamford Plaza Melbourne

Little Collins St.

Alfred Pl.

Exhibition St.

PARLIAMENT STATION

The Hotel Windsor

Cathedral Pl.

Park Hyatt Melbourne

St. Andrews Pl.

Jasper Hotel

Collins St.

Macarthur St.

Treasury Pl.

FITZROY GARDENS

InterContinental Melbourne the Rialto

Chin Chin

5

The Sebel Melbourne Flinders Lane

ezard

MoVida Next Door

Flinders La.

FEDERATION SQUARE

Hotel Lindrum

Flinders St.

TREASURY GARDENS

0   1/8 mile

0   200 meter

Taxi Kitchen

30

FLINDERS STREET STATION

St. Kilda Rd.

Yarra

Riverside Ave.

Batman Ave.

River

3

KEY

☐	*Hotels*
◼	*Restaurants*
⬦	*following reviews indicates a map-grid coordinate*
┼┼┼	*Rail Lines*
---	*Tram Lines*
▰▰▰	*Pedestrian Mall*

6

ALEXANDRA GARDENS

Wayside Inn

A

B

C

D

$$ ✕**HuTong Dumpling Bar.** The name means "alleyway" and in a sea of
CHINESE dumpling houses in Melbourne, down this little alleyway, you'll find
Fodor's Choice the best of them all. The boiled pork dumplings are popular (A$14.20
★ for eight), though the panfried variations of pork, chicken, prawn,
and chives hold up well, too. Signature dish, wantons with Hot Chilli
Sauce (A$10.80), packs a punch and is great on a cold day. The staff is
highly trained, and if the space on the ground floor is too snug, ask to
go upstairs where there's room to breathe. Bookings are essential, but
if you're feeling lucky, arrive at 11:30 am on the dot to try for a table—
there will probably be a line of hopefuls already. $ *Average main: A$26*
✉ *14–16 Market La., City Center* ☎ *03/9650–8128* ⊕ *www.hutong.
com.au* ✛ *1:B4.*

$ ✕**Krimper.** Designed to showcase the building's warehouse origins,
AUSTRALIAN Krimper's design is rough-hewn but warm. In the center of the large
space is a huge box that once held the elevator; now it's a cozy dining
space for four. Hidden away among former motorcycle repair shops
and a burgeoning dining street, Krimper serves innovative food, excel-
lent coffee, and hot chocolate from local company, Mork. Breakfast
may include a baked tartiflette of Jerusalem artichoke, potato hash
brown and melted cheese, or Duck in Pan—duck prosciutto, a duck
egg, and kale chips. Lunches include a Wagyu burger and pan fried
barramundi. $ *Average main: A$19* ✉ *20 Guildford La., City Center*
☎ *03/9043–8844* ⊕ *www.krimper.com.au* ✛ *1:A3.*

$ ✕**The Little Mule Cafe.** Melburnians love to head out for breakfast, and
AUSTRALIAN Little Mule is one of many popular laneway cafés satisfying the hun-
ger. Excellent coffee is teamed with simple meals made in the tiny,
open kitchen. Look for the fresh muffins as well as the breakfast favor-
ite, smashed avocado and feta cheese on toast. $ *Average main: A$13*
✉ *19 Somerset Pl., City Center* ☎ *03/9670–4904* ⊕ *thelittlemule.com*
⊗ *Closed Sun.* ✛ *1:A4.*

$ ✕**MoVida Next Door.** As the name suggests, this popular Spanish tapas
SPANISH restaurant is next door to something—in this case the grown-up parent
restaurant called MoVida. This is the casual little sister (or daughter)
for those who don't want to linger too long over their dinner. Dishes
range from tapas (from A$3.50 to A$9.50), like chorizo-filled Catalan
potato bomb with spicy sauce, to *racion* (bigger plates ranging from
A$13.50 to A$30), which might include pig's ear *a la plancha* (grilled)
with Guindillas. Finish the meal off with *churros con chocolate* (Spanish
fried dough served with a hot, thick chocolate drink). If you're after a
bigger meal, book table space at MoVida next door. Both eateries are
owned by Frank Camorra, a big name in the Melbourne dining scene.
$ *Average main: A$17* ✉ *1 Hosier La., City Center* ☎ *03/9663–3038*
⊕ *www.movida.com.au* ⊗ *No lunch Tues.–Thurs. Closed Mon.* ✛ *1:B5.*

$$ ✕**Seamstress Restaurant & Bar.** This bar-restaurant occupies a heritage-
MODERN ASIAN listed four-story building that has housed an undergarment manufac-
turer, a 1930s sweatshop, a brothel, and even a Buddhist temple (but
not at the same time). Asian dishes, in small, medium, and large por-
tions, are designed to be shared. Everything is served in an atmospheric
brick-walled first-floor dining area decorated with swaths of fabric and
sewing machines; the wine selection is stored in battered metal luggage

4

lockers. Small dishes include pods of snake bean and golden sweet kumaro poached in wanton pastry, green pea, and coriander puree. Favorite medium dishes include seafood yellow curry and honey soy braised Wagyu shin. $ *Average main: A$34* ⊠ *113 Lonsdale St., City Center* ☎ *03/9663–6363* ⊕ *www.seamstress.com.au* ⊙ *Closed Sun. No lunch Sat.* ⊹ *1:B4.*

$$$ ✕ **Taxi Kitchen.** Occupying an innovatively designed steel-and-glass space
MODERN above Federation Square, Taxi boasts both extraordinary food and
AUSTRALIAN spectacular views over Melbourne. East meets West on a menu that combines Japanese flavors—tempura prawn tails with yuzu and nori salt—with such European-inspired fare as slow-roasted lamb with root vegetables and jus. There is also an impressive list of new- and old-world wines. To taste some of Australia's best craft beers, have a pre-meal drink at the Transport Bar on the ground floor. $ *Average main: A$45* ⊠ *Level 1, Transport Hotel, Federation Sq., Flinders St. at St. Kilda Rd., City Center* ☎ *03/9654–8808* ⊕ *www.taxikitchen.com.au* ⌂ *Reservations essential* ⊹ *1:A5.*

$$$ ✕ **Wayside Inn.** Another addition to the city's gastropubs, this fully reno-
STEAKHOUSE vated historic building is a pleasant walk from bustling Southbank. The menu concentrates on high-quality aged cuts of steak from rural Victoria and Tasmania (A$32–A$140), but the daily rotisserie, which features a different meat or poultry on the spit, is also popular (Friday's suckling pig is a winner). There's an impressive local craft beer list, knowledgeable staff, and a comfortable beer garden that round out the awesome experience. $ *Average main: A$42* ⊠ *446 City Rd., South Melbourne* ☎ *03/9682–9119* ⊕ *www.waysideinn.com.au* ⊙ *Closed Sun.* ⊹ *1:A6.*

CARLTON

$$ ✕ **Abla's.** Matriarch Abla Amad has been re-creating the much loved
LEBANESE family recipes from her homeland of Lebanon since 1979. This intimate restaurant resembles a lounge room of a family house, which with Abla walking around talking to diners, adds to the feeling of being looked after. The signature dish, and one of the most well-known in the city, is the exquisitely flavored rice pilaf with minced lamb, chicken, almonds, and pine nuts (A$27); it's also part of a 12-course banquet (A$60) for those hungry enough. Bookings are recommended and you can BYO wine. $ *Average main: A$30* ⊠ *109 Elgin St., Carlton* ☎ *03/9347–0006* ⊕ *www.ablas.com.au* ⊙ *No lunch Sat.–Wed.* ⊹ *1:D1.*

$$ ✕ **Brunetti.** First opened in 1974, this iconic Romanesque bakery has
CAFÉ moved around Carlton on several occasions, and the masses have fol-lowed. Its biggest undertaking is in the heart of Lygon Street and still filled with perfect biscotti, mouthwatering cakes, and great service. In addition to an expanded lunch menu, a wood-fire oven—specially imported from Italy—makes pizzas, and you can finish it all off with a perfect espresso, or a thick European-style hot chocolate with a *cornetto con crema* (custard-filled croissant). Enjoy the same tempting delights at branches in Flinders Lane and Myer department store in Bourke Street. $ *Average main: A$23* ⊠ *380 Lygon St., Carlton* ☎ *03/9347–2801* ⊕ *www.brunetti.com.au* ⊹ *1:C1.*

$$ ✕**D.O.C.** A major player in Melbourne's pizza wars, D.O.C. has per-
ITALIAN fected the art of using fresh, simple ingredients to create something spe-
cial. The real treats lie in their pizza of the day. One with scampi, salsa
verde, buffalo mozzarella, and mentuccia (a type of mint) might be on
offer, or perhaps another with pork and venison sausage, wild mush-
room, and green chili (around A$25). Whatever is in season or comes
in, they will use. A chocolate pizza is at the ready for those with a sweet
tooth. They also have a delicatessen around the corner (*330 Lygon St.*),
which could be a good option for a packed lunch, and there's another
location in the picturesque seaside town of Mornington. ⑤ *Average
main: A$25* ✉ *295 Drummond St., Carlton* ☏ *03/9347–2998* ⊕ *www.
docgroup.net* ✚ *1:C1.*

ST. KILDA

$$$ ✕**Café di Stasio.** This upscale bistro treads a very fine line between
ITALIAN mannered elegance and decadence. A sleek marble bar and modishly
ravaged walls contribute to the sense that you've stepped into a scene
from *La Dolce Vita.* Happily, the restaurant is as serious about its food
as its sense of style. Crisply roasted duck is now a local legend, and the
pasta is always al dente. If the amazingly delicate crayfish omelet is on
the menu, do yourself a favor and order it. A lunch special (two courses
with wine and coffee) for A$35 is a great value if you're nearby. For
an informal drink before your meal, an adjoining bar has local wines
and a snack menu. ⑤ *Average main: A$39* ✉ *31 Fitzroy St., St. Kilda*
☏ *03/9525–3999* ⌦ *Reservations essential* ✚ *2:A6.*

$$$ ✕**Circa the Prince.** This light-filled space with a central, glass-roofed
AUSTRALIAN courtyard and seasonal menu draws on Victorian fisheries, farms, and
Fodor's Choice other local producers. Sustainable and organic ingredients include line-
★ caught fish, Milawa free-range poultry, and pasture-fed Black Angus
beef. You can also join the sommelier in the see-through cellar to select
a bottle from the exhaustive and tempting wine list. ⑤ *Average main:
A$39* ✉ *2 Acland St., St. Kilda* ☏ *03/9536–1122* ⊕ *www.circa.com.au/
food* ⌦ *Reservations essential* ✚ *2:A6.*

$$ ✕**Dog's Bar.** With its blazing fires, artfully smoky walls, and striking,
MEDITERRANEAN art deco–ish wrought-iron ceiling lights, this two-decade-old restaurant
has a lived-in, neighborly look. The food is good, its Australian wine
is taken very seriously, and the kitchen is open until late each night.
⑤ *Average main: A$22* ✉ *54 Acland St., St. Kilda* ☏ *03/9593–9535*
⊕ *www.dogsbar.com.au* ✚ *2:A6.*

$$$ ✕**Donovan's.** Grab a window table at this very popular bayside restau-
AUSTRALIAN rant (housed in the former 1920s bathing pavilion), and enjoy wide-
open views of St. Kilda beach and its passing parade of in-line skaters,
skateboarders, dog walkers, and ice-cream lickers. As you'd expect,
seafood is the highlight, and it's expertly woven into wonderful pastas
and risottos. Espresso soufflé, mandarin and rose petal sorbet, or Sicil-
ian pistachio ice cream finish the meal off nicely. Owners Kevin and
Gail Donovan are such natural hosts you may feel like bunking down
on the plush cushions near the cozy fireplace. ⑤ *Average main: A$47*
✉ *40 Jacka Blvd., St. Kilda* ☏ *03/9534–8221* ⊕ *www.donovanshouse.
com.au* ⌦ *Reservations essential* ✚ *2:A6.*

Melbourne's restaurant scene is a global potpourri of ethnic influences.

$
AUSTRALIAN ✗ **Dr Jekyll.** Primarily a place for breakfast and brunch, Dr Jekyll serves variations on the breakfast classics. From chai-spiced, five-grain porridge to its own Jekyll eggs, served with chorizo and feta, this family-friendly restaurant serves local, seasonal produce with flair. Dr Jekyll also sells premade meals and a range of cheeses and cured meats, in case you'd like to picnic on the beach at St. Kilda. ⓢ *Average main: A$16* ✉ *107 Grey St., St. Kilda* ☎ *03/9525–5999* ⊕ *www.drjekyll.com. au* ⊗ *No dinner Sun.–Thurs.* ✛ *2:A6.*

SOUTH YARRA–PRAHRAN

$$
ITALIAN ✗ **Caffe e Cucina.** If you're looking for a quintessential Italian dining experience in a place where it's easy to imagine yourself back in the old country, this is it. Fashionable, look-at-me types flock here for coffee and pastries downstairs, or more-leisurely meals upstairs in the warm, woody dining room. Try the melt-in-your-mouth gnocchi, or calamari Sant' Andrea (lightly floured and shallow fried). Save room for dessert—the tiramisu is even better-looking than the crowd. ⓢ *Average main: A$35* ✉ *581 Chapel St., South Yarra* ☎ *03/9827–4139* ⊕ *www. caffeecucina.com.au* ✛ *2:D5.*

RICHMOND

$
VIETNAMESE
Fodor's Choice
★ ✗ **I Love Pho 264.** Tucking into a steaming bowl of *phở* (traditional noodle soup) at this Victoria Street restaurant is like channeling the backstreets of Hanoi and Saigon. While they also serve crunchy, deep-fried spring rolls and flavor-packed ricepaper rolls, the mainstay of the

menu (a blackboard on the wall) is various combinations of *bò* (beef) and *gà* (chicken) with noodles in aromatic stock. Each order comes with a piled plate of Vietnamese mint, bean shoots, and lemon wedges, and there are bottles of chili paste and fish sauce on every mock-marble plastic table. This restaurant is crowded with Vietnamese and other *phŏ* lovers on weekends, so you often have to line up on the footpath, but turnover is fast so its never long before you are seated and eating some of Melbourne's best—and cheapest—food. I Love Pho also has an outlet at the Melbourne Emporium food hall in the city center. ⑤ *Average main: A$10* ✉ *264 Victoria St., Richmond* ☎ *03/9427–7749* ⊕ *pholove.com.au* ✛ *2:C1.*

$$ ╳ **Richmond Hill Café and Larder.** This bright and buzzy café–cum–pro-
CAFÉ duce store is popular with those seeking a late breakfast and brunch that extends well into the day. It's so popular you might have to wait briefly if you haven't booked a table. The bistro fare brims with wonderful flavors, from house-made dips and charcuterie boards to seasonal salads, seafood, and burgers. Desserts are mouthwateringly simple and impossible to resist. After you've eaten, pick up some marvelous cheese and country-style bread from the adjoining cheese room and grocery. ⑤ *Average main: A$25* ✉ *48–50 Bridge Rd., Richmond* ☎ *03/9421–2808* ⊕ *www.rhcl.com.au* ☾ *No dinner* ✛ *2:C2.*

FITZROY

$$ ╳ **Anada.** A chalkboard on the exposed brick wall lists eight dry and six
SPANISH sweet sherries to start (or finish), and there are Spanish and Portuguese
Fodor's Choice wines to accompany your selection of tapas and *raciones* (larger shared
★ plates). Seated at a table or on a stool at the bar, begin with chargrilled mussels, and go on to confit pork belly, or put in a request for the paella. Just leave room for dessert; the churros and chocolate are sinful. If you really can't decide, a dessert tasting plate for two absolves you of making a decision. ⑤ *Average main: A$25* ✉ *197 Gertrude St., Fitzroy* ☎ *03/9415–6101* ⊕ *anada.com.au* ☾ *No lunch weekdays* ✛ *2:B1.*

$ ╳ **Babka.** Food lovers in the know are often found loitering at this tiny,
CAFÉ bustling café. Try the excellent pastries, fresh-baked breads, or more substantial offerings like the Russian borscht (beetroot and cabbage soup) or menemen—scrambled eggs with chili, mint, tomato, and a sprinkling of feta cheese. The corned beef sandwich is also a favorite. It's an all-day brunch-style café, and there are often lines, so be prepared to wait for a table. Some complain that the busy staff can be brusque. ⑤ *Average main: A$13* ✉ *358 Brunswick St., Fitzroy* ☎ *03/9416–0091* ☾ *Closed Mon. No dinner* ✛ *1:D3.*

$ ╳ **Bimbo Deluxe.** This bohemian bar, with deep comfy sofas and the feel
CAFÉ of a local student hangout, has the cheapest and possibly the most delicious pizzas in town. On weekdays between noon and 4 pm, Saturday 7 to 9 pm and Monday–Thursday from 7 to 11 pm you can order a dinner-plate-size pizza (from 23 choices) for a mere A$4. The queues of students and hungry lunchers start to form outside around 11:55. If you miss the special, fear not: the same great pizzas are only A$8–A$10 at other times. Try the Agnello (tomato, mozzarella, spiced lamb, arugula, pine nuts, and sultanas). If you're hankering for a sugar rush, there are

also sweet pizzas such as Belgian chocolate with mascarpone. A range of chilled infused vodkas—including watermelon and lychee—is available, as well as local craft beers. ⑤ *Average main: A$9* ⊠ *376 Brunswick St., Fitzroy* ☏ *03/9419–8600* ⊕ *www.bimbodeluxe.com.au* ✛ *1:D3*.

$$ ✕ **Charcoal Lane.** This restaurant could be described as taking a leaf from
AUSTRALIAN celebrity chef Jamie Oliver's book. It is a social enterprise restaurant providing vulnerable young people with an opportunity to transform their lives by gaining a traineeship in the restaurant business. Named after a song by acclaimed Aboriginal singer/songwriter Archie Roach, it is housed in the former health service community center, dubbed Charcoal Lane by the many Aboriginal people, who for decades would drop in and swap stories and wisdom. The menu includes many Australian bushland ingredients, and the dishes have an Aboriginal influence. They might include starters of wild foraged mushroom consommé or a wild food tasting plate of native produce. Mains include wallaby wrapped in Parma ham and twice-cooked saltbush lamb with rivermint. Desserts also have a "bush tucker" influence. ⑤ *Average main: A$35* ⊠ *136 Gertrude St., Fitzroy* ☏ *03/9235–9200* ⊕ *www.charcoallane.com.au* ☾ *Closed Sun. and Mon.* ✛ *1:D3*.

$$ ✕ **The Commoner.** The street-facing dining room here is packed with
MODERN BRITISH young couples enjoying some of the town's best and most eclectic U.K.-inspired food. The menu features "small food" taste sensations like wallaby tartare and citrus-cured kingfish, and larger dishes like pressed suckling pig and beef cheek with brassicas. A five-course "Feed Me" degustation menu is A$75 per person, or A$100 for an even flasher version. The wine list has depth in both Aussie and international selections. The space itself is cozy, featuring original art, and there's an enclosed garden out the back. ⑤ *Average main: A$32* ⊠ *122 Johnston St., Fitzroy* ☏ *03/9415–6876* ⊕ *www.thecommoner.com.au* ☾ *Closed Mon. and Tues. No dinner Wed. and Thurs.* ✛ *1:D3*.

$$ ✕ **Ladro.** A local favorite, this stellar Italian bistro emphasizes flavor
ITALIAN over starchy linen and stuffy attitude. Here, lamb rump is scented with garlic and parsley and slow-roasted to impossible tenderness, and the service is as upbeat as the wine list. Delicious wood-fired pizzas, that some insist are the best in the city, are yet another reason to visit this suburban gem (thankfully, it's only a short walk from the city). ⑤ *Average main: A$26* ⊠ *224 Gertrude St., Fitzroy* ☏ *03/9415–7575* ⊕ *ladro.com.au* ☾ *No lunch Mon.–Sat.* ⌸ *Reservations essential* ✛ *2:B1*.

BRUNSWICK

$$ ✕ **400 Gradi.** This is the place for authentic Italian pizza: chef Johnny Di
ITALIAN Francesco trained in Naples to make pizza to the Associazione Verace Pizza Napoletana rules. Besides pizza, the restaurant serves pasta and other Italian dishes. ⑤ *Average main: A$30* ⊠ *99 Lygon St., Brunswick East* ☏ *03/9380–2320* ⊕ *www.400gradi.com.au* ✛ *1:A1*.

$$ ✕ **Hellenic Republic.** Owned by well-known TV chef George Calombaris,
MODERN GREEK Hellenic Republic pays homage to Calombaris's Greek heritage, creating a lively taverna type setting with a focus on communal food. We suggest the Trapezi Menu (A$59), which consists of numerous courses including meat from the omnipresent spit, whose mouthwatering scent

Map 2: Where to Eat and Stay in the Melbourne Suburbs

KEY

☐ Hotels
■ Restaurants
✛ following reviews indicates a map-grid coordinate
┼─┼─┼ Rail Lines
- - - - Tram Lines

A   **B**   **C**   **D**

Smith St.
Wellington St.
Gertrude St.
■ Ladro
Anada
George St.
Little Victoria St.
FITZROY
Langridge St.
I Love
Pho 264 ■ →
Victoria Parade

CARLTON
Nicholson St.
Brunswick St.
Young St.
Albert St.
Powlett St.
Clarendon St.
Simpson St.
Hoddle St.

Baden
Powell
Hotel

Exhibition St.
Spring St.
MacArthur St.
Lansdowne St.
FITZROY
GARDENS

CITY
CENTER
Russell St.
TREASURY
GARDENS
EAST
MELBOURNE
29

Collins St.
Swanston St.
30
Wellington   Parade
YARRA
PARK
Richmond Hill
Café and Larder
Bridge Rd.
30
Church St.

Flinders Street
3
Batman   Ave.
Yarra River
ALEXANDRA
GARDENS
MELBOURNE
CRICKET
GROUND ◆
Brunton   Ave.
Punt Rd.
Rowena Pde.
Richmond Terr.
Lennox St.
Richmond Hill
Hotel

Crown
Metropol
2
3
QUEEN
VICTORIA
GARDENS
2
Swan St.
OLYMPIC
PARK
RICHMOND

SOUTHBANK
Grant St.
Sturt Street
1
Linlithgow Ave.
St. Kilda Road
Birdwood
Ave.
Alexandra Ave.
South Eastern Frwy.
Ornamental
Lake
Anderson St.
Punt Rd.
Kelso
Balmain St.
Yarra River
29
1

Dorcas St.
Bank St.
Park St.
2
Kings
Way
SOUTH
MELBOURNE
26
Queens St.
Adams St.
Arthur St.
Hope St.
Domain Rd.
Toorak Rd. West
26
Toorak Rd.
The Lyall
Hotel and Spa
SOUTH
YARRA
The
Como
Melbourne

Cobden
Clarendon St.
Church St.
26
Albert
Albert
Road
Lakeside Dr.
Road Dr.
1
FAWKNER
PARK
Leopold St.
St. Kilda Rd.
Caffe e
Cucina

■ Circa, The Prince
■ Café di Stasio
■ Dog's Bar
■ Donovan's
■ Dr. Jekyll
☐ The Prince
☐ Tolarno Hotel

Gunn
Island
Albert Park
Lake
ALBERT
PARK
Queens Road
Roy
St.
Argo St.
Commercial Rd.
Baker Lane
Moubray St.
PRAHRAN

Aughtie Drive
Canterbury Rd.
☐ Middle Park
↓ Hotel

0   1/4 mile
0   400 meters

1
2
3
4
5
6

envelopes the room upon entering. Naturally the friendly staff will try to entice you into having a sip of ouzo, and since everyone else seems to be doing it, we suggest you do, too. ⑤ *Average main: A$30* ⊠ *434 Lygon St., Brunswick East* ☎ *03/9381–1222* ⊕ *hellenicrepublic.com.au* ⊘ *Closed for lunch Mon.–Thurs.* ✛ *1:C1.*

WHERE TO STAY

CITY CENTER

$$ 🏨 **Crossley Hotel.** There's an unexpected sense of space and lots of light
HOTEL in this compact boutique hotel half a block from Chinatown. **Pros:** great location; good restaurant; reasonable price. **Cons:** some rooms being refurbished over the next year. ⑤ *Rooms from: A$180* ⊠ *51 Little Bourke St., City Center* ☎ *03/9639–1639* 🛏 *84 rooms, 4 apartments* ⑩ *Breakfast* ✛ *1:B4.*

$$$ 🏨 **Crown Metropol.** Crown Casino's newest hotel may be huge (it has
HOTEL 665 rooms, making it one of the country's biggest), but it still retains an elegant boutique-type feel. **Pros:** professional service; great spa center. **Cons:** casino area might not appeal to all. ⑤ *Rooms from: A$255* ⊠ *8 Whiteman St., City Center* ☎ *03/9292–6211* ⊕ *www. crownmetropolmelbourne.com.au* 🛏 *632 rooms, 33 apartments* ⑩ *Breakfast* ✛ *2:A3.*

$$$ 🏨 **Hotel Lindrum.** Housed in the Heritage-listed Lindrum family billiards
HOTEL center, a short walk from Federation Square, this is one of Melbourne's savviest boutique properties. **Pros:** warm feel; exceptional service; full in-room entertainment systems. **Cons:** on busy thoroughfare. ⑤ *Rooms from: A$265* ⊠ *26 Flinders St., City Center* ☎ *03/9668–1111* ⊕ *www. hotellindrum.com.au* 🛏 *59 rooms* ⑩ *Breakfast* ✛ *1:C5.*

$$$$ 🏨 **The Hotel Windsor.** Built in 1883, this aristocrat of Melbourne
HOTEL hotels combines Victorian-era character with modern comforts, and is a must for history lovers. **Pros:** elegant heritage feel; central location. **Cons:** heritage rooms are fittingly old world in decor. ⑤ *Rooms from: A$399* ⊠ *111 Spring St., City Center* ☎ *03/9633–6000* ⊕ *www. thehotelwindsor.com.au* 🛏 *160 rooms, 20 suites* ⑩ *Breakfast* ✛ *1:C4.*

$$$$ 🏨 **InterContinental Melbourne The Rialto.** Tucked behind one of Mel-
HOTEL bourne's most iconic Gothic facades, The Rialto is a five-star luxury hotel designed by William Pitt, the architect behind many Melbourne landmarks. **Pros:** spectacular, historic facade; great bar and club lounge. **Cons:** slightly corporate feel; fee for in-room Wi-Fi. ⑤ *Rooms from: A$315* ⊠ *495 Collins St., City Center* ☎ *03/8627–1400* ⊕ *www. melbourne.intercontinental.com* 🛏 *244 rooms, 9 suites* ⑩ *No meals* ✛ *1:A5.*

$$$$ 🏨 **Jasper Hotel.** A former YWCA, the Jasper has undergone a radical
HOTEL face-lift, redesigned and polished to a shine. **Pros:** close to the Victoria Markets; entire hotel is nonsmoking. **Cons:** may be noisy in the morning, being near the markets. ⑤ *Rooms from: A$337* ⊠ *489 Elizabeth St., City Center* ☎ *03/8327–2777, 1800/468359* ⊕ *www.jasperhotel. com.au* 🛏 *80 rooms, 10 suites* ⑩ *No meals* ✛ *1:A5.*

$$ 🛏 **Middle Park Hotel.** In the picturesque suburb of Middle Park, toward
HOTEL the lively St. Kilda area, this 25-room hotel has been stylishly designed
by renowned local architects Six Degrees, giving the 125-year-old build-
ing new life. **Pros:** historic surroundings; warm service. **Cons:** might be
too far from city for some. ⑤ *Rooms from: A$200* ⊠ *102 Canterbury
Rd., City Center* ☎ *03/9690–1958* ⊕ *middleparkhotel.com.au* ⟿ *23
rooms, 1 suite, 1 apartment* ⍟ *Breakfast* ✛ *2:A6.*

$$$ 🛏 **Ovolo Hotel.** Much effort has gone into making this 43-room boutique
HOTEL hotel uniquely stylish and comfortable, including its laneway location,
which is ideal for those who want to be in the heart of the action.
Pros: latest entertainment technology in the rooms; central location.
Cons: area can be noisy late at night. ⑤ *Rooms from: A$240* ⊠ *19
Little Bourke St., City Center* ☎ *03/8692–0777* ⊕ *www.ovolohotels.
com* ⟿ *40 rooms, 3 penthouse suites* ⍟ *Breakfast* ✛ *1:C4.*

$$$$ 🛏 **Park Hyatt Melbourne.** Set right next to Fitzroy Gardens and opposite
HOTEL St. Patrick's Cathedral, this is one of Melbourne's most elegant hotels.
Fodor's Choice **Pros:** lavish appointments; world-class service; free Wi-Fi in rooms.
★ **Cons:** a little removed from the city center. ⑤ *Rooms from: A$325* ⊠ *1
Parliament Sq., City Center* ☎ *03/9224–1234* ⊕ *melbourne.park.hyatt.
com* ⟿ *216 rooms, 24 suites* ⍟ *Breakfast* ✛ *1:C4.*

$$ 🛏 **Quest Gordon Place.** This National Trust–listed 1884 lodging house
HOTEL is one of the most interesting and comfortable apartment hotels in the
city. **Pros:** modern apartment-style furnishings; great location. **Cons:**
homey feel. ⑤ *Rooms from: A$179* ⊠ *24 Little Bourke St., City Center*
☎ *03/9663–2888* ⊕ *www.questgordonplace.com.au* ⟿ *54 apartments*
⍟ *No meals* ✛ *1:C4.*

$$$$ 🛏 **The Sebel Melbourne Flinders Lane.** The smallest of the city's upscale
HOTEL hotels, the Sebel has a central location and a mix of lovely one- and
two-bedroom suites, which sleep four to eight people. **Pros:** elegant
design. **Cons:** not for the budget-conscious. ⑤ *Rooms from: A$360*
⊠ *321 Flinders La., City Center* ☎ *03/9629–4088* ⊕ *www.accorhotels.
com* ⟿ *58 suites* ⍟ *No meals* ✛ *1:A5.*

$$ 🛏 **Space Hotel.** Located just minutes from bustling Lygon Street, Carlton
HOTEL Gardens, and Queen Victoria Market, this family-run venue targets bud-
get travelers who like a bit more comfort. **Pros:** central location; newly
appointed rooms. **Cons:** can get noisy with lively patrons. ⑤ *Rooms
from: A$159* ⊠ *380 Russell St., City Center* ☎ *03/9662–3888* ⊕ *www.
spacehotel.com.au* ⟿ *128 rooms* ⍟ *No meals* ✛ *1:B3.*

$$$$ 🛏 **Stamford Plaza Melbourne.** Diamond-faceted glass elevators carry
HOTEL guests from the marble lobby of this "Paris-end," all-suite hotel to
rooms decorated with plush, rich hued velvets and art deco–ish crystal
lamps. **Pros:** lush decor; great restaurant; central location. **Cons:** might
not appeal to lovers of minimalist contemporary decor. ⑤ *Rooms from:
A$365* ⊠ *111 Little Collins St., City Center* ☎ *03/9659–1000* ⊕ *www.
stamford.com.au* ⟿ *283 rooms* ⍟ *Breakfast* ✛ *1:B4.*

CARLTON

$ | **Arrow on Swanston.** Location and great value make up for the limited
HOTEL | space in this CBD-edge hotel. **Pros:** easy walk to eateries and CBD attractions; inexpensive. **Cons:** limited space. *Rooms from: A$110 488 Swanston St., Carlton 03/9225–9000 www.arrowonswanston. com.au 47 rooms, 38 apartments No meals 1:A2.*

ST. KILDA

$$$ | **The Prince.** Cutting-edge design, contemporary artworks and sculptural furniture, and spare yet inviting luxury make this boutique hotel
HOTEL | perfect for aficionados of unfussy elegance. **Pros:** super comfortable rooms; gallery feel; great location. **Cons:** the modern shapes and neutral hues might not appeal to some. *Rooms from: A$220 2 Acland St., St. Kilda 03/9536–1111 www.theprince.com.au 39 rooms Breakfast 2:A6.*

$$ | **Tolarno Hotel.** Set in the heart of St. Kilda's café, bar, and club precinct, Tolarno Hotel was once owned by artists who ran a gallery out
HOTEL | of the space, and it still has an idiosyncratic artistic bent. **Pros:** great restaurant; cool vibe; heart-of-breezy-St. Kilda location. **Cons:** area can have a dubious crowd; can be noisy late at night; no elevator. *Rooms from: A$165 42 Fitzroy St., St. Kilda 03/9537–0200 www. hoteltolarno.com.au 32 rooms, 5 suites No meals 2:A6.*

SOUTH YARRA–PRAHRAN

$$$ | **The Como Melbourne.** With its opulent and funky modern furnishings,
HOTEL | this luxury hotel is as popular with business travelers as it is with visiting artists and musicians. **Pros:** lavishly appointed rooms; great shopping and restaurants nearby. **Cons:** outside the city center. *Rooms from: A$225 630 Chapel St., South Yarra 03/9825–2222 www. comomelbourne.com.au 107 suites Breakfast 2:D5.*

$$$$ | **The Lyall Hotel and Spa.** The spacious one- and two-bedroom suites
HOTEL | at this exclusive hotel make an art form of understated elegance, and they come with all the luxuries: CD and DVD players, velour bathrobes and slippers, gourmet minibars, and a pillow "menu." The in-house spa administers a full range of massages, facials, and body treatments (try the organic green tea exfoliation). **Pros:** an extravagant spa; 24-hour bistro; 24-hour gym. **Cons:** outside city center. *Rooms from: A$360 14 Murphy St., South Yarra 03/9868–8222, 1800/388234 www. thelyall.com 40 suites Breakfast 2:D5.*

RICHMOND

$ | **Richmond Hill Hotel.** Just a short ride from the city center (on the No.
HOTEL | 70 tram), this inexpensive boutique hotel occupies a garden-fronted 1918 mansion. **Pros:** city-fringe location; friendly service. **Cons:** somewhat Spartan digs; a bit mazelike; front rooms get peak-hour traffic noise. *Rooms from: A$140 353 Church St., Richmond 03/9428– 6501, 1800/801618 www.richmondhillhotel.com.au 42 rooms Breakfast 2:D3.*

EAST MELBOURNE

$ 📺 **Baden Powell Hotel.** One of the best ways to experience Melbourne's
HOTEL historic pubs is to stay inside one, and the well-appointed Baden Powell
Hotel is an ideal fit. **Pros:** good location for sport and nightlife; good
value. **Cons:** strict check-in times; can be noisy on weekends. ⑤ *Rooms
from: A$140* ✉ *61 Victoria Parade, Collingwood* ☎ *03/9486–0811*
⊕ *www.badenpowellhotel.com.au* ⤵ *11 rooms* ⏏ *No meals* ✛ *2:C1.*

NIGHTLIFE AND PERFORMING ARTS

PERFORMING ARTS

4

Time Out Melbourne, available from tourist outlets, is a comprehensive
monthly guide to what's happening in town. For a complete listing of
performing arts events, galleries, and films, consult the "Shortlist" supplement in the Friday edition of *The Age* newspaper. Tourism Victoria
hosts a fantastic website (⊕ *www.visitmelbourne.com*) detailing all of
Melbourne's upcoming and current events. The free local music magazine *Beat* is available at cafés, stores, markets, and bars. *Melbourne
Community Voice (MCV)* and *Star Observer* are the local LGBT papers.

MUSIC AND DANCE

Australian Ballet. In the 2,000-seat State Theatre at the Arts Centre,
the Australian Ballet stages five programs annually, and presents visiting celebrity dancers from around the world. ✉ *The Arts Centre, 100
St. Kilda Rd., Southbank* ☎ *03/9669–2700, 136–100 Ticketmaster*
⊕ *www.australianballet.com.au.*

Hamer Hall. This is Melbourne's premier concert venue and home to
Melbourne Symphony Orchestra. ✉ *The Arts Centre, 100 St. Kilda
Rd., Southbank* ☎ *03/9281–8000.*

Melbourne Symphony Orchestra. The Melbourne Symphony Orchestra
performs year-round in the 2,600-seat Hamer Hall. ✉ *The Arts Centre, 100 St. Kilda Rd., Southbank* ☎ *9929–9600 box office* ⊕ *www.
mso.com.au.*

Sidney Myer Music Bowl. Open-air concerts take place December through
March at the Sidney Myer Music Bowl. ✉ *King's Domain near Swan
St. Bridge, City Center* ☎ *136–100 Ticketmaster.*

THEATER

Comedy Theatre. Revues and plays are staged at the Comedy Theatre,
which along with the Princess, Regent, and Forum theaters is owned
by the Marriner Group and uses the same telephone numbers. ✉ *240
Exhibition St., City Center* ☎ *03/9299–9800, 1300/111011* ⊕ *www.
marrinergroup.com.au.*

fortyfivedownstairs. Cutting-edge independent theater, cabaret acts,
and exhibitions are featured here. ✉ *45 Flinders La., City Center*
☎ *03/9662–9966* ⊕ *www.fortyfivedownstairs.com.*

Half-Tix. This ticket booth in the Melbourne Town Hall sells tickets to
theater attractions at half price on performance days. It's open Monday

10–2, Tuesday–Thursday 11–6, Friday 11–6:30, and Saturday 10–4. Phone for information about shows on sale (recorded message), or see listings on the website. Sales are cash only, and only from the booth. The booth also sells tickets for bus tours. ⊠ *Melbourne Town Hall, Swanston and Collins Sts., City Center* ☎ *03/9650–9420* ⊕ *www. halftixmelbourne.com.*

Melbourne Theatre Company. Australia's oldest professional theater company stages up to 12 productions per year in various venues around the city, including the Southbank Theatre and the Arts Centre in St. Kilda Road. ⊠ *Southbank Theatre, 140 Southbank Blvd., Southbank* ☎ *03/8688–0800 box office* ⊕ *www.mtc.com.au.*

Playbox at the CUB Malthouse Company. The city's second-largest company, the **Malthouse Theatre**, stages about 10 new or contemporary productions a year. The CUB Malthouse is a flexible theater space designed for drama, dance, and circus performances. ⊠ *113 Sturt St., Southbank* ☎ *03/9685–5111* ⊕ *www.malthousetheatre.com.au.*

Regent Theatre. An ornate 1920s building, the Regent originally opened to screen movies but nowadays presents mainstream productions, including *The Lion King* and Andrew Lloyd Webber's *Cats.* ⊠ *191 Collins St., City Center* ☎ *03/9299–9800, 1300/111011 box office* ⊕ *www. marrinergroup.com.au.*

Theatre Works. This theater concentrates on contemporary Australian plays. ⊠ *14 Acland St., St. Kilda* ☎ *03/9534–3388* ⊕ *www. theatreworks.org.au.*

NIGHTLIFE

Most of the central city's dance clubs are along the King Street strip, or near the corner of Queen Street and Little Collins Street. Clubs usually open at 9 or 10 weekends and some weeknights, and stay open until the early-morning hours. Expect to pay a small cover at most clubs—between A$15 and A$20.

CITY CENTER
BARS
The Atrium Bar on 35. This cocktail bar on the 35th floor of the Sofitel Melbourne on Collins has spectacular views. ⊠ *25 Collins St., City Center* ☎ *03/9653–0000* ⊕ *www.sofitel-melbourne.com.*

Cookie. Located in a lofty warehouse-style space with exposed ceiling pipes and a balcony, Cookie focuses on domestic and international craft beer and great Thai food. ⊠ *Curtin House, 252 Swanston St., 1st fl., City Center* ☎ *03/9663–7660* ⊕ *cookie.net.au.*

Gin Palace. Reminiscent of Hollywood's golden era, Gin Palace has more than enough types of martinis to satisfy any taste. ⊠ *10 Russell Pl., off Bourke St., City Center* ☎ *03/9654–0533* ⊕ *www.ginpalace.com.au.*

Melbourne Supper Club. Age-buffed leather sofas, cigars, and an exhaustive wine list characterize the classy Melbourne Supper Club. ⊠ *161 Spring St., 1st fl., City Center* ☎ *03/9654–6300.*

Mitre Tavern. One of the oldest pubs in town, locals love the unpretentious vibe, and U.K.-like surrounding. It's especially popular with nine-to-fivers who like an after-work beer. ⊠ *5 Bank Pl., City Center* ☎ *03/9670–5644* ⊕ *www. mitretavern.com.au.*

Ms Collins. A bar from Tuesday to Saturday, with food designed by some of Melbourne's top chefs, Ms Collins turns Latin American on Thursday and R&B club on Friday night. ⊠ *425 Collins St., City Center* ☎ *03/8614–2222* ⊕ *www. mscollins.com.au.*

Section 8. Located in a car park, and housed in a shipping container, Section 8 is a reliably trendy bar, popular with the artsy student crowd. ⊠ *27–29 Tattersalls La., City Center* ☎ *0430/291–588* ⊕ *www.section8.com.au.*

A FUNNY NIGHT OUT

Melburnians love a laugh, and the annual Melbourne International Comedy Festival is a great opportunity to enjoy top Australian and international comedians. The month-long event takes place in the Melbourne Town Hall and venues across town, with free events in open spaces. In addition to hosting comedy stars, the festival seeks out new talent and culminates with the Raw Comedy award for the best new Australian stand-up performer. If you're in town in April, you won't be laughing if you miss it. ⊕ *www. comedyfestival.com.au.*

COMEDY CLUBS
Last Laugh Comedy Club. This is a popular place to see top-class Australian and international comedy acts. ⊠ *Upstairs at the Athenaeum Theatre, 188 Collins St., City Center* ☎ *03/9650–1977* ⊕ *www.thecomedyclub. com.au.*

MUSIC CLUBS
Bennetts Lane. One of Melbourne's jazz mainstays, Bennetts has international acts and the occasional megastar (like Prince) popping in. ⊠ *25 Bennetts La., City Center* ☎ *03/9663–2856* ⊕ *www.bennettslane.com.*

Cherry Bar. This small and intimate rock 'n' roll bar is located on AC/DC Lane. The address alone says it all. ⊠ *AC/DC La., City Center* ☎ *03/9639–8122* ⊕ *www.cherrybar.com.au.*

Ding Dong Lounge. You can catch headline rock acts at the Ding Dong Lounge. ⊠ *Level 1, 18 Market La., City Center* ⊕ *www.dingdonglounge. com.au.*

Max Watt's House of Music. This popular venue is known for live local and lesser-known international rock bands, and as a stand-up venue during the International Comedy Festival. ⊠ *125 Swanston St., City Center* ☎ *1300/843–443 tickets* ⊕ *maxwatts.com.au.*

RICHMOND
MUSIC CLUBS
Corner Hotel. The Corner Hotel has alternative, reggae, rock, blues, and jazz acts with an emphasis on homegrown bands. Tasty pub meals can be had on the rooftop for a pre-gig dinner. ⊠ *57 Swan St., Richmond* ☎ *03/9427–7300 bar, 1300/724867 tickets* ⊕ *cornerhotel.com.*

ST. KILDA

BARS

Esplanade Hotel. Not only is this hallowed live music venue a great place to see local bands, but the Esplanade, or "Espy," is a historic pub—built in 1878—listed with the National Trust. ⌧ *11 Upper Esplanade, St. Kilda* ☎ *03/9534–0211* ⊕ *www.espy.com.au.*

CONCERT VENUE

Palais Theatre. This theater features film, music festival openings, and concerts by Australian and international acts such as the Soweto Gospel Choir and Joe Bonamassa. ⌧ *Lower Esplanade, St. Kilda* ☎ *03/9525–3240, 136–100 Ticketmaster* ⊕ *www.palaistheatre.net.au.*

MUSIC CLUBS

Prince of Wales. For rock and roll, punk, and grunge, head to the Prince Bandroom at the Prince of Wales, which attracts a straight and gay crowd. Ticket prices vary widely, depending on the gig. ⌧ *29 Fitzroy St., St. Kilda* ☎ *03/9536–1168* ⊕ *princebandroom.com.au.*

FITZROY

BARS

The Everleigh. One of the city's best cocktail bars, the Everleigh also makes a perfect spot for couples, with dark lighting and soft tunes ⌧ *150–156 Gertrude St., upstairs, Fitzroy* ☎ *03/9416–2229* ⊕ *www.theeverleigh.com.*

Polly. Mix with colorful and quirky clientele in an equally fun 1920s design with red-velvet lounges, gilt mirrors, and chandeliers. Also enjoy a traditional or contemporary cocktail—there are 55 concoctions to choose from. ⌧ *401 Brunswick St., Fitzroy* ☎ *03/9417–0880* ⊕ *www.pollybar.com.au.*

MUSIC CLUBS

Night Cat. Bands and DJ's play AfroCuban and disco dance music here Thursday to Saturday evening, and the Latin big band on Sunday night is legendary. ⌧ *141 Johnston St., Fitzroy* ☎ *03/9417–0090* ⊕ *www.thenightcat.com.au.*

The Rainbow. Most nights of the week, for the past few decades, this great pub, located down a backstreet, has been showcasing local acts. There's also a great range of craft beers available, which you can enjoy in the beer garden during the warmer months. ⌧ *27 St. David St., Fitzroy* ☎ *03/9419–4193* ⊕ *therainbow.com.au.*

SOUTH YARRA–PRAHRAN

BARS

Revolver Upstairs. This bar caters predominantly to the young party goers, with early morning recovery sessions—a time for revelers around town to keep on partying—that are especially popular. ⌧ *229 Chapel St., Prahran* ☎ *03/9521–5985* ⊕ *revolverupstairs.com.au.*

BRUNSWICK

MUSIC CLUBS

Spotted Mallard. In addition hosting live bands, this venue also has trivia nights and serves a range of microbrewery beers. ⌧ *314 Sydney Rd., Brunswick* ☎ *03/9380–8818* ⊕ *www.spottedmallard.com.*

BARS

Alehouse Project. Regarded as having one of the best beer lists in the city, this local favorite also has an excellent menu, matched especially to the beers on offer. Head to the beer garden out the back in the warmer months. ⊠ *98 Lygon St., Brunswick East* ☎ *03/9387–1218* ⊕ *www. thealehouseproject.com.au.*

Retreat Hotel. This expansive pub has local bands performing most nights of the week. It also has one of the city's best beer gardens. ⊠ *280 Sydney Rd., Brunswick* ☎ *03/9380–4090* ⊕ *retreathotelbrunswick.com.au.*

Union Hotel. This family-friendly pub showcases local music on weekends. The atmosphere is always friendly and welcoming. ⊠ *109 Union St., Brunswick West* ☎ *03/9388–2235* ⊕ *unionhotelbrunswick.com.au.*

SOUTH MELBOURNE AND SOUTHBANK

CASINO

Crown Casino. Melbourne's first gambling center has blackjack, roulette, and poker machines. The casino is part of the Crown Entertainment Complex, which also has dozens of restaurants, including branches of the famed Japanese chef Nobu and renowned Sydney chef Neil Perry's Rockpool, shops, bars, and two nightclubs open until late. The Palms at Crown hosts international and Australian headliners. The casino is on the south bank of the Yarra. ⊠ *8 Whiteman St., Southbank* ☎ *03/9292– 8888* ⊕ *www.crowncasino.com.au* ⊙ *Daily 24 hrs.*

SHOPPING

Melbourne has firmly established itself as the nation's fashion capital. Australian designer labels are available on High Street in Armadale, on Toorak Road and Chapel Street in South Yarra, and on Bridge Road in Richmond. High-quality vintage clothing abounds on Greville Street in Prahran. Discount hunters love the huge discount fashion shopping center attached to Southern Cross Station on Spencer Street, with its many stores. Most shops are open Monday–Thursday 9–5:30, Friday until 9, and Saturday until 5. Major city stores are open Sunday until 5.

CITY CENTER

BOOKS

Books for Cooks. A fantastic array of cookbooks stock the shelves of Books for Cooks, including many from local chefs. Now located at the Queen Victoria Market, the shop's only steps from plenty of fresh produce, meat, and fish to support any sudden inspirations. ⊠ *129 Therry St., City Center* ☎ *03/8415–1415* ⊕ *www.booksforcooks.com. au* ⊙ *Mon.–Sat. 10–6, Sun. 11–5.*

CLOTHING

Jack London. This trendy shop has British and European styled Mod Rocker gear, specializing in winter coats for men. Various locations are dotted around town including Shop 1/258 Flinders Lane in City Center, 238 Brunswick St., Fitzroy, and 246 Chapel St., Prahran. ⊠ *301 Swanston St., City Center* ☎ *03/9639–2144* ⊕ *www.jacklondon.com.au.*

Melbourne is known for its top-notch live theater.

DEPARTMENT STORES AND SHOPPING CENTERS

Block Arcade. An elegant 19th-century shopping plaza with mosaic-tile floors, Block Arcade contains the venerable Hopetoun Tea Rooms, the French Jewel Box, Dafel Dolls and Bears, Basement Discs, Gewurzhaus,and Australian By Design. ⊠ *282 Collins St., City Center* ☎ *03/9654–5244* ⊕ *www.theblockarcade.com.au.*

Bourke Street Mall. Once the busiest east–west thoroughfare in the city, Bourke Street Mall is a pedestrian-only zone—but watch out for those trams! Two of the city's biggest department stores are here; an essential part of growing up in Melbourne is being taken to Myer at Christmas to see the window displays. ⊠ *Bourke St., City Center.*

Myer. Myer is one of the country's largest department stores, carrying a myriad of both casual and luxury brands for men and women. ⊠ *314–336 Bourke St., between Elizabeth and Swanston Sts., City Center* ☎ *03/9661–1111.*

David Jones. This big department store has a large array of luxury brands for both men and women. ⊠ *310 Bourke St., between Elizabeth and Swanston Sts., City Center* ☎ *03/9643–2222.*

Bridge Road. In Richmond, east of the city, Bridge Road is a popular shopping strip for women's retail fashion that caters to all budgets. ⊠ *Bridge Rd., Richmond* ⊕ *www.bridgerd.com.au.*

Emporium Melbourne. Many international brands established their first Australian outlets at this major shopping mall in the city center. The mall is filled with fashion, technology, food, and art outlets, and joined via above-ground walkways to the Myer and David Jones department stores and Melbourne Central shopping center. Stores include Michael Kors, Jones the Grocer, and Victoria's Secret. ⊠ *Lonsdale St., City Center* ☎ *03/8609–8221* ⊕ *emporiummelbourne.com.au.*

Flinders Lane. Dotted with chic boutiques, many of them selling merchandise by up-and-coming Australian designers, Flinders Lane makes fashionistas happy. Between Swanston and Elizabeth streets, look for Cathedral Arcade, home to vintage and designer stores, in the bottom of the Nicholas Building. The lift leads to an eclectic collection of tiny shops full of unique fashion and accessories. ⊠ *Flinders La., City Center.*

Little Collins Street. A precinct of stores frequented by shoppers with perhaps more money than sense, Little Collins Street is still worth a visit. In between frock shops you'll find musty stores selling classic film posters, antique and estate jewelry, and Australian opals. At the eastern end of **Collins Street,** beyond the cream-and-red Romanesque facade of St. Michael's Uniting Church, is the **Paris End,** a name coined by Melburnians to identify the elegance of its fashionable shops as well as its general hauteur. Here you find big-name international designer clothing, bags and jewelry. ⊠ *Little Collins St., City Center.*

Melbourne Central. Here you'll find a dizzying complex huge enough to enclose an 1880s redbrick shot tower (once used to make bullets) in its atrium. ⊠ *300 Lonsdale St., City Center* ☎ *03/9922–1100* ⊕ *www.melbournecentral.com.au.*

Royal Arcade. Built in 1846, this is Melbourne's oldest shopping plaza. It remains a lovely place to browse and is home to the splendid Gaunt's Clock, which tolls away the hours. ⊠ *355 Bourke St., City Center* ⊕ *www.royalarcade.com.au.*

Southgate. The shops and eateries at this spectacular riverside location are a short walk from both the city center, across the Ponyfish Island pedestrian bridge, and the Arts Center. There's outdoor seating next to the Southbank promenade. ⊠ *4 Southbank Promenade, City Center* ☎ *03/9686–1000* ⊕ *www.southgatemelbourne.com.au.*

MARKETS

Fodor's Choice ★ **Queen Victoria Market.** This market has buzzed with food and bargain shoppers since 1878. With more than 1,000 mostly open-air stalls, this sprawling, spirited bazaar is the city's prime produce outlet—many Melburnians come here to buy strawberries, fresh flowers, imported cheeses, meat, and eye-bright fresh fish. On Sunday there is less food and more great deals on jeans, T-shirts, and souvenirs. It's open Tuesday and Thursday 6–2, Friday 6–5, Saturday 6–3, and Sunday 9–4. Market tours take you deep inside the labyrinth, and cooking classes are conducted by well-known chefs. Wandering entertainers and aromatic hot food stalls add to the vibe at the Summer Night Market, open 5:30 to 10 pm on Wednesday from November to late-FebruaryThese markets focus on art, crafts, food, and gifts. ⊠ *Elizabeth and Victoria Sts., City Center* ☎ *03/9320–5822* ⊕ *www.qvm.com.au.*

SHOES AND LEATHER GOODS

Roberts and Hassett. If you're looking for something special in leather goods, bespoke shoemakers Roberts and Hassett sell handmade shoes, belts, satchels, and wallets made mostly from kangaroo leather. Much of their leather is sourced from Greenhalgh Tannery, which specializes in tanning with wattle tree bark. The business operates out of the "Gentleman's Outfitter," Captains of Industry, which also has a café, a barbershop, and a jeweler. ⊠ *Captains of Industry, 2 Somerset Pl., Levels 1/2, City Center ✛ Off Little Bourke St.* ☏ *03/9670–4405* ⊕ *roberts-hassett.com.au.*

ST. KILDA

MARKETS

The Esplanade Market St. Kilda. Open since 1970, this market started as an outlet for local artists. Today, it has up to 200 stalls selling contemporary paintings, crafts, pottery, jewelry, and homemade gifts. It's open every Sunday from 10 to 5 from October to April and 10 to 4 in the colder months. ⊠ *Upper Esplanade, St. Kilda* ☏ *03/9209–6634* ⊕ *www. stkildaesplanademarket.com.au.*

FITZROY

ART AND CRAFT GALLERIES

Gallery Gabrielle Pizzi. The gallery shows and sells the work of established and new Aboriginal artists from the communities of Balgo Hills, Papunya, Maningrida, Turkey Creek (Warmun), the Tiwi Islands and others in the Central Desert, Top End and Kimberley regions. Visits are by appointment only. ⊠ *51 Victoria St., Fitzroy* ☏ *0424/337–669* ⊕ *www.gabriellepizzi.com.au* ⊗ *By appointment only.*

BOOKS

CLOTHING

The Social Studio. This nonprofit store provides work experience, employment, and passageways for refugee youth. Limited-edition women's fashion designs are made using only reclaimed materials sourced from the local fashion industry. ⊠ *128 Smith St., Collingwood* ☏ *03/9417–2143* ⊕ *www.thesocialstudio.org* ⊗ *Mon.–Sat. 10:30–6.*

DEPARTMENT STORES AND SHOPPING CENTERS

Brunswick Street. Northeast of the city in Fitzroy, Brunswick Street has hip and grungy restaurants, coffee shops, gift stores, and clothing outlets selling the latest look. ⊠ *Brunswick St., Fitzroy.*

Smith Street. Perhaps Melbourne hippest street, this colorful strip is dotted with bars, restaurants, and many vintage-style clothing shops. Toward the northern end are clothing factory outlets. ⊠ *Smith St., Fitzroy.*

SOUTH YARRA–PRAHRAN

ART

Signed and Numbered. Melbourne is famous for its street art, and this purveyor of limited edition prints sells work by well-known local street artists like Ghostpatrol and Kaff-eine, as well as other national and international artists. ⊠ *Greville Print Shop, 153 Greville St., South Yarra* ☎ *02/9077–6468* ⊕ *signedandnumbered.com.au.*

CLOTHING

Eco D. International and Australian designers mix and mingle here, so you can find local fashion icons like Cable Melbourne, LIFEwithBIRD, and Camilla and Marc here. ⊠ *1064 High St., Windsor* ☎ *03/9500–0004* ⊕ *shop.ecod.com.au.*

DEPARTMENT STORES AND SHOPPING CENTERS

Chapel Street. This street is where you can find some of the ritziest boutiques in Melbourne, as well as cafés, art galleries, bars, and restaurants. ⊠ *Chapel St., between Toorak and Dandenong Rds., Prahran.*

High Street. Located between the suburbs of Prahran and Armadale, to the east of Chapel Street, High Street has the best collection of antiques shops in Australia. ⊠ *High St., between Chapel Orrong Sts., Prahran.*

Jam Factory. This historic redbrick brewery-turned-factory complex houses cinemas, fashion, food, and gift shops. ⊠ *500 Chapel St., South Yarra* ☎ *03/9860–8500* ⊕ *www.thejamfactory.com.au.*

MARKETS

Camberwell Sunday Market. A popular haunt for seekers of the old and odd, this market, about 6 km (4 miles) northeast of Chapel Street, South Yarra, has more than 300 stalls selling antiques, preloved clothing, books, and knickknacks. Food vans provide sustenance. ⊠ *Station St., Camberwell* ⊕ *camberwellsundaymarket.org.*

Chapel Street Bazaar. Everything from estate jewelry and stylish secondhand clothes to porcelain and curios is on sale at these wooden cubicles and glass-fronted counters. ⊠ *217–223 Chapel St., Prahran* ☎ *03/9529–1727* ⊕ *www.chapelstreet.com.au.*

Prahran Market. A fantastic, mouthwatering array imported from all over the world is available at this food market. ⊠ *163 Commercial Rd., South Yarra* ☎ *03/8290–8220* ⊕ *www.prahranmarket.com.au.*

SOUTH MELBOURNE AND SOUTHBANK

DEPARTMENT STORES AND SHOPPING CENTERS

South Wharf. This shopping precinct near the Exhibition Centre and the Polly Woodside historic ship hosts riverside restaurants and cafés in heritage sheds, along with discount outlet shopping of brands like Billabong, Kathmandu, Sass & Bide, and Tigerlilly Swimwear. ⊠ *South Wharf Promenade, Southbank* ⊕ *southwharf.com.au.*

MARKETS

South Melbourne Market. Established in 1867, South Melbourne Market is Melbourne's second-oldest market. You'll find a huge selection of fresh produce and foodstuffs (the Dim Sims are famous). ✉ *Cecil and Coventry Sts., South Melbourne* ☎ *03/9209–6295* ⊕ *www.southmelbournemarket.com.au.*

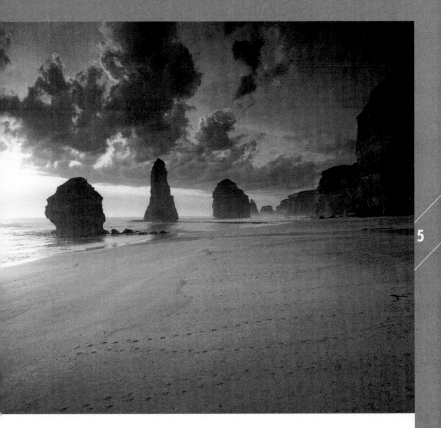

VICTORIA

5

WELCOME TO VICTORIA

TOP REASONS TO GO

★ **The Amazing Outdoors:** Victoria has outstanding national parks. Bushwalking, canoeing, fishing, rafting, and horse riding are all on the menu.

★ **Golden Country:** You can still pan for gold—and find it—in rivers northwest of Melbourne. But the gold-rush era's most attractive remnants are beautiful 19th-century towns constructed from its riches.

★ **Wonderful Wineries:** You'll find hundreds of wineries across the state, particularly in the Yarra Valley, Rutherglen, and on the Mornington Peninsula.

★ **Unique Wildlife:** Parrots in Sherbrooke, Phillip Island's penguin parade, and platypuses and dingoes at the Healesville Sanctuary, Victoria teems with native fauna.

★ **Foodie Heaven:** Victoria has a reputation for excellent local produce and wine. Even in rural towns, cafés and restaurants focus on fresh seasonal items.

1 Side Trips from Melbourne. On the city's doorstep are dozens of wineries with fabulous restaurants, mist-swathed hills dotted with charming B&Bs and curio shops, forested walking trails noisy with multicolor parrots, gold-era towns flush with grand, boom-time buildings, and glorious beaches.
It's a breeze to visit the Yarra Valley, Mornington Peninsula, the Goldfields, or the Dandenong Ranges on day trips.

2 Great Ocean Road. This is the ultimate road trip along the wave-lashed Southern Ocean. From Melbourne it's a 450-km (280-mile) coastal journey, with occasional detours into wooded hills dotted with fern gullies. Lighthouses, surfing beaches, and lively towns punctuate the road, but the headline attractions are the amazing shapes carved from the coastline, including the Twelve Apostles and the smaller rock stacks on show in this amazing natural sculpture park.

NEW SOUTH WALES

0 — 60 mi
0 — 60 km

River

Albury

4

Echuca

A39

Rutherglen

Wodonga

B400

Shepparton

B75

Wangaratta

B500

Nagambie

M31

Bright

Bendigo

B300

Mansfield

Kyneton

Seymour

Eildon

Yea

M79

1

GREAT DIVIDING RANGE

Sunbury

YARRA VALLEY

Healesville

Alpine Nat'l Park

MELBOURNE

DANDENONG RANGE

Sherbrooke

Werribee

M1

A1

Geelong

Mornington

Traralgon

Sale

Queenscliff Peninsula

M1

Sorrento

Torquay

PHILLIP ISLAND

Cowes

Leongatha

Gippsland Lakes Coastal Park

Yarram

A440

Bass Strait

Corner Inlet

Cape Liptrap

Wilsons Promontory

South Point

Wilsons Promontory

GETTING ORIENTED

This compact state is a patchwork of spectacular landscapes just waiting to be explored. The Yarra Valley wineries and the Dandenong Ranges are an hour's drive east of Melbourne, while the beaches and vineyards of the Mornington Peninsula are a 90-minute drive south of the city. The Great Ocean Road begins at Torquay, southwest of Melbourne, and continues along the Southern Ocean coast to Portland, a distance of about 350 km (220 miles). The Goldfields and spa country are between one and two hours northwest of Melbourne. The Grampians and the Murray River region and its wineries are about a three-hour drive north to northeast of the city.

5

3 The Grampians.
Encompassing a series of rugged sandstone ranges covered with native bushland, Grampians National Park is a wilderness area three hours from the heart of Melbourne. Spectacular rock formations including the Balconies, the Pinnacle, and the Fortress can be visited via walking trails. The Wonderland Range forms a wall behind the township of Halls Gap, which is a popular hangout for kangaroos.

4 Murray River Region.
The mighty Murray River forms the border between Victoria and New South Wales, and is an aquatic playground. Houseboats, speedboats, and old paddle wheelers share the river, and golf courses, farms, historic towns, and stands of majestic eucalyptus trees hug its banks. Wineries produce internationally acclaimed fortified wines and full-bodied reds.

Updated by
Tim Richards
and Narrelle
Harris

Separated from New South Wales by the mighty Murray River and fronted by a beautiful coastline, Victoria boasts terrain as varied as any in Australia. Without venturing too far from the Melbourne city limits you can indulge in all sorts of pastimes—exploring the spectacular western coastline as far as the stunning Twelve Apostles; walking among the rocky outcrops, waterfalls, and fauna of the Grampians; visiting historic inland gold-mining communities; toasting the sunrise over the Yarra Valley vineyards from the basket of a hot-air balloon; or taking in a Murray River sunset from the deck of a paddle steamer.

Sweeping landscapes are quilted together in this compact state. Many of the state's best sights are within a day's drive of Melbourne. Go farther afield and you can experience the high-country solitude of Alpine National Park.

PLANNER

WHEN TO GO
Victoria is at its most beautiful in fall, March through May, when days are crisp, sunny, and clear and the foliage in parks and gardens is glorious. Winter, with its wild seas and leaden skies, stretches June through August in this region, providing a suitable backdrop for the dramatic coastal scenery. It's dry and sunny in the northeast, however, thanks to the cloud-blocking bulk of the Great Dividing Range. Northeast summers, December through February, are extremely hot, so it's best to travel here and through the Gold Country in spring (September through November) and fall.

PLANNING YOUR TIME

From Melbourne, head for the town of Belgrave. Here you can ride the Puffing Billy train through the fern gullies and forests of the Dandenongs. In the afternoon, travel to Phillip Island for the endearing sunset penguin parade. Stay the night, and on the third morning meander along the coastal roads of the Mornington Peninsula through such stately towns as Sorrento and Portsea. Stop at a beach, or pick a Melbourne neighborhood or two to explore in the afternoon.

If you have more time to spend in the area, make your way west from Melbourne, stopping at Queenscliff on the Bellarine Peninsula, before setting off down the Great Ocean Road. (If you are starting from the Mornington Peninsula, you take the Sorrento-Queenscliff car and passenger ferry, which crosses Port Phillip Bay in 45 minutes.) The Great Ocean Road is one of the world's finest scenic drives, with stops at some irresistible beaches. Overnight in Lorne, beneath the Otway Ranges, then drive west to Port Campbell National Park. Here you can view the Twelve Apostles rock formations and stroll along the beach. Continue to Port Fairy for the night, making sure that you check out the wonderful Bay of Islands and Bay of Martyrs rock stacks (in the sea) along the way. On Day 4 wander along the banks of Port Ferry's Moyne River and amble around Griffiths Island. You can then drive northeast to the Goldfields center of Ballarat. That evening you can explore the town's 19th-century streetscapes, then catch the sound-and-light show at Sovereign Hill. Spend the night here, and in the morning head to the wineries and spas around Daylesford before returning to Melbourne.

GETTING HERE AND AROUND

The best way to explore Victoria is by car. The state's road system is excellent, with clearly marked highways linking the Great Ocean Road to Wilson's Promontory, the Yarra Valley, the Murray River region, and the Mornington Peninsula. Distances are not as extreme as in other states. Many scenic places (Bendigo, Ballarat, Beechworth, and Echuca, for instance) are less than three hours from Melbourne; the vineyards of the Yarra Valley and the Mornington Peninsula are an easy 90-minute drive. Buses and trains, which cost less but take more time, also run between most regional centers.

RESTAURANTS

Chefs in Victoria take pride in their trendsetting preparations of fresh local produce. International flavors are found in both casual and upscale spots—and some of the best bargains can be found in local cafés. On Sunday be sure to join in the Victorian tradition of an all-day "brekky."

HOTELS

Accommodations in Victoria include grand country hotels, simple roadside motels, secluded bushland or seaside cabins, friendly bed-and-breakfasts, and backpacker hostels. Although you don't find many sprawling resorts in this state, most of the grand old mansions and country homes have air-conditioning, home-cooked meals, and free parking. Rates are usually reduced after school and national holidays. Melbourne Visitor Centre (⊕ *www.visitvictoria.com*) has a list of the state's accommodations to help you plan. *Hotel reviews have been shortened. For full information, visit Fodors.com.*

WHAT IT COSTS (IN AUSTRALIAN DOLLARS)			
$	**$$**	**$$$**	**$$$$**
Restaurants	Under A$21	A$21–A$35	A$36–A$50	over A$50
Hotels	Under A$151	A$151–A$200	A$201–A$300	over A$300

Restaurant prices are the average cost of a main course at dinner or, if dinner is not served, at lunch. Hotel prices are the lowest cost of a standard double room in high season, excluding service.

SIDE TRIPS FROM MELBOURNE

Victoria's relatively compact size makes the state's principal attractions appealingly easy to reach, and the state's excellent road system makes driving the best option. There are a handful of enticing destinations within a 60- to 90-minute drive from Melbourne. Victoria is blessed with 21 distinct wine regions (and around 650 cellar doors, where you can try and buy the product). The Yarra Valley, 40 km (25 miles) east of Melbourne, is Victoria's oldest wine region and a pleasant place to spend a day on an organized tour. About 35 km (22 miles) south of the Yarra Valley is Olinda, a cute village at the heart of the Dandenong Ranges. This area of beautifully forested hills and valleys is a favorite weekend escape for Melburnians. The Mornington Peninsula is famous for its wineries and beaches. On the western shore of Port Phillip Bay, the Bellarine Peninsula also has a winery industry, but it's the grand 19th-century hotels of Queenscliff that most attract day-trippers.

YARRA VALLEY AND HEALESVILLE

65 km (40 miles) northeast of Melbourne.

Fodor's Choice The Yarra Valley spreads eastward from Melbourne's suburban fringe,
★ and is a popular area with both locals and international visitors. Because Melburnians often use the valley for weekend breaks, the best time to visit is on working weekdays when the crowds are thinner. The small, attractive towns are dotted with good cafés, restaurants, and shops; in the rolling countryside between them you'll find numerous fine wineries that have excellent restaurants with impressive food and views.

Healesville is a good base for travel to Yarra Valley wineries and the Dandenongs Region, as it's an easy drive from both. This pleasant town with a tree-shaded main street is also home to the Healesville Sanctuary, an open-plan zoo that showcases all manner of Australian native wildlife. Two popular areas within Yarra Ranges National Park—Badger Weir Walk and Maroondah Reservoir—are ideal for bushwalking and picnics.

Side Trips From Melbourne

GETTING HERE AND AROUND

Healesville, on the eastern side of the Yarra Valley, is 65 km (40 miles) from Melbourne. Take the Eastern Freeway from Melbourne to its junction with the Maroondah Highway and follow the signs to Lilydale and on to Healesville. Trains, operated by Metro, travel from central Melbourne to Lilydale, and McKenzie's buses connect Lilydale with Yarra Glen and Healesville via Route 685. It's advisable to have a car to explore the wineries, or take a half- or full-day tour. Most tours will pick you up at your hotel.

Transportation Contacts McKenzie's Tourist Services. ☎ 03/5962–5088 ⊕ www.mckenzies.com.au. **Metro.** ☎ 1800/800007 ⊕ www.metrotrains.com.au.

TOURS

Several companies operate winery tours from Melbourne or the Yarra Valley itself. Tours generally include visits to four to five wineries and lunch.

Swans on Doongalla Horse Drawn Carriages. Daily from 11 to 4, visit four wineries in horse-drawn carriages along St. Huberts Road in a stretched horse-drawn carriage. A light lunch is served at Yering Farm winery. The meeting place is St. Huberts Winery. ☎ 03/9762–1910, 0419/877–093 ⊕ www.swansondoongalla.com.au ☎ From A$110.

Wine Tours Victoria. These full-day tours depart from Melbourne and visit four to five wineries in the four winery regions surrounding Port Phillip Bay. Lunch is included. ☎ *03/5428–8500, 1800/946386 toll-free in Australia ⊕ www.winetours.com.au ✉ From A$165.*

Yarra Valley Railway. Rail enthusiasts can still enjoy the tracks even though regular passenger train services to Healesville ceased in 1980. You can travel along part of the track in railmotors (all-in-one motor and carriage) operated by the Yarra Valley Railway. The railmotors travel from Healesville through picturesque country, over Watts River, under bridges, and through the historic Tarrawarra brick tunnel and back again—a round trip of about 8 km (5 miles) that takes about 45 minutes. ⊠ *Healesville-Kinglake Rd., Healesville ☎ 03/5962–4429 reservations ⊕ www.yvr.com.au ✉ From A$15 ⊗ Sun. 10–4.*

Yarra Valley Winery Tours. Take public and private tours of wineries in the region with this operator. It also has accommodation packages. ☎ *03/5966–2372, 1300/496766 ⊕ www.yarravalleywinerytours.com. au ✉ From A$105 per person.*

ESSENTIALS

Visitor Information Yarra Valley Visitor Information Centre. ⊠ *The Old Courthouse, Harker St., Healesville ☎ 03/5962–2600 ⊕ www.visityarravalley.com.au.*

EXPLORING

The Yarra Valley is known for its wonderful produce—fruit, vegetables, herbs, bread, and cheeses—on sale at the monthly regional farmers' markets, including one at Yering Station *(see listing below).*

De Bortoli. A family winery for three generations, De Bortoli was established (in New South Wales) in 1928, four years after the founder Vittorio De Bortoli and his wife Giuseppina migrated to Australia from northern Italy. Today, this Yarra Valley winery specializes in Chardonnay, Pinot Noir, and Riesling, along with a changing array of less-famous wines including Gamays, Pinot Blanc, and Sangiovese. Wine tastings cost A$5, which includes the famous Noble One, De Bortoli's most awarded wine since its release in 1982. The restaurant, which has stunning views of the surrounding vines, landscaped gardens, and mountains, serves delectable dishes using Yarra Valley produce; on Saturdays the fixed price two-course lunch is A$55 a head and the three-course option on weekends is A$68. Trophy Room cheese and wine tastings for a minimum of four people include De Bertoli classics for A$30 a head. The winery also hosts other events, including special lunches and packages, throughout the year. ⊠ *58 Pinnacle La., Dixon's Creek ☎ 03/5965–2271 ⊕ www.debortoliyarra.com.au ⊗ Daily 10–5; restaurant lunch Thurs.–Mon., dinner Sat. only.*

Fodor's Choice ★ **Domaine Chandon.** This vineyard has one of the most spectacular settings in the Yarra Valley; its Chandon tasting bar has enormous floor-to-ceiling windows providing fantastic views over the vineyards and the Yarra Ranges. Apart from sparkling wines, the winery produces Shiraz, Pinot Noir, Chardonnay, Sauvignon Blanc, and Rosé. Take a free self-guided tour of the winery's history and production methods from 10:30 to 4:30 daily, or sign up for a A$75 wine discovery class on Sunday with a maximum of 12 people (bookings essential) to get a closer look at wine appreciation. Seasonal platters, tapas, and mains (A\$16–A\$38) are served in the Greenpoint Brasserie Monday and Friday from noon, and from 11 am on weekends. Each dish has a recommended accompanying wine (from A\$10.50 a glass). Selections include a charcuterie board with the 2010 Chandon Les Trois Rosé and sea scallops paired with a Chandon Blanc de Blancs. ⊠ 727 *Maroondah Hwy., Coldstream* ☎ *03/9738–9200, 03/9738–9245 cellar door* ⊕ *www.chandon.com. au* ☽ *Daily 10:30–4:30.*

FAMILY **Healesville Sanctuary.** Come face-to-face with wedge-tailed eagles, grumpy wombats, nimble sugar gliders, and shy platypuses at Healesville Sanctuary, a lovely, leafy, native wildlife sanctuary. Don't miss the twice-daily Spirits of the Sky show, during which raptors and parrots fly close overhead; and the daily Tales from Platypus Creek session, which features Australia's most unusual critter. You can pat a dingo or feed an emu on a Magic Moments experience (A\$12 extra), and for A\$199 you can join a platypus in the water via the Wade with the Platypus option. Another highlight is the Land of Parrots aviary, where you can feed and interact with colorful birds. You can also view the animal hospital to see wildlife recovering from injury or illness. The Future Vets play space lets kids—and their parents—dress up as vets and role-play caring for animals. Take a break and refuel at the Sanctuary Harvest café, which serves snacks and meals made with local and seasonal produce. ⊠ *Badger Creek Rd., Healesville* ☎ *03/5957–2800, 1300/966784* ⊕ *www.zoo.org.au* ▣ *A\$31.60* ☽ *Daily 9–5* ☞ *Children free on weekends.*

Rochford Wines. This winery occupies a striking-looking property; its cellar door building crafted almost entirely of glass overlooks the vineyards and rolling green paddocks. The family-owned winery produces renowned Pinot Noir and Chardonnay, and in recent years, has become the most happening place in the Yarra Valley—its huge amphitheater plays host to international and local performers during the annual A Day on the Green concert series (acts have included Alicia Keys and Billy Idol). You can also book two-hour Segway tours of the winery on weekends (A\$145 per person), which include training and lunch. The wine-tasting bar is open daily 9–5. Isabella's café serves light meals all day, seven days a week. The restaurant is open on weekends, serving two courses for A\$55 and three courses for \$A65 per person on Saturday; and A\$62/A\$73 on Sunday. ⊠ *878 Maroondah Hwy., Coldstream* ☎ *03/5957–3333* ⊕ *www.rochfordwines.com.au* ☽ *Daily 9–5.*

WINE AND SONG

Catch a little jazz at lunch or spend the whole day watching great performances from local and international headline acts; Victoria's wineries provide an array of entertainment for music connoisseurs. Vineyards come alive in summer, so check out the events with local tourist offices. Make sure you book early for the popular Day on the Green concert series held at Rochford Wines in the Yarra Valley, Mt. Duneed Estate near Geelong, All Saints Winery in Rutherglen, and Mitchelton Wines in Nagambie.

Yering Station. Victoria's first vineyard still has plenty of rustic charm, and it's a delightful place to eat, drink, and stay. An 1859 redbrick building is home to the cellar door, a wine-and-produce store, and the casual upstairs Matt's Bar ($$), where on weekends, you can relax all day sipping wine and dining from a tasty menu beneath an arched timber ceiling. The property's architectural and gastronomical pièce de résistance is the winery building, which houses the Wine Bar Restaurant ($$$). It's a sweeping, hand-hewn stone building with floor-to-ceiling windows overlooking spectacular valley scenery. Yering hosts an annual sculpture exhibition from October to December, and a farmers' market takes place on the third Sunday of the month. ✉ *38 Melba Hwy., Yarra Glen* ☎ *03/9730–0100* ⊕ *www.yering.com* ☉ *Cellar Door: 10–5 weekdays, 10–6 weekends; restaurant: lunch daily from noon (no dinner).*

SPORTS AND THE OUTDOORS

There are plenty of opportunities to get out in the fresh air in the Yarra Valley. Those with cash to spare can go ballooning; others may just like to walk or ride a bike along the trails or play golf at the three golf courses in the valley. Wine tasting is a given.

BALLOONING

Global Ballooning. This hot-air ballooning operation runs flights over the Yarra Valley. You can take off at dawn and drift peacefully over the vineyards for an hour. For A$30 extra, enjoy a Champagne breakfast after the flight at Rochford Wines. Check the website for accommodation packages. ☎ *1800/627661* ⊕ *www.globalballooning.com.au* ✉ *From A$365.*

BIKING

Yarra Valley Cycles. You can rent a bike (and compulsory helmet) from A$40 a day and Yarra Valley Cycles will point you in the right direction for the best cycling routes in the valley and nearby scenic regions. ✉ *108 Main St., Lilydale* ⚓ *Across road from Lilydale Railway Station* ☎ *03/9735–1483* ⊕ *www.yarravalleycycles.com.*

BUSHWALKING

Yarra Ranges National Park. About 50 miles east of Melbourne, this nearly 200,000-acre national park extending north of the Yarra River has plenty to keep your legs busy. Cross a 1,148-foot long elevated walkway (known as the Rainforest Gallery) to see 400-year-old Mountain Ash and Myrtle Beech trees, trek the 18-mile O'Shannassy Aqueduct Trail, or climb the lookout tower at the peak of Mt. Donna. Afterward, unpack lunch at one of several picnic areas. For more advice, stop into the Yarra Valley Visitor Information Centre in Healesville. ✉ *Yarra Ranges National Park* ☎ *13–1963* ⊕ *www.parkweb.vic.gov.au.*

GOLFING

Warburton Golf Club. This gem of a course is hidden among the Yarra Ranges. For A$30 for 18 holes on weekends (A$24 on weekdays), you can golf over meandering streams and bushland blooming with wildflowers. Although it's a semiprivate club, visitors are very welcome to come and play 9 or 18 holes if they call and book in advance. Rental clubs are available (A$15) if you didn't pack your own. The course is hilly and golf carts can be hired for A$35. Warburton is 30 km

"Just a short drive from Melbourne is the captivating beauty of the Yarra Valley." —photo by lisargold, Fodors.com member

(19 miles) southeast of Healesville. ⊠ *17 Dammans Rd., Warburton* ☎ *03/5966–2306* ⊕ *www.warburtongolf.com.au* ✉ *18 holes: weekdays A$20, weekends A$30; 9 holes: A$18/A$21* ⛳ *18 holes, 5925 yards, par 69.*

WHERE TO EAT AND STAY

$$
PIZZA
✕ **Innocent Bystander.** Despite the lofty modern steel and glass interior, this spacious contemporary restaurant in the town of Healesville has a warm, welcoming feel, and serves excellent food. It also hosts a winery's cellar door, along with a gourmet food shop and bakery. Star of the menu is the pizza selection—try the Puttanesca pizza with Spanish white anchovies, tomatoes, capers, black olives, dill, and buffalo mozzarella (A$25), and wash it down with wine or beer from the region. The "not pizza" category includes sharing plates and mains like the ale-braised beef cheek (A$23). Don't overlook the spectacularly good house-made bread. The place is popular, especially on the weekend, so it's wise to book ahead. $ *Average main: A$25* ⊠ *336 Maroondah Hwy., Healesville* ☎ *03/5962–6111* ⊕ *www.innocentbystander.com.au.*

$$$$
MODERN
AUSTRALIAN
✕ **Stones of the Yarra Valley.** Housed in an old weather-beaten barn that has been beautifully restored, Stones of the Yarra Valley is set amid 50 acres of Cabernet vines and surrounded by century-old oak trees and views of the Yarra Ranges. The Barn is a great place to have weekend lunch (two courses for A$60 or three for A$75), and the Stables restaurant also serves weekend lunch and dinner on Friday and Saturday from 6:30 pm. The café next door, Meletos, also has a 23-room boutique guesthouse (from A$320 per night) created in a former farm building. $ *Average main: A$60* ⊠ *14 St. Huberts Rd., Coldstream*

☎ 03/9739–0900 ⊕ stonesoftheyarravalley.com ☯ No lunch weekdays. No dinner Sun.–Thurs. ⊜ Reservations essential.

$$$$ 　🖭 **Balgownie Estate Vineyard Resort and Spa.** This resort has it all—stylish
HOTEL 　suites and apartment-style accommodations with balconies overlooking
　the Yarra Valley and Dandenong Ranges, plus a ton of other ameni-
　ties. **Pros:** excellent facilities; on-site cellar door; great day spa. **Cons:**
　holds conferences, so may get busy at times. **$** *Rooms from: A$320*
　⊠ *Melba Hwy. and Gulf Rd., Yarra Glen ☎ 03/9730–0700 ⊕ www.*
　balgownieestate.com.au ⇝ 15 rooms, 55 spa suites ⎸○⎹ *Breakfast.*

$$$$ 　🖭 **Chateau Yering.** Once an 1860s homestead, whose grounds later
HOTEL 　became the Yarra Valley's first vineyard, this luxury hotel features
Fodor's Choice 　opulent suites that have antique furniture and deep claw-foot bath-
★ 　tubs. **Pros:** grand living; delicious food. **Cons:** this lifestyle comes at a
　luxurious price. **$** *Rooms from: A$415* ⊠ *42 Melba Hwy., Yarra Glen*
　☎ 03/9237–3333, 1800/237333 ⊕ www.chateauyering.com.au ⇝ 32
　suites ⎸○⎹ *Some meals.*

$ 　🖭 **Healesville Hotel.** This famous local lodge in a restored 1910 pub has
HOTEL 　seven colorful, modern upstairs rooms (A$175 for a Saturday night in
　high season, less on other nights) with high ceilings, tall windows, and
　genteel touches such as handmade soaps. **Pros:** funky accommodation;
　great food; historic hotel. **Cons:** limited facilities; shared bathrooms
　within the main building. **$** *Rooms from: A$135* ⊠ *256 Maroondah*
　Hwy., Healesville ☎ 03/5962–4002 ⊕ www.yarravalleyharvest.com.au
　⇝ *7 rooms, 1 house* ⎸○⎹ *No meals.*

SHOPPING

FAMILY **Yarra Valley Chocolaterie.** Resident European chocolatiers create a vast
array of high-quality treats in all shapes and styles—over 250 of them,
in fact—at this specialist chocolate and ice-cream maker. Many items
include locally grown ingredients such as rosemary and lavender, and
there's a bush tucker range of chocolates incorporating native plant
products such as lemon myrtle, jindilli nut, and wattle seed. They even
have a range of beauty products, if the adults want an excuse to smear
chocolate-inspired goodness all over their faces. The Chocolaterie has
year-round events including kids' chocolate-making classes. ■**TIP**➔ **The
on-site café ($) has a beautiful view over hilly green farmland and is a
great place to eat chocolate and made-on-the-premises ice cream, and
also serves light meals; we also suggest you buy a selection of chocolates to enjoy later.** ⊠ *35 Old Healesville Rd., Yarra Glen ☎ 03/9730–
2777 ⊕ www.yvci.com.au ☯ Daily 9–5.*

THE DANDENONG RANGES

Melburnians come to the beautiful Dandenong Ranges, also known
simply as the Dandenongs, for a breath of fresh air, especially in fall
when the deciduous trees turn golden and in spring when the public
gardens explode into color with tulip, daffodil, azalea, and rhododendron blooms. At Mt. Dandenong, the highest point (2,077 feet), a scenic
lookout known as SkyHigh Mt. Dandenong affords spectacular views
over Melbourne and the bay beyond. Dandenong Ranges National

Park, which encompasses five smaller parks, including Sherbrooke Forest and Ferntree Gully, has dozens of walking trails.

The many villages (which include Olinda, Sassafras, Kalorama, Sherbrooke, and Kallista) have curio shops, art galleries, food emporiums, cafés, and restaurants, and are dotted with lovely B&Bs. Visitors should be aware that the Dandenong Ranges and the high point of Mt. Dandenong are completely different from Dandenong, an outer suburb of Melbourne (30 km [19 miles] southeast of the downtown and on the Pakenham railway line).

GETTING HERE AND AROUND

Motorists can either take the Yarra Valley route *(see above)*, turn off at Lilydale, and head south to Montrose and on to Olinda, or take the South Eastern Freeway or M1 (a toll applies) and exit at Ferntree Gully Road. From there, take the Mt. Dandenong Tourist Road and follow it to Olinda, arriving from the south. Trains travel from Flinders Street Station to Belgrave on the Belgrave line. This town is on the southern edge of the Dandenongs and is the home of the steam train called *Puffing Billy*. Other towns on the same railway line are Ferntree Gully and Upper Ferntree Gully.

Bus 688 runs from Upper Ferntree Gully Station through the trees to Sassafras and Olinda, then passes William Ricketts Sanctuary; while Bus 694 links Belgrave Station to the Mt. Dandenong Lookout, via the villages of Sherbrooke, Sassafras, and Olinda. Alternatively, take the train from Flinders Street Station to Croydon (on the Lilydale line), then take the 688 bus south to William Ricketts Sanctuary and Olinda.

TOURS

Gray Line. This operator runs about a dozen tours in the region, including a half-day to the steam-powered Puffing Billy train, which can be combined with visits to wineries or Healesville Sanctuary. ⊠ *Federation Sq., Flinders and Russell Sts., City Center* ☎ *1300/858687* ⊕ *www.grayline.com.au* 🚅 *From A$93.*

Melbourne's Best Day Tours. This tour company takes visitors to major sights in the region, including the 12 Apostles, Sovereign Hill, and Mt. Buller, among others. Combine a trip on the Puffing Billy steam train with a full-day visit to the penguin parade on Phillip Island or with lunch at a winery. ⊠ *Federation Sq., Flinders and Russell Sts., City Center* ☎ *1300/130550* ⊕ *www.melbournetours.com.au* 🚅 *From A$110.*

ESSENTIALS

Visitor Information Dandenong Ranges Information Centre.
⊠ *1211 Burwood Hwy., Upper Ferntree Gully* ☎ *03/9758–7522* ⊕ *www. experiencethedandenongs.com.au.*

EXPLORING

Cloudehill Gardens & Nursery. These glorious gardens are divided into 20 "garden rooms" that include the Maple Court, the Azalea Steps, and 87-year-old European beech trees. They were first established in the late 1890s as commercial and cut-flower gardens by the Woolrich family. The gardens are dotted with artworks and the Diggers Garden Shop hosts workshops, as well as selling plants and books. A central terraced area, with manicured hedges and a sculpture of a huge vase, is stunning, as is the view across the mountain ranges from the garden café. The café serves breakfast, lunch, and afternoon tea daily, with some ingredients coming from its own kitchen garden. A popular dish is the "Chatter Platter" for two, with a selection of cheeses, dips, garlic prawns, and salad (A$50). ⊠ *89 Olinda-Monbulk Rd., Olinda* ☎ *03/9751–1009* ⊕ *www.cloudehill.com.au* 🖃 *A$10* ⊗ *Gardens daily 9–5, café daily 9:30–5.*

George Tindale Memorial Garden. Azaleas, camellias, and hydrangeas spill down the hillsides in this 6-acre garden. While at its most colorful in spring, when the flowers are in bloom, and in autumn, when the trees turn gold and yellow, it is also beautiful in winter with a touch of snow. It's located just 8 km (5 miles) north of Belgrave in the little forest settlement of Sherbrooke, where whipbird calls echo through the trees. ⊠ *33 Sherbrooke Rd., Sherbrook* ☎ *13–1963* ⊕ *parkweb.vic.gov.au* 🖃 *Free* ⊗ *Daily 10–5, last entry 4:30.*

Fodor's Choice ★ **National Rhododendron Gardens.** The expansive gardens contain thousands of rhododendrons, azaleas, and camellias; in spring they put on spectacular white, mauve, yellow, and pink blooms. Several miles of walking trails lead to vistas over the Yarra Valley, and the small Garden Explorer bus also provides transportation around the property in the springtime peak from mid-September to early November. The gardens are a short stroll from Olinda village. For a perfect afternoon, combine your visit with tea and scones in one of the little cafés around town. ⊠ *The Georgian Rd., Olinda* ☎ *131–963* ⊕ *parkweb.vic.gov.au* 🖃 *Free* ⊗ *Daily 10–5, last entry 4:30.*

FAMILY **Puffing Billy.** This gleaming narrow-gauge steam train, based 40 km (25 miles) from Healesville in the town of Belgrave, runs on a line originally built in the early 1900s to open up the Dandenong Ranges to 20th-century pioneers. It's a great way to see the foothill landscapes. Daily trips between Belgrave and Emerald Lake pass through picturesque forests and over spectacular wooden trestle bridges. The 13-km (8-mile) trip takes an hour; it's another hour if you continue to the historic town of Gembrook. There are also lunch and dinner trips, plus special music and children's events. ⊠ *1 Old Monbulk Rd., Belgrave* ☎ *03/9757–0700* ⊕ *www.puffingbilly.com.au* 🖃 *One-way from A$22.50, round-trip from A$30.50* ⊗ *Daily, hrs vary.*

FAMILY **SkyHigh Mount Dandenong.** This lookout at the top of Mt. Dandenong has breathtaking views over Melbourne to the Mornington Peninsula and Port Phillip Bay. You can picnic or barbecue on the grounds, eat at the bistro (lunch and dinner), or stroll along the pleasant English Garden Walk while the kids get lost in the hedge maze. Other fun attractions include a Wishing Tree and the Giant's Chair. ⊠ *26 Observatory Rd., Mt. Dandenong* ☎ *03/9751–0443* ⊕ *www.skyhighmtdandenong. com.au* 🖃 *A$6 per car; maze A$6 adults, A$4 children* ⊗ *Weekdays 9 am–10 pm, weekends 8 am–10:30 pm; bistro open for lunch and dinner daily, breakfast on weekends.*

Fodor's Choice ★ **William Ricketts Sanctuary.** Fern gardens, moss-covered rocks, waterfalls, towering mountain ash, and kiln-fired sculptures of Aborigines and

All aboard the *Puffing Billy* steam train

Australian native animals fill this 4-acre property on Mt. Dandenong. William Ricketts, who established the sanctuary in the 1930s, meant it to stand as an embodiment of his philosophy: that people must act as custodians of the natural environment as Australia's Aborigines have for many millennia. ⊠ *1402 Mt. Dandenong Tourist Rd., Mt. Dandenong* ☎ *13–1963 Parks Victoria* ⊕ *parkweb.vic.gov.au* ⊠ *Free* ☉ *Daily 10–4:30.*

SPORTS AND THE OUTDOORS
HIKING
Dandenong Ranges National Park. Several reserves, including the Sherbrooke Forest—home to Sherbrooke Falls—make up this beautiful leafy and hilly national park. Trails include the Olinda Forest Trail (from Mt. Dandenong to Kallista), the Western Trail from the top of Mt. Dandenong to Ferntree Gully, the Sherbrooke Loop, and the Tourist Track from Sassafras to Emerald. Brochures and a trail map are available from the visitor information center at Upper Ferntree Gully and some cafés in the area. Trail maps can also be found on the park's website. ⊠ *Dandenong Ranges, Olinda* ☎ *13–1963* ⊕ *www.parkweb.vic.gov.au.*

Heidelberg School Artists' Trail. Stay fit and brush up on Australian art by following the trail that commemorates famous Melbourne artists of the late 19th century, including Arthur Streeton, Tom Roberts, and Frederick McCubbin. These artists all painted around the Heidelberg area east of Melbourne. The Dandenongs section of this 40-km (25-mile) trail (which begins in Templestowe, Melbourne) displays nine of the route's 57 interpretive signs explaining the artists' work. ⊠ *Chalet Rd., Olinda* ☎ *13–1963.*

WHERE TO EAT AND STAY

Olinda is the main village in the Dandenong Ranges region and a good base for exploring the area. It's actually two villages (Lower and Upper Olinda, though Lower Olinda is better known by the name of the peak it sits beneath, Mt. Dandenong). The two are connected by Monash Road, along which you'll find a lot of the town's B&Bs and self-catering cottages. Olinda has a handful of good restaurants and cafés, and many specialty boutique stores selling curios and gifts. It's a short drive from here to the National Rhododendron Gardens, Olinda Falls picnic grounds, Cloudehill Gardens, and various hiking trails.

PERFECT PICNICS

The Dandenongs are heaven for fresh-air freaks and foodies. Pick up some goodies at Olinda's Saturday morning market and work up an appetite taking the 2-km (1½-mile) loop walk to Sherbrooke Falls from Donohue Picnic Grounds. Ask the tourist office about other great walks and picnic spots.

$ ✕ **Miss Marple's Tea Room.** This determinedly old-fashioned and charm-
CAFÉ ing establishment is modeled after an English tearoom and is renowned for its afternoon teas. Named after the famous Agatha Christie detective, this place is a holdout from the era when the Dandenong Ranges were visited by genteel folk looking for polite conversation over a civilized cup of tea. On the menu are classic light meals such as Quiche Lorraine and cottage pie, but what this tearoom is really known for is its scones. The large light, fluffy square-cut scones are served in sets of two (A$9.50), accompanied by homemade raspberry jam and whipped cream. They go nicely with the house tea blend, Yorkshire Gold. $ *Average main: A$17* ✉ *382 Mt. Dandenong Tourist Rd., Sassafras* ☎ *03/9755–1610* ⊕ *www.missmarplestearoom.com* ⟳ *Reservations not accepted.*

$$ ✕ **Ranges.** This popular café-restaurant, right in the heart of Olinda,
EUROPEAN buzzes all day and is the perfect place for a snack or meal after browsing the adjacent curio shops or gardens. It's open daily for breakfast, lunch, and morning and afternoon tea, and for dinner Tuesday to Saturday. Lunchtime fare includes an Asian-style salt and pepper calamari salad (A$22) and a daily homemade savory pie; at night you might want to begin with a cocktail while browsing the menu of hearty steaks and other tasty choices such as the barramundi fillet served with a caramelized garlic soy sauce (A$32). $ *Average main: A$30* ✉ *5 Olinda-Monbulk Rd., Olinda* ☎ *03/9751–2133* ⊕ *ranges.com.au* ☾ *No dinner Sun. and Mon.*

$$ ✕ **Ripe.** With crackling open fires in winter and a covered deck for sum-
AUSTRALIAN mer grazing, this buzzy cottage café-cum-providore is the perfect place for a heartwarming casual lunch or afternoon tea. The menu changes daily, but may include baguettes, fish, or pasta. Vegan, vegetarian, and gluten-free choices are available as well. And while the Dandenongs have a long tradition of Devonshire teas, temptation here mainly comes in the shape of mouthwatering cakes, all made with free-range eggs. You can also buy relishes, cheeses, and fresh Yarra Valley pasta to cook yourself. Look out for the prawn and macadamia ravioli. $ *Average main:*

A$22 ✉376 Mt. Dandenong Tourist Rd., Sassafras ☎03/9755–2100 ⊕ripecafe.net ⊗ No dinner ⌕ Reservations not accepted.

\$\$
EUROPEAN
✕ **Wild Oak Restaurant and Bar.** Warm up the taste buds with items from the restaurant's popular small dishes menu, which includes such treats as Thai scallops (A$13.90) or pork belly with wombok salad (A$15.90) alongside the house-baked sourdough bread. A heartier main dish is the pan-seared kangaroo fillet with ratatouille (A$38). Chef and owner Ben Higgs also conducts hands-on cooking classes with different themes for groups (minimum four people). Jazz performers play on the last Friday night of every month. $ *Average main: A$34 ✉232 Ridge Rd., Olinda ☎03/9751–2033 ⊕ www.wildoak.com.au ⊗ Closed Mon. and Tues.*

\$\$\$
RENTAL
☷ **Candlelight Cottage.** Curl up with a book in front of the open fire in this charming 1880s cottage, and you might be tempted not to do anything else in the Dandenongs. **Pros:** historic property. **Cons:** two-night minimum stay on weekends. $ *Rooms from: A$295 ✉7 Monash Ave., Olinda ☎03/9751–2464, 1300/488448 ⊕ www.candlelightcottages. com.au ⇄ 10 cottages ⦿Breakfast.*

MORNINGTON PENINSULA

The Mornington Peninsula circles the southeastern half of Port Phillip Bay. A much larger piece of land than it first appears, the peninsula is lapped by water on three sides and measures about 65 km (40 miles) by 35 km (22 miles). Along the bay's coast is a string of seaside villages stretching from the larger towns of Frankston and Mornington to the summer holiday towns of Mount Martha, Rosebud, Rye, Sorrento, and Portsea (which has one of the most dramatic—and hazardous—beaches in the region). On the Western Port Bay side the smaller settlements of Flinders, Somers, and Hastings have quieter beaches without the crowds.

Together with Main Ridge and Merricks, Red Hill is one of the state's premium producers of cool-climate wines, particularly Pinot Noir and Shiraz. The majority of the peninsula's 60 wineries are clustered around Red Hill and Red Hill South; however, there are another dozen or more dotted around areas farther north, including Moorooduc, Dromana, and Mount Martha. For an afternoon of fine wine, excellent seafood, and spectacular coastal views, plan a route that winds between vineyards. Red Hill has a busy produce-and-crafts market, which has been operating for decades and shows no signs of abating. It's held on the first Saturday morning of each month from September to May. A good website for getting all the lowdown on peninsular wineries is ⊕ *www. visitmorningtonvineyards.com.*

Sorrento is one of the region's prettiest beach towns and one of the most popular day-tripper spots on the peninsula. It's also the peninsula's oldest settlement, and thus is dotted with numerous historic buildings and National Trust sites (among them the Collins Settlement Historical Site, which marks the first settlement site at Sullivan Bay; and the Nepean Historical Society Museum, with its displays of Aboriginal artifacts and settlers' tools). In summer the town transforms from a sleepy seaside village into a hectic holiday hot spot. Sorrento Back Beach, with its rock pools and cliff-side trails, and Point King, with its piers and boathouses, are the two most popular hangouts.

GETTING HERE AND AROUND

Renting a car in Melbourne and driving south along the Nepean Highway is the most practical way of seeing the Mornington Peninsula. At Frankston you can take the Frankston-Moorooduc Highway or stay on the Nepean Highway—eventually they both merge into the Mornington Peninsula Highway, which continues south to the various bayside towns. A train runs from Flinders Street Station to Frankston. At Frankston, connect with a diesel-train service to towns on the east of the peninsula including Hastings, Bittern, Point Crib, and Stony Point. Buses also run from Frankston to the bay-side towns; the No. 781 bus goes to Mornington and Mount Martha and the No. 782 and 783 buses travel to Hastings and Flinders on the Western Port side.

Ferries run passenger services to Phillip Island from Stony Point, and a car and passenger ferry services Queenscliff and Sorrento. A shuttle bus runs from Melbourne Airport's international terminal to Frankston and the Mornington Peninsula.

Transportation Frankston and Peninsula Airport Shuttle. ☎ *03/9783–1199* ⊕ *www.fapas.com.au.* **Inter Island Ferries.** ☎ *03/9585–5730* ⊕ *www.interislandferries.com.au.* **Sorrento-Queenscliff Ferry.** ☎ *03/5258–3244* ⊕ *www.searoad.com.au.*

WINERY TOURS

Amour of the Grape. Set winery tours for groups of two to seven passengers, and personal tours for those who want to devise their own itinerary, are run by this company. The day's outing includes tastings at four or five preselected cellar doors, and a gourmet lunch and a glass of wine at a boutique winery café. Golf tours and spa packages are also available. ☎ *0414/704–801* ⊕ *www.amourofthegrape.com.au* ✉ *A$175 per person Mornington Peninsula pick-up; central Melbourne pick-up A$220 per person (for 4 to 7 people).*

Wine Tours Victoria. This Melbourne-based operator runs tours of four to five wineries using minivans for up to 10 people. Lunch with wine and coffee are also on the menu. ✉ *9 The Willows, Gisborne, Melbourne* ☎ *03/5428–8500, 1300/946386* ⊕ *www.winetours.com.au* ✉ *From A$165.*

ESSENTIALS

Visitor Information Mornington Community Information and Support Centre. ✉ *320 Main St., Mornington* ☎ *03/5975–1644* ⊕ *www.morninfo.org.au.* **Mornington Peninsula Visitor Information Centre.** ✉ *359B Point Nepean Rd., Dromana* ☎ *03/5987–3078, 1800/804009* ⊕ *www.visitmorningtonpeninsula.org.*

EXPLORING

TOP ATTRACTIONS

Crittenden Estate. One of the region's most picturesque wineries with a lovely lakeside setting, Crittenden Estate produces Chardonnay, Pinot Noir, Pinot Grigio, and some Spanish styles. The flagship Crittenden Estate Pinot Noir and Chardonnay are made from vines that are among the oldest on the peninsula. The cellar door is open for tastings daily, and winery tours can be arranged by appointment. The cellar door also contains a produce store selling olives, olive oil, dukkah, and other food that goes well with wine. The tasting room is wonderfully warm in winter. The restaurant, Stillwater at Crittenden ($$$), is lovely year-round, and when the weather is fine, diners sit out on a terrace under shady umbrellas while enjoying views over the lake. It is open weekends for dinner and daily for lunch, except in winter when it closes Monday and Tuesday. ⊠ *25 Harrisons Rd., Dromana* ☎ *03/5981–8322 winery, 03/5981–9555 restaurant, 03/5987–3800 cellar door* ⊕ *www. crittendenwines.com.au* ⊗ *Cellar door: daily 10:30–4:30. restaurant: lunch daily noon–3, dinner Fri. and Sat. 6–11.*

Red Hill Estate. This winery, which has won numerous medals for its Chardonnay, Pinot Noir, and Shiraz, has an equally impressive view. Not only are there sweeping vistas over the 22-acre vineyard, but the magnificent waters of Western Port Bay are spread out in the distance. On clear days you can see as far as Phillip Island and Wilsons Promontory as you wander around the gardens. The award-winning cuisine and fabulous floor-to-ceiling windows make **Max's Restaurant** ($$$, *No dinner Sun.–Thurs.*) the perfect place to while away at least half the day. In spring, Max's tasting plate presents all-local ingredients and is served with a glass of Red Hill Estate wine. Six days a week a two-course meal is A$70. On Sunday, you get three courses for A$80, and A$100 if you want matching wines for each course. Although it may be a little chilly, winter is a good time to visit, as several events are staged, including art shows and the region's Winter Wine Weekend in June. ⊠ *53 Shoreham Rd., Red Hill South* ☎ *03/5989–2838 cellar door, 03/5931–0177 restaurant* ⊕ *www.redhillestate.com.au* ⊗ *Daily 11–5.*

Stonier Winery. This preeminent Mornington Peninsula producer of wines uses grapes from the region's oldest vines. The establishment specializes in Chardonnay and Pinot Noir (from vines first planted in 1978 and 1982, respectively) and also makes a sparkling Pinot Noir Chardonnay, as well as a Cuvée Rosé. Although there's no restaurant, platters of local Red Hill cheeses accompany the daily tastings. If time permits, visitors may be invited on an informal tour of the fermentation and barrel rooms. Several events take place during the year, such as the Pie and Pinot day in winter (part of the regional Winter Wine Weekend), and a dedicated Sparkling day in December. ⊠ *2 Thompsons La., Merricks* ☎ *03/5989–8300* ⊕ *www.stonier.com.au* ⊗ *Daily 11–5.*

Fodor's Choice ★ **T'Gallant Winemakers.** Home to the peninsula's first Pinot Grigio vines, this popular Italian-themed winery also contains a restaurant. T'Gallant produces excellent Pinot Noir, Chardonnay, and Muscat. If you're an art lover as well as an wine fan, you'll also admire the beautiful artwork on its bottle labels. The on-site restaurant La Baracca Trattoria ($$) and the alfresco Spuntino Bar ($) are always buzzing and the food is exceptional, with dishes made from local ingredients, including items from the house herb garden. Tuck into one of the trattoria's signature Italian wood-fired pizzas or a chocolate ganache brownie paired with the Romeo Shiraz. The cellar door and restaurant/bar are open seven days a week, and there's live music every weekend at lunchtime. Their annual

Continued on page 286

In recent decades Australia has emerged as an international wine powerhouse. The country's varied climate has proven favorable for growing high-quality grapes, and winemakers now produce some of the world's best Shiraz (Syrah) wines, as well as acclaimed Pinot Noirs and Rieslings. Wine sales currently contribute about $5.5 billion to the country's economy, and Australia is the third largest supplier to the United States behind France and Italy.

Touring wineries here is easy, as most properties have tasting rooms with regular hours. Whether you're sipping *in situ* at a winery or tasting wines at a shop in Sydney, here's how to get the most from your wine experience.

By Erica Watson

(top) Pinot noir grapes (right) Vineyard in One Tree Hill, South Australia

Wines of
Australia

WINE TRENDS: THEN AND NOW

(top left) Wine bottles await labels, (bottom left) Hunter Valley vista, (right) tasting in Barossa Valley

Although the first grapes in Australia arrived with British settlers in 1787, it really wasn't until the mid 1960s that a more refined tradition of wine making began to take hold. Prior to 1960, Australia's wine repertoire extended little beyond sherry and port, but after WWII, an influx of European immigrants, notably from Germany and Italy, opened the country's eyes to new tastes and production methods.

Australia now produces many classic varietals at prices from A$10 to A$40,000 (for a 1951 Penfolds Grange Hermitage, made by Australian pioneer Max Schubert). There are more than 60 wine regions dotted across the country and many of the smaller producers in lesser-known areas are beginning to flourish.

Although the industry has experienced rapid growth, it hasn't been without its problems. The health of the global economy, international competition, global warming, disease, drought, and bushfire have each presented challenges along the way.

These days, Australian vintners are known for combining old traditions with new ideas and technical innovations. While oak barrels are still widely used, stainless steel and plastic tanks are now recognized as suitable fermentation and storage methods. Screw caps, introduced more than a decade ago, are becoming more popular with winemakers and consumers.

The industry's lastest trends also include a growing interest in environmental sustainability, with organic and biodynamic wines appearing from numerous producers. The internet has revolutionized business, giving even the smallest vintners access to an international stage.

Like well-cellared wine, the palate of modern Australia is continually maturing. Whether your taste is for robust reds from Coonawarra and Barossa or the delicate and versatile whites of the Hunter Valley and Margaret River, Australia's winemakers are producing beautiful wines perfect to enjoy now or later.

AUSTRALIA'S DOMINANT VARIETALS

REDS

SHIRAZ
Australia's classic varietal. A full-bodied wine that, in hot areas, makes an earthy expression with softer acidity. Cooler regions produce a leaner, peppery style.

CABERNET SAUVIGNON
Dark red with black-currant and black cherry flavors, often with firm tannins and more acidity than Shiraz.

MERLOT
Intensely purple colored, full-bodied wine character-ized by moderate tannins, aromas of plum, and a velvety mouth-feel.

PINOT NOIR
Lighter-bodied with gentle tannins and fruity aromas of red berries.

WHITES

CHARDONNAY
Full-bodied wine that is often high in alcohol and low in acidity. Most Austra-lian versions are oaked.

RIESLING
Lighter-bodied wines with citrus and honey notes. Most are unoaked and dry or slightly off-dry.

SAUVIGNON BLANC
Makes crisp, dry wines with high acid and aromas of peach and lime.

SEMILLON
Light-bodied wines that have crisp acidity and complex flavors, including herbs, nuts, and honey.

WHITE BLENDS
Chardonnay-Semillon and Sauvignon Blanc-Semillon blends are popular. Semil-lon adds bright notes.

5

IN FOCUS WINES OF AUSTRALIA

WINE TOURING TIPS

Large vintners like Rosemount, McGuigan Wines, Jacobs Creek, Yalumba, and Wolf Blass are well equipped for visitors and many offer vineyard tours, as well as restaurants or cafes. Some require appointments.

Many boutique producers also have "cellar doors," a.k.a. tast-ing rooms, open seven days a week, but it is advisable to check their websites for de-tails. The average tastings cost around A$10 to A$15 for a flight of up to five different styles. Some include cheese, cracker, and fruit plates.

Winery in Clare Valley

AUSSIE WINE REGIONS

SOUTH AUSTRALIA

Barossa Vallery

❶ BAROSSA VALLEY The country's best-known wine region, Barossa Valley has more than 550 grape growers, including some fifth- and sixth-generation families. Shiraz is highly celebrated, particularly the lauded Penfolds Grange. Cabernet Sauvignon, Grenache, Merlot, Riesling, Semillon, and Chardonnay are all well suited to Barossa's temperate climate, which is slightly cooler on its peaks and in neighboring Eden Valley. Big producers Jacobs Creek and Wolf Blass both have visitors centers with modern tasting rooms and restaurants. For a history lesson, take a tour at Langmeil Winery. An impressive property is Yalumba, with a stone winery and clock tower. So, too, is the well-established Peter Lehmann Estate on the banks of the North Para River.

❷ ADELAIDE HILLS For world-class Chardonnays, Sauvignon Blancs, Rieslings, and sparkling wines, look to the Adelaide Hills. Just 25 minutes from the center of Adelaide, this high-altitude region, amid Mount Lofty and down through the Piccadilly Valley, has nurtured elegantly refined white wines. The cooler climate also means that it's one of South Australia's leading producers of the temperamental Pinot Noir. There are about 25 cellars that offer tastings, including Petaluma Cellar, well known for its sparkling wines, Rieslings, and Chardonnays as well as its modern Bridgewater Mill restaurant. To try Italian varietals, head to Chain of Ponds. For excellent Sauvignon Blanc, stop into Shaw and Smith's 46-hectare estate.

❸ MCLAREN VALE Situated in the Fleurieu Peninsula region, McLaren Vale is an easy 40-minute trip south of Adelaide. Uniquely located by the coast, it's regarded as one of the more unpretentious regions thanks to laid-back beach lifestyle, passionate vintners, and family-owned wineries. This fusion of ideals, together with its warm climate, has most likely sparked its interest in experimenting with more exotic varieties such as Tempranillo, Zinfandel, and Mourvedre, as well as Viognier and Sangiovese. There are more than 60 cellar tasting rooms, ranging from the large producers such as Rosemount Estate and Tintara Winery to boutique producers such as Wirra Wirra, D'Arenberg, and Gemtree, each offering sales and wine flights that include the chance to sample local foods.

Adelaide Hills

Hunter Valley

④ LIMESTONE COAST

Coonawarra's long ripening season coupled with the region's "terra rossa" soil atop rich limestone beds is responsible for some of Australia's most famed wines, notably full-bodied reds. Often described as the Bordeaux of Australia, Coonawarra is a top spot for Cabernet Sauvignon, Cabernet blends, and spicy Shiraz. And they don't come any better than at places like Penley, Katnook Estate, Hollick, and Wynns Coonawarra Estate. Sixty kilometers to the north is Padthaway. While reds still prevail, the region's slightly warmer climate produces fruity Chardonnay and enjoyable Sauvignon Blanc, Verdelho, and Riesling. Built from limestone in 1882, the historic Padthaway Estate provides the perfect backdrop to sample some of the region's finest. Stonehaven and Henry's Drive are also worth a visit.

VICTORIA

⑤ YARRA VALLEY Close

proximity to Melbourne makes the Yarra an easy choice if your touring time is limited. A cool climate and diverse mix of volcanic and clay soils have allowed Chardonnay and Pinot Noir to flourish. Other notable varieties here include Viognier, Gewürztraminer, Pinot Gris, and Sauvignon Blanc, as well as Malbec, Sangiovese, and Nebbiolo. Sparkling wine is also a winner and Domaine Chandon is a magnificent spot to enjoy some perfect bubbly. For a laidback experience, Lillydale is also a good choice. But upping the style stakes is the magnificent Yering Station with its modern Australian restaurant and gallery space. Elsewhere, De Bortoli sells delicious top-end wines.

Yarra Valley

NEW SOUTH WALES
⑥ HUNTER VALLEY

Despite being a producer of award-winning Chardonnay, Verdelho, and Shiraz, it's the honeyed Semillon, which can mature for up to two decades, that Hunter Valley does best. Split into upper and lower regions, it has more that 150 years of winemaking up its sleeve and 120 cellar doors. It's safe to say the Hunter knows how to entertain. From large-scale music concerts at Bimbadgen Estate and Tempus Two to the annual Jazz in the Vines event and other small food and wine festivals year-round, the region is constantly buzzing. Pokolbin, Broke, Wollombi, Lovedale, Rothbury and Mt View are the main areas to sample the regions best offerings. Autumn is an excellent time to visit.

AUSSIE WINE REGIONS

Margaret River

WESTERN AUSTRALIA

❼ MARGARET RIVER REGION

With the first vines planted in 1967, Margaret River might be one of the country's younger wine areas but that hasn't stopped it from producing exceptionally high quality vintages. Cool breezes from the Indian Ocean and a steady, Mediterranean-style climate offer perfect conditions for developing complex styles of Chardonnay and minty-toned Cabernet Sauvignons. Shiraz, Merlot, Semillon, Sauvignon Blanc, and Chenin Blanc also thrive. Although the area produces about 20% of Australia's premium wines, it only accounts for about 3% of the nation's grapes. Try the West Australian Marron—or crayfish—with a crisp glass of Leeuwin Estate chardonnay. Cape Mentelle and Evans & Tate are also among the region's highlights, with many of their special releases sold only through their cellar doors.

READING THE LABEL

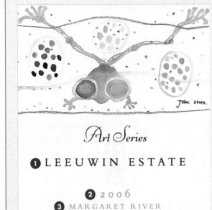

According to Australia's Label Integrity Program, when a wine label states region, grape variety, or vintage, then 85% of the wine contained in the bottle must come from that region, variety, or vintage.

❶ The producer of the wine.

❷ The vintage year, meaning the year the grapes were picked, crushed, and bottled.

❸ Australian GIs, or Geographic Indications, identify the region where the wine grapes were grown.

❹ The varietal, or type of grapes used to make the wine.

❺ The wine in this bottle contains 12% alcohol content by volume.

❻ The wine's country of origin.

❼ The volume of wine in the bottle.

MORE TASTING OPPORTUNITIES

Wine tasting at Mitchell Winery, Clare Valley

SIPPING IN SHOPS AND BARS

Even when you're not ensconced in the country's lush vineyards, high-quality wine isn't far away. The capital cities serve as a gateway for many of the wine country's top tastes.

In Sydney, try wine bars like the **Ivy's Ash Street Cellar**, **Glass Brasserie** wine bar at the Hilton Hotel and the **Gazebo Wine Garden** in Elizabeth Bay. **The Australian Wine Centre** in Circular Quay offers private tastings (with prior notice) and the **Ultimo Wine Centre** has free tastings each Saturday.

Heading south, visit Melbourne's **Prince Wine Store** at one of its three locations. Or soak up the atmosphere at **The Melbourne Supper Club** or **Melbourne Wine Room**. The bar of the award-winning **Press Club** restaurant also has an excellent Australian and international selection.

Apothecary 1878 on Adelaide's Hindley Street and **The Wine Underground**, just a few blocks away, both have a cosmopolitan ambience. Smaller vineyards are well represented at the city's **East End Cellars**.

In Perth, wine and dine alfresco at **Must Winebar** in Highgate. And **Amphoras Bar** in West Perth also has a long list of the country's best wines by the glass and bottle. No visit would be complete without heading to East Fremantle's **Wine Store**, for regular tastings and an extensive range of bottles. It also has an online store.

WINE FESTIVALS

Festivals offer chance to interact with the winemakers as well as sample local produce, especially cheese, fruit, and seafood. **The Barossa Vintage Festival** is one of the largest and longest running wine events in South Australia. Held in April each year it has everything from rare wine auctions to family friendly events. Other notables are **Adelaide's Tasting Australia** (April), **Coonawarra After Dark Weekend** (April), and **McLaren Vale Sea and Vines Festival** (June). In Western Australia, the **Margaret River Gourmet Escape** (April) celebrates culinary and winemaking talents.

RESEARCH & PLANNING

A little planning will allow you to make the perfect choices when it comes to deciding which regions to visit and where to taste. The websites of Australia's tourism commissions are filled with helpful planning informations. Not only do they offer winery information but also options for tours, accommodation and other sights to see while in the area. These include
⊕ www.visitvictoria.com,
⊕ www.southaustralia.com,
www.winecountry.com.au,
⊕ www.westernaustralia.com

Once on the ground, visitors centers such as the **Margaret River Wine Centre**, Adelaide's **National Wine Centre of Australia**, and **Hunter Valley Wine Country Tourism** can offer sound advice, especially on the best varietals and history of the regions.

Barossa Vintage Festival

winter Mushroom Festival is very popular and bookings for it are essential. ✉ *1385 Mornington–Flinders Rd., Main Ridge* ☎ *03/5931–1300* ⊕ *www.tgallant.com.au* ⊘ *Daily 9–5.*

WORTH NOTING

FAMILY **Arthurs Seat State Park.** Sweeping views of the surrounding countryside can be seen from this park, taking in Port Phillip Bay, Port Phillip Heads, and—on a clear day—the city skyline, the You Yangs, and Mt. Macedon. The mountain, which gives Arthurs Seat State Park its name, is the highest point on the Mornington Peninsula and named after Arthurs Seat in Edinburgh. A marked scenic drive snakes its way up to the summit, and walking tracks meander through the park's stands of eucalyptus. Seawinds, a public garden established by a local gardener in the 1940s, also forms part of the park and is a 10-minute walk or about 500 yards away. The road from Mornington is open at all times, so you can enjoy the spectacular mountaintop view by day or at night to see the lights. ✉ *Arthurs Seat Rd., Arthur's Seat* ☎ *13–1963* ⊕ *www.parkweb.vic.gov.au* ✉ *Free.*

BEACHES

Rosebud Beach. Backing onto the suburb of Rosebud, this popular beach has been rated one of the safest in Victoria. The white sand flats extend a long way offshore and sand bars keep the area protected for swimming,

BE AMAZED

Victorians do love their mazes, and you'll find these quaint English-garden features dotted around the Mornington Peninsula. There are topiary and sculptured mazes, mystery lawn puzzles, and big garden chess sets.

Ashcombe Maze & Lavender Gardens. Check out the world's first circular rose maze, a Cypress-hedge maze, a lavender labyrinth, and a "legendary" Great Gnome Hunt at this attraction, handily located east of T'Gallant Winery. ⊠ *15 Shoreham Rd., Shoreham* ☎ *03/5989–8387*

⊕ *www.ashcombemaze.com.au* 🖃 *A$18.50* ⊗ *Daily 8–5.*

Enchanted Maze Garden. Find your way through a traditional hedge maze or test your navigational skills in the indoor 3-D maze at this delightful attraction. The property also has "tree surfing," in which participants make their way through an aboveground obstacle course. ⊠ *55 Purves Rd., Arthur's Seat* ☎ *03/5981–8449* ⊕ *www. enchantedmaze.com.au* 🖃 *Gardens A$29, gardens and tree surfing A$59* ⊗ *Daily 10–6.*

while trees provide natural shade. The beach reserve includes a jetty (from which many locals fish), boat ramp, camping ground, and even a swimming pool. A picnic and barbecue area and playground in the adjacent Tom Salt Park make the beach a hit with families, and the nearby Bay Trail walking and cycling track is popular. Nearby accommodation tends to be motels and cottages for rent. **Amenities:** food and drink; lifeguards; parking (free); restrooms; showers. **Best for:** swimming; walking. ⊠ *Point Nepean Rd., end of Jetty Rd., Rosebud.*

SPORTS AND THE OUTDOORS
DIVING AND SNORKELING

Bayplay Adventure Tours. This adventure tour company runs a variety of activities, including diving, snorkelling, bike riding, and sea kayaking. You can explore colonies of weedy seadragons, dive through an octopus's garden, or feel the wash when dolphins leap over your kayak. Dives start from A$55, while a three-hour sea kayaking tour to a dolphin sanctuary costs A$99 per person. ⊠ *3755 Port Nepean Rd., Portsea* ☎ *03/5984–0888* ⊕ *www.bayplay.com.au.*

GOLF

Rosebud Park Public Golf Course. Situated on the steep slopes of Arthurs Seat overlooking Rosebud and Port Phillip Bay, this course provides spectacular views of greenery and water. The course has some extremely challenging holes, a resident teaching professional, plenty of parking, and excellent picnic facilities. Club hire (A$19) and motorized carts (A$40 for 18 holes) are available. Golfers can get light refreshments at the pro shop. ⊠ *Elizabeth Dr., Rosebud* ☎ *03/5981–2833* ⊕ *www. rosebudcountryclub.com.au* 🖃 *9 holes A$24, 18 holes A$36* 🏌 *18 holes, 5800 yards, par 70.*

HIKING

The Mornington Peninsula is a memorable walking destination. There are walks for all levels of fitness and interest, from cliff-top strolls to the ultimate 26-km (16-mile) Two Bays Walking Track. Stop in at the visitor information center at Dromana or Mornington to see what walking maps they have on hand, or contact Parks Victoria, the government body that manages the state's national parks.

Arthurs Seat State Park: There is a one-hour circuit walk to Kings Falls, and the relaxing Seawinds Gardens walk is less than a mile in length and takes only about half an hour.

Bushrangers Bay Walk: An exhilarating 6-km (4-mile) return walk along Western Port Bay begins at Cape Schanck Lighthouse and winds past basalt cliffs and Bushranger Bay, to finish at Main Creek.

Coppin's Track: A pleasant 3-km (2-mile) round-trip walk that stretches from Sorrento ocean beach (or Back Beach as it's known) to Jubilee Point along the Bass Strait coastline.

Two Bays Walking Track: A hardcore 26-km (16-mile) walking track that links Dromana, on Port Phillip Bay, with Cape Schanck on Western Port Bay.

HORSEBACK RIDING

FAMILY   **Ace-Hi Beach Rides.** Catering to both beginners and experienced riders, Ace-Hi has horse and pony rides on weekends and during school holidays (which includes the December to January summer vacation). One-hour scenic rides traverse the 200 acre property, while the Forest and Bush'n'Beach rides go farther afield. Short and simple pony rides give the under-sixes some fun as well. ⊠ *810 Boneo Rd., Cape Schanck* ☎ *03/5988–6262* ⊕ *www.ace-hi.com.au* 🖃 *From A$55 per hr.*

WHERE TO EAT AND STAY

$ ✕ **Cellar & Pantry.** Busy produce store-cum-deli, this is the perfect place
DELI   to pick up the makings of a picnic lunch or a dinner in self-contained accommodation. It is packed full of crusty loaves, cured and fresh meats, fruits and vegetables, aromatic cheeses, olives, relishes and chutneys, and countless other goodies. Most are grown or made on the Mornington Peninsula. The veranda is a popular spot for a light breakfast or lunch, or coffee and cake; coffee beans and local wines are also sold. Ⓢ *Average main: A$11* ⊠ *141 Shoreham Rd., Red Hill South* ☎ *03/5989–2411* ⊕ *www.cellarandpantry.com.au.*

$$$ ✕ **Montalto Vineyard & Olive Grove.** Overlooking a vineyard of rolling
FRENCH   green hills, this restaurant serves excellent French-inspired cuisine. Open
Fodor's Choice   daily for lunch (though closed Wednesday in winter), the restaurant has
★   an à la carte weekday menu, and on weekends diners choose either a two-course (A$75) or three-course (A$88) meal. The menu changes regularly, based on available local produce. The wine list borrows from the best of the estate's vintages, as well as classic wines from other regions. The open-air Piazza Café (open weekends) dishes up casual dining. From October to April, you can picnic on the grounds from hampers prepared by the restaurant. The picnics are hugely popular, so book well in advance. Take a moment to check out the herb garden and the nut and berry orchard, and admire the sculptures on permanent display. If

you're visiting from mid-February to late April you'll be able to see the entries in the Montalto Sculpture Prize and vote for your favorite. The expansive property also includes a natural wetlands and specially built boardwalks, from which visitors have a chance of spotting more than 90 bird species. The Cellar Door is open daily from 11 to 5. $ *Average main: A$36* ⊠ *33 Shoreham Rd., Red Hill South* ☎ *03/5989–8412* ⊕ *www.montalto.com.au* ✆ *No dinner Sun.–Thurs.*

$$$
HOTEL
Hotel Sorrento. Built in 1871, this historic hotel has attractive rooms with exposed limestone, funky interiors, and water views. **Pros:** great location; impressive views from some rooms. **Cons:** limited facilities. $ *Rooms from: A$280* ⊠ *15 Hotham Rd., Sorrento* ☎ *03/5984–8000* ⊕ *www.hotelsorrento.com.au* ✆ *3 rooms, 28 suites, 6 apartments* ⍾ *Breakfast.*

$$$$
B&B/INN
Fodor's Choice
★
Lakeside Villas at Crittenden Estate. Wine and dine to your heart's content, then amble home to this accommodation next to a tranquil lake. **Pros:** fantastic position; stylish and snug; all villas are wheelchair accessible. **Cons:** nearby Stillwater Restaurant is open for dinner only on Friday and Saturday. $ *Rooms from: A$320* ⊠ *25 Harrisons Rd., Dromana* ☎ *03/5987–3275* ⊕ *www.lakesidevillas.com.au* ✆ *3 villas* ⍾ *Breakfast.*

PHILLIP ISLAND

124 km (78 miles) southeast of Melbourne.

South of Melbourne and just off the Mornington Peninsula, Phillip Island has long been a playground for Victorians. Both the coast and the interior are appealing, with beaches and native animals such as koalas among the attractions. The perennial highlight, however, is the famous Penguin Parade, in which the seabirds march ashore to the delight of onlookers.

At low tide you can walk across a basalt causeway to the Nobbies (rugged coastal rocks); a boardwalk here takes you around the windswept coastline to a blowhole. Thousands of shearwaters (also known as mutton birds) nest here from September to April, when they return north to the Bering Strait in the Arctic. Farther out, Seal Rocks host Australia's largest colony of fur seals; up to 20,000 creatures bask on the rocky platforms and cavort in the water here in midsummer. Boat tours cruise past these playful creatures in all but the coldest months.

GETTING HERE AND AROUND

To reach the island from Melbourne, take the Princes Freeway (M1) southeast to the South Gippsland Highway (M420), and follow this to the Bass Highway (A420). V/Line runs combined train and bus service directly to Cowes, or a train to Stony Point, where a daily passenger ferry runs to Phillip Island.

Transportation Inter Island Ferries. ☎ *03/9585–5730* ⊕ *www. interislandferries.com.au.* **V/Line.** ☎ *1800/800007* ⊕ *www.vline.com.au.*

TOURS

Gray Line. This operator runs various day tours of the penguin parade, often combined with other sights, including Seal Rocks or *Puffing Billy* in the hills. ☏ *1300/858687* ⊕ *www.grayline.com.au* ✉ *From A$139.*

FAMILY   **Melbourne's Best Day Tours.** Take a day tour to see the penguin parade, or sign up for the full Phillip Island Wildlife and Penguin Experience, which includes a visit to Seal Rocks and the Koala Conservation Centre. ☏ *1300/130550* ⊕ *www.melbournetours.com.au* ✉ *From A$125.*

Wildlife Coast Cruises. This operator runs two-hour cruises from Cowes Jetty to the Nobbies and Seal Rocks, spending 20–30 minutes viewing the seal colony. Cruises run year-round with varying frequency, depending on the season. The company also has full-day and half-day cruises, and one-hour trips to Cape Woolamai from September to May. ✉ *13 The Esplanade, Cowes* ☏ *1300/763739* ⊕ *www.wildlifecoastcruises. com.au* ✉ *From A$25.*

ESSENTIALS

Visitor Information Phillip Island Visitor Information Centre. ✉ *895 Phillip Island Rd., Newhaven* ☏ *03/5956–7447, 1300/366422* ⊕ *www.visitphillipisland.com.*

EXPLORING

Cowes. The seaside town of Cowes is the hub of Phillip Island; the pier is where you can board sightseeing cruises and the passenger ferry that travels across Western Port Bay to Stony Point on the Mornington Peninsula. It has a lively café scene and several quality gift shops interspersed with the traditionally cheaper tourist fare. Restaurant and hotel bookings are essential in the busy summer months. ✉ *Cowes.*

FAMILY   **Koala Conservation Centre.** At this excellent wildlife center you can stroll along treetop-high boardwalks and view koalas in their natural habitat. At the visitor center, learn some fascinating things about the cute furry creatures—such as how they sleep 21 hours a day. It is located just a short drive from the tourist information center at Newhaven; follow the signs along Phillip Island Tourist Road. ✉ *1810 Phillip Island Tourist Rd., Cowes* ☏ *03/5951–2800* ⊕ *www.penguins.org.au/attractions/ koala-conservation-centre* ✉ *A$12.25* ☉ *Daily 10–5.*

FAMILY
Fodor's Choice
★

Penguin Parade. Phillip Island's main draw is the nightly parade of Little Penguins, also called Fairy Penguins, waddling from the sea to their burrows in nearby dunes. The parade of miniature penguins attracts onlookers year-round and crowds on summer weekends and holidays. There are several ways to view the Penguin Parade: general admission, with viewing from concrete bleachers; the Penguin Plus experience, which puts you on a smaller viewing platform that is closer to the action. There's even a small underground section to watch the penguins as they go to their nests. The Guided Ranger Tour puts you on the sand with a ranger, while the VIP Tour gets you into a private, elevated "Skybox" overlooking the beach. The Ultimate Adventure Tour, for private groups, includes headphones and night-vision equipment and a secluded spot on a separate beach. The spectacle begins at around sunset each night; booking ahead is essential in summer and during public holidays. Wear closed shoes and warm clothing—even in summer—and rain protection gear. Make sure to arrive an hour before the tour begins. A good deal for visitors staying for a day is the 3 Park Pass, giving admission to the Penguin Parade, the Koala Conservation Centre, and Churchill Island. ⊠ *1019 Ventnor Rd.* ☎ *03/5951–2800* ⊕ *www. penguins.org.au* ✉ *General admission A$24.50; Penguin Plus viewing platform A$47.20; Underground Viewing A$60; VIP and Guided Ranger Tours A$75.90; Ultimate Adventure Tour A$86.40; 3 Parks Pass from A$41.60* ⊗ *Daily, time changes throughout yr.*

BEACHES

Cape Woolamai Surf Beach. Phillip Island's only surf lifesaving club is based on this long, exposed stretch of prime surfing beach. The 4.2-km (2.6-mile) beach can be hazardous, with strong undertows, so it's a spot for experienced surfers and swimmers only. All beachgoers are encouraged to swim between the safety flags that mark the patrolled area. Check with the club (*03/5956–7311*) for patrol times. The Woolamai Beach Road runs off Phillip Island Road and is 14 km (9 miles) from Cowes. The nearest accommodation is generally cottage-style, with several places closer to the main road but none on the beach. Black Dolphin has a luxury penthouse and a cottage on the Cape, on Corona Road. **Amenities:** food and drink; lifeguards; parking (free); restrooms; showers. **Best for:** surfing; swimming. ⊠ *Woolamai Beach Rd., Cape Woolamai.*

Kitty Miller Bay. Regarded as one of Australia's best beaches, this south-facing beach provides excellent swimming and snorkeling, and a walking trail to view the remains of the wreck of the SS *Speke* at low tide. Sheltered by Watts Point and Kennon Head, the curved beach has low waves, with undertows only appearing when the waves whip up at high tide, which is the best time for surfing. There's not much shade and no kiosk, so bring water, food, and sunscreen with you. The beach is at the intersection with Watts Road. From Cowes, go either via Ventnor Road to Back Beach Road, or via Phillip Island Road and Back Beach Road, turning onto Kitty Miller Road. The beach is around 10 km (6 miles) from Cowes. The low key nature of Phillip Island and the remote nature of the beach means that accommodation is usually B&B-style. Try the Kitty Miller Bay B&B on Watts Road. **Amenities:** parking (free). **Best for:** snorkeling; surfing; swimming; walking. ⊠ *Kitty Miller Rd.*

SPORTS AND THE OUTDOORS

AUTO-RACING

FAMILY **Phillip Island Grand Prix Circuit.** This racing circuit continues the island's long involvement with motor sports, dating back to 1928 when the Australian Grand Prix was run on local unpaved roads. The circuit was completely redeveloped in the 1980s, and in 1989 hosted the first Australian Motorcycle Grand Prix. The circuit holds regular races as well as big-ticket events, such as the MotoGP in October and Superbike World Championships in February. Speed freaks can buckle-up for hot laps in a racing car (from A$330 for 30 minutes) driven by a professional driver year round (dates and times vary, see website), or drive a go-kart (A$35 for 10 minutes) around a scale replica of the actual track. There are 60-minute guided walking tours of the track daily at 2 (subject to availability); a 45-meter slot car Grand Prix Circuit replica racing track; and a museum showcasing the Island's motor racing history. ⊠ *Back Beach Rd.* ☎ *03/5952–9400* ⊕ *www.phillipislandcircuit. com.au* ✉ *Tours A$22, museum A$15, slot cars A$8* ⊘ *Nov.–Apr. 9–7; May–Oct. 9:30–5; track tours at 2.*

WHERE TO EAT AND STAY

$$$

ECLECTIC

✕ **Harry's on the Esplanade.** Spilling onto an upstairs terrace above the main Cowes beach, Harry's is a Phillip Island institution. Its menu, which changes regularly, draws heavily on seafood bought fresh from local trawlers, along with locally raised beef and lamb. Don't pass up the crayfish if it's on the menu. The wine list has an Australian emphasis and includes local wines. The bread is made on the premises, as are the pastries and ice cream. ⑤ *Average main: A$38* ⊠ *Upper level, 17 The Esplanade, Cowes* ☎ *03/5952–6226* ⊕ *www.harrysrestaurant.com.au* ⊘ *Closed Mon.*

$$$$

B&B/INN

🛏 **Glen Isla House.** A beautiful, safe swimming beach is right at the doorstep of this luxurious B&B, which contains six individually themed rooms. **Pros:** gorgeous furnishings; on a pristine beach; short drive to penguins. **Cons:** the heritage style may be too traditional for some. ⑤ *Rooms from: A$305* ⊠ *230 Church St., Cowes* ☎ *03/5952–1882* ⊕ *www.glenisla.com* ➽ *6 rooms, 1 suite, 1 cottage* ⦿ *Breakfast.*

QUEENSCLIFF

103 km (64 miles) southwest of Melbourne.

In the late 19th century Queenscliff was a favorite weekend destination for well-to-do Melburnians, who traveled by paddle steamer or train to stay at the area's grand hotels, some of which are still in business today. Be sure to check out Fort Queenscliff, another landmark from bygone days. Good restaurants and quiet charm are also traits of Queenscliff. The playground of families during the day and dog walkers come dusk, Queenscliff is a restful alternative to the resort towns of Sorrento and Portsea on the other side of the bay. At the end of November the annual Queenscliff Music Festival (⊕ *www.qmf.net.au*) draws thousands of visitors to town.

GETTING HERE AND AROUND

The lovely coastal village of Queenscliff and nearby smaller sibling Point Lonsdale make for a worthy—and well-signposted—detour on the drive from Melbourne to the start of the Great Ocean Road.

It's about a 60- to 90-minute drive from Melbourne to Geelong via the Princes Freeway (M1), then to Queenscliff via the Bellarine Highway (B110). Trains run from Melbourne's Southern Cross Station to Geelong, where buses (Nos. 75 and 76) continue on to Queenscliff. The Queenscliff–Sorrento Ferry departs on the hour (in both directions) from 7 am to 6 pm and to 7 pm in the summer months. The journey takes 40 minutes and costs A$10 for pedestrians, A$69 for cars including two passengers in the high season.

It's easy to walk around Queenscliff's main attractions; ask at the visitor center in Hesse Street for maps.

Transportation Bellarine Railway. ✉ *Queenscliff Railway Station, 20 Symonds St.* ☎ *03/5258–2069* ⊕ *bellarinerailway.com.au.* **Queenscliff–Sorrento Ferry.** ✉ *Queenscliff* ☎ *03/5258–3244* ⊕ *www.searoad.com.au.* **V/Line.** ☎ *1800/800007* ⊕ *www.vline.com.au.*

ESSENTIALS

Visitor Information Queenscliffe Visitor Information Centre. ✉ *55 Hesse St.* ☎ *03/5258–4843, 1300/884843* ⊕ *www.queenscliffe.vic.gov.au.*

WHERE TO STAY

$$$
HOTEL
Fodor's Choice
★

Vue Grand Hotel. Built in 1881, this stylish hotel blends old world elegance with modern touches in its recently restored grand premises. **Pros:** grand experience; wonderful dining room. **Cons:** not on the seaside. ⓢ *Rooms from: A$250* ✉ *46 Hesse St.* ☎ *03/5258–1544* ⊕ *www.vuegrand.com.au* ⤳ *29 rooms, 3 suites* ⫿◯⫿ *Breakfast.*

> ## LIGHT UP YOUR TRIP
>
> If you're into lighthouses, then this coast is a must-see. Here you can find seven historic lighthouses of varying shapes and sizes—from Point Lonsdale in the east to Portland in the west. Don't miss the tall red-capped white **Split Point Lighthouse** at Aireys Inlet, while **Cape Otway Lighthouse**, the oldest on mainland Australia, marks the point where the Southern Ocean and Bass Strait collide. Farther west at Portland is majestic **Cape Nelson Lighthouse**, high above ferocious seas. Guided tours are available.

EN ROUTE
From Queenscliff, follow Great Ocean Road signs for 45 km (28 miles) to **Torquay,** Australia's premier surfing and windsurfing resort, and Bell's Beach, famous for its Easter surfing contests and its October international windsurfing competitions. The Great Ocean Road, a positively magnificent coastal drive, officially begins at Eastern View, 10 km (6 miles) east of Lorne. The seaside towns of Anglesea, Aireys Inlet, and Fairhaven are other good warm-weather swimming spots.

GREAT OCEAN ROAD

The Great Ocean Road, which snakes along Victoria's rugged and windswept southwestern coast, is arguably Australia's most spectacular coastal drive. The road, built by returned soldiers after World War I along majestic cliffs, occasionally dips down to sea level. Here, in championship surfing country, some of the world's finest waves pound mile after mile of uninhabited, golden, sandy beaches and rocky headlands.

Although this region is actually on the southeast coast of the Australian mainland, it lies to the west of Melbourne, and so Melburnians refer to it as the "West Coast." From the city, you should allow two or more days for a West Coast sojourn.

Driving is the most convenient way to see the region, and the only way to really enjoy the Great Ocean Road. Although the route is officially deemed to be 243 km (152 miles), and runs between the towns of Torquay in the east and Allansford (near Warnambool) in the west, most people think of it as the much longer route that continues farther west to Port Fairy and Portland. Its many twists and turns and wonderful sights along the way take many hours to explore.

Sea kayaking in Apollo Bay

The going may be slow on the most scenic routes, especially during the summer holiday period. The winding road is notorious for its motor accidents (you'll notice roadside signs along the route reminding visitors that Australia drives on the left), so take care on the bends and slow down.

TOURS

AAT Kings. This operator has a six-day tour from Melbourne to Adelaide that travels the length of the Great Ocean Road and also includes visits to Mt. Gambier and Kangaroo Island. ⊠ *Melbourne Day Tours, Federation Sq., Flinders and Russell Sts., City Center* ☎ *1300/228546* ⊕ *www. aatkings.com.au* ✉ *From A$2195.*

Adventure Tours Australia. Find adventure on one-day tours to both the Great Ocean Road and the Grampians National Park (A$125 each), or you can take longer tours going on to Adelaide. The two-day option (A$295) visits the Great Ocean Road and the Grampians before arriving in Adelaide, and the four-day tour (A$780) includes an overnight stay on Kangaroo Island in South Australia. Some meals are included. Young backpackers are the target market, but anyone can join the tours, and there's a choice between dorm accommodation and singles or doubles. ☎ *03/8102–7800, 1300/654604* ⊕ *www.adventuretours. com.au* ✉ *From A$125.*

Auswalk. This tour company runs guided (seven-day) and self-guided (five- or eight-day) Great Ocean Walk tours. The short self-guided walk takes you from Apollo Bay to the Twelve Apostles over five days, taking in Wreck Beach and Loch Ard Gorge. The longer self-guided trip covers more beaches, Rainbow Falls and koala habitats. Walkers carry a day pack only; a support vehicle carries the luggage by car from hotel (or B&B) to hotel. Some tours include a night in the 19th-century Cape Otway Lighthouse cottages, and most meals are provided. Both guided and self-guided tours can be arranged year-round and generally require a minimum of two people. The seven-day group guided tour starts from A$2,595 per person (double) depending on the season, with a A$375 singles supplement. Each day's walking can range from five to seven hours, although the support vehicle can drive those who feel they have had enough walking for one day. ☎ *03/9530–8800* ⊕ *www.auswalk. com.au* ⊠ *From $A2245*.

Great Ocean Road Adventure Tours. GORATS, as this operator's called, runs mountain-bike tours across the region. Many tours run to the town of Forrest, considered a mountain-bike mecca, and numerous trails in the area showcase the natural beauty of the Otway Ranges. GORATS specializes in school groups but can tailor-make trips for a minimum of two people. Fees cover a two-hour trip, including bike, helmet, map, transport, and guide; pickups from local accommodations can be arranged. Flat-water canoe tours on the Barwon, Anglesea, and Aire rivers are also available. ☎ *0417/576–973* ⊕ *www.gorats.com.au* ⊠ *From A$85*.

Melbourne's Best Day Tours. This operator's 4WD tour of the Great Ocean Road from Melbourne starts at 7:30 am and includes breakfast and lunch, a lighthouse tour, rain-forest walks, the Otway Fly treetop walk, and sightseeing in Port Campbell National Park. The 12-hour tour takes a minimum of four people. ⊠ *Federation Square, Flinders and Russell Sts., City Center* ☎ *1300/130550* ⊕ *www.melbournetours.com. au* ⊠ *From A$326*.

Mulloka Cruises. Explore Port Fairy Bay on half-hour cruises—a quick way to get your sea legs and see Port Fairy from a different angle and learn more about it from the boat's owner. It's best to book in advance. ⊠ *Martins Point, end of wharf, Port Fairy* ☎ *0408/514–382* ⊠ *From A$10*.

Port Campbell Boat Charters. Dive to see famous wrecks (from A$60 per person), or relax above water on scenic cruises (from A$50 per person) and fishing trips (from A$70 per person), all for a minimum of five people. ⊠ *32 Lord St., Port Campbell* ☎ *0428/986–366* ⊕ *www. portcampbellboatcharters.com.au* ⊠ *From A$40*.

Southern Exposure Adventure Sports. Southern Exposure Adventure Sports runs mountain-bike tours along the coast and in the nearby Great Otway National Park, kayaking tours, and surfing lessons. Surfing lessons are A$85 for two hours, and combined bike and kayaking tours can be arranged. Bookings are essential. ⊠ *31 Baines Crescent* ☎ *03/5261–9170, 0425/784–643 mobile* ⊕ *www.southernexposure. com.au* ⊠ *From A$85*.

Split Point Lighthouse tours. Explore the majestic, and still operational, Split Point Lighthouse at Aireys Inlet, also known as the White Queen. You can see her for miles as you approach this section of the Great Ocean Road west of Anglesea—just look for the huge white tower with the red cap—and the views from the top are amazing. The 45-minute tours operate year-round, but bookings are required on weekdays. ✉ *Split Point lighthouse, Federal St., Aireys Inlet* ☎ *1800/174045* ⊕ *www.splitpointlighthouse.com.au* ✉ *From A$14.*

Spring Creek Horse Rides. Ride through beautiful Otway National Park on horseback for a leisurely hour or two. ✉ *245 Portreath Rd., Bellbrae* ☎ *03/5266–1541, 0403/167–590 mobile* ⊕ *www.springcreekhorserides. com.au* ✉ *From A$45.*

12 Apostles Helicopters. One exciting way to appreciate the awesome force of the Southern Ocean and this amazing natural sculpture park is by helicopter. Fifteen-minute flights take in the Twelve Apostles and Loch Ard Gorge; longer flights travel farther up the coast to the west and inland. ✉ *Twelve Apostles Information Centre, Great Ocean Rd., at Booringa Rd., Port Campbell* ☎ *03/5598–8283* ⊕ *www.12apostleshelicopters. com.au* ✉ *From A$145.*

ESSENTIALS

Visitor Information Geelong and Great Ocean Road Visitor Information Centre. ✉ *Princes Hwy., at the gas station, 20 km (12 miles) before Geelong, Little River* ☎ *03/5283–1735, 1800/755611* ⊕ *www.visitgeelongbellarine.com.au.* **Torquay Visitor Information Centre.** ✉ *Surf City Plaza, Beach Rd., Melbourne* ☎ *03/5261–4219, 1300/614219* ⊕ *www.visittorquay.org.*

LORNE

148 km (92 miles) southwest of Melbourne, 95 km (59 miles) southwest of Queenscliff, 50 km (31 miles) southwest of Torquay.

Located between sweeping Loutit Bay and the Otway Mountain Range, Lorne is one of the main towns on the Great Ocean Road, with a definite surf-and-holiday feel. It's the site of both a wild celebration every New Year's Eve and the popular Pier-to-Pub Swim held on the first weekend in January. Some people make their reservations a year or more in advance. It's also the starting point for the Great Ocean Road International Marathon held each May (the footrace ends in Apollo Bay). The town has a lively café and pub scene, as well as several upscale restaurants, trendy boutiques, and a day spa.

GETTING HERE AND AROUND

You really need a car to get to Lorne and other Great Ocean Road towns; the next best option is to take an organized tour. Public transport is available, but it's a long process: take the V/Line train to Geelong, then transfer to a bus to Apollo Bay, which stops at Lorne (about five hours). If driving, take the Princes Highway west from Melbourne across the Westgate Bridge to Geelong. From there, follow signs along the Surf Coast Highway to Torquay, where you'll connect with the Great Ocean Road.

ESSENTIALS

Visitor Information Lorne Visitor Information Centre. ✉ *15 Mountjoy Parade* ☎ *03/5289–1152, 1300/891152* ⊕ *www.visitlorne.org.*

Great Ocean Road and the Gold Country

BEACHES

Lorne Beach. This stretch of the Victorian coast is also called The Shipwreck Coast, with reputedly up to 700 ships at rest offshore. Lorne itself has a shipwreck plaque walk along the foreshore, giving the history of local disasters and near-misses dating from 1854. The Lorne Surf Life Saving Club patrols the southern end of popular Lorne Beach, which runs south from the Erskine River for 1.2 km (¾ mile). Although a fairly safe beach, especially in summer, care must be taken when the waves are high as the undertow can be dangerous. The beach has parking for 250 cars, a lookout, shade trees and shelters, barbecue and play areas, and a cycle track. The Lorne Beach Pavilion has a swimming pool and skate park as well. A camping ground and caravan park are also near the beach. Parking is available at the junction of Bay Street, Mountjoy Parade, and the Great Ocean Road, or along the Great Ocean Road itself. Other entrances to the beach are via **Grove Street** or **William Street**. The Mantra Lorne resort, with 12 acres of gardens and a range of rooms and apartments, is directly on the beach. **Amenities:** food and drink; lifeguards; parking (free); restrooms; showers. **Best for:** surfing; swimming; walking. ⊠ *Great Ocean Rd., at Bay St.*

SPORTS AND THE OUTDOORS

HIKING

The Great Ocean Road and the "Surf Coast" section of it around Torquay, Lorne, and Aireys Inlet have fantastic walks providing great cliff-top views, while inland a little way there are waterfalls and picnic grounds to explore.

The 30-km (19-mile) Surf Coast Walk, which begins near Jan Juc car park (1 mile west of Torquay) and ends around Moggs Creek Picnic Area at Aireys, can be done in short segments.

Inland from the towns of Fairweather and Eastern View is the vast Great Otway National Park, which has many picturesque walks, including the 12-km (7½-mile) walk from Aireys Inlet to Distillery Creek, which can be quite strenuous. There are also shorter and easier walks to Erskine Falls and Sheoak Falls just inland from Lorne. The Torquay and Lorne visitor centers have trail maps.

WHERE TO EAT AND STAY

$$ ✕ **Marks.** Fresh seafood—from fried calamari to roasted flathead—is
SEAFOOD the draw at this Lorne institution, which has been going strong since 1989. The design is "funky seaside," with bright walls, blue chairs, and a smattering of local art and sculpture for sale. The menu changes daily depending on what the fishermen have caught and what's growing in the restaurant's garden, but you'll always find oysters and steak on the menu, along with Atlantic salmon, and perhaps Sicilian seafood soup. For dessert there's nothing more delicious than the chocolate mousse served between vanilla biscuits with Kahlúa cream. Opening hours are extended during the summer months. $ *Average main: A$34* ⊠ *122 Mountjoy Parade* ☎ *03/5289–2787* ⊕ *www.marksrestaurant.com.au* ⊗ *Closed Sun. and Mon. and in July and Aug. No lunch Sun.–Thurs.*

$$$$ ▥ **Mantra Lorne.** You can fall asleep listening to waves rolling ashore at
RESORT this huge complex on 12 acres near the water's edge in Lorne. **Pros:** close to the beach; lots of facilities. **Cons:** fee for Internet. $ *Rooms from: A$379* ⊠ *Mountjoy Parade* ☎ *03/5228–9777* ⊕ *www.mantralorne. com.au* ⇨ *142 rooms, 135 apartments* ⦿|*Breakfast.*

EN
ROUTE **Otway Fly Treetop Adventures.** A spectacular 1,969-foot-long elevated treetop walk allows you to stroll a steel walkway above the rain forest canopy. One section is springboard-cantilevered, and gently bounces as you pass over Young's Creek. The entrance is about an hour's drive and 70 km (43 miles) from Lorne. To get there, follow the Great Ocean Road until it joins Skenes Creek Road, then take Forrest Apollo Bay Road to Beech Forest Road, then Colac Lavers Hill Road until you reach the signed turnoff to Phillips Track. From the Fly you'll see the tops of giant myrtle beech, blackwood, and mountain ash trees, as well as spectacular views of the surrounding region. ⊠ *360 Phillips Track* ☎ *03/5235–9200, 1800/300477* ⊕ *www.otwayflytreetopadventures. com.au* ▱ *A$25* ⊗ *Daily 9–5; last entry to treetop walk 4 pm.*

APOLLO BAY

45 km (28 miles) west of Lorne.

A small attractive town on a wide curving bay, Apollo Bay is a quieter alternative to busy Great Ocean Road towns like Lorne. There's enough diversity to entertain visitors, with several places to eat and plenty of opportunities for aquatic activities. It's most popular as a jumping-off point for the famous rock formations of the Twelve Apostles Marine National Park, and the greenery of Great Otway National Park.

GETTING HERE AND AROUND

Driving is the most convenient way to get here. Otherwise take the combined V/Line train-bus option, which involves riding a train from Melbourne's Southern Cross Station to Geelong and then a bus along the Great Ocean Road to Apollo Bay, via Lorne and other Surf Coast towns.

BEACHES

Apollo Bay Beach. At the far reaches of the Great Ocean Road, 195 km (121 miles) from Melbourne, you'll find one of Victoria's most popular holiday beaches. Protected by sea walls and Point Bunbury, Apollo Bay has low waves at the south end with a shallow sand bar, although care must be taken with an undertow that gets stronger as you go north. The local surf lifesaving club patrols between flags at the southern end. The 3-km (almost 2-mile) beach runs parallel to the Great Ocean Road and Collingwood Street, and at the latter end there is a reserve with shade trees and a picnic area. Behind the street is a row of shops and cafés, and on most Saturdays, the Apollo Bay market sees stall holders lining the foreshore path to sell local produce and crafts. Behind the town, the green hills of the Otways provide a change of scenery. A lookout up a mountain pathway gives a view of a sunken steamship when the weather is clear. If you want to get closer to the sea, Apollo Bay Surf and Kayak runs kayaking tours to see the local seal colony, as well as providing surfing and paddleboarding lessons. The Seaview Motel and Apartments are near the beach, and some rooms have balconies looking over the view. **Amenities:** food and drink; lifeguards; parking (free); restrooms; showers. **Best for:** surfing; swimming; walking. ✉ *Collingwood St.*

SPORTS AND THE OUTDOORS

DIVING

The Twelve Apostles Marine National Park and the nearby Arches Marine Sanctuary both provide fantastic diving opportunities. Local wrecks that can be explored with experienced guides include the *Napier* at Port Campbell, the famous *Loch Ard* (off Muttonbird Island), the *Schomberg* at Peterborough, and the *Fiji* near Moonlight Head. All wrecks are protected by federal law, and are not to be disturbed in any way. *(See Port Campbell boat charters in Tours, above.)*

HIKING

The Port Campbell National Park area, which is home to the Twelve Apostles, Loch Ard George, and other amazing landforms, has many good walks. Most are along wooden boardwalks; some also include

5

steep stairs down to the beach. The Visitor Centre at Port Campbell has all the details.

Inland from Port Campbell is the Camperdown-Timboon Rail Trail (also known as the Coast to Crater Rail Trail). It passes by lakes and streams and open volcanic plains. It is suitable for walkers and mountain bikers. The 36-km (22-mile) trail has good signage. Ask at the tourist offices for details.

WHERE TO STAY

$$$ **Beachfront Motel.** You couldn't hope for better placement at this seaside
HOTEL   town accommodation, which is located near beaches and shops. **Pros:** convenient location. **Cons:** there may be some noise from the adjacent main road. $ *Rooms from: A$280* ✉ *163 Great Ocean Rd.* ☏ *03/5237–6666* ⊕ *www.beachfrontmotel.com.au* ⇆ *10 rooms* ⦿ *No meals.*

$$$$ **Chris's Beacon Point Restaurant and Villas.** Set high in the Otway Ranges
HOTEL   overlooking the Great Ocean Road and the sea, this is a wonderful place
Fodor's Choice   to dine or bed down for the night. **Pros:** sensational views. **Cons:** pricey;
★   steep walk to some rooms. $ *Rooms from: A$330* ✉ *280 Skenes Creek Rd.* ⊕ *Take Skenes Creek Rd. turnoff about 3 km (2 miles) from Apollo Bay and wind up hill to Beacon Point.* ☏ *03/5237–6411* ⊕ *www.chriss.com.au* ⇆ *4 villas, 5 studios* ⦿ *Breakfast.*

PORT CAMPBELL NATIONAL PARK

283 km (75 miles) southwest of Melbourne via the Great Ocean Rd., 90 km (56 miles) west of Apollo Bay, 135 km (83 miles) west of Lorne.

It is possible to visit Port Campbell National Park on an organized day trip from Melbourne, but a better alternative is to stay overnight at one of the nearby towns and explore the region over a half or full day. Port Campbell township is the logical place to base yourself, providing a range of accommodation and dining options. The 30-km (19-mile) coastal drive is crammed with amazing sea sculptures, and you'll be stopping in the car parks along the way to get out and walk along the boardwalks to viewing platforms and steps that lead down to the coast.

GETTING HERE AND AROUND

The scenic route to Port Campbell National Park (which is actually a few miles east of the town of Port Campbell) is via the Great Ocean Road from Torquay, via Lorne and Apollo Bay. A car is the best way to go. A shorter drive is via the Princes Highway (M1) from Melbourne to Warrnambool, then the Great Ocean Road east to Port Campbell. A V/Line train operates to Warrnambool, and then a bus can be taken to Port Campbell. The journey takes about five hours.

Transportation V/Line. ☏ *1800/800007* ⊕ *www.vline.com.au.*

EXPLORING

Fodor's Choice   **Port Campbell National Park.** Stretching some 30 km (19 miles) along
★   Victoria's southern coastline, Port Campbell National Park is the site of some of the most famous and most beautiful geological formations in Australia. The ferocious Southern Ocean has gnawed at the limestone cliffs along this coast for eons, creating a sort of badlands-by-the-sea, where strangely shaped formations stand offshore amid the surf. The

most famous of these formations is the Twelve Apostles, as much a symbol for Victoria as the Sydney Opera House is for New South Wales (the name has always been a misnomer, as there were originally only nine of these stone columns—or sea stacks as they are correctly termed. Collapses in 2005 and 2009 mean that eight remain). If you happen to be visiting the Twelve Apostles just after sunset, you're likely to see bands of Little Penguins returning to their burrows on the beach. There's a population of around 3,000 of these cute creatures in the area.

Loch Ard Gorge, named after the iron-hulled clipper that wrecked on the shores of nearby Mutton Bird Island in 1878, is another spectacular place to walk. Four of the *Loch Ard*'s victims are buried in a nearby cemetery, while a sign by the gorge tells the story of the ship and its crew. This stretch of coast is often called the Shipwreck Coast for the hundreds of vessels that have met untimely ends in the treacherous waters. The Historic Shipwreck Trail, with landmarks describing 25 of the disasters, stretches from Moonlight Head to Port Fairy.

The best time to visit the park is late September to April, when you can also witness the boisterous birdlife on nearby Mutton Bird Island. Toward nightfall, hundreds of hawks and kites circle the island in search of baby mutton birds emerging from their protective burrows. The birds of prey beat a hasty retreat at the sight of thousands of adult shearwaters approaching with food for their chicks as the last light fades from the sky. Other amazing sea stacks and stone formations farther west along the Great Ocean Road are also not to be missed. These include the Grotto, London Bridge (now an arch after an earlier collapse), and the spectacular Bay of Islands and Bay of Martyrs.

The Twelve Apostles Information Centre is open daily 9 to 5. A self-guided, 1½-hour Discovery Walk begins near Port Campbell Beach, where it's safe to swim. The pounding surf and undertow are treacherous at other nearby beaches. ⊠ *Port Campbell National Park, Port Campbell.*

WHERE TO EAT AND STAY

$$
AUSTRALIAN
✕ **Waves.** A relaxed main street eatery with a spacious sundeck and friendly staff, Waves serves enormous breakfasts and fireside seafood dinners. Daily fish and curry specials are served, and the regular menu provides such dishes as a half-chicken cooked in a master stock and served with Asian vegetables, or chargrilled barramundi. Meat eaters can tuck into Angus scotch fillet and pork loin with caramelized apple. ⑤ *Average main: A$30* ⊠ *29 Lord St., Port Campbell* ☎ *03/5598–6111* ⊕ *www.wavesportcampbell.com.au.*

$$
RENTAL
⊤ **Daysy Hill Country Cottages.** Set in manicured gardens with lavender-lined walkways, these five attractive sandstone-and-cedar cottages look over the Newfield Valley. **Pros:** good price; good location. **Cons:** limited facilities; minimum stay required. ⑤ *Rooms from: A$200* ⊠ *2585 Cobden-Port Campbell Rd., Port Campbell* ☎ *03/5598–6226* ⊕ *www. daysyhillcottages.com.au* ⟿ *5 cottages, 4 suites, 3 cabins* ⊙I *No meals.*

$$$
RENTAL
⊤ **Southern Ocean Villas.** Ideally situated on the edge of Port Campbell National Park, within short walking distance of the town center and beach, these villas are stylishly furnished and fitted with polished

Loch Ard Gorge in Port Campbell National Park, Great Ocean Road

wood floors, picture windows, and high ceilings. **Pros:** good location near Twelve Apostles. **Cons:** located in sleepy town; difficult to find. $ *Rooms from: A$280* ✉ *2 McCue St., Port Campbell* ☎ *03/5598–4200* ⊕ *www.southernoceanvillas.com* ⇨ *15 villas* ⦿ *No meals.*

EN ROUTE **Warrnambool.** About 66 km (41 miles) west of Port Campbell, Warrnambool is Victoria's southern right whale nursery. Platforms at Logan's Beach, about 3 km (2 miles) east of the city, provide views of an amazing marine show from June to September. Whales return to this beach every year to calve, with the females and young staying close to the shore and the males playing about 150 yards out to sea. ✉ *Warrnambool.*

PORT FAIRY

377 km (215 miles) southwest of Melbourne via the Great Ocean Rd.; it is shorter if you take the Princes Hwy. (M1).

Port Fairy is widely considered to be the state's prettiest village. The second-oldest town in Victoria, it was originally known as Belfast, and there are indeed echoes of Ireland in the landscape and architecture. More than 50 of the cottages and sturdy bluestone buildings that line the banks of the River Moyne have been classified as landmarks by the National Trust, and few towns repay a leisurely stroll so richly. Huge Norfolk Island pines line many of the streets, particularly Gipps Street, and the town is dotted with good cafés, pubs, and art galleries.

The town still thrives as the base for a fishing fleet, and as host to the Port Fairy Folk Festival, one of Australia's most famous musical events, held every March. The town has a large colony of short-tailed shearwaters that nest on Griffiths Island. Amazingly, these birds travel here from the Aleutian Islands near Alaska, always arriving within three days of September 22. You can take a 45-minute walk around the island on marked trails to the historic lighthouse.

GETTING HERE AND AROUND

The most convenient form of transport is by car; the 377-km (234-mile) trip along the Great Ocean Road from Melbourne takes about 6½ hours, and it's advisable to break up the journey, as there's so much to see along the way. It's a shorter trip if you take the Princes Highway (M1).

Transportation V/Line. ☎ *1800/800007* ⊕ *www.vline.com.au.*

ESSENTIALS

Visitor Information Port Fairy Visitor Information Centre. ⊠ *Railway Pl., Bank St.* ☎ *03/5568–2682* ⊕ *www.port-fairy.com/vic.*

EXPLORING

Mott's Cottage. This National Trust-listed restored limestone-and-timber cottage was built by Sam Mott, a member of the 1830s whaling crew from the cutter *Fairy* who founded the town. ⊠ *5 Sackville St.* ☎ *03/5568–2682* 🎫 *A$2 donation* ⊗ *Wed. and Sat. 2–4, or by appointment June–Aug.*

Port Fairy Historical Society. The historical society's museum contains relics from the 19th-century whaling days, when Port Fairy was a whaling station with one of the largest ports in Victoria. It also highlights the stories of the many ships that have come to grief along this dangerous coast. ⊠ *Old Courthouse, 30 Gipps St.* ☎ *03/5568–2263* ⊕ *www. historicalsociety.port-fairy.com* 🎫 *A$4* ⊗ *Sept.–June Wed., Sat., and public holidays 2–5, Sun. 10:30–12:30; mid-July and Aug. Sat. 2–4.*

Tower Hill State Game Reserve. This reserve is packed with native Australian animals in their natural state. The Worn Gundidj Visitor Centre in the reserve conducts cultural interpretative walks. Take its one-hour personalized bush and nature walk to learn about indigenous lifestyles, bush food, and medicine, and hear about the local inhabitants, which include emus, sugar gliders, koalas, kangaroos, birds, and reptiles. The standard tour is A$23; also ask about the availability of other occasional specialist tours, including nighttime visits. Parks Victoria's website also has a map of the reserve and self-guided walking trails. ⊠ *Tower Hill State Game Reserve, Princes Hwy., between Port Fairy and Warrnambool, Tower Hill* ☎ *13/1963 Parks Victoria, 03/5561–5315 Tower Hill Tours* ⊕ *parkweb.vic.gov.au* ☞ *See www.towerhill. org.au for tour information.*

SPORTS AND THE OUTDOORS
HIKING

There are several walks around Port Fairy that highlight the town's historical aspects and the area's great beauty. Pick up a Historic Walks map from the visitor center and follow a trail past some 30 beautiful buildings; it takes about an hour. The Port Fairy Maritime & Shipwreck Heritage Walk is a 2-km (1-mile) trail that passes the sites of several shipwrecks: the bark *Socrates*, which was battered by huge seas in 1843;

the bark *Lydia,* which was wrecked off the coast in 1847; the schooner *Thistle,* which went down in 1837; and the brigantine *Essington,* which sank while moored at Port Fairy in 1852. Other historic attractions en route include the town port, the lifeboat station, riverside warehouses, cannons and gun emplacements at Battery Hill, and Griffiths Island Lighthouse. The walk is well marked.

Ten minutes or 14 km (9 miles) east of Port Fairy is Tower Hill State Game Reserve, nested in an extinct volcano. There are several walking trails and plenty of chances to see emus and kangaroos. About 40 minutes northeast is Mount Eccles National Park, another extinct volcano. Here there are four walks, including one to the crater rim and lava caves.

WHERE TO EAT AND STAY

$$$$
CAFÉ
✕ **Time & Tide.** "High Tea by the High Sea" is the menu highlight of this luscious café, which has an appetite-stimulating Southern Ocean view. Take a seat on a high-backed chair and indulge in three tiers of savory tarts, finger sandwiches, brownies, filled meringues, and more, including tea or coffee. The Grand High Tea (A$55 per person) includes a glass of sparkling Rosé, and there's also the Mini Grand High Tea (two tiers, A$39). It's a good idea to book ahead. ⑤ *Average main: A$55* ✉ *21 Thistle Pl.* ☎ *03/5568–2134* ⊕ *www.timeandtidehightea.com* ☾ *Closed weekdays. No dinner.*

$
B&B/INN
⌂ **Merrijig Inn.** One of Victoria's oldest inns, this beautifully restored 1841 Georgian-style building overlooks Port Fairy's working wharf from King George Square. **Pros:** cute and cozy; great food. **Cons:** upstairs rooms have character, but they're small. ⑤ *Rooms from: A$150* ✉ *1 Campbell St.* ☎ *03/5568–2324* ⊕ *www.merrijiginn.com* ⇆ *4 rooms, 4 suites* ⧉| *Breakfast.*

$$$$
B&B/INN
Fodor'sChoice
★
⌂ **Oscars Waterfront Boutique Hotel.** Overlooking the waterfront and a marina of yachts, this hotel gives French provincial style an Australian edge. **Pros:** fantastic location; great breakfasts. **Cons:** town is dead in the off season. ⑤ *Rooms from: A$325* ✉ *41B Gipps St.* ☎ *03/5568–3022* ⊕ *www.oscarswaterfront.com* ⇆ *6 rooms, 1 suite* ⧉| *Breakfast.*

THE GOLD COUNTRY

Victoria was changed forever in the early 1850s by the discovery of gold in the center of the state. News of fantastic gold deposits caused immigrants from every corner of the world to pour into Victoria to seek their fortunes as "diggers"—a name that has become synonymous with Australians ever since. Few miners became wealthy from their searches, however. The real money was made by those supplying goods and services to the thousands who had succumbed to gold fever.

Gold towns like Ballarat, Castlemaine, Maldon, and Bendigo sprang up like mushrooms to accommodate these fortune seekers, and prospered until the gold rush receded. Afterward, they became ghost towns or turned to agriculture to survive. However, many beautiful buildings were constructed from the spoils of gold, and these gracious old public buildings and grand hotels survive today and make a visit to Bendigo and Ballarat a pleasure for those who love classic architecture. Victoria's gold is again being mined in limited quantities, while these historic old towns remain interesting relics of Australia's past.

Although Victoria was not the first Australian state to experience a gold rush, when gold was discovered here in 1851 it became a veritable El Dorado. During the boom years of the 19th century, 90% of the gold mined in Australia came from the then British colony. The biggest finds were at Ballarat and then Bendigo, and the Ballarat diggings proved to be among the richest alluvial goldfields in the world.

For leisurely exploration of the Gold Country, a car is essential. Public transportation adequately serves the main centers, but access to smaller towns is less assured and even in the bigger towns attractions are spread out.

TOURS

AAT Kings. The one-day Sovereign Hill Gold Rush Tour visits the gold rush-era historical re-enactment village within Ballarat. An additional A\$20 gets you a visit to the Ballarat Wildlife Park as well. ⊠ *Melbourne Day Tours, Federation Sq., Flinders and Russell Sts., City Center* ☎ *1300/228–546* ⊕ *www.aatkings.com.au* ✉ *A\$159.*

Gray Line. This operator runs three-day tours to the historical re-enactment town, Sovereign Hill. ⊠ *Federation Sq. East, Flinders and Russell Sts., City Center* ☎ *1300/858687* ⊕ *www.grayline.com.au* ✉ *From A\$149.*

BALLARAT

106 km (66 miles) northwest of Melbourne.

In the local Aboriginal language, the name Ballarat means "resting place." In pre-gold-rush days, nearby Lake Wendouree provided the area with a plentiful supply of food. Once the gold boom hit, however, the town became much less restful; in 1854 Ballarat was the scene of the Battle of the Eureka Stockade, a skirmish that took place between miners and authorities over gold license fees that miners were forced to pay, though they had no vote. More than 20 men died in the battle. Today their flag—the Southern Cross—is a symbol of Australia's egalitarian spirit and can be viewed in the new Museum of Australian Democracy at Eureka (MADE).

Despite the harsh times, fortunes made from the mines (and from the miners) resulted in the grand Victorian architecture on Sturt and Lydiard streets—note the post office, the town hall, Craig's Royal Hotel, and Her Majesty's Theatre. The Old Colonists' Hall and the Mining Exchange (at 20 and 26 Lydiard Street, respectively) now house shops and cafés. The visitor center has a self-guided heritage walk.

GETTING HERE AND AROUND

It's an easy 80-minute drive to Ballarat along the Western Highway (M8) from Melbourne. The road, however, is the main artery between Melbourne and Adelaide, and many huge trucks also use the road. Take care and drive within the speed limit. From Ballarat you can easily drive north to the spa-country towns of Daylesford–Hepburn Springs and

Bendigo on the Midland Highway. The city itself is well signposted. The city center is built around a well-planned grid and has ample parking. Local bus services run from Sturt Street, the main thoroughfare, to most of Ballarat's attractions.

Transportation V/Line. ☎ 1800/800007 ⊕ www.vline.com.au.

ESSENTIALS

Visitor Information Ballarat Visitor Information Centre. ⊠ 225 Sturt St. ☎ 1800/446633 ⊕ www.visitballarat.com.au.

EXPLORING

Art Gallery of Ballarat. This impressive art museum has a large collection of Australian art, from 19th-century works to contemporary pieces. Keep an eye out for its paintings by landscape artist Eugene von Guerard, who captured Ballarat as it appeared in the raucous early gold rush days. ⊠ 40 Lydiard St. ☎ 03/5320–5858 ⊕ www.artgalleryofballarat. com.au ⊙ Daily 10–5.

Ballarat Botanical Gardens. On the shores of Lake Wendouree, the Ballarat Botanical Gardens are identifiable by the brilliant blooms and classical statuary. At the rear of the gardens, the Conservatory hosts events during the town's Begonia Festival held each March, with other events taking place near the lake. ⊠ Gillies St. North and Lake Gardens Ave. ☎ 03/5320–5135 ⊕ www.ballarat.vic.gov.au ⊙ Daily 7:30–6, conservatory 9–5.

FAMILY **Ballarat Wildlife Park.** All sorts of native animals, including kangaroos and emus (which roam free), saltwater crocodiles, snakes, Tasmanian devils, wombats, tree kangaroos, and echidnas can be found at this wildlife sanctuary. Daily tours of the park are led at 11, with a koala show at 2 and a wombat show at 2:30. On Sunday there's a crocodile feeding at 3. The park also has a café and picnic areas. ⊠ Fussel and York Sts., Ballarat East ☎ 03/5333–5933 ⊕ www.wildlifepark.com.au ⊠ A$29.50 ⊙ Daily 9–5:30.

Fodor'sChoice ★ **MADE.** The Museum of Australian Democracy at Eureka (MADE) opened in 2013 on the site of the 1854 Eureka Stockade revolt, in which gold miners staged an armed rebellion against police corruption and for the establishment of democracy in Victoria. The museum brings history to life via impressive interactive technology. Visitors learn about democracy around the world and can admire the tattered but beautiful remains of the original Eureka Flag, which flew above the site of the battle. The on-site café, Saltbush Kitchen, serves tasty food incorporating native Australian ingredients such as pepperberry and lemon myrtle. ⊠ 102 Stawell St. S ☎ 1800/287113 ⊕ www.made.org ⊠ A$12 ⊙ Daily 10–5.

FAMILY
Fodor'sChoice ★ **Sovereign Hill.** Built on the site of the former Sovereign Hill Quartz Mining Company's mines, this replica town provides an authentic look at life, work, and play during Ballarat's gold rush era. Highlights of the main street include a hotel, blacksmith's shop, bakery, and post office—all perfectly preserved relics of their time. You can have your photo taken in period costumes, take a mineshaft tour, pan for gold (and find some), ride in a stagecoach, or head to the "lolly shop" to

taste old-fashioned candy. Return at night for "Blood on the Southern Cross," a 90-minute sound-and-light spectacular that tells the story of the Eureka uprising. Your entry ticket also gets you into the **Gold Museum,** across Bradshaw Street, which displays an extensive collection of nuggets from the Ballarat diggings. ⊠ *Bradshaw St.* ☎ *03/5337–1100* ⊕ *www.sovereignhill.com.au* 🖃 *A$52.50; A$111.50 (entry and Blood on the Southern Cross show)* ⊘ *Daily 10–5; 2 show sessions, times vary.*

WHERE TO EAT AND STAY

$$ ✕ **The Forge.** This former industrial building now houses a pizzeria that

PIZZA   serves top-notch wood-fired pizzas in a big dining room with long

FAMILY   timber tables, wooden beams, and exposed brick walls. The pizzas are excellent, with light crusts and tasty toppings; try the Volcano (hot salami, chili pepper, Gorgonzola, feta, olives, and anchovies) for an entrée with a zing. An unusual appetizer is the Oliver Twist, a stack of baked pizza strips bearing olives, chili pepper, and Victorian goat's cheese. $ *Average main: A$21* ⊠ *14 Armstrong St. N* ☎ *03/5337–6635* ⊕ *www.theforgepizzeria.com.au.*

$ ✕ **L'Espresso.** Meals at this low-lighted local institution taste like they're

MEDITERRANEAN   from your grandmother's kitchen. It's open for breakfast and lunch daily and dinner (more expensive) on Friday, with specials like linguini alla Bolognese; or a risotto with beets, walnuts, and goat cheese. The corn fritters with salmon are a great way to start the day, as is the classic Aussie breakfast dish of smashed avocado with feta cheese and poached eggs. This was a popular record shop back in the 1970s, and decades later you can still buy blues, jazz, and interesting contemporary music CDs here. $ *Average main: A$17* ⊠ *417 Sturt St.* ☎ *03/5333–1789.*

$$ 🛏 **The Ansonia.** Built in the 1870s as professional offices, this building

HOTEL   now houses an excellent boutique hotel. **Pros:** cozy; arty; free parking. **Cons:** rooms opening onto the atrium lack privacy. $ *Rooms from: A$199* ⊠ *32 Lydiard St.* ☎ *03/5332–4678* ⊕ *www.theansoniaonlydiard. com.au* 🛏 *16 rooms, 3 apartments* ❙○❙ *Breakfast.*

$$ 🛏 **Mercure Ballarat Hotel.** This single-story accommodation is spread out

HOTEL   over a large property dotted with gum trees next to Sovereign Hill;

FAMILY   rooms are furnished in classic style, with dark green and timber notes. **Pros:** spacious; atmospheric. **Cons:** about 1½ miles from the city center. $ *Rooms from: A$189* ⊠ *613 Main Rd.* ☎ *03/5327–1200* ⊕ *www. mercureballarat.com.au* 🛏 *71 rooms, 9 apartments* ❙○❙ *No meals.*

DAYLESFORD AND HEPBURN SPRINGS

109 km (68 miles) northwest of Melbourne, 45 km (28 miles) northeast of Ballarat.

Nestled in the slopes of the Great Dividing Range, Daylesford and its nearby twin, Hepburn Springs, are a spa-lover's paradise. The water table here is naturally aerated with carbon dioxide and rich in soluble mineral salts, making it ideal for indulging in mineral baths and other rejuvenating treatments. The natural springs were first noted during the gold rush, and Swiss-Italian immigrants established a spa at Hepburn Springs in 1875. There are now about 70 natural springs in the area. The best time to visit the area is autumn, when the deciduous trees turn bronze and you can finish up a relaxing day next to an open fire with a glass of local red.

GETTING HERE AND AROUND

The twin towns of Daylesford and Hepburn Springs are easily reached by car from Melbourne. Take the Western Highway (M8) to Ballarat, then take the Midland Highway for another 40 km (25 miles) to Daylesford (via Creswick). Hepburn Springs is a mile or two from Daylesford. V/Line operates trains from Southern Cross Station, Melbourne, to Ballarat or Woodend (near Mount Macedon), and V/Line buses connect with the trains to take passengers to Daylesford.

Transportation V/Line.
☎ *1800/800007* ⊕ *www.vline.com.au.*

LIQUID GOLD

The promise of gold "in them thar hills" drew mobs of prospectors in the 1850s, but today's visitors aren't looking to quench their thirst for riches. The "Great Grape Touring Route" (⊕ *www.greatgraperoute. com.au*) and the "Vine to Vintage Trail" (⊕ *www.bendigotourism. com*) are wonderful itineraries for those who love fine wine and food. Ballarat's climate produces great Pinot Noir and Chardonnay, while the Grampians is the birthplace of Great Western, Australia's first and best-known sparkling wine. The Pyrenees region is known for its classic Shiraz.

ESSENTIALS

Visitor Information Daylesford Regional Visitor Information Centre. ✉ *98 Vincent St., Daylesford* ☎ *03/5321–6123* ⊕ *www.visitdaylesford.com.*

EXPLORING

Bromley & Co. This impressive art gallery inside a vast former industrial building displays the stylish, contemporary work of David Bromley, along with other artists. The fascinating space scatters the art pieces throughout several divided sections within the interior. Outside is an equally interesting garden filled with large works, including enormous colorful dolls and complex statues of animals constructed from small pieces of wood. ✉ *39 East St., Daylesford* ☎ *03/5348–3979* ⊕ *www. bromleyandco.com* ⊙ *Weekends 10–5.*

Convent Gallery. Perched on a hillside overlooking Daylesford, this gallery occupies a former nunnery that has been restored to its lovely Victorian-era state. It houses three levels of fine art and a nun-related museum, and occasionally stages live arts performances. At the front of the gallery is Bad Habits, a sunny café that serves light lunches and snacks. Altar Bar is a hip place for a drink. The second-story penthouse suite is the ultimate in decadence, with its own hydrotherapy bath and a boudoir-style bedroom ($$$). ✉ *7 Daly St., Daylesford* ☎ *03/5348–3211* ⊕ *www.theconvent.com.au* 🎟 *A$5* ⊙ *Daily 10–4.*

Mineral Springs Reserve. Above the Hepburn Bathhouse and Spa, a path winds past a series of mineral springs in this 74-acre reserve. Each spring has a slightly different chemical composition—and a significantly different taste. You can bring empty bottles, if you like, and fill them for free with the mineral water of your choice. ✉ *Mineral Springs Reserve, Hepburn Springs* ⊙ *Mon.–Thurs. 9–6:30, Fri. 9–8, Sat. 8–8, Sun. 8–6:30.*

WHERE TO STAY

$$$$
B&B/INN
Fodor'sChoice
★

The Dudley Boutique Hotel. This fine example of timber Federation-style architecture sits behind a neat hedge and picket gate on the main street of Hepburn Springs. **Pros:** tranquil garden setting; great heritage character. **Cons:** limited number of rooms may limit available booking dates. $ *Rooms from: A$395* ✉ *101 Main Rd., Hepburn Springs* ☎ *03/5348–3033* ⊕ *www.thedudley.com.au* ⇗ *7 rooms* ⦿*Breakfast.*

$$$$
HOTEL
Fodor'sChoice
★

Lake House. Featuring one of Victoria's best restaurants, this rambling lakeside hotel adds a distinct glamor to spa country. The accommodation, set in 6 acres of gardens, comprise standard rooms in the original homestead, plush waterfront rooms and suites, all of which have balconies, and the fully inclusive and luxurious two-villa retreat. A day spa administers some treatments specifically for men and expectant mothers, as well as those for couples, along with the more-traditional pampering. **Pros:** renowned food; tranquil garden setting. **Cons:** two-night minimum stay at weekends. $ *Rooms from: A$456* ✉ *King St., Daylesford* ☎ *03/5348–3329* ⊕ *www.lakehouse.com.au* ⇗ *16 rooms, 18 suites* ⦿*Breakfast.*

SHOPPING

SPAS

Fodor'sChoice
★

Hepburn Bathhouse & Spa. A destination for relaxation and wellness since the 19th century, this facility is the centerpiece of Australia's premier spa destination, and one of the largest and most spectacular spas in the country. The complex encompasses the original Edwardian Bathhouse (circa 1895), which houses private mineral baths and more than 20 wet-and-dry treatment rooms, and a stunning, contemporary building, where you find the public Bathhouse and the private Sanctuary area. Patrons can buy two-hour passes for the Bathhouse or the Sanctuary. The Bathhouse includes a relaxation mineral pool and a spa pool (A$32, Tuesday–Thursday and A$40 Friday–Monday), while the Sanctuary has underwater spa couches (for the ultimate in hydrotherapy), an aroma steam room, and a salt therapy pool (A$67 Tuesday–Thursday and A$87 Friday–Monday). There is also the day spa area, where you can choose from a long list of therapies, including body wraps and polishes, facials, and other treatments using the mineral waters. Products used in the spa include Kerstin Florian and a Hepburn Collection range specifically designed for Hepburn Bathhouse & Spa. ✉ *1 Mineral Springs Crescent, Hepburn Springs* ☎ *03/5321–6000* ⊕ *www. hepburnbathhouse.com* ⊘ *Sun.–Thurs. 9–6:30, Fri. 9–8, Sat. 8–8.*

BENDIGO

150 km (93 miles) northwest of Melbourne, 92 km (57 miles) south of Echuca.

Gold was discovered in the Bendigo district in 1851, and its boom lasted well into the 1880s. The city's magnificent public buildings bear witness to the richness of its mines. Today Bendigo is a bustling, enterprising small city, with distinguished buildings lining both sides of Pall Mall in the city center. These include the Shamrock Hotel, the General Post Office, and the Law Courts, all majestic examples of late-Victorian architecture. Although these glorious relics of a golden age dominate the landscape, the city is far from old-fashioned. You'll also find a lively café and restaurant scene, 30 boutique wineries, some of which can be visited on organized winery tours, and one of the best regional art galleries in Australia.

GETTING HERE AND AROUND

To reach Bendigo, take the Calder Highway northwest from Melbourne; the trip takes about 1 hour and 40 minutes. V/Line operates trains to Bendigo from Melbourne's Southern Cross Station, a journey of about two hours.

Transportation V/Line. ☎ *1800/800007* ⊕ *www.vline.com.au.*

TOURS

Fodor'sChoice ★ **Food Fossicking Tour.** The food scene in Bendigo has improved greatly in recent years, and this weekly walking tour highlights the best of the city's eating. Departing from the Bendigo Visitor Centre, the tour visits a chocolate shop, a sourdough bakery, and an Italian delicatessen, among other stops. In addition, you'll hear directly from the makers and taste samples along the way. The tour fee includes a light lunch and a glass of local wine at its conclusion. ⊠ *Bendigo Visitor Centre, 51 Pall Mall* ☎ *1800/813–153* ⊠ *A$75* ☞ *Departs 10 am Sat.*

Vintage Talking Tram. A good introduction to Bendigo is a tour aboard this hop-on, hop-off streetcar tour, which includes a taped commentary on the town's history. The half-hourly tram runs on an 8-km (5-mile) circuit between the Central Deborah Gold Mine and the Joss House temple, making six stops at historic sites. ⊠ *Bendigo* ☎ *03/5442–2821* ⊕ *www.bendigotramways.com* ⊠ *From A$17.50* ⊗ *Daily 10–5.*

ESSENTIALS

Visitor Information Bendigo Visitor Centre. ⊠ *51 Pall Mall* ☎ *03/5434–6060, 1800/813153* ⊕ *www.bendigotourism.com.au.*

EXPLORING

Fodor'sChoice ★ **Bendigo Art Gallery.** A notable collection of contemporary Australian painting can be found in this beautiful gallery, including the work of Rupert Bunny, Emily Kame Kngwarreye, and Arthur Boyd. The gallery also has some significant 19th-century French realist and impressionist works, bequeathed by a local surgeon. International exhibitions are regularly hosted. There's a free guided tour every day at 2 pm. ⊠ *42 View St.* ☎ *03/5434–6088* ⊕ *www.bendigoartgallery.com.au* ⊠ *Entry to permanent exhibition free; touring exhibitions A$20* ⊗ *Tues.–Sun. 10–5.*

Bendigo Pottery. Australia's oldest working pottery turns out distinctive brown-and-cream style pieces that many Australians have in their kitchens. Founded in 1858, the historic workshop hosts demonstrations. You can even get your hands dirty creating your own clay piece during an affordable wheel-throwing lesson (bookings essential during school holidays); there's also a clay play area for small children. Impressive beehive brick kilns, which you can step inside, are star exhibits in the museum. It's 6½ km (4 miles) northeast of Bendigo on the way to Echuca. ⊠ *146 Midland Hwy., Epsom* ☎ *03/5448–4404* ⊕ *www.bendigopottery.com.au* ⊠ *Free, museum A$8, wheel-throwing lessons A$15 per ½ hr* ⊗ *Daily 9–5.*

FAMILY

Fodor'sChoice

★

Central Deborah Gold Mine. This historic mine, with a 1,665-foot shaft, yielded almost a ton of gold before it closed in 1954. Above ground you can pan for gold, see the old stamper battery, and climb up the poppet head, but the thrill of mining is felt below ground. Three underground tours explore different mine levels; on the Mine Experience you descend 200 feet to widened tunnels, while the Underground Adventure puts you another 78 feet deeper. Nine Levels of Darkness is the ultimate adventure here; over 3½ hours you sign on as a "new chum" and ride a tiny cage lift 748 feet down to dripping original tunnels, where you work a drill, "set" explosives, and climb ladders. ⊠ *76 Violet St.* ☎ *03/5443–8322* ⊕ *www.central-deborah.com* ⛁ *A$6.50 (above ground only); tours (including entry): Mine Experience A$30, Underground Adventure A$85, Nine Levels of Darkness A$199* ☉ *Daily 9–5 (last tour at 3:30).*

Golden Dragon Museum. The Chinese community's important role in Bendigo life, past and present, is explored within this museum. Its centerpieces are the century-old Loong imperial ceremonial dragon and the Sun Loong imperial dragon, which, at more than 106 yards in length, is said to be the world's longest. When carried in procession, the body alone requires 52 carriers and 52 relievers, and more to carry the head, neck and tail; the head alone weighs 64 pounds. Also on display are other ceremonial objects, costumes, and historic artifacts. The lovely Yi Yuan Gardens, opposite, with ponds and bridges, are part of the museum and close at 4:30. ⊠ *5 Bridge St.* ☎ *03/5441–5044* ⊕ *www. goldendragonmuseum.org* ⛁ *A$11* ☉ *Daily 9:30–5.*

Joss House. An active place of worship on the outskirts of the city, this small Chinese temple was built during the gold rush days by Chinese miners. At the height of the boom in the 1850s and 1860s, about a quarter of Bendigo's miners were Chinese. These men were usually dispatched from villages on the Chinese mainland, and they were expected to work hard and return as quickly as possible with their fortunes. Sadly, tensions with white miners were a feature of that era, along with anti-Chinese riots. Luckily this attractive element of their presence has endured from those turbulent times. ⊠ *3 Finn St.* ☎ *03/5442–1685* ⊕ *www.bendigojosshouse.com* ⛁ *A$6* ☉ *Daily 11–4.*

WHERE TO EAT AND STAY

$$

STEAKHOUSE

Fodor'sChoice

★

✕ **The Woodhouse.** This excellent restaurant in a former blacksmith's workshop serves quality food in a casual dining environment. The atmospheric interior has exposed brick walls and timber beams, with a wood-fired pizza oven visible at one end of the bar. In addition to pizza, there are fine steaks on the menu from local producers, and a selection of craft beers. There are reasonable vegetarian options to choose from as well. If you have room, the dessert tasting plate comprises six tasty confections suitable for sharing. $ *Average main: A$33* ⊠ *101 Williamson St.* ☎ *03/5443–8671* ⊕ *www.thewoodhouse.com.au* ☉ *Closed Sun., no lunch Mon. and Sat.* ⊟ *No credit cards.*

$

HOTEL

⌂ **Hotel Shamrock.** The lodgings at this landmark Victorian hotel in the city center range from traditional guest rooms to spacious suites. **Pros:** historic gold-era building; central location. **Cons:** limited facilities.

⑤ *Rooms from: A$140* ✉ *Pall Mall, at Williamson St.* ☎ *03/5443–0333*
⊕ *www.hotelshamrock.com.au* ⤳ *24 rooms, 4 suites* ❢⊘ *Breakfast.*

$ 🔲 **The Schaller Studio.** Named after artist Mark Schaller, this property of
HOTEL the Melbourne-based Art Series Hotels is a cutting-edge addition to the
Fodor'sChoice Bendigo accommodation scene. **Pros:** stylish design; lively lobby; walk-
★ ing distance to the city center. **Cons:** small rooms; queen beds are the
largest size available. ⑤ *Rooms from: A$135* ✉ *Lucan St., at Bayne St.*
☎ *1800/278–468* ⊕ *www.artserieshotels.com.au/schaller* ⤳ *120 rooms*
❢⊘ *No meals.*

THE GRAMPIANS

About 93 km (79 miles) north of Port Fairy are the Grampians, sometimes referred to by their Aboriginal name Gariwerd. This 415,000-acre
region combines stunning mountain scenery, abundant native wildlife,
and invigorating outdoor activities. The sharp sandstone peaks here
were long ago forced up from an ancient seabed, and sculpted by aeons
of wind and rain.

Today the park has more than 160 km (100 miles) of walking trails, as
well as some 900 wildflower species, 200 species of birds, and 35 species of native mammals. The best time to visit is October–December,
when wildflowers carpet the landscape, the weather is mild, and summer crowds have yet to arrive. There are several wineries in the region,
including the historic Seppelt vineyard and winery, which runs fascinating tours of its underground wine cellars, at Great Western, about 38
km (24 miles) east of Halls Gap.

GRAMPIANS NATIONAL PARK

*260 km (162 miles) west of Melbourne, 100 km (62 miles) north of
Hamilton.*

Bushwalking is by far the most popular activity in the national park.
Some of the best walks include Mackenzie Falls, the walk to Mt. Abrupt
(or Mt. Murdadjoog in the Aboriginal language), the Hollow Mountain
walk, and another to Silverband Falls. Even if you're not a big walker
you can still see many of the best-known rock formations. Elephant
Hide, the Balconies, the Pinnacle, and the Fortress are only a short walk
from a car park. Canoeing is another great way to get away from the
crowds and experience the lakes and rivers of the Grampians.

The most popular attractions of the central Grampians region can
be visited in one day. However, if you want to visit the fascinating
Brambuk Aboriginal Cultural Centre and take in a few wineries, allow
yourself another day or two. From the town of Halls Gap it's a 15-km
(9-mile) drive (plus a 100-yard walk from the car park) to the spectacular Boroka Lookout.

GETTING HERE AND AROUND

Halls Gap (the base town for the Grampians National Park) is reached
via Ballarat and Ararat on the Western Highway (Highway 8). The
town is 260 km (162 miles) northwest of Melbourne, 97 km (60 miles)

Grampians
National Park

northeast of Hamilton, and 140 km (87 miles) west of Ballarat. V/Line
operates trains to Ballarat from Melbourne. V/Line buses connect with
the trains to take passengers to Halls Gap. For timetables and fares,
contact V/Line.

TOURS

Hangin' Out. For those who love experiencing the great outdoors from
different angles, Hangin' Out runs rock climbing and abseiling tours
to suit beginners and more experienced climbers; they also have an
all-day guided adventure walk (A$135) from Mt. Stapylton to Hol-
low Mountain in the north of the Grampians. A four-hour taste of
real rock climbing and rappelling costs A$75 (minimum two people);
a full-day introduction to the rope sports is A$130. Private guided sin-
gle- and multi-pitch climbs can be arranged. ☎ 0407/684–831 ⊕ www.
hanginout.com.au 🖂 From A$100.

ESSENTIALS

Visitor Information Halls Gap Visitor Information Centre. ✉ 117 Grampians Rd., Halls Gap ☎ 1800/065599 ⊕ www.visitgrampians.com.au. **Stawell and
Grampians Visitor Information Centre.** ✉ 8 Main St., Stawell ☎ 03/5358–
2314, 1800/330080 ⊕ www.visitgrampians.com.au.

EXPLORING

Brambuk National Park & Cultural Centre. Owned and operated by Aboriginal people, this park and center provide a unique living history of indigenous culture in this part of Victoria. Displays of artwork, weapons, clothes, and tools give a glimpse into the life of Koori people (Aboriginal people of southeastern Australia). A film screened in the Dreaming Theatre describes the Creation legends of the Grampians mountains. Educational programs, including boomerang throwing, painting, and didgeridoo workshops, are presented daily and there is a bush tucker discovery walk and tasting most days. Ceremonial music and dances are performed weekly. Visitors can learn the significance of paintings at nearby Bunjil's Shelter on the Bunjil Creation tour, conducted on weekdays at 9:30 am. ✉ *277 Grampians Tourist Rd., Halls Gap* ☎ *03/5361–4000* ⊕ *www.brambuk.com.au* ✉ *Free; films and activities A$6, bush discovery walks A$9, Bunjil Creation Tour A$70* ⊙ *Daily 9–5.*

Fodor'sChoice
★

Grampians National Park. Comprising four mountain ranges—Mt. Difficult, Mt. William, Serra, and Victoria—the impressive Grampians National Park spills over 412,000 acres. Its rugged peaks, towering trees, waterfalls, creeks, and plethora of wildlife attract bushwalkers, rock climbers, and nature lovers. Spectacular wildflowers carpet the region in spring, while a number of significant Aboriginal rock art sites make it an ideal place to learn about Victoria's indigenous history. The township of Halls Creek (population 600) sits within the national park, and with its 10,000 tourist beds it becomes quite a busy place in summer and at Easter. If you're staying in a self-catering accommodation, it's wise to stock up on groceries and wine in the big towns of Ballarat, Ararat, Hamilton, or Horsham, since prices at the Halls Gap general store are inflated. One of the most picturesque drives in the park is the 60 km (37 miles) stretch from Halls Gap to Dunkeld.

Some areas in the park can be affected by fire and flood from year to year, so check with Parks Victoria for current road and camping conditions. ✉ *Grampians National Park, Halls Gap* ☎ *131–963* ⊕ *parkweb. vic.gov.au.*

**▌OFF THE
BEATEN
PATH**

Seppelt Great Western Winery. This old winery is also one of Australia's most famous, the name Great Western being associated with a long-lived sparkling wine. The winery makes the Salinger and Fleur de Lys ranges as well as a Sparkling Shiraz and various table wines. Beneath the winery is an underground labyrinth of tunnels, known as the Drives, dating back to 1868 and originally built by goldminers. This is where the best sparkling wines are kept. You can take a day tour of these tunnels and the nearby shaft house and taste 20 Seppelt wines, or enjoy a barbecue and evening tour. Packages to tour and dine in the Drives, including cheese platters, two or three courses, and wine tastings, are also available from A$120 per person. The barbecue and dining options require a minimum of 15 people. ✉ *36 Cemetery Rd., Great Western* ☎ *03/5361–2239* ⊕ *www.seppelt.com.au* ✉ *Cellar door free; tours A$15, night tour and barbecue A$70* ⊙ *Tastings daily 10–5; tunnel tours daily at 11 and 2.*

Sitting on edge of Boroka Lookout in the Grampians National Park

SPORTS AND THE OUTDOORS
CANOEING
Absolute Outdoors. If you want to experience the Grampians wilderness via its serene lakes, a half-day canoeing trip with this company that operates from a shop that sells outdoor equipment in Halls Gap may be the answer. It hosts outings on Lake Bellfield, a little to the southeast of the township. It also runs rock climbing, abseiling, and mountain bike adventures within the park. ✉ *105 Main Rd., (aka Grampians Rd.), Halls Gap* ☎ *03/5356–4556, 1300/526258* ⊕ *www.absoluteoutdoors. com.au* ✆ *From A$60 for ½-day tour.*

HIKING
Auswalk. This long-established walking tour specialist operates guided and self-guided five-night inn-to-inn hikes. Luggage is transported between accommodation stops, a mix of B&Bs and motels. Maps and other information are provided for self-guided walkers, and only two participants are needed for a tour to take place. The terrain of the self-guided walk is graded "moderate" for up to 85% of the walk, with about 15% rated strenuous. Wildlife, particularly kangaroos and wallabies, is abundant in many areas transited, and wildflowers festoon the park from August to November. Trips usually run year-round. ☎ *03/9530–8800* ⊕ *www.auswalk.com.au* ✆ *From A$1,750.*

WHERE TO EAT AND STAY
$$
AUSTRALIAN
✕ **Kookaburra Hotel.** In the heart of Halls Gap, this is one of the town's best dining options and serves an imaginative range of dishes. The restaurant and bar provides a casual, gastropub experience, with signature dishes like the spinach crepe, baked duckling, blackened barramundi,

and the kangaroo fillet. Kookaburra's homemade ice cream is a particular treat. The wine list includes regional wines. Bookings are recommended. $ *Average main: A$33* ⊠ *125 Grampian Rd., Halls Gap* ☎ *03/5356–4222* ⊕ *www.kookaburrahotel.com.au* ⊗ *Closed Mon., no lunch Tues.–Fri.*

$$$
MODERN
AUSTRALIAN
Fodor'sChoice
★

✕ **Royal Mail Hotel.** Expansive views of the southern Grampians peaks are almost an unwelcome distraction from the extraordinary food plated up at the only hotel in the tiny town of Dunkeld, 64 km (40 miles) south of Halls Gap. The menu changes daily depending on the harvest from the kitchen gardens, specializing in organic and heirloom vegetables. Other produce comes from local beehives, free-range laying hens, nearby orchards, and an olive grove. Chef Robin Wickens continues the tradition of culinary innovation to create tasting and degustation dinner menus from A$115. There is also an à la carte bistro ($$$), and an excellent bar menu ($). With fine accommodation on-site, too ($$$), after dinner you can stroll to a spacious Mountain View or Garden View room, or apartment, all fitted with every modern convenience, or drive the 3 km (2 miles) to the hotel's historic Mt. Sturgeon farm, and sleep in a luxurious, period-furnished homestead bedroom or cozy stone cottage. $ *Average main: A$46* ⊠ *98 Parker St., Dunkeld* ☎ *03/5577–2241* ⊕ *www.royalmail.com.au* ⌦ *Reservations essential* ☞ *Sat. dinner degustation only.*

$$$$
HOTEL
Fodor'sChoice
★

Boroka Downs. On 300 acres of bush, scrub, and grassland, bordering the Grampians National Park, Boroka's six villas are nothing short of spectacular. **Pros:** luxurious; eco-friendly. **Cons:** all of this beauty comes at a high price. $ *Rooms from: A$595* ⊠ *51 Birdswing Rd., Halls Gap* ☎ *03/5356–6243* ⊕ *www.borokadowns.com.au* ⇥ *5 villas, 1 bungalow* ⊚ *Breakfast.*

MURRAY RIVER REGION

From its birthplace in the folds of the Great Dividing Range in southern New South Wales, the Mighty Murray winds 2,574 km (1,596 miles) northwest and then south before it empties into Lake Alexandrina, south of Adelaide. But it is not as mighty as it once was. Recent droughts and overreliance on—and exploitation of—the Murray and its tributaries by irrigators, river towns, and the city of Adelaide have threatened the river's health and the livelihoods of the people who rely on it.

Water—its supply, collection, and use—is a subject on almost everyone's lips. A revamped but still controversial water-trading and buy-out system based on water access entitlements, which promises to reallocate precious Murray-Darling water, is one of a range of measures being implemented by Australia's federal and state governments to reduce the impact of climate change and improve and supplement existing water sources. Making the right decisions for the river and those dependent on it is a challenging balancing act.

Victoria exports more than A$200 million worth of wine annually, and Murray River Muscats and Ports are legendary. The Rutherglen area, in particular, produces the country's finest fortified wine (dessert wine or "stickies").

Steeped in history and natural beauty, the eastern Murray River valley and High Country region is a gourmet foodies' heaven known for its fruit, olives, honey, and cheeses, as well as a renowned wine region. The lovely town of Beechworth is an ideal place to break the drive between Sydney and Melbourne.

GETTING HERE AND AROUND

The wide-open spaces of the region surrounding the Murray River make driving the most sensible and feasible means of exploration. Rutherglen is 274 km (170 miles) north of Melbourne, about a 3½- to 4-hour drive up the Hume Freeway; Echuca is 204 km (127 miles) northwest of Melbourne, about a 2½-hour drive. These two Murray River towns are 194 km (121 miles) apart. V/Line trains (☎ *1800/800007 ⊕ www. vline.com.au*) run to most of the major towns in the region, including Echuca, Wangaratta, and Albury-Wodonga, with bus connections to Beechworth and Rutherglen; this access is useful if you do not have a car or want to avoid the long-distance drives. As with most country Victorian areas, direct train access from Melbourne to the main centers is reasonable, but getting between towns isn't as easy.

BEECHWORTH

271 km (168 miles) northeast of Melbourne, 96 km (60 miles) northwest of Alpine National Park, 44 km (26 miles) south of Rutherglen.

One of the prettiest towns in Victoria, Beechworth flourished during the gold rush. When gold ran out, the town of 30,000 was left with all the trappings of prosperity—fine banks, imposing public buildings, breweries, parks, and hotels wrapped in wrought iron—but with scarcely two nuggets to rub together. However, poverty protected the town from such modern improvements as aluminum window frames, and many historic treasures that might have been destroyed in the name of progress have been retained.

GETTING HERE AND AROUND

Beechworth and Rutherglen are on opposite sides of the Hume Freeway, the main Sydney–Melbourne artery. The 44-km (26-mile) Rutherglen-Beechworth Road (C377) connects both towns. Beechworth is about a three-hour drive from Melbourne, twice that from Sydney. Beechworth can also be reached by taking a train from Melbourne's Southern Cross Station to Wangaratta, then changing to a bus service to the town; it's about a 3½-hour journey.

ESSENTIALS

Visitor Information Beechworth Tourist Information Centre. ⊠ *Old Town Hall, 103 Ford St.* ☎ *03/5728–8065, 1300/366321 ⊕ www.beechworthonline.com.au.*

EXPLORING

Burke Museum. This 150-year-old museum takes its name from Robert O'Hara Burke who, with William Wills, became one of the first white explorers to cross Australia from south to north in 1861. Burke served as superintendent of police in Beechworth from 1856 to 1859. Not surprisingly, the small area dedicated to Burke is overshadowed by the Ned Kelly collection: his death mask, replicas of the Kelly Gang's armor,

Murray River Wine Region

and some memorabilia that give insight into the man and his misdeeds. The museum also displays a reconstructed streetscape of Beechworth in the 1880s. ☒ *Loch St.* ☏ *03/5728–8067* ⊕ *www.burkemuseum.com. au* ☞ *A$8* ⊗ *Daily 10–5.*

Ford Street. A stroll along Ford Street is the best way to absorb the historic character and charm of Beechworth. Among the distinguished buildings are **Tanswell's Commercial Hotel,** the **Town Hall,** and the **Courthouse.** It was in the latter that the committal hearing for the famous bushranger Ned Kelly took place in August 1880. His feisty mother, Ellen Kelly, was also sentenced to three years in jail at this court. ☒ *Ford St.* ⊕ *www.beechworthonline.com.au.*

Murray Breweries. The 1920s temperance movement helped to turn this brewery's focus to the brewing of nonalcoholic cordials. The cordials are produced using old-time recipes and seasonal flavors, such as Sicilian blood orange, using the area's natural spring water. You'll find a display of antique brewing equipment, worldwide beer labels, and rare bottles. On the same site is the Beechworth Carriage Museum, a collection of 20 horse-drawn vehicles and Australian Light Horse Infantry memorabilia from World War I. Tastings are free. ☒ *29 Last St.* ☏ *03/5728–1304, 1800/990098* ⊕ *www.murraybreweries.com.au* ☞ *Free* ⊗ *Weekdays 10–4.*

CLOSE UP

Ned Kelly

The English have Robin Hood, the Americans Jesse James. Australians have Ned Kelly, an Irish-descended working-class youth whose struggles against police injustice and governmental indifference made him a legend (though whether he was a hero or villain can still be a hot topic of conversation). The best way to learn about this local legend is to visit the town of Beechworth, where a Ned Kelly Guided Walking Tour (A$10) departs from the visitor information center every day at 1:15 pm. You'll see the courthouse where he was tried and the jail where he was imprisoned during his many scrapes with the law.

The Burke Museum displays one of his death masks, made shortly after he was hanged at Melbourne Gaol. If you long to hear more, visit Glenrowan (40 km [25 miles] southwest of Beechworth), the scene of his famous "last stand." It was here that Kelly, dressed in his legendary iron armor, walked alone down the main street fending off police bullets. He was finally shot in the leg and arrested. A huge statue, and a sound-and-light show that has received rather mixed reviews and is said to be "quite loud," commemorate Australia's most infamous outlaw.

SPORTS AND THE OUTDOORS
BICYCLING
The area from the Murray River to the mountains of northeast Victoria is ideal for mountain bike enthusiasts.

Beechworth Cycle & Saws. Rent a bicycle at this outlet on Beechworth's main street for A$25 for half a day and A$35 for a full day. ☒ 17 Camp St. ☎ 03/5728–1402 ☉ Weekdays 9–5:30, Sat. 9–1, Sun. during school holidays.

Murray to Mountains Rail Trail. A 98-km (61-mile) paved trail stretches from Wangaratta to Bright, with a branch line to Beechworth and recent extensions to Milawa and Wandiligong. Bicycle rentals are available at Wangaratta, Beechworth, Bright, and Myrtleford. A trail map is available from the visitor centers at each of these towns, and can also be downloaded from the trail website. ☒ Albert Rd. ☎ 1800/801065 Wangaratta Visitor Information Centre ⊕ www.murraytomountains.com.au.

HIKING
There are several national parks within easy reach of Beechworth: Chiltern-Mt. Pilot National Park, Beechworth Historic Park, Mount Buffalo National Park, Mount Granya State Park, and Warby Range State Park. The Beechworth visitor center and Parks Victoria have information on bushwalks. The town of Beechworth is the perfect place to get out and about and stretch your legs while admiring late 19th-century architecture. You can pick up a copy of "Echoes of History," a self-guided walking tour of the town from the visitor information center.

Parks Victoria. This government organization has information on Victoria's National Parks and walking trails. ☎ 13–1963 ⊕ www.parkweb.vic.gov.au.

The mighty Murray River is the lifeblood of the region.

WHERE TO STAY

$$ **RENTAL** 🏠 **Country Charm Cottages.** Landscaped gardens overlooking Beechworth Gorge surround these charming pine and cedar cottages. **Pros:** tranquil setting; great views. **Cons:** minimum two-night stay on weekends. 💲 *Rooms from: A$195* ✉ *24 Malakoff Rd.* ☎ *03/5728–2435, 0488/440–101* ⊕ *www.countrycharmcottages.com.au* 🛏 *4 cottages* ⦿ *No meals.*

RUTHERGLEN

274 km (170 miles) northeast of Melbourne, 40 km (25 miles) northwest of Beechworth.

The surrounding red-loam soil signifies the beginning of the Rutherglen wine district, the source of Australia's finest fortified wines. If the term conjures up visions of cloying Ports, you're in for a surprise. In his authoritative *Australian Wine Compendium*, James Halliday says, "Like Narcissus drowning in his own reflection, one can lose oneself in the aroma of a great old muscat."

The main event in the region is Tastes of Rutherglen, held over two consecutive weekends in March. The festival is a celebration of food, wine, and music—in particular jazz, folk, and country. Events are held in town and at all surrounding wineries. Another popular day in the vineyards is the Rutherglen Winery Walkabout held in June, when wine, food, and music are again on the menu.

GETTING HERE AND AROUND

See Beechworth above. Rutherglen is 274 km (170 miles) north of Melbourne, about a 3½- to 4-hour drive along the Hume Freeway. V/Line train and bus services also come to Rutherglen.

Transportation V/Line. ☎ *1800/800007* ⊕ *www.vline.com.au.*

TOURS

Rutherglen Bus and Tour. Rutherglen Bus and Tour has winery tours for a minimum of six people, with visits to five to six wineries on half-day tours and eight to nine estates on day tours. Half-day tours cost A$40 per person, and day tours cost from A$55 per person (with pickup from Rutherglen accommodation only, though pickups from other towns can be arranged for A$15 per person). ☎ *02/6032–8774* ⊕ *www.rutherglenbusandtour.com* 🖘 *From A$40.*

ESSENTIALS

Visitor Information Rutherglen Wine Experience and Visitor Information Centre. ⊠ *57 Main St.* ☎ *1800/622871* ⊕ *www.rutherglenvic.com.*

EXPLORING

All Saints Estate. In business since 1864, this winery has a splendid, turreted castle that was built in the 1880s with capacious storage areas for its product. The old bottling hall and cellar have been revamped as a cheese tasting room, and a corrugated iron former Chinese dormitory is the property's third heritage-listed building. Guided tours of the winery are conducted at 11 am on weekends: just let them know at the cellar door. The winery produces Muscat and Muscadelle from 50-year-old vines, and a range of crisp whites and full-bodied reds. The onsite Indigo Food Company sells regional cheeses and condiments. The menu at the Terrace restaurant changes seasonally; desserts are excellent, especially when combined with a formidable northeast fortified wine. The cellar door and cheese room are open daily; the restaurant is open for lunch from Wednesday to Sunday and for dinner on Saturday only. ⊠ *All Saints Rd., Wahgunyah* ✛ *9 km (5½ miles) southeast of Rutherglen* ☎ *02/6035–2222, 1800/021621* ⊕ *www.allsaintswine.com.au* 🖘 *Free* ⊗ *Cellar door: Mon.–Sat. 9–5:30, Sun. 10–5:30; cheese room: 10–4.*

Campbell's Rutherglen Wines. Wines have been made here by five generations of the Campbell family, dating back to 1870. Brothers Colin and Malcolm Campbell, the winemaker and viticulturist respectively, have been at the helm for the past 40 years. Famed for its award-winning Bobbie Burns Shiraz and Merchant Prince Rare Rutherglen Muscat, the property covers a picturesque 160 acres. You can wander freely through the winery on a self-guided tour and taste wines at the cellar door, including rare and aged vintages. Vintage Reserve wines are available only at the cellar door. Private tastings and guided tours can be booked. The winery does not have a restaurant but sells baskets of local gourmet goodies. The winery also takes part in the annual Tastes of Rutherglen wine festival, when food and music are on the agenda. ⊠ *4603 Murray Valley Hwy.* ✛ *3 km (2 miles) west of Rutherglen* ☎ *02/6033–6000, 1800/359458* ⊕ *www.campbellswines.com.au* 🖘 *Free* ⊗ *Mon.–Sat. 9–5, Sun. 10–5.*

5

Chambers Rosewood Winery. Established in the 1850s, this is one of Australia's heavyweight producers of fortified wines. Stephen Chambers's Muscats are legendary, with blending stocks that go back more than a century. Stephen runs a very relaxed winery, which is genuinely rustic, being just a few corrugated iron sheds in an off-the-beaten-track road. The cellar door is renowned for great value and plenty of tastings; you can take home reasonably priced red and white wine and a full range of fortified wines—from the clean-skin variety (no-label stock) to big two-liter flagons. There's no restaurant, just a cellar door, which also sells homemade jams and condiments. ⊠ *Barkley St., off Corowa Rd.* ☎ *02/6032–8641* ⊕ *www.chambersrosewood.com.au* ☒ *Free* ⊗ *Mon.–Sat. 9–5, Sun. 10–5.*

Pfeiffer Wines. Since its first vines were planted in 1895, this winery has made exceptional fortified wines and varietal wines, including Chardonnay. It also has one of the few Australian plantings of Gamay, the classic French grape used to make Beaujolais. At this small rustic winery you can pre-order (with at least 24 hours' notice) picnic baskets for each season stuffed with gourmet products, cake, and a bottle of table wine for A$90 for two, including plates and cutlery. Vegetarian baskets for two are A$90, and children's are A$12.50 per child. Cheese platters (A$30) are available any time. Winemaker Jen Pfeiffer makes an aperitif called Pfeiffer Seriously Pink, along with a Chardonnay Marsanne, Shiraz, Merlot, and fortifieds such as Muscat, Muscadelle, and Topaque. ⊠ *167 Distillery Rd., Wahgunyah* ✛ *9 km (5½ miles) southeast of Rutherglen* ☎ *02/6033–2805* ⊕ *www.pfeifferwinesrutherglen. com.au* ☒ *Free* ⊗ *Mon.–Sat. 9–5, Sun. 10–5.*

Buller Wines. Established by Reginald Langdon Buller in 1921, this winery in Rutherglen produces delicious fortified wines and gutsy, fullbodied reds, the flagship being its Shiraz. As the old Shiraz vines are not irrigated, the annual yields are low, but the fruit produced has intense flavor, which winemaker Andrew Buller crafts into wines of great depth and elegance. There are also small plantings of rarer varieties such as Mondeuse. Tastings and sales are at the cellar door, but there's no restaurant. ⊠ *2804 Federation Way* ☎ *02/6032–9660* ⊕ *www.bullerwines. com.au* ☒ *Free* ⊗ *Daily 10–5.*

WHERE TO STAY

$$ ⛳ **Tuileries.** Incorporating a vineyard, olive groves, and a renowned
HOTEL restaurant, this accommodation feels like an exclusive retreat. **Pros:** beautifully appointed suites; tranquil country setting. **Cons:** next-to-no nightlife in Rutherglen. ⑤ *Rooms from: A$199* ⊠ *13 Drummond St.* ☎ *02/6032–9033* ⊕ *www.tuileriesrutherglen.com.au* ⤴ *16 rooms* ⊙| *Breakfast.*

ALPINE NATIONAL PARK

323 km (200 miles) northeast of Melbourne, 40–50 km (25–31 miles) south to southeast of Mt. Buffalo.

Alpine National Park is popular year-round, attracting campers and hikers in the warm months and skiers in the winter time. The High Country, as the region is commonly called, has gorgeous alpine scenery—mountain peaks, waterfalls, grassy plains, and summer wildflowers—and plenty of outdoor activities, from walking, cycling, and fishing to horse riding, canoeing, and cross-country skiing.

GETTING HERE AND AROUND

Bus services to Alpine National Park operate from Albury on the New South Wales border in the north. In ski season the Falls Creek Coach Service departs from Melbourne for Falls Creek via Mt. Beauty. V/Line's services also come here.

Transportation Falls Creek Coach Service. ☎ *03/5754-4024* ⊕ *www. fallscreekcoachservice.com.au.* **V/Line.** ☎ *1800/800007* ⊕ *www.vline.com.au.*

EXPLORING

Alpine National Park. This national park covers three loosely connected areas in eastern Victoria, which follow the peaks of the Great Dividing Range. One of these areas, formerly Bogong National Park, contains some of the highest mountains on the continent. As such, it is a wintertime destination for skiers who flock to the resorts at Falls Creek, Mt. Buller, and Mt. Hotham.

The land around here is rich in history. *Bogong* is an Aboriginal word for "big moth," and it was to Mt. Bogong that Aborigines came each year after the winter thaw in search of bogong moths, considered a delicacy. Aborigines were eventually displaced by cattle ranchers who brought their cattle here to graze. The main townships in the area are Bright and Mount Beauty, both of which have visitor information centers. ⊠ *Alpine National Park* ☎ *13–1963* ⊕ *parkweb.vic.gov.au.*

WHERE TO EAT

$$$ ✕ **Simones Restaurant.** A new generation of the Simone family is head-
ITALIAN ing this renowned restaurant, which has won numerous awards and made founder, Patrizia Simone, a legend of the Melbourne food and wine scene. Simones serves its blend of traditional Italian cuisine with creativity in a 19th-century cottage in the middle of town. The menu shows off the family's passion for cooking rustic Italian food and using seasonal local produce, from stuffed zucchini flowers and handmade pastas to Welsh Black beef sourced from a local cattle farmer. Herbs and some seasonal vegetables come from the kitchen garden. Simones also has an eight-course degustation menu (A$110). Patrizia runs cooking classes as well. ⑤ *Average main: A$40* ⊠ *98 Gavan St., Bright* ☎ *03/5755–2266* ⊕ *www.simonesbright.com.au* ⊘ *Closed Sun. and Mon.* ⚑ *Reservations essential.*

Snow Gum trees on the Bogong High Plains in Alpine National Park

ECHUCA

206 km (128 miles) north of Melbourne, 194 km (120 miles) west of Rutherglen, 92 km (57 miles) north of Bendigo.

The name Echuca comes from a local Aboriginal word meaning "meeting of the waters," a reference to the town's location at the confluence of the Murray, Campaspe, and Goulburn rivers. In the second half of the 19th century Echuca was Australia's largest inland port. Many reminders of Echuca's colorful heyday remain in the restored paddle steamers, barges, and historic hotels, and in the Red Gum Works, the town's sawmill, now a working museum.

GETTING HERE AND AROUND

Echuca is a three-hour drive from Melbourne, reached most directly by the Northern Highway (Highway 75). V/Line trains take 3½ hours to reach Echuca from Melbourne's Southern Cross Station once or twice a day; at other times trains connect at Bendigo or Murchison East with bus services to Echuca.

ESSENTIALS

Visitor Information Echuca Moama Visitor Information Centre. ⊠ *Old Pump Station, 2 Heygarth St.* ☎ *1800/804446* ⊕ *www.echucamoama.com.*

EXPLORING

Historic River Precinct. The inland river port of Echuca is a heritage town, home to a large paddle steamer fleet and its historic wharf. Among the vessels docked at the wharf is the PS *Adelaide* (built in 1866), the world's oldest operating wooden-hulled paddle steamer. Other historic buildings include the **Bridge Hotel**, built by ex-convict Henry Hopwood and the "father of Echuca," who had the foresight to establish a punt, and then to build a bridge at this commercially strategic point on the river. The **Star Hotel**, built in the 1860s, has an underground bar and escape tunnel, which was used by after-hours drinkers in the 19th century to evade the police. The **Port of Echuca Discovery Centre** is now open and full of historical displays. It's also a booking office, where you can get tickets to paddle steamer cruises and other historic sights, plus a spooky Port After Dark tour. The center itself runs daily tours (A$14) covering its displays and the recently revitalized wharf areas (warehouses, old railroad tracks, and riverboats included), and the Star Hotel.

One-hour river excursions are a refreshing treat at the end of a hot summer's day. Step aboard the historic *Pevensey,* and the *Alexander Arbuthnot* (⊕ *www.echucapaddlesteamers.net.au*) or the *Canberra* and *Emmylou* (⊕ *www.emmylou.com.au*), a 19th-century style boat built in 1980–82 for a television series (Murray River Paddle Steamers). The paddle wheelers depart daily from 10:15 am to 2:45 pm, with a 4 pm cruise sailing in peak periods; a one-hour cruise on the PS *Emmylou* costs A$28.50. ⊠ *74 Murray Esplanade* ☎ *03/5481–0500, 1300/942737* ⊕ *www.portofechuca.org.au* ☉ *Daily 9–5.*

SPORTS AND THE OUTDOORS
BOATING
Murray River Houseboats. A popular pursuit on the Murray is to rent a houseboat and drift slowly down the river, and this operator's vessels are five-star floating experiences with Jacuzzis, state-of-the-art kitchens, and the latest appliances. They can sleep from 2 to 12 people and be rented from three days to a week and longer. There are six boats for rent. Prices start from A$1,720 for three nights in the peak late-December/January period, for two to seven people. ⊠ *Riverboat Dock* ☎ *03/5480–2343* ⊕ *www.murrayriverhouseboats.com.au.*

CANOEING
River Country Adventours. If you want to canoe up a lazy river—the Goulburn, which is a tributary of the Murray— you can arrange for a half- or full-day trip with this tour company. ⊠ *Kyabram* ☎ *03/5852–2736, 0428/585–227 mobile* ⊕ *www.adventours.com.au* 🛏 *From A$65.*

WHERE TO EAT AND STAY
$$ ✗ **Ceres.** Housed in a circa 1922 pharmacy, this restaurant has some
ITALIAN history on top of the river views from its upstairs balcony. New owners have renovated the heritage-listed building to highlight its architectural features. Pasta is made fresh in the kitchen from local produce, and the signature breakfast dish is a twist on the Australian favorite of smashed avocado on toast—this version comes on an English muffin with an egg that's been poached and then fried. Ⓢ *Average main: A$26* ⊠ *554 High St.* ☎ *03/5482–5599* ⊕ *www.ceresechuca.com.au.*

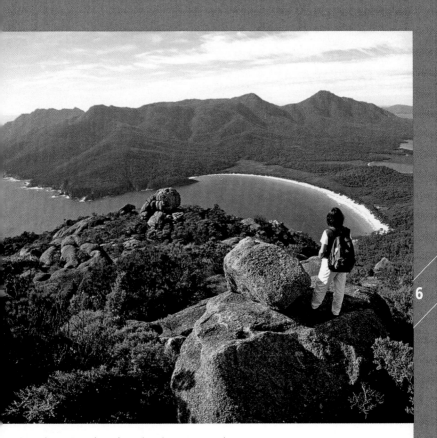

6

TASMANIA

WELCOME TO TASMANIA

TOP REASONS TO GO

★ **Beautiful Walks:** Tasmania has some of Australia's best walking terrain. Stunning walks can be taken around Cradle Mountain or on Freycinet Peninsula.

★ **Colonial Homes and Cottages:** Many of the Georgian mansions and charming cottages from Tasmania's early days as a colony are lovely lodging options.

★ **Tassie Tastes:** Hungry Tasmanian's are well served, thanks to the regions beautiful produce and excellent wine.

★ **Stunning Capital:** Hobart, nestled beneath Mt. Wellington and hugging the Derwent Estuary, has long attracted nature lovers.

★ **Living History:** The World Heritage-listed Port Arthur Historic Site is Australia's most famous penal settlement.

1 **Hobart.** Perhaps Australia's most beautiful state capital, the compact city has history and beautifully preserved colonial architecture in genteel surroundings.

2 **Port Arthur and the Tasman Peninsula.** The horrors of Tasmania's convict past are there to discover in the notorious penal settlement, which has been sensitively converted into an absorbing museum.

3 **Freycinet National Park and East Coast Resorts.** Deserted white-sand beaches, including the legendary Wineglass Bay, as well as some superb wineries, make the east coast a must-visit.

GETTING ORIENTED

About the size of West Virginia, and with a population of just over a half million, the island of Tasmania contains geographical diversity in stunning, easily navigable scenery. Surrounded by sea, the climate is, of course, maritime, with the west coast the wettest thanks to the roaring forties winds. On the other hand, the island's capital of Hobart, a proud port city that is Australia's second-oldest settlement, is Australia's second-driest city. The beautiful east coast is nearly always warmer and milder than the rest of the isle. This diversity has contributed to an amazing variety of vegetation, from eucalypt forest and alpine heathlands to large areas of cool temperate rain forests and moorlands.

6

4 Launceston. Tasmania's second-biggest city is a pleasant place to while away time thanks to its attractive parks and historic colonial mansions.

5 The Northwest. A nearly deserted rugged coastline and the dramatic landscapes of Cradle Mountain National Park make this area a must-visit for walkers.

Updated by Leah McLennan

Wild and dramatic landscapes, empty white beaches, heavenly food and wine—Tasmania's charms have been overlooked for too long by international travelers. Hikers have always known about the island's wilderness trails, which lead you through deserted forests and national parks, but now gourmands are discovering Tassie's superb local produce, making it a world-class gourmet destination, too.

Tasmania's attractions encompass the historic, the healthy, and the hedonistic. Although Tasmania now is an unspoiled reminder of a simpler, slower lifestyle away from the rat race, its bloody history is never far from the surface. Today, walking through the lovely grounds in Port Arthur, the notorious penal colony, or the unhurried streets of Australia's smallest capital city, Hobart, with its profusion of Georgian buildings, it's difficult to picture Tasmania as a land of turmoil and tragedy. But the destruction of the Aboriginal population, who are thought to have crossed into Tasmania approximately 36,000 years ago, is a dark stain on the island's memory.

In many ways Tasmania is still untamed, making it a hiker's delight. The island's 19 national parks encompass impenetrable rain forests and deep river gorges that cut through the massive mountain valleys. The coastlines are scalloped with endless desolate beaches—some pristine white, fronting serene turquoise bays, and some rugged and rocky, facing churning, choppy seas.

These beautiful surrounds have led to Tasmania's newest claim to fame as a gourmet haven. Thanks to the island's many microclimates, you can grow or harvest virtually anything from superb dairy produce to wonderful meat, and its clear seas abound in wonderful seafood. Oenophiles have also discovered the island's wines, and the island's wine routes are worth a slow meander.

PLANNER

WHEN TO GO

Cold weather–phobes beware: Tasmanian winters can draw freezing blasts from the Antarctic, so this is not the season to explore the high-lands or wilderness areas. It's better in the colder months to enjoy the cozy interiors of colonial cottages and the open fireplaces of welcoming pubs.

Summer can be hot—bushfires do occasionally occur—but temperatures tend to be lower than on the Australian mainland.

The best seasons to visit are autumn, summer, and spring; early autumn is beautiful, with deciduous trees in full color. Spring, with its splashes of pastel wildflowers and mild weather, is equally lovely. Tassie really comes alive in summer, when it's warm enough to swim at the many gorgeous beaches, the fresh summer fruits are ripe, and the lavender is in bloom.

Tasmania is a relaxing island with few crowds, except during the mid-December to mid-February school holiday period and at the end of the annual Sydney-to-Hobart yacht race just after Christmas. Most attractions and sights are open year-round.

PLANNING YOUR TIME

If you have limited time in Tasmania, spend your first morning in Hobart, where you can stroll around the docks, Salamanca Place, and Battery Point, and have some fish-and-chips from the harbor's floating chippies. After lunch, drive to Richmond and explore its 19th-century streetscape, then stay in a local B&B. On the second day head for Port Arthur, and spend the morning exploring the town's historic park, the site of the island's former penal colony. Take the afternoon to drive through the dramatic scenery of the Tasman Peninsula, noting the tessellated pavement and Tasman Arch blowhole near Eaglehawk Neck. Return to Hobart for the night, then on the third morning take a leisurely drive around the scenic Huon Valley. On return to Hobart, finish your tour with a trip to the summit of Mt. Wellington.

If you have more time, continue on to Freycinet National Park. Climb the steep path to the outlook over Wineglass Bay, then descend to the sands for a picnic and swim. Stay two nights in the park, then meander back through the east-coast wine regions. Return to the capital, topping off the day with city views from Mt. Wellington.

GETTING HERE AND AROUND

Tasmania is compact—the drive from southern Hobart to northern Launceston takes little more than two hours. The easiest way to see the state is by car, as you can plan a somewhat circular route around the island. Begin in Hobart or Launceston, where car rentals are available from the airport and city agencies, or in Devonport if you arrive on the ferry from Melbourne. Allow plenty of time for stops along the way, as there are some fabulous views to be seen. Bring a sturdy pair of shoes for impromptu mountain and seaside walks; you'll most often have huge patches of forest and long expanses of white beaches all to yourself.

In some cases the street addresses for attractions may not include building numbers (in other words, only the name of the street will be given). Don't worry—this just means either that the street is short and the attractions are clearly visible or that signposts will clearly lead you there.

If you are exploring several national parks in the space of a few weeks or months it is recommended to buy a Holiday Park Pass that is valid for two months for A$60 per vehicle in the National Parks of Tasmania.

AIR TRAVEL

Hobart International Airport is 22 km (14 miles) east of Hobart, one hour by air from Melbourne or two hours from Sydney. Although most interstate flights connect through Melbourne, Qantas, Jetstar, and Virgin Australia also run direct flights to other mainland cities. Launceston airport is at Western Junction, 16 km (10 miles) south of central Launceston. It's served by Jetstar, Tiger Airways, and Virgin Australia.

On the island, King Island Airlines can get you to the northwest and King Island. Tickets can be booked through the airlines or through the Tasmanian Travel and Information Centre. Tasmanian Redline Coaches has an airport shuttle service for A$18 per person between the airport and its downtown depot. Metered taxis are available at the stand in front of the terminal. The fare to downtown Hobart is approximately A$45.

CAR TRAVEL

Port Arthur is an easy 90-minute drive from Hobart via the Arthur Highway. A private vehicle is essential if you want to explore parts of the Tasman Peninsula beyond the historic settlement. A vehicle is absolutely essential on the west coast. The road from Hobart travels through the Derwent Valley and past lovely historic towns before rising to the plateau of central Tasmania. Many of the northwest roads are twisty and even unpaved in the more remote areas, but two-wheel drive is sufficient for most touring. Be prepared for sudden weather changes: snow in the summertime is not uncommon in the highest areas. Lake St. Clair is 173 km (107 miles) northwest of Hobart, and can be reached via the Lyell Highway, or from Launceston via Deloraine or Poatina. Cradle Mountain is 85 km (53 miles) south of Devonport, and can be reached by car via Claude Road from Sheffield or via Wilmot. Both lead 30 km (19 miles) along Route C132 to Cradle Valley.

RESTAURANTS

Although there are elegant dining options in the larger towns—especially Hobart—most eateries serve meals in a casual setting. Fiercely proud of their local produce, Tasmania's restaurateurs have packed their menus with home-grown seafood, beef, and cheeses, washed down with their famous cold-climate wines. Tasmanian wine is nearly unknown in the rest of the world, but that's not a comment on its quality; it's because Tasmanians tend to drink the vast majority of it themselves, leaving next to nothing to export.

HOTELS

The hospitality industry is thriving in Tasmania, so in popular areas you'll find a wide range of accommodation options, from inexpensive motels to genteel B&Bs, rustic lodges to luxury hotels. Most hotels will have air-conditioning, but bed-and-breakfast lodgings often do not. Apart from a few hotels right in the main city center, most Hobart accommodations have free parking. In many smaller places, especially the colonial-style cottages, no smoking is allowed inside. *Hotel reviews have been shortened. For full information, visit Fodors.com.*

WHAT IT COSTS (IN AUSTRALIAN DOLLARS)			
	$	$$	$$$	$$$$
Restaurants	Under A$21	A$21–A$35	A$36–A$50	over A$50
Hotels	Under A$151	A$151–A$200	A$201–A$300	over A$300

Restaurant prices are the average cost of a main course at dinner or, if dinner is not served, at lunch. Hotel prices are the lowest cost of a standard double room in high season, including tax and service.

HOBART

Straddling the Derwent River at the foot of Mt. Wellington's forested slopes, Hobart was founded as a penal settlement in 1803. It's the second-oldest city in the country after Sydney, and it certainly rivals its mainland counterpart as Australia's most beautiful state capital. Close-set colonial brick-and-sandstone shops and homes line the narrow, quiet streets, creating a genteel setting for this historic city of 215,000. Life revolves around the broad Derwent River port, one of the deepest harbors in the world. Here warehouses that once stored Hobart's major exports of fruit, wool, corn, and products from the city's former whaling fleet still stand alongside the wharf today.

Hobart sparkles between Christmas and New Year's—summer Down Under—during the annual Sydney-to-Hobart yacht race. The event dominates conversations among Hobart's citizens, who descend on Constitution Dock to welcome the yachts and join in the boisterous festivities of the crews. The New Year also coincides with the Tastes of Tasmania Festival, when the dockside area comes alive with the best of Tasmanian food and wine on offer in numerous cafés, bars, and waterfront stalls. Otherwise, Hobart is a placid city whose nightlife is largely confined to excellent restaurants, jazz clubs, and the action at the Wrest Point Casino in Sandy Bay.

GETTING HERE AND AROUND

Hobart, being teeny-tiny, is eminently walkable; once you're in the city center, no attraction is more than 15 minutes' walk away, apart from the Cascade Brewery and the Museum of Old and New Art (MONA). Because of the many one-way streets, it's best to park a car and leave it for the day as you explore. If you prefer two wheels to two legs, you can hire trendy electric bicycles from the Henry Jones Art Hotel on Hunter Street for A$35 for the day.

Hobart

KEY

⛴ *Ferry*

ESSENTIALS

Visitor Information Tasmanian Travel and Information Centre. ✉ *20 Davey St., at Elizabeth St., Hobart Waterfront* ☎ *03/6238–4222,* ⊕ *www. hobarttravelcentre.com.au.*

EXPLORING

TOP ATTRACTIONS

Cascade Brewery. This is Australia's oldest and most picturesque brewery, producing fine Tasmanian beers since 1824. You can see its inner workings on the 90-minute tours, which require lots of walking and climbing, but you're rewarded with three free drinks at the end. Note that appropriate attire (long pants and closed-toe shoes only) is required, and tour reservations are essential. It's a 30-minute walk from the city center, or buses leave from Franklin Square every 35 minutes from 9:15 am. ✉ *140 Cascade Rd., South Hobart* ☎ *03/6224–1117* ⊕ *www. cascadebreweryco.com.au* 🎫 *A$25.*

Constitution Dock. Yachts competing in the annual Sydney-to-Hobart race moor at this colorful marina dock from the end of December through the first week of January. Buildings fronting the dock are century-old reminders of Hobart's trading history. Nearby Hunter

Street is the original spot where British ships anchored. ⊠ *Argyle and Davey Sts., Hobart Waterfront* ☒ *Free* ☉ *Daily 24 hrs.*

Fodor'sChoice **Museum of Old and New Art (MONA).**
★ Australia's largest privately funded museum is home to a diverse array of exhibits from Tasmanian millionaire David Walsh's private collection. The unusual collection of more than 400 often provocative pieces, including Sidney Nolan's *Snake*—an impressive mural made of more than 1,500 individual

paintings—and Wim Delvoye's *Cloaca Professional*, an interesting contraption that transforms food into excrement. Each year, the museum also hosts the MOFO festival, Tasmania's largest contemporary musical festival. Sometimes compared with Bilbao's Guggenheim Museum, MONA has an eclectic mix of antiquities and contemporary art. The unusual building itself is set into cliffs on the Berriedale peninsula, and visitors to the museum use touch-screen devices to learn about the exhibits as they wander around. To reach MONA, it's a 15-minute drive, or you can take the MONA-ROMA minibus from the Hobart waterfront or airport. There is also the MONA fast catamaran from the Hobart waterfront. ⊠ *651–655 Main Rd., Berriedale* ☎ *03/6277–9900* ⊕ *www.mona.net.au* ☒ *A$25* ☉ *Dec. and Feb.– Apr., Wed.–Mon. 10–6; Jan., daily 10–6; May–Nov., Wed.–Mon. 10–5.*

Fodor'sChoice **Salamanca Place.** Many of the warehouses once used by whalers from
★ ships docking at Salamanca Place have been converted into delightful crafts shops, art galleries, and restaurants. At the boisterous Saturday market, which attracts all elements of Tasmanian society, from hippies to the well-heeled, dealers in Tasmanian arts and crafts, antiques, old records, and books—and a fair bit of appalling junk—display their wares between 8:30 and 3. Keep an eye open for items made from beautiful Tasmanian timber, particularly Huon pine. ⊠ *Salamanca Pl., Hobart Waterfront* ⊕ *www.salamanca.com.au.*

WORTH NOTING

Arthur Circus. Hobart's best-preserved street is a charming collection of tiny houses and cottages in a circle around a village green on Runnymede Street, in the heart of historic Battery Point. Most of these private houses, which were built in the 1840s and 1850s, have been nicely restored. ⊠ *Arthur Circus, Battery Point.*

Brooke Street Pier. The busy waterfront at Brooke Street Pier is the city's key departure point for harbor cruises. Nearby **Elizabeth Street Pier** has trendy restaurants and bars. ⊠ *Franklin Wharf.*

**OFF THE
BEATEN
PATH** **Bonorong Wildlife Sanctuary.** About 25 km (16 miles) north of Hobart on the highway toward Launceston, this sanctuary hosts a diverse selection of Australian species—many of which have been rescued—including koalas, wombats, quolls, and the adorable Tasmanian devil. Free feeding

tours take place daily at 11:30 and 2. The private dusk tours are highly recommended and provide a rare opportunity to experience Tassie's beautiful nocturnal animals at their most active. ✉ *593 Briggs Rd., Brighton* ☎ *03/6268–1184* ⊕ *www.bonorong.com.au* 🖾 *A$30, dusk tours A$149* ⊙ *Daily 9–5.*

Penitentiary Chapel Historic Sight. "The Tench," as it was known by its inhabitants, was the prisoners' barracks for Hobart Town. The buildings, only a short walk from Hobart's CBD, vividly portray Tasmania's penal, judicial, and religious heritage in their courtrooms, old cells, and underground tunnels. If you want to get spooked, come for the nighttime ghost tour (reservations necessary). ✉ *Brisbane and Campbell Sts., City Center* ☎ *03/6231–0911* ⊕ *nationaltrusttas.rezdy.com* 🖾 *A$15, ghost tour A$20* ⊙ *Tours Sun.–Fri. at 10, 11:30, 1, and 2:30 and Sat. at 1 and 2:30; ghost tour Mon. and Fri. at 8 pm in winter and 9 pm in summer.*

FAMILY **Royal Tasmanian Botanical Gardens.** The largest area of open land in Hobart, these well-tended gardens are rarely crowded and provide a welcome relief from the city. Plants from all over the world are here—more than 6,000 exotic and native species in all. The collection of Tasmania's unique native flora is especially impressive. ✉ *Lower Domain Rd., Queen's Domain* ☎ *03/6236–3075* ⊕ *www.rtbg.tas.gov.au* 🖾 *Free* ⊙ *Apr. and Sept., daily 8–5:30; May–Aug., daily 8–5; Oct.–Mar., daily 8–6:30.*

Tasmanian Museum and Art Gallery. In a building overlooking Constitution Dock, this art gallery is a good starting point for uncovering Tasmania's rich history. It's a great place in Hobart to learn about the island's Aboriginal culture and unique wildlife. There are free guided tours Wednesday to Sunday at 11, 1, and 2. ✉ *Dunn Pl., Hobart Waterfront* ☎ *03/6165–7000* ⊕ *www.tmag.tas.gov.au* 🖾 *Free* ⊙ *Tues.–Sun. 10–4.*

BEACHES

Hobart, which is surrounded by water, has a number of spectacular sandy beaches, most of them close to the city center or Derwent estuary.

Cornelian Bay Beach. Just five minutes' drive from Hobart's city center, this safe and quiet beach lies immediately north of the Queen's Domain urban parkland. Assorted sailing boats sit offshore in Cornelian Bay, while a popular trail, the Queen's Walk, runs directly behind the beach. The Cornelian Bay trail is popular among the locals. Charming heritage-listed boathouses, picnic sites, and barbecues line the shore. The waterfront-facing Cornelian Bay Boathouse Restaurant is known for creative locally caught seafood and fresh Tasmanian produce. **Amenities:** food and drink; parking (free). **Best for:** solitude; walking. ✉ *Cornelian Bay, Queen's Domain.*

> ## BELLERIVE VILLAGE
> Take the ferry across the River Derwent to Bellerive, a lovely little village-like suburb that will make you feel as if you've stepped back in history. There are great restaurants, and the view back to the city with Mt. Wellington looming in the background is impressive.

Continued on page 342

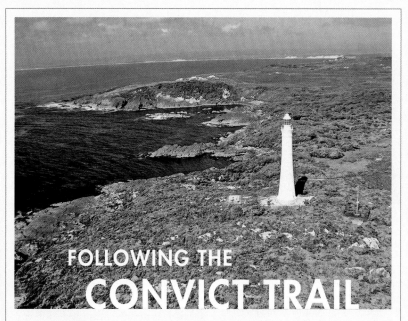

FOLLOWING THE
CONVICT TRAIL

For many, Tasmania conjures up grim images of chain-ganged prisoners: British convicts banished from the motherland to languish on a distant island in a faraway colony.

Its humble (and brutal) beginning as a penal colony is a point of pride for many Australians. It's no small feat that a colony comprised of, among others, poor Irish, Scottish, and Welsh convicts— many imprisoned for crimes as petty as stealing a loaf of bread—were able to build what is now Australia. It epitomizes a toughness of character that Australians prize. Many here can accurately trace their lineage back to the incarcerated. Kevin Rudd, the country's former Prime Minister, is himself descended from six convicts, including Mary Wade, the youngest female prisoner transported to Australia at the age of 11.

Tasmania has a number of remarkably well-preserved convict sites, most of which are set on the isolated Tasman Peninsula, some 75 km (47 miles) southeast of Hobart. Here, the region's beautifully rugged landscape belies the horrors of the past. Exploring Tasmania's convict heritage and the dramatic beauty of the island are two sides of the same coin. The region's isolation, impenetrable rain forests, and sheer cliffs falling into the sea made it a perfect island prison. By following signs on what's called the Convict Trail, you'll go home with provocative insight into what life was like for the almost 75,000 souls sent to Tasmania between 1803 and 1853.

by Helena Iveson

The rugged and beautiful Tasmanian Coast.

TASMANIA'S CONVICT PAST

Port Arthur Historic Site

"It is impossible to convey, in words, any idea of the hideous phantasmagoria of shifting limbs and faces which moved through the evil-smelling twilight of this terrible prison-house. Callot might have drawn it, Dante might have suggested it, but a minute attempt to describe its horrors would but disgust. There are depths in humanity which one cannot explore, as there are mephitic caverns into which one dare not penetrate."

—Marcus Clarke's description of
Port Arthur's Separate Prison in his famous
novel *For the Term of his Natural Life.*

They came in chains to this hostile island, where the seasons were all the wrong way around and the sights and smells were unfamiliar. In the 50 years following the establishment of the first settlement in Tasmania (Van Diemen's Land) in 1803, 57,909 male and 13,392 female prisoners were sent to the island. From 1830 on, many ended up at the newly built penal settlement at Port Arthur, where the slightest infraction would be punished by 100 lashes or weeks of solitary confinement

on a diet of bread and water. Life was spent in chains, breaking up rocks or doing other menial tasks—all meant to keep criminal tendencies at bay.

The location of the settlement on the Tasman Peninsula was ideal for a prison. Joined to the rest of the island by a narrow neck of land with steep cliffs pounded by surging surf, it was easy to isolate and guard with half-starved dogs on the infamous dogline. Even though convicts were sentenced for a specific number of years, conditions were so brutal that even a few years could become a life sentence. With no chance of escape, some prisoners saw suicide as the only way out.

As the number of prisoners increased, more buildings went up. In time, the penal colony became a self-sufficient industrial center where prisoners sawed timber, built ships, laid bricks, cut stone, and made tiles, shoes, iron castings, and clothing.

A sculpture representing
the infamous dogline
at Eaglehawk Neck,
Tasman Peninsula

HOW TO EXPLORE

GETTING HERE

To fully experience the trail, you'll need a car. It's possible to get to Port Arthur via operators such as Tassielink, but you can't access the whole trail by public transportation.

From Hobart head north to the well-preserved village of Richmond before continuing southeast on the Arthur Highway (A9) to the small town of Sorrell. Not far from here is the infamous Eaglehawk neck, marking the start of the Tasman Peninsula. The Convict Trail runs in a circle around the peninsula, with signs clearly marking the many sites along the way.

TIMING

Port Arthur is 120 km (75 miles) or an hour and a half away from Hobart, but will take longer if you intend on making stops at Richmond and Sorell (which you should).

This trip can be done in one long day, but if you want to thoroughly explore the Tasman Peninsula, allow for two or three days. The Convict Trail booklet is available from visitor information centers across Tasmania and details the key sites and attractions along the route.

Richmond Bridge and Church

EXPLORING

It's easy to forget that Port Arthur wasn't an isolated settlement. The whole of the Tasman Peninsula was part of a larger penal colony, so, for the full experience, don't overlook the smaller sights. There are plenty of cafés and accommodations along the way, so take your time.

STUNNING VIEWS

Don't miss the vistas at the Tasman National Park Lookout. The walk along dramatic sea cliffs, which are among the highest and most spectacular in Australia, is easy and rewarding. The views of Pirates Bay, Cape Hauy, and the two islands just off the coast called The Lanterns are spectacular.

EN ROUTE

Take a break at the famous Sorell Fruit Farm where from November to May it's pick-you-own-berry season (✉ *174 Pawleena Road, Sorell* ☎ *03/6265–2744* ⊕ *www.sorellfruitfarm.com* ⊗ *Oct., Mar., Apr., and May 10–4; Nov., Dec., Jan., and Feb. 8:30–5*).

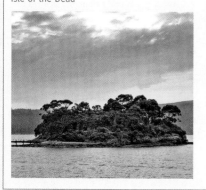
Isle of the Dead

TOURING THE CONVICT TRAIL

It's hard to absorb this disturbing story of human suffering. Around 73,000 convicts were transported here, and about 1 in 5 served time in Port Arthur, on Tasmania's southernmost tip.

Stone bridge at Richmond

① RICHMOND BRIDGE.

Australia's oldest bridge was built by convict labor in 1825 and is a lasting symbol of the island's convict heritage. Don't miss the village's gaol, which predates Port Arthur by five years.

② SORELL. This early settle-

ment is where bloody bushranger battles were fought in the colony's formative years. Bushrangers were actually

Sorell Berry Farm

outlaws who lived in the bush. A walk around the town reveals some interesting heritage buildings; there are also plenty of antiques shops and cafes to keep you occupied.

③ THE DOGLINE. Statues

of snarling hounds represent the dogs that prevented the convicts from escaping and mark the infamous dogline along the narrow strip of land linking the Tasman Peninsula with the rest of Tasmania.

Old wooden jetty in Norfolk Bay

④ NORFOLK BAY. This is

the site of a human-powered tramway. Goods were unloaded from ships at the Convict Station and then transported to Port Arthur by a tram dragged by convicts across the peninsula. This saved the ship a dangerous journey across the peninsula's stormy bays.

⑤ PORT ARTHUR. Walking

among the peaceful ruins and quiet gardens, it's difficult to imagine that this place was hell-on-earth for the convicts. When the settlement closed in 1877, the area was renamed Carnarvon in an attempt to disconnect the land from the horrors associated with its former name. However, in 1927 it was reinstated as Port Arthur and opened to a public keen to embrace this aspect of the Australian story.

TRAIL MARKERS

The Convict Trail is marked with a broad arrow symbol that was stamped on convict-made goods. It's framed in yellow to reference the color of convict clothing.

Sandstone church at Port Arthur

7 ISLE OF THE DEAD CONVICT CEMETERY. A small island in the harbor near Port Arthur is the final resting place for about a thousand people, most of them convicts and ex-convict paupers who were buried mostly in unmarked graves.

8 NUBEENA was established as an outstation of Port Arthur and for many years was an important convict farming community. It was also the sight of a semaphore station, used to raise the alarm if a convict made a bid for freedom.

9 SALTWATER RIVER. Exploring the abandoned mines reveals the terrible conditions in which the convicts suffered: restored tiny underground cells, totally without light and filled with fetid air give horrifying insight.

10 KOONYA. The probation station here was once an important convict outpost known as the Cascades. It operated between 1843 and 1846 and you'll find a few isolated houses and a well-restored penitentiary that once held 400 men, at least a quarter of them in chains.

6 POINT PUER BOYS PRISON. More than 3,000 boys, some as young as age nine, passed through here from 1834 to 1849. Located just across the harbor from the main Port Arthur settlement, this was the first jail in the British Empire built exclusively for juvenile male convicts. But just because they were young doesn't mean they were spared from hard labor like stone-cutting and construction. The prison was also infamous for its stern discipline—solitary

The Penitentiary Block

confinement, days at a time on a tread wheel, and whipping were standard punishments for even a trivial breach of the rules.

Seven Mile Beach. One of Tassie's favorite beaches, this long, sandy stretch of sand is less than a 20-minute drive outside of Hobart, close to the airport. It is both isolated and stunning to look at, although it can be noisy with planes taking off and landing nearby. Considered a great family beach, it's rarely crowded and ideal for long walks along sand that's peppered with many unusual shells. The small surrounding community includes a playgrounds, golf courses, and restaurants. Seven Mile Beach Cabin and Caravan Park is set withing a beautiful park alongside the beach. There are numerous day-use areas—No. 1 has unsheltered tables and a lawn area suitable for picnicking. **Amenities:** food and drink; parking (free); showers; toilets. **Best for:** solitude; swimming; walking. ⊠ *Seven Mile Beach*.

SPORTS AND THE OUTDOORS

Hobartians are an outdoorsy lot who make the most of the city's waterfront location by fishing, cruising, and sailing or heading inland to Mt. Wellington to explore the many trails that start there.

BICYCLING

FAMILY **Hobart Bike Hire.** This conveniently located outfitter for renting bikes makes for a fun way to get around the city, particularly via the old railway lines along the western bank of the Derwent River. In addition to pedal bikes for adults and kids, tandem bikes and automatic motor scooters are available. ⊠ *35 Hunter St., Hobart Waterfront* ☎ *0447/556–189* ⊕ *www.hobartbikehire.com.au* ✎ *A$25 daily*.

BOAT TOURS

FAMILY **Hobart Historic Cruises.** Travelers love this old-fashioned red boat, the "Emmalisa," which takes you on a leisurely cruise around the harbor as the friendly tour guide points out the sights. ⊠ *6 Franklin Wharf, Hobart Waterfront* ☎ *03/6223–5893* ⊕ *www.hobarthistoriccruises. com.au* ✎ *A$20*.

FAMILY **Pennicott Wilderness Journeys.** From Hobart, this operator runs a range of cruises, including a two-and-a-half-hour trip that explores Hobart's waterways, and a full-day seafood-focused tour, on which you cruise down to Bruny Island, taste oysters shucked straight from the water, and watch your guide dive for abalone and sea urchin. You can also choose to drive yourself to Adventure Bay on Bruny Island (the Bruny Island Ferry can take any size vehicle) and join a three-hour wilderness cruise, where you can spot seals and, if you're lucky, dolphins and whales. ⊠ *Dock Head Bldg., Franklin Wharf, Hobart Waterfront* ☎ *03/6234–4270* ⊕ *www.pennicottjourneys.com.au* ✎ *A$125*.

FAMILY **Peppermint Bay Cruises.** This catamaran races through the majestic waterways of the Derwent River and the D'Entrecasteaux Channel to Peppermint Bay at Woodbridge and provides a fantastic way to spy some of Tasmania's epic wildlife. And it is abundant, from sea eagles and falcons soaring above the weathered cliffs to pods of dolphins swimming alongside the boat. Underwater cameras explore kelp forests and salmon in the floating fish farms. ⊠ *Brooke St. Pier, Sulivans Cove, Hobart Waterfront* ☎ *03/6231–5114* ⊕ *www.peppermintbay.com.au* ✎ *A$98* ⊙ *Daily 10:30.*

FISHING

Tasmania's well-stocked lakes and streams are among the world's best for trout fishing. The season runs from August through May, and licensed trips can be arranged through the Tasmanian Travel and Information Centre.

Several professional fishing guides are based on the island. For information on these guides, as well as related tours, accommodations, and sea charters, check out ⊕ *www.troutguidestasmania.com.au* or inquire at the Tasmanian Travel and Information Centre for a professional guide in the area you are visiting.

Mr Flathead. If you fancy taking to the ocean to explore local fishing hot spots, check with this company that runs half- and full-day tours on which you'll find scores of flathead, whiting, and salmon. All rods, reels, and equipment are supplied. ⊠ *Dodges Ferry boat ramp, Tiger Head Rd., Dodges Ferry* ☎ *0439/617–200* ⊕ *www.mrflathead.com. au* ✉ *$A150.*

Rod & Fly Tasmania. Tasmania is home to some world-class fishing, and if you'd like to catch some local trout in the region's wonderfully clear rivers, this friendly operator is a good choice for setting up an outing, with more than 30 years of experience. ⊠ *35 Misty Hill Rd., Mountain River* ☎ *03/6266–4480, 0408/469–771* ⊕ *www.rodandfly.com.au.*

HIKING

Pick up a Mt. Wellington Walk Map from the tourist office on Elizabeth Street in Hobart to make the most out of the park that towers over Hobart. Although shops around town stock outdoor equipment, you should bring your own gear if you're planning any serious bushwalking. Sneakers are adequate for walking around Mt. Wellington and along beaches. A car is necessary to access several of the trails around the peak.

Tasmanian Hikes. Go hiking with this guide company—you can choose from a range of breathtaking hikes around Tasmania. A nine-day South Coast trek starts in Hobart and explores the wild southern shoreline, but they conduct much shorter trips, too. ☎ *0400/882–742* ⊕ *www. tasmanianhikes.com.au.*

WALKING TOURS

Hobart Historic Tours. This tour company leads walks through old Hobart, around the waterfront and maritime precinct, and to historic pubs Wednesday to Sunday at 3 and 5. ⊠ *Hobart Travel Centre, Davey and Elizabeth Sts., Hobart Waterfront* ☎ *03/6238–4222* ⊕ *www. hobarthistorictours.com.au* ✉ *A$30.*

WHERE TO EAT

Constitution Dock is the perfect place for yacht-watching, as well as gobbling fresh fish-and-chips from one of the punts (floating fish-and-chips shops) moored on the water. Ask for the daily specials, such as local blue grenadier or trevally, which cost A$7–A$16, or go for some freshly shucked oysters. The city's main restaurant areas include the docks and the streets around Salamanca Place.

The extremely popular Saturday Salamanca Market

$
INDIAN
FAMILY

✕ **Annapurna.** In the bustling restaurant strip of North Hobart, this local favorite has maintained an enviable reputation for many years thanks to its consistently good-value Indian food. Tandoori, curries (take care, they can be searingly hot), and a wide selection of other Indian delicacies keep people coming back. Inexpensive lunch boxes are available. There is a second location in Salamanca Place. ⑤ *Average main: A$16* ⊠ *305 Elizabeth St., North Hobart* ☎ *03/6236–9500* ⊕ *www.annapurnaindiancuisine.com* ⊘ *No lunch weekends.*

$$
STEAKHOUSE

✕ **Ball and Chain Grill.** Set in an old sandstone warehouse, this eatery is the place to go to sample delicious meat and game cooked over a charcoal fire. The huge, succulent hunks of meat here leave even the biggest eater satisfied. Try the uniquely Australian carpetbag steak stuffed with oyster meat; there's also a self-serve salad bar. ⑤ *Average main: A$30* ⊠ *87 Salamanca Pl., Battery Point* ☎ *03/6223–2655* ⊕ *www. ballandchain.com.au* ⊘ *No lunch Sat.*

$$$$
MODERN
AUSTRALIAN
Fodor's Choice
★

✕ **Ethos Eat Drink.** Operated by one of Hobart's most trusted restaurateurs, the dishes at this lively spot feature a daily-changing list of seasonal ingredients available as a six-course set menu (A$90, with matched wines A$165). Housed in a historic former stable in the heart of the city, the dining rooms exude charm. Typical tantalizing dishes include slow-cooked duck egg with pancetta, potatoes, and breadcrumbs; and roasted goat served alongside eggplant, turnips, radishes, and leeks. There's also an excellent wine list and stellar desserts, including housemade chocolates. ⑤ *Average main: A$90* ⊠ *100 Elizabeth St., City Center* ☎ *03/6231–1165* ⊕ *www.ethoseatdrink.com* ⊘ *Closed Sun. and Mon.* ⌦ *Reservations essential.*

$$$
ECLECTIC
✕ Henry's Restaurant. Part of the Henry Jones Art Hotel, this small restaurant has some of Hobart's best fine dining in arty surroundings. The food isn't overshadowed by the contemporary art on the walls thanks to the focus on seasonal produce in hearty dishes like slow-cooked beef cheek with beetroot, horseradish, and chard. The wine list features selections from only the finest Tasmanian, mainland Australian, and overseas wineries. ⑤ *Average main: A$40* ✉ *25 Hunter St., Hobart Waterfront* ☎ *03/6210–7700* ⊕ *www.thehenryjones.com* ⊗ *Lunch by appointment.*

$$$
AUSTRALIAN
✕ Lebrina. Elegant surroundings in an 1840 brick colonial home inspire classic Tasmanian cooking in Hobart's most formal dining room. The best of the island's fresh produce is well utilized in such dishes as the twice-cooked Gruyère soufflé appetizer, or the seared loin of venison with fresh horseradish, served with a chestnut puree. Leave room for the superb Tasmanian cheese plate. The wine list includes many fine Tasmanian vintages. ⑤ *Average main: A$50* ✉ *155 New Town Rd., New Town* ☎ *03/6228–7775* ⊕ *lebrina.com* ⊗ *Closed Sun. and Mon. No lunch* ⚒ *Reservations essential.*

$$
ITALIAN
✕ Maldini Café Restaurant. Reminiscent of an Italian café in a charming country village, this popular (and occasionally cramped) spot lets you watch the parade of Salamanca Place shoppers as you dine on appetizers like antipasto or chargrilled sardines. Heartier fare includes pastas, Sicilian fish stew, and free-range-chicken breast with ricotta, basil, and lemon stuffing. Although Australian wines dominate the list, there are a few Italian labels to match the setting. ⑤ *Average main: A$30* ✉ *47 Salamanca Pl., Hobart Waterfront* ☎ *03/6223–4460* ⊕ *www. maldinirestaurant.com.au.*

$$
CHINESE
FAMILY
✕ Me Wah. Featuring a superb range of wines from around the world, this sumptuously decorated Sandy Bay eatery rivals many of the better Chinese restaurants in Sydney and Melbourne. There is a broad menu, ranging from the pricey long-cooked dish of braised abalone cooked with Chinese mushrooms to traditional favorites, such as Me Wah's delicious steamed dumplings. The *yum cha* (traditional Cantonese tea service) available on weekends at lunch time is worth the short journey from the city center. ⑤ *Average main: A$30* ✉ *16 Magnet Ct., Sandy Bay* ☎ *03/6223–3688* ⊕ *www.mewah.com.au* ⊗ *Closed Mon.*

$$$
SEAFOOD
✕ Mures Fish Centre. On the top floor of this complex at Franklin wharf, the Upper Deck section has superb indoor and alfresco views of the harbor. Downstairs, Mures Lower Deck is a bistro-style alternative, where you can order, take a number, pick up your food, and eat at tables outside. Also in the complex is Mures Sushi Bar, where you can find fresh-out-of-water sushi and sashimi. ⑤ *Average main: A$38* ✉ *Victoria Dock* ☎ *03/6231–1999 upper deck, 03/6231–2009 lower deck, 03/6231–1790 sushi bar* ⊕ *www.murestasmania.com.au.*

$$$$
MODERN
AUSTRALIAN
✕ The Point. This revolving restaurant atop one of Hobart's tallest buildings (it's also home to the city's casino) has breathtaking views, and the food is equally rewarding. The smoked Tasmanian salmon appetizer is a wonderful starter; for a main course, try the braised Robbins Island Wagyu beef brisket with buffalo curd, smoked carrot, farro, and dried olive oil. Meals here aren't cheap, so you might want to give the

6

tables a try before heading up here. $ *Average main: A\$55* ⊠ *Wrest Point Hotel, 410 Sandy Bay Rd., Sandy Bay* ☎ *03/6221–1888* ⊕ *www. pointrevolving.com.au* ⊘ *Closed Sun. and Mon. No lunch Sat.–Thurs.* ⌂ *Reservations essential.*

\$\$
BISTRO
✕ **Remi de Provence.** At Tasmania's leading classic French bistro you can sample authentic classic and contemporary Provençal fare accompanied by superb wines. Add to that the elegant dining room aglow with mirrors and a lovely mural. This nicely valued bistro also has a terrific wine bar along with *cave à manger* where an extensive selection of cheeses, pâtés, and terrines are available. Be sure to try one of Remi's braised dishes, such as coq au vin, which are particularly popular. Save room for the crème brûlée. $ *Average main: A\$30* ⊠ *252 Macquarie St., City Center* ☎ *03/6223–3933* ⊕ *www.remideprovence.com.au* ⊘ *Closed Sun. and Mon. No lunch Sat.–Tues.*

WHERE TO STAY

Hobart has some lovely lodgings in old, historic houses and cottages, most of which have been beautifully restored. If you're seeking more modern conveniences, there are plenty of newer hotels, too.

\$\$\$
B&B/INN
▦ **Corinda's Cottages.** This complex comprises a charming residence built in the 1880s for Alfred Crisp, a wealthy timber merchant who later became Lord Mayor of Hobart, as well as three lovingly restored outbuildings in which each of the accommodations are located—these include a gardener's residence, servants' quarters, and coach house. **Pros:** wonderfully restored historic accommodation; generous buffet breakfast. **Cons:** no leisure facilities; steep steps in the Gardener's Cottage. $ *Rooms from: A\$265* ⊠ *17 Glebe St., Glebe* ☎ *03/6234–1590* ⊕ *www.corindascottages.com.au* ⇙ *3 cottages* ⦿ *Breakfast.*

\$\$\$
HOTEL
Fodor's Choice
★
▦ **Henry Jones Art Hotel.** Arguably one of Australia's best hotels, right on the Hobart waterfront, this row of historic warehouses and a former jam factory have been transformed into a sensational, art-theme hotel, where the work of Tasmania's finest visual and performing artists is displayed. **Pros:** unstuffy and friendly staff despite the arty surrounds; stunning rooms worth lingering in; excellent location. **Cons:** excellent but pricey breakfast at A\$35. $ *Rooms from: A\$280* ⊠ *25 Hunter St., City Center* ☎ *03/6210–7700* ⊕ *www.thehenryjones.com* ⇙ *52 rooms, 4 suites* ⦿ *No meals.*

\$\$\$
HOTEL
▦ **Hotel Grand Chancellor.** Across the street from the old wharves and steps from some of the most exciting restaurants in Hobart, this imposing glass-and-stone building offers sumptuous accommodation in one of the city's best locations. **Pros:** steps away from the city's museums; offers familiar chain comforts. **Cons:** some traffic noise; stark lobby; fee for parking. $ *Rooms from: A\$245* ⊠ *1 Davey St., Hobart Waterfront* ☎ *03/6235–4535, 1800/753379* ⊕ *www.ghihotels.com* ⇙ *232 rooms, 12 suites* ⦿ *No meals.*

\$\$\$\$
HOTEL
Fodor's Choice
★
▦ **Islington Hotel.** Built in 1847, this elegant Regency mansion was converted to a five-star luxury boutique hotel and is now one of the finest lodgings in Australia. **Pros:** fully tailored hospitality experience; sophisticated service from staff. **Cons:** 20-minute walk to city center;

only accommodates children 15 years and over. [$] *Rooms from: A$395* ✉ *321 Davey St., South Hobart* ☎ *03/6220–2123* ⊕ *www.islingtonhotel. com* ➡ *11 rooms* |○| *Breakfast.*

$
HOTEL

🏨 **Lodge on Elizabeth.** This opulent grand manor, convict-built in 1829 and home over the years to many Hobart notables, is within walking distance of the city center, but far enough removed to feel like a sanctuary. **Pros:** hearty continental buffet breakfast; convenient option for groups. **Cons:** a few bedrooms are on the small side; some street noise. [$] *Rooms from: A$150* ✉ *249 Elizabeth St., City Center* ☎ *03/6231–3830* ⊕ *www.thelodge.com.au* ➡ *14 rooms* |○| *Breakfast.*

$$$$
HOTEL
Fodor'sChoice
★

🏨 **MONA Pavilions.** These eight high-style pavilions are easily Tasmania's most cutting-edge accommodations—the property is near Tasmania's world-class experimental art museum, the Museum of Old and New Art (MONA). **Pros:** breathtaking indoor infinity pool with views of the Derwent; check-in staff helpful and pleasant; parking right outside your pavilion. **Cons:** lots of high-tech features that can be confusing to operate; this level of luxury doesn't come cheap. [$] *Rooms from: A$500* ✉ *655 Main Rd., Berriedale* ☎ *03/6277–9900* ⊕ *www.mona. net.au* ➡ *8 chalets* |○| *Breakfast.*

$$
HOTEL
FAMILY

🏨 **Old Woolstore Apartment Hotel.** With a mix of standard rooms as well studios and one- and two-bedroom apartments, this property just a block from Hobart's iconic waterfront occupies one of the city's oldest and most historic buildings, the Roberts Limited Woolstore. **Pros:** central location; complimentary parking; historic ambience. **Cons:** small balconies; confusing drive-in entrance; busy neighborhood. [$] *Rooms from: A$155* ✉ *1 Macquarie St., City Center* ☎ *1800/814676, 03/6235–5355* ⊕ *www.oldwoolstore.com.au* ➡ *59 rooms, 177 apartments, 6 suites* |○| *No meals.*

$$$
RENTAL
FAMILY

🏨 **Sullivans Cove Apartments.** This is an impressive collection of 17 handsome, self-catered apartments spread across five waterfront precincts in Hobart. **Pros:** close to Salamanca Place shops and waterfront; stunning interiors. **Cons:** need to book early to reserve; some noise from adjoining businesses in waterfront precincts. [$] *Rooms from: A$260* ✉ *Sullivans Cove Apartments & Check-in, 5/19a Hunter St., Hobart Waterfront* ☎ *03/6234–5063* ⊕ *www.sullivanscoveapartments.com.au* ➡ *17 apartments* |○| *No meals.*

$$$$
HOTEL

🏨 **Villa Howden.** Just a 15-minute drive from Hobart and along the edge of the renowned Huon Valley tourist route, this new and swanky 10-room boutique hotel has a distinctly Provençal feel. **Pros:** intimate setting; heated indoor saltwater pool; lots of fancy in-room amenities. **Cons:** short drive away from the city; a bit pricey. [$] *Rooms from: A$355* ✉ *77 Howden Rd., Howden* ☎ *03/6267–1161* ⊕ *www. villahowden.com.au* ➡ *10 suites* |○| *Breakfast.*

NIGHTLIFE AND PERFORMING ARTS

Although Hobart has the only true nightlife scene in Tasmania, it's extremely tame compared to what's in Melbourne and Sydney. There are few dance clubs, and evenings out tend to revolve around a bottle of excellent local wine. Consult the Friday or Saturday editions of the *Mercury* newspaper before heading out. *This Week in Tasmania,* available at most hotels, is a comprehensive guide to current stage performances and contemporary music concerts.

BARS AND DANCE CLUBS

Atrium Bar. Hotel Grand Chancellor's piano bar is a relaxing spot by the harbor where local professionals mingle alongside hotel guests. Adjoining the hotel lobby, the bar has comfy chairs with waterfront views—an ideal setting for enjoying the fine cocktails, cold beers on tap, and enticing Tasmanian wines. ✉ *1 Davey St., Hobart Waterfront* ☎ *03/6235–4547* ⊕ *www.grandchancellorhotels.com.*

Cargo Bar Pizza Lounge. This beautifully furnished bar has inviting booth-style seats toward the back—a peaceful refuge during the busy dinner hour. Note the generous wine selection, with plenty of notable beers and spirits, too, and the tasty pizzas. In winter, sit outside under a heater and catch one of the occasional live acoustic performances. ✉ *51 Salamanca Pl., Battery Point* ☎ *03/6223–7788* ⊕ *www.cargobarsalamanca. com.au.*

Grape Wine Food Bar. This popular wine and tapas bar has a wonderful shop where you can browse among 300 types of Tasmanian wines and pick up a cheese platter for an impromptu picnic. Choose to sit outside and watch the world go by or enjoy the intimate, laid-back indoor space. Wines are served in trendy Reidel O tumblers. There's live music in the evening toward the end of the week. ✉ *55 Salamanca Pl., Battery Point* ☎ *03/6224–0611* ⊕ *www.grapebar.com.au.*

Republic Bar and Cafe. The cool kids head to this raucous, art deco pub warmed by roaring log fires to watch nightly live music, including plenty of top Tasmanian bands. ✉ *299 Elizabeth St., North Hobart* ☎ *03/6234–6954* ⊕ *www.republicbar.com.*

Round Midnight. Set in a former brothel that dates back more than a century, this spacious nightclub hosts top local and international DJs as well as live bands, with music ranging from blues to rock to dance. ✉ *39 Salamanca Pl., Battery Point* ☎ *03/6223–2491.*

T42. Officially called Tavern 42 Degrees South, this lively waterfront spot is popular for both dining and drinking—it's something of a Hobart institution. Patrons have the choice of sitting inside or out, noshing on tapas, sipping wine, and looking out over the harbor. The breakfast is enjoyable as well. For something a bit different, try the duck brioche bun with fried eggs and chili jam to start the day. ✉ *Elizabeth St. Pier, Hobart Waterfront* ☎ *03/6224–7742* ⊕ *www.tav42.com.au.*

SHOPPING

Tasmanian artisans and craftspeople work with diverse materials to fashion unusual pottery, metalwork, and wool garments. Items made from regional timber, including myrtle, sassafras, and Huon pine, are popular. The wonderful scenery around the island is an inspiration for numerous artists.

Along the Hobart waterfront at Salamanca Place are a large number of shops that sell arts and crafts. On Saturday (between 8 and 3) the area

Side Trips
from Hobart

turns into a giant market, where still more local artists join produce growers, bric-a-brac sellers, and itinerant musicians to sell their wares.

SIDE TRIPS FROM HOBART

Hobart is a perfect base for short trips to some of Tasmania's most historic and scenic places. Although you can visit them in a day, if you can, stay a night or two and experience their delights at a leisurely pace.

THE HUON VALLEY

40 km (25 miles) south of Hobart.

Fodor's Choice
★

En route to the vast wilderness of South West National Park is the tranquil Huon Valley. Sheltered coasts and sandy beaches are pocketed with thick forests and small farms. William Bligh planted the first apple tree here, founding one of the region's major industries. Salmon and trout caught fresh from churning blue rivers are also delicious regional delicacies.

The valley is also famous for the Huon pine, much of which has been logged over the decades. The trees that remain are strictly protected, so other local timbers are used by the region's craftspeople.

EXPLORING

The Apple Shed. En route to Huonville, this museum, cider house, and café showcases the best of local product. It's housed in a former apple-packing shed and is a remarkable time capsule, depicting the lives of the early Huon Valley settlers. The museum displays farming artifacts, picking and processing equipment, and early settler memorabilia from the area's orchards. There's also an art gallery. ⊠ *2064 Huon Hwy., Grove* ☎ *03/6266–4345* ⊕ *www.williesmiths.com.au* ✉ *Free* ☉ *Daily 10–6.*

Hastings Caves and Thermal Springs. Spectacular cave formations and thermal pools amid a fern glade await at the Hastings Caves and Thermal Springs. The caves are about 125 km (78 miles) south of Hobart, past Huonville and Dover. You can take a tour of the chambers, or just relax at the well-equipped picnic areas and make use of the thermal pool. The route to the site is well marked from the town of Dover. Hours vary seasonally, so check ahead. ⊠ *754 Hastings Caves Rd., Hastings* ☎ *03/6298–3209,* ⊕ *www.parks.tas.gov.au* ✉ *A$24* ☉ *Daily Feb.–Apr. and Oct.–Dec. 10–4, Jan. 9–5.*

FAMILY **Tahune AirWalk Tasmania.** Beyond Geeveston, the cantilevered, 1,880-foot-long Tahune AirWalk rises to 150 feet above the forest floor, providing a stunning panorama of the Huon and Picton rivers and the Hartz Mountains. The best views are from the platform at the end of the walkway, and if you have time, follow one of the trails that lead from the center through the surrounding forests. If one day isn't enough you can stay the night on-site in the reasonably priced Tahune Lodge or in a self-contained cabin. There's also a shop and a café with free Wi-Fi. ⊠ *Arve Rd., Geeveston* ☎ *1300/720507* ⊕ *tahuneairwalk.com. au* ✉ *A$28* ☉ *Summer, daily 9–5; winter, daily 10–4.*

BEACHES

Carlton Beach. Situated in the southeast of Tasmania in Frederick Henry Bay, this is a lovely beach well-regarded by surfers—almost 3 km (2 miles) in length and offers easy access from Carlton Beach Road. A 50-foot-high dune backs the beach, and residential properties line the beach road behind it. You'll find plenty of walking trails, and the Carlton Park Surf Life Saving Club lies at the eastern end, with lifeguards on duty in summer. **Amenities:** lifeguards; parking (free); showers; toilets. **Best for:** surfing; swimming; walking. ⊠ *1 Raprinner St., Carlton.*

Kingston Beach. This is the first main swimming beach southwest of Hobart—it's less than 30 minutes' drive from the Huon Valley. The beach sits in front of the fairly developed town of Kingston, on the Derwent River at the mouth of Browns Rivulet. Shopping and housing sit behind and to the south of the beach, and a narrow reserve, picnic area, and playground back the sand. Kingston Beach is patrolled by the local Surf Life Saving Club; however, you should still keep clear of any boating activity in the south corner; the waters are quite deep directly off the beach. **Amenities:** food and drink; lifeguards; parking (free); showers; toilets. **Best for:** surfing; swimming; walking. ⊠ *Beach Rd. at Osbourne Esplanade, Kingston Beach.*

WHERE TO EAT AND STAY

$$ ✕ **Home Hill Winery Restaurant.** Large plate-glass windows open to the
AUSTRALIAN Home Hill winery's endless hillside vineyards at this boutique vineyard,
cellar door, and restaurant—a true Tasmanian country retreat. The
seasonal menu includes such delicacies as pan-seared Huon Atlantic
salmon served with vanilla potatoes, mushrooms, and a butter emul-
sion. After lunch, you can head down to the cellar to sample the win-
ery's excellent cool-climate wines. Besides lunch, morning and afternoon
tea is also available. ⑤ *Average main: A$35* ⊠ *38 Nairn St., Ranelagh*
☎ *03/6264–1200* ⊕ *homehillwines.com.au* ⊗ *No lunch Tues. and Wed.*

$$ ⊡ **Herons Rise Vineyard.** Mornings in any of the vineyard's three self-
B&B/INN contained cottages are bucolic and gorgeous; you'll wake to glorious
water views out over the flower gardens, where you might see rabbits
nibbling while you soak up the tranquillity of this peaceful environment.
Pros: peaceful surrounds; owners pride themselves on their eco-friendly
accommodation. **Cons:** no leisure facilities; smoke from fireplaces might
be a problem for the asthmatic. ⑤ *Rooms from: A$170* ⊠ *Saddle Rd.,*
Kettering ☎ *03/6267–4339* ⊕ *www.heronsrise.com.au* ⇆ *3 cottages*
⑩ *Breakfast.*

RICHMOND

24 km (15 miles) northeast of Hobart.

Fodor's Choice Twenty minutes' drive from Hobart and a century behind the big city,
★ this colonial village in the Coal River valley is a major tourist magnet.
Visitors stroll and browse through the craft shops, antiques stores, and
cafés along the main street. Richmond is also home to a number of
vineyards, all of which produce excellent cool-climate wines.

WHERE TO EAT AND STAY

$ ✕ **Ashmore on Bridge Street.** Once you've perused all of Richmond's cute
CAFÉ shops and historic sights, be sure to recharge in this surprisingly trendy
café with an open roaring fire and a friendly owner. The creamy scrambled eggs on sourdough toast with Tasmanian cold smoked salmon and
house relish is delicious for breakfast, and in the afternoon the huge and
delectable Devonshire teas will have you sighing with pleasure. Dinner
with a changing menu is served Tuesday and Wednesday. ⑤ *Average*
main: A$15 ⊠ *34 Bridge St.* ☎ *03/6260–2238.*

$$ ✕ **Frogmore Creek.** Wine tasting and an art gallery complement this
AUSTRALIAN unpretentious but upscale restaurant with floor-to-ceiling windows
Fodor's Choice looking out to views over the vineyards of Frogmore Creek and Bari-
★ lla Bay. In the restaurant world-class chef Ruben Koopman creates
incredible and unique dishes from local produce, such as venison from
Doo Town, a quaint seaside village on the Tasman Peninsula. You can
choose from an informal tapas-style menu or a multicourse degustation
(A$85 per person). Make sure to save room for the green tea and coco-
nut panna cotta with lemon and tea sherbet, lemon gel, and lime and
coconut sorbet. ⑤ *Average main: A$35* ⊠ *699 Richmond Rd., Cam-*
bridge ☎ *03/6274–5844* ⊕ *www.frogmorecreek.com.au* ⊗ *No dinner*
⚖ *Reservations essential.*

6

$ Mrs Currie's House B&B. This gracious Georgian house, built between
B&B/INN   1820 and 1860, is set in a peaceful garden with lovely views over the village of Richmond and the surrounding countryside. **Pros:** quaint accommodation and friendly owners; spotlessly clean. **Cons:** not particularly child-friendly; showers are on the old-fashioned side. $ *Rooms from: A$150 ✉ 4 Franklin St. ☎ 03/6260–2766 ➿ 4 rooms ⛧ Breakfast.*

PORT ARTHUR AND THE TASMAN PENINSULA

102 km (63 miles) southeast of Hobart.

When Governor George Arthur, lieutenant-governor of Van Diemen's Land (now Tasmania), was looking for a site to dump his worst convict offenders in 1830, the Tasman Peninsula was a natural choice. Joined to the rest of Tasmania only by the narrow Eaglehawk Neck, the spit was easy to isolate and guard. Between 1830 and 1877, more than 12,000 convicts served sentences at Port Arthur in Britain's equivalent of Devil's Island. Dogs patrolled the narrow causeway, and guards spread rumors that sharks infested the waters. Reminders of those dark days remain in some of the area names—Dauntless Point, Stinking Point, Isle of the Dead.

EXPLORING

FAMILY   **Port Arthur Historic Site.** This property, formerly the grounds of the Port
Fodor's Choice   Arthur Penal Settlement, is now a lovely—and quite large—historical
★   park with a fascinating convict past central to Tasmania's history. Be prepared to do some walking between widely scattered sites. Begin at the excellent visitor center, which introduces you to the experience by "sentencing, transporting, and assigning" you before you set foot in the colony. Most of the original buildings were damaged by bushfires in 1895 and 1897, shortly after the settlement was abandoned, but you can still see the beautiful church, round guardhouse, commandant's residence, model prison, hospital, and government cottages.

The old **lunatic asylum** is now an excellent museum, with a scale model of the Port Arthur settlement, a video history, and a collection of tools, leg irons, and chains. Along with a walking tour of the grounds and entrance to the museum, admission includes a harbor cruise, of which there are eight scheduled daily in summer. There's a separate twice-daily cruise to and tour of the **Isle of the Dead,** which sits in the middle of the bay. It's estimated that 1,769 convicts and 180 others are buried here, mostly in communal pits. Ghost tours (reservations are essential) leave the visitor center at dusk and last about 90 minutes. Buy your tickets at the site, or at the Brooke Street Pier, at Franklin Wharf in Hobart. ✉ *Arthur Hwy., Port Arthur* ☎ *03/6251–2300, 1800/659101* ⊕ *www. portarthur.org.au* ✑ *A$37; Site Entry and Isle of the Dead Tour A$50; Ghost Tour $25; After Dark Pass A$69 (includes a 2-course dinner)* ☉ *Daily 9–dusk.*

FAMILY   **Tasmanian Devil Conservation Park.** This park is one of the best places to come face to face with real live Tasmanian devils. Spot these burrowing carnivorous marsupials (about the size of a small dog), as well as quolls, boobooks (small, spotted brown owls), masked owls, eagles,

Historic buildings from Tasmania's convict past can be seen in Port Arthur.

and other native fauna. The devils are fed six times throughout the day, with the first taking at 10 and the last at 5. ✉ 5990 Port Arthur Hwy., Taranna ✛ 11 km (7 miles) north of Port Arthur ☎ 1800/641–641 ⊕ www.tasmaniandevilpark.com ✉ A$33 ⊙ Daily 9–5.

BEACHES

FAMILY **White Beach.** It's less than a 10-minute drive from the historic former penal colony of Port Arthur to the pristine white sands of beautiful White Beach, a wild, unspoiled, crescent-shape beach often named one of the most beautiful beaches in Australia. The breathtaking views from the beach are the most beautiful in all of Tasmania, stretching as far as the eye can see across Wedge Bay to Storm Bay and then beyond to the Hartz. The local trails are worth exploring, not far from the usually deserted 3 km (2 mile) beach, although world-class diving is also available at Eaglehawk Neck and decent surfing at Roaring Beach. White Beach Tourist Park fronts directly onto the beach, and the general area has a number of cafés and restaurants offering excellent local Tasmanian cuisine. **Amenities:** food and drink; parking (free); toilets. **Best for:** snorkeling; solitude; sunrise; sunset; surfing; swimming; walking. ✉ White Beach Rd., Port Arthur.

WHERE TO EAT

$$ ✗ **Felons Bistro.** Feast on wonderfully fresh Tasmanian seafood and game
AUSTRALIAN in the heart of the Port Arthur Historic Site at this small but lovely
FAMILY restaurant. Standout appetizers include the area's local oysters. At teatime (dinner), pop in for one of the rich desserts. If you've built up an appetite during the day's visit, you'll relish the two-course meal prior to your spooky encounters on the Ghost Tour. There is also an inexpensive

café in the visitor center. $ *Average main: A$30* ⊠ *Port Arthur Historic Site, Port Arthur* ☎ *03/6251–2314, 1800/659101* ⊕ *www.portarthur. org.au* ⌕ *Reservations essential.*

FREYCINET NATIONAL PARK AND EAST-COAST RESORTS

The east coast enjoys Tasmania's mildest climate, pristine beaches, and excellent fishing spots. The stretches of white sand here are often so deserted that you can pretend you're Robinson Crusoe. The towns in this region are quiet but historically interesting; in Louisville, for example, you can catch a ferry to the Maria Island National Park, which was a whaling station and penal settlement in the mid-19th century. Farther north, the town of Swansea has numerous stone colonial buildings that have been restored as hotels and restaurants, as well as the unusual Spiky Bridge (so named because of its vertically placed sandstone "spikes") and the convict-built Three Arch Bridge, both of which date from 1845.

The jewel of the eastern coast is Freycinet National Park, renowned among adventure seekers and those who appreciate stunning scenery. The spectacular granite peaks of the Hazards and the idyllic protected beach at Wineglass Bay have been dazzling visitors to this peninsula since it became a park in 1916.

EAST-COAST RESORTS

Fodor'sChoice From Hobart, the east-coast Tasman Highway travels cross country to
★ Orford, then passes through beautiful coastal scenery with spectacular white-sand beaches, usually completely deserted, before reaching Swansea. Bicheno, just north of Freycinet National Park, and St. Helens, which is farther north, are both fishing and holiday towns with quiet, sheltered harbors.

EXPLORING

Fodor'sChoice **Bay of Fires Lodge Walk.** Taking the four-day guided Bay of Fires Walk
★ along the coast north of St. Helens is a wonderful way to enjoy the rugged beauty and tranquility of the coast. The walk, which is about 27 km (18 miles) long, winds along the edge of Mt. William National Park and allows you to visit stunning beaches, heathlands, Aboriginal sites, and peppermint forests, where a profusion of plant and animal life flourishes. During part of the relatively easy walk you'll stay at an ecologically sound campsite, which is as luxurious as it can get, with timber floors and kitchen facilities, and two nights at the dramatic, remote, and ecologically sustainable **Bay of Fires Lodge.** All meals and most beverages are provided, as well as return transfers between Launceston and the walk base, two qualified guides, a backpack and jacket, National Park pass, and optional kayaking day. ⊠ *Bay of Fires* ☎ *03/6392–2211* ⊕ *www.bayoffires.com.au* ⊟ *A$2,300* ☉ *Oct.–May.*

BEACHES

FAMILY **Bicheno Beach.** Extending 650 feet along the southern shore of Waubs Bay, this gentle beach is in the heart of pretty Bicheno. A secondary north-facing beach sits on the western side of the bay. Rounded granite rocks border and separate the two beaches. There is a car park and toilet facilities at the middle of the beach where Beach Street meets the sand, while the town itself sits on the slopes at the south end. A popular shoreline walking track follows the rocky coast around the headland. **Amenities:** food and drink; parking (free); toilets. **Best for:** surfing; swimming; walking. ⊠ *Bicheno.*

FAMILY **Friendly Beaches.** Contained within the boundaries of the Freycinet National Park, this long, sweeping, beautiful beach is accessed from Coles Bay Road, 9 km (6 miles) south of the turnoff on the Tasman Highway. Enjoy going barefoot as the sand is extremely soft, fine, and bright as a result of its high silicon content. The waves are excellent for surfers, but there are strong rip and tidal currents, so exercise care. Start at the small parking area, take the short stroll to the beach, and bring water and sunscreen, as there are no nearby facilities. **Amenities:** parking (free). **Best for:** solitude; surfing; swimming; walking. ⊠ *Coles Bay Rd., Coles Bay.*

SPORTS AND THE OUTDOORS

DIVING

Bicheno Dive Centre. The spectacular coastline and clear, cool-temperate waters make this a great destination for diving, and this well-established company leads a range of spectacular boat and beach dives. Boat dives leave twice daily at 9 and 1, while beach dives can be arranged any time of day. A full set of dive gear is available for hire. ⊠ *2 Scuba Ct., Bicheno* ☎ *03/6375–1138* ⊕ *www.bichenodive.com.au* ⊠ *From A$50.*

KAYAKING

Frecyinet is Tasmania's premier sea-kayaking destination, and it's possible to do guided tours or hire your own kayak and cruise around at your own pace.

FAMILY **Freycinet Adventures.** Providing a memorable way to explore the spec-
Fodor's Choice tacular coastline at a leisurely pace, this family-run company runs half-
★ day kayaking tours around the peninsula, as well as two- and four-day trips. Along the way guides point out local marine life, such as sea eagles. Tour packages aim at all skill levels. ⊠ *2 Freycinet Dr., Coles Bay* ☎ *03/6257–0500* ⊕ *www.freycinetadventures.com.au* ⊠ *From A$95.*

WILDLIFE WATCHING

FAMILY **Bicheno Penguin Tours.** At Bicheno, a very popular tour is the nightly hour-long vigil to see the penguins emerge from the water and clamber up to their nesting area. The daily tours begin at dusk, and penguin numbers often exceed 50. It's a magical opportunity to view these creatures up-close. ⊠ *70 Burgess St., Bicheno* ☎ *03/6375–1333* ⊕ *www. bichenopenguintours.com.au* ⊠ *A$30.*

WHERE TO STAY

$$$$ ⊡ **Avalon Coastal Retreat.** This gorgeous three-bedroom house is the ulti-
RENTAL mate in exclusivity: it sits entirely alone on Tasmania's east coast, with just the occasional passing white-bellied sea eagle for company. **Pros:**

unadulterated privacy; gorgeous views; fully stocked. **Cons:** there's only one house, and it books up quickly. ⑤ *Rooms from: A$900* ✉ *11922 Tasman Hwy., Swansea* ☏ *1300/361136 Australia, 0428/250–399 International* ⊕ *www.avalonretreats.com.au/coastal* ↘ *1 3-bedroom house* ⑥ *Breakfast.*

$$$ ⛺ **Diamond Island Resort.** Direct access to a deserted beach, island walks,
RESORT and penguin-viewing platforms are among the draws of this peaceful hideaway 1½ km (1 mile) north of Bicheno and overlooking the Tasman Sea. Twelve two-bedroom duplexes are nestled within 7 acres of landscaped gardens; there are also 14 smaller one-bedroom units. **Pros:** minutes from a superb beach; kitchenettes in all units. **Cons:** not great value for what you get. ⑤ *Rooms from: A$220* ✉ *69 Tasman Hwy., Bicheno* ☏ *03/6375–0100, 1800/030299* ⊕ *www.diamondisland.com. au* ↘ *27 rooms* ⑥ *Breakfast.*

$$ ⛺ **Eastcoast Central Watersedge Resort.** This seaside complex in the town
RESORT of Louisville is a great jumping-off point for exploring Maria Island
FAMILY National Park; the resort's catamaran, the *Eastcoaster Express,* makes three or four trips a day to the island. **Pros:** family-friendly resort; inexpensive and unpretentious. **Cons:** somewhat dated design. ⑤ *Rooms from: A$180* ✉ *1 Louisville Rd., Orford* ☏ *03/6257–1172* ⊕ *eastcoastcentral. com.au* ↘ *48 rooms, 8 cabins, 30 caravan sites* ⑥ *No meals.*

$$$ ⛺ **Hamptons on the Bay.** These seven water-facing cabins have dramatic
HOTEL views over Great Oyster Bay and the Freycinet Peninsula through fulllength windows in living and bedroom areas. **Pros:** friendly property manager; incredible views over the ocean; 10-minute drive to Swansea's restaurants. **Cons:** BBQ area is between cabins five and six, which could impact privacy; no Wi-Fi in rooms. ⑤ *Rooms from: A$240* ✉ *12164 Tasman Hwy., Swansea* ☏ *0417/481–777* ⊕ *www.hamptonsonthebay. com.au* ↘ *6 1-bedroom cabins, 1 2-bedroom cabin, 1 3-bedroom house* ⑥ *No meals* ▭ *No credit cards.*

$$ ⛺ **Meredith House and Mews.** Exquisite red-cedar furnishings and
B&B/INN antiques decorate this grand 1853 refurbished residence in the center of Swansea. **Pros:** excellent service from affable hosts; superb freshly cooked breakfasts. **Cons:** books up well in advance. ⑤ *Rooms from: A$180* ✉ *15 Noyes St., Swansea* ☏ *03/6257–8119* ⊕ *www.meredithhouse.com.au* ↘ *11 rooms* ⑥ *Breakfast.*

FREYCINET NATIONAL PARK

238 km (149 miles) north of Port Arthur, 214 km (133 miles) southwest of Launceston, 206 km (128 miles) northeast of Hobart.

The road onto the Freycinet Peninsula ends just past the township of Coles Bay; from that point the Freycinet National Park begins and covers 24,700 acres.

ESSENTIALS

Contact Freycinet National Park Offices. ✉ *Coles Bay Rd., Coles Bay* ☏ *03/6256–7000* ⊕ *www.parks.tas.gov.au.*

"We had driven from Friendly Beach further into the Park when we came across this beautiful area." —photo by Gary Ott, Fodors.com member

EXPLORING

Fodor's Choice
★

Freycinet National Park. Highlights of the dramatic scenery here include the mountain-size granite formations known as the **Hazards.** On the ocean side of the peninsula there are also sheer cliffs that drop into the deep-blue ocean; views from the lighthouse at Cape Tourville (reached by a narrow dirt road) are unforgettable. A series of tiny coves called the Honeymoon Bays provide a quieter perspective on the Great Oyster Bay side. **Wineglass Bay,** a perfect crescent of dazzling white sand, is best viewed from the lookout platform, about a 30-minute walk up a gentle hill from the parking lot; if you're feeling energetic, though, the view from the top of Mt. Amos, one of the Hazards, is worth the effort. A round-trip walk from the parking lot to Wineglass Bay takes about 2½ hours. The park's many trails are well signposted. Daily entry to the park costs A$12 per person and A$24 per vehicle. ✉ *Coles Bay Rd., Coles Bay* ☎ *03/6256–7000* ⊕ *www.parks.tas.gov.au.*

BEACHES

FAMILY

Nine Mile Beach. A stone's throw from the historic town of Swansea, this long, sweeping beach is a favorite for swimming, fishing, and simply soaking up the views and peaceful surroundings—visitors enjoy uninterrupted views across Great Oyster Bay to Schouten Island, The Hazards, and the Freycinet Peninsula. Dangerous rips can be a concern here—take care, especially near the sand bar. The western end of the beach has a variety of lodgings and holiday rentals. Great Swanport lagoon and wetlands form the back side of the beach. There's parking for about 100 cars in the lot. **Amenities:** parking (free). **Best for:** solitude; surfing; swimming; walking. ✉ *Dolphin Sands Rd., Swansea.*

WHERE TO STAY

$$$
RENTAL

⊡ **Edge of the Bay.** The outstanding views from these modern, minimal-ist-style waterview suites and cottages set along 27 acres of untouched wilderness stretch for miles across Great Oyster Bay to the Hazards. **Pros:** animals wander freely around the resort; idyllic setting. **Cons:** two-night minimum; no breakfast is served but breakfast baskets can be ordered. ⑤ *Rooms from: A$260* ⊠ *2308 Main Rd., Coles Bay* ☎ *03/6257–0102* ⊕ *www.edgeofthebay.com.au* ⊐ *14 suites, 7 cottages* ⦿| *No meals.*

$$$
RENTAL
Fodor's Choice
★

⊡ **Freycinet Lodge.** With cabin-style accommodation scattered through the densely wooded forest overlooking Great Oyster Bay, this cushy eco-lodge has a remote setting that allows for an intimate connection with the surrounding scenic environment. **Pros:** superb food in fine-dining restaurant; perfect for getting away from it all. **Cons:** utilitarian furniture for the price; only the premier spa cabin has a TV; rooms can be on the cold side. ⑤ *Rooms from: A$275* ⊠ *Freycinet National Park, Coles Bay Rd., Coles Bay* ☎ *03/6256–7222* ⊕ *www.freycinetlodge.com. au* ⊐ *60 cabins* ⦿| *Breakfast; Some meals.*

$$$$
RESORT
Fodor's Choice
★

⊡ **Saffire Freycinet.** Blame it on jaw-dropping views of Wineglass Bay and the Hazards Mountains that frame the resort, or the eco-friendly space-age architecture fit for the likes of James Bond—a far-flung luxe getaway doesn't get much better than this. **Pros:** views from every inch of the property; comfy, modern suites; great excursions; all-inclusive rates. **Cons:** extremely remote (transfers are not included); one restaurant; very pricey. ⑤ *Rooms from: A$1950* ⊠ *Coles Bay Rd., Freycinet Peninsula, Coles Bay* ☎ *03/6256–7888* ⊕ *www.saffire-freycinet.com.au* ⊐ *20 suites* ⦿| *All-inclusive; Breakfast; Some meals.*

LAUNCESTON

200 km (124 miles) north of Hobart.

Nestled in a fertile agricultural basin where the South Esk and North Esk rivers join to form the Tamar, the city of Launceston (pronounced *Lon*-sess-tun), or Lonie to locals, is the commercial center of Tasmania's northern region. Many unusual markets and shops are concentrated downtown (unlike Hobart, which has most of its stores in the historic center, set apart from the commercial district).

Launceston is far from bustling, and has a notable number of pleasant parks, late-19th-century homes, historic mansions, and private gardens. The sumptuous countryside that surrounds the city—rolling farmland and the rich loam of English-looking landscapes—set off by the South Esk River meandering through towering gorges, is also appealing.

EXPLORING

FAMILY

Cataract Gorge. Almost in the heart of the city, the South Esk River flows through the stunningly beautiful Cataract Gorge on its way toward the Tamar River. A 1-km (½-mile) path leads along the face of the precipices to the **Cliff Gardens Reserve,** where there are picnic tables, a pool, and a restaurant. Take the chairlift in the first basin for a thrill-ing aerial view of the gorge—at just over 900 feet, it's the longest single span in the world. Self-guided nature trails wind through the park, and it's a great place for a picnic. ⊠ *Basin Rd.* ☎ *03/6331–5915* ⊕ *www. launcestoncataractgorge.com.au* 🎟 *Gorge free, chairlift A$15* ⊙ *Daily 9–4:30 (until 6 in summer).*

FAMILY **Franklin House.** Built in 1838 by noted a local businessman and brewer, who had once been a convict, this fine late-Georgian house is notable for its beautiful cedar architecture and collection of period English furniture, clocks, and fine china. The tearoom serves light meals and refreshments. ⊠ *413 Hobart Rd., Franklin Village* ☎ *03/6344–7824* ⊕ *www. discovertasmania.com/attraction/franklinhouse* 🎟 *A$10* ⊙ *Summer, Mon.–Sat. 9–5, Sun. noon–4; winter, Mon.–Sat. 9–4, Sun. noon–4.*

FAMILY **Queen Victoria Museum and Art Gallery.** Opened in 1891, the gallery presents fascinating insights into the city's history, including the rich Aboriginal and colonial past. There's also a large natural-history collection of stuffed birds and animals (including the now-extinct thylacine, or Tasmanian tiger). ⊠ *2 Invermay Rd.* ☎ *03/6323–3777* ⊕ *www.qvmag. tas.gov.au* 🎟 *Free* ⊙ *Daily 10–4.*

Fodor'sChoice
★
Tamar Valley Wine Route. Along both sides of the Tamar River north of Launceston, the soil and cool weather are perfect for grape growing. Here in the Tamar Valley wine region, some of the outstanding varieties grown include Pinot Noir, Riesling, and Chardonnay; the sparkling wines produced here are world-leading. A map of the route, available for download at their website, will help you to plan your visit. Noteworthy stops along the route are Pipers Brook Vineyard, Strathlynn Wine Centre, Moores Hill, Holyman wines at Stoney Rise, Clover Hill, and The Jansz Wine Room. ⊠ *Launceston* ⊕ *www.tamarvalleywineroute.com.au.*

SPORTS AND THE OUTDOORS

There are plenty of opportunities to spot wildlife, fish, or birds in the lovely countryside surrounding Launceston and the Tamar Valley.

BIRD-WATCHING

FAMILY **Tamar Island Wetlands.** This bird sanctuary on the banks of the Tamar River just outside Launceston is the ideal place to see purple swamp hens and black swans from boardwalks over the wetlands while scanning the sky for white-breasted sea eagles or forest ravens. ⊠ *West Tamar Hwy., Riverside* ☎ *03/6327–3964* ⊕ *www.parks.tas.gov.au* 🎟 *Free* ⊙ *Daily dawn–dusk.*

RIVER CRUISES

FAMILY **Tamar River Cruises.** This company conducts relaxing trips on the Tamar, past many wineries and into Cataract Gorge. The Tamar Odyssey catamaran, which has an upper and lower deck and spacious lounges is used for the longer cruises, while the gorgeous, old-fashioned Lady Launceston takes visitors on the shorter Cataract Gorge cruises. ⊠ *Home Point Cruise Terminal, Home Point Parade* ☎ *03/6334–9900* ⊕ *www. tamarrivercruises.com.au* 🎟 *From A$29.*

WALKING

FAMILY **Launceston Historic Walks.** This professional outfit conducts a leisurely one-hour sightseeing stroll through the historic heart of the city. The guided walks leave from the 1842 Gallery and present an engaging look at Launceston's charming architecture and the city's colorful past. ⊠ *Cimitiere St.* ☎ *03/6331–2213* ⊕ *www.1842.com.au* 🎟 *A$15* ⊙ *Tues.– Sat. at 10, Mon. at 4.*

WILDLIFE-WATCHING

FAMILY **Pepperbush Adventures.** This husband-and-wife team runs tours out of Scottsdale, but the majority of tours depart from Launceston and cover Tasmania's northeast, looking at local wildlife in its natural habitat. The full-day Quoll Patrol takes you to view the "bandit of the Bush," as well as wallabies, platypuses, and, if you're lucky, some devils. Trout fishing and full-day wine tasting tours are also available, as well as several multiday excursions, including a six-day experience that visits the Bay of Fires on the northeast coast and the Tarkine, the greatest expanse of cool temperate rain forest in Australia. ⊠ *65 King St.* ⊕ *www.pepperbush.com.au* ✉ *From A$195.*

ZIP LINING

FAMILY
Fodor'sChoice
★
Hollybank Treetops Adventure. Just 15 minutes' drive northeast of Launceston, this popular attraction that's especially appealing to kids offers three-hour zip-lining tours through a verdant forest canopy high above the Pipers River. ⊠ *66 Hollybank Rd., Underwood* ☎ *03/6395–1390* ⊕ *www.treetopsadventure.com.au* ✉ *From A$120* ☉ *Daily 9–5.*

WHERE TO EAT AND STAY

$$
STEAKHOUSE
FAMILY
✕ **Jailhouse Grill.** If you have to go to jail, this is the place to do it—in a 130-year-old historic building where you'll dine on succulent grass-fed beef, typically of the Angus or Hereford breed. Despite being furnished with chains and bars, it was never actually a place for incarceration, so relax and feast on prime beef cuts (or fish and chicken), and an all-you-can-eat salad bar. The wine list is comprehensive. ⑤ *Average main: A$30* ⊠ *32 Wellington St.* ☎ *03/6331–0466* ⊕ *www.jailhousegrill. au* ☉ *No lunch Mon.–Wed.*

$$$
AUSTRALIAN
Fodor'sChoice
★
✕ **Stillwater.** Part of Ritchie's Mill—a beautifully restored 1830s flour mill beside the Tamar River—this much-lauded restaurant serves wonderfully creative seafood dishes, usually with an Asian twist, such as the confit of Macquarie Harbour ocean trout with wasabi mash, trout crackle, and citrus and flying fish roe emulsion. The five-course tasting menu includes wine pairings from the great selection of Tasmanian wines. A produce shop, café, wine bar, and art gallery are part of the same complex. ⑤ *Average main: A$40* ⊠ *Ritchie's Mill, 2 Bridge Rd.* ☎ *03/6331–4153* ⊕ *www.stillwater.com.au* ☉ *No dinner Sun. and Mon.*

$$
B&B/INN
⌂ **Alice's Cottages.** Constructed from the remains of three 1840s buildings, this delightful B&B is full of whimsical touches. **Pros:** perfect for a romantic getaway, especially the "boudoir"-themed room; spa bathrooms are luxurious and decadent. **Cons:** not child-friendly. ⑤ *Rooms from: A$160* ⊠ *129 Balfour St.* ☎ *03/6334–2231* ⊕ *www.alicescottages. com.au* ✍ *8 cottages* �� *Breakfast.*

$
B&B/INN
⌂ **Old Bakery Inn.** History comes alive at this colonial complex made up of a converted stable, the former baker's cottage, and the old bakery. **Pros:** quaint and sensitively restored rooms; great value; walking distance to downtown Launceston. **Cons:** some noise from busy road; breakfast ends at 9 am sharp. ⑤ *Rooms from: A$90* ⊠ *York St.* ☎ *03/6331–7900, 1800/641264* ⊕ *www.oldbakeryinn.com.au* ✍ *24 rooms* ⳨ *Breakfast.*

$$$
HOTEL
⌂ **Peppers Seaport Hotel.** Superbly situated on the Tamar riverfront, this popular urban-chic hotel is part of the Seaport Dock area and is

shaped like a ship. **Pros:** lovely waterfront views from some rooms; immaculate lobby and service; free Wi-Fi. **Cons:** parking costs extra; the waterfront scene isn't very lively. ⑤ *Rooms from: A$240* ✉ *28 Seaport Blvd.* ☎ *03/6345–3333* ⊕ *www.peppers.com.au* ⤵ *24 rooms, 36 suites* ⦿ *No meals.*

$$$
RENTAL
🛏 **TwoFourTwo.** Three contemporary apartments and a townhouse built within a historic Launceston property have all modern conveniences, including espresso machines and iPod docks, plus the wonderful timber design work of Alan Livermore, one of the owners. **Pros:** rooms are stylish and well laid out; personal touches like fresh flowers and a thoughtfully stocked in-room wine selection. **Cons:** not particularly child-friendly; no leisure facilities. ⑤ *Rooms from: A$220* ✉ *242 Charles St.* ☎ *03/6331–9242,* ⊕ *www.twofourtwo.com.au* ⤵ *4 apartments* ⦿ *No meals.*

$
B&B/INN
🛏 **Waratah on York.** Built in 1862, this grand Italianate mansion has been superbly restored with spacious modern rooms tastefully decorated to reflect the era in which the building was constructed; six rooms have hot tubs. **Pros:** complimentary port in guest sitting rooms ; helpful staff. **Cons:** a lot of stairs to climb; rooms are on the dark side. ⑤ *Rooms from: A$135* ✉ *12 York St.* ☎ *03/6331–2081* ⊕ *www.waratahonyork. com.au* ⤵ *9 rooms, 1 apartment* ⦿ *Breakfast.*

THE NORTHWEST

Tasmania's northwestern region is one of the most beautiful and least explored areas of the state. For its sheer range of landscapes, from jagged mountain contours to ancient rain forests and alpine heathlands in the Cradle Mountain area alone, the northwest can't be matched. The region's beauty saw it designated the Tasmanian Wilderness World Heritage Area, protecting one of the last true wilderness regions on Earth.

These regions are a major draw for hikers and sightseers. The western side of the northwest tip of Tasmania bears the full force of the roaring forties winds coming across the Indian Ocean, and this part of Tasmania contains some of the island's most dramatic scenery. Mining was a major industry a century ago, and although some mines still operate, the townships have a rather forlorn look.

GETTING HERE AND AROUND

This region is not the easiest to get to (the nearest airport is as much as two hours away at Launceston) but the destination is certainly rewarding enough to make the journey worthwhile. Driving to Cradle Mountain from Launceston takes 2 hours, and 1½ hours from Devonport. It is possible to take public transport through coach operator Tassie Link, which connects the major transportation hubs with Cradle Mountain and Strahan, but for convenience, nothing beats renting your own car. It should be noted that the northern part of the Cradle Mountain–Lake St. Clair National Park (that is, Cradle Mountain itself) is accessed by roads inland from Devonport and the nearby town of Sheffield. The southerly Lake St. Clair end of the park, though, is reached by the Lyell Highway between Hobart and Queenstown at Derwent Bridge.

STANLEY

140 km (87 miles) northwest of Devonport, 400 km (248 miles) north-west of Hobart.

Stanley is one of the prettiest villages in Tasmania, and a must for any-one traveling in the northwest. A gathering of historic cottages at the foot of the Nut, Tasmania's version of Uluru (Ayers Rock), it's filled with friendly tearooms, interesting shops, and old country inns.

EXPLORING

FAMILY **Highfield Historic Site.** At this atmospheric site you can explore the town's history at the fully restored Regency house and grounds where Van Diemen's Land Company, who settled the estate in 1824, once stood. Day tours are self-guided, but guides in period costumes are on hand to answer any questions. ⊠ *Green Hills Rd.* ☎ *03/6458–1100* ⊕ *www. historic-highfield.com.au* ⊠ *A$12* ⊙ *Sept.–May, daily 9:30–4:30; June–Aug., weekdays 9:30–4:30.*

FAMILY **The Nut.** This sheer volcanic plug that's some 12.5 million years old rears up right behind the village—it's almost totally surrounded by the sea. You can ride a chairlift to the top of the 500-foot-high headland, where the views are breathtaking; or, you can make the 20-minute trek on a footpath leading to the summit, where walking trails lead in all directions. ⊠ *Browns Rd.* ☎ *03/6458–1286* ⊠ *Chairlift A$10* ⊙ *Chairlift daily 9:30–5.*

BEACHES

FAMILY **Godfreys Beach.** Just north of the Nut is Stanley's curving Godfreys Beach, at which you can detect how elements of the region have formed by volcanic activity—note the basalt rock formations. The 1-km (½-mile) beach is largely protected from the region's strong westerly winds, which can lead to waves of 3 feet or higher. This is a lovely stretch of sand for strolling, but it's a bit chilly for swimming. You can park at the lot near town, at the south end of the sand, where you'll also find a playground. **Amenities:** parking (free); showers; toilets. **Best for:** solitude; walking. ⊠ *Green Hill Rd.*

SPORTS AND THE OUTDOORS

FISHING

Murray's Day Out. The exuberant owner of this tour service takes guests out on a full day's fishing expedition, providing everything necessary, including lunch and refreshments, and imparting his fantastic knowledge of Tasmania. Some of his recommended common fishing spots include Stanley Wharf, Beauty Point, and Garden Island. Murray also runs personalized shopping and scenic day tours, overnight trips, and other customized excursions. ⊠ *2/15–19 King St., Devonport* ☎ *03/6424–2439* ⊕ *www.murraysdayout.com.au* ☒ *From A$150.*

WILDLIFE WATCHING

FAMILY **Stanley Seal Cruises.** Twice a day (except in winter), the motor cruiser *Sylvia C* leads passengers on 75-minute journeys from Stanley's dock to Bull Rock, where they view delightful Australian fur seals basking on the Bass Strait rocks. Southern Right Whales are also sometimes spotted in the waters near the Nut. ⊠ *Dockside, Wharf Rd.* ☎ *0419/550–134* ⊕ *www.stanleysealcruises.com.au* ☒ *A$55* ⊗ *Closed mid-May–Aug 31.*

FAMILY **Wing's Wildlife Park.** This park, a 50-minute drive from Devonport, has one of the larger collections of Tasmanian wildlife in Australia, which as well as all the usual suspects includes an aquatic section where you can view albino rainbow trout and Atlantic salmon. Excellent guided tours can be tailored to your interests. ⊠ *137 Winduss Rd., Gunns Plains* ☎ *03/6429–1151* ⊕ *www.wingswildlife.com.au* ☒ *A$22* ⊗ *Daily 10–4.*

WHERE TO EAT AND STAY

$$ ✕ **Stanley's on the Bay.** Set on the waterfront in the fully restored old
AUSTRALIAN Bond Store, this unpretentious restaurant specializes in succulent steaks and freshly cooked seafood. Try the eye fillet of beef—Australian terminology for the top-quality beef cut—topped with prawns, scallops, and fish fillets, served in a creamy white-wine sauce. $ *Average main: A$30* ⊠ *15 Wharf Rd.* ☎ *03/6458–1404* ⊕ *www.stanleyvillage.com.au* ⊗ *Closed Sun. and July and Aug. No lunch* ⚲ *Reservations essential.*

$$ ⌂ **Beachside Retreat West Inlet.** These modern, environmentally friendly
B&B/INN cabins are located directly on waterfront sand dunes overlooking the sea
FAMILY with kilometers of absolutely private beach frontage. **Pros:** guests with special needs are well catered to; breathtaking views from cabins. **Cons:** two-night minimum; limited food availability on-site. $ *Rooms from: A$200* ⊠ *253 Stanley Hwy.* ☎ *03/6458–1350* ⊕ *www.beachsideretreat.com* ⊲ *4 cabins* ◯ *No meals.*

6

$$ **Touchwood Cottages.** Built in 1840 right near the Nut, this is one
RENTAL of Stanley's oldest homes, furnished with plenty of period pieces and
known for its doorways of different sizes and an oddly shaped living room. **Pros:** relaxing and romantic play to stay. **Cons:** no baths in
two of the cottages; no leisure facilities. $ *Rooms from: A$185* ✉ *31
Church St.* ☎ *03/6458–1348* ⊕ *www.touchwoodstanley.com.au* ⤺ *3
rooms* ⦿ *Breakfast.*

CRADLE MOUNTAIN–LAKE ST. CLAIR NATIONAL PARK

*173 km (107 miles) northwest of Hobart to Lake St. Clair at the southern end of the park, 85 km (53 miles) southwest of Devonport, 181 km
(113 miles) from Launceston, 155 km (97 miles) northeast from Strahan
to Cradle Mountain at the northern end of the park.*

This expansive, remote park contains some of the most spectacular
alpine scenery and mountain trails in Australia. Popular with hikers of
all abilities, the park has several high peaks, including Mt. Ossa, the
highest in Tasmania (more than 5,300 feet).

ESSENTIALS

Contacts Cradle Mountain Visitor Centre. ✉ *4057 Cradle Mountain Rd.,
Cradle Mountain* ☎ *03/6492–1110* ⊕ *www.parks.tas.gov.au.* **Lake St. Clair
Visitor Centre.** ✉ *Lake St. Clair National Park, Derwent Bridge* ☎ *03/6289–
1172* ⊕ *www.parks.tas.gov.au.*

EXPLORING

FAMILY **Cradle Mountain–Lake St. Clair National Park.** The Cradle Mountain section
of the park lies in the north. The southern section of the park, centered
on Lake St. Clair, is popular for boating and hiking. Many walking trails
lead from the settlement at the southern end of the lake, which is surrounded by low hills and dense forest. Visitors are advised to park their
cars in the free lot and then make use of the shuttle bus that runs from
the Cradle Mountain Visitor Centre and makes stops at all the trails.
In summer the bus runs every 15 minutes, in winter every 30 minutes.

One of the most famous trails in Australia, the **Overland Track** traverses
65 km (40 miles) between the park's northern and southern boundaries.
The walk usually takes six days, depending on the weather, and on clear
days the mountain scenery seems to stretch forever. Hikers are charged
A$200 to do the Overland during peak walking season (October to
May), and Tasmania's Parks and Wildlife Service has provided several
basic sleeping huts that are available on a first-come, first-served basis.
Because space in the huts is limited, hikers are advised to bring their
own tents. If you prefer to do the walk in comfort, you can use well-equipped, heated private structures managed by Cradle Mountain Huts
✉ *Cradle Mountain–Lake St. Clair National Park, Cradle Mountain*
☎ *03/6492–1110* ⊕ *www.cradlehuts.com.au* ⤺ *A$16.50 per person.*

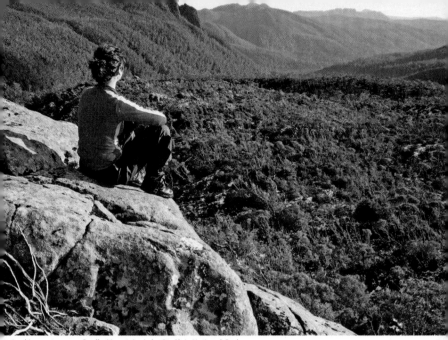

Looking out across Cradle Mountain–Lake St. Clair National Park

SPORTS AND THE OUTDOORS

AIR TOURS

FAMILY **Cradle Mountain Helicopters.** The views are magnificent on this company's scenic helicopter flights from Cradle Mountain village to the country's deepest gorge, Fury Gorge, and then on to picture-postcard Dove Lake, set against epic Cradle Mountain itself. The panoramas over the rugged Tasmanian landscape are breathtaking. ⊠ *Cradle Mountain* ⊕ *www. cradlemountainhelicopters.com.au* ✉ *From A$250.*

HIKING

Cradle Mountain Coaches. This Devonport-based company provides bus transport to Cradle Mountain, Lake St. Clair, Walls of Jerusalem, Frenchmans Cap, and many other popular bushwalking destinations. ⊠ *283 Port Sorell Rd., Wesley Vale* ☎ *03/6427–7626* ⊕ *www. cradlemountaincoaches.com.au.*

HORSEBACK RIDING

FAMILY **Cradle Country Adventures.** Choose from half-day, full-day, and multi-day horse rides through stunning natural vistas—available packages are suitable for both novices and experienced riders. All equipment, guides, and transfers are included. ⊠ *Cradle Mountain* ☎ *1300/656069* ⊕ *www.cradleadventures.com.au* ✉ *From A$120.*

QUAD BIKING

Cradle Mountain Quad Bikes. Year-round you can hire a Suzuki Ozark 250 quad bike and ride it on a special track that winds up through ancient myrtle forests and alpine eucalypt forest. Four-wheel-drives are also available. Rides go for 2½ hours, including transfers. ⊠ *Cradle Mountain* ☎ *1300/656–0069* ⊕ *www.cradlemountainquadbikes.com.au* ✉ *A$129.*

WHERE TO STAY

$$
RESORT
⛄ **Cradle Mountain Hotel.** Five minutes' drive from the entrance to the national park is this upmarket lodge, complete with rooms that face the woods and have perching posts for local birds. **Pros:** delicious meals in fine dining restaurant. **Cons:** can be packed with corporate events. ⑤ *Rooms from: A$200* ⊠ *3718 Cradle Mountain Rd., Cradle Mountain* ☎ *1800/420155, 03/6492–1404* ⊕ *www.cradlemountainchateau.com. au* ⇲ *60 rooms* ⦿ *No meals.*

$
RENTAL
FAMILY
⛄ **Discovery Holiday Parks, Cradle Mountain.** Near the forest at the northern edge of the park, Discovery Holiday Parks is the best budget accommodation in the area, with campgrounds, RV sites, four-bed bunkhouses with cooking facilities, and self-contained cabins with kitchens. **Pros:** family-friendly and good-value accommodation; free Internet. **Cons:** reception closes early; most expensive spa cabins are pricey. ⑤ *Rooms from: A$120* ⊠ *3832 Cradle Mountain Rd., Cradle Mountain* ☎ *03/6492–1395* ⊕ *www.discoveryholidayparks.com.au* ⇲ *38 unpowered sites, 10 powered sites, 75 bunkhouse beds, 36 cabins* ⦿ *No meals.*

$$$
RESORT
FAMILY
Fodor's Choice
★
⛄ **Peppers Cradle Mountain Lodge.** This charming lodge with its collection of wood cabins dotted around the wilderness of Cradle Mountain Valley is a firm favorite with park visitors. **Pros:** good range of food options, including a restaurant, bistro, and bar; fireplaces are a hit in winter. **Cons:** some might rue the lack of home comforts—no room service, TV, or Internet (except in the lobby). ⑤ *Rooms from: A$250* ⊠ *4038 Cradle Mountain Rd., Cradle Mountain* ☎ *1300/806192* ⊕ *www. cradlemountainlodge.com.au* ⇲ *58 rooms, 28 suites* ⦿ *Breakfast.*

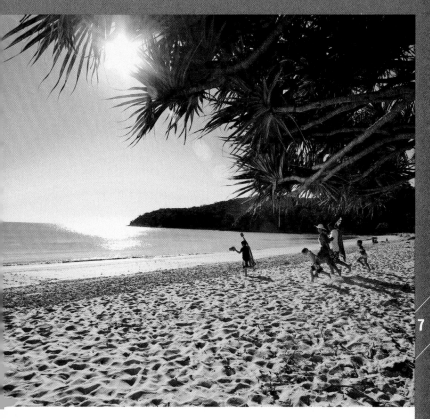

BRISBANE AND
ITS BEACHES

WELCOME TO
BRISBANE AND ITS BEACHES

TOP REASONS TO GO

★ **Enjoying the Outdoors:** From rain forests and reefs, unspoiled beaches and islands, rushing rivers, dramatic gorges, distinctive wildlife, hiking, and water sports.

★ **Experiencing the Laid-Back Vibe:** Queensland is renowned for its relaxed and welcoming feel, even at the upmarket hotels and fine-dining restaurants.

★ **Releasing Your Inner Child:** Queensland's Gold Coast is abuzz with world-class theme parks—from thrill rides and water parks to Outback-inspired extravaganzas.

★ **Seeing Wildlife:** Head out to the Reef for fish, rays, turtles, and cetaceans; on the mainland, watch for rare birds and mammals, endangered frogs, dingoes, and koalas.

★ **Savoring the Arts:** Brisbane's world-renowned Gallery of Modern Art (GoMA) and galleries and art spaces are transforming this former cultural backwater into an emerging arts hub.

1 **Brisbane.** Affectionately dubbed Brisvegas, Queensland's capital city is a breezily cheerful, increasingly sophisticated city with a thriving casino, cultural attractions, and some terrific restaurants, galleries, nightspots, and markets all centered around the city's sprawling river.

2 **The Gold Coast.** An hour's drive south of Brisbane, Queensland's first coastal resort has expanded into a busy strip of high-rise hotels, action-packed theme parks, casinos, bars, eateries, and nightclubs. If you need a break from the bustle, walk down to the beach and curl your toes in the sand; alternatively, drive west and spend a day (or several) exploring the lush, mountainous hinterland.

3 **The Sunshine Coast.** This stretch of coastline about an hour north of Brisbane is known for its glorious beaches, stunning national parks, and mountain hinterland dotted with charming, heritage-style townships. In recent years, new roads and infrastructure have spurred a boom in accommodation, eateries, markets, and other attractions.

4 **Mackay-Capricorn Islands.** This smattering of coral cays along the southern end of the Great Barrier Reef—including Heron, Wilson, Lady Musgrave, and Lady Elliot islands—is home to a host of marine wildlife, including seabirds, turtles, rays, sharks, and millions of dazzling tropical fish.

5 **Fraser Island.** A gigantic sand island off Hervey Bay, Fraser Island is paradise for the active visitor. What it lacks in luxe amenities it makes up for in scenery: miles of white-sand beaches, deep-blue lakes, and bushland bristling with wildlife—including some of the world's most purebred dingoes.

GETTING ORIENTED

At 1,727,999 square km (667,180 square miles) and more than four times the size of California, Queensland has enormous geographic variety. Its eastern seaboard stretches 5,200 km (3,224 miles) from the subtropical Gold Coast to the wild and steamy rain forests of the far north. Away from the coastal sugar and banana plantations, west of the Great Dividing Range, Queensland looks as arid as any other part of Australia's interior. Not surprisingly, most of the state's 4.6 million inhabitants live on the coast. Brisbane and the beach resorts toward the south of the coast have experienced dramatic expansion over the past decade. The region's main attractions are its glorious coastline, the fertile hinterland, and the reefs and islands that lie offshore.

South Pacific Ocean

MACKAY-CAPRICORN ISALNDS

4

Great Barrier Reef Marine Park

GREAT BARRIER REEF

CURTIS COAST

CAPRICORN COAST

HINTERLAND

Gladstone

BUNKER GROUP

Round Hill Head

CORAL COAST

Miriam Vale

Moore Park

Sandy Cape

16

A1

Monto

Bundaberg

Waddy Point

Gin Gin

Hervey Bay

3

Childers

Hervey Bay

5 FRASER ISLAND

Howard

Mundubbera

Biggenden

Maryborough

Gayndah

A1

Great Sandy National Park

Tin Can Beach

A3

49

Rainbow Beach

Murgon

Gympie

SUNSHINE COAST

Kingaroy

Nambour

Noosa Heads

49

Nanango

Maroochydore

Yarraman

Caloundra

Wutul

Harlin

85

Bongaree

Cape Moreton

17

Caboolture

Moreton Island National Park

Dalby

A3

MORETON ISLAND

Point Lookout

BRISBANE

A1

Amity

Toowoomba

A2

1

Logan

Ipswich

Beenleigh

13

M1

GOLD COAST

Beaudesert

Southport

A3

15

2

Surfers Paradise

Warwick

Nerang

Coolangatta

NEW SOUTH WALES

7

SUNSHINE COAST'S TOP BEACHES

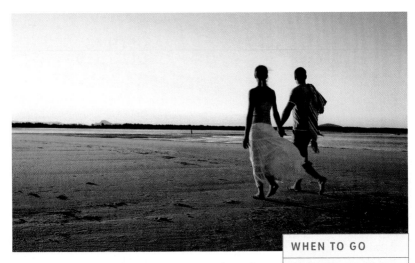

Queensland's Sunshine Coast stretches from Caloundra in the south to Noosa Heads in the north. Along it you'll find everything from family-friendly beaches to thundering surf breaks to pretty sheltered coves ideal for snorkeling.

The Sunshine Coast has been developed more slowly and sensitively than its southern counterpart, the Gold Coast. Although it has its share of shops, cafés, and resorts, there are still dozens of clean, uncrowded beaches where you can sunbathe, stroll, cast a line, or jump in the unspoiled waters to swim, snorkel, and surf.

Some beaches are perfect for water sports such as sailing, windsurfing, kayaking, or wakeboarding. Others are known for their reliable surf breaks. You'll find secluded rocky coves where you can "fossick" (Australian for beachcomb) among rock pools, or don a mask and snorkel to come face-to-face with colorful fish, rays, sea stars, and squid. There are also safe, lifeguard-patrolled swimming beaches with playgrounds, skate parks, kiosks, changing rooms, and picnic facilities ideal for families.

WHEN TO GO

The Sunshine Coast has sunny skies and year-round balmy temperatures, but beaches can get crowded at peak season, and prices are higher. Crowds are smaller and the weather is still summery in November and early December and March and April (except Easter week when school is out). January and February bring the most rain.

SUNSHINE BEACH

Lovely Sunshine Beach, the last easterly facing beach before Noosa, is patrolled year-round. Beach breaks, reliable swell, a rocky headland sheltering it from winds, and clear, glassy water make Sunshine popular with surfers. When northeast-erlies blow, surf the northern pocket. Fish off the beach year-round for dart, bream, and flathead, or cast a long line into deep water to hook numerous seasonal species. Use covered picnic areas, barbecues, toilets, and parking.

MOOLOOLABA BEACH

This super-safe, family-friendly swimming beach is patrolled year-round, and has just enough swell to make it fun. Surfers might want to check out the left-hand break that sometimes forms off the rocks at the northern end. There are shady picnic areas with barbecues, playgrounds, showers, toilets, public phones, exercise areas, and parking—as well as the local meeting point, the Loo with a View. Stroll south along the coastal path to the river mouth and rock wall (off which you can fish, year-round, for bream); north to Alexandra Headland for views of the bay; or along Mooloolaba Espla-nade, lined with casual eateries and boutiques.

COOLUM BEACH

Coolum Beach is a popular choice for families, boasting a surf club, skate park, playgrounds, changing rooms, toilets, kiosks, shorefront parks, and picnic areas. A long, white-sand beach, Coolum is patrolled year-round, and has a nice beach break and some decent waves off the headland. Fish from the beach in the evening for grouper, tailor, bream, and dart; catch bream around the headland, especially in winter. Walk south along the boardwalk to the headland park for magnificent coastal views, or north to quieter Peregian Beach with its patrolled surf, playground, and adjacent Environmental Park.

SAFETY

Most popular Sunshine Coast beaches are patrolled by lifeguards in school holiday and peak periods and on weekends throughout the warmer months. On some Sunshine Coast beaches, sandbanks, strong currents, and riptides make surf conditions challenging. Even on patrolled beaches, swimming unaccompanied is not recommended. Swim between the red-and-yellow flags, and follow lifeguards' direc-tives. Locals are often the best sources of advice on where and when to dive in.

Sharks are rarely a problem; however, lifeguards keep watch and issue warnings if they're sighted. A more constant hazard is the harsh Queensland sun: apply SPF30-plus sunscreen at regular intervals. Get information on local beaches at ⊕ *coastalwatch.com*, and surf reports on Surf Life Saving Queensland's website, ⊕ *www. lifesaving.com.au.* Contact SLSQ Lifeguards on ☎ *07/3846–8000.*

7

COASTAL AND WILDERNESS WALKS

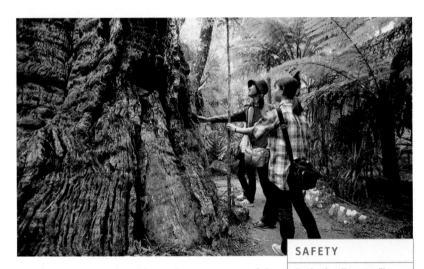

Southeast Queensland lays claim to some of the world's most superb wilderness areas, and the best way to explore them is on foot. Behind the Gold and Sunshine coasts are national parks, forests, and nature reserves dense with trails and walkways. Several also trace scenic sections of the coastline.

Coastal trails wind along the beachfront, trace rainforest-clad headlands, and meander through waterfront reserves from the Gold Coast to the national parkland north of Noosa.

A string of national parks and wilderness areas connects the Gold and Sunshine Coast hinterlands, with trails of varying lengths and degrees of difficulty. Walkers are rewarded with memorable sights: dramatic waterfalls and pristine pools, tracts of ancient rain forest, and glow-worm caves; wildflowers, wildlife, and exceptional views, some stretching as far as the coast.

SAFETY

For bushwalking you'll need sturdy shoes with grip, a hat, sunscreen, insect repellent, wet- and cold-weather gear, drinking water, food, camping equipment and permits (if overnighting), and a map and compass. Leech-proof yourself by wearing long socks over your pant legs and carrying a lighter to burn off any hitchhikers. Let others know your planned route and timing, even for day hikes.

QUEENSLAND'S GREAT WALKS

If your schedule allows it, tackle one of Queensland's Great Walks. A A$10-million state government initiative, the Great Walks aim to allow visitors of all ages and of average fitness to explore significant wilderness areas in a safe, eco-sensitive way.

A standout is the 54-km (34-mile) Gold Coast Hinterland Great Walk, linking the species-rich, Gondwana Rainforests of Australia World Heritage Area of Lamington and Springbrook plateaus via the glorious Numinbah Valley. En route, you'll traverse ancient volcanic terrain and pristine rain forest, passing torrential streams and waterfalls and 3,000-year-old hoop pines. Allow three days for the full walk, camping at designated sites en route, or trek just one section.

The Sunshine Coast Hinterland Great Walk, a 58-km (36-mile) hike traversing the Blackall Range northwest of Brisbane, includes sections of Kondalilla and Mapleton Falls national parks, Maleny Forest Reserve, and Delicia Road Conservation Park. The four- to six-day hike takes you past waterfalls and through open eucalypt and lush subtropical rain forest teeming with native birds, reptiles, and frogs.

The Cooloola Great Walk meanders through Great Sandy National Park north of Noosa. A 90-km (55-mile) network of graded walking tracks passes the spectacular multihue sand dunes of Rainbow Beach, and includes walks of varying distances and difficulty across a range of conditions.

Fraser Island Great Walk rewards hikers with exceptional scenery—wide, white-sand beaches, pristine deep-blue lakes, rain-forest tracts, and plenty of birds, reptiles, wallabies, and dingoes.

SHORTER OPTIONS

Coastal Trails. Compact Burleigh Head National Park, midway between Surfer's Paradise and Coolangatta, includes coastal rain forest and heath that's home to wallabies, koalas, lizards, snakes, and brush turkeys. Trek the 2.3-km (1.43-mile) Rainforest Circuit for excellent views, or the shadier, shorter, 1.2-km (0.75-mile) Oceanview Walk.

Hinterland Trails. Mt. Tamborine, Springwood, Witches Falls-Joalah, and Lamington national parks in the Gold Coast hinterland are all ideal for exploring on foot. Several wilderness retreats in the region include guided bushwalks as part of the package. West of the Sunshine Coast, short scenic walking trails in Kondalilla National Park near Montville take you past waterfalls, boulder-strewn streams, and lush rain forest abuzz with local wildlife. Or stroll along easy trails through Mary Cairncross Scenic Reserve, near Montville.

7

Updated by
Tess Curran

A fusion of Florida, Las Vegas, and the Caribbean, southern Queensland attracts crowd-lovers and escapists alike. Whether you want to surf or soak in the Pacific Ocean, stroll from cabana to casino with your favorite cocktail, hike through subtropical rain forests, or join seabirds and turtles on a pristine coral isle—it's all here.

Local license plates deem Queensland "The Sunshine State"—a laid-back stretch of beaches and sun where many Australians head for their vacations. The state has actively promoted tourism, and areas such as the Gold Coast, an hour south of Brisbane, and the Sunshine Coast, a roughly equivalent distance north of the capital, have expanded exponentially in recent years, with high-rise hotels, nightclubs, trendy bars and cafés, shopping precincts, and beachfront amusements popping up on nearly every block. These thriving coastal strips are the major attraction of southern Queensland for Australians and foreign tourists alike—along with a scattering of islands, notably Fraser Island, off Hervey Bay, and the Mackay-Capricorn islands lying on the southern end of the Great Barrier Reef.

Queensland was thrust into the spotlight when Brisbane hosted the Commonwealth Games in 1982. The World Expo '88 and the 2001 Goodwill Games have ensured that it's remained there. Such big-name competitions exposed Brisbane to the wider world and helped to bring the city, along with other provincial capitals, to social and cultural maturity. Queensland is now a vibrant and cosmopolitan place to visit, and Sunshine Staters are far more likely to be urbane city slickers than the "bushie" stereotype of decades past. Still, as with many regions blessed with abundant sunshine, the lifestyle here is relaxed.

PLANNER

WHEN TO GO

Temperatures average 15.6°C (60°F) between May and September with chillier nights, and 20°C (68°F) to 29°C (80°F) December to February. From December through March, expect high humidity and periods of heavy rain. Temperatures run slightly cooler inland. Sea- and reef-side Queensland tends to fill up from mid-December through January and can also be heavily booked in July, September, and throughout Easter. There's no daylight saving time in the state.

PLANNING YOUR TIME

If you're after a quick, Miami Beach–style holiday, fly into Brisbane and head straight for the glitzy Gold Coast, overnighting in Surfers Paradise. You could end the spree with a final night and morning in nearby Lamington National Park, renowned for its subtropical wilderness and birdlife.

If you have a bit more time, do three days on shore and two days on the reef. Stay a night in Brisbane, then head to the Sunshine Coast for a hike in the Glasshouse Mountains on the way to Noosa Heads. When you've had your fill of beaches and surf, take a leisurely drive through the Sunshine Coast's lovely hinterland villages for quaint shops and cafés and stunning natural scenery. Then make your way north to Bundaberg or Gladstone for a flight to Lady Elliot, Heron, or Wilson islands to wildlife-watch, dive, and snorkel; or a ferry to Fraser Island, off Hervey Bay, where you can swim in pristine lakes, 4WD along beaches stretching 80 km (50 miles), and see wild dingoes.

GETTING HERE AND AROUND

AIR TRAVEL

Qantas (⊕ *www.qantas.com.au*), Virgin Australia (⊕ *www.virginaustralia. com*), and a number of other carriers fly direct from U.S. cities to Australian capitals and regional tourist hubs. Qantas, Virgin Australia, and Jetstar (⊕ *www.jetstar.com.au*) link several regional centers throughout Queensland. Budget carrier Tigerair (⊕ *www.tigerair.com.au*) also covers most major centers, including Cairns, Mackay, and the Whitsunday Coast.

BOAT TRAVEL

Ferries and charter boats ply the waters between the southeast Queensland mainland and its various islands and offshore resorts. Most make daily or more frequent return trips; some carry vehicles as well as passengers.

BUS TRAVEL

Buses service most major towns and tourist areas around southeast Queensland, and are reliable and affordable—though on many routes it's as cheap, and faster, to fly. During holiday periods on popular routes buses are often heavily booked; buy tickets in advance, and don't expect to stretch out, even on overnight services. Tourist offices can advise which companies go where.

CAR TRAVEL

Traveling outside of cities is often simplest and most comfortable by car. Roads are generally good, but signage varies in clarity; study maps and work out highway exits in advance (although most hire cars will have GPS installed). Be prepared for heavy traffic between Brisbane and the Gold and Sunshine coasts in peak periods. Expect temporary road closures and detours after heavy rains. Roads are narrow and winding in some parts of the hinterlands. You'll need a 4X4 to get around Fraser Island, the sand islands of Moreton Bay, and some national park roads and Outback tracks. You can rent a small runabout from about A\$30 per day; a decent touring car from about A\$40 a day, and a 4X4 from about A\$65 per day (based on a weekly rental period). Gas costs vary, and tend to be pricier away from major towns and highways.

TRAIN TRAVEL

Frequent trains service routes between the capital and the Gold and Sunshine coasts. The Queensland Rail network links regional towns and tourist centers, and is a scenic way to travel (though on longer routes it's often cheaper to fly). The *Sunlander* and high-speed *Tilt Train* ply the coast between Brisbane and Rockhampton or Cairns, servicing towns that act as launching pads for island resorts.

RESTAURANTS

Once largely unfamiliar with the concept of specialized cuisine, Queensland is coming into its own as a new foodie hub. Cosmopolitan Brisbane boasts its share of modern Australian, Mediterranean, and Asian-influenced menus capitalizing on fresh regional produce, and the cuisine at many of Queensland's high-end resorts now rivals the standards of big-city fine-dining. Coastal tourist towns are full of casual open-air restaurants that take advantage of the tropical climate—an increasing number of them helmed by city-class chefs. Away from tourist hubs, steak, seafood, and the occasional Asian restaurant still tend to dominate. If you're on the road, an old-fashioned pub meal is more than satisfying and a great way to get to know the locals.

HOTELS

Accommodations in this state run the gamut from rain-forest lodges, Outback pubs, backpacker hostels, and colonial "Queenslander" bed-and-breakfasts—beautiful timber houses built high on stilts, with wrap-around verandas and character windows—to deluxe beachside resorts and big-city hotels. The luxury resorts are clustered around the major tourist areas of the Gold and Sunshine coasts and nearby islands such as Heron and Wilson. In smaller coastal towns, accommodation is mostly in motels, apartments, and B&Bs. There is also an increasing number of eco-friendly accommodation options, which utilize green technologies such as renewable energy and water conservation systems to minimize their impact on the environs. Many of Queensland's island resorts fall into this category. *Hotel reviews have been shortened. For full information, visit Fodors.com.*

WHAT IT COSTS IN AUSTRALIAN DOLLARS			
$	**$$**	**$$$**	**$$$$**
Restaurants	Under A$21	A$21–A$35	A$36–A$50	over A$50
Hotels	Under A$151	A$151–A$200	A$201–A$300	over A$300

Restaurant prices are the average cost of a main course at dinner or, if dinner is not served, at lunch. Hotel prices are the lowest cost of a standard double room in high season, inclusive of tax (10%).

TOURS

Guided day tours are a simple way to see Brisbane if your schedule is tight. View the city's many attractions from the comfort of a chauffeured coach, with a driver giving insider information. Buses are also great for covering the relatively short distances between Brisbane and nearly all of the mainland attractions. Within an hour or two you can be taste-testing your way through the Tambourine or Scenic Rim wineries, or practicing your poker face at a Gold Coast casino.

Most day tours include admission to sights, refreshments, and on full-day tours, lunch, as well as commentary en route and time to explore.

JPT Tour Group. Also known as Australian Day Tours, this company conducts half-, full-, and multiday tours across popular sites in Brisbane, Moreton Island, the Gold and Sunshine coasts, Fraser Island, and more. ✉ *2 Elkhorn Ave., Shop 18, Surfers Paradise* ☎ *07/5630–1602 outside Australia, 1300/781362* ⊕ *www.daytours.com.au* ✈ *From A$35.*

Queensland Day Tours. This group runs day tours to some of southeast Queensland's most popular beach and hinterland destinations, including the Gold Coast; Springbrook; Mt. Tamborine; and Fraser, Moreton, and Stradbroke Islands. Tour options include wildlife encounters, whale and dolphin watching, wine tastings, and more. ☎ *0488/332–257* ⊕ *www.qdtours.com.au* ✈ *From A$139.*

BRISBANE

Founded in 1824 on the banks of the wide, meandering Brisbane River, the former penal colony of Brisbane was for many years regarded as just a big country town. Many beautiful timber Queenslander homes, built in the 1800s, still dot the riverbanks and inner suburbs, and in spring the city's numerous parks erupt in a riot of colorful jacaranda, poinciana, and bougainvillea blossoms. Today the Queensland capital is one of Australia's most up-and-coming cities: glittering high-rises mark its polished business center, slick fashion boutiques and restaurants abound, and numerous outdoor attractions beckon. In summer, temperatures here are broilingly hot and days are often humid, a reminder that this city is part of a subtropical region. Wear SPF 30-plus sunscreen and a broad-brimmed hat outdoors, even on overcast days.

Brisbane's inner suburbs, a 5- to 10-minute drive or 15- to 20-minute walk from the city center, have a mix of intriguing eateries and quiet accommodations. Fortitude Valley combines Chinatown with a cosmopolitan mix of clubs, cafés, and boutiques. Spring Hill has several high-quality hotels, and Paddington, New Farm, Petrie Terrace, West End, and Woolloongabba are full of an eclectic mix of restaurants and bars. Brisbane is also a convenient base for trips to the Sunshine and Gold coasts, the mountainous hinterlands, and the Moreton Bay islands.

GETTING HERE AND AROUND
AIR TRAVEL
Brisbane is Queensland's major transit hub. Qantas, Virgin Australia, Jetstar, and Tigerair fly to all Australian capital cities and many regional hubs around Queensland, including the Gold, Sunshine, and Whitsunday coasts.

Brisbane International Airport is 9 km (5½ miles) from the city center. Con-x-ion operates a bus service to meet all flights and drops passengers door to door at major hotels throughout Brisbane and the Gold Coast. The one-way fare is A$15 to Brisbane, A$49 to Gold Coast hotels, with cheaper deals available for families.

Airtrain has rail services to stations throughout Brisbane and the Gold Coast. The one-way fare is A$17 per person, or A$32 for a round-trip from the airport to the city (discounts apply for groups and tickets purchased online). Trains depart up to four times an hour, taking 20 minutes to reach the city center. Kids (5–14 years) travel free. Taxis to downtown Brisbane cost A$40 to A$50, depending on time of day.

Airport Information and Transfers Brisbane Airtrain. ☎ *07/3216–3308, 1800/119091* ⊕ *www.airtrain.com.au.* **Brisbane International Airport.** ✉ *Airport Dr., Brisbane Airport* ☎ *07/3406–3000* ⊕ *www.bne.com.au.*

BOAT AND FERRY TRAVEL
Speedy CityCat boats and City Ferries dock at 25 points along the Brisbane River from Hamilton to St. Lucia, running every 15 minutes or more for most of the day (the last service is at 11:45 pm). The ferries are terrific for a quick survey of the Brisbane waterfront, from the city skyline to luxury homes and beautiful parkland. If you're staying within the CBD and South Bank, try the free CityHopper ferry, which runs every 30 minutes between 6 am and midnight every day.

Boat and Ferry Information CityCat ferries. ☎ *13–1230* ⊕ *www.translink.com.au.*

BUS TRAVEL
Greyhound Australia, the country's only nationwide bus line, travels to around 1,100 destinations. Bus stops are well signposted, and vehicles usually run on schedule. It's 1,716 km (1,064 miles), a 30-hour journey, between Brisbane and Cairns. Book in person at Greyhound's Roma Street office, by phone, or online. Purchase point-to-point tickets or flexible passes that allow multiple stops. Most buses are also equipped with USB ports and Wi-Fi.

Crisps Coaches operates a morning and afternoon service from Brisbane to the Southern Downs and towns to the city's south and west. TransLink's help line and website can help you find bus lines that run to your destination.

Brisbane

Bus Information Con-x-ion. ☎ 1300/266946 ⊕ www.con-x-ion.com. **Crisps Coaches.** ✉ 78 Grafton St., Warwick ☎ 07/4661–8333 ⊕ www.crisps.com. au. **Greyhound Australia.** ✉ Level 3, Brisbane Transit Centre, Roma St., City Center ☎ 7/4690–9850, 1300/473946 ⊕ www.greyhound.com.au. **TransLink.** ☎ 13–1230 ⊕ www.translink.com.au.

RENTAL CAR TRAVEL

Most major car rental companies have offices in Brisbane, including Avis, Thrifty, Budget, and Hertz. Four-wheel-drive vehicles, motor homes, and camper vans (sleeping two to six people) are available from Britz, Maui Rentals, and KEA Campers. If you're heading north along the coast or northwest into the bush, you can rent in Brisbane and drop off in Cairns or other towns. One-way rental fees usually apply.

Brisbane is 1,002 km (621 miles) from Sydney, a 12-hour drive along the Pacific Highway (Highway 1). Another route follows Highway 1 to Newcastle, then heads inland on the New England Highway (Highway 15). Either drive can be made in a long day, although two days or more are recommended for ample time to rest and sightsee.

Rental Cars Britz Australia Campervan Hire and Car Rentals. ✉ 21 Industry Ct., Eagle Farm ☎ 07/3868–1248, 1300/738087 ⊕ www.britz.com.au. **KEA Campers.** ✉ 348 Nudgee Rd., Eagle Farm ☎ 07/3868–4500, 1800/664825 ⊕ aurentals.keacampers.com. **Maui Australia Motorhome Rentals and Car Hire.** ✉ 21 Industry Ct., Eagle Farm ☎ 03/8398–8829, 1800/827821 ⊕ www. maui.com.au.

TAXI TRAVEL

Taxis are metered and relatively inexpensive. They are usually available at designated taxi stands outside hotels, downtown, and at Brisbane Transit and Roma Street stations, although it is often best to phone for one. New ride-sharing service Uber is also available to anyone with the smartphone app. The service is usually comfortable and reliable, with fares often cheaper than traditional taxis.

Taxis Black and White Cabs. ☎ 13–3222 ⊕ www.blackandwhitecabs.com.au. **Uber.** ✉ Brisbane ⊕ www.uber.com/cities/brisbane. **Yellow Cab Co.** ✉ Brisbane ☎ 13–1924 ⊕ www.yellowcab.com.au.

TRAIN TRAVEL

CountryLink trains make the 14-hour journey between Sydney and Brisbane. Rail services from Brisbane city and airport to the Gold Coast run regularly from 5:30 am until midnight. The *Spirit of Queensland* makes the 24-hour trip along the state's coast from Brisbane to Cairns five times a week, with stops at Mackay, Townsville, the Whitsunday coast, and more. All trains include the option of luxurious RailBed carriages with convertible lie-down bed seats, personal entertainment systems, and meals. The speedy, state-of-the-art *Tilt Train* runs from Brisbane to Bundaberg and Brisbane to Rockhampton six days a week, passing through various regional centers along the way.

Other long-distance passenger trains from Brisbane include the *Westlander,* to and from Charleville (twice weekly); and the *Spirit of the Outback,* to and from Longreach, via Rockhampton (twice weekly). Trains depart from Roma Street Station.

Trains Queensland Rail Travel. ✉ *Central Railway Station Concourse, 305 Edward St.* ☎ *07/3072–2222, 13–1617* ⊕ *www.queenslandrail.com.au.*

ESSENTIALS

Visitor Information Brisbane City Council. ✉ *266 George St., City Center* ☎ *07/3403–8888* ⊕ *www.brisbane.qld.gov.au.*

TOURS

At the Brisbane City Council office, pick up a self-guided Brisbane City-Walk map (also available from tourist information offices and online), as well as brochures and maps detailing other designated Brisbane walking trails.

FAMILY **The Brisbane Explorer.** The Brisbane Explorer operates air-conditioned, double decker, hop-on, hop-off tour buses that make circuits of city landmarks and other points of interest, including South Bank, China-town, and Mt. Coot-tha lookout. They leave from Post Office Square every 45 minutes, starting at 9 am; last departure is 5:15 pm. You can buy tickets online or from agents, and get on or off at any of the 20 stops all day for A$35 (or $60 for two days). ✉ *Post Office Sq., 280 Queen St., City Center* ☎ *02/9567–8400* ⊕ *www.brisbanecityexplorer. com.au* ✆ *From A$35.*

JPT Tours. JPT Tours (also known as Australian Day Tours) conducts half- and full-day tours of Brisbane, Moreton Island, Fraser Island, Springbrook National Park, Mt. Tamborine, Byron Bay, and north-wards to Australia Zoo in Beerwah, with options to include meals and attractions. Check online to view current rates, last minute specials, and promotions, including buy two tours, get one free. Buses depart both the Gold Coast and Brisbane. ✉ *2 Elkhorn Ave., Shop 18, Surfers Paradise* ☎ *07/5630–1602, 1300/781362* ⊕ *www.jpttours.com* ✆ *From A$70.*

Kookaburra Showboat Cruises. This tour company runs lunch, dinner, high tea, and special event cruises along the Brisbane River on board its iconic paddle wheelers. Lunch cruises include scenic and historic commentary; live entertainment and dancing are highlights of dinner cruises. The weekend jazz lunch cruise is especially popular. ✉ *Eagle St. Pier, 45 Eagle St., City Center* ☎ *07/3221–1300* ⊕ *www. kookaburrariverqueens.com* ✆ *From A$49.*

FAMILY **River City Cruises.** This operator runs daily sightseeing tours through and around South Bank, the City Center, and Kangaroo Point cliffs, including morning and afternoon tea options. It departs from Jetty A at South Bank Parklands, in front of the Wheel of Brisbane. ✉ *Jetty A, South Bank Parklands* ☎ *0428/278–473* ⊕ *www.rivercitycruises.com. au* ✆ *From A$29.*

Story Bridge Adventure Climb. Energetic visitors might want to scale Brisbane's Story Bridge for a 360-degree city overview; the climb takes around two hours and goes during the day, twilight, and evening. ✉ *Wharf and Main Sts., Kangaroo Point* ☎ *1300/254627* ⊕ *www.sbac. net.au* ✆ *From A$119.*

EXPLORING

Brisbane's city-center landmarks—a mix of Victorian, Edwardian, and slick contemporary architecture—are best explored on foot. Most lie within the triangle formed by Ann Street and the bends of the Brisbane River. ■TIP→ Streets running toward the river are named after female British royalty; those parallel to the river after male royalty. The well-tended South Bank precinct has riverfront parklands and cultural centers, alfresco cafés, and weekend markets. Upriver, the quiet, leafy suburb of Fig Tree Pocket is home to Australia's best-known koala sanctuary.

TOP ATTRACTIONS

FAMILY
Fodor'sChoice
★
Lone Pine Koala Sanctuary. Founded in 1927, Queensland's most famous fauna park is recognized by the *Guinness Book of World Records* as the world's first and largest koala sanctuary. The attractions for most people are the koalas themselves (130 in all), although emus, wombats, crocs, bats, platypuses, and lorikeets also reside here. You can hand-feed baby kangaroos in the free-range 'roo and wallaby enclosure, have a snake wrapped around you, or cuddle a koala and have your photo taken with one (for A$18, until 4:30 pm). There's also a thrice-daily sheepdog show, regular bird feedings, and animal presentations. Intimate encounters and behind-the-scenes tours can also be arranged for small groups. Book ahead online for 10% off ticket prices. To make your visit extra special, book a combo ticket (A$72) via Mirimar Cruises (⊕ *www.mirimar.com*) and travel to Lone Pine along the Brisbane River, leaving from South Bank Parklands at 10 am and Lone Pine at 1:30 pm. ⊠ *708 Jesmond Rd., Fig Tree Pocket* ☎ *07/3378–1366 Lone Pine Sanctuary, 0412/749–426 Mirimar Cruises* ⊕ *www.koala.net* ⊠ *A$35* ⊙ *Daily 9–5.*

Fodor'sChoice
★
Queensland Cultural Centre. This sunny riverside hub is literally the cultural center of Brisbane, with a variety of world-class facilities nestled together amongst landscaped lawns and cafés. The world famous Gallery of Modern Art (GoMA) with its ever-changing exhibitions and events is a must-visit, while a short stroll away the equally impressive Queensland Art Gallery, Queensland Museum, and Sciencentre have attractions for both young and old. Meanwhile, you can't miss the green walls of the architecturally renowned State Library of Queensland (find many free, interactive children's activities inside at The Corner). Across the road, the Queensland Performing Arts Centre (QPAC) bustles with concerts and stage shows. There's also a host of restaurants, cafés, gift and book shops, a ticketing agent (in QPAC), public-access computer terminals, and various public spaces. Regular special events and festivals are also held in the Cultural Centre forecourt, particularly on weekends. Green Cabs (modern rickshaws) are a fun and unique way to get around and sightsee in this area. Starting at the Wheel of Brisbane adjacent QPAC, they'll ferry passengers anywhere between West End and Fortitude Valley. ⊠ *Melbourne and Grey Sts., South Bank, South Brisbane* ☎ *07/3840–7303 Galleries, 07/3840–7555 Museum and Sciencentre, 07/3840–7666 State Library, 07/3840–7444 QPAC* ⊕ *www.qagoma.qld.gov.au* ⊠ *Free (excluding Sciencentre and certain*

Lone Pine Koala Sanctuary, Brisbane

GoMA exhibitions) ⊙ *Galleries daily 10–5; Museum and Sciencentre daily 9:30–5; library Mon.–Thurs. 10–8, Fri.–Sun. 10–5.*

FAMILY **Roma Street Parkland.** The world's largest subtropical garden within a city is a gentle mix of forest paths, floral displays, and structured plantings surrounding a fish-stocked lake. Highlights include the Lilly Pilly Garden, with native evergreen rain forest plants, interesting children's play areas, and the friendly resident birds and lizards. A range of public art pieces are also dotted throughout the park. Pack a picnic, take advantage of the free grills, or stop for lunch at elegant on-site café Melange. Free hour-long guided garden tours begin daily at 11 am and 1 pm, or from Wednesday to Sunday, hop on the Parkland Explorer, a trackless train that gives guests a full tour of the gardens for a gold coin donation. There are also specialist art, heritage, curator's, or sensory tours (prebook these) and brochures for self-guided walks available online or from Colin Campbell Place. Regular special events add to the fun. ⊠ *1 Parkland Blvd., City Center* ☎ *1300/137468* ⊕ *www.visitbrisbane. com.au/Roma-Street-Parkland-and-Spring-Hill* ☐ *Free* ⊙ *Daily 24 hrs.*

FAMILY **South Bank Parklands.** One of the most appealing urban parks in Austra-
Fodor's Choice lia, this massive complex along the banks of the Brisbane River includes
★ parklands, shops, hotels, a maritime museum, walking and cycling paths, a sprawling man-made beach, a stunning Nepalese pagoda, and excellent city views. The weekend Collective Markets bristle with hand-made goods, live entertainers, buskers, artists, and emerging designers. Almost every week you'll find a new festival or event lighting up the Cultural Forecourt. Nearby Grey Street is lined with trendy shops and cafés, as well as contemporary international restaurants, bars, and a

cinema. The Wheel of Brisbane (A$17.50), a giant Ferris wheel at the northern entrance of South Bank, has some of the most spectacular views of the city. South Bank Parklands stretches along the riverbank south of the Queensland Cultural Centre. ⊠ *Grey St. south of Melbourne St.* ☎ *07/3156–6366 Parklands, 07/3844–3464 Wheel of Brisbane, 07/3844–5361 Maritime Museum* ⊕ *www.visitbrisbane.com.au/south-bank* ⊠ *Parklands free, museum A$16* ☉ *Parklands daily 5 am–midnight; info center daily 9–5; museum daily 9:30–4:30 (last entry at 3:30); markets Fri. 5–9, Sat. 10–9, Sun. 9–4.*

WORTH NOTING

Anzac Square and the Shrine of Remembrance. Paths stretch across manicured lawns toward the Doric Greek Revival shrine made of Queensland sandstone. An eternal flame burns here for Australian soldiers who died in World War I. In the Shrine of Remembrance, a subsurface crypt stores soil samples from key battlefields. On April 25, Anzac Day, a moving dawn service is held here in remembrance of Australia's fallen soldiers. ⊠ *Adelaide St., between Edward and Creek Sts., City Center* ⊠ *Free* ☉ *Public square daily 9–5; shrine weekdays 9–3.*

The Commissariat Store. Convict-built in 1829 on the site of the city's original timber wharf, this was Brisbane's first stone building and remains the oldest occupied one in Queensland. It has served as a customs house, storehouse, and immigrants' shelter, and is currently the headquarters of The Royal Historical Society of Queensland. The RHSQ library and Commissariat Store museum is open to visitors and holds exhibitions, historical documents, manuscripts, and artifacts dating back to Brisbane's early colonial days. Group tours of the museum are welcome. ⊠ *115 William St., City Center* ☎ *07/3221–4198* ⊕ *www.queenslandhistory.org.au* ⊠ *A$7* ☉ *Tues.–Fri. 10–4.*

Old Windmill & Observatory. This 1824 construction is the oldest remaining convict-built structure in Brisbane, dubbed the "Tower of Torture" by convicts forced to power a treadmill to crush the colony's grain on windless days. When fire razed part of the city in 1864 the windmill survived, later repurposed as an observatory. Stripped of its blades, the tower now resembles a lighthouse. ⊠ *Wickham Park, Wickham Terr., City Center* ⊕ *www.brisbanehistory.com/windmill_and_treadmill.html* ⊠ *Free.*

Parliament House. Opened in 1868, this splendid, stone-clad, French Renaissance building with a Mount Isa copper roof earned its colonial designer a meager 200-guinea (A$440) fee. A legislative annex was added in the late 1970s. The interior is fitted with polished timber, brass, and frosted and engraved glass. There are free half-hour tours on weekday afternoons, depending on demand. High Tea is served in the elegant Strangers' Dining Room from 10:30 am to noon the first Friday of every month (A$41 per person). The adjacent, kid-friendly City Botanic Gardens have native and exotic plants and theme areas, including the Bamboo Grove and Weeping Fig Avenue, along with sculptures, ponds, and an on-site café. ⊠ *George and Alice Sts., City Center* ☎ *07/3553–6000* ⊕ *www.parliament.qld.gov.au* ⊠ *Free* ☉ *Parliament House weekdays 9–5 (last tour 4 pm), gardens daily 24 hrs.*

Modern sculpture at the Queensland Cultural Centre, South Bank, Brisbane

Treasury Casino & Hotel. This Edwardian baroque edifice overlooking the river stands on the site of military barracks from the original penal settlement, flanked by bronze statuary. Constructed between 1885 and 1889, the former treasury is now a popular **hotel, casino, and entertainment complex.** In addition to three floors of gaming, the casino houses six eateries, five bars, and lavish suites for overnight stay. ⊠ *Queen St. Mall, William and Elizabeth Sts., City Center* ☎ *07/3306–8888* ⊕ *www. treasurybrisbane.com.au* ✉ *Free* ☉ *Daily 24 hrs.*

SPORTS AND THE OUTDOORS

BICYCLING

An extensive network of bicycle paths crisscrosses Brisbane. One of the best paths follows the level and impeccably maintained Bicentennial Bikeway southeast along the Brisbane River, across the Goodwill Bridge, then along to South Bank Parklands or Kangaroo Point cliffs. The new Kurilpa Bridge and Go Between Bridge are also both cyclist-friendly ways to cross the river between the city and South Brisbane. The city's famous Riverwalk gives cyclists and pedestrians a scenic route from New Farm to the CBD.

Bike Obsession. Rent bikes here from A\$25 for two hours. Pick yours up nearby the Brisbane Botanic Gardens or arrange to have the bike dropped off at CBD hotels. Books, maps, and cycling advice are also available. ⊠ *133 Mary St., City Center* ☎ *07/3221–7228* ⊕ *www. bikeobsession.com.au/bike-hire.*

Brisbane City Council. The Brisbane City Council website includes downloadable maps and lets you search for bikeways. Visitors can pick up Council-operated CityCycle bikes from 150 designated points around the inner city, returning them when they're done. ⊠ *Brisbane* ⊕ *www. brisbane.qld.gov.au.*

CLIMBING

Kangaroo Point cliffs, near the city center, are ideal for climbing and abseiling. You can kayak or paddleboard on the Brisbane River, and numerous scenic bushwalking, climbing, and rappelling sites lie less than 90 minutes by car from Brisbane. Government-run Outdoors Queensland (QORF) (⊕ *www.qorf.org.au*) gives regional information and lists businesses offering adventure activities from hiking to horse riding.

Adventures Around Brisbane. Adventures Around Brisbane runs daily rock-climbing and abseiling sessions off Kangaroo Point cliffs, as well as bushwalks and adventure day trips to the scenic Glass House Mountains and Mt. Maroon. ⊠ *River Terr., Kangaroo Point* ☎ *07/3367–0130* ⌨ *Rock climbing and abseiling from A$79.*

GOLF

St. Lucia Golf Links and Golf World. One of Brisbane's oldest golf courses, St. Lucia Golf Links and Golf World is an 18-hole, par-70, pay-and-play course open to visitors. Work up an appetite on the fairways, then dine on-site at the Hillstone clubhouse's recently refurbished Hundred Acre Bar, overlooking the 18th green. ⊠ *Indooroopilly Rd., at Carawa St., St. Lucia* ☎ *07/3403–2556 golf course, 07/3870–3433 Hillstone Clubhouse* ⊕ *www.hillstonestlucia.com.au* ⌨ *Weekdays A$34; weekends A$40* ⌦ *18 holes, 5917 yards, par 69.*

MULTISPORT OUTFITTERS

FAMILY **Riverlife Adventure Centre.** A one-stop-shop for adventure in the inner city, Riverlife runs guided rock-climbing and abseiling sessions off Kangaroo Point cliffs, cycling and Segway tours around Brisbane attractions, day and night kayaking and stand up paddle boarding trips on the Brisbane River (followed by BBQ dinner and seafood options). The Mirrabooka Aboriginal Cultural Experience includes a traditional performance by the Yuggera Aboriginal Dancers and hands-on instruction in fire-starting, instrument playing, boomerang throwing, and painting. The center also rents bicycles, rollerblades, kick bikes, and scooters. ⊠ *Naval Stores, Lower River Terr., Kangaroo Point* ☎ *07/3891–5766* ⊕ *www. riverlife.com.au* ⌨ *From A$20.*

WATER SPORTS

Moreton Bay. A half-hour's drive east of Brisbane city brings you to Moreton Bay, stretching 125 km (78 miles) from the Gold Coast to the Sunshine Coast. A number of operators based in Brisbane's bayside suburbs—Manly, Redcliffe, Sandgate—run sailing, diving, sightseeing, and whale- and dolphin-watching trips around the Bay, and trips to its various islands. Some cruises include tours of St. Helena Island's historic prison ruins; others visit Moreton Island, where you can toboggan down massive white sand-dunes. ⊠ *Moreton Island National Park* ⊕ *www.moretonbay.qld.gov.au.*

FAMILY **Moreton Bay Escapes.** This operator runs tours and charters around Moreton Island National Park that includes 4WD driving, snorkeling, kayaking, body-boarding, hiking, and sand-boarding. Tailored excursions incorporate bird-watching, fishing, swimming with dolphins, and more. Admission includes ferry trip, park entry fees, and meals. ☒ *Brisbane* ☎ *1300/559355* ⊕ *www.moretonbayescapes.com.au* ✆ *From A$189.*

WHERE TO EAT

In the past decade Brisbane has transformed from a culinary backwater into a city full of inventive dining options. Top chefs have decamped to Brisbane's best eateries and are busy putting put a fresh subtropical spin on Modern Australian, pan-Asian, and Mediterranean cuisine.

Imaginative dishes capitalize on abundant regional produce: fine fresh seafood—notably the local delicacy, the Moreton Bay bug (a sweet-fleshed crustacean)—premium steak, Darling Downs lamb, cheeses, macadamia nuts, avocados, olives, and fruit, matched with fine regional wines.

Most of the city's hip cafés, bars, and smart fine dining establishments are clustered in the CBD, West End, Fortitude Valley, New Farm, Teneriffe, and Petrie Terrace; you'll also find some excellent eateries in the riverfront South Bank precinct, and a smattering around the suburbs, particularly Rosalie, Paddington, Milton, Ascot and Woolloongabba. For terrific fresh seafood, head for Brisbane's bayside suburbs, such as Manly, Redcliffe, and Sandgate.

Typically, dining ambience is relaxed, seating is alfresco, and well-mannered children are welcomed.

Use the coordinate (✛ B2) at the end of each listing to locate a site on the corresponding map.

$$ ✕ **Alfred & Constance.** Combining a café, restaurant, three bars, and a
CAFÉ beer garden, this hip Fortitude Valley establishment is as much worth a visit for its trendy design and upbeat vibe as it is for its hearty, locally sourced fare. Stylish young waiters slide between the various quirkily designed seating "houses," where your steak, burger, or salad may appear from beneath giant elephant wall art or collections of suspended vintage lanterns. Chefs work enthusiastically in open view of patrons, using only the finest ingredients and premium free range and organic meats. As the sun sets, the extensive cocktail menu comes out to play, with fresh, tropical flavors like Plantation Punch and Tiki Mai Tai making the perfect nightcap (or beginning!). Ⓢ *Average main: A$25* ☒ *Alfred and Constance Sts., Fortitude Valley* ☎ *07/3251–6500* ⊕ *www.alfredandconstance.com.au* ✛ *D1.*

$$$ ✕ **Breakfast Creek Hotel.** Perched on the wharf at Breakfast Creek, this
AUSTRALIAN iconic, heritage–listed, French-Renaissance-style hotel is renowned for its breezy tropical beer garden and superb trademark steaks. Nonsteak eaters also have plenty of options, including vegetarian dishes, salads, and fresh seafood. As well as its famous five bars, the hotel also boasts a new on-site coffee cart and café, and live entertainment on the

weekends. $ *Average main: A$38* ⊠ *2 Kingsford Smith Dr., Albion* ☎ *07/3262–5988* ⊕ *www.breakfastcreekhotel.com* ✛ *C1.*

$$
TURKISH

✕ **Caravanserai.** Decked out in traditional woven kilims and Mediterranean lanterns, this ambient Turkish restaurant is a treat for the senses, with its rich, generously portioned servings of contemporary Middle Eastern fare served amongst cozy nooks of candlelit tables and breezy views over West End. Start your meal with a delicious garlic pide bread (dripping with garlic butter) or a share platter of gourmet olives, dips, cheeses, nuts, cured meats, and regional condiments, before moving on to the fragrant mains, including the signature köfte (spiced meatballs), harissa seafood risotto, marinated chicken breast, and chargrilled "Sultan's Steak." Vegetarian dishes like grilled mushrooms, polenta, and haloumi cheese, and lentil and fennel soup, are available, as well as and a selection of deluxe banquets, which also feature the restaurant's must-try desserts: mint fig mousse, house-made baklava, and, of course, Turkish delight. $ *Average main: A$27* ⊠ *1–3 Dornoch Terr., West End* ☎ *07/3217–2617* ⊕ *www.caravanserairestaurant.com.au* ⊘ *Closed Mon. No lunch Tues.–Fri.* ⌂ *Reservations essential* ✛ *A3.*

$$
MODERN
AUSTRALIAN

✕ **The Charming Squire.** Named after legendary convict brewmaster James Squire, this stylish new brewery and restaurant in South Bank's cultural precinct pairs contemporary design with modern Australian pub cuisine and a tempting selection of more than 20 craft beers and ciders. The large, open-plan bar area—featuring sweeping ceilings, polished concrete flooring, repurposed timber, and trendy copper accents—encourages patrons to get to know the process and personality of the venue's namesake via floor-to-ceiling glass windows that capture the whole process from keg to glass. The surrounding restaurant serves local beef, lamb, pork, and seafood slow-cooked on an exposed coal-fired spit, alongside traditional pub favorites like fish-and-chips, burgers, pizza, salads, and antipasto-style share plates. Nonbeer drinkers still find plenty to wet their lips, and a decent selection of spirits and wines is also available. The venue's own deli, The Brewer's Pantry, is also open for breakfast, lunch, and coffee. $ *Average main: A$24* ⊠ *133 Grey St., Southbank* ☎ *07/3077–7254* ⊕ *www.thecharmingsquire.com.au* ☞ *Bookings recommended, especially on weekends* ✛ *B3.*

$$$
AUSTRALIAN-
MEDITERRANEAN
Fodor's Choice
★

✕ **e'cco.** Consistently ranked among the best restaurants in town, this petite, city-edge bistro in a converted tea warehouse serves innovative fare to a loyal following. Completely refurbished in 2014, e'cco's clean, contemporary design makes the perfect backdrop for the seasonally changing Mediterranean and Asian-inspired Mod Oz dishes, where the focus is on fresh, local ingredients and simple, yet bold, cuisine. Start with vine-wrapped quail or smoked pancetta with watermelon, and follow with black cardamom beef or duck breast with caramelized pear. The dessert selection is equally delectable: banana and hazelnut ice cream, strawberry, rhubarb, and rosewater cheesecake, and carrot cake with pistachio and orange blossom. For a bit of everything, order the excellent tasting menu; it showcases five dishes (A$89) and can be paired with top wines by the restaurant's sommelier (A$139). $ *Average main: A$45* ⊠ *100 Boundary St., City Center* ☎ *07/3831–8344* ⊕ *www.*

eccobistro.com ⊗ *Closed Sun. and Mon. No lunch Sat.* ⌲ *Reservations essential* ✛ *D1.*

$$ ✕ **The Gunshop Café.** Named after its previous life as an actual gun shop,
CAFÉ this trendy West End café is the place to go for breakfast and brunch on weekends (the potato-feta hash cakes with spinach, house-dried tomato, and herbed sour cream are locally famous). Unfinished brick walls where guns once hung help create a rustic ambience and set the stage for flavorsome Merlo coffee, freshly squeezed juices, and spicy chai tea with honey from the café's own rooftop bees. Dine around wooden tables near the open kitchen or request a seat out on the sidewalk to people watch. A select but eclectic Mod Oz menu fuses Mediterranean and Asian flavors in dishes like Margaret River lamb, Angus beef, duck, and seafood. Vegetarian dishes and exciting salads, with produce sourced daily from local markets, are also available. Foodies flock here for lunch, dinner, or even just a coffee and dessert; the flourless chocolate fudge cake is particularly unforgettable. $ *Average main: A$28* ✉ *53 Mollison St., West End* ☎ *07/3844–2241* ⊕ *www.thegunshopcafe.com* ⊗ *No dinner Sun.–Thurs.* ✛ *A3.*

$ ✕ **Happy Boy.** With exposed brick walls and industrial-style Edison bulb
CHINESE lighting, this bustling little wine bar and eatery in downtown Spring Hill is not your average Chinese restaurant. Locals and foodies alike flock to experience its delicious, regional Chinese fare cooked by a Michelin-trained chef. Most mains fall under the A$20 mark, and A$10 will get you a glass of wine from a curated list of boutique Australian makers. Munch on dishes like the mouthwatering salt and pepper quail eggs and the perfectly crisp crispy-skinned chicken, wash them down with a South Australia Riesling, and you'll be sure to finish the evening very happy indeed. $ *Average main: A$20* ✉ *2/36 Mein St., City Center* ☎ *0413/246–890* ⊕ *www.happyboy.com.au* ⊗ *No breakfast or lunch on weekends* ✛ *C1.*

$ ✕ **The Himalayan Cafe.** An Aladdin's cave of candles and spices, this tra-
NEPALESE ditional Tibetan-Nepalese sanctuary is one of Brisbane's most popular
Fodor's Choice inner-city eats. While its famous Sherpa chicken and goat curries cer-
★ tainly impress, it's the restaurant's heavenly homemade entrée breads that keep patrons coming back—divinely moist and fluffy, each is served with a minted yogurt dipping sauce in the traditional Himalayan style. When it comes to mains, there's something for everyone, from vegans and vegetarians to the most committed carnivores: spicy noodle soups, tofu and vegetable curries; and tender lamb, beef, chicken, and goat dishes in a range of flavors and intensities. For an extra treat, ask for a seat in one of the traditional Himalayan raised rooms. $ *Average main: A$20* ✉ *640 Brunswick St., New Farm* ☎ *07/3358–4015* ⊗ *Closed Mon. No lunch* ✛ *D1.*

$$$ ✕ **Jellyfish.** At this upmarket riverside eatery, you can sit indoors on
SEAFOOD smart black-and-white chairs under low-slung, jellyfish-shape lights, or outside on the breezy terrace with views, and choose from a Modern Australian menu that changes daily but always features 8–14 different species of fish—panfried or oven-roasted, steamed, seared, or with your choice of six available batters and a range of side dishes. Try the signature tempura soft-shell mud crab with green chili, shallots,

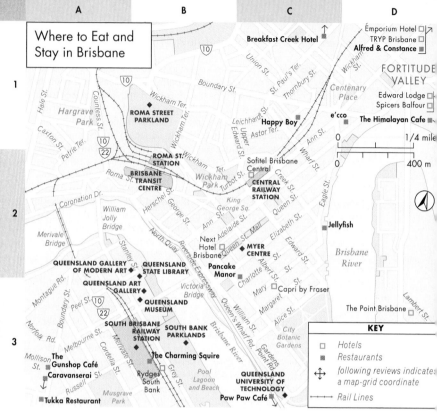

Where to Eat and
Stay in Brisbane

and wasabi mayo; or the kingfish delicately flavored with watermelon and mint. The fresh, interesting menu also includes eye fillet steak, pork belly, and vegetarian options, as well as desserts such as Valrhona chocolate fondant and strawberry and basil seed compote. The attached bar pours a selection of boutique wines by the glass. $ *Average main: A$42* ⊠ *Boardwalk, Riverside Centre, 123 Eagle St., Brisbane* ☎ *07/3220–2202* ⊕ *www.jellyfishrestaurant.com.au* ☾ *No lunch weekends* ⌂ *Reservations essential* ⟷ *C2.*

$ ✕ **Pancake Manor.** Housed inside the historic, heritage-listed St. Luke's
CAFÉ Cathedral, this elegant 24-hour pancake parlor is a Brisbane institution.
FAMILY Guests can take a seat in one of the Manor's converted church pew booths and chow down on a tempting menu of snacks, salads, steaks, and sweets beneath the building's grand redbrick arches. For breakfast try the simple eggs Benedict or the hearty Aussie Sunrise, while dinner patrons will find a range of savory crepes and pancake dishes to please the palate. But it's desserts that Pancake Manor is really famous for: grilled bananas drizzled in creamy butterscotch sauce, set upon a fluffy short stack of pancakes with rich vanilla ice cream directly hits the sweet spot. The bar downstairs has an all-day drinks menu of local and imported beers and wines; with its swift, attentive service, this is the place to venture when jet lag kicks in. $ *Average main: A$16* ⊠ *18 Charlotte St., City Center* ☎ *07/3221–6433* ⊕ *www.pancakemanor.com.au* ⟷ *C2.*

$$ ✕ **Pawpaw Cafe.** The small selection of simple dishes here is beauti-
ASIAN FUSION   fully prepared from 90% local ingredients in a modern Vietnamese and Balinese style. Popular choices include the crispy fish taco, macadamia chicken, chili caramel pork belly, and classic yellow or red curry. A curated selection of desserts and wines rounds out the menu, while the adjacent café area makes a tempting range of smoothies, pressed juices, and classic, all-day breakfast options. It's a little far from the CBD, but if you're out this way anyway, it's a delicious stop. $ *Average main: A$24* ✉ *898 Stanley St., at Potts St., East Brisbane* ☎ *07/3891–5100* ⊕ *www.pawpawcafe.com.au* ◷ *No dinner Mon. and Tues.* ✛ *C3.*

$$ ✕ **Tukka Restaurant.** Earth-tone walls lined with Aboriginal artworks
MODERN   are a fitting backdrop for native-inspired Modern Australian cuisine,
AUSTRALIAN   including a range of lean local meats like seared wallaby, kangaroo, emu, croc tail, and possum, deliciously fused with seasonal produce and native Australian herbs and spices. One excellent option is the entrée platter of cured meats and flavorful indigenous berries and flowers, all served on a rustic wooden camphor platter. The "Discovery" (A$75) and "Great Escape" (A$115) degustation menus let you taste your way through a curated selection of interesting and impeccably presented native delicacies, perfect for pairing with the restaurant's top vintages from boutique Australian wineries. You can also buy Tukka's own line of spices, cured meats, glazed fruits and sorbets, or ask for a "taste and talk" tour of the restaurants thriving garden. $ *Average main: A$32* ✉ *145 Boundary St., West End* ☎ *07/3846–6333* ⊕ *www. tukkarestaurant.com.au* ◷ *No dinner Mon. No brunch weekdays* ✛ *A3.*

WHERE TO STAY

Twenty years ago Brisbane's accommodation options consisted of a few big hotels and some welcoming but nondescript motels and B&Bs. These days the inner-city area bristles with luxury hotels and smart serviced-apartment complexes. There are also a few excellent boutique hotels, some cut-above B&Bs, and modern backpacker hotels giving pricier digs a run for their money. Many have good-value packages and seasonal and last-minute specials. Jump online for the best deals.

Use the coordinate (✛ B2) at the end of each listing to locate a site on the corresponding map.

For expanded hotel reviews, facilities, and current deals, visit Fodors.com.

$$$ 🏨 **Capri by Fraser.** Contemporary design meets superior comfort at this
HOTEL   newly completed, health-focused hotel, perfectly positioned between the Queen Street Mall and the Botanic Gardens in CBD. **Pros:** great service and location; free, fast Wi-Fi; quality, healthy buffet breakfast. **Cons:** pricey parking; niche restaurant may not appeal to all. $ *Rooms from: A$229* ✉ *80 Albert St., City Center* ☎ *07/3013–0088* ⊕ *brisbane. capribyfraser.com* ⇌ *239 rooms* ❝◎❞ *Breakfast* ✛ *C3.*

$ 🏨 **Edward Lodge.** This charming, inner-suburban, art deco B&B is set
B&B/INN   among Asian-style tropical gardens and close to cafés and restaurants, New Farm Park, Brisbane Powerhouse, and the CityCat ferry. **Pros:** free Wi-Fi; guest kitchen and laundry; vibrant area; free continental breakfast. **Cons:** 15-minute walk from the city; no room service.

$ *Rooms from: A$135* ✉ *75 Sydney St., New Farm* ☎ *07/3358–2680, 07/3358–3583* ⊕ *www.edwardlodge.com.au* 🛏 *9 rooms, 1 apartment* ⦿I *Breakfast* ✢ *D1.*

$$$
HOTEL

🛏 **Emporium Hotel.** Billing itself as a luxury boutique hotel, this contemporary, vibrantly designed establishment in lively Fortitude Valley boasts a rooftop swimming pool, exquisite cocktail bar, and easy access to some of the city's best restaurants. **Pros:** superb design and facilities; close to nightlife; wheelchair-accessible suite; free Wi-Fi. **Cons:** outside the city center; expensive parking; can be noisy—ask for a room away from street. $ *Rooms from: A$299* ✉ *1000 Ann St., Fortitude Valley* ☎ *07/3253–6999* ⊕ *www.emporiumhotels.com.au* 🛏 *102 suites* ⦿I *Breakfast* ✢ *D1.*

$$$
HOTEL
Fodor's Choice
★

🛏 **Next Hotel Brisbane.** Modern technology is the order of the day at this state-of-the-art, high-tech, high-rise hotel, merging innovative, plush design and an unbeatable location on the Queen Street Mall. **Pros:** clean, comfortable and quiet; central location; free Wi-Fi, movies, and minibar items. **Cons:** limited and pricey parking; technology may be off-putting to some. $ *Rooms from: A$259* ✉ *72 Queen St., City Center* ☎ *07/3222–3222* ⊕ *www.silverneedlehotels.com/next/brisbane* 🛏 *304 rooms* ⦿I *Breakfast* ✢ *B2.*

$$
HOTEL
🛏 **The Point Brisbane.** Across the river from the central business district, this modern hotel on picturesque Kangaroo Point has great city skyline and river views from each balcony. **Pros:** terrific on-site facilities; free Wi-Fi and parking; wheelchair accessible rooms. **Cons:** a 20-minute walk to the city. $ *Rooms from: A$174* ✉ *21 Lambert St., Kangaroo Point* ☎ *07/3240–0888, 1800/088388* ⊕ *www.thepointbrisbane.com.au* 🛏 *137 rooms, 64 suites* ⦿I *Breakfast* ✢ *D3.*

$$$
HOTEL
FAMILY
🛏 **Rydges South Bank.** Surrounded by Brisbane's famous South Bank Parklands and Cultural Precinct, within walking distance of numerous attractions, this tasteful, well-maintained hotel is an excellent choice if location's your focus. **Pros:** lively location; excellent restaurant and facilities. **Cons:** steep fees for parking; not all rooms have balconies so be sure to request one. $ *Rooms from: A$249* ✉ *9 Glenelg St., at Grey St., South Brisbane* ☎ *07/3364–0800* ⊕ *www.rydges.com/southbank* 🛏 *240 rooms, 64 suites* ⦿I *Breakfast* ✢ *B3.*

$$$
HOTEL
🛏 **Sofitel Brisbane Central.** Despite its position above the city's main rail station, this decadent, French-flavored hotel is a quiet and classy choice when it comes to city-center accommodations and feels worlds away from the rush below with its sophisticated, Parisian atmosphere that begins in the soaring lobby. **Pros:** prompt, pleasant service; luxurious rooms and facilities; superb buffet breakfast. **Cons:** pricey meals and minibar; expensive Wi-Fi and parking; compact bathrooms. $ *Rooms from: A$284* ✉ *249 Turbot St., City Center* ☎ *07/3835–4444* ⊕ *www.sofitelbrisbane.com.au* 🛏 *409 rooms, 21 suites* ⦿I *Breakfast; No meals; Some meals* ✢ *C2.*

$$$
HOTEL
Fodor's Choice
★
🛏 **Spicers Balfour.** With service, style, and hospitality above and beyond the call of duty, this hotel is a distinctly local and wonderfully welcoming experience, perfect for weary travelers looking for a home away from home. **Pros:** attentive and personalized service; close to public transport and ferry; free Wi-Fi and parking; à la carte breakfast included

in rate. **Cons:** outside the city center. $ *Rooms from: A$279* ⊠ *37 Balfour St., New Farm* ☎ *07/3358–8888* ⊕ *www.spicersgroup.com.au* ☞ *9 rooms, 8 suites* |⊙| *Breakfast; Some meals* ✛ *D1.*

$ 🚇 **TRYP Brisbane.** This young, vibrant art hotel in downtown Fortitude
HOTEL   Valley is perfect for energetic travelers looking to take advantage of Brisbane's nightclub and dining precinct. **Pros:** lively location; upbeat vibe; free Wi-Fi. **Cons:** limited facilities; no on-site parking; some street noise. $ *Rooms from: A$149* ⊠ *14–20 Constance St., Fortitude Valley* ☎ *07/3319–7888* ⊕ *www.trypbrisbane.com* ☞ *61 rooms, 4 spa suites* |⊙| *Breakfast* ✛ *D1.*

NIGHTLIFE AND PERFORMING ARTS

The Saturday edition of the *Courier–Mail* newspaper (⊕ *www.couriermail.com.au*) lists live gigs and concerts, ballet, opera, theater, jazz, and other events in its Life section, while Friday's *CM2* insert has a comprehensive entertainment guide for the weekend ahead. *The Weekend Edition* (⊕ *www.theweekendedition.com.au*) has suburb-by-suburb listings of Brisbane's best cafés, restaurants, shopping, and nightlife spots, as well as weekly updates on new events and establishments around the city. Alternately, visit *Brisbane Art* (⊕ *www.bneart.com*) for up-to-date listings of arts events and galleries around the city.

PERFORMING ARTS
ARTS CENTERS
Brisbane Powerhouse. Housed in a grand, former coal power station, the Heritage-listed Brisbane Powerhouse hosts frequent, often-free, art exhibitions, live performances, and children's events in its flexible 200- and 400-seat theaters. Cafés, restaurants, bikeways, boardwalks, and picnic areas complement the spacious, contemporary riverside hub, which also adjoins beautiful New Farm Park. A recent renovation added a new café-bar, a roof terrace, and enlarged theater spaces. ⊠ *119 Lamington St., New Farm* ☎ *07/3358–8600 box office, 07/3358–8622 reception* ⊕ *www.brisbanepowerhouse.org.*

NIGHTLIFE
BARS
Cloudland. An "urban oasis" with fanciful design, a retractable glass roof, and street-front waterfall flowing over its contemporary architectural facade, Cloudland restaurant and nightclub woos well-heeled locals and tourists alike with an extensive drinks menu, cut-above food, and an exciting, expensive ambience. ⊠ *641 Ann St., Fortitude Valley* ☎ *07/3872–6600* ⊕ *www.katarzyna.com.au/venues/cloudland.*

Cru Bar + Cellar. Sleek and sophisticated, Cru Bar + Cellar has leather ottomans, a long onyx bar, circa 1800 French chandeliers, and a fine-wine-loving clientele. Cru's huge cellar houses hundreds of top Australian vintages, to drink on-site or later; the cocktail menu is also extensive and impressive. Cheese tasting plates are available all day. It's a good ideal to book in advance for dinner. ⊠ *James St. Market, 22 James St., Fortitude Valley* ☎ *07/3252–2400* ⊕ *www.crubar.com.*

Fodor's Choice ★ **Lefty's Old Time Music Hall.** This trendy, saloon-style bar on bustling Caxton Street mixes old school American charm with modern craft brews and a hefty range of spirits (including more than 100 rye whiskies). Decked out in vintage taxidermy and moody chandeliers, the retro Americana vibe continues with the Southern-themed bar food, including po'boys, corn dogs, and popcorn shrimp (all available until 3 am). A rollicking mix of country and rockabilly tunes burst from the stage and speakers. ⊠ *15 Caxton St., Petrie Terrace* ⊕ *www.leftysmusichall. com* ☞ *Closed Mon. and Tues.*

EARTH'S FASTEST MOVING ISLAND

Moreton Island lies just 35 km (20 miles) offshore. This 38-km-long (23-mile-long) mass is shifting at an estimated 3¼ feet a year toward the Queensland coast. Attractions include tobogganing down sand dunes, bird-watching, dolphin spotting, water sports, and cetacean- and dugong-watching. Camping within Moreton Island National Park is possible (A\$5.95 per person permit; information available at ⊕ *www.parks.nprsr. qld.gov.au/permits*).

CASINOS

Treasury Casino & Hotel. With a "neat and tidy" dress code geared to securing an upscale clientele, The Treasury is a European-style casino with three levels of gaming beneath a stunning four-story atrium. Beneath a seduction of light and color, the facility comes alive at night with more than 80 gaming tables and more than 1,300 machines, as well as six restaurants and six bars. It's open 24 hours. ⊠ *130 William St., City Center* ☎ *07/3306–8888* ⊕ *www. treasurybrisbane.com.au.*

SHOPPING

For more information on shopping in Brisbane, visit ⊕ *www. visitbrisbane.com.au/things-to-do/shopping.*

ANTIQUES

Paddington Antique Centre. Located in a converted theater, the Paddington Antique Centre is brimming with antiques, furniture, collectibles, various bric-a-brac as well as colorful vintage clothing. Around 50 dealers operate within the center, alongside an on-site café. It's open daily 10–5, closing an hour earlier on Sunday. ⊠ *167 Latrobe Terr., Paddington* ☎ *07/3369–8088* ⊕ *www.paddingtonantiquecentre.com.au.*

Woolloongabba Antique Centre. This vibrant, retro-themed warehouse includes 60-plus stalls, an on-site vintage café, and enough antiques and treats to excite the nostalgia in all of us. From fine china, collectibles, and the kitschiest of curiosities, to clothing, records, prints, paintings, home wares, games, and a vast collection of Australiana, it's the perfect place to pick up something unique. It's open every day, 9–5. ⊠ *22 Wellington Rd., Woolloongabba* ☎ *07/3392–1114* ⊕ *www. woolloongabbaantiquecentre.com.*

MALLS AND ARCADES

James Street. This new upmarket lifestyle precinct in Fortitude Valley has an ever-growing array of local fashion, homewares, jewelry, and design stores, alongside trendy cafés and bars. ⊠ *James St., Fortitude Valley* ☎ *07/3850–0111* ⊕ *www.jamesst.com.au.*

MacArthur Central. Historic MacArthur Central, the WWII headquarters of U.S. General Douglas MacArthur, houses boutiques and specialty shops, a food court, and a museum. Located at the bottom of the Queen Street Mall, the streets surrounding the center also feature a range of high-end fashion boutiques including Louis Vuitton, Hermès, and Tiffany & Co. The MacArthur Museum is open to the public Tuesday, Thursday, and Sunday 10–3. ⊠ *201 Edward St., City Center* ☎ *07/3211–7052 museum* ⊕ *www.mmb.org.au.*

FAMILY **Queen Street Mall.** Fun and lively Queen Street Mall, considered Brisbane's best downtown shopping area, attracts around 26 million visitors a year. Nearly a third of a mile long, the mall incorporates 700 retailers and five major shopping centers, including the Myer Centre, Wintergarden, and Queens Plaza, as well as two large department stores, Myer and David Jones, and four arcades: historic Tattersall's Arcade and MacArthur Central, Heritage-listed Brisbane Arcade, and Broadway on the Mall, all housing designer boutiques and a range of specialty stores. On weekends, free entertainment and performances can often be found on the Mall's two open stages. ⊠ *Queen St., City Center* ☎ *07/3006–6200* ⊕ *www.visitbrisbane.com.au/the-city.*

MARKETS

Brisbane Powerhouse Farmers Market. The Brisbane Powerhouse hosts a local produce farmers' market from 6 am to noon every Saturday. Enjoy a fresh, leisurely breakfast on the lawn by the river, and afterward, stroll through nearby New Farm Park. ⊠ *119 Lamington St., New Farm* ☎ *07/3358–8600* ⊕ *www.brisbanepowerhouse.org.*

The Collective Market South Bank. South Bank Parklands hosts a weekend Collective Market, showcasing high-quality and emerging designer clothing, accessories, artwork, craft, food, and music. It runs Friday 5–9, Saturday 10–9, and Sunday 9–4 in Stanley Street Plaza. ⊠ *Grey St., at Stanley St. Plaza, City Center* ☎ *07/3844–2440* ⊕ *www.collectivemarkets.com.au.*

Eat Street Markets. Located on a revamped shipping wharf at riverside Hamilton, this bustling interactive market gives visitors a taste of Brisbane's best street food from over sixty funky shipping container "restaurants." Open Friday and Saturday evening 4–10 and Sunday 10 am–3 pm, there's also a regular line up of live music and entertainment, and hip wares from local artists and makers. Entry costs A$2. ⊠ *Macarthur Ave., Brisbane* ☎ *07/3358–2500* ⊕ *www.eatstreetmarkets.com.*

FAMILY **Riverside Markets.** This eclectic arts-and-crafts bazaar meandering along the Brisbane River sells everything from pressed flowers to hand-painted didgeridoos and homemade treats and clothing. It's open Sunday 7–3. ⊠ *Riverside Centre, 123 Eagle St., City Center* ☎ *07/3870–2807* ⊕ *www.riversidemarkets.com.au.*

State library, Queensland Cultural Centre

OUTDOOR GEAR OUTFITTERS

Kathmandu. This one-stop-shop for outdoor clothing and equipment has camping, climbing, hiking, and traveling goods. ✉ *193 Albert St., Brisbane* ☎ *07/3210–2777* ⊕ *www.kathmandu.com.au.*

Paddy Pallin. With stores throughout Australia, Paddy Pallin sells quality outdoor and travel gear, including hats, footwear, clothing, backpacks, and equipment. On staff are dedicated bushwalkers, rock climbers, and travelers. ✉ *108 Wickham St., Fortitude Valley* ☎ *07/3839–3811* ⊕ *www.paddypallin.com.au.*

WINERY TOURS FROM BRISBANE: SOUTHERN DOWNS

From Brisbane, the Granite Belt is 225 km (140 miles) west, Mt. Tamborine is 62 km (39 miles) southwest, and Scenic Rim wineries are around 135 km (85 miles) southwest.

If the Brisbane cityscape has given you a thirst for pastoral rolling hills—and fabulous wine—you're in luck, because some of Queensland's best viticultural regions lie within a two-hour drive of the city.

Drive two hours west on the Cunningham Highway and you'll reach the Southern Downs, where spring brings the scent of peach and apple blossoms and fall finds the region's 50-plus vineyards, concentrated around Stanthorpe, ripe for harvest. Winter is ideal for wine-country excursions, with clear days and tastings by fireplace by night. This area, extending from Cunninghams Gap in the east to Goondiwindi in the west, Allora in the north to Wallangarra in the south, is known as the Granite Belt.

The local Italian community pioneered viticulture here, planting the first Shiraz grapes in 1965. Today the Granite Belt is the state's largest wine region, with nearly 2,000 acres under vines and more than 50 cellar doors, most attached to family-run and boutique wineries. Thanks to its altitude (2,500–4,000 feet above sea level) and decomposed-granite soils, the region enjoys unique growing and ripening conditions, enabling the production of outstanding, full-bodied reds and extra-crisp whites.

Just over an hour's drive southwest of Brisbane, inland from the Gold Coast, you'll find the world's largest caldera and one of the state's most exciting emerging wine regions: the Scenic Rim. The region's rich volcanic soils, first planted with vines in the late 19th century, now produce fine red and white varieties. On the region's easterly edge, you'll find a dozen wineries and a distillery within a compact area around Mt. Tamborine.

GETTING HERE AND AROUND

Driving yourself is an option but may not be the best idea if you plan to skip the spit bucket on your tasting stops. However, for the self-guiders out there, the Granite Belt and Scenic Rim tourism boards provide downloadable maps. Find Granite Belt winery and walking trails at ⊕ *www.granitebeltwinecountry.com.au*, and Scenic Rim winery and trail maps at ⊕ *www.visitscenicrim.com.au*.

Arguably, the safest way to sample the offerings of the region's wineries is via guided tour. More than half a dozen companies run tours of wineries in the Scenic Rim and Mt. Tamborine areas, but some require groups of at least six people.

TOURS

Cork 'n Fork Winery Tours. Family-run Cork 'n Fork Winery Tours runs daily and overnight viticultural tours for couples and small groups to Mt. Tamborine and the Scenic Rim. Their popular full-day tour includes hotel pickups from the Gold Coast or Brisbane, lunch, and five winery visits with guided tastings. ☎ *07/5543–6584* ⊕ *www.corknfork.com* 🍴 *From A$150.*

Filippo's Tours. This popular operator runs an assortment of specialist food, wine, and brewery tours across the Granite Belt, with departures from both Stanthorpe and Brisbane. Small, customized, group tours are also available. ☎ *07/4681–3130* ⊕ *www.filippostours.com. au* 🍴 *From A$99.*

Granite Highlands Maxi Tours. This local operator runs half-, full-day, and weekend tours of Granite Belt wineries, specializing in the verdant vineyards of Stanthorpe. Departing Brisbane, the Sunshine Coast, and various regional centers, most tours also include meals, sightseeing, and local attractions. ✉ *19 Amosfield Rd., Stanthorpe* ☎ *07/4681–3969, 1800/852969* ⊕ *www.maxitours.com.au* 🍴 *From A$75.*

EXPLORING

Ballandean Estate Wines. Just south of Glen Aplin is the town of Ballandean, home to award-winning Ballandean Estate Wines, the oldest family-owned and -operated vineyard and winery in Queensland. The first grapes were grown on the Granite Belt site in 1931, and the tasting room is the original brick shed built in 1950. The Barrel Room Cafe behind it—with massive, 125-year-old wooden barrels lining one wall—serves modern Italian cuisine, showcasing local produce and quality coffee (lunch Wednesday–Monday, dinner Thursday–Sunday). There are free 45-minute tours of the facility daily at 11 am. ☒ *354 Sundown Rd., Ballandean* ☎ *07/4684–1226* ⊕ *www.ballandeanestate. com* ☒ *Free* ☉ *Cellar door daily 9–5.*

FAMILY **Girraween National Park.** One of the most popular parks in southeast Queensland—meaning "place of flowers"—sits at the end of the New England Tableland, a stepped plateau area with elevations ranging from 1,968 to 4,921 feet. The 17 km (11 miles) of walking tracks, most starting near the information center and picnic area, wind past granite outcrops, giant boulders, eucalyptus forests, and spectacular wildflowers in spring. Along the way you might encounter kangaroos, echidnas, brush-tailed possums, and turquoise parrots. To camp, you'll need a permit from the NPRSR (⊕ *www.qld.gov.au/camping*). ☒ *Ballandean ✛ 11 km (7 miles) north of Wallangarra or 26 km (16 miles) south of Stanthorpe, off the New England Hwy.* ☎ *07/4684–5157* ⊕ *www.nprsr. qld.gov.au/parks/girraween.*

Normanby Wines. This friendly, family-run winery-vineyard hand picks all the grapes on its property. There are seven to choose from, including Verdelho, Shiraz, Durif, Chambourcin, Veraz, Merlot, and traditional fortified varieties. Taste and buy them—including many medal winners—at the cellar door, then wander through the vineyard and native gardens or enjoy a barbecue under the trees. Guided vineyard tours are available for a small extra charge, if staff are available. ☒ *178 Dunns Ave., Harrisville* ☎ *07/5467–1214* ☒ *Free; A$3 tasting* ☉ *Daily 10–5.*

Sirromet Wines at Mount Cotton. Queensland's largest winery sits midway between Brisbane and the Gold Coast. Sirromet's much-lauded wines—distinctive reds, crisp whites, and some terrific blended varieties—can be sampled at their impressive cellar door, alongside coffee and cake, Devonshire tea, and lunchtime platters (bookings required). Elegant on-site restaurant Lurleen's; open at select times Wednesday–Sunday for breakfast, lunch, and dinner; has an alfresco dining area with superb views to Moreton Bay. Live jazz livens things up on weekend afternoons. ☒ *850–938 Mount Cotton Rd., Mount Cotton* ☎ *07/3206–2999* ⊕ *www.sirromet.com* ☒ *Tastings (up to 8 wines) A$5; premium tasting A$30; guided tours from A$20 (Wed.–Sun.)* ☉ *Cellar door daily 9–4:30.*

WHERE TO STAY

$$$$ **Spicers Peak Lodge.** If you're looking for a luxurious, all-inclusive

RESORT mountain retreat with an entire mountaintop to itself and the views to match, look no further. **Pros:** world-class restaurant with terrific wine list; thoughtful, impeccable service; stunning, serene location. **Cons:** all-inclusive package pricey; no public transport to lodge. Ⓢ *Rooms from: A$1199* ✉ *Wilkinsons Rd., Maryvale* ☎ *1300/198386* ⊕ *www. spicersretreats.com/spicers-peak-lodge* ⇄ *10 suites, 2 private lodges* ⏉❘ *All-inclusive.*

$$
B&B/INN
Fodor's Choice
★
🖻 **Vineyard Cottages and Café.** Built around a turn-of-the-20th-century church that's now the Vineyard Cafe and restaurant, this popular property boasts seven period-style cottages set amid 2 acres of manicured gardens, only two blocks from Ballandean village. **Pros:** excellent food and wine; warm, friendly ambience; close to top wineries; disabled friendly. **Cons:** 20 minutes to Stanthorpe; some road noise—request a cottage in back to avoid. Ⓢ *Rooms from: A$230* ✉ *New England Hwy., near Bents Rd., Ballandean* ☎ *07/4684–1270* ⊕ *www.vineyardcottages. com.au* ⇄ *4 cottages, 3 suites* ⏉❘ *Breakfast; No meals; Some meals.*

THE GOLD COAST

Resorts, theme parks, and 300 days of sunshine a year ensure the Gold Coast, the most developed tourist destination and one of the fastest-growing regions in Australia, remains a popular destination year-round. Easter weekend and December through the last week of January and Australian school holidays are peak seasons. Around 80 km (50 miles)—an hour's drive—south of Brisbane, the Gold Coast stretches some 70 km (43 miles) from Labrador in the north to Coolangatta-Tweed Heads in the south, and has now sprawled as far inland as Nerang. Boasting an average daily temperature of 24°C (75°F), it has around three dozen patrolled beaches and 446 km (277 miles) of canals and tidal rivers: nine times the length of the canals of Venice.

GETTING HERE AND AROUND

Gold Coast Airport, also known as Coolangatta Airport, is the region's main transit point.

Access Hope Island via bridges from the west (Oxenford and Coomera) or from the eastern, coastal side (via Paradise Point, Hollywell, and Runaway Bay). Route 4, the Oxenford–Southport Road, begins in Oxenford at the Pacific Motorway's (M1's) Exit 57 and travels through Hope Island on its way to Hope Harbour, on the coast.

Driving distances and times from the Gold Coast via the Pacific Highway are 859 km (533 miles) and 12–13 hours to Sydney; 65 km (40 miles) and less than an hour to Brisbane's outskirts; and 1,815 km (1,125 miles) and 22 hours to Cairns.

The Gold Coast begins 65 km (40 miles) south of Brisbane. The Pacific Motorway, or M1, bypasses Gold Coast towns, but well-marked exits guide you to your destination. If you're coming from Brisbane International Airport by car, take the toll road over Gateway Bridge to avoid traversing Brisbane, then follow the signs to the Gold Coast. Long-distance buses traveling between Sydney and Brisbane also stop at Coolangatta and Surfers Paradise.

Queensland Rail service connects Brisbane to Coomera, Helensvale, Nerang, Robina, and Varsity Lakes stations on the Gold Coast from

4:30 am until midnight. Alight at Coomera or Helensvale for the theme parks and northern suburbs; Nerang for Surfer's Paradise; and Robina or Varsity Lakes for Main Beach and all suburbs south of it. From rail stations, cabs and shuttle buses ferry visitors to nearby beaches, tourist centers, theme parks, and the airport. From any of these stations, it's a short (A$20–A$30) cab ride to the nearest Gold Coast town.

The Gold Coast's own light-rail tram service, G:link, ferries passengers between the tourist hubs of Southport, Surfers Paradise, and Broadbeach. As part of the new service, special go explore cards allow unlimited all-day travel on TransLink's G:link and bus services—including to and from the airport and theme parks—for only A$10. For more information or to purchase a pass, visit ⊕ *www.translink.com.au/goexplore*.

Alternately, Surfside Buslines' Gold Coast Tourist Shuttle runs services around the clock between Gold Coast attractions, theme parks, and the airport, along the strip between Tweed Heads and Southport. Services run at five-minute intervals during the day and at least half-hourly after dark. Buy single tickets or a 3-, 5-, 7-, or 10-day Gold Pass (A$59–A$129) or Freedom Pass (A$79–A$149), which give you unlimited shuttle travel and theme park transfers; the Freedom Pass also includes a return Gold Coast airport transfer.

Approximate taxi fare from Gold Coast Airport to Currumbin is A$35; to Burleigh Heads, A$45; to Broadbeach, A$60; to Surfers Paradise, A$65; to Main Beach, A$70; and to the northern suburbs, more than A$95. Shuttle buses can be cheaper than cabs at A$5–A$35, depending on your destination. Before boarding, confirm that the bus stops near your accommodation.

Rental cars are a cost-effective option if you plan to tour the area. Most major car rental agencies have offices in Brisbane, Surfers Paradise, and at Gold Coast Airport. Companies operating on the Gold Coast include Avis, Budget, and Thrifty. Four-wheel-drive vehicles are available. It's strongly recommended that you prebook.

Airport Gold Coast Airport (*Coolangatta Airport*). ⊠ *1 Eastern Ave., Bilinga* ☎ *07/5589–1100* ⊕ *www.goldcoastairport.com.au.*

Car Rental Avis. ⊠ *Cypress Ave., Surfers Paradise* ☎ *07/5583–6477, 13–6333 reservations* ⊕ *www.avis.com.au.* **Budget.** ⊠ *1 Ferny Ave., Surfers Paradise* ☎ *07/5538–1344, 1300/362848 reservations* ⊕ *www.budget.com.au.* **Thrifty.** ⊠ *1006 Surfers Paradise Blvd., Surfers Paradise* ☎ *07/5570–9999, 1300/139009 reservations* ⊕ *www.thrifty.com.au.*

Ferry Zane's Water Taxi. ⊠ *Runaway Bay Marina, 247 Bayview St., Runaway Bay* ☎ *0404/905–970* ⊕ *www.inzanewatertaxis.com.au.*

Public Bus and Train Con-x-ion. ☎ *1300/266946* ⊕ *www.con-x-ion.com.* **Gold Coast Tourist Shuttle.** ☎ *1300/655655* ⊕ *www.gcshuttle.com.au.* **Greyhound Australia.** ⊠ *Surfers Paradise Transit Centre, 10 Beach Rd., Surfers Paradise* ☎ *1300/473946, 07/5531–6677* ⊕ *www.greyhound.com.au.* **Queensland Rail.** ☎ *13–1617* ⊕ *www.queenslandrail.com.au.* **Surfside Buslines.** ⊠ *43 Commerce Dr., Surfers Paradise* ☎ *13–1230* ⊕ *www.surfside.com.au.* **Translink.** ☎ *13–1230* ⊕ *www.translink.com.au.*

Taxi Gold Coast Cabs. ☎ *13–1008* ⊕ *www.gccabs.com.au.*

The Gold Coast

TO BRISBANE · Jacobs Well
Luscombe
Southern Moreton Bays Islands National Park
Pimpama
92
Tamborine National Park
Dreamworld / White Water World
Sanctuary Cove
South Stradbroke Island
Tamborine
Mt. Tamborine
Warner Bros. Movie World
Coomera · Hope Island
Oxenford
Paradise Country · Helensvale
Eagle Heights
Australian Outback Spectacular
Boyland
Labrador
The Spit
Wet 'n' Wild Water World
Sea World
North Tamborine
Nerang
2
20
Main Beach
Southport
90
GOLD COAST
Canungra
40
Surfers Paradise
Beaudesert
Wonglepong
BEECHMONT RANGE
Broadbeach
50
Mermaid Beach
3
Nobby Beach
Mudgeeraba
97
Burleigh Heads
99
David Fleay Wildlife Park
Palm Beach
Beechmont
Reedy Creek
Tallebudgera Beach
Currumbin Beach
Currumbin Wildlife Sanctuary
Tugun
Point Danger
Gold Coast Hinterland
Springbrook Nat'l Park
Coolangatta
1
Tweed Heads
Darlington
Lamington National Park
98
Springbrook
MCPHERSON RANGE
Banora Point
Fingal Head
NEW SOUTH WALES
Kingscliff

0 ___ 10 mi
0 ___ 10 km

South Pacific Ocean

COOMERA AND OXENFORD

48–51 km (30–32 miles) south of Brisbane.

The biggest draws of these two northern Gold Coast suburbs are their family-oriented theme parks—Dreamworld, Warner Bros. Movie World, Wet 'n' Wild Water World, Paradise Country, the Australian Outback Spectacular, and WhiteWater World. The sprawling complexes have many attractions: each takes about a day for a leisurely visit.

EXPLORING

FAMILY **Australian Outback Spectacular.** The Australian Outback Spectacular, one of six Village Roadshow theme parks in the area, lets visitors experience "the heart and soul of the Australian Outback." The evening show, High Country Legends, features state-of-the-art visual effects and performances from top local stunt riders, interactive team racing, and live country and orchestral music. Guests get a hearty, three-course dinner and complimentary drinks during the 90-minute, A$23-million production, plus a souvenir stockman's hat. Doors open at 6:15 pm;

showtime is at 7:30 pm. A special Sunday matinee show takes place at 12:30 pm once a month, more frequently in high season. Return transfers from Gold Coast hotels cost around A$20; on-site parking is free. This park (and neighboring theme parks Paradise Country, Warner Bros Movie World, and Wet 'N,' Wild Water World) is a short taxi ride from Helensvale station. If driving, take Exit 60 at Oxenford off the M1 Pacific Motorway. ⊠ *Pacific Motorway, Oxenford* ☎ *13–3386, 07/5519–6200 bookings* ⊕ *outbackspectacular.com.au* ✉ *A$99.99, Sat. A$109.99* ⊙ *Tues.–Sat. 7:30 pm, Sun. 12:30 pm (once a month)*.

FAMILY   **Dreamworld.** At Coomera's Dreamworld, the main draw is the "big

Fodor'sChoice   nine": high-tech thrill rides including the aptly-named Giant Drop,

★   a nearly 400-foot vertical plummet akin to skydiving; the nine-story, 360-degree pendulum swing of Claw; the turbulent Wipeout and screamingly fast, scarily high Tower of Terror; and Tail Spin, a soaring mini airplane adventure; plus five roller coasters and an all-new interactive motorsports precinct. But it's certainly not all thrills and spills. Take a leisurely walk through Tiger Island where Bengal tigers and their gorgeous cubs swim, play, and even let you pet (and feed!) them; or get your picture taken with a cuddly koala in Koala Country. See more than 800 other native animals at the conservation-focused on-site Wildlife Sanctuary (including crocs), cool off in the artificial lagoon, or cruise the park's waterways on a paddle wheeler. Kids enjoy the ABC Kids World and DreamWorks Experience, alongside classic favorites like bumper cars, river rapids, and the Rocky Hollow Log Ride. Book ahead and you can also try the Flowrider (A$7.50), an amalgam of surfing and skateboarding, or, at the end of the day, join a guided, two-hour Sunset Safari (A$29) for close-up encounters with tigers and native wildlife (from 4:45 pm, in season). Make the most of your day by signing up for Q4U virtual queueing on your smartphone (A$15), which saves you from waiting in line for popular rides. The park is 45 minutes outside Brisbane and 20-25 minutes from Surfers Paradise along the M1 Pacific Motorway: take Exit 54 at Coomera. Purchase tickets online for discounts and specials. ⊠ *1 Dreamworld Pkwy., Coomera* ☎ *07/5588–1111, 1800/073300* ⊕ *www.dreamworld. com.au* ✉ *Entry (includes WhiteWater World and Dream World) A$85; 7-day pass A$89; 21-day pass A$105* ⊙ *Daily 10–5*.

FAMILY   **Paradise Country.** Billed as "an authentic Australian farm experience," the park appeals to families with wildlife tours, farmyard and bird feedings, sheep shearing, boomerang throwing, and displays of horsemanship. Meanwhile, adults can book a private wine tasting session, while kids enjoy koala cuddling, kangaroo feeding, wagon rides, and the baby animal nursery. An optional barbecue lunch is also available. The park is directly behind the Australian Outback Spectacular. Car parking spaces are limited. ⊠ *Pacific Motorway, Oxenford* ☎ *13–3386, 07/5519–6200* ⊕ *paradisecountry.com.au* ✉ *A$29.99; A$39.99 (tour and lunch)* ⊙ *Daily 9:30–4:30*.

FAMILY   **Warner Bros. Movie World.** One of the few movie theme parks outside the United States, Warner Bros. Movie World mixes an old Hollywood ambiance with live character shows, interactive adventures, and thrill rides for young and old. Get airborne on the Batwing Spaceshot, accelerate to 100 km (62 miles) an hour in two seconds on the awesome Superman Escape, or fight alien invasion in the new Justice League 3D. You can also check out vehicles, props, and costumes from the Batman blockbuster *Dark Knight*; enter a custom-built "immersive" movie set to watch precision driving and action-film-style stunts in the new *Hollywood Stunt Driver* show; and rocket through the air on the new Green Lantern coaster (with the steepest drop in the world). Little kids love to see the daily Main Street Star Parade (3:30 pm) and Looney Toons Dance Party (10:45 am), visit Bugs Bunny and friends in the WB Fun Zone, or get behind the wheel at the new Junior Driving School. With a large portion of its area now covered by a 43,055-square-foot roof, this park is a smart choice in bad weather. It's adjacent to Australian Outback Spectacular. ⊠ *Pacific Motorway, Oxenford* ☎ *13–3386, 07/5573–8399* ⊕ *www.movieworld.com.au* ✑ *General admission A\$89; multipark Holiday Pass (consecutive entry to SeaWorld, Movie World, and Wet'n'Wild) A\$94 7-day pass, A\$99 21-day pass* ⊗ *Daily 10–5.*

FAMILY **Wet 'n' Wild Water World.** Oxenford's Wet 'n' Wild Water World boasts magnificent, adrenaline-pumping water slides; a wave pool with a 3-foot-high surf; tandem, entwined-tube and family-friendly slides; and the new Surfrider that simulates the sensation of surfing the world's biggest waves. In the Extreme H20 zone, you can plunge down pitch-black spirals of water in the Black Hole, hang on through the churning Tornado, race your friends on the Mach 5, or survive the scary Kamikaze: a giant, U-shape, friction-free slide with a near-vertical 36-foot drop. Enough aquatic thrills? Take it easy on Calypso Beach, a "tropical island" fringed with white-sand beaches, or relax in the rolling surf of the 3-million-liter Giant Wave Pool. Kids love Buccaneer Bay, a pirate-themed aquatic playground with multiple levels, and the new Wet 'n' Wild Junior area, featuring another eight kid-friendly slides, including mini versions of the park's most popular thrill rides. Select pools and slides are heated May through September, when days are often still sunny and warm. The park is ½ km (¼ mile) down the Pacific Highway from Warner Bros. Movie World. ⊠ *Pacific Hwy., Oxenford* ☎ *13–3386, 07/5556–1660* ⊕ *www.wetnwild.com.au* ✑ *General admission A\$64; multipark Holiday Pass (entry to SeaWorld, Movie World, and Wet'n'Wild) 7-day pass A\$84, 21-day pass A\$89* ⊗ *Oct.–Apr. 10–5; May.–Sept. 10–3:30, 10–4 weekends.*

FAMILY
Fodor's Choice
★
WhiteWater World. Directly adjacent to Dreamworld, and included in all Dreamworld ticket purchases, is the Gold Coast's latest thrill-seeker's water park, WhiteWater World. Here you'll find state-of-the-art water rides including the Blue Ringed Octopus (BRO), a convoluted eight-lane racer slide; The Rip, Australia's biggest corkscrew-cored whirl-pool; the dual-bowl Little Rippers ride; the Temple of Huey inner-tube "aquacoaster"; and the mat-free "drop and loop" of The Wedgie. Small kids will enjoy Pipeline Plunge, an enormous aquatic tree fort, while under-fives are taken care of at shady, fully supervised Wiggle Bay. Relax and let the current take you away in the Cave of Waves, or learn to surf before or after public park hours by booking into Get Wet Surf School (A\$75, including photos, transfers, and a guaranteed

7

board stand-up). The park is close to Coomera railway station; from there, catch a Surfside bus to the park. Prepurchase tickets online for discounts and specials. ⊠ *Dreamworld Pkwy., Coomera* ☎ *07/5588–1111, 1800/438938 Get Wet Surf School* ⊕ *www.whitewaterworld.com.au* ⊠ *A$49 single entry; A$85 1-day World Pass (Dreamworld and WhiteWater World); Holiday World Pass (unlimited entry to Dreamworld, WhiteWater World, and Skypoint Observation Deck) A$89 7-day pass, A$95 21-day pass* ⊗ *Daily 10–3, subject to weather. Hrs extended in summer and school holidays.*

WHERE TO STAY

$$$$ ▦ **Peppers Ruffles Lodge & Spa.** Set
RESORT high on a hill in manicured gardens, this luxurious retreat boasts six private villas, three tree houses, and an executive lodge suite, all with sweeping views of Gold Coast beaches and the surrounding bushland. **Pros:** architecturally superb; breathtaking setting and views; terrific food. **Cons:** must book well ahead; off the beaten track. ⑤ *Rooms from: A$479* ⊠ *423 Ruffles Rd., Willow Vale* ☎ *07/5546–7411* ⊕ *www.peppers.com.au/ruffles-lodge* ⟿ *10 villas, including 3 tree houses and 1 suite* ⑩ *Breakfast* ☞ *Restaurant closed Mon. and Tues.*

HOPE ISLAND

This isn't your average island. Like several Gold Coast islands, it is actually a mile or two inland and circled by the Coomera River and a series of canals. The resort has a marina full of luxury launches and yachts, two golf courses, a swanky hotel, beautiful condos, and upscale restaurants, nightclubs, and shops. Stop by if you're passing through for a glimpse into jet-set culture, Queensland style.

Hope Island is accessed via bridges from the west or east. Route 4, also known as the Oxenford–Southport Road, passes straight through.

SOUTHPORT AND MAIN BEACH

16 km (10 miles) southeast of Oxenford.

South of Southport, look for the turnoff to the Spit, a natural peninsula that stretches 4 km (2½ miles) north, almost to the tip of South Stradbroke Island. Seaworld Drive runs the full length of the Spit, from Mariner's Cove (a popular covered area with affordable restaurants and fast-food outlets) to a nature reserve. This narrow peninsula is bordered by the Pacific Ocean to the east and the calm waters of the Broadwater (a long lagoon) to the west. Two of the Gold Coast's most opulent hotels face each other across Seaworld Drive and are connected to Marina Mirage, arguably the most elegant shopping precinct on the Gold Coast. An assortment of adventure sports operators can also be found in this area, including jet boating and skiing, helicopter flights, fishing charters, electric bike rentals, surf schools, and sailing lessons, Farther up the road is the SeaWorld theme park itself.

EXPLORING

FAMILY **SeaWorld.** Australia's largest marine theme park, SeaWorld lets visitors get up close and personal with its resident dolphins, fur seals, sea lions, Fairy penguins, and polar bears. Hand-feed the 100-plus eagle, manta,

Main beach in Byron Bay, Queensland's Gold Coast

and sting rays at Ray Reef, or take a walk through Shark Bay, the world's largest artificial lagoon system for sharks, where a state-of-the-art dual enclosure system keeps dangerous tiger sharks in one section and harmless reef sharks, rays, and fish in another. Patrons can dive in the latter, and get close-up views of the former through the massive windows that separate the lagoons. If you're after even more of a thrill, jump on board the Sea Viper, Jet Rescue, or new Storm roller coasters, or make a splash at the park's various waterslides and interactive pool areas. Take a break and take in the view from the Sky High cable cars, or speed around the park on SeaWorld Monorail. Whatever you do, don't miss the daily Jet Stunt Extreme show, featuring the gravity-defying talents of the world's top Jet Ski stunt performers. Accommodation packages are offered at the adjacent SeaWorld Resort. ⊠ *Seaworld Dr., oceanside end of this long street, The Spit, Main Beach, South-port* ☎ *13–3386, 07/5588–2222* ⊕ *www.seaworld.com.au* ✉ *General admission A$79; multipark Holiday Pass (consecutive entry to Sea-World, Movie World, and Wet'n'Wild) 7-day pass A$84, 21-day pass A$89* ⊙ *Daily 10–5.*

SPORTS AND THE OUTDOORS

BOAT TOURS

FAMILY

Fodor'sChoice

★

Paradise Jet Boating. The thrill-seekers way to sightsee, these high-speed jet boats rocket through the Gold Coast's scenic beaches and water-ways, treating passengers to 360-degree spins, high speed drifting, and other exciting maneuvers along the way. Tours pass through SeaWorld theme park, the mansions of Sovereign Island, and the open waters of Moreton Bay Marine Park and South Stradbroke Island, where dolphins, wallabies, and other wildlife can often be spotted. Customized tours are also available on request. ⊠ *Shop 7B, Mariners Cove Marina, 60 Seaworld Dr., Southport* ☎ *07/5526–3089, 1300/538262* ⊕ *www.paradisejetboating.com.au* ⊠ *From A$59.*

CYCLING

Gold Coast Bike Tours. The Gold Coast's first on-beach cycling experience, this group runs daily tours for up to 13 people and is a great way to stay active while taking in the beauty of the region's famous coastline. The half-day guided rides start at Surfers Paradise and run 12 km (7 miles) in length, encompassing various stops and points of interest along the way (including swim breaks), before finishing with a bite to eat overlooking the luxury marina. You may also simply rent a bike and go your own way. ☎ *0405/327–004* ⊠ *Guided tour A$89, bike rental A$25–A$35.*

SURFING

Get Wet Surf School. The Gold Coast, renowned for long, white, sandy beaches and reliable breaks, is a terrific place to surf. Of the patrolled beaches, Main Beach, Surfers Paradise, Broadbeach, Mermaid, Miami, and Nobby are the most popular; Kirra Beach, in the south, is arguably the area's best surf beach. Though the challenging break at Kirra is perhaps best left to the pros, most Gold Coast beaches are suitable for grommets (beginners). There are plenty of local surf schools happy to teach you, and board and wetsuit hire outlets flank popular beaches. Local surfers and lifeguards are good sources of information about surf conditions and hazards—just remember to stay between the red and yellow flags! Get Wet Surf School holds twice-daily group lessons (up to six students per coach) at a sheltered, crowd-free beach off the Spit, just north of Surfers Paradise, as well as lessons outside park hours in the controlled environment of WhiteWater World's large wave pool (heated in winter). They also host private lessons and multiday surf tours. ⊠ *Seaworld Dr., Main Beach, Southport* ☎ *1800/438938* ⊕ *www. getwetsurf.com* ⊠ *A$55 (beach), A$110 (private), A$75 (wave pool)* ☉ *Daily 10 am and 1 pm (beach); wave pool according to demand.*

WHERE TO EAT AND STAY

$$$$
JAPANESE
FAMILY
✕ **Misono Japanese Steakhouse.** Run by charismatic chefs, who clearly love to please a crowd, this popular Teppanyaki restaurant is as much about the spectacle of their meal as the quality ingredients and perfectly executed flavors. Try the succulent fillet steak with teriyaki chicken, traditional tofu and hibachi vegetables, or salmon and lobster tail. A deluxe seafood banquet includes fresh local prawns, scallops, bugs, and fish. Wash it all down with your pick of six blends of sake or a signature cocktail, and before you know it you'll be joining in the end-of-night sing-along led by restaurant "Rock Star" Nobu, topping off what truly has to be one of the Gold Coast's most unique and fun-filled dining experiences. ■ TIP➜ Take advantage of the early bird special (A$39.95) Sunday–Friday at 5:30 and 6 pm, and all night Wednesday. $ *Average main: A$65* ⊠ *Marriott Hotel, 158 Ferny Ave., Level 3, Surfers Paradise* ☎ *07/5592–9770* ☉ *No lunch* ⌂ *Reservations essential.*

$$$
SEAFOOD
✕ **Omeros Bros Seafood Restaurant.** This iconic seafood restaurant perched on the waterfront at the lovely Marina Mirage center has dishes spanning the seafood spectrum—from Bouillabaisse and classic surf-and-turf

to local barramundi, lobster, oysters, mud crab, and Moreton Bay bugs. But it's not just creatures of the deep available; there is also a tempting selection of meat, vegetarian, and pasta dishes, and an extensive dessert menu and wine list. ⑤ *Average main: A$36* ✉ *Marina Mirage, Seaworld Dr., Shop 55/74, Southport* ☎ *07/5591–7222* ⊕ *www.omerosbros.com.*

$$$$ ⟁ **Palazzo Versace.** The famous Italian fashion house lent its flair to
HOTEL this expansive, opulent waterfront hotel—the first of its kind in the
Fodor's Choice world. **Pros:** five-star service and dining; free self parking; refurbished in
★ 2015; all rooms include a spa bath. **Cons:** pricey; in-room Wi-Fi extra. ⑤ *Rooms from: A$474* ✉ *94 Seaworld Dr., adjoining Marina Mirage, Southport* ☎ *07/5509–8000* ⊕ *www.palazzoversace.com* ⟿ *146 rooms, 54 suites* ⏏ *Breakfast.*

SHOPPING

Marina Mirage Gold Coast. The sleek Marina Mirage Gold Coast is perhaps the most beautiful shopping and dining complex on the Gold Coast. Among its 80-plus stores are high-end gift and homewares, jewelry, and designer fashion boutiques, including Hermès, Christensen Copenhagen, and Calvin Klein, along with famous Australian brands, fine waterfront restaurants, beauty salons and day spas, and marina facilities. On Saturday morning (7–11 am), buy fresh gourmet produce at the Marina Mirage Gourmet Farmers' Markets. Surfside buses 750 and 715 stop at the door. ✉ *74 Seaworld Dr., Main Beach, Southport* ☎ *07/5555–6400, 07/3103–2325 market* ⊕ *www.marinamirage.com.au.*

BROADBEACH

8 km (5 miles) south of Southport.

With clean beaches, great cafés, and trendy nightspots, Broadbeach is one of the most popular areas on the Gold Coast, especially with locals. It's also home to mega-shopping mall Pacific Fair and a good base for visiting the wildlife parks south of town.

EXPLORING

FAMILY **Currumbin Wildlife Sanctuary.** A Gold Coast institution and perhaps the
Fodor's Choice most ecologically minded wildlife facility in the region, Currumbin
★ Wildlife Sanctuary is a 70-acre, not-for-profit National Trust Reserve featuring more than 60 koalas and an on-site wildlife hospital. Established in 1947 as a lorikeet sanctuary, it now shelters a wide variety of Australian species, including kangaroos, crocodiles, wombats, dingoes, Tasmanian devils, echidnas, emus, and rare birds. Ride the on-site mini train between the Park's different precincts, or take in one of the more than 10 daily animal feedings, shows, and performances. Currumbin's friendly 'roos (often with joeys in their pouches!) love to be petted and hand-fed, and the fleet of young koalas make for perfect cuddle and photo opportunities. Come at 8 am or 4 pm when the lorikeets are fed, or book a Segway Safari tour (A$45 for 50 minutes). Kids also enjoy the new Blinky Bill show, twice daily. The park also provides return transfers to and from the Gold Coast (book at ☎ *07/5534–0879*). All revenue goes toward Currumbin's work protecting, treating, and rehabilitating local wildlife. ■ **TIP➜ Tickets are much cheaper if bought online in advance, especially in low season.** ✉ *28 Tomewin St., off*

SURFERS PARADISE

Before the Gold Coast existed as a tourism entity, there was Surfers Paradise: a stunning 3-km (2-mile) stretch of beach with great surf, 5 km (3 miles) south of Southport. Now overrun with high-rises, it's still a vibrant beachside town, with plentiful shopping options and an emergent arts and fine-dining culture (check out the 4217 for some of the region's up and coming artisans and providores (⊕ www.the4217. com). Regardless, nightlife is still the main draw: head to Orchid, Elkhorn, and Cavill avenues. Or, for stunning 360-degree views of the entire coast and hinterland, venture up to the SkyPoint observation deck and Seventy7 Café + Bar located on the 77th floor of Surfers' famous Q1 Tower, the tallest building in the southern hemisphere.

Surfers Paradise Beachfront Markets. Thrice weekly, crowds flock to haggle for handmade crafts and gifts at the busy Surfers Paradise Beachfront Markets. ⊠ *The Esplanade, between Hanlan St. and Elkhorn Ave., Surfers Paradise* ☉ *Wed., Fri., and Sun. 3–8 pm.*

Gold Coast Hwy., Currumbin ⊹ 14 km (8½ miles) south of Broadbeach ☎ *07/5534–1266, 1300/886511* ⊕ *www.cws.org.au* ⊠ *General admission A$49; Koala Experience Pass A$79* ☉ *Daily 8–5.*

FAMILY **David Fleay Wildlife Park.** Located in the town of Burleigh Heads—7 km (4½ miles) south of Broadbeach—and named for an Australian wildlife naturalist, the park features a boardwalk trail through pristine wetlands and rain forests. Koalas, kangaroos, dingoes, platypuses, and crocodiles, grouped together in separate zones according to their natural habitat, are just some of the creatures you might see. A state-of-the-art nocturnal house displays threatened species and the elusive platypus. There's also a café and a gift shop. Family passes give a significant discount on admission. ■TIP➜ Daily presentations are free; the platypus feeding at 2:45 pm is a must-see. ⊠ *Tallebudgera Creek Rd., near W. Burleigh Rd., Burleigh Heads* ☎ *07/5576–2411* ⊕ *www.nprsr.qld.gov. au* ⊠ *A$20.80* ☉ *Daily 9–5.*

WHERE TO STAY

$$ 🛏 **Jupiters Hotel & Casino.** This massive, glitzy resort in central Broad-
RESORT beach has a lot more going for it than its bustling, 24-hour casino and entertainment center. **Pros:** modern, luxury furnishings and facilities; close to shopping centers; free parking for guests. **Cons:** expensive in-room Wi-Fi; can be noisy on weekends. $ *Rooms from: A$299* ⊠ *Broadbeach Island, Casino Dr., off Gold Coast Hwy.* ☎ *07/5592–8100, 1800/074344* ⊕ *www.jupitersgoldcoast.com.au* ⇄ *561 rooms, 29 suites, 2 penthouses* ❍ *Breakfast.*

$$ 🛏 **QT Gold Coast.** One of Queensland's most popular destination hotels,
HOTEL this vibrant retro-meets-modern resort boasts 360-degree views of the
Fodor'sChoice beach and hinterland, on-site restaurants and bars, and enough quirk
★ and energy to make it stand brightly apart in a glut of beachside high rises. **Pros:** lively atmosphere and design; excellent on-site food options; close to beach; free (though not very fast) Wi-Fi. **Cons:** design getting a

little tired; parking costs A$8 per night; area can be noisy at night (ask for a room on a higher level). ⑤ *Rooms from: A$199* ⊠ *7 Staghorn Ave., Surfers Paradise* ☎ *07/5584–1200* ⊕ *www.qtgoldcoast.com.au* ⏎ *282 rooms, 15 suites* ⑩ *Breakfast; No meals; Some meals.*

$$$ ⛱ **The Wave Resort.** This ultramodern high-rise apartment resort is one of
RESORT Broadbeach's most luxurious. **Pros:** free parking, Wi-Fi, and cable TV; helpful staff; well-maintained and sound-proofed rooms. **Cons:** minimum three-night (or, in peak periods, five-night) stay; no meal plans. ⑤ *Rooms from: A$230* ⊠ *89–91 Surf Parade* ☎ *07/5555–9200* ⊕ *www.thewaveresort.com.au* ⏎ *118 apartments* ⑩ *No meals.*

NIGHTLIFE

Howl at the Moon. This lively lounge bar is fun if you like sing-alongs and know the words to hits from the '80s, '90s, and today. Every night, pianists with vocal skills belt out a medley of tunes (some requested by patrons) on baby grands to an appreciative crowd of thirty- and fortysomethings. Share a plate of tapas, book a private karaoke room, or grab a cosmo and hit the dance floor. ⊠ *58 Cavill Ave., Surfers Paradise* ☎ *1300/004695* ⊕ *www.howlatthemoon.com.au.*

Jupiters Casino. Find flamboyant, round-the-clock entertainment alongside 70-plus blackjack, baccarat, craps, sic bo, Texas Hold'em poker, and keno tables, and more than 1,400 gaming machines at this casino. There are also several private gaming and members' club rooms. Thanks to the casino's ongoing A$345-million expansion, there are seven more restaurants and eight bars to come. The elaborate new 2,300-seat showroom hosts glitzy stage shows, touring acts, and a range of concerts. ⊠ *Casino Dr., off Gold Coast Hwy.* ☎ *07/5592–8100* ⊕ *www.jupitersgoldcoast.com.au.*

SHOPPING

Fodor's Choice **Pacific Fair.** A sprawling indoor/outdoor shopping hub, the recently rede-
★ veloped Pacific Fair is Queensland's largest mall, featuring Myer and David Jones department stores, major retailers, and more than 400 specialty stores and services (including travel agencies, fashion outlets, and sports and outdoor gear). For a breather, head to the landscaped grounds with restaurants and cafés dotted around sparkling pools and water features, a children's park, and village green, or take in a movie at the 12-screen cinema complex. Pacific Fair is open Monday–Wednesday, and Friday and Saturday until 5:30 pm, Sunday until 4 pm, and Thursday until 9 pm, with select stores, supermarkets, and restaurants extending beyond. ⊠ *Hooker Blvd., at Gold Coast Hwy., opposite Jupiters Casino* ☎ *07/5581–5100* ⊕ *www.pacificfair.com.au.*

GOLD COAST HINTERLAND

No visit to the Gold Coast would be complete without an excursion to the region's verdant hinterland. The natural grandeur of the area lies in dramatic contrast to the human-made excesses of the coastal strip. The Gold Coast Hinterland's superb national parks and nature reserves protect magnificent waterfalls, natural rock pools, mountain lookouts with expansive views of the surrounding terrain and coast, and an array of wildlife. Walking trails traverse rain forest dense with ancient trees.

Among the parks lie boutique wineries and quaint villages where a high-rise is anything over one story. The parks form part of a unique, ancient geological region known as the Scenic Rim: a chain of mountains running parallel to the coast through southeast Queensland and northern New South Wales. Because it rises to 3,000 feet above sea level, some parts of the hinterland are 4°C–6°C (7°F–11°F) cooler than the coast.

GETTING HERE AND AROUND

The Hinterland's main areas—Tamborine Mountain, Lamington National Park, and Springbrook—can be reached from the Pacific Highway or via Beaudesert from Brisbane, and are a 30- to 40-minute drive inland from the Gold Coast. To reach Tamborine, around 80 km (50 miles) south of Brisbane and 36 km (24 miles) from Southport, take Exit 57 off the Pacific Motorway to the Oxenford–Tamborine Road; or take Exit 71 off the Pacific Motorway, the Nerang–Beaudesert Road, to Canungra. From Canungra, follow the signs to Tamborine, 4 km (2½ miles) along Tamborine Mountain Road. The Gold Coast Hinterland is ideal for touring by car: rent a vehicle, arm yourself with local maps, fill the tank, and take to the hills.

TOURS

Araucaria Ecotours. Departing Brisbane, this eco-certified company runs single and multiday guided tours of Mt. Tamborine and the Scenic Rim, taking in its rich diversity of wildlife and habitat. Travel options include camping, bird-watching, glowworm cave tours, wine tasting, and more. ☎ *07/5544–1283* ⊕ *www.learnaboutwildlife.com* ✉ *From A$99.*

JPT Tour Group. This tour company (also known as Australian Day Tours) picks up passengers from Gold Coast hotels and the Brisbane Transit Centre daily at 8:45 am and travels via Tamborine Mountain to the Hinterland and O'Reilly's Rainforest Retreat, before returning to the Gold Coast at 5:30 pm (Brisbane at 6 pm). Tour highlights include the Mt. Tamborine Gallery Walk, Mountain View Alpaca Farm, and lunch, and bird-feeding at O'Reilly's. The company also runs nightly tours and guided walks through local Hinterland caves, which, when the sun is down, light up spectacularly with populations of glowworms. ⊠ *Shop 18, 2 Elkhorn Ave., Surfers Paradise* ☎ *1300/781362, 07/5630–1602* ⊕ *www.jpttours.com* ✉ *From A$110.*

Southern Cross Day Tours. Keeping a good distance from the crowds, this father and son team leads expeditions to the natural wonders of the area, including several national parks, plus wildlife spotting and cultural activities along the way. ⊠ *5a/3078 Surfers Paradise Blvd., Surfers Paradise* ☎ *1300/762665* ⊕ *southerncrossdaytours.com.au* ✉ *From A$58.*

EXPLORING

Fodor's Choice ★ **Lamington National Park.** Part of the Gondwana Rainforests of Australia World Heritage Area, beautiful Lamington National Park is a lush, subtropical-temperate zone that shelters abundant and highly diverse plant and animal life. Forming part of the largest subtropical rain forest in the world, its 50,600-acre expanse comprises two sections: Binna Burra and Green Mountains. Find Antarctic beech trees dating back more than 3,000 years, as well as waterfalls, mountain pools, breathtaking views, bright wildflowers, and more than 160 native bird species. The Park

Luke's Bluff Lookout on O'Reilly's Plateau, Lamington National Park

is laced with 160 km (100 miles) of bushwalking tracks, ranging from 1.2 km (¾ mile) to 54 km (34 miles), with campsites along the way. All park camping areas require nightly permits (A$5.95 per person), obtained in advance. ⊠ *Binna Burra* ☎ *13–7468* ⊕ *www.nprsr.qld.gov. au* ✉ *Free* ⊗ *Daily 24 hrs.*

Springbrook National Park. The peaks of Springbrook National Park rise to around 3,000 feet, dominating the skyline west of the Gold Coast. The World Heritage-listed park has four regions: scenic Springbrook plateau, Mt. Cougal, Natural Bridge, and Numinbah. Highlights include waterfalls and cascades, Jurassic-Age hoop pines, ancient rain forest, and abundant native birds and wildlife. Thanks to steep, winding roads and longish distances between sections, it takes at least a full day to explore this large park. It's about 30 km (19 miles) from the tiny hamlet of Springbrook to Natural Bridge—a waterfall that cascades through a cavern roof into an icy pool (reach it via a half-mile circuit track, an hour round-trip). This cavern is home to Australia's largest glowworm colony, which at night illuminates the rock walls to stunning effect. Several waterfalls, including the area's largest, Purling Brook Falls, can be reached via a steepish 4-km (2½-mile) path (allow 15 minutes for each half-mile). The 54-km Gold Coast Hinterland Great Walk extends from the Settlement campground to Green Mountains campsite in Tamborine National Park. For those short on time or energy, the lookout near the parking lot has beautiful waterfall views. Camping is permitted only in designated private campgrounds. ⊠ *Springbrook* ☎ *13–7468* ⊕ *www. explorespringbrook.com* ✉ *Free* ⊗ *Daily dawn–dusk.*

Tamborine National Park. More than 20 million years ago, volcanic eruptions created rugged landscapes, while fertile volcanic soils produced the luxuriant tracts of rain forest that make up the enchanting Tamborine National Park. This is the most developed region of the Gold Coast Hinterland, and it's worth spending at least a day or two here. Apart from the natural environment, there are wineries, lodges, restaurants, and the famed Gallery Walk, a 1-km-long (½-mile-long) street lined with art galleries. Some of the simplest (under two hours) and best trails here are the Cedar Creek Falls Track, with waterfall views; Palm Grove Rainforest Circuit; and Macdonald Rainforest Circuit, a quieter walk popular with bird-watchers. Start your visit with a stop at Tamborine Mountain Visitor Information Centre, open 10 am to 4 pm daily, and don't forget to stop by the local Botantic Gardens for a rest and a picnic. Several fragmented parks make up Tamborine National Park, including Cedar Creek, Palm Grove, Joalah, The Knoll, Witches Falls and MacDonald. To the east of Witches Falls is **Joalah National Park,** where a 1½-km (1-mile) circuit takes you to a rocky pool at the base of Curtis Falls. ✉ *Main Western Rd., Mt. Tamborine* ☎ *07/5545–3200 information center* ⊕ *www.tamborinemtncc.org.au* 🖃 *Free.*

SPORTS AND THE OUTDOORS
HIKING
Bushwalking is a popular pastime in the national parks and nature reserves of the Gold Coast Hinterland, where an extensive network of well-maintained scenic trails caters to recreational walkers, serious hikers, campers, and wildlife lovers. The region's many protected wilderness tracts, including World Heritage–listed Gondwana Rainforests of Australia (within Springbook National Park), contain hundreds of well-marked trails that vary from easy half-hour strolls to steep half-day hikes and multiday treks. Most Hinterland walks offer spectacular views and sights.

However, conditions can be challenging and changeable, so before setting out on longer hikes, get suitably equipped. Download local trail maps and detailed park info from NPRSR's website or regional visitor information offices, and follow NPRSR guidelines.

When walking, wear sturdy shoes, sunscreen, and protective gear; carry maps and a compass; and pack drinking water, emergency food supplies, and a well-charged mobile phone. If possible, walk in a group, especially on long hikes. Check local weather conditions with the Bureau of Meteorology and trail conditions on NPRSR's website before you go.

If exploring the national parks by car, check road conditions with the RACQ's website and be sure you have local maps, good tires, sound brakes, water, and a full tank of gas before setting out.

Contacts Department of National Parks, Sport and Racing (NPRSR). ☎ *13–7468 camping permits and information* ⊕ *www.nprsr.qld.gov.au.* **Royal Automobile Club of Queensland (RACQ).** ☎ *1300/888449* ⊕ *www.racq.com.au.*

WHERE TO STAY

$$
B&B/INN
FAMILY

🏨 **Binna Burra Mountain Lodge & Campsite.** At the doorstep of Lamington National Park, this historic, eco-certified, back-to-basics mountain lodge and campground is a birdwatcher's paradise, with sweeping views across Heritage-listed rain forest and more than 160 km (99 miles) of walking trails. **Pros:** beautiful setting and wildlife; easy, interesting drive up mountain; old-fashioned, communal atmosphere; great choice for families. **Cons:** very basic meals for the price; mountain lodge in need of refurbishment. $ *Rooms from: A$169* ⊠ *Binna Burra Rd., via Beechmont, Lamington National Park* ☎ *07/5533–3622, 1300/246622* ⊕ *www.binnaburralodge.com.au* ⇄ *35 cabins (9 with shared bath), 3 studios, 5 apartments* ⦿ *Breakfast; No meals; Some meals.*

$$
RESORT
FAMILY
Fodor's Choice
★

🏨 **O'Reilly's Rainforest Retreat, Villas & Lost World Spa.** One thousand meters (3,280 feet) above sea level and immersed in the subtropical rain forests of World Heritage–listed Lamington National Park, the iconic, eco-certified O'Reilly's Rainforest Retreat provides atmosphere and adventure in equal doses. **Pros:** breathtaking location; plenty of activities; excellent facilities. **Cons:** long drive up mountain—use a coach or transfer service if you're not confident on Australian roads; fee for Wi-Fi. $ *Rooms from: A$179* ⊠ *Lamington National Park Rd., Canungra* ☎ *07/5544–0644, 1800/688722* ⊕ *www.oreillys.com. au* ⇄ *67 rooms, 5 suites, 48 villas* ⦿ *Some meals; Breakfast.*

$$$$
RESORT

🏨 **Pethers Rainforest Retreat.** Set on 12 acres of privately owned rain forest, this secluded, couples-only resort comprises 10 spacious tree houses with timber floors, French doors opening onto verandas, fireplaces, hot tubs, and open-plan interiors furnished with Asian antiques. **Pros:** luxurious appointments; glorious environs; complimentary Wi-Fi, parking, and breakfast; no kids. **Cons:** no on-site dinner Sunday to Wednesday; limited mobile phone coverage. $ *Rooms from: A$315* ⊠ *28B Geissmann St., North Tamborine* ☎ *07/5545–4577* ⊕ *www.pethers.com.au* ⇄ *10 tree houses* ⦿ *Breakfast.*

THE SUNSHINE COAST

60 km (37 miles) north of Brisbane.

The Sunshine Coast is a 60-km (37-mile) stretch of white-sand beaches, inlets, lakes, and mountains that begins at the Glass House Mountains, an hour's drive north of Brisbane, and extends to Rainbow Beach in the north. Kenilworth is its inland extreme, 40 km (25 miles) from the ocean. For the most part, the Sunshine Coast has avoided the high-rise glitz of its southern cousin, the Gold Coast. Although there are plenty of stylish restaurants and luxurious hotels, this coast is best loved for its national parks, secluded coves, and relaxed beachside towns.

GETTING HERE AND AROUND

From Brisbane, drive 60 km (35 miles) north on the Bruce Highway, taking the Caloundra Road exit to get to the Sunshine Coast's southernmost beach town, Caloundra. Another 5 km (3 miles) along the highway, there's a well-marked exit to the Sunshine Motorway, which funnels you through to Sunshine Coast towns farther north via a series of large roundabouts (stay tuned for the appropriate exit). Follow the motorway north for 9½ km (6 miles) to get to the Brisbane Road–Mooloolaba exit; 15 km (9 miles) to reach the turn-off to Maroochydore; 29 km (18 miles) to the Yandina-Coolum Road exit for Coolum Beach; and 34 km (21 miles) to reach the Noosa turnoff.

Visit Sunshine Coast has information centers at the Sunshine Coast Airport, Caloundra, Maroochydore, Mooloolaba, Coolum, Glasshouse Mountains, and Montville.

AIR TRAVEL

Sunshine Coast Airport is the main airport for the area, servicing several flights a day by Jetstar, Qantas, and Virgin Australia from Sydney and Melbourne. By air from Maroochydore it's 2 hours 25 minutes to Melbourne, 2 hours 15 minutes to Adelaide, and 1 hour 35 minutes to Sydney. Park at the airport for around A$25 a day, A$79 a week.

Airport Contacts Sunshine Coast Airport. ⌂ *10 Electra La., Marcoola* ☎ *07/5453–1500* ⊕ *www.sunshinecoastairport.com.au.*

BUS TRAVEL

Con-x-ion runs daily buses from Brisbane Airport and the Roma Street Transit Centre in Brisbane to all the main Sunshine Coast towns. Distances between towns are short (10- to 30-minute drive). Con-x-ion also runs regular services from Brisbane International Airport to Sunshine Coast and Hinterland towns (from A$49), and shuttles prebooked, prepaid passengers from the Sunshine Coast Airport to surrounding towns including Maroochydore, Mooloolaba, and Caloundra (from A$20 one-way). Book online at ⊕ *www.con-x-ion.com.*

Henry's Transport Group meets all flights, running buses from Sunshine Coast Airport to Noosa and the northern Sunshine Coast (A$15–A$30) and, on market days, to Eumundi.

Bus Contacts Con-x-ion. ☎ *1300/266946* ⊕ *www.con-x-ion.com.* **Henry's Transport Group.** ☎ *07/5474–0199* ⊕ *www.henrys.com.au.*

CAR TRAVEL

A car is a virtual necessity on the Sunshine Coast. The traditional route to the coast from Brisbane is along the Bruce Highway (Highway 1) to the Glass House Mountains, with a turnoff at Cooroy. Taking the Sunshine Motorway may be faster, however: after 65 km (40 miles), turn off the Bruce Highway at Tanawha (toward Mooloolaba) and follow the signs. On either route, allow 1½ hours to get to the central coastal town of Coolum, a further half hour to reach Noosa, on the northern Sunshine Coast. The most scenic route is to turn off the Bruce Highway at the exit to Caloundra, then follow the coast to Noosa Heads.

TRAIN TRAVEL

Trains leave regularly from Roma Street Transit Centre in Brisbane en route to Landsborough and Nambour, the business hub of the Sunshine Coast. They continue on to Yandina, Eumundi, and other noncoastal towns. Once in Nambour, however, a car is a necessity, so it may make more sense to drive from Brisbane.

Train Contacts Queensland Rail. ☎ *13–1617* ⊕ *www.queenslandrail.com.au.*

ESSENTIALS

Visitor Information Tourism Noosa. ⊠ *61 Hastings St., Noosa Heads* ☎ *07/5430–5000* ⊕ *www.visitnoosa.com.au.* **Visit Sunshine Coast.** ☎ *07/5458–8800, 1300/847481* ⊕ *www.visitsunshinecoast.com.au.*

NOOSA

39 km (24 miles) northeast of Nambour, 17 km (11 miles) north of Coolum, 140 km (87 miles) north of Brisbane.

Set along the calm waters of Laguna Bay at the northern tip of the Sunshine Coast, Noosa is one of Australia's most stylish resort areas. Until the mid-1980s the town consisted of little more than a few shacks—then surfers discovered the spectacular waves that curl around the sheltering headland of Noosa National Park. Today Noosa is an enticing mix of surf, sand, and sophistication, with a serious reputation for distinctive, always-evolving cuisine. Views along the trail from Laguna Lookout to the top of the headland north of Main Street take in miles of magnificent beaches, ocean, and dense vegetation.

EXPLORING

Teewah Coloured Sands. About 3 km (2 miles) northeast of Noosa Heads you'll find the Teewah Coloured Sands, an area of multicolored dunes created in the Ice Age by natural chemicals in the soil. Teewah's sands stretch inland from the beach to a distance of about 17 km (11 miles); some of the 72 distinctly hued sands even form cliffs rising to 600 feet. A four-wheel-drive vehicle is essential for exploring this area and interesting sites to the north, such as Cooloola National Park—home to 1,300-plus species of plants, 700 native animals, and 44% of Australia's bird species—and Great Sandy National Park. Access is by ferry across the Noosa River at Tewantin.

Tour operators run day trips via cruise boat and four-wheel drive that take in these sights; some include visits to Fraser Island, north of Rainbow Beach. You can also explore the area on foot. One of Queensland's latest Great Walks winds through Cooloola National Park. ⊠ *Noosa Heads.*

BEACHES

FAMILY **Noosa Main Beach.** With gentle waves and year-round lifeguard patrol, Noosa's Main Beach is a perfect swimming spot, ideal for families or those who aren't confident in the bigger swells. One of only a handful of beaches along Australia's coastline that faces north, Main Beach also hosts surfing lessons for beginners with Go Ride A Wave surf school (A$65–A$80, two-hour lesson). The beach backs onto leafy Hastings Street with its bustle of upmarket cafés, bars, restaurants, and shopping spots. For a quieter scene, adventure around the corner to **Noosa Spit**, a popular picnic spot and off-leash dog beach. **Amenities:** food and drink; lifeguards; parking; showers; toilets. **Best for:** sunrise; sunset; swimming; walking. ⊠ *Hastings St., Noosa Heads* ⊕ *www.visitnoosa.com.au.*

Fodor's Choice ★ **Sunshine Beach.** Incorporating 16 km (10 miles) of beachfront that stretches north to Noosa national park, lovely Sunshine Beach is patrolled year-round. Beach breaks, reliable swell, a rocky headland sheltering it from winds, and clear, glassy water make Sunshine popular with surfers. When northeasterlies blow, surf the northern pocket. Fish off the beach year-round for dart, bream, and flathead, or cast a long line into deep water to hook numerous seasonal species. From here, hike past nudist-friendly Alexandria Bay to Noosa, or end a long day of swimming with a beer or a meal at The Sunshine Beach Surf Club. **Amenities:** food and drink; lifeguards; parking; showers; toilets. **Best for:** sunrise; sunset; surfing; swimming; walking. ⊠ *Belmore Terr., Sunshine Beach.*

SPORTS AND THE OUTDOORS

RIVER CRUISING

Noosa Everglades Discovery. Eco-accredited Noosa Everglades Discovery runs half- and full-day river cruises and guided canoe trips through the glassy waters of the Noosa Everglades. ⊠ *Noosa Everglades, 186 Gympie Terr., Noosaville* ☎ *07/5449–0393* ⊕ *www.thediscoverygroup. com.au* ⊠ *6-hr BBQ Lunch Cruise A$110; 6-hr Canoe Safari & BBQ Lunch A$125.*

SURFING

Go Ride a Wave. This operator rents equipment and runs surfing lessons for beginners in the sheltered warmth of Noosa Heads Beach. Book in advance to secure two-hour beginner, group, or private lessons, with surfboard, wet suit, and all other equipment included in the fee (A$65). Make the most of your holiday with a Go All Day pass (just A$20 more to use the equipment all day after your lesson), or a five-lesson Go Carve It Up pack from A$260. Book online in advance to save. ⊠ *On the beach, Hastings St., near Haul St., Noosa Heads* ☎ *1300/132441* ⊕ *www.gorideawave.com.au.*

WHERE TO EAT AND STAY

$$
MODERN
AUSTRALIAN
✕ **Bistro C.** Spectacular views of the bay from the open dining area make a stunning backdrop for this fashionable restaurant's Mod Oz cuisine. The fresh, tropical menu highlights local seafood, though landlubbers can partake of several meat and vegetarian dishes (think 12-hour lamb, caramelized pork belly, duck confit, or risotto verde). Start with the melt-in-your-mouth calamari with chili lime dipping sauce, before moving onto the signature seafood spaghetti served in pan, or local favorite: beer-battered flathead with lemon and tartar sauce. Sweet tooths don't just have the divine desserts to be tempted by; there are also six flavors of Espresso Martinis to try, including chai, chocolate mint, jaffa, and tiramisu. ⑤ *Average main: A$35* ⊠ *49 Hastings St., on the Beach Complex, Noosa Heads* ☎ *07/5447–2855* ⊕ *www.bistroc.com.au.*

$$$
MODERN
AUSTRALIAN
✕ **Ricky's River Bar + Restaurant.** A dining room overlooking the Noosa River makes this picturesque restaurant the perfect spot for a relaxed lunch or a romantic dinner. The menu features "modern Noosa cuisine," which mingles Mediterranean flavors beautifully with Australian ingredients. Sip a lime daiquiri or classic margarita, and polish off a plate of tapas before moving on to a main course of baby barramundi, roast duck with rhubarb, or chargrilled eye-filet. Alternately, treat your palate to a five- or six-course tasting menu with matching wines (A$85–A$145). The adjacent River Bar serves a lighter menu, including cheese plates, and has

an extensive wine list. $ *Average main: A$42* ✉ *Noosa Wharf, Quamby Pl., Noosa Heads* ☎ *07/5447–2455* ⊕ *www.rickys.com.au.*

$$$
RESORT
🏨 **Sheraton Noosa Resort & Spa.** Facing fashionable Hastings Street on one side, the river on the other, you can't miss this elaborate, six-story, horseshoe-shape complex as you drive into Noosa Heads; it's painted a simple, chic white to highlight the sparkling central pool. **Pros:** close to beach and shops; beautiful pool area; spacious, well-kept rooms; generous noon check out. **Cons:** pricey; A$25 a day parking fee; free Wi-Fi only if room booked through hotel's website. $ *Rooms from: A$281* ✉ *14–16 Hastings St., Noosa Heads* ☎ *07/5449–4888* ⊕ *www.sheratonnoosaresort.com* ⤳ *140 rooms, 29 suites, 7 spa studios, 1 apartment* ⦿ *No meals.*

PEREGIAN AND COOLUM

Peregian is 11 km (7 miles) south of Noosa, with Coolum 17 km (11 miles) south of Noosa and 25 km (16 miles) northeast of Nambour.

At the center of the Sunshine Coast, Coolum makes an ideal base for exploring the countryside. It has one of the finest beaches in the region, a growing reputation for good food and quality accommodation, and all the services you might need: banks with ATMs, medical centers, gas stations, pharmacies, supermarkets, gyms, beauty salons, and day spas—even a beachfront playground, kiosk, and skate park. Ten minutes north of Coolum is Peregian, a quaint little seaside town with numerous fashionable shops, eateries, and facilities, a string of stunning beaches, and a local produce and crafts market on the first and third Sunday of the month.

BEACHES

FAMILY
Fodor'sChoice
★
Coolum Beach. A popular choice for families, beautiful **Coolum Beach** boasts a surf club, skate park, playgrounds, change rooms, toilets, kiosk, shore-front parks, and well-maintained picnic areas. A long, white-sand beach, Coolum is patrolled year-round and has a nice beach break and some decent, uncrowded waves off the headland. Fish from the beach in the evening for grouper, tailor, bream, and dart; catch bream around the headland, especially in winter. Walk south along the boardwalk to the headland park for magnificent coastal views, or north to quieter **Peregian Beach** with its patrolled surf, playground, and adjacent Environmental Park. For a break from the sun, head down David Low Way for shops, cafés, and restaurants. **Amenities:** food and drink; lifeguards; parking; showers; toilets. **Best for:** sunset; surfing; swimming; walking. ✉ *David Low Way, Coolum* ⊕ *www.visitsunshinecoast.com.au.*

SPORTS AND THE OUTDOORS

SURFING

Coolum Surf School. Run by an expert surfer and local lifeguard, Coolum Surf School runs two-hour group and 90-minute private lessons, as well as board and gear hire. It's the only surf school in the area: find it 164 feet north of Coolum Surf Lifesaving Club, next to the skate park. ✉ *Coolum Boardriders Clubhouse, Tickle Park, David Low Way, Coolum* ☎ *0438/731–503* ⊕ *www.coolumsurfschool.com.au* 🏄 *Single* *private lesson A$110, beginner class A$55 (prices include gear) ⊙ Daily dawn–dusk; lessons by appointment.*

WHERE TO EAT AND STAY

$$
AUSTRALIAN
FAMILY

✕ **Coolum Surf Club.** This lively oceanfront restaurant serves fresh seafood and simple, pub-style fare in its large dining room overlooking Coolum Beach. Reasonable prices, rotating meal specials, live entertainment, and a friendly, casual atmosphere ensure it is always well attended by locals and visitors alike. Chow down on a classic beef burger, fish-and-chips, or surf and turf, or opt for something more upmarket like a juicy Angus sirloin or wood-fired Atlantic salmon. A range of vegetarian options, as well as gourmet share plates, is also available. Kids are also well looked after, with their own menu and activities provided. Booking ahead is highly recommended, especially to secure a table with a view. ⑤ *Average main: A$24* ✉ *1775–1779 David Low Way, Coolum* ☎ *07/5446–1148* ⊕ *www.coolumsurfclub.com.*

$$
MODERN
AUSTRALIAN
Fodor's Choice
★

✕ **Pitchfork.** Positioned within the café and shopping strip along Peregian Beach, this contemporary seaside bistro entices crowds with its imaginative, subtropical Mod Oz cuisine and modern, rustic styling. Highlights include the lightly fried stuffed zucchini flowers or baby squid to start, and the Hervey Bay scallop fusilli with smoked pancetta for main. However, keep an eye out for their specials board—their duck pie is one to request. Gluten-free and vegetarian diners are well looked after with their own special, seasonally changing menus, and kids enjoy the mini meals designed especially for them. Booking in advance is highly recommended. ⑤ *Average main: A$33* ✉ *5/4 Kingfisher Dr., Peregian Beach* ☎ *07/5471–3697* ⊙ *Closed Mon.* ⌂ *Reservations essential.*

$$$
RENTAL
FAMILY

🏠 **Coolum Seaside Holiday Apartments.** These sleek and spacious self-contained studios and one- to four-bedroom apartments are just around the corner from Coolum's restaurants, shops, and beach. **Pros:** good on-site facilities; complimentary Wi-Fi, cable TV, and parking; central to beach and restaurants. **Cons:** dated design in some units; no meals; about a 10-minute walk to the beach. ⑤ *Rooms from: A$278* ✉ *6–8 Perry St., Coolum* ☎ *07/5455–7200, 1800/809062* ⊕ *www.coolumseaside.com* ⤳ *44 apartments* ⧉ *No meals.*

MAROOCHYDORE

18 km (11 miles) south of Coolum, 18 km (11 miles) east of Nambour.

Maroochydore, at the mouth of the Maroochy River, has been a popular beach resort town for years, and has its fair share of high-rise towers. Its draw is excellent surfing and swimming beaches.

BEACHES

FAMILY
Alexandra Headland. South of Maroochydoore's main beach and just north of Mooloolaba, Alexandra Headland offers a reliable surf break in moderate to high swell. The beach is patrolled year-round, but swimmers need to take care to avoid the headland rocks at the southern end of the beach where there is often a strong rip. A shady park, barbecue and picnic area, kiosk, playground, skate park, and walking and cycling tracks color the foreshore, with many alfresco cafés and restaurants also nearby. Cast a line at the river mouth or off the headland for bream,

dart, whiting, and flathead, or take advantage of rip holes for beach fishing. **Amenities:** food and drink; lifeguards; parking; showers; toilets. **Best for:** sunset; surfing; swimming; walking. ⊠ *Alexandra Parade, Alexandra Headland* ⊕ *www.visitsunshinecoast.com.au.*

FAMILY **Maroochydore Beach.** Averaging waves around 3 feet, this long, picturesque white-sand beach is a great option for swimmers and amateur surfers alike. Patrolled year-round by one of Queensland's oldest surf lifesaving clubs, rips are common along this strip, so stay in the central area between the red-and-yellow flags. A busy walking and cycling track runs adjacent to the beachfront, connecting visitors to both Cotton Tree and Alexandra Headland. A few minutes north is Maroochy River, a popular fishing spot and water sports activities hub. As with almost all Sunshine Coast beaches, an array of shops, cafés, and eateries line the esplanade. **Amenities:** food and drink; lifeguards; parking; showers; toilets; water sports. **Best for:** sunset; surfing; swimming; walking. ⊠ *Alexandra Parade* ⊕ *www.visitsunshinecoast.com.au.*

WHERE TO EAT AND STAY

$$$ ✕ **ebb Waterfront.** Faux-suede sofas and ottomans in varying shades
AUSTRALIAN of cool blue set the mood at this riverside restaurant specializing in top-quality regional produce, particularly sustainably farmed local seafood. Floor-to-ceiling windows line one side of the long, open dining room, while the large, breezy outdoor area offers stunning views across the water. The award-winning Mod Oz menu changes seasonally, but always highlights fresh seafood and quality cuts of meat. Try the turmeric scallops or stuffed zucchini flowers before moving on to duck, lamb, or locally farmed barramundi. Complement your meal with a choice of wines from Australia's finest producers, and make sure to leave room for the excellent cheese plates and desserts. A degustation menu is also available upon request. ⑤ *Average main: A$40* ⊠ *6 Wharf St.* ☎ *07/5452–7771* ⊕ *www.ebbwaterfront.com* ⊗ *No dinner Sun.– Thurs.* ⚑ *Reservations essential.*

$ ✕ **Raw Energy.** Keep your fuel up for long days of swimming and surfing
CAFÉ with a stop at Raw Energy, where freshly made smoothies and juices, hearty burgers and wraps, and fair trade coffee will give you just the boost you need. Popular with locals and tourists alike, the light-and-healthy fare includes protein- and superfood-packed smoothies; seasonal, locally flavored fruit, veggie and green juices; and an array of burgers stacked sky-high with fresh ingredients. For breakfast, try the famous Poached Eggs, delicious Potato Fritter Stack or Acai Breakfast Bowl; or grab a homemade organic muffin and takeaway coffee and meander down to the seaside to watch the waves roll in. More branches of the chain are opening along the Sunshine Coast. ⑤ *Average main: A$13* ⊠ *20 Memorial Ave.* ☎ *07/5443–1777* ⊕ *www.rawenergy.com.au.*

$$$ 🏨 **Novotel Twin Waters Resort.** About 9 km (5½ miles) north of Maroochy-
RESORT dore, this family-friendly, activity-packed resort is built around a 15-acre
FAMILY saltwater lagoon bordering Maroochy River and Mudjimba Beach. **Pros:** great grounds and lagoon; free use of water-sports equipment; terrific kids' programs. **Cons:** housekeeping standards vary; buffet meals pricey; many rooms in need of maintenance and updating; free Wi-Fi only available to Accor & Club members. ⑤ *Rooms from: A$209* ⊠ *Ocean Dr.,*

Twin Waters ☎ *07/5448–8000, 1800/072277* ⊕ *www.twinwatersresort. com.au* ⤵ *235 rooms, 126 suites* ⊙|*Breakfast; Some meals.*

$$$ ▦ **The Sebel Maroochydore.** Each spacious one- or two-bedroom apart-
RENTAL ment in this stylish, view-rich, 15-level hotel has a curved feature wall
FAMILY and full gourmet kitchen bristling with modern European appliances.
Pros: 25-meter (82-foot) pool and separate kids pool; hot tub in every
room; free parking; good service. **Cons:** noise from pool area and traffic
at night; beach is across a four-lane road; some apartments in need of
updating; charge for Wi-Fi. ⑤ *Rooms from: A$239* ⊠ *20 Aerodrome
Rd.* ☎ *07/5479–8000* ⤵ *28 apartments* ⊙|*No meals.*

MOOLOOLABA

5 km (3 miles) south of Maroochydore.

Mooloolaba stretches along a lovely beach and riverbank, both an easy
walk from town. The Esplanade has many casual cafés, upscale res-
taurants, and fashionable shops. Head to the town outskirts for picnic
spots and prime coastal views.

EXPLORING

FAMILY **UnderWater World SEA LIFE Mooloolaba.** The largest tropical oceanarium
in the southern hemisphere, this all-weather sea life sanctuary has back-
to-back marine presentations, including stingray feedings, guided shark
tours, and seal and otter shows, all accompanied by informative talks.
Sixteen themed zones spread over three levels, including Australia's
largest and most interactive jellyfish display, a seahorse sanctuary, and
a famous underwater tunnel that gets you face-to-face with the majestic
creatures of the deep. Roll up your sleeves and tickle a starfish or a sea
cucumber in the touch pool; or swim with seals (A$90), snorkel the
reef (A$90), or scuba dive with resident sharks (A$255 for beginners,
A$195 for certified divers). A souvenir shop and a café are also on-site,
as well as a new, three-level indoor playground for kids. The aquarium
is part of Mooloolaba's Wharf Complex, which features a marina, res-
taurants, and a tavern. ■**TIP**➜ **Don't forget to get your hand stamped
so you can reenter the park. Save up to 20% by booking tickets online
in advance.** ⊠ *10 Parkyn Parade, The Wharf* ☎ *07/5458–6280* ⊕ *www.
underwaterworld.com.au* ⧖ *A$39* ⊙ *Daily 10–5; last entry at 4.*

BEACHES

FAMILY **Mooloolaba Beach.** A super-safe, family-friendly swimming beach,
Fodor's Choice Mooloolaba Beach is patrolled year-round and has just enough swell
★ to make it fun. Surfers might want to check out the left-hand break that
sometimes forms off the rocks at the northern end. There are shady
picnic areas with barbecues, playgrounds, and exercise areas—as well
as the local meeting point, the Loo with a View. Stroll south along the
coastal path to the river mouth and rock wall (off which you can fish,
year-round, for bream); north to Alexandra Headland for views of the
bay; or along Mooloolaba Esplanade, lined with casual eateries and
boutiques. **Amenities:** food and drink; lifeguards; parking; showers; toi-
lets. **Best for:** sunrise; sunset; swimming; walking. ⊠ *Beach Terr.* ⊕ *www.
visitsunshinecoast.com.au.*

WHERE TO EAT AND STAY

$$ ✕ **Bella Venezia Italian Restaurant & Bar.** A large mural of Venice, simple
ITALIAN wooden tables, and terra-cotta floor tiles decorate this popular res-
taurant in an arcade off the Esplanade. You can eat in or take out
traditional and modern Italian cuisine, such as the *Pesce del giorno*
(fish of the day served with garlic chat potatoes and seasoned greens);
Saltimbocca alla Romana (prime cut veal topped with prosciutto and
sage); or fresh Coffin Bay oysters with lime, mint, and chili dressing.
There's an extensive selection of pizza, pasta, and risotto, as well as
wine and cocktails. Open daily from noon to late, the restaurant also
delivers to local hotels. ⑤ *Average main: A$35* ✉ *95 The Esplanade*
☎ *07/5444–5844* ⊕ *www.bellav.com.au.*

$$$$ 🛏 **Mantra Sirocco.** Located across the road from the beach and sur-
RENTAL rounded by trendy restaurants and cafés, this popular, upscale apart-
ment complex on Mooloolaba's main drag has spacious, self-contained
two- and three-bedroom apartments, an impressive pool and Jacuzzi
area, and a large fitness center. **Pros:** fantastic views from big balconies;
in-room Jacuzzis; friendly staff; free parking. **Cons:** minimum two-night
stay; Wi-Fi costs extra. ⑤ *Rooms from: A$329* ✉ *59–75 The Esplanade*
☎ *07/5444–1400, 1800/811454 reservations* ⊕ *www.mantrasirocco.
com.au* 🛏 *41 apartments, 2 penthouses* ❅ *No meals.*

CALOUNDRA

*29 km (18 miles) south of Maroochydore, 63 km (39 miles) south of
Noosa, 91 km (56 miles) north of Brisbane.*

This unassuming southern seaside town has nine beaches of its own,
which include everything from placid wading beaches (King's Beach
and Bulcock Beach are best for families) to bays with thundering surf,
such as Dicky, Buddina, and Wurtulla beaches.

BEACHES

Bulcock Beach. Flanked by a timber boardwalk with stunning views
across the coastline, Bulcock Beach is one of Caloundra's most popular
surfing spots. Children enjoy the small paddling pools that form across
the sand at low tide, while nearby Happy Valley parkland creates the
perfect canvas for games of Frisbee and traditional "Aussie" beachside
cricket. Surf the break off Deepwater Point, or enjoy boogie-boarding
or bodysurfing in the swell closer to shore. Rips can form through
the channel, so stay between the flags and only swim when the beach
is patrolled (September–May). When you've had too much sun, head
across the road for cafés, restaurants, shops, and a place to cool off.
Amenities: lifeguards; parking; toilets. **Best for:** sunrise; sunset; surfing;
walking. ✉ *The Esplanade.*

FAMILY **King's Beach.** With rockpools, water fountains, an oceanfront saltwater
Fodor'sChoice swimming pool, and gentle, patrolled swimming areas, it's no surprise
★ that festive King's Beach is one of the Sunshine Coast's most popu-
lar choices for families. The region's closest beach to Brisbane, it also
attracts plenty of surfers chasing the breaks toward the beach edges.
King's foreshore is well landscaped, with seating and shade areas, as
well as a bustling boardwalk. A grassy reserve, fronted by a seawall,

runs alongside the beach, peppered with children's playgrounds, picnic spots, and barbecue areas. A range of beachside cafés and eateries surround. Deep rip holes run off the rocks for fishing. **Amenities:** food and drink; lifeguards; parking; showers; toilets. **Best for:** sunset; surfing; swimming; walking. ⊠ *Ormond Terr.*

WHERE TO EAT AND STAY

$$
AUSTRALIAN

✕ **Alfie's Mooo Char & Bar.** Owned by legendary (and now retired) Queensland Rugby League footballer Allen "Alfie" Langer, this airy, steak-centric restaurant has an ideal setting right on Bulcock Beach, overlooking the sheltered inlet known as Pumicestone Passage. The design is light and bright, and there's both indoor and outdoor dining. Try the restaurant's deservedly popular steak, baked barramundi, signature oysters, local king prawns, or take advantage of the popular A$15 lunch menu. ⑤ *Average main: A$35* ⊠ *Esplanade and Otranto Aves.* ☎ *07/5492–8155* ⊕ *www.alfies.net.au* ⌕ *Reservations essential.*

$$$
RESORT
Fodor's Choice
★

Rolling Surf Resort. The stunning white sands of Kings Beach front this modern, airy resort comprised of well-equipped one- to three-bedroom oceanfront and poolside apartments enveloped in tropical gardens. **Pros:** huge pool; good on-site food options; right on the beach; free parking. **Cons:** two-night minimum stay in high season; steep charge for basic supplies; limited complimentary Wi-Fi. ⑤ *Rooms from: A$240* ⊠ *10 Levuka Ave., Kings Beach* ☎ *07/5491–9777, 1800/775559* ⊕ *www.rollingsurfresort.com.au* ⇥ *66 apartments* ⑩ *No meals.*

SUNSHINE COAST HINTERLAND

The Sunshine Coast Hinterland, extending from the Glass House Mountains just northwest of Brisbane to Eumundi and Yandina, west of the northern Sunshine Coast town of Noosa, is ideal terrain for daytrippers. Tracts of subtropical rain forest and mountainous areas linked by scenic drives and walking trails are interspersed with charming hillside villages, their main streets lined with cafés, galleries, gift shops, and guesthouses. Here you'll also find thriving markets; renowned restaurants and cooking schools; ginger, nut, and pineapple farms; theme and wildlife parks; and luxury B&Bs.

The Hinterland's southerly extent is the nine distinctive conical outcrops of the Glass House Mountains—the eroded remnants of ancient volcanoes—rising dramatically from a flattish landscape 45 km (27 miles) northwest of Brisbane. Get a great view of the mountains from Glass House Mountains Lookout, also the starting point for a scenic, 25-minute walk. Several longer trails begin from nearby vantage points, such as Mt. Beerburrum and Wild Horse Mountain Lookout. Nearby, you'll find Aussie World amusement park, and the late Steve Irwin's famous Australia Zoo.

Meander north through the mountains to reach the arty village of Maleny, quaint, European-style Montville, and food-friendly Mapleton. Nearby lies tranquil Baroon Lake and easy walking trails in Kondalilla National Park and Mary Cairncross Scenic Reserve.

The Sunshine Coast and Sunshine Coast Hinterland

Continue north to Yandina, where you'll find much-lauded restaurant Spirit House and the Ginger Factory, and Eumundi, known for its thriving twice-weekly markets. Hinterland hub Nambour, east of Mapleton, has shops, banks, and local attractions.

GETTING HERE AND AROUND

To get to the Sunshine Coast Hinterland from Brisbane, follow the Bruce Highway north for around 35 km (22 miles), taking the Glass House Mountains Road exit. A 10-km (6-mile) drive along Glass House Mountains Road brings you to the quaint Glass House Mountains Village. Access Glass House Mountains Lookout, 10 km (6 miles) from the village, via Glass House Mountains Tourist Route. Drive 10 km (6 miles) north along Glass House Mountains Road from the village to reach Maleny.

From Maleny, take the Landsborough-Maleny Road for 10 km (6 miles), turning right at Maleny–Montville Road, to get to Montville. From Montville it's a five-minute drive west on Western Avenue to Kondallilla National Park. A further 10 km (6 miles) drive northwest brings you to Mapleton, from which it's a 12-km (7-mile), 15-minute drive east to Nambour, en route to the Sunshine Coast.

From Nambour, a 20-minute drive east along Petrie Creek Road and David Low Way brings you to the mid-Sunshine Coast town of

Fishing at Bulcock Beach, Caloundra, Sunshine Coast

Maroochydore. Or drive 20 minutes north along the Bruce Highway to reach Eumundi, 20 km (12 miles) away. From here it's a half-hour, 20-km (12-mile) drive east along the Eumundi–Noosa Road to Noosa, the northernmost town on the Sunshine Coast.

From Nambour it's an 8-km (5-mile) drive north along the Nambour Connection Road, then Old Bruce Highway, to reach Yandina. From Brisbane, it's an hour's drive north along the Bruce Highway: take the Coolum/Yandina exit.

It's around 60 km (35 miles) to Glass House Mountains Village; just under 100 km (60 miles) to Montville; and nearly 110 km (65 miles) to Maleny from Brisbane. Driving time is 60 minutes to the Glasshouse Mountains; around 1½ hours to Maleny and Montville, and a further 15-minute drive to Nambour and another 12-minute drive to Yandina. From the Sunshine Coast most parts of the Hinterland are less than an hour's drive inland.

You'll find few banks and money exchanges around the Sunshine Coast Hinterland. ■TIP➔ Get cash in advance from ATMs in larger coastal towns such as Noosa. Alternatively, several are available at service stations along the Bruce Highway, or at stores and pubs in the Hinterland.

ESSENTIALS

Visitor Information Maleny Hinterland Visitor Information Centre. ✉ *Shop 2, 23 Maple St., Maleny* ☎ *07/5499–9033* ⊕ *www.maleny.qld.au.* **Montville Visitors Information Centre.** ✉ *198 Main St., Montville* ☎ *07/5458–8845* ⊕ *www.hinterlandtourism.com.au.*

GLASS HOUSE MOUNTAINS AREA

35 km (22 miles) north of Brisbane on Bruce Hwy. to the Glass House Mountains Rd. exit; 4 km (2.5 miles) south of Beerwah.

More than 20 million years old, the Glass House Mountains consist of nine conical outcrops—the eroded remnants of volcanoes—that rise dramatically from a flattish landscape northwest of Brisbane. Get a great view of the mountains from Glass House Mountains Lookout. Access is 10 km (6 miles) from the village via Glass House Mountains Tourist Route. The lookout is also the starting point for a scenic 25-minute walk. Several longer walks begin from nearby vantage points, such as Mt. Beerburrum and Wild Horse Mountain Lookout.

EXPLORING

FAMILY **Aussie World.** The Sunshine Coast's colorful Aussie World amusement park features several games rooms, a hall for "Funnybone Flicks," and a bustling fairground with 30-plus rides, including bumper cars, a retro merry-go-round, Ferris wheel, roller coaster, log ride, minigolf—even a sideshow alley. Admission is cheap, the "old school" carnival vibe is fun and friendly, and the park is far less crowded than its Gold Coast equivalents. An eclectic range of specialty stores are also housed within the complex, as well as the iconic Aussie World Pub (formerly Ettamogah Pub): a quirky, much-photographed watering hole full of kitsch Australiana and classic Aussie pub meals. ⊠ *73 Frizzo Rd., Palmview* ☎ *07/5494–5444* ⊕ *www.aussieworld.com.au* ✉ *General admission A$37 (A$34 online), family pass A$131* ⊘ *Daily 9–5, pub open late.*

FAMILY **Australia Zoo.** Made famous by the late Steve Irwin, this popular, Fodor's Choice 110-acre park is home to all manner of Australian animals: koalas, ★ kangaroos, wallabies, dingoes, Tasmanian devils, snakes, wombats, lizards—and, naturally, crocodiles. There are also otters, lemurs, tigers, red pandas, and a giant rain forest aviary. Daily shows feature crocs, birds of prey, koalas, and more. There are also plenty of extras that let you get up close and personal with the residents, including petting and hand-feeding red pandas (A$80), getting cozy with cheetahs (A$60–A$150) and rhinos (A$80), cuddling a koala (A$40), or partaking in an Outback-style camel ride (A$80). Get around the park on foot or try the free hop-on, hop-off mini-trains. Private guided tours and Segway adventures (A$60) are also available. ⊠ *1638 Steve Irwin Way, 5 km (3 miles) north of Glass House Mountains, Beerwah* ☎ *07/5436–2000* ⊕ *www.australiazoo.com.au* ✉ *General admission A$59; two-day pass A$87* ⊘ *Daily 9–5 (last entry 4:30).*

MONTVILLE

16 km (10 miles) northwest of Forest Glen.

This charming mountain village, settled in 1887, is known as the creative heart of the Sunshine Coast, as many artists live here. There are panoramic views of the coast from the main street, a charming mix of Tudor, Irish, and English cottages constructed of log or stone; Bavarian and Swiss houses; quaint B&Bs; and old Queenslander homes. Shops are a browser's delight, full of curiosities and locally made crafts, while galleries showcase more serious pieces by local artists. Note that the nearest major banks are in Nambour.

EXPLORING

FAMILY   **Kondalilla National Park.** With its swimming hole, 295-foot waterfall, picnic grounds, and walking trails, Kondalilla National Park is a popular local attraction. Three bushwalks begin near the grassy picnic area: Picnic Creek Circuit, Rock Pools Walk, and the Kondalilla Falls Circuit. They're all rated easy to moderate and range from 2 km (1 mile) to 5 km (3 miles) in length. The **Sunshine Coast Hinterland Great Walk** (58 km [34 miles]) is accessible from the Falls Loop track, and links with parks farther north. Download maps from the Department of National Parks, Sport and Racing (NPRSR) website. Camping is not permitted within the park. ⊠ *Kondalilla Falls Rd., off Montville–Mapleton Rd., near Flaxton* ☎ *13/5494–3983* ⊕ *www.nprsr.qld.gov.au* 🖼 *Free.*

WHERE TO EAT AND STAY

$$ ✕**Montville Café Bar Grill.** Twinkling with fairy lights by night and win-
AUSTRALIAN   dow-box blooms by day, this friendly, "ye olde English"–style family pub on Montville's main street provides a free courtesy bus to and from local accommodations every evening. Start with the salt-and-pepper calamari, and work your way up to a generous 10-ounce Black Angus rib fillet sourced from Queensland's own Channel Country, with a quality range of Australian wines to accompany. Live entertainment adds to the wholesome country feel on Friday and Saturday evenings, and Sunday afternoon starting at noon. The venue's alfresco café serves a lighter lunch menu, as well as coffee and cakes. $ *Average main: A$28* ⊠ *Main St.* ☎ *07/5278–5535* ⊕ *www.montvillepub.com.au.*

$$ ✕**Poets Cafe.** A leafy rain forest garden, quaint tearoom decor, and
CAFÉ   views of the Pacific Ocean combine to make this iconic, federation-style café a popular stop for visitors passing through the Hinterland. With a prime position overlooking the main street, Poet's eclectic menu includes gourmet open sandwiches, seafood risotto, garlic prawns, eye fillet steak, pasta dishes, and delectable cakes and desserts (save room for the caramel macadamia tart). The Main Street Gallery below sells contemporary Australian artwork, including glassware and pottery, and a new wedding chapel rounds out the picturesque property. $ *Average main: A$29* ⊠ *167 Main St.* ☎ *07/5478–5479 café, 07/5478–5050 gallery* ⊕ *www.weddingsatpoets.com.au* ☾ *No dinner Sun.–Thurs.*

$$$$ 🖼**Narrows Escape Rainforest Retreat.** In the midst of a verdant valley
B&B/INN   overlooking beautiful Lake Baroon, this tranquil, couples-only retreat
Fodor's Choice   features six self-contained, generously appointed cottages nestled deep
★   in the Hinterland Rain forest. **Pros:** beautiful, peaceful setting; excellent service; no children or large groups; free Wi-Fi. **Cons:** a little way out of town. $ *Rooms from: A$330* ⊠ *78 Narrows Rd.* ☎ *07/5478–5000* ⊕ *www.narrowsescape.com.au* ⇗ *6 cottages* ⏐⏐ *Breakfast; Some meals.*

$$$ 🖼 **The Spotted Chook & Amelie's Petite Maison.** Just over a mile from Mont-
B&B/INN   ville, this whimsical, French-provincial-style B&B feels a world away with
FAMILY   its picturesque country gardens and sweeping views over Obi Obi Gorge. **Pros:** warm and welcoming ambience; delicious French-style country breakfasts included in rate; excellent service; wheelchair-friendly cottage, ramps, and walkways. **Cons:** two-night minimum stay on weekends; Wi-Fi

only in public areas; books up quickly in wedding season. $ *Rooms from: A$245* ✉ *176 Western Ave.* ☎ *07/5442–9242* ⊕ *www.spottedchook.com.au* ⤵ *4 suites, 1 cottage* ⦿ *Breakfast; Some meals.*

$$
B&B/INN **Treetops Montville.** Nearby beautiful Kondalilla Falls, these cutting-edge-design tree houses perched on an escarpment are the ideal location for a romantic escape. **Pros:** stunning views; peaceful setting; close to town and walking tracks. **Cons:** minimum two-night stay on weekends; no Wi-Fi in rooms; limited phone reception. $ *Rooms from: A$220* ✉ *4 Cynthia Hunt Dr., off Kondalilla Falls Rd., Flaxton* ☎ *07/5478–6618, 1800/087330* ⊕ *www.treetopsmontville.com.au* ⤵ *4 tree houses, 4 cabins* ⦿ *Breakfast; Some meals.*

MALENY

14 km (8½ miles) west of Montville.

The Hinterland village of Maleny is a lively mix of rural life, the arts, wineries, cafés, and cooperative ventures. First settled around 1880, eclectic Maleny is now a popular tourist center with a strong community spirit, as well as a working dairy town.

EXPLORING

Mary Cairncross Scenic Reserve. One of the area's most popular picnic spots, Mary Cairncross Scenic Reserve is 5 km (3 miles) southeast of Maleny at the intersection of the Landsborough–Maleny Road and Mountain View Road. The 130 acres of subtropical rain forest shelter an array of wildlife that includes bandicoots, goannas, echidnas, wallabies—and even pythons. There's an excellent information center and two easy walks. Eat in the café (serving fair-trade coffee and homemade cakes) or at picnic tables for magnificent views of the Glass House Mountains. ✉ *148 Mountain View Rd.* ☎ *07/5429–6122* ⊕ *www.marycairncross.com.au.*

WHERE TO EAT AND STAY

$ ✕ **Maple 3 Café.** Renowned for its great coffee and hearty breakfasts,
CAFÉ this local favorite changes its menu daily, but there are always fresh salads, focaccias, pastas, and plenty of dessert options, including terrific cheesecake and special Maleny "mud pie." Come in for breakfast or brunch, grab a sandwich and a huge slice of homemade cake, and head down to Lake Baroon for a picnic. Or just sit out front on the deck and watch affable Maleny townsfolk go about their day. $ *Average main: A$19* ✉ *3 Maple St.* ☎ *07/5499–9177.*

$$$
B&B/INN **Blue Summit Cottages.** These three luxurious cottages on a view-rich mountaintop property are set among 10 acres of immaculate gardens and rolling hills, making it the perfect place to check in when you want to get away from it all. **Pros:** breathtaking location; complete privacy and serenity; free Wi-Fi. **Cons:** a 10-minute drive to town; books out quickly in high season. $ *Rooms from: A$270* ✉ *547 Maleny-Kenilworth Rd.* ☎ *07/5435–8410* ⊕ *www.bluesummitcottages.com.au* ⤵ *3 cottages, 1 house* ⦿ *Breakfast; Some meals.*

$$$$
B&B/INN **Maleny Tropical Retreat.** At the end of a steep driveway, ensconced in a misty rain forest valley, lies this romantic B&B retreat. **Pros:** top location and service; quality cooked breakfast; large DVD & games library;

no kids. **Cons:** higher rates and two-night minimum stay on weekends; patchy phone reception. ⓢ *Rooms from: A$325* ✉ *540 Maleny–Montville Rd.* ☎ *07/5435–2113* ⊕ *www.malenytropicalretreat.com* ⤳ *3 rooms, 4 villas, 1 cabin* ⍾ *Breakfast.*

YANDINA, EUMUNDI, AND COOROY

Yandina is 110 km (68 miles) north of Brisbane on the Bruce Hwy., Eumundi is 12 km (7½ miles) north of Yandina.

Yandina and Eumundi, just 12 km (7½ miles) apart, are home to some of the most iconic attractions in the area. Don't miss the Ginger Factory in Yandina, where you can learn—and eat—lots while enjoying the mini-amusement parklike attractions; or stop in at the tranquil Spirit House for a meal or cooking class. The Eumundi Market (on Wednesday and Saturday) is also a must.

EXPLORING

FAMILY
Fodor'sChoice
★

Eumundi Market. The big attraction of this area is the twice-weekly Eumundi Market—the best and largest street market on the Sunshine Coast. More than 600 stall-holders gather along Memorial Drive in the picturesque town of Eumundi to sell arts, crafts, clothing, accessories, and fresh and gourmet produce. Buses run to Eumundi from Noosa and other Sunshine Coast towns on market days, when the town swells to near-cosmopolitan proportions. Live musicians, poets, and masseurs keep the crowd relaxed. ✉ *80 Memorial Dr., Eumundi* ☎ *07/5442–7106* ⊕ *www.eumundimarkets.com.au* ۞ *Sat. 7 am–2 pm, Wed. 8 am–1:30 pm.*

FAMILY
The Ginger Factory. This legendary Queensland establishment goes far beyond its original factory-door sale of ginger. You can still take a 40-minute guided tour of the world's only publicly accessible ginger processing plant. A café and shop sell ginger in all forms—incorporated into jams, cookies, chocolates, ice cream, wine, and herbal products. There's also a train trip and a boat ride, a miniature rain forest for kids, a live beehive tour that includes a honey tasting, and plenty of shops to browse. Just up the road, you'll find the beautiful Yandina Historic House. ✉ *50 Pioneer Rd., Yandina* ☎ *07/5446–7100, 1800/067686* ⊕ *www.gingerfactory.com.au* ⍓ *Free entry; tours, demos, and rides A$8–A$43* ۞ *Daily 9–5.*

WHERE TO EAT

$
BISTRO
Fodor'sChoice
★

✕ **Maison de Provence.** Run by a French couple, the charming Maison de Provence is one part patisserie and one part French homewares shop. Find light meals like quiches, baguettes, and the delectable pastries and cakes, including tarte aux fruits, eclairs, and brioche. They also make their own tempting range of chocolates and macarons. At the back of a large corner balcony, this little café is a great spot to soak up some sun and fresh Hinterland air while treating yourself to a little bit of French delight. ⓢ *Average main: A$17* ✉ *9/13 Garnet St., Cooroy* ☎ *07/5472–0077* ۞ *Closed Mon.*

$$$
MODERN ASIAN
Fodor'sChoice
★

✕ Spirit House. Headed up by a trio of credentialed chefs who travel annually to Asia for inspiration, this iconic Yandina restaurant does a remarkable job re-creating contemporary Thai cuisine on Queensland soil. The menu, designed around plates to share, changes seasonally, with most ingredients sourced locally; a worthy signature dish is the whole crispy reef fish with tamarind-chili sauce. Save room for delectable desserts, best sampled in the tasting plate for two. The tranquil garden setting includes a lagoon and Buddhist shrines, and lights up magically at night with fairy lights. Spirit House also runs a popular cooking school with lively, learn-and-dine classes held Wednesday–Sunday. ⑤ *Average main: A$39* ✉ *20 Ninderry Rd., Yandina* ☎ *07/5446–8977* ⊕ *www.spirithouse.com.au* ☾ *No dinner Sun.–Tues.* ⌂ *Reservations essential.*

MACKAY–CAPRICORN ISLANDS

Despite its name, this group of islands lying offshore between Bundaberg and Rockhampton is closer to the southern half of Queensland than it is to the city of Mackay. The Mackay–Capricorn Islands comprise the section of the Great Barrier Reef known as Capricorn Marine Park, which stretches for 140 km (87 miles) and cuts through the Tropic of Capricorn, Heron Island being the closest point. This is a great area for wildlife: turtles use several of the islands as breeding grounds; seabirds nest here; and humpback whales pass through on their migration to Antarctica each spring—generally between July and October.

LADY ELLIOT ISLAND

80 km (50 miles) off the Queensland coast.

The closest Great Barrier Reef island to Brisbane, Lady Elliot Island is a highly protected coral cay approximately 85 km (53 miles) northeast of Bundaberg. The 111-acre island is a sanctuary for more than 1,200 species of marine life, which—along with its crystal clear waters and healthy coral—make it one of the top snorkeling and diving destinations on the reef.

GETTING HERE AND AROUND

Lady Elliot is the only coral cay with its own airstrip. Small aircraft generally make the flight from Hervey Bay (40 minutes) or Bundaberg (30 minutes), though pickups can be arranged from as far south in Queensland as Coolangatta, on the Gold Coast (two hours). You can day-trip to Lady Elliot with Seair Pacific, too. The cost includes scenic flight, buffet lunch, reef walking, glass-bottom boat ride, snorkeling, and island tour.

Tours require a minimum of 2 passengers and use planes that can carry up to 12. Strict luggage limits for both hand and checked baggage allow 10 kilograms (22 pounds) per person (for a small charge, divers can take an extra 10 kilograms in dive gear). If you exceed this limit, you can repack at the ticket-counter scale or wave good-bye to the plane.

Airlines Seair Pacific. ☎ *07/5599–4509* ⊕ *www.seairpacific.com.au.*

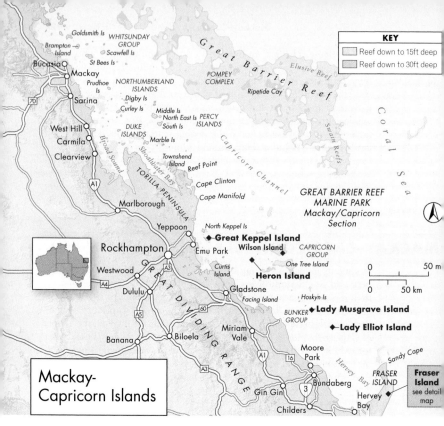

EXPLORING

Fodor's Choice ★ **Lady Elliot Island.** Positioned 80 km (50 miles) off the Queensland coast, Lady Elliot Island is a 104-acre coral cay on the southern tip of the Great Barrier Reef, within easy reach of Bundaberg and Hervey Bay. One of just six island resorts actually on the reef, it's a high-level Marine National Park Zone. Wildlife here easily outnumbers the guests (a maximum of 100 can visit at any one time)—and that reality is underscored by the ammoniacal odor of hundreds of nesting seabirds and, in season, the sounds and sights of them courting, mating, and nesting.

Divers enjoy the easy access to the reef and the variety of diving sites around Lady Elliot. Fringed on all sides by coral reefs and blessed with a stunning white-sand, coral-strewn shore and bright azure waters, this oval isle seems to have been made for diving. There's a busy dive shop and a reef education center with marine-theme exhibits (plus an educational video library—great for rainy days). Inclement weather and choppy waves can lead to canceled dives and washed-out underwater visibility. When the waters are calm, you'll see turtles, morays, sharks, rays, and millions of tropical fish. Many divers visit Lady Elliot specifically to encounter the resident population of manta rays that feed off the coral.

From October to April, Lady Elliot becomes a busy breeding ground for crested and bridled terns, silver gulls, lesser frigate birds, and the rare red-tailed tropic bird. Between November and March, green and loggerhead turtles emerge from the water to lay their eggs; hatching takes place after January. During the hatching season, staff biologists host guided turtle-watching night hikes. From about July through October, pods of humpback whales are visible from the beachfront restaurant.

Lady Elliot is one of the few islands in the area where camping—albeit modified—is part of the resort, and a back-to-basics, eco-friendly philosophy dominates the accommodations. ⊠ *Lady Elliot Island* ⊕ *www. ladyelliot.com.au.*

SPORTS AND THE OUTDOORS

At the resort dive shop you can rent equipment and arrange dive courses to more than a dozen excellent sites, including Lighthouse Bommie, home to a 40-strong manta ray colony, and the Blow Hole and Hiro's Cave. Refresher pool dives, a shore snorkeling trip, and guided reef, nature, and historical walks are free for resort guests. Off-boat snorkeling and glass-bottom boat rides are A$30. Boat dives and night dives range A$65–A$90, but all guests are entitled to one complimentary combined tour during their stay. Open-water certification courses cost A$550; "Discover Scuba Diving" short courses are A$165; and referral courses, available to those who've completed the classroom and pool portions of a certification course prior to arrival, are A$450.

Diving here is weather-dependent, so plan accordingly if you intend to do a dive course over multiple days. Special five-night packages, including buffet breakfast and dinner, a glass-bottom boat tour, snorkeling tours, and reef tax, start at A$680 per person. Flights (from Hervey Bay, Fraser coast, Bundaberg, the Gold and Sunshine coasts, or Brisbane) are extra. Several other special deals and packages are available. There is a one-time A$20 environmental management charge for all nonpackage guests.

WHERE TO STAY

$$$ 🏕 **Lady Elliot Island Eco Resort.** On this pristine reef island you're more like a marine biologist at an island field camp than a tourist enjoying a luxury resort. **Pros:** eco-friendly; unbeatable proximity to nature; friendly, knowledgeable staff; hearty meals; plenty of activities. **Cons:** no Wi-Fi or phone reception in rooms; limited leisure options for rainy, nondiving days; minimum three-night stay during peak times. ⑤ *Rooms from: A$272* ⊠ *Lady Elliot Island* ☎ *07/5536–3644 head office, 07/4156–4444 resort* ⊕ *www.ladyelliot.com.au* ⟿ *13 reef units, 11 garden units, 5 2-bedroom suites, 12 eco tents* ⑪ *Breakfast; Some meals.*

RESORT
FAMILY

LADY MUSGRAVE ISLAND

40 km (25 nautical miles) north of Lady Elliot Island, 96 km (53 nautical miles) northeast of Bundaberg.

This island sits at the southern end of the Great Barrier Reef Marine Park, about 40 km (25 miles) north of Lady Elliot Island and 96 km (60 miles) northeast of Bundaberg. The cay has a 2,945-acre surrounding

432 < **Brisbane and Its Beaches**

reef, about one-third of which is a massive yet calm lagoon, a true coral cay of 39.5 acres. Here day-trippers, yachties, divers, and campers converge, and, like nearby Lady Elliot Island, it has some of the best diving and snorkeling in Queensland. Campers have a chance to view the myriad sea life surrounding this tiny speck of land in the Pacific.

From October through April the island is a bird and turtle rookery, with black noddies, wedge-tailed shearwaters, bridled terns, more timid black-naped and roseate terns, and green and loggerhead turtles. There's also an abundance of flora, including casuarina and pisonia trees.

GETTING HERE AND AROUND

Lady Musgrave Barrier Reef Cruises. This is the only carrier servicing Lady Musgrave Island. It primarily operates as a day-cruise service, but also ferries campers to the island. Boats depart daily at 8:30 am (board from 8 am) from the Town of 1770 marina on Captain Cook Drive, arriving around 75 minutes later. Baggage is limited to 12 cubic feet per person, as space on board is tight. You'll be expected to load most of your gear at least an hour before departure; on the island, use wheelbarrows to haul it to the campground from the island drop-off point, 250 meters (275 yards) away. If you're carrying a dinghy for getting around the island, it costs an extra A\$400 in transfer fees (rent dinghies from Burnett Boat Hire (☎ 0414/721–883). Campers must have a NPRSR permit at time of boarding (A\$5.95 per person, per night). If you're camping, you get substantial discounts on boat transfers April through June. In low season and bad weather, ring ahead to make sure the boat is leaving as scheduled. ☎ 07/4974–9077 ⊕ www.lmcruises. com.au ✉ A\$190.

SPORTS AND THE OUTDOORS

WATER SPORTS

FAMILY **Lady Musgrave Barrier Reef Cruises.** This company operates a pontoon in the vast deep-water coral lagoon off Lady Musgrave Island, with an underwater observatory, snorkeling deck, changing rooms, and sheltered seating. Their Lady Musgrave day cruises get you out to the reef in 75 minutes. Day Cruise passengers can enjoy more than 5 hours on the reef, including a buffet lunch and a 90-minute stopover on the Outer Reef, at a pontoon within a sheltered lagoon where you can snorkel, view 350 varieties of colorful live coral and 1,300 species of tropical fish year-round from a submersible or glass-bottom boat, take a guided island walk, see migrating whales in season, swim with turtles, or do some scuba diving or reef fishing before the boat cruises back to the mainland in the afternoon. Reef fishing and scuba diving are extra (for novice and certified divers, with or without gear). Cruises depart daily from the Town of 1770 and include a tropical buffet lunch, morning and afternoon tea, activities on the reef, and most gear. The day trip, including most extras, is A\$190 per person (including an A\$10 reef tax); campers staying on-island pay A\$450 return—but get to take the cruise twice. ✉ Town of 1770 marina, Captain Cook Dr., Seventeen Seventy ☎ 07/4974–9077 ⊕ www.lmcruises.com.au ✉ A\$190 day cruise; A\$40 reef fishing; A\$70 or A\$90 for 1 or 2 dives; A\$95 introductory lesson and 1 dive with gear.

HERON ISLAND

72 km (45 miles) northeast of the mainland port of Gladstone.

Most resort islands lie well inside the shelter of the distant reef, but Heron Island, some 72 km (45 miles) northeast of the mainland port of Gladstone, is actually part of the reef. The waters off this 40-acre island are spectacular, teeming with fish and coral, and ideal for snorkeling and scuba diving. The water is generally clearest in June and July and cloudiest during the rainy season, January and February. Heron Island operates on "island time"—an hour ahead of Eastern Standard Time—and at its own leisurely pace. You won't find much in the way of nightlife, as the island's single resort accepts a cozy maximum of 250 people—and there are no day-trippers. But these might be reasons why you decide to come here.

GETTING HERE AND AROUND

Once in Gladstone, passengers can board the high-speed, 112-foot Heron Islander from the city's marina. The launch makes the two-hour run to Heron Island from Gladstone, on the Queensland coast, for A$60 one-way, departing at 2 pm daily and arriving at 4:30 pm. The return boat departs from Heron Island for the mainland at 10 am EST (9 am island time) and arrives at 12:30 pm. This can be a rough journey: take ginger or antinausea medicine ½ hour before departure. A courtesy shuttle bus transfers guests from Gladstone Airport, leaving at 12:40 pm daily, and meets all afternoon boats. (Fly to Gladstone from Brisbane, Mackay, Rockhampton, Townsville, and Cairns with Qantas or Virgin Australia.) You can also arrange transfers to and from Gladstone Station; get here on Queensland Rail's fast *Tilt Train* or *Spirit of Queensland* from the north or south (⊕ *www.queenslandrail.com.au*).

Australia by Seaplane. Australia by Seaplane makes scenic, 25-minute flights to Heron Island from Gladstone from A$338 one-way, with more services October through April. The baggage restriction is 33 pounds per person. Lockup facilities for excess baggage are free (or get it brought over on the daily launch for free). You can charter a helicopter to the island from Gladstone for A$2,450 (maximum five adults, one infant). ⊠ *Heron Island* ☎ *07/4972–1940* ⊕ *www. australiabyseaplane.com.au.*

EXPLORING

Wilson Island. Only guests of the Heron Island Resort can visit uninhabited Wilson Island, a coral cay 15 km (9 miles) north of (and a 45-minute trip) Heron Island. In January and February Wilson Island becomes the breeding ground for roseate terns and green and loggerhead turtles. The island also has its own exclusive, six-suite, premium tented resort, catering to a maximum of 12 guests (and no children under 13), with all meals and transfers included in the rate—from A$463 per person, per night (more nights mean lower rates). Combination packages allow for nights at both Heron and Wilson islands, including meals. Guest accommodation is only available certain months to guests not wishing to "book the whole island." ⊠ *Wilson Island* ☎ *1300/863–248* ⊕ *www. wilsonisland.com.*

Coral and Lighthouse, Lady Elliot Island

SPORTS AND THE OUTDOORS

You can book snorkeling, scuba diving, and fishing excursions as well as turtle-watching tours and sunset cruises through Heron Island Marine Centre & Dive Shop. Snorkeling lessons are free, refresher dive courses are A$10. Snorkeling trips are A$50.

DIVING

Various diving options include a resort diving course for beginners, including training and one guided dive, for A$199 (subsequent dives, A$160). For certified divers it's A$75 per dive, and just A$55 per dive upward of five dives. Night dives, including light stick and flashlight, are A$90. Three-, five-, and seven-night dive packages include multiple dives throughout Heron and Wistari reefs, as well as accommodation, breakfast, buffet lunch, dinner, and all tanks and weights. Price is upon application. Half- and full-day dive boat charters are also available.

For all dives, prebooking is essential, and gear costs you extra. Children under 8 aren't permitted on snorkeling trips, under-12s can't go diving, and under-14s must be accompanied by an adult (and if diving, must be certified).

FISHING

Heron Island Marine Centre & Dive Shop. In addition to diving, snorkeling, and semisubmersible trips (A$50), Heron Island Marine Centre & Dive Shop runs three-hour fishing trips (A$115) and half- (A$920) and full-day (A$1,400) guided reef-fishing charters for up to 10 passengers, with gear, tackle, and optional stops for snorkeling. Toast the sunset on an hour-long wine-and-cheese cruise (A$60) or book a charter cruise for up to eight people (A$600–A$800). ⊠ *Heron Island* ☎ *07/4972–9055* ⊕ *www.heronisland.com* ☽ *Daily 8–5:30.*

SNORKELING AND SEMISUBMERSIBLE

Nondivers wanting to explore their underwater environs can take a half-day snorkeling tour of Heron and Wistari reefs, or an hour-long, naturalist-guided semisubmersible tour. Guided reef and birdlife walks, movies under the stars, and visits to the island's Marine Research Station are free.

WHERE TO STAY

$$$$
RESORT
☷ **Heron Island Resort.** Set among palm trees and connected by sand paths, this secluded, eco-certified resort has six accommodation types, from the deluxe Beach House with private outdoor shower and beach boardwalk to the comparatively compact, garden-level Turtle Rooms. **Pros:** lots of activities; eco-friendly; under-12s stay and eat free (most packages). **Cons:** no mobile phone coverage; limited Wi-Fi; no TVs in rooms. ⑤ *Rooms from: A$330* ⊠ *Heron Island* ☎ *1300/731551* ⊕ *www.heronisland.com* ⤳ *32 rooms, 76 suites, 1 house* ⑲ *Breakfast.*

GREAT KEPPEL ISLAND

40 km (25 miles) from the Great Barrier Reef.

Positioned at the southern end of the Great Barrier Reef near the Tropic of Capricorn, idyllic Great Keppel Island boasts crystal clear waters, palm-fringed white sand beaches, scenic hiking trails, and some of the most diverse and unspoiled coral on the reef. The 593-acre island is also home to a rich diversity of flora and fauna, including over 90 species of birds.

GETTING HERE AND AROUND

AIR TRAVEL
Low-cost carrier Virgin Australia flies to Rockhampton from Brisbane, with connections to all major Australian cities. Qantas has direct flights to Rockhampton from Brisbane, Townsville, and Mackay, connecting to other capitals.

Airlines Peace Aviation. ☎ *07/4927–4355, 0429/616–758* ⊕ *www. peaceaviation.com.* **Qantas.** ☎ *13–1313* ⊕ *www.qantas.com.au.* **Virgin Australia.** ☎ *13–6789* ⊕ *www.virginaustralia.com.*

BOAT AND
FERRY TRAVEL
Freedom Fast Cats. These ferries transfer guests to the island from Pier 1 at Rosslyn Bay Harbour, near Yeppoon (across the bay from the marina). Departures are early- to mid-morning (check schedules) daily, and return trips back to the mainland are Tuesday to Sunday early- to mid-afternoon. The cost is A$55 per person, round-trip. Glass bottom boat tours (A$50) and various cruise packages are also available. Depending on the time of your flight arrival, you may need to stay overnight in Rockhampton or Yeppoon before and after your island stay. ⊠ *Great Keppel Island* ☎ *07/4933–6888* ⊕ *www.freedomfastcats.com.*

Keppel Bay Marina. Keppel Bay Marina runs day cruises to secluded coves and beaches: choose a romantic sunset cruise (A$55) or a full-day cruise including snorkeling, fishing, beachcombing, and a full buffet lunch on board (A$125). Three-day adventure cruises

Scuba diving off Heron Island

(including accommodation), as well as private charters, are also available by request. ✉ *Great Keppel Island* ☎ *07/4933–6244* ⊕ *www. keppelbaymarina.com.au.*

EXPLORING

Great Keppel Island. Although Great Keppel is large, at 8 km (5 miles) by 11 km (7 miles), it lies 40 km (25 miles) from the Great Barrier Reef, which makes for a long trip from the mainland. There's lots to do, with walking trails, 17 stunning safe swimming beaches, excellent coral gardens in many sheltered coves, plenty of friendly local wildlife, and dozens of beach and water-sports activities available. A refurbished underwater observatory at nearby Middle Island lets you stay dry while viewing the local marine life from 6 meters below the ocean surface, including a confiscated Taiwanese fishing boat that was deliberately sunk alongside the observatory to shelter tropical fish. An abundance of bushwalking tracks allows visitors to explore the island's interior and access secluded beaches. Several major resorts have closed down on Great Keppel in recent years, but a redevelopment plan is underway for the construction of a multimillion-dollar, solar-powered eco-luxury resort and villa complex, with a 250-berth marina, retail village, day spa, golf course, and commercial airstrip. ✉ *Great Keppel Island.*

SPORTS AND THE OUTDOORS

WATER SPORTS

The Watersports Activities Hut. In Great Keppel Island Holiday Village (open weekends and school holidays), this operator runs guided kayak and motorized canoe trips, and water taxi drop-offs to and pickups from surrounding beaches and islands. They also rent out water-sports equipment, including kayaks and paddle boards, and have banana and tube rides. ⊠ *Fisherman's Beach* ⊕ *www.gkiholidayvillage.com.au.*

WHERE TO STAY

$ 🛏 **Great Keppel Island Holiday Village.** Surrounded by stunning beaches

RENTAL and untouched bush, this is a modest, quiet alternative for travelers

FAMILY looking to get back to basics and enjoy the environs the "old fashioned" way. **Pros:** beautiful and peaceful location; relaxed and friendly atmosphere; helpful staff; great value. **Cons:** patchy mobile phone coverage; no Wi-Fi or TV (except in Keppel House); some design getting quite dated; wildlife can be noisy at night. ⑤ *Rooms from: A$100* ⊠ *Great Keppel Island* ☎ *07/4939–8655, 1800/537735* ⊕ *www. gkiholidayvillage.com.au* ⊅ *4 rooms, 2 houses, 2 cabins, 9 tents, 1 campground* ⊘❘ *No meals.*

FRASER ISLAND

200 km (125 miles) north of Brisbane

Fraser Island, at 1,014 square km (391 square miles), is the largest of Queensland's islands and the most unusual. Fraser is the world's largest sand island—instead of coral reefs and coconut palms, it has wildflower-dotted meadows; 100-plus freshwater lakes; dense, tall stands of rain forest; towering dunes; sculpted, multicolor sand cliffs; up to 40,000 migratory shorebirds; and rare and endangered species including dugongs, turtles, Illidge's ant-blue butterfly, and eastern curlews—a lineup that won the island a place on UNESCO's World Heritage list.

The surf fishing is legendary, and humpback whales and their calves winter in Hervey Bay between May and September. The island also has Aboriginal sites dating back more than a millennium.

Hervey Bay is the name given to the expanse of water between Fraser Island and the Queensland coast, and to four nearby coastal towns—Urangan, Pialba, Scarness, and Torquay—that have merged into a single settlement. Hervey Bay and Rainbow Beach are the main jumping-off points for offshore excursions. (Maps and road signs usually refer to individual town names.)

GETTING HERE AND AROUND

AIR TRAVEL

Several direct air services on Jetstar, Qantas, and Virgin Australia connect Sydney and Fraser Coast (Hervey Bay) Airport. Bay 2 Dore shuttle buses link the airport to Urangan, meeting flights upon request.

Airport Contact Fraser Coast (Hervey Bay) Airport. ⊠ *Don Adams Dr., Hervey Bay* ☎ *07/4194–8100* ⊕ *www.frasercoastairport.com.au.*

Shuttle Bay 2 Dore Airport Shuttle. ☎ *07/4124–3516, 0417/637–447* ⊕ *www. bay2dore.com.au.*

BOAT AND FERRY TRAVEL

Numerous vehicular ferries service Fraser Island from Rainbow Beach and Hervey Bay. Manta Ray Fraser Island Barges runs a regular service from 6 am to 5:30 pm between Inskip Point, near Rainbow Beach, and

Fraser Island

Hook Point at the island's southern end. The company's two to three barges make up to 40 round-trips daily, so if you miss one barge, the next will be along soon. Buy tickets online (recommended) or as you board.

Fraser Island Barges' *Fraser Venture* makes the half-hour trip between River Heads, 20 minutes' drive south of Hervey Bay, and Wanggoolba Creek, opposite Eurong Bay Resort on the island's west coast, three times a day. The Kingfisher Bay Passenger and Vehicle Ferry also connects River Heads with Kingfisher Bay Resort in 50 minutes up to six times a day.

Boat and Ferry Contacts Fraser Island Barges. ☏ *07/4194–9300, 1800/227437* ⊕ *www.fraserislandferry.com.au.* **Kingfisher Bay Ferry.** ✉ *Urangan* ☏ *07/4194–9300, 1800/227437* ⊕ *www.fraserislandferry.com.au.* **Manta Ray Fraser Island Barges.** ☏ *07/5486–3935, 0418/872–599* ⊕ *www. mantarayfraserislandbarge.com.au.*

CAR AND BUGGY TRAVEL
Fraser's east coast favors two Australian passions: beaches and vehicles. Unrestricted access has made this coast a giant sandbox for four-wheel-drive vehicles, busiest in school-holiday periods.

The southernmost tip of Fraser Island is just more than 200 km (125 miles) north of Brisbane. The simplest access is via barge from Rainbow Beach or Hervey Bay, 90 km (56 miles) farther north. For Rainbow Beach, take the Bruce Highway toward Gympie, then follow signs to Rainbow Beach. For Hervey Bay, head to Maryborough, then follow the signs to River Heads.

Every vehicle entering the island by barge from the mainland must have a one-month Vehicle Access Permit (A$46.65). To obtain these and island camping permits (A$5.95 per person, per night), contact NPRSR ⊕ *www.nprsr.qld.gov.au.*

You can rent four-wheel-drive vehicles from Aussie Trax 4WD Hire at Kingfisher Bay Resort and Village for upward of A$295 a day, or from various rental companies at Urangan and Hervey Bay Airport for considerably less.

Four-wheel-drive rentals may be cheaper on the mainland, but factoring in the ferry ticket makes rental on-island a viable option. Most commodities, including gas, are pricier on-island.

Wet weather and sandy surfaces can make island driving challenging and hazardous. Consult NPRSR's website for detailed information on safe driving and local hazards. Basic mechanical assistance and tow-truck services are available from Eurong. Orchid Beach has emergency towing only. If you can't get the mechanical assistance you need, phone Eurong Police.

Car Rental Budget Car Rental. ✉ *Hervey Bay Airport, Airport Terminal, Hervey Bay* ☎ *07/4125–3633* ⊕ *www.budget.com.au.*

ESSENTIALS

Vehicle Permits Department of National Parks, Sport and Racing. ☎ *13–7468 for info and permits* ⊕ *www.nprsr.qld.gov.au.*

Visitor Information Hervey Bay Visitor Information Centre. ✉ *227 Maryborough-Hervey Bay Rd., Hervey Bay* ☎ *1800/811728* ⊕ *www.visitfrasercoast.com.*

TOURS

Air Fraser Island. Air Fraser Island runs day trips, transfers, and scenic and whale watching flights (in season) from Hervey Bay, using the pristine beaches of Fraser Island as its landing strip. Overnight packages, including 4WD rentals, are also available. ✉ *Fraser Island* ☎ *07/4125–3600* ⊕ *www.airfraserisland.com.au* ✈ *From A$75.*

Fraser Explorer Tours. This group operates one- and two-day 4WD tours across World Heritage-Listed Fraser Island, taking in its pristine beaches and colored sands, fresh water lakes, verdant forests, and abundant marine life. Departing both Hervey Bay and Rainbow Beach, tours include barge transfers, meals, National Park fees, and audio guides in various languages. ✉ *1 Eastern St.* ☎ *07/4194–9222, 1800/678431* ⊕ *www.fraserexplorertours.com.au* ✈ *From A$185.*

EXPLORING

Highlights of a drive along the east coast, which is known as Seventy-Five Mile Beach for its sheer distance, include **Eli Creek**, a great freshwater swimming hole. North of this popular spot lies the rusting hulk of the *Maheno*, half buried in the sand, a roost for seagulls and a prime hunting ground for anglers when the tailor are running. Once a luxury passenger steamship that operated between Australia and New Zealand (and served as a hospital ship during World War I), it was wrecked during a cyclone in 1935 as it was being towed to Japan to be sold for scrap metal. North of the wreck are the **Pinnacles**—dramatic, deep-red cliff formations. About 20 km (12 miles) south of Eli Creek, and surrounded by massive sand-blow (or dune), is **Lake Wabby**, the deepest of the island's lakes.

GETTING HELP

Fraser Island does not have a resident doctor. Emergency medical assistance can be obtained at the ranger stations in Eurong, Waddy Point, and Dundubara, but these have variable hours—if no answer, phone the base station at Nambour on the mainland. Kingfisher Bay Resort has first-aid facilities and resident nursing staff.

Note that swimming in the ocean off the island is not recommended because of the rough conditions and sharks that hunt close to shore. Stick to the inland lakes.

Fraser Island, Sandy Cape Conservation Park. This park covers the top third of Fraser Island. Beaches around Indian Head are known for their shell middens—shell heaps that were left behind after Aboriginal feasting. The head's name is another kind of relic: Captain James Cook saw Aborigines standing on the headland as he sailed past, and he therefore named the area after inhabitants he believed to be "Indians." Farther north, past Waddy Point, is one of Fraser Island's most magnificent variations on sand: wind and time have created enormous dunes. Nearby at Orchid Beach are a series of bubbling craters known as the Champagne Pools. ✉ *Fraser Island* ☎ *13–7468* ⊕ *www.nprsr.qld.gov.au.*

Wanggoolba Creek. A boardwalk heads south from Central Station to Wanggoolba Creek, a favorite spot for photographers. The little stream snakes through a green palm forest, trickling over a bed of white sand between clumps of rare angiopteris fern. The 1 km (½-mile) circuit takes 30 minutes to an hour. ✉ *Fraser Island.*

SPORTS AND THE OUTDOORS

FISHING

Hervey Bay Fishing Charters. This family-run business caters to all levels of experience with its half- and full-day fishing trips through the waters off Fraser Island. Morning tea, lunch, refreshments, bait, tackle, and fish cleaning is all included. Private and overnight charters are also available upon request. ✉ *51 Tristania Crescent, Urangan* ☎ *07/4125–3958, 0427/621–623* ⊕ *www.herveybayfishingcharters.com.au* 🚢 *From A$150.*

Offshore, Fraser Island. All freshwater fish are protected on Fraser Island, so you can't fish in lakes or streams, but just offshore is one of Australia's richest, most diverse fishing areas, with whiting, flathead, trevally, red emperor, snapper, sea perch, coronation trout, cod, and, in summer, mackerel, cobia, amberjack, and more. This is partly due to the diversity of habitat; choose between estuary, surf beach, reef, sport, and game fishing. On reef-fishing trips dolphins are commonly sighted, as are whales in season.

When angling off Fraser Island beaches and jetties, follow NPRSR guidelines. To discourage dingoes and other undesirable visitors, clean fish away from campsites and dispose of scraps carefully (bury fish scraps at least a foot below the tide line). Some beaches are closed to fishing during August and September, and bag and size limits apply to some species: for details, go to ⊕ *www.nprsr.qld.gov.au.* ⊠ *Fraser Island* ⊕ *www.nprsr.qld.gov.au.*

HIKING

Central Station. The island's excellent network of walking trails converges at Central Station, a former logging camp at the center of the island. Services here are limited to a map board, parking lot, and campground. It's a promising place for spotting dingoes. Comparative isolation has meant that Fraser Island's dingoes are the most purebred in Australia. They're also wild animals, so remember: don't feed them, watch from a distance, don't walk alone after dark, store food and dispose of rubbish carefully, and keep a close eye on children, especially between late afternoon and early morning.

Most of the island's well-marked trails are sandy tracks. Guides advise wearing sturdy shoes, wearing sunscreen, and carrying first-aid supplies and drinking water on all walks. ⊠ *Central Station* ⊕ *www.tourfraser. com.au.*

Pile Valley. One trail from Central Station leads through rain forest—growing, incredibly enough, straight out of the sand—to Pile Valley, which has a stand of giant satinay trees. Allow two hours to walk the full 4½-km (2¼-mile) circuit. ⊠ *Fraser Island.*

SWIMMING

Lake McKenzie. The center of Fraser Island is a quiet, natural garden of paperbark swamps, giant satinay and brush box forests, wildflower heaths, and 40 freshwater lakes. The spectacularly clear Lake McKenzie, ringed by a beach of incandescent white sand, is arguably the most stunning of the lakes and is the perfect place for a refreshing swim, day or night. ⊠ *Lake McKenzie.*

CLOSE UP

Camping on Fraser Island

The Queensland Parks and Wildlife Service manages the island and maintains ranger bases at Dundubara and Eurong. You can pitch a tent anywhere you don't see a "no camping" sign; there are four main public campgrounds—Central Station, Dundubara, Lake Boomanjin, and Waddy Point—though all sites on the Island require you to book your permit in advance. These campgrounds have fenced sites to protect from dingoes (advised if you have kids under 14), toilet blocks, drinking water, hot showers (some coin-operated), gas grills, phones, and other amenities. There are also smaller designated camping areas along Fraser Island's Great Walk, and a number of established beach campsites, all run by The Queensland Parks and Wildlife Service. They have toilet blocks, picnic tables, and walking trails. Most lack drinking water, so bring plenty with you. Because the entire island is a World Heritage site, permits for camping (A\$5.95 per person, per night) are required.

WHERE TO STAY

\$\$
RESORT
Eurong Beach Resort. This simple-but-comfortable, east-coast resort has the best of Fraser Island at its doorstep. **Pros:** on-site general store; great location and facilities; large pool; good value. **Cons:** rooms in need of updating; slow, pricey Internet; spotty mobile phone reception; air conditioning not available in all rooms. $ *Rooms from: A\$135* ⊠ *75 Mile Beach Rd.* ☎ *07/4120–1600, 1800/111808* ⊕ *www.eurong. au* ⤳ *124 rooms, including 16 apartments* ⫶ *No meals; Breakfast; Some meals.*

\$\$\$
RESORT
FAMILY
Fodor's Choice
★
Kingfisher Bay Resort. This stylish, high-tech marriage of glass, stainless steel, dark timber, and corrugated iron nestles in tree-covered dunes on the island's west coast. **Pros:** terrific facilities, tours, and activities; eco-friendly; excellent location; child sitting available. **Cons:** many rooms in need of updating; housekeeping standards vary; west-coast beaches unsuitable for 4WD vehicles; charge for Wi-Fi. $ *Rooms from: A\$208* ⊠ *North White Cliffs, 75 Mile Beach* ☎ *07/4120–3333, 1800/072555* ⊕ *www.kingfisherbay.com* ⤳ *152 rooms, 109 villas, 184 beds in lodges (for 18–35s)* ⫶ *No meals; Breakfast.*

THE GREAT
BARRIER REEF

WELCOME TO THE GREAT BARRIER REEF

TOP REASONS TO GO

★ **Reef Explorations:** There are thousands of spectacular dive sites scattered along the coral spine of the Great Barrier Reef.

★ **Wildlife Watching:** Flora and fauna on the islands themselves can be fascinating: rain forests, hills and rocky areas, and postcard-perfect beaches provide diverse habitat.

★ **Cultural Immersion:** The Kuku Yalanji people have lived in the area between Port Douglas and Cookdown for millennia. A highlight of visiting the region is experiencing this unique landscape from the perspective of its traditional owners.

★ **Ancient Rain Forest:** The UNESCO World Heritage–listed Daintree rain forest is a rich and ancient ecosystem in which you'll find sustainable resorts, jungle zip lines, and deserted beaches.

★ **Outback Adventures:** West of Port Douglas lie vast tracts of savannah dotted with termite mounds and teeming with kangaroos, wallabies, reptiles, and birds.

1 Cairns. A laid-back tropical tourist hub built around a busy marina and swimming lagoon, Cairns bristles with hotels, tour agencies, dive-cruise boats, and travelers en route to the rain forest and reef. It has some fine retail stores and markets, plus an extensive waterfront park and entertainment precinct.

2 North of Cairns. The pristine coastline north of Cairns is punctuated by charming villages and tourist towns, including Palm Cove, with its European Riviera ambience, and bustling Port Douglas, with its sparkling marina, sprawling resorts, and hip café scene. North of the Daintree River, World Heritage–listed wilderness extends to Cape Tribulation and beyond; here you'll find few services but some terrific, eco-friendly rain-forest retreats.

3 Whitsundays/Airlie Beach. The glorious Whitsunday Islands, just off the mid-north-Queensland coast, lure holidaymakers with world-class water sports, sheltered yacht anchorages, and resorts catering to every taste. Airlie Beach, the closest mainland town, buzzes with backpackers, who flock to its man-made lagoon, markets, bars, and budget digs. Well-heeled travelers might prefer the boutique retreats and resorts that hug the hillsides above the main drag.

4 North Coast islands. The upscale, eco-conscious boutique resort on Orpheus and Bedarra islands, off Ingham and Mission Beach, are tailored to foodies and honeymooners, reclusive VIPs, and nature-loving travelers. Lizard and Fitzroy islands, off Cairns, offer ready access to world-class dive and game-fishing sites.

5 Townsville and Magnetic Island. Regional city Townsville has gracious heritage buildings, excellent museums and marine centers, and a well-maintained waterfront with a man-made swimming lagoon. Offshore, Magnetic Island is a popular holiday spot, with high-end and budget accommodation and an array of aquatic activities, including sea kayaking and scuba diving.

GETTING ORIENTED

A map linking all of northern Queensland's coastal ports and offshore resorts from the Whitsundays north to Lizard Island would look like a lace-up boot 1,600 km (1,000 miles) long. However, you'd only see less than half the reef, which extends south to Lady Elliot Island and as far north as the near-roadless wilderness of Cape York and the shores of Papua New Guinea.

If you're visiting the reef only briefly, it's simplest and most economical to day-trip from the mainland. Some reef-island resorts are accessible by boat; others can be reached only by plane, and both airfare and rates can be expensive. Day trips depart from major coastal cities including Cairns, Port Douglas, Townsville, and Airlie Beach.

8

SAILING THE WHITSUNDAY ISLANDS

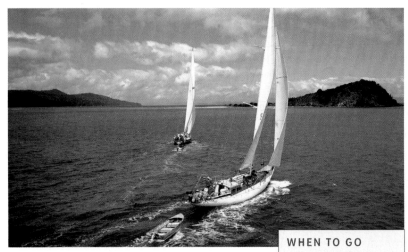

The Whitsundays, 74 islands and dozens of islets scattered along Queensland's central coast off Airlie Beach, are favorite destinations among yachties and beach-lovers—and with good reason.

The Whitsunday islands, protected from Coral Sea swells by sheltering reefs and cooled by trade winds, offer hundreds of yacht anchorages in close proximity, making this ideal cruising territory. The aquamarine waters shimmer and sparkle—a light-scattering effect that results when fine sediment run-off from river systems is stirred up by the 3- to 5-meter tides that sweep the coast.

Island resorts offer safe moorings for passing yachts, and an array of water sports and facilities. Farther out, on the Barrier Reef, you'll find fine snorkeling, diving, and fishing sites. Most Whitsunday Islands are unspoiled national parks; just a few—Hayman, Hamilton, Daydream, South Molle, and South Long—have resorts.

WHEN TO GO

With a climate moderated by cooling trade winds, the Whitsundays are typically balmy year-round, though summer days can sometimes exceed 100° Fahrenheit. Over winter (June–August) it's warm, clear, and sunny by day and cool—even chilly—at night. Steer clear of Australia's summer holidays to avoid hordes of local families who, despite often wet and stormy weather, flock here December to February. Spring and fall weather can be perfect, and these seasons are often the quietest, if you avoid school and Easter holidays. Migrating southern right and humpback whales traverse these waters between July and September.

WHERE CAN I FIND . . .

Underwater adventure? Most Whitsunday resorts have dedicated dive shops offering scuba and snorkeling lessons and gear hire; all either run or can organize day trips to dive and snorkeling spots nearby. Highlights include Heart Reef and vast Knuckle Reef Lagoon, where a purpose-built pontoon floats in sheltered waters teeming with tropical fish, turtles, and rays. Not keen to get wet? Take a semisubmersible coral-viewing tour, guided reef walk, or scenic heli-flight. Sheltered coves and coral-fringed beaches around many Whitsunday islands also offer good snorkeling. Many cruises stop to snorkel off Whitehaven Beach and the northern end of Long Island.

Luxury? At Qualia, Hamilton Island's most lavish accommodation, sleek suites have infinity pools and alfresco areas, artfully lighted after dark, and fine food and wine brought in from Hamilton's best restaurants. Bedarra, Orpheus, and Lizard Island resorts serve up gourmet meals and exclusive accommodations, while Paradise Bay Island Resort pampers its select group of guests with top-quality, all-natural furnishings and fabrics, Molton Brown toiletries, and cruises on the resort's own sailing cat. The lavish The One & Only Hayman Resort, a magnificent sprawl of public areas and opulent suites, is solid enough to withstand a Category 5 cyclone and luxurious enough to satisfy the fussiest visitor. Here your needs are more than met: they're often spookily anticipated.

Family-friendliness? BreakFree Long Island Resort's jam-packed sports and activities program offers dozens of aquatic and land-based sports, most included in the rates. Daydream and Hamilton islands have dedicated kids' clubs, playgrounds, and myriad kid-at-heart features and activities. At Fitzroy Island Resort, children's activity programs mean parents can relax or join in the fun, while nature-based activities on Lizard and Hayman islands are great for older kids.

TOP REASONS TO GO

Aquatic Playground
This is a snorkelers' and divers' paradise and one of the world's top sailing and cruising areas. It's also great for kayaking, windsurfing, and paragliding—and most resorts include the use of nonmotorized water sports equipment in their rates.

Tropical Paradise
Enjoy a mild climate and warm, clear waters whatever the season, plus beautiful fine-white-sand beaches.

Gourmet Destination
Several Whitsunday and Barrier Reef island resorts offer cuisine to rival that of high-end city establishments. Island-resort food runs the gamut from four-star gourmet fare to regional cuisine presented with site-specific twists.

Resort Variety
You can divide your time easily between luxurious, leisurely resorts (such as those on Hayman and Lizard islands, or Paradise Bay Island Resort on South Long Island) and a gregarious, activity-oriented isle (such as Hamilton or Daydream).

8

OUTDOOR ADVENTURES IN DAINTREE

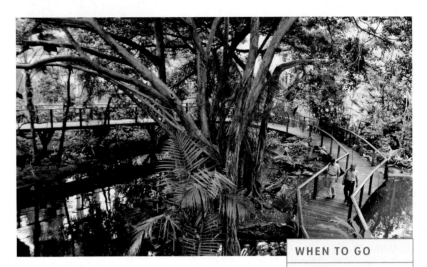

Cape Tribulation, Daintree National Park is an ecological wonderland. Here you can see several of the world's most ancient plants and some of Australia's rarest creatures, protected by the Daintree's traditional owners, the Eastern Kuku Yalanji, for thousands of years.

The park extends over approximately 22,000 acres, although the entire Wet Tropics region—which stretches from Townsville to Cooktown and covers 1,200 square km (463 square miles)—was declared a UNESCO World Heritage site in 1988. Within it, experts have identified several species of angiosperms, the most primitive flowering plants in existence, many of which are found nowhere else on the planet.

WHEN TO GO

Clear, sunny days, comfortably cool nights, no stingers in the ocean and mud-free rain forest and mangrove trails: "the Dry" season is the most pleasant time to visit.

"The Wet"—roughly November through April—can be wonderful, too: foliage is lush and green; buds turn to hothouse blooms. Drawbacks include occasional flash flooding and road closures, high humidity, slippery tracks, and leeches and mosquitoes.

Spring and late fall can be a good compromise: the weather—and the water—are typically warm and clear, and activities are less heavily booked than during the dry season.

A SACRED SITE

With diverse plant and animal life, abundant fresh water, and tracts of fertile coastal lowland, the Daintree rain forest is rich terrain for the resourceful. Its traditional custodians are the Eastern Kuku Yalanji, a peaceable people who've been coexisting with and subsisting on the forest's abundant flora and fauna for tens of thousands of years. Their tribal lands stretch north almost as far as Cooktown, south as far as Mossman and west to the Palmer River, with the Kuku Yalanji traveling seasonally throughout the region.

Designating five rather than four seasons in a year, the Eastern Kuku Yalanji used changes in weather and growth cycles to guide hunting and foraging expeditions into the rain forest: when the *jun jun* (blue ginger) came into fruit, they'd catch *diwan* (Australian brush-turkey); when *jilngan* (mat grass) flowered, they'd collect *jarruka* (orange-footed scrubfowl) eggs; and year-round, they'd track tree-dwelling animals—*yawa* (possum), *kambi* (flying fox), and *murral* (tree kangaroo). Even today, members of the Kuku Yalanji can tell you which local plants can be eaten, used as medicines, and made into utensils, weapons, and shelter.

The Daintree's indigenous inhabitants believe many of the area's natural sites have spiritual significance, attributing particular power to Wundu (Thornton Peak), Manjal Dimbi (Mt. Demi), Wurrmbu (The Bluff), and Kulki (Cape Tribulation). Dozens of spots in the rain forest—waterfalls, crags, peaks, and creeks—are deemed by the Kuku Yalanji to have spiritual, healing, or regenerative powers. Take a walk with one of the area's traditional custodians to get an intimate, intriguing perspective on this extraordinary terrain.

Various indigenous-guided tours and experiences in the Daintree area focus on bush tucker and medicines, wildlife and hunting techniques, culture, history, and ritual. A waterhole just behind Daintree Eco Lodge & Spa is deemed a site of special significance for women: a dip in its healing waters is a female-only ritual.

TOP REASONS TO GO

Animals. Watch for the rare Bennett's tree kangaroo, believed to have evolved from possums; the endangered, spotted-tailed quoll, a marsupial carnivore; a giant white-tailed rat (prone to raiding campsites); and the Daintree River ringtail possum, found only around Thornton Peak and the upper reaches of the Daintree and Mossman rivers.

Birds. Daintree National Park shelters hundreds of bird species: azure kingfishers swoop on crabs in the creeks, white-rumped swiftlets dart above the canopy. The pied imperial pigeon flies south from Papua New Guinea to breed here—as does the glorious buff-breasted paradise kingfisher, distinguished by its orange underbelly, blue wings, and long white tail. Year-round, you'll see orange-footed scrubfowl foraging or building gigantic leaf-litter nest-mounds. If you're very lucky, you might even spot the 6-foot-tall, flightless southern cassowary.

8

Updated by
Merran White

A maze of 3,000 individual reefs and 900 islands stretching for 2,600 km (1,616 miles), the Great Barrier Reef is among the world's most spectacular natural attractions. Known as Australia's "Blue Outback," the reef is a haven for thousands of species of marine creatures as well as turtles and birds. Most visitors explore this section of Australia from one of the dozen-plus resorts strung along the coasts of islands in the southern half of the marine park, most of them in or north of the Whitsunday Islands group. Although most Barrier Reef islands are closer to the mainland than they are to the spectacular outer reef, all island resorts offer (or can organize) boat excursions to various outer-reef sites.

The reef was established as a marine park in 1975, and the United Nations designated the Great Barrier Reef a World Heritage site in 1981. Strict legislation was enacted in 2004, prohibiting fishing along most of the reef—a further attempt to protect the underwater treasures of this vast, delicate ecosystem. Any visitor over the age of four must pay a A$6 per day Environmental Management Charge ("reef tax") to support ongoing efforts to preserve the reef.

The Great Barrier Reef system began to form approximately 6,000–7,000 years ago, say marine scientists. It's comprised of individual reefs and islands, which lie to the east of the Coral Sea and extend south into the Pacific Ocean. Most of the reef is about 65 km (40 miles) off the Queensland coast, although some parts extend as far as 300 km (186 miles) offshore. Altogether, it covers an area bigger than Great Britain, forming the largest living feature on Earth and the only one visible from space.

PLANNER

WHEN TO GO

The bulk of the Great Barrier Reef islands lie north of the tropic of Capricorn in a monsoonal climate zone. In the hot, wet season (roughly December–April), expect tropical downpours that can limit outdoor activities and mar underwater visibility.

The warm days, clear skies, and pleasantly cool nights of the dry season, especially June–August, are ideal for traveling around and above Cairns. In the Whitsundays, some winter days may be too cool for swimming and nights can be chilly (pack a sweater and long pants).

The islands are warm, even in winter; during the summer months, temperatures regularly top 35° Celsius (95° Fahrenheit), and the farther north you go, the hotter it gets. The water temperature is mild to cool year-round; however, in jellyfish season (typically, November through May), you'll need to wear a full-body stinger suit to swim anywhere but within patrolled, netted areas.

PLANNING YOUR TIME

Most visitors to the Great Barrier Reef combine stays on one or more islands with time in Queensland's coastal towns and national parks. With a week or more, you could stay at two very different Barrier Reef island resorts: perhaps at an activities-packed Whitsundays resort and one of the more remote northerly islands, allowing a day or two to travel between them. If you want to resort-hop, opt for the Whitsundays, where island resorts lie in relatively close proximity and are well serviced by water and air transport.

If you have limited time, take a boat from Cairns or Port Douglas to a pontoon on the outer reef for a day on the water. A helicopter flight back to the mainland will give you an exhilarating aerial view of the reef and its islands. Alternatively, catch an early boat from Cairns to Fitzroy Island or from Shute Harbour to Daydream Island. Spend a couple of hours snorkeling, take a walk around, then relax on a quiet beach or in the resort bar.

GETTING HERE AND AROUND

AIR TRAVEL

Jetstar, Virgin Australia, and Qantas have daily direct flights linking capital cities around Australia to Cairns Airport (which also handles international flights). These airlines also have flights to Townsville, Whitsundays Coast (Proserpine), Hamilton Island, and Mackay airports, linking with east-coast capitals and major regional cities throughout Queensland. From these hubs, regular boat and charter air services are available to most of the Great Barrier Reef resorts. Generally, island charter flights are timed to connect with domestic flights, but double-check. *For information about reaching the islands, see Getting Here and Around under each island's heading.*

BOAT TRAVEL

Usually, island launches are timed to connect with charter flights from island or mainland airports, but do ask. Crossings can be choppy; take ginger tablets for motion sickness ahead of time. If you're based on the mainland or in a hurry, many operators run day trips out to the reef and resort islands.

Several operators provide skipper-yourself (bareboat) and crewed charters to explore the Whitsundays. Almost all have five-day minimum charter periods; most offer discounts for multiday hire and optional extras such as catering. Packages start from around A$120 per person, per night, but can be several times that on crewed or luxury vessels.

BUS TRAVEL

Long-distance buses are an economical but often cramped way to travel along the North Queensland coast; don't expect to get much sleep on board. Shuttle buses transfer visitors from regional airports, Cairns, and beaches and towns to as far north as Cape Tribulation. They link airports, railway stations, and local towns to island ferry services departing from Mission Beach, Airlie Beach, and Shute Harbour. Hotel pickups are usually available; call ahead to confirm.

CAR TRAVEL

If you're visiting several North Queensland destinations, it may be simplest to drive. Most popular North Queensland routes are paved, though roads may be flooded in the wet season. A 4WD vehicle is advised. Leave extra time if you're crossing the Daintree River or driving between Port Douglas and Cairns—peak-season traffic and roadwork may create congestion. If you're heading farther north, fill up with gas at or before Wonga Beach, and carry water, tools, and supplies. Past this point, services are infrequent, and gas and goods can be pricey.

RESTAURANTS

Typically, restaurants on Barrier Reef islands are part of each island's main resort, so many resorts' rates include some or all meals. Some larger resorts have a range of restaurants, with formal dining rooms, outdoor barbecues, and seafood buffets; some have premium dining options for which you pay extra. Dress is generally "island casual." Some upscale restaurants—such as those on Hayman Island—require men to wear jackets for dinner and frown on flip-flop sandals. On the mainland you'll find plenty of casual, open-air restaurants, serving mainly Modern Australian–style meals that showcase seafood and regional produce. With a few notable exceptions, Cairns, Palm Cove, and Port Douglas are your best bets for upscale dining.

HOTELS

Most inhabited islands have just one main resort, typically offering a range of lodging types and prices. Choose island destinations based on your budget and the kind of vacation you want—active or relaxed, sociable or quiet, or a mix. Offerings range from luxurious enclaves with upscale facilities (Lizard, Orpheus, Bedarra, Hayman islands) to small, eco-focused retreats (Long Island) to activity-packed, family-friendly resorts (Long, South Molle, Daydream, and Fitzroy islands). The more rustic, remote resorts may lack modern conveniences such as telephones, televisions, and Internet access. Even on some Barrier Reef resorts close to the mainland, Internet connections can be slow and mobile phone coverage limited or nonexistent, and critters may infiltrate your room. *Hotel reviews have been shortened. For full information, visit Fodors.com.*

WHAT IT COSTS (IN AUSTRALIAN DOLLARS)			
	$	$$	$$$	$$$$
Restaurants	Under A$36	A$36–A$45	A$46–A$65	over A$65
Hotels	Under A$201	A$201–A$300	A$301–A$450	over A$450

Restaurant prices are the average cost of a main course at dinner or, if dinner is not served, at lunch. Hotel prices are the lowest cost of a standard double room in high season, excluding service and tax (10%).

HEALTH AND SAFETY

You'll find large, well-equipped hospitals in Cairns, Townsville, and Mackay; doctors and medical centers in Port Douglas and Airlie Beach, and nearby towns. Emergency services are scarce between the Daintree River and Cooktown. Island resort front-desk staff typically handle emergencies and can summon doctors and aerial ambulance services. Remote islands have "flying doctor" kits; Hamilton Island has its own doctors and Hayman has an on-site medical center. Contact Cairns Health Online (⊕ *www.cairnshealthonline.com*) for a list of GPs, hospitals, and pharmacies in the region.

Avoid midday rays, even in winter, and wear a hat and SPF15-plus sunscreen to prevent sunburn. Rehydrate often and take it easy in the heat.

Avoid touching coral: it is easily damaged, and can cut and sting. Clean cuts thoroughly, scrubbing with a brush and flushing the affected area with saline solution. Toxic and stinging jellyfish frequent waters off the mainland and some Barrier Reef islands over the warmer months. Avoid the ocean at these times, unless you're wearing a stinger suit. If in doubt, ask a local.

Mosquitoes, midges, and leeches can be a problem in wet summer months. Wear insect repellent to avoid being bitten; check extremities, especially between your toes, after walking in damp, forested areas, and remove leeches by applying a flame or salt.

Estuarine crocodiles live in rivers and coastal waters along the North Queensland coast and on some Barrier Reef islands. Don't swim where crocs live (ask a local), especially in breeding season, September to April—and never dangle your limbs over the sides of boats.

CAIRNS

Tourism is the lifeblood of Cairns (pronounced *Caans*). The city makes a good base for exploring the wild top half of Queensland, and tens of thousands of international travelers use it as a jumping-off point for activities such as scuba diving and snorkeling trips to the Barrier Reef, as well as boating, fishing, parasailing, scenic flights, and rainforest treks.

It's a tough environment, with intense heat and fierce wildlife. Along with wallabies and gray kangaroos in the savanna and tree kangaroos in the rain forest, you'll find stealthy saltwater crocodiles, venomous snakes, and jellyfish so deadly they put the region's stunning beaches off-limits to swimmers for nearly half the year. Yet despite this formidable setting, Cairns and tropical North Queensland are far from intimidating places. The people are warm and friendly, the sights spectacular, and—at the right time of year—the beachside lounging is world-class.

GETTING HERE AND AROUND

AIR TRAVEL

Cairns Airport is a major international gateway, and a connection point for flights to other parts of Queensland, including Townsville, Mackay, Rockhampton, Hamilton Island, and the Northern Territory, as well as all Australia's capital cities.

Airport Connections runs coaches between Cairns International Airport and town—an 8-km (5-mile) trip that takes about 10 minutes and costs A$17. The company also services Cairns's northern beaches, Palm Cove, Port Douglas, Silky Oaks Lodge (near Mossman), and Daintree Village (A$25 to A$77). Port Douglas–based Exemplar Chauffeured Coaches and Limousines provides services direct from the airport to Cairns CBD (A$15), Palm Cove (A$22), and Port Douglas (A$41), just over an hour's drive north of Cairns, by coach or limousine. Private taxis make these trips as well (A$26–A$32, airport to Cairns).

Airport and Transfers Airport Connections. ☎ 07/4098–2800 ⊕ www.tnqshuttle.com. **Cairns Airport.** ✉ Mick Borzi Dr. off Airport Ave., Aeroglen ☎ 07/4080–6703 ⊕ www.cairnsairport.com.au.

CAR TRAVEL

Between Brisbane and Cairns, the Bruce Highway rarely touches the coast. Unless you're planning to stop off en route or explore the Great Green Way, fly or take the *Spirit of Queenslander* (⊕ www.queenslandrailtravel.com.au) train to Cairns, renting a vehicle on arrival. Avis, Budget, Hertz, and Europcar all have rental cars and four-wheel-drive vehicles available.

ESSENTIALS

Visitor Information Cairns & Tropical North Visitor Information Centre (TTNQ). ✉ 51 The Esplanade, between Spence and Shield Sts., CBD ☎ 07/4051–3588, 1800/093300 ⊕ www.cairnsgreatbarrierreef.org.au.

TOURS

FAMILY

Fodor's Choice
★

Adventure North Australia: Daintree Dreaming Day Tour. On Adventure North's Daintree Dreaming Day Tours, you can explore Cooya Beach and coastal mangroves, World Heritage–listed Daintree rain-forest trails, and Mossman Gorge with the area's traditional owners. ✉ 36 Aplin St. ☎ 07/4028–3376 ⊕ www.adventurenorthaustralia.com 🖾 From A$225.

FAMILY

Blazing Saddles Adventures. Blazing Saddles Adventures organizes two-hour horse rides and all-terrain vehicle tours. A full-day horse-riding and ATV touring is A$195, and includes transfers, morning tea, gear, and a barbecue lunch. Each rider pays insurance of A$15. ⊠ *154 Yorkeys Knob Rd., Kuranda* ☎ *07/4055–7400* ⊕ *www.blazingsaddles.com. au* ⊠ *From A$125.*

FAMILY **BTS Tours.** BTS Tours runs various trips out of Cairns and Port Douglas, including a popular full-day Daintree tour and half-day Mossman Gorge trip. The Daintree itinerary includes a croc-spotting river cruise, canoeing, swimming in rain-forest pools, guided walks, and a barbecue lunch (A$165–A$175). The Mossman Gorge tour includes a 90-minute Kuku Yalanji–guided rain-forest walk, bush tea, and free time to swim, sightsee, and explore the Gorge (A$83). ⊠ *49 Macrossan St., Port Douglas* ☎ *07/4099–5665* ⊕ *www.btstours.com.au* ⊠ *From A$83.*

FAMILY **Coral Expeditions.** This established operator's comfortable expedition-style ships take no more than 50 passengers on three-, four-, and seven-day live-aboard trips, departing Cairns twice a week. Exclusive outer Barrier Reef moorings mean you see more of the marine life. Stops at Lizard, Dunk, and Fitzroy islands as well as Coral Expedition own idyllic island, Pelorus, allow you ample time to relax and explore. Friendly crew, dive guides, and an onboard marine biologist ensure scuba novices are up to speed and snorkelers are catered to. The per-person fare includes a glass-bottom coral-viewing tour, complimentary scuba skills sessions, snorkeling gear, twin-berth accommodation, all meals, and most activities. ⊠ *Coral Expeditions head office, 24 Redden St., Portsmith* ☎ *07/4040–9999, 1800/079545 toll-free in Australia* ⊕ *www.coralexpeditions.com* ⊠ *From A$1596.*

FAMILY **Down Under Tours.** Eco-certified Down Under Tours makes half- and full-day trips and four-wheel-drive excursions, as well as reef trips, river cruises, white-water rafting, bungee jumping, and hot-air ballooning adventures, most departing from Cairns. Popular guided half- and full-day excursions take in the attractions of Kuranda, Hartley's Crocodile Adventures, and Mossman Gorge, the Daintree, and Cape Tribulation. ⊠ *26 Redden St., CBD* ☎ *07/4035–5566* ⊕ *www.downundertours.com* ⊠ *From A$89.*

FAMILY **Heritage 4WD Safari Tours - Wilderness Challenge.** Advanced eco–certified Heritage Tours - Wilderness Challenge runs nine-day Gulf Savannah tours departing Cairns (A$3,495 per person, twin-share, or A$3,830 sole use), and seven-day fly/drive to 12-day overland trips to Cape York Peninsula during the dry season, May through early October. Two popular seven-day, fly/drive camping safaris between Cairns and Cape York each cost A$2,449 twin-share, or A$2,549 sole use. On all tours, you get to stand on top of mainland Australia and stay in bush cabins and/or safari tents. All tours have a maximum of 25 guests and are accompanied by a senior guide. ⊠ *21 Salter Close* ☎ *07/4054–7750, 1800/775533* ⊕ *www.heritagetours.com.au* ⊠ *From A$2449.*

FAMILY **Kuku Yalanji Cultural Habitat Tours.** The Eastern Kuku Yalanji people have called the Daintree area home for tens of thousands of years, and have an intimate understanding of the terrain. Today, the Kubirri Warra brothers pass on a little of that boundless ancestral wisdom on two-hour beach, mudflat, and mangrove walks (daily, 9:30 am and 1:30 pm,

8

A$75) with Adventure North's Kuku Yalanji Cultural Habitat Tours. Learn techniques for throwing spears, tracking coastal food sources, and much more from your knowledgeable, skillful guides. Transfers between the Port Douglas area and Cooya Beach, a 25-minute drive north, are A$30. ☏ 07/4028–3376 ⊕ *www.adventurenorthaustralia. com* 🖃 *A$75.*

FAMILY

Fodor'sChoice

★

Ocean Spirit Cruises. Long-established Ocean Spirit Cruises runs full-day tours to glorious Michaelmas Cay, a remote Great Barrier Reef sand isle encircled by fish- and turtle-filled coral gardens. It's also a protected sanctuary for migratory seabirds. Cruise out to the cay on *Ocean Spirit*, a 105-foot luxury sailing catamaran, for four hours of snorkeling, semi-submersible coral-viewing tours, and marine biologist presentations, with a full buffet lunch, morning and afternoon tea, snorkeling gear, and reef tax included in the A$202.50 per person cost. *Ocean Spirit* departs daily from Cairns Reef Fleet Terminal. Transfers from Cairns and the Northern Beaches are available. ⊠ *Shangri-La Marina, 1 Spence St., Office 3–Level 1, CBD* ☏ 07/4031–9944 ⊕ *www.oceanspirit.com. au* 🖃 *From A$151.*

EXPLORING

Cosmopolitan Cairns, the unofficial capital of Far North Queensland, is Australia's 14th-largest city, with a burgeoning population pushing 1,435,000—double that when you include the thriving hinterland. Once a sleepy tropical town sprawled around Trinity Bay and Inlet, the city has expanded hugely in recent decades, and now extends north to Ellis Beach, west to the Atherton Tablelands, and south along the Great Green Way as far as Edmonton.

TOP ATTRACTIONS

FAMILY

Australian Butterfly Sanctuary. More than 1,500 tropical butterflies— including dozens of the electric-blue Ulysses species and Australia's largest butterfly, the green-and-gold Cairns Birdwing—flutter within a compact rain-forest aviary, alighting on foliage, interpretative signage, and feeding stations. About 24,000 pupae are released into the aviary each year, ensuring the colorful spectacle continues. Free half-hour guided tours of the aviary and caterpillar breeding area are full of fascinating tidbits. ⊠ *8 Rob Veivers Dr., Kuranda* ☏ 07/4093–7575 ⊕ *www.australianbutterflies.com* 🖃 *A$19.50 entry and guided tour; A$58 2-park package (Australian Butterfly Sanctuary and Rainforestation); A$85 4-park package (Australian Butterfly Sanctuary, Rainforestation, Cairns Dome Zoo, and Wildlife Habitat in Port Douglas)* ☉ *Daily 9:45–4, tours 10:15–3:15.*

FAMILY

Cairns Regional Gallery. Occupying the impressive former Public Office Building constructed in the 1930s, Cairns Regional Gallery houses a hodgepodge of local, national, international, and indigenous art-works, including a fine collection of Australian photography, in its wood-paneled rooms. The shop stocks high-quality Australian giftware, toys, jewelry, prints, books, and cards. Prebook a 45-minute guided tour; there are also kids' programs, classes, talks, and workshops. ⊠ *City Pl., Shields and Abbott Sts., CBD* ☏ 07/4046–4800 ⊕ *www.*

Exploring
Cairns

KEY

⊷⊷ *Rail Lines*

cairnsregionalgallery.com.au ✉ *A$5 (free for kids 16 and under)* ⊗ *Weekdays 9–5, Sat. 10–5, Sun. 10–2.*

FAMILY   **The Esplanade.** Fronting Cairns Harbour, this busy boardwalk and rec-
Fodor'sChoice   reational zone is the focal point of life in Cairns. Along the walk you'll
★   encounter shady trees and public art, picnic and barbecue facilities,
a large saltwater swimming lagoon, volleyball courts, an imaginative kids' playground, a state-of-the-art skate plaza, and areas for fitness, markets, and live entertainment. A shallow, 4,800-square-meter
(51,667-square-foot) filtered saltwater lagoon swimming pool with a
sandy shore, decking, and shelters, patrolled by lifeguards year-round,
provides free, convenient relief from the often sticky air. Along the
street opposite and along the marina at the boardwalk's southern end,
you'll find hotels, shops, galleries, bars, and eateries. ✉ *Between Spence
and Upward Sts., CBD* ☎ *07/4044–3715* ⊕ *www.cairnsesplanade.com*
✉ *Free* ⊗ *Pool: Thurs.–Tues. 6 am–9 pm, Wed. noon–9 pm; Mud-
dy's playground: daily 9 am–7 pm; volleyball courts: Thurs.–Tues. 9
am–9:30 pm, Wed. 4–9:30 pm; Esplanade Market: Sat. 8–4.*

FAMILY   **Kuranda Scenic Railway.** The historic Kuranda Scenic Railway makes a
115-minute ascent through rain forest and 15 hand-hewn tunnels to
pretty Kuranda village, gateway to the Atherton Tableland. Book a
simple Heritage Class seat; get snacks, drinks, cool towels, and souvenir

SCENIC DRIVE: THE GREAT GREEN WAY

Babinda Boulders. About an hour's drive from Cairns, Babinda Boulders is a popular swimming hole—and a sacred Aboriginal site. It's 7 km (5 miles) inland on The Boulders Road from the town of Babinda, accessible via the Bruce Highway about 60 km (37 miles) south of Cairns. You can also hike to the boulders, taking the 19-km (12-mile) **Goldfield Track (Wooroonooran National Park)** that starts in Goldsborough Valley, southwest of Cairns, and ends in Babinda Boulders car park. Babinda is kid-friendly, yet not overrun with offspring. ⊠ *Babinda Information Centre, 1 Munro St., Babinda* ☎ *07/4067–1008 info center, 07/4067–6304 park ranger* ⊕ *www.babindainfocentre.com.au* ⊙ *Information center daily 9–4.*

Great Green Way. A scenic section of the Bruce Highway locals call the Great Green Way links Cairns with Townsville, taking you through sugarcane, papaya, and banana plantations, past white-sand beaches and an island-dotted ocean. The 348-km (216-mile) drive takes about 4½ hours. Add a few more hours to explore towns, parks, waterfalls, and rain-forest tracts along the way. ⊹ *Bruce Hwy., between Cairns and Townsville.*

Paronella Park. A sprawling Spanish-style castle and gardens grace this offbeat National Trust site in the Mena Creek Falls rain forest. Explore the park on a self-guided botanical walk or 45-minute guided tour, enjoy Devonshire tea on the café's deck, buy local arts and crafts, and cool off under a 40-foot waterfall. On hour-long flashlight-lit evening tours (a must-do if you're traveling with kids) starting nightly at 6:15, you might spot eels, water dragons, fireflies, and glowworms. Allow at least three hours to explore. It's around 1½ hours' (about 60 miles) drive south of Cairns via the Bruce Highway. ⊠ *1671 Japoonvale Rd. (Old Bruce Hwy.), Mena Creek* ☎ *07/4065–0000* ⊕ *www.paronellapark.com.au* 🎟 *A$43* ⊙ *Daily 9–7:30.*

Tully Gorge National Park. In the wettest zone of the Wet Tropics World Heritage area, the mighty Tully River is a magnet for white-water rafters, while the gorge's scenic, often mist-shrouded trails suit walkers of all levels. Access Tully Gorge National Park via the town of Tully, 141 km (88 miles) or about two hours' drive south of Cairns, then continue for 54 km (34 miles)—approximately 40 minutes—along Jarra Creek and Cardstone roads to Kareeya Hydroelectric Station parking lot and viewing platform. Other excellent vantage points are the Tully Falls lookout, 24 km (15 miles) south of Ravenshoe, and the Flip Wilson and Frank Roberts lookouts. September to February, the short, wheelchair-accessible Rainforest Butterfly walk is filled with brilliant creatures. Rafting trips can be booked through operators in Tully and Cairns. ⊠ *Tully Falls Rd., Koombooloomba* ☎ *07/4068–2288 Tully visitor information, 13/7468 ParksQ camping permits and general inquiries* ⊕ *www.nprsr.qld.gov.au/parks/tully-gorge.*

pack in Royale Class; or splurge on a Gold Class ticket with fine local food and wine, table service, swanky decor, and souvenirs. Several tour packages are available, from full-day rain-forest safaris and visits to local Aboriginal centers and wildlife parks to simple round-trips combining rail and cable-car journeys. ⊠ *Cairns Railway Station, Bunda St., CBD* ☎ *07/4036–9333, 1800/577245* ⊕ *www.ksr.com.au* ✉ *1-way ticket A$50–$A99, round-trip A$76–$174; combined railway/cable-car/wildlife or aboriginal culture packages A$158–A$170* ☉ *Departs from Cairns daily 8:30 and 9:30 am, from Kuranda at 2 and 3:30; Gold Class only on 9:30 and 3:30 services.*

FAMILY
Fodor'sChoice
★
Reef Teach. Knowledgeable marine biologists and conservationists give entertaining talks and multimedia presentations, usually to packed houses, about everything Great Barrier Reef–related, from sea turtles' sleep cycles to coral-killing starfish. Expect to learn more than you thought possible about the reef's evolution and the diverse inhabitants of this delicate marine ecosystem. The attached Marine Shop sells an array of reef-themed merchandise: T-shirts, DVDs, books, field guides, and souvenirs. Sign up for a Reef Teach seat by midday. ⊠ *Boland's Centre, 81–85 Lake St., Level 2, CBD* ☎ *07/4031–7794* ⊕ *www.reefteach. com.au* ✉ *A$23* ☉ *Shows Tues.–Sat. 6:30–8:30.*

FAMILY
Fodor'sChoice
★
Skyrail Rainforest Cableway. From the Skyrail terminal just north of Cairns, take a six-person cable car on a breathtaking 7½-km (5-mile) journey across pristine, World Heritage–listed rain-forest canopy to the highland village of Kuranda, where you can visit local wildlife parks and shop for local craft and Aboriginal art. At two stations along the way, you can hop off and explore (the Skyrail ticket price includes a short ranger-guided rain-forest tour at Red Peak, and there's an info center and lookout at Barron Falls). The cableway base station is 15 km (9 miles) north of Cairns. Many visitors take the Scenic Railway to Kuranda, the cableway on the return trip. ⊠ *Captain Cook Hwy., at Cairns Western Arterial Rd., Smithfield* ☎ *07/4038–5555* ⊕ *www. skyrail.com.au* ✉ *1-way A$50, round-trip A$75 (self-drive); A98– A$120 (with transfers); cable car with scenic railway/cultural/rain forest/wildlife experiences A$99–A$194.50* ☉ *Daily 9–5:15 at 15-min intervals, last round-trip boards at 2:45; last 1-way trip at 3:30.*

FAMILY
Fodor'sChoice
★
Tanks Arts Centre. This vibrant arts center is housed in a trio of repurposed World War II–era oil storage tanks in Cairns's lush Flecker Botanic Gardens, 4 km (2 miles) north of the Cairns city center. It has become a vital creative hub for the region, showcasing everything from dance and theater troupes to local folk, blues, jazz, and indigenous artists. The Centre hosts a colorful arts and food market, with live music and free kids' activities, on the last Sunday of the month from April to November. ⊠ *46 Collins Ave., Edge Hill* ☎ *07/4032–6600* ⊕ *www. tanksartscentre.com* ✉ *Galleries free, venue ticket prices vary.*

FAMILY
Tjapukai Aboriginal Cultural Park. At the base of the Skyrail Rainforest Cableway, this park offers many opportunities to learn about indigenous Djabugay people through exhilarating dance performances, hands-on workshops in traditional fire-making, spear and boomerang throwing, arts and crafts, didgeridoo lessons, and talks on bush tucker and natural

8

The Skyrail Rainforest Cableway outside Cairns

medicines. You can buy Aboriginal artworks, artifacts, and instruments (including didgeridoos) at the retail gallery on-site (open daily 10 am–5 pm and 6:45–10 pm); café fare, buffet lunches, and dinners are also available. One of Australia's most informative cultural attractions, it's also one of the few that returns profits to the indigenous community. Ticket options include Tjapukai by Day and Tjapukai by Night, the latter a nightly four-course buffet dinner/performance package. ✉ *Cairns Western Arterial Rd., next to Skyrail terminal, Cavaronica* ✛ *15 km (9 miles) north of Cairns* ☎ *07/4042-9999* ⊕ *www.tjapukai.com.au* ✉ *Tjapukai by Day: A$60 self-drive, A$58 with Cairns transfers, A$85 with Northern Beaches transfers, Tjapukai by Night: A$120 self-drive, A$145 with transfers* ⊘ *Daily 9–5, night show 7–9:30 pm.*

WORTH NOTING

FAMILY
Fodor's Choice
★

Birdworld Kuranda. One of your best chances to see the endangered Southern cassowary, a prehistoric emu-like bird, is at Birdworld Kuranda. It's home to hundreds of colorful birds from nearly 60 species, more than 20 of them native to vanishing rain-forest areas—walking and flying freely in a gigantic aviary. Many of them are tame enough to perch on your shoulders. Wear a hat and sleeved shirt: birds' claws are scratchy. ✉ *Kuranda Heritage Village, Rob Vievers Dr., Kuranda* ☎ *07/4093-9188* ⊕ *www.birdworldkuranda.com* ✉ *A$18, Birdworld/Koala Park (self-drive) A$31, Birdworld/Koala Park/Butterfly Park (self-drive) A$48.50* ⊘ *Daily 9–4.*

Cairns Marlin Marina. This floating marina's 261 berths bristle with charter fishing, diving, and private vessels, including superyachts up to 60 meters (197 feet) long. At the Reef Fleet Terminal off Marlin Wharf, you'll find tour offices, shops, cafés, and Wi-Fi connectivity. Big-game fishing is a big business here; fish weighing more than 1,000 pounds have been caught in the waters off the reef. Most of the dive boats and catamarans that ply the Great Barrier Reef dock here or at nearby Trinity Wharf. ⊠ *1 Spence St., CBD* ☎ *07/4052–3866* ⊕ *www. portsnorth.com.au/marina.*

FAMILY **City Centre Alive.** Cairns's throbbing heart is City Centre Alive, a pedestrian mall and mini-rain forest that extends along the city's main shopping drag on Shields Street between Lake and Grafton streets. There is

KURANDA WILDLIFE EXPERIENCE

Tropical Kuranda offers several nature-oriented attractions, including the Australian Butterfly Sanctuary, Birdworld Kuranda, and Kuranda Koala Gardens. See these sites individually, visit on a Kuranda Wildlife Experience pass (A$48.50), which gives entry to all three, or buy a return Skyrail & Kuranda Wildlife Experience package that includes return Skyrail tickets (from A$123.50).

construction underway for a further extension as far as Abbott Street. The shady precinct has lawn areas, art installations, and plenty of shops and cafés. ⊠ *Shield St. between Lake St. and Grafton St., CBD* ☎ *07/4044–3715* ⊕ *www.cairns.qld.gov.au.*

FAMILY **Kuranda Koala Gardens.** All kinds of Australian wildlife are housed here, but the namesake marsupials are star attractions. A half-hour stroll through the compact park also puts you eye-to-eye with wombats, wallabies, freshwater crocs, lizards, and snakes in open walk-through enclosures. For an extra fee, have your photo taken with a tame koala. ⊠ *Kuranda Heritage Village, Rob Vievers Dr., Kuranda* ☎ *07/4093–9953* ⊕ *www.koalagardens.com* ⎙ *A$18; Koala Gardens/ Birdworld pass: A$31; Koala Gardens/Birdworld/Butterfly Sanctuary pass A$48.50* ☉ *Daily 9–4.*

OFF THE BEATEN PATH

Undara Volcanic National Park. The lava tubes here are a fascinating geological oddity in the Outback: a volcanic outpouring 190,000 years ago created the hollow basalt, tubelike tunnels, many of which you can trek through on guided tours. Undara is the Aboriginal word for "a long way," and it's apt: one of the original lava tubes extended for 100 miles in total, and several sections of it can be explored on tours led by well-trained, informative guides. The lava tubes extend over an area of 580-odd square miles; some are 62 feet high and half a mile long. ⊠ *Off the Gulf Developmenatal Rd. (Savannah Way), Mt. Surprise* ⊹ *Take Gulf Developmental Rd. (Savannah Way) past turnoff to Undara Experience, 17 km (10.6 miles) from turnoff. Six km (3.7 miles) farther, take right-hand fork and drive another 9 km (5.6 miles), then turn left at fork and drive 6 km (3.7 miles) on an all-weather gravel road to reach Kalkani day-use area* ☎ *13-7468 NPRSR parks, 07/4097–7700 Ravenshoe Visitor Information* ⊕ *www.nprsr.qld.gov. au* ⎙ *Free* ☉ *Daily 24 hrs.*

Undara Experience. This extraordinary complex on the edge of Undara Volcanic National Park, 275 km (171 miles) or a four-hour scenic drive or rail trip from Cairns, supplies the complete Outback experience: bush breakfasts, campfire activities, lava-tube tours, and guided evening wildlife walks, plus a range of distinctive accommodation. Vintage railway cars have been converted into comfortable (if compact), fan-cooled motel rooms with their own en suites. You can also stay in a modern, air-conditioned "Pioneer Hut" with private veranda, fridge, and bathroom (A$160 per night in high season), in a safari tent; or at a powered or unpowered site with shared amenities. One-night "budget" self-drive packages that incorporate tours, campfire activities, and swag-tent accommodation cost A$110 per person in high season, A$167 per person with meals; or from A$259 to A$309 per person with swankier accommodation. Two-night packages including meals, rail-carriage or Pioneer Hut accommodation, and tours range from A$405 to A$471 per person in high season. Other packages include transfers to and from Cairns via coach or on heritage train *The Savannahlander*. Drink and dine on site at Fettler's Iron Pot Bistro; breakfast at the Ringer's Camp. ⊠ *Undara Volcanic Park, Savannah Way, Mt. Surprise* ☎ *07/4097–1900, 1800/990992* ⊕ *www.undara.com.au.*

SPORTS AND THE OUTDOORS

It's no surprise that lots of tours out of Cairns focus on the Great Barrier Reef. Half-day snorkeling, diving, and fishing trips out of Cairns, most departing from the Reef Fleet Terminal, start from around A$100; full-day trips start from about A$200. Scuba dives and gear generally cost extra. Typically you'll pay an additional admin fee that includes the A$6 per person, per day Environmental Management Charge (EMC) or "reef tax," and you may also be hit with a Port Authority charge of around A$9 per person, per day.

Ask a few pertinent questions before booking diving tours: dive trips vary in size, and some cater specifically to, say, sightseers; others to experienced divers. If you're a beginner or Open Water diver, ensure that you book excursions that visit suitable dive sites, with certified staff on hand to assist you.

Cairns is also a great base for adventure activities and horse riding on the Atherton Tableland, ballooning over the Mareeba Valley, and day tours to the UNESCO World Heritage–listed Daintree rain forest. The offices of adventure-tour companies, tourist offices and booking agents are concentrated around the Esplanade.

MULTISPORT OPERATORS

FAMILY   **Raging Thunder Adventures.** This operator has various adventure pack-
Fodor'sChoice ages: snorkel and kayak around the Barrier Reef's Fitzroy Island; glide
★   over the Mareeba Valley or Atherton Tablelands in a hot-air balloon;
or white-water raft through the hinterland's rugged gorges. ⊠ *52–54 Fearnley St., Portsmith* ☎ *07/4030–7990* ⊕ *www.ragingthunder.com. au* ▭ *From A$74.*

FAMILY   **RnR White Water Rafting.** This operator runs white-water rafting expeditions for adults on the Barron, North Johnstone, and Tully rivers. They also offer snorkeling trips, ATV adventure tours, balloon rides, and packages combining a half-day's Barron River rafting with a half-day on Fitzroy Island. All gear and safety equipment is provided. ⊠ *52 Fearnley*

St., CBD ☎ *07/4030–7944* ⊕ *www.*
raft.com.au ✉ *From A$103.*

SNORKELING AND DIVING

FAMILY **Deep Sea Divers Den.** Long-established, PADI-five-star-rated Deep
Sea Divers Den has a roaming permit that allows its guides to visit
any part of the Great Barrier Reef,
including 17 exclusive moorings
on the reef's outer edge frequented
by turtles, rays, and colorful reef
fish. Four- to six-day open water
and advanced PADI dive courses
include one- or two-night live-
aboard trips. Three- and four-night
dive expeditions on sleek dive boat
Taka take you to world-renowned
sites on the pristine Ribbon Reefs.
Day trips include up to three dives
or snorkeling opportunities; gear

BEACHES
Because Cairns lacks city beaches, most people head out to the reef to swim and snorkel. North of the airport, neighboring areas including **Machans Beach, Holloways Beach, Yorkey's Knob, Trinity Beach**, and **Clifton Beach** are perfect for swimming from June through September and sometimes even October; check local weather reports. Avoid the ocean at other times, however, when deadly box jellyfish (marine stingers) and invisible-to-the-eye Irukandji jellyfish float in the waters along the coast.

and lunch is included in the price, but reef tax (A$20) and photos cost
extra. ✉ *319 Draper St., CBD* ☎ *07/4046–7333* ⊕ *www.diversden.com.
au* ✉ *From A$265.*

Fodor's Choice **Mike Ball Dive Expeditions.** Mike Ball, an enthusiastic American who's
★ been diving the Great Barrier Reef since 1969, runs multiday, multidive
trips along the Queensland coastline on which novice divers are given
expert guidance and experienced divers get to set their own bottom
times and dive their own plans. Custom-built, twin-hulled live-aboard
boats loaded with top-end gear, serious divers, and qualified chefs
depart twice-weekly to visit renowned dive sites and spot minke whales
and sharks. Dive courses cost extra but there are several available, and
the quality of instruction's high. ✉ *3 Abbott St., CBD* ☎ *07/4053–0500,
0407/146–834* ⊕ *www.mikeball.com* ✉ *From A$1827, with standard
gear hire fees (A$44 per day) and nitrox (A$25 per day), personal guides
(A$250 per day plus berth cost for guide), and reef tax (A$20 per day).*

FAMILY **Ocean Spirit Cruises.** This operator offers daily trips on its sleek sailing
Fodor's Choice catamaran that include four hours at Michaelmas Cay on the Great
★ Barrier Reef, a marine biologist presentation, snorkeling gear, guided
snorkeling, a fish-feeding demonstration, a semi-submersible tour,
morning and afternoon tea, a buffet lunch, and a glass of wine on the
return journey. Reef and port charges are an extra A$6. If you're a
beginner, have mobility issues, or aren't a strong swimmer, this might
be the best operator for you. ✉ *Reef Fleet Terminal, 1 Spence St., CBD*
☎ *07/4044–9944* ⊕ *www.oceanspirit.com.au* ✉ *From A$188.*

Pro Dive Cairns. This Advanced Ecotourism–certified operator runs multiday, live-aboard trips on three custom-built dive boats, and offers
PADI-five-star-accredited courses at their state-of-the-art training facility in Cairns. Three-, four-, and seven-day trips take a maximum of
28 divers and snorkelers to Outer Barrier Reef, Cod Hole, Ribbon

Reefs, and Coral Sea sites, where they can dive ecologically diverse sites with optimal visibility. Trips include accommodation in serviced quad-share, twin, or double cabins, TVs, and private en suites. You also get chef-prepared meals, top-end gear, and guided dives. ⊠ *Pro Dive Cairns Training Centre, 116 Spence St., CBD* ☎ *07/4031–5255* ⊕ *www.prodivecairns.com* ⬚ *From A$190.*

FAMILY **Tusa Dive.** Among Cairns's best dive boats are the custom-built fast cats
Fodor'sChoice run by Tusa Dive, a PADI-, SSI-, and Advanced Ecotourism–accredited
★ outfit that whisks passengers out to two sites on the Great Barrier Reef. Get dive briefs and info en route, along with continual refreshments including a big lunch. In the water, people of all ages and experience levels can dive or snorkel under the watchful gaze of well-trained guides. Every passenger pays a A$10 per day reef tax; other extras include guided dives (A$10), nitrox (A$15 per fill), and underwater digital camera rental. ⊠ *Shield St., at The Esplanade, CBD* ☎ *07/4047–9100* ⊕ *www.tusadive.com* ⬚ *From A$260.*

WHERE TO EAT

Use the coordinate (✛ B2) at the end of each listing to locate a site on the corresponding map.

$ ✕ **Barnacle Bill's Seafood Inn.** Complete with netting and mounted, shel-
SEAFOOD lacked fish on the walls, Barnacle Bill's is an Esplanade institution,
FAMILY serving fresh, mainly local seafood to throngs of tourists. Lunch and dinner menus are packed with dishes showcasing mud crabs, crayfish, prawns, oysters, wild barramundi, mahimahi, salmon, and coral trout. The wine list favors mid-range Australian and New Zealand vintages. Diners who order before 6 pm and depart by 7:30 get a 20% discount. ⑤ *Average main: A$16* ⊠ *103 The Esplanade, near Aplin St., CBD* ☎ *07/4051–2241* ⊕ *www.barnaclebills.com.au* ⚮ *Reservations essential* ✛ *B3.*

$ ✕ **Bayleaf Balinese Restaurant.** Dining in the open-sided restaurant or
INDONESIAN alfresco under the light of tiki torches, you can enjoy some of the most
Fodor'sChoice delicious, innovative cuisine in North Queensland. Choose from an
★ expansive menu that combines traditional Balinese spices and recipes with native Australian ingredients—try the crocodile satay. The *be celeng base manis* (pork in sweet soy sauce) sounds simple, but is mouthwatering. The traditional rijsttafel feast for two includes rice with lots of curries, salads, fish dishes, stews, pickle sides, and, if you can squeeze them in, desserts. There's a long, tropically themed cocktail menu and a well-priced wine list. ■**TIP**➜ Don't eat lunch if you're planning to order the rijstaffel at dinner—it's huge. ⑤ *Average main: A$25* ⊠ *Bay Village Tropical Retreat, 227 Lake St., at Gatton St., CBD* ☎ *07/4047–7955* ⊕ *www.bayvillage.com.au/bayleaf* ☾ *No lunch weekends* ⚮ *Reservations essential* ✛ *A1.*

$ ✕ **Cairns Night Markets Food Court.** The food court in these lively, night
FAST FOOD owl–friendly markets offers something for every palate, from Korean
FAMILY BBQ to sweet-and-sour chicken, sushi, Thai, and Italian. You can also max out on desserts, with outlets offering crepes, waffles, churros, gelato, ice cream, and Italian-style coffee. The food court's open

daily from 10 am to 11 pm; the night markets, 5 to 11 pm. ⓢ *Average main: A$14* ✉ *71–75 The Esplanade, between Shield and Spence Sts., CBD* ☎ *07/4051–7666* ⊕ *www.nightmarkets.com.au* ⚮ *Reservations not accepted* ⌁ *Most food stalls accept credit cards but bring cash in case* ✛ *B3.*

$ ✕ **Ochre Restaurant.** Local seafood and native ingredients take top bill-
AUSTRALIAN ing at this upscale yet relaxed Cairns institution that specializes in
Fodor's Choice bush dining. Try the popular Australian antipasto platter: 'roo terrine,
★ emu carpaccio, and smoked crocodile, with fine Antipodean wines to
match. Most dishes incorporate native foods and seasonal ingredients:
sample wild-caught baby barramundi or order a vegetarian, Australian
game, or seafood platter to share. The signature dessert, wattle-seed
pavlova with Davidson plum sorbet and macadamia biscotti, makes
a fine finish. ⓢ *Average main: A$33* ✉ *43 Shields St., at Sheridan St.,
CBD* ☎ *07/4051–0100* ⊕ *www.ochrerestaurant.com.au* ☽ *No lunch
weekends* ⚮ *Reservations essential* ✛ *A3.*

$ ✕ **Perrotta's at the Gallery.** This outdoor café and wine bar at Cairns
MODERN Regional Gallery serves sumptuous breakfasts and brunches. Lunch fare
AUSTRALIAN includes warm duck and roast chicken salads, pasta and seafood dishes,
FAMILY and various sandwiches. At dinner, you can tuck into Italian and Modern Australian dishes: antipasto, pasta, and such dishes as slow-cooked
lamb shoulder or roast barramundi with eggplant and an onion-herb
salad. Dessert might be buttermilk panna cotta with blueberries, dulce
de leche, sbrisolona crumbs, and mint. ⓢ *Average main: A$33* ✉ *Gal-
lery Deck, Cairns Regional Gallery, 38 Abbott St., at Shield St., CBD*
☎ *07/4031–5899* ⊕ *www.perrottasatg.com* ✛ *B3.*

$$ ✕ **Restaurant M Yogo.** Occupying a prime pier-front position, Restaurant
MODERN FRENCH M Yogo offers refined dining in relaxed environs. Chef Masa puts a deft,
modern-Japanese spin on classic French dishes. Enjoy his tiger prawns
sautéed in pie pastry with garlic cream sauce, or sautéed fish, prawns,
scallops, and squid with lobster Américaine sauce. The food is as inspir-
ing as the marina, inlet, and mountain views. The waitstaff can help you
select the perfect match from a well-chosen Antipodean wine list. If you
have room, desserts are equally delectable: a green tea trio of "opera"
cake, pudding, and ice cream; a gluten-free Belgian chocolate tasting
plate; or a fluffy cream-cheese soufflé cake with Chantilly cream and
seasonal fruits. The set-price lunch specials are a good value. ⓢ *Average
main: A$39* ✉ *Pier Shopping, Pierpoint Rd., Shop G9* ☎ *07/4051–0522*
⊕ *www.matureyogo.com* ⚮ *Reservations essential* ✛ *B3.*

$$ ✕ **Waterbar & Grill Steakhouse.** At this busy waterfront eatery, you can
SEAFOOD- gaze at Cairns's bustling marina while chowing down on a locally
STEAKHOUSE sourced, chargrilled steak. The steaks come in all cuts and sizes, with
thick fries on the side. There's also a nice selection of barbecued pork
and lamb ribs, burgers, and seafood. Lunches offer lighter fare, such
as pita wraps and salads. There's a hearty kids' menu, and a long wine,
beer, and cocktail list. Even though Waterbar is often packed, the airy
open-plan design makes it seem less crowded. ⓢ *Average main: A$39*
✉ *Pier Shopping Centre, Pier Point Rd., Shop G1A, CBD* ☎ *07/4031–
1199* ⊕ *www.waterbarandgrill.com.au* ⚮ *Reservations essential* ✛ *B3.*

8

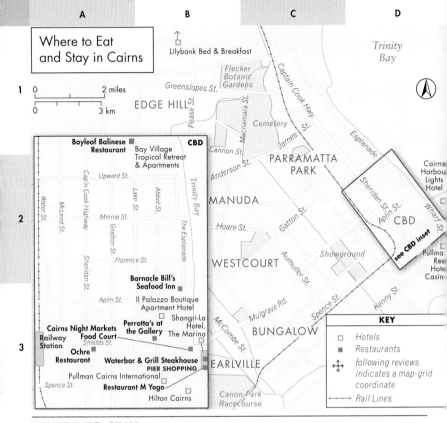

Where to Eat and Stay in Cairns

A B C D

Trinity Bay

1 0 — 2 miles
0 — 3 km

Lilybank Bed & Breakfast

Flecker Botanic Gardens

Greenslopes St.

EDGE HILL

Cemetery

Captain Cook Hwy.

James St.

PARRAMATTA PARK

Esplanade

Cairns Harbour Lights Hotel

CBD

Bayleaf Balinese Restaurant

Bay Village Tropical Retreat & Apartments

Cannon St.

Anderson St.

Upward St.

Cap'n Cook Highway

Lake St.

Abbot St.

Trinity Bay

MANUDA

Hoare St.

Gatton St.

Sheridan St.

Aplin St.

CBD

see CBD inset

2 Water St.

McLeod St.

Minnie St.

Grafton St.

Florence St.

The Esplanade

Sheridan St.

WESTCOURT

Aumuller St.

Showground

Wharf St.

Pullman Reef Hotel Casino

Barnacle Bill's Seafood Inn

Il Palazzo Boutique Apartment Hotel

Aplin St.

Perrotta's at the Gallery

Shangri-La Hotel, The Marina

Mulgrave Rd.

McCombe St.

BUNGALOW

Spence St.

Kenny St.

3 Cairns Night Markets Food Court

Railway Station

Ochre Restaurant

Shields St.

Waterbar & Grill Steakhouse

PIER SHOPPING

EARLVILLE

Spence St.

Pullman Cairns International

Restaurant M Yogo

Hilton Cairns

Canon Park Racecourse

KEY

☐ Hotels
■ Restaurants
⊕ following reviews indicates a map-grid coordinate
┄┄┄ Rail Lines

WHERE TO STAY

$
RESORT
FAMILY
Bay Village Tropical Retreat & Apartments. The sociable public areas at this family-friendly complex include a lovely lagoon pool, an Internet area, a guest laundry, and the terrific Bayleaf Balinese Restaurant & Bar. The main complex offers simple but spacious double, family, and studio rooms, some with balconies. **Pros:** handy guest laundry; sociable atmosphere and helpful, friendly staff; free Wi-Fi. **Cons:** pool area and ground-floor rooms can be noisy; standard rooms lack ambient lighting and all but simple amenities; no elevator access to second floor; 15 minute walk from Cairns's downtown. ⑤ *Rooms from: A$150* ✉ *227 Lake St., at Gatton St., CBD* ☎ *07/4051–4622* ⊕ *www.bayvillage.com. au* ➐ *62 suites, 28 apartments* ℝ *No meals* ⊕ *A1.*

$$
HOTEL
Cairns Harbour Lights Hotel. The refurbished hotel rooms and one- and two-bedroom apartments at this hotel on Cairns's waterfront are a two-minute stroll to Reef Fleet Terminal, making them ideal for early-morning reef trips. **Pros:** terrific central location; good on-site dining options; great views. **Cons:** fees for parking and Wi-Fi; pool small, and can be chilly in cooler months; rooms on lower floors can be noisy. ⑤ *Rooms from: A$275* ✉ *1 Marlin Parade* ☎ *07/4057–0800* ⊕ *www. cairnsharbourlightshotel.com.au* ➐ *94 studios and apartments* ℝ *No meals* ☞ *Takeout available from Dundee's on ground floor of site* ⊕ *D2.*

$$ ▦**Hilton Cairns.** This attractive hotel has an enviable location near the
HOTEL waterfront, a flotilla of services, and classy on-site drinking and dining
Fodor'sChoice options. **Pros:** modern rooms with comfortable beds; expansive break-
★ fast buffet; free Wi-Fi for Hilton members; friendly, helpful service.
Cons: pricey Internet access for non-Hilton members; steep fees for
parking; large tour groups can create crowds in public areas. ⑤ *Rooms
from: A$299* ✉ *34 Esplanade* ☎ *07/4050–2000* ⊕ *www3.hilton.com*
↪ *264 rooms* ⦿❘ *No meals* ✛ *B3.*

$$ ▦**Il Palazzo Boutique Apartment Hotel.** Cairns is a long way from Europe
HOTEL but you can imagine yourself on the Riviera at this intimate, centrally
located continental-style hotel. **Pros:** free on-site parking; helpful staff;
clean, quiet rooms. **Cons:** dated decor; slow in-room Internet; free Wi-Fi
only in public areas. ⑤ *Rooms from: A$250* ✉ *62 Abbott St., CBD*
☎ *07/4041–2155, 1800/813222* ⊕ *www.ilpalazzo.com.au* ↪ *38 suites*
⦿❘ *No meals* ✛ *B3.*

$ ▦**Lilybank Bed & Breakfast.** Built in 1887, this two-story Queenslander
B&B/INN is a relaxed six-guestroom B&B with spacious communal areas and
an alfresco breakfast area. **Pros:** clean, well-appointed rooms; relaxed,
quiet environs; free airport pickups daily. **Cons:** a fair distance from
the CBD; no meals offered apart from breakfast, although there are
cooking facilities on-site; can be too quiet. ⑤ *Rooms from: A$100* ✉ *75
Kamerunga Rd., Stratford* ☎ *07/4053–1123* ⊕ *www.lilybank.com.au*
↪ *6 suites* ⦿❘ *Breakfast* ✛ *B1.*

$$ ▦**Pullmann Cairns International.** This practicality-meets-luxury hotel near
HOTEL Cairns's waterfront has an impressive three-story lobby, an elegant day
spa, and smartly outfitted guest rooms and suites, all with furnished bal-
conies. **Pros:** central location; good on-site services and facilities; comfort-
able beds. **Cons:** thin walls; fees for Internet access and parking; main pool
can be chilly. ⑤ *Rooms from: A$218* ✉ *17 Abbot St., at Spence St., CBD*
☎ *07/4031–1300, 1800/079100* ⊕ *www.pullmancairnsinternational.
com.au* ↪ *321 rooms/suites* ⦿❘ *No meals* ✛ *B3.*

$$$ ▦**Pullmann Reef Hotel Casino.** Part of a lively entertainment complex
HOTEL in the heart of Cairns, this high-end hotel has spacious rooms and
Fodor'sChoice suites—as well as several restaurants and bars, a nightclub, a casino, an
★ outdoor swimming pool, and a small wildlife sanctuary and zip-lining
operation in its rooftop dome. **Pros:** several on-site entertainment and
dining options; helpful, high-end service. **Cons:** chilly pool. ⑤ *Rooms
from: A$ 350* ✉ *35–41 Wharf St., CBD* ☎ *07/4030–8888* ⊕ *www.
pullmannhotels.com* ↪ *128 rooms and suites* ⦿❘ *No meals* ✛ *D2.*

$$$ ▦**Shangri-La Hotel, The Marina.** With chic modern decor and buzzing
HOTEL on-site bars and eateries, this marina-side resort is among Cairns's
hippest refurbished outdoor areas are suitably sleek, with extensive
wooden decking, palm-shaded swimming pools, a Jacuzzi, and a pool-
side cocktail bar. **Pros:** great views; free Wi-Fi; 24-hour room service
and gym; proximity to the marina. **Cons:** lower-floor pier-side rooms
above the bar can be noisy. ⑤ *Rooms from: A$365* ✉ *Pierpoint Rd.,
CBD* ☎ *07/4031–1411, 1800/222448* ⊕ *www.shangri-la.com/cairns/
shangrila* ↪ *230 rooms, 25 suites* ⦿❘ *No meals* ✛ *B3.*

8

NIGHTLIFE

Cairns's Esplanade and the CBD streets leading off it come alive at night, with most restaurants serving until late, and wine or a cold beer is a staple with evening meals. Several rowdy pubs catering to backpackers and younger travelers line the central section of City Place; a few bars and hotel venues manage to be upscale while remaining true to the city's easygoing spirit. Unless noted, bars are open nightly and there's no cover charge.

The Pier Bar. A prime waterside location and a big, breezy deck draw an upbeat, mixed crowd to The Pier Bar. They flock here for woodfired pizzas, well-priced drinks, and laid-back Sunday sessions with live music and DJs. The bar gets noisier, younger, and more crowded as the night wears on, but service is friendly and food is palatable, even when the bar's jam-packed. ⊠ *The Pier Shopping Centre, 1 Pierpoint Rd.* ☎ *07/4031–4677* ⊕ *www.thepierbar.com.au.*

Vertigo Cocktail Bar & Lounge. This sleek bar-lounge off the main foyer of Pullman Reef Hotel Casino has live bands (including big-name acts) Thursday through Saturday, karaoke on Sunday, and big production shows two or three nights a week, followed by DJs and dancing. ⊠ *Pullmann Reef Hotel Casino, 35–41 Wharf St., ground-floor foyer, CBD* ☎ *07/4030–8888* ⊕ *www.reefcasino.com.au/vertigo.*

SHOPPING

MALLS

Cairns Central. Adjacent to Cairns Railway Station, Cairns Central houses 180-plus specialty stores, a supermarket, department stores, a food court, several coffee shops, and a cinema complex. Stroller hire is available. It also has the only free parking in Cairns CBD: three hours' free Monday through Saturday, and all day Sunday. ⊠ *McLeod and Spence Sts., CBD* ☎ *07/4041–4111* ⊕ *www.cairnscentral.com.au.*

The Pier at the Marina. Overlooking Trinity Bay and Marlin Marina in the Shangri-La Hotel complex, this low-rise waterfront mini-mall houses outlets of top Australian and international designers as well as galleries, salons, fitness facilities, and a visitor information center. Many of The Pier's bars and restaurants open onto waterfront verandas and the marina boardwalk. ⊠ *Pier Point Rd., CBD* ☎ *07/4052–7749* ⊕ *www. thepier.com.au.*

MARKETS

FAMILY **Cairns Night Markets.** If you're looking for bargain beachwear, local jewelery, art and crafts, a massage, a meal, a coffee, or souvenirs, The Cairns Night Markets, open daily 5–11 pm, are the place to go. Bring cash—several of the 70-plus merchants charge additional fees for credit cards. ⊠ *71–75 The Esplanade, at Aplin St., CBD* ☎ *01/4051–7666* ⊕ *www.nightmarkets.com.au.*

FAMILY **Rusty's Markets.** Cairns's iconic weekend "street" market, Rusty's attracts 180-plus stallholders, who peddle everything from fresh tropical produce to art and crafts, jewelry, clothing, natural health and skin-care products, and food. The market is covered, offering a pleasant respite from the sun. Take advantage of two hours' free parking in Gilligan's/Rusty's carpark, above Rusty's on Sheridan Street. ✉ *57–89 Grafton St., CBD* 📞 *07/4040–2705, 0438/753–460 market manager Justin Welch* ⊕ *www. rustysmarkets.com.au* ☽ *Fri. and Sat. 5 am–6 pm; Sun. 5 am–3 pm.*

SPORTING GOODS

Tusa Dive Shop. This store stocks a wide range of big-name dive gear as well as stinger and wet suits, swimwear, kids' gear, and accessories such as snorkels and sunscreen. ✉ *The Esplanade, at Shields St., CBD* 📞 *07/4047–9120* ⊕ *www.tusadive.com/shop* ☽ *Daily 7:30 am–9 pm.*

NORTH OF CAIRNS

The Captain Cook Highway runs from Cairns to Mossman, a relatively civilized stretch known mostly for the resort towns of Palm Cove and Port Douglas. Past the Daintree River, wildlife parks and sunny coastal villages fade into sensationally wild terrain. If you came to Australia seeking high-octane sun, pristine coral cays, steamy jungles filled with exotic birdcalls and riotous vegetation, and a languid beachcomber lifestyle, head for the coast between Daintree and Cooktown.

The southern half of this coastline lies within Cape Tribulation, Daintree National Park, part of the Greater Daintree Wilderness Area, a region named to UNESCO's World Heritage list because of its unique ecology. To experience the area's natural splendor, there's no need to go past Cape Tribulation. However, the Bloomfield Track continues on to Cooktown, a frontier destination that tacks two days onto your itinerary. This rugged country breeds some maverick personalities offering fresh perspectives on Far North Queensland.

8

Prime time for visiting is May through September, when daily maximum temperatures average around 27°C (80°F) and the water is comfortably warm. During the wet season, November through April, expect rain, humidity, and lots of bugs. Highly poisonous box and Irukandji jellyfish make the coastline unsafe for swimming from October through May, but "jellies" hardly ever drift out as far as the reefs, so you're safe to get wet there.

PALM COVE

23 km (14 miles) north of Cairns.

A 35-minute drive north of Cairns, Palm Cove is one of Queensland's jewels: an idyllic, albeit pricey, base from which to explore the far north. It's a quiet place, sought out by those in the know for its magnificent trees, calm waters, exceptionally clean beach, and excellent restaurants.

GETTING HERE AND AROUND

Getting here from Cairns is a cinch: by car, follow the signs from the city center to Captain Cook Highway, then head north, taking the Palm Cove turnoff after about 25 km (16 miles). Regular shuttle buses service Palm Cove from the airport, Cairns, and Port Douglas, farther north. Around this compact beach area, though, most people walk or cycle.

EXPLORING

A charming beachside village that sprawls back toward the highway, Palm Cove is navigated easily on foot. Many of the best accommodations, bars, and eateries are strung along the oceanfront strip of Williams Esplanade, fronting what has been dubbed Australia's cleanest beach. At its far north end, a five-minute stroll from the "village," there's a jetty and a small marina.

TOP ATTRACTIONS

FAMILY **Cairns Tropical Zoo.** At this 10-acre zoo, visitors can hand-feed tame kangaroos, cuddle with koalas, enjoy breakfast with the wildlife, and attend daily snake, crocodile, and bird shows. You'll also be able to see wombats, dingoes, echidnas, cassowaries, and the zoo's star resident—Sarge, a 17-foot, 660-pound centenarian croc. Have a souvenir photo taken with a koala, boa, or baby croc for A$18. Breakfast at the zoo runs daily from 8 am (groups) or 8:30 am (self-drivers) and includes park entry, full breakfast, and a wildlife presentation. ⊠ *Captain Cook Hwy.* ✢ *Between Clifton Beach and Palm Cove, just south of Bokissa Rd./Argentea Blvd.* ☎ *07/4055–3669* ⊕ *www.cairnstropicalzoo.com.au* ⊠*Entry A$34; 2-park pass (Cairns Tropical Zoo/Hartley's Crocodile Adventure)* ⊙ *Daily 8:30–4.*

FAMILY **Hartley's Crocodile Adventures.** Hartley's houses thousands of crocodiles as well as koalas, wallabies, quolls, snakes, lizards, southern cassowaries, and tropical birds in natural environs, accessible via boardwalks and boat tours. A lagoon cruise, on which keepers feed big crocs at close range, is included in your entry price. There are daily cassowary, wallaby, quoll, and koala feedings, croc and snake shows, and croc farm tours. Most thrilling is the Big Croc Experience, held daily at 10:30 and 1 (book 24 hours ahead). It's your chance to handle squirming baby crocs and pole-feed gigantic ones, and includes a guided tour and commemorative photo. The Gondwana Grill showcases local delicacies, including crocodile, of course. If you don't feel like driving, **Down Under Tours** (☎ *07/4035–5566*), **Tropical Horizons Tours** (☎ *07/4047–9049*), and several other operators include Hartley's on their day-tour itineraries. ⊠ *Captain Cook Hwy., Wangetti* ☎ *07/4055–3576* ⊕ *www.crocodileadventures.com* ⊠*Entry A$36; Croc Encounter A$125, self-drive; 2-park pass to Hartley's and Cairns Tropical Zoo A$64* ⊙ *Daily 8:30–5.*

FAMILY
Fodor's Choice
★
Mareeba Tropical Savanna and Wetlands Reserve. If you drive 70 km (44 miles) west of Palm Cove you'll encounter another world: giant termite mounds dot savanna scrub, and vast reclaimed wetlands give refuge to hundreds of bird species, including Australia's only stork, the Jabiru. In the midst of all this sits open-sided Clancy's Lagoon Visitor Centre and Jabiru Safari Lodge, a cluster of luxurious tented accommodation with decks, lighting, insect screens, and attached en suites. There's a well-equipped guests' camp kitchen (barbecue dinner packs available), a communal campfire area, and outdoor Jacuzzi. Knowledgable, enthusiastic staff run nature-based excursions on and around the vast, lily-littered lagoons and savanna: wildlife and birdwatching tours, bushwalking, fly fishing, canoeing, and photography sessions. A 2½-hour Sunset Reserve Safari departing 3:30 pm daily combines

Palm Cove is one of many pristine beaches along the tropical Queensland coast.

a bird-watching cruise, ranger-guided savanna drive on which you'll spot wallabies and kangaroos, a "billy" tea and bird-hide stop, and fine Aussie wine and cheese. Consider Jabiru's all-inclusive overnight and multiday packages A$490 per night, for two persons; it includes deluxe safari-tent accommodation, continental breakfast, BBQ dinner, and various guided site tours, walks, and cruises. Daily transfers to and from Cairns are available. All proceeds feed back into the Wetlands' environmental work. ✉ *Clancy's Lagoon Visitor Centre, 142 Pickford Rd., Biboohra ✛ Take Pickford Rd. turnoff from Biboohra, 7 km (4.4 miles) north of Mareeba on Peninsula Development Rd.* ☎ *07/4093–2514* ⊕ *www.mareebawetlands.org; www.jabirusafarilodge.com* ✉ *From A$278 (Jabiru deluxe safari-tent accomm., 2 people, incl. breakfast).*

SPORTS AND THE OUTDOORS

Palm Cove makes a great base for rain-forest and reef activities—hiking, biking, horseback riding, rafting, ballooning, and ATV adventures on the Atherton Tableland; snorkeling, diving, and sailing around the Low Isles and Barrier Reef; sea kayaking just offshore; and scenic flights over just about anywhere a small plane can get on a tank of gas. Though few cruise or tour companies are based in this beachside enclave, many Cairns and Port Douglas–based operators offer Palm Cove transfers.

KAYAKING

FAMILY **Palm Cove Watersports.** Paddling around history-rich Double Island, off
Fodor's Choice Palm Cove Jetty, in a kayak or on a paddleboard is a tranquil, eco-
★ friendly way to get close to the local marine life: you'll often spot dolphins, stingrays, turtles, and colorful fish on this local operator's terrific sunrise tours and half-day snorkeling excursions. Helpful guides impart

safety briefings and labor-saving tips on technique before you set out, and there are frequent stops for refreshments, snorkeling (May–November), and wildlife-watching en route. Even if you've never paddled a kayak before you're unlikely to capsize; the single and double kayaks are super-stable. Half-day trips circumnavigate Double Island, stopping off on the fringing reef about 600 meters (½ mile) from shore and on a secluded beach. Transfers from Cairns (A$25 per person) and Port Douglas (A$30 per person) are available; bookings are essential. ■ TIP→ Safety and snorkeling gear is provided, but bring sunglasses, a hat, and sunscreen. ✉ *79 Williams Esplanade ✛ 100 meters south of Palm Cove Jetty* ☎ *0402/861–011* ⊕ *www.palmcovewatersports.com* ⌛ *From A$55.*

WHERE TO EAT

$$

SEAFOOD

Fodor's Choice

★

✕ **Beach Almond Beach House.** This low-key eatery's simple beach-shack setting on Palm Cove's seafront underplays the freshness and flavor of its Modern Asian food. Seafood's the specialty here, and signature dishes include whole Singaporean chill mud crab and a lavish two-person seafood platter. The small but satisfying menu is full of fresh spins on favorite dishes from around Southeast Asia, including green papaya salad, banana leaf–wrapped barramundi with a coconut-lime dressing, and "tropical" lobster with tumeric, coconut, and mild chili. Beach Almond also serves leisurely lunches and coffee, and stays open later than many of its Palm Cove competitors at night. ⑤ *Average main: A$38* ✉ *145 Williams Esplanade* ☎ *07/4059–1908, 0488/145–147* ⊕ *www.beachalmond.com.*

$$

INTERNATIONAL

✕ **Lime & Pepper Restaurant and Bar.** European flair meets great local produce at this upscale beachfront restaurant and bar. Lime & Pepper mixes fresh seafood, tropical fruits, and bush-tucker ingredients, such as native finger limes and Davidson plums, in innovative dishes, with a worthy wine list and tropical cocktails. Menu options for lunch, dinner, and the five-course degustation (A$159 per person, with matched wines) change seasonally. Stand-out entrées might include grilled Gulf of Carpentaria tiger prawns with a coffee-lime dressing, or lemon-myrtle-marinated Grimaud duck breast on orange risotto, with asparagus and vanilla foam. Desserts are suitably elegant. The cuisine might be sophisticated, but kids are catered for with their own menu. Lime & Pepper also serves elegant high teas (from A$35, glass of bubbly included). Service, with the odd exception in peak periods, is attentive and knowledgeable. ⑤ *Average main: A$36* ✉ *Peppers Beach Club & Spa, 123 Williams Esplanade* ☎ *07/4059–9200* ⊕ *www.peppers.com. au/beach-club-spa/dining* 🪑 *Reservations essential.*

$$

MODERN

AUSTRALIAN

✕ **NuNu Restaurant.** Sexy suede lounges, intimate banquettes, and unbroken views of the Coral Sea make lingering easy at this Palm Cove eatery. The menus showcase the region's best and freshest produce. Start with a vanilla-ginger mojito or lime-coconut daiquiri, then select tapas-style tasting plates, such as baby barramundi, or wok-fried north Queensland mud crab with chili tamarind, sweet pork, and market greens. Those with large appetites may want to book a four- or seven-course degustation dinner (A$70/A$110) with matched wines. Tropical desserts are deceptively simple: a plum soufflé with dragon

8

fruit and pink wine sorbet, or coconut snow eggs with sticky black rice and passionfruit ice-cream. $ *Average main: A$43* ⊠ *Alamanda Palm Cove by Lancemore, 1 Veivers Rd.* ☎ *07/4059–1880* ⊕ *www. nunu.com.au* ♠ *Reservations essential.*

$$
MODERN ASIAN
✕ **Temple of Tastes.** Knowledgeable staff, an impressive wine and cocktail list, and a torchlit waterfront terrace are among the many reasons to dine at this excellent resort restaurant. You can expect generous servings of fresh modern Australian food infused with Asian and South Pacific flavors. Mains might include local barramundi, fish pot curry, or twice-cooked pulled pork. If you're feeling indulgent, save room for a sinful caramel brûlée or coconut cake. Temple's varied menu includes gluten-free and vegetarian options and changes seasonally. $ *Average main: A$37* ⊠ *Hotel Pullmann Palm Cove Sea Temple Resort and Spa, 5 Triton St.* ☎ *07/4059–9600* ⊕ *www.pullmanhotels.com* ♠ *Reservations essential.*

$$
MODERN
AUSTRALIAN
FAMILY
Fodor's Choice
★
✕ **Vivo Bar and Grill.** Diners at this classy beachside eatery enjoy Coral Sea views framed by palms and melaleucas along with Mod Oz dishes. Housemade muesli and freshly baked breads make this a favorite breakfast spot; panini, pasta, salads, and calamari pack in the crowds at lunch. At dinner, the chefs transforms fresh seasonal produce, along with seafood, into inventive contemporary food in a gleaming open kitchen. Try the delectable spanner crab linguine, chargrilled black Angus eye fillet, or seafood platter for two (A$95 per person). Then indulge in a caramelized fig, cinnamon, and chocolate pudding or a flourless mandarin cake with mascarpone ice cream. The two- to three-course prix-fixe menu comes with a glass of fine wine (A$39/A$49 per person). A chic sunken bar forms the hub of this sociable haunt; between meals, Vivo's a popular spot for city-strong coffee, tapas, and cocktails. $ *Average main: A$36* ⊠ *49 Williams Esplanade* ☎ *07/4059–0944* ⊕ *www.vivo.com.au.*

WHERE TO STAY

$$$$
RESORT
Fodor's Choice
★
▦ **Alamanda Palm Cove by Lancemore.** Fine landscaping, pools, barbecues, and sunny areas for relaxation enhance this classy colonial-style vacation complex fronting a palm-shaded white-sand beach. **Pros:** terrific location; upscale restaurant; free Wi-Fi. **Cons:** no elevators; pools on the chilly side. $ *Rooms from: A$499* ⊠ *1 Veivers Rd.* ☎ *07/4055–3000* ⊕ *www.lancemore.com.au/alamanda* ⇨ *67 apartments* ❤|*Breakfast.*

$$$
RESORT
▦ **Hotel Pullman Palm Cove Sea Temple Resort and Spa.** The well-appointed studio rooms and apartments at Pullman's gorgeous Palm Cove property have private balcony or terrace areas, high-definition flat-screen TVs, Nespresso coffee machines, and comfortable beds with memory-foam pillows. **Pros:** glorious grounds and pools; excellent on-site restaurant; five-star service. **Cons:** occasional noise from wedding parties; five-minute walk from Palm Cove's main strip and beach. $ *Rooms from: A$332* ⊠ *5 Triton St.* ☎ *07/4059–9600* ⊕ *www.pullmanhotels. com* ⇨ *126 studio rooms, suites, and penthouses* ❤|*No meals.*

$$
RESORT
FAMILY
Fodor's Choice
★
▦ **Kewarra Beach Resort & Spa.** This beachfront property just south of Palm Cove has its priorities right: Kewarra's sensitively designed, sleekly appointed bungalows and restored pioneer's cottage overlook rain forests teeming with wildlife, free-form pools, or a private white-sand beach. **Pros:** high-end facilities and service; eco-friendly ethos;

spectacular grounds; free Wi-Fi (even on the beach). **Cons:** a drive from Palm Cove's cafés; no on-site gym; rain-forest environs can mean the odd critter gets into your room. [$] *Rooms from: A$299* ⊠ *Kewarra Beach, 80 Kewarra St.* ☎ *07/4058–4000* ⊕ *www.kewarra.com* ⇆ *44 rooms* ⏐⏐ *No meals.*

$$$
RESORT
FAMILY

🛏 **Peppers Beach Club & Spa.** Its beachfront location, excellent on-site dining, and tropical suites make this laid-back resort popular with city dwellers seeking upscale relaxation. **Pros:** terrific on-site dining; multiple pools including a quiet pool zone and Serenity wing; well-equipped, air-conditioned gym; tennis court; free underground parking. **Cons:** fee for Internet use (limit); main pool area can be noisy. [$] *Rooms from: A$351* ⊠ *123 Williams Esplanade* ☎ *07/4059–9200 direct line, 1300/737444 toll-free in Australia, 07/5665–4426 Australia-wide reservations* ⊕ *www.peppers.com.au/beach-club-spa* ⇆ *150 rooms and suites* ⏐⏐ *No meals; Breakfast.*

$$$
RESORT

🛏 **The Reef House.** This centrally located small resort, once a private residence, feels positively quaint, and that's a good thing when you're looking for a low-key escape in this resort area. **Pros:** large, well appointed rooms; complimentary sunset punch and canapes; free in-room Wi-Fi and movies. **Cons:** pools can be cold; breakfast is pricey; grounds relatively small. [$] *Rooms from: A$329* ⊠ *99 Williams Esplanade* ☎ *07/4080–2600* ⊕ *www.reefhouse.com.au* ⇆ *69 rooms* ⏐⏐ *Some meals.*

PORT DOUGLAS

67½ km (42 miles) northwest of Cairns.

8

Known simply as "Port" to locals, Port Douglas offers almost as broad a range of outdoor adventures as Cairns, but in a more compact, laid-back setting. In this burgeoning tourist town there's a palpable buzz, despite tropical haze and humidity. Travelers from all over the world base themselves here, making excursions to the north's wild rain forests, the savanna and wetlands west of Mareeba, and the Great Barrier Reef. Varied lodgings, restaurants, and bars center on and around Port's main strip, Macrossan Street.

Like much of North Queensland, Port Douglas was settled after gold was discovered nearby. When local ore deposits dwindled in the 1880s, it became a port for sugar milled in nearby Mossman until the 1950s. The town's many old "Queenslander" buildings give it the feel of a simple seaside settlement, despite its modern resorts and overbuilt landscape. The rain forests and beaches that envelop the town are, for the most part, World Heritage sites—so while Port continues to grow in popularity, the extraordinary environs that draw people here are protected from development.

GETTING HERE AND AROUND

By car, it's a scenic, 75-minute drive north to Port Douglas from Cairns: take Sheridan Street to the Captain Cook Highway, following it for around 60 km (35 miles) to the Port Douglas turnoff. North of Palm Cove, along the 30-km (19-mile) Marlin Coast, the road plays hide-and-seek with an idyllic stretch of shoreline, ducking inland through tunnels of tropical coastal forest and curving back to the surf to reach Port Douglas.

Around town, most people drive, walk, or cycle. It's about 5½ km (3½ miles), or an hour's level walk from the highway to the main street. Regular shuttle buses call in at major hotels and resorts day and night, ferrying travelers to and from Cairns, the airport, and nearby towns and attractions.

EXPLORING

Port Douglas is actually an isthmus, bounded by Four Mile Beach on one side, Dickson Inlet on the other, with the town's main retail, café, and restaurant strip, Macrossan Street, running up the center. The town sprawls as far as the highway, 5½ km (3½ miles) to the west, along Port Douglas Road, which is lined with upmarket resorts and holiday apartment complexes. At the far end of Macrossan Street, on Wharf Street, there's a busy marina.

FAMILY **Wildlife Habitat.** This world-class wildlife sanctuary just off the Captain
Fodor's Choice   Cook Highway is divided into "immersion" wetland, rain forest, grass-
★   land, and savanna habitats, enabling close creature encounters with everything from koalas to cassowaries and crocs. The park shelters more than 180 species of native wildlife in its 8-acre expanse, including technicolor parrots, emus, kangaroos, echidnas, and reptiles. The buffet breakfast with the birds, served daily 8–10:30 (A$52, including sanctuary entry and a guided tour) is accompanied by avian residents so tame they'll perch on your shoulders—and may steal your food if you're distracted. You can also lunch with the lorikeets from noon to 2 daily (A$55), then join one of the sanctuary's free expert-guided tours, held several times daily, or book a VIP behind-scenes version (A$25). ⊠ *Port Douglas Rd., at Agincourt St.* ☎ *07/4099–3235* ⊕ *www.wildlifehabitat.com.au* ⊡ *A$33 park entry; A$52 Breakfast with the Birds; A$55 Lunch with the Lorikeets; A$85 4-park pass; A$25 VIP tour* ☉ *Daily 8–5, last admission at 4.*

SPORTS AND THE OUTDOORS

Port Douglas is a great base for activities on the mainland and reef. Several tour companies conduct day trips into the rain forest and beyond in four-wheel-drive buses and vans; most include river cruises for crocodile-spotting and stops at local attractions. Various reef operators either base vessels at or pick up from Port Douglas Marina. You can also horseback ride, bungee jump, raft, go off-roading, hike, mountain-bike, and balloon on and around the Atherton Tablelands, or go Outback for excellent bird- and wildlife-watching west of Mareeba, just over an hour's drive from Port.

FISHING

FAMILY **MV Norseman.** Long-established MV *Norseman* is one of the best game-fishing boats on the Great Barrier Reef for novice and experienced anglers alike. Head out to the best spots on the reef's edge on a 60-foot, purpose-designed, high-tech vessel to fish for large pelagic species including Spanish mackerel, tuna, wahoo, and the elusive giant trevally. Closer in, find sea perch, mangrove Jack, red and spangeled emperor, and coral trout. It's A$246 per adult for a full day on the water (bait, equipment, instruction, refreshments, fuel levy, and reef taxes included; rod and reel hire is an additional A$45 per day). Port Douglas accommodation transfers are free; it costs extra for transfers from Cairns, the Northern Beaches, and Palm Cove. ⊠ *The Reef Marina, 44 Wharf St., Berth E11, at Inlet Rd.* ☎ *0419/015–262* ⊕ *www.mvnorseman.com.au* ☞ *From A$246 per person.*

RIVER CRUISES

FAMILY **Crocodile Express.** Bird-watchers and photographers flock to Crocodile Express's flat-bottom boats to cruise the Daintree River on crocodile-spotting excursions; you may also see rare birds and outsize butterflies, flying foxes, snakes, and lizards en route. Sixty-minute cruises leave the Daintree Gateway, 500 meters before the ferry crossing, at regular intervals from 8:30 am to 2:30 pm; or you can board at Daintree Village Jetty and cruise the Upper Daintree regularly between 10 and 3:30. Extra cruises from both access points are scheduled in peak periods. ⊠ *5 Stewart St., end of Mossman–Daintree Rd., Daintree* ☎ *07/4098–6120* ⊕ *www.crocodileexpress.com* ☞ *From A$28.*

RAIN FOREST AND REEF TOURS

FAMILY
Fodor's Choice
★
Back Country Bliss Adventures. Amazing wilderness locations, high-quality equipment, excellent staff (including, when available, local indigenous guides), and Wet Tropic World Heritage Tour Operator accreditation give the Bliss team the edge. Based in Port Douglas but ranging much farther afield, the company runs customized, culturally and eco-sensitive small-group day and multiday trips that take you to nature and adventure hotspots from the Atherton Tablelands, Mossman Gorge, and Mareeba Wetlands to Cape Tribulation and Cooktown. They'll take you sea kayaking, wakeboarding, kite-surfing, rafting, hiking, mountain biking, drift-snorkeling in rain-forest streams, and "jungle surfing" in the rain-forest canopy. ☎ *07/4099–3677* ⊕ *www.backcountrybliss.com. au* ☞ *From A$99* ☞ *Tour prices include pickups from and drop-offs to local accommodations and resorts.*

FAMILY **Daintree Tours.** This operator conducts day-long, well-guided trips in top-of-the-line 4WD vehicles and custom-built trucks to the Daintree rain forest and beyond, with plenty of stop-offs en route to eat, drink, swim, and explore. Visit the Mossman Gorge, the Daintree rain forest, and Cape Tribulation. You can also arrange a daylong private wildlife-spotting charter to the Outback west of Mareeba, the Atherton Tablelands, and the rugged track to Bloomfield Falls. Ample lunch and refreshments, included in all excursions, ensure you keep your strength up. Port Douglas pick-ups and drop-offs make the early-morning starts simple. ⊠ *Tropical Journeys, 21–23 Warner St., Shop 3A, at Macrossan St.* ☎ *07/4099–6999, 1800/055966* ⊕ *www.daintreetours.com* ☞ *From A$190.*

FAMILY **Reef and Rainforest Connections.** This long-established, eco-friendly operator offers day trips exploring Kuranda's attractions and local wildlife parks; excursions to Cape Tribulation, the Daintree rain forest, and Mossman Gorge; and Great Barrier Reef cruises with Quicksilver Connections. The popular Kuranda day tour includes trips on the historic Scenic Railway and Skyrail Rainforest Cableway; a stroll around charming Kuranda Village, with its markets, curio stores, and wildlife attractions; and a visit to Tjapukai Aboriginal Cultural Park or Rainforestation. ✉ *40 Macrossan St.* ☎ *1300/780–455 reservations, 07/4047–9085 administration* ⊕ *www.reefandrainforest.com.au* ✈ *From A$155.*

FAMILY

Fodor's Choice

★

Tony's Tropical Tours. This company gives entertaining small-group day tours in luxe Land Cruisers that take in rain-forest sights and attractions as far as Cape Tribulation or, if you're prepared to get up earlier, the renowned and ruggedly beautiful Bloomfield Track. Well-informed, witty commentary from local experts, and non-rushed, well-chosen stops and activities—from interpretative rain-forest walks and Daintree River wildlife (croc) cruises, to handmade ice-cream and tropical-fruit tasting—make these trips crowd-pleasers. Refreshments, included in the cost, are a cut above the norm. Tony's also runs off-road tours through the Daintree as far as the Bloomfield Falls and terrific charter tours to the crater lakes, Atherton Tablelands, and Mareeba Wetlands, on which you might see kangaroos, birdlife, and the famed Curtain Fig tree. ✉ *Port Douglas* ☎ *07/4099–3230* ⊕ *www.tropicaltours.com. au* ✈ *From A$185.*

SNORKELING AND DIVING

Eye to Eye Marine Encounters. On these all-inclusive, dive/snorkel liveaboard trips, you visit world-renowned northern Great Barrier Reef and Coral Sea sites, including 2,000-foot drop-offs and pristine coral gardens, top shark-spotting sites, and turtle-nesting grounds. John Rumney, who pioneered swim-with-whales in Queensland, brings 30-plus years of experience on the Reef and extensive ecological knowledge and nautical expertise to the expeditions, working with highly skilled divers, scientists, and skippers to ensure each trip is as exciting as it is eco-friendly. ✉ *10 Captain Cook Hwy.* ☎ *07/4098–5417, 0417/726–622* ⊕ *www.marineencounters.com.au.*

FAMILY

Fodor's Choice

★

Poseidon. Excellent pre-dive briefings from a marine naturalist, high safety standards, and a wide choice of dive and snorkeling sites make this advanced eco-certified operator a smart choice. Poseidon runs guided snorkeling and PADI-style diving trips to sites at three separate reef sites at the Agincourt Ribbon Reef on a small, usually uncrowded boat. A day's cruise to three Agincourt sites includes a marine biologist–guided snorkel tour, lycra suits, masks, snorkels, fins, and flotation devices; wet suits for snorkelers can be rented at A$7 per day. For certified divers, a full day in the water includes dive gear. Morning and afternoon tea and a buffet lunch are provided for all guests. Port Douglas transfers are free; from Cairns or the Northern Beaches, it's A$28. ✉ *Reef Marina, Wharf St., off Inlet Dr.* ☎ *07/4087–2100* ⊕ *www. poseidon-cruises.com.au* ✈ *From A$232 (cruise and snorkeling), from A$278 (with diving), A$6.50 reef/admin tax* ☉ *Daily 8:30–4:30.*

FAMILY **Quicksilver Cruises.** Quicksilver's fast, modern catamarans speed you from Port Douglas's marina to a large commercial activity platform on the outer Barrier Reef. There, you can dive and snorkel with the reef residents, and make leisurely sail-and-snorkel trips to Low Isle coral cays. Options at Agincourt Reef include marine-biologist-guided snorkeling tours (A$60–A$78), introductory or certified scuba dives (extra

A$118–A$166), 10-minute scenic heli-tours (A$175), and "Ocean Walker" sea-bed explorations (A$166). There's also a semi-submersible underwater observatory, included in the A$238 rate. A quieter sailing trip to a Low Isles coral cay, closer to shore (A$188), includes a biologist-guided glass-bottom-boat trip and snorkeling. Everyone pays a A$6.50 reef tax. The trip includes a varied lunch buffet and dive/snorkel gear. Transfers are available from Port Douglas accommodations and farther afield (A$12–A$28). ⊠ *The Reef Marina, Wharf St., off Inlet Dr.* ☎ *07/4087–2100* ⊕ *www.quicksilver-cruises.com* 🖾 *From A$118.*

FAMILY **The Silver Series: Silversonic.** High-end, high-speed catamaran *Silversonic* whisks visitors to three pristine dive-snorkel sites on Agincourt Reef, known for its high-visibility waters. There, you can spend five hours amid spectacular corals on the edge of the Coral Sea trench, with turtles, rays, tropical fish, large pelagic species, and, in season, the odd Minke whale. Full-day outer reef cruises run daily, weather permitting; the A$232 tariff includes a "tropical smorgasbord" lunch, morning and afternoon tea, Wi-Fi, snorkeling, and gear; all scuba dives are guided at no extra cost, and everyone pays a A$6.50 reef tax. Coach transfers from local accommodations are included in the cruise fare; transfers to and from Palm Cove, the Northern Beaches, and Cairns are available for a surcharge. ⊠ *The Reef Marina, 1 Wharf St., off Inlet Dve.* ☎ *07/4087–2100* ⊕ *www.silverseries.com.au* 🖾 *From A$232, with EMC charge of A$6.50.*

WHERE TO EAT

$$ ✕**Harrisons.** A classic "Queenslander" with a lovely outdoor cocktails area shaded by century-old mango trees and fine-dining inside, Harrisons impresses with deftly executed dishes that showcase fresh seafood and small-batch ingredients, sourced locally. You might start with Moreton Bay bugs and move on to roasted barramundi; Hiramasa yellowtail kingfish with artichokes, sorrell, clams, succulents, and mushrooms; or a tender Chateaubriand of Victorian Black Angus steak (A$98 for two). Harrison's dessert menu is limited but seductive: it might be lemon meringue pie or a decadent Valrhona white chocolate and amaretto zabaglione with honeycomb. There's a six-course "menu gourmande" at A$80 per person, A$140 with matched wines. On the wine list, you'll find plenty of good mid-priced Antipodean drops and a smattering of French ones. ⑤ *Average main: A$40* ⊠ *22 Wharf St.* ☎ *07/4099–4011* ⊕ *www.harrisonsrestaurant.com.au* ☺ *Reservations essential.*

FRENCH FUSION

Fodor's Choice
★

$ ✕**On The Inlet Seafood Restaurant.** Choose your own live mud crab from holding tanks at this much-lauded seafood restaurant fronting Dickson Inlet. Watch yachts dock as you sit on the deck and down the sunset special: a generous bucket of prawns and a choice of Aussie beer or wine. Modern Australian dishes put the focus on fresh North Queensland produce and seafood, which is delivered direct from local fishing boats to the restaurant's pontoon. You can start with freshly shucked oysters or chili-salt calamari, then move on to beer-battered Spanish mackerel, crispy-skinned barramundi, or the restaurant's famed fish curry. There's also a kids' menu (A$15, two courses), and a terrific wine and cocktail list. If you're planning to come during peak dinner hours, a

SEAFOOD

FAMILY

Fodor's Choice
★

reservation is highly recommended. $ *Average main: A$34* ✉ *3 Inlet St.* ☎ *07/4099–5255* ⊕ *www.ontheinlet.com.au.*

$

MODERN
AUSTRALIAN
FAMILY
Fodor's Choice
★

✗ **Salsa Bar & Grill.** Rub shoulders with local foodies on the deck of this lively waterside institution that serves tropical Modern Australian fare. The large wooden deck overlooking Dickson Inlet becomes an intimate dining area after sunset. The dinner menu offers something for everyone, from kangaroo loin to herb-crusted wild barramundi, yellowfin tuna, or Jambalaya loaded with yabbies (local crayfish), tiger prawns, squid, and crocodile sausage. Happy hour comes daily between 3 and 5, just right for a daiquiri or two. Prebooking is strongly advised. $ *Average main: A$34* ✉ *26 Wharf St.* ☎ *07/4099–4922* ⊕ *www.salsaportdouglas. com.au* ⌲ *Reservations essential.*

$

MODERN
AUSTRALIAN

✗ **Watergate Restaurant & Lounge Bar.** Atmospheric indoor-outdoor dining, attentive service, and a well-stocked bar are nice, but the primary draw at this relaxed restaurant is the food, which highlights the freshest local ingredients: reef fish and prawns straight off Port Douglas's fishing boats, and seasonal fruit, vegetables, and herbs from the Atherton Tableland. The seasonal menu might include dukkah-crusted kangaroo loin with beetroot-goat's cheese tart; prawn-scallop ravioli in a creamy chardonnay-leek sauce; apple-infused Tableland pork; or eye fillet with a smoked-crocodile croquette and Daintree coffee jus. Book ahead for dinner, especially in peak periods. $ *Average main: A$35* ✉ *5/31 Macrossan St.* ☎ *07/4099–5544* ⊕ *www.watergateportdouglas.com.au.*

WHERE TO STAY

$

HOTEL
FAMILY
Fodor's Choice
★

🏨 **Best Western Lazy Lizard Motor Inn.** The clean, spacious, self-contained studio at this friendly low-rise motel just outside of town make it a practical base for those who don't mind a short walk or cycle to Port Douglas's center. **Pros:** friendly hosts; great rates; free cable TV and Wi-Fi; easy parking outside your door (or guest bikes to get around town on). **Cons:** reception closes at 7 pm; no on-site bar or restaurant. $ *Rooms from: A$199* ✉ *121 Davidson St.* ☎ *07/4099–5900, 1800/995950 toll-free in Australia* ⊕ *www.bestwestern.com.au* ⇴ *22 studios* ⏴⊙⏵ *Breakfast.*

$$$$

RENTAL

🏨 **Coconut Grove Port Douglas.** These well-appointed luxe apartments and penthouses perched above Port Douglas's main strip have state-of-the-art furnishings and appliances, free-standing spa baths, and large entertaining spaces including big, furnished balconies or decks, some with outdoor barbecues and plunge pools. **Pros:** immaculate living areas; central location; free undercover parking. **Cons:** fees for Wi-Fi and daily housekeeping; reception closes after business hours; 10 am check-out. $ *Rooms from: A$470* ✉ *56 Macrossan St.* ☎ *07/4099–0600* ⊕ *www. coconutgroveportdouglas.com.au* ☽ *Reception closes daily 5 pm–8 am* ⇴ *31 apartments, 2 penthouses* ⏴⊙⏵ *No meals.*

$$$

RENTAL
FAMILY
Fodor's Choice
★

🏨 **Mandalay Luxury Beachfront Apartments.** With beautiful Four-Mile Beach just outside and shops and eateries a brisk walk away, these comfortable, expansive, fully equipped apartments are in an excellent location. **Pros:** reasonable rates; plenty of space; close to the beach. **Cons:** street outside is poorly lit at night; no reception in off-peak hours; closest restaurants are a 10-minute walk away. $ *Rooms from: A$365*

⌧ *Garrick and Beryl Sts.* ☎ *07/4099–0100* ⊕ *www.mandalay.com.au* ⤶ *41 apartments* ⦿*No meals.*

$ ⌂ **Pink Flamingo Resort.** This gay-friendly, adults-only boutique resort,
RESORT set amid tropical gardens around a large, heated lagoon pool, is a perfect mix of hip and affordable, gregarious and relaxed. **Pros:** terrific
grounds, facilities, and hosts; free public-area Wi-Fi and parking; A$10
per night discount for "eco-stays" (no housekeeping) and 2-plus-day
stays. **Cons:** 15- to 20-minute walk to beaches and Port Douglas's main
strip; only the two garden studios have in-room Wi-Fi; reception hours
limited. **$** *Rooms from: A$145* ⌧ *115 Davidson St.* ☎ *07/4099–6622
9–5 daily, 0419/213–228 after hours* ⊕ *www.pinkflamingo.com.au*
⊙ *Reception closed Mon.–Sat. 5 pm–8 am, and Sun. after 1 pm* ⤶ *10
villas, 2 studios* ⦿*No meals.*

$$$ ⌂ **Thala Beach Nature Reserve.** Set on 145 acres of private beach, coco-
RESORT nut groves, and forest, this eco-certified nature lodge is about low-
Fodor'sChoice key luxury. **Pros:** eco-friendly ethos; multiday packages; free activities
★ include guided walks and wildlife- and bird-watching; gourmet hampers
available for private picnics. **Cons:** no in-room Internet access; hilly
property is unsuitable for guests with limited mobility; 15-minute drive
to Port Douglas. **$** *Rooms from: A$339* ⌧ *5078 Captain Cook Hwy.*
⤴ *Oak Beach, 38½ km (24 miles) north of Cairns, just south of Port
Douglas* ☎ *07/4098–5700, 866/998–4252 toll-free from U.S.* ⊕ *www.
thalabeach.com.au* ⤶ *83 individual cabins (bungalows and suites)*
⦿*All-inclusive; Breakfast; No meals.*

SHOPPING

FAMILY **Port Douglas markets.** Local growers and artisans gather on Sunday morn-
Fodor'sChoice ings in Port Douglas's waterfront park to sell fresh tropical produce and
★ gourmet goodies, arts and crafts, handmade garments, precious-stone
jewelry, books, and souvenirs. The atmosphere is relaxed, the crowd is
colorful, and there's plenty of variety. ⌧ *Anzac Park, Wharf St., end of
Macrossan St.* ⊕ *www.douglas.qld.gov.au/markets/communitymarkets*
⊙ *Pt. Douglas Market, Sun. 8 am–1:30 pm; Sunset Markets, Wed. 2–7 pm.*

MOSSMAN

*14 km (8½ miles) northwest of Port Douglas, 75 km (47 miles) north
of Cairns.*

This sleepy sugarcane town of just a couple of thousand residents has
shops, a medical center, and gas stations, but most visitors merely pass
through en route to Mossman Gorge, the Daintree, and rain-forest
accommodations.

GETTING HERE AND AROUND

From Port Douglas, it's 20 km (12 miles) or about 20 minutes' drive
northwest to Mossman. From Cairns it's a 75-km (47-mile) drive along
the Captain Cook Highway. There's little here to explore, but it's a good
place to stop for supplies and has a few good eateries.

ESSENTIALS

Visitor Information Destination Daintree. ⌧ *Daintree* ⊕ *www.
destinationdaintree.com.*

8

EXPLORING

Daintree Village, a half-hour drive north along the Mossman-Daintree Road, has restaurants, cafés, galleries, and access to croc river cruises. Drive 20 minutes northeast of Mossman to reach Wonga Beach, where you can stroll along the sand or go walkabout with indigenous guides.

FAMILY

Fodor'sChoice

★

Mossman Gorge. Just 5 km (3 miles) outside Mossman are the spectacular waterfalls and swimming-hole-studded river that tumble through sheer-walled Mossman Gorge. The Kuku Yalanji-run Mossman Gorge Centre is the starting-point for various aborigine-led walks, tours, and activities. There are several boulder-studded, croc-free swimming holes within the Gorge, and a 2½-km (1½-mile) rain-forest walking track and suspension bridge. (Swimming in the river itself is hazardous, crocs or no, due to swift currents, slippery rocks, and flash flooding.) Keep your eyes peeled for tree and musky rat-kangaroos, Boyd's water dragons, scrub fowl, turtles, and big, bright butterflies—and try to avoid stinging vines (plants with serrated-edge, heart-shaped leaves, found at rain-forest edges). If you intend to hike beyond the river and rain-forest circuits, inform the information desk staff at the Mossman Gorge Centre, which also has café/restaurant, gift shop, indigenous art gallery, restrooms, showers, and visitor parking. ⊠ *Mossman Gorge Centre, 212r Mossman Gorge Rd.* ☎ *07/4099–7000* ⊕ *www.mossmangorge. com.au* ✉ *Free entry (Mossman Gorge Centre); tour prices vary.*

SPORTS AND THE OUTDOORS

The spectacular wilderness around Mossman is ideal terrain for adventure sports and outdoor activities. If you have a day—or even a few hours—to spare, you can explore beaches, rain forest, and bushland trails on horseback, mountain bike, or ATV; take a scenic trek through Mossman Gorge; or drift-snorkel in the Upper Mossman River. The region's indigenous guardians, the Kuku Yalanji, run guided tours of Mossman Gorge and their coastal hunting grounds near Wonga Beach, in the World Heritage–listed Daintree rain forest.

ABORIGINAL TOURS

FAMILY

Fodor'sChoice

★

Kuku Yalanji Cultural Habitat Tours (*Daintree Dreaming tour*). On these relaxed, two-hour coastal walks, Kubirri Warra brothers Linc and Brandon Walker, members of the Kuku Yalanji *bama* (people), take turns guiding groups through three diverse ecosystems along Cooya Beach, demonstrating traditional plant use, pointing out bush tucker ingredients, recounting Dreamtime legends, and sharing their prodigious cultural and local knowledge, with plenty of jokes thrown in. Wear wading shoes, light clothing, a hat, insect repellent, and sunscreen. Return transfers to the Port Douglas area are A$30. ⊠ *Mossman Gorge Rd.* ☎ *07/4098–3376* ⊕ *www.bamaway.com.au/kuku-yalanji-cultural-habitat-tours* ✉ *From A$230.*

FAMILY

Walkabout Adventures. Personable indigenous guide Juan Walker takes small groups on fascinating half- and full-day rain-forest safari and coastal hunting trips, and personalized tours on request. These excursions visit the world's oldest rain forest, Mossman Gorge, and coastal mudflats, mangroves, and beaches, with swims in rain-forest streams, foraging beach and mangrove walks, and lessons on spear-throwing. ✉ *Daintree* ☏ *0429/478–206 Juan Walker* ⊕ *www. walkaboutadventures.com.au* 🎫 *From A$75, transfers extra* ☉ *Daily, morning pick-ups 8–9 am, afternoon pickups 12:30–1:30 pm.*

HELICOPTER EXCURSIONS

FAMILY

Fodor's Choice

★

Vertical Adventures. The half- and full-day helicopter tours whisk you from Great Barrier Reef sites to Daintree National Park and Mossman Gorge for guided kayak, mountain-bike, hiking, river-snorkeling, and jungle surfing adventures. Options include a half-day helicopter-kayak tour, and a half-day helicopter-river-snorkeling option. The Daintree Adventure Day includes a helicopter flight into the Daintree rain forest, zip-lining opportunities, and a crocodile-spotting river cruise. Helicopters depart from the Sheraton Mirage Country Club helipad near GBR's Sunbird Centre. Rates include flights, refreshments, all safety gear and equipment, entry fees, insurance, and transfers from Port Douglas, Mossman and Oak (Thala) Beach; from Palm Cove or the Northern Beaches, it's A$35/A$50 return. ✉ *4 Davidson St.* ☏ *07/4099–6310* ⊕ *www.backcountrybliss.com.au/heli-adventures* 🎫 *From A$333 per person.*

HORSEBACK RIDING

FAMILY

Daintree Station. Impressive displays of horsemanship and "jackeroo" (cowboy) skills are the draw at Daintree Station, which offers a daily Stockmans Lunch Muster complete with whip-cracking, cattle-driving, a bull catcher, ATVs, cattle dogs, stunt horses, and various other animals. It's all delivered with dry Outback humor and followed by a barbecue lunch, live music, and bush tales. Daily shows are staged in a 19th-century-inspired "Outback station shed" arena in rain-forest environs 12½ km (8 miles) north of Mossman or a 35-minute drive north of Port Douglas. After lunch, you can test your rodeo skills on a mechanical bull, or amuse the kids at the farm-animal petting zoo. ✉ *Kingston Rd., Whyanbeel* ✣ *Via Miallo, in Whyanbeel Valley* ☏ *07/4098–1149* ⊕ *www.daintreestation.com* 🎫 *From A$63.*

WHERE TO STAY

$$$

RESORT

🏨 **Daintree EcoLodge & Spa.** At this 30-acre boutique eco-resort in the ancient Daintree rain forest, elevated boardwalks protect the fragile environs and link the day spa, heated pool, restaurant/bar, and 15 freestanding tree houses or "bayans." All are air-conditioned and equipped with ceiling fans, satellite TVs, and king-size canopy beds. **Pros:** alfresco spa treatments; luxe, house-made bathroom amenities; eco-friendly; lower rates with longer stays. **Cons:** some rooms lack seclusion; no in-room Internet access; noise from public areas carries to proximate rooms and spa. ⑤ *Rooms from: A$345* ✉ *3189 Mossman-Daintree Rd.* ✣ *3 km (2 miles) past Daintree village, 110 km (68 miles) north of Cairns* ☏ *07/4098–6100* ⊕ *www.daintree-ecolodge.com.au* ☉ *Reception closed daily 5 pm–8 am* ➟ *15 individual bayans* ⎜Ⓞ⎜*Breakfast; All-inclusive.*

$$$

RESORT

Fodor's Choice

★

🏨 **Silky Oaks Lodge.** Cocooned in national parkland, this Advanced Ecotourism–certified hotel has luxe tree houses and suites clustered around an expansive open-sided lodge, day spa, and lagoon pool. **Pros:** lovely spa and grounds; free Wi-Fi in public areas; helpful tour desk and lots

8

Silky Oaks Lodge, near Daintree National Park

of included activities; well-marked walking trails around the resort. **Cons:** no in-room Internet; steep paths to some rooms (though you can call for a buggy pickup); occasional critters; access road can flood after heavy rain, Jan.–Mar. $ *Rooms from: A$398* ✉ *Finlayvale Rd.* ☎ *07/4098–1666* ⊕ *www.silkyoakslodge.com.au* ⤶ *40 rooms, 3 suites* ⦿ *Breakfast; All-inclusive.*

CAPE TRIBULATION

35 km (22 miles) north of the Daintree River crossing, 140 km (87 miles) north of Cairns.

Set dramatically at the base of Mount Sorrow, Cape Tribulation was named by Captain James Cook after a nearby reef snagged the HMS *Endeavour,* forcing him to seek refuge at the site of present-day Cooktown. Today, the tiny settlement, little more than a general store and a few lodges, is the activities and accommodations base for the surrounding national park.

GETTING HERE AND AROUND

Daintree Ferry. The Daintree–Mossman Road winds through sugarcane plantations and towering green hills to the Daintree River, a short waterway fed by monsoonal rains that make it a favorite inland haunt for saltwater crocodiles. On the river's northerly side, a sign announces Cape Tribulation National Park. There's just one cable ferry, carrying a maximum 27 vehicles, so although the crossing takes five minutes, the wait can be 15 or more, especially between 11 am and 1 pm, and all afternoon during holidays. There's no need to prebook your passage, but bring cash if you'll be crossing after dark. Return fare for a car is A$25 (one-way A$14); for a motorbike, it's A$10/A$5; a multiday car pass (five trips) is A$50; and walk-on passengers pay just A$2. ✉ *Daintree River ferry crossing, Daintree–Mossman Rd., Daintree ⚓ Ferry turnoff is just under 30 kms (18 miles) north of Mossman on Daintree-Mossman Rd.* ☎ *07/4099–9444 Douglas Shire Council offices ⊕ www.douglas.qld.gov.au/community/daintree-ferry 🖃 Round-trip: A$23 per car, A$9.50 motorbike, A$2 walk-on passenger/bicycle, A$46 multiday car pass (5 return trips) ⊙ Daily 6 am–midnight.*

The 140-km (86-mile) drive from Cairns to Cape Tribulation takes just under three hours. If you're renting a car, it's simplest to do so in Cairns or Port Douglas. This can be tough driving territory. The "highway" is narrow with just two lanes; many minor roads are rough and unpaved; and even major thruways in this area may be closed in the wet season due to flooding.

Mason's Cape Tribulation Tourist Information Centre, grocery store, bottle shop, and PK's Jungle Village, a little farther north on the opposite side of Cape Tribulation Road, are the last stops for food, supplies, and fuel as you head north. At PK's there's a supermarket, a bar serving meals and drinks, and an ATM.

ATMs are scarce beyond Mossman. Get cash and gas at the service station and convenience store on the Mossman-Daintree Road at Wonga Beach, or at PK's. North of the Daintree River, mobile phone coverage is limited (except in and around Mossman and Daintree Village and around Thornton Beach Kiosk), and you'll be lucky to get any signal once you get as far as Cape Tribulation.

Public transport is limited throughout the region. Coral Reef Coaches runs several daily services between Cairns, Port Douglas, and Mossman/Silky Oaks Lodge. Sun Palm Transport's daily services link Cairns airport with Cairns, Palm Cove, and Port Douglas. Charter services to Mossman, Daintree, Cow Bay, and Cape Trib can also be arranged. The journey from Cairns to Port Douglas takes around two hours, with stops at most resorts on request.

Bus Contacts Coral Reef Coaches. ☎ *07/4098–2800* ⊕ *www.coralreefcoaches.com.au.* **Sun Palm Transport Group.** ☎ *07/4099–1191* ⊕ *www.sunpalmtransport.com.au.*

ESSENTIALS

Tours and Visitor Information Mason's Cape Tribulation Tourist Information Centre, Shop, & Mason's Tours. ✉ *3781 Cape Tribulation Rd.* ☎ *07/4098–0070* ⊕ *www.masonstours.com.au.* **PK's Jungle Village.** ✉ *Cape Tribulation Rd., Lot 7* ☎ *07/4098–0040* ⊕ *www.pksjunglevillage.com.au.*

EXPLORING

Cape Tribulation Road winds through rain forest north of Cow Bay, veering east to join the coast at Thornton Beach, then skirting a string of near-deserted beaches en route to Cape Trib. Accommodations, attractions, and access points for beaches, croc cruise boats, and mangrove and rain-forest boardwalks are well signposted from the main road.

These rugged-looking yet fragile environs, Kuku Yalanji tribal lands, are best explored with experienced, culturally sensitive and eco-conscious guides. Excursions by 4WD and on horseback, bicycle, boat, and foot are offered by a few dozen local operators and resorts.

If exploring off-road on your own, arm yourself with detailed local maps, supplies, and up-to-date information. Let a reliable person know your intended route and return time, and don't underestimate the wildness of this terrain.

Fodor's Choice ★ **Daintree National Park.** The world's oldest tropical rain forest is an ecological wonderland: 85 of the 120 rarest species on earth are found here, and new ones are still being discovered. The 22,000-acre park, part of the UNESCO World Heritage–listed Wet Tropics region, stretches along the coast and west into the jungle from Cow Bay, 40 km (25 miles) or around an hour's drive northwest of Mossman. The traditional owners, the Eastern Kuku Yalanji, who live in well-honed harmony with their rain-forest environs, attribute powerful properties to many local sites—so tread sensitively. Prime hiking season here is May through September, and many local operators offer guided Daintree rain-forest walks, longer hikes, and nighttime wildlife-spotting excursions. Gather information and maps from local rangers or the Queensland Parks and Wildlife Service's **ParksQ** website before hiking unguided, and stay on marked trails and boardwalks to avoid damaging your fragile surroundings. Whatever season you go, bring insect repellent. ⊠ *Daintree* 🕾 *13-7468* ⊕ *www.nprsr.qld.gov.au/parks/daintree.*

FAMILY **Daintree Discovery Centre.** This World Heritage–accredited Wet Tropics Visitor Centre's elevated boardwalks and a high viewing tower enable you to overlook an astoundingly diverse tract of ancient rain forest. You can acquire information en route from handheld audio guides, expert talks, and the on-site interpretive center. Four audio-guided trails include a Bush Tucker Trail and a Cassowary Circuit, on which you might spot one of these large but well-camouflaged birds. Take the Aerial Walkway across part of the bush, then the stairs to the top of the 76-foot-high Canopy Tower. Keen students of botany and ecology might want to prebook a guided group tour. The shop sells books, cards, souvenirs, and clothing. There's also an on-site café. ⊠ *Tulip Oak Rd., off Cape Tribulation Rd., Cow Bay* 🕾 *07/4098–9171* ⊕ *www.daintree-rec.com.au* 🖃 *A$32 (includes 48-page guidebook/return entry for 7 days)* ☺ *Daily 8:30–5.*

SPORTS AND THE OUTDOORS
CANOPY TOURS

FAMILY **Jungle Surfing Canopy Tours.** It's an exhilarating perspective on the rain forest and reef: suspended above the canopy on flying-fox zip lines, your speed controlled by guides as you whiz along over lush rain forest and Mason's Creek, stopping at tree platforms for killer bird's-eye views. Sessions last 1½ to 2 hours and depart eight times a day starting at 7:45 am. Nightly guided Jungle Adventures Nightwalks explore the critter-filled 45-acre grounds, departing PK's Jungle Village reception at 7:30 pm. You can also buy tickets covering zip-lining and the night tour. Transfers from most local accommodations are free, or self-drive to the central departure point. Day-tour packages from Port Douglas include lunch. Note that Jungle Surfing is unsuitable for anyone weighing more than 120 kilograms (260 pounds), and that anyone under 18 needs a medical certificate and waiver before they'll be allowed to zip-line. ⊠ *The Snake House, Cape Tribulation Rd., Lot 2* ⊹ *Free parking at pickup point. Arrive 10 min prior to designated departure time to complete paperwork* ☎ *07/4098–0043* ⊕ *www.junglesurfing.com.au* ⊠ *From A$45.*

GREAT BARRIER REEF TOURS

FAMILY

Fodor's Choice

★

Ocean Safari. Eco-certified Ocean Safari runs half-day small-group tours that include snorkeling two pristine sites on the Great Barrier Reef, just half an hour's thrilling motorboat ride off Cape Trib Beach. Well-chosen sites on magnificent Mackay and Undine reefs teem with "Nemos" (clown anemone fish), turtles, rays, barracuda, potato cod, giant clams, nudibranchs, and an astounding array of corals. A maximum of 25 passengers and a rigid inflatable boat (with covered seating area and bathroom facilities). Snorkeling equipment, expert guidance, and EMC (reef) tax are included in the price; you can hire wet suits/sunsuits (A$8) and prescription masks (A$15), and buy soft drinks, chocolate, and underwater cameras on board. Meet at Ocean Safari's office, on-site at the Turtle Rock Cafe opposite PK's; pickups from Cape Trib accommodations are free. Package deals that include safari-hut accommodation at Jungle Lodge and an Ocean Safari excursion are available. ⊠ *Ocean Safari office (on-site at Turtle Rock Cafe), Cape Tribulation Rd., Lot 4* ⊹ *opposite PK's Jungle Village* ☎ *07/4098–0006* ⊕ *www.oceansafari.com.au* ⊠ *From A$139* ⊙ *Daily 9–12:30 and 1–4:30, weather permitting.*

WHERE TO EAT

$

MEDITERRANEAN

✕ **On The Turps Bar & Restaurant.** At this open-air restaurant in the Daintree rain forest, wallabies, bandicoots, and musky rat kangaroos might join you at the table as you tuck into Mod-Oz-meets-Mediterranean food that highlights local, seasonal ingredients including fresh seafood, and wines from the well-stocked bar. On The Turps also does "tropical Continental" breakfasts and varied, good-value lunches, as well as leisurely morning and afternoon Devonshire teas. Arrive early for a dip in the creek, a rain-forest stroll, or a spa treatment. $ *Average main: A$33* ⊠ *Daintree-Cape Tribulation Heritage Lodge & Spa, Lot 236, R36, Turpentine Rd.* ⊹ *18 km (about 11 miles) north of Daintree River crossing, turn left at Turpentine Rd.* ☎ *07/4098–9321* ⊕ *www.heritagelodge.net.au.*

$

MODERN
AUSTRALIAN

FAMILY

Fodor's Choice

★

✕ **Whet Cafe, Bar and Restaurant.** Stylish and hip yet comfortable, Whet Cafe, Bar and Restaurant draws visitors and locals with its outdoor deck, perfect for long lunches, sunset cocktails, and romantic dinners. It has Modern Australian food, friendly service, and an on-site boutique cinema. Regional and seasonal ingredients, including plenty of local seafood are combined in fresh, simple dishes with Asian and Mediterranean influences. Gluten-free, vegetarian, and kid-size meals are available. Booking ahead is a good idea at peak visitor times. Whet Flicks, a laid-back, licensed, 24-seat cinema upstairs, runs daily sessions of pre-DVD-release movies for A$10 a pop. Relax in air-conditioned comfort on beanbags, recliners, or leather lounges and enjoy tapas-style snacks with the film. ⑤ *Average main: A$23* ✉ *Cape Tribulation Rd., Lot 1* ☎ *07/4098–0007* ⊕ *www.whet.net.au.*

WHERE TO STAY

Privately run campgrounds and small resorts can be found along Daintree Road at Myall Creek and Cape Tribulation.

$$$
B&B/INN

🏚 **Cockatoo Hill Retreat.** The elegant solar-powered tree houses at this impeccably run boutique retreat invite relaxation and romance. **Pros:** helpful, thoughtful host; eco-friendly; magnificent views. **Cons:** phone/Internet access only if you have Telstra service; 4WD required during or after heavy rain to get up the resort's steep driveway; no on-site food apart from breakfast. ⑤ *Rooms from: A$395* ✉ *2060 Cape Tribulation Rd., Diwan* ✛ *Midway between Daintree and Cape Tribulation* ☎ *07/4098–9277* ⊕ *www.cockatoohillretreat.com.au* ↩ *4 rooms* ⦿I *Breakfast.*

$
B&B/INN
FAMILY

🏚 **Daintree Wild Zoo and B&B.** At this well-run B&B adjoining Daintree Zoo, wallabies, kangaroos, cockatoos, emus, and Southern cassowaries wander the grounds, often joining guests for tropical breakfasts in the open-sided dining area. **Pros:** friendly, knowledgeable, wildlife-loving hosts; free tropical breakfasts and buffet BBQ dinners (in peak periods); half-price unlimited zoo entry. **Cons:** budget rooms share facilities and public Wi-Fi; Sunbird Room can get communal shower noise; unsuitable for those who aren't fond of birds and animals. ⑤ *Rooms from: A$185* ✉ *2054 Mossman-Daintree Rd., Wonga* ☎ *07/4098–7272* ⊕ *www.daintreewildbnb.com.au* ↩ *6 motel rooms, 4 budget rooms with shared bath* ⦿I *Breakfast.*

$$$
RESORT
FAMILY

🏚 **Heritage Lodge & Spa.** Nestled in World Heritage–listed rain forest beside Cooper Creek, this secluded spa resort is a great antidote to stress. **Pros:** friendly fauna; lots of on-site facilities; tranquil rain-forest environs. **Cons:** limited cell-phone coverage; drive or longish trek to beach; occasional critters; Internet only through roaming Wi-Fi hotspot. ⑤ *Rooms from: A$330* ✉ *Turpentine Rd., Lot 236/R96, Diwan* ✛ *15 km (10 miles) north of Daintree River ferry crossing* ☎ *07/4098–9321* ⊕ *www.heritagelodge.net.au* ↩ *20 cabins* ⦿I *Breakfast.*

COOKTOWN

103 km (64 miles), around 3½-hours' drive, north of Cape Tribulation; 324 km (203-mile) or 5½-hours' drive north of Cairns.

Traveling north, Cooktown is the last major settlement on the east coast of the continent, sitting at the edge of a difficult wilderness. Its wide main street consists mainly of two-story pubs with four-wheel-drive vehicles parked out front. Despite the frontier air, Cooktown has an impressive history. It was here in 1770 that Captain James Cook beached HMS *Endeavour* to repair her hull. Any tour of Cooktown should begin at the waterfront, where a statue of Cook gazes out to sea, overlooking the spot where he landed.

GETTING HERE AND AROUND

By car from Cairns, take the inland highway, Peninsula Developmental Road, a 200-odd-mile stretch of fully paved road that barrels you through Australia's Outback—watch for errant cattle and 'roos on the drive. From Cape Tribulation, head up the Cooktown Developmental Road, or take the 4WD-only Bloomfield Track, just 97 km (60 miles), but challenging and sometimes flooded in the Wet. The Bloomfield Track journey, which roughly traces a series of indigenous story-line trails known as the Bama (People's) Way, takes around three hours, longer in wet weather; the Developmental Road is smoother but less scenic. Getting around Cooktown, a compact town, is a comparative cinch: drive, walk, or cycle.

EXPLORING

Cooktown has some lovely old buildings and a cemetery dating from the 1870s gold rush. Stroll along botanic garden trails and uncrowded beaches, check out the environment interpretative center and visitor info-hub Nature's Powerhouse, cool off in the public swimming pool, and scale Grassy Hill around sunset for stupendous views.

Black Mountain (Kalkajaka) National Park. Just south of Cooktown within the Wet Tropics World Heritage Area, Black Mountain (Kalkajaka) National Park protects a unique mix of gigantic granite boulders, wet-tropics species, and savanna woodland vegetation harboring abundant wildlife, including threatened species. Lucky visitors might spot the scanty frog, rainbow skink, Black Mountain gecko, Godman's rock-wallaby, or a rare ghost bat. Kalkajaka means "place of the spear"; Black Mountain was a significant meeting place for the Eastern Kuku Yalanji tribe. The boulders are treacherous, so climbing and hiking is not allowed, but the lookout point provides a fairly close-up view. ⌂ *Mulligan Hwy., Rossville* ☎ *13/7468 ParksQ hotline* ⊕ *www.nprsr. qld.gov.au/parks/black-mountain.*

James Cook Museum. Cooktown, in its heyday, was a gold-mining port, with 64 pubs lining the 3-km-long (2-mile-long) main street; a significant slice of this colorful history, including mementos of Cook's voyage and Aboriginal artifacts, is preserved at this National Trust–run museum. The former convent houses relics of the Palmer gold-mining and pastoral eras, including a Chinese joss house; canoes, and the anchor and one of six cannons jettisoned when the HMS *Endeavour* ran aground. The surprisingly good on-site shop sells books and souvenirs. It's recommended that you allow at least an hour to pore over the exhibits. ⌂ *Helen St. at Furneaux St.* ☎ *07/4069–5386* ⊕ *www. nationaltrust.org.au/qld/JamesCookMuseum* ⌑ *A$10; A$5 souvenir handbook* ⊘ *Apr.–Oct., daily 9–4; Nov.–Jan. and Mar., daily 9:30–4; Feb., Mon.–Sat. 10–1.*

Nature's Powerhouse & Cooktown Botanic Gardens. This interpretive center and museum at the entrance to Cooktown's heritage-listed Botanic Gardens is home to a valuable collection of local botanical illustrations by internationally recognized artist Vera Scarth-Johnson, and impressive displays of Cape York Peninsula wildlife, bequeathed by local fauna expert Charlie Tanner. Take extra time to wander through the Gardens, which, with its stone-pitched waterways and shady paths, include 154 acres of colorful native and exotic plants. A popular attraction in the gardens is a 7-meter python carved locally from ironwood. You can enjoy afternoon tea or a light lunch at the Vera Café; browse the shop of botanically themed gifts and souvenirs, including beautiful scarves, prints and postcards, wooden bowls, and authentic Aboriginal art; and get regional travel tips from the on-site Cooktown and Cape York Peninsula Visitor Information Centre. ⊠ *Walker St.* ✛ *follow road to end of Walker St.* ☎ *07/4069–6004* ⊕ *www.naturespowerhouse.com.au* 🖂 *Botanic Gardens free, Nature's Powerhouse A$3.50* ⊙ *Powerhouse hrs vary seasonally; gardens Tues.–Sun. 9–5.*

SPORTS AND THE OUTDOORS

There's plenty of outdoorsy fun to be had in and around Cooktown. Book a diving, snorkeling, or game-fishing cruise to the outer Barrier Reef or Lizard Island; take a guided rock-art or rain-forest walk; go Outback on a multiday 4WD Cape York excursion; or charter a scenic heli-flight over both World Heritage areas.

CULTURAL TOURS

FAMILY
Fodor's Choice
★

Guurrbi Tours. A 45-minute drive inland of Cooktown lie ancient Aboriginal rock-art sites of immense significance, the exact locations of which are a closely guarded secret—so who better to guide you than Nugalwarra elder Willie Gordon, a designated storyteller? During the dry season, Willie guides guests around his ancestral rock-art sites, set high in the hills behind Hope Vale, on scheduled weekday tours that pick up from accommodations around Cooktown. The 5½-hour Rainbow Serpent tour takes in half a dozen sites including the renowned Rainbow Serpent Cave and an ancestral birthing site. En route, Willie shares the Dreamtime stories and traditional lore behind this extraordinary cave art, some of which was painted by his own grandfather. If you're self-driving to the Guurrbi Meeting Point, near Hope Vale Aboriginal Community (about 45 minutes from town): request a map and directions when you book. It's recommended you wear sunscreen and insect protection; closed-toe shoes are mandatory. ⊠ *9 Boundary St.* ☎ *07/4034–5020* ⊕ *www.guurrbitours.com* 🖂 *From A$135* ⊙ *Apr.–Jan., weekdays 7:45 am–1:30 pm.*

WHERE TO STAY

$
RESORT

Milkwood Lodge Rainforest Retreat. Six pole cabins oriented for seclusion provide breezy, split-level accommodation overlooking rain forest and bushland at this user-friendly tropical retreat. **Pros:** free airport pickups; breakfast packs; discounts for on-site vehicle hire and longer stays. **Cons:** small TVs; some rooms lack Wi-Fi access; no restaurant; fair way out of town. $ *Rooms from: A$145* ⊠ *Annan Rd.* ☎ *07/4069–5007* ⊕ *www.milkwoodlodge.com* ⤴ *6 treehouses* ⦿⦿ *Breakfast.*

$
HOTEL
FAMILY

The Seaview Motel. This clean, quiet seafront establishment has five categories of accommodation, some newer than others and some with magnificent views. **Pros:** friendly atmosphere; takeout drinks and breakfast packs/toasters (for a fee); scenic location. **Cons:** no screens on sliding doors to motel-room balconies; small pool; breakfast restaurant may close outside of peak periods. $ *Rooms from: A$110* ⊠ *178*

Charlotte St. ☎ *07/4069–5377* ⊕ *www.cooktownseaviewmotel.com.au* ⇌ *38 motel rooms, 1 family unit, 3 townhouses* ⦿ *Breakfast.*

$ ⛳ **The Sovereign Resort Hotel.** This attractive, two-story colonial-style
HOTEL   hotel in the heart of town is the best bet in Cooktown. **Pros:** good-
FAMILY   value apartments; free in-room Wi-Fi; airport/wharf transfers; terrific
Fodor'sChoice   gardens, BBQ area, and pool. **Cons:** restaurant not open for dinner in
★   wet season (Nov.–Mar.). $ *Rooms from: A$195* ⊠ *128 Charlotte St.,
at Green St.* ☎ *07/4043–0500* ⊕ *www.sovereignresort.com.au* ☽ *Café
closed Sun. No dinner Sun. and Nov.–Mar.* ⇌ *31 rooms, 7 apartments*
⦿ *No meals.*

THE WHITSUNDAY ISLANDS AND AIRLIE BEACH

The Whitsundays are a group of 74 islands situated within 161 km
(100 miles) of each other and around 50 km (31 miles) from Shute
Harbour, the principal mainland departure point, though some boats
depart from Airlie Beach marina nearby. Discovered in 1770 by Captain
James Cook of the HMS *Endeavour*—though in fact not on Whitsunday itself, thanks to a time-zone change oversight on Cook's part—the
Whitsundays are a favorite sailing destination and an easy-access base
from which to explore the midsection of the Great Barrier Reef. Some of
the islands' beaches—notably, famous Whitehaven Beach—are picture-
postcard gorgeous, though vegetation on the islands themselves looks
more scrubby than tropical. In fact, the entire region is subtropical,
making for moderate air and water temperatures year-round. Most of
the Whitsunday Islands are designated national parks and, although
you'll spot few animals on them, birds are plentiful—more than 150
species make their homes here. Only a few of the islands have resorts;
others serve as destinations for day trips, beach time, and bushwalks,
or simply as backdrop at scenic moorings.

Camping is popular on the myriad islands of the Whitsunday group. To
pitch a tent on islands lying within national parks you need a A$5.95
per-person, per-night permit from the ParksQ (Queensland Department
of National Parks, Recreation, Sport & Racing [NPRSR]). The Whitsunday Region Information Centre, on the Bruce Highway at Proserpine, is open daily 9–5.

AIRLIE BEACH

*1,119 km (695 miles) or 13½ hours' drive north of Brisbane, 623 km
(387 miles) south of Cairns via the Bruce Hwy.*

Airlie Beach's balmy climate and its proximity to the Whitsunday
Islands, a resort and water-sports playground, make it hugely popular
with partying backpackers and holidaymakers en route to the islands
and reef.

The Whitsunday Islands and Airlie Beach

GETTING HERE AND AROUND

Whitsunday Coast Airport, near Proserpine, 36 km (23 miles) southeast of Airlie Beach, has direct daily flights to and from Brisbane and less frequent services to Sydney, on Virgin Blue and Jetstar. Whitsunday Transit buses connect the airport and Proserpine Railway Station to Airlie Beach, Cannonvale, and Shute Harbour, with services timed to meet all flights and passenger trains (drive time 30–40 minutes). It's A$12.10, one way, to or from Proserpine railway station. Greyhound Australia and Oz Experience offer daily services into Airlie Beach from Sydney, Brisbane, and towns between, and from Cairns. Queensland Rail operates several long-distance trains weekly, northbound and southbound, that stop at Proserpine Railway Station, about 25 km (15 miles) from Airlie Beach.

Airport Whitsunday Coast Airport. ⊠ *Sir Reginald Ansett Dr., Proserpine* ☎ *07/4945–0200 airport.*

Boat Contacts Cumberland Charter Yachts. ⊠ *Abel Point Marina, Shingley Dve.* ☎ *07/4946–7500, 1800/075101* ⊕ *www.ccy.com.au.* **Queensland Yacht Charters** (*Whitsunday Yacht Charters*). ⊠ *Abel Point Marina* ☎ *07/4946–7400, 1800/075013 toll-free in Australia* ⊕ *www.yachtcharters.com.au.* **Whitsunday Rent A Yacht.** ⊠ *Shute Harbour, 6 Bay Terr.* ☎ *07/4946–9232, 1800/075000 toll-free in Australia* ⊕ *www.rentayacht.com.au.*

Bus Contacts Greyhound Australia.
☎ 1300/473–946 toll-free in Australia,
07/4690–9850 ⊕ www.greyhound.com.
au. **Whitsunday Transit.** ☎ 07/4946–
1800 ⊕ www.whitsundaytransit.com.au.

Train Contacts Proserpine Railway
Station. ✉ Hinschen St., Proserpine
☎ 13–1617 in Australia, 07/4945–1013

BEWARE

From October to May the ocean
off beaches north of Rockhampton
is rendered virtually unswimmable
by toxic-tentacled box jellyfish.

⊕ www.qr.com.au. **Queensland Rail.** ☎ 13-1617 toll-free in Australia, 07/3072–
2222 ⊕ www.qr.com.au.

TOURS

Whitsunday Sailing Adventures. Whitsunday Sailing Adventures runs several sailing, scuba, and snorkeling trips around the islands and Great Barrier Reef on a dozen-plus owner-operated vessels, including modern sailing cats and tall ships. Choose from sailing, diving, kayaking, and snorkeling excursions. A two-night, three-day live-aboard outer reef trip starts at A$799 per person in a private double room, A$699 in a shared room, with one scuba dive and all gear and meals included. One- and two-night performance sailing adventures start at A$380. If time is limited, there's an eco-friendly sail-and-snorkel day-trip (A$1,955). Book well ahead for holiday periods. ✉ 402 Shute Harbour Rd. ☎ 07/4940–2000, 1300/653100 toll-free in Australia ⊕ www. whitsundaysailingadventures.com.au ⌁ From A$380.

EXPLORING

Airlie's main street is packed with cafés, bars, tour agencies, and hotels, with homes and higher-end accommodations extending up the steep hills behind it. The waterfront Esplanade, with its boardwalk, landscaped gardens, swimming lagoon, and weekend markets, is generally lively.

FAMILY **Conway National Park.** Ten minutes' drive southeast of Airlie, Conway National Park is a 54,000-acre expanse of mangroves, woodlands, rocky cliffs, and tropical lowland rain forest that shelters the endangered Proserpine rock wallaby and other rare species, as well as sulphur-crested cockatoos, emerald doves, Australian brush-turkeys, and orange-footed scrubfowl. Most walking trails start at the park's picnic area at the end of Forestry Road, about 10 km (6 miles) from Airlie. Mount Rooper Walking Track, a 5.4-km (3-mile) circuit, meanders uphill through bushland to a lookout with breathtaking Whitsundays views. If time permits, and you're sufficiently fit, you can cycle, run, or walk the 27-km (17-mile) Conway circuit, starting at Forestry Road carpark and ending in Airlie Beach. Swamp Bay track follows the creek to a coral-strewn beach with a bush camping area. ✉ Shute Harbour Rd., at Mandalay Rd. ⊕ Travel 10 km (6 miles) west along Shute Harbour Rd., then turn left onto Brandy Creek Rd. Follow it to Forestry Rd. and carpark (start of the Conway circuit) ☎ 07/4945–3967 Whitsunday Visitor Information, 13–7468 ParksQ hotline/camping permits ⊕ www. nprsr.qld.gov.au/parks/conway ⌁ Camping permits, A$5.95 per person, per night ☞ Camping permits must be pre-booked via ParksQ.

Shute Harbour. Ten kilometers (6 miles) southeast of Airlie Beach along Shute Harbour Road, Shute Harbour is the main ferry terminal and gateway to the Whitsunday islands and the reef. The large, sheltered inlet teems with boats—it's one of the busiest commuter ports in Australia. Though accommodation is available, the harbor is geared toward transferring visitors. For a great view over Shute Harbour and the Whitsunday Passage, drive to the top of Coral Point. ⊠ *Shute Harbour Rd., Shute Harbour.*

BEACHES

FAMILY

Fodor's Choice

★

Airlie Beach Lagoon. This stinger-free swimming enclosure on Airlie's shorefront has dedicated lap-swimming lanes, real-sand "beaches," adjoining children's pools, and sensor-activated lighting after dark. There are toilets, showers, and change rooms nearby, and all pools are patrolled by trained lifeguards year-round. A tropical garden, crisscrossed with walkways and dotted with public art, picnic tables, and free electric BBQs, surround the lagoon, and there's a playground for the kids. Not surprisingly, it's hugely popular with locals and visitors, especially in stinger season. **Amenities:** food and drink; lifeguards; showers; toilets. **Best for:** swimming. ⊠ *The Esplanade, at Broadwater Ave., parallel to Shute Harbor Rd.* ☎ *07/4945–0200* ⊕ *www.whitsunday.qld. gov.au* ⊗ *Patroled daily 8 am–9 pm (summer), 9–7 (winter).*

WHERE TO EAT

$

MODERN
AUSTRALIAN

⨯ **Easy Cafe.** Tucked away in an arcade off the main strip, Easy Cafe whips up relaxed breakfasts, brunches, and light lunches, drawing a sociable mix of travelers and locals with well-priced, tasty food, great coffee, free Wi-Fi, and friendly service. Join the crowd that flocks here weekdays for the good-value Easy Breakfast. Come here before your dive for a healthy fruit salad with yogurt and maple, or eggs Benedict on homemade herb-Parmesan bread. Pop in later in the day for a burger, sandwich, or coffee and cake (a steal at around A$4 a slice). $ *Average main: A$16* ⊠ *Pavilion Arcade, 287 Shute Harbour Rd.* ☎ *07/4946–5559* ⊗ *No dinner* ⌂ *Reservations not accepted.*

$

SEAFOOD

⨯ **Fish D'Vine and Rum Bar.** The menu here showcases seafood in all its forms—from beer-battered fish-and-chips to seafood chowder and wild-caught barramundi (the chef will even cook your catch). The bar is stocked with 500-plus rums and has a mean cocktail list. Signature D'Vine dishes include the seafood indulgence, which is loaded with local marine produce (tiger prawns, reef fish, salmon, scallops, oysters, mussels, and calamari) and chips; and, in season, mud crab, served chilled with house-made cocktail sauce and crusty bread. You can also get vegetarian dishes. Good choices for dessert include lemon-and-lime tart with mixed berry compote and chantilly cream; or banana fritters with spiced rum maple syrup, vanilla bean ice cream, and a dark-chocolate swirl. $ *Average main: A$33* ⊠ *303 Shute Harbour Rd.* ☎ *07 /4948–0088* ⊕ *www.fishdvine.com.au* ⊗ *No lunch.*

$

TAPAS

⨯ **Mr Bones.** Red plastic bar stools line the open front of this well-run Airlie café/bar overlooking the water. Three big attractions here are thin-crust pizzas, tapas-style dishes, and ice-cold beer. Small dishes include chicken-laced spring rolls, lamb croquettes, and corn fritters. The delectable lamb pizza, topped with slow-roasted lamb, halloumi, salsa verde, olives, and lemon, is a deserved house favorite; you can also order generous salads, burgers, and strong coffee. There's a good selection of chilled beer and wine available at the bar. ⑤ *Average main: A$23* ✉ *263 Shute Harbour Rd.* ☎ *0416/011–615.*

WHERE TO STAY

$ · 🖼 **Airlie Beach Hotel.** With the town's small beach at its doorstep, three
HOTEL · eateries and bars downstairs, and the main street directly behind it, this
FAMILY · hotel makes a comfy and convenient base. **Pros:** free Wi-Fi and undercover parking; lots of on-site food and drink options; close to main
strip, Airlie Lagoon, and waterfront. **Cons:** no room service; rooms
can be noisy. ⑤ *Rooms from: A$189* ✉ *16 The Esplanade, at Coconut
Grove* ☎ *07/4964–1999, 1800/466233 toll-free in Australia* ⊕ *www.
airliebeachhotel.com.au* ↪ *80 rooms and suites* ⅋ *No meals.*

$$$ · 🖼 **Peppers Airlie Beach.** The expansive one- to three-bedroom apart-
RESORT · ments at this high-end hillside resort are tailored for comfort, with
spa baths the size of small cars, designer decor and appliances, high-
end entertainment systems, free Wi-Fi, and big, furnished balconies
with great views of the bay and yacht club. **Pros:** classy decor, food,
and service; quiet location; buggies to ferry you up the resort's steep
driveways; free undercover parking. **Cons:** fee for Wi-Fi use; a walk
from Airlie's main street; 2% surcharge on credit-card payments; no in-
room heating in winter. ⑤ *Rooms from: A$398* ✉ *Mt. Whitsunday Dr.*
☎ *07/4962–5100, 1300/737444 toll-free in Australia* ⊕ *www.peppers.
com.au* ↪ *102 apartments* ⅋ *No meals.*

$ · 🖼 **Whitsunday Moorings B&B.** Overlooking Abel Point Marina, this metic-
B&B/INN · ulously run B&B has everything you need: stupendous marina views,
Fodor's Choice · charming hosts, and terrific gourmet breakfasts, often accompanied
★ · by colorful chirping parrots. **Pros:** charming, knowledgeable hosts;
fab breakfasts; upmarket toiletries; free Wi-Fi. **Cons:** uphill walk from
main street; open-room plan best suited to couples; reception closed
between 7 pm and 6 am. ⑤ *Rooms from: A$195* ✉ *37 Airlie Crescent*
☎ *07/4946–4692* ⊕ *www.whitsundaymooringsbb.com.au* ↪ *3 rooms*
⅋ *Breakfast.*

NIGHTLIFE

Shute Harbour Road, the main strip, is where it all happens in Airlie
Beach. Most main-street establishments cater to the backpacker crowd,
with boisterous, college-style entertainment, live music, and a late-open-
ing dance club. Older and more sophisticated visitors gravitate to qui-
eter establishments with pleasant outdoor areas, such as the bars and
restaurants attached to some of the hillside resorts.

Beaches Bar & Grill. The crowd is gregarious at Beaches Bar & Grill, part
of the attached hostel. You can catch live bands here on weekends, eat
hearty food cheaply, play pool, mingle in the beer garden, and watch
sports on big-screen TVs. ✉ *356 Shute Harbour Rd.* ☎ *07/4946–6244*
⊕ *www.beaches.com.au.*

Mama Africa Bar & Niteclub. When the main-street watering holes close
around midnight, Airlie's party kicks on till late at hot Mama Africa.
There's a zebra-striped dance floor, and DJs spin trance, house, and
old-school beats. Friendly bartenders create tropically themed cocktails
and dress up for the club's frequent theme nights. ✉ *263 Shute Harbour
Rd., 2nd level* ☎ *07/4948–0599* ⊕ *www.mamaafrica.com.au* 🎟 *A$5.*

LONG ISLAND

12 km (7 miles) west of Hamilton Island, 13 km (7½ miles) east of the mainland

Although it's 9 km (5½ miles) long and no more than 2 km (1 mile) wide—around 3,000 acres total—this aptly named island has several walking trails through tracts of dense rain forest. Most of the island is national parkland, sheltering birds, butterflies, goannas, and wallabies. Some of its beaches are picturesque; others rocky and windblown. Though its waters are less clear than those off the outer reef islands, there are some excellent snorkeling spots on the island's fringing reef, where you'll share the balmy water with soft and hard corals, tropical fish, and turtles. You may also see dolphins and migrating humpback whales July through September.

GETTING HERE AND AROUND

You can reach Long Island via water taxi from Shute Harbour or private watercraft. The trip takes around 20 minutes by water taxi, and is cheaper if you have more passengers.

Various regional operators, including Air Whitsunday and Hamilton Island Air, offer seaplane or helicopter transfers to Long Island resorts from regional airports including Great Barrier Reef (Hamilton Island), Whitsundays Airport near Airlie Beach, and Whitsunday Coast (Proserpine) Airport. Transfers are scheduled to coincide with incoming and outgoing flights. If your vacation time is limited, this is the fastest way to get here—but per-person costs can be steep. Trips require minimum passenger numbers, strict baggage limits apply, and prebooking is essential.

If you're keen to visit other resort isles from Hamilton Island, the on-island helicopter service, Hamilton Island Air, can transport you there. Helicopters take off on demand from Great Barrier Reef (Hamilton Island) Airport, flying to Long, Daydream, and Hayman islands, and to Airlie Beach on the mainland. Prebookings are essential for all charter flights; baggage is limited to 15 kg (33 pounds) per passenger, in soft-sided bags, and anyone weighing more than 110 kg (250 pounds) pays a seat surcharge.

Virgin Australia and Jetstar have direct daily flights between Hamilton Island and Melbourne, Sydney, and Brisbane.

Air Contacts Air Whitsunday. ⊠ *Air Whitsunday Airport, 12 Whitsunday Rd., Terminal One, Flametree* ☎ *07/4946–9111 Air Whitsundays, 0477/770–133 Palm Bay Resort* ⊕ *www.airwhitsunday.com.au.* **Hamilton Island Air.** ⊠ *Great Barrier Reef (Hamilton Island) Airport, Palm Valley Way, Hamilton Island* ☎ *07/4969–9599* ⊕ *hamiltonislandair.com.* **Heli Taxi.** ⊠ *Shute Harbour* ☎ *1300/668716 Heli Taxi* ⊕ *www.helitaxi.com.au.*

Boat Contact Island Transfers (*Shute Harbour Water Taxi*). ⊠ *Shute Harbour* ☎ *0488/022–868* ⊕ *www.islandtransfers.com.*

WHERE TO STAY

$$ 🛏 **Palm Bay Resort.** This beachfront property houses self-catering trav-
RESORT elers at alluringly reasonable rates. **Pros:** friendly, helpful staff; island grocery/food store and bottle shop; lovely accommodations in glorious

tranquil environs. **Cons:** curlews can be noisy at night; self-catering, though staff clean your dishes; no resort Wi-Fi or TV. $ *Rooms from: A$249* ⊠ *Long Island* ⚓ *Get to and from Palm Bay Resort via Island Transfers water-taxi scheduled services (A$50 per person, minimum 2)* ☎ *1300/655126 toll-free in Australia* ⊕ *www.palmbayresort.com.au* ⤵ *7 bures, 8 bungalows, 6 villas, 2 suites* ⵙ *No meals.*

HAMILTON ISLAND

16 km (10 miles) southeast of Shute Harbour.

Though it's the most heavily populated and developed island in the Whitsunday group, more than 70% of Hamilton Island has been preserved in its natural state. The 1,482-acre island abounds in beautiful beaches (such as long, curving, palm-dotted Catseye Beach), bush trails, and spectacular lookouts. Yet for all its natural beauty, Hamilton's is more an action-packed, sociable holiday isle than a place to get away from it all.

Around 35 minutes by ferry from Shute Harbour, Hamilton buzzes with activity. Guests of the resort, and its various types of accommodation, including hotel-style and self-catering establishments, make up most of the itinerant population, but there are private residences here—as well as throngs of day-trippers from the mainland, other islands, and cruising yachts, who wander the island's bustling marina and village each day.

For a family-friendly, one-stop Whitsundays experience, Hamilton Island is a smart choice. Many of the resort accommodations allow kids under age 13 to stay free, provided they stay with parents and use existing beds (no roll-aways or cribs). Under-13s can even eat free at some island restaurants when staying at resort hotels, choosing from kids' menus.

The resort's set up like a small city, with its own school, post office and banking outlets, medical center, pharmacy, supermarket, and DVD-rental store, plus shops, restaurants, bars, and a nightclub, all open to island guests and day-trippers. There's also an island hair and beauty salon, and a day spa (open daily 9–7) that offers massages, facials, and aromatherapy treatments using natural Australian-made products. But little on Hamilton is free; prices—for food, activities, Internet use, even grocery items—can be steep. The ubiquitous golf carts that visitors hire to zip around the island are A$46 an hour, A$62 for three hours, and A$87 for 24 hours from Hamilton Island Buggy Rentals (7:30 am to 6 pm). Save a few bucks by using the free Island Shuttle service that runs around the island on three set routes at regular (15–40 minute) intervals between 7 am and 11 pm.

GETTING HERE AND AROUND

Virgin Australia and Jetstar fly directly to Hamilton Island from Sydney, Melbourne, and Brisbane. You can take a Cruise Whitsundays ferry to the island from Abel Point Marina, Airlie Beach, or nearby Shute Harbour (A$56), or arrange a seaplane transfer from regional mainland airports at Proserpine or Mackay, or from Airlie Beach's Whitsunday

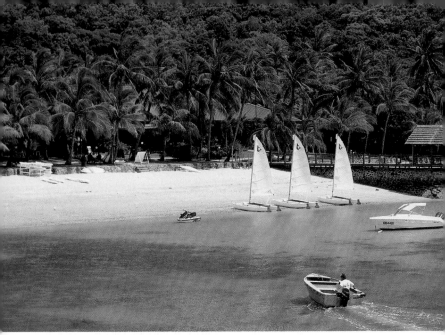
Wind- and motor-powered water sports are popular on many Whitsunday Islands.

Airport with Air Whitsunday. From Hamilton Island, the "hub" of the Whitsundays, you can catch a ferry to neighboring resort isles Daydream and Hayman via fast ferry with Cruise Whitsundays Resort Connections, timed to coincide with incoming and outgoing flights from Hamilton's airport. You can get there faster by seaplane with Air Whitsunday or helicopter with Hamilton Island Air.

FAMILY **Sunsail Australia.** This operator has various yachts available for bareboat charter at Hamilton Island's marina. You can book a five-day-minimum charter yacht and sail around the Whitsundays' sheltered waters. Optional extras include professional skipper and cook, kayaks, and dinghy. Rates vary according to the number of days, number of passengers, vessel, and season. Sunsail Whitsundays also offers certified sailing courses. ⊠ *Front St.* ☎ *07/4948–8250, 1800/803988 toll-free in Australia* ⊕ *www.sunsail.com.au.*

Buggy Rental Hamilton Island Buggy Rental. ⊠ *Front St.* ☎ *07/9433–9444, 13-7333 toll-free in Australia, 866/209–0891 in U.S., 424/206–5274 toll-free in U.S.* ⊕ *www.hamiltonisland.com.au/getting-around-island/buggy-hire.*

Ferry Cruise Whitsundays. ⊠ *Cruise Whitsundays Bldg., 2 Abel Point Marina, Airlie Beach* ☎ *07/4846–7000, 1800/426403 toll-free in Australia* ⊕ *www.cruisewhitsundays.com.*

Helicopter Hamilton Island Air. ⊠ *Great Barrier Reef (Hamilton Island) Airport, Palm Valley Way* ☎ *07/4969–9599* ⊕ *hamiltonislandair.com.*

Seaplane Air Whitsunday. ⊠ *Whitsunday Airport, 12 Air Whitsunday Ave., Terminal One, Flametree* ☎ *07/4946–9111* ⊕ *www.airwhitsunday.com.au.*

EXPLORING

FAMILY **WILD LIFE Hamilton Island.** This charming wildlife sanctuary houses kangaroos, wallabies, wombats, dingoes, birds, and reptiles, including a resident croc. There are daily breakfasts with the koalas (7–10) and daily guided tours. ⊠ *1 Resort Dve.* ☎ *07/4946–9078 sanctuary, 07/4946–8305 HI tour desk* ⊕ *www.wildlifehamiltonisland.com.au* ⊡ *A$22, unlimited entry for duration of HI stay; Breakfast with the Koalas, A$34* ⊙ *Daily 8:30–5; Breakfast with the Koalas, 7 am; guided walks, 10 and 4.*

SPORTS AND THE OUTDOORS

FISHING

FAMILY **Renegade Sports Fishing & Charters.** The outer Great Barrier Reef offers world-class fishing for species like coral trout, mackerel, and tuna—and you have a better-than-average chance of landing one off the deck of a 38-foot flybridge game boat. Hamilton Island can arrange small-group sportfishing trips with Renegade Sports Fishing & Charters, with all equipment included. A full-day excursion is A$2750 (private charter) or A$300 per person (shared); a half-day trip (8–noon or 1–5) costs A$1750 (private charter) or A$190 per person (shared). Full-day tours also include morning and afternoon tea and a cheese/fruit platter at lunch. If time or your budget is tight, you can hire a dinghy for puttering about closer to shore. Organize it all through Hamilton Island's Tour Desk. ⊠ *Hamilton Island Marina, Front St., D Arm, D WS berth* ☎ *07/4946–8305 HI tour desk* ⊕ *www.renegadecharters.com.au* ⊡ *From A$190 per person.*

GOLF

Fodor'sChoice ★ **Dent Island Golf Course.** This Peter Thomson–designed championship course has sweeping Whitsundays views from all 18 holes. You can hire clubs, take lessons, and practice your swing on the golf driving range at the Hamilton Island–run complex, which incorporates a swanky clubhouse, pro shop, restaurant, and bar. Clubs, shoes, caddy services, and lessons are also available. Ferries to Dent Island depart all day from 7:30 am from Hamilton Island Marina; allow five hours to play 18 holes and half that to play nine. Prices include GPS-fitted golf carts and ferry transfers. ⊠ *Main St., Dent Island* ☎ *07/4949–9760* ⊕ *www.hamiltonislandgolfclub.com.au* ⊡ *A$180* ⅃ *18 holes, 6692 yards, par 71.*

GREAT BARRIER REEF TOURS

FAMILY Fodor'sChoice ★ **Cruise Whitsundays Reefworld.** On the outer edge of the Great Barrier Reef sits magnificent Hardy Reef Lagoon, and within it sits Reefworld, a state-of-the-art pontoon around which you can snorkel and dive along easy coral trails. There's a large underwater viewing chamber, a spacious sun deck, change rooms and fresh-water showers, a kid-friendly snorkeling area, and a child-minding service. There's even a massage hut and accommodation for Reefsleep guests. There are many ways to explore the underwater environs: take a semisubmersible coral-viewing tour, guided snorkel safari (A$45), or an introductory (A$119) or certified dive (A$99) with gear included. A scenic heli-flight over famed Heart Reef starts from A$135 per person. ⊠ *Depart Hamilton Island Airport and Airport Jetty, Palm Valley Way* ☎ *07/4946–7000*

8

Cruise Whitsundays, 07/4969–9599 Hamilton Island Air ⊕ www. cruisewhitsundays.com or www.helireef.com.au ✉ From A$225.

MULTISPORT OPERATORS

FAMILY   **Hamilton Island Activities.** Hamilton Island Resort has the widest selection of activities in the Whitsundays: game fishing, snorkeling, scuba diving, waterskiing, parasailing, jet skiing, wakeboarding, sea kayaking, speedboat adventure rides, and fish-feeding tours are all on the agenda. Everything can be booked through the island's central tour desk. The use of nonmotorized watercraft is free to resort guests through the Beach Hut (Hamilton Island Beach Sports) on Catseye Beach, with Beach Hut staff ready to give assistance, tips, and—for a fee—lessons. If the Coral Sea doesn't tempt you, there are well-marked walking trails, quad-bike and ATV tours, twilight 4WD "bush safaris," go-karts, a nine-pin bowling center, a target-shooting range, an aquatic driving range, public-access swimming pools, and an 18-hole golf course on nearby Dent Island. The island's sports and fitness complex incorporates a state-of-the-art gym, a whirlpool spa and sauna, squash and floodlit tennis courts, and a mini-golf course. You can also sign up for various tours, cruises, and special events. ⊠ *Main resort complex, off Resort Dve.* ☎ *07/4946–8305 HI tour desk, 13-7333 toll-free in Australia* ⊕ *www.hamiltonisland.com.au.*

WHERE TO EAT

$$$ ✕ **Bommie Restaurant.** With sail-shaped tables, chic Eames chairs, and
MODERN   marina views, Bommie has a sophisticated, upmarket ambience and
AUSTRALIAN   smart-casual dress code (collared shirts for men and no singlets, boardshorts, or flip-flops). It proves the ideal setting for fine Modern Australian cuisine. Tuck into a tasty kangaroo fillet or a perfect seafood risotto, but leave space for tropically inspired desserts; standouts include bloodpeach soufflé and house-made sorbets. A private dining room seats up to 14 (minimum 24 hours' notice required). ■TIP➔ **Book well ahead to secure a table on the deck.** ⑤ *Average main: A$48* ⊠ *Hamilton Island Yacht Club, Front St.* ☎ *07/4948–9433, 13–3777 toll-free in Australia* ⊕ *www.hamiltonisland.com.au/restaurants/bommie* ⊗ *No lunch. Closed Sun. and Mon.*

$ ✕ **coca chu.** Hamilton Island's only Asian eatery, coca chu appeals to all
ASIAN FUSION   comers with its relaxed vibe, Catseye Beach views, busy Sunday yum chas, and a varied dinner menu that showcases regional produce and Southeast Asian flavors. The twice-cooked Sichuan duck with chili, coriander, ginger, and soy black vinegar sauce is a worthy signature dish. Families with young children should be aware there's only one "designated" kid's dish: simple soy chicken and rice. ⑤ *Average main: A$33* ⊠ *Main resort complex, Catseye Beach* ☎ *07/4946–8580 HI tour desk* ⊕ *www.hamiltonisland.com.au/coca-chu-restaurant* ⊗ *No lunch Mon.–Sat. No dinner Sun.*

$ ✕ **Manta Ray.** This could be the island's best all-round dining establish-
ECLECTIC   ment. It's great for breezy alfresco lunches, sunset drinks on the deck,
FAMILY   and wood-fired pizzas. Dine right by the marina on salads and pasta,
Fodor'sChoice   or join the queue for the pizzas (also available as takeout or delivery).
★   There's plenty on Manta Ray's menu to suit all tastes. The wine list is also a crowd-pleaser (though for a corkage charge of A$15, you can

CASTAWAY CUISINE

On Hamilton, the Whitsundays' largest inhabited island, guests can eat and drink at a variety of restaurants and bars. Virtually all of them are managed by the Hamilton Island consortium, whose owners, the Oatley family, made their millions out of wine. The Oatleys are keen to further the island's reputation for quality wining and dining—recruiting big-city chefs, improving supply lines, scheduling epicurean events, and adding to the island's vast central cellar and produce store. Opportunities for young guns to work their way up through Hamilton's hierarchy, training under culinary heavyweights, bring a continuing stream of fresh talent to the island. The bad news? Staff don't always stay and as a result, food and service standards can be inconsistent—and as there's a virtual monopoly on dining options, prices tend to be steep.

BYO special bottle). $ *Average main: A$26* ⊠ *Front St.* ☎ *07/4946–8536 resort restaurant reservations, 07/4946–8213 takeout and delivery* ⊕ *www.hamiltonisland.com.au/restaurants/manta-ray.*

$$
SEAFOOD
Fodor'sChoice
★
✕ **Mariners.** This breezy, upscale eatery turns the local catch into fresh contemporary dishes: artfully arranged sashimi, house-made tagliatelle marinara, Thai-style jumbo prawn curry, and a terrific hot and cold seafood platter (A$220 for two). You can also get vegetarian and nonseafood options, and wine from a bar stocked mainly with mid-price Antipodean vintages. Book a balcony table and watch yachts dock as you dine. $ *Average main: A$42* ⊠ *Marina Village, Front St.* ☎ *07/4946–8628* ⊗ *No lunch* ⌂ *Reservations essential.*

$$
ITALIAN
✕ **Romano's.** The full-frontal marina views from the broad balconies of this two-level waterfront eatery make it a favorite for family celebrations and romantic dining. The menu is loaded with traditional Italian fare like osso buco as well as more inventive dishes, such as black linguini with Moreton Bay bug (crayfish) tails in a roasted-tomato-shellfish sauce. Dessert might be gelato, panna cotta, or tiramisu. There's a steep corkage charge (A$25) if you BYOB. $ *Average main: A$37* ⊠ *Marina Village, Front St.* ☎ *07/4946–8212* ⊕ *www.hamiltonisland.com.au/romanos-restaurant* ⊗ *No lunch* ⌂ *Reservations essential.*

$$$$
MODERN
AUSTRALIAN
✕ **Sunset Cruise & Dine on the Denison Star.** The *Denison Star*, a magnificent 107-foot motor cruiser hewn from Tasmanian Huon pine, glides out of Hamilton Island Marina most evenings for Cruise Indigo's small-group, starlit dinner cruise around the island's sheltered waters. As night falls, the skipper drops anchor in a scenic, secluded spot so that there's no rocking as you dine. You can start with sunset daiquiris and canapés, and then order from a four-course à la carte menu of Modern Australian dishes as your complimentary bottle of wine is uncorked. Stargaze from the upper deck as you cruise back to base. ■**TIP**➔ **Leave your high-heels at home and bring a jacket; it can get chilly on deck during the cooler months.** $ *Average main: A$150* ⊠ *Cruise Indigo Jetty, Hamilton Island Marina, Front St.* ☎ *07/4946–8305 HI tour desk, 13-7333 toll-free in Australia* ⊕ *www.hamiltonisland.com.au/dinner-cruise-denison-star* ⊗ *No lunch* ⌂ *Reservations essential.*

8

WHERE TO STAY

$$$$ ⬚ **Hamilton Island Beach Club.** The upscale amenities and no-kids policy
RESORT   mean this hotel swarms with couples, who can cool off in the infin-
ity-edge pool, enjoy meals poolside, or admire the Catseye Beach and
Coral Sea views from their balconies (all rooms have ocean vistas).
Pros: beachfront location; free Wi-Fi; reasonably priced lunch menu.
Cons: service standards vary. $ *Rooms from: A$690 ⊠ 9 Resort Dr.*
☎ *02/9433–0444, 13-7333 toll-free in Australia* ⊕ *www.hamiltonisland.*
com.au ⮑ 57 rooms ❑ *No meals; Breakfast.*

$$$ ⬚ **Hamilton Island Holiday Homes.** Part of the Hamilton Island resort,
RENTAL   Hamilton Island Holiday Homes manages more than 100 self-catered
FAMILY   one- to five-bedroom vacation properties in prime locations around the
island, including studio, split-level, and two-story designs. **Pros:** privacy;
full kitchen and laundry facilities; complimentary use of many resort
facilities; kids under 13 can eat free with their parents at selected HI
restaurants. **Cons:** minimum four-day stays in holiday periods, two-
or three-night minimum at other times; no housekeeping. $ *Rooms*
from: A$400 ⊠ Bookings office, Front St. ☎ *02/9433–0444, 13-7333*
toll-free in Australia ⊕ *www.hihh.com.au ⮑ More than 100 properties*
❑ *No meals.*

$$$ ⬚ **Hamilton Island Palm Bungalows.** Spacious, self-contained, and with a
RESORT   relaxed island vibe, these steep-roofed, freestanding bungalows are great
FAMILY   for families and self-sufficient travelers. **Pros:** free use of the resort's
gym/sports complex and nonmotorized watercraft; complimentary air-
port transfers; close to main pool, beach, and wildlife park. **Cons:** some
bungalows can be musty; buggy hire not included; up a steepish hill;
no Wi-Fi in rooms. $ *Rooms from: A$445 ⊠ 3 Resort Dr.* ☎ *02/9433–*
0444, 13-7333 toll-free in Australia ⊕ *www.hamiltonisland.com.au*
⮑ *49 bungalows* ❑ *No meals; Some meals.*

$$$$ ⬚ **Hamilton Island Reef View Hotel.** Only rooms on higher floors of this
HOTEL   hotel live up to the name—those on the fifth floor and above have
FAMILY   unbroken Coral Sea vistas, while rooms on lower levels overlook a
landscaped, tropical garden and pool. **Pros:** good breakfasts (included
with stays of four-plus days); in higher-floor rooms, beds face the views;
better-than-usual service. **Cons:** lower-level rooms can be noisy; cockatoos fly in open windows. $ *Rooms from: A$470 ⊠ 12 Resort Dr.*
☎ *02/9433–0444, 13-7333 toll-free in Australia* ⊕ *www.hamiltonisland.*
com.au ⮑ 382 rooms and suites ❑ *Breakfast; No meals.*

$$$$ ⬚ **Qualia.** With its private beach, infinity-edge pools, and complex of
RESORT   luxe freestanding pavilions, Hamilton Island's most exclusive resort has
Fodor'sChoice   a tranquil, decadent ambience and impeccable service standards. **Pros:**
★   glorious, tranquil location; fine food and wine; high-end everything.
Cons: two-night minimum stay in peak periods; pricey. $ *Rooms from:*
A$1150 ⊠ 20 Whitsunday Blvd., Lot 10 ☎ *02/9433–0444, 13-7777*
toll-free in Australia ⊕ *www.qualia.com.au ⮑ 60 suites* ❑ *Breakfast.*

NIGHTLIFE

Bohemes Nightclub. At Bohemes, Hamilton Island's only dedicated late-
night bar and dance-spot, you can drink and boogie till the wee hours
to DJ-spun classic and contemporary music, and occasional live acts. It's
usually open Thursday to Saturday until well after midnight, but opening

hours, days, and entertainment line-ups vary with the season. ✉ *Marina Village, Front St.* ☏ *07/4946–9999* ⊕ *www.hamiltonisland.com.au.*

DAYDREAM ISLAND

5 km (3 miles) from Shute Harbour.

The resort on this small, 42-acre island is especially welcoming to day-trippers. Around 30 minutes' boat ride from Shute Harbour Abel Point Marina, or Hamilton Island, it's a perfect place to relax or pursue outdoor activities such as snorkeling and water sports—which are comparatively affordable here. The resort's lush gardens blend into a small tract of rain forest, frequented by tame wallabies and big-eyed, stilt-legged Stone curlews. The island is surrounded by clear blue water and coral reefs.

GETTING HERE AND AROUND

Most visitors get to Daydream Island by boat from Great Barrier Reef (Hamilton Island) Airport, but they can also fly to Whitsunday Coast (Proserpine) Airport on the mainland, catch a bus to the Port of Airlie, and then take a Cruise Whitsundays ferry direct to the island. Cruise Whitsundays Resort Connections also operates several direct daily services between Daydream Island and Hamilton Island's airport jetty on modern, air-conditioned catamaran cruisers. Cruise Whitsundays ferry services are scheduled to coincide with incoming flight and trains, and coach transfers from Proserpine to the ferry port are available.

Domestic airlines Virgin Australia and Jetstar have daily scheduled flights from Melbourne, Sydney, and Brisbane to both Great Barrier Reef (Hamilton Island) and Whitsunday Coast (Proserpine) airports. Queensland Rail (QR) long-distance rail services stop at Proserpine Rail Station, near Airlie Beach. If you've prebooked an air transfer to the island, a representative from Air Whitsunday will generally greet your incoming flight at the airport. Check with each carrier for weight and baggage restrictions.

SPORTS AND THE OUTDOORS

At Daydream Island Resort and Spa, many activities, such as water polo, beach volleyball, basketball, tennis, and bocce, snorkeling, scavenger hunting, and fish-feeding, and the use of resort kayaks, paddleboards, and catamarans, are included in room rates. Guided fishing, snorkeling, and scuba-diving day trips, parasailing, jet skiing, waterskiing and wakeboarding sessions, guided sea kayak and ocean rafting excursions, glass-bottom boat tours, banana-boat tube rides, and more can be arranged through the resort's Tour Desk for an additional charge. Nonguests can also book activities through the resort.

Daydream offers day trips to Whitehaven Beach on catamaran *Camira*; snorkel and dive cruises to Knuckle Reef Lagoon with classy local operator Cruise Whitsundays for A\$230; fishing trips with Sea Fever Sportfishing; and HeliReef scenic flights and excursions; as well as leisurely snorkeling and beach trips with Ocean Rafting. To prebook on- or offshore activities prior to your arrival, phone ☏ *07/4948–8477* or email *discovery@daydreamisland.com.*

8

FISHING

FAMILY **Sea Fever Sportfishing Whitsundays.** The custom-built game-fishing boat *Sea Fever* picks up at Daydream Island's jetty at 6:20 am for a fast two-hour boat-ride to the outer Great Barrier Reef. There, you can cast poppers and jig for feisty giant trevally, coral trout, shark, and red emperor; or sport-fish for large pelagics (Spanish and scaly mackerel, tuna, and barracuda), and, on the way back, troll with light tackle for sailfish and the elusive juvenile black marlin. The rate includes expert guidance as well as bait, tackle, and lines. Lunch and nonalcoholic drinks and snacks are provided; BYO alcohol (limits apply) along with sunscreen, a brimmed hat, and sunglasses. ✉ *Pickups from Daydream Island Jetty* ☎ *07/4948–8477 Discovery Desk, Daydream Island, 07/4948–2798 Sea Fever, 0427/524–975 Sea Fever (cell)* ⊕ *www.seafever.com.au* 🖃 *From A$420 per person.*

SNORKELING AND DIVING

FAMILY **Camira.** The purple catamaran *Camira* offers sociable day cruises to Whitehaven Beach that include time to swim and sunbathe, a stop to snorkel off Hook Island on the way back, a big barbecue lunch, and all beverages (including beer and wine from 11 am). The boat picks guests up and drops them off at Daydream Island Jetty. ✉ *Daydream Island* ☎ *07/4948–8477 Discovery Desk, Daydream Island, 07/4946–7000 Cruise Whitsundays* ⊕ *www.cruisewhitsundays.com/camira.aspx* 🖃 *From A$199 per person.*

FAMILY
Fodor's Choice
★
Cruise Whitsundays. This reliable local operator runs day-long snorkel and dive cruises to Knuckle Reef Lagoon, a large, activities-laden pontoon that floats in the balmy, translucent waters of the outer Great Barrier Reef. The popular reef-snorkel cruise includes a big buffet lunch, snorkeling gear and guidance, and plenty of time to take advantage of the excellent pontoon facilities, from massages and reef talks to semisubmersible boat rides, scenic heli-flights, and Queensland's largest underwater viewing chamber. Keen to get your feet wet? Take a guided or self-guided snorkeling tour in the sheltered lagoon, or go scuba diving for an extra fee to see several marine species, including large pelagic fish. ✉ *Pickups from Daydream Island Resort Jetty* ☎ *07/4948–8477 Discovery Desk, Daydream Island, 07/4946–7000 Cruise Whitsundays* ⊕ *www.daydreamisland.com or www.cruisewhitsundays.com* 🖃 *From A$235* ⚲ *Departs Daydream Island Jetty at 8:50 am.*

FAMILY **Ocean Rafting.** Long-established Ocean Rafting has access permits to visit protected areas in the Great Barrier Reef Marine Park, exclusive direct access to iconic Hill Inlet beach, and top reef sites off uninhabited Hook and Border islands, where you can snorkel in spectacular subtropical environs. The "rafts"—11-meter-long former rescue crafts with undercover seating, powered by 500-horsepower engines, and crewed by a skipper and eco-guide—carry a maximum 28 people, so you're never snorkeling in a crowd. Choose from two tours: the Northern Exposure, with more time to snorkel, and the Southern Lights, with more beach time. ✉ *Pickups from Daydream Island Jetty* ☎ *07/4948–8477 Discovery Desk, Daydream Island, 07/4946–6848 Ocean Rafting* ⊕ *www.oceanrafting.com.au* 🖃 *From A$139 per person.*

WHERE TO STAY

$$$
RESORT
FAMILY

Daydream Island Resort and Spa. Colorfully decorated, with whimsical touches—starfish-and-shell-embedded toilet seats, mermaid and dolphin statues, a giant chess set, an outsize marine mobiles and murals, and an ocean-fed living aquarium that meanders through the grounds—this family-focused resort has youthful, cheerful staff; many kid-friendly activities; and several public areas. **Pros:** large, well-run spa; numerous activities, including mini-golf and outdoor movie screenings; snorkeling off Lovers' Cove. **Cons:** teeming with kids; buffet food lackluster; steep fees for kids' club and babysitting. $ *Rooms from: A$385 ⊠ Daydream Island Rd., Lot 1 ☎ 07/3259–2350, 1800/075040 toll-free in Australia ⊕ www.daydreamisland.com ⬏ 280 rooms, 9 suites* ⦿| *Breakfast.*

HAYMAN ISLAND

Fodor's Choice
★

Hayman Island, in the northern Whitsunday Passage, is the closest of the Whitsunday resort isles to the outer Barrier Reef. The island, a 900-acre crescent with a series of hills along its spine, has just one resort, one of the oldest and most opulent in the region and popular with jet-setters who take their leisure seriously. The service—understated yet attentive—merits the price you pay for it; staff members even traverse the resort via tunnels so they're less of a "presence."

Reflecting pools, sandstone walkways, manicured tropical gardens, statuary, and waterfalls provide the feel of an exclusive club, while beautiful walking trails crisscross the island, leading to pristine coves and vantage points. The main beach sits right in front of the resort complex, but more secluded sands and fringing coral can be reached by boat or on foot.

8

GETTING HERE AND AROUND

Hayman has its own heliport, and can arrange helicopter or seaplane transfers from airports at Hamilton Island, Proserpine, Airlie Beach, and Mackay. From Hamilton Island, you can also transfer onto one of Hayman's luxury motor yachts. Tea, coffee, and Australian sparkling wine are served during the 60-minute trip to the island; on the return journey, you'll get full bar service, platters of food, tea, and espresso coffee. On board, you can complete your resort check-in and book tours, reef excursions, and island-based activities. Make sure you're ticketed all the way to Hayman Island, including the motor-yacht leg, as purchasing the round-trip yacht journey from Hamilton Island to Hayman separately costs more.

Air Whitsunday provides seaplane connections from various regional airports: Airlie Beach, to Hamilton Island, and on request, Proserpine and Mackay. The resort can also arrange helicopter transfers for guests (minimum two). On all air transfers, baggage restrictions apply.

Flying by seaplane over Whitsunday and Hook islands, Langford Reef, and Hayman itself, is an exhilarating introduction to your Hayman Island vacation. Prebook through the resort or Air Whitsunday for a seamless charter seaplane connection from Great Barrier Reef (Hamilton Island) Airport; the cost is A$790, with up to four passengers, A$1,590 with up to six (though you can fit a few more people if everyone takes less baggage). Air Whitsunday can also arrange seaplane transfers to Hayman from mainland airports including Whitsunday (Airlie Beach), Whitsunday Coast (Proserpine), and Mackay. The flight takes approximately 15 minutes; baggage is strictly limited to 30 kilograms (66 pounds) per person, in soft-sided bags only; excess baggage can be safely stored at airports prior to departure if you've overpacked.

TOURS

One&Only Hayman Island Guest Services. One&Only Hayman Island Guest Services provides information and can book all tours and activities on the island as well as various excursions offshore. ⊠ *One&Only Hayman Island* ☎ *07/4940–1234, 1800/075175 toll-free in Australia* ⊕ *www.hayman.com.au.*

SPORTS AND THE OUTDOORS

All nonmotorized water sports on Hayman Island—well-maintained catamarans, windsurfers, and paddleboards, lined up for guests' use on Hayman Beach—are included in the room rates. So is the use of Hayman's swimming pools, well-equipped indoor-outdoor gym, five floodlit tennis courts, squash and basketball facilities, and badminton, Ping-Pong, and croquet equipment. There's a complimentary golf driving range and 9-hole putting green; aqua-fitness, Zumba and "box fit" classes; and self-guided art and garden walks. You can also order a picnic hamper and arrange a beach drop-off—or take a hike along one of the island's well-maintained bush trails, which take you to lookouts, wildlife hotspots, and pristine beaches, coves, and coral gardens.

Some on-site activities cost extra: personal training sessions (A$85), Pilates and yoga classes (A$20); tennis lessons and clinics (A$20); inflatable-tube rides (from A$70); waterskiing and wakeboarding sessions; scuba training; and guided local tours. The five-star PADI-accredited Marine Centre at Hayman Marina has a training tank for diving lessons, and runs various dive courses, trips, and packages. It also hires and sells everything from snorkel and dive accessories to wet suits. All local aquatic tours and excursions, including guided local sea kayaking, snorkeling, and dive tours, can be booked through the Marine Centre at Hayman Marina. Arrange fitness sessions and off-site excursions— sailing, game-fishing, dive-snorkel outer reef excursions, scenic flights, and heli-golf tours to nearby Dent Island—through the resort or the individual operators (most pick up from Hayman on request).

DIVING AND SNORKELING

Cruise Whitsundays, Hayman Island. Hayman is the closest of the Whitsundays islands to the Great Barrier Reef—from here, it's a speedy ride on Cruise Whitsundays's wave-piercer craft to Knuckle Reef Lagoon pontoon on the outer Reef. There, you can snorkel and dive over myriad corals alongside rainbow-hued wrasse and clownfish, reef sharks, rays, and green sea turtles. Picking up from Hayman daily, the daylong dive-and-snorkel cruise includes the use of paddleboards, snorkeling gear, a giant waterslide, and a vast underwater viewing chamber. You also get priority access to coral-viewing tours and various optional extras: guided snorkel safaris, scuba diving, scenic helicopter flights over Heart Reef, even massages. Cruise Whitsundays also runs shorter cruises

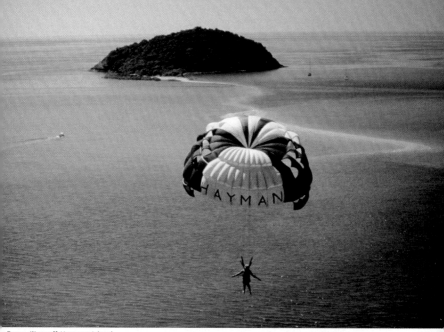

Parasailing off Hayman Island

around the Whitsundays and to glorious Whitehaven Beach. ✉ *Hayman Island Jetty, off Raintree Ave.* ☎ *07/4946–9102 Cruise Whitsundays, 07/4940–1234 Hayman Island resort* ⊕ *www.cruisewhitsundays. com* ✉ *A$225 cruise, incl. buffet lunch; A$45 guided snorkeling safari, A$99 certified scuba dive, A$119 beginner dive, A$59 second dive.*

FAMILY
Fodor's Choice
★

Hayman Island Diving and Snorkeling. The only Whitsundays resort within the Great Barrier Reef Marine Park, Hayman offers fast access to some of the world's best underwater sites. Hayman's dedicated dive/snorkel center has an array of guided excursions to the inner and outer reef, available on demand. Local hot spots include Hayman's own Bali Hai (a green sea turtle hangout), and beautiful Blue Pearl Bay, where you can swim among 1,500-odd species of fishes and 400 hard and soft corals. A guided shore-dive tour of inner Barrier Reef sites nearby offers certified divers the chance to swim alongside green turtles, manta rays, and more. Hayman has expert dive instructors on-site and offers PADI scuba courses and introductory sessions. You can buy dive and snorkel accessories at Hayman's Marine Centre. Prices and excursion times vary and are weather dependent; pre-book through Hayman's Marine Centre (daily 8-4:30) at the marina. ✉ *One&Only Hayman Island Diving and Snorkelling Centre, Raintree Ave.* ☎ *07/4940–1234* ⊕ *hayman. oneandonlyresorts.com* ✉ *From A$80* ☞ *Divers need to bring certification card and current dive medical certificate.*

FAMILY
Hayman Marine Centre. Handily located at Hayman's marina, a short stroll or buggy ride from the resort complex, this scuba training facility—also the place to inquire about and book local dive, snorkel, and sea kayaking tours and beach drop-offs—sells and rents out equipment,

including dive and snorkel gear, accessories, and stinger suits. Nonmotorized water-sports equipment—catamarans, kayaks, windsurfers, and the like—can be found lined up along Hayman Beach in front of the main resort pool. ⊠ *Hayman Marina, off Raintree Ave.* ☎ *07/4940–1234 guest services* ⊕ *www.hayman.com.au.*

FISHING

FAMILY   **Hayman Island Sportfishing.** The outer edge of the Great Barrier Reef, with its abundant marine life, claims some of the best fishing grounds on the planet. This could be your chance to catch tuna, sailfish, wahoo, mahimahi, Spanish mackerel, giant trevally, or, if you're really lucky, black marlin. Hayman's Marine Centre runs game and bottom fishing trips on the resort's game-fishing boat, its large deck perfect for landing the "big one." You can have your catch cleaned and cooked by Hayman's chefs that night. Note that species vary by season, and trips are dependent on numbers and weather. ■TIP➔ **If you're set on snagging a really big fish, visit September through February, when warmer waters attract larger species, including black marlin; March to August is prime time for tasty table fish.** ⊠ *Excursions depart from Hayman Island Jetty, Raintree Ave.* ☎ *07/4940–1234 guest services* ⊕ *hayman. oneandonlyresorts.com* ⊠ *From A$260 per person.*

HELICOPTER TOURS

FAMILY
Fodor'sChoice
★

Hayman Island Seaplane Adventures. This operator flies guests over Bait and renowned Heart reefs en route to Hardy Reef on the outer Great Barrier Reef, where you have a couple of hours to explore your underwater environs via glass-bottom boat and snorkel with tropical fish and turtles. Experience the dazzling white sands of Whitehaven Beach on a two-hour air-and-land excursion; or take a 2½-hour Wonders of the World tour for spectacular aerial views of Bait, Hook, Heart, and Hardy reefs, with a stop at Whitehaven Beach. On all tours, the resort can organize gourmet picnic lunches: prebook via In-Room Dining. ⊠ *One&Only Hayman Island Seaplane Base, off Raintree Ave.* ☎ *07/4940–1234 guest services* ⊕ *hayman.oneandonlyresorts.com* ⊠ *From A$399.*

FAMILY
Fodor'sChoice
★

Hayman Island Helicopter Adventures. Time-pressed guests can pack in the region's attractions on heli-tours of the Whitsundays and Great Barrier Reef. Short, scenic tours over Hayman Island, Heart Reef, and Whitehaven Beach start at A$199 per person for 15 minutes. A two-hour escapade that includes a Heart Reef flyover and inner-reef snorkeling off Whitehaven Beach or Hook Island is A$899 per person, gear included. On all tours, refreshments are complimentary. ⊠ *Hayman Island Resort Seaplane Base, Raintree Ave.* ☎ *07/4940–1234* ⊠ *From A$199.*

WILDLIFE WATCHING

Hayman Island Wildlife. Largely free of human traffic besides the odd hiker or snorkeler, Hayman Island gives sanctuary to numerous wild creatures, including the world's largest colony of endangered Proserpine rock wallabies. There are also lizards, butterflies, and many native birds, such as cockatoos, rainbow lorikeets, kookaburras, stone curlews, egrets, and sea eagles. The resort ponds and lagoons are home to barramundi, swans, and ducks; under the marina live tropical fish, rays, and turtles, especially evident at feeding time. The resort can suggest the best birdwatching and wildlife-spotting walks, and offers guided excursions to local snorkeling and dive sites. ⊠ *Hayman Island* ☎ *07/4940–1234* ⊕ *hayman.oneandonlyresorts.com.*

WHERE TO EAT

All restaurants are within the resort complex. Reservations are recommended and in some cases essential: they can be made with ease through the resort's concierge. Dress for all Hayman's evening restaurants is "smart resort wear"—no jerseys, shorts, or flip-flops.

Restaurant opening times are staggered so you always have at least two dining options; guests can breakfast in their rooms or at Azure. During the day, eat at the Beach Pavilion, snack by the Pool Bar, or preorder a picnic hamper.

Hayman offers various epicurean events, including design-your-own dinners, with tables set up on Hayman Beach or in Rainforest Grove; and exclusive degustation dining experiences that include up to 12 courses, matched wines, culinary tips from your chef, and behind-scenes tours of Hayman's vast wine cellar.

$$
ITALIAN
FAMILY
✕ **Amici.** A classic Italian-style eatery with a crowd-pleasing menu of antipasto, pasta, seafood, and traditional dishes, family-friendly Amici also whips up terrific wood-fired pizzas. Seafood—fresh oysters, succulent prawns, yellowfin tuna, reef fish, calamari, and spanner crab—is well represented, as are meat and vegetarian dishes. Terra-cotta-tiled floors and rustic furnishings add to the homely ambience. $ *Average main: A$39* ⊠ *Main resort complex, Raintree Ave.* ☎ *07/4940– 1234* ⊕ *hayman.oneandonlyresorts.com* ☷ *No lunch* ⚠ *Reservations essential.*

$
ASIAN
✕ **Bamboo.** This lovely pan-Asian establishment overlooks a tranquil Japanese garden with rock pools, waterfalls, and a teahouse. Menu choices include Thai, Korean, Chinese, Japanese, and Indian cuisine. Try the whole steamed baby reef fish with ginger, chili, and shallot; wok-fried Wagyu beef; or a Goan-style coconut chicken curry. There's a long wine list and several different types of sake, many available by the glass. $ *Average main: A$33* ⊠ *Hayman resort complex, Raintree Ave.* ☎ *07/4940–1838* ⊕ *www.hayman.com.au* ☷ *No lunch* ⚠ *Reservations essential.*

$$$$
MODERN
AUSTRALIAN
Fodor's Choice
★
✕ **Fire.** This elegant restaurant, refurbished in rich ruby hues, is the resort's culinary showpiece. Its imaginative dishes are built around premium ingredients, sourced locally and from around the world. Its cellar is filled with exciting new wines and acclaimed vintages. $ *Average main: A$73* ⊠ *Main resort complex, Raintree Ave.* ⊕ *www.hayman. oneandonlyresorts.com* ☷ *No lunch* ⚠ *Reservations essential* ⌂ *Jacket required.*

WHERE TO STAY

$$$$
RESORT
☷ **One&Only Hayman Island.** This magnificent resort is the grande dame of the Whitsundays, attracting worldly, high-flying guests seeking precious downtime and five-star services and facilities. **Pros:** fine food and wine; impeccable interiors and grounds; wide array of on- and off-island activities; PADI dive center on-site, and proximity to outer Barrier Reef

8

sites. **Cons:** service standards patchy; a fair hike from some rooms to restaurants and public areas; room-raiding cockatoos fly through open balcony doors. ⑤ *Rooms from: A$930* ⊠ *Raintree Ave.* ☎ *07/4940–1234 guest services, 02/9308–0500 reservations, 1800/075175 toll-free in Australia, 866/552–0001 within U.S.* ⊕ *hayman.oneandonlyresorts.com* ⌁ *160 rooms, suites, penthouses, and beach houses* ⍩ *Breakfast.*

SHOPPING

Hayman has its own chichi shopping arcade next to the spa. Prices aren't cheap, but the merchandise is high-quality and well chosen. There are a couple of lovely boutiques stocked with designer clothes and accessories, swimwear, and resort wear for men, women, and kids, including enough stylish pieces to ensure you meet Hayman's "smart-resort-wear-for-dinner" dress code. There's a small high-end jeweler, a news agency that also sells photographic accessories and prints images, a medical center that fills pharmacy prescriptions, and a gift shop stocked with quality Australian-made merchandise, art, and crafts. If you're lucky, you'll visit during a sale: in the low season you might snare a bargain designer swimsuit, caftan, or beach bag. Stores are open daily until 5 or 6, depending on the season.

NORTH COAST ISLANDS

ORPHEUS ISLAND

24 km (15 miles) offshore of Ingham, 80 km (50 miles) northeast of Townsville, 190 km (118 miles) south of Cairns.

Volcanic in origin, this narrow island—11 km (7 miles) long and 1 km (½ mile) wide, 3,500 acres total—uncoils like a snake in the waters between Halifax Bay and the Barrier Reef. It's part of the Palm Island Group, which consists of 10 islands, 8 of which are Aboriginal reservations. Orpheus is a national park, occupied only by a marine research station and the island's resort, which has a large vegetable garden, a solar hot-water system, and a 21,134-gallon water tank, as well as an infinity-edge pool and several beachfront villas linked by a rear boardwalk.

Although there are patches of rain forest in the island's deeper gullies and around its sheltered bays, Orpheus is a true Barrier Reef island, ringed by seven unspoiled sandy beaches and superb coral reefs. Amazingly, 340 of the known 359 species of coral inhabit these waters, as do more than 1,100 types of tropical fish and the biggest giant clams in the southern hemisphere. The local marine life is easily accessed and extraordinary.

GETTING HERE AND AROUND

Nautilus Aviation helicopters depart daily at 2 pm from Townsville Airport's Domestic Gate Lounge 10, returning Orpheus guests to the mainland from 2:30 (A$275 per person, one way); and from Cairns airport at 11 am daily, with return flights departing at noon (A$670 per person, one way). You can also charter flights from other mainland ports and islands. Baggage should be soft-sided and is strictly limited to a maximum of 15 kilograms (33 pounds) per person. Excess baggage can be stored at Townsville Airport for free, and the resort offers complimentary laundry (excluding dry cleaning). Book flights with Orpheus Island Resort.

Seaplane Nautilus Aviation. ✉ *Townsville Airport, Gypsy Moth Crt., Hangar 15, Townsville* ☎ *07/4034–9000 Nautilus Aviation, 07/4725–6056 Nautilus Aviation Townsville Airport Base* ⊕ *www.nautilusaviation.com.au.*

SPORTS AND THE OUTDOORS

Orpheus Island Resort is surrounded by walking trails, and there are spectacular snorkeling and diving sites right off the beaches, with manta rays (July to early November), humpback whale migration (June to September), and the annual coral spawning (mid- to late October to late November) among the underwater highlights. Resort guests get complimentary use of snorkeling and light fishing gear, as well as kayaks, stand-up paddleboards, catamarans, and motorized dinghies in which to buzz from cove to cove. The coral around Orpheus is some of the best in the area, and cruises to the outer reef can be arranged through the resort for an additional fee. Whereas most Great Barrier Reef resort islands are more than 50 km (31 miles) from the reef, Orpheus is just 15 km (9 miles) away. Dive operators on the island provide scuba courses and various boat-diving options.

BOAT CRUISES

Hinchinbrook and Palm Islands Tours. Orpheus Island resort guests can take helicopter flights over Hinchinbrook Island National Park, Australia's largest protected island wilderness; or cruise the Hinchinbrook-Cardwell channel, and nearby Palm Islands, with stops for wildlife-spotting, snorkeling, and bushwalks. On a daylong Hinchinbrook-Cardwell channel cruise, you'll seek out saltwater crocs in island estuaries and anchor in secluded coves for guided rain-forest treks to Zoe and Mulligan waterfalls. Or take a leisurely cruise around the Palm Islands on the resort's own vessel, the *Maree Ann*, with stops to snorkel, explore significant sites, and take guided nature walks. Sunset cruises on the *Maree Ann* include drinks and canapés on deck. ✉ *Orpheus Island* ☎ *07/4777–7377* ⊕ *www.orpheus.com.au* 🛥 *From A$386 per person.*

FISHING

Orpheus Island Fishing. The tropical waters off Orpheus Island offer prized game and reef fish species. On group trips or solo dinghy excursions via motorized dinghy (free for guests' use, as is light tackle), tasty reef fish (red emperor and coral trout, sweetlip and giant trevally) can be caught right off the island. On excursions to the outer reef, you'll get the chance to land large pelagics including wahoo, Spanish mackerel, and dog-tooth tuna. Prebooking fishing charters is essential and all expeditions are subject to weather and tidal conditions. ✉ *Orpheus Island Jetty* ☎ *07/4777–7377* ⊕ *www.orpheus.com.au* 🛥 *From A$915.*

GREAT BARRIER REEF EXCURSIONS

FAMILY **Orpheus Island Diving & Snorkeling.** Orpheus Island is encircled by fringing reef, with world-class dive and snorkeling sites an easy boat or dinghy ride away; free pool scuba refresher courses and various off-island

Continued on page 522

WHAT LIVES ON THE REEF?

Equivalent to the Amazon Rainforest in its biodiversity, the Reef hosts the earth's most abundant collection of sea life. Resident species include (but aren't limited to):

- More than 1,500 species of fish
- 5,000 species of mollusk
- 400 species of hard and soft coral
- 30 whale and dolphin species
- More than 500 species of sea plants and grasses
- 14 sea-snake species
- Six sea-turtle species
- 200 sea-bird species
- More than 150 species of shark

DIVING THE REEF

To astronauts who've seen it from space, the Great Barrier Reef resembles a vast, snaking wall—like a moat running parallel to Australia's entire northeastern coast. Almost unimaginably long at 1,430-odd miles, it's one of the few organic structures that can be seen from above the earth's atmosphere without a telescope.

(left) purple anthias; (above) pink coral

Up close, though, what looks (and from its name, sounds) like a barrier is in fact a labyrinthine complex with millions of points of entry. Mind-boggling in size and scope, encompassing more than 4,000 separate reefs, cays, and islands, the Reef could rightly be called its own subaqueous country.

An undersea enthusiast could spend a lifetime exploring this terrain—which ranges from dizzying chasms to sepulchral coral caves, and from lush underwater "gardens" to sandy sun-dappled shallows—without ever mapping all its resident wonders. Not only is the Reef system home to thousands upon thousands of sea-life species, the populations are changing all the time.

So how is a visitor—especially one with only a week to spend—supposed to plan a trip to this underwater Eden? How to choose among the seemingly endless spots for dropping anchor, donning fins and tanks, and plunging in?

With this many options, figuring out what you want to experience on the Reef is essential. If you've dreamed of floating among sea turtles, you'll likely need to head to a different location than if you want to swim with sharks; if you're an experienced deep-water diver with a taste for shipwrecks, you'll probably need to make separate arrangements from your friends who prefer to hover near the surface. There really is a spot for every kind of diver on the Reef; the trick is knowing where they are.

Luckily, many veteran divers agree about some of the Reef's most reliably excellent sites (and the best ways to access them). The selection compiled here should help you to—ahem—get your feet wet.

by Sarah Gold

BEST DIVING EXPERIENCES

Potato Cod and diver at Cod Hole

BEST WRECK DIVE

The coral formations of the Reef, while dazzling for divers, have proven treacherous to ship captains for centuries. More than 1,500 shipwrecks have been found on the Reef thus far—and there are almost certainly more waiting to be discovered.

S.S. YONGALA

The hulk of this 360-foot steamship, which sank during a cyclone in 1911, is easily the most popular wreck dive on the Reef. Part of the appeal is its easy accessibility; the Yongala lies just a half-hour's boat ride off the coast of Townsville, and though some sections are fairly deep (around 90 feet), others are just 45 feet below the surface. The entire wreck is now encrusted with coral, and swarms with a profusion of species including giant grouper, sea snakes, green sea turtles, and spotted eagle rays.

Difficulty level: Intermediate. Divers should have some previous deep-water experience before visiting this site.

How to get there: Yongala Dive (www.yongaladive.com.au), based in Alva Beach (south of Townsville), runs trips to the wreck several times per week.

BEST SITE TO GET YOUR HEART RATE UP

For some thrill-seeking divers, the wonders of the Great Barrier Reef are even better when accompanied by an extra shot of adrenaline—and a few dozen sharks.

OSPREY REEF

More than 200 miles north of Cairns (and only accessible via a live-aboard dive trip), Osprey is peerless for divers hell-bent on a rendezvous with the ocean's most famous predators. The northernmost section of the reef, where two ocean currents converge (it's known as the North Horn), is an especially thronged feeding ground for white-tipped reef, gray reef, hammerhead, and tiger sharks.

Difficulty level: Intermediate. Though the North Horn's best shark-viewing areas are only at about 60 feet, even seasoned divers may feel understandably anxious.

How to get there: Mike Ball Dive Expeditions (www.mikeball.com) offers multi-day packages to Osprey Reef from Cairns and Port Douglas.

PAPUA
NEW GUINEA

Dwarf Minke Whale

Ribbon Reef

Cuttlefish

rres Strait

York

Denham
Group

⚑ **Raine Island**

Cape Grenville

Sir Charles Hardy
Group

Far North Section

Claremont
Isles   *Cape Melville*

Howick
Group

⚑ *Osprey Reef*

Ribbon Reef #10

⚑⚑ **Cod Hole**

Lizard Island   *Cape Flattery*

Turtle
Group

GREAT BARRIER REEF
MARINE PARK

Cooktown

Cape Tribulation

Mossman

Port Douglas

Cairns

⚑ **Cathedral**
Cape Grafton

Cairns
Section

Flinders Reefs

Coral Sea

Coral Sea
Islands

Innisfail

Cardwell

Ingham

Hinchinbrook
Island

Townsville

Ayr

⚑ **S.S. Yongala**

Bowen

Proserpine

Airlie
Beach

Whitsunday Island

Whitsunday
Group

Central Section

Northumberland
Islands

Swam Reefs

Mackay

Percy Islands

Duke Islands

Cape Manifold

Marlborough

Rockhampton

TORILLA
PENINSULA

Macay/Capricorn
Section

Capricorn
Group

Bunker
Group

Blow
Hole

Lighthouse Bommies ⚑⚑

Bundaberg

Lady Elliot
Island

Fraser
Island

Hervey Bay

Maryborough

Gympie

BRISBANE ★

KEY	
	Reef down to 15ft deep
	Reef down to 30ft deep

8

0 ___ 100 mi
0 ___ 100 km

RAINE ISLAND

Thousands of green sea turtles migrate
each year to lay eggs on the protected
shores of Raine Island.

Scuba isn't the only option; snorkelers have plenty of opportunities to get up close to coral, too.

BEST CORAL-FORMATION SITES

Whether they're hard formations that mimic the shapes of antlers, brains, and stacked plates, or soft feathery Gorgonians and anemones, the building blocks of Reef ecology are compelling in their own right.

BLOW HOLE

Set off the eastern coast of Lady Elliot Island, this cavern-like coral tube is almost 60 feet in length. Divers can enter from either end, and swim through an interior festooned with Technicolor hard and soft corals—and swarming with banded coral shrimp, crayon-bright nudibranchs (sea slugs), and fluttery lionfish.

Difficulty level: Easy. Unless you're claustrophobic. Divers need only be Open-Water certified to visit this site, which ranges in depth from about 40 to 65 feet.

How to get there: The dive center at Lady Elliot Island Resort (www.ladyelliot.com.au) runs dives to the Blow Hole several times daily.

CATHEDRAL

Part of Thetford Reef, which lies within day-tripping distance of coastal Cairns, Cathedral is a wonderland of coral spires and swim-through chasms. The towering coral heads include thick forests of blue staghorn, sea fans, and sea whips; in between are sandy-bottomed canyons where shafts of sunlight play over giant clam beds.

Difficulty level: Intermediate. Though many coral peaks lie just 15 to 20 feet below the surface, the deeper channels (which go down to 85 feet) can be disorienting.

How to get there: Silverseries (www.silverseries.com.au) runs day-long trips from Cairns that visit several Thetford sites.

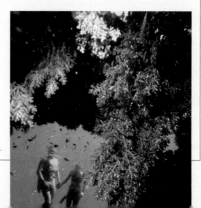

Divers explore a swim-through coral formation.

BEST GUARANTEED CLOSE-ENCOUNTER SITES

While just about any dive site on the Reef will bring you face-to-face with fantastic marine creatures, a few particular spots maximize your chances.

RIBBON REEF NUMBER 10

The northernmost of the Ribbon Reefs (a group that extends off the Cairns coast all the way to the Torres Strait) is home to some famously curious sea creatures. At Cod Hole, divers have been hand-feeding the enormous, 70-pound resident potato cod for decades. Ribbon Reef Number 10 is also one of the only places on earth where visitors can have breathtakingly close contact with wild dwarf minke whales. These small, playful baleen whales stop here every June and July—and they often approach within a few feet of respectful divers.

Difficulty level: Easy. Divers need only be Open-Water certified to dive at the 50-foot Cod Hole; dwarf minke encounters are open to snorkelers.

How to get there: Several dive operators run live-aboard trips to the Ribbon Reefs, including Mike Ball Expeditions (www.mikeball.com), Pro Dive Cairns (www.prodivecairns.com), and Eye to Eye Marine Encounters (www.marineencounters.com.au).

LIGHTHOUSE BOMMIES

Part of the southerly Whitsunday group, Lady Elliot Island is surrounded by shallow, pristine waters that teem with life. In particular, the Lighthouse Bommies— freestanding coral formations set off the island's northwest coast—host a large population of manta rays, some of which have a wingspan twelve feet across.

Difficulty level: Easy. Divers need only be Open-Water certified to visit this site; the depth averages about 50 feet.

How to get there: The dive center at Lady Elliot Island Resort (www.ladyelliot.com.au) runs dives to the Bommies daily.

Sea turtle and diver

RAINE ISLAND

In the far north reaches of the Coral Sea off Cape York, this coral cay is one of the Reef's greatest—and most inaccessible—treasures. Its beaches comprise the world's largest nesting ground for endangered green sea turtles; during November and December more than 20,000 turtles per week mob the shores to lay their eggs. Because Raine is a strictly protected preserve, seeing this annual phenomenon is an exceedingly rare privilege. In fact, only one dive operator, Eye to Eye Marine Encounters, is sanctioned by the Marine Park Authority to visit the site—and only twice a year.

Difficulty level: Intermediate to Expert. The dive trips involve a heavy research component; participants not only dive among the turtles, but also collect data on them and fit them with satellite tags (some also tag tiger sharks, another rare endemic species).

How to get there: The 18 spots on these ten-day trips are in high demand; learn more at www.marineencounters.com.au.

SCUBA DIVING 101

(left) ProDive is one of several great dive companies on the Reef; (right) snorkelers receive instruction.

Visiting the Reef can be a snap even if you've never dived before; most local dive operators offer Open Water (entry-level) certification courses that can be completed in just three to five days. The course involves both classroom and pool training, followed by a written test and one or more open-water dives on the Reef. Once you're certified, you'll be able to dive to depths of up to 60 feet; you'll also be eligible to rent equipment and book dive trips all over the world.

TIGHT SCHEDULE?

If time is of the essence, ask about doing your Open Water class and in-pool training near home; some Reef operators may allow you to complete your certification (and get right to the good part—the actual ocean dives) once you arrive in Australia.

Though most serious divers insist that certification is necessary for scuba safety, if you're short on time you may find yourself tempted to take advantage of what are generally called "resort courses"—single-day instruction programs that allow you to dive at limited depths under strict supervision. As long as you choose a reputable operator

(like Mike Ball Dive Expeditions, www. mikeball.com) and do exactly as your dive guides say, you'll likely be fine.

FLYING

No matter how you get yourself underwater, you'll need to make sure you don't schedule a flight and a dive in the same day. Flying too soon after diving can lead to "the bends"—an excruciating buildup of nitrogen bubbles in the bloodstream that requires a decompression chamber to alleviate. Since that's not anything you'd want to develop at the beginning of a transatlantic flight, be sure to wait 12 hours before flying after a single dive, 18 hours after multiple dives, and 24 hours if your dive(s) required decompression stops.

Regulators up! Reef visitors learn Scuba basics.

LOGISTICS

CERTIFYING ORGANIZATIONS

You'll find that all reliable dive operators—on the Reef and elsewhere—are affiliated with one of the three major international dive-training organizations: PADI (www.padi.com), NAUI (www.naui.org), or SSI (www.divessi.com). The certification requirements for all three are similar, and most dive shops and outfitters consider them interchangeable (i.e., they'll honor a certification from any of the three).

COSTS

The price for taking a full Open Water certification course (usually over four or five days of training) averages around A$500—but in many cases, rental equipment, wetsuits, and instruction manuals cost extra. Some dive shops have relationships with hotels, and offer dive/stay packages. One-day scuba resort courses usually cost around $200-$300, with all gear included.

EMERGENCIES

Before diving on the Reef, it's a good idea to purchase divers' insurance through the Divers Alert Network (DAN), an international organization that provides emergency medical assistance to divers. (Learn more about the different plans at www.diversalertnetwork.org). DAN also has a 24-hour emergency hotline staffed by doctors, emergency medical technicians, and nurses; for help with diving injuries or immediate medical advice, call (001) 919-684-4326 from Australia.

SNORKELING TIPS

Snorkelers explore Fitzroy Reef Lagoon.

■ If you're a beginner, avoid snorkeling in areas where there's chop or strong currents.

■ Every few minutes, look up and check what's floating ahead of you—you'll want to avoid boats, jellyfish, and other surface-swimmers.

■ Give corals, plants, and sea creatures a wide berth—for their protection and yours.

■ Coat every part of your back with high-SPF, waterproof sunscreen; the water's reflection greatly intensifies the sun's rays.

DIVING TIPS

■ Before heading off on a dive trip, have your doctor rule out any possible health complications.

■ Be sure your dive operator is affiliated with an internationally known training organization, such as PADI or NAUI.

■ Stick to dive trips and sites that are within your expertise level—the Reef is not the place to push safety limits.

■ Remember that in Australia, depths and weights use the metric system—so bring a conversion table if you need to.

■ Always dive with a partner, and always keep your partner in sight.

■ Never dive when you're feeling ill—especially if you're experiencing sinus congestion.

■ Never dive after consuming alcohol.

■ If you feel unwell or disoriented while diving, signal to your partner that you need to surface so she or he can accompany you.

DANGERS OF THE REEF

(left) The Irukandji box jellyfish sting causes severe pain; (right) small sharks inhabit areas of the Reef.

Like any other wild natural habitat, the Reef is home to creatures that are capable of causing you harm—and possibly even killing you. But surprisingly, the most lethal Reef inhabitants aren't of the Shark Week variety. In fact, they're just about invisible.

THE DEADLIEST REEF DWELLER

Chironex fleckeri—better known as box jellyfish—are native to the same waters as the Reef. They also just happen to be the most poisonous sea creatures on the planet. Cube-shaped and transparent (which makes them almost impossible to see in the water), these jellies have tentacles whose stinging cells release an enormously potent venom on contact. A box-jelly sting causes excruciating pain, often followed very quickly (within three or four minutes) by death.

The good news about box jellies is that they're only rarely encountered on the outer Reef and islands (they're much more prevalent close to the mainland shore, especially in summer—which is why you may see beautiful North Queensland beaches completely empty

on a hot December day). While the only sure way to prevent a box jellyfish sting is to stay out of the sea altogether, there are measures you can take to lessen the already minimal risks. First, consider wearing a full-length Lycra "sting suit" when you dive. Second, make sure your dive operator carries a supply of Chironex antivenom onboard your dive boat, just in case.

OTHER (LESS DEADLY) DANGERS

Although box jellyfish are by far the most dangerous creatures on the Reef, there are other "biteys" and "nasties" to be aware of. In particular, you should try to stay clear of a smaller box-jelly variety called Irukandji (whose sting causes delayed but often intense pain); Millepora, or stinging coral (which causes irritation and welts when it touches bare skin); sea snakes (who seldom bite humans, but whose poison can cause paralysis); and, yes, sharks (although you'll likely only see small ones on the Reef—the much more hyped Hammerheads, Tiger Sharks, and Great Whites prefer deeper and colder waters).

PROTECTING THE REEF

(left) Even the tiniest coral can serve as protective habitat; (right) divers explore a large coral formation.

Enormous though it may be, the Great Barrier Reef's ecosystem is one that requires a delicate balance. The interdependence of species here means that harming even a single food source—like a particular type of plankton—can have wide-ranging and even devastating effects.

The majority of the Reef is an official marine preserve that's managed and protected by the Great Barrier Reef Marine Park Authority. This govern-ment agency has developed a series of long-range programs to help protect the Reef—including population-monitoring of sealife species, water-temperature and salinity studies, and screening of all commercial fishing and tourism/recreational operations.

Since almost 2 million tourists visit the Reef each year, even day-trippers should be mindful of their impact on this fragile environment. Specifically, if you're planning to dive and snorkel here, you should:

■ Make sure your dive gear is secure, with no loose straps or dangling hoses that might snag on corals.

■ Swim slowly to avoid brushing against corals (and be especially mindful when wearing swim fins).

■ Avoid picking up or touching any corals, plants, or creatures (for your protection and theirs). No souvenirs, even empty shells or dead-looking coral.

■ Keep clear of all free-swimming sea creatures like sea turtles, dolphins, dugongs, or whales.

VOLUNTEERING ON THE REEF

If you'd like to do more to protect the Reef, the following organizations offer volunteer programs that allow you to help collect study data and monitor the health of reef species:

■ The Australian Marine Conservation Society: www.amcs.org.au

■ Reef Check Australia: www.reefcheckaustralia.org

■ UNESCO (United Nations Educational, Scientific, and Cultural Organization): whc.unesco.org boat-diving options are available for beginner and PADI-certified divers. The resort can arrange half-day dive and snorkeling trips around the neighboring Palm Islands, and full-day charter dive and snorkeling excursions to sites on the Outer Barrier Reef teeming with turtles, colorful fish, and coral species—and, in season, massive manta rays and masses of coral spawning. Costs depend on passenger numbers and inclusions; booking ahead is essential. Resort guests can also preorder gourmet picnic hampers and use the resort's motorized dinghies to visit secluded, boulder-strewn coves and snorkeling spots on the island's fringing reef. Often, you can snorkel directly off the beach into fish-filled coral gardens. ⊠ *Orpheus Island Resort jetty* ☎ *07/4777–7377* ⊕ *www. orpheus.com.au* ⌨ *From A$200.*

WHERE TO STAY

$$$$
RESORT
Fodor's Choice
★

🖼 **Orpheus Island.** This unpretentious, eco-friendly resort epitomizes laid-back luxury, with sleekly appointed beachfront rooms, suites, and villas; romantic alfresco dining; boutique wines; and numerous outdoor activities included in the rate. **Pros:** idyllic environs; wonderful food and wine; free Wi-Fi in public areas; excellent underwater sites nearby. **Cons:** no in-room Internet; occasional geckos and insects indoors; three-night minimum stay over Christmas and New Year period. $ *Rooms from: A$1,400* ⊠ *Orpheus Island Resort* ✈ *accessible via air from Townsville or Cairns* ☎ *07/4777–7377* ⊕ *www.orpheus.com.au* ⌨ *14 rooms, suites, and villas* ⏀ *All-inclusive.*

LIZARD ISLAND

240 km (150 miles) off the North Queensland coast.

The small, upscale resort on secluded Lizard Island is the farthest north of any Barrier Reef hideaway. At 2,500 acres, virtually all of it protected as a national park, it's larger than and quite different from other islands in the region. Composed mostly of granite, Lizard has a remarkable diversity of vegetation and terrain: grassy hills give way to rocky slabs interspersed with valleys of rain forest.

Ringed by two-dozen white-sand beaches, the island has some of the best fringing coral in the region. Excellent walking trails lead to lookouts with spectacular views of the coast. The island's highest point, Cook's Look (1,180 feet), is the historic spot from which, in August 1770, Captain Cook finally spotted a safe passage through the reef that had held his vessel captive for a thousand miles. Large monitor lizards, after which the island is named, often bask in this area.

GETTING HERE AND AROUND

Lizard Island has its own small airstrip served by Hinterland Aviation. Hour-long flights to the island depart up to twice a day from Cairns, at 11 and 2, returning at 12:30 and 3:25; taking an hour and costing A$315 per person each way. Allow two hours' transit time for connecting international flights, one for domestic flight transits: check-in is 30 minutes prior to flight time at the Hinterland Aviation Terminal. You can also arrange charter flights to the island, with prices varying depending on the size of aircraft available (☎ *07/4043–1999 resort, 03/9426–7550 bookings*).

North Coast Islands, Townsville, and Magnetic Island

KEY
Reef down to 15ft deep
Reef down to 30ft deep

Air Contacts Hinterland Aviation. ☎ 07/4040–1333, 1800/359428 toll-free in Australia ⊕ www.hinterlandaviation.com.au.

EXPLORING

Fodor's Choice **Cod Hole.** For divers and snorkelers, the usually crystal-clear waters off
★ Lizard Island are a dream. Cod Hole, 20 km (12 miles) from Lizard Island, ranks among the best dive sites on Earth. Massive potato cod swim up to divers like hungry puppies; it's an awesome experience, considering that these fish can weigh 300 pounds and reach around two meters (6 feet) in length. The island lures big-game anglers from all over the world from September to December, when black marlin are running. ⊠ *Lizard Island.*

SPORTS AND THE OUTDOORS

The lodge has catamarans, outboard dinghies, paddle-skis (including glass-bottom ones), fishing supplies, snorkeling gear, and lessons. There is superb snorkeling around the island's fringing coral, or you can cruise over it on a glass-bottom paddle-ski tour. Self-guided bushwalking trails and nature slide shows get guests in touch with the local flora and fauna. Arrange a picnic hamper with the kitchen staff and take a dinghy out for an afternoon on your own private beach. All these activities are included in your room rate.

Other activities cost extra: inner and outer reef dive/snorkel trips, night dives, scuba courses, and game- and bottom-fishing excursions (black marlin season runs September through December). For pricing, details, and to prebook activities, contact Lizard Island Activities Desk (☎ *1300/863248 or 07/9426–7550 ⊕ www.lizardisland.com.au*).

FISHING

Lizard Island is one of the big game-fishing centers in Australia, with several world records set here since the mid-1990s. Game fishing is generally best in spring and early summer, and giant black marlin weighing more than 1,000 pounds are no rarity. September through December, the folk from Lizard Island run full-day game-fishing trips to the outer reef; January through August, you can book half-day bottom-fishing excursions.

Fodor'sChoice   **Lizard Island Sportfishing.** Even though fishing is banned in the waters
★   immediately off Lizard Island, world-renowned fishing grounds lie less than an hour away. From September through December, fishing enthusiasts arrive in droves to land tuna, sailfish, mahimahi, and, if they're lucky, the legendary "Grander" black marlin. From January to August, you might nab trevally, mackerel, or queenfish. Lizard Island Resort arranges small-group, high-adrenaline trips to the outer reef and half- and full-day inner reef excursions on its 51-foot Riviera Platinum Model Flybridge cruiser, *Fascination III*. An outer-reef game-fishing day trip, including heavy tackle, lunch, and light refreshments, costs from A$2,995 for up to four people; a half-day bottom-fishing excursion, with bait, light tackle, and refreshments, is from A$1,995. For all fishing trips, prebooking is essential. ⊠ *Lizard Island Resort jetty* ☎ *03/9426–7550 bookings, 1300/8876724 toll-free in Australia, 884/731–551 in U.S. ⊕ www.lizardisland.com.au* ✆ *From A$1995.*

SCUBA DIVING

The reefs around Lizard Island have some of the best marine life and coral on the planet. The resort runs expertly guided scuba-diving and snorkeling trips on its custom-built dive boat to pristine sites on the Great Barrier Reef, including the Ribbon Reefs and globally renowned Cod Hole, as well as local dives, snorkeling excursions, and scuba courses.

Fodor'sChoice   **Lizard Island Snorkeling & Diving.** Lizard Island is a short boat ride from
★   some of the richest, least spoiled sites on the Great Barrier Reef. Within an hour, you can dive the ribbon reefs or renowned Cod Hole, eyeballing giant potato cod, pelagic fish, turtles, rays, and sharks. You can also take guided day or night dives to explore fish-filled coral gardens just offshore. Lizard Island Resort's 55-foot dive boat MV *Serranidae* makes reef excursions as well as dive-snorkel trips, and privately guided dives to local fringing reefs and the Cobia Hole. Need scuba skills or gear? The resort has nonaccredited Discover Scuba and PADI Referral courses, and a wide range of modern dive equipment for hire. Use of snorkeling masks, snorkels, and fins is complimentary. ⊠ *Lizard Island Resort* ☎ *03/9426–7550 bookings, 1300/731551 toll-free in Australia, 884/887–6724 in U.S. ⊕ www.lizardisland.com.au* ✆ *From A$45* ⟳ *All divers must bring certification card and current dive medical certificate.*

WHERE TO STAY

$$$$
RESORT
Fodor's Choice
★

☒ **Lizard Island Resort.** Beloved by honeymooners, divers, and well-heeled travelers, this outer Great Barrier Reef resort ticks all the high-end tropical-island vacation boxes: luxurious beachfront accommodation, fine food and wine, and world-class diving and fishing. **Pros:** superb diving and fishing; quality food and wine; use of nonmotorized watercraft and dinghies. **Cons:** successive cyclones have damaged the island's vegetation; lighting inadequate for reading; no cell-phone coverage. ⑤ *Rooms from: A$1759* ☒ *Lizard Island* ☎ *1300/731551 bookings (toll-free in Australia), 07/4043–1999 resort, 844/887–6724 toll-free in U.S.* ⊕ *www.lizardisland.com.au* ⤴ *39 villas, 1 pavilion* ⑪ *All-inclusive.*

TOWNSVILLE AND MAGNETIC ISLAND

Townsville and adjacent twin city Thuringowa make up Australia's largest tropical city, with a combined population of just under 200,000. It's the commercial capital of the north, and a major center for education, scientific research, and defense. Spread along the banks of Ross Creek and around the pink granite outcrop of Castle Hill, Townsville is a pleasant city of palm-fringed malls, historic colonial buildings, extensive parkland, and gardens. It's also the stepping-off point for Magnetic Island, one of the state's largest islands and a haven for wildlife.

GETTING HERE AND AROUND

Qantas flies frequently from Townsville Airport to Brisbane, Cairns, Cloncurry, Mount Isa, and Mackay, as well as to capital cities around Australia and overseas destinations. Jetstar has services to Brisbane, Sydney, and Melbourne; Virgin Australia connects Townsville with Cairns, Brisbane, the Gold Coast, Rockhampton, Sydney, Melbourne, and Canberra. There are no air connections to Magnetic Island; you need to take a ferry from Townsville (one-way, it's A$12.50 for a walk-on passenger; A$90 for a vehicle with up to four passengers). Townsville Taxis are available at the airport. The average cost of the ride to a city hotel is between A$20 and A$25, more after 7 pm.

Townsville is a flat, somewhat dull 1,358-km (844-mile), 16-hour drive from Brisbane. The 348-km (216-mile), 4½-hour journey from here to Cairns, with occasional Hinchinbrook Island views, is more scenic. Greyhound Australia coaches travel regularly to Cairns, Mount Isa, Rockhampton, Brisbane, and other destinations throughout Australia from the SeaLink Terminal on Townsville's Breakwater, also the departure point for Magnetic Island ferries, day cruises, and dive trips. Regular long-distance Queensland Rail services, offering reclining seats or pod-like RailBeds, connect Townsville with Brisbane, Cairns, Mount Isa, and dozens of towns en route.

Once in town, you can flag a Townsville Taxis cab on the street, find one at taxi stands, hotels, and the island's ferry terminal, or book one online.

Ferry Contacts SeaLink Queensland. ☒ *Breakwater Terminal, 18 Sir Leslie Thiess Dr., Townsville* ☎ *07/4726–0800* ⊕ *www.sealinkqld.com.au.*

Taxi Contacts Townsville Taxis. ☒ *11–15 Yeatman St., Townsville* ☎ *13–1008 local bookings, 07/4778–9555 interstate bookings* ⊕ *www.tsvtaxi.com.au.*

8

TOURS

Tropicana Guided Adventure Company. The knowledgeable guides from this local tour outfit run small-group expeditions to normally inaccessible bays and beaches around Magnetic Island in a stretch jeep. The company's signature tour is its five-hour Remote Area Adventure (A$132 per person), accessing permit-only areas around Florence Bay and West Point. The excursion allows time to explore remote beaches, hike to lookouts, photograph wildlife, and watch the sun set over the sea from West Point. The tour leaves Nelly Bay Harbour daily at 2:30, returning in time for the 7:50 SeaLink ferry to Townsville (or dropping guests off at Magnetic Island accommodations). It's A$79 per person for a three-hour eco-orientation tour, departing daily at 11 from Nelly Bay near the taxi stand (catch the 10:30 SeaLink ferry from the mainland). An 8½-hour sightseeing tour of the island, including its wildlife hot spots and remote and tourist areas, leaves daily at 11 am from Magnetic Harbour (A$198, including lunch and refreshments). ⊠ *Taxi cab rank, Nelly Bay Harbour, Magnetic Island* ☎ *07/4758–1800* ⊕ *www. tropicanatours.com.au* ☞ *From A$79.*

ESSENTIALS

Visitor Information Flinders Square Visitor Information Centre. ⊠ *Flinders Mall, 334A Flinders St., near Stanley St., Townsville* ☎ *07/4721–3660* ⊕ *www. townsvillenorthqueensland.com.au.*

TOWNSVILLE

1,358 km (844 miles) north of Brisbane, 348 km (216 mile) south of Cairns.

This coastal city has little in the way of sandy beaches or surf, but it does have shady parks, charming colonial buildings, and a boardwalk-flanked waterfront esplanade with a terrific man-made beach and picnic facilities. The historic town center has thrived in the past decade, with an influx of lively eateries and bars. There is also an excellent museum and a world-class aquarium.

Queensland Parks and Wildlife Service (ParksQ) has an office on Magnetic Island, but Tourism Townsville's information kiosk in Flinders Square and the Townsville Bulletin Square Visitor Information Centre near the Museum of Tropical Queensland (MTQ), on the mainland, are the best sources of visitor info about the island.

EXPLORING

FAMILY **Billabong Sanctuary.** This eco-friendly, interactive sanctuary on 22 acres of bushland shelters koalas, wombats, dingoes, wallabies, endangered bilbies, snakes, crocodiles, lizards, and numerous birds, most featuring in daily wildlife shows, presentations, and feedings. The sanctuary has daily free-flight birds of prey shows, crocodile and cassowary feedings, venomous snake presentations, and turtle racing. This is one of the few places in Australia at which you can cuddle a koala (and get your photo taken as a memento). You can also get your photo taken holding a wombat, snake, or baby croc. Thrill-seekers can book a personal croc-feeding experience, with or without souvenir photo. ⊠ *Bruce*

Hwy., Nome ⊹ 17 km (11 miles) south of Townsville ☎ 07/4778–8344 ⊕ www.billabongsanctuary.com.au ☒ A$34 entry ⊙ Daily 9–5.

Castle Hill. The summit of pink-granite monolith Castle Hill, 1 km (½ miles) from the city center, provides great views of the city and Magnetic Island. While you're perched on top, think about the proud local resident who, with the aid of several scout troops, spent years in the 1970s piling rubble onto the peak to try to add the 23 feet that would make Castle Hill a mountain, officially speaking—which means a rise of at least 1,000 feet. These days, most people trek to the top along a steep walking track that doubles as one of Queensland's most scenic jogging routes. ☒ *Castle Hill Lookout, Castle Hill Rd.* ☎ *07/4721–3660 Townsville Visitor Information* ⊕ *www.townsvillenorthqueensland.com.au.*

Flinders Street. A stroll along Flinders Street from the Strand to Stanley Street takes you past some of Townsville's most impressive turn-of-the-20th-century colonial structures. **Magnetic House** and several other historic buildings along the strip have been beautifully restored. The grand old **Queens Hotel** is a fine example of the early Victorian Classical Revival style, as is the **Perc Tucker Regional Gallery,** circa 1885, originally a bank. **Tattersalls Hotel,** circa 1865, is typical of its era, with wide verandas and fancy wrought-iron balustrades; today, it houses the rambunctious **Molly Malones** Irish pub. Once the town's post office, what's now **The Brewery** had an impressive masonry clock tower when it was erected in 1889. The tower was dismantled in 1942 so it wouldn't be a target during World War II air raids, and re-erected in 1964. **The Exchange,** Townsville's oldest pub, was built in 1869, burned down in 1881, and was rebuilt the following year. ☒ *Flinders St.*

FAMILY **Museum of Tropical Queensland.** Centuries-old relics from the HMS *Pandora* (the ship sent by the British Admiralty to capture the mutinous *Bounty* crew), which sank in 1791 carrying 14 crew members of Captain Bligh's infamous ship, are among the exhibits at this repository of the region's maritime, natural, and indigenous history. There's a fun introduction to North Queensland's culture and lifestyle, a shipwreck exhibit, and the ecology-focused Enchanted Rainforest. Displays of tropical wildlife, dinosaur fossils, local corals, and deep-sea creatures round out a diverse public collection. ☒ *70–102 Flinders St. E* ☎ *07/4726–0600* ⊕ *www.mtq.qm.qld.gov.au* ☒ *A$15* ⊙ *Daily 9:30–5.*

FAMILY **Queens Gardens.** Offering shade and serenity less than a mile from the CBD, Townsville's colonial-era botanic gardens occupies 10 verdant acres at the base of Castle Hill. Bordered by frangipani (plumeria) and towering Moreton Bay fig trees, whose unique dangling roots veil the entry to the grounds, the gardens are a wonderful place to picnic, stroll, or amuse the kids. There are play areas, a hedge maze, formal rose garden, fountains, and a lovely rain-forest walk. A compact aviary houses bright-plumed peacocks, lorikeets, and sulfur-crested cockatoos. ☒ *Gregory St. at Paxton St., North Ward* ☎ *1300/878001 toll-free in Australia* ⊕ *www.townsville.qld.gov.au* ☒ *Free* ⊙ *Daily dawn–dusk.*

FAMILY
Fodor's Choice
★ **Reef HQ Aquarium.** Come eye-to-eye with sharks, rays, giant trevally, and green sea turtles at the Reef HQ Aquarium. It houses a 200,000-gallon predator tank, a hands-on discovery lagoon, and a vast aquarium, open

to the elements. The main oceanarium is populated with 120 species of hard and soft coral, as well as sea stars, spiky urchins, sponges, and more than 150 species of tropical fish. There's also a 20-meter (65-foot) Perspex underwater walkway. Time your visit to coincide with the aquarium's daily predator dive show (10:30 am), twice-daily turtle talks (noon and 3:30), guided tours, or thrice-weekly shark feeds (2:30 on Tuesday, Thursday, and Sunday). ⊠ *2–68 Flinders St. E* ☏ *07/4750–0800* ⊕ *www.reefhq.com.au* ⊠ *A$28* ⊙ *Daily 9:30–5.*

FAMILY **Townsville Town Common Conservation Park.** Spot wallabies, echidnas, dingoes, goannas, and hundreds of bird species at this terrific wetlands conservation park crisscrossed by walking and biking trails, and dotted with bird blinds and a wildlife-viewing tower. You can take the easy, hour-long Forest Walk to see kingfishers and honey-eaters, the Pallarenda to Tegoora Rock circuit for wetlands overviews, or several other walking and biking trails (with estimated walk times ranging from 30 minutes to five hours). The 5-km (3-mile), two-plus-hour-long trail from Bald Rock to Mount Marlowl is worth the uphill trek for the glorious regional panorama at the summit. Most trails start from Bald Rock parking lot, 7 km (4½ miles) from the park entrance on unpaved roads. ⊠ *Freshwater Lagoon Rd., off Cape Pallarenda Rd., near Rowes Bay Golf Club, Pallarenda* ☏ *07/4721–3660 Townsville Tourist Information, 13–7468 ParksQ infoline* ⊕ *www.nprsr.qld.gov.au/parks/townsville* ⊙ *Daily 6:30–6:30.*

FAMILY **Wallaman Falls.** Surrounding the highest sheer-drop waterfall in Australia is glorious Girringun National Park, in which ancient rain forests accessible via scenic walking trails shelter rare plants and animals that include the endangered southern cassowary, platypus, and musky rat-kangaroo. You might also spot eastern water dragons, saw-shelled turtles, and crocodiles here. The park is the start of the Wet Tropics Great Walk, suitable for experienced hikers. For day-trippers, there are two spectacular lookouts and some scenic short walks, such as the 45-minute Banggurru circuit along Stony Creek's bank, or the steeper, two-hour walk to the base of the falls. ⊠ *Lava Plains Mount Fox Rd.* ✛ *From Townsville, take Bruce Hwy. (A1) north for just under 100 km (60 miles), then turn left onto Lannercost St. (signposted for Abergowrie/Wallaman Falls), taking Abergowrie-Ingham Rd. to Abergowrie, then Stone Rd. and Mount Fox Rd. to park entrance* ☏ *07/4776–4792 GBR region QPWS office, 13–7468 ParksQ infoline* ⊕ *www.nprsr.qld.gov.au/parks.*

BEACHES

Townsville is blessed with a golden, 2-km (1-mile) beach that stretches along the city's northern edge. The beach, with its associated pools, water park, and adjacent parklands, is hugely popular with the locals, especially over school holidays and summer.

FAMILY
Fodor's Choice
★
The Strand. Dubbed Australia's Cleanest Beach, this palm-flanked stretch of sand—lined with jogging tracks and cycleways, picnic-friendly parklands, and hip beachfront bars—has two swimming enclosures and a long pier perfect for fishing. The beach and its permanent swimming enclosure, Strand Rock Pool, are fitted with temporary nets during

box-jellyfish season, November–May. There's also a free, kid-friendly Strand Water Park. All are patrolled by lifeguards daily, with hours varying seasonally. **Amenities:** food and drink; lifeguards; toilets. **Best for:** swimming. ⊠ *The Strand* ☎ *1300/878001 Townsville City Council* ⊕ *www.townsville.qld.gov.au* ☉ *Lifeguard patrol: Strand & Rock Pool 9–5 (6 in summer); Water Park 10–5 (later in peak seasons/summer). Rock Pool closed Wed., Water Park closed Tues. and Wed. except school holiday periods.*

SPORTS AND THE OUTDOORS

KAYAKING

FAMILY **Magnetic Island Sea Kayaks.** On these eco-friendly kayaking trips around Magnetic Island's quieter bays, you might spot turtles, dolphins, dugongs, sea eagles, ospreys, and, mid-July through mid-September, migrating whales and their calves. The company runs three different excursions: a leisurely 4½-hour morning tour of beaches, coves, and bays (A$85); a twilight paddle around Horseshoe Bay with a stop for drinks (A$60); and a daylong kayaking tour of the island (A$155). Rates include the use of single or double kayaks and safety gear, expert truition and guidance, commentary on the island's ecology, breakfast or sunset drinks, lunch (on daylong tours), reef tax, and National Park entry fees. Experienced kayakers can also rent out single or double kayaks by the day, with safety gear included in the rate. ⊠ *Horseshoe Bay boat ramp, end of Pacific Dr., off Horseshoe Bay Rd., Magnetic Island* ☎ *07/4778–5424* ⊕ *www.seakayak.com.au* ◱ *From A$60* ☉ *Morning tour: Daily from 8. Sunset tour: Wed., Fri., and Sat. from 2 hrs before sunset.*

SCUBA DIVING

Surrounded by tropical islands and warm waters, Townsville is a top-notch diving center. Diving courses, day trips, and multiday excursions tend to be less crowded than those in the hot spots of Cairns or the Whitsunday Islands.

About 16 km (10 miles) offshore, a 60-km (37-mile) boat ride southeast of Townsville, is the wreck of the mighty SS *Yongala,* a steamship that sank in 1911 and now lies 49 to 91 feet beneath the surface. It teems with marine life and is considered one of Australia's best dive sites. It can be explored on one- and two-day trips. All local dive operators conduct excursions to the wreck.

Adrenalin Dive. This local outfit runs day and live-aboard trips to diverse sites on the Great Barrier Reef, including the wreck of the SS *Yongala.* The *Yongala* trip includes weight belt, tanks, two dives, and lunch; it's an extra A$40 for dive gear and A$10 for the introductory guided dive that's compulsory for novice divers. Snorkel/dive day trips to sheltered sites on the GBR's Lodestone Reef are A$220 for snorkelers, A$250 for certified divers (A$290 with gear); for introductory divers, it's A$295 with one dive and snorkeling, A$335 with two dives. On a three-night, live-aboard eco-trip, you can make up to 10 dives, including two night dives and two dives on the *Yongala* (A$815 for a snorkeler, A$935 for a diver in a double room, including diving, gear, and meals). Cheaper twin and dorm berths are available. On all dive trips, optional extras include PADI Adventure Dives (A$25 per dive); enriched-air nitrox (A$50 for two tanks, Nitrox-certified divers only); and camera hire (A$65). ✉ *252 Walker St.* ☎ *07/4724–0600, 1300/664600 toll-free in Australia* ⊕ *www.adrenalindive.com.au* ✉ *From A$220.*

WHERE TO EAT

$$
MODERN
AUSTRALIAN

✕ **JAM Corner.** This fine-dining restaurant sources terrific organic and tropical produce for its modern Australian menus, which change seasonally, but always feature fresh seafood and premium Australian meats in artful, beautifully balanced dishes, with fine Antipodean wines to complement them. Ingredients are top-notch: free-range chicken, Victorian spring lamb, Tasmanian fillet steak, Western Plains pork, Sunshine Coast crab, Coffin Bay oysters, and North Queensland seafood, with a smattering of bush tucker and heirloom vegetables. Leave room for memorable desserts: a lemon myrtle panna cotta with a chocolate sphere, or passionfruit parfait with honeycomb, sugared macadamia, and seasonal berries. For special occasions, there's a luxurious, chandelier-lighted private dining room. ∎**TIP**➔ Reservations aren't essential, but it's a smart idea to book ahead. ⑤ *Average main: A$36* ✉ *1 Palmer St., South Townsville* ☎ *07/4721–4900* ⊕ *www.jamcorner.com. au* ⊙ *Closed Mon. No dinner Sun.*

$
MODERN
AUSTRALIAN
Fodor'sChoice
★

✕ **A Touch of Salt.** This Modern Australian eatery ticks all the boxes: location (riverfront), service (impeccable), ambience (relaxed), food (exciting and flavorful), and wine (top-flight). Mains are divided into "sea," "earth," and "land." Dishes on the "sea" selection might include tempura soft shell crab, seared chipotle prawns, or spiced Spanish mackerel. "Land" dishes could be Schezuan-style duck, or a premium eye-fillet steak. On the constantly changing "earth" list of vegan options, you might find goats' cheese gnocchi, or mushroom and sweet-corn gyoza. Small but artfully presented desserts taste as good as they look. There's also an excellent, largely Australian wine list. Prebooking is strongly recommended, especially if you want to sit outside on the expansive waterfront deck. ⑤ *Average main: A$34* ✉ *86 Ogden St.* ☎ *07/4724–4441* ⊕ *www.atouchofsalt.com.au* ⊙ *Closed Sun. and Mon. No lunch Sat.–Thurs.*

WHERE TO STAY

$
HOTEL

🏨 **Grand Hotel Townsville.** With a terrific location in Townsville's liveliest bar-restaurant precinct, this stylish, secure, and spotless hotel-apartment complex has everything you need: chic, well-appointed accommodation; a clean pool and terrific gym; business center; accommodating staff; and charge-back arrangements with local eateries. **Pros:** close to many bars, eateries, and attractions; helpful, friendly staff; well-equipped apartments; 24-hour room service. **Cons:** lower-floor rooms are small and lack views; Palmer Street-facing rooms can be noisy, especially on weekends; free on-site car-parking spots limited. ⑤ *Rooms from: A$199* ✉ *8–10 Palmer St.* ☎ *07/4753–2800* ⊕ *www.grandhoteltownsville.com. au* ⌥ *106 rooms* ⦿*No meals.*

$$$
HOTEL

🏨 **Oaks M on Palmer.** The smartly configured studios and suites at this hotel are a five-minute walk from Palmer Street's bar and dining precinct, and an easy stroll across the footbridge from Flinders Street and the ferry port. **Pros:** excellent in-room facilities; central location; 15% discount for 2-plus-day stays. **Cons:** feels a tad clinical; service standards vary; fee for in-room Wi-Fi after first 30 minutes. $ *Rooms from: A$395* ⊠ *81 Palmer St.* ☎ *07/4753–2900 reception, 1300/559129 toll-free in Australia* ⊕ *www.theoaksgroup.com.au* ⌁ *104 rooms* ⦿ *No meals.*

NIGHTLIFE

Fodor'sChoice
★ **The Brewery.** Townsville's historic post office now houses this sociable gastropub, which serves upmarket, bistro-style meals and boutique beers brewed on-site. The owners have combined modern finishes with the building's original design, incorporating old post-office fittings, such as the main bar, once the stamp counter, to create a venue with character and polish. ⊠ *Flinders Mall, 252 Flinders St.* ☎ *07/4724–2999* ⊕ *www.townsvillebrewery.com.au.*

The Ville Resort Casino. Dominating Townsville's waterfront, this high-rise casino-hotel complex is an entertainment hub: a luxury hotel, three on-site restaurants, four bars, regular live shows, and more than 370 slot machines and 20-plus gaming tables. If you choose to stay over, the 198-room hotel has well-appointed rooms, suites, and a two-bedroom apartment. Good-value package deals and online specials are available. ⊠ *Sir Leslie Thiess Dr., Box 1223* ☎ *07/4722–2333* ⊕ *www.the-ville.com.au.*

MAGNETIC ISLAND

10 km (6 miles) from Townsville.

More than half of Magnetic Island's 52 square km (20 square miles) is national parkland, laced with miles of walking trails and rising to 1,640 feet at the Mt. Cook summit. The terrain is littered with huge granite boulders and softened by tall hoop pines, eucalyptus forest, and rainforest gullies. A haven for wildlife, the island shelters rock wallabies, echidnas, frogs, possums, fruit bats, nonvenomous green tree snakes, and Northern Australia's largest population of wild koalas. Its beaches, mangroves, sea-grass beds, and fringing reefs support turtles nesting, fish hatching, and a significant dugong (manatee) population. You can take time out on 23 island beaches and dive nine offshore shipwrecks.

More than 2,500 people call "Maggie" home; most live on the island's eastern shore at Picnic Bay, Arcadia, Nelly Bay, and Horseshoe Bay. Many artists and craftspeople reside here, drawn by the serenity and scenic environs; you can see and buy their work at studios and galleries around the island.

GETTING HERE AND AROUND

Fantasea Cruising Magnetic. The 40-minute Fantasea Cruising Magnetic ferry service has several scheduled services daily from the mainland to Maggie's Nelly Bay Ferry Terminal, 10 km (6 miles) offshore. The first ferry leaves Townsville at 5:20 am weekdays, 7:10 on weekends, with the last return service departing the island at 6:55 pm. One-way fares are A$89 for a vehicle with up to six people, A$14.50 for a person with no vehicle (bicycles free). SeaLink Queensland has a daily 25-minute catamaran service linking Townsville and Nelly Bay on Magnetic

Island. Bus and island transfers meet the ferry during daylight hours. Up to 18 SeaLink ferries a day cruise out of Townsville between 5:30 am (6:30 Sunday) and 10:30 pm (11:30 pm Friday and Saturday), returning between 6:20 am (7:10 Sunday) and 11 pm (midnight Friday and Saturday); a one-way ticket costs A$16. ⊠ *22 Ross St., Townsville* ☏ *07/4796–9300* ⊕ *www.fantaseacruisingmagnetic.com.au.*

Magnetic Island Sunbus. Get an overview of Magnetic Island riding the cheap, reliable local buses, which ply the coast road between Picnic Point, Nelly Bay, Arcadia, and Horseshoe Bay from dawn till late, and can be hailed from the roadside. Single-fare tickets (A$1.70 to A$3.50) as well as unlimited-travel day and weekly passes are available from the driver. The bus departs Picnic Bay Jetty at regular intervals throughout the week. Hail it between designated stops simply by standing at the roadside and raising your hand. ⊠ *Nelly Bay, 44 Mandalay Ave.* ☏ *07/4778–5130* ⊕ *www.sunbus.com.au.*

Magnetic Island Taxi Service. This local taxi company services the entire island. Go to its website to prebook cabs and get fare estimates. ⊠ *Magnetic Island* ☏ *13–1008 toll-free in Australia, 07/4778–9566* ⊕ *www.131008.com.*

MI Wheels. The tiny Mini Moke, a soft-top convertible version of the Mini-Minor car, is an ideal means by which to explore Magnetic Island. MI Wheels, next to the IGA supermarket near Nelly Bay Ferry Terminal, rents out Mokes, including fuel; a driver's license is required. ⊠ *Nelly Bay, 138 Sooning St., opposite Ferry Terminal, Nelly Bay* ☏ *07/4758–1111* ⊕ *www.miwheels.com.au.*

ESSENTIALS

Visitor Information Queensland Parks and Wildlife Service, Magnetic Island. ⊠ *22 Hurst St., Picnic Bay* ☏ *13/7468 ParksQ hotline, toll-free in Australia* ⊕ *www.nprsr.qld.gov.au/parks/magnetic-island.*

SPORTS AND THE OUTDOORS

The island has 24 km (15 miles) of hiking trails, most of which are relatively easy. The popular Forts Walk leads to World War II gun emplacements overlooking Horseshoe and Florence bays. At a leisurely pace, it takes about 45 minutes each way from the Horseshoe–Radical Bay Road. Look up en route and you may spot a sleepy koala.

Some of the island's best views are on the 5-km (3-mile) Nelly Bay to Arcadia Walk. Look out for shell middens created over thousands of years by the island's Aboriginal owners, the Wulgurukaba, or "Canoe People."

Swimming and snorkeling are other popular activities, but from November to May, box jellyfish ("stingers") are a hazard: swim at Picnic and Horseshoe bays, which have stinger nets, and wear a protective suit. At other times, Alma Bay and Nelly Bay, as well as Picnic, Florence, Radical, Horseshoe, and Balding bays, are all suitable for swimming. Horseshoe has daily lifeguard patrols and a stinger-free swimming enclosure; Alma and Picnic bays are patrolled over weekends and school holiday periods, September to May.

MIGALOO THE ALBINO WHALE

Migaloo was the world's only documented white humpback whale when he was first spotted in 1991, making his way up the Queensland coastline. A witty indigenous elder suggested the name Migaloo, an Aboriginal word for "white fella."

Every year, thousands eagerly watch for a glimpse of Migaloo's distinctive pure-white dorsal fin, as the 14-meter (46-foot) whale makes his annual migration from the Antarctic to tropical waters in June and July. He's been spotted as far up Australia's east coast as Port Douglas, north of Cairns—usually from the decks of dive and cruise boats (which are forbidden by law from going within 500 meters of the rare cetacean). Sometimes Migaloo travels solo; on other journeys, he's accompanied by dolphins or fellow humpbacks.

Migaloo's not the only albino marine creature you might spot on your visit to Queensland: in early 2006, a tiny white sea turtle was found on Blacks Beach, Mackay, and shipped off to Reef HQ in nearby Townsville for rehab. Today he's doing well—and is a great deal larger.

Geoffrey Bay has a well-trafficked unofficial snorkel trail. Other good snorkeling spots include Nelly Bay, Alma Bay (which has its own snorkel trail), and the northern ends of Florence and Arthur bays. Near the northeastern corner of the island, Radical Bay has a small, idyllic beach flanked by tree-covered rock outcrops. Horseshoe Bay, the island's largest beach, is lined with boat-rental outlets and water-sports equipment.

HORSEBACK RIDING

FAMILY

Fodor's Choice

★

Horseshoe Bay Ranch. Leaving only hoof prints on Magnetic Island's white-sand beaches, these eco-friendly horse rides offer the chance to go bareback swimming with your well-trained steed. Two-hour rides (A\$120) depart Horseshoe Bay Ranch daily at 8:30 am and 2:30 pm, wending their way along bush trails to a secluded beach, where you get to unsaddle and take the horses for a Coral Sea swim. Wear a bathing suit, shirt, long pants, socks, and closed shoes, and BYO drinking water and sunscreen. Safety helmets are provided, as are stinger suits in season, and a minimum of two guides accompanies each ride. Ten-minute kids' pony rides are A\$20. ⊠ *38 Gifford St., Horseshoe Bay* ☎ *07/4778–5109* ⊕ *www.horseshoebayranch.com.au* ⛴ *From A\$20.*

SNORKELING AND SCUBA DIVING

FAMILY

Pleasure Divers. The local guides at Pleasure Divers run good-value dive trips to the SS *Yongala* shipwreck and pristine Lodestone Reef on the outer Barrier Reef as well as snorkeling and diving in the waters off Magnetic Island. Day trips include two dives and buffet lunch. Optional introductory dives, adventure diving, and guided dives (compulsory for those with fewer than 15 logged dives) cost extra. Reef dive and snorkel trips run Tuesday, Thursday, Friday, and Sunday; *Yongala* trips run Wednesday and Saturday, departing Nelly Bay Ferry Terminal and Townsville. Pleasure Divers run various SSI/PADI-accredited courses from the island, including refresher sessions and three-day, four-dive

Open Water courses. ✉ *10 Marine Parade, Arcadia* ☎ *07/4778–5788* ⊕ *www.pleasuredivers.com.au* ✉ *From A$125.*

TOAD RACES

FAMILY **Arcadia Village Motel Toad Races.** A Magnetic Island institution, the Arcadia Village Motel weekly toad races offer cut-price, Aussie-style hilarity. After each race, the winners kiss their toads and collect the proceeds, with funds raised going to the Arcadia Surf Life Saving Club. The Arcadia's cane-toad races have been held every Wednesday night from 8 pm for nearly three decades, despite several changes in the hotel's ownership. Even when the toads aren't racing, the hotel is pumping, with three well-patronized bars, regular live bands, pool tables, and bistro meals. ✉ *Arcadia Village Motel, 7 Marine Parade, Arcadia* ☎ *07/4778–5177* ⊕ *www.arcadiavillage.com.au.*

WATER SPORTS

FAMILY **Adrenalin Jet Ski Tours.** This operator offers tours through Magnetic Island's clear waters on SeaDoo 4-stroke Jet Skis. Choose between the three-hour island circumnavigation and the 90-minute "Top End" tour, with up to two people on each ski. All equipment and instruction are included in the rate; no licenses required. ✉ *9 Pacific Dve., Horseshoe Bay* ☎ *07/4778–5533, 0407/785–533 after hrs.*

FAMILY **Horseshoe Bay Watersports.** This outfitter can take you tube-riding, wakeboarding, waterskiing, and sailing on a Hobie cat in the translucent waters of Horseshoe Bay. All tube rides are for a minimum of two people and start from A$15 per person for an exhilarating 10 minutes; an extra person can ride for free in the ski boat to take pictures. Horseshoe Bay Watersports also rents out an array of water-sports gear and equipment. Find them beside the boat ramp at the center of Horseshoe Bay, weather permitting. ✉ *Boat ramp, Pacific Dr., at Horseshoe Bay Rd., Horseshoe Bay* ☎ *07/4758–1336* ⊕ *www.sailsonhorseshoe.com. au* ✉ *From A$15.*

8

WHERE TO STAY

Magnetic Island began "life" as a holiday-home getaway for Townsville residents; only in the past decade has it attracted the kind of large-scale development that has transformed other islands near the Barrier Reef. Accommodations here are a mix of functional 1970s properties; small budget lodges; and newer, upmarket but relatively small apartment complexes and resorts. Luxurious Peppers Blue on Blue Resort is one of a handful of exceptions to the rule.

$$ 🏨 **Peppers Blue On Blue Resort.** The hotel and studio rooms, apartments, RESORT and penthouse suites at waterfront Blue on Blue are stylishly designed, FAMILY with high-end entertainment systems, luxe amenities, and balconies overlooking the ferry port, pool or the island's private marina. **Pros:** fine on-site food and wine; terrific pools; convenient launchpad for excursions. **Cons:** some suites lack full elevator access; lower-floor, ferry-side rooms can be noisy; limited Wi-Fi access. ⑤ *Rooms from: A$240* ✉ *123 Sooning St., adjacent to ferry terminal, Nelly Bay* ☎ *07/4758–2400 reception, 1300/663786 reservations (toll-free in Australia)* ⊕ *www. peppers.com.au/blue-on-blue* ⇲ *60 twin rooms, 127 apartment suites and penthouses* ⧚ *No meals.*

$$ ⛴ **Sails on Horseshoe.** This unassuming low-rise complex has a prime
HOTEL   location on Horseshoe Bay, where visitors can stroll across the road to
FAMILY   snorkel, hire kayaks, take Jet Ski tours, and ride horses along the sand.
Pros: welcoming, helpful hosts; terrific beachfront location; free use of
pool toys, beach chairs, umbrellas, a mini-Moke, and two motor scoot-
ers; palm-shaded grounds full of rainbow lorikeets. **Cons:** dated fur-
nishings; fee for Wi-Fi; pool area can be noisy. ⑤ *Rooms from: A$230*
✉ *13–15 Pacific Dr., opposite beach, Horseshoe Bay* ☎ *07/4778–5117*
⊕ *www.sailsonhorseshoe.com.au* ⟲ *2 studios, 2 villas, 10 townhouse
apartments* ⏺ *No meals.*

ADELAIDE AND SOUTH AUSTRALIA

WELCOME TO ADELAIDE AND SOUTH AUSTRALIA

TOP REASONS TO GO

★ **Arts and Music:** South Australia has fantastic events: the Adelaide Fringe Festival, Come Out Children's Festival, and the WOMADelaide celebration to name a few.

★ **Bush Tucker:** The Australian palate has been reeducated in the pleasures of bush tucker: kangaroo, crocodile, and emu, are now embraced by all.

★ **Historic Homes:** Stay in the historic properties in North Adelaide and the Adelaide Hills, with easy access to the city, rustic villages, and the vineyards.

★ **Wonderful Wines:** The top-notch wines of the Barossa Region, Clare Valley, McLaren Vale, Adelaide Hills, and Coonawarra are treasured by connoisseurs.

★ **Wildlife:** Kangaroo Island is Australia's third largest island and home to colonies of fur seals, sea lions and penguins, thousands of koalas, and roughly half a million wallabies.

1 Adelaide. Heritage buildings line the small but perfectly formed center of South Australia's capital city. A diverse range of attractions, eateries, and bars makes the city a livelier option than its reputation would suggest.

2 The Barossa Wine Region. One of the country's best-known wine regions—expect rolling hills, delicious local produce, and some of the best Shiraz in the world.

3 The Clare Valley. Less visited than the Barossa. Riesling fans should meander through the valley, tasting as they go while enjoying some spectacular views of the Flinders Ranges.

4 Fleurieu Peninsula. Wine buffs on a short time frame shouldn't miss beautiful McLaren Vale and its amenable cellar doors, while beautiful beaches and dramatic cliff walks are only a short drive away.

GETTING ORIENTED

South Australia encompasses both the dry hot north of the Outback and the greener, more temperate south coast. The green belt includes Adelaide and its surrounding hills and orchards, the Barossa and Clare Valley vineyards, the beautiful Fleurieu Peninsula, and the cliffs and lagoons of the mighty Murray, Australia's longest river. Offshore, residents of Kangaroo Island live at a delightfully old-fashioned pace, savoring their domestic nature haven.

9

5 Kangaroo Island.
Remote, beautiful, and just verging on the right side of isolated, Australia's third-largest island is a paradise for animal lovers, and also offers some of the world's coolest accommodation.

6 The Outback. Heading north, a trip to South Australia's Outback gives visitors a glimpse into an arid and dramatic landscape that is unmistakably Australian.

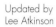
Updated by
Lee Atkinson

Renowned for its celebrations of the arts, its multiple cultures, and its bountiful harvests from vines, land, and sea, South Australia is both diverse and divine. Here you can taste some of the country's finest wines, sample its best restaurants, and admire some of the world's most valuable gems. Or skip the state's sophisticated options and unwind on wildlife-rich Kangaroo Island, hike in the Flinders Ranges, or live underground like opal miners in the vast Outback.

Spread across a flat saucer of land between the Mt. Lofty ranges and the sea, the capital city of Adelaide is easy to explore. The wide streets of its 1½-square-km (½-square-mile) city center are organized in a simple grid that's ringed with parklands. The plan was laid out in 1836 by William Light, the colony's first surveyor-general, making Adelaide the only early-Australian capital not built by English convict labor. Today Light's plan is recognized as being far ahead of its time. This city of 1.25 million still moves at a leisurely pace, free of the typical urban menace of traffic jams thanks to Light's insistence that all roads be wide enough to turn a cannon.

Nearly 90% of South Australians live in the fertile south around Adelaide, because the region stands on the very doorstep of the harshest, driest land in the most arid of Earth's populated continents. Jagged hills and stony deserts fill the parched interior, which is virtually unchanged since the first settlers arrived. Desolate terrain and temperatures that top 48°C (118°F) have thwarted all but the most determined efforts to conquer the land. People who survive this region's challenges do so only through drastic measures, such as in the far-northern opal-mining town of Coober Pedy, where residents live underground.

Still, the deserts hold great surprises, and many clues to the country's history before European settlement. The ruggedly beautiful Flinders Ranges north of Adelaide hold Aboriginal cave paintings and fossil remains from when the area was an ancient seabed. Lake Eyre, a great salt lake, fills with water, on average, only four times each century, but when it does hundreds of thousands of birds flock to the area to breed, creating quite a spectacle. The Nullarbor ("treeless") Plain stretches west across state lines in its tirelessly flat, ruthlessly arid march into Western Australia.

Yet South Australia is, perhaps ironically, gifted with the good life. It produces most of the nation's wine, and the sea ensures a plentiful supply of lobster and famed King George whiting. Cottages and guesthouses tucked away in the countryside around Adelaide are among the most charming and relaxing in Australia. Farther afield, unique experiences like watching seal pups cuddle with their mothers on Kangaroo Island would warm any heart. South Australia may not be grand in reputation, but its attractions are extraordinary, and after a visit you'll know you've indulged in one of Australia's best-kept secrets.

PLANNER

WHEN TO GO

Adelaide has the least rainfall of all Australian capital cities, and the midday summer heat is oppressive. The Outback in particular is too hot for comfortable touring during this time, but Outback winters are pleasantly warm. South Australia's national parks are open year-round. The best times to visit are in spring and autumn. In summer extreme fire danger may close walking tracks, and in winter heavy rain can make some roads impassable. Boating on the Murray River and Lake Alexandrina is best from October to March, when the long evenings are bathed in soft light. The ocean is warmest from December to March.

PLANNING YOUR TIME

Many of the state's attractions are an easy drive from Adelaide. However, for a taste of the real South Australia a trip to a national park or to the Outback is definitely worth the extra travel time. Short flights between destinations make any journey possible within a day or overnight, but the more time you leave yourself to explore the virtues of this underrated state, the better.

If you have limited time, spend your first day in Adelaide enjoying the museums and historic sights, as well as the bustling Central Market. Take a sunset stroll along the Torrens, then have dinner and drinks at one of the city's vibrant restaurants or wine bars. Spend the night, then on Day 2 tour the Adelaide Hills, strolling the streets of 19th-century villages and taking in the panorama from atop Mt. Lofty. Stay the night in a charming bed-and-breakfast in one of the region's small towns, or come back down to North Adelaide and rest among the beautiful sandstone homes. Save Day 3 for wine tasting in the Barossa Region.

If you have more time, expand your horizons beyond Adelaide and take a tram-car ride to the beach at touristy Glenelg or its neighbors at laid back Brighton or posher Henley Beach, where you can laze on the white sands and dine at tasty outposts. Spend the night here or at a B&B on the Fleurieu Peninsula, then take Day 3 to explore the vineyards and catch the ferry to Kangaroo Island. After a night here, use Day 4 to explore and appreciate the island's wildlife and untamed beauty. Return to Adelaide in the afternoon on Day 5 and drive up to the Adelaide Hills for sunset at Mt. Lofty.

GETTING HERE AND AROUND
AIR TRAVEL
Adelaide Airport, 15 minutes from the city center, is a pleasant place to fly into and the state's main hub. The international and domestic terminals share a modern building complete with cafés, a tourist office, and free Wi-Fi.

International airlines serving Adelaide include Singapore Airlines, Malaysia Airlines, Cathay Pacific, Air New Zealand, Virgin Australia, Jetstar, and Emirates. Qantas also connects Adelaide with many international cities (usually via Melbourne or Sydney). Domestic airlines flying into Adelaide include Qantas, Jetstar, REX/Regional Express, Tigerair, and Virgin Australia. You can also fly to Coober Pedy and Kangaroo Island from here.

BUS TRAVEL
Adelaide's Central Bus Station is the state's main hub for travel across the region as well as interstate services to Melbourne and Sydney. It's difficult and time-consuming to travel by bus to the wine regions, however; we recommend either renting a car or taking a tour.

CAR TRAVEL
The best way to experience this diverse state is by road. In general, driving conditions are excellent, although minor lanes are unpaved. It's two hours from Adelaide to the Barossa and Clare, the southern coast, and most other major sights, and less than an hour to McLaren Vale's wineries. The most direct route to the Flinders Ranges is via the Princes Highway and Port Augusta, but a more interesting route takes you through the Clare Valley vineyards.

TRAIN TRAVEL
If you love train travel, you might find yourself stopping in Adelaide, as two classic train journeys also wind through this state: the *Ghan*, which runs north via Alice Springs to Darwin, and the *Indian Pacific*, which crosses the Nullarbor Plain to reach Perth. More prosaically, you can catch a train to Sydney or Melbourne, though often budget airlines are much cheaper.

RESTAURANTS
Foodies are spoiled for choice in South Australia; the region is famous throughout the country for its excellent produce. Make sure you try some of Adelaide's Mod Oz cuisine, with dishes showcasing oysters, crayfish, and King George whiting prepared with Asian and Mediterranean flavors. Bush foods are also available in some eateries; look for kangaroo, emu, and wattle seed.

Many restaurants close for a few days a week, so call ahead to check. Some upscale institutions require booking well in advance, and tables are tight during major city festivals and holidays.

HOTELS

As well as all the standard chains, South Australia is packed with delightful lodgings in contemporary studios, converted cottages, and grand mansions. Modern resorts sprawl along the coastal suburbs, the Barossa Valley, and other tourist centers, but intimate properties for 10 or fewer guests can easily be found.

There is plenty of competition in Adelaide, so shop around for great deals. Outside the city, weekday nights are usually less expensive and two-night minimum bookings often apply. *Hotel reviews have been shortened. For full information, visit Fodors.com.*

WHAT IT COSTS (IN AUSTRALIAN DOLLARS)			
$	**$$**	**$$$**	**$$$$**
Restaurants	Under A$21	A$21–A$35	A$36–A$50	over A$50
Hotels	Under A$151	A$151–A$200	A$201–A$300	over A$300

Restaurant prices are the average cost of a main course at dinner or, if dinner is not served, at lunch. Hotel prices are the lowest cost of a standard double room in high season, excluding service and tax.

WINERIES

Oenophiles rejoice: in South Australia you've arrived in wine heaven. SA is the country's wine powerhouse, producing most of the nation's wine and boasting some of the oldest vineyards in the world. Thanks to its diverse geography and climate, the region produces a huge range of grape varieties—from cool-climate Rieslings in the Clare Valley to the big, full-bodied Shiraz wines of the world-famous Barossa. Less well known, McLaren Vale now punches above its weight with an exceptional variety of grapes, including Merlot, Chardonnay, and Cabernet Sauvignon, while just a 20-minute drive from Adelaide is Adelaide Hills, where temperatures are lower than the rest of the region, leading to great sparkling wines and Pinot Noir.

Although you can drive yourself to any of these regions, strict drunk driving laws mean that the unfortunate designated driver will be restricted to a few sips, if that. We highly recommend that you leave the driving to professionals.

Fodor's Choice ★ **A Taste of South Australia.** For a luxurious tour option in the region, go with Mary Anne Kennedy, the owner of A Taste of South Australia, who is one of the most knowledgeable regional food and wine guides. Her boutique tours of any region you choose with lunch (four hours A$596; minimum two people, max four) are a taste treat. ☎ 08/8371–3553, 0419/861–588 ⊕ www.tastesa.com.au.

ADELAIDE

Australians think of Adelaide as a city of churches, but Adelaide has outgrown its reputation as a sleepy country town dotted with cathedrals and spires. The Adelaide of this millennium is infinitely more complex, with a large, multiethnic population and thriving urban art and music scenes supported by a "space activation program" that encourages pop-up shops, markets, performances, street food, minifestivals, art exhibitions, and other "off-the-cuff" experiences in the city's underutilized streets and public spaces.

Bright and clean, leafy and beautiful Adelaide is a breeze to explore, with a grid pattern of streets encircled by parkland. The heart of the greenbelt is divided by the meandering River Torrens, which passes the Festival Centre in its prettiest stretch.

GETTING HERE AND AROUND

A car gives you the freedom to discover the country lanes and villages in the hills region outside the city, and Adelaide also has excellent road connections with other states. But South Australia is a big place, and we recommend flying if you're looking to save time. Adelaide has an excellent bus system, including the no-cost Adelaide Free City Connector buses, which make about 30 downtown stops. Free guides to Adelaide's public bus lines are available from the Adelaide Metro Info Centre. The city's only surviving tram route now runs between the Entertainment Centre in Hindmarsh through the city to the beach at Glenelg. Ticketing is identical to that on city buses; travel between South Terrace and the Entertainment Centre on Port Road is free.

Taxi Suburban Taxis. ☎ *13–1008* ⊕ *www.suburbantaxis.com.au.* **Yellow Cabs.** ☎ *13–2227* ⊕ *www.yellowadelaide.com.au.*

TOURS

Adelaide Sightseeing. Adelaide Sightseeing operates a morning city sights tour. The company also runs a daily afternoon bus tour of the Adelaide Hills and the German village of Hahndorf. ✉ *85 Franklin St.* ☎ *1300/769762* ⊕ *www.adelaidesightseeing.com.au* 🎫 *From A$66.*

Adelaide Visitor Information Centre. Free 30- to 45-minute city orientation walking tours depart from here on weekdays at 9:30 am. No bookings needed. ✉ *James Pl., just off Rundle Mall, City Center* ☎ *1300/588140* ⊕ *www.rundlemall.com* 🎫 *Free.*

Gray Line Adelaide. Gray Line Adelaide provides morning city tours that take in all the highlights. ✉ *85 Franklin St.* ☎ *1300/858687* ⊕ *www.grayline.com.au* 🎫 *Morning tours from A$65; full-day tours from A$99.*

Tourabout Adelaide. Tourabout Adelaide has private tours with tailored itineraries. Prices run from around A$100 per person for a two-hour city heritage walk to A$600 for a daylong excursion to the Barossa Valley, which includes private wine tastings and lunch. ✉ *Wellington Business Centre, 2 Portrush Rd., Suite 24, Payneham* ☎ *08/8365–1115, 0408/809–232* ⊕ *www.touraboutadelaide.com.au* 🎫 *From A$100.*

EXPLORING

CITY CENTER

The compact city center is where you'll find most of Adelaide's sights, shops, and grand stately buildings: staying here means you're in the heart of the action. North of the Torrens River is North Adelaide, which is dominated by the spires of St. Peter's Cathedral. This genteel

Adelaide

suburb has some great neighborhood restaurants. For fun in the sun, head to touristy Glenelg and its cooler near neighbors, Henley Beach and Brighton. Greater Adelaide has great views over the city at Mt. Lofty and in Port Adelaide; seafaring fans will enjoy the South Australian Maritime Museum.

TOP ATTRACTIONS

FAMILY **Adelaide Zoo.** Australia's second-oldest zoo still retains much of its original architecture. Enter through the 1883 cast-iron gates to see such animals as the giant pandas, Sumatran tigers, Australian rain-forest birds, and chimpanzees housed in modern, natural settings. The zoo is world renowned for its captive breeding and release programs, and rare species including the red panda and South Australia's own yellow-footed rock wallaby are among its successes. In June 2008, the Australian government and Adelaide zoo signed a cooperative agreement to help secure the long-term survival of the giant panda, and in late 2009 Wang Wang and Fu Ni arrived on loan from China to become the only giant pandas in the Southern Hemisphere, and the first to live permanently in Australia. Special VIP panda tours are now also available. Ask at the ticket office about tours and feeding times. ⊠ *Frome Rd., near War Memorial Dr., City Center* ☎ *08/8267–3255* ⊕ *www.adelaidezoo.com.au* ⊠ *A$33.50, kids under 14 A$18.50, families (2 adults, 2–3 kids) A$87.50* ☉ *Daily 9:30–5.*

Art Gallery of South Australia. Many famous Australian painters, including Charles Conder, Margaret Preston, Clifford Possum Tjapaltjarri, Russell Drysdale, and Sidney Nolan, are represented in here. Extensive Renaissance and British artworks are on display, and the atrium houses Aboriginal pieces. There is usually a visiting exhibition, too. A café and bookshop are also on-site. ⊠ *North Terrace, near Pulteney St., City Center* ☎ *08/8207–7000* ⊕ *www.artgallery.sa.gov.au* ☉ *Daily 10–5.*

FAMILY
Fodor'sChoice
★
Botanic Gardens of Adelaide. These magnificent formal gardens include an international rose garden, giant water lilies, an avenue of Moreton Bay fig trees, acres of green lawns, and duck ponds. The Bicentennial Conservatory—the largest single-span glass house in the southern hemisphere—provides an environment for lowland rain-forest species such as the cassowary palm and torch ginger. Daily free guided tours leave from the Visitor Information Centre in the Schomburgk Pavilion at 10:30; or download the free app for a self-guided tour. In summer the Moonlight Cinema series (⊕ *www.moonlight.com.au*) screens new, classic, and cult films in Botanic Park, adjacent the garden at sunset; bring a picnic blanket and a bottle of wine. Tickets sell fast, so plan ahead. ⊠ *Botanic Rd., North Terr., City Center* ☎ *08/8222–9311* ⊕ *www.botanicgardens. sa.gov.au* ⊠ *Gardens/Conservatory Free* ☉ *Gardens: weekdays 7:15 am, weekends 9 am, closing times vary seasonally. Bicentennial Conservatory: daily 10–4 (5 during daylight saving).*

Botanic Gardens of Adelaide

Migration Museum. Chronicled in this converted 19th-century Destitute Asylum, which later in the 19th century served as a school where Aboriginal children were forced to train as servants to the British, are the origins, hopes, and fates of some of the millions of immigrants who settled in Australia during the past two centuries. The museum is starkly realistic, and the bleak welcome that awaited many migrants is graphically illustrated. ⊠ *82 Kintore Ave., City Center* ☎ *08/8207–7580* ⊕ *migration.history.sa.gov.au* ⊘ *Weekdays 10–5, weekends 1–5.*

Parliament House. Ten Corinthian columns are the most striking features of this classical parliament building. It was completed in two stages 50 years apart: the west wing in 1889 and the east wing in 1939. Alongside is **Old Parliament House,** which dates from 1843. There's a free guided tour of both houses weekdays at 10 and 2 during nonsitting days. The viewing gallery is open to the public when parliament is sitting. ⊠ *North Terrace, at King William St., City Center* ☎ *08/8237–9467* ⊕ *www.parliament.sa.gov.au.*

St. Peter's Cathedral. The spires and towers of this cathedral dramatically contrast with the nearby city skyline. St. Peter's is the epitome of Anglican architecture in Australia, and an important example of grand Gothic Revival. Free 45-minute guided tours are available Wednesday at 11 and Sunday at 12:30. ⊠ *27 King William St., North Adelaide* ☎ *08/8267–4551* ⊕ *www.stpeters-cathedral.org.au* ⊘ *Daily services Sun.–Fri.*

South Australian Museum. This museum's Australian Aboriginal Cultures Gallery houses 3,000 items, including ceremonial dress and paintings from the Pacific Islands. Old black-and-white films show traditional

An exhibition at the Pacific Cultures Gallery, Adelaide

dancing, and touch screens convey desert life. Also in the museum are an exhibit commemorating renowned Antarctic explorer Sir Douglas Mawson, after whom Australia's main Antarctic research station is named; an Opal-Fossils Gallery housing the fantastic opalized partial skeleton of a 19-foot-long plesiosaur; and a biodiversity gallery. There's also a café overlooking a grassy lawn. If you are traveling during local school holidays, there are fantastic interactive craft and education activities for children for a small fee. ⊠ *North Terrace, near Gawler Pl., City Center* ☎ *08/8207–7500* ⊕ *www.samuseum.sa.gov.au* ⊙ *Daily 10–5; tours weekdays at 11, weekends at 2 and 3.*

Fodor's Choice
★

Tandanya Aboriginal Cultural Institute. A must-see, Tandanya is the first major Aboriginal cultural facility of its kind in Australia. You'll find high-quality changing exhibitions of works by Aboriginal artists and a theater where you can watch cultural performances and shows by visiting artists from around the country and Pacific Islands. A highlight is the Spirit Festival in March. There's a great gift shop, too, where you can buy CDs of local music. ⊠ *253 Grenfell St., City Center* ☎ *08/8224–3200* ⊕ *www.tandanya.com.au* ✉ *Free entry to galleries; fee for performances* ⊙ *Mon.–Sat. 10–5.*

Victoria Square/Tarntanyangga. The geographical center of the city this newly made-over public space is the city's focal point and a popular meeting spot. The fountain in the square, which is floodlighted at night, celebrates the three rivers that supply Adelaide's water: the Torrens, Onkaparinga, and Murray are each represented by a stylized man or woman paired with an Australian native bird. The park hosts many events and attracts lunching office workers while shoppers and tourists come and go from the Glenelg-City Tram, which stops here on its way through the city. ☒ *King William, Grote, and Wakefield Sts., City Center* ⊕ *www.adelaidecitycouncil.com.*

WORTH NOTING

Adelaide Town Hall. An imposing building constructed in 1863 in Renaissance style, the Town Hall was modeled after buildings in Genoa and Florence. Tours visit the Colonel Light Room, where objects used to map and plan Adelaide are exhibited, and there are frequently traveling art exhibitions. The balcony of the Town Hall is famous for the appearance of the Beatles in 1964, which attracted the venue's largest crowd to date: approximately 300,000 screaming fans. ☒ *128 King William St., City Center* ☎ *08/8203–7590* ⊕ *www.adelaidetownhall. com.au* ☉ *Weekdays 9–5; free tours available on select Mon. at 10, bookings required.*

Ayers House. Between 1855 and 1897 this sprawling colonial structure was the home of Sir Henry Ayers, South Australia's premier and the man for whom Uluru was originally named Ayers Rock. Most rooms—including the unusual Summer Sitting Room, in the cool of the basement—have been restored with period furnishings and the state's best examples of 19th-century costumes and lifestyle. Guided tours cost A$10 and depart on the hour, every hour. ☒ *288 North Terr., City Center* ☎ *08/8223–1234* ⊕ *www.ayershousemuseum.org.au* 🏷 *A$5, kids under 12 free* ☉ *Daily 10–5.*

National Wine Centre of Australia. Timber, steel, and glass evoke the ribs of a huge wine barrel, and a soaring, open-plan concourse make this a spectacular showcase for Australian wines set in the Botanic Gardens. The Wine Discovery Journey takes you from neolithic pottery jars to a stainless-steel tank; you can even make your own virtual wine on a touch-screen computer. The Centre's Cellar Door offers tastings of more than 120 of Australia's most iconic wines, including the famous Penfold's Grange and Henschke's Hill of Grace: tastings start at A$2.50 per pour. The Wined Bar has a good all-day menu, including a great selection of local cheeses and smoked meats. ☒ *Corner of Hackney and Botanic Rds., City Center* ☎ *08/8313–3355* ⊕ *www.wineaustralia.com. au* ☉ *Weekdays 8–7, weekends 9–5.*

St. Francis Xavier's Cathedral. This church faced a bitter battle over construction after the 1848 decision to build a Catholic cathedral. It's now a prominent, decorative church with a soaring nave, stone arches through to side aisles with dark-wood ceilings, and beautiful stained-glass windows. ☒ *17 Wakefield St., at Victoria Sq., City Center* ☎ *08/8232–8688* ⊕ *www.adelcathparish.org* ☉ *Mass weekdays 8 am, 12:10, and 5:45 pm; Sat. 8 and 11:30 am; Sun. 7, 9, 11 am, and 6 pm.*

GREATER ADELAIDE

TOP ATTRACTIONS

Coopers Brewery. Founded by Thomas Cooper in 1862, this is Australia's only large-scale, independent, family-owned brewery. The Coopers beer story began when Thomas tried to create a tonic for his ailing wife, Ann, but instead created his first batch of beer. Customers grew in numbers as Thomas hand-delivered his all-natural ales and stout by horse and cart; the tradition lives on with guest appearances at special events by Clydesdayles drawing the very same cart that Thomas once used. You can take guided tours (A$27.50) of the brewhouse and enjoy tastings of the award-winning signature Coopers ales, including Coopers Pale Ale, Coopers Sparkling Ale, and Coopers Stout, in the museum posttour. The museum features a display of the historic horse and cart, vintage Coopers delivery truck, and pictorials showcasing the history of the brewery. ⊠ *461 South Rd., Regency Park* ☎ *08/8440–1800* ⊕ *www. coopers.com.au* ⊡ *A$27.50 (A$25 is donated to charity)* ☉ *Guided tours Tues.–Fri. 1 pm* ☞ *Must be over 18 and wearing closed-toe shoes.*

FAMILY **National Railway Museum.** Steam-train buffs will love this collection of locomotives and rolling stock in the former Port Adelaide railway yard. The largest of its kind in Australia, the collection includes enormous "mountain"-class engines and the "Tea and Sugar" train, once the lifeline for camps scattered across the deserts of South and Western Australia. For an additional cost take a ride on the historic Semaphore to Fort Glanville Tourist Railway; it runs every Sunday and public holiday from October to end of April and daily during school holidays. ⊠ *76 Lipson St., Port Adelaide* ☎ *08/8341–1690* ⊕ *www.natrailmuseum.org.au* ⊡ *A$12, kids 3–15 A$6, family (2 adults plus 2–3 kids) A$32* ☉ *Daily 10–4:30.*

Fodor's Choice **Penfolds Magill Estate.** Founded in 1844 by immigrant English doctor
★ Christopher Rawson Penfold, this is the birthplace of Australia's most famous wine, Penfolds Grange, and one of the world's only city wineries. Introduced in 1951, Grange is the flagship of a huge stable of wines priced from everyday to special-occasion (collectors pay thousands of dollars to complete sets of Grange). Take the Magill Estate Heritage Tour (10 am, 1, and 4 daily); if you're a serious wine lover take the Ultimate Penfolds Tour and visit the original Penfold family cottage and the winery to enjoy some premium wine tastings. ⊠ *78 Penfold Rd., Magill* ☎ *08/8301–5400* ⊕ *www.penfolds.com* ⊡ *Magill Heritage Tour A$20, Ultimate Penfold Experience A$150* ☉ *Daily 9–6.*

WORTH NOTING

FAMILY **The Beachouse.** This theme park, located on the Glenelg foreshore overlooking Holdfast Bay, is fun for children of all ages. There are waterslides, bumper cars, bumper boats, arcade games, minigolf, a miniature train (that children under 35 inches can ride), a modest Ferris wheel, and a carousel serving visitors to Glenelg for more than 120 years. Admission is free but Fun Cards are used to purchase credits for use on the rides. ⊠ *Colley Terr., Glenelg* ☎ *08/8295–1511* ⊕ *www.thebeachouse. com.au* ⊡ *Power Hour of amusement rides from A$39 (70 minutes)* ☉ *Mon. 9:30–6, Tues.–Thurs. 10–6, Fri. 10–10, Sat. 9–10, Sun. 9–9.*

FAMILY **South Australian Maritime Museum.** Inside a restored stone warehouse, this museum brings maritime history vividly to life with ships' figureheads, shipwreck relics, and intricate scale models. In the basement you can lie in a bunk bed aboard an 1840s immigrant ship and hear passengers telling of life and death on their journeys to South Australia. In addition to the warehouse displays, the museum includes a lighthouse (worth climbing the 75 steps up to see the view), restored steam tug, and a WWII tender at the nearby wharf. ⊠ *126 Lipson St., Port Adelaide*

☎ *08/8207–6255* ✉ *A$10, children A$5, family A$25 (2 adults and up to 5 children) includes lighthouse entry* ☼ *Museum, daily 10–5; lighthouse, weekdays 10–2, weekends 10:30–4.*

BEACHES

Adelaide's beaches offer something for everyone. From North Haven in the north to Sellicks Beach in the south, most beaches are located less than 30 minutes from the city center. Glenelg Beach is the main tourist attraction framed by restaurants, bars, and attractions. Farther south the hills meet the sea as beaches jut out from cliff faces providing great swimming, fishing, and surfing spots.

FAMILY

Fodor's Choice

★

Glenelg Beach. Located just 10 km (6 miles) from the Adelaide city center, Glenelg is a charming beachside suburb known for its sandy beach, historic jetty, serene marinas, bustling shops, hotels, restaurants, bars, and The Beachhouse entertainment complex. Trams lead the way to the beach carrying passengers along Jetty Road from the city while pedestrians weave in and out of the various retail outlets that line the strip. A day trip to Glenelg is a must, but this seaside resort setting offers plenty of options for backpackers to more discerning travelers to make this their Adelaide base. The beach is large, sandy, and the waters are calm. But expect to see large crowds on hotter days and, depending on the season, seaweed can be a problem. **Amenities:** food and drink; lifeguards; parking; showers; toilets; water sports. **Best for:** sunrise; sunset; swimming; walking; windsurfing. ⊠ *Jetty Rd., Glenelg* ⊹ *Trams run approximately every 20 min from downtown* ☎ *08/8294–5833 Glenelg Visitor's Centre* ⊕ *www.glenelgsa.com.au.*

FAMILY

Henley Beach. The beach in this quiet coastal suburb offers white sand, gently lapping waves, summer entertainment, and a square known for popular dining spots. You'll find families spread out along the sand, and there are places on the grassy areas to enjoy picnics. The jetty is perfect for walking or fishing—drop a line in the water and try your luck. During summer, Henley Beach Square bordering the center of the beach itself comes alive with live music and festivals while eateries along Henley Beach Road bring the world to your plate—Asian, African, Mediterranean, and Indian mix with local cuisine. **Amenities:** food and drink; parking; toilets. **Best for:** swimming; sunrise; sunset; walking; windsurfing. ⊠ *Esplanade, Henley Beach* ☎ *08/8408–1111 City of Charles Sturt.*

9

SPORTS AND THE OUTDOORS

AUSTRALIAN RULES FOOTBALL

Adelaide Oval. The stadium received a state-of-the-art upgrade in 2013 and is now the dual home for cricket and Australian Rules Football—South Australia's most popular winter sport. The Aussie Rules season runs March to September. Cricket season is October–March. Tours of the historic stadium operate on nonevent days. ⊠ *War Memorial Dr., North Adelaide* ☎ *08/8205–4700* ⊕ *www.adelaideoval.com.au* ✉ *Tours: adults A$22, children A$12* ☼ *Tours depart weekdays 10, 11, and 2, extra tour on weekends at 1 pm.*

BASKETBALL

Adelaide Arena (Titanium Security Arena). The home stadium for the Adelaide 36ers of the National Basketball League and the Adelaide Lightning of the Womens National Basketball League. Located in Findon, an inner western suburb of Adelaide, Adelaide Arena is the largest purpose-built basketball arena in Australia. The NBL season runs from October to February. ⊠ *44A Crittenden Rd., Findon* ☎ *08/8268–3592* ⊕ *www.titaniumarena.com.au.*

BICYCLING

Adelaide's parks, flat terrain, and uncluttered streets make it a perfect city for two-wheel exploring.

Tour Down Under. The first stop on the world cycling calendar, in January, the Tour Down Under attracts riders from all over the world as part of the UCI Pro Tour. Outside of the Tour de France, the event attracts the biggest crowds in the world for eight days, taking in metropolitan and regional South Australia. ⊠ *Victoria Sq.* ☎ *08/8463–4701* ⊕ *www. tourdownunder.com.au.*

CRICKET

Bradman Collection Museum. Cricket season is October–March, and the main venue for interstate and international competition is the Adelaide Oval. It's also home to the new purpose-built Bradman Collection Museum, dedicated to the legendary Sir Donald Bradman. He's celebrated as the greatest batsman in the history of cricket and he lived in Adelaide for much of his life. ⊠ *Adelaide Oval, War Memorial Dr. and King William St., North Adelaide* ☎ *08/8300–3800* ⊕ *www. adelaideoval.com.au* ⊗ *Closed weekends and event days.*

GOLF

North Adelaide Golf Course. A 10-minute walk outside of the city, the North Adelaide Golf Course—reputed to be one of the most picturesque golf settings in the country with game-distracting views of the city— runs one short (par 3) and two 18-hole courses. You can rent clubs and carts from the pro shop. Playing hours are dawn to dusk daily. ⊠ *Strangways Terr., North Adelaide* ☎ *08/8203–7888* ⊕ *northadelaidegolf.com. au* ⌦ *Greens fees: North Course: From A$23 weekdays, A$27 weekends; South Course: A$28 weekdays, A$35 weekends* ⚐. *North Course: 18 holes, 4958 yards, par 69; South Course: 18 holes, 6435 yards, par 71.*

SOCCER

Coopers Stadium. Also known as Hindmarsh Stadium, this is a multipurpose venue and the first purpose-built soccer stadium in Australia. It's the home of the Australian A-League soccer team, Adelaide United. The national A-League season runs from October to March; finals are in April. ⊠ *Holden St., Hindmarsh* ☎ *08/8241–7122* ⊕ *www. coopersstadium.com.au.*

WATER SPORTS

The Dolphin Boat. The Dolphin Boat, also known as Temptation, is the first vessel in South Australia to be given a dolphin swim license, which allows you to swim with the cute and friendly animals. The dolphins and tour guides have developed a close relationship over the years, so you're guaranteed to get up close. In fact, if you don't get into the water to swim with the dolphins, they will refund the difference between the watch and the swim. ⊠ *Marina Pier, Holdfast Shores Marina, Glenelg* ☎ *0412/811–838* ⊕ *www.dolphinboat.com.au* 🖃 *From A$24; dolphin swims from A$98.*

FAMILY **SA Aquatic & Leisure Centre.** Located next to Marion Shopping Centre, this state of the art aquatic and recreation facility is designed to bring elite aquatic sport to South Australia. However, the FINA-accredited pools, waterslides, and health club are open to visitors of all ages; there's even dedicated pools for the little ones. ⊠ *443 Morphett Rd., Oaklands Park* ☎ *08/8198–0198* ⊕ *www.saaquatic.ymca.org.au* 🖃 *Adults A$7.70, kids A$6.20, family passes A$23, waterslides A$2 per slide* ⊙ *Weekdays 5 am–10 pm, Sat. 5 am–8 pm, Sun. and holidays 7 am–8 pm.*

WHERE TO EAT

Melbourne, Gouger, O'Connell, and Rundle streets, along with the Norwood Parade and Glenelg neighborhoods, are the main eating strips. In any of these areas it's fun to stroll around until a restaurant or café takes your fancy. Chinatown is also lively, and if you feel like an alfresco picnic, pick some delicious local produce from Central Market.

Use the coordinate (✛ B2) at the end of each listing to locate a site on the corresponding map.

CITY CENTER

$$ ✕ **Amalfi Pizzeria Ristorante.** This place is rustic and noisy. The terrazzo-ITALIAN tile dining room is furnished with bare wooden tables, around which sit professionals and university students in enthusiastic conversation. The paper place-mat menu lists traditional pizza and pasta dishes in two sizes—appetizer and entrée—a must-order is the spaghetti marinara. As this is one of the most popular (read: packed) restaurants in the East End of Rundle Street, reservations are a good idea. Because the restaurant stays open late, it's also popular after a show or a movie. ⑤ *Average main: A$25* ⊠ *29 Frome St., City Center* ☎ *08/8223–1948* ⊙ *Closed Sun. No lunch Sat.* ✛ *C2.*

$ ✕ **Big Table.** Simply the best breakfast choice in Adelaide, Big Table has CAFÉ been at the Central Market for over 20 years, and regulars know to **Fodor's**Choice get there early for a chance at one of the few tables. Sitting up at the ★ counter isn't too bad an option, however, especially when you have treats like fresh banana bread with rhubarb conserve and ricotta to look forward to. The enormous Big Brekkie lives up to its name, and offers quality as well as quantity with delicious thick-sliced local bacon and field mushrooms cooked with pesto and served on Turkish bread. ⑤ *Average main: A$14* ⊠ *Adelaide Central Market, Southern Roadway, Stall 39/40, City Center* ☎ *08/8212–3899* ▬ *No credit cards* ⊙ *Closed Mon. and Sun. No dinner.* ✛ *B3.*

$$$ ✕ **Chianti.** Family-run since 1985, Chianti is all things to all people. ITALIAN Breakfast, lunch, or dinner. Big or small groups. Inside or outside dining. Families mix with business people in the mornings for the

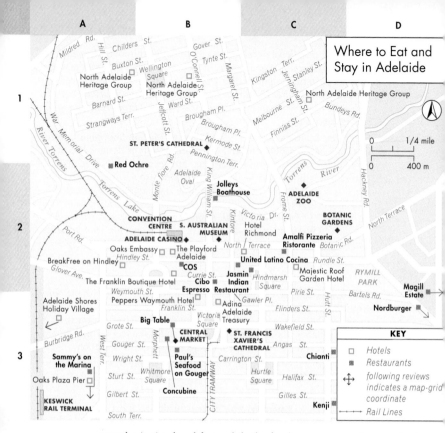

Where to Eat and Stay in Adelaide

KEY

☐	Hotels
■	Restaurants
✛	following reviews indicates a map-grid coordinate
⊢⊢⊢⊢	Rail Lines

award-winning breakfasts while the food connoisseurs show up in the evenings. The northern Italian cuisine is highlighted by the Genovese-style stuffed veal breast and the tagliolini with local blue swimmer crab and chili. But if it's a signature dish you're after, try the sumptuous slow-roasted rabbit with pancetta, port, and sage. ⑤ *Average main: A$38* ⊠ *160 Hutt St., City Center* ☎ *08/8232–7955* ⊕ *chianti.net.au* ✛ *C3.*

$ ✕**Cibo Espresso.** Caffeine addicts head here for a little taste of Italy in
CAFÉ stylish fun surroundings. The small local chain has branches dotted around the city, and in each one you are guaranteed a fabulous espresso from their Wega machines and irresistible sweet treats. If you're there at lunchtime, the freshly baked panini are good, too. All branches have free Wi-Fi. ⑤ *Average main: A$10* ⊠ *82 King William St., Shop 7, City Center* ☎ *08/8410–4088* ⊕ *www.ciboespresso.com.au* ☾ *No dinner. Closed Sun.* ✛ *B2.*

$$ ✕**Concubine.** This restaurant, located in Adelaide's premier Asian dining
CHINESE FUSION strip, features a fusion of modern Chinese dishes with traditional spices and fresh local produce. The food here is sensational; the wine and cocktail lists are intriguing; the service is flawless and friendly; and the ambience is second to none thanks to the funky decor and trendy vibe. The tangy tamarind duck keeps the customers coming back. ⑤ *Average main: A$30* ⊠ *132 Gouger St., City Center* ☎ *08/8212–8288* ⊕ *www. concubine.com.au* ☾ *Closed Mon. No lunch Sat.* ✛ *B3.*

$$$
STEAKHOUSE

✗ **COS.** If you're in need of a fine steak, look no further. Located on trendy Leigh Street, COS is one of Adelaide's best spots for steak and seafood. The simplicity of these steaks—select from a 250-gram grain-fed yearling eye-fillet to a 500-gram rib-eye fillet—served with frites and side salad ensure even lunchers are not too gastronomically challenged. An excellent selection of local and international boutique wines rounds out a complete meal. If seafood is your fancy, there are some excellent oyster options, not to mention signature dishes featuring king prawns, rock lobster, and King George whiting. ⑤ *Average main: A$39* ✉ *18 Leigh St., City Center* ☎ *08/8231–7611* ⊕ *www.18leigh.com.au* ⊗ *Closed Sun.* ✦ *B2.*

$$
INDIAN
Fodor's Choice
★

✗ **Jasmin Indian Restaurant.** Located in a basement off Hindmarsh Square, this elegant establishment is beautifully decorated with stylish timber furniture and local artwork. The dim lighting and relaxing background music really set the mood for some quality Indian cuisine, which is what you'll get in spades—visiting Indian and English cricket teams dine here and you know those guys know a thing or two about good Indian food. You might want to try everything on the menu, and the Feed Me Menu allows for just that, but the Punjabi tandoori lamb and prawn sambal are perennial favorites. The staff are friendly and the service is exceptional. ⑤ *Average main: A$27* ✉ *31 Hindmarsh Sq., City Center* ☎ *08/8223–7837* ⊕ *www.jasmin.com.au* ⊗ *Closed Sun. and Mon. No lunch Sat.–Wed.* ⊜ *Reservations essential* ✦ *C2.*

$$$
MODERN
AUSTRALIAN

✗ **Jolleys Boathouse.** Blue canvas directors' chairs and white-clothed wooden tables create a relaxed, nautical air here—which perfectly suits the location on the south bank of the River Torrens. Sliding glass doors open onto a full-width front balcony for alfresco dining. The imaginative modern Australian menu changes seasonally, but might include a salad of grilled Kangaroo Island marron, green mango, basil, and shallots, or sweet pork belly with red dates. Executives make up most lunch crowds, and warm evenings attract couples. ⑤ *Average main: A$36* ✉ *1 Jolleys La., Corner of Victoria Dr. and King William Rd., City Center* ☎ *08/8223–2891* ⊕ *www.jolleysboathouse.com* ⊗ *No lunch Sat. No dinner Sun.* ⊜ *Reservations essential* ✦ *B2.*

$$
JAPANESE
Fodor's Choice
★

✗ **Kenji.** Kenji, the chef and owner, is one of the few in Australia to hold a license to prepare fugu (pufferfish), so it goes without saying this should be first on your list—you'll experience a great amalgamation of taste, texture, and presentation. Other famous dishes include the extremely fresh sushi and sashimi boat (oysters, sushi, sashimi, pickled fish, etc.), which serves 2–3 people. It's not cheap, but the quality of the food is worth the price, and the daily changing kaiseki eight-course degustation menu is pure genius. ⑤ *Average main: A$35* ✉ *5/242 Hutt St., City Center* ☎ *08/8232–0944* ⊗ *No lunch. Closed Sun.* ✦ *C3.*

$$
CAFÉ

✗ **Paul's Seafood on Gouger.** It may look like your run-of-the-mill fish-and-chip shop, but this Gouger Street veteran of more than 60 years is the place to get hooked on King George whiting. It's been hailed as one of Adelaide's best—and best-priced—seafood restaurants. The salt-and-pepper squid is another local favorite. For a great view of the bustle in the open kitchen, request a table upstairs on the ship's-deck-like mezzanine floor. ⑤ *Average main: A$29* ✉ *79 Gouger St., City Center* ☎ *08/8231–9778* ⊕ *www.paulsongouger.com.au* ✣ *B3.*

$$ ✕**Red Ochre.** A sweeping view of Adelaide is the backdrop for contem-
MODERN porary workings of traditional bush meats such as kangaroo, emu and
AUSTRALIAN wild boar, herbs, and fruits at this riverfront restaurant. The downstairs
River Café, the restaurant's sister venue, is more informal, and offers a
modern Italian menu for lunch weekdays, while Red Ochre is only open
for dinner. For a splurge, head upstairs; if you like your steaks, you'll
love these, served with onion puree and broccolini, bush tomato chim-
michurri, wattle-seeded mustard, pepper berry jam, and confit garlic.
Don't miss the wattle-seed pavlova, Red Ochre's version of Australia's
famous meringue dessert. ⑤ *Average main: A$35* ✉ *War Memorial Dr.,
North Adelaide* ☎ *08/8211–8555* ⊕ *www.redochre.com.au* ☾ *Closed
Sun. No lunch* ⌔ *Reservations essential* ✣ *A2.*

$ ✕**United Latino Cocina.** Long communal tables, funky artwork, and
MEXICAN Mexican tunes typify this tucked-away little restaurant along the side
FAMILY of the new Rundle Place development. Stylishly modern with Mexican
slant, United Latino Cocina (known locally as ULC) is rapidly gaining
momentum. The menu isn't long, but there is a nice variety that ranges
from quesadillas and tacos to chicken wings and less traditional items
such as loose-leaf green tea. Daily specials are always on offer and can
be hard to look past, but the tostadas are well known, as are the fish
taco and the ULC Dog—a chorizo sausage nestled in creamy jalapeño
coleslaw, bean mash, cheese, and onion strings. ⑤ *Average main: A$20*
✉ *off Rundle Mall, 14-16 Francis St., City Center* ☎ *08/8232–0674*
☾ *No dinner Sat.–Thurs.* ✣ *B2.*

GREATER ADELAIDE

$$$$ ✕**Magill Estate.** Do you inhale deeply from your wine glass before drink-
MODERN ing? Do you know your back palate from your front? Then you're ready
AUSTRALIAN to join the wine buffs at this pavilion-style vineyard restaurant that has
the critics across the country raving. The restaurant overlooks vineyards
and the distant city skyline and coast but the food is just as special as
the view. The seasonal menu might include such local delights as KI
marron (a delicious lobster-looking creature typically harvested near
Kangaroo Island), chick weed, young shoots, peas, wood sorrel, and
organic honey, or South Australian abalone with quail or perhaps even
Mayura Wagyu with a sesame emulsion followed by a mouth-water-
ing selection of desserts all made from local produce. The 10-course
tasting menu is A$175 per person; opt to have accompanying wines
selected for you; it costs extra but the experience is well worth it (this
is a vineyard after all). ⑤ *Average main: A$175* ✉ *78 Penfold Rd.,
Magill* ☎ *08/8301–5551* ⊕ *www.magillestaterestaurant.com* ☾ *Closed
Sun–Tues. No lunch Wed. and Thurs.* ⌔ *Reservations essential* ✣ *D3.*

$ ✕**Nordburger.** You won't find too many burgers better than those at
BURGER Nordburger. Just a five-minute drive from the center of town, you'll
find queues of people waiting to sink their teeth into the signature
American-style cheeseburgers and hot dogs—it's so popular that there
are now branches in Hindmarsh and Frewville. The staff are friendly,
service is fast, and people sit at the counter or eat standing up by tall
tables in the back, which combines for quick turnover. Be sure to try the

PB&J milk shake! $ *Average main: A$10* ⊠ *168 The Parade, Norwood* ☎ *08/8331–9923* ⊕ *www.nordburger.com* ✛ *D3.*

$$$ ✕ **Sammy's on the Marina.** Enormous fishbowl windows frame views of
SEAFOOD million-dollar yachts at this restaurant—one of Adelaide's top seafood eateries—at the far end of Glenelg's glitzy Holdfast Marina. Watch the setting sun silhouette playing dolphins or a storm rolling across Gulf St. Vincent as you tuck into skewered scallops or crispy-skin Atlantic salmon wrapped in prosciutto and served over broccolini and baby carrots with salsa verde. The menu here charts South Australia's ocean bounty, and the hot seafood platter (for two people) would feed a school of sharks. $ *Average main: A$38* ⊠ *1–12 Holdfast Promenade, Glenelg* ☎ *08/8376–8211* ⊕ *www.sammys.net.au* ⚓ *Reservations essential* ✛ *A3.*

WHERE TO STAY

At first glance, large international, business-style hotels seem to dominate Adelaide—there's a Hilton, a Hyatt, and a Crowne Plaza—but there's actually a wide choice of places to rest your head. Adelaide's accommodations are a mix of traditional mid-rise hotels, backpacker hostels, an abundance of self-contained apartments, and charming bed-and-breakfasts, many in century-old sandstone buildings. With a car you'll be within easy reach of a Glenelg beach house or an Adelaide Hills B&B.

Use the coordinate (✛ 1:B2) at the end of each listing to locate a site on the corresponding map. For expanded hotel reviews, visit Fodors.com.

CITY CENTER

$$ ☷ **Adina Adelaide Treasury.** Contemporary Italian furnishings in white,
HOTEL slate-gray, and ocher are juxtaposed with 19th-century Adelaide archi-
Fodor's Choice tecture in this stylish Victoria Square hotel. **Pros:** beautiful, classic build-
★ ing with light and airy reception rooms. **Cons:** no on-site parking but parking station nearby. $ *Rooms from: A$195* ⊠ *2 Flinders St., City Center* ☎ *08/8112–0000, 1300/633462* ⊕ *www.tfehotels.com* ⇄ *20 studio rooms, 59 apartments* ❤️ *Some meals* ✛ *B3.*

$ ☷ **BreakFree on Hindley.** Step out your door at this three-story redbrick
HOTEL complex and you might think you're in the tropics; open-air walkways and palm trees suggest you're closer to the beach than the western-parkland end of Hindley Street. **Pros:** great value for money; kitchens are fully equipped for self-catering. **Cons:** basic furnishings; bathrooms could do with a face-lift. $ *Rooms from: A$145* ⊠ *255 Hindley St., City Center* ☎ *08/8217–2500* ⊕ *www.breakfree.com.au* ⇄ *48 studios, 94 2-bedroom apartments* ❤️ *Some meals* ✛ *A2.*

$ ☷ **The Franklin Boutique Hotel.** Situated above the Franklin Hotel—a pub
B&B/INN known for its relaxed, but quirky atmosphere and good food and micro-
Fodor's Choice beers—this hotel is also a little bit different. **Pros:** free in-room snacks
★ (including beer) and Wi-Fi; fun boutique experience; close to Central Market; Franklin Hotel pub is downstairs. **Cons:** limited capacity; potential for noise from the downstairs pub; finding free parking can be difficult. $ *Rooms from: A$150* ⊠ *92 Franklin St., City Center* ☎ *08/8410–0036* ⊕ *www.thefranklinhotel.com.au* ⇄ *7 rooms* ❤️ *Some meals* ✛ *B2.*

9

$ ⛱ **Hotel Richmond.** Situated in the center of Rundle Mall, the city's main
HOTEL shopping strip, the hotel is an original, 1920s art deco building and
Fodor's Choice offers a boutique experience, trendy rooms, and luxurious suites. **Pros:**
★ beautiful, classic building; undercover valet parking; Rundle Mall is
right outside the door; free Wi-Fi. **Cons:** foot traffic in Rundle Mall
and the lively Lounge Bar can be noisy. ⑤ *Rooms from: A$140* ⊠ *128*
Rundle Mall, City Center ☎ *08/8215–4444* ⊕ *www.hotelrichmond.*
com.au ⇌ *30 rooms* ⦿⊘ *All meals* ✛ *B2.*

$$ ⛱ **Majestic Roof Garden Hotel.** Modern and stylish, each room features
HOTEL modern bathrooms, king-size beds, and free Wi-Fi. **Pros:** 50 meters from
FAMILY the restaurants, bars, and shops of Rundle Street; the rooftop garden has
uninterrupted views of the famous Adelaide Hills and East End. **Cons:**
rooms are nondescript. ⑤ *Rooms from: A$165* ⊠ *55 Frome St., City*
Center ☎ *08/8100–4400* ⊕ *www.roofgardenhoteladelaide.com* ⇌ *120*
suites ⦿⊘ *All meals* ✛ *C2.*

$$$ ⛱ **Oaks Embassy.** This hotel is ideally positioned to explore the River
HOTEL Torrens, visit the Adelaide Casino and Adelaide Convention Centre, or
take in the many restaurants and nightlife spots along or surrounding
Hindley Street. **Pros:** good city views; well serviced by public transport;
opposite Adelaide Casino and Adelaide Convention Centre; minutes
from River Torrens, parklands, and Hindley Street entertainment precinct. **Cons:** expensive Wi-Fi. ⑤ *Rooms from: A$215* ⊠ *96 North Terr.,*
Glenelg ☎ *08/8124–9900* ⊕ *www.oakshotelsresorts.com* ⇌ *122 apart-*
ments ⦿⊘ *Some meals* ✛ *B2.*

$$$ ⛱ **Peppers Waymouth Hotel.** Black-tile-and-timber columns frame the
HOTEL Hollywood-glamorous marble lobby of this ultrasleek upscale hotel.
Fodor's Choice **Pros:** five-star facilities; excellent wine list at the restaurant; good loca-
★ tion. **Cons:** tiny gym; more corporate than boutique in feel. ⑤ *Rooms*
from: A$229 ⊠ *55 Waymouth St., City Center* ☎ *08/8115–8888* ⊕ *www.*
peppers.com.au/waymouth ⇌ *167 rooms, 35 suites* ⦿⊘ *Some meals* ✛ *B2.*

$$$ ⛱ **The Playford Adelaide.** MGallery Hotels are always a bit special and
HOTEL the Playford proves the rule with showy chandeliers that illuminate a
Fodor's Choice movie-set-like celebration of art nouveau in the lobby of this luxury
★ hotel. **Pros:** excellent breakfast spread; convivial bar; affordable luxury.
Cons: expensive Internet and parking. ⑤ *Rooms from: A$210* ⊠ *120*
North Terr., City Center ☎ *08/8213–8888* ⊕ *www.accorhotels.com*
⇌ *110 rooms, 72 suites* ⦿⊘ *Some meals* ✛ *B2.*

GREATER ADELAIDE

$$ ⛱ **Adelaide Shores Holiday Village.** The breeze is salty, the lawns are green,
RESORT and white sand is only a few lazy steps from this summery resort on the
FAMILY city's coastal fringe. **Pros:** very family-friendly, with plenty of activities
for kids and well-planned family rooms. **Cons:** bad choice for a roman-
tic break; in peak season service levels drop. ⑤ *Rooms from: A$189*
⊠ *Military Rd., West Beach* ☎ *08/8355–7360* ⊕ *www.adelaideshores.*
com.au ⇌ *22 bungalows, 30 villas, 32 units* ⦿⊘ *No meals* ✛ *A3.*

$$$ ⛱ **North Adelaide Heritage Group.** Tucked into the city's leafy, oldest sec-
RENTAL tion, these 19 lodgings are both beautiful and unique. **Pros:** historic
Fodor's Choice properties in Adelaide's most upscale suburb; friendly owners give help-
★ ful tips on what to do. **Cons:** some properties can be on the dark side;
not child-friendly. ⑤ *Rooms from: A$225* ⊠ *82 Hill St., North Adelaide*

☎ *08/8267–2020* ⊕ *www.adelaideheritage.com* ⌁ *8 cottages, 3 suites, 8 apartments* ⦿*Breakfast* ✛ *A1, B1, C1.*

$$$
RENTAL
⛫ **Oaks Plaza Pier.** Sea air wafts through open balcony doors in this all-apartment complex on Adelaide's favorite beach. **Pros:** steps from the beach; helpful reception staff who are full of advice. **Cons:** corporate feel to the lobby; the bars can get noisy and messy at peak times; expensive Internet. ⑤ *Rooms from: A$206* ⊠ *16 Holdfast Promenade, Glenelg* ☎ *08/8350–6688, 1300/551111* ⊕ *www.oakshotelsresorts.com/oaks-plaza-pier* ⌁ *121 1-bedroom apartments, 34 2-bedroom apartments* ⦿*Some meals* ✛ *A3.*

PERFORMING ARTS

Adelaide truly is the festival state, and with the majority of the major events running at the end of summer in "Mad March," this is the best time to visit, as the city takes on an extra festive feel.

For a listing of performances and exhibitions, look to the entertainment pages of *The Advertiser,* Adelaide's daily newspaper. The *Adelaide Review,* a free monthly arts paper, reviews exhibitions, galleries, and performances, and lists forthcoming events.

BASS Ticket Agency. This agency sells tickets for most live performances. ⊠ *Adelaide Festival Centre, King William St., City Center* ☎ *13–1246* ⊕ *www.bass.net.au.*

ARTS CENTERS

Adelaide Entertainment Centre. Opened in 1991, most major concerts are held here but it also features a mix of everything from music, theater, and other performing arts to conventions and sporting events. ⊠ *98 Port Rd., Hindmarsh* ☎ *08/8208–2222* ⊕ *www.theaec.net.*

Adelaide Festival Centre. This city's major venue for the performing arts. The State Opera, the State Theatre Company of South Australia, and the Adelaide Symphony Orchestra perform here regularly. Performances are in the Playhouse, the Festival and Space theaters, the outdoor amphitheater, and Her Majesty's Theatre at 58 Grote Street. The box office is open weekdays 9–6. ⊠ *King William St., near North Terr., City Center* ☎ *13–1246* ⊕ *www.adelaidefestivalcentre.com.au.*

FESTIVALS

Adelaide Festival of Arts. Australia's oldest arts festival takes place annually for three weeks in February and March. It's a cultural smorgasbord of outdoor opera, classical music, jazz, art exhibitions, film, a writer's festival, and cabaret presented by some of the world's top artists; it's held across the city at a variety of venues. ⊠ *City Center* ☎ *08/8216–4444* ⊕ *www.adelaidefestival.com.au.*

Adelaide Fringe Festival. The Fringe Festival, held over four weeks during mid-February and mid-March, is the second largest of its kind in the world. It's an open-access arts festival featuring cabaret, street performances, comedy, circus, music, visual art, theater, puppetry, dance, and design, all across Adelaide and its surroundings. ⊠ *City Center* ☎ *08/8100–2000* ⊕ *www.adelaidefringe.com.au.*

9

WOMADelaide Festival. The annual four-day festival of world music, arts, and dance takes place in early March and attracts top musicians from all over the world to its stages in the picturesque Botanic Park. ☒ *Botanic Park, Hackney Rd.* ☎ *08/8271–1488* ⊕ *www.womadelaide.com.au.*

NIGHTLIFE

There's something going on every evening in Adelaide, although clubs are especially packed on weekends. Cover charges vary according to the night and time of entry. Nightlife for the coming week is listed in Hit, a pull-out section of Thursday's edition of the *Advertiser.* ⊕ *Ripitup.com.au* is an online music-and-club publication aimed at the younger market.

Bars along Rundle Street, the west end of Hindley Street, and Gouger Street are trendy, while Hindley and Waymouth streets are lined with traditional pubs. North Adelaide's O'Connell Street buzzes every night, and the popular Sunday-evening beer-and-banter sessions really pack in the crowds. There are also a number of vibrant pubs on The Parade at Norwood and the Glenelg precinct, especially popular on a Sunday afternoon in the sun.

CITY CENTER
BARS AND CLUBS
Austral Hotel. The first bar in South Australia to put Coopers beer on tap, the Austral is a local favorite and a great place to drink outdoors. You can down shooters or sip cocktails from a long list while listening to a band play or a DJ spin groovy tunes. It's open daily 11 am–3 am. ☒ *205 Rundle St., City Center* ☎ *08/8223–4660* ⊕ *www.theaustral.com.au.*

Botanic Bar. This cool city cocktail lounge features leather banquettes that encircle the U-shape, marble-top bar. Muddlers (crushed ice drinks) are the specialty, and bring in mostly young professionals, including off-duty medics from the nearby hospital. The menu focuses on Thai street food. Botanic Bar is open until late Tuesday to Sunday. ☒ *309 North Terr., City Center* ☎ *08/8227–0799* ⊕ *www.botanicbar.com.au* ☉ *Closed Mon.*

Casablabla. You'll find this multicultural tapas and lounge bar along trendy Leigh Street, the first of Adelaide's laneways to be rejuvenated. The atmosphere and live entertainment line-up is as unique as the contemporary fusion of South East Asian and Middle Eastern decor. Wednesday night is live Latin night with free salsa lessons. A mild-mannered restaurant by day, it's a pumping club by night. ☒ *12 Leigh St., City Center* ☎ *08/8231–3939* ⊕ *www.casablabla.com* ☉ *Closed Sun. and Mon.*

Fodor's Choice ★ **Clever Little Tailor.** Adelaide has a fascination with small bars and hole-in-the-wall-style venues, and the Clever Little Tailor was one of the city's first. Named after a German fairy tale, the warmth of this place is undeniable. The bar staff is welcoming and helpful and the venue is cozy and charming with its contemporary interior, exposed red bricks, and hanging ferns. The cocktails are delicious, too, and the boutique wine and beer list is impressive. Plus, the music is soft

The Art Gallery of South Australia

enough to chat to your heart's content. ✉ *19 Peel St., City Center* ⊕ *www.cleverlittletailor.com.au* ⊙ *Closed Sun.*

The Curious Squire. Here you can taste freshly brewed beer from the local Australian James Squire range, which is brewed on the premises. Beer is the main game here, although there is also a short cocktail and wine list. The menu is full of pub snacks and bar food with a good choice of BBQ platters, pizzas, and burgers. ✉ *10 O'Connell St., City Center* ☎ *08/7071-5767* ⊕ *www.thecurioussquire.com.au* ⊙ *Closed Mon.*

Grace Emily Hotel. A classic old-school pub, you'll find bartenders spouting the mantra "No pokies, no TAB, no food"—pokies are the poker machines found in many pubs, and TAB, Australia's version of OTB, lets you place bets on horse races—at this multilevel music-lover's watering hole. Instead, there's live music nightly. The beer garden is one of the city's best, with secluded spots for those wanting a quiet tipple and big round tables for groups to drink en masse and alfresco. It's open daily 4 pm until the wee hours. ✉ *232 Waymouth St., City Center* ☎ *08/8231-5500.*

The Grace Establishment. This place is part bar, part restaurant, and part beer garden. At night things get lively and you'll see your fair share of hipsters, posh locals, and the manicured set. The food's good, too. ✉ *127 The Parade, City Center* ☎ *08/8333-1007* ⊕ *www.thegrace.net.au.*

Jack Ruby. Underground, convivial, and very lively, this speakeasy-meets-Mississippi juke joint also has a hint of American diner thanks to the Americana menu. This spot is named after the man who shot Lee Harvey Oswald. Craft beer from the United States and Australia dominate the drinks menu, but if beer isn't your thing, try the spiked milk shakes or the various cocktails on offer. ⊠ *Basement, 89 King William St., City Center* ☎ *08/8231–5795* ⊕ *www.jackruby.com.au* ☾ *Closed Sun.*

The Loft Oyster & Wine Bar. Perched above Gouger Street, The Loft is an eye-catching space that features a beautiful barrel vault ceiling and a stunning mix of dim lighting, heritage fixtures, and modern decor. Oysters come in multiple styles, matched with an international wine list including some hard to find Australian gems. Cocktails here are inspired by recent trends and evoke the feeling of being transported back to the 1920s. ⊠ *128 Gouger St., Level 1, City Center* ☎ *08/8211–8887* ⊕ *www.loftbar.com.au* ☾ *Closed Mon. and Tues.*

Rhino Room. This is the home of Adelaide comedy, featuring an open mike night on Thursday and live shows Friday and Saturday night. Some of Australia's best comedians as well as overseas acts grace the tiny stage; during the annual Fringe Festival you can catch a glimpse of some verified superstars. But it's also a funky little club in its own right, and DJs fill the void when the laughs take a break on other nights. ⊠ *13 Frome St., City Center* ☎ *08/8227–1611* ⊕ *www.rhinoroom.com. au* ☒ *From A$10* ☾ *Closed Sun.–Tues.*

Fodor'sChoice **Udaberri.** One of the first of Adelaide's growing trend of "small bars,"
★ Udaberri is a cozy, intimate setting where some of the city's best wine and beer is served. The narrow space is reminiscent of a barn, but it's a very chic barn. DJs spin their groovy house beats but the music is never overpowering as interaction and conversation is encouraged. If you're lucky enough to beat the crowds to the loft, you can unwind on the sofas while enjoying the view and snacking on Basque-style tapas. ⊠ *11-13 Leigh St., City Center* ☎ *08/8410–5733* ⊕ *www.udaberri.com.au.*

CASINO

SKYCITY Adelaide Casino. Housed in the former railway station, SkyCity is the place to go for big-time casino gaming, including the highly animated Australian Two-up, in which you bet against the house on the fall of two coins. Four bars, including the elegant Chandelier Bar, and six restaurants are also within the complex. It's one of a handful of places in Adelaide that keep pumping until dawn. ⊠ *City Center* ☎ *08/8212–2811* ⊕ *www.adelaidecasino.com.au.*

GREATER ADELAIDE
BARS AND CLUBS

The Gov. The favorite venue of a mixed crowd, young homeowners and long-term regulars come for Irish music sessions, all-weekend metal fests, and everything in between. Cabaret, comedy, Latin music—if you can name it, you can probably hear it here. There's good pub grub, too. ⊠ *59 Port Rd.* ☎ *08/8340–0744* ⊕ *www.thegov.com.au* ☾ *Closed Sun. unless there's a show.*

SHOPPING

If you are wondering where everyone in Adelaide is, you'll find them at Rundle Mall, the city's main shopping strip. Shops in the City Center are generally open Monday–Thursday 9–5:30, Friday 9–9, Saturday 9–5, and Sunday 11–5. Suburban shops are often open until 9 pm on Thursday night instead of Friday. As the center of the world's opal industry, Adelaide has many opal shops, which are around King William Street. Other good buys are South Australian regional wines, crafts, and Aboriginal artwork. The trendiest area to browse is King William Road in Hyde Park, a 20-minute walk south from Victoria Square. Outside of the city, the Marion Shopping Centre is packed with current trends, and Harbour Town next to Adelaide Airport is a great place to find a bargain.

CITY CENTER

ARTS AND CRAFTS GALLERIES

Fodor'sChoice ★ **Jam Factory.** A contemporary craft-and-design center at the Lion's Arts Centre, Jam Factory exhibits and sells unique Australian glassware, ceramics, wood, and metal work and you can often see the artists at work. Its fantastic gift shop is the place to pick up a unique handmade piece of art, including a description from the artist. ⊠ *19 Morphett St., City Center* ☎ *08/8231–0005* ⊕ *www.jamfactory.com.au.*

Urban Cow Studio. For quirky locally made jewelry, pottery, glass, and sculptures, visit Urban Cow Studio, which exhibits more than 150 South Australian artists and designers. ⊠ *11 Frome St., City Center* ☎ *08/8232–6126* ⊕ *www.urbancow.com.au.*

DEPARTMENT STORES AND SHOPPING CENTERS

Fodor'sChoice ★ **Rundle Mall.** Adelaide's main shopping area is Rundle Mall, a pedestrian plaza lined with boutiques, department stores, and arcades, including Australia's two best-known stores, Myer and David Jones, as well as some of the world's big name and luxury brands sprinkled among the local product. Heritage-listed Adelaide Arcade is a Victorian-era jewel, with a decorative tiled floor, skylights, and dozens of shops behind huge timber-framed windows. ⊠ *Rundle St., between King William and Pulteney Sts., City Center* ☎ *08/8203–7611* ⊕ *www.rundlemall.com.au.*

FOOD

Fodor'sChoice ★ **Haigh's Chocolates.** Ask anyone who no longer lives in Adelaide what they miss most about the city and chances are they'll say "Haigh's." Australia's oldest chocolate manufacturer has tempted people with corner shop displays since 1915, and although there are now Haigh's stores in several locations across the city and in other capitals, the Beehive Corner store is the original, and a local icon. The family-owned South Australian company produces exquisite truffles, pralines, and creams— as well as the chocolate bilby (an endangered Australian marsupial), Haigh's answer to the Easter bunny. No trip to Adelaide is complete without at least one chocolate indulgence. ■TIP➜ **Free chocolate-making tours at the Haigh's Visitor Center at 154 Greenhill Road in Parkside run Monday–Saturday from 9 am. Bookings are essential.** ⊠ *2 Rundle Mall, at King William St., City Center* ☎ *08/8372–7070* ⊕ *www. haighschocolates.com.*

JEWELRY AND ACCESSORIES

Adelaide Exchange Jewellers. Located just off Rundle Mall, the exchange sells high-quality antique jewelry. They can also be found in Glenelg and Modbury. ⊠ *10 Stephens Pl., City Center* ☎ *08/8212–2496* ⊕ *www. adelaide-exchange.com.au.*

Australian Opal and Diamond Collection. One of Australia's leading Opal merchants, wholesalers, exporters, and manufacturing jewelers, Australian Opal and Diamond Collection sells superb handcrafted one-of-a-kind opal jewelry. ⊠ *14 King William St., City Center* ☎ *08/8211–9995* ⊕ *www.aodc.net.au.*

MARKETS

Fodor'sChoice   **Central Market.** One of the largest produce markets in the southern hemi-
★   sphere, and Adelaide's pride and joy, the Central Market is chock-full of stellar local foods, including glistening-fresh fish, meat, crusty Vietnamese and Continental breads, German baked goods, cheeses of every shape and color, and old-fashioned lollies (candy). You can also buy souvenir T-shirts, CDs, books, cut flowers, and a great cup of coffee. The enthusiastic couple behind Adelaide's Top Food and Wine Tours (⊕ *www.topfoodandwinetours.com.au*) showcases Adelaide's food-and-wine lifestyle—as in the behind-the-scenes guided tour of the Central Market (A$55), which lets you meet stall holders, share their knowledge, and taste the wares. Tours are scheduled Tuesday and Thursday through Saturday at 9:30 am; reservations are essential. ⊠ *Gouger St., City Center* ☎ *08/8203–7494* ⊕ *www.adelaidecentralmarket.com.au.*

GREATER ADELAIDE

DEPARTMENT STORES AND SHOPPING CENTERS

Harbour Town Adelaide. For discount shopping, hop off the plane and head straight to nearby Harbourtown. You'll find Morrissey, JAG, Levi's, Esprit, Cue, RM Williams, Authentic Factory Outlet (Converse), and Woolworths among the 100 outlets. ⊠ *727 Tapleys Hill Rd., West Beach* ☎ *08/8355–1144* ⊕ *www.harbourtownadelaide.com.au.*

Marion Shopping Centre. Adelaide's largest shopping complex is easily accessible via public transport and contains more than 300 stores, including major department stores and boutiques, bars, restaurants, and the largest cinema complex in the state. ⊠ *297 Diagonal Rd., Marion* ☎ *08/8298–1188* ⊕ *www.westfield.com.au.*

SIDE TRIPS TO THE ADELAIDE HILLS

With their secluded green slopes and flowery gardens, the Adelaide Hills are a pastoral vision in this desert state. The patchwork quilt of vast orchards, neat vineyards, and avenues of tall conifers resembles the Bavarian countryside, a likeness fashioned by the many German immigrants who settled here in the 19th century. In summer the Hills are consistently cooler than the city, although the charming towns and wineries are pleasant to visit any time of year. To reach the region from Adelaide, head toward the M1 Princes Highway or drive down Pulteney Street and on to Glen Osmond Road, which becomes the M1. From here signs point to Crafers and the freeway.

MT. LOFTY

16 km (10 miles) southeast of Adelaide.

There are splendid views of Adelaide from the lookout atop 2,300-foot Mt. Lofty, the coldest location in Adelaide, where snow is not uncommon in winter months. The energetic can follow some of the many trails that lead from the summit, or alternatively, have a cup of coffee in the café and enjoy the view in the warmth.

> ### NICE VIEWS
>
> There is no better view of Adelaide—day or night—than the city-and-sea sweep from atop 2,300-foot Mt. Lofty. There's an appropriately named glass-front restaurant here called the Summit, though prices at both the café and restaurant are sky-high.

GETTING HERE AND AROUND

By car from Adelaide, take the Crafers exit off the South Eastern Freeway and follow Summit Road or from the eastern suburbs via Greenhill Road. You can get to the summit as well as the Mt. Lofty Botanic Gardens and Cleland Wildlife Park in about 40 minutes by catching Bus 842, 865, or 865F from Currie or Grenfell Street in the city center. Alight at bus stop 24A and connect to Bus 823.

A 3½-km (2-mile) round-trip walk from the Waterfall Gully parking lot in Cleland Conservation Park (15-minute drive from Adelaide) takes you along Waterfall Creek before climbing steeply to the white surveying tower on the summit; the track is closed on Total Fire Ban days.

Transportation Adelaide Metro Info Centre. ⊠ *Currie and King William Sts., Adelaide* ☎ *08/8210–1000* ⊕ *www.adelaidemetro.com.au.*

EXPLORING

FAMILY
Fodor'sChoice
★

Cleland Wildlife Park. A short drive from Mt. Lofty Summit brings you to delightful Cleland Wildlife Park, where many animals roam free in three different forest habitats. Walking trails crisscross the park and its surroundings, and you're guaranteed to see emus and kangaroos in the grasslands and pelicans around the swampy billabongs. There are also enclosures for wombats and other less sociable animals. Koala cuddling is a highlight of koala close-up sessions (daily 2–3:30, plus Sunday 11–noon). Two-hour night walks (A$50 for adult, A$40 for children 3–14) let you wander among nocturnal species such as potoroos and brush-tailed bettongs: check the website for the next scheduled walk. Private guided tours can be arranged for A$120 per hour weekdays, A$180 per hour on the weekends. ■TIP→ **Reservations 48 hours prior are essential for tours.** The park is closed when there's a fire ban (usually between December and February). ⊠ *365 Mount Lofty Summit Rd., Mount Lofty* ☎ *08/8339–2444* ⊕ *www.cleland.sa.gov.au* ⊠ *A$22, A$11 children 3–14, A$50 family pass* ☉ *Daily 9:30–5.*

Mt. Lofty Botanic Gardens. With its rhododendrons, magnolias, ferns, and exotic trees, these gardens are glorious in fall and spring; during these seasons, free guided walks leave the lower parking lot on Thursday at 10:30. ⊠ *Picadilly entrance, 16 Lampert Rd., Mount*

9

Lofty ☎ *08/8370–8370* ⊕ *www.environment.sa.gov.au/botanicgardens* ⊗ *Weekdays 8:30–4, weekends 10–5, 6 during summer.*

WHERE TO EAT AND STAY

$$$
ECLECTIC

✕ **The Summit.** If you suffer from vertigo, think twice about dining here; this glass-front building atop Mt. Lofty is all about dining with altitude. Café by morning and lunch, intimate candlelit restaurant by night, the menu here includes a local delicacy—kangaroo fillet with seasonal vegetables as well as plenty of other local specialties, including Woodside cheese. The wine list promotes Adelaide Hills vintages. While the food is good, you pay a premium for the view. ⑤ *Average main: A$39* ⊠ *Mt. Lofty Lookout, Mt. Lofty Summit Rd., Mount Lofty* ☎ *08/8339–2600* ⊕ *www.mtloftysummit.com* ⊗ *No dinner Sun.–Tues in summer, Sun.– Thurs. in winter* ⚋ *Reservations essential.*

$$$
B&B/INN

🛏 **Mt. Lofty House.** From very English garden terraces below the summit of Mt. Lofty, this refined country house overlooks a patchwork of vineyards, farms, and bushland. **Pros:** peaceful location in stunning surroundings; free Wi-Fi. **Cons:** popular with groups, so book ahead at the restaurant. ⑤ *Rooms from: A$299* ⊠ *74 Summit Rd., Crafers* ☎ *08/8339–6777* ⊕ *www.mtloftyhouse.com.au* ⮐ *33 rooms, 3 cottages* ⑪ *Breakfast.*

BRIDGEWATER

6 km (4 miles) north of Mylor, 22 km (14 miles) southeast of Adelaide.

Bridgewater came into existence in 1841 as a refreshment stop for bullock teams fording Cock's Creek. More English than German, with its flowing creek and flower-filled gardens, this leafy, tranquil village was officially planned in 1859 by the builder of the first Bridgewater flour mill.

GETTING HERE AND AROUND

From the city center, drive onto the Mount Barker Expressway until you see the Stirling exit. From there, travel through lush countryside following the signs to Bridgewater. The town itself is small and walkable. By public transport, take Bus 864 or 864F from Currie Street in the city to stop 46.

WHERE TO EAT AND STAY

$$
ECLECTIC
FAMILY

✕ **Aldgate Pump Hotel.** You get a leisurely glimpse of local culture at this friendly two-story country pub. There is an extensive selection of hearty pub fare such as platters with everything from chicken wings to spring rolls to oysters. Breakfast is served only on Sunday. Warmed by log fires in winter, the dining room overlooks a shaded beer garden. The place is 2 km (1 mile) from Bridgewater, in the delightful village of Aldgate. ⑤ *Average main: A$26* ⊠ *1 Strathalbyn Rd., Aldgate* ☎ *08/8339–2015* ⊕ *www.aldgatepumphotel.com.au.*

$$$
AUSTRALIAN
Fodor's Choice
★

✕ **Bridgewater Mill Restaurant.** A stylish yet charmingly casual restaurant in a converted 1860s flour mill, this is a great spot to linger over a long lunch, especially in winter when you can cozy up beside the open fire. Using mostly local produce, chef Zac Ronayne creates an imaginative contemporary menu that is a mix of French, Japanese, Middle

Eastern and modern Australian. Lunch is a selection of regional platters designed to share, dinner is à la carte, and the wine list has an extensive range of local wines. In summer, book ahead to get a table on the deck beside the waterwheel. $ *Average main: A$38* ✉ *386 Mt. Barker Rd.* ☎ *08/8339–9200* ⊕ *thebridgewatermill.com.au* ⊗ *Closed Tues. No dinner Sun.–Thurs.*

$
CAFÉ
FAMILY
✕ **Organic Market and Café.** Pram-wheeling parents, hikers resting their walking poles, and friends catching up on gossip keep this red-and-blue café and adjoining organic supermarket buzzing all day. Reasons to linger include focaccias, soups, home-baked muffins and cakes, and all kinds of purportedly healthy and unquestionably delicious drinks. While this establishment is in Stirling, about 3 km (2 miles) from Bridgewater, it's worth the short drive. $ *Average main: A$16* ✉ *5 Druid Ave., Stirling* ☎ *08/8339–4835 café* ⊕ *www.organicmarket.com.au* ⊗ *No dinner.*

$$$$
B&B/INN
🏨 **Thorngrove Manor Hotel.** This romantic Gothic folly of turrets and towers is *Lifestyles of the Rich and Famous* writ large. **Pros:** perfect for the archetypal romantic getaway. **Cons:** if you have to ask how expensive it is, you can't afford it. $ *Rooms from: A$899* ✉ *2 Glenside La., Crafers* ☎ *08/8339–6748* ⊕ *www.thorngrove.com.au* ⤵ *2 rooms, 4 suites* ⦿ *Breakfast.*

THE BAROSSA WINE REGION

Some of Australia's most famous vineyards are in the Barossa, just over an hour's drive northeast of Adelaide. More than 200 wineries across the two wide, shallow valleys that make up the region produce some of Australia's most celebrated wines, including aromatic Rhine Riesling, Seppeltsfield's unique, century-old Para Port—and Penfolds Grange, which sells for more than A$750: a bottle of the 1951 Grange Hermitage costs A$65,000, if you can find one (most were given away by the winemaker).

Cultural roots set the Barossa apart. The area was settled by Silesian immigrants who left the German–Polish border region in the 1840s to escape religious persecution. These farmers brought traditions that you can't miss in the solid bluestone architecture, the tall slender spires of the Lutheran churches, and the *kuchen*, a cake as popular as the Devonshire tea introduced by British settlers. Together, these elements give the Barossa a charm that is unique among Australian wine-growing areas.

Most wineries in the Barossa operate sale rooms—called cellar doors—that usually have 6 to 12 varieties of wine available for tasting. You are not expected to sample the entire selection; to do so would overpower your taste buds. It's far better to give the tasting-room staff some idea of your personal preferences and let them suggest wine for you to sample. Some cellar doors charge a A$5 tasting fee, refundable against any purchase.

9

The vineyards of the Barossa Valley

GETTING HERE AND AROUND

The most direct route from Adelaide to the Barossa is via the town of Gawler. From Adelaide, drive north on King William Street. About 1 km (½ mile) past the Torrens River Bridge, take the right fork onto Main North Road. After 6 km (4 miles) this road forks to the right—follow signs to the Sturt Highway and the town of Gawler. At Gawler leave the highway and follow the signs to Lyndoch on the Barossa's southern border. The 50-km (31-mile) journey should take just more than an hour. A more attractive, if circuitous, route to Lyndoch takes you through the Adelaide Hills' Chain of Ponds and Williamstown.

Because the Barossa wineries are relatively far apart, a car is by far the best way to get around. But keep in mind that there are stiff penalties for driving under the influence of alcohol—the legal blood-alcohol limit is 0.05g/100ml. Police in patrol cars can pull you over for a random breath test anywhere in the state, and roadside mobile breath-testing stations—locally known as "Booze Buses"—are particularly visible during special events, such as the biennial Barossa Vintage Festival, held during mid-April in odd-numbered years. The best advice is to take a tour.

TOURS

Barossa Taste Sensations. Host Jonathon Milne is an excellent guide to the region's best wineries as well as where to buy some excellent local produce. He's happy to make suggestions or will take you wherever you fancy. Full- and half-day tours are available. ☎ 08/8564–3130 ⊕ barossatastesensations.com ✉ From A$200.

Enjoy Adelaide. Enjoy Adelaide runs a full-day Barossa tour that visits its four vineyards and includes lunch. ☎ *08/8332–1401* ⊕ *www.enjoyadelaide.com.au* ✉ *From A$110.*

Gray Line Adelaide. Gray Line Adelaide's full-day tour of the Barossa Region leaves from Adelaide Central Bus Station. It includes lunch at a winery. ☎ *08/8410–8800* ⊕ *www.grayline.com.au/adelaide* ✉ *From A$140.*

Groovy Grape Getaways. Groovy Grape Getaways offers full-day Barossa tours with a visit to the Adelaide Hills and a barbecue lunch. ☎ *08/8440–1640, 1800/661177* ⊕ *www.groovygrape.com.au* ✉ *From A$99.*

ESSENTIALS

Visitor Information Barossa Visitors Centre. ✉ *66–68 Murray St., Tanunda* ☎ *08/8563–0600, 1300/852982* ⊕ *www.barossa.com.*

LYNDOCH

58 km (36 miles) northeast of Adelaide.

This pleasant little town surrounded by vineyards was established in 1840 and is the Barossa's oldest settlement site. It owes the spelling of its name to a draftsman's error—it was meant to be named after the British soldier Lord Lynedoch.

EXPLORING

Burge Family Winemakers. You can drink in a leafy vineyard view while tasting from the wine barrels in this understated cellar door. Winemaker Rick Burge's best include the powerful yet elegant Draycott Shiraz and Olive Hill Shiraz-Grenache-Mourvedre blend. ✉ *Barossa Valley Way near Hermann Thumm Dr.* ☎ *08/8524–4644* ⊕ *www.burgefamily.com.au* ⊗ *Fri., Sat., and Mon. 10–5 (call ahead).*

Lyndoch Lavender Farm. A family-friendly tribute to the purple flower that adorns the hills, Lyndoch Lavender Farm grows more than 90 varieties on 6 lush acres high above Lyndoch. Light café meals are available, and the farm shop sells essential oils, creams, and other products, including wine from their adjacent vineyard. ✉ *At Hoffnungsthal and Tweedies Gully Rds.* ☎ *08/8524–4538* ⊕ *www.lyndochlavenderfarm.com.au* ✉ *A$2 during flowering season (Aug.–Jan.)* ⊗ *Daily 10–4:30.*

WHERE TO STAY

$$$$
B&B/INN
Fodor's Choice
★

⊞ **Abbotsford Country House.** Tranquility reigns at this property on 50 acres of rolling beef farm with Barossa views. **Pros:** a serene and luxurious place to recover from all the wine tasting; very welcoming hosts. **Cons:** dining in the restaurant is expensive; health nuts might rue the lack of gym and leisure facilities. ⑤ *Rooms from: A$415* ✉ *Yaldara Dr. at Fuss Rd.* ☎ *08/8524–4662* ⊕ *www.abbotsfordhouse.com* ⤳ *8 suites* ⦿*Breakfast.*

$$$
B&B/INN

⊞ **Belle Cottages.** Rose-filled gardens or sweeping rural acres surround these classic Australian accommodations. **Pros:** great discounts available for groups; comfortable and homey accommodation. **Cons:** not the

The Barossa Wine Region

TO THE CLARE VALLEY

KEY

Rail Lines

Roberts Rd.

Seppeltsfield Rd.

Sturt Hwy.

Barossa Valley Highway

Stockwell Rd.

Nuriootpa

Banrock Station Wine & Wetland Station

Gerald

Marananga

Penfolds Barossa Valley ◆

TO GAWLER

Seppeltsfield Winery ◆ ○ Seppeltsfield

Maggie Beer's Farm Shop ◆

Dorrien

Siegersdorf Rd.

Saltram ◆

Two Hands Wines ◆

Greenock Ck.

Magnolia Rd.

Vine Vale Rd.

Angaston ○

Both Rd.

Heinze Rd.

Stonewell Rd.

North Para Rd.

Peter Lehmann ◆ Wines

Yalumba ◆

Rosedale Rd.

Gomersale Rd.

Tanunda ○

Basedow Rd.

Angaston Rd.

Lyndoch Rd.

Brock Rd.

Barossa Visitors ◆ Centre

○ Gomersal

Bethany ○

Bethany Rd.

Scenic Drive

Tanunda Ck.

Rockford ◆

Grant Burge ◆

Krondorf Rd.

Jacob's Creek ◆ Visitor Centre

Kabminye ◆ Wines

Barossa Valley Way

Charles Melton Wines

North Para R.

Burge Family Winemakers ◆

○ **Lyndoch**

Lyndoch ◆ Lavender Farm

0 ——— 2 miles

0 ——— 3 km

place for an anonymous stay; some quirks to the plumbing. $ *Rooms from: A$240* ✉ *8 King St.* ☎ *08/8524–4825, 0411/108–800* ⊕ *www.bellescapes.com* ⤳ *11 cottages, 3 suites* ⟨○⟩ *Breakfast.*

$$$$
B&B/INN
Fodor's Choice
★

🏠 **Kingsford Homestead.** Set in a historic 1856 homestead on a 225-acre authentic sheep station, Kingsford Homestead offers one of the Barossa Valley's most exquisite experiences. **Pros:** personable hosts make you feel like family; gourmet farm-to-table seasonal menus; secluded feel yet easily accessible. **Cons:** two-night minimum; lunch not included. $ *Rooms from: A$920* ✉ *Kingsford Rd., Kingsford* ☎ *08/8524–8120* ⊕ *www.kingsfordhomestead.com.au* ⤳ *6 suites, 1 cottage* ⟨○⟩ *All-inclusive; Some meals.*

TANUNDA

13 km (8 miles) northeast of Lyndoch, 70 km (43 miles) northeast of Adelaide.

The cultural heart of the Barossa, Tanunda is its most German settlement. The four Lutheran churches in the town testify to its heritage, and dozens of shops selling German pastries, breads, and wursts (sausages)—not to mention wine—line the main street. Many of the valley's best wineries are close by.

EXPLORING

Charles Melton Wines. Tasting here is relaxed and casual in a brick-floor, timber-wall cellar door, which is warmed by a log fire in winter. After making sure the resident cats have vacated it first, settle into a director's chair at the long wooden table and let the staff pour. Nine Popes, a huge, decadent red blend, is the flagship wine, and the ruby-red Rose of Virginia is arguably Australia's best rosé. You can enjoy a glass of either with a cheese platter or game pie on the veranda. ⊠ *Krondorf Rd. near Nitschke Rd.* ☎ *08/8563–3606* ⊕ *www.charlesmeltonwines. com.au* ⊗ *Daily 11–5.*

Grant Burge. This is one of the most successful of the Barossa's young, independent wine labels. Wines include impressive Chardonnays, crisp Rieslings, and powerful reds such as Meshach Shiraz. Don't miss the Holy Trinity—a highly acclaimed Rhône blend of Grenache, Shiraz, and Mourvedre. The cellar door is at Krondorf, 5 km (3 miles) south of Tanunda and has a small café overlooking the vines. ⊠ *279 Krondorf Rd.* ☎ *08/8563–3700* ⊕ *www.grantburgewines.com.au* ⊗ *Daily 10–5.*

Jacob's Creek Visitor Centre. An impressive block of glass, steel, and recycled timber, Jacob's Creek Visitor Centre overlooks the creek whose name is familiar to wine drinkers around the world, as they export to more than 60 countries. It can sometimes be overrun with tour groups, but the informative staff makes the place well worth a visit—it's certainly more than your run-of-the-mill visitor center. Inside the building, plasma screens and pictorial displays tell the history of the label. Cabernet Sauvignon, Merlot, Chardonnay, and the Shiraz-rosé, served chilled, can be tasted at a 60-foot-long counter. There is a lunch-only restaurant with broad glass doors opening onto a grassy lawn edged with towering eucalyptus trees, and there are workshops and tours you can join, including food and wine matching (A$150) and behind the scenes tours (A$300): bookings are essential. ⊠ *2129 Barossa Valley Way near Jacob's Creek* ☎ *08/8521–3000* ⊕ *www.jacobscreek.com* ⊗ *Daily 10–5.*

Kabminye Wines. Each wine at Kabminye has its own unique and surprising taste, particularly the excellent Ilona rosé and the full-frontal flagship Hubert Shiraz. ⊠ *179 Krondorf Rd.* ☎ *08/8563–0889* ⊕ *www. kabminye.com* ⊗ *Sat. 11–5.*

Peter Lehmann Wines. This winery is owned by a larger-than-life Barossa character whose wine consistently wins international awards. Art-hung stonework and a wood-burning fireplace make the tasting room one of the most pleasant in the valley. This is the only place to find Black Queen Sparkling Shiraz. Wooden tables on a shady lawn encourage picnicking on the Weighbridge platter, a selection of local smoked meats, cheeses, and condiments. Served daily, it's big enough for two. They also offer VIP tastings in a private room with food matchings, but you must book in advance. ⊠ *Para Rd. off Stelzer Rd.* ☎ *08/8565–9555* ⊕ *www.peterlehmannwines. com.au* ⊗ *Weekdays 9:30–5, Sat. 10:30–4:30, Sun. 9:30–4:30.*

Fodor's Choice
★

Rockford. Nestled in a lovely cobbled stable yard, Rockford is a small winery with a tasting room in an old stone barn. The specialties are heavy, rich wines made from some of the region's oldest vines. Several notable labels have appeared under the Rockford name—be sure to try the Cabernet Sauvignon and the Basket Press Shiraz (at cellar door from March until sold out), outstanding examples of these most traditional of Australian varieties. The owners pride themselves on their old-school methods. The same equipment (you can see in the yard) has been used for more than a century. ⊠ *131 Krondorf Rd. near Nitschke Rd.* ☎ *08/8563–2720* ⊕ *www.rockfordwines.com.au* ⊗ *Daily 11–5.*

> **PACE YOURSELF**
>
> Home-smoked meats, organic farmhouse cheeses, and mouth-filling Shiraz—the Barossa is the ultimate picnic basket. Use this fact as an excuse for a long lunch, which will give you time to recover from all that wine tasting. Remember to pace yourself as you taste, and wherever possible, make use of those spit buckets you see at each winery. You'll be glad you did.

WHERE TO EAT AND STAY

$
GERMAN
✕ **Die Barossa Wurst Haus & Bakery.** For a hearty German lunch at a reasonable price, no place beats this small, friendly café and shop. The wurst is fresh from local butchers, the sauerkraut is direct from Germany, and the potato salad is made on-site from a secret recipe. ⑤ *Average main: A$11* ⊠ *86A Murray St.* ☎ *08/8563–3598* ▭ *No credit cards* ⊗ *No dinner.*

$$
AUSTRALIAN
✕ **1918 Bistro & Grill.** This rustic and whimsical restaurant in a restored villa makes exemplary use of the Barossa's distinctive regional produce in a seasonal Oz menu flavored with tastes from Asia and the Middle East. Local olive oil and seasonal fruits and vegetables influence dishes like the delicious chargrilled octopus with cauliflower skordalia, pancetta, ruby grapefruit, and truffle oil. Meals are served beside a two-sided fireplace in winter and alfresco in the garden in summer. The mostly Barossa wine list includes rare classics and newcomers. ⑤ *Average main: A$35* ⊠ *94 Murray St.* ☎ *08/8563–0405* ⊕ *www.1918.com.au* ⌂ *Reservations essential.*

$$
B&B/INN
▦ **Blickinstal Barossa Valley Retreat.** Its name means "view into the valley," which understates the breathtaking panoramas from this lovely B&B. **Pros:** great-value rooms with superb views across the valley; complimentary port in the evening. **Cons:** don't expect corporate-office facilities or an anonymous stay. ⑤ *Rooms from: A$180* ⊠ *Rifle Range Rd.* ☎ *08/8563–2716* ⊕ *www.blickinstal.com.au* ⇆ *4 studios, 2 lodges* ⑩ *Breakfast.*

$$
B&B/INN
▦ **Lawley Farm.** Amid 20 acres of grapes, in a courtyard shaded by gnarled peppercorn trees, these delightful stone cottage-style suites were assembled from the remains of barns dating from the Barossa's pioneering days. **Pros:** original buildings have been lovingly preserved; the breakfasts are legendary. **Cons:** no exercise facilities for working off all the local wine and produce. ⑤ *Rooms from: A$195* ⊠ *Krondorf and Grocke Rds.* ☎ *08/8563–2141* ⊕ *www.lawleyfarm.com.au* ⇆ *4 suites* ⑩ *Breakfast.*

ANGASTON

16 km (10 miles) northeast of Tanunda via Menglers Hill Rd. Scenic Drive, 86 km (53 miles) northeast of Adelaide.

Named after George Fife Angas, the Englishman who founded the town and sponsored many of the German and British immigrants who came here, Angaston is full of jacaranda trees, and its main street is lined with stately stone buildings and tiny shops. Schulz Butchers has been making and selling wurst since 1939; 17 varieties hang above the counter. You can buy other delicious regional produce every Saturday morning at the Barossa Farmers Market, behind Vintners Bar & Grill.

EXPLORING

Saltram. Low-beamed ceilings and ivy-covered trellises give Saltram an urbanized sort of rustic charm. The vineyard's robust wine list includes the Pepperjack Barossa Grenache Rosé, a delightful vintage available only in summer. It's a delicious accompaniment to the Italian-influenced menu at the adjacent—and excellent—Salter's Kitchen restaurant. ⊠ *Murray St.* ☎ *08/8561–0200* ⊕ *www.saltramwines.com.au* ☾ *Daily 10–5.*

Yalumba. Australia's oldest family-owned winery, Yalumba sits within a hugely impressive compound resembling an Italian monastery. The cellar door is decorated with mission-style furniture, antique winemaking materials, and mementos of the Hill Smith family, who first planted vines in the Barossa in 1849. The Octavius Shiraz are superb, and the "Y Series" Viognier is thoroughly enjoyable. ⊠ *40 Eden Valley Rd. just south of Valley Rd.* ☎ *08/8561–3200* ⊕ *www.yalumba.com* ☾ *Daily 10–5.*

WHERE TO EAT

$$$ ✕ **Vintners Bar & Grill.** The Barossa region is at its best in this sophisti-
AUSTRALIAN cated spot, where vivid contemporary artworks adorn the walls and
Fodor's Choice wide windows look out on rows of vineyards. The short menu blends
★ Australian, Mediterranean, and Asian flavors in such dishes as delicious truffled leek risotto with confit duck leg, roasted apple, and pinot jus. Scarlet and charcoal suede chairs and an upbeat jazz sound track make it easy to relax; top winemakers often come here to sample from the cellar's 160 wines. Ⓢ *Average main: A$38* ⊠ *Stockwell Rd.* ☎ *08/8564–2488* ⊕ *www.vintners.com.au* ☾ *No dinner Sun.* ⬗ *Reservations essential.*

NURIOOTPA

8 km (5 miles) northwest of Angaston, 74 km (46 miles) northeast of Adelaide.

Long before it was the Barossa's commercial center, Nuriootpa was used as a bartering place by local Aboriginal tribes, hence its name: Nuriootpa means "meeting place." Most locals call it Nurie.

EXPLORING

Fodor's Choice **Maggie Beer's Farm Shop.** Renowned cook and food writer Maggie Beer
★ is an icon of Australian cuisine. Burned-fig jam, ice cream, *verjuice* (a
golden liquid made from unfermented grape juice and used for flavor-
ing), and her signature Pheasant Farm Pâté are some of the delights
you can taste and buy at Maggie Beer's Farm Shop. Treat-filled picnic
baskets are available all day to take out or dip into on the deck overlooking a tree-fringed pond full of turtles. Don't miss the daily cooking
demonstrations at 2 pm. ✉ *50 Pheasant Farm Rd.* ☎ *08/8562–4477*
⊕ *www.maggiebeer.com.au* ⊙ *Daily 10:30–5* ☞ *Bookings are required
for cooking demonstrations for groups of 10 or more.*

Penfolds Barossa Valley. A very big brother to the 19th-century Magill
Estate in Adelaide, this massive wine-making outfit in the center of
Nuriootpa lets you taste Shiraz, Cabernet, Merlot, Chardonnay, and
Riesling blends—but not the celebrated Grange—at the cellar door. To
savor the flagship wine and other premium vintages, book a Taste of
Grange Tour (A$150 per person, minimum of two, 24-hour advance
notice needed). ✉ *30 Tanunda Rd.* ☎ *08/8568–8408* ⊕ *www.penfolds.
com* ⊙ *Daily 9–5.*

OFF THE BEATEN PATH

Banrock Station Wine & Wetland Centre. The salt-scrub-patched Murray
River floodplain 150 km (94 miles) east of Nuriootpa is an unlikely
setting for a winery, but it is worth making the journey to this spot at
Kingston-on-Murray. Within the stilted, mud-brick building perched
above the vineyard and river lagoons you can select a wine to accompany an all-day grazing platter or lunch on the outdoor deck—try the
pan seared Murray Cod with corn puree, braised spring onions, and
beetroot chips. Afterward, you can take one of three self-guided walks
(ranging from 2.5 km [1.5 miles] up to 8 km [5-mile]); trail access is by
donation) to view the surrounding wetlands (which can be "drylands"
during a drought), and learn about the ongoing wildlife habitat restoration and conservation work funded by Banrock Station wine sales and
walkers' donations. ✉ *Holmes Rd. just off Sturt Hwy., Kingston-on-
Murray* ☎ *08/8583–0299* ⊕ *www.banrockstation.com.au* ⊙ *Daily 9–5.*

MARANANGA

*6 km (4 miles) west of Nuriootpa, 68 km (42 miles) northeast of
Adelaide.*

The tiny hamlet of Marananga inhabits one of the prettiest corners of
the Barossa. This area's original name was Gnadenfrei, which means
"freed by the grace of God"—a reference to the religious persecution the German settlers suffered before they emigrated to Australia.
Marananga, the Aboriginal name, was adopted in 1918, when a wave
of anti-German sentiment spurred many name changes in the closing
days of World War I.

EXPLORING

Seppeltsfield Winery. Joseph Seppelt was a Silesian farmer who purchased
land in the Barossa after arriving in Australia in 1849. Under the control of his son, Benno, the wine-making business flourished, and today
Seppelt Winery and its splendid grounds are a tribute to the family's

CLOSE UP

Fish Tales

With nearly 4,800 km (3,000 miles) of coastline and hundreds of miles of rivers, South Australia has almost as many opportunities for fishing as it has varieties of fish. You can join local anglers of all ages dangling hand lines from a jetty, casting into the surf from coastal rocks, hopping aboard charter boats, or spending a day sitting on a riverside log.

The Murray River is the place to head for callop (also called yellow belly or golden perch) and elusive Murray cod. In the river's backwaters you can also net a feed of yabbies, a type of freshwater crayfish, which make a wonderful appetizer before you tuck into the one that didn't get away. In the ocean King George whiting reigns supreme, but there is also excellent eating with mulloway, bream, snapper, snook, salmon, and sweep. The yellowtail kingfish, a great fighter usually found in deep water, prefers the shallower waters of Coffin Bay, off the Eyre Peninsula.

Baird Bay Ocean Eco Experience. Most well known for their Swim with Wild Sea Lions and Dolphin tours on the Eyre Peninsula—a truly awesome once-in-a-lifetime experience worth every penny of the A$150—this charter company also runs fishing charters to Coffin Bay and other top spots on request. Children are welcome. ✉ *Baird Bay Rd., Baird Bay* ☎ *08/8626–5017* ⊕ *www.bairdbay. com* ✉ *A$150.*

Another popular destination is the Yorke Peninsula.

S.A. Fishing Adventures. Owners Herbie and Kirsty Glacken know just about everything there is to know about fishing the southern gulf waters and this charter takes anglers to great spots around the Yorke Peninsula, as well as Wedge, Neptune, and Kangaroo islands. Typical catches feature the delicious Nannigai, famous Whiting and lots of other instagram-worthy big fish. ✉ *7 Gannet Crescent, Marion Bay* ☎ *08/8854–4098.*

Last, but certainly not least, is legendary Kangaroo Island.

Kangaroo Island Fishing Adventures. This tour operator has fast, clean boats and a live-aboard mother ship; the company takes groups in a 30-foot cruiser out in the Western River region (the island's north coast) and into the Investigator Strait, which is rarely fished by private fishing boats. ✉ *Western River Rd., Parndana* ☎ *08/8559–3232* ⊕ *www. kangarooislandadventures.com.au.*

9

industry and enthusiasm. Fortified wine is a Seppelt specialty; this is the only winery in the world that has ports for every year as far back as 1878. Most notable is the 100-year-old Para Liqueur Tawny. The Grenache, Chardonnay, Cabernet, and sparkling Shiraz are also worth tasting. Tours of the 19th-century distillery are run daily; you can also book 24 hours ahead for the Centenary Tour where you get to taste four of the six paramount wines as well a 100-year-old wine and one that was 100 years old in your birth year. There's a small café that offers delicious cakes and afternoon teas. ✉ *Seppeltsfield Rd., 3 km (2 miles) west of Marananga, Seppeltsfield* ☎ *08/8568–6217* ⊕ *www.seppeltsfield.com. au* ✉ *Heritage Tour A$15, Taste Your Birth Year Tour A$60, Centenary*

Tour A$100 ⊙ *Daily 10–5. Heritage Tours daily 11:30 and 3:30; Taste Your Birth Year Tour daily (by appointment) 2:30, Centenary Tour daily (by appointment).*

Two Hands Wines. The interior of this 19th-century sandstone cottage is every bit as surprising as the wines produced here. Polished wood and glass surround the contemporary counter where the excellent staff leads you through the tasting of several "out of the box" red and white varietals and blends. The main event is Shiraz sourced from six wine regions. Compare and contrast Shiraz from Victoria and Padthaway (South Australia); and try the Barossa-grown Bad Impersonator. ✉ *273 Neldner Rd.* ☎ *08/8562–4566* ⊕ *www.twohandswines.com* 🍷 *General tastings A$5 (refundable with purchase)* ⊙ *Daily 10–5.*

WHERE TO STAY

$$$$ **The Lodge Country House.** Rambling and aristocratic, this bluestone
B&B/INN homestead 3 km (2 miles) south of Marananga was built in 1903 for one of the 13 children of Joseph Seppelt, founder of the showpiece winery across the road. **Pros:** beautiful gardens; informative hosts who delight in telling guests about the history of the place. **Cons:** not particularly suitable for kids. ⑤ *Rooms from: A$360* ✉ *743 Seppeltsfield Rd., Seppeltsfield* ☎ *08/8562–8277* ⊕ *www.thelodgecountryhouse.com.au* 🛏 *4 double rooms* ⑩ *Breakfast; Some meals.*

$$$$ **The Louise.** Prepare for pampering and privacy at this country estate
RESORT on a quiet back road with glorious valley views. **Pros:** stunning rooms with beautiful private gardens; destination dining at its best. **Cons:** pricey; no children under 10; need to book well ahead at restaurant. ⑤ *Rooms from: A$600* ✉ *Seppeltsfield and Stonewell Rds.* ☎ *08/8562–2722, 08/8562–4144 restaurant* ⊕ *www.thelouise.com.au; restaurant www.appellation.com.au* 🛏 *15 suites* ⑩ *Breakfast.*

THE CLARE VALLEY

Smaller and less well known than the Barossa, the Clare Valley nonetheless holds its own among Australia's wine-producing regions. Its robust reds and delicate whites are among the country's finest, and the Clare is generally regarded as the best area in Australia for fragrant, flavorsome Rieslings. On the fringe of the vast inland deserts, the Clare is a narrow sliver of fertile soil about 30 km (19 miles) long and 5 km (3 miles) wide, with a microclimate that makes it ideal for premium wine making.

The first vines were planted here as early as 1842, but it took a century and a half for the Clare Valley to take its deserved place on the national stage. The mix of small family wineries and large-scale producers, 150-year-old settlements and grand country houses, snug valleys and dense native forests, has rare charm.

GETTING HERE AND AROUND

The Clare Valley is about a 90-minute drive from Adelaide via Main North Road. From the center of Adelaide, head north on King William Street through the heart of North Adelaide. King William becomes O'Connell Street. After crossing Barton Terrace, look for Main North Road signs on the right. The road passes through the satellite town of

Elizabeth, bypasses the center of Gawler, and then runs due north to Auburn, the first town of the Clare Valley when approaching from the capital. Main North Road continues down the middle of the valley to Clare.

As with the Barossa, a car is essential for exploring the Clare Valley in any depth. Taste wine in moderation if you're driving; as well as keeping yourself and others safe, you'll avoid paying the extremely high penalties for driving while intoxicated.

TOURS

Clare Valley Experiences. Clare Valley Experiences combines wine and beer tasting with food, culture, and cycling on its tour of the region's major wineries and sites (A$215 each for two people including lunch), departing from Clare. ⊠ *29 Hope St., Clare* ☎ *08/8842–1880* ⊕ *www. clarevalleyexperiences.com* ⊠ *A$215 each for two people including lunch.*

ESSENTIALS

Visitor Information Clare Valley Visitor Information Centre. ⊠ *8 Spring Gully Rd., 6 km (4 miles) south of Clare, Clare* ☎ *1800/242–131, 08/8842–2131* ⊕ *www.clarevalley.com.au.*

SEVENHILL

126 km (78 miles) north of Adelaide.

Sevenhill is the Clare Valley's geographic center, and the location of the region's first winery, established by Jesuit priests in 1851 to produce altar wine. The area had been settled three years earlier by Austrian Jesuits who named their seminary after the seven hills of Rome.

The Riesling Trail, a walking and cycling track that follows an old Clare Valley railway line, runs through Sevenhill. The 36-km (22-mile) trail passes wineries and villages in gently rolling country between Auburn and Clare, and three loop trails take you to vineyards off the main track.

EXPLORING

Clare Valley Cycle Hire. Riding the Reisling Trail from Clare to Auburn is one of the best ways to explore the valley—it takes around 2½ hours to cycle the whole thing (one way), unless, of course, you get distracted by the wineries along the way. Bikes (including helmets, which are mandatory in Australia) for both adults and kids (and baby seats) can be rented from Clare Valley Cycle Hire. ⊠ *32 Victoria Rd., Clare* ☎ *0418/802–077* ⊕ *www.clarevalleycyclehire.com.au* ⊠ *A$20 4 hrs, A$30 up to 8 hrs* ⟳ *Cash only.*

Kilikanoon Wines. Award-winning Kilikanoon is renowned for multilayered reds, such as the dense, richly colored Oracle Shiraz (occasionally available for tasting); Prodigal Grenache is another beauty. A$5 tasting fee (five wines), refundable on any purchase, premium wine tasting packages are also available. ⊠ *Penna La., 2 km (1 mile) off Main North Rd., Penwortham* ☎ *08/8843–4206* ⊕ *www.kilikanoon.com.au* ⊘ *Daily 11–5.*

9

Fodor'sChoice
★

Sevenhill Cellars. The area's first winery, Sevenhill Cellars was created by the Jesuits, and they still run the show, with any profits going to education, mission work, and the needy within Australia. In the 1940s the winery branched out from sacramental wine to commercial production, and today 21 wine varieties, including Riesling (try the St. Aloysius label), Verdelho, Grenache, and fortified wines, account for 75% of its business. Book a guided tour with the charming Brother John May, Jesuit winemaker emeritus, who takes you to the cellars, the cemetery, and the church crypt where Jesuits have been interred since 1865. You can also rent bicycles here to explore the rolling hills and vineyards and there are toys for the kids. ⊠ *College Rd., just off Main North Rd.* ☎ *08/8843–4222* ⊕ *www.sevenhillcellars.com.au* ☏ *Tours A$10* ⏱ *10–5; tours Tues. and Thurs. at 2.*

Skillogalee Winery. Known for its excellent Riesling, Gewürztraminer, and Shiraz, the winery is also known for its wonderful restaurant (see listing below). Wine tasting takes place in a small room in the 1850s cottage (the restaurant occupies the others). Don't miss the sparkling Riesling. ⊠ *Trevarrick Rd.* ☎ *08/8843–4311* ⊕ *www.skillogalee.com* ⏱ *Daily 10–5.*

WHERE TO EAT

$$
AUSTRALIAN

✕**The Rising Sun Hotel.** People have watched the world go by from the veranda of this landmark hotel in Auburn, 16 km (10 miles) south of Sevenhill, since it was built in 1849. Pull up a chair overlooking the street and partake of the delicious modern Australian food, perhaps kangaroo fillet with quandong (a native fruit) and sweet-potato mash, or butterfish in a batter of Coopers Pale Ale (Adelaide's own beer). The wine list shows off the Clare Valley's best. ⑤ *Average main: A$30* ⊠ *19 Main North Road, Auburn* ☎ *08/8849–2015* ⊕ *www.therisingsunhotel.com.au.*

$$
AUSTRALIAN

✕**Skillogalee Winery.** The dining area here spills from a 1850s cottage onto a beautiful veranda overlooking a flower-filled garden and rows of grapevines. The menu changes seasonally, but you can't go wrong with the "vine pruner's lunch," chef Diana Palmer's spin on the British plowman's meal, a platter of rum-glazed local ham, cheddar cheese, chutney, and crusty bread. Entrées might include fish tagine with olives, apricots, and Skillogalee figs with saffron and lemon couscous or dukkah-crusted chicken breast. While most Clare restaurants have limited hours, Skillogalee is so popular it's open seven days a week and even serves breakfast, as well as lovely morning and afternoon teas. Gourmet picnic baskets can be ordered (24 hours notice required), and group dinners are available by prior arrangement. Skillogalee also has self-contained cottage accommodation. ⑤ *Average main: A$35* ⊠ *Trevarrick Rd.* ☎ *08/8843–4311* ⊕ *www.skillogalee.com.au* ⏱ *No dinner* ⌂ *Reservations essential.*

CLARE

10 km (6 miles) north of Sevenhill, 136 km (84 miles) north of Adelaide.

The bustling town of Clare is the Clare Valley's commercial center. Unusual for ultra-English South Australia, many of its early settlers were Irish—hence the valley's name, after the Irish county Clare, and place-names such as Armagh and Donnybrook.

EXPLORING

Knappstein Enterprise Winery & Brewery. One of the most recognizable and popular wineries in the Clare Valley, Knappstein is located in the original 19th-century Enterprise Brewery, a heritage-listed building and a well-known landmark of a township that's oozing with history. Knappstein Hand Picked Riesling is consistently rated among Australia's finest, though the same could be said for any of the wines lovingly handcrafted here. There's also a microbrewery on-site that produces the award-winning Knappstein Reserve Lager, a premium Bavarian-style lager. ⌂ *2 Pioneer Ave.* ☎ *08/8841–2100* ⊕ *www.knappstein.com.au* ⊙ *Weekdays 9–5, Sat. 11–5, Sun. 11–4.*

Tim Adams Wines. The small, no-frills tasting room means there is nothing to distract you from discovering why Tim Adams Wines has a big reputation. The standout in an impressive collection of reds and whites, which includes a celebrated Riesling and delicious Pinot Gris, is the purple-red Aberfeldy Shiraz, made from 100-year-old vines. You can buy wine by the glass and bottle to enjoy with a bring-your-own-picnic on the veranda. ⌂ *Warenda Rd. just off Main North Rd., 5 km (3 miles) south of Clare* ☎ *08/8842–2429* ⊕ *www.timadamswines.com. au* ⊙ *Weekdays 10:30–5, weekends 11–5.*

WHERE TO STAY

$$

B&B/INN

FAMILY

Bungaree Station. Your journey back to colonial Australia begins at check-in at this family-owned farm; the reception area is in the original station store. **Pros:** fascinating insight into a working homestead; accommodation options for all budgets; great family option. **Cons:** city types might find it too rustic; food options are limited. Ⓢ *Rooms from: A$168* ⌂ *Main North Rd., 12 km (7 miles) north of Clare* ☎ *08/8842–2677* ⊕ *www.bungareestation.com.au* 🛏 *7 cottages, 3 rooms with shared bathrooms* ⦿| *Breakfast.*

FLEURIEU PENINSULA

The Fleurieu has traditionally been seen as Adelaide's backyard. Generations of local families have vacationed in the string of beachside resorts between Victor Harbor and Goolwa, near the mouth of the Murray River. McLaren Vale wineries attract connoisseurs, and the beaches and bays bring in surfers, swimmers, and sun-seekers. The countryside, with its rolling hills and dramatic cliff scenery, is a joy to drive through.

Although the region is within easy reach of Adelaide, you should consider spending the night if you want to enjoy all it has to offer. You can also easily combine a visit here with one or more nights on Kangaroo Island. The ferry from Cape Jervis, at the southern tip of the peninsula, takes less than an hour to reach Penneshaw on the island, and there are coach connections from Victor Harbor and Goolwa.

GETTING HERE AND AROUND

Renting a car in Adelaide and driving south is the best way to visit the Fleurieu Peninsula, especially if you wish to tour the wineries, which aren't served by public transportation.

Fleurieu Peninsula and Kangaroo Island

The Fleurieu is an easy drive south from Adelaide. McLaren Vale itself is less than an hour away. Leave central Adelaide along South Terrace or West Terrace, linking with the Anzac Highway, which heads toward Glenelg. At the Gallipoli Underpass intersection with Main South Road, turn left. This road takes you almost to McLaren Vale. After a detour to visit the wineries, watch for signs for Victor Harbor Road. About 20 km (12 miles) south the highway splits. One road heads for Victor Harbor, the other for Goolwa. Those two places are connected by a major road that follows the coastline. Drivers heading to Cape Jervis and the Kangaroo Island ferries should stay on Main South Road.

ESSENTIALS

Visitor Information McLaren Vale and Fleurieu Visitor Centre. ✉ *796 Main Rd., McLaren Vale* ☎ *08/8323–9944* ⊕ *www.mclarenvale.info.* **Victor Harbor Visitor Information Centre.** ✉ *The Causeway, Victor Harbor* ☎ *08/8557–0777, 1800/557094* ⊕ *holidayatvictorharbor.com.au.*

MCLAREN VALE

39 km (24 miles) south of Adelaide.

The nearest wine region to Adelaide, this area has a distinctly modern, upscale look, even though many of the more than 80 wineries in and around town are as old as their Barossa peers. The first vines were planted in 1838 at northern Reynella by Englishman John Reynell, who had collected them en route from the Cape of Good Hope. The McLaren Vale region has always been known for its big—and softer—reds, including Shiraz, as well as a few white varietals. Local microbrewed beer is also becoming an increasingly popular attraction in the region.

EXPLORING

Coriole Vineyards. The 1860s stone cellar door at Coriole Vineyards sits among nasturtiums and hollyhocks on a hill with stunning St. Vincent Gulf views. From the surrounding vines, winemakers Simon White and Mark Lloyd make some of Australia's best Italian varietal wines, such as Sangiovese and Nebbiolo. Coriole grows olives, too, and you can taste olive oils as well as wine. Enjoy a platter of estate-grown and local produce—cheese, smoked kangaroo, roasted vegetables, and chutney—in the flagstone courtyard (lunch Thursday to Monday). The hosted tastings are excellent and should be booked ahead. ⊠ *Chaffeys Rd. near Kays Rd.* ☎ *08/8323–8305* ⊕ *www.coriole.com* ⊙ *Weekdays 10–5, weekends 11–5.*

d'Arenberg Wines. A fine restaurant complements excellent wine at d'Arenberg Wines, family-run since 1912. Winemaker Chester d'Arenberg Osborn is known for his quality whites, including the luscious Noble Riesling dessert wine, as well as powerful reds and fortified wines with equally compelling names. Reservations are essential for d'Arry's fine-dining veranda restaurant, which overlooks the vineyards, the valley, and the sea. The tempting seasonal lunch-only menu ($$$) uses local produce for its Mod Oz dishes. ⊠ *Osborn Rd.* ☎ *08/8829–4822 cellar door, 08/8329–4848 restaurant* ⊕ *www.darenberg.com.au* ⊙ *Daily 10–5.*

Pertaringa Wines. On a quiet, unpaved back road, boutique winery Pertaringa (meaning "belonging to the hills") makes limited quantities of mouth-filling reds and several whites. At the cellar door, facing the vines, you can sip Two Gentlemen's Grenache and Scarecrow Sauvignon Blanc, a great accompaniment to a bring-your-own picnic or make up a platter from the selection of cheese and other goodies sold at the cellar door. It is worth buying some of the premium Over the Top Shiraz even without tasting—you won't be disappointed. ⊠ *Hunt and Rifle Range Rd.* ☎ *08/8383–2700* ⊕ *www.pertaringa.com.au* ⊙ *Daily 11–5.*

WHERE TO EAT AND STAY

$ × **Blessed Cheese.** It's hard to disappoint when cheese and chocolate are
AUSTRALIAN your specialties, particularly when they're adeptly paired with local wines. Blessed cheese is a unique combination of cheese shop, licensed café, and provedore specializing in artisan cheeses, local and imported gourmet foods, and regional produce. You can pack a picnic for the

day with platters for two available from A$50, dine in their licensed café with a regional breakfast or lunch, relax with cake and coffee, or sample their delicious range of cheese. ⑤ *Average main: A$15* ⊠ *150 Main Rd.* ☎ *08/8323–7958* ⊕ *www.blessedcheese.com.au* ☾ *No dinner*.

$$ ✕ **Bracegirdles at 190.** With its worn floorboards and pressed-metal ceil-
AUSTRALIAN   ings, this café feels like a country corner store, but you'll also find a large alfresco area and undercover courtyard, perfect in spring. Come early for a cup of coffee, a piece of chocolate, and the best breakfast outside Adelaide. The menu shows off Fleurieu Peninsula produce: for a taste of McLaren Vale, order a tasting plate for two, and for something spicier, tuck into gluten-free salt-and-pepper squid (in season). ■ **TIP➜** Book ahead for weekends. ⑤ *Average main: A$23* ⊠ *190 Main Rd.* ☎ *08/8323–8558* ⊕ *www.bracegirdles.com.au/mclaren-vale.html* ☾ *No dinner Sun.–Thurs.*

$$ ✕ **Star of Greece.** More for the linen-slacks-and-deck-shoes set than the
AUSTRALIAN   board-shorts-and-sunscreen crowd, this extended weatherboard kiosk
Fodor's Choice on the cliffs at Port Willunga, 10 km (6 miles) southwest of McLaren
★   Vale, is beach-ball bright and extremely popular. Wooden chairs painted in mandarin, lime, and sky-blue stripes sit at paper-draped tables, and windows frame the aqua sea. (The offshore buoy marks where the three-masted *Star of Greece* foundered in 1888.) Reading the menu nets mostly seafood, and depending on the season, you might find seared scallops wrapped in octopus bacon, or crispy skinned ocean trout on prawn salsa. ⑤ *Average main: A$34* ⊠ *1 Esplanade, Port Willunga* ☎ *08/8557–7420* ⊕ *www.starofgreece.com.au* ☾ *No dinner Sun.–Wed. No lunch Mon. and Tues.* ⌲ *Reservations essential.*

$$$ ⌅ **Wine & Roses B&B.** It may look like a regular residential house from
B&B/INN   the outside, but this luxury B&B has an interior that's far from ordinary. **Pros:** perfect for a romantic getaway; the complimentary port is delicious. **Cons:** if all four suites are booked it's a little cramped; not child-friendly. ⑤ *Rooms from: A$249* ⊠ *39 Caffrey St.* ☎ *08/8323–7654* ⊕ *www.wineandroses.com.au* ⥬ *4 suites* ⎮⊙⎮ *Breakfast.*

GOOLWA

44 km (27 miles) southeast of McLaren Vale, 83 km (51 miles) south of Adelaide.

Beautifully situated near the mouth of the mighty Murray River, which travels some 2,415 km (1,594 miles) from its source in New South Wales, Goolwa grew fat on the 19th-century river paddle-steamer trade. Today, with its enviable position close to the sea and the combined attractions of Lake Alexandrina and Coorong National Park, tourism has replaced river trade as the main source of income.

EXPLORING

FAMILY   **Goolwa Wharf.** Set sail from here for daily tour cruises upon the *Spirit of the Coorong,* a fully equipped motorboat that offers a four-and-a-half-hour (A$90) or six-hour cruise (A$105) to Coorong National Park. Both include guided walks, lunch, and afternoon tea. Visitors can also enjoy locally brewed craft beer at the Steam Exchange Brewery located in the old railway goods shed on the wharf or go shopping at the Goolwa Wharf Markets on the first and third Sunday of each month. ⊠ *Goolwa Wharf* ☎ *08/8555–2203, 1800/442203 tour cruises* ⊕ *www.coorongcruises.com.au.*

FAMILY **Oscar W.** Goolwa is also the home port of paddle-steamer *Oscar W.* Built in 1908, it's one of the few remaining wood-fired boiler ships. This boat holds the record for bringing the most bales of wool (2,500) along the Darling River, which flows into the Murray River. When not participating in commemorative cruises and paddleboat races, the boat is open for inspection and cruises. ⊠ *Goolwa Wharf* ☎ *1300/466592* ⊕ *www.oscar-w.info* 🖃 *Donation requested to inspect boat; 1-hr cruises A$20* ☉ *Daily 10–3* ☞ *See website for cruising dates (weekends only).*

VICTOR HARBOR

18 km (11 miles) west of Goolwa, 83 km (51 miles) south of Adelaide.

As famous for its natural beauty and wildlife as for its resorts, Victor Harbor is South Australia's favorite seaside getaway. In 1802 English and French explorers Matthew Flinders and Nicolas Baudin met here at Encounter Bay, and by 1830 the harbor was a major whaling center. Pods of southern right whales came here to breed in winter, and they made for a profitable trade through the mid-1800s. By 1878 the whales were hunted nearly to extinction, but the return of these majestic creatures to Victor Harbor in recent decades has established the city as a premier source of information on whales and whaling history.

EXPLORING

Bluff. Seven km (4½ miles) west of Victor Harbor, the Bluff is where whalers once stood lookout for their prey. Today the granite outcrop, also known as Rosetta Head, serves the same purpose in very different circumstances. It's a steep, 1,400-foot climb to the top, on a formed trail, to enjoy the bluff views. ⊠ *The Bluff.*

FAMILY **Cockle Train.** Traveling the route of South Australia's first railway line— originally laid between Goolwa and Port Elliot, and extended to Victor Harbor in 1864—the line traces the lovely Southern Ocean beaches on its 16-km (10-mile), half-hour journey. The train runs by steam power, subject to availability and weather conditions, daily during summer school holidays (late December to late January), on Easter weekend, and on the third Sunday of each month from June to November. A diesel locomotive pulls the heritage passenger cars (or a diesel railcar operates) on other Sundays and public holidays, and days of Total Fire Ban. ⊠ *Railway Terr. near Coral St.* ☎ *08/8263–5621 on days the train is operating, 1300/655991* ⊕ *www.steamrangerheritagerailway. org* 🖃 *Round-trip A$29.*

FAMILY **Granite Island.** This island is linked to the mainland by a 650-yard causeway, along which Clydesdales pull a double-decker tram. Within Granite Island Nature Park a self-guided walk leads around the island, and guided walking tours to view the colony of about 500 fairy penguins are run each night at dusk; book at the Victor Harbor Visitor Centre before 4 pm. Look out for seals in the shallows. ⊠ *Granite Island*

☎ *1800/557–094* ⊕ *www.graniteisland.com.au* ⊠ *Round-trip tram A$9, penguin tours A$15* ⊙ *Daily; penguin tours at dusk.*

FAMILY   **South Australian Whale Centre.** The center tells the often graphic story of the whaling industry along South Australia's coast, particularly in Encounter Bay. Excellent interpretive displays spread over three floors focus on dolphins, seals, penguins, and whales—all of which can be seen in these waters. In whale-watching season the center has a 24-hour information hotline on sightings. There's a Discovery Trail and craft area for children. ⊠ *2 Railway Terr.* ☎ *08/8551–0750, 1900/942537 whale information* ⊕ *www.sawhalecentre.com* ⊠ *A$9; combined tickets with tramway A$15* ⊙ *Daily 10:30–5.*

OFF THE
BEATEN
PATH

Coorong National Park. A sliver of land stretching southeast of the Fleurieu Peninsula and completely separate from it, this park hugs the South Australian coast for more than 150 km (94 miles). Many Australians became aware of the Coorong's beauty from the 1970s film *Storm Boy*, which told the story of a boy's friendship with a pelican. These curious birds are one reason why the Coorong is a wetland area of world standing. ⊠ *Accessible via Goolwa, Meningie, and Salt Creek off Hwy. 1, Coorong National Park* ☎ *08/8575–1200* ⊕ *www.environment.sa.gov.au.*

BEACHES

Boomer Beach. The surf here is very big thanks to the exposed reef break. Most waves are dumpers, hence the name Boomer, and can get up to 15 feet high. As a result, this is a beach for surfers and strong swimmers. Waves decrease toward Victor Harbor, providing lower surf and usually calm conditions. In summer the surf tends to be mostly flat, but you need to be vigilant of rocks, rips, and sharks year-round. There is an excellent view down the entire beach from the headland at Port Elliot; from here you can spot the southern right whale, which in winter claims this area as its territory. **Amenities:** lifeguards; parking; toilets. **Best for:** fishing; surfing; swimming. ⊠ *Port Elliot.*

Horseshoe Bay, Port Elliot. This 2,300-foot-long beach faces east at the jetty and swings round to face south against Commodore Point. Thanks to the protection on either side, the waves are relatively low, making this a great swimming destination. However, the waves can be heavy during a high swell and surge up the steep beach. The safest swimming is at the western surf club end, where waves are always smallest. Fishing is popular around jetty and boundary rocks. **Amenities:** parking; toilets. **Best for:** swimming; walking. ⊠ *Basham Parade, Port Elliot.*

Middleton. One of South Australia's most popular surfing beaches is also one of its most hazardous due to the persistent high waves. The entire beach is composed of fine sand and waves averaging more than 2 meters breaking across a 500-meter-wide double bar surf zone. Numerous spilling breakers, substantial wave setup and set-down at the shoreline, and widely spaced rips during lower wave conditions are common characteristics here. Thanks to the very wide surf zone, it is moderately safe to swim in the inner surf zone on the bar but it is advised that swimmers do not venture beyond the first line of breakers as strong currents occupy the trough between the sand bars. **Amenities:** parking; toilets. **Best for:** surfing; walking. ⊠ *Esplanade, Middleton.*

SPORTS AND THE OUTDOORS
BICYCLING
Encounter Bikeway. For cycling enthusiasts, there's Encounter Bikeway, a paved track that runs 30 km (19 miles) from the Bluff along a scenic coastal route to Laffin Point (east of Goolwa). Almost flat, the bikeway is suitable for riders of most ages and experience levels. ■ **TIP**➔ When the Cockle Train is operating the Encounter Bikeway users can combine their trip with a journey on the train, traveling one-way on the bike path and returning on the train. ✉ *Encounter Bikeway* ⊕ *holidayatvictorharbor. com.au.*

WHERE TO STAY
$$$ 🏨 **The Bluff Resort Apartments.** The vibe is more tropical than maritime at
HOTEL   Victor Harbor's upscale resort complex, with palm trees and spectacular surf as the backdrop for spacious, well-equipped rooms of varying configurations. **Pros:** stunning views of three islands from some suites; real "getaway" feel; free Wi-Fi. **Cons:** 10-minute drive from downtown. ⑤ *Rooms from: A$229* ✉ *123 Franklin Parade* ☎ *08/8552–1200* ⊕ *www.bluffresort.com.au* 🛏 *12 suites, 14 apartments, 12 upper studios, 4 poolside studios* ❙⊘❙ *No meals.*

KANGAROO ISLAND

Kangaroo Island, Australia's third largest (after Tasmania and Melville), is barely 16 km (10 miles) from the Australian mainland. Yet the island belongs to another age—a folksy, friendly, less sophisticated time when you'd leave your car unlocked and knew everyone by name.

The island is most beautiful along the coastline, where the land is sculpted into a series of bays and inlets teeming with bird and marine life. The stark interior has its own charm, however, with pockets of red earth between stretches of bush and farmland. Wildlife is probably the island's greatest attraction; in a single day you can stroll along a beach crowded with sea lions and watch kangaroos, koalas, pelicans, and little penguins in their native environments.

Its towns and most of its accommodations are on the island's eastern third. The standout sights are on the southern coast, so if you've only one day—you could easily spend a week—it's best to tour the island in a clockwise direction, leaving the north-coast beaches for the afternoon. Before heading out, fill your gas tank and pack a picnic lunch. Shops are few and far between outside the towns, general stores being the main outlets for food and gas.

GETTING HERE AND AROUND
REX/Regional Express flies two times daily between Adelaide and Kingscote, the island's main airport. Ask about holiday packages in conjunction with SeaLink. Flights to the island take about 30 minutes.

SeaLink ferries allow access for cars through Penneshaw from Cape Jervis, at the tip of the Fleurieu Peninsula, a two-hour drive from Adelaide. There are four daily sailings each way, with additional crossings at peak times. SeaLink operates the vehicular passenger ferry *Sea Lion 2000* and *Spirit of Kangaroo Island*, a designated freight boat with passenger

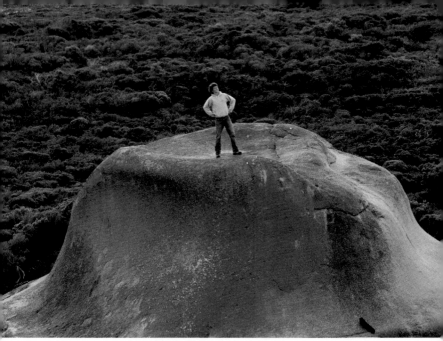
Remarkable Rocks are one of Kangaroo island's signature landmarks.

facilities. These ferries make 45-minute crossings between Cape Jervis and Penneshaw. Ferries are the favored means of transportation between the island and the mainland, and reservations are necessary. Adelaide Sightseeing operates coach tours of Kangaroo Island out of Adelaide in conjunction with the SeaLink ferry services from A$269 for a (very long) day trip.

Kangaroo Island's main attractions are widely scattered; you can see them best on a guided tour or by car. The main roads form a paved loop, which branches off to such major sites as Seal Bay and Admirals Arch and Remarkable Rocks in Flinders Chase National Park. Stretches of unpaved road lead to lighthouses at Cape Borda and Cape Willoughby, South Australia's oldest. Roads to the island's northern beaches, bays, and camping areas are also unpaved. These become very rutted in summer, but they can be driven carefully in a conventional vehicle. Be alert for wildlife, especially at dawn, dusk, and after dark. Slow down and dip your lights so you don't blind the animals you see.

Transportation Adelaide Sightseeing. ☒ *85 Franklin St., City Center* ☎ *1300/769762* ⊕ *www.adelaidesightseeing.com.au.* **REX/Regional Express.** ☎ *13–1713* ⊕ *www.regionalexpress.com.au.* **SeaLink.** ☎ *13–1301* ⊕ *www.sealink.com.au.*

TOURS

Exceptional Kangaroo Island. Exceptional Kangaroo Island has quality four-wheel-drive and bushwalking tours. Tailor-made itineraries, including bird-watching and photography, and flight-accommodation packages can also be arranged. ☎ *08/8553–9119* ⊕ *www.exceptionalkangarooisland. com* ✈ *From A$425.*

Kangaroo Island Odysseys. Kangaroo Island Odysseys operates luxury four-wheel-drive nature tours from one to three days; expect lots of wildlife and lots of great food. ☎ *08/8553–0386* ⊕ *www. kangarooislandodysseys.com.au* ✈ *From A$440.*

HOW REMARKABLE

Balanced precariously on the promontory of Kirkpatrick Point in Flinders Chase National Park, the Remarkable Rocks are aptly named. Sitting with your back against one of these fantastically shaped boulders is the best way to view sunset or sunrise on Kangaroo Island.

Kangaroo Island Wilderness Tours. Kangaroo Island Wilderness Tours has five personalized four-wheel-drive wilderness tours from one to four days; a range of accommodation packages is available. ☎ *08/8559– 5033* ⊕ *www.wildernesstours.com.au* ✈ *From A$451.*

SeaLink Kangaroo Island. SeaLink Kangaroo Island operates one-day (A$269) bus tours of the island, departing from Adelaide, in conjunction with the ferry service from Cape Jervis. They also can arrange fishing and self-drive tours and extended packages. Two-day/one-night tours are A$387 and up per person; three-day/two-night self-drive tours start at A$255 per person. ✉ *440 King William St., Adelaide* ☎ *13– 1301* ⊕ *www.sealink.com.au* ✈ *From A$157.*

ESSENTIALS

Visitor Information Department of Environment, Water and Natural Resources Office. ✉ *Natural Resources Centre Kangaroo Island, 37 Dauncey St., Kingscote* ☎ *08/8553–4444* ⊕ *www.environment.sa.gov.au/parks.* **Kangaroo Island Gateway Visitor Information Centre.** ✉ *Howard Dr., Penneshaw* ☎ *1800/8553–1185* ⊕ *www.tourkangarooisland.com.au.*

KINGSCOTE

121 km (75 miles) southwest of Adelaide.

Kangaroo Island's largest town, Kingscote is a good base for exploring. Reeves Point, at the town's northern end, is where South Australia's colonial history began. Settlers landed here in 1836 and established the first official town in the new colony. Little remains of the original settlement except Hope Cottage, now a small museum; several graves; and a huge, twisted mulberry tree that grew from a cutting the settlers brought from England—locals still use the fruit to make jam. Today American River, about halfway between Kingscote and Penneshaw, the island's second-largest town, is another accommodation and restaurant hub.

WHERE TO STAY

$$$
RENTAL
FAMILY

🏠 **Acacia Apartments.** A huge movie collection in the reception area confirms that the self-contained one- and two-bedroom units at this Reeve's Point complex are family-friendly. **Pros:** kid-friendly; very amenable owner. **Cons:** slightly overpriced; 10 am check-out time. ⑤ *Rooms from: A$265* ✉ *3-5 Rawson St.* ☎ *08/8553–0088, 1800/247007* ⊕ *www. acacia-apartments.com.au* ⇝ *10 apartments* ⦿�| *Breakfast.*

$$
HOTEL

Ozone Hotel. The original Victorian facade on this two-story 1920s hotel, directly opposite the new section across the road, hides surprisingly modern and spacious rooms that overlook Nepean Bay. The choicest accommodations, however, are in the newer adjoining wing. **Pros:** across the street from the waterfront; friendly staff. **Cons:** older rooms are old-fashioned, as is the breakfast. $ *Rooms from: A$159 ⊠ Commercial St.* ☎ *08/8553–2011, 1800/083133* ⊕ *www.auroraresorts.com. au* ↻ *75 rooms* ⍾ *All meals.*

$$
RENTAL
FAMILY

Kangaroo Island Bayview Villas. Located on a hillside overlooking Nepean Bay and the town of Kingscote, these bayview villas are fully equipped, self-contained style accommodations with a private patio and barbecue facilities. **Pros:** panoramic views; self-contained; modern and spacious; good for groups and/or families. **Cons:** single-night surcharge is included for one-night stays. $ *Rooms from: A$199 ⊠ 20 Reeves St.* ☎ *08/8553–0149* ⊕ *www.bayview-villas.com.au* ↻ *4 villas* ⍾ *No meals.*

$$$
RESORT

Mercure Kangaroo Island Lodge. Facing beautiful Eastern Cove at American River, the island's oldest resort has rooms that overlook open water or the saltwater pool; the most attractive are the "waterview" rooms, which have mud-brick walls, warm terra-cotta tones, and king-size beds. **Pros:** set in beautiful and peaceful surroundings; nearby trails lead to kangaroos and pelicans. **Cons:** dated rooms and basic breakfast. $ *Rooms from: A$225 ⊠ Scenic Dr., American River* ☎ *08/8553–7053, 1800/355581* ⊕ *www.kilodge.com.au* ↻ *38 rooms* ⍾ *Some meals.*

$$$
B&B/INN

Wanderers Rest. Delightful local artworks dot the walls in this country inn's stylish units, all of which have king-size beds. **Pros:** simple, high-quality accommodation with stunning views. **Cons:** kids under 10 aren't allowed; tours and extras quickly add up. $ *Rooms from: A$246 ⊠ Bayview Rd., Lot 2, American River* ☎ *08/8553–7140* ⊕ *www. wanderersrest.com.au* ↻ *8 suites* ⍾ *Breakfast.*

PENNESHAW

62 km (39 miles) east of Kingscote.

This tiny ferry port once had a huge population of penguins—locals would complain about the birds burrowing in their gardens and you'd often see them around town after dark—but sadly, the colony's numbers have decreased in recent years due to an increased number of seals (and domestic cats and dogs) who prey on the flightless birds. You can still see some on nocturnal tours, but other reasons to visit Penneshaw include a gorgeous shoreline, views of spectacularly blue water, and rolling green hills.

EXPLORING

FAMILY **Penneshaw Penguin Centre.** There are now only around 15 pairs of the delightful little (formally called fairy) penguins in the colony here at Penneshaw. From the indoor interpretive center, where you can read about bird activity—including mating, nesting, and feeding—a boardwalk leads to a viewing platform above rocks and sand riddled with burrows. Because the penguins spend most of the day fishing at sea or inside their burrows, the best viewing is after sunset. The informative guided tour starts with a talk and video at the center. You might see penguins waddling ashore, chicks emerging from their burrows to feed, or scruffy adults molting—although sadly, sometimes you may not see any at all. ✉ *Middle and Bay Terr.* ☎ *08/8553–7407* ⊕ *www.users.on.net/~nickpike/ penguins.html* ✍ *Guided tours A$13, bookings essential* ⊙ *Mar.–Jan., tour times vary, check when booking* ⊙ *Closed Feb. 1–21.*

Sunset Winery. Sip smooth Chardonnay while overlooking Eastern Cove at this calm, cool, and pristine addition to Kangaroo Island's thriving wine industry. You can sample wines for free at the cellar door, and opt for the Savoury Platter: a selection of Kangaroo Island and regional cheeses, KI Source Relish, South Rock Salami, local olives, crackers, and more for A$28. Alternately, try a Dukkah Plate from the Fleurieu, served with local Wild olive oil and delicious local bread for A$15. ✉ *4564 Hog Bay Rd.* ☎ *08/8553–1378* ⊙ *Daily 11–5.*

OFF THE BEATEN PATH South Australia's oldest lighthouse stands on Kangaroo Island's easternmost point, Cape Willoughby, 27 km (17 miles) from Penneshaw, on a mostly unpaved road. You can explore the property around the towering, white lighthouse, but only guided tours (A$14.50 or KI Pass) can enter the 1852 building itself. Tours depart from the National Parks office in one of the three 1920s lighthouse keepers' cottages. The other two cottages have been converted into self-contained accommodations that let you experience Kangaroo Island at its most remote and wildest—it's always windy here!

BEACHES

Island Beach. Known locally as Millionaires' Row for its fabulous real estate, Island Beach is the quintessential beach holiday location. Framed by dense bushland, the sandy beach is secluded and stretches almost as far as the eye can see and provides very safe swimming. Walking along the coast towards American River yields plenty of bird-watching opportunities. **Amenities:** parking; food and drink. **Best for:** swimming; walking; solitude. ✉ *Off Island Beach Rd., Island Beach.*

WHERE TO EAT AND STAY

$$
SEAFOOD ✕ **Fish of Penneshaw.** Belly up to the counter in this tiny shop for cheap local seafood, to take out or enjoy with a glass of wine in the seating area next door. Choose your fish—whiting, John Dory, garfish—from the blackboard menu and have it beer-battered, crumbed, or grilled. Or you might prefer a paper-wrapped parcel of scallops, prawns, lobster, and oysters (in season) shucked to order. ⑤ *Average main: A$25* ✉ *43 North Terr.* ☎ *08/8553–1177 Fish of Penneshaw, 08/8553–7406 2 Birds & A Squid* ⊕ *www.2birds1squid.com/fish-of-penneshaw* ☰ *No credit cards* ⊙ *Closed May–mid-Oct. No lunch.*

$$
HOTEL ⊞ **Kangaroo Island Seafront Resort.** This hotel has an ideal position near the ferry terminal and overlooking Penneshaw Bay. You can choose an ocean-view room or stay amid tropical gardens in freestanding chalets. **Pros:** steps away from ferry terminal and penguin viewing; spacious rooms; free Wi-Fi. **Cons:** older parts of the hotel are showing their age; no air-conditioning in rooms. ⑤ *Rooms from: A$187* ✉ *49 North Terr.* ☎ *08/8553–1028, 1800/624624* ⊕ *www.seafront.com.au* ⌁ *6 rooms, 12 villas* ⫯◎⫰ *Breakfast.*

9

"Naptime on the beach at Kangaroo Island" —photo by Istarr, Fodors.com member

SEAL BAY CONSERVATION PARK

60 km (37 miles) southwest of Kingscote via South Coast Rd.

There are no seals in Seal Bay, but a visit to Seal Bay is a highlight of most people's time on Kangaroo Island—it's one of the only places in the world where you can walk along a beach crowded with wild sea lions. The endangered Australian sea lion is one of the rarest species in the world, Seal Bay is home to around 1,000—the misleading name is thanks to whalers who couldn't tell the difference between seals and sea lions (the latter have ear flaps and can use their back flippers to 'walk' on land, unlike seals). The tours here are some of the best close-up animal encounters of their kind.

EXPLORING

FAMILY

Fodor's Choice

★

Seal Bay Conservation Park. This top Kangaroo Island attraction gives you the chance to visit one of the state's largest Australian sea lion colonies. About 300 animals usually lounge on the beach, except on stormy days, when they shelter in the dunes. You can only visit the beach, and get surprisingly close to females, pups, and bulls, on a 45-minute tour with an interpretive officer; otherwise, you can follow the self-guided boardwalk to a lookout over the sand. ■ TIP→ **Two-hour twilight tours are only available during South Australian Daylight Savings times and visitors must call ahead.** The park visitor center has fun and educational displays, and a touch table covered in sea-lion skins and bones. There is also a shop. ⊠ *End of Seal Bay Rd.* ☎ *08/8553–4463* ⊕ *www. environment.sa.gov.au/sealbay/home* ☒ *Tour A$33 per person, twilight tour A$60, boardwalk A$16* ☾ *Tours Dec. and Jan., daily 9–5, every 15–45 min; Feb.–Nov., daily 9–5, every 45 min.*

BEACHES

Vivonne Bay. This is one of the most popular surfing beaches on the island's south coast; the 5-km (3-mile) white-sand beach is also one of the most pristine to swim. Safe swimming areas can be found near the jetty and boat ramp, or the sandy-bottomed Harriet River entering the bay. On the other side of the river, Point Ellen provides photographers with spectacular views of the Southern Ocean. Vivonne Bay is billed as the only safe harbor on the south coast of Kangaroo Island and is the base for crayfishing boats from November to May. You'll also find barbecue and picnic areas, toilets, and a camping area. The beach can be reached by taking the road just past the Vivonne Bay store. **Amenities:** parking; toilets; food and drink. **Best for:** swimming; surfing; solitude; walking. ⊠ *Bayview Rd., Vivonne Bay.*

OFF THE BEATEN PATH

Hanson Bay. A narrow, winding, unsealed road off South Coast Road, 46 km (29 miles) west of Seal Bay Road, ends at this perfect little sandy cove. Rocky headlands on either side protect the gently sloping beach so swimming is safe. To the east are several secluded beaches; these are more exposed, though, and riptides make swimming dangerous. **Amenities:** parking; toilets. **Best for:** swimming; walking; surfing. ⊠ *West River Rd., off South Coast Rd., Karatta.*

FLINDERS CHASE NATIONAL PARK

102 km (64 miles) west of Kingscote.

Some of Australia's most beautiful coastal scenery is in Flinders Chase National Park on Kangaroo Island.

EXPLORING

Fodor's Choice ★

Flinders Chase National Park. The effects of seas crashing mercilessly onto Australia's southern coast are visible in the oddly shaped rocks on the island's shores. A limestone promontory was carved from beneath at Cape du Couedic on the southwestern coast, producing what is known as **Admiral's Arch.** From the boardwalk you can see the New Zealand fur seals that have colonized the area around the rock formation. About 4 km (2½ miles) farther east are the aptly named **Remarkable Rocks,** huge, fantastically shaped boulders balanced precariously on the promontory of Kirkpatrick Point. This is a great place to watch the sun set or rise.

Much of Kangaroo Island has been cultivated since settlement, but after being declared a national treasure in 1919, a huge area of original vegetation has been protected in Flinders Chase and the park has several 1½-km to 9-km (1-mile to 5½-mile) loop walking trails, which take one to three hours to complete. The trails meander along the rivers to the coast, passing mallee scrub and sugar gum forests, and explore the rugged shoreline. The 4-km (2½-mile) Snake Lagoon Hike follows Rocky River over and through a series of broad rocky terraces to the remote sandy beach where it meets the sea. The sign warning of freak waves is not just for show.

The park is on the island's western end, bounded by the Playford and West End highways. The state-of-the-art visitor center, open daily 9–5,

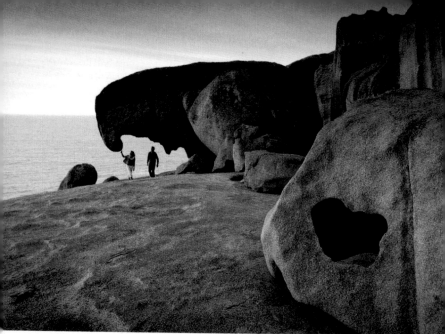

Lots of Remarkable Rocks, Flinders Chase National Park

is the largest National Parks and Wildlife office. Displays and touch screens explore the park's history and the different habitats and wildlife in Flinders Chase. The center provides park entry tickets and camping permits, and books stays at the Heritage cabins. A shop sells souvenirs and provisions, and there is also a café. ✉ *South Coast Rd.* ⊕ *www. environment.sa.gov.au* ✉ *A$11 entry fee; 2-day pass A$16.*

SPORTS AND THE OUTDOORS

FISHING

Fishing is excellent on Kangaroo Island's beaches, bays, and rivers. The island's deep-sea fishing fleet holds several world records for tuna. No permit is required for recreational fishing, but minimum lengths and bag limits apply. You can pick up a fishing guide from the information center in Penneshaw.

Cooinda Fishing Charters. Cooinda runs fishing charters from half a day to three days out of American River. ✉ *American River Wharf, Muston* ☎ *08/8553–7236* ⊕ *www.cooindafishingcharters.com.*

Turner Fuel. This spot sells fishing tackle and bait. ✉ *26 Telegraph Rd., Kingscote* ☎ *08/8553–2725.*

WHERE TO STAY

$$
RESORT
🏨 **Kangaroo Island Wilderness Retreat.** With wallabies and possums treating the grounds as their own domain, this eco-friendly retreat is everything a wildlife-loving traveler could want. **Pros:** wonderful experience for animal lovers; free Internet access and DVDs. **Cons:** only two time slots for dinner; basic rooms might disappoint city slickers. ⑤ *Rooms from: A$190*

✉ *1 South Coast Rd.* ☎ *08/8559–7275* ⊕ *www.kiwr.com* ⇆ *18 courtyard rooms, 2 suites, 4 apartments, 7 lodge rooms* ❧ *All meals.*

$$$$
HOTEL
Fodor's Choice
★

🏨 **Southern Ocean Lodge.** This truly remarkable hotel might be the highlight of your trip—if money is no object. **Pros:** superb restaurant; simple but stunning decor exudes luxury and class. **Cons:** if you have to ask the price, you can't afford this place; sophisticated surroundings are not really suitable for children, though kids over 6 years are welcome. ⑤ *Rooms from: A$1100* ✉ *Hanson Bay Rd., Kingscote* ☎ *08/8559–7347* ⊕ *www.southernoceanlodge.com.au* ⇆ *21 suites* ❧ *All-inclusive.*

THE OUTBACK

South Australia is the country's driest state, and its Outback is an expanse of desert vegetation. But this land of scrubby salt bush and hardy eucalyptus trees is brightened after rain by wildflowers—including the state's floral emblem, the blood-red Sturt's desert pea, with its black, olive-like heart. The terrain is marked by geological uplifts, abrupt transitions between plateaus broken at the edges of ancient, long-inactive fault lines. Few roads track through this desert wilderness—the main highway is the Stuart, which runs all the way to Alice Springs in the Northern Territory.

The people of the Outback are as hardy as their surroundings. They are also often eccentric, colorful characters who happily bend your ear over a drink in the local pub. Remote, isolated communities attract loners, adventurers, fortune-seekers, and people simply on the run. In this unyielding country, you must be tough to survive.

COOBER PEDY

850 km (527 miles) northwest of Adelaide.

Known as much for the way most of its 1,700 inhabitants live—underground in dugouts gouged into the hills to escape the relentless heat—as for its opal riches, Coober Pedy is arguably Australia's most singular place. The town is ringed by mullock heaps, pyramids of rock and sand left over after mine shafts are dug.

Opals are Coober Pedy's reason for existence. Australia has 95% of the world's opal deposits, and Coober Pedy has the bulk of that wealth; this is the world's richest opal field.

Coober Pedy is a brick-and-corrugated-iron settlement propped unceremoniously on a scarred desert landscape. It's a town built for efficiency, not beauty. However, its ugliness has a kind of bizarre appeal. There's a feeling that you're in the last lawless outpost in the modern world, helped in no small part by the local film lore—*Priscilla Queen of the Desert, Pitch Black, Kangaroo Jack,* and *Mad Max 3* were filmed here. Once you go off the main street, you get an immediate sense of the apocalyptic.

GETTING HERE AND AROUND

REX/Regional Express Airlines flies direct to Coober Pedy from Adelaide Sunday–Friday. Because it's the only public carrier flying to Coober Pedy, prices are sometimes steep. The airport is open only when a flight is arriving or departing. At other times, contact the Desert Cave Hotel.

Greyhound Australia buses leave Adelaide's Central Bus Station for Coober Pedy daily. Tickets for the 12-hour overnight ride can cost A$148–A$180 each way.

The main road to Coober Pedy is the Sturt Highway from Adelaide, 850 km (527 miles) to the south. Alice Springs is 700 km (434 miles) north of Coober Pedy. The drive from Adelaide to Coober Pedy takes about nine hours. From Alice Springs it's about seven hours.

A rental car enables you to see what lies beyond Hutchison Street, but an organized tour is a better way to do so. Thrifty and Budget have rental-car outlets in Coober Pedy. Although some roads are unpaved—those to the Breakaways and the Dog Fence, for example—surfaces are generally suitable for conventional vehicles. Check on road conditions with the police if there has been substantial rain.

The most interesting route to Flinders Ranges National Park from Adelaide takes you north through the Clare Valley vineyards and Burra's copper-mining villages. For a more direct journey to Wilpena Pound, follow the Princes Highway (A1) north to Port Augusta, and then head east toward Quorn and Hawker. A four-wheel-drive vehicle is highly recommended for traveling on the many gravel roads around the national park.

Transportation Coober Pedy Airport. ✉ *Airport Rd., off Stuart Hwy., 2 km (1 mile) north of town* ☎ *08/8672–5688.* **Greyhound Australia.** ✉ *Hutchinson St.* ☎ *1800/801294, 1300/4739–46863* ⊕ *www.greyhound.com.au.* **REX/Regional Express.** ☎ *13–1713* ⊕ *www.rex.com.au.*

ESSENTIALS

Visitor Information Coober Pedy Tourist Information Centre. ✉ *Coober Pedy District Council Bldg., Hutchison St., LOT 773* ☎ *1800/637076* ⊕ *www. cooberpedy.sa.gov.au.* **Wilpena Pound Visitor Centre.** ✉ *1 Wilpena Rd., Hawker* ☎ *08/8648–0048* ⊕ *www.environment.sa.gov.au.*

EXPLORING

Fossicking for opal gemstones—locally called noodling—requires no permit at the Jewellers Shop mining area at the edge of town. Take care in unmarked areas, and always watch your step, as the area is littered with abandoned opal mines down which you might fall. (Working mines are off-limits to visitors.)

Although most of Coober Pedy's devotions are decidedly material in nature, the town does have its share of spiritual houses of worship. In keeping with the town's layout, they, too, are underground. **St. Peter and St. Paul's Catholic Church** is a National Heritage–listed building, and the Anglican **Catacomb Church** is notable for its altar fashioned from a windlass (a winch) and lectern made from a log of mulga wood. The **Serbian Orthodox Church** is striking, with its scalloped ceiling, rock-carved icons, and brilliant stained-glass windows.

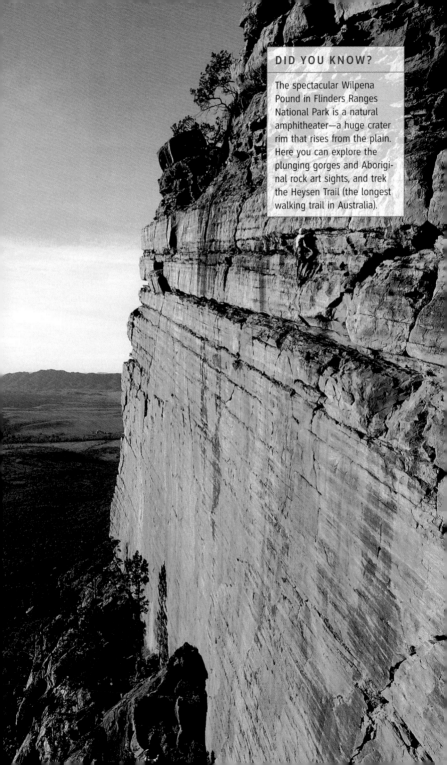

IN TOWN

Old Timers Mine. This is a genuine opal mine turned into a museum. Two underground houses, furnished in 1920s and 1980s styles, are part of the complex, where mining memorabilia is exhibited in an extensive network of hand-dug tunnels and shafts. You can also watch demonstrations of opal-mining machines. Tours are self-guided. ⊠ *Crowders Gully Rd. near Umoona Rd.* ☎ *08/8672–5555* ⌨ *A$15* ⊙ *Daily 9–5.*

Umoona Opal Mine & Museum. This is an enormous underground complex with an original mine, a noteworthy video on the history of opal mining, an Aboriginal Interpretive Center, and clean, underground bunk camping and cooking facilities. Guided tours of the mine are available. ⊠ *14 Hutchison St.* ☎ *08/8672–5288* ⊕ *www.umoonaopalmine.com. au* ⌨ *Tour A$10* ⊙ *Daily 8–6; tours at 10, 2, and 4.*

AROUND TOWN

Breakaways. A striking series of buttes and jagged hills centered on the Moon Plain is reminiscent of the American West. There are fossils and patches of petrified forest in this strange landscape, which has appealed to makers of apocalyptic films. *Mad Max 3—Beyond Thunderdome* was filmed here, as was *Ground Zero*. The scenery is especially evocative early in the morning or at sunset. The Breakaways area is 30 km (19 miles) northeast of Coober Pedy. ■**TIP**➜ **Permits to explore the area cost A$10 per vehicle and can be purchased at the Coober Pedy Tourist Information Centre in the District Council Office on Hutchinson Street.** ⊠ *Off Stuart Hwy. 33 km (20 miles) north of Coober Pedy* ⊕ *www. cooberpedy.sa.gov.au* ⌨ *Permits A$10 per vehicle.*

Fodor'sChoice **Mail Run Tour.** This 12-hour, 600-km (372-mile) tour through the Out-
★   back (A$195) is one of the most unusual experiences anywhere, with stops at outback cattle stations, bush pubs, and the world's longest manmade structure, the Dingo Fence. Tours depart Monday and Thursday at 8:45 am from Underground Books on Post Office Hill Road. ⊠ *Lot 374, Post Office Hill Rd.* ☎ *08/8672–5226, 1800/069911* ⊕ *www. mailruntour.com* ⌨ *A$195 per seat (no children's or concession prices).*

WHERE TO EAT AND STAY

$$ ✕**Nostimo Pizza.** Locals swear that the pizzas at the popular Stuart
PIZZA Range outback resort and caravan park are among Australia's best—maybe, maybe not, but they are certainly the best in Coober Pedy. The toppings combinations can be classic, creative, or gourmet, such as the Noon (with tomato, mushrooms, and onions) and the Garlic Prawn (with basil pesto and semi-dried tomatoes). Ⓢ *Average main: A$25* ⊠ *Stuart Hwy. at Hutchison St.* ☎ *08/8672–5179, 1800/067787* ⊕ *www.stuartrangecaravanpark.com.au* ⊙ *No lunch.*

$$ ✕**Umbertos.** Perched atop the underground Desert Cave Hotel, this eat-
AUSTRALIAN ery named after the hotel's founding developer is Coober Pedy's most urbane restaurant. The Mod Oz menu takes you from the Outback (oven-baked kangaroo loin with grilled figs) to the sea (lemon sole). Ⓢ *Average main: A$30* ⊠ *Hutchison St.* ☎ *08/8672–5688* ⊕ *www. desertcave.com.au* ⊙ *No lunch.*

$$$ ⚏ **Desert Cave Hotel.** This underground hotel presents a contemporary,
HOTEL blocky face to the desert town. **Pros:** unique place to stay; pool is wel-
Fodor's Choice come relief in the heat; underground rooms are very quiet. **Cons:** not for
★ the claustrophobic; overpriced for what you get. ⑤ *Rooms from: A$259*
✉ *Lot 1, Hutchison St. at Post Office Hill Rd.* ☎ *08/8672–5688* ⊕ *www.
desertcave.com.au* ⥲ *50 rooms, with 19 underground* ⧀ *Some meals.*

$ ⚏ **The Underground Motel.** The Breakaways sometimes seem close enough
HOTEL to touch at this hilltop motel, where you can lounge on a veranda
watching the sun set on the rock formations 30 km (19 miles) across the
desert. **Pros:** lovely patio to sit out on and watch the stars; very helpful
owners. **Cons:** slightly out of town, which in the heat is a disadvantage;
rooms are a little dated. ⑤ *Rooms from: A$135* ✉ *1185 Catacomb Rd.*
☎ *08/8672–5324* ⊕ *www.theundergroundmotel.com.au* ⥲ *6 rooms, 2
suites* ⧀ *Breakfast.*

IKARA-FLINDERS RANGES NATIONAL PARK

*690 km (430 miles) southeast of Coober Pedy, 460 km (285 miles)
northeast of Adelaide.*

Extending north from Spencer Gulf, the Flinders Ranges mountain
chain includes one of Australia's most impressive Outback parks. These
dry, folded, and cracked mountains, once the bed of an ancient sea, have
been sculpted by millions of years of rain and sun. Cypress pine and
casuarina cover this furrowed landscape of deep valleys, which slope
into creeks lined with river red gums. The area is utterly fascinating—
both for geologists and for anyone else who revels in wild, raw scenery
and exotic plant and animal life.

EXPLORING

Ikara-Flinders Ranges National Park. The numerous steep trails make the
Flinders Ranges ideal for bushwalking, even though the park has few
amenities. Water in this region is scarce, and should be carried at all
times. The best time for walking is during the relatively cool months
between April and October. This is also the wettest time of year, so you
should be prepared for rain. Wildflowers, including the spectacular
Sturt's desert pea, are abundant between September and late October.

The park's most spectacular walking trail leads to the summit of 3,840-
foot **St. Mary's Peak,** the highest point on the Pound's rim and South
Australia's second-tallest peak. The more scenic of the two routes to the
top is the outside trail (15-km [9-mile] return); give yourself a full day
to get up and back. The midsection of the ascent is steep and strenu-
ous, but views from the summit—including the distant white glitter of
the salt flats on Lake Frome—make the climb worthwhile. ✉ *End of
Wilpena Rd., Hawker* ☎ *08/8648–0048* ⧀ *A$10 entry fee per vehicle.*

Wilpena Pound. The scenic center of the Flinders Ranges is the
crater-like Wilpena Pound, an 80-square-km (31-square-mile) bowl
ringed by hills that curve gently upward, only to fall away from the
rims of sheer cliffs. The only entrance to the Pound is a narrow cleft
through which Wilpena Creek sometimes runs. The best way to see it
is from above—scenic flights are available at Wilpena Pound Resort

(from A\$169) and are well worth the splurge. ⊠ *Wilpena Rd., Hawker* ⊕ *www.wilpenapound.com.au.*

Wilpena Pound Visitor Information Centre. A mud-brick visitor center, part of the Wilpena Pound Resort, has information about hiking trails and campsites within the park. ⊠ *1 Wilpena Rd., Hawker* ☎ *08/8648–0048* ⊕ *www.wilpenapound.com.au.*

WHERE TO STAY

\$\$\$

RESORT

⟨⟩ **Wilpena Pound Resort.** You couldn't ask for a more idyllic and civilized nature outpost than this popular resort at the entrance to Wilpena Pound. **Pros:** quiet and peaceful rooms; perfect for animal lovers. **Cons:** campsites can be overrun with school groups; permanent tents are overpriced. ⑤ *Rooms from: A\$227* ⊠ *1 Wilpena Rd., Hawker* ✛ *156 km (97 miles) off the Princes Hwy. via town of Hawker* ☎ *08/8648–0004* ⊕ *www.wilpenapound.com.au* ⤳ *60 rooms including 10 suites, 15 safari tents, 2 permanent tents, 44 powered sites, unlimited unpowered sites* ❙❍❙ *Some meals.*

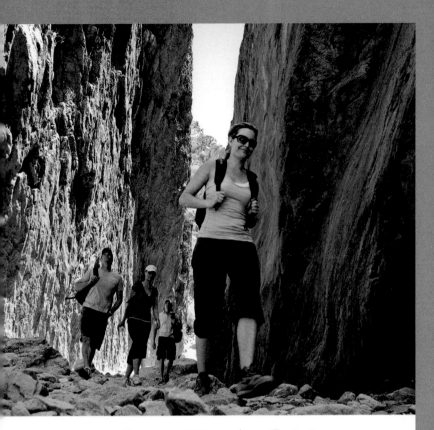

THE OUTBACK

WELCOME TO THE OUTBACK

TOP REASONS TO GO

★ **Red Heart:** Watching the sun rise and set at Uluru (Ayers Rock) is a once-in-a-lifetime experience you'll never forget.

★ **Old Culture:** The Red Centre, Top End, and the Kimberley are the best places to experience one of the oldest cultures in the world, that of Australia's Aborigines.

★ **National Parks:** With spectacular terrain and one-of-a-kind plant and animal species, rugged national parks tell the story of Australia's age-old landforms, especially across the gorge-pocked Kimberley region.

★ **Wild Rivers:** The waterways and billabongs of the Top End teem with wildlife, including saltwater crocodiles and a multitude of birdlife.

★ **Cable Beach:** It may be touristy, but riding a camel into the sunset on one of Australia's most beautiful beaches is hard to resist.

1 Red Centre. Uluru (Ayers Rock) is one of Australia's iconic images, and the main reason people visit the Red Centre. A striking sight, it is one of the world's largest monoliths, the last vestige of an ancient mountain range that looms 1,100 feet above the surrounding plain. But, there is more than just "the Rock" in the Red Centre—traditional Aboriginal "Dreamtime" stories overlie a region rich in geological wonders.

2 The Top End. The "Top End" of Australia packs in some of the world's great natural environments—and with few people to crowd the views. Add in modern and ancient Aboriginal art and locals with a definite individualistic attitude, and

Cape Wessel

Arafura Sea

Jabiru　Nhulunbuy

Gulf of Carpentaria

Katherine
Mataranka

Daly Waters　Borroloola

11

0 ——— 200 mi
0 ——— 200 km

Tennant Creek　66

Barrow Creek

87

Alice Springs

QUEENSLAND

SOUTH AUSTRALIA

GETTING ORIENTED

Big, vast, expansive, huge—whichever way you cut it, the Northern Territory is daunting. This, in many respects, is the "real Australia" as you imagine it—remote, mostly uninhabited, the landscape ground down over millennia. Getting around by road will absorb days, if not weeks, but fortunately air services can cut the travel times between the gems of this vast area—the Red Centre, the Top End, and the Kimberley—to hours not days.

10

you have an Australia so different from Sydney and Melbourne that you'll think you're in another country entirely.

3 **The Kimberley.** Look no further than the Kimberley for a genuine Outback experience. This remote area contains several of Australia's most spectacular national parks, and numerous tropical forests, croc-infested rivers, and soaring cliffs.

ABORIGINAL CULTURE

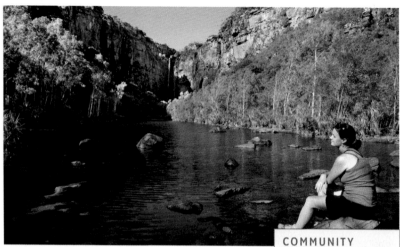

When Europeans arrived to establish a permanent colony in what was to become New South Wales, Aboriginal people had been living across the continent for at least 50,000 years.

Perhaps 600 different "clan groups" or "nations"—each with its own distinctive culture and beliefs—greeted the new settlers in a clash of civilizations that remains largely unresolved today. Despite the efforts of governments of all persuasions and society at large, Aboriginal people by all measures—economic, health, social, education—remain an underprivileged group.

But Aboriginal culture as expressed in oral tradition, art, and lifestyle and by sacred sites such as Uluru is of growing interest to travelers. Experiences range from organized tours to dance performances, shopping for traditional Aboriginal artifacts and art, and the opportunity to visit Aboriginal land to experience the daily lives of Aboriginal people. Tourism represents an important source of income ensuring that Aboriginal communities prosper and that their heritage is preserved.

COMMUNITY VALUES

Welcome to Country is an important ritual. Protocol dictates that people are welcomed when entering and learning about Country; for many this is simply good manners and respect. It's likely you will enjoy a Welcome to Country if you join any Aboriginal-guided tour.

In some cultures there were once strict rules about eye contact; you may find that some people follow this practice and won't make eye contact with you. This, or lowering the eyes, are two actions that are often a show of respect toward older people.

SACRED SITES

Uluru (Ayers Rock) is probably Australia's best-known natural site, but it also has significant cultural meaning for the traditional owners, the Anangu people. They believe they are direct descendants of the beings—which include a python, an emu, a blue-tongue lizard, and a poisonous snake—who formed the land and its physical features during the Tjukurpa (the "Dreamtime," or creation period). Rising more than 1,100 feet from the surrounding plain, Uluru is one of the world's largest monoliths, though such a classification belies the otherworldly, spiritual energy surrounding it.

Kakadu National Park contains some of the best ancient rock art accessible to visitors in Australia. The Anbangbang Gallery has a frieze of Aboriginal rock painting dating back thousands of years, while among the six galleries at Ubirr there is a 49-foot frieze of X-ray paintings depicting animals, birds, and fish. Warradjan Aboriginal Cultural Centre's large display, developed by the local Bininj/Mungguy people, provides detailed information about Aboriginal culture in Kakadu.

Purnululu National Park (the Bungle Bungles) is an amazing geological wonder and a site for Aboriginal culture. Although the Bungle Bungle Range was extensively used by Aboriginal people during the wet season, when plant and animal life was abundant, few Europeans knew of its existence until the mid-1980s. The area is rich in Aboriginal rock art, and there are also many burial sites, although these are not typically open to visitors.

Farther west in the **Kimberley Region** the pearling town of **Broome** is the starting point for many adventure tours into the remote Outback, and visiting Aboriginal communities such as Bardi Creek, Biridu Community, and One Arm Point Community with local Aboriginal guides. Geickie Gorge, Windjana Gorge, and Tunnel Creek combine wilderness scenery with indigenous rock art, lifestyles, and stories from the Dreamtime.

TOP SIGHTS

By far the best way to experience Aboriginal culture is on foot and with an experienced guide, though at some national parks, interpretive centers, signage, and—occasionally—self-guided audio equipment mean you can visit on your own. On foot generally requires a level of fitness and surefootedness for trails and pathways; even the best locations are uneven and stony, and can include steep climbs. Boats provide an alternative, such as at Geikie Gorge and Kakadu, where guided tours along the waterways include information about Aboriginal culture. From Broome, four-wheel-drive safaris can get you into remote Aboriginal communities where you can meet the locals and listen to campfire stories. If mobility is an issue, there are easily accessible interpretive centers at places like Uluru and Kakadu national parks that have extensive displays describing Aboriginal life.

10

Updated by
Lee Atkinson

Few visitors who explore Australia's remote Red Centre and wild Top End are left unmoved by the stark, expansive beauty of the landscape. The Outback's amazing World Heritage national parks, many on the ancestral homelands of the traditional indigenous owners, are home to some of Australia's most fascinating and iconic natural attractions, such as Ulruru (Ayers Rock), the magnificent Bungle Bungles, and the vast bird-filled wetlands and raging waterfalls of Kakadu. The Outback contains deeply carved rock canyons, deserts with unending horizons, and prolific wildlife. It is Australia at its wildest, rawest, and most sublime, and it's a landscape that will sear itself onto your memory forever.

The Top End of Australia is a geographic description—but it's also a state of mind. Isolated from the rest of Australia by thousands of miles of desert and lonely scrubland, Top Enders are different and proud of it, making the most of their isolation with a strongly independent and individualistic attitude. The region is a melting pot of cultures and traditions. Darwin and Broome—closer geographically to the cities of Southeast Asia than to any Australian counterparts—host the nation's most racially diverse populations: Aborigines, Anglos, and Asians share a tropical lifestyle.

In the west, the Kimberley offers some of the most dramatic landscapes in Australia. A land of rugged ranges and vast cattle stations, the Kimberley is still the frontier, a place even few Australians get to see. Like Top Enders, the people of the Kimberley region see themselves as living in a land apart from the rest of the nation, and it's easy to see why: climate extremes, inaccessibility of the landscape, and great distances combine to make the Kimberley one of the world's few uniquely unpeopled spaces.

For thousands of years this area of northern and central Australia has been home to Aboriginal communities that have undiminished ties to the land. Stunning examples of ancient Aboriginal rock art remain—on cliffs, in hidden valleys, and in city art galleries and cooperative art centers in remote communities. Aboriginal artwork has now moved into Australia's mainstream art movement, and some expensive canvases by Aboriginal artists decorate galleries, homes, and corporate boardrooms around the world. But there is more to Aboriginal culture than art, and there is no better place to try and understand it than here, on a guided tour of some of the country's most spiritually significant Aboriginal sites.

PLANNER

WHEN TO GO

May through September (Australia's winter) are the best months to visit the Red Centre and the Top End; nights are crisp and cold and days are pleasantly warm. Summer temperatures in the Centre—which can rise above 43°C (110°F)—are oppressive, while the wet season (December–April) means that Darwin and surroundings are hot, humid, and, well, wet. In the Kimberley May–November is the preferred season, with usually clear skies and balmy days and nights.

In the Top End the year is divided into the wet season (the Wet; December–April) and the dry season (the Dry; May–November). The Dry is a period of idyllic weather with warm days and cool nights, while the Wet brings monsoonal storms that dump an average of 52 inches of rain in a few months and result in widespread road closures. You can also catch spectacular electrical storms, particularly over the ocean. The "Build Up," in October, is the Top End's most oppressive weather period and should be avoided. The Kimberley has a similar wet season; however, the rainfall is less and generally comes in short, heavy storms. Cyclones also occur during this period and can disrupt travel arrangements.

PLANNING YOUR TIME

The sheer size of the Northern Territory means it is impossible to cover it all on a short visit. You will need to be selective.

If you choose one of Australia's great icons—Uluru—you could fly directly to Ayers Rock Airport and spend two days there, taking a hike around the rock followed by a look at the Uluru–Kata Tjuta Cultural Centre near its base.

The next day take a sightseeing flight by helicopter or fixed-wing aircraft, then visit Kata Tjuta (the Olgas) to explore its extraordinary domes and end the day with sunset at the rock. A flight will get you to Alice Springs, where you can tour out to either the Eastern or Western MacDonnell Ranges to explore the gorges and take a dip in a waterhole.

If you make Darwin your starting point, head east early on the Arnhem Highway to Fogg Dam to view the birdlife. Continue into Kakadu National Park and picnic at the rock-art site at Ubirr. Take a scenic flight in the afternoon, then a trip to the Bowali Visitors Centre, and you can overnight in Jabiru.

10

On the second day, head to Nourlangie Rock; then continue to the Yellow Water Billabong cruise at Cooinda and stay there for the night. The next day, drive to Litchfield National Park and visit Florence, Tjaynera, or Wangi Falls.

The easiest way to see Purnululu's amazing "beehive" rock formations is from the air. To do this you'll need to fly to Kununurra from Darwin or Broome, then take a sightseeing flight.

GETTING HERE AND AROUND

AIR TRAVEL

Darwin is the main international arrival point. Qantas and Virgin Australia are Australia's main domestic airlines, and both operate an extensive network and regular services crisscrossing the country from all the major cities to regional centers like Alice Springs and Broome. Both airlines also have budget subsidiaries, Jetstar (Qantas) and Tigerair (Virgin Australia). Air North has an extensive network throughout the Top End and covers some Western Australia legs.

CAR AND BUS TRAVEL

Driving around the Northern Territory is relatively easy, with mostly good paved roads and light traffic outside Darwin. But distances can be daunting. For example, Adelaide to Alice Springs via the Stuart Highway is 1,000 miles, and can take 24 hours. From Darwin to Broome is 1,152 miles, a tiring three-day drive, but you really want to take a week as there is much to see and do along the way. Greyhound Australia operates an extensive network of long-distance coaches. Although major highways usually remain open, many regional roads are closed during the wet season due to flooding.

TRAIN TRAVEL

Great Southern Railways operates the *Ghan* from Adelaide north to Alice Springs, then on to Darwin twice a week; return services from Darwin to Adelaide are also twice a week.

RESTAURANTS

Restaurants and cafés in the Northern Territory are largely reflective of their location: in the Red Centre you'll find "bush tucker" menus with crocodile, kangaroo, camel, and native fruits, berries, and plants; in Darwin and Broome locally caught seafood is prepared with flavor influences from Asia. Many restaurants and cafés offer alfresco dining. Tips aren't expected, but an extra 10% for exceptional service is welcome.

HOTELS

From five-star to basic, you'll find suitable accommodations throughout the region. The well-known international chains are largely in Darwin, but there are also sublime boutique accommodations set in wilderness or natural settings outside these centers, especially in the Kimberley. You can also experience Outback Australia at homesteads and working cattle stations, while owner-run bed-and-breakfasts provide comfort, charm, and a glimpse of local life. In the cities and the Outback there are plenty of less-than-memorable motels where you can at least get a clean bed for the night. Popular options—especially for families and small groups—are self-contained apartments, villas, and chalets. With two or three bedrooms, living areas, and kitchens, they allow you to save on dining costs by cooking your own meals; these are best if staying more than one night. *Hotel reviews have been shortened. For full information, visit Fodors.com.*

WHAT IT COSTS (IN AUSTRALIAN DOLLARS)			
	$	$$	$$$	$$$$
Restaurants	Under A$21	A$21–A$35	A$36–A$50	over A$50
Hotels	Under A$151	A$151–A$200	A$201–A$300	over A$300

Restaurant prices are the average cost of a main course at dinner or, if dinner isn't served, at lunch. Hotel prices are the lowest cost of a standard double room in high season, excluding service and tax.

HEALTH AND SAFETY

If you are self-driving—especially in remote areas—make sure you have enough fuel, water, and food and carry a first-aid kit. Let others know where you are going and for how long. If you go off bushwalking or hiking, bring adequate supplies and directions, and let others know your plan.

There are "critters" to avoid—snakes, crocodiles, and box jellyfish, for example. Mosquitoes are prevalent, so cover up and use a good insect repellent; the worst times for mosquitoes are dawn and dusk.

Respect the Australian sun, especially in summer. Sunburn is a real danger if you don't do what the Australians are urged to do: slip, slap, slop—that is, slip on a hat, slap on sunglasses, and slop on sunscreen. On popular beaches around major cities and towns, lifesavers (lifeguards) are usually on duty and put up flags to swim between, but generally most beaches are unguarded. Take extra care, especially where there are strong currents. Crocodiles are active in many of the Territory's waterways, so obey warning signs and check before swimming.

The emergency contact number for police, fire, and ambulance is ☎ *000*. From a GSM mobile (cell) phone you can also dial ☎ *112*, although triple zero will still get through. Telstra is the only service provider that has reliable network coverage outside of major cities; however, be aware that mobile phone coverage outside of town limits is almost nonexistent in the Outback. If traveling in remote areas by car consider renting a satellite phone, which you can find at many outback tourist information centers.

TOURS

If you want to avoid the hassles of getting yourself around this vast region, then a tour group is certainly an option. Hundreds of tours and tour operators cover Western Australia and the Northern Territory, and can introduce you to the many experiences on offer here: four-wheel-drive treks, helicopter flights, bush-tucker-gathering expeditions, Aboriginal-guided walks, fishing safaris, and national park tours to name a few.

You can also take a day tour or shorter overnight tours up to, say, five days. Most of these operate from Darwin, Broome, Perth, and Alice

Springs. The benefit is that all your transport, accommodation, meals, and sightseeing arrangements are preset, and you will get to see and do things you may otherwise miss if you try to organize them yourself.

Australian Adventure Travel. This company offers comfortable camping safaris for small groups through the Kimberley, using four-wheel-drive vehicles. Highlights of their 11-day Broome to Darwin safari include Gibb River Road, Cable Beach, Broome, Derby, Windjana Gorge, Tunnel Creek, Bells Gorge, the King Leopold Ranges, Aboriginal rock art, wildlife, El Questro Station, Kununurra, Bungle Bungles, and Darwin. ☎ *0434/923–274* ⊕ *www.safaris.net.au* ✉ *From A$1295.*

Fodor'sChoice
★
Bill Peach Journeys. This agency runs Aircruising Australia, using private aircraft to fly you to the icon attractions of central Australia, staying overnight in best-available hotels and motels. Their 12-day Great Australian Aircruise departs from and returns to Sydney, and includes stops at Longreach (Queensland), Katherine, Kakadu, and Darwin in the Northern Territory, Kununurra and Broome in Western Australia, and finally Uluru and Alice Springs in the Northern Territory. ☎ *02/9693–2233* ⊕ *www.billpeachjourneys.com.au* ✉ *From A$16,495.*

North Star Cruises. North Star Cruises operates the small luxury-expedition cruise ship *True North,* which takes just 36 passengers on 7-, 10-, and 13-night cruises between Broome and Wyndham along the inaccessible Kimberley coastline. The cruises are adventure oriented, with daily activities including scenic walks, fishing, diving, snorkeling, and on-shore picnics. The ship has six expedition craft and its own helicopter for scenic flights. ✉ *25 Carnarvon St., Shop 2, Broome* ☎ *08/9192–1829* ⊕ *www.northstarcruises.com.au* ✉ *From A$11,995.*

RED CENTRE

The light in the Red Centre—named for the deep color of its desert soils—has a purity and vitality that photographs only begin to approach. For tens of thousands of years this vast desert territory in the south of the Northern Territory has been home to Australia's Aboriginal people. Uluru, also known as Ayers Rock, is a great symbol in Aboriginal traditions, as are many sacred sites among the Centre's mountain ranges, gorges, dry riverbeds, and spinifex plains.

The essence of this ancient land is epitomized in the paintings of the renowned Aboriginal landscape artist Albert Namatjira and his followers. Viewed away from the desert, their images of the MacDonnell Ranges may appear at first to be garish and unreal in their depiction of purple-and-red mountain ranges and stark-white ghost gum trees. Seeing the real thing makes it difficult to imagine executing the paintings in any other way.

Uluru (pronounced *oo*-loo-*roo*), that magnificent stone monolith rising from the plains, is but one focus in the Red Centre. Kata Tjuta (*ka*-ta *tchoo*-ta), also known as The Olgas, are another. Watarrka National Park and Kings Canyon, Mt. Conner, and the cliffs, gorges, and mountain chains of the MacDonnell Ranges are other worlds to explore.

The Red Centre

TO DARWIN

Stuart Hwy.

TO ADELAIDE →

Stuart Hwy.

Lasseter Hwy.

Ross River

Trephina Gorge Nat'l Park

Santa Teresa

Alice Springs

Emily Gap

Ewaninga Rock Carvings Conservation Reserve

Maryvale

Titjikala

Chambers Pillar Historical Reserve

Simpsons Gap

John Flynn's Grave

Standley Chasm

Between Uluru and Alice Springs

Rainbow Valley Conservation Reserve

Hugh River

Owen Springs Reserve

West Macdonnell National Park

Ellery Creek Big Hole

Serpentine Gorge

Wallace Rockhole

Camels Australia

Henbury

Impadna

Ormiston Gorge

Hermannsburg

Henbury Meteorites Conservation Reserve

Glen Helen Gorge

Glen Helen Resort

PALM VALLEY

Finke Gorge Nat'l Park

Mount Ebenezer

Tnorala (Goose Bluff) Conservation Reserve

West MacDonnell Ranges

Areyonga

Wallara Ranch

30 mi

30 km

IDIRRIKI RANGE

KRICHAUFF RANGE

MIDDLE RANGE

Kings Canyon

Watarrka National Park

Mt. Conner

Uluru (Ayers Rock)

Uluru-Kata-Tjuta National Park

Ayers Rock Resort

Kata Tjuta (The Olgas)

Cultural Centre

The primary areas of interest are Alice Springs, which is flanked by the intriguing Eastern and Western MacDonnell Ranges; Kings Canyon; and Uluru–Kata Tjuta National Park, with neighboring Ayers Rock Resort. Unless you have more than three days, focus on only one of these areas.

ALICE SPRINGS

2,021 km (1,256 miles) northwest of Sydney, 1,319 km (820 miles) north of Adelaide, 1,976 km (1,228 miles) northeast of Perth

Once a ramshackle collection of buildings on dusty streets, Alice Springs—known colloquially as "the Alice" or just "Alice"—is today an incongruously suburban tourist center with a population of more than 30,000 (including about 2,000 Americans, many employed at Pine Gap, a joint Australian and U.S. satellite tracking station) in the middle of the desert. Alice derives most of its income from tourism, and more than 300,000 tourists visit annually. The town's ancient sites, a focus for the Arrernte Aboriginal people's ceremonial activities, lie cheek-by-jowl with air-conditioned shops and hotels. The MacDonnell Ranges dominate Alice Springs, changing color according to the time of day from brick red to purple.

> **ART HUNT**
>
> If you're looking for Aboriginal art, galleries abound along Todd Mall (the main shopping street); they're filled with canvas and bark paintings, as well as handcrafted didgeridoos and other artifacts. You can also buy art directly from Aborigines on weekends outside Flynn Memorial Church in the mall.

GETTING HERE AND AROUND

Alice Springs Airport is 15 km (9 miles) southeast of town. Qantas flies in and out of Alice Springs daily with direct flights from Brisbane, Sydney, Melbourne, Adelaide, Perth, Darwin, and Cairns, as well as Ayers Rock. Virgin Australia flies direct from Adelaide and Darwin. It's three hours' flying time from Sydney, Melbourne, and Brisbane; two hours from Adelaide and Darwin; and about 40 minutes from Ayers Rock. Flights run less frequently in the "Wet" summer months.

Alice Springs Airport Shuttle Bus meets every flight. The ride to all hotels and residential addresses in town costs A$16 each way. On request, the bus will also pick you up at your hotel and take you back to the airport, though you must give four hours' notice (☎ 08/8952–2111). From the airport, taxi fare to most parts of town is about A$35.

The Stuart Highway, commonly called the Track, is the only road into Alice Springs. The town center lies east of the highway. The 1,693-km (1,000-mile) drive from Adelaide takes about 24 hours. The drive from Darwin is about 160 km (100 miles) shorter, and takes about 21 hours. Bus tours run between all Red Centre sites, as well as between Alice Springs and Ayers Rock Resort, which will take around 6 hours.

Traveling by car will give you the most flexible itinerary—although the trade-off is that you'll travel many long, lonely stretches of one-lane

The Outback just outside Alice Springs

highway through the red-dust desert. Vehicles can be rented at Alice Springs and Ayers Rock Resort. The Central Australian Tourism Industry Association in Alice Springs books tours and rental cars, and provides motoring information.

Ghan. The *Ghan* train leaves Adelaide at 12:15 pm Sunday and Wednesday, arriving in Alice Springs at 1:45 pm Monday and Thursday. Return trains leave Alice Springs at 12:45 pm Thursday and 10 pm Sunday, arriving in Adelaide at 11:30 am on Friday and 1:10 pm Tuesday. On Monday and Thursday at 6 pm the *Ghan* continues to Darwin via Katherine, arriving at 5:30 pm Tuesday and 6:30 pm Friday. Trains from Darwin depart Wednesday at 10 am and Saturday at 9 am. The Alice Springs railway station is 2½ km (1½ miles) west of Todd Mall. ✉ *Alice Springs* ☎ *08/13–2147 bookings* ⊕ *www.greatsouthernrail. com.au* ☞ *From A$469.*

Taxi Alice Springs Taxis. ✉ *Alice Springs* ☎ *08/8952–1877.*

SAFETY AND PRECAUTIONS
Please note that many Aborigines living in or around Alice Springs have been asked to leave their native villages by tribal elders because of their problems with alcohol. Crime and violence stemming from alcohol abuse can make Alice unsafe at night, and it's recommended you travel only by taxi after dark. Sections of the dry Todd riverbed function as makeshift campsites for some Aborigines, so caution is advised when traversing it.

10

TIMING

The best time to visit is between May and August, when the weather is mild during the day, although often freezing at night; the summer months can be blisteringly hot, and some tourism services are less frequent or stop altogether. Alice Springs is pleasant enough, but most of the Red Centre's attractions are outside the town. If visiting Uluru is the main reason for your visit to the Red Centre, you can skip Alice Springs and go directly to Uluru–Kata Tjuta National Park.

TOURS

AAT Kings. This well-known bus company operates half-day tours that include visits to the Royal Flying Doctor Service Base, School of the Air, Telegraph Station, and Anzac Hill scenic lookout as well as day tours to Palm Valley and the West MacDonnell Ranges. ⊠ *74 Todd St.* ☎ *08/8952–1700, 1300/228546* ⊕ *www.aatkings.com.au* ✉ *From A$99.*

ESSENTIALS

Visitor Information Tourism Central Australia. ⊠ *Todd Mall at Parsons St.* ☎ *08/8952–5800, 1800/645199* ⊕ *www.discovercentralaustralia.com.*

EXPLORING
IN ALICE SPRINGS

FAMILY **Alice Springs Reptile Centre.** Thorny devils, frill-neck lizards, some of the world's deadliest snakes, and "Terry" the saltwater crocodile inhabit this park in the heart of town, opposite the Royal Flying Doctor Service. May to August (winter) the viewing is best from 11 to 3, when the reptiles are most active. There's also a gecko cave. Free talks are conducted daily at 11, 1, and 3:30, during which you can learn to pick up the pythons. ⊠ *9 Stuart Terr.* ☎ *08/8952–8900* ⊕ *www.reptilecentre. com.au* ✉ *A$16.50* ☉ *Daily 9:30–5.*

Royal Flying Doctor Service (RFDS). This much-visited tourist attraction in Alice Springs has a theater, interactive displays, and a full-scale replica of the fuselage of the service's current Pilatus PC12 aircraft. The site has long been the radio base for the Royal Flying Doctor Service, which directs doctors (using aircraft) on their house calls to remote settlements and homes hundreds of miles apart. The RFDS is a vital part of Outback life and fascinating to visitors. The center has historical displays and an audiovisual show. Tours run every half hour throughout the year, and there's a good café at the back. ⊠ *8–10 Stuart Terr.* ☎ *08/8958–8412* ⊕ *www.rfdsalicesprings.com.au* ✉ *A$15* ☉ *Mon.–Sat. 9–5, Sun. 1–5.*

FAMILY **School of the Air.** What do children who live hundreds of miles from the nearest school do for education? Find out at this informative visitor center, which harbors a working school within its walls. You can discover how distance education has been delivered to the country's most remote parts since 1951; from pedal-operated radio systems to interactive online classes, it's come a long way. The best time to visit is before 3 pm on a school day so that you can watch a live lesson; outside of school hours you can see a recorded lesson. ⊠ *80 Head St.* ☎ *08/8951–6834* ⊕ *www.assoa.nt.edu.au* ✉ *A$7.50* ☉ *Mon.–Sat. 8:30–4:30, Sun. 1–4:30.*

OUTSIDE ALICE SPRINGS

FAMILY

Fodor'sChoice

★

Alice Springs Desert Park. Focusing on the desert, which makes up 70% of the Australian landmass, this 75-acre site contains 320 types of plants and 120 animal species in several Australian ecosystems—including the largest nocturnal-animal house in the southern hemisphere. An open-air habitat is also open at night, when animals are most active. Local Aboriginal guides share their native stories about the wildlife and the land. Don't miss the twice daily birds of prey presentation. Allow about four hours to explore the park; it's 6½ km (4 miles) west of Alice Springs. ⊠ *Larapinta Dr.* ☎ *08/8951–8788* ⊕ *www.alicespringsdesertpark.com. au* ⊠ *A$25* ⊗ *Daily 7:30–6.*

Araluen Cultural Precinct. The most distinctive building in this complex is the Museum of Central Australia, which charts the evolution of the land and its inhabitants—human and animal—around central Australia. Exhibits include a skeleton of the 10½-foot-tall *Dromornis stirtoni*, the largest bird to walk on earth, which was found northeast of Alice. Also in the precinct are the (free) Aviation Museum, Central Craft, and Araluen Centre, home to the Araluen Art Galleries and the Namatjira Gallery, a collection of renowned Aboriginal landscapes, and the Yeperenye Sculpture—a 3-meter-high caterpillar that you can walk through, representing the sacred Dreamtime creator of the country around Alice

Springs. The precinct is 2 km (1 mile) southwest of town, and is on most tourist bus itineraries. The entry pass is good for two days. ✉ 61 Larapinta Dr. ☎ 08/8951–1120 ⊕ artsandmuseums.nt.gov.au/araluen-cultural-precinct ☛ A$15 ◷ Weekdays 10–4, weekends 11–4.

OFF THE BEATEN PATH

Spectacular scenery and Aboriginal rock art in the MacDonnell Ranges east of the Alice are well worth a day or more of exploration. Emily Gap (a sacred Aboriginal site), Jessie Gap, and Corroboree Rock, once a setting for important men-only Aboriginal ceremonies, are within the first 44 km (27 miles) east of Alice Springs. Beyond these are Trephina Gorge, John Hayes Rockhole, and N'Dhala Gorge Nature Park (with numerous Aboriginal rock carvings).

Arltunga Historical Reserve, 110 km (69 miles) northeast of Alice, contains the ruins of a 19th-century gold-rush site. If you fancy fossicking (prospecting) for your own semiprecious stones, you can take your pick—and shovel—at Gemtree in the Harts Ranges, 140 km (87 miles) northeast of Alice. Ranger stations (☎ 08/8956–9765) are at Trephina Gorge and John Hayes Rockhole.

SPORTS AND THE OUTDOORS

CAMEL RIDING

Pyndan Camel Tracks. Daily one-hour camel rides are offered by this company at 9, noon, 2:30, and sunset. They explore a valley of diverse habitat about 15 km (9 miles) from Alice Springs and surrounded by the ancient MacDonnell Ranges. ✉ Alice Springs ☎ 0416/170–164 ⊕ www.cameltracks.com ☛ From A$60.

HIKING

The MacDonnell Ranges, the craggy desert mountains that frame Alice Springs, are rich with desert landscapes and Aboriginal significance. The **Emily and Jessie Gaps Nature Park,** located in the Eastern MacDonnells, just 10 km (6 miles) east of Alice Springs along the Ross Highway, contains registered sacred Aboriginal sites, including rock paintings depicting the caterpillar story of the Dreamtime—the Aboriginal stories of the world's creation.

The **Larapinta Trail** is a 223-km-long (145-mile-long) walking track that runs west from Alice Springs into the Western MacDonnell Ranges. It's a spectacular, though challenging, track that takes hikers through classically rugged and dry central Australian landscape. Hikers are encouraged to participate in the voluntary Overnight Walker Registration Scheme, designed to ensure that all trekkers on the trail can be tracked and accounted for in case of emergency. Contact the **Northern Territory Parks & Wildlife Service** (☎ 08/8951–8250) for more information. **Tourism Central Australia** in Alice Springs (☎ 08/8952–5800) can also advise you if you're interested in planning bushwalking itineraries. **World Expeditions** runs guided and self-guided, multiday hikes on the best sections of the trail, ranging from 3 to 14 days, with accommodation in permanent campsites and all meals. ⊕ www.worldexpeditions.com

HOT-AIR BALLOONING

Fodor's Choice ★ **Outback Ballooning.** Floating over the desert spinifex in a hot-air balloon while the sun comes up is a once-in-a-lifetime experience. Outback Ballooning makes hotel pickups about an hour before dawn and returns between 9 am and 10 am. The A$290 fee covers 30 minutes of flying time, insurance, and a champagne breakfast. A 60-minute flight costs A$385. ■**TIP**→ **Take warm clothes to beat the predawn chill.** ⊠ *35 Kennett Ct.* ☏ *1800/809790* ⊕ *www.outbackballooning. com.au* ✉ *From A$290.*

QUAD-BIKE RIDING

Outback Quad Adventures. Hop aboard a motorbike with four huge wheels and explore the Northern Territory's oldest working cattle station with Outback Quad Adventures. The company collects you from Alice Springs and takes you to the station, 17 km (10 miles) out of town on the edge of the MacDonnell Ranges. No special license is needed, and all tours are escorted by guides with two-way radios. Rides operate year-round and range from 2½ hours (A$138) to 6 hours (A$299). ⊠ *Alice Springs* ☏ *08/8953–0697* ⊕ *outbackquadadventures.com.au* ✉ *From A$138* ⊘ *Closed Feb.*

WHERE TO EAT

$$$
AUSTRALIAN

✕**Barra on Todd.** As the name suggests, barramundi is the name of the game at this venerable and popular restaurant on the banks of the dry Todd River. You can try Thai-style barramundi spring rolls, saltbush dukkah-crusted barramundi, and herb and macadamia nut over roasted barramundi, to name a few. The restaurant and bar, which are part of the Chifley Alice Springs Resort, are popular with locals, too. Other delicious dishes on offer include black-pepper crusted kangaroo fillet, wild clover lamb rack, and mango-glazed pork cutlet. And why not try the distinctly Australia dessert of banana Mars bar (yes, a Mars candy bar and a banana wrapped in pastry, deep fried, and served with macadamia nut ice cream and chocolate sauce? $ *Average main: A$36* ⊠ *34 Stott Terr.* ☏ *08/8952–3523* ⊕ *www.silverneedlehotels.com/ chifley/alice-springs/dining.*

$$
ITALIAN

✕**Casa Nostra.** Red-and-white checkered tablecloths, Chianti bottles, and plastic grapes festoon this family-run Alice old-timer. Locals crowd in for traditional meat dishes, pizza, and pasta, including Al's Special, a dish of chicken parmigiana paired with pasta in a cream-and-black-pepper sauce that the chef took 15 years to perfect. Take a tip from the regulars and preorder a serving of vanilla slice for dessert, or you might miss out on this scrumptious cake of layered papery pastry and custard cream. It's BYO beer and wine. $ *Average main: A$29* ⊠ *Undoolya Rd., at Sturt Terr.* ☏ *08/8952–6749* ⊘ *Closed Sun. and late Dec.–mid-Jan. No lunch.*

$$
ASIAN
Fodor's Choice
★

✕**Hanuman Thai.** With its Thai, Nonya (Malaysian), and Indian-flavored menu, this lovely spot is the only place in the desert to offer a range of big-city-quality southeast Asian food. The trumpet mushrooms topped with prawn and pork mince are popular, as is the barramundi poached in coconut sauce. Desserts include black-rice brûlée, and banana spring rolls with butterscotch sauce. This place is as popular with the locals as it is the tourists—which means you should book a day or two ahead. $ *Average main: A$30* ⊠ *DoubleTree by Hilton Hotel Alice Springs, 82 Barrett Dr.* ☏ *08/8953–7188* ⊕ *www.hanuman.com.au* ⊘ *No lunch weekends* ⚟ *Reservations essential.*

10

WHERE TO STAY

$$
HOTEL
Chifley Alice Springs Resort. This convenient spot might make you forget that you're surrounded by desert; the palm trees and broad, foliage-fringed lawns and pool area provide respite from the region's red dirt. **Pros:** short walk to shops; tour desk can book variety of tours; great beds; free Wi-Fi in rooms. **Cons:** convention facilities attract tour groups; no views. $ *Rooms from: A$159* ⊠ *34 Stott Terr.* ☎ *08/8951–4545* ⊕ *www.silverneedlehotels.com/chifley/alice-springs* ⤳ *139 rooms* ⦿*Some meals.*

$
RESORT
Desert Palms Resort. At Desert Palms Resort, you can escape the dust and the dry desert heat by dipping your toes in the island pool with a waterfall or just lounging underneath the umbrella-like palm trees and red-and-pink bougainvillea. **Pros:** private, comfortable villas; great value; adjacent golf course; free Wi-Fi in all villas and by the pool. **Cons:** no restaurant; villas aren't fancy. $ *Rooms from: A$140* ⊠ *74 Barrett Dr.* ☎ *08/8952–5977, 1800/678037 reservations* ⊕ *www.desertpalms. com.au* ⤳ *80 cabins* ⦿*No meals.*

$$
HOTEL
DoubleTree by Hilton Hotel Alice Springs. Landscaped lawns with elegant eucalyptus and palm trees greet you at this upscale international chain about a mile outside town. **Pros:** excellent restaurant; many rooms have views of MacDonnell Ranges; winner of environmental awards. **Cons:** in suburban area; no shopping nearby; expensive Internet. $ *Rooms from: A$169* ⊠ *82 Barrett Dr.* ☎ *08/8950–8000* ⊕ *doubletree3.hilton. com* ⤳ *229 rooms, 7 suites* ⦿*No meals.*

$$
HOTEL
Fodor's Choice
★
Lasseters Hotel Casino. A popular place thanks to the great views of the MacDonnell Ranges from guest rooms and the nightlife provided by the adjacent casino, Lasseters is the most luxurious resort in Alice Springs. **Pros:** mountain bikes are complimentary; excellent views of MacDonnell Ranges; casino and nightlife on-site; free in-room Wi-Fi. **Cons:** adjacent convention center attracts big groups; 30-minute walk to town center. $ *Rooms from: A$200* ⊠ *93 Barrett Dr.* ☎ *08/8950–7777* ⊕ *www.lhc.com.au* ⤳ *205 rooms* ⦿*No meals.*

NIGHTLIFE AND PERFORMING ARTS

PERFORMING ARTS

Sounds of Starlight. This is the place to enjoy evocative Outback theater performances and didgeridoo music accompanied by a slide show of Red Centre images. Ninety-minute concerts (A$30) are held at 8 pm Tuesday, Friday, and Saturday; A$85 dinner and show packages are also available. Free didgeridoo classes are held at the venue during the day. ⊠ *40 Todd Mall* ☎ *08/8953–0826* ⊕ *www.soundsofstarlight.com* ⤇ *From A$30.*

NIGHTLIFE

Lasseters Casino. Entry is free at Lasseters Casino, where the action goes late into the night. More than 300 slot machines sit here, plus blackjack, roulette, craps, and baccarat tables. The two bars have entertainment on weekends—the Juicy Rump is a favorite for its live music. ⊠ *93 Barrett Dr.* ☎ *08/8950–7777, 1800/808975* ⊕ *lasseters.com.au/casino.*

SHOPPING

Shopping in Alice Springs is all about Aboriginal art and artifacts. Central Australian Aboriginal paintings are characterized by intricate patterns of dots—and are commonly called sand paintings because they were originally drawn on sand as ceremonial devices.

Papunya Tula Artists. Encouraged to paint a mural on a blank building wall by a local school teacher in 1971, the Papunya Tula artists were the founders of the modern western and central desert art movement. This gallery showcases the work of some of the area's best artists. ⊠ *63 Todd Mall* ☎ *08/8952–4731* ⊕ *www.papunyatula.com.au.*

Fodor's Choice ★ **Red Kangaroo Books.** From bush poetry and traditional bush tucker recipes to anthropological texts on Aborigines and their culture, Red Kangaroo Books has an outstanding collection of literature pertaining to all things Australian. ⊠ *79 Todd Mall* ☎ *08/8953–2137* ⊕ *www. redkangaroobooks.com.*

Todd Mall Markets. Held every other Sunday morning from 9 am until around 1 pm, mid-February to December (until 2 pm, June to August), the markets feature more than 100 stalls of local arts, crafts, and food, which are displayed while musicians entertain. ■**TIP➔** Search out the mango smoothie stall; they are quite possibly the best in the country. ⊠ *Todd St.* ☎ *0458/555–506* ⊕ *www.toddmallmarkets.com.au.*

WEST MACDONNELL RANGES

The West MacDonnell Ranges—stretching westward from just a few kilometers outside Alice Springs for around 200 km (125 miles)—are a spectacular series of red-rock mountains interspersed by canyons and narrow gorges. Each of the chasms and gorges has its own unique character, and in many there are waterholes where you can swim. Black-footed rock wallabies are among the wildlife to be spotted. The 223-km (139-mile) Larapinta Trail in the park is the showpiece of central Australian bushwalking. The trail is broken into 12 sections, each a one- to two-day walk.

GETTING HERE AND AROUND

To reach all the major sights, the Red Centre Way follows Larapinta Drive (the western continuation of Stott Terrace) from Alice Springs and Namatjira Drive westward to Glen Helen, about 130 km (81 miles) from Alice Springs. Roads leading off it access the highlights.

SAFETY AND PRECAUTIONS

Take care when bushwalking or hiking, as paths are usually rocky and uneven. Snakes inhabit most areas, so be cautious when walking through tall grass. You should always carry and drink plenty of water; at least one liter of water for every hour of walking in hot weather.

TOURS

Emu Run Tours. One-day tours are offered by air-conditioned bus to all the major sights in the park, including Simpsons Gap, Standley Chasm, the Ochre Pits, and Ormiston Gorge. ⊠ *72 Todd St., Alice Springs* ☎ *08/8953–7057* ⊕ *www.emurun.com.au* ⊡ *From A$99.*

10

Trek Larapinta. Small-group guided bushwalks are available along the Larapinta Trail. Their six-day tour costs from A$2,295; a longer tour completing the whole trail is 15 days (A$3,595). ⊠ *Alice Springs* ☎ *1300/133278* ⊕ *www.treklarapinta.com.au* ⬚ *From A$1295.*

ESSENTIALS

Visitor Information Simpsons Gap Visitor Information Centre. ☎ *08/8951–8250.*

EXPLORING

These sights are organized by distance—from closest to farthest—from Alice Springs.

Fodor's Choice ★ **Simpsons Gap.** This is the closest gorge to Alice Springs. There is a bicycle track that winds from the city center to the Gap. Stark-white ghost gums (Australian evergreen trees), red rocks, and the purple-haze mountains provide a taste of the scenery to be seen farther into the ranges. The gap can be crowded in the morning and late afternoon, since these are the best times to see rock wallabies. ⊠ *Larapinta Dr., Alice Springs* ✛ *18 km (11 miles) west of Alice Springs, then 6 km (4 miles) on side road* ☎ *08/8951–8250* ⬚ *Free.*

Fodor's Choice ★ **Standley Chasm.** This is one of the most impressive canyons in the MacDonnell Ranges. At midday, when the sun is directly overhead, the 10-yard-wide canyon glows red from the reflected light—this lasts for just 15 minutes. The walk from the parking lot takes about 20 minutes, and is rocky toward the end. For a greater challenge, climb to the top via the steep trail that branches off to the left at the end of the gorge; the views are spectacular. There's a kiosk selling snacks and drinks at the park entrance. ⊠ *Larapinta Dr., Alice Springs* ✛ *40 km (25 miles) west of Alice Springs, then 9 km (5½ miles) on Standley Chasm Rd.* ☎ *08/8956–7440* ⊕ *www.standleychasm.com.au* ⬚ *A$10* ☉ *Daily 8–6.*

Ellery Creek Big Hole. This is one of the prettiest (and coldest) swimming holes in the Red Centre. It's also the deepest and most permanent water hole in the area, so you may glimpse wild creatures like wallabies or goannas (monitor lizards) quenching their thirst. Take the 3-km (2-mile) Dolomite Walk for a close-up look at this fascinating geological site. ⊠ *Namatjira Dr., Alice Springs* ✛ *88 km (55 miles) west of Alice Springs* ☎ *08/8951–8250.*

Serpentine Gorge. This site is best experienced by taking a refreshing swim through the narrow, winding gorge. According to an Aboriginal myth a fierce serpent makes its home in the pool, hence the name. ⊠ *Namatjira Dr., Alice Springs* ✛ *99 km (61 miles) west of Alice Springs* ☎ *08/8951–8250.*

Glen Helen Gorge. This gorge slices through the MacDonnell Ranges, revealing dramatic rock layering and tilting. The gorge was cut by the sporadic Finke River, often described as the oldest river in the world. Here the river forms a broad, cold, permanent water hole that's great for a bracing swim. ⊠ *Namatjira Dr., Alice Springs* ✛ *132 km (82 miles) west of Alice Springs* ☎ *08/8951–8250.*

Ormiston Gorge. This gorge is breathtaking. A short climb takes you to Gum Tree Lookout, where you can see the spectacular 820-foot-high

The Australian Heartland

For most Australians the Red Centre is the mystical and legendary core of the continent, and Uluru is its beautiful focal point. Whether they have been there or not, locals believe its image symbolizes a steady pulse that radiates deep through the red earth, through the heartland, and all the way to the coasts.

Little more than a thumbprint within the vast Australian continent, the Red Centre is harsh and isolated. Its hard, relentless topography (and lack of conveniences) makes this one of the most difficult areas of the country to survive in, much less explore. But the early pioneers—some foolish, some hardy—managed to set up bases that thrived. They created cattle stations, introduced electricity, and implemented telegraph services, enabling them to maintain a lifestyle that, if not luxurious, was at least reasonably comfortable.

The people who now sparsely populate the Red Centre are a breed of their own. Many were born and grew up here, but many others were "blow-ins," immigrants from far-flung countries and folk from other Australian states who took up the challenge to make a life in the desert and stayed on as they succeeded. Either way, folks out here have a few common characteristics. They're laconic and down-to-earth, canny and astute, and likely to try to pull your leg when you least expect it.

No one could survive the isolation without a good sense of humor: Where else in the world would you hold a bottomless-boat race in a dry riverbed? The Henley-on-Todd Regatta, as it is known, is a sight to behold in Alice Springs, with dozens of would-be skippers bumbling along within the bottomless-boat frames.

As the small towns grew and businesses quietly prospered in the mid-1800s, a rail link between Alice Springs and Adelaide was planned. However, the undercurrent of challenge and humor that touches all life here ran through this project as well. Construction began in 1877, but things went wrong from the start. No one had seen rain for ages, and no one expected it; hence, the track was laid right across a floodplain. It wasn't long before locals realized their mistake, when intermittent heavy floods regularly washed the tracks away. The railway is still in operation today, and all works well, but its history is one of many local jokes here.

The Red Centre is a special place where you will meet people whose generous and sincere hospitality may move you. The land and all its riches offer some of the most spectacular and unique sights on the planet, along with a sense of timelessness that will slow you down and fill your spirit. Take a moment to shade your eyes from the sun and pick up on the subtleties that nature has carefully protected and camouflaged here, and you will soon discover that the Red Centre is not the dead center.

10

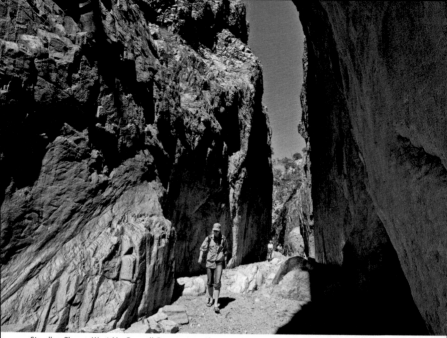

Standley Chasm, West MacDonnell Ranges near Alice Springs

red gorge walls rising from the permanent pool below. There is a water hole suitable for swimming. Trails include the 7-km (4½-mile) Ormiston Pound Walk. ⊠ *Namatjira Dr., Alice Springs* ✛ *135 km (84 miles) west of Alice Springs* ☎ *08/8956–7799.*

WHERE TO STAY

$$ ⌕ **Glen Helen Resort.** Better described as an Outback lodge, Glen Helen
RESORT   Resort earns its charm from its traditional bush welcome and atmosphere. **Pros:** traditional Outback Australia atmosphere; easy access to Larapinta Walking Trail; plenty of opportunities to see local fauna. **Cons:** limited amenities in motel rooms; rooms 10–17 are next to the generator and very noisy. Ⓢ *Rooms from: A$160* ⊠ *1 Namatjira Dr., Alice Springs* ✛ *135 km (84 miles) west of Alice Springs* ☎ *08/8956– 7489* ⊕ *www.glenhelen.com.au* ⇋ *25 motel rooms, 10 bunkhouse rooms, 105 unpowered sites, 38 powered sites* ⦅◎⦆ *Some meals.*

BETWEEN ULURU AND ALICE SPRINGS

The 440-km (273-mile) drive to Uluru from Alice Springs along the Stuart and Lasseter highways takes about five hours—or longer if you veer off the track to see some other impressive geological sites.

EXPLORING

Camels Australia. En route from Alice Springs you'll find Camels Australia, a fun stop on the way to Uluru. Owners Neil and Jayne Waters offer everything from quick jaunts to whole-day safaris. Phone beforehand for all rides; 72 hours' notice for day treks is required. It's A$30 for a half-hour ride and A$50 for a one-hour ride. Take-away food and gifts are also available at the farm shop—the camel burger is pretty tasty. ⊠ *Stuart Hwy, Alice Springs* ✚ *90 km (56 miles) south of Alice Springs* ☎ *08/8956–0925* ⊕ *www.camels-australia.com.au.*

Ewaninga Rock Carvings Conservation Reserve. More than 3,000 ancient Aboriginal rock engravings (petroglyphs) are etched into sandstone outcrops in Ewaninga Rock Carvings Conservation Reserve, 39 km (24 miles) south of Alice on the road to Chamber's Pillar. Early-morning and late-afternoon light are best for photographing the lines, circles, and animal tracks. A 2-km (1-mile) trail leads to several art sites. The reserve is open all day year-round and is accessible by regular (rather than four-wheel-drive) cars. ⊠ *Old South Rd.* ✚ *39 km (24 miles) south of Alice Springs* ☎ *08/8951–8250* 🗏 *Free.*

Henbury Meteorites Conservation Reserve. The Henbury Meteorites craters, 12 depressions between 6 feet and 600 feet across, are believed to have been formed by a meteorite shower about 5,000 years ago. One is 60 feet deep. To get here, you must travel 13 km (8 miles) off the highway on an unpaved road—conventional 2WD sedans will be fine. ⊠ *Ernest Giles Rd.* ✚ *114 km (71 miles) south of Alice Springs and 13 km (8 miles) west of Stuart Hwy.* ☎ *08/8951–8250.*

Fodor's Choice ★ **Kings Canyon.** In Watarrka National Park, Kings Canyon is one of the most spectacular sights in central Australia. Sprawling in scope, the canyon's sheer cliff walls shelter a world of ferns and woodlands, permanent springs, and rock pools. The main path is the 6-km (4-mile) Canyon Walk, which starts with a short but steep climb from the parking lot to the top of the escarpment; the view 886 feet down to the base of the canyon is amazing. An easier walk, called the Creek Walk, which starts at the parking lot and winds through the base of the canyon, is just as worthwhile. Alternatively, see it all from above during the half-hour scenic helicopter flight over the canyon and range from Kings Canyon Resort (A$275 or A$145 for 15 minutes). ⊠ *Luritja Rd., Alice Springs* ✚ *167 km (104 miles) from turnoff on Lasseter Hwy.*

Rainbow Valley Conservation Reserve. Amazing formations in the sandstone cliffs of the James Range take on rainbow colors in the early-morning and late-afternoon light. The colors have been caused by water dissolving the red iron in the sandstone, and further erosion has created dramatic rock faces and squared towers. To reach the reserve, turn left off the Stuart Highway 75 km (46 miles) south of Alice. The next 22 km (13 miles) are on a dirt track, requiring a four-wheel-drive vehicle. ⊠ *Stuart Hwy., Alice Springs* ☎ *08/8951–8250* ⊕ *www.nt.gov.au* 🗏 *Free.*

WHERE TO STAY

$$$$
RESORT
Fodor's Choice ★
🛏 **Kings Canyon Resort.** The best place to stay near Watarrka National Park, this resort is 7 km (4½ miles) from Kings Canyon. **Pros:** deluxe rooms offer floodlit views of adjacent ranges at night; bush entertainment at the Outback BBQ dinner. **Cons:** unless you opt for a guided tour you'll need your own transport to get to the canyon. ⑤ *Rooms from: A$303* ⊠ *Luritja Rd., Watarrka National Park* ☎ *08/8956–7442* ⊕ *www.kingscanyonresort.com.au* ⇝ *32 deluxe rooms, 96 standard rooms, 35 budget rooms, 72 powered caravan sites, unlimited tent sites* ❘⊙❘ *Some meals.*

10

ULURU AND KATA TJUTA

It's easy to see why the Aborigines attach spiritual significance to Uluru (Ayers Rock). It rises magnificently above the plain and dramatically changes color throughout the day. At more than 1,100 feet, Uluru is one of the world's largest monoliths, though such a classification belies the otherworldly, spiritual energy surrounding it. The Anangu people are the traditional owners of the land around Uluru and Kata Tjuta. They believe they are direct descendants of the beings—which include a python, an emu, a blue-tongue lizard, and a poisonous snake—who formed the land and its physical features during the Tjukurpa (the "Dreamtime," or creation period).

Kata Tjuta (the Olgas), 53 km (33 miles) west of Uluru, is a series of 36 gigantic rock domes hiding a maze of fascinating gorges and crevasses. The names Ayers Rock and the Olgas are used out of familiarity alone; at the sites themselves, the Aboriginal Uluru and Kata Tjuta are the respective names of preference. The entire area is called Yulara, though the airport is still known as Ayers Rock.

Uluru and Kata Tjuta have very different compositions. Monolithic Uluru is a type of sandstone called arkose, while the rock domes at Kata Tjuta are composed of conglomerate. Both of these intriguing sights lie within Uluru–Kata Tjuta National Park, which is protected as a World Heritage site. The whole experience is a bit like seeing the Grand Canyon turned inside out, and a visit here will be remembered for a lifetime.

In terms of where to eat and stay, Ayers Rock Resort, officially known as the township of Yulara, is a complex of lodgings, restaurants, and facilities, and is base camp for exploring Uluru and Kata Tjuta. The accommodations and services here are the only ones in the vicinity of the national park. Uluru is about a 20-minute drive from the resort area (there's a sunset-viewing area on the way); driving to Kata Tjuta will take another 30 minutes. The park entrance fee of A$25 is valid for three days.

The resort "village" includes a bank, newsstand, supermarket, several souvenir shops, Aboriginal art gallery, hair salon, and child-care center.

The accommodations at the resort, which range from luxury hotels to a campground, are all run by Voyages Indigenous Tourism Australia and share many of the same facilities. Indoor dining is limited to each hotel's restaurants and the less-expensive Geckos Cafe, all of which can be charged back to your room. All reservations can be made through Voyages Indigenous Tourism Australia (⊕ *www.voyages.com.au*) on-site, or their central reservations service in Sydney.

GETTING HERE AND AROUND

Qantas, along with its budget subsidiary, Jetstar, operates direct flights from Sydney, Melbourne, and Cairns; and Virgin Australia flies direct from Sydney to Ayers Rock Airport, which is 5 km (3 miles) north of the resort complex. Passengers from other capital cities fly to Alice Springs to connect with flights to Ayers Rock Airport. Qantas flies daily 40-minute flights from Alice Springs to Ayers Rock.

AAT Kings runs a complimentary shuttle bus between the airport and Yulara, which meets every flight. If you have reservations at the resort, representatives wait outside the baggage-claim area of the airport to whisk you and other guests away on the 10-minute drive.

If you're driving from Alice Springs, it's a five-hour-plus, 440-km (273-mile) trip to Ayers Rock Resort. The road is paved, but lacks a shoulder, and is one lane in each direction for the duration, making it challenging and risky to overtake the four-trailer-long road trains. The route often induces fatigue; avoid driving at night as wildlife is prolific and you've a good chance of colliding with a kangaroo.

From the resort it's 19 km (12 miles) to Uluru or 53 km (33 miles) to Kata Tjuta. The road to Kata Tjuta is paved.

If you prefer to explore Uluru and Kata Tjuta on your own schedule, then renting your own car is a good idea; the only other ways to get to the national park are on group bus tours or by chauffeured taxi or coach. Avis, Hertz, and Thrifty all rent cars at Ayers Rock Resort. Arrange for your rental early, since cars are limited.

Taxi Uluru Express. ✉ *Yulara* ☎ *08/8956–2019* ⊕ *www.uluruexpress.com.au.*

Transportation Contacts AAT Kings. ☎ *08/8956–2171, 1300/228546* ⊕ *www.aatkings.com.* **Automobile Association of the Northern Territory.** ☎ *08/8956–2188, 13–1111 emergency road assistance* ⊕ *www.aant.com.au.* **N.T. Road Report.** ☎ *1800/246199* ⊕ *www.ntlis.nt.gov.au/roadreport.*

SAFETY AND PRECAUTIONS

Water is vital in the Red Centre. It is easy to forget, but the dry atmosphere and the temperatures can make you prone to dehydration. If you are walking or climbing, you will need to consume additional water at regular intervals. You should carry at least 2 liters of water for every hour. Regardless of where you plan to travel, it is essential to carry plenty of water, 20 liters minimum.

TIMING

If seeing Uluru is your reason for visiting the Red Centre, there are tours that fly in and out, stopping just long enough to watch the rock at sunset. However, for a more leisurely visit, allow two days so you can also visit Kata Tjuta (The Olgas) nearby.

TOURS

AIR TOURS **Ayers Rock Helicopters.** Helicopter flights are A$150 per person for 15 minutes over Uluru, or A$285 for 30 minutes over Kata Tjuta and Uluru. ✉ *Yulara* ☎ *1300/134044* ⊕ *www.ayersrockresort.com.au* ✈ *From A$150.*

WATCH THE SKY

More stars and other astronomical sights, such as the fascinating Magellanic Clouds, are visible in the southern hemisphere than in the northern, and the desert night sky shows off their glory with diamond-like clarity. Look out for the Southern Cross, the constellation that navigators used for many centuries to find their way—most Australians will proudly point it out for you.

10

Ayers Rock Scenic Flights. The best views of Uluru and Kata Tjuta are from the air. Light-plane tours, with courtesy hotel pickup from Ayers Rock Resort hotels, include 40-minute flights over Ayers Rock and The Olgas, and day tours to Kings Canyon and a huge meteorite crater known as Gosses Bluff. For options, contact Ayers Rock Resort. ☎ *1300/134044* ⊕ *www.ayersrockresort.com.au* ✆ *From A$115.*

ABORIGINAL TOURS   Ayers Rock Resort organizes trips through the Uluru and Kata Tjuta region led by local Aboriginal people. Tours, which leave from the resort, include the guided bush tucker tours (A$92) and full-day 4WD trips to Cave Hill and into the desert of the Pitjantjatjara Lands of Central Australia (A$280), as well as sunrise tours at the base of Uluru (A$165 with breakfast). Guides are Aborigines who work with interpreters. Aboriginal art aficionados can attend dot-painting workshops (A$69).

CAMEL TOURS   **Uluru Camel Tours.** A great way to get out in the open and see the sights
Fodor's Choice   is from the back of one of the desert's creatures. Uluru Camel Tours
★   has sunrise and sunset tours that last for 2½ hours; tours leave from the Ayers Rock Resort. ☎ *08/8956–3333* ⊕ *ulurucameltours.com.au* ✆ *From A$80.*

ESSENTIALS

Visitor Information The Uluru–Kata Tjuta Cultural Centre is on the park road just before you reach the rock. It also contains the park's ranger station. The Cultural Centre is open daily 7–6. The Ayers Rock Visitor Centre in the town Square at Yulara is open daily 8–7 and includes an interesting free museum.

Ayers Rock Resort Visitor Centre. ⊠ *Yulara* ☎ *08/8957–7324.* **Central reservations service.** ⊠ *Yulara* ☎ *1300/134044* ⊕ *www.ayersrockresort.com.au.* **Uluru–Kata Tjuta Cultural Centre.** ⊠ *Yulara* ☎ *08/8956–1128.*

EXPLORING

Fodor's Choice   **Kata Tjuta.** Many visitors feel that Kata Tjuta (formerly known as The
★   Olgas) is more satisfying to explore than Uluru. Uluru is one immense block, so you feel as if you're always on the outside looking in. Kata Tjuta, as its Aboriginal name ("many heads") suggests, is a collection of huge rocks hiding numerous gorges and chasms that you can enter and explore.

There are three main walks, the first from the parking lot into Walpa Gorge, the deepest valley between the rocks. This is a 2-km (1-mile) walk, and the round-trip journey takes about one hour. The gorge is a desert refuge for plants and animals. The rocky track gently rises along a moisture-rich gully, passing inconspicuous rare plants and ending at a grove of flourishing spearwood.

More rewarding, but also more difficult, is the Valley of the Winds Walk. This 7½-km (4½-mile) walk is along a stony track to two spectacular lookouts—Karu and Karingana. Experienced walkers can complete this walk in about three hours. The Valley of the Winds walk is closed when temperatures rise above 36°C (97°F), which is after 11 am most days in summer.

The Kata Tjuta Viewing Area, 25 km (16 miles) along the Kata Tjuta Road, offers a magnificent vista, and is a relaxing place for a break. It's 600 meters from the car park, and interpretive panels explain the natural life around you. ⊠ *Lasseter Hwy., Yulara ✛ 53 km (33 miles) west of Yulara* ⊕ *www.parksaustralia.gov.au/uluru.*

Fodor's Choice **Uluru.** An inevitable sensation of excitement builds as you approach ★ this great monolith. If you drive toward it in a rental car, you may find yourself gasping at the first glimpse through the windshield; if you're on a tour bus, you'll likely want to grab the person sitting next to you and point out the window as it looms larger and larger. Rising like an enormous red mountain in the middle of an otherwise completely flat desert, Uluru (formerly called Ayers Rock) is a marvel to behold.

Uluru is circled by a road and walking trails. Two car parks—Mala and Kuniya—provide access for several of the walks, or you can choose to do the full circle of the Rock on the Base Walk.

As you work your way around Uluru, your perspective of the great rock changes significantly. You should allow four hours to walk the 10 km (6 miles) around the rock and explore the several deep crevices along the way. Some places are Aboriginal sacred sites and cannot be entered, nor can they be photographed. These are clearly signposted. Aboriginal art can be found in caves at the rock's base.

If you're looking for an easy walk that takes you just partway around the base, the **Mala Walk** is 2 km (1 mile) in length and almost all on flat land. The walk goes to the Kanju Gorge from the base of the climbing trail; park rangers provide free tours daily at 8 am from October to April and at 10 am from May to September.

The **Liru Walk** starts at the cultural center and takes you to the base of the Rock. Along the way are stands of mulga trees and—after rain— wildflowers. The track is wheelchair accessible, and the walk is an easy 1½ hours.

On the southern side of Uluru, the Kuniya Walk and Mutitjulu Water-hole trail starts at the Kuniya car park and is an easy 45-minute walk along a wheelchair-accessible trail to the water hole, home of Wanampi, an ancestral snake. A rock shelter used by Aborigines houses rock art.

Another popular way to experience Uluru is far less taxing but no less intense: watching the natural light reflect on it from one of the two sunset-viewing areas. As the last rays of daylight strike, the rock positively glows as if lighted from within. Just as quickly, the light is extinguished and the color changes to a somber mauve and finally to black. ⊠ *Lasseter Hwy., Yulara* ⊕ *www.parksaustralia.gov.au/uluru.*

Uluru–Kata Tjuta Cultural Centre. The cultural center is the first thing you'll see after entering the park through a tollgate. The two buildings are built in a serpentine style, reflecting the Kuniya and Liru stories about two ancestral snakes who fought a long-ago battle on the southern side of Uluru. Inside, you can learn about Aboriginal history and the return of the park to Aboriginal ownership in 1983. There's also an excellent park ranger's station where you can get maps and hiking guides, as well as two art shops where you'll likely see indigenous artists at work. ⊠ *Off*

10

The monumental Uluru as seen from the air

Lasseter Hwy., Yulara 🕾 *08/8956–1128* ⊕ *www.parksaustralia.gov.au/uluru/do/cultural-centre.html* 📧 *Free* ⊙ *Daily 7 am–6 pm.*

WHERE TO EAT

$$
MEDITERRANEAN

✕ **Geckos Cafe.** In the resort's main shopping center, this is the most casual dining option on-site, and relative to other eateries, it's reasonably priced. The all-day dining options include affordable appetizers, hamburgers, pastas, and pizzas. $ *Average main: A$26* ⊠ *Yulara Centre, Town Sq., Yulara* 🕾 *08/8957–7722.*

$$$$
AUSTRALIAN

✕ **Ilkari Restaurant.** A cut above your standard hotel buffet, Ilkari Restaurant has specialties that include barramundi and kangaroo, prepared with a combination of traditional and Mod Oz flavors. The decor reflects local legends with a Kuniya Dreaming mural covering the rear wall. The buffet changes nightly, but make sure you leave room for the wonderful array of desserts, including the perennially popular chocolate fountain. $ *Average main: A$68* ⊠ *Sails in the Desert hotel, Yulara Dr., Yulara* 🕾 *08/8957–7714* ⊙ *No lunch* 🍴 *Reservations essential.*

$$
AUSTRALIAN

✕ **Pioneer BBQ and Bar.** You'll see why Australians love cooking and dining outdoors at this eatery at the hostel-style Outback Pioneer Hotel & Lodge. You can order steak, prawn skewers, or a kangaroo kebab from the server, and then cook it to your liking on huge barbecues. $ *Average main: A$25* ⊠ *Outback Pioneer Hotel & Lodge, Yulara Dr., Yulara* 🕾 *08/8957–7605* ⊙ *No lunch.*

$$
ECLECTIC

✕ **Pira Pool Bar.** A casual poolside bar at Sails in the Desert hotel, Pira offers an all-day menu, serving simple meals from 10 am to 7 pm; there's also a children's menu available. It's a nice spot for a late afternoon cocktail. $ *Average main: A$25* ⊠ *Sails in the Desert Hotel, Yulara Dr., Yulara* 🕾 *08/8957–7417* ⊙ *No dinner.*

CLOSE UP

Climbing Uluru . . . or Not

There's only one trail that leads to the top of the rock. Though many people visit Uluru with the explicit intention of climbing it, there are a few things you should bear in mind before attempting this. First, Aboriginal people consider climbing the rock to be sacrilege—so if you believe in preserving the sanctity of sacred native sites, you should be content with admiring it from below. Your entry pass into the park even says, "It is requested that you respect the wishes of the Anangu by not climbing Uluru." The climb is not closed; the

Aboriginal people prefer that you choose to respect their law and culture by not climbing.

Second, if you do decide to make the climb, be aware that it's a strenuous hike, and not suitable for those who aren't physically fit. The ascent is about 1½ km (1 mile), and the round-trip climb takes about three hours. Sturdy hiking boots, a hat, sunscreen, and drinking water are absolute necessities. The climb is closed when temperatures rise above 36°C (97°F)—which means after 9 am most mornings in summertime.

$$$$ **✕ Sounds of Silence.** The most memorable group-dining experience in the
AUSTRALIAN region is the unique but expensive (A$195 including transfers) Sounds
Fodor's Choice of Silence, an elegant (although heavily attended) outdoor dinner served
★ on a dune that provides sunset views of either Uluru or Kata Tjuta. Australian wines and Northern Territory specialty dishes—including bush salads and Australian game—are served at a lookout before you progress to a buffet meal on tables covered with crisp white linens, right in the desert. An astronomer takes you on a stargazing tour of the southern sky while you dine. A more intimate small-group *table d'hôte* four-course dinner (maximum 20 diners) is also available, called Tali Wiru, at a different vantage point where tables are set for two, four, or six (A$325). The dining tour includes transport to and from your hotel at Yulara. ⑤ *Average main: A$195* ✉ *Yulara* ⊕ *www.ayersrockresort. com.au* ☾ *No lunch* ⚏ *Reservations essential.*

WHERE TO STAY

$$$$ ⌂ **Desert Gardens Hotel.** This is the only hotel-style accommodation in
HOTEL the area that offers views of Uluru from (some) rooms. **Pros:** a relatively affordable view of Uluru; free Wi-Fi; shady gardens among gum trees. **Cons:** busy resort entrance road passes hotel. ⑤ *Rooms from: A$332* ✉ *Yulara Dr., Yulara* ☎ *08/8957–7701* ⊕ *www.ayersrockresort.com. au/accommodation/desert-gardens-hotel* ⇲ *218 rooms* ⦿⎮ *Some meals.*

$$$$ ⌂ **Emu Walk Apartments.** Self-catering one- and two-bedroom apartments
HOTEL with fully equipped kitchens, separate living rooms, and daily maid ser-
FAMILY vice are available at Emu Walk Apartments. **Pros:** extra beds ideal for families or traveling companions; kitchen allows for self-catering; adjacent to resort dining options and shops. **Cons:** room rates are pricey; limited amenities in rooms. ⑤ *Rooms from: A$344* ✉ *Yulara Dr., Yulara* ☎ *08/8957–7701* ⊕ *www.ayersrockresort.com.au* ⇲ *40 1-bedroom, 20 2-bedroom apartments* ⦿⎮ *Some meals.*

10

$$$$ **Longitude 131°.** In the desert 3 km (2 miles) from Ayers Rock Resort,
RESORT Longitude 131° is the be-all and end-all of Outback luxury, with 15
Fodor'sChoice elevated hard-floored "tents" with uninterrupted views of Uluru. **Pros:**
★ luxury tented accommodation, some convertible to twin share; din-
ner under the stars; touring included; attentive staff. **Cons:** the price is
steep; no bathtubs; minimum two-night stay. ⑤ *Rooms from: A$1200*
⊠ *Yulara* ☎ *08/8957–7131* ⊕ *www.longitude131.com.au* ⤴ *15 tents*
⑩ *All-inclusive.*

$$$ **Outback Pioneer Hotel & Lodge.** The theme at this affordable and popu-
HOTEL lar hotel is the 1860s Outback, complete with corrugated iron, timber
FAMILY beams, and camel saddles; but you won't be roughing it here—not
with a pool and two restaurants. **Pros:** lodge rooms are cheapest in the
resort; swimming-pool area. **Cons:** resort shuttle bus to shops; hotel
rooms are basic for the price. ⑤ *Rooms from: A$276* ⊠ *Yulara Dr.,
Yulara* ☎ *08/8957–7606* ⊕ *www.ayersrockresort.com.au* ⤴ *125 hotel
rooms, 42 budget rooms (30 with bathroom, 12 without bathroom),
168 lodge bunk beds* ⑩ *Some meals.*

$$$$ **Sails in the Desert.** Architectural shade sails, ghost-gum-fringed lawns,
RESORT Aboriginal art, and numerous facilities distinguish this upscale hotel
option. **Pros:** Aboriginal artworks featured throughout; kids under 12
stay free. **Cons:** pricey. ⑤ *Rooms from: A$452* ⊠ *Yulara Dr., Yulara*
☎ *08/8957–7417*   ⊕ *www.ayersrockresort.com.au/accommodation/
sails-in-the-desert* ⤴ *214 rooms, 18 suites* ⑩ *Some meals.*

SHOPPING

Uluru–Kata Tjuta Cultural Centre. The cultural center not only has informa-
tion about the Anangu people and their culture, it also houses beautiful
art for purchase. The Ininti Cafe (☎ *08/8956–2214*) carries souvenirs
and light food. The nearby Maruku Arts (☎ *08/8956–2558*) is owned
by Aborigines, and sells Aboriginal paintings and handicrafts. The Cul-
tural Centre itself is open daily 7–6 (information desk 8–5); Ininti Cafe
is open daily 7–5; Maruku Arts is open daily 7:30–5:30. ⊠ *Uluru–Kata
Tjuta National Park, Yulara* ☎ *08/8956–1128.*

THE TOP END

From Arnhem Land in the east—home to remote Aborigines—to the
lush tropical city of Darwin and on to Broome in the west, the Top
End offers some of the most dramatic landscapes in Australia. It's a
landscape of rugged ranges, tropical wetlands, and desert, of vast cattle
stations and wonderful national parks, including the bizarre, beau-
tiful, red-and-black-stripe sandstone domes and towers of Purnululu
National Park and Kakadu National Park, a wilderness area that is
one of Australia's natural jewels and the reason many people come to
the Top End.

The Top End and the Kimberley

DARWIN

3,146 km (1,955 miles) northwest of Sydney, 2,609 km (1,621 miles) north of Adelaide.

Darwin is Australia's most colorful, and exotic, capital city. Surrounded on three sides by the turquoise waters of the Timor Sea, the streets are lined with tropical flowers and trees. Warm and dry in winter, hot and steamy in summer, it's a relaxed and casual place, as well as a beguiling blend of tropical frontier outpost and Outback hardiness. Thanks to its close proximity to Southeast Asia and its multicultural population it also seems more like Asia than the rest of Australia.

Darwin is a city that has always had to fight for its survival. The seductiveness of contemporary Darwin lifestyles belies a history of failed attempts that date from 1824 when Europeans attempted to establish an enclave in this harsh, unyielding climate. The original 1869 settlement, called Palmerston, was built on a parcel of mangrove wetlands and scrub forest that had changed little in 15 million years. It was not until 1911, after it had already weathered the disastrous cyclones of 1878, 1882, and 1897, that the town was named after the scientist who had visited Australia's shores aboard the *Beagle* in 1839. During World War II it was bombed more than 60 times, as the harbor full of warships was a prime target for the Japanese war planes. Then, on the night of Christmas Eve 1974, the city was almost completely destroyed by Cyclone Tracy, Australia's greatest natural disaster.

It's a tribute to those who stayed and to those who have come to live here after Tracy that the rebuilt city now thrives as an administrative and commercial center for northern Australia. Old Darwin has been replaced by something of an edifice complex—such buildings as Parliament House and the Supreme Court all seem very grand for such a small city, especially one that prides itself on its casual, outdoor-centric lifestyle.

Today Darwin is the best place from which to explore Australia's Top End, with its wonders of Kakadu and the Kimberley region.

GETTING HERE AND AROUND

Darwin's International Airport is serviced from overseas by Qantas, Jetstar, Philippine Airlines, Air Asia, and Air North. Qantas flies from Darwin to Bali several times a week, SilkAir and Jetstar connect Darwin with Singapore, and Air North flies to East Timor.

Qantas, Air North, Virgin Australia, Tigerair, and Jetstar fly into Darwin regularly from other parts of Australia and operate regional flights within the Top End. Air North flies west to Kununurra and Broome, and east to Gove. The Darwin Airport Shuttle has regular service between the airport and the city's hotels. The cost is A$18 one-way, A$30 round-trip; book a day in advance for hotel pickup. Taxis await at the airport's taxi rank. The journey downtown costs about A$25–A$30.

The *Ghan* train connects Darwin with Adelaide via Alice Springs on a two-night 2,979-km (1,861-mile) journey a couple of times a week (⊕ *www.greatsouthernrail.com.au*).

The best way to get around Darwin is by car. The Stuart Highway is Darwin's land connection with the rest of Australia. By road Darwin

Darwin

Dudley Point

FANNIE

Fannie Bay

BAY

Vesteys Beach

Gregory St.

Dick Ward Dr.

Playford

Wells St.

Smith Ave.

Stuart Hwy.

Pr. Parade Rd.

East Point Rd.

TO AIRPORT

Bullocky Point

STUART PARK

Westralia St.

Mindil Beach

Myilly Point

Emery Point

Cullen Bay

Palmerston Park

Gardens Rd.

Giruuth Ave.

Stuart Hwy.

Frances Bay Dr.

Dinah Beach

Beach Rd.

Frances Bay

LARRAKEYAH

Packard St.

Mitchell St.

Smith St.

Esplanade

Woods St.

Cavenagh St.

Smith St.

Mitchell St.

McMinn St.

Knuckey St.

Clair St.

Bennett St.

The Mall

CITY CENTER

Elliott Point

Lameroo Beach

Herbert St.

Port Darwin

Fort Hill Wharf

0   1/8 mile

0   400 meters

KEY

Beaches

is 15 hours from Alice Springs (1,491 km [926 miles]), 2½ days from Broome via the Great Northern Highway (1,875 km [1,165 miles]), 4–5 days from Brisbane (3,387 km [2,105 miles]), and 5–6 days from Perth (3,981 km [2,474 miles]).

For drivers headed outside the Northern Territory, one-way drop-off fees for rental vehicles are often twice as much as a weekly rental. If you don't feel like driving, the bus network in Darwin links the city with its far-flung suburbs, and a choice of minibus operators, including the 24-hour Metro minibuses, run all over town for fixed prices starting at A$4 per person. The main bus terminal (Darwin Bus) is on Harry Chan Avenue, near the Bennett Street end of Smith Street Mall. A minibus stand is also located at the front of Darwin's airport terminal.

Taxis Blue Taxi Company. ⊠ *Darwin* ☎ *08/8981–3777* ⊕ *www.bluetaxi.com.au.* **Darwin Radio Taxis.** ⊠ *Darwin* ☎ *13–1008 in local area, 08/8985–0720.*

SAFETY AND PRECAUTIONS

Swimming in the ocean is not recommended because of the box jellyfish, commonly known as "stingers." Salt and freshwater crocodiles are found in most Top End billabongs and rivers, and are occasionally seen even on Darwin beaches. The accessible rivers and billabongs are generally signposted if saltwater crocodiles are known to inhabit the area, but if you are not sure, don't swim.

Avoid driving outside towns after dark due to the dangers presented by buffalo, cattle, horses, donkeys, and kangaroos on the road. If your vehicle breaks down, stay with it; it is easier to find a missing vehicle than missing people. If you are going for a bushwalk, always tells someone your plan and when you expect to return.

TIMING

Although Darwin has some attractions, many people view the city as the entry point to the Top End's national parks, in particular Kakadu and Litchfield. Two days in the city will be enough to see the main attractions, after which you will want to head to Kakadu.

TOURS

Darwin Day Tours. Every day but Sunday, Darwin Day Tours conducts afternoon trips. Tours include historic buildings, the main harbor, the Botanic Gardens, the Northern Territory Museum of Arts and Sciences, East Point Reserve, and Stokes Hill Wharf. ⊠ *Darwin* ☎ *1300/228546* ⊕ *www.darwindaytours.com.au* ⊠ *From A$79.*

FAMILY **Duck About Tours.** The quirky Duck About tour uses an amphibious vehicle to deliver you from land to water while seeing the sights. ⊠ *Darwin* ☎ *1300/382522* ⊕ *www.duckabout.com.au* ⊠ *From A$38.*

Spirit of Darwin. Daytime and sunset cruises explore a harbor five times the size of Sydney's. Trips depart daily from Stokes Hilll Wharf between April and October. ⊠ *Darwin* ☎ *0417/381–977* ⊕ *spiritofdarwin.com. au* ⊠ *From A$65.*

Tour Tub. You can take a five-hour guided tour of Darwin on the Tour Tub bus that includes entry to six attractions. ⊠ *Darwin* ☎ *08/8985–6322* ⊕ *www.tourtub.com.au* ⊠ *From A$110.*

ESSENTIALS

Visitor Information Top End Tourism. ⊠ *6 Bennett St., City Center* ☎ *08/8980–6000, 1300/138886* ⊕ *www.tourismtopend.com.au.*

EXPLORING: CITY CENTER

TOP ATTRACTIONS

FAMILY **Crocosaurus Cove.** Right in the heart of Darwin, this is the place to go swimming with saltwater crocodiles and live to tell the tale. Feeding times and the Cage of Death, where visitors are lowered into croc-infested pools in a perspex container (A$165), are the highlights. Feeding happens at different times throughout the day in the four main sections: fish, big crocs, turtles, and nocturnal reptiles. ⊠ *58 Mitchell St.* ☎ *08/8981–7522* ⊕ *www.crocosauruscove.com* 🎫 *A$35* 🕐 *Daily 9–6.*

> ## CROCS BITE!
>
> The crocodile has long been a dominant predator in the wetland regions of Australia. Powerful and stealthy, the saltwater (estuarine) crocodile has little to fear—and that includes humans. More than 80,000 crocodiles are found in the coastal and tidal areas of rivers, as well as floodplains and freshwater reaches of rivers. In fact, they can be found in the larger rivers, lagoons, and billabongs right across northern Australia. Attacks on people are rare and deaths few (an average of one a year), but you should observe all no-swimming and warning signs and treat crocs with respect.

Stokes Hill Wharf. The best views of Darwin Harbour are from this working pier, which receives cargo ships, trawlers, defense vessels, and, occasionally, huge cruise liners. It's also a favorite spot for Darwinites to fish, and when the mackerel are running you can join scores of locals over a few beers. The cluster of cafés becomes crowded on weekends and when cruise ships arrive. On the city side, in the Waterfront Precinct, is the Wave Lagoon (entry $7; open daily 10–6) and a free, stinger-free (safe from jellyfish) swimming lagoon. Both are popular on hot days. ⊠ *McMinn St., Darwin Harbour* ☎ *08/8981–4268.*

WORTH NOTING

Indo Pacific Marine. This marine interpretative center houses a large open tank with one of the few self-contained coral-reef ecosystems in the southern hemisphere—and it's been growing on its own for almost 20 years. Other exhibits include a static display of rare, deepwater coral skeletons and an exhibit explaining the effects of global warming on the planet. Night tours, which begin at 6:30 on Wednesday, Friday, and Sunday, take you by ultraviolet flashlight to view the biodiversity of the fluorescing reef and live venomous animals; the colors the coral produce are astounding. The tours include a four-course seafood dinner, followed by a nocturnal coral reef tour of the exhibitions. Bookings are essential. ⊠ *29 Stokes Hill Rd., Wharf Precinct* ☎ *08/8981–1294* ⊕ *www.indopacificmarine.com.au* 🎫 *A$24, night tours A$110* 🕐 *Apr.–Oct., daily 10–4; Nov.–Mar. call for opening times.*

10

AROUND DARWIN
TOP ATTRACTIONS

FAMILY   **Crocodylus Park and Zoo.** This research facility has an excellent air-conditioned crocodile museum and education center. There are more than 1,200 crocodiles here, from babies to giants up to 5 meters long. The saurian section of the zoo includes the croc-infested Bellairs Lagoon and pens for breeding and raising. The park also has enclosures with lions, tigers, cassowaries, primates, and turtles, and it holds one of the biggest snakes in Australia: a Burmese python weighing 140 kg (308 lbs). Tours and feedings are at 10, noon, 2, and 3:30. ⊠ *815 McMillans Rd., opposite Berrimah Police Centre, Berrimah* ☎ *08/8922–4500* ⊕ *www.crocodyluspark.com.au* 🖾 *A$40* ⊙ *Daily 9–5.*

FAMILY   **George Brown Darwin Botanic Gardens.** First planted in 1886 and largely destroyed by Cyclone Tracy, the 92-acre site today displays rain forest, mangroves, and open woodland environments. There are more than 450 species of palms growing in the gardens. A popular walk takes visitors on a self-guided tour of plants Aborigines used for medicinal purposes. The Children's Evolutionary Playground traces the changes in plant groups through time, while the plant display house has tropical ferns, orchids, and other exotic plants. ⊠ *Gardens Rd. at Geranium St., Mindil Beach* ☎ *08/8981–1958* ⊕ *www.nt.gov.au* 🖾 *Free* ⊙ *Geranium St. gates daily 7–7, Gardens Rd. gates daily 7–7; information center daily 8–4.*

Fodor's Choice   **Museum and Art Gallery of the Northern Territory.** Collections at this excel-
★   lent museum and art gallery encompass Aboriginal art and culture, maritime archaeology, Northern Territory history, and natural sciences. One gallery is devoted to Cyclone Tracy where you can listen to a terrifying recording of the howling winds. You can also see "Sweetheart," a 16-foot 10-inch stuffed saltwater crocodile that attacked fishing boats on the Finniss River in the 1970s. The Cornucopia Museum Café overlooks tropical gardens and the Darwin harbor and is open all day for meals. ⊠ *19 Conacher St., Bullocky Point, Fannie Bay* ☎ *08/8999–8264* ⊕ *www.magnt.net.au* 🖾 *Free* ⊙ *Weekdays 9–5, weekends and public holidays 10–5.*

FAMILY   **Territory Wildlife Park.** In 1,000 acres of natural bushland, this impressive park is dedicated to the Northern Territory's native fauna and flora. In addition to saltwater crocodiles, water buffalo, dingoes, and waterbirds, it also has an underwater viewing area for observing freshwater fish and a nocturnal house kept dark for late night creatures. The treetop-level walkway through the huge aviary allows you to watch native birds from the swamps and forests at close range. Daily events include feedings, guided walks, and a birds of prey display: see the website for daily schedules. ⌧ *Cox Peninsula Rd, Berry Springs* ✛ *47 km (29 miles) south of Darwin* ☎ *08/8988–7200* ⊕ *www.territorywildlifepark.com. au* ⌫ *A$26* ☉ *Daily 8:30–4; exit open until 6.*

<table>
<tr><td>

OFF THE
BEATEN
PATH

</td><td>

Litchfield National Park. This beautiful park lies just 122 km (76 miles) south of Darwin off the Stuart Highway. Its 1,340 square km (515 square miles) are an untouched wilderness of monsoonal rain forests, rivers, and striking rock formations. The highlights are four separate, spectacular waterfalls—**Florence, Tjaynera, Wangi, and Tolmer Falls**—all of which have secluded plunge pools. ⚠ **The pools are suitable for swimming but occasionally there are crocs here, so observe any "no swimming" signs.** There is also a dramatic group of large, freestanding sandstone pillars known as the **Lost City,** and the **Magnetic Termite Mounds,** which have an eerie resemblance to eroded grave markers, dot the black-soiled plains of the park's northern area. You'll need to camp if you want to stay in the park; campgrounds and RV sites are near several of the major sights (call the Parks and Wildlife Service of the Northern Territory at ☎ 08/8976–0282 for information). There are also a few restaurants and a modest hotel (the Batchelor Resort ☎ 08/8976–0123, which has comfortable hotel rooms, as well as RV and camping facilities) in the nearby town of Batchelor. ⌧ *Litchfield Park Rd., Litchfield Park.*

</td></tr>
</table>

WORTH NOTING

Australian Aviation Heritage Centre. Due to its isolation and sparse population, the Northern Territory played an important role in the expansion of aviation in Australia, and this impressive museum traces the history of flight Down Under. Planes on exhibition include a massive B-52 bomber on permanent loan from the United States, a recently retired RAAF F-111 fighter jet as well as a Japanese Zero shot down on the first day of bombing raids in 1942. ⌧ *557 Stuart Hwy., Winnellie* ✛ *8 km (5 miles) northeast of city center* ☎ *08/8947–2145* ⊕ *www.darwinsairwar. com.au* ⌫ *A$14* ☉ *Daily 9–5.*

Defence of Darwin Experience. WWII came to Australia when 188 Japanese planes bombed Darwin on February 19, 1942, killing almost 1,000 people. This high-tech museum at East Point—opened in 2012 to commemorate the 70th anniversary of the attack—tells the story of the day and Darwin's role in the war. It's next door to the older Darwin Military Museum (included in entry fee), which has lots of guns and other military equipment on show. ⌧ *5434 Alec Fong Lim Dr., East Point* ☎ *08/8981–9702* ⊕ *www.defenceofdarwin.nt.gov.au* ⌫ *A$14* ☉ *Daily 9:30–5.*

SPORTS AND THE OUTDOORS

FISHING

Barramundi, the best-known fish of the Top End, can weigh up to 110 pounds and are excellent fighting fish that taste great on the barbecue afterward.

10

Equinox Fishing Charters. Equinox Fishing Charters has half-day, full-day, and extended fishing trips using the 38-foot *Tsar*, which is licensed to carry 12 passengers and two crew, and *Equinox II*, which can carry 18–20 people. Full-day fishing charters with all meals and tackle provided are from A\$260 per person; shorter five- and seven-hour trips are also available. ⊠ *64 Marina Blvd., Shop 2, Cullen Bay* ☎ *08/8942–2199* ⊕ *www.equinoxcharters.com.au* ⊡ *From A\$160.*

Northern Territory Fisheries Division's Recreational Fishing Office. The office has information on licenses and catch limits. ⊠ *Berrimah Research Farm, Makagon Rd., Berrimah* ☎ *08/8999–2144* ⊕ *www.nt.gov.au/dpifm/Fisheries.*

WHERE TO EAT

\$\$
SEAFOOD
FAMILY

✕ Crustaceans on the Wharf. In a corrugated-iron storage shed at the end of a commercial pier, this is a good place to dine on local fish-and-chips on outdoor tables. Don't expect silver service, though. This is more like a glorified take away in a fabulous location than a full-service restaurant. Seafood takes center stage here; standout choices include the Moreton Bay bugs (which are like small lobsters), calamari, and chili mud crabs. Kids under 10 eat free and they can feed the fish that gather in the water under the lights. ⑤ *Average main: A\$30* ⊠ *Stokes Hill Wharf, Wharf Precinct* ☎ *08/8981–8658* ⊕ *www.crustaceans.net.au.*

\$\$
THAI
Fodor'sChoice
★

✕ Hanuman Darwin. Excellent food and a wine list that includes the best from every grape-growing region in Australia are served against a backdrop of furnishings, tableware, and artworks from around the world in Hanuman's indoor and alfresco dining areas. By drawing on Thai, Nonya (Malaysian), and Indian tandoori culinary traditions, Hanuman's chefs turn local herbs, vegetables, and seafood into sumptuous and innovative dishes. Of special note are Hanuman oysters, lightly cooked in a spicy coriander-and-lemongrass sauce; Hanuman prawns; and any of the curries. ⑤ *Average main: A\$30* ⊠ *93 Mitchell St., City Center* ☎ *08/8941–3500* ⊕ *www.hanuman.com.au* ☾ *No lunch weekends* ⚑ *Reservations essential.*

\$\$
ITALIAN

✕ il lido barpizza. This polished pizzeria and bar is in Darwin's waterfront precinct and provides reflective views as you drink and dine in the open air, with live music on Friday evening. The pizzas are better than average, with toppings like truffled mushrooms and roast pork belly with smoked bacon, toffee apple, and crackling. They also make burgers, upscale hot dogs, and a range of skewered bar snacks. It's worth coming here for the cocktails alone. ⑤ *Average main: A\$25* ⊠ *Wharf One, Kitchener Dr., Darwin Harbour* ☎ *08/8941–0900* ⊕ *www.illidodarwin.com.au.*

$$ ✕ **Manoli's Greek Taverna.** Darwin has a large Greek community and
GREEK this unassuming family-run restaurant does a great souvlaki and other
authentic Greek fare. Don't be put off by the outside appearance, which
looks like a takeaway food store, or the basic decor, because the focus
is all about the food. It gets lively on Friday and Saturday nights with
live Greek music. $ *Average main: A$28* ⊠ *4/64 Smith St.* ☎ *08/8981–
9120* ⊕ *www.manolisgreektaverna.com.au* ☾ *Closed Sun. No lunch
Sat. and Mon.*

$$$ ✕ **Pee Wee's at the Point.** Uninterrupted views of Darwin Harbour at
MODERN East Point Reserve make this restaurant a favorite with locals and visi-
AUSTRALIAN tors wanting a special night out. Dine inside with views of the harbor
through large glass doors, or out on the tiered timber decks beneath the
stars. The cooking is modern Australian, and the carefully considered
wine list has good values. Highlights include soft shell mud crabs, Thai
fried gold band snapper, and pan-roasted wild saltwater barramundi.
$ *Average main: A$45* ⊠ *East Point Reserve, Alec Fong Ling Dr., Fannie Bay* ☎ *08/8981–6868* ⊕ *www.peewees.com.au* ☾ *No lunch. Closed
late Jan.–mid-Mar.* ⚇ *Reservations essential.*

WHERE TO STAY

$$$ ⌂ **DoubleTree by Hilton Hotel Esplanade Darwin.** Most rooms have good
HOTEL views over Darwin harbor from this hotel next door to the Darwin
Entertainment Center. **Pros:** city center location; large swimming pool;
free parking. **Cons:** convention center attracts tour groups. $ *Rooms
from: A$289* ⊠ *116 The Esplanade* ☎ *08/8980–0800* ⊕ *doubletree3.
hilton.com* ⇲ *163 rooms, 34 suites* ⎮◯⎮ *Some meals.*

$$$ ⌂ **Novotel Atrium.** The hotel's bar and restaurant are set around a tiny
HOTEL artificial stream that flows through tropical plants in the middle of the
lobby, which also features a central, vine-hung atrium. **Pros:** tropical
garden in the atrium; some rooms have views over Darwin Harbor;
close to shopping precinct. **Cons:** some rooms are noisy; standard rooms
are small, especially bathrooms. $ *Rooms from: A$219* ⊠ *100 Esplanade* ☎ *08/8941–0755* ⊕ *www.novotel.com* ⇲ *138 rooms, 2 suites*
⎮◯⎮ *Some meals.*

$$$ ⌂ **Sky City Darwin.** The most luxurious place to stay in Darwin, the
RESORT three-story hotel adjacent to the SkyCity Darwin Casino has beachfront
Fodor's Choice accommodations set amid lush lawns and gardens and a huge lagoon-
★ style swimming pool, complete with Darwin's only swim-up bar. **Pros:**
close to Mindil Beach Sunset Market; excellent lagoon-style swimming
pool. **Cons:** casino operates 24 hours, so nights can be noisy; conven-
tion center attracts big groups. $ *Rooms from: A$239* ⊠ *Gilruth Ave.,
Mindil Beach* ☎ *08/8943–8888, 1800/891118* ⊕ *www.skycitydarwin.
com.au* ⇲ *154 rooms* ⎮◯⎮ *Some meals.*

$$$$ ⌂ **Vibe Hotel Darwin Waterfront.** This good-value hotel overlooks the
HOTEL wave pool and lagoon in the heart of the busy waterfront restaurant
Fodor's Choice strip. **Pros:** great location; free Wi-Fi for first 100MB. **Cons:** 10-min-
★ ute walk to city center; no free parking (A$10 per day). $ *Rooms
from: A$356* ⊠ *7 Kitchener Dr., Waterfront* ☎ *08/8982–9998* ⊕ *www.
tfehotels.com* ⇲ *120 rooms* ⎮◯⎮ *Some meals.*

10

Tiwi islands sculptures at a gallery in Darwin

NIGHTLIFE AND PERFORMING ARTS
PERFORMING ARTS

Fodor's Choice
★
Deckchair Cinema. Watching a movie beneath the stars while relaxing on canvas deckchairs with a glass of wine at this outdoor, 350-seat movie theater is one of Darwin's quintessential experiences. Australian, foreign, art house, or classic films are screened every night April–November. Gates open at 6:30 for the sunset, and picnic baskets (no BYO alcohol) are permitted, although there is a snack kiosk and a bar. The first movie screens at 7:30; second showing at 9:30 pm. ⊠ *Jervois Rd., off Kitchener Dr., Wharf Precinct* ☎ *08/8981–0700* ⊕ *www. deckchaircinema.com* ⊑ *A$16* ☼ *Mid-Apr.–mid-Nov.*

NIGHTLIFE

Bogarts Bar and Grill. Named after Humphrey, this small bar and restaurant is adorned with posters and memorabilia in a shabby chic kind of way, complete with couches and a fantastic atmosphere. It's a favorite cocktail haunt for locals and a touch more sophisticated than the bars in the city center. ⊠ *52 Gregory St., Parap* ☎ *08/8981–3561* ⊕ *www. bogartsbarandgrill.com.au* ☼ *Closed Sun. and Mon.*

Monsoons. This establishment has an 80-foot-long granite bar with 20 different beers on tap and wines from Australia and New Zealand and a party-all-night-every-night vibe. The kitchen serves up seafood, pastas, burgers, and steaks, and there is occasional live music. ⊠ *46 Mitchell St., City Center* ☎ *08/8941–7171* ⊕ *www.monsoons.net.au.*

Shenannigans Irish Pub. This pub has Guinness on tap, along with Kilkenny and Harp. Traditional Irish pub food is served, with meat roasts on Sunday. ⊠ *69 Mitchell St., City Center* ☏ *08/8981–2100* ⊕ *www.shenannigans.com.au.*

Fodor's Choice
★ **Ski Club.** This favorite local spot is *the* place to go for a sunset beer in the tropics, and it's right next to the Museum and Art Gallery of the Northern Territory. Its plastic white chairs and tables add to the laid back, "old Darwin" vibe. There's live music on Friday and Saturday nights. ⊠ *20 Conacher St., Fannie Bay* ☏ *08/8981–6630* ⊕ *www.darwinskiclub.com.au.*

SkyCity Darwin Casino. SkyCity Darwin Casino is one of Darwin's most popular evening spots. The 700 gaming machines are open 24 hours, while gaming tables are open from noon until 4 am Thursday and Sunday and until 6 am Friday and Saturday. ⊠ *Gilruth Ave., Mindil Beach* ☏ *08/8943–8888* ⊕ *www.skycitydarwin.com.au.*

Throb. Renowned for its floor shows and drag acts, Throb is Darwin's only gay nightclub. Open Friday and Saturday only from 11 pm, the shows start around 12:30 am and the fun doesn't end until 4 am. Cover charge is A$10–A$15. ⊠ *64 Smith St., City Center* ☏ *08/8942–3435* ⊕ *www.throbnightclub.com.*

SHOPPING
MARKETS

Fodor's Choice
★ **Mindil Beach Sunset Market.** The Mindil Beach Sunset Market is an extravaganza that takes place every Thursday 5 pm–10 pm and every Sunday 4 pm–9 pm from April to October; the Sunday market is smaller than Thursday. Come in the late afternoon to snack at a choice of 60 stalls offering food from more than 25 different countries. You can shop at more than 200 artisans' booths, and enjoy singers, dancers, and musicians. Or join the other Darwinites with a bottle of wine to watch the sun plunge into the sea. ⊠ *Beach Rd., Mindil Beach* ☏ *08/8981–3454* ⊕ *www.mindil.com.au.*

Nightcliff Market. One of the few markets here open year-round, Nightcliff Market takes place on Sunday morning and lasts until around 2 pm in Nightcliff Village, with craft and food stalls and entertainers; it's a great spot for breakfast. ⊠ *Pavonia Pl., Nightcliff* ☏ *0414/368–773* ⊕ *www.nightcliffmarkets.com.au.*

Parap Markets. Located north of the city center, the Parap Markets is where the locals shop. The stalls are open Saturday 8 am–2 pm and have a terrific selection of ethnic Asian food, including some of the best laksa in the country. ⊠ *Parap Sq., Parap* ☏ *0438/882–373, 08/8942–0805* ⊕ *parapvillagemarkets.com.au.*

10

THE INDIGENOUS ARTS SCENE

Start at the Museum and Art Gallery of the Northern Territory for a comprehensive understanding of indigenous art and artifacts. Then head to one of many arts and crafts outlets in and around Darwin to purchase an authentic and unique piece of art. In many indigenous communities throughout the tropical Outback—including Maningrida, Oenpelli, Tiwi islands, and Yirrikala—you can buy direct from the artist.

Rapid Creek Markets. Open Sunday morning, the Rapid Creek Markets are Darwin's oldest and have fresh food produce, as well as locally made handicrafts. ⊠ *Rapid Creek Shopping Centre, Trower Rd., Rapid Creek* ☎ *08/8948–4866.*

KAKADU NATIONAL PARK

Begins 117 km (73 miles) east of Darwin.

This national park is a jewel among the Top End parks, and many visitors come to the region just to experience this tropical wilderness. Beginning east of Darwin, and covering some 19,800 square km (7,645 square miles), the park protects a large system of unspoiled rivers and creeks, as well as a rich Aboriginal heritage that extends back to the earliest days of humankind.

GETTING HERE AND AROUND

From Darwin it's a two- to three-hour drive along the Arnhem Highway east to the entrance to the park at Bowali Visitor Center. Although four-wheel-drive vehicles are not necessary to travel to the park, they are required for many of the unpaved roads within, including the track to Jim Jim Falls. Entry is free, but you must buy a A$25 National Park permit, which is good for 14 days.

SAFETY AND PRECAUTIONS

If you are driving, watch out for road trains—large trucks up to 160 feet in length with up to four trailers behind a prime mover. They are common on Northern Territory roads, and you should give them plenty of room. Avoid driving after dark outside towns because of the high likelihood of straying animals—kangaroos and cattle in particular. It is a good idea to always tell someone of your plans if you intend traveling to remote places; the same applies when bushwalking. Always make sure you have adequate water and food.

TIMING

The best time to visit is between May and September during the Dry. The shortest time you should allow is a three-day, two-night itinerary from Darwin. This will provide opportunities to visit the major sights—a cruise on the East Alligator River; Ubirr, a major Aboriginal rock-art site; a flight-seeing flight from Jabiru Airport; Nourlangie Rock, another Aboriginal rock-art site; the Warradjan Aboriginal Cultural Centre, to learn about traditional Aboriginal people; and a sunset cruise on Yellow Water Billabong to see birds, crocodiles, and other wildlife. On the return to Darwin, you can visit Mamukala Wetlands for an abundance of birds and wildlife. A five-day itinerary will give you time to visit Jim Jim Falls and Twin Falls, a four-wheel-drive excursion.

TOURS

During the Dry, park rangers conduct free walks and tours at several popular locations. You can pick up a program at the entry station or at either of the visitor centers.

Far Out Adventures. Far Out Adventures runs customized tours of Kakadu, as well as other regions of the Top End, for small groups. ☎ *04/2715–2288* ⊕ *www.farout.com.au* ✉ *Price on request.*

Fodor's Choice
★ **Kakadu Air.** Well worth the splurge, the best way to see Kakadu's famous waterfalls is from the air, during the wet season or early in the dry season around April. This company makes scenic hour (A$250) and half-hour (A$150) flights out of Jabiru. In the Dry the flight encompasses the northern region, including Arnhem Land escarpment, Nourlangie and Mamakala Wetlands, East Alligator River, and Jabiru Township. During the Wet only, a similarly priced half-hour or one-hour flight takes in the Jim Jim and Twin falls, when they are most spectacular. Heli tours are also available. ☎ 1800/089113, 08/8941–9611 ⊕ www.kakaduair. com.au 🖾 From A$150.

Fodor's Choice
★ **Kakadu Tourism.** The Cooinda Lodge arranges magical boat tours of Yellow Water Billabong, one of the major waterholes in Kakadu, where innumerable birds and crocodiles gather. There are six tours throughout the day as well as a night tour (no children under 8 on the night tour); the sunrise and sunset cruises are best—both in terms of temperature and animal activity. ☎ 08/8979–1500 ⊕ www.kakadutourism. com 🖾 From A$72.

ESSENTIALS

Visitor Information Bowali Visitor Centre. The visitor center has state-of-the-art audiovisual displays and traditional exhibits that give an introduction to the park's ecosystems and its bird population, the world's most diverse. Kids love the giant crocodile skeleton. ⊠ Arnhem and Kakadu Hwys. ☎ 08/8938–1120 🖾 Free ☯ Daily 8–5.

Kakadu National Park. ⊠ Kakadu National Park ☎ 08/8938–1120 ⊕ www. environment.gov.au/parks/kakadu. **Tourism Top End.** ⊠ 6 Bennett St., Darwin ☎ 1300/138886 ⊕ www.tourismtopend.com.au. **Warradjan Cultural Centre.** ⊠ Kakadu National Park ⊹ 5 km (3 miles) off Kakadu Hwy. on road to Cooinda Lodge ☎ 08/8979–0145.

EXPLORING

Jim Jim Falls. The best way to gain a true appreciation of the natural beauty of Kakadu is to visit the waterfalls running off the escarpment. Some 39 km (24 miles) south of the park headquarters along the Kakadu Highway, a track leads off to the left toward Jim Jim Falls, 60 km (37 miles) away (about a two-hour drive). The track is rough and unpaved, and you'll need a four-wheel-drive vehicle to navigate it. From the parking lot you have to scramble 1 km (½ mile) over boulders to reach the falls and the plunge pools they have created at the base of the escarpment. After May, the water flow over the falls may cease, and the unpaved road is closed in the Wet. ■ TIP➜ **The best way to see these falls at their best is on a scenic flight from Jabiru during the wet season.** ⊠ Jim Jim Falls Track, Kakadu Hwy.

10

FodorśChoice
★
Kakadu National Park. The superb gathering of Aboriginal rock art is one of Kakadu National Park's major highlights. Two main types of Aboriginal artwork can be seen here. The Mimi style, which is the oldest, is believed to be up to 20,000 years old. Aborigines believe that Mimi spirits created the red-ocher stick figures to depict hunting scenes and other pictures of life at the time. The more recent artwork, known as X-ray painting, dates back fewer than 9,000 years and depicts freshwater animals—especially fish, turtles, and geese—living in floodplains created after the last ice age.

As the dry season progresses, billabongs (waterholes) become increasingly important to the more than 280 species of birds that inhabit the park. Huge flocks often gather at Yellow Water, South Alligator River, and Magela Creek. Scenic flights over the wetlands and Arnhem Land escarpment provide unforgettable moments in the wet season. ⊠ *Kakadu National Park* ⊕ *www.environment.gov.au/parks/kakadu* ⊡ *A$25 for up to 14 days.*

FodorśChoice
★
Nourlangie Rock. Like the main Kakadu escarpment, Nourlangie Rock is a remnant of an ancient plateau that is slowly eroding, leaving sheer cliffs rising high above the floodplains. The main attraction is the **Anbangbang Gallery,** an excellent frieze of Aboriginal rock paintings. ⊠ *Kakadu National Park* ⊹ *19 km (12 miles) from park headquarters on Kakadu Hwy.; turn left toward Nourlangie Rock, then follow paved road, accessible yr-round, 11 km (7 miles) to parking area* ⊕ *www. environment.gov.au/parks/kakadu* ⊙ *Daily 7 am–sunset.*

Twin Falls. As you approach the Twin Falls, the ravine opens up dramatically to reveal a beautiful sandy beach scattered with palm trees, as well as the crystal waters of the falls spilling onto the end of the beach. This spot is a bit difficult to reach, but the trip is rewarding. Take the road to Jim Jim Falls, turn off just before the parking lot, and travel 10 km (6 miles) farther to the Twin Falls parking lot. A regular boat shuttle (A$12.50; buy your tickets before you go at Bowali Visitor Centre or Garnamarr campground) operates a return service up the Twin Falls gorge, and then you need to walk over boulders, sand, and a boardwalk to the falls. Saltwater crocodiles may be in the water in the gorge, so visitors are urged not to enter the water. The round-trip, including the boat shuttle, takes around two hours. ⊠ *Off Jim Jim Rd.*

Ubirr. Ubirr has an impressive display of Aboriginal paintings scattered through six shelters in the rock. The main gallery contains a 49-foot frieze of X-ray paintings depicting animals, birds, and fish. A 1-km (½-mile) path around the rock leads to all the galleries. It's just a short clamber to the top for wonderful views over the surrounding wetlands, particularly at sunset. ■TIP➜ **Take a flashlight to help you get down after sunset.** Stop in at the Border Store and Cafe on your way in; they do lunch and a postsunset Thai dinner and sell arts and crafts. Beware of wildlife on the roads if driving after dark. ⊠ *43 km (27 miles) north of park headquarters along paved road* ☏ *08/8979–2474 for Border Store and Cafe* ⊕ *www.kakadu.com.au; www.environment.gov.au/parks/ kakadu* ⊙ *Apr.–Nov., daily 8:30–sunset; Dec.–Mar., daily 2–sunset.*

Gunlom Falls in the Kakadu National Park

WHERE TO STAY

There are several lodges in the park, and campgrounds at Merl, Muire-lla Park, Mardugal, and Gunlom have toilets, showers, and water. Sites are A$10 per night. Alcohol is not available in Jabiru, so stock up in Darwin.

$$$ **Aurora Kakadu.** This comfortable hotel has doubles and family rooms—
HOTEL which sleep up to five—spread through lush tropical gardens; the rooms and campgrounds are clean and provide good value for the money. **Pros:** fauna is abundant; tropical garden setting; free bottled water in rooms. **Cons:** some distance from park attractions; limited amenities in rooms; thin walls; own transport essential. *$ Rooms from: A$204 ⊠ Arnhem Hwy. ✣ 2½ km (1½ miles) before highway crosses South Alligator River ☎ 08/8979–0166, 1800/818845 ⊕ www.auroraresorts.com.au ⤳ 138 rooms, 36 powered sites, 250 tent sites ⊺⊙⊺ Some meals.*

$$$$ **Cooinda Lodge.** Near Yellow Water Billabong, this facility has light,
HOTEL airy lodgings looking out over tropical gardens. **Pros:** center for Yellow Water Cruises; close to Aboriginal cultural center. **Cons:** 30 minutes from Jabiru shops; limited amenities in rooms; limited dining options. *$ Rooms from: A$335 ⊠ Kakadu Hwy., Cooinda ✣ 2 km (1 mile) toward Yellow Water Wetlands ☎ 08/8979–1500 ⊕ www.kakadutourism.com ⤳ 48 rooms ⊺⊙⊺ No meals.*

$$$$ **Mercure Kakadu Crocodile Hotel.** Shaped like a crocodile, this unusual
HOTEL hotel with spacious, refurbished rooms is the best of the area's accom-
Fodor's Choice modation options. **Pros:** friendly, helpful staff; Aboriginal artwork on
★ sale; Jabiru village within walking distance. **Cons:** pool area is small;

10

ground-floor rooms can have "critters". $ *Rooms from: A$329* ⊠ *1 Flinders St., Jabiru* ☎ *08/8979–9000* ⊕ *www.kakadutourism.com* ⌂ *110 rooms* ❍❘ *Some meals.*

KATHERINE GORGE

30 km (18 miles) east of Katherine, 346 km (215 miles) southeast of Darwin, 543 km (337 miles) northeast of Kununurra.

Officially called Nitmiluk, the Aboriginal or Jawoyn name for the cicadas associated with the creation stories of the area, this stunning canyon formed by the Katherine River in Nitmiluk National Park is actually a series of 13 gorges, each separated by a jumble of boulders. The gorge is 12 km (7½ miles) long and in many places the red rocky walls are almost 230 feet high. During the wet season (November through to April), the gorge is full of raging water and saltwater crocodiles, but during the dry season you can hire canoes or take one of several cruises to explore the gorges. Rangers clear the river of dangerous crocodiles at the start of each season so you can also swim, if the harmless freshwater crocodiles don't bother you.

ANCIENT ART AND NATURE

Almost the size of West Virginia, Kakadu National Park is an ancient landform, with wetlands, gorges, waterfalls, and rugged escarpments. It also has one of the highest concentrations of accessible Aboriginal rock-art sites in the world. Take a tour with an Aboriginal guide from one of the cultural centers near Jabiru or Cooinda. The art sites date back 20,000 years.

GETTING HERE AND AROUND

There are no commercial flight services that fly direct into Katherine; the closest airport is Darwin, which is about a three-hour drive.

TOURS

Nitmiluk Tours. Although you can explore Katherine Gorge on foot on one of the many bushwalking trails, the best way to see the gorge is to hit the water. Jawoyn-owned Nitmiluk Tours offer a range of cruises, starting at A$84 for a two-hour trip that departs several times each day. Wear comfortable walking shoes as there is some walking involved between gorges. ■ TIP→ The best time to go is during the late afternoon, when you'll get the best photo opportunities as the walls of the gorge glow a deep red. Canoe hire is A$55 for half a day, A$75 for a full day. Helicopter flights over the gorge start at A$99. ⊠ *Nitmiluk National Park, Gorge Rd., Katherine* ☎ *08/8972–1253* ⊕ *www.nitmiluktours.com.au* ⌂ *From A$84.*

WHERE TO STAY

$$$$　**Cicada Lodge.** The stylish air-conditioned rooms at the luxury Cicada
RESORT　Lodge are decorated with Aboriginal artwork, and each has a private balcony overlooking the gorge from which you can enjoy the sunset. **Pros:** great location; excellent food and service; open during the wet season; complimentary drink and snack each evening. **Cons:** expensive; tours and meals cost extra. $ *Rooms from: A$495* ⊠ *Nitmiluk National Park, Katherine* ☎ *08/8974–3100* ⊕ *cicadalodge.com.au* ⌂ *18 rooms* ❍❘ *Breakfast.*

THE KIMBERLEY

Perched on the northwestern hump of the loneliest Australian state, only half as far from Indonesia as it is from Sydney, the Kimberley remains a frontier of sorts. The first European explorers, dubbed by one of their descendants as "cattle kings in grass castles," ventured into the heart of the region in 1879 to establish cattle stations. They subsequently became embroiled in one of the country's longest-lasting conflicts between white settlers and Aborigines, led by Jandamarra of the Bunuba people.

The Kimberley remains sparsely populated, with only 35,000 people living in an area of 351,200 square km (135,600 square miles). That's about 12 square km (4½ square miles) per person. The region is dotted with cattle stations and raked with craggy ocher ranges, croc-infested rivers, tropical forests, and towering cliffs. Several of the country's most spectacular national parks are here, including Purnululu (Bungle Bungle) National Park, a vast area of bizarrely shaped and colored rock formations that became widely known to white Australians only in 1983. Facilities in this remote region are few, but if you're looking for a genuine Outback experience, the Kimberley represents the opportunity of a lifetime.

KUNUNURRA

516 km (322 miles) west of Katherine, 840 km (525 miles) southwest of Darwin.

Kununurra is the eastern gateway to the Kimberley. With a population of around 6,000, it's a modern, planned town developed in the 1960s for the nearby Lake Argyle and Ord River irrigation scheme. It's a convenient base from which to explore local attractions such as Mirima National Park (a mini–Bungle Bungle on the edge of town), Lake Argyle, and the River Ord. The town is also one starting point for adventure tours of the Kimberley; the other option is to start from Broome.

GETTING HERE AND AROUND

Distances in this part of the continent are colossal. Flying is the fastest and easiest way to get to the Kimberley. Both Virgin Australia and Air North have extensive air networks throughout the Top End, linking Kununurra to Broome, Perth, and Darwin.

From Darwin to Kununurra and the eastern extent of the Kimberley it's 827 km (513 miles). The route runs from Darwin to Katherine along the Stuart Highway, and then along the Victoria Highway to Kununurra. The entire road is paved but narrow in parts—especially so, it may seem, when a road train (a long truck towing three or four trailers) is coming the other way. Drive with care. Fuel and supplies can be bought at small settlements along the way, but you should always keep supplies in abundance and expect to pay a pretty penny.

Taxis Spud's Taxis. ✉ *Kununurra* ☎ *08/9168–2553.* **Taxi Services Kununurra.** ✉ *Kununurra* ☎ *13–1008, 08/9168–1521.*

10

SAFETY AND PRECAUTIONS

Driving long distances through the Kimberley can be an adventure, but also carries risks. For drivers not used to the conditions, and not taking adequate rest breaks, the combination of warm sun through the windshield, long sections of road, and lack of traffic can have a hypnotic effect. Take regular breaks every two hours to walk and have a stretch, and get plenty of sleep the night before. If you are feeling sleepy, stop immediately and take a break. Many vehicle crashes in this area are vehicle versus animal, often a kangaroo or straying cattle. Dusk and dawn are when animals are most active. If you see an animal on the road in front of you, brake firmly in a straight line and sound your horn. Do not swerve: it is safer to stay on the road.

TIMING

You should allow at least five days to see Kununurra and the East Kimberley, including your arrival and departure days. That will allow enough to visit the Ord River and cruise Lake Argyle, take a scenic flight to the Bungle Bungles and hike the area with a guide, and take a four-wheel-drive excursion to El Questro Wilderness Park. Winter—May to September—is the most popular time to visit, as days are warm and there is little rain. October to April is the wet season, and temperatures can be a lot higher—up to 45°C (113°F).

TOURS

APT Kimberley Wilderness Adventures. This agency conducts tours from Broome and Kununurra, which include excursions along Gibb River Road and into Purnululu National Park. A two-day self-drive tour from Kununurra includes the Mitchell Plateau and Mitchell Falls, with an overnight in a wilderness camp. Longer four-wheel-drive bus and flight tours are also available. ⊠ *Kununurra* ☎ *1300/334872, 1800/889389* ⊕ *www.kimberleywilderness.com.au* ⌂ *From A$295 self-drive, A$1495 by bus.*

Aviair. This company conducts both fixed-wing and helicopter flights from Kununurra and Purnululu National Park. A two-hour fixed-wing flight over the Bungle Bungle and Lake Argyle is A$399. ☎ *08/9166–9300* ⊕ *www.aviair.com.au* ⌂ *From A$399.*

East Kimberley Tours. This company's most popular day tour includes an eye-popping flight to Purnululu National Park, a four-wheel-drive tour to the famous "beehive domes" and Cathederal Gorge, lunch, and a return scenic flight over Argyle Diamond mine. ⊠ *Kununurra* ☎ *08/9168–2213* ⊕ *www.eastkimberleytours.com.au* ⌂ *From A$790.*

Fodor's Choice ★ **Kingfisher Tours.** This company operates scenic flights from Kununurra Airport. A two-hour scenic flight over the Bungle Bungles and other sights costs A$360. ⊠ *Kununurra* ☎ *08/9148–2630* ⊕ *kingfishertours. net* ⌂ *From A$360.*

Lake Argyle Cruises. Excellent trips on Australia's largest expanse of freshwater, the man-made Lake Argyle, start with a bus trip, which run daily March to October. It's A$70 for the two-hour morning cruise, A$155 for the six-hour cruise, and A$90 for the sunset cruise (which starts around 2:45). ☎ *08/9168–7687* ⊕ *www.lakeargylecruises.com* ⌂ *From A$70.*

ESSENTIALS
Visitor Information Kununurra Visitor Centre. ⊠ 75 Coolibah Dr.
☎ 08/9168–1177, 1800/586868 ⊕ www.visitkununurra.com.

EXPLORING

OFF THE BEATEN PATH

El Questro Wilderness Park. This 1-million acre property features some of the most ruggedly beautiful country in the East Kimberley. El Questro has a full complement of recreational activities like fishing, swimming, and horse and helicopter rides. It also offers individually tailored walking and four-wheel-drive tours. Four independent accommodation facilities are on-site, each different in style and budget: the luxury Homestead; the safari-style tented cabins at Emma Gorge Resort; and air-conditioned Riverside Bungalows and Riverside Campgrounds at the Station Township. Each has a restaurant, and rates (minimum two nights) at the Homestead include drinks and food, laundry, and activities. Transportation from Kununurra is available from A$98 per person. ⊠ 1 Gibb River Rd. ⌖ 100 km (60 miles) west of Kununurra, via Great Northern Hwy.; take Gibb River Rd. for 42 km (14 miles) from highway exit ☎ 03/9169–1777 reservations, 08/9161–4388 Emma Gorge Resort, 1300/233432 ⊕ www.elquestro.com.au ⊠ El Questro Wilderness Park permit (required) A$20 for 1- to 7-day pass with access to gorge walks, thermal springs, fishing holes, rivers, and use of the Emma Gorge Resort swimming pool ⊗ Daily Apr.–Oct. ⇆ 6 suites, 60 tented cabins, 12 bungalows, 28 campsites, 6 lodge cabins.

Home Valley Station. If you've ever fancied being a cowboy (or cowgirl) this massive 3.5-million-acre working cattle farm at the foot of the majestic Cockburn (pronounced co-burn) is the place to do it. Owned and operated by the traditional owners of the land, the Balanggarra people through the Indigenous Land Corporation, you can join a cattle muster or just take a half-day horse trek. Other activities include fishing and 4WD trips. There's a bar and restaurant on-site and a range of accommodations, from stylish bungalows complete with cow-skin rugs, air-conditioning, fully stocked minibar, flat-screen cable TV, huge walk-in rain shower, and resident tree frogs. For those on a tighter budget there's the motel-style guesthouse rooms, eco-tents with a raised wooden floor and queen-size bed, and remote bush camping beside the Pentecost River, 4 km (2½ miles) from the homestead. Transfers from Kununurra cost A$240; A$100 from neighboring El Questro. ⊠ Kununurra ⌖ 120 km (75 miles) from Kununurra on Gibb River Rd. ☎ 08/9161–4322, 02/8296–8010 reservations ⊕ www.hvstation.com.au ⊗ Closed Nov.–end of Apr.

10

WHERE TO STAY

$$
HOTEL

Ibis Styles Kununurra Hotel. Set in tropical gardens, the brightly furnished rooms here provide a comfortable base from which to explore the eastern Kimberley. **Pros:** walking distance to downtown; colorful Aboriginal art theme in rooms; swimming pool in tropical gardens setting. **Cons:** limited amenities in rooms; limited dining options. $ Rooms from: A$169 ⊠ Victoria Hwy. and Messmate Way ☎ 08/9168–4000 ⊕ www.accorhotels.com.au ⇆ 60 rooms ⊙ Breakfast.

$$$ **Kununurra Country Club Resort.**
HOTEL   In the center of town, this hotel is encircled by its own little rain forest of tropical gardens. **Pros:** complimentary airport shuttle; poolside dining and bars; easy walk to downtown. **Cons:** tour groups stay here. $ *Rooms from: A$235* ✉ *47 Coolibah Dr.* ☎ *08/9168–1024* ⊕ *www.kununurracountryclub.com.au* ⤴ *90 rooms* �

Some meals.

$$$ **Kununurra Lakeside Resort.** On the
RESORT   shores of Lake Kununurra sits this understated, tranquil resort, where you can see stunning sunsets over the water and watch for fruit bats flying overhead. **Pros:** lakeside location; courtesy bus available; crocodile spotting at night. **Cons:** rooms are basic. $ *Rooms from: A$230* ✉ *50 Casuarina Way, off Victoria Hwy.* ☎ *08/9169–1092, 1800/786692* ⊕ *www.lakeside.com.au* ⤴ *42 rooms* ☐ *No meals.*

> **A FANTASY LANDSCAPE**
>
> For millions of years nature has savaged the rocks of Purnululu National Park with water and wind, creating one of the most unusual landscapes in the world. Traveling into the area is a remarkable experience—the timelessness of the ancient rocks draws you back across the millennia. All around, the conically weathered formations cluster together like a meeting of some metamorphic executives.

PURNULULU (BUNGLE BUNGLE) NATIONAL PARK

252 km (156 miles) southwest of Kununurra.

This park covers nearly 3,120 square km (1,200 square miles) in the southeast corner of the Kimberley. Australians of European descent first "discovered" its great beehive-shaped domes—their English name is the Bungle Bungle—in 1983, proving how much of this vast continent remains outside of "white" experience. The local Kidja Aboriginal tribe, who knew about these scenic wonders long ago, called the area Purnululu, meaning sandstone.

The striking, black-and-orange-stripe mounds seem to bubble up from the landscape. Climbing on them is not permitted, because the sandstone layer beneath their thin crust of lichen and silica is fragile, and would quickly erode without protection. Walking tracks follow rocky, dry creek beds. One popular walk leads hikers along the **Piccaninny Creek** to **Piccaninny Gorge**, passing through gorges with towering 328-foot cliffs to which slender fan palms cling.

GETTING HERE AND AROUND

The Bungle Bungles are 252 km (156 miles) south of Kununurra along the Great Northern Highway. A very rough, 55-km (34-mile) unpaved road, negotiable only in a four-wheel-drive vehicle, is the last stretch of road leading to the park from the turnoff near the Turkey Creek–Warmum Community. That part of the drive can take two to three hours, depending on the condition of the road. It's farther on to one of the three campgrounds, two public and one used by tour operators that is also available to self-drivers who prefer hot showers, flushing toilets, and regular beds. The most-visited section of the park is in the south, where there are rough walking trails to the main sights.

SAFETY AND PRECAUTIONS

The park is usually open from April to December (depending on whether the road is passable after the wet season); however, temperatures in April, October, November, and December can be blisteringly hot. If you travel in these months, make sure you have plenty of water and be sun-smart.

TIMING

Purnululu National Park can be visited in a day from Kununurra, but only with a flight and safari package. There are also tours available that include overnight camping, but the road trip from Kununurra takes the best part of a day. Driving yourself to the park is not recommended, as the last section is a very rough track suitable only for four-wheel-drive vehicles; it has been kept deliberately so to limit visitation. If you do decide to drive in yourself, be aware that there are few facilities in the park's public campgrounds; you need to take in all your own food and camping equipment.

ESSENTIALS

Visitor Information Purnululu Visitor Centre. ⊠ *Purnululu National Park* ☎ *08/9168–7300* ⊕ *parks.dpaw.wa.gov.au/park/purnululu.*

EXPLORING

The most popular walking trails are in the south of the park, where the famous "beehives" are located. From Piccaninny Creek car park you can hike in to Cathedral Gorge; the walk takes about an hour. Take a 20-minute detour on the Domes Walk to see more of the famous sandstone "beehives." If you have more time, you can follow the Piccaninny Creek walk into Piccaninny Gorge, following an eroded riverbed and sandstone ledges. This will take all day, but you can return at any time. In the north of the park there are walks to Echidna Gorge (about one hour), where dinosaur-era livistona palms cling to the cliffs and the gorge narrows to about 3 feet across, and Mini Palms Gorge, a rock-strewn gorge again filled with livistona palms. At the end there is a viewing platform overlooking the valley. Allow an hour for this walk.

WHERE TO STAY

Although there are two designated campsites in the area, neither has many facilities. Both the Bellburn Creek and Walardi campgrounds have simple chemical toilets; fresh drinking water is at both campgrounds. Kununurra Visitor Centre has information about the campsites. The two tour operators who fly clients in from Kununurra, Broome, and Halls Creek, and drive them around in four-wheel-drive vehicles, have comfortable bush camps that regular visitors can also pay to use and eat at. April through December, the most popular tours include an overnight stay. The mounds are closed from January through March.

GEIKIE GORGE NATIONAL PARK

416 km (258 miles) southwest of Purnululu National Park, 416 km (258 miles) east of Broome.

Halfway between Purnululu and Broome, Geikie Gorge, an ancient flooded reef, is one of the highlights of a trip through the Kimberley.

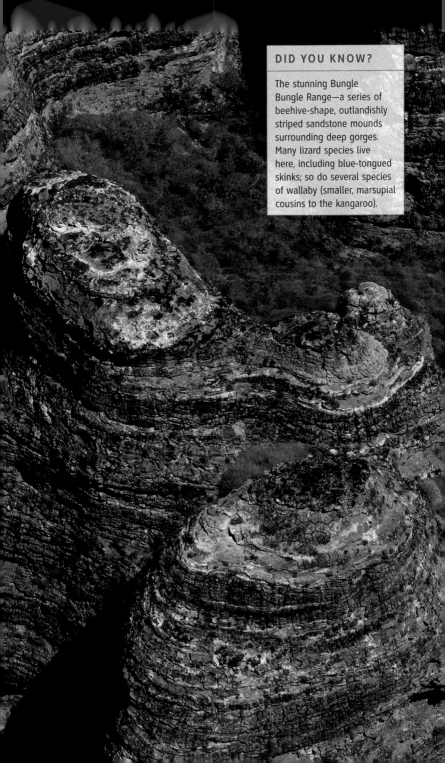

TOURS

National Park Ranger Station. The best way to see the gorge is aboard one of the 90-minute boat tours led by a ranger from the National Park Ranger Station, departing at 8, 9:30, 11, and 3. The knowledgeable rangers are helpful in pointing out the vegetation, strange limestone formations, and many freshwater crocodiles along the way. You may also see part of the noisy fruit-bat colony that inhabits the region. The park is open for day visits daily from 6:30 am to 6:30 pm between April and November. Entry is restricted during the wet season, from December to March when the Fitzroy River floods. ⊠ *Great Northern Hwy., King Leopold Ranges* ☎ *08/9191–5121* ⊕ *parks.dpaw.wa.gov. au/park/geikie-gorge* 🖃 *From A$40.*

EXPLORING

Geikie Gorge National Park. Twenty km (12.5 miles) northeast of the township of Fitzroy Crossing, Geikie Gorge is part of a 350-million-year-old reef system formed from fossilized layers of algae—evolutionary precursors of coral reefs—when this area was still part of the Indian Ocean. The limestone walls you see today were cut and shaped by the mighty Fitzroy River; during the wet season, the normally placid waters roar through the region. The walls of the gorge are stained red from iron oxide, except where they have been leached of the mineral and turned white by the floods, which have washed as high as 52 feet from the bottom of the gorge.

When the Indian Ocean receded, it stranded a number of sea creatures, which managed to adapt to their altered conditions. Geikie is one of the few places in the world where freshwater barramundi, mussels, stingrays, and prawns swim. The park is also home to the freshwater archerfish, which can spit water as far as a yard to knock insects out of the air. Aborigines call this place Kangu, meaning "big fishing hole."

Although there's a 5-km (3-mile) walking trail along the west side of the gorge, the opposite side is off-limits because it's a wildlife sanctuary. ⊠ *Great Northern Hwy., King Leopold Ranges* ⊕ *parks.dpaw.wa.gov. au/park/geikie-gorge.*

BROOME

1,032 km (640 miles) southwest of Kununurra via Halls Creek, 1,544 km (957 miles) southwest of Katherine, 1,859 km (1,152 miles) southwest of Darwin.

Broome is the holiday capital of the Kimberley. It's the only town in the region with sandy beaches, and is the base from which most strike out to see more of the region. In some ways, with its wooden sidewalks and charming Chinatown, it still retains the air of its past as a boisterous shantytown. However, with tourism increasing every year it is becoming noticeably upscale.

Long ago, Broome depended on pearling for its livelihood. By the early 20th century 300 to 400 sailing boats employing 3,000 men provided most of the world's mother-of-pearl shell. Many of the pearlers were Japanese, Malay, and Filipino, and the town is still a wonderful multicultural center today with the modern pearling industry very much at its heart. Each August during the famous Shinju Matsuri (Festival of the Pearl), Broome commemorates its early pearling years and heritage. The 10-day festival features many traditional Japanese ceremonies. Because of the popularity of the festival, advance bookings for accommodations are highly recommended. Several tour operators have multiday cruises out of Broome along the magnificent Kimberley coast. The myriad deserted islands and beaches, with 35-foot tides that create horizontal waterfalls and whirlpools, make it an adventurer's delight.

Broome marks the western extent of the Kimberley. From here it's another 2,250 km (1,395 miles) south to Perth, or 1,859 km (1,152 miles) back to Darwin.

GETTING HERE AND AROUND

Qantas and its subsidiaries fly to Broome from Brisbane, Sydney, Melbourne, and Adelaide via Perth. Direct flights from Sydney, Melbourne, and Brisbane are twice a week. Air North has an extensive air network throughout the Top End, linking Broome to Kununurra and Darwin. Virgin Australia also services Broome from Perth. Broome's airport is right next to the center of town, on the northern side. Though it's called Broome International Airport, there are no scheduled overseas flights, but charter flights and private flights arrive there.

SAFETY AND PRECAUTIONS

From November to April there is a possibility of cyclones off the Kimberley coast. It is important that visitors are aware of the procedures to follow in the event of a cyclone alert. These procedures are provided in all accommodations and are also at the Broome Visitor Centre or the Shire of Broome office. Call ☎ *1300/659210* for cyclone watch and warning messages, or go online at ⊕ *www.bom.gov.au.*

November to April is also when mosquitoes are at their most prevalent. To avoid the discomfort of mosquito bites and any risk of infection, it is advisable to cover up at dawn and dusk and apply insect repellent, which is supplied in most hotels. Sand flies become more active in Broome on high tides; use the same prevention methods.

Tropical waters can contain various stingers. The two types of dangerous jellyfish are the chironex box jellyfish (a large but almost transparent jellyfish up to 12 inches across with ribbonlike tentacles from each of the four corners) and Irukandji (a tiny transparent jellyfish less than 1 inch across with four thin tentacles). Both are found during the summer months of November to May. Take care when swimming (wear protective clothing—a wet suit or lycra stinger suit to reduce exposure to potential stings) and obey signs displayed on the beaches at all times. Medical attention (pour vinegar onto the sting and call ☎ *000* for an ambulance) should be sought if someone is stung.

Saltwater crocodiles live in estuaries throughout the Kimberley, and freshwater Johnsons crocodiles hang out in freshwater gorges and lakes. Look for warning signs. Even if not signposted, advice from a reliable local authority should always be sought before swimming in rivers and waterholes.

10

TIMING

Ideally, you need at least five days in Broome and the West Kimberley, including your arrival and departure days. This will give you time to go swimming and sunbathing on Cable Beach, take a camel ride, and cruise on a restored pearl lugger. A scenic flight will show you the pristine Kimberley coastline and the horizontal waterfalls of Buccaneer Archipelago. A day tour will get you to Cape Leveque or Windjana Gorge. To go farther afield, join a four-wheel-drive safari; a two-day tour will show you the gorges of the area, including Geikie Gorge.

The most popular time to visit is from May to October, during the dry season.

TOURS

APT Kimberley Wilderness Adventures. APT Kimberley Wilderness Adventures conducts tours from Broome, which include excursions along Gibb River Road and into Purnululu National Park as well as cruises to Darwin. Their 15-day Kimberley Complete tour includes the gorges along the Gibb River Road, the Aboriginal culture of the Mitchell Plateau, a scenic flight over the Mitchell Falls, Purnululu National Park, and an Aboriginal-guided tour through Geikie Gorge. ☎ *1300/334872* ⊕ *www.kimberleywilderness.com.au* ✉ *From A$8995.*

Astro Tours. Astro Tours organizes entertaining, informative night-sky tours of the Broome area. Two-hour shows (offered four nights a week) cost A$85, including transfers from your hotel, folding-stool seating, hot beverages, and cookies. The company also offers four-wheel-drive Outback stargazing adventures farther afield. ✉ *Broome* ☎ *0417/949–958* ⊕ *www.astrotours.net* ✉ *From A$85.*

Broome Sightseeing Tours. Broome Sightseeing Tours has a 2½-hour Broome town tour (A$80) that includes visits to Cable Beach, Gantheaume Point, Chinatown, Roebuck Bay, Sun Pictures, and the Japanese cemetery. It ends at Pearl Luggers in time for the attraction's next tour. ✉ *Broome* ☎ *08/9192–0000* ⊕ *www.thebroomeexperience. com.au* ✉ *From A$80.*

Broome Top Deck Tours. See the sights of Broome from the top of a double-decker bus; 90-minute tours depart at 4 pm daily except Sunday. Pick-up points include the visitor center and various Cable Beach resorts. ✉ *Broome* ☎ *1800/858985* ⊕ *www.broometopdecktours.com.au* ✉ *From A$40.*

Fodor's Choice **Kimberley Quest.** Much of the Kimberley coast is inaccessible by land
★ and can be visited only by boat. Kimberley Quest has multiday Kimberley adventures along the region's magnificent coastline in their luxury *Kimberley Quest 11* cruiser. All meals and excursions (including fishing trips) are included in the cost of A$9,639 for 8 days to A$13,970 for 14 days. Cruising season runs from March to September. ☎ *08/9193–6131* ⊕ *www.kimberleyquest.com.au* ✉ *From A$9639.*

ESSENTIALS

Visitor Information Broome Visitor Centre. ✉ *1 Hamersley St.* ☎ *08/9195–2200* ⊕ *www.broomevisitorcentre.com.au.*

Broome By Camelback

Though not native to Australia, camels played a large part in exploring and opening up the country's big, dry, and empty interior. In the 1800s, around 20,000 camels were imported from the Middle East to use for cross-country travel—along with handlers (many from Afghanistan) who cared for them.

When railways and roads became the prime methods of transport in the early 20th century, many camels were simply set free in the desert. A steady population of wild camels—some 1,000,000 of them—now roams across the Australian Outback.

Broome has for many years been a place where people enjoy camel rides—especially along the broad, desertlike sands of Cable Beach. Two tour companies in town now offer camel "adventures" on a daily basis;

yes, it's touristy, but it's great fun and a wonderful way to see the coast and get a taste of history.

Broome Camel Safaris. Open Monday–Saturday, Broome Camel Safaris offers 30-minute rides (A$30) or one-hour sunset rides (A$80). ⊠ *Broome* ☎ *0419/916-101* ⊕ *www.broomecamelsafaris.com.au* ▨ *From A$30.*

Red Sun Camels. Morning and sunset rides are available every day on Cable Beach. The morning ride lasts for 40 minutes and costs A$60; the presunset ride runs for 30 minutes and costs A$40; the sunset ride takes an hour and costs A$85. ⊠ *Broome* ☎ *08/9193-7423, 1800/184488* ⊕ *www.redsuncamels. com.au* ▨ *From A$40.*

EXPLORING

Broome is a small, compact town that's easy to explore on foot—you can even walk to the airport on the edge of town. You will need transportation to get to and from Cable Beach, which is around 7 km (4½ miles) from the town center. Chinatown, with its historic buildings, pearl showrooms, and art galleries, is in the middle of the main street shopping strip, and Roebuck Bay is only a few blocks to the south.

10

TOP ATTRACTIONS

FAMILY **The Malcolm Douglas Wilderness Wildlife Park.** Entering via the jaws of a giant crocodile, this huge park opens up to reveal the Kimberley's native species in a variety of habitats. There are rare western quolls and bilbies to dingoes, flying foxes, barking owls, several types of kangaroo, and, of course, hundreds of crocodiles. Don't miss the nocturnal sanctuary, which houses endangered species that are part of an important breeding program. Beware the replica croc at the entry—many people have been fooled and frightened by its lifelike appearance. Don't miss the famous croc feeding at 3 pm daily. ⊠ *Great Northern Hwy.* ✛ *Go 16 km (10 miles) out of Broome on Great Northern Hwy. and see sign pointing to right* ☎ *08/9193-6580* ⊕ *www.malcolmdouglas.com.au* ▨ *A$35* ☉ *Daily 2–5.*

Fodor'sChoice **Pearl Luggers.** This historical display sheds light on the difficulties and ★ immense skill involved in pearl harvesting. It has two restored luggers along with other such pearling equipment as diving suits and an

A$100,000 pearl you can hold. Get an insight into the risky lives of pearl divers, who spent years aboard pearling luggers and diving for pearl shells, on the regular tours (allow 1 hour). This is a must-see for those interested in Broome's history. ✉ *31 Dampier Terr.* ☎ *08/9192– 0022* ⊕ *www.pearlluggers.com.au* ✉ *A$25* ☉ *Daily 9–5; Apr.–Sept. tours run on the hr, Oct.–Mar. tours at 10 and 3.*

FAMILY
Fodor's Choice
★ **Sun Pictures.** Opened in 1916, Sun Pictures is the world's oldest oper- ating outdoor movie theater. Here silent movies—accompanied by a pianist—were once shown to the public. These days current releases are shown in the very pleasant outdoors. Historical tours of the theater are also available during the dry season weekdays at 10:30 am and 1 pm for A$5 per person. ✉ *8 Carnarvon St.* ☎ *08/9192–1077* ⊕ *www. broomemovies.com.au* ✉ *A$17* ☉ *Daily 6 pm–11 pm.*

Willie Creek Pearl Farm. You can watch demonstrations of the cultured pearling process—including the seeding of a live oyster and a boat ride to the marine farm—at Willie Creek Pearl Farm, 38 km (23½ miles) north of Broome. Drive out to the farm yourself (you must make res- ervations first and a 4WD is recommended), or join a four-hour tour bus leaving from town. There's also the option of taking a scenic heli- copter ride while on the property. ✉ *Willie Creek Rd.* ⊹ *Drive 9 km (5½ miles) east from Broome on Broome Hwy., turn left onto Cape Leveque Rd. for 15 km (9 miles), turn left onto Manari Rd. for 5 km (3 miles), turn left and follow signs for 2½ km (1½ mile). Allow about 1 hr* ☎ *08/9192–0000* ⊕ *www.williecreekpearls.com.au* ✉ *A$65, bus tour A$105* ☉ *Guided tours daily every hr 9–3; less often in wet sea- son, Oct.–Mar.*

WORTH NOTING

Broome Bird Observatory. A nonprofit research, education, and accom- modation facility, the Broome Bird Observatory provides the perfect opportunity to see the Kimberley's numerous bird species, some of which migrate annually from Siberia. On the shores of Roebuck Bay, 25 km (15 miles) east of Broome, the observatory has a prolific number of migratory waders. The observatory offers a variety of daily guided tours in the dry season (from May to around September) costing A$70 per person for a half-day tour departing from the observatory. Pick-up from Broome can also be arranged. A full-day tour costs A$150 from the observatory and A$195 from Broome. Start times depend on the day of the week and the tides and season, but are typically from 8 am to 3 pm. ✉ *Crab Creek Rd.* ⊹ *15 km (9 miles) from Broome Hwy.* ☎ *08/9193–5600* ⊕ *www.broomebirdobservatory.com* ✉ *A$5 recom- mended donation for day visitors* ☉ *Day visitors: 8–4; tour reserva- tions essential.*

Cultured Pearling Monument. The life-size bronze statues of the Cultured Pearling Monument are near Chinatown. The monument depicts three pioneers of the cultured pearling industry that is so intertwined with the city's development and history. ✉ *Carnarvon St.*

Japanese Cemetery. More than 900 pearl divers are buried in the Japa- nese Cemetery, on the road out to Broome's deepwater port. The graves testify to the contribution of the Japanese to the development of the

Camel riding on Cable Beach, Broome

industry in Broome, as well as to the perils of pearl gathering in the industry's early days. ⊠ *Port Dr.* 🎟 *Free.*

BEACHES

Fodor's Choice
★

Cable Beach. Watching the sun sink into the sea on Cable Beach is a nightly ritual for almost all visitors to Broome, who flock to the 22-km (14-mile) stretch of dazzling white sand lapped by turquoise water 7 km (4½ miles) from the center of town. The most popular way to watch the sunset is from the back of a swaying camel, but you can also unpack a picnic at the beachside park, drive a 4WD onto the sand, or sip a cocktail from the beachside bar at Cable Beach Resort. By day it's a lot less crowded, and north of the vehicle access ramp is a declared nude beach. It's good for swimming, but low tide can mean a long walk across sand to get to the water. Beware of marine stingers (deadly Box and Irukandji jellyfish) in the water from December through to April. **Amenities:** lifeguard; parking (free); toilets. **Best for:** sunset; swimming; walking. ⊠ *Cable Beach Rd. W.*

WHERE TO EAT

$$
AUSTRALIAN

✕**Matso's Broome Brewery.** One of the most popular spots to eat and drink in Broome, this micro-brewery in an old bank building overlooking Roebuck Bay serves bar snacks, burgers, steaks, and fish-and-chips. The fan-cooled bar is full of pearling memorabilia and historic photographs, although most people choose to sit on the breezy veranda or in the shady beer garden. The brewery produces eight craft beers and a very refreshing alcoholic ginger beer. $ *Average main: A$30* ⊠ *60 Hammersley St.* 🕾 *08/9193–5811* ⊕ *www.matsos.com.au.*

10

WHERE TO STAY

$$$$ 🕎 **Cable Beach Club Resort and Spa.** Broome's only accommodation that
RESORT   faces the famous Cable Beach, this resort is the area's most luxuri-
Fodor'sChoice   ous place to stay. **Pros:** easy walk to Cable Beach; peaceful, tropi-
★   cal atmosphere; distinctive architecture; separate swimming pool for
adults. **Cons:** no shopping nearby; need transport to get into town.
Ⓢ *Rooms from: A$415* ⊠ *Cable Beach Rd.* ☎ *08/9192–0400* ⊕ *www.
cablebeachclub.com* ⬐ *176 rooms, 45 bungalows, 7 villas, 3 suites*
†◎† *Some meals.*

$$$$ 🕎 **Eco Beach.** This wilderness retreat peers over a cliff edge and gazes
RESORT   into the ocean, giving the impression it's incredibly remote while only
being about an hour and a half drive—or a shorter helicopter flight—
away. **Pros:** lots of activities; beautiful waterfront location; can self-
cater. **Cons:** no shopping nearby; isolated location; expensive dining.
Ⓢ *Rooms from: A$345* ⊠ *Roebuck Bay* ☎ *08/9193–8015* ⊕ *www.
ecobeach.com.au* ⬐ *29 eco tents, 24 villas (garden or ocean views), 2
beach houses* †◎† *No meals.*

$$$$ 🕎 **Kimberley Sands Resort.** This glam resort seduces with its stunning
RESORT   pool, spa facilities, and chic bar that sit at the heart of the luxurious
rooms and suites. **Pros:** great lap pool; great food; all rooms have private balcony or courtyard. **Cons:** 10-minute walk to beach; parking-
lot-facing rooms are noisy. Ⓢ *Rooms from: A$350* ⊠ *Cable Beach, 10
Murray Rd.* ☎ *08/9193–8388* ⊕ *kimberleysands.com.au* ⬐ *72 rooms*
†◎† *Some meals.*

$$$$ 🕎 **McAlpine House.** Originally built for a pearling master, this luxury
B&B/INN   guesthouse in tropical gardens is full of exquisite Javanese teak furniture. **Pros:** restored pearling master's residence; luxurious suites; intimate, private spaces; complimentary airport transfers. **Cons:** limited
leisure facilities; no children under 16. Ⓢ *Rooms from: A$365* ⊠ *55
Herbert St.* ☎ *08/9192–0510* ⊕ *www.mcalpinehouse.com* ⬐ *8 rooms;
1 5-bedroom villa* †◎† *Breakfast.*

SHOPPING

Broome has an abundance of jewelry stores.

Allure South Sea Pearls. This store sells high-end jewelry. They also have
an outlet at Cable Beach Club Resort and Spa. ⊠ *25 Dampier Terr.*
☎ *08/9192–2430* ⊕ *www.alluresouthseapearls.com.au.*

Kailis Australian Pearls. This shop specializes in high-quality, expensive pearls and jewelry. ⊠ *23 Dampier Terr., Shop 3* ☎ *08/9192–2061*
⊕ *www.kailisjewellery.com.au.*

Paspaley Pearling. Family-owned Paspaley Pearling, in Chinatown, sells
pearls and stylish local jewelry. ⊠ *2 Short St.* ☎ *08/9192–2203* ⊕ *www.
paspaley.com.*

PERTH AND WESTERN AUSTRALIA

WELCOME TO PERTH AND WESTERN AUSTRALIA

TOP REASONS TO GO

★ **Beach Heaven:** Some of Australia's finest beaches are in Western Australia. Hundreds of kilometers of virtually deserted sandy stretches and bays invite you to swim, surf, snorkel, or laze about.

★ **National Parks:** With spectacular terrain and one-of-a-kind plant and animal species, rugged national parks tell the story of Australia's age-old landforms, especially across the gorge-pocked Kimberley region.

★ **Slick Eats:** Perth's modern food revolution has made way for a smorgasbord of small bars and edgy restaurants excelling at local, seasonal fare.

★ **Wine Trails:** Follow the beautiful wine trails from Perth to the south coast to enjoy free tastings of internationally renowned drops at the cellar doors.

★ **Foodie Culture Clash:** Waves of immigrants to Australia have delivered some of the finest multicultural cuisine around.

1 Perth. A population boom has led to a significant urban revitalization in Western Australia's capital, with the inner-city's beating heart now matching the wow-factor of its Caribbean-style coastline.

2 Fremantle. The port town has charm in spades, both for its curving, colonial streets and the quirky vibe of its residents.

GREAT SANDY DESERT

LITTLE SANDY DESERT

WESTERN
AUSTRALIA

GREAT VICTORIA DESERT

NORTHERN TERRITORY

QUEENSLAND

○Laverton

eonara

0   200 mi

0   200 km

algoorlie

①

Norseman

Esperance

outhern Ocean

GETTING ORIENTED

Glance at a map of Australia and you'll see that the state of Western Australia (aka WA) encompasses one-third of the country. It's a massive slab, all 1 million square miles of it, so it may take longer than you expect to reach your destination. But efforts are rewarded with fewer tourists and unadulterated nature. The state's glamour girl is undoubtedly the Margaret River wine region, as rich in native forests and rugged beaches as it is vineyards. The once sleepy capital city of Perth is now a vibrant eating and drinking scene. Fremantle and Rottnest Island are mere day trips away. Journeying up the sparsely populated but beautiful northern coast is made easier with air travel—only tackle the roads if you have ample time.

3 Rottnest Island. The ultimate escape, with no cars—bikes are the dominant mode of transport—no pretension, and no cares in the world. The promise of 63 beaches just 19 km (12 miles) from Perth has people flocking.

4 The South West Wine Region. Towering native trees, epic surf, delightful winery-restaurants, and vineyards comb the coastal countryside. It's no wonder this area is regarded as one of the world's great wine regions.

Updated by
Fleur Bainger

Western Australia is a stunningly diverse place, with rugged interior deserts, endless, untrammeled white-sand beaches, a northern tropical wilderness, and a temperate forested south. The scenery here is magnificent; whether you travel through the rugged gorges and rock formations of the north; the green pastures, vineyards, and tall-tree forests of the south; or the coastline's vast, pristine beaches, you'll be struck by how much space there is here. If the crowds and crush of big-city life aren't your thing, this is the Australia you may never want to leave.

Perth, the capital city and home to nearly 70% of the state's 2.47 million residents, is a modern, pleasant metropolis with an easygoing, welcoming attitude. However, at 3,000 km (1,864 miles) from any other major city in the world, it has fondly been dubbed "the most isolated city on Earth." Its remoteness is part of what makes Western Australia so awe-inspiring.

It took more than 200 years after Dutch seafarer Dirk Hartog first landed on the coast of "New Holland" in 1616 in today's Shark Bay before British colonists arrived to establish the Swan River Colony (now Perth) in 1829. Progress was slow for half a century, but the discovery of gold around Kalgoorlie and Coolgardie in the 1890s brought people and wealth, especially to the fledgling city of Perth; much later, in the 1970s, the discovery of massive mineral deposits throughout the state began an economic upswing that still continues.

Western Australia produces much of Australia's mineral, energy, and agricultural wealth, though recent falls in resources prices have slowed development, curbed employment figures, and reduced the population flow to WA, with fewer people chasing the highs of its boom-and-bust cycle. Nonetheless, development continues: a number of the state's airports are being expanded; central train lines are being sunk, linking the city's divided heart; and the long-term riverside development known as Elizabeth Quay continues to evolve (expect road delays). The cooling economy has delivered a boon for travelers: hotel prices are falling, making for a more affordable experience in this land of oft-inflated prices.

PLANNER

WHEN TO GO

You can visit Western Australia year-round, though the weather will influence your activities and sightseeing. Perth enjoys more sunny days than any other Australian capital city. Summer (December–February) in Perth is *hot* and temperatures can rise to 40°C (100°F), but the locals love it and flock to the beaches. Be aware major school and university holidays occur at this time. The Perth International Arts Festival (PIAF) in February is an excellent reason to visit. Weather-wise, March, April, November, and December are most pleasant, with sunny days and warm, comfortable temperatures. July and August are traditionally cool and wet.

PLANNING YOUR TIME

Fly into Perth and spend most of the first day exploring the city center, especially King's Park and, by night, the restaurants of the CBD and small bars of Northbridge. The following day, take the train to Cottesloe Beach and gaze at the translucent water. As the sun's rays strengthen, continue along the tracks to charmingly preserved Fremantle and stroll through the heritage precinct, stopping for breaks at sidewalk cafés and the bustling markets. On day three, take a ferry to Rottnest Island and rent a bike or walk around to the lovely beaches. Keep an eye open for small local marsupials called quokkas. For the following days, take a wine-touring excursion to the glamorous Margaret River region.

GETTING HERE AND AROUND

AIR TRAVEL

Perth is the main international arrival point on this side of the country and is serviced by a dozen or more airlines. Qantas is Australia's main domestic airline, and with its budget subsidiary Jetstar operates an extensive network and regular services crisscrossing the country from all the major cities to regional centers like Exmouth and Broome. Virgin Australia competes with Qantas in major cities, and, after purchasing local carrier Skywest, now covers many regional centers such as Albany, Kununurra, Esperance, and Broome. Air North has an extensive network throughout the Top End and covers some WA legs in the north.

CAR AND BUS TRAVEL

Driving around Western Australia is relatively easy, with mostly good paved roads and light traffic outside Perth. While the distances in the Outback are daunting (Perth to Broome is 2,230 km [1,386 miles]), Perth to the Margaret River in the South West is just over three hours along good roads. Always be aware of wildlife on the roadsides, particularly at dawn and dusk. Greyhound Australia and Integrity Coach

Lines operate an extensive network of long-distance coaches. From Perth to Adelaide, expect to be on the road for 36 hours.

TRAIN TRAVEL

The *Indian Pacific*, operated by Great Southern Rail, links Sydney and Perth via Kalgoorlie and Adelaide, with once-weekly services each way. The trip takes around four days.

From Perth, TransWA operates train services to Bunbury twice daily and to Northam and Kalgoorlie, with coaches linking to other destinations including Geraldton, Kalbarri, Albany, and Esperance.

Getting around Perth by train is quick and easy, with lines to Armadale/Thornlie, Midland, Butler, Fremantle, Mandurah, and Rockingham.

RESTAURANTS

A number of talented chefs have recently returned to Perth from overseas, bringing international trends, abilities, and standards with them. This influence, coupled with a healthy push for seasonal, local produce, has given the Perth dining scene an exciting shot in the arm. Throughout the young city's history, waves of immigrants from Italy, the former Yugoslavia, and Asia have also delivered cultural authenticity to the more traditional eateries. A British handover, fish-and-chips, remains one of the beach-going state's favorite picnic meals.

Expect to find Western Australian wines on the wine list when dining in most licensed restaurants in Perth and, of course, in the Margaret River wine region, where first-class food is matched with highly regarded vino.

Many restaurants and cafés have alfresco dining. Tips aren't expected, but an extra 10% for exceptional service is welcome, particularly since Perth suffers from a sometimes justified reputation for below-par service.

HOTELS

From five-star to basic, you'll find suitable accommodations throughout the region. The well-known international chains are all in Perth but there are also sublime boutique accommodations. Perth once had some of the highest occupancy rates in Australia, largely due to business travelers, but a cooling of this has reduced room rates. Ideally, book ahead, though last-minute bargains can be had, especially for weekends. Other popular options—especially for families and small groups—are self-contained apartments or villas. With two or three bedrooms, living areas, and kitchens, they allow you to save on dining costs by cooking your own meals; these are best if staying more than one night. *Hotel reviews have been shortened. For full information, visit Fodors.com.*

WHAT IT COSTS (IN AUSTRALIAN DOLLARS)			
$	**$$**	**$$$**	**$$$$**
Restaurants	Under A$21	A$21–A$35	A$36–A$50	over A$50
Hotels	Under A$151	A$151–A$200	A$201–A$300	over A$300

Restaurant prices are the average cost of a main course at dinner or, if dinner is not served, at lunch. Hotel prices are the lowest cost of a standard double room in high season, excluding service and tax.

HEALTH AND SAFETY

If you are self-driving—especially in remote areas—make sure you have enough fuel, water, and food and carry a first-aid kit. Let others know where you are going and for how long. Mosquitoes are prevalent, so cover up and use a good insect repellent; the worst times for mosquitoes are dawn and dusk.

Respect the Australian sun, especially in summer. Sunburn is a real danger if you don't follow the Australian mantra: slip, slap, slop—that is, slip on a hat, slap on sunglasses, and slop on sunscreen. On popular beaches around major cities and towns, lifesavers (lifeguards) are usually on duty and put up flags to swim between, but generally most beaches are unguarded. Take extra care, especially where there are strong currents.

The emergency contact number for police, fire, and ambulance is ☎ *000*. From a GSM mobile (cell) phone the number is ☎ *112*.

PERTH

Buoyed by a history of mineral wealth and foreign investment, Perth has high-rise buildings dotting the skyline, and an influx of immigrants gives the city a healthy diversity. Some of Australia's finest sandy beaches, sailing, and fishing are within 15 minutes' drive of the city; the best seaside villages and postcard beaches lie just north of bohemian Fremantle. The main business thoroughfare is St. Georges Terrace, an elegant street lined with skyscrapers and an excellent set-back entertainment precinct, while urban villages such as Leederville and Mt. Lawley deliver chic-yet-welcoming community vibes. Perth's literal highlight is King's Park, 1,000 acres of greenery atop Mt. Eliza, which affords panoramic city views.

GETTING HERE AND AROUND

The main gateway to Western Australia is Perth's busy airport. It has three separate terminals—the original domestic terminal (about 11 km [7 miles] from Perth's central business district), and a secondary domestic terminal near the international hub (about 16 km [10 miles] away). A free shuttle bus connects the terminals 24 hours a day.

Taxis are at the airport around the clock. Trips to the city cost about A\$40 and take around a half hour. Perth Airport Connect (☎ *08/9277–4666*) operates frequent coach services from the terminals to Perth city hotels, and the East Perth train station (no need to book ahead). The cost to downtown Perth is A\$15 from the domestic terminal; you must transfer there from the international terminal to take it.

Fewer people arrive by road or rail from the east. Crossing the Nullarbor Plain from the eastern states is one of the great rail journeys of the world. Great Southern Railways' *Indian Pacific* makes runs from Sydney and Adelaide, arriving at the East Perth Terminal. Greyhound Australia has long-distance coaches to Perth from eastern states capitals.

Driving in Perth is relatively easy; just remember to stay on the left-hand side of the road, give way to traffic on your right, and avoid peak periods. All major car-rental companies have branches at the international and domestic airport terminals, while motor home and caravan hubs lie near airports.

Perth

NORTHBRIDGE

Swan River

King's Park

KEY

→← Rail Lines

🛈 Tourist Information

0   1/8 mile

0   200 meters

AQWA: Aquarium of
Western Australia **8**

Art Gallery of
Western Australia **5**

Batavia Coast **12**

The Bell Tower **2**

Cohunu Koala Park **9**

King's Park **1**

London Court **3**

Nambung National Park .. **13**

Perth Mint **4**

Perth Zoo **10**

Scitech Discovery
Center **7**

Western Australian
Museum and Old
Perth Gaol **6**

Yanchep National Park ... **11**

Perth and its environs are well connected by Transperth buses. The main terminals are at the Esplanade Bus Port on Mounts Bay Road and the Roe Street Bus Station. Buses run daily 6 am–11:30 pm, with reduced service on weekends and holidays. Rides within the city center are free. CAT (Central Area Transit) buses circle the city center, running frequently on weekdays 7–6 and Saturday 9–5. Routes and timetables are available from Transperth (☎ *13–6213* ⊕ *www.transperth.wa.gov.au*).

Transperth tickets are valid for two hours and can be used on Transperth trains and ferries. The ferries make daily runs from 6:50 am to 7:15 pm between Barrack Street Jetty in Perth to Mends Street, across the Swan River in South Perth. Reduced services run on weekends and holidays.

Transperth trains also provide a quick way to get around the city. Most attractions are accessed via the Fremantle line, which traces the coast via Perth's most affluent suburbs. Other lines run east to Midland, north to Butler, southeast to Armadale/Thornlie, and south to Mandurah. Central-city trains depart from Wellington Street and Perth Underground at the corner of William and Murray streets. Tickets must be purchased at vending machines before boarding.

South West Coachlines. Daily services depart Perth Central Bus Station at the Esplanade Bus Port on Mounts Bay Road—as well as from Perth domestic and international airports—to South West towns, including Dunsborough, Busselton, Manjimup, and as far as Augusta. Services may vary according to season. ☎ *08/9261–7600 Perth office* ⊕ *www. southwestcoachlines.com.au*.

Taxi Information Black & White. ☎ *13–1222* ⊕ *blackandwhitecabs.com.au/ perth.* **Swan Taxis.** ☎ *13–1330* ⊕ *www.swantaxis.com.au.*

TIMING

Perth and surroundings can be visited in two to three days, if you're short on time and plan to explore farther afield. Spend the first day in central Perth, visiting Kings Park, the Perth Cultural Centre, the Hay Street and Murray Street shopping malls, great restaurants, and small bars, and, perhaps, the Swan Bells Tower. On the second day, head to Perth's most stunning piece of coastline, Cottesloe Beach. Continue on to Fremantle, about 30 minutes from the city by train, where you can spend the rest of the day exploring this heritage port city. On the third day, take a day trip to Rottnest Island by ferry (30–60 minutes each way from the city center, Fremantle, or Hillarys). An upriver cruise to the Swan Valley that includes a visit to a winery and lunch also makes for a relaxing day.

ESSENTIALS

Visitor Information Western Australia Visitor Centre. ✉ *55 William St., CBD* ☎ *08/9483–1111 outside Australia, 1800/812808* ⊕ *www.westernaustralia.com.*

TOURS

Australian Pacific Touring. Commonly known as APT, this national group runs extended 4WD adventure coach trips around Western Australia for groups of 20, and one very special cruise. Comfortable, multiday tours travel from Perth to Monkey Mia, via wildflower country and Shark Bay; and from Broome to Perth, stopping in at Ningaloo Reef and the Pinnacles. APT specializes in the Kimberley, crossing the fabled Gibb River Road, and staying in their own wilderness lodges at numerous locations including Purnululu National Park. The most popular tour is the 15-day Kimberley Complete. You can also cruise the Kimberley coastline by boat. Tours run from five days and up. ⊠ *Perth* ☎ *1300/336932 call center* ⊕ *www.aptouring.com.au* ☑ *From A$8,995 (twin share), A$11,345 for solo travelers.*

Australian Pinnacle Tours. This local outfit conducts day tours of Perth and its major attractions. You can also take a day or multiday trip of outer sights like Nambung National Park—with its weird limestone formations—Margaret River and its wineries, or, with more time, Monkey Mia, Wave Rock near Hyden, and the Treetop Walk near Walpole (be aware that this is a long 14½-hour tour). ⊠ *Shop 1, Barrack St. Jetty, CBD* ☎ *08/6270–6060 outside Australia, 1300/551687* ⊕ *www. australianpinnacletours.com.au* ☑ *From A$79.*

Captain Cook Cruises. A scenic glide on the flat water of the Swan River with this tour company makes for an excellent afternoon, especially if you want to travel from Perth to the Indian Ocean at Fremantle. Optional 1½-hour stopovers are included. Cruises cost A$28 one-way, A$38 return, or A$69 with lunch included. It also has tours upriver to the Swan Valley vineyards. ⊠ *Pier 3, Barrack St. Jetty, CBD* ☎ *08/9325–3341* ⊕ *www.captaincookcruises.com.au* ☑ *From A$28.*

Casey Australia Tours. A range of extended tours departing from Perth covers nearly every inch of the state, including a 14-day four-wheel-drive tour that traverses the iconic Gibb River Road and covers the Bungle Bungle Range in Purnululu National Park, plus an optional flight over Mitchell Falls. Some accommodation is in motels, but it's mostly camping—this is an Outback tour, after all! Shorter tours visit the southwest's apple and truffle growing region in four days. ⊠ *63 Birdwood Circus W, Bicton* ☎ *08/9339–4291, 1800/999677* ⊕ *www. caseytours.com.au* ☑ *From A$1140.*

Golden Sun Cruises. This ferry operator provides round-trip passage along the Swan River; thrice-daily (except winter) between Perth and Fremantle (one-way trips are also available), or daily to Guildford and the Swan Valley. ⊠ *Barrack St. Jetty, Pier 4, CBD* ☎ *08/9325–1616 office, 0418/816–166 bookings line* ⊕ *www.goldensuncruises.com.au* ☑ *From A$15.*

Perth Explorer. This open-top bus company runs hop-on, hop-off trips around central Perth and to Kings Park on a typical red double-decker. Tickets (A$35) are valid for 48 hours, and you can get on and off as you choose, or stay on for the full two-hour tour. Book online for discounts or upgrade your ticket to a Triple Tour (A$95), which includes a Swan River cruise and tour of Fremantle in a wooden replica tram. ☎ *08/9203–8882* ⊕ *www.citysightseeingperth.com* ☑ *From A$35.*

Fodor'sChoice
★
Rottnest Express. Rottnest Express runs excursions to Rottnest Island once daily from Perth and six to eight times daily from Fremantle, depending on the season. It also runs whale-watching tours in season, September and October, as does Rottnest Fast Ferries and Mills Charters. Fares are cheapest on Tuesday, and several package options are available, including with bike rentals. ⊠ *Pier 2, Barrack St. Jetty, CBD* ☎ *1300/467688* ⊕ *www.rottnestexpress.com.au* ☑ *From $A31.*

Fodor's Choice **Two Feet and a Heartbeat.** These guys are award-winning for several
★ reasons: their walking tours are fun, informative, and wrap in elements that reveal the personality of a city, such as street art, small
bars, sculptures, history, and hidden relics. You can also take a small
bar and laneways (side alleys) tour; a walk through the CBD's grit-
tier cousin, Northbridge; plus sailor- and convict-themed tours in Fremantle. There's a bike riding excursion on Rottnest Island, too. Book
early for a "Tight Arse Tuesday" tour, which is half price (only A$20).
✉ *CBD* ☎ *08/6143–4620 outside Australia, 1800/459388* ⊕ *www.
twofeet.com.au* ✍ *From A$40.*

EXPLORING

Because of its relative colonial youth, Perth has an advantage over most
other capital cities in that it was laid out with foresight. Streets were
planned so that pedestrian traffic could flow smoothly from one avenue
to the next, and this compact city remains easy to negotiate on foot.
Many points of interest are in the downtown area close to the banks
of the Swan River, while shopping arcades and pedestrian malls are a
short stroll away.

The city center (CBD, or Central Business District), a pleasant blend
of old and new, runs along Perth's major business thoroughfare, St.
Georges Terrace, as well as on parallel Hay and Murray streets.

TOP ATTRACTIONS

FAMILY **AQWA: Aquarium of Western Australia.** Huge, colorful aquariums filled
with some 400 different species of local sea creatures—including sharks
that are 13 feet long—from along the 12,000 km (7,456 miles) of Western Australia's variable coastline are the fascinating draws of this boutique aquarium in northern Perth. Sharp toothed sharks, stingrays,
turtles, and schools of fish swim overhead as you take the moving
walkway beneath a transparent acrylic tunnel. You can even do a guided
snorkel or scuba dive with the sharks for 30–45 minutes; bookings are
essential. Perhaps most interesting is the change in habitats and species
as you move from colder, southern waters to the tropics of Western Australia's north—AQWA boasts one of the largest living coral reef displays
in the world. Check it out from above and then below in the underwater gallery. Other highlights include the rare seadragons and DAN-
GERzone, featuring a deadly line up of sea creatures. ✉ *Hillarys Boat
Harbour, 91 Southside Dr., Hillarys* ✛ *AQWA is a 20-min drive north
of Perth's CBD via the Mitchell Freeway, turn left at Hepburn Ave. and
continue to Hillarys Boat Harbour. Or, take northern Joondalup train
line. Alight at Warwick station and take bus No. 423* ☎ *08/9447–7500*
⊕ *www.aqwa.com.au* ✍ *A$29; shark experience A$159, plus A$20
snorkel or A$40 scuba equipment rental* ☉ *Daily 10–5.*

Art Gallery of Western Australia. Founded in 1895, the Art Gallery of
Western Australia is home to more than 17,000 treasures and numerous free exhibitions of Indigenous and modern art, which makes it
worth an afternoon's devotion. The collection of Indigenous art is
impressive, while other works include Australian and international
paintings, sculpture, prints, crafts, and decorative arts. Free guided

tours run regularly, though times vary. Generally, they're held at 11, 1, and 2, Wednesday to Monday. Family-friendly tours and activities are held during school holidays. There are also special tours for the vision impaired—phone or email ahead for bookings. Check the website for details. Admission is free although donations are appreciated. An entry charge usually applies to special exhibitions. ■TIP→ There are also many seasonal, ticketed events, from intimate rock and pop concerts to late night viewings with a bar. ⊠ *Perth Cultural Centre, James St., at Beaufort and Roe Sts., CBD* ☎ *08/9492–6600* ⊕ *www.artgallery.wa.gov.au* ☜ *Free* ☾ *Wed.–Mon. 10–5 and until 9 pm on ARTBAR event nights.*

> ### THE VIEW FROM KING'S PARK
>
> The best spot is the manicured eastern edge of the park, past the border of tall, white-bark trees and overlooking Perth's Central Business District and the Swan River. While it's a jubilant place buzzing with friends and families picnicking, it also has a somber edge, home to the State War Memorial and its eternal flame, as well as the memorial to local victims of the 2002 terrorist bombing in Bali.

FAMILY
Fodor'sChoice
★

King's Park. Locals boast that this is one of the few inner-city parks to dwarf New York City's Central Park; it covers 1,000-acres and grants eye-popping views of downtown Perth and its riverfront at sunrise, sunset, and all times in between. Once a gathering place for Aboriginal people, and established as a public space in 1890, it's favored for picnics, parties, and weddings, as well as regular musical and theater presentations, plus the excellent summer Moonlight Cinema (in Synergy Parkland, on the western side). Each September, when spring arrives, the park holds a wildflower festival and the gardens blaze with orchids, kangaroo paw, banksias, and other native wildflowers, making it ideal for a walk in the curated bushland. The steel-and-glass **Lotterywest Federation Walkway** takes you into the treetops and the 17-acre botanic garden of Australian flora. The **Lotterywest Family Area** has a shaded playground for youngsters ages 1–5, and a café for parents. The Rio Tinto Naturescape is fun for bigger kids who enjoy climbing and exploring in nature. Free walking tours, which depart from the Aspects Gift Shop on Fraser Avenue, take place daily at 10 am and 2 pm; September–June there's also a walk at noon. Details on seasonal and themed tours are available from the information kiosk near Fraser's Restaurant. ⊠ *Fraser Ave., at King's Park Rd., West Perth* ☎ *08/9480–3634* ⊕ *www.bgpa.wa.gov.au* ☜ *Free* ☾ *Daily 24 hrs.*

FAMILY
Yanchep National Park. Sure, it's nice to cuddle a koala in an enclosure, but it's far more exciting to see them in the wild, just above your head. Take the 240-meter (787-foot) Koala Board Walk through native bush with your eyes raised skyward to see some of the state's largest populations of koalas. Watch for western grey kangaroos on the 2-km (1.2-mile) wetland walking trail around Loch McNess lake and then escape summer's heat by joining one of several daily underground tours of Crystal Cave (A$10.80 or A$27 for a family pass), where cooling caverns open up to impressive stalactite galleries and clear water pools. The

park is also a lovely picnic spot, and there's a pub within the grounds. ■ TIP→ Yanchep National Park is a 45-minute drive north of Perth and is open every day of the year; book tours and get walk trail information at McNess House Visitor Centre. National park entry is A$12 per vehicle. ✉ *3499 Wanneroo Rd., Yanchep* ☎ *08/9303–7759 McNess House Visitor Centre* ⊕ *www.dpaw.wa.gov.au.*

WORTH NOTING

The Bell Tower. The spirelike Bell Tower is home to one of the world's largest musical instruments, the 12 antique Swan Bells, which have surprising historical links. Originally from St. Martin-in-the-Fields Church of London, England, these same bells were rung to celebrate the destruction of the Spanish Armada in 1588, the homecoming of Captain James Cook in 1771, and the coronation of every British monarch. The tower contains fascinating displays on the history of the bells and bell ringing, and provides stunning views of the Perth skyline and the nearby Swan River. ■ TIP→ Head to the lofty heights of the observation deck on Level 6 for the Wow factor. Flat, closed shoes must be worn for access to the observation deck; stroller and wheelchair access are available via the elevator. ✉ *Barrack Sq., Barrack St., at Riverside Dr., CBD* ☎ *08/6210–0444* ⊕ *www.thebelltower.com.au* ✉ *A$14* ⊘ *Daily 10–4; bell-handling demonstrations (single bell) Wed. and Fri. 11:30 am–12:30 pm; full bell ringing Mon., Thurs., and weekends noon–1 pm.*

FAMILY **Cohunu Koala Park.** The main lure at this 30-acre property is the joy of cuddling a koala (for an additional A$25 fee). But the other native animals, such as emus, dingoes, wallabies, kangaroos, and wombats are worth visiting, too. Remember that Cohunu (pronounced co-hu-na) is an attraction park, rather than a natural habitat, and some wildlife are caged. A miniature steam railway (A$4 per ride) operates mostly on weekends and school and public holidays. ✉ *Lot 802, Nettleton Rd., Byford* ✛ *Cohuna is a 40-min drive south of Perth's CBD. Take South Western Hwy. to Byford, turn left at Nettleton Rd. for 500 meters* ☎ *08/9526–2966* ⊕ *www.cohunu.com.au* ✉ *A$15* ⊘ *Daily 10–5.*

London Court. Gold-mining entrepreneur Claude de Bernales built this quaint outdoor shopping arcade in 1937. Today it's a magnet for anyone with a camera wanting to recapture the atmosphere and architecture of Tudor England, and for those looking for Australian souvenirs. Along its length are statues of Sir Walter Raleigh and Dick Whittington, the legendary lord mayor of London. Above the arcade entry, costumed mechanical knights joust with one another when the clock strikes the quarter hour. ■ TIP→ The Genuine UGG boot store is popular with tourists; John Walker Chocolatier is another must-see (and sample!). ✉ *St. Georges Terr. and Hay St., CBD* ⊕ *www.londoncourt.com.au.*

FAMILY **Perth Mint.** All that glitters is gold at the Perth Mint, one of the oldest mints in the world still operating from its original premises, and a reminder of the great gold rush days at the turn of the century. Established in 1899, it first refined gold from Western Australia's newly discovered goldfields, striking gold sovereigns for the British Empire. Today it still produces Australia's legal tender in pure gold, silver, and platinum bullion and commemorative coins for investors and collectors.

King's Park with downtown Perth in the distance

Visitors can have a hands-on experience at the Mint—watch 200 ounces of molten gold being poured in time-honored fashion to form a gold bar; eye off the biggest coin ever made, weighing 1 ton; get close to more than A$700,000 worth of gold bullion; see Australia's best collection of natural gold nuggets, including the 369-ounce Golden Beauty, one of the largest natural nuggets in the world and discover your own weight in gold. ⊠ *310 Hay St., CBD* ☎ *08/9421–7223* ⊕ *www.perthmint.com. au* ☒ *A$19* ⊗ *Daily 9–5 except on some public holidays; guided talks every ½-hr 9:30–3:30; gold pour every hr 10–4.*

FAMILY **Perth Zoo.** From kangaroos to crocodiles and venomous Aussie snakes to Asian sun bears and orangutans, this expansive, more than century-old zoo is an easy 10-minute drive from Perth's CBD. Expect lush gardens—perfect for a BYO picnic—and different native habitats of various animals from around the world. Walk among Australian animals in an environment depicting the diversity of Australia's native landscape, including a bird-filled wetland. Discover the Reptile Encounter, Rainforest Retreat, and the Australian Bushwalk. For something a little more exotic, there's the African Savannah; with rhinoceros, giraffe, lions, cheetahs, and baboons; and the Asian Rainforest, with elephants, tigers, otters, gibbons, and a komodo dragon. A number of special encounters are available, such as joining a keeper as they feed the lions, which is best booked and paid for in advance. Free guided walks depart daily at 11:30 am and 1:30 pm, and there are more than a dozen free talks and presentations each day. A one-hour guided tour around the zoo on an electric Zebra Car, seating seven passengers and the driver, costs A$5 per person. ⊠ *20 Labouchere Rd., South Perth* ⊕ *Catch No. 30* *or 31 bus at Esplanade Busport or take ferry ride across Swan River from bottom of Barrack St. and then 10-min walk following signs* ☎ *08/9474–0444, 08/9474–0333 weekend inquiries* ⊕ *www.perthzoo. wa.gov.au* 🎫 *A$29* 🕙 *Daily 9–5.*

FAMILY **Scitech Discovery Centre.** Interactive science and technology displays educate and entertain visitors of all ages—particularly the younger ones—in this excellent facility. There are more than 100 hands-on general science exhibits, as well as in-depth feature exhibitions. Daily science and puppet shows present science in an entertaining way, and the space shows in the newly refurbished planetarium should stretch your imagination as they take you to the far edges of the known Universe. ■ **TIP→ Keep an eye out for the quirky facts that dot the space, including the fact that the heart of a giraffe is two feet long.** ✉ *City West Centre, Sutherland St., West Perth* ☎ *08/9215–0700* ⊕ *www. scitech.org.au* 🎫 *A$17* 🕙 *Weekends, school holidays, and public holidays 10–5; weekdays 9:30–4.*

FAMILY **Western Australian Museum and Old Perth Gaol.** Whether you fancy getting close to a taxidermied wallaby, dinosaur fossils, meteorites, or hundreds of colorful butterflies, you'll find it all contained in the state's most comprehensive museum. The site also includes some of Perth's oldest structures, such as the Old Perth Gaol. Built of stone in 1856, this was Perth's first and only prison until 1888. After being decommissioned as a gaol it became Perth's first museum. Get a feeling for Perth's criminal past and have a coffee at the Muse Café in the leafy courtyard close to where executions once took place. Today it is part of a much larger museum where permanent exhibitions include "Diamonds to Dinosaurs," which uses fossils, rocks, and gemstones to take you back 3.5 billion years. "Katta Djinoong: First Peoples of Western Australia" has a fascinating collection of primitive tools and lifestyle artifacts used thousands of years ago by Australia's Aboriginals. International and national visiting exhibitions, though ticketed, are a highlight. ✉ *Perth Cultural Centre, James and William Sts., CBD* ☎ *08/9212–3700* ⊕ *www.museum. wa.gov.au* 🎫 *Free; suggested donation A$5* 🕙 *Daily 9:30–5.*

OFF THE BEATEN PATH **Batavia Coast.** A drive along this part of the coast, which starts at Green Head, 285 km (178 miles) north of Perth, and runs up to Kalbarri, takes you past white sands and emerald seas, and some lovely small towns. Among them are the fig-shaded, seaside village of **Dongara** and the more northerly **Central Greenough Historical Settlement,** whose restored colonial buildings—including a jail with original leg irons—date from 1858. A few miles north is **Geraldton,** whose skyline is dominated by the beautiful Byzantine St. Francis Xavier Cathedral. Its foreshore playground is great for kids; also worth a visit is the haunting HMAS Sydney II Memorial, which is the only recognized national war memorial outside of Canberra and has expansive views. The huge Batavia Coast Marina has a pedestrian plaza, shopping arcades, and the fascinating Western Australian Museum, which houses a collection of artifacts from the *Batavia,* a Dutch vessel shipwrecked in 1629. ✉ *Batavia Coast.*

Nambung National Park. Imagine an eerie moonscape where pale yellow limestone formations loom as high as 15 feet: this is Nambung

The Pinnacles of Nambung National Park, Western Australia

National Park and its most famous attraction, the **Pinnacles Desert.**
Set on the Swan coastal plain 200 km (125 miles) north of Perth, it's
now accessible in just under two hours along the scenic Indian Ocean
Drive. Formed 200,000 years ago, the pinnacles are one of the world's
most spectacular karst landscapes created by the dissolving action of
water on exposed limestone beds that formed under wind-blown sand
dunes. Only a tiny proportion of them have been uncovered. You can
walk among them along a 1.2-km (0.7-mile) return walk that starts
at the parking area. There's also a 4-km (2½-mile) one-way Pinnacles
Desert Loop scenic drive (not suitable for large RVs or buses). Stop
in to the Pinnacles Desert Discovery Centre to see interpretative displays focused on the region's unique geology, flora, and fauna. August
through October the heath blazes with wildflowers. Note the "no's":
no pinnacle climbing, no dogs, no bins, no drinking water, although
water is available to purchase at the interpretative center and gift shop.
✉ *Nambung National Park* ☎ *08/9652–7913, 08/9652–1911* ⊕ *www.
parks.dpaw.wa.gov.au* ✉ *$12 per vehicle.*

BEACHES

FAMILY
Fodor's Choice
★
Cottesloe. Perth's poster beach is as beguiling as it is relaxing, what with
its soft cream sand, transparent blue waters, and strip of beachy pubs
and restaurants. Naturally, it's very popular, particularly on Sunday,
when people of all ages picnic on grass beneath the row of Norfolk pines
that also hosts masses of squawking birds. The water is fairly calm,

though punchy waves can roll through, crashing mainly in shallow depths. "Sunday sessions"—afternoon beer drinking in two local pubs at the Ocean Beach Hotel and the swanky Cottesloe Beach Hotel, both of which have good, ocean-facing accommodations—are also held here. South of the Cottesloe groyne is a reasonable reef surf break, but it's often crowded. ■ TIP→ Time your visit for the annual Sculptures by the Sea event, a shore-side exhibition of huge sculptures each March. **Amenities:** food and drink; lifeguards; parking (free); showers; toilets. **Best for:** swimming; sunset; walking. ⊠ *Marine Parade, Cottesloe* ⊕ *www. cottesloe.wa.gov.au* ☞ *Parking is free but don't overstay the time limits—inspectors are vigilant, and fines are high.*

FAMILY **North Cottesloe.** This is the quieter end of Cottesloe, where local residents go to walk their dogs (a section by Grant Street is a designated dog beach), dive in for an early morning dip, or share a sunset wine on the sand. The concrete walking path looks over the sandy beach and affords impressive views of the coastal mansions that look out to sea. Coastal reef fans out to the right of Grant Street and makes for good snorkeling, particularly as the water is calm and there are no rips or currents. Beware invisible jellyfish, known as stingers, which cause pain but pose little other threat. **Amenities:** lifeguards; showers. **Best for:** snorkeling; solitude; sunset; swimming; walking. ⊠ *365 Marine Parade, North Cottesloe.*

Swanbourne. While lovely, Swanbourne tends to keep a lower profile within Perth's beach scene, largely due to its nudist-friendly stretch dominated by men. The southern end is popular thanks to the aptly named ocean-facing café, The Naked Fig, which serves breakfasts and light meals and is family friendly; there's a playground nearby. The sand is soft and the surf rises somewhat along this section, with parts favored by body boarders. It's just north of Cottesloe and is about 20 minutes from Perth's City Center. **Amenities:** food and drink; parking (limited); showers; toilets. **Best for:** nudists; sunset. ⊠ *Marine Parade 278, Swanbourne.*

FAMILY **Trigg.** Surfers and body boarders favor this beach, riding the transparent blue waves from Trigg Point and Trigg Island, sometimes crashing into the sandy bottom. Swimmers don masks and paddle to the snorkeling spot of Mettams Pool that is lovely on calm days but should be avoided when the swell is up. A hip coffee haunt, Yelo, is the best café in the area. Across the road away from the ocean, the Trigg Bushland Reserve makes for interesting, paved bush walking—just follow the trail and its interpretive signage. ■ TIP→ There is sometimes a strong undertow off this beach, and swimmers have struck trouble. **Amenities:** food and drink; lifeguards; parking; toilets. **Best for:** snorkeling; sunset; surfing. ⊠ *361 West Coast Dr., Trigg.*

SPORTS AND THE OUTDOORS

BICYCLING

Perth's climate and its network of excellent trails make cycling a safe and enjoyable way to discover the city. But beware: summer temperatures can exceed 40°C (100°F) in the shade. A bicycle helmet is required by law, and carrying water is prudent. About Bike Hire, which rents bikes for A$10 an hour, A$24 a day, or A$64 a week, is open daily 9–5 with extended hours on weekends and in high season. Free brochures detailing trails, including stops at historic spots, are available from the Western Australia Visitor Centre.

FAMILY **About Bike Hire.** Rent everything from regular bicycles to tandems, family quads, and caboose carriers for the kids. Helmets cost only A$1 and it's A$3 for child seats. The company also does drop-offs and pick-ups for those wanting to trail ride or venture further afield. ⊠ *Point Fraser Reserve, 305 Riverside Dr., East Perth* ☎ *08/9221–2665* ⊕ *www.aboutbikehire.com.au.*

> **CATCHING WAVES**
>
> Western Australians adore the beach. During the summer months you'll find thousands of them lazing on sandy beaches, swimming, and surfing. There are popular beaches on Perth's doorstep, but serious board surfers head south to the rugged coastline from Cape Naturaliste to Cape Leeuwin. Favorite big surf breaks are Surfer's Point, Lefthanders, Three Bears, Grunters, Cow Bombie, Bunker Bay Bombie, Moses Rock, the Guillotine, the Farm, Boneyards, and Supertubes. There are some 50 recognized surf breaks along this coast. Check ⊕ www.surf-forecast.com for up-to-date surf reports.

SURFING

Western Australians take to the surf from a young age—and with world-famous surfing beaches right on the city's doorstep, it's no wonder. The most popular year-round beaches for body and board surfing are Scarborough and Trigg, where waves can reach 6–9 feet. There are also more than a dozen beaches heading north from Leighton (near Fremantle), including the Cables Artificial Reef (near Leighton) and Watermans (in the northern suburbs of Perth). Cottesloe Beach is favored by novice surfers and children; south of the groyne (a man-made breakwater or jetty) is popular with stand-up paddleboard riders.

If you venture outside the city, Rottnest Island's west end has powerful surf, and if you head south on the mainland coast, you'll find more than 20 surf locations from Cape Naturaliste to Cape Leeuwin. The Main Break at Margaret River is the best known, where waves often roll in at more than 12 feet, setting the scene for the annual Margaret River Pro, a World Championship Tour event on the official Association of Surfing Professionals circuit, held in April at Surfers Point.

Wet suits are de rigueur for the colder months (May–September), when the surf is usually at its best.

FAMILY **Scarborough Beach Surf School.** These surfer dudes have been pushing beginners out into the white water for more than 20 years. They specialize in adult lessons on Scarborough beach but also provide separate kiddy lessons, or family groups too (11 years and up). If you want to get serious, there are several levels you can complete, and when you do, you'll be presented with a Surfing Australia Certificate. Single lessons are A$60 or a five-lesson course costs A$225. Courses run daily in summer (weekends in winter) 7:15–9:30 and 9:45–noon. ■TIP→ **Courses sell out one week in advance so book ahead.** ⊠ *The Esplanade, Scarborough* ☎ *08/9447–5637, 08/9448–9937* ⊕ *www.surfschool.com.*

WATER SPORTS

FAMILY **Funcats Surfcat Hire.** If you want to enjoy the Swan River at a leisurely pace and possibly spot its resident dolphins, rent a 14-foot catamaran (A$40 per hour), kayak (A$20 per hour for a single, A$30 for a double), or a stand-up paddle board (A$20 per hour) from Funcats Surfcat Hire. Funcats operates from the end of September through April, and life jackets are included. ⊠ *Coode St. Jetty, South Perth* ☎ *0408/926–003,* ⊕ *www.funcats.com.au.*

WA Surf. Perth has consistent winds, particularly in the afternoons, so it's one of the best places to learn to kite surf. WA Surf gives lessons in both kite surfing (from A$89) and stand-up paddleboarding (from A$45) year-round on the shores of Safety Bay, just south of Perth, where the water is flat and calm. As people improve, kites increase in size, adding more power to their ride, so it can be as extreme or as mellow as you like. Safety systems are built-in, so you can be detached from your kite in a couple of seconds if you get into trouble. Most people opt for a series of three, two-hour lessons, but tricks can be taught to old hands, too. ⊠ *Safety Bay Yacht Club, Safety Bay Rd. at Arcadia Dr., Safety Bay* ☎ *08/9592–1657* ⊕ *www.wasurf.com.au* ⊗ *Closed Apr.–Sept.*

WHERE TO EAT

Northbridge, northwest of the railway station, is *the* dining, bar-hopping, and nightclubbing center of Perth, and reasonably priced restaurants are everywhere. Elsewhere around Perth, particularly in Mount Lawley, Leederville, and Fremantle, are seafood and international restaurants, some with stunning views over the Swan River, beachside, or city, and cantilevered windows that make for a seamless transition between indoor and alfresco dining.

For those on a budget, the noisy fun of a dim sum lunch at one of Perth's many traditional Asian teahouses (especially in Northbridge) is cheap and delicious; expect long lines on Sunday morning. Along with a cup of green tea, you can enjoy steamed pork buns, fried chicken feet, and dumplings served at your table from a trolley. Food halls in Perth, Northbridge, and Fremantle are other budget options.

Use the coordinate (✛ B2) at the end of each listing to locate a site on the corresponding map.

$$ ✕ **Brookfield Place.** Like bees swarming a hive, once the clock hits 5 pm,
MODERN   punters flood Perth's CBD's main thoroughfare, St. Georges Terrace,
AUSTRALIAN and its strip of hip new venues. The nebulous is at Brookfield Place,
Fodor's Choice where the swanky Print Hall development hugs the huge new BHP
★   tower. Print Hall is credited with dishing up some of the city's best

modern Australian fare, while Bob's Bar is a happening rooftop venue focusing on simple, tasty, Mexican-inspired eats. In between the two is The Apple Daily, which focuses on Asian street food and more refined fare. At the toes of the BHP tower are some serious contenders in Bar Lafayette, a boho cocktail bar; The Trustee, a classy wine bar and restaurant; and Sushia, a Japanese restaurant with ocean-fresh food prepared in the huge open kitchen. During the day there's a bakery, café, burger bar, and food hall (hidden behind the BHP tower) serving plenty of lunch options. ⑤ *Average main: A$35* ✉ *123–137 St. Georges Terr., CBD* ☎ *08/9428–6400 general number* ⊕ *brookfieldplaceperth. com/eat-drink-shop* ✛ *C3.*

$$$
AUSTRALIAN

✕ **Coco's Riverside Bar and Restaurant.** Appealing to the glitzy, moneyed, cosmetically conscious crowd in Perth, you'll be lucky to get a table on Friday, when rollicking long lunches can extend well past sunset—unless you book in advance. The views are as good as the people watching, and though the classic food is expensive, it's beautifully executed. The diverse menu includes a Pernod-cured salmon with fried capers, slow-brazed Black Angus beef; pea risotto with truffle oil; and for dessert, macadamia bombe Alaska. It should ideally be washed down with a selection from the extensive wine list that includes many of the best labels from the Margaret River region. ⑤ *Average main: A$45* ✉ *Southshore Centre, 85 Esplanade, South Perth* ☎ *08/9474–3030* ⊕ *westvalley.com.au* ⚬ *Reservations essential* ✛ *D2.*

$$
THAI

✕ **Dusit Thai Restaurant.** Come here for authentic Thai food, lovingly prepared and served among traditional sculptures and artwork. Starters include *kra thong tong* (stir-fried diced prawns, minced chicken, and sweet corn in deep-fried cups); or *ma hor* (fruit slices topped with a mixture of minced chicken, shallots, peanuts, palm sugar, and coriander roots). Main-course specialties include *gang keaw-whan* (green curry chicken) and *gang-phed-dang* (hot and spicy red curry with green peas, bamboo strips, roast duck, and pineapple). Attentive service placing accent on detail—note the linen napkins elaborately folded liked winged birds. Dusit Thai has been in Northbridge for nearly 30 years. ⑤ *Average main: A$25* ✉ *249 James St., Northbridge* ☎ *08/9328–7647* ⊕ *www.dusitthai.com.au* ⊘ *No lunch Mon.–Sat.* ✛ *A3.*

$$$
MODERN
AUSTRALIAN

✕ **Fraser's Restaurant.** In fair weather the large outdoor area at this Kings Park restaurant fills with people enjoying food and views of the city and Swan River. At night, the outlook over the glittering city is memorable. The ever-changing menu of share plates or larger dishes highlights fresh Western Australian produce. Look for tuna tartare, glazed duck breast with pastrami spice, or grilled local octopus with chickpea fritters. ⑤ *Average main: A$45* ✉ *King's Park, Fraser Ave., West Perth* ☎ *08/9481–7100* ⊕ *www.frasersrestaurant.com.au* ⚬ *Reservations essential* ✛ *D1.*

$$
MODERN
AUSTRALIAN
Fodor's Choice
★

✕ **Il Lido Italian Canteen.** With a window seat onto iconic Cottesloe beach, this whitewashed canteen scores with simple, seasonal food delivered with finesse. Handmade pasta is a specialty—spaghetti ribboned around sweet Shark Bay crab meat, flecked with baby capers and chili, is a dish to die for. The house favorite, seared slices of pork and fennel seed sausage strewn on roasted cauliflower, is made from the owner's family recipe, as the knowledgeable staff attest. The wine list favors local producers and pleasingly sells quarts as well as bottles. Communal tables are de rigueur; the convivial alfresco area looks out to a coastal conga line of walkers, joggers, and cyclists. By night candles and '50s films projected silently on the wall deliver a romantic feel. $ *Average main: A$30* ⊠ *88 Marine Parade, Cottesloe* ☎ *08/9286–1111* ⊕ *www. illido.com.au* ✛ *B1.*

$$ ✕ **Jamie's Italian.** The British celebrity chef and good food crusader Jamie
ITALIAN Oliver opened his biggest restaurant worldwide in Perth. Fun, fresh, and
FAMILY fabulous, Jamie's Italian serves up fantastic value with every dish. The queues may be a battle, but the polenta chips make up for it, chased with a side of crunchy apple slaw. Once your table is ready, settle in for the fennel sausage pappardelle pasta or the creamy blue swimmer crab risotto. Servings are generous enough to opt for the appetizer size (unless you're ravenous). Plan to dine during nonpeak times. $ *Average main: A$26* ⊠ *140 William St., CBD* ☎ *08/9363–8600* ⊕ *www. jamieoliver.com/italian/australia/restaurants/perth* ✍ *Reservations essential* ✛ *B4.*

$$ ✕ **Joe's Oriental Diner.** On the street level of the Hyatt Regency Hotel,
ASIAN Joe's serves a wide range of dishes from Indonesia, Thailand, Malaysia, and Singapore, and makes for a convenient option if you're staying there. The rattan-and-bamboo interior is reminiscent of the many noodle houses throughout Southeast Asia, and meals are prepared in the spectacular open kitchen. Hearty soups and delicious noodle dishes, like *laksa* (rice noodles in a spicy coconut-milk broth with chicken, bean curd, fish cakes, fish balls, and prawns), are the standouts. Each dish carries a chili coding indicating its relative spiciness—so you won't breathe fire unless you want to. $ *Average main: A$28* ⊠ *Hyatt Regency, 99 Adelaide Terr., CBD* ☎ *08/9225–1268* ⊕ *www.perth.regency.hyatt.com/en/hotel/dining/ JoesOrientalDiner.html* ☾ *Closed Sun. No lunch Sat.* ✛ *D6.*

$$ ✕ **Lalla Rookh.** Anywhere that takes its name from a Kalgoorlie showgirl
MODERN has got to have spunk, and Lalla Rookh has it in spades. The below-
AUSTRALIAN street-level venue on Perth's business strip is a real find, and combines a
Fodor'sChoice slick restaurant and tiny wine bar that introduces quaffers to local and
★ "untampered with grape" varieties. The restaurant is headed up by chef Joel Valvasori, who describes his food as "Cucina Westraliana," combining the Italian influence of his nonna with seasonal, local produce. Think kumquat-glazed buffalo mozzarella with pickled fennel; ravioli stuffed with spinach, ricotta, figs, and walnuts; and braised rabbit with polenta. Consider going for the "Il Capo" chef's selection of six dishes for A$58. The quality of the consumables is matched by the generous, informed service. $ *Average main: A$30* ⊠ *77 St. Georges Terr., CBD* ☎ *08/9325–7077* ⊕ *www.lallarookh.com.au* ✛ *C3.*

$$ ✕ **The Old Crow.** The delectable slow-roasted and smoked brisket, char-
MODERN grilled Brussels sprouts, and Cajun spiced fried chicken ensure that
AUSTRALIAN this delectable Northbridge venue is packed come sundown. Housed
Fodor'sChoice in an old-school cottage complete with a bullnose veranda, it's heavy
★ on charm—staff wear suspenders. Prices will please, too, with Southern American influenced appetizers set at A$16.50 a pop, and nothing over A$35 in the mains department. On Monday and Tuesday, there's

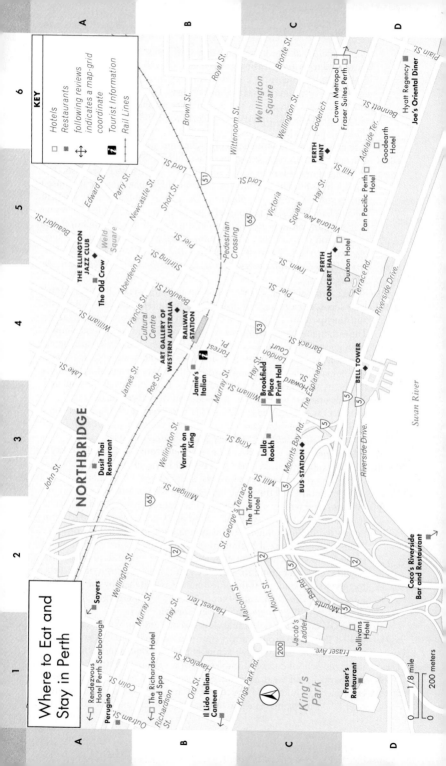

Where to Eat and Stay in Perth

KEY

☐ Hotels

■ Restaurants

↕ following reviews indicates a map-grid coordinate

🛈 Tourist Information

—— Rail Lines

NORTHBRIDGE

← Rendezvous Hotel Perth Scarborough

Sayers

Perugino

← The Richardson Hotel and Spa

Il Lido Italian Canteen

Dusit Thai Restaurant

THE ELLINGTON JAZZ CLUB

The Old Crow

Weld Square

ART GALLERY OF WESTERN AUSTRALIA

Cultural Centre

RAILWAY STATION

Jamie's Italian

Varnish on King

The Terrace Hotel

Lalla Rookh

Brookfield Place
Print Hall

BUS STATION

PERTH MINT

Crown Metropol
Fraser Suites Perth

Pan Pacific Perth Hotel

Goodearth Hotel

Hyatt Regency

Joe's Oriental Diner

PERTH CONCERT HALL

Duxton Hotel

BELL TOWER

Swan River

Sullivans Hotel

Fraser's Restaurant

King's Park

Coco's Riverside Bar and Restaurant

Riverside Drive

0   1/8 mile

0   200 meters

a wine-matched dinner for two for A$55. While it's open for lunch weekends, dinner is when the atmosphere is best. $ *Average main: A$30 ☒ 172 Newcastle St., Northbridge* ☎ *08/9227–9995* ☾ *No lunch weekdays* ⌲ *Reservations essential* ✛ *A4.*

$$
ITALIAN

✕ **Perugino.** For 30 years, chef and owner Giuseppe Pagliaricci has taken an imaginative yet simple approach to the cuisine of his native Umbria, dishing up typical, homemade Italian fare to his loyal customers. Popular in old-school business and political circles, the restaurant has set price lunches, including *saltimbocca alla romana* (veal scallops with sage and prosciutto); or *pesce spada alla griglia* (herb and lemon-marinated swordfish). While there is an à la carte menu for dinner, the seven-course degustation menu (booked in advance) highlights the best of the house. $ *Average main: A$32 ☒ 77 Outram St., West Perth* ☎ *08/9321–5420* ⊕ *www.perugino.com.au* ☾ *Closed Sun. and Mon. No lunch Sat.* ⌲ *Reservations essential* ✛ *A1.*

$$
MODERN
AUSTRALIAN
Fodor's Choice
★

✕ **Print Hall.** For the most refined food in town, head to Print Hall, a classy, perennially packed restaurant in a city-center heritage building. It wows with dishes like snow crab with kaffir lime, camel tartare with wattle seed and wild sorrel, and pan-roasted ocean trout with octopus and white anchovy, all served with house-baked bread. The latter comes from Small Print, a separate, casual café downstairs. The A$110 degustation is popular, or there's a bar section with a more casual and moderately priced menu. Service is polished, the wine list is smashing and satisfaction is all but guaranteed. Many come solely for the sexy bar with high ceilings, backed by a vertical fern garden. $ *Average main: A$30 ☒ Brookfield Place, 125 St. Georges Terr., CBD* ☎ *08/6282–0000* ⊕ *www.printhall.com.au* ☾ *Closed Sun. No lunch Sat.* ✛ *C3.*

$
MODERN
AUSTRALIAN

✕ **Sayers.** When an overseas visitor asks, "Where should I go for breakfast?" the local response is often: "Sayers." The original Sayers in Leederville has long been Perth's go-to spot for flavor-rich breakfast dishes created with primo local/organic/seasonal ingredients. The simple chocolate and banana bread has achieved cult status, with the poached eggs and potato rosti, coriander and cumin-spiked bean tagine, and Italian sausage with lemony wilted spinach not far behind. ■ TIP➜ Expect queues and a possible wait for food. Breakfast is served until 2 pm on weekends. $ *Average main: A$19 ☒ 224 Carr Pl., Leederville* ☎ *08/9227–0429* ⊕ *www.sayersfood.com.au* ☾ *No dinner* ✛ *A2.*

$$
MODERN
AUSTRALIAN
Fodor's Choice
★

✕ **Varnish on King.** Since American whiskey is the specialty at this hard-to-find basement bar, you might expect the food to play second fiddle, but it gets just as much love. Fluffy mac and cheese comes with bone marrow and speck; pigs' ears are pressed, fried, and served with house-made bacon salt; and sweet prawns are split in two and grilled to perfection. Artisan grunge may be the theme, but foodie heaven could be another descriptor. If you've got a huge appetite or are there with a group, Allison does a few big plates to share. The place is often busy, so be prepared for close quarters. Oh, and the whiskey? Choose from more than 150 styles. ■ TIP➜ The venue packs out on a Friday, so book ahead, even for lunch. $ *Average main: A$30 ☒ 75 King St., downstairs, Northbridge* ☎ *08/9324–2237* ⊕ *varnishonking.com* ☾ *Closed Sun. No lunch Sat.* ✛ *B3.*

WHERE TO STAY

During the week, businesspeople from eastern Australia and all parts of Asia flock to Western Australia, and consequently hotel rooms in Perth are often full. But the flow is slowing, and several new hotels have been built recently, so prices are coming down. Weekends still provide the best rates. ■**TIP→ The wise will book early.**

Use the coordinate (✛ jB2) at the end of each listing to locate a site on the corresponding map. For expanded hotel reviews, visit Fodors.com.

$$$
RESORT
Fodor's Choice
★
Crown Metropol. While across the river from the city center, Crown is like an island where everything is self-contained: myriad restaurants and bars, a theater, resort-style pool, 18-hole golf course, casino, nightclub, and, of course, the pyramid-shape hotel. **Pros:** impressive lobby rises the full height of the building; Isika Spa adds luxury; some free parking; free Wi-Fi for two devices. **Cons:** adjacent casino and nightclub attracts a boisterous crowd; atrium-style lobby creates noise to some rooms. ⑤ *Rooms from: A$298* ⊠ *Great Eastern Hwy., at Bolton Ave., Burswood* ☎ *08/9362–8888, 1800/999667* ⊕ *www.crownperth.com. au* ⇗ *397 rooms, 19 suites* ⑩| *No meals* ✛ *C6.*

$$$
HOTEL
Duxton Hotel. Facing the Swan River and adjacent to the Perth Concert Hall, this elegant hotel sits at the eastern end of the business district, within easy walking distance of the city center. **Pros:** free Wi-Fi; minutes' walk to city-center shopping malls; popular restaurant with alfresco terrace; some rooms have river views; easy access to free bus. **Cons:** valet parking fee of A$48 applies. ⑤ *Rooms from: A$269* ⊠ *1 St. Georges Terr., CBD* ☎ *08/9261–8000, 1800/681118* ⊕ *www.duxtonhotels.com/ perth* ⇗ *291 rooms, 15 suites* ⑩| *No meals* ✛ *C5.*

$$$$
HOTEL
Fraser Suites Perth. This flashy, executive-style hotel impresses guests with its good value, modern design, corporate standards, and the fact that every room is a self-contained suite. **Pros:** free Wi-Fi; free bikes; free city bus stop out front; excellent restaurant; fantastic views. **Cons:** far eastern end of the CBD; perfunctory reception. ⑤ *Rooms from: A$330* ⊠ *10 Adelaide Terr., East Perth* ☎ *08/9261–0000* ⊕ *perth. frasershospitality.com* ⇗ *236 suites* ⑩| *No meals* ✛ *C6.*

$$
HOTEL
FAMILY
Goodearth Hotel. Tourist accommodation at a reasonable price can be hard to find close to Perth's CBD, which is why this business district, full-service apartment-style hotel is favored not only by regional Western Australians and their families, but also by dollar-conscious tourists. **Pros:** 24-hour lobby shop; free satellite TV; free Wi-Fi throughout hotel; Internet kiosk; complimentary bathroom facilities for early and late departures; on-site bar and restaurant. **Cons:** hair dryers only on request; small bathrooms; rooms near elevators can be noisy. ⑤ *Rooms from: A$160* ⊠ *195 Adelaide Terr., CBD* ☎ *08/9492–7777, 1800/098863* ⊕ *www.goodearthhotel.com.au* ⇗ *24 rooms, 156 apartments* ⑩| *Breakfast; Some meals* ✛ *D6.*

$$$
HOTEL
Hyatt Regency. Big rooms, great river views, and an easy walk into Perth's central business district make this glamorous hotel a worthy choice, particularly if you score a weekend deal. **Pros:** river views from many rooms; evening nibbles and drinks in the executive lounge; café, bar, and restaurants in hotel; free Wi-Fi. **Cons:** primarily a business

market hotel with corporate design; just east of the city center; few dining options nearby. $ *Rooms from: A$205* ⊠ *99 Adelaide Terr., CBD* ☎ *08/9225–1234* ⊕ *www.perth.hyatt.com* ⤳ *367 rooms, 32 suites* ⊗ *No meals* ⊹ *D6.*

$$$ 🏨 **Pan Pacific Perth Hotel.** Sweeping views over the Swan River from many
HOTEL guest rooms—a quarter of which have just been remodeled—are a feature of this 23-story, five-star hotel, a 10-minute walk from downtown. **Pros:** many rooms have river views; day spa and in-room spa services available; heated outdoor pool; 24-hour gym with steam rooms; Wi-Fi is complimentary in public areas; Premier Rooms and suites remodeled in 2015. **Cons:** hotel is in an office area; parking and Internet access cost extra. $ *Rooms from: A$280* ⊠ *207 Adelaide Terr., CBD* ☎ *08/9224–7777, 1877/324–4856 toll-free from U.S.* ⊕ *www.panpacific.com/perth* ⤳ *436 rooms, 50 suites* ⊗ *No meals* ⊹ *D5.*

$$$ 🏨 **Rendezvous Hotel Perth Scarborough.** If all you want to do is swim and
HOTEL surf, and a 20-minute drive into the city doesn't bother you, this multi-
FAMILY story beach-front hotel may be the ticket. **Pros:** great views of the Indian Ocean; walk straight on to Scarborough Beach; on-site bar; newly renovated pool; tennis courts; shuttle to the city. **Cons:** few other attractions nearby; breakfast and parking cost extra; limited shopping facilities; dubious nightlife. $ *Rooms from: A$259* ⊠ *The Esplanade, Scarborough Beach* ☎ *08/9245–1000, 1800/067680* ⊕ *www.rendezvoushotels.com* ⤳ *330 rooms, 6 suites* ⊗ *No meals* ⊹ *A1.*

$$$$ 🏨 **The Richardson Hotel and Spa.** Tucked away in a quiet, tree-lined street
HOTEL in West Perth, The Richardson provides a discrete and indulgent stay without forgoing any of the amenities of the bigger downtown hotels— it's no surprise that this is where visiting celebrities often stay. **Pros:** large rooms and suites; balconies, fridges, microwaves, Nespresso coffee machines, and evening turn-down service in all rooms; quiet; complimentary Wi-Fi and movies; convenient frozen meal packs in modestly priced minibar. **Cons:** views mostly of surrounding buildings; Subiaco and shopping areas a short walk away. $ *Rooms from: A$420* ⊠ *32 Richardson St., West Perth* ☎ *08/9217–8888* ⊕ *www.therichardson.com.au* ⤳ *54 rooms, 20 suites* ⊗ *No meals* ⊹ *B1.*

$$ 🏨 **Sullivans Hotel.** With the city's free CAT buses stopping right out
HOTEL front, this friendly, family-run hotel opposite waterfront parkland at the foot of King's Park manages to combine natural charms with city proximity. **Pros:** good-value beds for the area; close to King's Park; free public bus service at front; free Wi-Fi. **Cons:** no night service for free public bus; free parking subject to availability. $ *Rooms from: A$200* ⊠ *166 Mounts Bay Rd., CBD* ☎ *08/9321–8022* ⊕ *www.sullivans.com.au* ⤳ *71 rooms* ⊗ *No meals* ⊹ *D1.*

$$$ 🏨 **The Terrace Hotel.** Set in a fantastic location, this boutique hotel is a
HOTEL glamorous, heritage-listed, luxury home away from home with an on-site
Fodor's Choice bar and restaurant. **Pros:** good online price specials; free Wi-Fi; glamor-
★ ous on-site restaurant and bar; leafy alfresco terrace; opulent surroundings; five-minute walk to city. **Cons:** valet parking costs extra. $ *Rooms from: A$269* ⊠ *237 St. Georges Terr., CBD* ☎ *08/9214–4444* ⊕ *www.terracehotelperth.com.au* ⤳ *9 rooms, 6 suites* ⊗ *No meals* ⊹ *C2.*

NIGHTLIFE AND PERFORMING ARTS

Details on cultural events in Perth are published in *Weekend West Australian* and *The Sunday Times*. A free weekly, *X-Press Magazine*, lists music, concerts, movies, entertainment reviews, and who's playing at pubs, clubs, and hotels. *SCOOP* magazine (⊕ *www.scoop.com.au*), published quarterly, is an excellent guide to the essential Western Australian lifestyle.

PERFORMING ARTS

Ticketek. This is the main booking agent in Perth for the performing arts. It operates solely online, though there are several physical box offices at arts venues such as the Art Gallery of WA, the State Theatre, and His Majesty's Theatre in the CBD. ⊠ *Perth* ⊕ *premier.ticketek.com.au.*

BALLET

West Australian Ballet Company. This world-class ballet company has a diverse repertoire that includes new, full-length story ballets, cutting-edge contemporary dance, and classical and neoclassical ballets. The company has earned an international reputation for excellence due to its overall innovation and creativity and performances are held throughout Perth, including His Majesty's Theatre, the atmospheric Quarry Amphitheatre, and the State Theatre Centre. ⊠ *134 Whatley Crescent, Maylands* ☎ *08/9214–0707* ⊕ *www.waballet.com.au.*

CINEMA

FAMILY **Rooftop Movies.** Perth's first—and only—rooftop cinema opened after a summer trial run sold out night after night. Crowning a seven-story car park, it shows cult films, old blockbusters, and cherished classics, with a few arthouse and family-friendly selections thrown in, on a giant movie screen rigged up on sea containers. Colorful vintage caravans serve "dude food" on a carpet of faux grass and palm trees, while booze and pizzas can be delivered, but self-packed picnic baskets are equally welcome. Tickets are A$16. ■TIP➜ Movies run each night, except Monday, during the warmer months of October–April. ⊠ *Roe St. car park, access off 129 James St., Northbridge* ✛ *Drive in at 68 Roe St., Northbridge; walk in off James St., opposite Northbridge Piazza, and take elevator to top* ☎ *08/9227–6288* ⊕ *rooftopmovies.com.au.*

CONCERTS

Perth Concert Hall. A starkly rectangular building overlooking the Swan River in the city center, the Perth Concert Hall stages regular plays, comedy acts, musicals, and recitals by the excellent West Australian Symphony Orchestra, as well as Australian and international performers. It's particularly busy during the Perth International Arts Festival. Adding to the appeal of the fine auditorium is the 3,000-pipe organ surrounded by a 160-person choir gallery. ■TIP➜ The hall is said to have the best acoustics in Australia. ⊠ *5 St. Georges Terr., CBD* ☎ *08/9231–9900* ⊕ *www.perthconcerthall.com.au.*

FESTIVALS

Perth International Arts Festival (PIAF). If you can, time your trip to attend this energetic, big-name summer festival that sees the city come alive with open air music, fireworks spectaculars, indigenous performances, and world-famous artists. PIAF is held February and March in venues throughout the city, and its more highbrow shows are tempered with the raucousness of the Perth Fringe World Festival, which runs in January and February. While most shows for both festivals are ticketed, there are also plenty of free outdoor performances. PIAF is Australia's oldest and biggest annual arts festival, running for more than 50 years. As part of the festival, the Lotterywest Festival Films screens films outdoors at The University of Western Australia's beautiful Somerville Auditorium from November to April. ✉ *Perth* ☎ *08/6488–2000 for information and tickets* ⊕ *www. perthfestival.com.au.*

> ### ROCKIN' IN PERTH
>
> Thanks to pop, rock, and metal bands like Eskimo Joe, the John Butler Trio, the Waifs, Karnivool, Little Birdy, San Cisco, and the Sleepy Jackson—who all started in Perth—the music scene here is thriving. Despite—or perhaps because of—their isolation from the rest of Australia, Western Australian musicians are turning out some top-notch material. Music commentators claim there isn't a "Perth sound" as such, just a talented bunch of artists writing and performing original music. Check out ⊕ *www. xpressmag.com.au* for an up-to-date guide on live shows.

OPERA

West Australian Opera Company. The West Australian Opera Company presents three seasons annually—in February, July, and October—at His Majesty's Theatre. It also performs the free Opera in the Park in Perth's Supreme Court Gardens each February. The company's repertoire includes classic opera, Gilbert and Sullivan operettas, and occasional musicals. ✉ *His Majesty's Theatre, 825 Hay St., CBD* ☎ *08/9278–8999, 1300/795012 box office* ⊕ *www.waopera.asn.au.*

THEATER

Crown Theatre Perth. This 2,300-seat venue has regular mainstream theatrical and musical productions from around the world—think *Cats, Wicked,* and *The Lion King.* Note that parking can be difficult on weekends. ✉ *Great Eastern Hwy., Burswood* ☎ *13–2849 box office, 08/9362–7685* ⊕ *www.crownperth.com.au.*

His Majesty's Theatre. The opulent Edwardian His Majesty's Theatre, which opened in 1904, is admired by those who step inside. His Maj, as it's locally known, is home to the West Australian Opera company and the West Australian Ballet, and hosts most theatrical productions in Perth; there's also a comedy lounge downstairs. Purchase tickets at the box office on-site, or via ⊕ *www.ticketek.com.au.* ✉ *825 Hay St., CBD* ☎ *08/9265–0900* ⊕ *www.hismajestystheatre.com.au.*

Quarry Amphitheatre. For outdoor performances, the grass terraced Quarry Amphitheatre is a unique and popular venue, particularly during the Perth International Arts Festival and warmer months. ✉ *Waldron Dr., off Oceanic Dr., City Beach* ☎ *08/9385–7144* ⊕ *www.cambridge.wa.gov.au.*

Regal Theatre. The 1930s-era Regal Theatre hosts local and visiting performances, ranging from comedy to musicals. ✉ *474 Hay St., at Rokeby Rd., Subiaco* ☎ *08/9388–2066, 1300/795012 theater bookings* ⊕ *www. regaltheatre.com.au.*

State Theatre Centre of Western Australia. The flashy, gilded State Theatre Centre of Western Australia is home to the 575-seat Heath Ledger Theatre and Studio Underground, a flexible performance space. Outdoor events are held in the multipurpose Courtyard. The State Theatre Centre presents contemporary performing arts, both theater and dance, and is the home of the Perth Theatre Company and Black Swan State Theatre Company. ✉ *174–176 William St., Northbridge* ☎ *08/6212–9200* ⊕ *www.statetheatrecentrewa.com.au.*

NIGHTLIFE

Perth's inner city has gone through a significant revitalization; it's now a hotbed of classy small bars that buzz until midnight and later. Twenty- and thirtysomethings also flock to Northbridge, Leederville, Mount Lawley, Subiaco, or Fremantle. Pubs generally close by midnight, which is when the crowds start arriving at the nightclubs; these tend to stay open until around 5 am.

BARS

The Brass Monkey. This pub is in a huge, crimson-painted building with antique verandas and a lively, blokey vibe; it claims to be one of the oldest and most photographed pubs in WA. It has several areas with different moods, such as the beer garden, the rooftop bar, the balcony couch zone, the sports bar, and the adjoining Grapeskin wine bar. Open-mike nights on Tuesday, DJ mixes on Wednesday, and acoustic covers on the balcony on Friday appeal to the fun-loving—though we suggest you avoid backpacker night on Monday. ■TIP➔ There's no cover charge. ✉ *William and James Sts., Northbridge* ☎ *08/9227–9596* ⊕ *www.thebrassmonkey.com.au.*

Mechanics Institute. Perched above a gourmet burger bistro called Flip Side—yes, they deliver upstairs—this rooftop haunt is furnished with market umbrellas, upcycled bench tables, and retro couches, which make it both welcoming and hip. Access to the cocktail, wine, and craft beer bar is via a rear lane coated in street art, adding to the intrigue. Owners of both top and bottom businesses—husband and wife team—aimed to create a neighborhood atmosphere when they moved into the gritty urban suburb of Northbridge, and they have. ✉ *222 William St., at rear, Northbridge* ☎ *08/9228–4189* ⊕ *mechanicsinstitutebar.com.au.*

Queen's Tavern. The Queen's, as it's known locally, has an excellent, thriving outdoor beer garden that features plenty of local and international craft brews. The upstairs bar has a relaxed lounge vibe, with DJs on Friday, Saturday, and Sunday. There is also free Wi-Fi throughout. ✉ *520 Beaufort St., Highgate* ☎ *08/9328–7267* ⊕ *www.thequeens.com.au.*

Subiaco Hotel. This hotel attracts a lively after-work crowd during the week—especially on Friday—and has an excellent, busy restaurant with a covered balcony perfect for people-watching. An extensive renovation, finishing in 2015, has added new spaces that are as smart and chic as its clientele, plus the new chef is getting rave reviews. ■TIP➔ You'll get one of the best steaks in town here. ✉ *465 Hay St., Subiaco* ☎ *08/9381–3069* ⊕ *www.subiacohotel.com.au.*

The London Court shopping mall facade at Hay Walking Street, Perth

Universal Bar. This bar has live jazz and blues Thursday–Sunday, usually from 9 pm till late, and attracts an exuberant, middle-aged crowd, who love to shake their booty. ✉ *221 William St., Northbridge* ☎ *08/9227–6771* ⊕ *www.universalbar.com.au.*

JAZZ AND BLUES

The Ellington Jazz Club. Inspired by the New York jazz scene, the Ellington is *the* place for jazz in Perth. Catch live music seven nights a week in an intimate and sophisticated setting. A tapas and pizza menu is available. General entry is A$15 weekdays or A$20 weekends for a table or A$10 at the bar. National and international acts attract a higher entry fee—check the website for details, and book your spot online. ✉ *191 Beaufort St., Northbridge* ☎ *08/9228–1088* ⊕ *www.ellingtonjazz.com.au.*

The Laneway Lounge. This sexy little number is as sultry as the jazzy tunes that fill the discreet laneway space each night. A number of the cocktails use smoked ice cubes—not to be confused with tacky dry ice—giving the liquor a heavenly, charred dimension. Retire to the dining room for the dude-food inspired menu, with prawn and pork dumplings, truffle arancini, and satay chicken wings on the starters list. Then head to the back lounge where live jazz plays most nights. ■ **TIP→ The bar is accessed down a laneway off Murray Street—look out for the "red carpet" painted on the pavement.** ✉ *414A Murray St., Northbridge* ☎ *08/9321–2508* ⊕ *www.thelanewaylounge.com.au* ☾ *Closed Mon.*

NIGHTCLUBS

Connections Nightclub. This is Perth's number one gay-friendly nightclub, but it's far more dimensional than its drag queen shows, party beats, and mirror balls. The venue has a classy, industrial-chic lounge bar within the club that opens two hours earlier, at 8 pm. It's like a small bar hidden in the busy core. The bar opens out to a fantastic open-air deck that has whistle-worthy views of the CBD. It's a great place to marvel at the skyline with a bespoke cocktail in hand. ■**TIP**➔**The club and lounge bar stay open till 5 am on Friday and Saturday nights, making it one of the latest late-night venues in Perth.** ⊠ *81 James St., Northbridge* ☎ *08/9328–1870* ⊕ *connectionsnightclub.com* ⊗ *Closed Mon. and Tues.*

Eve. Eve is a glitzy, two-story venue done up with stainless steel and retro fittings. Thursday through Sunday, the five bars, cozy lounge areas, stage, and dance floor with sound-and-light show reverberate to the sounds of renowned DJs spinning the latest dance tunes. Doors open at 9 pm. There's free entry Friday through Sunday before 10 pm. ⊠ *Crown Perth, Great Eastern Hwy. at Bolton Ave., Burswood* ☎ *08/9362–7699* ⊕ *www.crownperth.com.au.*

Hip-e Club. This Perth institution popular with young things in Leederville plays one-hit-wonders from the 1980s, the latest commercial hits, and favorite retro remixes. The famed student/backpacker night takes place on Tuesday; it's been running for nearly 25 years. ⊠ *663 Newcastle St., Leederville* ☎ *08/9227–8899* ⊕ *www.hipeclub.com.au.*

SHOPPING

Shopping in Perth, with its pedestrian-friendly central business district, vehicle-free malls, and many covered arcades, is a delight. Hay Street Mall and Murray Street Mall are the main city shopping areas with large department stores, linked by numerous arcades with small shops; up the far western end is King Street and its glitzy international stores including Louis Vuitton, Tiffany & Co., and Gucci. Head to Northbridge's William Street for hipster and local designer boutiques. In the suburbs, top retail strips include Napoleon Street in Cottesloe for classic, beachy clothing, and homewares; Claremont Quarter in Claremont for fashion-forward garments; Oxford Street in Leederville for edgy threads and unique knickknacks; and Beaufort Street in Mount Lawley for idiosyncratic finds.

Australian souvenirs and iconic buys are on sale at small shops throughout the city and suburbs.

ART AND CRAFT GALLERIES

Creative Native. You can find authentic Aboriginal artifacts at Creative Native; their selection of Aboriginal art is extensive. Each piece of original artwork comes with a certificate of authenticity. ⊠ *Forrest Chase, Forrest Pl., Shop 58, CBD* ☎ *08/9221–5800* ⊕ *www.creativenative.com.au.*

The Mossenson Galleries. Get your fill of authentic Aboriginal art—far more than just dot paintings—by viewing one of the solo or group curated exhibitions by emerging and established artists and communities at the Mossenson Galleries, which has been around since 1993 and is one of Australia's leading Indigenous commercial galleries. ⊠ *115 Hay St., Subiaco* ☎ *08/9388–2899* ⊕ *mossensongalleries.com.au.*

Maalinup Aboriginal Gallery. Find true Aboriginal art here, as well as gifts and souvenirs, including soaps, bath, and beauty products, featuring Australian native plants. Oils and clays are made on-site. The gallery is owned and operated by local Aboriginal people. ⊠ *10070 W. Swan Rd., Henley Brook* ☎ *041/111–2450* ⊕ *www.maalinup.com.au.*

CLOTHING

R. M. Williams. This shop sells everything for the Australian bushman—and woman—including moleskin pants, hand-tooled leather boots, Akubra hats, and their characteristic cobalt blue shirts. ■**TIP➔ They have a discount store at Watertown Brand Outlet Centre on Welling-ton St. in West Perth.** ⊠ *Hay St. Mall, Shop 38, CBD* ☎ *08/9321–7786* ⊕ *www.rmwilliams.com.au.*

DEPARTMENT STORES AND SHOPPING CENTERS

Claremont Quarter. For a mix of designer threads, high fashion, and comfy staples, head to this shiny enclosed shopping center. You'll find gorgeous Australian beauty products by Aesop and Jurlique; classic garments at Country Road; mature but glam women's wear at Carla Zampatti; cosmetics at Napoleon Perdis; and electrical goods and gadgets at Dick Smith—they're all Australian. For international brands, seek out Calvin Klein, French Connection, Karren Millen, and Mecca Cosmetica. There are half a dozen chic cafés, too—get a chocolate hit at Koko Black and great yum cha at Yamato Sushi. ⊠ *9 Bayview Terr., Claremont* ☎ *08/286–5888* ⊕ *www.claremontquarter.com.au.*

FAMILY **Forrest Place.** Flanked by the post office and the Forrest Chase Shopping Plaza, Forrest Place is the largest mall area in the city. It has a lovely fountain designed by artist Jeppe Hein, where children love to play on warm days. ■**TIP➔ There's a large cactus sculpture, opposite Perth Central Train Station, which makes for a good meeting spot.** ⊠ *Forrest Pl., CBD* ⊕ *visitperthcity.com/tags/forrest-place.*

David Jones. This classy department store opens onto the Murray Street pedestrian mall. ⊠ *Murray St. Mall, CBD* ☎ *08/9210–4000.*

Myer. This popular department store carries all manner of goods and sundries. ⊠ *Murray St. Mall, at Forrest Pl., CBD* ☎ *08/9265–5600* ⊕ *www.myer.com.au.*

Hay Street Mall. Running parallel to Murray Street and linked by numer-ous arcades, the Hay Street Mall is another extensive, mainstream shop-ping area. Make sure you wander through the arcades that connect Hay and Murray streets, such as the **Carillion** and **Piccadilly Arcades,** which have many more shops. ⊠ *Hay St., CBD.*

Watertown Brand Outlet Centre. If you feel the need for retail therapy, here's a great spot to let loose, as every store—and there are a lot of them—sells discounted goods here. There are clothes for all ages and styles, shoes, sneakers, gifts, books, sporting gear, beauty products, and more. There are cafés on-site to refuel in, but the food is nothing special. ⊠ *840 Wellington St., West Perth* ☎ *08/9321–2282 general number* ⊕ *www.watertownbrandoutlet.com.au.*

FREMANTLE

About 19 km (12 miles) southwest of Perth.

The port city of Fremantle is a jewel in Western Australia's crown, largely because of its colonial architectural heritage and hippy vibe. Freo (as the locals call it) is a city of largely friendly, interesting, and sometimes eccentric residents supportive of busking, street art, and alfresco dining. Like all great port cities, Freo is cosmopolitan, with mariners from all parts of the world strolling the streets—including thousands of U.S. Navy personnel on rest and recreation throughout the year. It's also a good jumping-off point for a day trip to Rottnest Island, where lovely beaches, rocky coves, and unique wallaby-like inhabitants called quokkas set the scene.

Modern Fremantle is a far cry from the barren, sandy plain that greeted the first wave of English settlers back in 1829 at the newly constituted Swan River Colony. Most were city dwellers, and after five months at sea in sailing ships they landed on salt-marsh flats that sorely tested their fortitude. Living in tents with packing cases for chairs, they found no edible crops, and the nearest freshwater was a distant 51 km (32 miles)—and a tortuous trip up the waters of the Swan. As a result they soon moved the settlement upriver to the vicinity of present-day Perth.

Fremantle remained the principal port, and many attractive limestone buildings were built to service the port traders. Australia's 1987 defense of the America's Cup—held in waters off Fremantle—triggered a major restoration of the colonial streetscapes. In the leafy suburbs nearly every other house is a restored 19th-century gem.

GETTING HERE AND AROUND

Bus information for service from Perth is available from Transperth (☎ 13–6213 ⊕ *www.transperth.wa.gov.au*). Their Central Area Bus Service (CAT) provides free transportation around Fremantle in orange buses. The route begins and ends outside the Fremantle Bus/Train Terminus, and stops include the Arts Centre, the cappuccino strip, and the Fremantle Market. CAT buses run every 10 minutes weekdays 7:30–6:30, and 10–6:30 on weekends and public holidays.

Trains bound for Fremantle depart from Perth approximately every 15–30 minutes from the Perth Central Station on Wellington Street. You can travel from Perth to Fremantle (or vice versa) in about 30 minutes. Tickets must be purchased at the ticket vending machines prior to travel.

If you are driving from downtown Perth, the most direct route is via Stirling Highway, from the foot of Kings Park; it will take about 35 minutes, depending on traffic.

Cab fare between 6 am and 6 pm weekdays is an initial A$4.20 plus A$1.72 every 1 km (½ mile). From 6 pm to 6 am and on weekends the rate rises to A$6.10 plus A$1.72 per 1 km (½ mile).

Taxi Contacts Black & White. ☎ *13–3222.* **Swan Taxis.** ☎ *13–1330.*

SAFETY AND PRECAUTIONS

Fremantle is a safe destination and popular with families, particularly on weekends and during the school holidays. It also has a lively night-life, and late-night crowds leaving pubs and clubs can—and do—cause problems. Taxis are in high demand late at night when other public transport stops operating.

TIMING

Fremantle can easily be visited in a day from Perth, though if you want to trip over to Rottnest Island you will have to add an extra day. Most of the sights are clustered in a relatively small area along Market Street and South Terrace, and close to the Fishing Boat Harbour, and you can take a walking tour or take a hop-on, hop-off tour tram.

TOURS

Dolphin Dive Fremantle. Got a budding diver in the family? Water babies will get a buzz from this beginner's experience, which departs Fremantle and heads to the subtropical waters of Rottnest Island. You get to swim through underwater archways flecked with electric-blue fish, inspect limestone caverns, and explore coral rimmed caves. If you're a newbie, opt for a "Discover Scuba" experience, which involves taking one person out with an instructor (A$385) or a maximum of two (ask about the discounted price). Trips are also available experienced divers—call the store for details. ✉ *256 Hampton Rd., South Fremantle* ☎ *08/9335–9969* ⊕ *www.dolphindiveshop.com* 🎫 *From A$385.*

Fremantle Tram Tours. This company runs hop-on-hop-off tours around the city daily from 9:45 am to approximately 3:30 pm, with six stops all close to the major sights. A tour around Fremantle is a great way to get to know each area of the port city. A full-day tour is the Triple Tour, which includes a guided tour of Fremantle, a cruise on the Swan River to Perth, and a sightseeing tour in Perth. The tour finishes in Perth, but you can catch a train or bus back to Fremantle. The cost is A$81, not including your return to Fremantle. On Friday night, "ghostly tours" take in suspected haunted premises, with a dinner of fish-and-chips included. The cost is A$80 per person. ✉ *Fremantle* ☎ *08/9433–6674* ⊕ *www.fremantletrams.com* 🎫 *From A$27.*

ESSENTIALS

Visitor Information Fremantle Visitor Centre. ✉ *Kings Sq., at High St.* ☎ *08/9431–7878* ⊕ *www.visitfremantle.com.au.*

EXPLORING

An ideal place to start a leisurely stroll is South Terrace, known as the Fremantle cappuccino strip. Wander alongside locals through sidewalk cafés or browse in bookstores, art galleries, and souvenir shops until you reach the Fremantle Markets. From South Terrace walk down to the Fishing Boat Harbour where there's always activity—commercial and pleasure craft bob about, and along the timber boardwalk is a cluster of outdoor eateries and a microbrewery.

Between Phillimore Street and Marine Terrace in the West End is a collection of some of the best-preserved heritage buildings in the state. The

Fremantle Railway Station on Elder Place is another good spot to start a walk. Maps and details for 11 different self-guided walks are available at the Fremantle Visitor Center; a popular heritage walk is the Convict Trail, passing by 18 different sights and locations from Fremantle's convict past.

TOP ATTRACTIONS

FAMILY   **Fremantle Market.** The eclectic, artsy, and always bustling Fremantle Market has been housed in this huge Victorian building since 1897 and sells everything from WA landscape photographs to incense, freshly roasted coffee, toys, baby clothes, and fruit and vegetables out the back. You can also get street food, such as Turkish gözleme, German sausages, corn on the cob, and fresh-squeezed orange juice in the Yard. Around 150 stalls attract a colorful mix of locals and tourists. On weekends and public holidays the market can get crowded, but the Market Bar is a nice, if slightly shabby, place to take a break and watch the buskers. Family-friendly events are also regularly held here. ⊠ *South Terr., at Henderson St.* ☎ *08/9335–2515* ⊕ *www.fremantlemarkets.com.au* ⊙ *Hall: Fri. 9–8, weekends 9–6. Yard: Fri. 8–6, weekends 8–8.*

FAMILY   **Fremantle Prison.** Built in the 1850s, this is where 44 inmates met their fate on the prison gallows between 1888 and 1964. One of the most popular tourist attractions in the state, prison day tours illustrate convict and prison life—including (successful) escapes and the classic-art cell, where a superb collection of drawings by convict James Walsh decorates his quarters. Reservations are required for the 90-minute, goosebump-inducing Torchlight Tours (evening tours by flashlight). For the 2½-hour Tunnels Tour, visitors are provided with hard hats, overalls, boots, and headlamps before descending 65 feet into the labyrinthine tunnels that run beneath the prison; some of the tour is by boat in underground waterways; reservations are also essential. Access to the Prison gatehouse complex, for a simple wander, is free. ⊠ *1 The Terrace* ☎ *08/9336–9200* ⊕ *www.fremantleprison.com.au* ⊠ *A$20, including a 75-min tour; Torchlight Tour A$26, Tunnels Tour A$60* ⊙ *Daily 9–5 with tours every 30 min 10–5. Torchlight Tours Wed. and Fri. regularly from 6:30 or 7 pm in summer; last tour usually at 9 pm. Tunnels Tour at 9, 9:45, 10:40, 12:20, 1:40, 2:40, 3:25.*

FAMILY
Fodor's Choice
★
Western Australian Maritime Museum. Resembling an upside-down boat, the Western Australian Maritime Museum sits at the edge of Fremantle Harbour. It houses *Australia II,* winner of the 1983 America's Cup, and has hands-on, rotating exhibits that are great fun for children. You can also take one-hour guided tours of the adjacent submarine *Ovens,* a former Royal Australian Navy World War II submarine. Tours depart from the maritime museum every 30 minutes between 10 am and 3:30 pm; reservations are recommended during school holidays. Another attraction is the Welcome Walls, a record of all those who immigrated to Western Australia via ship during the major postwar migration. A five-minute walk away on Cliff Street in a separate, heritage building, the Shipwreck Galleries house the recovered remains of Dutch wrecks, including the *Batavia* (wrecked offshore in 1629), and the 1872 SS *Xantho* steamer. ■ TIP➔ On the second Tuesday of every month there is entry to the Western Australian Maritime Museum by gold coin donation. ⊠ *West end of Victoria Quay* ☎ *1300/134081* ⊕ *www.museum.wa.gov.au/maritime*

⬚ *Museum and ovens A$10 each, combo museum and ovens A$16, shipwreck gallery A$5 suggested donation* ⊙ *Daily 9:30–5.*

WORTH NOTING

FAMILY

Fodor's Choice

★

Adventure World. Not far from Fremantle, Adventure World is every fun-loving kid's paradise—especially on a hot day, with water mountain mat slides, rapids navigated in an inflatable tube and bumper boats with water cannons. The 2,066-foot roller-coaster ride called Abyss is guaranteed to thrill: it heads skyward for 10 stories, drops more than 98 feet, and delivers G-force twists of up to 4.5 in its loops. Inspired by ancient Druid guardians, its thrusts are reportedly greater than those of a space shuttle launch. General entry tickets allow you access to everything and are discounted after 2 pm. ⊠ *179 Progress Dr., Bibra Lake* ☎ *08/9417–9666* ⊕ *adventureworld.net.au* ⬚ *A$57; family pass A$177* ⊙ *Feb.–Dec., Thurs.–Mon. 10–5; Jan., Thurs.–Mon. 10–7.*

Fremantle Arts Centre. Like most of Fremantle, the fine, Gothic Revival Fremantle Arts Centre (FAC) was built by convicts in the 19th century. First used as a lunatic asylum, by 1900 it was overcrowded and nearly shut down. It became a home for elderly women until 1942, when the U.S. Navy turned it into its local submarine base in WWII. This time has been captured in an augmented reality iPad tour, "Time Window," accessed via an app, which digitally overlays historic content over the present day site. IPads can be borrowed for free.

As one of Australia's leading arts organizations, FAC has an engaging cultural program year-round. Dynamic exhibitions, a gift shop, and an expansive live music and special events program feature throughout the year. FAC also has free live music on Sundays at 2 pm, from October to March; people like to bring picnics and watch. ⊠ *1 Finnerty St.* ☎ *08/9432–9555* ⊕ *www.fac.org.au* ⬚ *Free* ⊙ *Daily 10–5.*

FAMILY

Roundhouse. An eye-catching landmark of early Fremantle atop an ocean-facing cliff, the Roundhouse was built in 1831 by convicts to house other convicts. This curious, 12-sided building is the state's oldest surviving public structure. Its ramparts have great vistas spanning from High Street to the Indian Ocean. Underneath, a tunnel was carved through the cliffs in the mid-1800s to give ships lying at anchor easy access from town. From the tunnel you can walk to the calm and quiet Bathers Beach where there used to be a whaling station, and listen out for the firing of the cannon at 1 pm daily. Volunteer guides are on duty during opening hours. ⊠ *West end of High St.* ☎ *08/9336–6897* ⊕ *www.fremantleroundhouse.com.au* ⬚ *Donation suggested* ⊙ *Daily 10:30–3:30.*

BEACHES

FAMILY

Bathers Beach. Sometimes, good things come in small packages. This flat, soft-sand beach sits hidden between the Fishing Boat Harbour and the Roundhouse. It's an ideal spot to picnic, with take-away fish-and-chips. **Amenities:** food and drink. **Best for:** solitude; sunset; swimming; walking. ⊠ *Behind Roundhouse, accessed via Fleet St. or Mews Rd.*

FAMILY

Leighton Beach. South of busy Cottesloe and about 30 minutes from central Perth, Leighton is a relatively quiet beach loved for its sugarlike sand and flat, calm water, which is perfect for those who like to paddle. It's equally loved by wind and kite surfers on windy days, who tear across the table-top surface. At the northern end of the beach, dogs are allowed to be off-leash, so expect to see lots of happy pooches running around. ■TIP→ It's close to the North Fremantle train station. **Amenities:** lifeguards; parking; toilets. **Best for:** snorkeling; swimming; sunset; walking; windsurfing. ✉ *Leighton Beach Blvd., North Fremantle.*

FAMILY **Port Beach.** A local favorite, wide Port Beach has small, gentle waves; water the color of a Bombay Sapphire bottle; and pale white sand. It butts up against Fremantle Harbour's North Quay wharf and stretches towards Leighton. Like most of the western-facing coast, the sunsets are epic and the views of Rottnest charming. **Amenities:** lifeguards; parking. **Best for:** snorkeling; sunset; swimming; walking; windsurfing. ✉ *Port Beach Rd., North Fremantle.*

WHERE TO EAT

$$ ✕ **Bread in Common.** We challenge you not to fall in love with the funky
MODERN Bread in Common. This industrial-chic bakery-cum-restaurant wins
AUSTRALIAN the gong for hottest interior in town, with dozens of vintage-style
Fodor's Choice globes streaming from the warehouse ceiling or looping in red elec-
★ trical cord over suspended beams. Their warm light illuminates long, wooden tables backed by distressed brick, all with views of the giant open kitchen. Herb boxes line the 1890s heritage facade, while out back is the wood-fired oven that pumps out three styles of crunchy organic bread. It's great value at A$2 per person, improved only by a serve of tangy olive oil or the creamy, crunchy pork, fennel, and pistachio whip. That said, it's worth leaving room for the smoky lamb ribs and the heirloom carrots squished into lashings of labneh (soft cheese made from yogurt), not to mention the crispy spuds roasted in duck fat. ⑤ *Average main: A$25* ✉ *43 Pakenham St.* ☎ *08/9336–1032* ⊕ *www. breadincommon.com.au.*

$$ ✕ **Capri Restaurant.** You may need to wait for a table (they take limited
ITALIAN bookings), but the complimentary minestrone and crusty bread will tide you over at this Fremantle institution. You'll get a warm welcome from the Pizzale family, who have owned and run the restaurant for more than 50 years—the fourth generation is now in charge. Sit down to grilled calamari splashed with lemon, panfried scaloppini in white wine, rich spaghetti marinara, excellent steaks, and fresh salads. Simple white-linen tablecloths, carafes of chilled water—it's BYO—and the sounds of laughter and clinking glasses round out the experience. This is old-style Fremantle at its best. ⑤ *Average main: A$28* ✉ *21 South Terr.* ☎ *08/9335–1399* ⊕ *www.caprirestaurantfremantle.com.*

$$$ ✕ **Char Char Bull.** Waterfront Fremantle is renowned for its seafood res-
STEAKHOUSE taurants, so going to a harborside venue for steak seems almost irrev- erent—a bit like going to Italy for a curry—but meat lovers revel in the juicy steak selection at Char Char Bull. This lively restaurant, with full table service, specializes in chargrilled prime beef selected from year-old, grass-fed Murray Grey cattle. Choose from tender filet mignon, tender- loin, sirloin, and rib eye cooked exactly how you like it, with all the

trimmings. If you just can't go a day without fish, oysters, barramundi, garlic prawns, scallops, and wine-steamed mussels also feature on the menu, as does pizza. ■ **TIP→ Make reservations and ask for a table out on the deck.** ⑤ *Average main: A$40* ⊠ *Fishing Boat Harbour, 44 Mews Rd.* ☎ *08/9335–7666* ⊕ *www.charcharbull.com.au.*

$$
AUSTRALIAN-
SEAFOOD
FAMILY

✕ **Cicerello's.** No visit to Fremantle is complete without a stop at this locally famous fish-and-chippery which was once featured on a postage stamp. Housed in a boathouse-style building fronting Fremantle's lovely Fishing Boat Harbour, this joint serves the real thing: fresh oysters, mussels, crabs, fish, lobsters, and chips, all wrapped up in butcher paper (no cardboard boxes or plastic plates here). While you eat, you can check out the huge aquarium and touch pool: the restaurant has more than 50 species of local marine life. Better still, on Tuesday kids eat for free. Cicerello's also has a restaurant in Mandurah. ⑤ *Average main: A$25* ⊠ *Fisherman's Wharf, 44 Mews Rd.* ☎ *08/9335–1911* ⊕ *www.cicerellos.com.au.*

$$
ITALIAN

✕ **Gino's Café.** The original owner, Gino, was so passionate about coffee that he closed his tailor shop to open this cappuccino-strip property with a busy alfresco terrace. Among the most popular drinks are the house coffee (Gino's Blend), and the Baby Chino—a froth of milk dusted with chocolate powder that young children love. Gino's opens at 6 am to serve coffee, then cooks an extensive choice of reasonably priced breakfasts from 7 am. The lunch menu focuses on focaccias and panini while for dinner, more than two dozen different pasta dishes are available—many made with fresh pasta—including a superb penne alla vodka with chicken and spinach. ⑤ *Average main: A$25* ⊠ *South Terr., at Collie St.* ☎ *08/9336–1464* ⊕ *www.ginoscafe.com.au.*

$$
SEAFOOD
FAMILY

✕ **Joe's Fish Shack.** Fremantle's quirkiest restaurant looks like everyone's vision of a run-down, weather-beaten Maine diner. With uninterrupted harbor views, authentic nautical bric-a-brac, and great food, you can't go wrong. Recommendations include the salt-and-pepper squid, stuffed tiger prawns, and chili mussels. An outdoor section with umbrella-covered tables serves "Joe's to Go" takeaway food from a smaller, fish-and-chip-style menu. ⑤ *Average main: A$30* ⊠ *42 Mews Rd.* ☎ *08/9336–7161* ⊕ *www.joesfishshack.com.au.*

$
MODERN
AUSTRALIAN

✕ **Moore & Moore.** You'll know this clean-living café by the retro bikes stacked out front next to the potted garden, eclectic-looking people, and live music that often streams from the doorway. There's an art gallery up the creaky stairs, but continue straight ahead past up-cycled furniture to the garden seating out the back. Their food is as tasty as the vibe is charming. Hugely popular for its all-day breakfast (even though the kitchen has a "no scrambled eggs" rule), it also makes for a great lunch option. Expect poached organic eggs with nitrate-free bacon with chickpeas and spinach; smoked cod with wasabi yogurt and eggs; organic beef ribs; chicken club sandwich with Sriracha aioli; and more eco-focused but super yummy dishes. It's feel-good all around. ⑤ *Average main: A$19* ⊠ *46 Henry St.* ☎ *08/9335–8825* ⊕ *www.mooreandmoorecafe.com.*

$
MODERN
AUSTRALIAN
FAMILY

✕ **Ootong & Lincoln.** It says a lot about the café's style that they commissioned a local street artist to paint a giant, multicolor zebra mural on an external wall. Inside, colorful communal tables are surrounded by dividers made from plumbing pipes while vintage tricycles line a shelf below the ceiling. Just as much love is put into the food. Everything is made from scratch—even the jams—and the eggs in the breakfast dishes are, naturally, free range. Go for the poached egg and smoked salmon dish that's pumped up with diced avocado and a corn and zucchini fritter, dolloped with hollandaise. $ *Average main: A$17* ✉ *258 South Terr., South Fremantle* ☎ *08/9335–6109* ⊕ *www.ootongandlincoln.com.au.*

WHERE TO STAY

$$$ Esplanade Hotel Fremantle—By Rydges. Part of a colonial-era hotel, this huge, conveniently located establishment has balconies facing the park and nearby harbor, Essex Street, or the pool. **Pros:** central to Fremantle attractions; tropical garden setting around heated pool; three outdoor spas; ample dining and shopping options nearby. **Cons:** sea views are limited to some rooms; functions can make venues crowded; parking costs extra; rooms facing resort pool may encounter car park noise. $ *Rooms from: A$249* ✉ *Marine Terr., at Essex St.* ☎ *08/9432–4000* ⊕ *www.rydges.com* 🛏 *293 rooms, 7 suites* ⦿| *No meals.*
HOTEL

$$ Fothergills of Fremantle. Antiques, pottery, sculptures, bronzes, and paintings adorn these popular, two-story, 1892 limestone terrace houses opposite the old Fremantle prison. **Pros:** breakfast included; personalized service; good location; free Wi-Fi and parking. **Cons:** comfy shoes required for the walk to central Fremantle; limited facilities on-site. $ *Rooms from: A$180* ✉ *18–22 Ord St.* ☎ *08/9335–6784* ⊕ *www.fothergills.net.au* 🛏 *7 rooms* ⦿| *Breakfast.*
B&B/INN
Fodor's Choice ★

$$ Norfolk Hotel. With an excellent location, leafy beer garden, and basement live music bar all part of its assets, this central accommodation has a lot going for it. **Pros:** free parking in central location; free Wi-Fi; light and airy; Fremantle Train Station a 10-minute walk away; free CAT bus nearby. **Cons:** shared facilities in some rooms; potential noise from pub. $ *Rooms from: A$180* ✉ *47 South Terr.* ☎ *08/9335–5405* ⊕ *www.norfolkhotel.com.au* 🛏 *9 rooms* ⦿| *No meals.*
HOTEL

$$$ Port Mill Bed & Breakfast. Discreetly concealed in a picture postcard courtyard reminiscent of Provence, this flour mill-turned-bed-and-breakfast contains four sunny, individually decorated suites, each with its own Juliette balcony; two overlooking the courtyard garden. **Pros:** heritage-listed accommodation; free Wi-Fi; discounts offered for longer stays; close to shopping, dining, and tourist attractions. **Cons:** parking
B&B/INN

THE CUP

In 1848, Britain's Queen Victoria authorized the creation of a solid silver cup for a yacht race that would be "open to all nations." In 1851, the New York Yacht Club challenged 16 English yachts and won with the boat *America.* The United States continued to win for 132 years straight until the upstart *Australia 11* won 4–3 in sensational style, and the Cup came to Fremantle. Australia was euphoric. Fremantle spruced up for the defense of the Cup in 1987, but the fairy tale ended in a 4–0 loss to the San Diego Yacht Club entrant. Today *Australia 11* is a centerpiece display at the WA Maritime Museum.

nearby for a A$7 per day fee; two-story building has winding stairs, but no elevator. Ⓢ *Rooms from: A$269* ⊠ *3/17 Essex St.* ☎ *08/9433–3832, 0404/120–019* ⊕ *www.portmillbb.com.au* ⇆ *4 suites* ⫯◎⫯ *Breakfast.*

NIGHTLIFE

There's nothing more pleasant than relaxing in the evening at one of the sidewalk tables on the cappuccino strip. This area, along South Terrace, opens at 6 am and closes around 3 am.

Fly By Night Musicians Club. "The Fly," as it's locally known, has a great tradition of raw live music—including regular jazz and swing—comedy, and dance performances by excellent Australian and international artists, including Fremantle native John Butler. Many local bands and soloists owe their big breaks to Fly By Night Musicians Club, a not-for-profit, smoke-free venue. There is plenty of parking opposite. ⊠ *Victoria Hall, 179 High St.* ☎ *08/9430–5208* ⊕ *www.flybynight.org.*

Fodor'sChoice
★

Little Creatures. Fancy a tour of a brewery? How about borrowing a free, retro-red bike for the day? Little Creatures has got a lot going for it—including its harborside location and fun-loving, artsy vibe—and it won't cost an arm and a leg. Sign up for the A$12 tours that take you through every step on the beer-making process, running at 1, 2, and 3 pm every day. Then, leave a photo copy of your credit card and driver's licence or passport with the staff so you can borrow a bike. This is the best place in Fremantle to taste kangaroo—the skewers are excellent, as are the steamed mussels and thin-crust pizzas. Naturally, matching the food with beer is a must. Expect a pleasant surprise from the mid-strength Rogers beer. ⊠ *40 Mews Rd.* ☎ *08/6215–1000* ⊕ *www. littlecreatures.com.au.*

Metropolis Concert Club Fremantle. In the heart of Fremantle's cappuccino strip, Metropolis Concert Club Fremantle, a nonstop techno and funk dance venue, is a fun, if youth-dominated, place to go late on a Friday or Saturday night. ⊠ *58 South Terr.* ☎ *08/9336–1880* ⊕ *www. metropolisfremantle.com.au.*

Sail and Anchor Pub. Thanks to its selection of craft beers—40 on tap—and right-in-the-middle-of-it location, the heritage-listed Sail and Anchor Pub is one of Australia's most popular watering holes. Upstairs has comfy couches; you can watch buskers from the balcony; the front bar often has live music; and the bistro serves up no-nonsense pub grub. ⊠ *64 South Terr.* ☎ *08/9431–1666* ⊕ *www.sailandanchor.com.au.*

Who's Your Mumma. This city-style venue is on one of boho Fremantle's loveliest streets. Who's Your Mumma really comes alive at night. Its industrial globes put out warm light, and its wooden tables and chairs are packed with hip, fashionable, but friendly locals sipping on quirky cocktails and craft beers. ■TIP➔ **If you're peckish, the pork buns are divine.** ⊠ *142 South Terr.* ⊕ *www.whosyourmumma.com.au.*

SHOPPING

Kakulas Sisters. A strong supporter of both WA and international produce, this unique Greek-owned providore overflows with fragrances and sacks of goodies from across the globe. Delectable items such as Brazilian quince and guava pastries, goji berries, Tasmanian honey, Japanese teas, locally produced pestos and olives, roasted coffee beans, and European hard cheeses ensure that homesick, or simply nostalgic, visitors can enjoy a slice, sliver, or smell of home. ✉ *29–31 Market St.* ☎ *08/9430–4445* ⊕ *kakulassister.com.au.*

FAMILY **Pickled Fairy & Other Myths.** A fairy theme pervades the Pickled Fairy & Other Myths, making it a delight for children and elves, with themed activities to entertain all involved. All staff are dressed as fairies and kids get sprinkled with magic dust and a wish. Fairy dresses, fairy books, and mystical magical knickknacks make this a treasure trove of potential presents for lucky little girls, or anyone with a numinous streak. ✉ *South Terrace Piazza, Shop 7B* ☎ *08/9430–5827* ⊕ *www. pickledfairy.com.au.*

ROTTNEST ISLAND

19 km (12 miles) west of Fremantle.

An easy 30-minute cruise from Fremantle, or about one hour down the Swan River from Perth, sunny, quirky Rottnest Island makes an ideal day trip. Known to locals as "Rotto," the former penal colony, boys' reformatory, and war base is as much a part of Western Australia as mine sites, colorful entrepreneurs, and untouched beaches. Its strange moniker—translated to mean rat's nest—can be attributed to 17th-century Dutch explorers who mistook the native marsupials called quokkas for cat-size rats.

Much of the island's charm lies in the fact it's largely car free: rent a bike to make the most of it. The island has an interesting past, which is evident in its historic buildings. Though records of human occupation date back 6,500 years, when Aboriginal people inhabited the area, European settlement only dates back to 1829. Since then the island has been used for a variety of purposes, including attempts at agriculture, a boy's reformatory, a penal colony, and for military purposes in both the Great War and World War II. The Rottnest Museum is a great place to get the history of the place, further enhanced by the many free daily tours run by volunteers. You can also take a train trip and tour to Oliver Hill to see gun emplacements from World War II.

Of course, most West Australians go to the island for the beaches, the swimming, and the laid-back atmosphere on Perth's doorstep. A warm ocean current passes by Rottnest, allowing it to host an unusual mix of tropical and temperate marine life. In fact, it's home to 135 species of tropical fish and 20 species of coral, and even air temperature is warmer than on the mainland.

GETTING HERE AND AROUND

A number of operators run light plane and helicopter flights to Rottnest Island. Check the Rottnest Island Visitor Information Centre website for other options.

There are no taxis on Rottnest Island. Almost everyone rides bikes, which can either be rented when booking your ferry ticket, or once you arrive, at Rottnest Bike Hire.

Charter1 catamaran. Cuddle up on board a 41-foot, island-circling catamaran for snorkeling and seal- and dolphin-spotting adventures to Rottnest Island's isolated bays by day, and gently rocking accommodation complete with stargazing by night. The day tours head to a small rocky island where Australian fur seals like to loll about, but once they see you splash into the ocean, they're keen to swim around you and play in the water. From September to November, spot dolphins and humpback whales frolicking in the ocean. All-day snorkel tours depart from Fremantle and head to Rottnest September–March (A$129); half-day tours sail to Carnac Island (A$79) and twilight sails along the coast (A$98) make for another relaxing option. Bookings are recommended. ■ TIP➔ Snorkelling gear is provided. ⊠ *Rottnest Island* ☏ *0428/604–794* ⊕ *www.charter1.com.au.*

Rottnest Air Taxi. This speedy air service to Rottnest Island flies from Perth's Jandakot airport. Round-trip fare is from around A$127 per person for a fully occupied aircraft, and it includes Rottnest entry fees (fewer passengers means prices rise; there's a four-seater and a six-seater aircraft). The service operates on demand, anytime during the day, weather permitting. Flight time is around 12 minutes. Telephone for flight times. Joy flights provide 30-minute scenic spins over Perth and its surrounding beaches. ☏ *0411/264–547, 1800/500006 within Australia only* ⊕ *www.rottnestairtaxi.com.au.*

FAMILY
Fodor's Choice
★
Rottnest Express. Rottnest Express is the main operator running ferries to Rottnest Island from two locations in Fremantle (one outside Fremantle train station) and from central Perth (this includes a scenic cruise of the Swan River). Rottnest Express also runs a number of tours, from whale watching and snorkeling to adventure boat cruises along the rugged coastline. You can rent bikes and snorkel gear as part of your ticket. TIP: Ferry tickets are reduced on Tuesdays and it's cheaper to buy online, in advance. ☏ *1300/467688* ⊕ *www.rottnestexpress.com. au* ☞ *Ferry tickets include price of entry to island.*

Rottnest Fast Ferries. Rottnest Fast Ferries runs boats from Hillarys Boat Harbour. The ferries take approximately 45 minutes from Hillarys to Rottnest, with hotel pick-ups from Perth available. Round-trip prices, including entry to Rottnest are from A$85.50. Add bike rentals to the trip for a total fare of A$105, snorkel sets are A$15 extra. Whale watching tours, which are cheapest on weekdays and start from A$65 (early-September to early December), are also available. ☏ *08/9246–1039* ⊕ *rottnestfastferries.com.au* ☉ *Closed June, July (except school holidays), and Aug.*

SAFETY AND PRECAUTIONS

Be sun-smart, especially from October through April. Even on cloudy days people unused to being outdoors for any length of time can suffer severe sunburn. Wear a hat, long-sleeved shirt, and high-strength sunscreen. If you are a weak or novice swimmer, always swim with a friend; lifesavers (lifeguards) patrol certain beaches during peak holiday periods.

TIMING

Rottnest Island can be visited in a day. An early ferry gets you to the island with plenty of time to tour the main attractions or beaches, returning to Fremantle or Perth in the late afternoon. Staying an extra day or two gives you time to laze at a beach or go surfing or diving.

TOURS

There's a narrated 90-minute coach tour of the island's highlights, including convict-built cottages, World War II gun emplacements, salt lakes, and the remote West End. Tours depart daily from Main Bus Stop. The Oliver Hill Railway made its debut in the mid-1990s, utilizing 6 km (4 miles) of reconstructed railway line to reach the island's World War II gun batteries. Information is available from the Rottnest Island Visitor Centre.

Discovery Tour. For those not keen on biking or hop-on, hop-off buses, Rottnest Express runs a popular Discovery Tour that gives an overview of the island's activities, history, environment, and wildlife as it circumnavigates the island in about 90 minutes. Highlights of the tour are the salt lakes, Wadjemup Lighthouse, convict-built cottages, World War II gun emplacements, and the remote West End. Tours depart daily from the Main Bus Stop at 11 am and 1 pm; tickets are available online. ⊠ *Thompson Bay* ☎ *08/9372–9732* ⊕ *www.rottnestexpress. com.au* 🖃 *A$45.*

Island Explorer. This service, which runs on a continuous hop-on, hop-off island circuit, picks up and drops off passengers at the most beautiful bays and beaches. Day tickets are A$20 and can be purchased from the Rottnest Island Visitor Centre, online, at ticket machines on the Island, or through bus operator, Adams (⊕ *www.goadams.com.au*). Buses run 8:30–3:30, hourly in winter and half hourly in summer until 4:30. Timetables are posted at all bus stops and within the Essential Guide found on the Rottnest Island website. ■ **TIP→ The Island Explorer is free from Geordie Bay to the Main Bus Stop in Thomson Bay.** ⊠ *Thomson Bay, Henderson Ave.* ☎ *08/9372–9732* ⊕ *www.rottnestisland.com* 🖃 *A$20.*

FAMILY **The Oliver Hill Train.** Known as the *Captain Hussey,* the Oliver Hill train is an ideal way to see the island. The route from the Main Settlement to Oliver Hill runs daily at 1:30 and connects with a guided tour of the historic Oliver Hill gun battery. The fare is A$9 for train only and A$29 with a guided tour of the World War I tunnels. Tickets are available at the visitor information center. ⊠ *Thomson Bay* ☎ *08/9372–9732* ⊕ *www.rottnestisland.com* 🖃 *A$29.*

ESSENTIALS

Visitor Information Rottnest Island Visitor Centre. ⊠ *Thomson Bay beachfront, adjacent Dome Café* ☎ *08/9432–9111* ⊕ *www.rottnestisland.com.*

EXPLORING

The most convenient way to get around Rottnest is by bicycle, as private cars are not allowed on the island. A self-guided bicycle tour of the island covers 26 km (16 miles) and can take as little as three hours, although you really need an entire day to enjoy the beautiful surroundings.

Heading south from Thomson Bay, between Government House and Herschell Lakes, you'll find the Quokka Walk and a man-made causeway where you'll find a few quokka colonies. Continue south and to Oliver Hill and the Wadjemup Light House, where tours are run every half hour from 11 am until 2:30 pm. As you continue to Bickley Bay you can spot the wreckage of ships—the oldest dates from 1842—that came to rest on Rottnest's rocky coastline.

Follow the main road past Porpoise, Salmon, Strickland, and Wilson bays to West End, the windiest point on the island and another graveyard for unfortunate vessels. Heading back to Thomson Bay, the road passes a dozen rocky inlets and bays. Parakeet Bay, the prettiest, is at the northernmost tip of the island.

Rottnest Museum. At the Thomson Bay settlement, don't miss the Rottnest Museum, which includes mementos of the island's sometimes turbulent past. Staying true to local history, displays are housed in an old mill and hay store built in 1857, showing local geology, natural and social history, and maritime lore with a bunch of surprising facts. It's open daily 10:45–3:30 by gold coin donation. **Wadjemup Lighthouse Tours**—find out what goes on within the confines of a working lighthouse and climb to the top of this Heritage structure for fabulous 360-degree views. Tours depart daily, on demand, at 11 am and every half hour until 2:30 pm, and cost A$9. ⊠ *Thomson Bay, Digby Dr., at Kitson St.* ☎ *08/9372–9732* ⊕ *www.rottnestisland.com* ✉ *Donation suggested.*

BEACHES

There are some 63 beaches on Rottnest Island, suitable for swimming, surfing, snorkeling, and diving. The most popular include Geordie Bay, Little Parakeet, Parker Point, Little Salmon Bay, and the Basin.

Surfers and body-boarders will head for Stark Bay, Strickland Bay, and West End, while swimmers love the sandy white beaches at Pinkies Beach and the Basin. Beach spots for snorkeling and diving include Little Salmon Bay (it has underwater markers), and Parker Point.

FAMILY
Fodor's Choice
★

The Basin. This pool-like bay is one of Rottnest's most popular, both for its safe, shallow waters and proximity to the main settlement. Protected by an outer reef, the ocean is crystal clear, the waves are gentle, and little fish dart about. **Amenities:** lifeguards; showers; toilets. **Best for:** swimming. ⊠ *Rottnest Island* ⊹ *Northwest of Thompson Bay* ⊕ *www. rottnestisland.com.*

Geordie Bay. Over the dunes is the whitest of white sand and the most azure waters of Geordie Bay. Photographed by many, its flat, motionless ocean makes for safe swimming. A confetti of yachts spreads across the bay in summer months (there are protected, boat-free swimming zones), and beachside accommodation mirrors the cove. Nearby, next to a mini-mart, find Geordie's Cafe and Art Gallery (☎ 08/9292–5411), one of the best foodie options on the island. Open for breakfast, lunch and dinner, it also serves many gluten-free dishes. Expect to see furry quokkas looking for scraps. **Amenities:** showers; toilets. **Best for:** swimming. ⊠ *Geordie Bay Rd.*

Little Salmon Bay. Make sure you pack your snorkeling gear for this one—due to Rottnest's warmer waters, created by the passing Leeuwin Current, there's a fascinating mix of tropical and temperate fish species in the clear waters. Aim to go at low tide and look out for

bream, red-lipped morwong, zebrafish, and king wrasse, plus plenty of little colored fish. There are underwater plaques that guide you along a great snorkel trail and the waters are calm so you can enjoy flipping about. Coral reefs are about 330 feet out but worth checking out if you're a confident swimmer. ■TIP➜ If it's overcrowded, head to the next, bigger beach, Salmon Bay. **Amenities:** none. **Best for:** snorkeling; swimming. ⊠ *Rottnest Island ✛ Little Salmon Bay, southwest of Thompson Bay, off Parker Point Rd.*

SPORTS AND THE OUTDOORS

BIKING

FAMILY **Rottnest Island Pedal and Flipper.** You can rent one of this outfit's 1,300 bikes—the island's must-have item—from A\$30 per day, with a returnable deposit of A\$50 per bike. Tandem bikes and attachable buggies for little children can also be rented. Also for rent: snorkel sets, paddleboards, surfboards, bodyboards, wet suits, and beach cricket and soccer essentials. It's open daily 8:30–5:30, though hours vary according to the season (when there's no 6 pm ferry, it closes at 4 pm). Expect queues at ferry arrival times. ⊠ *Thomson Bay* ☎ *08/9292–5105* ⊕ *www.rottnestisland.com.*

WHERE TO STAY

Accommodation on the island ranges from basic camping sites to self-contained holiday villas and hotels. Space is at a premium during the summer months, Easter, and school holidays. November can be busy because of the so-called schoolies week, when high-school leavers celebrate the end of senior school. This time is best avoided. Outside these times, accommodation is easier to find. Check ⊕ *www.rottnestisland.com* for details.

Snorkeling at the Basin on Rottnest Island, Western Australia

$$$ **▪ Rottnest Lodge.** The largest hotel on Rottnest and the only one with a
HOTEL pool and spa facilities, its sturdy structure reveals an interesting past as
a colonial barracks and a prison. **Pros:** centrally located; some rooms
have lake views; some rooms ideal for families. **Cons:** not on beach-
front; limited leisure facilities; some design is dated. ⑤ *Rooms from:
A$225* ⊠ *Kitson St.* ☎ *08/9292–5161* ⊕ *www.rottnestlodge.com.au*
⤴ *80 rooms, including 12 premium rooms* ⏍ *Breakfast.*

THE SOUTH WEST WINE REGION

The South West—Western Australia's most popular destination, with
2.4 million visitors annually—should not be missed if you are coming
to this state, a fact well known by Perth residents, who flock here year-
round for the wines, beaches, surfing, marine wildlife, forests, locally
produced crafts and artisan products, and the country vistas.

The region stretches from the port city of Bunbury—about two hours
south of Perth by freeway and highway—through Busselton, Dunsbor-
ough, Margaret River (1½ hours farther south), and on to Augusta, at
the tip of Cape Leeuwin.

Margaret River is best known for its fabulous wines—Chardonnay and
Cabernet Sauvignon are the standout varieties—but the South West
has wineries from well north of Bunbury to the south coast. Busselton,
Dunsborough, Yallingup, Prevelly, and Margaret River are all suitable
places to stay if you want to visit wineries; all but Margaret River are
on the coast with easy beach access.

The South West Wine Region

The best surfing beaches are on the coast between Cape Naturaliste and Cape Leeuwin.

All major South West towns have visitor centers that can arrange tours, book accommodations, and provide free information.

EN ROUTE

Bunbury is a great stopover point where you can visit the Dolphin Discovery Centre to swim with wild dolphins (in season), or wade in shallow waters with them under the watchful eye of center volunteers and biologists. About 100 bottlenose dolphins make their permanent home in and around the waters of Koombana Bay off Bunbury, making your chances of seeing them in their natural habitat very high. You can also take a dolphin cruise with the Dolphin Discovery Centre, or an eco-conscious whale-watching excursion with Naturaliste Charters.

Dolphin Discovery Centre. Get up close to wild dolphins at the Dolphin Discovery Centre. Two-hundred dolphins have been identified in Koombana Bay—swim with them, book an eco-cruise, or stay on the beach and wade into the interaction zone. Enjoy the discovery center with its unique digital dolphinarium, interpretive panels and theater, dolphin skeleton, and café and gift shop. ■ TIP➔ Call first to book the weather-dependent swim and eco-cruises. Dolphin encounters are not guaranteed. ⊠ 830 Koombana Dr., Bunbury ☎ 08/9791–3088 ⊕ www.

dolphindiscovery.com.au ⌨ *Discovery Centre A\$10, Swim Encounter A\$165, Eco-Cruise A\$49* ⊙ *Oct.–May, daily 8–4; June–Sept., daily 9–2.*

Naturaliste Charters. This company runs eco-conscious whale watching tours along the south western coastline, relocating from Augusta to Dunsborough as the whale migration shifts north from late May to early December. You can expect to see playful humpbacks and surfacing southern right whales, and if you're lucky, rare blue and minke whales. The company also runs Eco Wilderness and Sunset Eco Tours from September to January, out of Dunsborough. For something really special, join a Bremer Canyon expedition from January to April, to see a killer whale and shark feeding ground in a remote and deep part of ocean off the Albany coast. ⌧ *Shop 1, Bayview Centro, Dunsborough* ☎ *08/9750–5500* ⊕ *www.whales-australia.com* ⌨ *A\$80; Sunset and Eco Wilderness Tours A\$90; Bremer Canyon expeditions A\$350.*

DUNSBOROUGH

252 km (157 miles) south of Perth.

The attractive and fashionable seaside town of Dunsborough is perfect for a few days of swimming, sunning, and fishing—which is why it's become a popular holiday destination for many Perth families. Onshore attractions include Meelup Beach, a protected cove encircled by native bush with calm swimming water, and the nearby wineries of Margaret River. Offshore, you can dive on the wreck of the HMAS *Swan,* the former Royal Australian Navy ship deliberately sunk in Geographe Bay at the end of its useful life, or take a cruise to see migrating humpback and southern right whales September–December.

GETTING HERE AND AROUND

From Perth, take the Kwinana Freeway south; it joins the Forrest Highway and then Highway 1 down the coast to Bunbury. Switch to Highway 10 through Busselton, then Caves Road to Dunsborough. If you drive from Perth, it will take around three hours. Alternatively, **South West Coachlines** (☎ *08/9261–7600* ⊕ *www.southwestcoachlines.com. au*) has daily South West Express coach service from Perth Central Bus Station at the Esplanade Bus Port on Mounts Bay Road to South West towns, including Dunsborough. Once here, a rental car is recommended, as there is limited public transport, and some accommodations are in bushland or beach settings, away from the towns.

Dunsborough Car Rentals. Late-model vehicles are available at reasonable rates for touring the Margaret River region. ⌧ *201 Geographe Bay Rd., Quindalup* ☎ *1800/449007* ⊕ *www.dunsboroughcarrentals.com.au.*

Taxi Contacts Busselton Taxis. ⌧ *Busselton* ☎ *13–1008.* **Dunsborough Taxis.** ⌧ *Dunsborough* ☎ *08/9756–8688* ⊕ *www.dunsboroughtaxis.com.au.*

SAFETY AND PRECAUTIONS

The calm waters of Geographe Bay are home to a jellyfish with a nasty sting—colloquially named "stingers." They are not deadly so don't panic, but they are painful and hard to spot—the main body of the stinger is translucent and only about 2 inches across, and the hard-to-see tentacles trailing are the cause for concern. While not common, the jellyfish like warm, very calm water, so still days in summer are when you are most likely to encounter them as they drift close to shore. Rubbing a sting is not recommended; try bathing in vinegar.

Mosquitoes are prevalent in summer, especially along the South West coast and in swamplands. To avoid being bitten by mosquitoes, cover up and use a repellent, especially around dawn and dusk, when mosquitoes are most active.

TIMING

Dunsborough (and the surrounding area) deserves at least two days, preferably three. Western Australian school holidays, especially the summer break over Christmas and New Year's Day, and Easter, are usually booked solid by Perth holidaymakers with families. One week in November is also crowded for "schoolies week," when teenage students boisterously celebrate the end of their schooling life. The summer months (December–March) are best for swimming and beaches, springtime (September–November) is ideal for bush and coastal walking and wildflower spotting, while the heaviest surfing conditions are often best during the winter months (May–September) when wet suits are required.

TOURS

FAMILY

Fodor's Choice

★

Busselton Jetty and Underwater Observatory. At almost 2-km (1¼-miles) long, the 148-year-old Busselton Jetty is the longest timber jetty in the southern hemisphere. You can visit the Interpretive Center and Heritage Museum at the start of the jetty, then either catch the miniature train (45-minute ride) or walk to the fascinating Underwater Observatory—one of only seven in the world—where you'll spy all manner of soft, colorful coral as you descend the cylindrical, windowed observatory. Tours for up to 40 people run every hour, taking you 26 feet below the water. The warm Leeuwin Current and the sheltering effect of the jetty above have created a unique microclimate rich with colorful tropical and subtropical corals, sponges, fish, and invertebrates—there are 300 marine species in all. ■TIP➔ Booking is essential. ⊠ *Beachfront, Queen St., Busselton* ☎ *08/9754-0900* ⊕ *www.busseltonjetty. com.au* ⊠ *1 Jetty Day Pass A$3; Jetty Train Ride A$12; Underwater Observatory (including tour) A$32* ☉ *Interpretive Center and Heritage Museum, May–Aug., daily 9–5; Sept.–Apr., daily 8:30–6. Underwater Observatory and Jetty Train Tour, May–Aug., on the hr 10–3; Sept.–Apr., on the hr 9–4.*

Cape Dive. This company has dive tours to the wreck of the HMAS *Swan,* a Royal Australian Navy River Class Destroyer Escort deliberately sunk in about 100 feet of water off Dunsborough to become an artificial reef and dive wreck. Dives are tailored to novices and experienced divers alike. Other dives go around the Busselton Jetty, where an abundance of corals and marine life have made their homes on the pylons. In spring, whale watching is added to its suite of experiences. ⊠ *Shop 1, 222 Naturaliste Terr.* ☎ *08/9756–8778* ⊕ *www.capedive. com* ⊠ *From A$160* ☉ *Thur.–Sun. 9–5 (reduced hrs in colder months).*

Cellar d'Or Winery Tours. Cellar d'Or Winery Tours has daily tours of Margaret River region wineries from A$88 per person. The tours include pick-up at your accommodation, wine tastings at five boutique wineries, platter lunch and beer tasting at a micro brewery, chocolate sampling, cheese and local produce tasting, and complimentary bottled water and wine glass. ☎ *0428/179–729* ⊕ *www.cellardortours.com.au* ◎ *From A$88.*

ESSENTIALS

MasterCard and Visa are always taken at restaurants, lodgings, and shops; American Express and Diners Club are less acceptable, and the merchant may add a small surcharge.

Visitor Information Busselton Visitor Centre. ⊠ *Busselton beachfront, Beach end of Queen St., Busselton* ☎ *08/9752–5800* ⊕ *www.margaretriver.com.* **Dunsborough Visitor Centre.** ⊠ *Shop 1 Dunn Bay Centre, 31 Dunn Bay Rd.* ☎ *08/ 9755–3517* ⊕ *www.margaretriver.com.*

EXPLORING

Clairault Streicker Wines. This winery is known for its award-winning Chardonnay, Cabernet Sauvignon, and Cabernet Merlot, and loved for its natural bushland setting, about 18 km (11 miles) south of Dunsborough. The cellar door is modern in style with polished timber floors, natural stone, and walls of glass overlooking the scrub. The spacious café (open daily, 11–4) has glass doors that open on to a large timber deck in warm weather—picnic blankets are available to borrow—while two huge stone fireplaces warm the tables in winter. The winery and restaurant are popular for weddings, especially during the spring and fall months. ⊠ *3277 Caves Rd., Wilyabrup* ☎ *08/9755–6225 cellar door café* ⊕ *www.clairaultstreickerwines.com.au* ◎ *Daily 10–5.*

Happs Pottery & Winery. Handmade mudbricks, recycled timbers, and stained-glass windows point to the origins of this family-owned and built winery. A few miles from Dunsborough you'll find a friendly welcome, huge range of wines to taste (33 at last reckoning) and an eclectic gallery of locally made products in the same building. Erl Happ began his pottery business in 1970 and planted his first vines eight years later, going against local wisdom by planting Merlot. Later, a second vineyard, with 31 varieties of grape, was established near Karridale some 90 km (55 miles) to the south, its wines produced under the Three Hills label. Free tastings allow you to try some wines only available at the cellar door, such as Fuchsia and preservative-free wines. His wife Roslyn has created a much photographed garden courtyard. To see the pottery created by Erl's son Myles), travel to nearby Happs Pottery (749 Caves Road, Anniebrook), where works are for sale and, if you're game, you can get your hands dirty during a pottery class. ⊠ *575 Commonage Rd.* ☎ *08/9755–3300* ⊕ *www.happs.com.au* ◎ *Daily 10–5.*

Wise Wines. The view from the hilltop overlooking Geographe Bay is almost as good as the wines and food at this northernmost winery in the region, about a 15-minute drive from Dunsborough towards Cape Naturaliste. This family-owned boutique vineyard has a history of producing award-winning Chardonnay, though other wines have received accolades as well. Try the Sea Urchin or Bead Sparkling wines, or the single vineyard Eagle Bay. The adjacent Wise Vineyard restaurant is open for breakfast and lunch as well as dinner on Friday and Saturday night. ■TIP→ If you can't bear to leave, a timber chalet called The Barn is available for a minimum stay of two nights. ⊠ *80 Eagle Bay Rd.* ☎ *08/9750–3100 cellar door* ⊕ *www.wisewine.com.au* ⊙ *Daily 11–5* ☞ *Accommodations begin at A$230 per night.*

NEED A BREAK?

Simmo's Ice Creamery and Fun Park. This institution for families and sweet tooths includes up to 60 different flavors of ice cream and sorbet, including apple pie, mascarpone with fig, mango macadamia, and caramel choc fudge. Everything is made fresh daily, including cones, waffles, and sundaes. There's coffee to go, and—for the kids—a great fun park with games including an 18-hole mini-golf course (A$10.50). You can have a picnic in the shady grounds and meet Edward, the ice cream–eating emu. ⊠ *161 Commonage Rd.* ☎ *08/9755-3745* ⊕ *www.simmos.com.au* ⊙ *Daily 10–5.*

BEACHES

FAMILY
Fodor's Choice
★

Meelup Beach. Sheltered from wind, this soft-sand haven makes for a gorgeous coastal escape. Its aquamarine blue waters attract many a visitor. Bring food with you because there are barbecue facilities and picnic tables. **Amenities:** showers; toilets. **Best for:** solitude; swimming; walking. ⊠ *Meelup Beach Rd.*

WHERE TO EAT

$$
MODERN
AUSTRALIAN
Fodor's Choice
★

✕ **Eagle Bay Brewery.** Fun is an essential ingredient in any restaurant, and the family-owned-and-run Eagle Bay Brewery champions it. Grab a six-beer tasting tray so you can sample its many creations, then have a ball seeing which ones best complement your meals you choose. The food is pure gastropub—the proper English gourmet sort—and the U.K.-born chef likes to dip in to the organic kitchen garden for a fresh kick. The wood-fired pizzas are hard to pass up: our pick is the pulled pork, topped with blue cheese and wicked chili caramel. For heartier appetites, beef burger with double smoked ham and cheddar is satisfying, but if you want to fit in dessert, opt for the lighter blackened salmon salad with nectarine slivers and cumin-candied almonds. ⑤ *Average main: A$26* ⊠ *236 Eagle Bay Rd.* ☎ *08/9755–3554* ⊕ *eaglebaybrewing. com.au* ⊙ *No dinner.*

$$$
MODERN
AUSTRALIAN

✕ **The Studio Bistro.** This is fancy pants food at its best: king oyster mushroom with slow-cooked hen's egg and raspberry on a radish salad; local fish paired with sautéed Chinese cabbage and pipis; and milk chocolate ganache textured with pistachio sponge and crystallized pistachios, finished with a dollop of tonka bean ice cream. Salivating yet? Better still is the presentation, perhaps inspired by the art coating the restaurant walls; the bistro hosts regularly changing art exhibitions. Degustations, available for lunch daily and for Friday and Saturday dinners (on request; A$135 with wine, A$95 without) are when the kitchen team really hits its stride, taking you to foodie nirvana with the six-course menu. ⑤ *Average main: A$36* ⊠ *7 Marrinup Dr., Yallingup* ☎ *08/9756–6164* ⊕ *www.thestudiobistro.com.au* ⊙ *Closed Tues.* ⌚ *Reservations essential.*

$$$
AUSTRALIAN

✕ **Wise Vineyard Restaurant.** Verdant bushland, manicured vineyards and expansive views all the way down to Geographe Bay are showstopping features of this modern restaurant. Expect the unexpected and be pleasantly surprised by culinary creations that change with the turning of each season. In keeping, the accent is on the use of fresh, local produce. Look out for house-cured salmon, crunchy edged pork belly with creamed truffle potatoes, or the Amelia Park lamb rack with polenta and pine nuts. The extensive dessert menu is just as appealing, so leave room for sweets. ■TIP➔ On Friday night, pasta and risotto dishes are featured. ⑤ *Average main: A$36* ⌧ *80 Eagle Bay Rd.* ☎ *08/9755–3331* ⊕ *www.wisefood.com* ☺ *No dinner Sun.–Thurs.* ⚐ *Reservations essential.*

WHERE TO STAY

$$
HOTEL
FAMILY
🏨 **Broadwater Beach Resort Busselton.** Sunny public areas and extensive sports facilities make this one of the best accommodation choices on the Geographe Bay beach strip, especially for families with energetic children. **Pros:** walk straight onto beach; apartments ideal for families; numerous leisure facilities. **Cons:** own transport essential; limited dining options nearby; no shopping (except convenience) nearby. ⑤ *Rooms from: A$199* ⌧ *At Bussell Hwy. and Holgate Rd., Busselton* ☎ *08/9754–1633* ⊕ *www.broadwaters.com.au* ⏎ *10 rooms, 15 apartments, 40 villas* ⑩ *No meals.*

$
HOTEL
🏨 **Dunsborough Central Motel.** With a swimming pool, heated spa, and barbecue area, this motel for the dollar-conscious provides convenient, comfortable accommodations with en suites, and proximity to town and the beach. **Pros:** good-value beds for the area; guest laundry; close to shops and dining options; Wi-Fi in all rooms (but there's a charge). **Cons:** not on the beachfront; no on-site restaurant. ⑤ *Rooms from: A$140* ⌧ *50 Dunn Bay Rd.* ☎ *08/9756–7711* ⊕ *www.dunsboroughmotel.com.au* ⏎ *47 rooms* ⑩ *No meals.*

$$$$
RESORT
Fodor's Choice
★
🏨 **Pullman Bunker Bay Resort.** Sprawling down the hillside of the Cape Naturaliste Ridge in bushland, this resort woos with its sexy infinity pool, swanky rooms, and easy access to one of the area's best beaches. **Pros:** large, luxurious rooms; quiet environment; walk straight onto the beach; infinity pool with ocean views; on-site restaurant and bar. **Cons:** limited sea views from rooms; own transport essential; no shopping nearby. ⑤ *Rooms from: A$489* ⌧ *Bunker Bay Rd., off Cape Naturaliste Rd.* ☎ *08/9756–9100* ⊕ *www.accorhotels.com* ⏎ *150 villas* ⑩ *No meals.*

LEEUWIN–NATURALISTE NATIONAL PARK

The northernmost part of the park is 266 km (165 miles) south of Perth, 25 km (16 miles) northwest of Dunsborough.

The 74.5-mile-long coast-hugging Leeuwin-Naturaliste National Park faces the cobalt Indian Ocean with honey-hued sands and people-free swimming spots. It's ribboned by the Cape to Cape Track, a popular 135-km (84-mile) walking trail; the signposted path weaves through tumbles of granite boulders saddling scrubby hills, limestone tracts, and tall forests. Granite in these parts is dated at between 600 and 1,500 million years old, while the limestone ridge the track follows ages only two million years.

GETTING HERE AND AROUND

From Perth take the Kwinana Freeway south; it joins the Forrest Highway and then Highway 1 to Bunbury; switch to Highway 10 via the Busselton bypass to Dunsborough. Because of its patchwork boundaries, Leeuwin-Naturaliste National Park can be accessed at many points along the coast. Caves Road, a tree-lined secondary road from Dunsborough to Augusta, provides the best access—all the side roads to the best coastal spots and many excellent wineries come off this road. Only on a section through the Boranup Karri Forest does Caves Road actually travel through the park for any distance. Marked trails are available from most of the coastal parking lots; they vary from an easy 1-km (½-mile) trail from the car park at Cape Naturaliste Lighthouse to a challenging 20-km (12-mile) full-day hike between Cosy Corner and Skippy Rock, near Augusta.

SAFETY AND PRECAUTIONS

Although the temptation is to climb all over the rocky outcrops, such as Canal Rocks, Sugarloaf Rock, and Skippy Rock, be aware of "king waves" that rise up with little warning from the ocean. Take note of the warning signs; at a few locations life buoys have been stationed for just such incidents.

TIMING

Any time of the year is suitable for visiting the park. You can picnic, go for a scenic drive, explore the caves, and go fishing, surfing, and bush-walking year-round. The summer months are best for swimming and snorkeling, while whale-watching months are usually June-December, starting in the south of the region and heading north as the season progresses.

TOURS

Bushtucker River and Wine Tours. This company runs canoe and cave, and bush-tucker tours daily from Margaret River. The tours give you an opportunity to see inaccessible parts of the Margaret River, Aboriginal sites, and caves while canoeing sections of the river down to the mouth at Surfers Point. A short walk shows you the rich variety of "bush tucker" Aboriginal people would have eaten, while lunch includes a selection of authentic bush-tucker foods. The canoe and cave tours (A$95) take about four hours. Winery and brewery tours (A$100) are also available, departing from Busselton, Dunsborough, or Margaret River (and Bunbury by special request). ✉ *20 Auger Way, Margaret River* ☎ *08/9757–9084, 0419/911–971* ⊕ *www.bushtuckertours.com* 🖾 *From A$95.*

EXPLORING

FAMILY **Cape Leeuwin Lighthouse.** The view from the top of the Cape Leeuwin Lighthouse, the tallest lighthouse on mainland Australia and only a 10-minute drive south of Augusta, allows you to witness the meeting of the Southern and the Indian oceans. In some places this alliance results in giant swells that crash against the rocks; in others, you'll spot whales surfacing (in season: May–September). While the ocean can be chilly, small coves are blessed with calm waters ideal for swimming. The lighthouse precinct is open daily 9–5 (last entry 4:30 pm, includes self-guided audio tour; A$8). Guided tours to the top of the lighthouse (via a lengthy stairway) cost A$20 and run daily every 40 minutes. The last tour is at 4:20 pm. ✉ *Leeuwin Rd., Augusta* ☎ *08/9758–1920* ⊕ *www.margaretriver.com.*

Cape Naturaliste Lighthouse. At the northern end of Leeuwin–Naturaliste National Park stands Cape Naturaliste Lighthouse. A 1½-km-long (1-mile-long) trail leads from Cape Naturaliste to Canal Rocks, passing rugged cliffs, quiet bays, and curving beaches. You can opt for guided tours, on request (various routes and costs); the cape to cave trail wraps in Ngilgi Cave and a stunning stretch of coastline. Migrating whales are often spotted along this stretch, and from the lighthouse. This is also the start of the coast-hugging 135-km (86-mile) Cape-to-Cape Track, for which there are also guided tours (Cape to Cape Tours are recommended for extended hikes; ☎ *0459/452–038,* ⊕ *capetocapetours. com.au).* Four major cave systems are easily accessible within Leeuwin–Naturaliste National Park. ✉ *1267 Cape Naturaliste Rd., Leeuwin–Naturaliste National Park* ☎ *08/9157–7411* ⊕ *www.margaretriver.com/ members/cape-naturaliste-lighthouse* 🎟 *Guided tour A$28* ⊙ *Daily 9–4:30 (first tour at 9:30; last entry at 4:30).*

Jewel Cave. The southernmost cave of the entire underground system, Jewel has one of the longest straw stalactites in any tourist cave in the world—measuring about 16 feet. There's also an interpretive center on-site and a café nearby. ✉ *Caves Rd., Augusta* ☎ *08/9757–7411* ⊕ *www. margaretriver.com/nature-adventure/caves* 🎟 *A$22.50; Lake, Jewel, and Mammoth caves combo A$55* ⊙ *Daily 9:30–3:30, tours every hr on the ½ hr (more frequent during school vacation).*

Lake Cave. Centered around a tranquil, eerie-looking underground lake, Lake Cave is the deepest of all the open caves in the region, and there are tearooms on-site. ✉ *Caves Rd., Forest Grove* ☎ *08/9757–7411* ⊕ *www.margaretriver.com/nature-adventure/caves* 🎟 *A$22.50; Lake, Jewel, and Mammoth caves combo A$55* ⊙ *Daily 9:30–3:30, with tours every hr on the ½ hr.*

Lake Cave Eco Centre. This eco display center at Lake Cave gives a good introduction to the whole cave system and how it was formed. There's a simulated cave tunnel called a cave crawl for kids to safely experience tight spaces. ✉ *Caves Rd., Forest Grove* ☎ *08/9757–7411* ⊕ *www.margaretriver.com/nature-adventure/caves/lake-cave-eco-centre* 🎟 *Free* ⊙ *Daily 9–5.*

FAMILY

Fodor'sChoice
★

Leeuwin-Naturaliste National Park. This national park clutches one of Western Australia's most spectacular coastlines, from Cape Naturaliste by Geographe Bay in the north, to Cape Leeuwin, close to Augusta in the south. The park is not a composite destination, rather a narrow patchwork of protected areas along the coast, intersected by beach access roads and small beachside villages, and traced by the Cape to Cape Track.

The mostly unspoiled coastal vistas are as awe-inspiring as any in the world—on a calm day the view northwards from Yallingup past Sugarloaf Rock towards Cape Naturaliste is nature at its best and it's often sprinkled with surfing dolphins. Farther south, between Cowaramup

Bay and Karridale, scenic lookouts allow you to access coastal cliffs and rocky shoreline that bear the brunt of giant ocean swells generated across thousands of miles of Indian Ocean.

In addition to the scenic attractions of the coast, the park sits over limestone ridges where numerous caves have formed over the millennia, leached out by dripping water. A number of these caves are open to the public year-round, including Lake, Mammoth, Jewel, and Ngilgi. Boranup Karri Forest, near Karridale, creates a contrast to the coast—the distinctive, pale-bark hardwood giants reach 190 feet or more and dominate the hills and valleys of this area. This is the farthest west that karri trees grow in Western Australia, and, interestingly, Boranup is a regrowth forest; it was cut over by loggers more than 100 years ago, and 1961 wildfire destroyed many trees. The most breathtaking stretch lies about 20 minutes' drive south of Margaret River on Caves Road—you'll know it when you hit it because the beauty is unmistakable. ⊠ *Off Caves Rd., Leeuwin-Naturaliste National Park* ⊕ *parks. dpaw.wa.gov.au/park/leeuwin-naturaliste.*

Mammoth Cave. Here you'll find ancient fossil remains of extinct animals and a tannin-stained stream. You can do a self-guided tour or opt for an audio experience, available in English, German, and Mandarin. Wheelchair access is possible to the first chamber. ⊠ *Caves Rd., Witchcliffe* ☎ *08/9757–7411* ⊕ *www.margaretriver.com* 🖃 *Self-guided tours A$22.50* ⊙ *Daily 9–5; last entry at 4.*

Ngilgi Cave. Near Yallingup, this is a main site for adventure caving. In between crawling through tight spots, sliding down smooth rock surfaces and gazing at stalactites, you'll learn about the fascinating history of this special cave, explored by candlelight in the 1900s. Semi-guided cave tours take about one hour, cost A$22.50 and run every half hour from 9:30 to 4. Highly recommended adventure caving tours operate at either 9:30 am or 1:30 pm on various weekdays. Prebooking at least 48 hours in advance is advised. Adventure tours cost from A$60 to A$158, and vary from 45 minutes to four hours in length, depending on the tour. ⊠ *76 Yallingup Caves Rd., Yallingup* ☎ *08/9755–2152* ⊕ *www. margaretriver.com/nature-adventure/caves.*

Vasse Virgin. This surprising artisanal producer smack dab in the middle of vineyards and olive trees is an aromatherapy feast. Inside a converted machinery shed (the soap factory), you'll find a chemical-free range of soaps and body care products hand blended with natural organic ingredients, as well as yummy olives, tapenades, dukkahs, and pestos all without preservatives or artificial additives. This is a place for gastronomes and purists. Sniff, rub, scrub, pamper, and taste to your heart's content! ⊠ *135 Puzey Rd., Wilyabrup* ☎ *08/9755–6111* ⊕ *vassevirgin. com.au* 🖃 *Free* ⊙ *Daily 10–5.*

BEACHES

Fodor's Choice **Smiths Beach.** In a state of extraordinary beaches, this one rates high on
★ the list. Bookended by rounded granite boulders, the caramel-hued sand sinks beneath your feet and the gentle, rolling waves beckon, daring you to cool off in the clean ocean. Edged by native bush, it's secluded and quiet but has plenty of accommodation options nearby, all hidden

Canal Rocks near Yallingup, Leeuwin-Naturaliste National Park, Western Australia

behind sand dunes. **Amenities:** food and drink; parking; toilets. **Best for:** solitude; sunset; swimming; walking. ⊠ *Smiths Beach Rd., Yallingup.*

FAMILY **Yallingup Beach.** Picture perfect views, transparent water, clean, honey-color sand, and a gentle pool of ocean that protects you from the waves beyond: what's not to love about this wide beach, out the front of the hillside town of Yallingup? Parts of the ocean have soft seaweed growing thick on the bottom, making for interesting snorkeling. Surf breaks are near but elsewhere, at Smiths, Three Bears, Super Tubes, Injidup, and Rabbits. Ask the locals for directions as only some are signposted. There are limited food and drink options nearby, so come prepared. **Amenities:** lifeguards; parking; showers; toilets. **Best for:** snorkeling; sunset; swimming; walking. ⊠ *Yallingup Beach Rd., Yallingup.*

WHERE TO EAT

$$ ╳ **Lamont's Smiths Beach.** Just off Smiths Beach is the chic eatery-cum-
AUSTRALIAN delicatessan-cum–cellar door, Lamont's. It does a fantastic break-fast—think cured salmon with scrambled eggs—and is popular for "sundowners," which is the local description for a glass of wine at sunset, often with tapas. Café lunches are lovely and simple, but more refined options are available in the restaurant. From noon till late, dine on sage and prosciutto-wrapped chicken breast with whipped feta; confit duck leg drizzled with vino cotto jus; or grilled local snapper with a side of organic quinoa salad. Executive chef Kate Lamont is CEO and ambassador for Lamont's (check out her cookbooks). You're welcome to pop in for wine tasting at the adjoined wine store and deli without eating at the restaurant. $ *Average main: A$28* ⊠ *Smiths*

Beach Resort, Smiths Beach Rd., Yallingup ☎ *08/9750–1299* ⊕ *www.lamonts.com.au* ⊙ *No dinner Tues. and Wed. in winter.*

MARGARET RIVER

181 km (112 miles) south of Perth, 38 km (24 miles) south of Cape Naturaliste.

The lovely town of Margaret River is considered the center of the South West's wine region, though vineyards and wineries stretch well beyond its pretty surroundings. Nevertheless, there are more than 140 wineries in the region that share the same name (to confuse things further, there's also a river called Margaret River), offering tastings and sales of some of the world's best wines. The region is often compared to France's Bordeaux for its similar climate and soils; it's gaining huge national and international acclaim for its exceptional red and white vintages, the most notable labels touting Chardonnay, Sauvignon Blanc, Shiraz, and Cabernet-Merlot blends.

GETTING HERE AND AROUND

From Perth take Kwinana Freeway south; it joins Forrest Highway and then Highway 1 to Bunbury. Switch to Highway 10 through Busselton and on to Margaret River. Your best option is to rent a car in Perth. Public transport is nonexistent around the area, and using taxis will soon blow the budget. Most accommodations—farmstays, bushland chalets, and boutique hotels—as well as the wineries, the beaches, and other attractions, are outside the town, and you need your own transportation to reach them, though there are also good options in Margaret River itself.

Taxi Contacts Margaret River Taxis. ✉ *Margaret River* ☎ *08/9757-3444.*

SAFETY AND PRECAUTIONS

You are unlikely to have any personal safety concerns in the Margaret River area, except, perhaps, on the roads. Many of the roads leading to the wineries, the beaches, and your accommodation are narrow and winding, though traffic is usually light. Caves Road in particular is known for car accidents.

TIMING

Margaret River is a year-round destination, with each season bringing different pleasures. Summer is busy, especially December and January, as families from Perth arrive during the school holidays. Winter (June–September) brings rain and cooler temperatures, but the paddocks are green and there are not too many days when the rain doesn't ease to showers with lengthy fine breaks in between. If you are traveling from Perth, you can easily spend a week in the region; at the least, try to schedule several days to truly appreciate the area's attractions.

TOURS

Margaret River Visitor Centre is the best starting point if you want to do a tour. They will find the right tour for you, make the booking, and arrange pickup at your accommodation if appropriate (many tours provide this service). Tour operators in the area run tours as diverse as wineries and food tasting, horseback riding, surfing, bushwalks, whale-watching, kayaking, scenic flights, mountain biking, stand-up paddle-boarding, rock climbing, and abseiling.

ESSENTIALS

Visitor Information Margaret River Visitor Centre. ✉ *100 Bussell Hwy.* ☎ *08/9780–5911* ⊕ *www.margaretriver.com.*

EXPLORING

Cape Mentelle. One of the "founding five" wineries in the area, Cape Mentelle planted its first vines in 1970 on a 16-hectare block just outside Margaret River. Today it's still one of the most notable wineries. The adobe-style rammed-earth building and tasting rooms, so typical of the buildings in the Margaret River district, are as handsome and memorable as the wine. The winery produces Chardonnay, Sauvignon Blanc/Semillon, Botrytis Viognier (dessert wine), Cabernet/Merlot, Cabernet Sauvignon, Shiraz, and Zinfandel wines. They also have a one-hour Behind the Scenes tour (A$25), and a degustation tour and tasting (A$80) Monday–Wednesday, and Friday and Saturday at 11:30 am (less frequent May–October). In summer enjoy a balmy evening of food, wine, and film at the winery's outdoor movie nights. ✉ *331 Wallcliffe Rd., 4 km (2 miles) west of Margaret River* ☎ *08/9757–0812 cellar door* ⊕ *www.capementelle.com.au* ☼ *Daily 10–5.*

Fodor's Choice ★ **Cullen Wines.** Biodynamic? Tick. Home-grown produce? Tick. Gorgeous vineyard setting? Tick. Stellar wines. Tick, tick, tick. Cullen isn't the flashiest winery in Margaret River, but its rustic, cottage feel is a strong part of the allure. Family owned since it began, it has long followed an ethos to care for the planet and exist sustainably, and it seems Mother Nature is returning the favor. Fresh, flavorsome ingredients from the organic kitchen garden (visit for free independently, or guided for a fee) give considerable sparkle to the dishes. Think organic beef sirloin with pureed spinach and pumpkin and white bean salad, or seared scallops with fennel and naked citrus salad. There's also a new spiral-form, biodynamic garden to wander through, with excellent information boards. Meanwhile, the cellar door serves crisp, clean, biodynamic wines with a pleasing flavor punch. Make a point of trying the exceptional Diana Madeline Cabernet Merlot. ■ TIP➔ Enjoy lunch outside under the peppermint trees in the sunshine. ✉ *4323 Caves Rd., Wilyabrup* ☎ *08/9755–5277 cellar door, 08/9755–5656 restaurant* ⊕ *www.cullenwines.com.au* ☼ *Daily 10–4:30.*

Hay Shed Hill. Winemaker and owner Michael Kerrigan—once chief winemaker at neighboring Howard Park and Madfish Wines—is on a mission to produce "modern wines from old vines" under several different labels. His hands-on approach, using the best grapes from the 30-year-old plantings, has won show awards and five-star endorsements by wine writers. The tasting room breaks from the usual Margaret River architecture—no rammed earth, timber, and stone here, rather a lovely white-painted clapboard building, polished concrete floors, and pitched ceiling. As the name suggests, the building is the original hay shed on what was a dairy farm. A pleasant café (open 9–3:30) overlooking the vineyards serves casual breakfast and lunch—pizzas, salads, fish, and duck dishes plus well-selected cheese platters.

✉ *511 Harmans Mill Rd., Wilyabrup* ☎ *08/9755–6046* ⊕ *hayshedhill. com.au* ☉ *Daily 9–5; cellar door daily 10–5.*

Howard Park Wines. One of the big pluses of stopping in at WA's largest boutique family-owned winery is that they have a number of labels you can taste, all fixed at different quality and price points. Beneath high ceilings and with views of vineyard rows, compare the Howard Park branded wines against the simpler MadFish and the elegant drops under their super premium offering, Marchand & Burch. Interestingly, feng shui principles were used to design the spacious tastings room. Floor-to-ceiling windows allow in plenty of light as well as giving views over the property, and even the door has specific measurements to allow good luck to flow through. Wines produced under the Howard Park label include Riesling, Chardonnay, Sauvignon Blanc, and Cabernet Sauvignon. ✉ *Miamup Rd., Cowaramup* ☎ *08/9756–5200* ⊕ *www. burchfamilywines.com.au* ☉ *Daily 10–5.*

Fodor's Choice **Leeuwin Estate.** This winery's Art Series wines—especially the Chardon-
★ nay and Cabernet Sauvignon—have a deserved reputation as some of the best in the country, and feature on Australia's "most collected" list. Free tastings and guided tours (A\$25) are conducted on the property daily, introducing you to the extensive art gallery in the cellar. Setting aside the entire afternoon is the way to go at Leeuwin's restaurant, open daily for lunch and for Saturday dinner. ■TIP➔ In January the estate holds it's iconic Leeuwin Concert Series; many international superstars—including Tom Jones, Diana Ross, Sting, and the late Ray Charles—have performed there against a backdrop of tall, floodlit karri trees. ✉ *Stevens Rd., off Gnarawary Rd.* ☎ *08/9759–0000* ⊕ *www. leeuwinestate.com.au* ☉ *Daily 10–5.*

Vasse Felix. Here you'll find a busy cellar door, excellent upstairs restaurant overlooking the vineyards, landscaped grounds, and an art gallery that houses regular exhibitions from the celebrated Holmes à Court Collection, featuring works from prominent Australian artists. In the winery, Virginia Willcock, who was awarded Australian Winemaker of the Year in 2012, is at the helm, perfecting the region's strong suits of Chardonnay and Cabernet Sauvignon, as well as developing clean, flavorsome Sauvignon Blanc, Semillon, and Shiraz. Grapes are plucked from vines planted as far back as 1967, when pioneer Dr. Tom Cullity established Vasse Felix as one of the first commercial wineries in the area. The award-winning, fine-dining restaurant (open noon–3 pm weekdays and 4 pm weekends) has been headed by executive chef Aaron Carr since 1995 and is regarded as one of the region's best. With its feature floating fireplace it's welcoming in winter—book in advance for a table on the outside balcony during summertime. ✉ *Tom Cullity Dr., at Caves Rd., Cowaramup* ☎ *08/9756–5000 cellar door, 08/9756–5050 restaurant* ⊕ *www.vassefelix.com.au* ☉ *Daily 10–5.*

SPORTS AND THE OUTDOORS
HIKING

Marked trails through the Leeuwin-Naturaliste National Park pro-vide many opportunities for hiking through the natural bushland and on coastal walks, with vistas along untouched rugged cliffs, rocky outcrops, and sandy bays. The Cape-to-Cape Track runs 135 km (85 miles) from Cape Naturaliste to Cape Leeuwin, but can be broken into shorter sections. You will find the start points generally at beach-side parking lots. A number of tour companies have guided walks of varying duration, or drop-off and pickup services (as do some accommodations). Canal Rocks to Wyadup is a two-hour return walk from the car park on Canal Rocks Road; a one-hour walk via beach, rocks, and bushland begins at the Leeuwin Waterwheel, near Cape Leeuwin Lighthouse in Augusta; and a four-hour walk with expansive coastal views starts at the Hamelin Bay boat ramp and heads to Cosy Corner.

Away from the coast, a popular short walk is from the historic homestead of Ellensbrook (Ellensbrook Road off Caves Road, 13 km [8 miles] from Margaret River). The walk takes about 40 minutes to the Meekadarabee Falls, known to Aboriginal people as the "bathing place of the moon," and is best in winter and spring.

Brochures and maps on all walk trails in the region are available from the Margaret River Visitor Centre.

WHERE TO EAT

$$
MODERN
AUSTRALIAN
Fodor'sChoice
★

× **Arimia Estate.** The newest kid on the Margaret River block, boutique winery Arimia Estate has a charming, tree-surrounded cellar door and restaurant with a wraparound veranda perfect for lazy afternoons. Make a beeline for the deck, and stay for a light lunch after sampling their award-winning wines. Savor the delicious pork shoulder rillette, before moving on to marinated cuttlefish with saffron dressing, braised goat ragout with gnocchi and chèvre, or a wood-fired pizza. Kids' meals are also available. Family-owned and -run since 1997 (the name Arimia is a combination of the owners' two daughter's names), the wines are described as "avant-garde" and aimed at the refined palette, categorized as Premium, Prestige, and Reserve. If you want to properly settle in, there's a guesthouse on-site. ■**TIP→** Don't be put off by the 2-km (1-mile) dirt road; it's well kept. $ *Average main: A$28* ⊠ *242 Quininup Rd., Yallingup* ☏ *08/9755-2528* ⊕ *www.arimia.com.au* ⊘ *No dinner.*

$$$
MODERN
AUSTRALIAN

× **Flutes Restaurant.** The pastoral setting over the dammed waters of Wilyabrup Brook, encircled by olive groves in the midst of the Brookland Valley Vineyard, is almost as compelling as the cuisine. French bistro fare is mixed with tropical influences from the northern Australian town of Broome. Executive chef and restaurant owner François Morvan makes use of prime local produce, executing a variety of mouthwatering dishes including the ever-popular Chinese-style shredded duck with Esperance scallops and candied chilies. You're unlikely to be disappointed by the "signature trio" of marron, salmon, and ocean-reared barramundi topped with goat cheese macadamia crumble, or the duck confit paired with slow-cooked peach. The beef fillet also goes down well with a glass of one of Brookland Valley's award-winning wines. ■**TIP→** Reserve a seat by the window, or on the wooden deck that juts out over the picturesque dam. $ *Average main: A$42* ⊠ *4070 Caves Rd., 5 km (3 miles) south of Metricup Rd., Wilyabrup* ☏ *08/9755-6250* ⊕ *www.flutes.com.au* ⊘ *No dinner* ⚖ *Reservations essential.*

$$
MODERN
AUSTRALIAN
FAMILY

✕ **Settler's Tavern.** Sometimes you don't need to dab foams or wipe purees across a plate to impress. Sometimes you just have to serve up consistently good, hearty fare that fills the belly and doesn't burn a hole in the pocket. That's the reliable party trick at Settler's Tavern, in the heart of Margaret River township where finding a good value meal can otherwise be challenging. The crowds are testament to the fact that the pub's got the formula right, be it a thick scotch fillet cooked to perfection or a sweet and spicy Malaysian laksa jammed with prawns and herbs. The lack of pretension and warm vibe seal the deal. Expect a lively crowd, and on really busy nights, a wait for food. Families are welcome. ■ TIP➔ Free Wi-Fi is available if you need to check emails over lunch. The kitchen often closes at 8:30 pm so get there earlier, before the live music starts. ⑤ *Average main: A$26* ✉ *114 Bussell Hwy.* ☎ *08/9757–2398* ⊕ *www.settlerstavern.com.*

$$$
CONTEMPORARY

✕ **Voyager Estate.** One of the appellation's grande dames, with its white-washed buildings and expansive, manicured gardens—featuring more than 1,000 roses—has a Wine Room to deliver quaffing experience with a difference. While swilling the estate's repertoire of wines, you'll also learn about the wine-making process in intimate surroundings. Opt for a seated tasting with tutelage from Voyager's team (A$25), or download their iPad app free from iTunes for a tour at your own pace. The tasting counter can take care of anyone looking for a more casual experience, with four wine tasters complimentary. The large restaurant with antique wooden furniture, brass chandeliers, and soaring cathedral ceilings is highly regarded. Dishes are inspired by the wine, naturally, and celebrate local, seasonal ingredients such as green asparagus, snow-white marron meat, ocean-fresh fish and Margaret River reared venison. High tea (A$39) is also served Saturday–Monday at 10:30 am and 3:30 pm. ■ TIP➔ Book an estate tour in the safari-style bus with a private wine tasting (A$35), with lunch (A$85) or add on a six-course, wine-matched menu for A$200 total. Tours run at 11 am daily. ⑤ *Average main: A$38* ✉ *Stevens Rd.* ☎ *08/9757–6354* ⊕ *www.voyagerestate. com.au* �8 *No dinner.*

$$$
AUSTRALIAN
FAMILY

✕ **Watershed.** Families are welcomed at this large vineyard restaurant and café with its impressive modern architecture: big windows, and a wraparound deck offer uninterrupted views. The main restaurant menu changes each season; choices like the local marron, sweet corn puree and roasted leek topped with mojito foam, or the lamb shoulder slow braised in red wine and served with confit garlic, smoked mash potato, and wild rice popcorn are show-stopping dishes. The adjacent café has an enclosed children's playground and caters to children with an appropriate, cheaper menu that still scores on the flavor scale in a casual setting. While the cellar door and restaurant are top-notch in terms of design and construction, it's the seriously award-winning wines that will hold your attention. ■ TIP➔ Try the signature dish—the chef's Taste Plate consisting of all five entrée choices for A$58. You can be really decadent and do the same with the dessert dishes, for A$36. ⑤ *Average main: A$38* ✉ *Cnr Bussell Hwy. at Darch Rd.* ☎ *08/9758–8633* ⊕ *www.watershedwines.com.au* �8 *No dinner.*

$ ✕ **White Elephant Beach Café.** The umbrella-topped tables are hot property
CAFÉ   at this ocean-facing gem, particularly at breakfast time. Precede your
FAMILY   bacon and eggs with a lovely beach stroll or strut along the walking
track, which traces the coast from Prevelly to the White Elephant Beach
Café. Lunch is equally impressive, with crispy baby calamari, Thai beef,
or harissa-spiced chickpea salad. A new glass-fronted addition with
an open fireplace has allowed the café to remain open year-round and
sheltered from winter winds. It's a prime position for watching the wild
ocean, particularly the region's main surf break, Surfers Point. ⑤ *Average main: A$20* ⊠ *Gnarabup Rd., Gnarabup* ☎ *08/9757–1990* ⊕ *www.
whiteelephantcafe.com.au* ⊘ *No dinner.*

WHERE TO STAY

$$$$ ☐ **Cape Lodge.** Regarded as the grandest boutique property in Margaret
RESORT   River wine country, the lodge's five-bedroom residence and 22 luxury
Fodor's Choice   suites deliver in service, space, and views of an 8-acre vineyard that
★   produces Sauvignon Blanc and Shiraz exclusively for guests. **Pros:** large,
luxurious rooms, some with spas; highly regarded restaurant. **Cons:** no
shopping nearby; limited evening dining options nearby; own transport essential. ⑤ *Rooms from: A$449* ⊠ *3341 Caves Rd., Yallingup*
☎ *08/9755–6311* ⊕ *www.capelodge.com.au* ↪ *22 suites, 5-bedroom
residence* ❏*♡❏ Breakfast.*

$$$$ ☐ **Forest Rise Eco Retreat.** King-size beds, fluffy robes, dreamy candlelit
RENTAL   spas with overhead windows looking up to the forest canopy and oh-so-
Fodor's Choice   private verandas make this eco-certified retreat a true sanctuary. **Pros:**
★   totally self-contained; two mountain bikes per chalet; private chef and
massage therapist on request; birds, possums, and kangaroos abound.
Cons: robes cost extra; free Wi-Fi in office area only; minimum stays
enforced; closest convenience store is 10-minute drive away, no shopping or dining nearby; not suitable for children. ⑤ *Rooms from: A$365*
⊠ *231 Yelverton Rd., Yelverton* ☎ *08/9755–7110* ⊕ *www.forestrise.
com.au* ↪ *10 chalets, 1 homestead* ❏*♡❏ No meals.*

$$$ ☐ **Gilgara Retreat.** The romantic rooms in this replica 1870 station home-
B&B/INN   stead have open fireplaces and access to a spacious, communal lounge,
but if you need to spread out, choose the modern, split-level, self-catering
garden suites with dreamy sunken spa baths, atriums, and private sitting areas that overlook the extensive woodland gardens. **Pros:** private
lounge with log fire; free Wi-Fi; continental breakfast included for main
house guests; lots of birds. **Cons:** standard main house rooms are small;
no shopping nearby; minimum stays of two nights; no children allowed.
⑤ *Rooms from: A$230* ⊠ *Caves and Carter Rds.* ☎ *08/9757–2705*
⊕ *www.gilgara.com.au* ↪ *5 rooms, 8 suites* ❏*♡❏ Breakfast.*

$$$$ ☐ **Grand Mercure Basildene Manor.** Each of the rooms in this grand,
RESORT   circa-1912 house has been lovingly refurbished, though history still
looms large in the main homestead, and due to its big-name chain
ownership, there are loads of extras on offer. **Pros:** heritage rooms
with new design; lavish breakfast; quiet location; horse riding, tennis, bushwalking and beach nearby. **Cons:** own transport essential; no
lunch or dinner; dining options 1½ km (1 mile) away. ⑤ *Rooms from:
A$339* ⊠ *187 Wallcliffe Rd.* ☎ *08/9757–3140* ⊕ *www.basildene.com.
au* ↪ *10 rooms, 9 suites* ❏*♡❏ Breakfast.*

$$$ ⛆ **Heritage Trail Lodge.** Nestled among the towering trees, this luxury
HOTEL   retreat is only about ½ km (¼ mile) from Margaret River township
and its spacious suites have hot tubs, king-size beds, and private bal-
conies overlooking the forest. **Pros:** free Wi-Fi; walking trails nearby;
10-minute walk to shops and restaurants; bushland setting. **Cons:**
no leisure facilities; children discouraged; two rooms face highway
meaning traffic noise during day. $ *Rooms from: A$259* ⊠ *31 Bus-
sell Hwy.* ☎ *08/9757–9595* ⊕ *www.heritage-trail-lodge.com.au* ⮧ *10
suites* ⦿ *Breakfast.*

$$ ⛆ **Riverglen Chalets.** In a magical woodland setting, Riverglen Chalets
B&B/INN   consists of modest, self-contained timber cabins interspersed among 7
FAMILY   acres of forest and gardens just a 10-minute stroll along the river into
Margaret River township. **Pros:** secluded chalets; breakfast hampers sup-
plied on request; some outdoor spas; communal games room; wildlife.
Cons: some road noise during the day. $ *Rooms from: A$190* ⊠ *Bussell
Hwy., at Carters Rd.* ☎ *08/9757–2101* ⊕ *www.riverglenchalets.com.au*
⮧ *14 chalets sleeping 2–8 persons* ⦿ *No meals.*

EN
ROUTE

Nannup. Rustic timber cottages and historic buildings characterize the
small town of Nannup, 100 km (62 miles) east of Margaret River.
Several scenic drives wind through the area, including the Blackwood
River Tourist Drive, a 10-km (6-mile) ride along a section of river surrounded by hills with karri and jarrah forests. You can also canoe on the
Blackwood River and wander through the Blythe Gardens. A map of the
buildings used in the 2013 surf movie, *Drift,* is also available from the
Nannup Visitor Centre (*open daily, 10–4;* ⊕ *www.everythingnannup.
com.au*). At various times of the year look out for Nannup's popular
festivals: music, flower and garden, and art and photography. The Festival of Country Gardens displays an artist's palette of WA's spring and
autumn colors. ⊠ *Nannup.*

Holberry House. If you'd like to spend the night, check out Holberry
House, a charming colonial B&B with exposed beams and stone fireplaces, overlooking Blackwood Valley. The gardens are peppered with
statues and sculptures set amongst a woodland of jarrah trees through
which Mount Folly Creek flows. For a small (courtesy) donation of
A$4 at the main gate you can explore the extensive gardens without
overnighting here. ■**TIP**➜ **Ask about the facts and myths surrounding
the legend of the Nannup Tiger.** ⊠ *14 Grange Rd., Nannup* ☎ *08/9756–
1276* ⊕ *www.holberryhouse.com.*

TRAVEL SMART AUSTRALIA

GETTING HERE AND AROUND

Australia is divided into six states and two territories—Northern Territory (NT) and Australian Capital Territory (ACT)—similar to the District of Columbia. Tasmania, the smallest state, is an island off mainland Australia's southeast point.

∎ AIR TRAVEL

Sydney is Australia's main international hub, though it is also easy to get international flights to Melbourne, Brisbane, Cairns, and Perth. You can catch nonstop or one-stop flights to Australia from New York (21 hours via Los Angeles); Chicago (19 hours via Los Angeles); Los Angeles (14 hours nonstop); Vancouver (14 hours nonstop); Toronto (20 hours via Los Angeles or Vancouver); and London (20–24 hours via Hong Kong, Singapore, Kuala Lumpur, Dubai, or Bangkok).

Because Pacific-route flights from the United States to Australia cross the international date line, you lose a day, but regain it on the journey home.

Air Pass Information Qantas Walkabout Air Pass. ☏ 800/227–4500 in U.S., 13–1313 in Australia ⊕ www.qantas.com.au. **Regional Express.** ☏ 13–1713 ⊕ www.rex.com.au. **Visit Australia and New Zealand Pass.** ⊕ www.oneworld.com.

Airline Security Issues Transportation Security Administration. ☏ 866/289–9673 ⊕ www.tsa.gov.

AIRPORTS

Sydney Airport (SYD) is Australia's main air hub and the first port of call for more than half of the country's visitors. Terminal 1 is for all international flights, Qantas and Qantaslink domestic flights operate out of Terminal 3, and Terminal 2 is for all other domestic flights (including Virgin Australia, Tigerair, and Jetstar). A rail link connects the terminals underground, and frequent shuttle buses run between them aboveground. There is

an excellent range of shops and restaurants in the international terminal.

Brisbane International Airport (BNE) is southern Queensland's main airport and rivals Sydney's in quality and services. There are separate domestic and international terminals. Cairns International Airport (CNS), in north Queensland, is the hub for northern Queensland and visits to the Great Barrier Reef.

Melbourne Airport (MEL) is sometimes known as "Tullamarine," after a neighboring suburb. International flights leave from Terminal 2; Qantas and Jetstar use Terminal 1 for their domestic operations. Virgin Australia makes up the bulk of the other domestic flights, which go from Terminal 3. Tigerair flies from Terminal 4.

South Australia's main airport is Adelaide International (ADL). Domestic flights and a few services to nearby Asian cities land at Darwin International Airport (DRW) in the Northern Territory. The hub for the Red Centre is Alice Springs Airport (ASP), which only receives domestic flights. Perth International Airport (PER) is the gateway to Western Australia. International flights operate from Terminal 1; most Qantas and Qantaslink domestic flights leave from Terminal 4. Terminal 2 and 3 host Virgin Australia, Jetstar, Tigerair, Alliance Airlines, and some Qantas regional services.

Airport Information Adelaide Airport. ☏ 08/8308–9211 ⊕ www.adelaideairport.com. au. **Alice Springs Airport.** ☏ 08/8951–1211 ⊕ www.alicespringsairport.com.au. **Brisbane Airport.** ☏ 07/3406–3000 ⊕ www.bne. com.au. **Cairns Airport.** ☏ 07/4080–6703 ⊕ www.cairnsairport.com. **Darwin International Airport.** ☏ 08/8920–1811 ⊕ www. darwinairport.com.au. **Melbourne Airport.** ☏ 03/9297–1600 ⊕ www.melbourneairport. com.au. **Perth Airport.** ☏ 08/9478–8888 ⊕ www.perthairport.com.au. **Sydney Airport.** ☏ 02/9667–9111 ⊕ www.sydneyairport.com.au.

FLIGHTS

TO AUSTRALIA

Qantas is Australia's flagship carrier. It operates direct flights to Sydney from New York, San Francisco, and Los Angeles, and from Los Angeles to Melbourne and Brisbane. There are connecting Qantas flights to many other North American cities, and direct flights from various Australian airports to many Asian and European destinations. It's part of Oneworld Alliance, and has excellent standards of safety and comfort. Qantas flights aren't always the cheapest, but their Walkabout Air Pass includes three stops within Australia for the same price as your ticket from North America.

Jetstar is a low-cost local airline owned by Qantas, and has flights from Sydney, Melbourne, Brisbane, Cairns, Perth, Adelaide, and Darwin to Bali, Japan, New Zealand, Singapore, Thailand, Vietnam, and Honolulu. Virgin Australia and Virgin Samoa fly to Tonga, Samoa, Fiji, Vanuatu, New Zealand, Indonesia, and the Cook Islands, while Virgin Australia-owned budget airline Tigerair Australia flies direct from select cities to Bali and to other Asian destinations through affiliate carriers.

Airline Contacts Air New Zealand. ☎ *1800/262–1234 in U.S., 13–2476 in Australia* ⊕ *www.airnewzealand.com. au.* **British Airways.** ☎ *1800/247–9297 in U.S., 1300/767177 in Australia* ⊕ *www. britishairways.com.* **Cathay Pacific.** ☎ *1800/233–2742 in U.S., 13–1747 in Australia* ⊕ *www.cathaypacific.com.* **Qantas.** ☎ *1800/227–4500 in U.S., 13–1313 in Australia* ⊕ *www.qantas.com.au.* **United.** ☎ *1800/864–8331 in U.S., 13–1777 in Australia* ⊕ *www.united.com.* **Virgin Australia.** ☎ *1855/253–8021 in U.S., 13–6789 in Australia* ⊕ *www.virginaustralia.com.*

WITHIN AUSTRALIA

Australia's large distances mean that flying is usually the locals' favorite way of getting from one city to another. In general, safety standards on domestic flights are high, flights are punctual, and there's plenty of timetable choice. On routes between popular destinations like Sydney, Melbourne, and Brisbane there are often several flights each hour.

Airline Contacts Airnorth. ☎ *1800/627474* ⊕ *www.airnorth.com.au.* **Jetstar.** ☎ *13–1538* ⊕ *www.jetstar.com.* **Qantas.** ☎ *13–1313* ⊕ *www.qantas.com.au.* **Regional Express.** ☎ *13–1713* ⊕ *www.rex.com.au.* **Tigerair.** ☎ *02/8073–3421* ⊕ *www.tigerair.com.*

▌ BOAT TRAVEL

Organized boat tours from the Queensland mainland are the only way to visit the Great Barrier Reef. Cairns is the number-one point of departure, but boats also leave from Mackay, Airlie Beach, Townsville, and Port Douglas. Boats also run between the Whitsunday Islands. The Great Barrier Reef Marine Park Authority website has helpful advice on how to choose a tour operator and lists which companies are ecotourism-certified.

The daily ferries *Spirit of Tasmania I* and *II* take 10 hours to connect Melbourne with Devonport on Tasmania's north coast. Make reservations as early as possible, particularly during the busy December and January school holidays.

Sealink Ferries transport passengers and vehicles between Cape Jervis on the South Australian coastline south of Adelaide, and Penneshaw on Kangaroo Island.

You can find out about ferry and cruise schedules for these and other scenic rides at most state tourism offices and on their websites. All operators accept major credit cards and cash.

Information Great Barrier Reef Marine Park Authority. ☎ *07/4750–0700* ⊕ *www. gbrmpa.gov.au.* **Sealink Ferries.** ☎ *13–1301* ⊕ *www.sealink.com.au.* **Spirit of Tasmania.** ☎ *1800/634906* ⊕ *www.spiritoftasmania.com.au.*

▌ BUS TRAVEL

Bus travel in Australia is comfortable and well organized. Long-distance buses, also called "coaches," have air-conditioning, onboard toilets, reclining seats, Wi-Fi, and even attendants and videos on longer routes. By law, all are required to provide seat belts, and you are required to use them. Smoking is prohibited on all buses.

Australia's national bus network is run by Greyhound Australia (no connection to Greyhound in the United States), which serves far more destinations than any plane or train services. However, Australia is a vast continent, and bus travel here requires plenty of time. The journey from Sydney to Melbourne takes 15 hours, Adelaide to Perth takes 39 hours, and Brisbane to Cairns takes 30 hours. If you plan to visit specific regions, it could be worthwhile considering flying to a major hub, then using buses to explore the region when you get there.

Oz Experience has hop-on, hop-off coach travel and tour packages aimed at budget travelers. Utilizing the Greyhound network, the packages take in both major cities and adventure destinations. Oz has a great selection of routes—you buy a pass, and then have unlimited stopovers along that route, booking each segment by telephone or online as you travel. For example, their Bruce Cobber Pass (A$599) takes you along the coast between Sydney and Cairns, including stops at Byron Bay, Magnetic Island, and the Atherton Tablelands, where you get a day tour.

You can book passes and individual tickets on Greyhound and Oz Experience online through their websites, over the telephone, or in person at their desks in bus terminals.

Bus Information Greyhound Australia.
☎ *1300/473946* ⊕ *www.greyhound.com.au.*
Oz Experience. ☎ *1300/300028* ⊕ *www. ozexperience.com.*

▌ CAR TRAVEL

Endless highways, fabulous scenery, eccentric little towns in the middle of nowhere: Australia is road-trip paradise. Even if you don't have time for major exploring, traveling by car can be a great way to explore a particular region at your own pace. Traffic in city centers can be terrible, so keep the car for the open road.

Driving is generally easy in Australia, once you adjust to traveling on the left side of the road. Road conditions on busy coastal highways usually pose few problems, though remote roads (even big highways) and routes through the desert are often a different story. When you're preparing a driving itinerary, it's vital to bear in mind the huge distances involved and calculate travel time and stopovers accordingly.

Most rental companies in Australia accept driving licenses from other countries, including the United States, provided that the information on the license is clear and in English. Otherwise, an International Driver's Permit is required (but they'll still want to see your regular license, too).

GASOLINE

Gas is known in Australia as "petrol." Self-service petrol stations are plentiful near major cities and in rural towns. In remote regions they can be few and far between, so fill up whenever you can. In really out-of-the-way places, carrying a spare petrol can is a good idea. Smaller petrol stations often close at night and on Sunday, though in major cities and on main highways there are plenty of stations open round the clock.

PARKING

On-street parking is usually plentiful in Australian cities, except in the traffic-heavy CBD (downtown area) of the big capitals. Electronic meters are the norm—you pay in advance, and there's usually a maximum stay, which you should respect, as Australian parking inspectors are very vigilant. Paid parking lots are also common and usually clearly signposted.

Outside the capitals, on-street parking is usually free, as are the lots outside malls and supermarkets.

RENTING A CAR

Australia's cities have good public transport, so there's not much point in renting a car if you're staying in an urban area, especially one popular with tourists. Step outside city limits, and a car is practically a necessity.

Rates for economy cars (a Hyundai Getz, Excel, or Accent or a Nissan Pulsar, for example) with unlimited mileage start at around A$60 a day (plus fees).

Intercity highways are usually in good condition, but more remote roads—even those that look important on maps—can often be unpaved or full of potholes. You can manage short distances on these in a car (for example, an access road to an attraction a few miles from the highway). For longer stretches and any Outback driving, a 4WD is necessary, as insurance generally doesn't cover damage to other types of cars traveling such roads. Only rent a 4WD if you're competent to drive one on tough surfaces like sand and bogs: rescue vehicles take a long time to get to the middle of nowhere.

Rental companies have varying policies and charges for unusual trips, such as lengthy cross-state expeditions around the Top End and Western Australia. Ask about additional mileage, fuel, and insurance charges if you're planning to cover a lot of ground.

Another popular way to see Australia is to rent a camper van (motor home). Nearly all have a toilet, shower, and cooking facilities; utensils and bed linen are usually included, too. Smaller vans for two can be rented for A$50–A$150 a day with unlimited mileage (there's usually a five-day minimum).

In Australia you must be 21 to rent a car, and rates may be higher if you're under 25. There is no upper age limit for rental so long as you have a valid international driver's license. Most companies charge

BUYING A CAR

For road trips longer than a couple of months, renting costs add up, so buying a car or van (and selling it at the end of your trip) might be more economical. Most camper-van agencies have a sales department; Sydney Travellers Car Market and Travellers Autobarn are two reputable agencies that specialize in selling to and rebuying from visitors.

extra for each additional driver. It's compulsory for children to use car seats, so be sure to notify your agency when you book—most charge around A$9 per day for a baby or booster seat, or find them for free as part of certain deals.

Your driver's license may not be recognized outside your home country. You may not be able to rent a car without an International Driving Permit (IDP), which can be used only in conjunction with a valid driver's license and which translates your license into 10 languages. Check the AAA website for more info as well as for IDPs ($15) themselves.

Car Rental Resources American Automobile Association (AAA). ☎ 315/797–5000 ⊕ www. aaa.com. **Australian Automobile Association.** ☎ 02/6247–7311 ⊕ www.aaa.asn.au.

Local Rental Agencies Redspot Car Rentals. ☎ 02/8303–2222 outside Australia, 1300/668810 in Australia ⊕ www.redspot. com.au. **Wicked Campers.** ☎ 1800/246869 in Australia, 07/3217–0100 outside Australia ⊕ www.wickedcampers.com.au.

Major Agencies Alamo. ☎ 1888/233–8749 in U.S. ⊕ www.alamo.com. **Avis.** ☎ 1800/331–1212 in U.S., 136–333 in Australia ⊕ www. avis.com.au. **Budget.** ☎ 800/472–3325 in U.S., 1300/362848 in Australia ⊕ www.budget.com. au. **Hertz.** ☎ 800/654–3001 in U.S., 13–3039 in Australia ⊕ www.hertz.com. **Thrifty.** ☎ 800/847–4389 in U.S., 1300/367227 in Australia ⊕ www.thrifty.com.au.

ROAD CONDITIONS

Except for some expressways in and around the major cities, most highways are two-lane roads with frequent passing lanes but no barrier separating the two directions of traffic. Main roads are usually paved and well maintained, though lanes are narrower than in the United States.

Outside big urban areas roundabouts are far more common than traffic lights—some towns have dozens of them. Remember that when driving on the left you go around a roundabout clockwise and give way to traffic entering from the left and already on the roundabout.

Potential road hazards multiply in rural areas. Driving standards, which are generally high in Australia, become more lax. Road surfaces deteriorate, becoming potholed or uneven. Fine sand sometimes fills the holes, making them hard to see. Windshield cracks caused by small stones are frequent. Flash floods are also common during the summer months in northern Australia. Locals advise never crossing a flooded road. When in doubt, turn back or seek advice from the police before crossing.

Animals—kangaroos and livestock, primarily—are common causes of road accidents in rural Australia, especially at night. If you see an animal near the edge of the road, slow down immediately, as it may just decide to step out in front of you. If it does, hitting the animal is generally preferable to swerving, as you can lose control of your car and roll. However, braking too suddenly into the animal can send it through your windshield. Ideally, you should report any livestock you kill to the nearest ranch, and should check dead kangaroos for joeys (babies carried in their pouches): if you find one, wrap it up and call animal rescue or take it to the nearest vet.

"Road trains" are another Outback hazard: they're truck convoys made of several connected trailers, totaling up to 170 feet. They take a *long* time to brake, so keep your distance and overtake them only with extreme caution.

Outback driving can be exhausting and potentially dangerous. Avoid driving alone, and rest often. Carry plenty of water with you (at least one gallon per person per day)—high temperatures make dehydration a common problem on the road. Don't count on your cell phone working in the middle of nowhere, and if an emergency occurs never leave your vehicle: it's visible, and provides you shelter from the sun and cold. Stick by the side of the road: sooner or later, someone will come along.

ROADSIDE EMERGENCIES

If you have an emergency requiring an ambulance, the fire department, or the police, dial 000.

Many major highways now have telephones for breakdown assistance; you can also use your cell phone if you have one. Otherwise, flag down and ask a passing motorist to call the nearest motoring service organization for you. Most Australian drivers are happy to assist, particularly in country areas.

Each state has its own motoring organization that provides assistance for vehicle breakdowns. When you rent a vehicle, check that you are entitled to assistance from the relevant motoring organization free of charge. A toll-free nationwide number is available for roadside assistance.

Emergency Services Emergency Services.
☏ *000.* **National Roadside Assistance.**
☏ *13-1111.*

RULES OF THE ROAD

Speed limits vary from state to state. As a rough guide, 50–60 kilometers per hour (30–37 mph) is the maximum in populated areas, reduced to 40 kph (25 mph) near schools. On open roads limits range from 100 to 130 kph (62–80 mph). Limits are usually signposted clearly and regularly, and are enforced by police speed checks and—in state capitals—by automatic cameras.

FROM	TO	DISTANCE	MAIN HIGHWAY NAMES
Sydney	Melbourne	873 km (542 miles) /1,043 km (648 miles)	Hume/Princes
Sydney	Brisbane	982 km (610 miles)	Pacific
Brisbane	Cairns	1,699 km (1,056 miles)	Bruce
Melbourne	Adelaide	732 km (455 miles) /912 km (567 miles)	Dukes/Pacific
Adelaide	Perth	2,716 km (1,688 miles)	Eyre and Great Eastern
Adelaide	Alice Springs	1,544 km (959 miles)	Stuart
Alice Springs	Darwin	1,503 km (934 miles)	Stuart
Darwin	Cairns	2,885 km (1,793 miles)	Bruce, Flinders, Barkley, and Stuart

Drunk driving, once a big problem in Australia, is controlled diligently. The legal limit is 0.05% blood-alcohol level, and penalties are so high that many Aussies just don't drink if they're driving. Seat belts are mandatory nationwide. Children must be restrained in a seat appropriate to their size. Car rental agencies can install these for about A$30 per week, with 24 hours' notice. It is illegal to use a mobile-phone handset when driving.

Traffic circles, called "roundabouts," are widely used at intersections; cars that have already entered the circle have the right-of-way. At designated intersections in Melbourne's central business district, you must get into the left lane to make a right-hand turn (called a "hook turn")—this is to facilitate crossing streetcar lines. Watch for the sign "right-hand turn from left lane only." Everywhere, watch for sudden changes in speed limits.

The Australian Automobile Association has a branch in each state, known as the National Roads and Motorists Association (NRMA) in New South Wales and Canberra, the Automobile Association in the Northern Territory (AANT), and the Royal Automobile Club (RAC) in all other states. It's affiliated with AAA worldwide, and has reciprocal services to American members, including emergency road service, road maps, copies of each state and territory's Highway Code, and discounts on car rental and accommodations.

∎ CRUISE SHIP TRAVEL

Coral Princess Cruises runs three- to seven-night cruises along the Great Barrier Reef; its Across the Top trip continues to Darwin. There's also a cruise between Darwin and Broome.

Pacific Dawn, Australia's biggest cruise liner sails various one- and two-week Pacific and New Zealand cruises out of Brisbane, while *Pacific Jewel* runs "Island Hopper" tours and a short Brisbane to Sydney cruise. The *Pacific Pearl* also cruises the Pacific, leaving from Sydney. All three are owned by P&O, known in the rest of the world as Princess Cruises.

Princess Cruises' huge *Sapphire Princess* sails between New Zealand and Australia at the end of its 33-day cruise from Seattle, Washington. The smaller *Dawn Princess* travels between the Australian east coast, New Zealand, and the South Pacific, departing Sydney and Brisbane.

Regent Seven Seas' *Seven Seas Voyager* docks at several points on Australia's east and north coasts; including Sydney, Brisbane, and Darwin; on cruises to Indonesia, Singapore, and Papua New Guinea. Crystal Cruises' Australia and New Zealand tours take in a range of popular destinations on the east coast and Top End, including Melbourne, Sydney, Brisbane, the Great Barrier Reef, Cairns, and Darwin. Some cruises even encompass the beautiful coastlines of Western Australia and Tasmania. Silversea's *Silver Whisper* follows a similar route plan and also encompasses Hong Kong.

Cunard's *Queen Elizabeth* sails from New York and San Francisco to Sydney, and calls at Australian ports on round-the-world cruises, too. So do its *Queen Mary 2* and *Queen Victoria.*

Information Great Southern Rail. ☎ *1800/703357 in Australia, 08/8213–4401 outside Australia ⊕ www.greatsouthernrail. com.au.* **NSW TrainLink.** ☎ *13–2232 ⊕ www.nswtrainlink.info.* **Queensland Rail.** ☎ *1800/872467 in Australia, 07/3606–6630 outside Australia ⊕ www.queenslandrailtravel. com.au.* **Rail Australia.** ☎ *1800/872467 in Australia, 07/3235–1122 outside Australia ⊕ www.railaustralia.com.au.*

▌ TRAIN TRAVEL

Australia has a network of long-distance trains providing first- and economy-class service along the east and south coasts, across the south of the country from Sydney to Perth, and through the middle of the country between Adelaide and Darwin.

Most long-distance trains are operated by various state-government-owned enterprises. The luxurious exceptions to the rule are the *Ghan, Indian Pacific,* and *Overland,* all run by the private company Great Southern Rail. Rail Australia is the umbrella organization for all of these services outside the country.

The state-owned trains are usually punctual and comfortable. Economy class has reclining seats, and on longer routes there are sleeper classes. Second-class sleepers have shared bathrooms and sometimes you share your cabin with strangers, too. In first class you have the cabin to yourself and a small en suite bathroom. Meals are sometimes included. Comfort levels increase in Premium Red Service on the *Overland,* and Gold and Platinum Service on the *Ghan* and *Indian Pacific* and in the *Spirit of Queensland's* RailBed carriages. The high-speed *Tilt Train* is aimed at business travelers and has business-class-style reclining seats.

ESSENTIALS

■ ACCOMMODATIONS

Australia operates a rating system of one to five stars. Five-star hotels include on-site dining options, concierge and valet services, a business center, and, of course, very luxurious rooms. Four stars denote an exceptional property that just doesn't have all the extras needed for five. Three stars means quality fittings and service. Always ask about additional costs when pricing your hotel room.

APARTMENT AND HOUSE RENTALS

Judging from the huge number of short-term rental properties in Australia, many locals prefer doing their own thing to being in a hotel. It's easy for you to do likewise. Serviced apartments and peer-to-peer accommodation options are plentiful in Australia for those who'd rather avoid the big hotel chains and live like the locals instead. Booking agency Move and Stay has an enormous range of properties, usually aimed at executives. Medina has top-end apartments and apart-hotels in all the big cities. Quest owns apartment complexes all around the country. Furnished Properties focuses on the Sydney area and has reasonable rates.

In beach areas, "units" are the thing: they're usually small detached houses or bungalows, often with a communal area with laundry facilities and a swimming pool. Maid service is usually optional here. In summer, units at popular beach resorts are often booked months in advance, so make reservations in plenty of time by searching online for holiday rental agents in the area you plan to visit.

In line with international trends, community marketplace Airbnb has emerged as a popular new type of accommodation in Australia. Register with Airbnb online to browse a variety of rentable rooms, apartments, B&Bs, and holiday houses, often with a much more intimate feel and at

significantly lower prices than traditional establishments. Here you'll also find properties off the beaten track, including farm stays, rain forest retreats, and houseboats. Stays usually involve some degree of interaction with hosts, however some lodgings have complete privacy.

Contacts Adina Apartment Hotels. ☎ 13–8642 ⊕ www.adinahotels.com.au. **Airbnb.** ⊕ www.airbnb.com. **Furnished Properties.** ☎ 02/9518–8828 ⊕ www.furnishedproperties. com.au. **Move and Stay.** ⊕ www.moveandstay. com. **Quest Serviced Apartments.** ☎ 03/9645–8357 outside Australia, 1800/334033 in Australia ⊕ www.questapartments.com.au.

BED-AND-BREAKFASTS

B&Bs are a big deal in Australia, and are popular in both urban and rural areas. The classic Aussie B&B is a family-run affair: expect clean, homey rooms, private bathrooms, and bountiful breakfasts, often showcasing local produce. A room for two usually ranges from A$80 to A$200 a night. The word "boutique" in conjunction with a B&B implies a higher level of luxury—decorative, gastronomic, or both—and facilities, but all at a higher price.

OzBedandBreakfast.com has comprehensive listings that include boutique properties. You'll also find locals offering the "B&B experience" in their homes through Airbnb.

Local tourist-information centers throughout Australia also have lists of B&Bs in their area.

Reservation Services Bed & Breakfast. com. ☎ 512/322–2710 in U.S. ⊕ www. bedandbreakfast.com. **Bed & Breakfast and Farmstay Association of NSW & ACT.** ☎ 1300/888862 ⊕ www. bbfaccommodation.com.au. **Hosted Accommodation Australia.** ☎ 1300/664707 in Australia, 03/9431–5417 outside Australia ⊕ www.australianbedandbreakfast.com. au. **OzBedandBreakfast.com.** ⊕ www. ozbedandbreakfast.com.

HOME AND FARM STAYS

Home and farm stays combine B&B-style accommodation with the chance to join in farm activities or explore the countryside. Some hosts run day trips, as well as horseback riding, hiking, and fishing trips. Accommodations vary from modest shearers' cabins to elegant homesteads; some include breakfast in the room price, others an evening meal. Families are usually welcomed. For two people the cost varies from A$100 to A$250 nightly. *Many of the B&B sites above also have farm-stay listings.*

Reservation Services Australian Farm Stays. ☎ 03/5824–3285 ⊕ *www. australianfarmstay.com.au.*

HOME EXCHANGES

With a direct home exchange, you stay in someone else's home while they stay in yours. Some outfits also deal with vacation homes, so you're not actually staying in someone's full-time residence, just their vacant weekend place.

Although home exchanges aren't a popular choice in Australia, there are still many options available, particularly on the east coast. Most organizations charge a small membership fee for use of their site.

Exchange Clubs HomeExchange. com. ☎ 800/877–8723 in U.S. ⊕ *www. homeexchange.com.* **HomeLink Australia.** ☎ 1800/853535 in Australia, 02/4947–9039 outside Australia ⊕ *www.homelink.com.au.* **Intervac.** ⊕ *intervac-homeexchange.com.*

▌ COMMUNICATIONS

INTERNET

Internet access is widely available to travelers in Australia. Top-end hotels always have some sort of in-room access for laptop users—usually Wi-Fi, otherwise there are data ports. Note that in some establishments, you are charged a hefty premium for using this service.

Australia's main telephone network, Telstra, has wireless hotspots all over the country, and 3G/4G coverage for smartphones

and tablets is reliable in most populated areas. Fast-food restaurants like McDonald's, as well as many cafés, offer free Wi-Fi for customers. Alternatively, you can buy prepaid data packages for your smartphone or tablet at news agencies and convenience stores, or purchase a prepaid mobile broadband USB or dongle from Telstra, Optus, Virgin, or Vodafone retailers. These services start at around A$40 for several gigabytes of data and act as a "portable modem," giving you Internet access wherever you go. In many cases, this may be more cost effective than using hotel and Internet cafés. However, make sure to take note of the expiry window for your data—most passes last only 30 days.

Contacts Telstra. ☎ 13–2200 ⊕ *www.telstra. com.au.*

PHONES

The country code for Australia is 61. To call Australia from the United States, dial the international access code (011), followed by the country code (61), the area or city code without the initial zero (e.g., 2), and the eight-digit phone number.

CALLING WITHIN AUSTRALIA

Australia's phone system is efficient and reliable. You can make local and long-distance calls from your hotel—usually with a surcharge—or from any public phone. There are usually public phones in shopping areas, at train stations, and outside rural post offices. You can use coins or phone cards in most public phones; credit-card phones are common at airports.

All regular telephone numbers in Australia have eight digits. There are five area codes: 02 (for New South Wales and Australian Capital Territory), 03 (Victoria and Tasmania), 04 (for cell phones), 07 (for Queensland), and 08 (for Western Australia, South Australia, and Northern Territory). Toll-free numbers begin with 1800, and numbers starting with 13 or 1300 are charged at local rates anywhere in the country.

Calls within the same area code are charged as local. Long-distance call rates vary by distance, and are timed. When you're calling long distance within Australia, remember to include the area code, even when you're calling from a number with the same area code. For example, when calling Canberra from Sydney, both of which have an 02 prefix, you still need to include the area code when you dial.

Directory Assistance Local Directory Assistance. ☎ *1223.*

CALLING OUTSIDE AUSTRALIA
To call overseas from Australia, dial 0011, then the country code and the number. Kiosks and groceries in major cities sell international calling cards. You can also use credit cards on public phones.

The country code for the United States is 1.

You can use AT&T, Sprint, and MCI services from Australian phones, though some pay phones require you to put coins in to make the call. Using a prepaid calling card is generally cheaper, and Skype calls can be made for free with a steady Internet connection.

Access Codes AT&T Direct. ☎ *1800/881011 from Telstra phones, 1800/551155 from Optus phones.* **MCI WorldPhone.** ☎ *1800/881100 from Telstra phones, 1800/551111 from Optus phones.* **Skype.** ⊕ *www.skype.com.*

Useful Numbers International Directory Assistance. ☎ *1225.*

CALLING CARDS
It's worth buying a phone card in Australia even if you plan to make just a few calls.

Telstra, Australia's main telephone company, has a prepaid phonecard you can use for local, long-distance, or international calls from public pay phones. There are many other calling cards in Australia as well, often with better rates than Telstra's, and many can now be used from your mobile phone. The best way to find one is to ask in a convenience store or newsagent's: they usually have a selection on hand, and you can compare rates to the country you're calling to. Access codes can also be purchased online.

Contacts Onesuite.com. ☎ *866/417-8483 in U.S.* ⊕ *www.onesuite.com.* **Phone Cards Selector Australia.** ☎ *1800/671823* ⊕ *www.phonecardselector.com.au.* **Telstra.** ☎ *13-2200* ⊕ *www.telstra.com.au.*

MOBILE PHONES
Unlike in previous decades, most modern mobile phones (particularly smartphones) have advanced, multiband technology, which means they can be used in virtually any country where mobile reception is available. However, do your research before you travel, as most providers charge hefty fees for standard international roaming. The best option is to contact your provider to see if they have special international roaming and data passes, which significantly reduce these costs. Be aware that you normally pay for incoming calls as well as outgoing calls, so when overseas, text messaging is usually much more economical. The other roaming expense to watch out for is data usage, which can be as much as several dollars to look at one Web page on your smart phone. To avoid exorbitant charges, keep data roaming switched off on your phone while overseas, and access local Wi-Fi spots instead.

If you just want to make local calls, consider buying a new SIM card (your provider may have to unlock your phone to use a different SIM card) and a prepaid service plan from a local provider (such as Telstra, Optus, Vodafone, or Virgin Mobile). New SIMs are usually inexpensive, and you'll then have a local number and can make local calls at local rates. Mobile data packages are also available. If your trip is extensive, you could also simply buy or rent a cell phone in your destination, as the initial cost will be offset over time.

Alternately, save on call and text costs by utilizing one of the many free instant messaging services now available on smart phones and tablets (such as WhatsApp, Viber, and Facebook's Messenger app). They'll deliver instant messages to your contacts anywhere in the world, wherever you have Internet access.

Nearly all Australian mobile phones use the GSM network. If you have an unlocked phone and intend to make calls to Australian numbers, it makes sense to buy a prepaid Australian SIM card on arrival—rates will be much better than using your U.S. network. Alternatively, you can rent a phone or a SIM card from companies like Vodafone. Rates start at A$5 per day for a handset and A$1 a day for a SIM. You can also buy a cheap, pay-as-you-go handset from Telstra, Virgin Mobile, or Optus. Cell-phone stores are abundant, and staff are used to assessing tourists' needs.

Contacts Cellular Abroad. ☎ 800/287–5072 in U.S. ⊕ www.cellularabroad.com. **Mobal.** ☎ 888/888–9162 in U.S. ⊕ www.mobal.com. **Optus.** ⊕ www.optus.com.au. **Virgin Mobile.** ☎ 1300/555100 ⊕ www.virginmobile.com.au. **Vodafone.** ☎ 1300/650410 ⊕ www.vodafone.com.au.

▌ CUSTOMS AND DUTIES

Australian customs regulations are unlike any other. As an island long isolated from the rest of the world, Australia is free from many pests and diseases endemic in other places, and it wants to stay that

way. Customs procedures are very thorough, and it can take up to an hour to clear them.

All animals are subject to quarantine. Many foodstuffs and natural products are forbidden, including meat, dairy products, fresh fruit and vegetables, and all food served on aircraft. Most canned or preserved foods may be imported, but you have to declare them on your customs statement and have them inspected, along with wooden artifacts and seeds.

Airport sniffer dogs patrol arrivals areas, and even an innocent dried flower forgotten between the pages of a book could cause problems. If in doubt, declare something—the worst-case scenario is that it will be taken from you, without a fine.

Otherwise, nonresidents over 18 may bring in 50 cigarettes (or 50 grams of cigars or tobacco) and 2¼ liters of alcohol. Adults can bring in other taxable goods (that is, luxury items like perfume and jewelry) to the value of A$900.

Information Australian Customs and Border Protection. ⊕ www.border.gov.au. **Department of Agriculture.** ☎ 1800/020504 ⊕ www.daff.gov.au.

U.S. Information U.S. Customs and Border Protection. ☎ 877/CBP–5511 ⊕ www.cbp.gov.

▌ EATING OUT

Fresh ingredients, friendly service, innovative flavor combinations, and great value for your money mean that eating out Down Under is usually a pleasant experience.

Australia's British heritage is evident in the hearty food served in pubs, roadhouses, and country hotels. It all seems to taste much better than food in Britain, though. Roast meat and potatoes; fish-and-chips; pasties and pies swimming in gravy; flaky sausage rolls; sticky teacakes and fluffy scones—all are cheap and tasty counter staples and give the big fast-food franchises a serious run for their money.

MEALS AND MEALTIMES

Australians eat relatively early. Breakfast is typically between 7 and 10, and eating it out (usually at a café) is popular. Options range from toast or cereal through fruit and yogurt and muffins, pastries, and hotcakes to a full fry-up—eggs, bacon, sausages, baked beans, hash browns, tomatoes, and mushrooms. Morning coffee and afternoon tea are popular in-between meals, and many cafés serve late or all-day breakfast and brunch on weekends.

For most locals, lunch is usually lighter than dinner: a salad or a sandwich, say, usually between 11:30 am and 2:30 pm. Dinner is the main meal and begins around 6:30. In the cities, dining options are available outside these hours, but the choices are far more restricted in the countryside and smaller towns, where even takeaways can close at 8:30 pm.

Unless otherwise noted, the restaurants listed in this guide are open daily for lunch and dinner.

PAYING

At most restaurants you ask for the bill at the end of the meal. At sandwich bars, burger joints, takeaways, and some cafés, you pay up front. Visa, MasterCard, and American Express are widely accepted in all but the simplest eateries.

RESERVATIONS AND DRESS

Regardless of where you are, it's a good idea to make a reservation if you can. In some places (Sydney, for example) it's expected. We only mention them specifically when reservations are essential (there's no other way you'll ever get a table) or when they are not accepted. For popular restaurants, book as far ahead as you can (often 30 days), and reconfirm as soon as you arrive. (Large parties should always call ahead to check the reservations policy.) We mention dress only when men are required to wear a jacket or a jacket and tie.

▌ELECTRICITY

The electrical current in Australia is 240 volts, 50 cycles alternating current (AC), so most American appliances can't be used without a transformer. Wall outlets take slanted three-prong plugs and plugs with two flat prongs set in a V.

Consider making a small investment in a universal adapter, which has several types of plugs in one lightweight, compact unit. Most laptops and mobile-phone chargers are dual voltage (i.e., they operate equally well on 110 and 220 volts), so require only an adapter. These days the same is true of small appliances such as hair dryers. Always check labels and manufacturer instructions to be sure. Don't use 110-volt outlets marked "for shavers only" for high-wattage appliances such as hair dryers. Many hotels can supply you with an adapter upon request.

▌HEALTH

The most common types of illnesses are caused by contaminated food and water. Mild cases of traveler's diarrhea may respond to Imodium (known generically as loperamide) or Pepto-Bismol. Be sure to drink plenty of fluids; if you can't keep fluids down, seek medical help immediately.

Infectious diseases can be airborne or passed via mosquitoes and ticks and through direct or indirect physical contact with animals or people. Some, including Norwalk-like viruses that affect your digestive tract, can be passed along through contaminated food. Speak with your physician and/or check the CDC or World Health Organization websites for health alerts, particularly if you're pregnant, traveling with children, or have a chronic illness.

SHOTS AND MEDICATIONS

Unless you're arriving from an area that has been infected with yellow fever, typhoid, or cholera, you don't need to get any shots or carry medical certificates to enter Australia.

Australia is relatively free from diseases prevalent in many countries. In the far north there have been occasional localized outbreaks of dengue and Ross River fever—just take the usual precautions against mosquito bites (cover up your arms and legs and use ample repellent), and you should be fine.

Familiar brands of nonprescription medications are available in pharmacies. Note that Tylenol is usually called paracetamol in Australia.

SPECIFIC ISSUES IN AUSTRALIA

Australian health care is excellent, with highly trained medical professionals and well-equipped hospitals. Hygiene standards are also high and well monitored, so you can drink tap water and eat fresh produce without worrying. You may take a four weeks' supply of prescribed medication into Australia (more with a doctor's certificate)—if you run out, pharmacies require a prescription from an Australian doctor. The quickest way to find one is to ask your hotel or look under "M" (for Medical Practitioner) in the Yellow Pages.

Sunburn and sunstroke are the greatest health hazards when visiting Australia. Remember that there's a big hole in the ozone layer over Australia, so even on cloudy days the rays of light coming through are harmful. Stay out of the sun in the middle of the day (the hottest hours are generally 11 am–2 pm) and, regardless of whether you normally burn, follow the locals' example and slather on the sunscreen. Protect your eyes with good-quality sunglasses, and try to cover up with a long-sleeve shirt, a hat, and pants or a beach wrap whenever possible. Keep in mind that you'll burn more easily at higher altitudes and in the water.

Dehydration is another concern, especially in the Outback. It's easy to avoid: carry plenty of water and drink it often.

No rural scene is complete without bush flies, a major annoyance. These tiny pests, found throughout Australia, are especially attracted to the eyes and mouth in search of the fluids that are secreted there. Some travelers resort to wearing a face net, which can be suspended from a hat with a drawstring device.

Some of the world's deadliest creatures call Australia home. The chances of running into one are low, particularly in urban areas, but wherever you go, pay close heed to any warnings given by hotel staff, tour operators, lifeguards, or locals in general. The Outback has snakes and spiders, while on the coast there's everything from sharks to octopi, stonefish, and jellyfish. In northern Australia, rivers, lakes, billabongs, and even flooded streams and creeks are home to estuarine crocodiles. The best advice is to always be cautious, and double-check the situation at each stop with the appropriate authority.

Australian coastal waters are also home to strong currents known as "rips." Pay close attention to the flags raised on beaches, and only swim in areas patrolled by lifeguards. If you get caught in a rip, the standard advice is never to swim against it, as you rapidly become exhausted. Instead, try to relax and float parallel to the shore: eventually the current will subside and you will be able to swim back to the shore, albeit farther down the coast.

▌ HOLIDAYS

New Year's Day; Australia Day, January 26; **Good Friday; Easter Monday; Anzac Day,** April 25; **Christmas,** December 25; **Boxing Day,** December 26. There are also several state- and territory-specific public holidays.

▌ MAIL

All regular mail services are run by the efficient Australia Post, which has offices all over the country. Post offices are usually open only during business hours weekdays, but stamps are available from newsagents at other times. Postboxes for regular mail in Australia are usually bright red; express postboxes are yellow. Postage rates are A0.70¢ for domestic letters and A$2.75 per 50-gram (28.35 grams = 1 ounce) air-mail letter or postcard. Allow at least a week for letters and postcards to arrive.

Contact Australia Post. ☎ 13–7678 ⊕ www. auspost.com.au.

▮ MONEY

The most expensive part of your trip to Australia will probably be getting there. Australian hotels are generally cheaper than similar establishments in North America, as is food.

Australians use debit cards or PayPass wherever possible to pay for things—you can use your credit card, or pay cash, always in Australian dollars. ATMs are ubiquitous; it's very hard to change trav-eler's checks.

Prices for goods and services can be vola-tile at times. A 10% Goods and Services Tax (or GST—similar to V.A.T. in other countries) applies to most activities and goods, though some unprocessed foods are exempt.

▮TIP→ Banks never have every foreign currency on hand, and it may take as long as a week to order. If you're planning to exchange funds before leaving home, don't wait until the last minute.

ATMS AND BANKS

Your own bank probably charges a fee for using ATMs abroad; the foreign bank you use may also charge a fee. Nevertheless, you usually get a better rate of exchange at an ATM than you do at a currency-exchange office or even when changing money in a bank. And extracting funds as you need them is a safer option than carrying around a large amount of cash.

▮TIP→ PIN numbers with more than four digits are not recognized at ATMs in many countries. If yours has five or more, remember to change it before you leave.

For most travelers to Australia, ATMs are the easiest—and often cheapest—way to obtain Australia dollars. Australia's big-gest banks are Westpac, ANZ, the Com-monwealth Bank of Australia, and the National Australia Bank. Their ATMs all accept Cirrus and Plus cards. Smaller state-based banks are also common, but some may not accept foreign cards. Major cities often have branches of international banks like Citibank or HSBC.

Before traveling, check if your bank has an agreement with any Australian banks for reduced ATM fees. For example, Bank of America customers can use Westpac ATMs to withdraw cash without incur-ring a fee.

CREDIT CARDS

It's a good idea to inform your credit-card company before you travel, especially if you're going abroad and don't travel internationally often. Otherwise, the credit-card company might put a hold on your card owing to unusual activity—not a good thing halfway through your trip. Record all your credit-card numbers— as well as the phone numbers to call if your cards are lost or stolen—in a safe place, so you're prepared should some-thing go wrong. Both MasterCard and Visa have general numbers you can call (collect if you're abroad) if your card is lost, but you're better off calling the num-ber of your issuing bank, since Master-Card and Visa usually just transfer you to your bank; your bank's number is usually printed on your card.

If you plan to use your credit card for cash advances, you'll need to apply for a PIN at least two weeks before your trip. Although it's usually cheaper (and safer) to use a credit card abroad for large pur-chases (so you can cancel payments or be reimbursed if there's a problem), note that some credit-card companies *and* the banks that issue them add substantial percentages to all foreign transactions, whether they're in a foreign currency or not. Check on these fees before leaving home, so there won't be any surprises when you get the bill.

■TIP➔ Before you charge something, ask the merchant whether he or she plans to do a dynamic currency conversion (DCC). In such a transaction the credit-card processor (shop, restaurant, or hotel, not Visa or MasterCard) converts the currency and charges you in dollars. In most cases you'll pay the merchant a 3% fee for this service in addition to any credit-card company and issuing-bank foreign-transaction surcharges.

Dynamic currency conversion programs are becoming increasingly widespread. Merchants who participate in them are supposed to ask whether you want to be charged in dollars or the local currency, but they don't always do so. And even if they do offer you a choice, they may well avoid mentioning the additional surcharges. The good news is that you *do* have a choice. And if this practice really gets your goat, you can avoid it entirely thanks to American Express; with its cards, DCC simply isn't an option.

Most Australian establishments take credit cards: Visa and MasterCard are the most widely accepted, American Express and Diners Club aren't always accepted outside the cities. Just in case, bring enough cash to cover your expenses if you're visiting a national park or a remote area.

Reporting Lost Cards American Express.
☎ *800/992–3404 in U.S., 336/393–1111 collect from abroad, 1300/132639 in Australia* ⊕ *www.americanexpress.com.* **Diners Club.**
☎ *800/234–6377 in the U.S., 303/799–1504 collect from abroad, 1300/360060 in Australia* ⊕ *www.dinersclub.com.* **MasterCard.**
☎ *800/627–8372 in U.S., 636/722–7111 collect from abroad, 1800/120113 in Australia* ⊕ *www.mastercard.com.* **Visa.** ☎ *800/847–2911 in U.S., 303/967–1090 collect from abroad, 1800/450346 in Australia* ⊕ *www.visa.com.*

CURRENCY AND EXCHANGE

Australia has its own dollar—assume all prices you see in Australia are quoted in Australian dollars. The currency operates on a decimal system, with the dollar (A$) as the basic unit and 100 cents (¢) equaling A$1. Bills, differentiated by color and size, come in A$100, A$50, A$20, A$10, and A$5 denominations, and are made of plastic rather than paper—you can even take them swimming with you. Coins are minted in A$2, A$1, A0.50¢, A0.20¢, A0.10¢, and A0.05¢ denominations.

At this writing, the exchange rate was about A$1.34 to the U.S. dollar.

■TIP➔ Even if a currency-exchange booth has a sign promising no commission, rest assured that there's some kind of huge, hidden fee. (Oh . . . that's right. The sign didn't say no fee.) And as for rates, you're almost always better off getting foreign currency at an ATM or exchanging money at a bank.

▌ PACKING

If Crocodile Dundee is your idea of an Aussie style icon, think again: Melburnians and Sydneysiders are as fashion-conscious as New Yorkers. In the big cities, slop around in shorts and you might as well wear an "I'm a tourist" badge. Instead, pack nicer jeans, Capri pants, skirts, or dress shorts for urban sightseeing. A jacket and tie or posh dress are only necessary if you plan on some seriously fine dining.

Things are a bit different out of town. No Aussie would be seen dead on the beach without their "thongs," as flip-flops are confusingly called here. Wherever you are, your accessories of choice are high-quality sunglasses and a hat with a brim—the sun is strong *and* dangerous. Carry insect repellent and avoid lotions or perfume in the tropics, as they attract mosquitoes and other insects.

A light sweater or jacket will keep you comfy in autumn, but winter in the southern states demands a heavier coat—ideally a raincoat with a zip-out wool lining. You should pack sturdy walking boots if you're planning any bushwalking, otherwise sneakers or flats are fine.

Australian pharmacies stock all the usual hygiene products (including tampons and condoms) and toiletries, plus a whole lot of fabulous local brands often not available overseas. There's also a mind-boggling range of sunscreens and insect repellents, so have no qualms about bringing everything in travel-size bottles and stocking up when you arrive. Oral contraceptive pills are usually prescription-only, though emergency contraceptive pills are available over the counter. Grocery stores and supermarkets frown on your using too many plastic bags—carry a foldable canvas tote or reusable shopping bag, and you'll blend in perfectly.

▌ PASSPORTS AND VISAS

To enter Australia for up to 90 days you need a valid passport and a visa (New Zealand nationals are the exception). These days, instead of a visa label or stamp in your passport, citizens of the United States (and many other countries) can get an Electronic Travel Authority (ETA). This is an electronically stored travel permit. It saves you time both when you apply—the process is all online—and when you arrive in Australia.

To obtain an ETA for Australia you must: (1) hold an ETA-eligible passport; (2) be visiting Australia for tourism, family, or business; (3) stay less than three months; (4) be in good health; and (5) have no criminal convictions. The Visitor ETA allows you as many visits of up to 90 days as you like within a 12-month period, but remember that no work in the country is allowed. If you're visiting Australia on business, a Short Validity Business ETA might be more appropriate. Technically, both are free of charge, but you need to pay a $A20 service charge by credit card. Children traveling on a parent's passport also need an ETA. You can apply for the

ETA yourself or your travel agent can do it for you.

If you don't meet the ETA requirements or need a different kind of visa, you should contact your nearest Australian diplomatic office well in advance of your trip, as processing other visas takes time. Equally, if you plan to stay longer than three months you must obtain a paper visa (there's a A$135 fee). If you travel to Australia on an under-three-month ETA and later decide to extend your visit, then you must apply for a visa at the nearest Australian Immigration regional office (there's an up-to A$340 fee).

At present, Australia doesn't require a notarized letter of permission if only one parent is traveling with a child, but it's always best to err on the side of caution and take along such a letter if you can.

▌ TAXES

Everyone leaving Australia pays a A$55 departure tax, euphemistically known as a Passenger Movement Charge. It's included in your airline ticket price. There's also a 10% V.A.T. equivalent known as Goods and Services Tax (GST), which is included in displayed prices. There is a GST refund for visitors on purchases totaling more than A$300 made in one store. You need to keep the receipts for these and present them at the Australian Customs Services booths that are after passport control in international airports. The tax is refunded to a credit card, even if you paid cash for the purchases. Allow an extra 30 minutes for this process.

▌ TIME

Without daylight saving time, Sydney is 14 hours ahead of New York and Toronto; 15 hours ahead of Chicago and Dallas; and 17 hours ahead of Los Angeles.

Australia has three major time zones. Eastern Standard Time (EST) applies in Tasmania, Victoria, New South Wales, and Queensland; Central Standard Time applies in South Australia and Northern Territory; and Western Standard Time applies in Western Australia. Central Standard Time is ½ hour behind EST, and Western Standard Time is 2 hours behind EST.

Within the EST zone, each state chooses a slightly different date on which to commence or end daylight saving—except for Queensland, where the powerful farm lobby has prevented the state from introducing daylight saving at all, since it would make the cows wake up an hour earlier. Western Australia and Northern Territory also decline to recognize daylight saving, which means that at certain times of the year Australia can have as many as six different time zones.

▌ TOURS

ABORIGINAL ART

Aboriginal Travel. This agency has several Aboriginal art tours, including a five-day collectors tour and shorter rock-art tours. ☎ *08/8234–8324* ⊕ *www.aboriginaltravel.com* ✉ *From A$69.*

Adventure Tours Australia. This company runs a host of both long and short trips, many of which are Aboriginal-culture centric, particularly the three-day Rock the Centre tour of Uluru and surroundings. ☎ *1300/654604 in Australia, 03/8102–7800 outside Australia* ⊕ *www.adventuretours.com.au* ✉ *From A$110.*

Palya Art Tours. Pilot and art lover Helen Read flies you and guides you on Palya Art Tours' small-group trips through remote indigenous communities in northwestern Australia. ⊕ *www.palya.com.au* ✉ *From $8800.*

BIKING

AllTrails. Discover Australia's hidden gems and untouched terrain with AllTrails' small-group and self-guided cycling tours throughout the country. ☎ *03/9645–3355* ⊕ *www.alltrails.com.au* ✉ *From A$450.*

Remote Outback Cycling Tours. Catering to those with a thirst for adventure, ROC runs cycling, bus, and 4WD tours through the Australian Outback, with camping and hiking along the way. ☎ *0418/633–106* ⊕ *www.remoteoutbackcycletours.com.au* ✉ *From A$800.*

BIRD-WATCHING

Birdwatch Australia. Led by expert birders, this company tailors individual and small-group guided birdwatching and nature tours throughout Australia. ☎ *02/4422–0616* ⊕ *www.birdwatch-australia.com.au* ✉ *From A$125.*

Follow That Bird. This Sydney-based company runs a variety of short birding trips, private included, in southeastern Australia. ✉ *3/59 Central Rd., Sydney* ☎ *02/9973–1865* ⊕ *www.followthatbird.com.au* ✉ *From A$135.*

Kimberley Birdwatching. Join leading Australian ornithologists for intimate bird-watching tours in the Kimberley and Northern Australia, with camping, boating, and farm-stay options. ✉ *Broome* ☎ *08/9192–1246, 0429/706–800 mobile* ⊕ *www.kimberleybirdwatching.com.au* ✉ *From A$90.*

CULTURE

National Geographic Expeditions. Local experts lead National Geographic's extensive Australia expeditions, which take in the Great Barrier Reef and Uluru, but that knowledge doesn't come cheap, nor does the private air transport they use. ☎ *888/966–8687 in U.S.* ⊕ *www.nationalgeographicexpeditions.com* ✉ *From $7,990.*

SEIT Outback Australia. Join SEIT to experience small-group tours and workshops in Central Australia, working in partnership with Aboriginal communities and operators. ☎ *08/8956–3156* ⊕ *www.seitoutbackaustralia.com.au* ✉ *From A$92.*

Smithsonian Journeys. Learning is the focus of Smithsonian Journeys' small-group tours, led by university professors. Their 22-day Splendors of Australia and New Zealand tour covers the best of Australia—and much of New

Zealand, too. ☎ *855/338–8687* ⊕ *www. smithsonianjourneys.org* ✉ *From $9057.*

DIVING

Daintree Air Services. Local flightseeing company Daintree Air Services' Ultimate Dive package includes 18 dives in nine days. The Great Barrier Reef, Coral Sea, and a wreck dive are included. ☎ *1800/246206 in Australia, 07/4034–9300 outside Australia* ⊕ *www. daintreeair.com.au* ✉ *From A$160.*

Diversion Dive Travel. Working with dive operators around Australia, Diversion connects you with Australia's diving hotspots including the Great Barrier Reef, Christmas Island, and the south and west Australian coasts. ☎ *1800/607913 within Australia, 07/4039–0200 outside Australia* ⊕ *www.diversiondivetravel.com.au* ✉ *From A$630.*

ECO-TOURS AND SAFARIS

Northern Experience Eco Tours. Experience the beauty of North Queensland's World Heritage-listed Wet Tropics Rain forests and the Atherton Tablelands with this family-owned, eco-tour operator. Trips include swimming in waterfalls, a lake cruise, visiting national parks, Aboriginal Dreamtime education and stories, as well as plentiful encounters with local flora and fauna. ☎ *07/4058–0268* ⊕ *www. northernexperience.com.au* ✉ *From A$125.*

Sacred Earth Safaris. This family-operated tour company specializes in 4WD tours through remote and Top End Australia, including the Kakadu and Kimberley frontiers, the Nullabor Plain, the Flinders Ranges, Kangaroo Island, and Pilbara. ☎ *0415/692–855* ⊕ *www. sacredearthsafaris.com.au* ✉ *From A$645.*

Tread Lightly Eco Tours. This Advanced Eco-tourism-certified operator runs guided bushwalking, 4WD, nighttime, and glowworm tours, among others, through the Blue Mountains National Park, west of Sydney. ☎ *0414/976–752* ⊕ *www. treadlightly.com.au* ✉ *From A$65.*

Wayoutback Australian Safaris. This tour company employs certified eco-tour operators who run camping and accommodated safaris, as well as Desert Walks, throughout Australia, with a strong focus on Aboriginal culture. ☎ *1300/551510 in Australia, 08/8952–4324 outside Australia* ⊕ *www.wayoutback.com.au* ✉ *From A$375.*

FOOD AND WINE

Adelaide's Top Food and Wine Tours. Eat and drink your way around the famous vineyards and providores of The Barossa Valley, McLaren Vale, Clare Valley, and Adelaide Hills on these personalized, small-group tours. ☎ *08/8386–0888* ⊕ *www. topfoodandwinetours.com.au* ✉ *From A$55.*

Artisans of Leisure. This company's indulgent nine-day Food and Wine Australia tour divides time between vineyards, markets, and luxurious hotels. ☎ *800/214–8144 in U.S.* ⊕ *www.artisansofleisure. com* ✉ *From A$12,710.*

Two Fat Blokes. Experience full- and half-day tours showcasing local wines and gourmet produce in the Hunter Valley region. ☎ *0414/316–859 in Australia, 2/4998–6699 outside Australia* ⊕ *www. twofatblokes.com.au* ✉ *From A$25.*

HIKING

Australian Walking Holidays. Mix hiking with other adventure activities with one of Australian Walking Holidays' guided trips. ☎ *1300/720000 in Australia* ⊕ *www.australianwalkingholidays.com. au* ✉ *From A$105.*

Auswalk. This company has a huge range of hiking expeditions all over Australia. There are group departures and customized self-guided tours, with accommodation and sightseeing included. ☎ *03/9530–8800* ⊕ *www.auswalk.com. au* ✉ *From A$1225.*

INDEX

PHOTO CREDITS

Front cover: imageBROKER / Alamy [Description: Sydney Opera House and Sydney Harbor Bridge, Sydney, Australia]. 1, Southern Grampians Shire/Tourism Victoria. 2, skateduck, Fodors. com member. 5, Pictor/age fotostock. Chapter 1: Experience Australia: 8-9, Konrad Wothe/age fotostock. 14 (left), Garry Moore/Tourism Tasmania . 14 (top right), Annie Doyle, Fodors.com member. 14 (bottom right), Gary Ott, Fodors.com member. 15 (left), Carol Matz, Fodors.com member. 15 (right), tab hauser, Fodors.com member. 16 (left), jonathanvlarocca/Flickr. 16 (right), The Rainforest Habitat Port Douglas. 17 (left), Tourism Australia. 17 (right), Barry Skipsey/Tourism NT. 20, Oliver Strewe/Tourism Australia. 21, Jamie MacFadyen/Tourism Australia. 32 (top), Peter Eve/Tourism NT. 32 (bottom), Alma Webou/Short St. Gallery. 33 (top), Penny Tweedie/Alamy. 33 (bottom), Peter Eve/Tourism NT. 34 (top left), emmettanderson/Flickr. 34 (top right), safaris/Flickr. 34 (bottom), David B. Simmonds/Tourism Australia. 35 (top left), Thomas Schoch/wikipedia.org. 35 (top right), Jochen Schlenker/age fotostock. 35 (bottom), Paul Blackmore/Tourism Australia. 36, Sheila Smart/Alamy. 38 (top left), Lydia Balbal / Short St. Gallery. 38 (top right), Courtesy of Kara Napangardi Ross and Warlukurlangu Artists Aboriginal Corporation www.warlu.com. 38 (right center), Daniel Walbidi/Short St. Gallery. 38 (right bottom), Barry Skipsey/Tourism NT. 39 (top), Penny Tweedie/Alamy. 39 (bottom), Iconsinternational. Com/Alamy. 40 (left), Penny Tweedie/Alamy. 40 (right), Donald Moko/Short St. Gallery. 41 (top), Steve Strike/Tourism Australia/Tourism NT. 41 (bottom), Weaver Jack/Short St. Gallery. Chapter 2: Sydney: 43, ARCO/Schulz, I/age fotostock. 45 (top), wizalt711, Fodors.com member. 45 (bottom), Kelly Kealy. 46, Tourism Australia/Robert Wallace. 55, Carly Miller, Fodors.com member. 58, ImageState/Alamy. 64-65, Jose Fuste Raga/age fotostock. 71, Norman Price/Alamy. 74, Gary Ott, Fodors.com member. 82, David Coleman/Alamy. 90, R1/Alamy. 96, Jose Fuste Raga/age fotostock. 99, Oliver Gerhard/age fotostock. 108, Tony Yeates/Tourism Australia. 109, Ming Pao Weekly/Tourism Australia. 110 (top), Oliver Strewe/Tourism Australia. 110 (bottom), Ron Hohenhaus/iStockphoto. 111 (top), Tony Yeates/Tourism Australia. 111 (bottom), CuboImages srl/Alamy. 112 (top), Murray Hilton/Sean's Panaroma. 112 (bottom), Matthew Cole/iStockphoto. 113 (top), Basquali Skamaachi/Tourism Australia. 113 (bottom), Dallas Events Inc/Shutterstock. 114 (top), Bon Appetit/Alamy. 114 (bottom), Christopher Meder - Photography/Shutterstock. 115 (top), Pack Shot/Shutterstock. 115 (bottom), Tom Keating/Tourism Australia. 137, Dominic Harcourt Webs/age fotostock. Chapter 3: New South Wales: 139, Tim Hester / Alamy. 140, Scott Sherrin, Fodors.com member. 141 (top), Sharyn Cairns/Tourism NSW. 141 (bottom), Mucky, Fodors.com member. 142, Melanie Ball. 149 (top), Susan Wright/Tourism NSW. 149 (bottom), Chris Jones/Tourism NSW. 150, Kitch Bain/Shutterstock. 151, Don Fuchs/Tourism NSW. 152, Jeff Davies/Shutterstock. 154, Vivian Zinc/Tourism Australia. 155, Chris Jones/Tourism NSW. 156 (left), LOOK Die Bildagentur der Fotografen GmbH/Alamy. 156 (top right), Keiichi Hiki/iStockphoto. 156 (bottom right), Inc/Shutterstock. 168, Oliver Strewe/Tourism. 177, David Wall/Alamy. 184, Grenville Turner/ Tourism NSW. 189, Sally Mayman/Tourism NSW. 198, Chris Howarth/Australia/Alamy. 200, Rob Walls/Alamy. 206, Wiskerke/Alamy. Chapter 4: Melbourne: 211, Mark Chew/Tourism Victoria. 212, Mojo Advertising Partners/Tourism Victoria. 213 (left), David Hannah/Tourism Victoria. 213 (right), sheldon Meyers, Fodors.com member. 214, Neale Cousland/Shutterstock. 222, Tktktk I Dreamstime.com. 225, Jose Fuste Raga/age fotostock. 230, Richard Nebesky/age fotostock. 242, David Wall/Alamy. 254, Tim Webster/Tourism Victoria. Chapter 5: Victoria: 259, Peter Dunphy/Tourism Victoria. 260, Southern Grampians Shire/Tourism Victoria. 261 (top), Tourism Victoria. 261 (bottom), lisargold, Fodors.com member. 262, Southern Grampians Shire/Tourism Victoria. 269, Alyssand I Dreamstime. com. 273, David Wall/Alamy. 278, Nick Osborne/Shutterstock. 279, kwest/Shutterstock. 280 (top left), iStockphoto. 280 (bottom left), Oliver Strewe/Tourism. 280 (right), Chris Kapa/Tourism Australia. 281 (top), kwest/Shutterstock. 281 (2nd from top), Phillip Minnis/iStockphoto. 281 (3rd from top), kwest/ Shutterstock. 281 (4th from top), Vidler Steve/age fotostock. 281 (5th from top), Alison Griffiths/ Campbell's Winery, Rutherglen. 281 (6th from top), giovannirivolta/age fotostock. 281 (7th from top and bottom), Claver Carroll/age fotostock. 282 (top), Tom Keating/Tourism Australia. 282 (bottom), kwest/Shutterstock. 283 (top), Oliver Strewe/Tourism Australia. 283 (bottom), Shoot/age fotostock. 284, Doug Pearson/age fotostock. 285 (top and bottom), Milton Wordley/Photolibrary. 294, Mark Watson/Tourism Victoria. 302, David Wall/Alamy. 315, Bill Bachman/ Alamy. 320, CuboImages srl/ Alamy. 324, Ern Mainka/Alamy. Chapter 6: Tasmania: 327, Mago World Image/age fotostock. 329 (top), logicaldog, Fodors.com member. 329 (bottom), Masha1, Fodors.com member. 330, Joe Shemesh /Tourism Tasmania. 337 (top), Tourism Tasmania. 337 (bottom), Rachael Bowes/Alamy. 338 (top), Tourism Tasmania. 338 (bottom), Lyndon Giffard/Alamy. 339 (top), Tourism Tasmania. 339 (bottom), Alistair Scott/Alamy. 340 (top), David Moore/Alamy. 340 (center), David Parker/Alamy. 340 (bottom), Nick Osborne/Tourism Tasmania. 341 (top), Alistair Scott/Alamy. 341 (bottom), David Parker/Alamy. 344, Tktktk I Dreamstime.com. 353, Chris Bell/Tourism Tasmania. 357, Gary Ott, Fodors.com mem-

NOTES

NOTES

NOTES

NOTES

NOTES

NOTES

NOTES

NOTES

NOTES

NOTES

NOTES

ABOUT OUR WRITERS

Lee Atkinson, freelance travel writer and author of 10 books and two smartphone apps about travelling in and around Australia, has been writing about her adventures on and off the road for major Australian newspapers and travel magazines since 1991. For this edition she updated the NSW, South Australia, and Outback chapters. You can follow her on twitter or instagram at @ OzyRoadTripper.

Perth-based journalist **Fleur Bainger** found her calling in freelance travel, food, and culture writing and podcasting. After many years reporting for ABC radio (Australia), she now crisscrosses Western Australia for *Australian Traveller, Australian Geographic,* and *The Sydney Morning Herald's Traveller.* She has commando-crawled remote sand dunes to watch turtles lay their eggs in Gnaraloo, scaled high trees in Pemberton, and surfed the white water at one of the world's best surf spots in Margaret River.

Tess Curran is a freelance journalist, writer, and editor hailing from the quiet sunshine of southeast Queensland. The deputy editor of *Peppermint* magazine for five years, her interests include ethical fashion, social enterprise, architecture and design, health, politics, and pop culture. She is also passionate about new trends in travel inspired by a "leave things better" philosophy: from sustainable and community-led tourism to peer-to-peer networks and the sharing economy. In her spare time she enjoys nothing more than lazy road trips through the countryside, discovering stunning landscapes, grand old homesteads, and honesty boxes bursting with fresh produce.

Narrelle Harris is a freelance writer and published author of horror, romance, and fantasy fiction, including the Melbourne vampire novels *The Opposite of Life* and *Walking Shadows.* Her latest book, *The Adventure of the Colonial Boy,* features Sherlock Holmes in Australia. She's travelled widely in Australia and overseas, and now lives in central Melbourne with fellow writer and husband Tim Richards. Narrelle and Tim jointly updated the Victoria and Melbourne chapters of this edition. Find out more about her work at www. mortalwords.com.au.

Leah McLennan is a freelance travel writer based in Broome, Western Australia. Her articles have appeared in Australia's top magazines, newspapers, and websites, such as *Luxury Travel, The Irish Independent, The Gold Coast Bulletin, The Canberra Times, The Australian,* and more. Leah worked as the full-time travel reporter in Sydney at news.com.au, Australia's number one news site. Prior to that, she was a senior reporter in Sydney at Australian Associated Press for over seven years.

Tim Richards fell into travel writing after living and teaching in Egypt and Poland. He's a light packing obsessive, and loves chasing down a story with a historical angle. Tim contributes travel articles regularly to the *Sydney Morning Herald* and *The Age* newspapers, has authored apps and ebooks, and writes about travel in his blog Aerohaveno at www.aerohaveno. com. In 2014 his debut novel, *Mind the Gap,* was published. He lives in Melbourne's lively downtown, and for this edition he and wife Narrelle Harris updated the Melbourne and Victoria chapters.

Merran White, a former national travel editor for Australia's *CitySearch*, has worked with *Time Out* guides in London, concierge.com, *Australia's Vacations & Travel*, and various cruise and in-flight publications, including Virgin Australia's *Voyeur*. She's authored two books for solo women travelers, and spends her vacations beachcombing, scuba diving, and communing with wildlife.